Government Contract Law
in the
Twenty-First Century

Government Contract Law in the Twenty-First Century

Charles Tiefer
PROFESSOR,
UNIVERSITY OF BALTIMORE SCHOOL OF LAW

William A. Shook
SENIOR PARTNER, SHOOK DORAN LLP
WASHINGTON, D.C.

Carolina Academic Press
Durham, North Carolina

ISBN 978-1-59460-804-9
LCCN 2011942304

Carolina Academic Press
700 Kent Street
Durham, NC 27701
Telephone (919) 489-7486
Fax (919) 493-5668
www.cap-press.com

Printed in the United States of America

Contents

Table of Principal Cases and Rulings

Preface and Acknowledgments

Government contracting matters more than ever. Government has grown, especially in what it does—and how it uses contracting to get its jobs done. As an example, for the wars in Iraq and Afghanistan, the government used contractors for everything from serving meals and repairing vehicles to providing interpreters and guarding convoys and bases. At times, in the theater of war the government had more contractors than it had military or civilian employees.

Like the business of government contracting, the law of government contracting matters more than ever, too. It provides the legal structure for the government to buy its enormous needs of goods and services. These are transactions with a far larger role for lawyers than contracts between purely private parties, because government contracting is far more regulated. Government contracting carries out the great range of policies by which Congress and Executive authorities seek to make procurement economical, efficient, competitive, practical, fair, and an instrument of diverse substantive national policies like support for small business. As a field of practice, it puts lawyers—both established and starting—to work where they can accomplish much for their clients, their country, the economy, and themselves.

Through this subject, such lawyers take on the challenges of a sophisticated legal specialty. As a subject, it is both intensely practical and intellectually stimulating. There is no point in memorizing or otherwise dully plodding away at government contract law. This body of law is too vast, too complex, and too rapidly evolving to be mastered entirely in a single semester course of study. Those who tackle it learn core concepts and then learn to follow the trail of study to specific advanced areas.

This book on government contracting law in the 2000s has roots in a predecessor volume, *Government Contracting Law: Cases and Materials*, first published in 1998. It is a very new book that follows a very new approach in key respects.

Reviewing its novel approach serves as an introduction to its contents. This book has adopted a new focus, so that instead of being heavily weighted just to traditional core topics, it covers a wide set of interesting emerging topics. The book has nineteen chapters, seven beyond the predecessor book, reflecting this diverse set of fresh topics. The new chapters, plus many new subchapters and current cases and notes even in the core chapters, reflect a whole new set of worlds in government contracting since the 1990s.

It helps to group all the new material into four largely or entirely new lines of practice reflected in this book's new chapters. One line of practice covers technology and health, which have the necessary new chapters. A few years back, issues of technology, and specifically intellectual property, were relatively simple. The government acquired the intellectual property it needed, on its terms. And, a government contracting book could omit contracting with health providers altogether, because government payment for medical goods and services did not matter so much.

Now the government acquires much of the intellectual property—such as word processing software like that with which this book, and millions of government documents a week, are written—in a "commercial" way that makes complex compromises with the commercial world about intellectual property. And, the government's purchases of health care are big business, with rapid evolution in the 2000s of how the government, particularly the Defense Department, buys health care.

Second, government contracting has new and complex litigation aspects. The book has the contemporary chapter on the False Claims Act and defective pricing suits. In the last century, the False Claims Act case law had only begun its development after the 1986 statutory amendments. Now that body of law is full-blown; and there have been a string of important Supreme Court rulings in the 2000s. The book has separate chapters on protests, and on claims, reflecting how each has rapidly evolved. Since 2000, protests no longer come to district courts, while the Court of Federal Claims has become their vital judicial forum. Claims now come through a consolidated Civilian Board of Contract Appeals.

Third, transactional government contracting has evolved, too. Commercial, IDIQ, and MAS contracting have mushroomed, with their unique bodies of law. Not until 2008 could a challenger even protest an IDIQ task order award; now IDIQ case law is a whole subject. Commercial and MAS contracting law have moved rapidly as the era of government-restricted procurement has given way to a commercial market. So these areas have the new chapter they need. And, construction law has its own chapter, reflecting how it increasingly emerges as a separate specialized body of law.

Fourth, government contracting has increasing connections with diverse policy realms. This book has the current chapter on international procurement, including the global wars from 2001 to the present. More than ever before, we live in a global world. We make war with the support of private contractors, and we have new government contracting law to deal with these challenges. This book has the needed chapter on government and contractor workforce, recognizing how developments reflect how much more they matter, with so much more procurement of services, rather than goods, and close oversight by government employees of what contractors provide. The 2000s shook up the government workforce issue, with the struggles over whether the defense and homeland security employees would be organized as in the past. And, the book has the contemporary chapter on government breach and takings, subjects more emphasized these days, in the wake of *Winstar*, than hitherto.

With these new lines of practice and so many new subjects, the book's cases have had to catch up to the present. A large majority of the book's cases come from the last decade or two. Whenever possible, the book has traded in older in favor of more recent cases. Among other benefits, this increases the likelihood that the cases will discuss a context familiar to the students of this generation. For example, almost none of this book's cases that relate to wartime procurement relate to the experience of past generations with World War II, the Korean War, the Vietnam War, or even the Persian Gulf War. The war-related cases have to do with the Iraq and Afghanistan wars. Very few of the cases in this book that relate to regulations, stop with the versions of the regulations before the Federal Acquisition Regulation (FAR) of 1984. These fresh cases focus on the implementation and evolution of the FAR and successor waves of regulations as the new development.

Does this mean that those who taught the predecessor volume must throw out their whole set of notes for their government contracting course and start all over from scratch when planning how to teach from this book? Of course not. The book has continuity for the core subjects of the government contracting curriculum. Those continuing basics include the limited authority of officials, competition, negotiated procurement, and protests of awards. So too do the basics continue of the core of contract types and administration, changes, claims, small businesses and subcontracts, and disputes. Termination for convenience and for default are as they were.

As to these subjects, this book uses fresh cases in place of those from decades ago, and delves into new aspects that have replaced old ones. But, those who taught the predecessor volume will have no unnecessary difficulty teaching the core of their course using the new one. Moreover, they will find their load lightened by their not having to supplement the book with explanations of what has changed in the years since the 1980s, the 1990s, or even the early 2000s.

As for the two authors, Charles Tiefer, Professor at University of Baltimore Law School, annually teaches a course in government contract law. He served as General Counsel (Acting), Deputy General Counsel, and Solicitor of the U.S. House of Representatives in 1984–95. In 2008–11, he served as Commissioner on the Commission on Wartime Contracting in Iraq and Afghanistan, a full-time federal commission created by Congress. He participated in its 25 televised hearings and major reports that delved deeply into state-of-the-art procurement issues.

William Shook is senior partner in the government contracting firm of Shook Doran in Washington, D.C. He came to that position after serving from 1979 through 1985 on various congressional investigations committees that focused on government contracting procedures and abuses. Since then, his practice has been at the cutting edge in fast-evolving areas such as commercial contracting and intellectual property. He lectures across the country regarding government contract law. It has been an effective, thought-provoking, and pleasant collaboration, with one party bringing the academic perspective, and the other, successful and extensive experience with a broad range of issues in practice.

Professor Tiefer acknowledges the assistance of his colleagues at the University of Baltimore Law School with whom he has had valuable discussions of the work, including: Dean Phillip J. Closius, who has inspired the school's intellectual flowering; former deans Gil Holmes and John Sebert; the current Acting Dean, Michael Higginbotham; and associate deans John Lynch, Jane C. Murphy, and Donald Stone, each of whom encouraged scholarship in many ways that made the book possible. A special thanks goes to Dean Closius and Associate Dean Lynch, who willingly supported the years of leave at the Commission and also provided the supportive welcome back.

Also providing valuable help were colleagues: Michael Meyerson, Steve Shapiro, and Fred Brown, who sat in on course sessions and gave important advice on their improvement; and Barbara Babb, Dick Bourne, Steve Davison, Eric Easton, Garrett Epps, Robert Lande, Audrey MacFarlane, Lynn McLain, Arnold Rochvarg, Rob Rubinson, Elizabeth Samuels, Mortimer Sellers, Amy Sloan, Angela Vellario, and Barbara White, all of whom gave advice and support over the years of development. Unique help came from his sister, Dr. Leonore Tiefer, whose own best-selling books, and internationally well-received talks, on sexual psychology, alas, could only have some of their aspects of interest smoothly melded into this book.

Principal credit for the skilled word processing on the book, including the patient massaging of countless very raw sources into polished form, goes to Mary Heywood Peterson. Also helping have been Will Tress, Robin Klein, Harvey Morrell, Robert Pool, and Elizabeth Rhodes, who miraculously retrieved library and computer resources, often from the most unexpected and inaccessible sources. And much help came from the students of government contracting law classes, who cheerfully learned the subject from predecessor materials and whose diplomatic yet urgent requests for improvement in those materials spurred the book's progress. A series of top-flight, creative, hard-working research assistants did high-quality work on the book, including Myshala Middleton, Melissa Goldmeier, and Michele Reichlin, and, including Aidan Smith who did deep research and superb work for the health care chapter.

Helping in countless ways were his wife, Hillary Burchuk, who leant tremendous strength of character, and her own insights into the workings of government and business from her years in advanced practice in both public and private sectors. This book could only be done with major support for Commissioner Tiefer on his wartime contracting commission, and the burden of that support fell heavily on Hillary's ability to juggle her own challenging legal career, the care of our two boys, and all the rest of the household load for three long years, especially during the trips to Iraq and Afghanistan,. She also gave wise counsel, both for the Commission and for the book, from her own years as a Justice Department trial lawyer. Also contributing were two promising young authors: Max David Tiefer, twelve, whose skills at creative writing and moviemaking inspired the better passages of this book; and Roy Bernard Tiefer, nine, whose exceptionally high level of reading interests kept the household's attention on the goal of quality writing.

Keith Sipe and Linda Lacy at Carolina Academic Press provided a high level of enthusiasm and professional counsel in getting the book to completion. They helped to visualize the book when it was only a thought in the minds of the authors, and generously used their own confidence and experience to bring it forth. The book's editors, especially Tim Colton, took the raw manuscript material and brought it to a high polish.

William Shook acknowledges the significant help, by his forebearance, of Stratton Shook, who somewhat willingly agreed to excuse his father from various duties; whose ability to excel in college and in learning abroad, and in commencing his career have been a source of constant inspiration and pleasure. William Shook also acknowledges the enormous contribution of his wife, Teri, whose boundless energy for adventure, and whose own challenging career as a government contractor, provide a world of inspiration.

And he recognizes the help of his colleague, Kelly Doran, who youthful professionalism helps keep him grounded in frontline happenings.

Copyright Acknowledgments

We gratefully acknowledge the permission granted by authors, publishers, and organizations to reprint portions of the following copyrighted materials:

Coburn, George, *Enlarged Bid Protest Jurisdiction of the United States Court of Federal Claims, The Procurement Lawyer*, Fall 1997. Published by the American Bar Association. Reprinted by permission.

Feldman, Steven, GOVERNMENT CONTRACT CASEBOOK (Thomson Reuters, 4th ed. 2010). Reprinted by permission.

Judge Advocate General's School, U.S. Army in Charlottesville, Virginia, Materials from the Contract Attorney's Courses (1995–1998). Reprinted with approval.

Livingston, Scott A., *Fair Treatment for Contractors Doing Business With the State of Maryland*, 15 University of Baltimore Law Review 215 (1986). Reprinted by permission.

Tiefer, Charles, *"Budgetized" Health Entitlements and the Fiscal Constitution in Congress's 1995–1996 Budget Battle*, 33 Harvard Journal on Legislation 411 (1996). Reprinted by permission.

Tiefer, Charles and Stroman, Ronald, *Congressional Intent and Commercial Products, The Procurement Lawyer*, Spring 1997. Published by the American Bar Association. Reprinted by permission.

Government Contract Law
in the
Twenty-First Century

Chapter 1

Government Contracting Doctrines

A. Introduction: The Challenge of the Different Culture of Government Contracting

Government contracting law has grown in interest and attraction for law students (and others who would study this casebook). Federal government contracting law directs the federal government's procurement of goods and services. It thereby governs an area of practice which accords a large role for lawyers because the federal government binds itself, and its contractors, by much more elaborate law than the comparatively simple law governing how private parties contract with each other. This has long been true.

Today, though, studying federal government contracting law has increased value. Most states model their state and local procurement, to a considerable degree, on federal government law. Aspects of government procurement law apply to the large amount of health care expenditures covered by Medicare and Medicaid and to other government programs such as government grants and loans. Finally, selected aspects of government contract law apply to, or influence contractual relations with, the subcontractors, suppliers, and others who aid those who contract directly with the government. Combining all these, government contracting law shapes legal work for procurement amounting to many hundreds of billions of dollars of commerce with intensive needs for lawyering.

Moreover, government contracting law presents a unique opportunity, being situated at the complex and ambiguous boundary zone between public and private law. On one side, government contract law draws on concepts familiar to students grounded in the introductory contracts course of the first year of law school, with its common law origins. Government contract formation law draws on the familiar concepts of offer and acceptance; government contract rules for accurate statements draw on the familiar concepts of mistake and fraud; government contract administration draws on the familiar concepts of interpretation, conditions, and excuse; government contract termination draws on the familiar concepts of breach and remedy.

However, government contract law deserves respectful attention for the large number of new concepts. Basic (private) contract law remains largely true to its common law roots, even when codified and, in the process, modified, by such developments as the Uniform Commercial Code. In contrast, government contract law ultimately derives only to a limited degree from court-made law, as distinguished from the overriding importance of statutes, regulations, and standard clauses. Today, the federal code of government contract rules, known as the Federal Acquisition Regulation (the "FAR"), more than any body of adjudications, answers the largest number of legal questions in government contract law.

Basic contract law contrasts with government contract law as to the economic "culture" in which they play the legal role. Basic contract law exists in the culture of the private economy, with its transactions between private parties, and its law made by those private parties, that is, its "private" law. It governs symmetric transactions in which the parties on both sides not only have solely private, not public, powers and responsibilities, but also solely economic, not governmental, motivations and interests. In contract, government contract law involves governmental powers and responsibilities, and, looking at the surrounding "culture," also governmental motivations and interests. The presence of governmental agencies and their contracting officers on one side of the transaction brings in an entire culture of public law. Contracting officers do not act from pure economic self-interest, as a private contracting party does; they implement public policy making, meaning that they must find their way through the sometimes clear, but sometimes mysterious, mix of instructions that govern the public world. Their instructions come from the elected Congress and President, the appointed heads of departments, the senior civil service above them, and the fellow governmental employees who are their colleagues and assistants. Their public law culture sets them apart in every respect from the private commercial world: in institutions, motives, rules, ethics, and language. Sometimes they even act in a particularly special sub-culture within the public world, such as military contracting officers whose procurement activity derives its shape in part from the unique military culture.

Hence, for learning this different culture and its different language, a casebook becomes just as vital a learning tool for government contract law as for basic (private) contract law. The cases supply the vital context that a reading of dry regulations would not: like a newspaper story, they tell, in discussing the legal issue, what is being purchased, by whom, when, where, and how. They place the new vocabulary, especially the wealth of acronyms from ACOs and the ASPR to TINA and the ASBCA, in comprehensible surroundings. Their stories show the interaction of the special motivations of government officials and government contractors, thereby revealing the meaning and purpose infusing the clauses, rules, and statutes.

So, this book depends heavily on its cases, not in defiance of the difference between the statutory origins of government contract law and the common law origins of private contract law, but in recognition and acknowledgement of that difference. The cases are needed to show the government contract culture, as well as its black-letter law. If government contract law were just another common law subject, similar to basic contract law but with different rules, perhaps then the graduate of a course in basic contract law could learn the differences from an abstraction of the specific rules in a Restatement or codification. As an entirely different culture, government contracting requires the contextual richness of cases to effectively transmit understanding.

Accordingly, this chapter starts with a case chosen not so much for its particular point of law, as to illustrate the different culture of government contracting. The chapter then continues with cases and discussion about the three doctrinal areas that most distinguish government contract law: the limited authority of government employees; the source of the law in statutes, regulations, and standard clauses; and, the role of public budgets as a separate formal constraint on contracting. Finally, the chapter uses some state materials to illustrate the similarities and differences between federal and state government contracting law.

As for the particular case that starts this chapter, the opinion has many passages of remarkably clear, helpful exposition of government contract law. Deriving full benefit from these involves a major effort that is its own reward: a first chance, in the context of a relatively comprehensible opinion, to encounter the differentiating aspects of government contract law. So, in reading the case, try not to rush past, or to glide over, the following new aspects; instead, begin acclimating to them, making it much easier to deal with them when they recur in subsequent opinions:

1. The government procurement context. In this first case the context consists of the government buying medical care for military dependents. The plaintiff sells those medical services to an Army hospital commanded by Colonel James Henry. Readers must learn how that context works from the opinion, unless for some unusual reason they may have independent knowledge of the context of military health care.

For example, some of the plaintiff's dealings concern Colonel Henry. But other of the plaintiff's dealings concern the "fiscal intermediary," the Associated Group. This reflects how government procurement works in this context. Colonel Henry, as the hospital commander who buys the services, makes some decisions. However, the Army has set up its medical system so that the plaintiff sends its bills not to Colonel Henry, but to a fiscal intermediary, namely, the Associated Group, which processes them on behalf of the Army. So, the Associated Group makes some decisions. It is a challenge for the reader without any previous background to come to understand the major different roles in this opinion assigned by this Army medical care procurement system to Colonel Henry and to the Associated Group. A host of persons or entities in the Department of Defense also have cameo roles in this opinion.

2. Acronyms. A reader of this opinion would usefully keep a chart as to what each of the following stands for: TMM, CHAMPUS, MOU, MEI, and CDA. Only CDA will recur later on, but the habit of dealing with acronyms as they arise will stand a reader of government contract law in good stead. Government contract law involves learning precisely this specialized new language.

3. Specialized procedures. The opinion's citation tells that this decision comes from the United States Court of Appeals for the Federal Circuit, a specialized tribunal. Almost immediately, the opinion's first sentence tells that the appeal comes up from the Court of Federal Claims, another specialized tribunal. Later, the "Procedural History" section indicates that the case began as a claim under the Contract Disputes Act ("CDA"), a specialized procedure. None of this will seem familiar from a course in basic contract law, which commonly gets litigated in general nonspecialized tribunals and begins without preliminary formalities like a claim under a special "Disputes Act." Yet all these specialized aspects will prove recurrent and important as the course proceeds. It will probably require reading several other cases occurring more or less the same way before beginning to feel at home with these specialized procedures.

4. Statutes. The opinion's "Background" section begins with Congress establishing this military health plan by statute. This statute, and other statutes, play a large part in the law of this opinion. Quite evidently, the health care system for military dependents, and the law regarding that system, did not arise by descent from the common law. It started with Congressional enactments, signified by the citation to 10 U.S.C. § 1071–1106, where the U.S.C. is the United States Code, the codification of federal statutes.

5. Regulations. Fairly quickly, it turns out that the details of the rate-setting dispute in this case between the Army and the medical provider (TMM) concern regulations. The Department of Defense, it seems, has provided the detailed law regarding this health care system in such regulations. Unless the readers have taken administrative law, this may be their first encounter with extensive resort to federal regulations. These regulations are signified by citation to 32 C.F.R. § 199, where the C.F.R. is the Code of Federal Regulations,

the codification of federal regulations. The wording of the regulations resolves this case. It is decisive. It is the law. So the opinion has an important lesson: regulations may make slow reading because of the concentrated style in which they are written, but they are where the law is.

For further discussion of the subjects of this chapter, see the cites in the specific subchapters, and see: Ralph Nash & Steven Feldman, *Government Contract Changes*, §§ 5.2– 5.12 (Thomson Reuters, 3rd ed. 2006); Steven Feldman, *Government Contract Guidebook*, § 2.21 (Thomson Reuters, 4th ed. 2010); John S. Pachter, *The Incredible Shrinking Contracting Officer*, 39 Pub. Cont. L.J. 705 (Summer 2010); Robert K. Tompkins, Elizabeth M. Gill, Lindsey D. Weber, *The Service Contract Act: A Primer For The New Decade*, 57 Fed. Law. 58 (Oct. 2010).

Total Medical Management, Inc., Plaintiff-Appellee, v. The United States, Defendant-Appellant

No. 96-5013
United States Court of Appeals, Federal Circuit
Jan. 16, 1997

Before ARCHER, Chief Judge, MICHEL and RADER, Circuit Judges.

MICHEL, Circuit Judge.

The United States ("government") appeals from the November 2, 1994 order of the United States Court of Federal Claims, No. 92-838C, granting summary judgment of contractual liability against the government in favor of Total Medical Management, Inc. ("TMM"). The order became final when, on August 31, 1995, the trial court entered judgment in TMM's favor in the amount of $57,197.50, plus interest. The appeal was submitted for our decision following oral argument on July 2, 1996. We hold that, because the applicable base reimbursement rate in this local contract conflicts with valid national regulations, the contract is void as beyond the authority of the government signatory. As such, we reverse and remand with instructions to dismiss for failure to state a claim upon which relief can be granted.

BACKGROUND

In 1956, Congress established a health plan for dependents of members of the uniformed services. This plan allowed for the provision of medical care at civilian medical facilities for those who could not be cared for at military medical facilities. See Dependents' Medical Care Act, Pub.L. No. 84-569, 70 Stat. 250 (1956) (codified as amended at 10 U.S.C. §§ 1071–1106) ("Act"). This plan has been implemented through the Civilian Health and Medical Program of the Uniformed Services ("CHAMPUS"). 10 U.S.C. § 1072(4) (1994). The plan allows military hospitals and private health care companies to create facility-sharing arrangements. Specifically, according to section 1096(a) of the Act,

> The Secretary of Defense may enter into an agreement providing for the sharing of resources between facilities of the uniformed services and facilities of a civilian health care provider or providers that the Secretary contracts with under section 1079, 1086, or 1097 of this title if the Secretary determines that such an agreement would result in the delivery of health care to which covered beneficiaries are entitled under this chapter in a more effective, efficient, or economical manner.

10 U.S.C. § 1096(a) (1994). The Secretary of Defense has implemented this general power granted by Congress by encouraging military hospital commanders to enter into facility-

sharing partnership agreements, upon approval of the Director of CHAMPUS and the Surgeon General of the appropriate military department, with private health care companies. See Department of Defense Instruction 6010.12, "Military-Civilian Health Services Partnership Program" (Oct. 22, 1987); 32 C.F.R. § 199.1(p) (1995) (permitting entry into agreements under "Military-Civilian Health Services Partnership Program"). These partnership agreements are typically memorialized in "Memoranda of Understanding" ("MOUs") or "Memoranda of Agreement" ("MOAs"). This arrangement saves the government the expense of reimbursement for treatment in expensive civilian medical facilities. This additional expense would otherwise be billed to CHAMPUS.

Instead of billing patients, the private health care companies that have entered into MOUs file claim forms with a fiscal intermediary (in TMM's case, the Associated Group) that processes and pays the claims. Prior to February 1989, the reimbursement rate scheme was as follows:

The allowable charge for authorized care shall be the lower of:

(A) The billed charge for the service;

(B) The prevailing charge level that does not exceed the amount equivalent to the 80th percentile of billed charges made for similar services in the same locality during the base period.

32 C.F.R. § 199.14(h)(1)(i) (1989).

Effective February 1, 1989, Congress modified the CHAMPUS payment rules. Department of Defense Appropriations Act of 1989, Pub.L. No. 100-463, § 8019, 102 Stat. 2270. The new reimbursement scheme is:

The allowable charge for authorized care shall be the lowest of the amounts identified … :

(A) The billed charge for the service.

(B) The prevailing charge level that does not exceed the amount equivalent to the 80th percentile of billed charges made for similar services in the same locality during the base period.

* * *

(C) For charges from physicians and other individual professional providers, the fiscal year 1988 prevailing charges adjusted by the Medicare Economic Index (MEI), as the MEI is applied to Medicare prevailing charge levels.

32 C.F.R. § 199.14(g)(1) (1990). The CHAMPUS Operating Manual and the Code of Federal Regulations both reflected this change in the reimbursement scheme, thus putting all program participants on constructive notice that the MEI could limit the reimbursement amount. 44 U.S.C. § 1507 (1994).

On November 10, 1988, TMM entered into an MOU with Ireland Army Hospital in Fort Knox, Kentucky, to provide internal medicine services for CHAMPUS beneficiaries. The MOU contained the following provision relating to reimbursement rates for services provided under the agreement:

… Billing rates are as follows:

(1) CHAMPUS eligibles at 75% of current CHAMPUS prevailing rate for outpatient services (current as of date of billing).

(2) All others (primarily active duty military) at 75% of current CHAMPUS prevailing rate for all outpatient services.

(3) All inpatient services at 80% of current CHAMPUS prevailing rate.

By letter dated February 10, 1989, the Associated Group informed TMM that the Internal Medicine MOU had been approved. In addition, the letter noted that "all payments are based on the CHAMPUS allowable charge methodology; payment for a procedure will not exceed the area prevailing charge." Similarly, the letter indicated that "Partnership claims will be processed in the same manner as CHAMPUS claims and are subject to program and policy limitations.... Payments may not exceed the CHAMPUS prevailing fees."

* * *

In 1990, the Associated Group began reimbursing TMM according to the limitation imposed by the use of the MEI. On February 22, 1990, TMM sent a letter to Colonel James Henry, the Commander at the Fort Knox hospital, reporting that the MEI had been used in determining the amount that TMM was reimbursed for certain medical services. TMM pointed out that the Internal Medicine MOU called for reimbursement based upon "75% of the current CHAMPUS prevailing rate" and made no mention of the use of the MEI to limit payments.

Colonel Henry conveyed TMM's concern to the Army Health Services Command. In his letter, Colonel Henry sought clarification regarding the MEI limitation. The Associated Group prepared a response and sent it to CHAMPUS on May 10, 1990. This response indicated that the payments made by the Associated Group were in accordance with the MEI limitation in the CHAMPUS regulations. CHAMPUS then sent a response to the Army.

TMM and the Army re-executed the ... MOUs at the end of each of the initial two year terms ... The re-executed contracts were silent as to the MEI limitation. On February 22, 1991, the Associated Group sent a letter to TMM stating:

> Per the agreement, the reimbursement of your Partnership claims will be based on a single percentage of the ... prevailing charge or the maximum allowable prevailing charge (also called the Medicare Economic Index adjusted prevailing charge), whichever is lower)....

* * *

PROCEDURAL HISTORY

On April 10, 1992, TMM sent a claim under the Contract Disputes Act ("CDA") for $52,746.28 to Colonel Thomas Clements at Ireland Army Community Hospital. This amount was calculated as the difference between the actually reimbursed MEI rate and TMM's calculation of the contract rate.

* * *

TMM filed a complaint against the government in the Court of Federal Claims on December 8, 1992.

* * *

On July 11, 1994, the parties filed cross-motions for summary judgment on the issue of liability. On November 2, 1994, the trial court granted TMM's summary judgment motion and denied the government's motion. In a ruling from the bench, the trial judge held that liability turned on the meaning of the term "current CHAMPUS prevailing rate" used in the MOU. The judge agreed with TMM that this was the same as the "current CHAMPUS prevailing charge" as used in 32 C.F.R. § 199.14 (1990), rather than the "allowable rate," which, under the CHAMPUS regulations, would have included the MEI limitation.

DISCUSSION

* * *

There is no question that TMM pleaded the existence of a valid contract here. The proper question, despite the government's label, is one of the merits: whether TMM failed to state a claim upon which relief can be granted. Id.

The requirements for a valid contract with the United States are: a mutual intent to contract including offer, acceptance, and consideration; and authority on the part of the government representative who entered or ratified the agreement to bind the United States in contract. Thermalon Indus., Ltd. v. United States, 34 Fed.Cl. 411, 414 (1995) (citing City of El Centro v. United States, 922 F.2d 816, 820 (Fed.Cir.1990) and Fincke v. United States, 230 Ct.Cl. 233, 244, 675 F.2d 289, 295 (1982)). In addition, government contracts must comply with statutorily sanctioned regulations. See, e.g., United States v. Amdahl Corp., 786 F.2d 387, 392 (Fed.Cir.1986) (holding that a procurement contract award in conflict with statute and regulation was void ab initio). A contract which is "plainly illegal" is a nullity and void ab initio. John Reiner & Co. v. United States, 163 Ct.Cl. 381, 325 F.2d 438, 440 (1963). A contract is "plainly illegal" when made contrary to statute or regulation either because of some action or statement by the contractor, or when the contractor is on "direct notice that the procedures being followed were violative of such requirements." Amdahl, 786 F.2d at 395 (quoting a decision of the Comptroller General, B-176393, 52 Comp. Gen. 214, 218 (1972) (citing Schoenbrod v. United States, 187 Ct.Cl. 627, 410 F.2d 400 (1969)).

Here, the existence of the negotiated, signed MOUs evidences offer and acceptance. There was also consideration in the mutuality of obligation: TMM is to provide discounted health care services; the Army is to provide support staff and free space in the military hospital.

The Contract Disputes Act defines a contracting officer as:

> any person who, by appointment in accordance with applicable regulations, has the authority to enter into and administer contracts and make determinations and findings with respect thereto. The term also includes the authorized representative of the contracting officer, acting within the limits of his authority.

41 U.S.C. § 601(3) (1994). The Secretary of Defense has authority to enter into resource sharing "agreements" with civilian health care providers. 10 U.S.C. § 1096 (1994). In Department of Defense Instruction 6010.12, the Secretary authorizes hospital commanders to administer the partnership agreements and to encourage civilian health care providers to participate in them. Hospital commanders may execute an agreement only after submitting it for approval to the Director, CHAMPUS, and the Surgeon General of the appropriate military department. Department of Defense Instruction 6010.12(F)(1). The MOUs here were forwarded to the Associated Group, the CHAMPUS approval designee, and were approved. Therefore, we hold that the MOU was ratified by a government representative with the authority to bind the United States in contract. Thus, we hold all elements for a contract were met by the MOUs.

* * *

However, even though the basic requirements for a government contract are met, the contract is void because the MOUs are in direct conflict with CHAMPUS regulations. This regulatory scheme in effect at the time each of the contracts was entered into (or renewed), explicitly limited health care provider reimbursement base rates to the lowest of three possibilities: the billed charge, the prevailing charge, or the MEI limited prevailing charge. 32 C.F.R. § 199.14(g)(1) (1990). Neither the Secretary of Defense nor any of his designated representatives had the authority to obligate CHAMPUS beyond these base rates set by regulation. The government "is not bound by its agents acting beyond their authority and contrary to regulation." Urban Data Sys., Inc. v. United States, 699 F.2d 1147, 1153 (Fed.Cir.1983) (quoting Yosemite Park & Curry Co. v. United States, 217 Ct.Cl. 360, 582 F.2d 552, 558 (1978)); see also Office of Personnel Management v. Richmond, 496 U.S. 414, 428, 110 S.Ct. 2465, 2473, 110 L.Ed.2d 387 (1990) (agencies' unauthorized statements to citizens cannot obligate the Treasury for the payment of funds). A contractor who enters into an arrangement with an agent of the government bears the risk that the agent is acting outside the bounds of his authority, even when the agent himself is unaware of the limitations on his authority. Federal Crop Ins. Corp. v. Merrill, 332 U.S. 380, 384, 68 S.Ct. 1, 3, 92 L.Ed. 10 (1947).

Furthermore, the illegality was "plain" under the Reiner test. 325 F.2d at 440. TMM was on constructive and actual notice that the CHAMPUS regulatory scheme would be used in determining payment rates. Each of the MOUs was either entered into or renewed after the new regulatory reimbursement scheme went into effect. Also, the Associated Group informed TMM in their approvals of the MOUs that "CHAMPUS allowable charge methodology" would be used in determining reimbursement rates. Since the contracts were "plainly illegal," they were void ab initio. A dismissal on this basis is one for failure to state a claim. Gould, 67 F.3d at 930.

Since the MOUs were void ab initio, TMM failed to state a claim upon which relief can be granted. We therefore reverse and remand with instructions to dismiss for failure to state a claim.

REVERSED AND REMANDED.

Notes and Questions

1. The two sides' opposing theories have surprising simplicity and intrinsic interest, revealed by peeling off the surrounding layers of acronyms and specialized vocabulary. Simple opposing theories underlie the arguments about the wording of statutes, regulations, and contracts. In 1990, Congress by statute, and the Defense Department by regulations, imposed a ceiling on medical rates. That ceiling capped contract rate increases at a level found by adding the "Medicare Economic Index" to the previous year "prevailing charges." Regardless of the precise calculation of that cap, what matters is that Congress intended to cap the increase of federal payments for medical care. However, TMM, the health provider, had a contract without any express mention of this new MEI cap, so it wanted to be paid at what it considers its contract's rate.

What would the health provider argue in such a case, in terms of fairness? What would the government, in opposing that claim, argue back? Evidently the court thinks it irrelevant whether what Congress intends is fair. Why does the court make the case turn on a textual reading of the wording of the statutes, regulations, and contract clauses, as opposed to dwelling on or even mentioning any notions of fairness, justice, or contractor expectations?

2. The government contracts context often reflects particular historical developments that statutes and regulations arise from but say little or nothing explicit about. Even the best judicial opinions often leave that context relatively undiscussed, although the judges probably understand it well, particularly when, as in this case, the statute and regulation arose within a few years of the case. By statute that became effective in 1990, Congress decided to cap federal payments for medical care. While the opinion does not discuss "why," from your own knowledge, why do you suppose Congress capped medical cost inflation at that time? To what extent does the whole elaborate machinery of government

contracting reflected in this opinion exist just so that Congress, for such reasons, can make such decisions?

3. Why is there a system of specialized tribunals and specialized procedures to handle a matter like this? As later cases in this book will reflect, often these matters do go before tribunals of general jurisdiction, one of which is the United States Supreme Court, yet most such matters stay within the administrative and judicial systems of specialized jurisdiction. By the same token, would it be expected that the lawyers working on these issues, either within the government or with the contractors, have specialized training (such as that imparted by studying this casebook)? Is such specialized training more necessary than, say, for some similar issue that might arise if TMM had a contract dispute with a private sector contracting party, like the insurance carrier for some private sector employer's policy for its private employees' dependents?

4. Note the distinction drawn in the opinion between the two types of issues that will come up next in this chapter: the limited authority of government agents and the decisive role of statutes, regulations, and standard clauses. TMM's contract with the government consisted of an MOU, which had been entered for the government when the Associated Group approved it. Did the court analyze whether the Associated Group had the authority to enter the MOU? What determines whether the Associated Group had that authority? The court separately analyzes whether the MOU conflicted with regulations. Evidently the court can separate these two questions, of the government agent's authority and the contract's conflict with regulations. Both these questions involve regulations and a dispute between the two sides on how to view those regulations. What separates the two questions so much that the court rules for one side on one question, and for the other side on the other?

5. Size up how difficult is the legal issue in this case by how the different specialized deciders and tribunals go different ways on it. When the Associated Group entered the MOU, it must have thought the MOU legal. Yet later, the Associated Group and the Army refused what TMM asked. Then, the Court of Federal Claims agreed with TMM, rejecting the position of the Associated Group and the Army. Whereupon on appeal, the Federal Circuit reversed the Court of Federal Claims, accepting the position of the Associated Group and the Army and rejecting TMM's. One moral of the story: it is complicated enough to figure out the answers to such government contracting law questions that practitioners in the field have a great deal to argue about and deal with.

B. Characteristic Doctrines

1. Limited Authority

A key characteristic doctrine of government contracting law concerns the limited authority of the government's agents. As made clear by the leading case, *OPM v. Richmond*, this doctrine has major significance at a number of levels. In the sphere of private contracts and other private interactions, the authority to act has sufficient significance to form an important part of the course taught under the various headings of "agency and partnership," "corporations," and "business organization." That is, in the private sector, whenever forming contracts and similar interactions between any private entities (other than two individuals acting directly for themselves), the legal question arises of the authority of the persons or entities communicating during the contract formation or similar interaction to bind the entities or other individuals that they represent. Concretely, private economic activity regularly turns on whether a corporation, partnership, or other entity is bound when an employee negotiates the contract, or when superior officers higher in the entity sanction it, or, perhaps, only when some central governing body like the corporation's board of directors expressly considers and approves it.

Even compared to the law of authority regarding private entities, the law of the limited authority of government agents has new and intriguing aspects. In the government sector, the issues carry much greater significance than in private sector relations. They go to the heart of the legal nature of the public sphere and, particularly, the public sphere in American law, as distinct from the private sphere. The twin notions underlying the nature of a federal government sphere consist of a Constitution constraining all arms of government and a set of democratic processes making Congress and the President representative institutions of a sovereign body of citizens. These notions make the entire system of government turn on a set of legal doctrines regarding authority, for this is how the Constitution and the representative Congress and President direct and control the actions of the government's employees. In a government contracting interaction, the authority on the private side follows the simple rules of the law of agency. By contract, the authority on the public side follows a much more complex, subtle, and important set of rules, intended to make the Constitution, its statutory implementation, and the activity of the Congress and the President relevant and decisive factors in what the entire government can and cannot do.

Calling this doctrine by its superficial terms, that "estoppel does not run against the government," or that government agents do not have "apparent authority," hardly begin to express the significance of this doctrine. Describing this as an estoppel issue makes it sound like it matters only insofar as some particular defense available in equity, an estoppel, is unavailable. Many government contracting officers could work for an entire career without their actions coming before a court of equity, and they might comfortably carry out an entire lifetime of responsibility without any need to think of the word *estoppel*. Yet rare is the responsible government contracting officer who does not act with considerable familiarity with both the content of some body of constraining regulations or the like (such as departmental or military-service guidelines, agency manuals, bureau instructions, or standard government forms), and an intimate feel for how that substantive body of constraining regulations defines that officer's sphere of activity. In a word, employees must go "by the book." The doctrine of limited authority of government agents defines what they do, carrying far more weight than simply preventing the private persons with whom they interact from raising the particular equitable issue of estoppel.

Thus, one of the great steps in the transition from familiarity with basic contract law to government contracting law is coming to understand the workings of the doctrine of the limited authority of government agents. Administrative law also involves the issues of the discretion of administrative agencies; the government's contracting officers in some respects act as merely another kind of administrator, like a licensing officer or an officer who manages administrative cases. Even from there, it is a new leap from the concept of an administrator's discretion in the regulatory and administrative sphere to the new sphere of contracting activity.

On the one hand, statutes and regulations confine a contracting officer's discretion so that even government officers who believe and act as though they could take a contracting action may turn out unable to do so. Their statements of agreement or advice, and even their signatures on agreements and orders, do not signify that the government who they appear to represent so agrees or so orders. On the other hand, within such contracting officers' sphere of discretion and authority these officers may well be able to take contracting actions which would draw disagreement from their superiors in the government, their colleagues, or even sound-thinking predecessors, colleagues, and successors in their own office. The lawyer practicing government contracting law develops an acute feel for what actions the subordinates of a contracting officer can take, what actions only a fully authorized contracting officer can take, and what actions even a contracting officer cannot take or takes without binding effect.

The high significance of this doctrine comes through in the leading case on this subject, *OPM v. Richmond*, at the start of today's government contracting book, just as the predecessor Supreme Court opinion, *Federal Crop Insurance Corp v. Merrill*, 332 U.S. 380 (1947)(discussed in a note after the *OPM* case), started government contracting courses from the 1940s to the 1990s. *OPM v. Richmond* develops the issue with emphasis on the Constitution's Appropriations Clause and the body of law regarding public money. That body of law, referred to herein as appropriations law, budget law, or fiscal law, will come up again later in this book.

Note that *OPM v. Richmond* concerns, in one respect, a type of government program that will not arise again in this book, namely a benefits program for disabled government employees. While many ties exist between the subjects of government contracting and government benefits, the line has to be drawn somewhere to keep the subject of government contracting manageable in size. However, the doctrine of the limited authority of government employees applies the same to the law of government contracts and the law of government benefits. Only the particular statutory system of retirement benefits will not recur.

The doctrine of the limited authority of government agents has another important variant: as for those actions which the government can take, even these can only be taken by the particular government agents, acting in the particular way, contemplated by the authorization, and not by other government agents acting in other ways. *Mil-Spec Contractors, Inc. v. United States* exemplifies this doctrinal variant. Just as the doctrine of *OPM v. Richmond* allows the law to define what a government agency can and cannot do, the doctrine in *Mil-Spec* allows the law to define who can do it and how it can be done. This has intriguing implications all throughout government contracting. Relatively few government agents have the authority of full "contracting officers," compared to the larger numbers of those who assist them and who frequently handle virtually all the actual details of contact with contractors. Conversely, questions also arise of the extent to which the superiors of contracting officers, from slightly higher-grade civil servants up to the President, can issue them commands about decisions that statutes put in the contracting officers' own hands, like the decisions to terminate a contract. Contracting decisions are power. In a word, these doctrines determine who has that power.

For further discussion of the issues in this section see: Michael Cameron Pitou, *Equitable Estoppel: Its Genesis, Development and Application in Government Contracting*, 19 Pub. Cont. L.J. 606 (1990); Joel P. Shedd, *Principles of Authority on Contracting Officers in Administration of Government Contracts*, 5 Pub. Cont. L.J. 88 (1972).

Office of Personnel Management, Petitioner v. Charles Richmond

No. 88-1943. Supreme Court of the United States
496 U.S. 414
Argued Feb. 21, 1990
Decided June 11, 1990

Justice KENNEDY delivered the opinion of the Court.

This case presents the question whether erroneous oral and written advice given by a Government employee to a benefits claimant may give rise to estoppel against the Government and so entitle the claimant to a monetary payment not otherwise permitted by law. We hold that payments of money from the Federal Treasury are limited to those authorized by statute, and we reverse the contrary holding of the Court of Appeals.

I

Not wishing to exceed a statutory limit on earnings that would disqualify him from a disability annuity, respondent Charles Richmond sought advice from a federal employee and received erroneous information. As a result he earned more than permitted by the eligibility requirements of the relevant statute and lost six months of benefits. Respondent now claims that the erroneous and unauthorized advice should give rise to equitable estoppel against the Government, and that we should order payment of the benefits contrary to the statutory terms. Even on the assumption that much equity subsists in respondent's claim, we cannot agree with him or the Court of Appeals that we have authority to order the payment he seeks.

Respondent was a welder at the Navy Public Works Center in San Diego, California. He left this position in 1981 after petitioner, the Office of Personnel Management (OPM), approved his application for a disability retirement. OPM determined that respondent's impaired eyesight prevented him from performing his job and made him eligible for a disability annuity under 5 U.S.C. § 8337(a). Section 8337(a) provides this benefit for disabled federal employees who have completed five years of service. The statute directs, however, that the entitlement to disability payments will end if the retired employee is "restored to an earning capacity fairly comparable to the current rate of pay of the position occupied at the time of retirement." § 8337(d).

The statutory rules for restoration of earning capacity are central to this case. Prior to 1982, an individual was deemed restored to earning capacity, and so rendered ineligible for a disability annuity, if

> in each of 2 succeeding calendar years the income of the annuitant from wages or self-employment ... equals at least 80 percent of the current rate of pay of the position occupied immediately before retirement." 5 U.S.C. § 8337(d) (1976 ed.) (emphasis added).

The provision was amended in 1982 by the Omnibus Budget Reconciliation Act, Pub.L. 97-253, 96 Stat. 792, to change the measuring period for restoration of earning capacity from two years to one:

> Earning capacity is deemed restored if in any calendar year the income of the annuitant from wages or self-employment or both equals at least 80 percent of the current rate of pay of the position occupied immediately before retirement. 5 U.S.C. § 8337(d) (emphasis added).

After taking disability retirement for his vision impairment, respondent undertook part-time employment as a schoolbus driver. From 1982 to 1985, respondent earned an average of $12,494 in this job, leaving him under the 80% limit for entitlement to continued annuity payments. In 1986, however, he had an opportunity to earn extra money by working overtime. Respondent asked an employee relations specialist at the Navy Public Works Center's Civilian Personnel Department for information about how much he could earn without exceeding the 80% eligibility limit. Relying upon the terms of the repealed pre-1982 statute, under which respondent could retain the annuity unless his income exceeded the 80% limit in two consecutive years, the specialist gave respondent incorrect advice. The specialist also gave respondent a copy of Attachment 4 to Federal Personnel Manual Letter 831-64, published by OPM, which also stated the former 2-year eligibility rule. The OPM form was correct when written in 1981; but when given to respondent, the form was out of date and therefore inaccurate. Respondent returned to the Navy in January 1987 and again was advised in error that eligibility would be determined under the old 2-year rule.

After receiving the erroneous information, respondent concluded that he could take on the extra work as a schoolbus driver in 1986 while still receiving full disability benefits for impaired vision so long as he kept his income for the previous and following years below the statutory level. He earned $19,936 during 1986, exceeding the statutory eligibility limit. OPM discontinued respondent's disability annuity on June 30, 1987. The annuity was restored on January 1, 1988, since respondent did not earn more than allowed by the statute in 1987. Respondent thus lost his disability payments for a 6-month period, for a total amount of $3,993.

Respondent appealed the denial of benefits to the Merit Systems Protection Board (MSPB).... The MSPB denied respondent's petition for review, and respondent appealed to the Court of Appeals for the Federal Circuit.

A divided panel of the Court of Appeals reversed, accepting respondent's contention that the misinformation from Navy personnel estopped the Government, and that the estoppel required payment of disability benefits despite the statutory provision to the contrary....

We granted certiorari, 493 U.S. 806, 110 S.Ct. 46, 107 L.Ed.2d 15 (1989).

II

From our earliest cases, we have recognized that equitable estoppel will not lie against the Government as it lies against private litigants. In Lee v. Munroe & Thornton, 7 Cranch 366, 3 L.Ed. 373 (1813), we held that the Government could not be bound of an agent unless it were clear that the representations were within the scope of the agent's authority. In The Floyd Acceptances, 7 Wall. 666, 19 L.Ed. 169 (1869), we held that the Government could not be compelled to honor bills of exchange issued by the Secretary of War where there was no statutory authority for the issuance of the bills. In Utah Power & Light Co. v. United States, 243 U.S. 389, 408–409, 37 S.Ct. 387, 391, 61 L.Ed. 791 (1917), we dismissed the argument that unauthorized representations by agents of the Government estopped the United States to prevent erection of power houses and transmission lines across a public forest in violation of a statute: "Of this it is enough to say that the United States is neither bound nor estopped by acts of its officers or agents in entering into an arrangement or agreement to do or cause to be done what the law does not sanction or permit."

The principles of these and many other cases were reiterated in Federal Crop Ins. Corporation v. Merrill, 332 U.S. 380, 68 S.Ct. 1, 92 L.Ed. 10 (1947), the leading case in our modern line of estoppel decisions. In Merrill, a farmer applied for insurance under the Federal Crop Insurance Act to cover his wheat farming operations. An agent of the Federal Crop Insurance Corporation advised the farmer that his entire crop qualified for insurance, and the farmer obtained insurance through the Corporation. After the crop was lost, it was discovered that the agent's advice had been in error, and that part of the farmer's crop was reseeded wheat, not eligible for federal insurance under the applicable regulation. While we recognized the serious hardship caused by the agent's misinformation, we nonetheless rejected the argument that his representations estopped the Government to deny insurance benefits. We recognized that "not even the temptations of a hard case" will provide a basis for ordering recovery contrary to the terms of the regulation, for to do so would disregard "the duty of all courts to observe the conditions defined by Congress for charging the public treasury." Id., at 385–386, 68 S.Ct., at 3–4.

Despite the clarity of these earlier decisions, dicta in our more recent cases have suggested the possibility that there might be some situation in which estoppel against the Government could be appropriate. The genesis of this idea appears to be an observation found at the end of our opinion in Montana v. Kennedy, 366 U.S. 308, 81 S.Ct. 1336, 6 L.Ed.2d 313 (1961). In that case, petitioner brought a declaratory judgment action seeking to establish his American citizenship. After discussing petitioner's two statutory claims at length, we rejected the final argument that a consular official's erroneous advice to petitioner's mother that she could not return to the United States while pregnant prevented petitioner from having been born in the United States and thus deprived him of United States citizenship. Our discussion was limited to the observation that in light of the fact that no legal obstacle prevented petitioner's mother from returning to the United States,

> what may have been only the consular official's well-meant advice — 'I am sorry, Mrs., you cannot [return to the United States] in that condition' — falls far short of misconduct such as might prevent the United States from relying on petitioner's foreign birth. In this situation, we need not stop to inquire whether, as some lower courts have held, there may be circumstances in which the United States is estopped to deny citizenship because of the conduct of its officials. Id., at 314–315, 81 S.Ct., at 1340–1341.

The proposition about which we did not "stop to inquire" in Kennedy has since taken on something of a life of its own. Our own opinions have continued to mention the possibility, in the course of rejecting estoppel arguments, that some type of "affirmative misconduct" might give rise to estoppel against the Government. See INS v. Hibi, 414 U.S. 5, 8, 94 S.Ct. 19, 21, 38 L.Ed.2d 7 (1973) (per curiam) ("While the issue of whether 'affirmative misconduct' on the part of the Government might estop it from denying citizenship was left open in Montana v. Kennedy, 366 U.S. 308, 314, 315, 81 S.Ct. 1336, 1340, 1341, 6 L.Ed.2d 313 (1961), no conduct of the sort there adverted to was involved here"); Schweiker v. Hansen, 450 U.S. 785, 788, 101 S.Ct. 1468, 1470, 67 L.Ed.2d 685 (1981) (per curiam) (denying an estoppel claim for Social Security benefits on the authority of Merrill, supra, but observing that the Court "has never decided what type of conduct by a Government employee will estop the Government from insisting upon compliance with valid regulations governing the distribution of welfare benefits"); INS v. Miranda, 459 U.S. 14, 19, 103 S.Ct. 281, 283, 74 L.Ed.2d 12 (1982) (per curiam) ("This case does not require us to reach the question we reserved in Hibi, whether affirmative misconduct in a particular case would estop the Government from enforcing the immigration laws"); Heckler v. Community Health Services, 467 U.S., at 60, 104 S.Ct., at 2224 ("We have left the issue open in the past, and do so again today").

The language in our decisions has spawned numerous claims for equitable estoppel in the lower courts....

The Solicitor General proposes to remedy the present confusion in this area of the law with a sweeping rule. As it has in the past, the Government asks us to adopt "a flat rule that estoppel may not in any circumstances run against the Government." Community Health Services, supra, 467 U.S., at 60, 104 S.Ct., at 2224.... Petitioner advances as a second basis for this rule the doctrine of separation of powers. Petitioner contends that to recognize estoppel based on the misrepresentations of Executive Branch officials would give those misrepresentations the force of law, and thereby invade the legislative province reserved to Congress. This rationale, too, supports the petitioner's contention that estoppel may never justify an order requiring executive action contrary to a relevant statute, no matter what statute or what facts are involved.

We have recognized before that the "arguments the Government advances for the rule are substantial." Community Health Services, supra, 467 U.S., at 60, 104 S.Ct., at 2224. And we agree that this case should be decided under a clearer form of analysis than "we will know an estoppel when we see one." Hansen, supra, at 792, 101 S.Ct., at 1473 (MARSHALL, J., dissenting). But it remains true that we need not embrace a rule that no estoppel will lie against the Government in any case in order to decide this case. We leave for another day whether an estoppel claim could ever succeed against the Government. A narrower ground of decision is sufficient to address the type of suit presented here, a claim for payment of money from the Public Treasury contrary to a statutory appropriation.

III

The Appropriations Clause of the Constitution, Art. I, § 9, cl. 7, provides that: "No Money shall be drawn from the Treasury, but in Consequence of Appropriations made by Law." For the particular type of claim at issue here, a claim for money from the Federal Treasury, the Clause provides an explicit rule of decision. Money may be paid out only through an appropriation made by law; in other words, the payment of money from the Treasury must be authorized by a statute. All parties here agree that the award respondent seeks would be in direct contravention of the federal statute upon which his ultimate claim to the funds must rest, 5 U.S.C. § 8337. The point is made clearer when the appropriation supporting the benefits sought by respondent is examined. In the same subchapter of the United States Code as the eligibility requirements, Congress established the Civil Service Retirement and Disability Fund. § 8348(a)(1)(A). That section states in pertinent part: "The Fund ... is appropriated for the payment of ... benefits as provided by this subchapter...." (Emphasis added.) The benefits respondent claims were not "provided by" the relevant provision of the subchapter; rather, they were specifically denied. It follows that Congress has appropriated no money for the payment of the benefits respondent seeks, and the Constitution prohibits that any money "be drawn from the Treasury" to pay them.

Our cases underscore the straightforward and explicit command of the Appropriations Clause. "It means simply that no money can be paid out of the Treasury unless it has been appropriated by an act of Congress." Cincinnati Soap Co. v. United States, 301 U.S. 308, 321, 57 S.Ct. 764, 770, 81 L.Ed. 1122 (1937) (citing Reeside v. Walker, 11 How. 272, 291, 13 L.Ed. 693 (1851)). In Reeside, supra, we addressed a claim brought by the holder of a judgment of indebtedness against the United States that the Secretary of the Treasury of the United States should be ordered to enter the claim upon the books of the Treasury so that the debt might be paid. In rejecting petitioner's claim for relief, we stated as an alternative ground for decision that if

> the petition in this case was allowed so far as to order the verdict against the United States to be entered on the books of the Treasury Department, the plaintiff would be as far from having a claim on the Secretary or Treasurer to pay it as now. The difficulty in the way is the want of any appropriation by Congress to pay this claim. It is a well-known constitutional provision, that no money can be taken or drawn from the Treasury except under an appropriation by Congress. See Constitution, art. 1, § 9 (1 Stat. at Large, 15).
>
> However much money may be in the Treasury at any one time, not a dollar of it can be used in the payment of any thing not thus previously sanctioned. Any other course would give to the fiscal officers a most dangerous discretion. Id., at 291.

The command of the Clause is not limited to the relief available in a judicial proceeding seeking payment of public funds. Any exercise of a power granted by the Constitution to one of the other branches of Government is limited by a valid reservation of congressional control over funds in the Treasury. ...

We have not had occasion in past cases presenting claims of estoppel against the Government to discuss the Appropriations Clause, for reasons that are apparent. Given the strict rule against estoppel applied as early as 1813 in Lee v. Munroe & Thornton, 7 Cranch 366, 3 L.Ed. 373, claims of estoppel could be dismissed on that ground without more. In our cases following Montana v. Kennedy, 366 U.S. 308, 81 S.Ct. 1336, 6 L.Ed.2d 313 (1961), reserving the possibility that estoppel might lie on some facts, we have held only that the particular facts presented were insufficient. As discussed, supra, at 2470–2471, we decline today to accept the Solicitor General's argument for an across-the-board no-estoppel rule. But this makes it all the more important to state the law and to settle the matter of estoppel as a basis for money claims against the Government.

Our decision is consistent with both the holdings and the rationale expressed in our estoppel precedents. Even our recent cases evince a most strict approach to estoppel claims involving public funds. See Community Health Services, 467 U.S., at 63, 104 S.Ct., at 2225 ("Protection of the public fisc requires that those who seek public funds act with scrupulous regard for the requirements of law"). The course of our jurisprudence shows why: Opinions have differed on whether this Court has ever accepted an estoppel claim in other contexts, see id., at 60, 104 S.Ct., at 224 (suggesting that United States v. Pennsylvania Industrial Chemical Corp., 411 U.S. 655, 93 S.Ct. 1804, 36 L.Ed.2d 567 (1973) (PICCO), was decided on estoppel grounds); id., at 68, 104 S.Ct., at 2228 (opinion of REHNQUIST, J.) (PICCO not an estoppel case), but not a single case has upheld an estoppel claim against the Government for the payment of money. And our cases denying estoppel are animated by the same concerns that prompted the Framers to include the Appropriations Clause in the Constitution. As Justice Story described the Clause:

> "The object is apparent upon the slightest examination. It is to secure regularity, punctuality, and fidelity, in the disbursements of the public money. As all the taxes raised from the people, as well as revenues arising from other sources, are to be applied to the discharge of the expenses, and debts, and other engagements of the government, it is highly proper, that congress should possess the power to decide how and when any money should be applied for these purposes. If it were otherwise, the executive would possess an unbounded power over the public purse of the nation; and might apply all its moneyed resources at his pleasure. The power to control and direct the appropriations, constitutes a most useful and salutary check upon profusion and extravagance, as well as upon corrupt influence and public peculation...."
> 2 Commentaries on the Constitution of the United States § 1348 (3d ed. 1858).

The obvious practical consideration cited by Justice Story for adherence to the requirement of the Clause is the necessity, existing now as much as at the time the Constitution was ratified, of preventing fraud and corruption. We have long ago accepted this ground as a reason that claims for estoppel cannot be entertained where public money is at stake, refusing to "introduce a rule against an abuse, of which, by improper collusions, it would be very difficult for the public to protect itself." Lee, supra, at 370. But the Clause has a more fundamental and comprehensive purpose, of direct relevance to the case before us. It is to assure that public funds will be spent according to the letter of the difficult judgments reached by Congress as to the common good and not according to the individual favor of Government agents or the individual pleas of litigants.

Extended to its logical conclusion, operation of estoppel against the Government in the context of payment of money from the Treasury could in fact render the Appropriations

Clause a nullity. If agents of the Executive were able, by their unauthorized oral or written statements to citizens, to obligate the Treasury for the payment of funds, the control over public funds that the Clause reposes in Congress in effect could be transferred to the Executive. If, for example, the President or Executive Branch officials were displeased with a new restriction on benefits imposed by Congress to ease burdens on the fisc (such as the restriction imposed by the statutory change in this case) and sought to evade them, agency officials could advise citizens that the restrictions were inapplicable. Estoppel would give this advice the practical force of law, in violation of the Constitution.

* * *

Respondent points to no authority in precedent or history for the type of claim he advances today. Whether there are any extreme circumstances that might support estoppel in a case not involving payment from the Treasury is a matter we need not address. As for monetary claims, it is enough to say that this Court has never upheld an assertion of estoppel against the Government by a claimant seeking public funds. In this context there can be no estoppel, for courts cannot estop the Constitution. The judgment of the Court of Appeals is

Reversed.

Justice WHITE, with whom Justice BLACKMUN joins, concurring.

I agree that the Government may not be estopped in cases such as this one and therefore join the opinion and judgment of the Court. I write separately to note two limitations to the Court's decision. First, the Court wisely does not decide that the Government may not be estopped under any circumstances. Ante, at 2471. In my view, the case principally relied on by respondent, United States v. Pennsylvania Industrial Chemical Corp., 411 U.S. 655, 93 S.Ct. 1804, 36 L.Ed.2d 567 (1973) (PICCO), may well have been decided on the basis of estoppel. But there is a world of difference between PICCO and this case: In PICCO, the courts were asked to prevent the Government from exercising its lawful discretionary authority in a particular case whereas here the courts have been asked to require the Executive Branch to violate a congressional statute. The Executive Branch does not have the dispensing power on its own, see Kendall v. United States ex rel. Stokes, 12 Pet. 524, 613, 9 L.Ed. 1181 (1838), and should not be granted such a power by judicial authorization.

Second, although the Court states that "[a]ny exercise of a power granted by the Constitution to one of the other branches of Government is limited by a valid reservation of congressional control over funds in the Treasury," ante, at 2472, the Court does not state that statutory restrictions on appropriations may never fall even if they violate a command of the Constitution such as the Just Compensation Clause, cf. Jacobs v. United States, 290 U.S. 13, 54 S.Ct. 26, 78 L.Ed. 142 (1933), or if they encroach on the powers reserved to another branch of the Federal Government. Although Knote v. United States, 95 U.S. 149, 154, 24 L.Ed. 442 (1877), held that the President's pardon power did not extend to the appropriation of moneys in the Treasury without authorization by law for the benefit of pardoned criminals, it did not hold that Congress could impair the President's pardon power by denying him appropriations for pen and paper.

[Other concurring and dissenting opinions are omitted.]

Notes and Questions

1. Cutting off the employee's disability benefits in this case struck the Ninth Circuit as so unfair that the court of appeals strained the law a long way — more, as it turned out,

than the Supreme Court would let it — to rule for the employee. Does cutting off the employee's benefits strike you, too, as extremely unfair? The doctrine that estoppel does not run against the government often seems cruel in operation. Some students of the law, particularly those who (to their credit) have been slow to abandon the basic notions of sympathy, fairness, and justice as guidance, may read this case and this doctrine as simply a harsh, mean, even absurdist statement that government contracting law excludes what would otherwise be essential elements of decency without anything in its place. Certainly the Supreme Court does not offer anything particularly sympathetic or emotionally "warm" even as dicta, recognizing that its kindler and gentler past dicta have spawned lower court elaborations that undermine the heart of its doctrine.

Could you portray the argument for the government, that is, for the limited authority of its agents, in ways that would appeal to more widely shared values than just an acceptance that law can sometimes be strict, rigid, and pitiless? The notions of a government of limited powers and of the "rule of law" rather than men, often appeals to libertarian and populist sentiments. The opinion's specific notion of a particularly tight requirement of authorization for decisions about spending appeals to particular libertarian and populist sentiments having to do with who, in Anglo-American democracy, wields the power of the purse. To put it differently, how much is this case about penalizing a (blameless) retired Navy welder as the only way to constrain the power of a (blameworthy) Navy employee relations specialist by rendering the specialist's advice ineffective? Focus on that mistaken Navy employee relations specialist. Even if you are very sympathetic to the welder, do you want that mistaken specialist empowered to override the law as made by a Congress authorized by the Constitution and responsible to the electorate? Tight statutory "pocketbook" control means that to the extent that individuals must yield up their money as taxes, it is spent only pursuant to the formally enacted collective decisions of their elected representatives. This means that Navy specialists, whether in the employee benefits or the artillery-firing departments, cannot act out either their merciful or their martial sentiments without public authorization. You might want Navy specialists to be able to give potent disability benefits advice, even without authorization; would you want them able to start wars that way?

2. Note how the Court draws a distinction between the limited sphere of Government agent decisions directly concerned with public money, for which it makes a strict rule against agent authority, and the sphere of other Government agent decisions, which it carefully does not, for now, address. Consider how this applies technically in government contracting. Some decisions of contracting officers directly concern money: the prices at which procurement occurs, or, many decisions on money that occur with changes, modifications, claims, and terminations. What about the decisions of contracting officers that do not directly concern money, but concern such matters as the timing of what is being provided or the details of reporting and disclosure duties? Suppose the employment specialist's advice had supplanted not a substantive element of the retired welder's right to disability payments, but rather the frequency with which the welder must submit some kind of required report to OPM? *See Joseph DeVito v. United States*, 188 Ct. Cl. 979 (1969)(waiver, by government employee delay, of opportunity to terminate for default).

3. Note the distinction between the doctrines of estoppel and finality. For example, the opinion mentions without further analysis that the retired welder exceeded the eligibility limit during 1986, but OPM did not discontinue his disability annuity until June 30, 1987. Suppose that means the retired welder got benefits to which he was not entitled from January through June of 1987, but, on the other hand, suppose the disability statute makes such payments relatively final so that there is no way to recoup wrong payments.

So the welder might have gotten and kept six months of benefits (January through July, 1987) to which he was not entitled. How do you square the retention on finality grounds by the welder of six months of benefits to which he was not entitled, with the Court's reasoning for his not getting, on estoppel grounds, six more months of benefits (July through December)? If it is a constitutional imperative that the taxpayer's money not end up without authorization in the private party's pocket, what is he doing with that six months of benefits?

4. Decisions since OPM v. Richmond have preserved a sphere for estoppel and the similar doctrine of laches. In *Burnside-Ott Aviation Training Ctr., Inc. v. United States*, 985 F.2d 1574, 1581 (Fed. Cir. 1993), the Court remanded the issue of equitable estoppel. It found that the Claims Court improperly relied on *OPM*, when Burnside-Ott's assertion was not based on a statutory entitlement, but rather on a contract with the Navy. However, the *Burnside-Ott* ruling did not negate the relevance of *OPM* when equitable estoppel against the government was sought to prevent conducting a competitive bid process. *Westinghouse Electric Corp. v. United States Dep't of Navy*, 894 F. Supp. 204 (W.D. Pa. 1995), 41 Fed. Cl. 229 (1998). The notion of asserting laches against the government remains unclear since *OPM*. In *JANA, Inc. v. United States*, 936 F.2d 1265 (Fed. Cir. 1991), *cert. denied*, 112 S. Ct. 869 (1992), the Court of Appeals reversed the Claims Court, holding that the government's actions in delaying an audit and the issuance of the contracting officer's assessment of overcharges by the contractor were not unreasonable and inexcusable so as to constitute laches.

5. Note on Federal Crop Ins. Corp. v. Merrill, 332 U.S. 680 (1947). OPM v. Richmond describes the case of FCIC v. Merrill as "the leading case in our modern line of estoppel decisions." In that case, farmers applied for and received federal crop insurance on government advice, and then, after their crop was destroyed by drought, the Court held that erroneous advice by the government's agents did not bind the government to admit coverage. A private insurer would not be allowed to deny coverage in a similar situation. In Merrill, besides the basic logic of the limited authority of government agents, the Court threw in that the public is "charged with knowledge" of limitations on authority in statutes and in regulations published in the Federal Register, which were incorporated by reference in the crop insurance application. But, Justice Jackson's dissent took on the Federal Register argument, lambasting the "absurdity" of expecting farmers to "peruse this voluminous and dull publication," and doubting, too, "that a reading of technically worded regulations would enlighten" the farmer "much in any event." If disabled navy welders and insurance-obtaining wheat farmers with every appropriate reason to rely on government advice cannot win on this issue, what chance does a government contractor have?

Mil-Spec Contractors, Inc., Plaintiff-Appellant, v. The United States, Defendant-Appellee

No. 87-1203

835 F.2d 865

United States Court of Appeals, Federal Circuit

Dec. 16, 1987

Before FRIEDMAN, SMITH, and MAYER, Circuit Judges.

FRIEDMAN, Circuit Judge.

This is an appeal from a decision of the Armed Services Board of Contract Appeals (Board), dismissing a contractor's claim for additional compensation on the ground that an oral agreement to settle the claims constituted an accord and satisfaction. Mil-Spec Contractors, Inc., 87-1 B.C.A. (CCH) ¶ 19,391 (Sept. 23, 1986). We hold that there was not a valid accord and satisfaction, and therefore reverse and remand.

I

The government awarded to the predecessor of the appellant Mil-Spec Contractors, Inc. (Mil-Spec), a contract to insulate certain buildings on Norton Air Force Base in California. The contract was funded from an Air Force general account for energy conservation. The Air Force allocated approximately $622,000 for the work. The contract price was $581,247, and a contingency fund of $6,000 to $7,000 was available for contract modifications.

After completing the work, Mil-Spec submitted to the government a series of increasing claims for additional costs it allegedly incurred. After Mil-Spec had rejected several of the government's proposals for additional payment, Mr. Hooppaw, the resident contracting officer (who was also the resident engineer), telephoned Mr. Barnes, Mil-Spec's principal officer, in late August or early September 1983. Mr. Hooppaw explained that he could not obtain extra funds for additional payment under the contract because the money came from an appropriation that would expire on September 30, 1983, and that after that date the $6,000–$7,000 in the contingency fund would not be available. Mr. Barnes was advised that if he did not agree to a settlement, "the only other way to get funds is to go to court."

Three days before the funds would expire, Mr. Barnes and Mr. Barker, a negotiator, had several telephone conversations during which they orally agreed upon a settlement. Mr. Barker's notes state that Mr. Barnes

> agreed to drop his proposal of [a] $70,956.00 increase in Contract amount and accept the Government estimate amount of $6,367.00. In doing so, the contractor requested that all remaining funds (less $100.00) be paid to him with this settlement.
>
> Both parties agreed to accept [a] $6367.00 increase in [the] Contract amount as fair and reasonable. The Contract time was extended 87 calendar days to a final completion date of 20 June 1980. The negotiated price of $6367.00 is hereby accepted subject to approval of the Contracting Officer.

The contracting officer, Mr. Hooppaw, then prepared a contract modification (standard form 30), signed it and mailed it to Mr. Barnes for his signature. In the interval, an Internal Revenue Service (IRS) employee had told Mr. Barnes that with a legitimate claim Mr. Barnes could have obtained more than the government had offered. Mr. Barnes telephoned Mr. Hooppaw and stated that he did not accept the government's settlement offer.

On September 30, 1983, the government issued a check for $6,367 to the IRS because of a previously filed tax lien.

Mil-Spec filed with the contracting officer a claim for its alleged additional costs. When the contracting officer failed to decide the claim within a reasonable time, Mil-Spec appealed to the Board. After a hearing, the Board held that the oral settlement agreement constituted an accord and satisfaction, and denied the appeal.

II

The Court of Claims, the decisions of which are binding precedents in this court, South Corp. v. United States, 690 F.2d 1368, 1370 (Fed.Cir.1982), has stated:

The essential elements of an effective accord and satisfaction are proper subject matter, competent parties, meeting of the minds of the parties, and consideration.

Brock & Blevins Co. v. United States, 343 F.2d 951, 955 (Ct.Cl.1965) (quoting Nevada Half Moon Mining Co. v. Combined Metals Reduction Co., 176 F.2d 73, 76 (10th Cir.1949), cert. denied, 338 U.S. 943, 70 S.Ct. 429, 94 L.Ed. 581 (1950)).

Relying on that decision, the Board held:

> These essential elements are fully met in this appeal. There is no question concerning either the propriety of subject matter or the competence of the parties. Both parties agree that there was a meeting of the minds and the fact that this was an oral agreement does not change its legal effect. Consideration was shown by the check which the Government issued and which, because of a prior tax lien, was paid to IRS for appellant's account thus diminishing its outstanding delinquent taxes. Appellant agreed to accept that amount for a full settlement of all outstanding claims.

Mil-Spec Contractors, Inc., 87-1 B.C.A. (CCH) ¶ 19,391 (Sept. 23, 1986).

The ruling of the Board has three fatal flaws: (A) There was no valid oral agreement because Mr. Barker, the negotiator, had no authority to bind the government to the settlement; (B) as the government recognized, the accord and satisfaction constituted a modification of the contract which was required to be in writing and signed by both parties; and (C) the government's "payment" to Mil-Spec of $6,367 by sending a check for that amount to the IRS did not comply with the terms of the oral agreement and therefore did not constitute consideration adequate to support the alleged accord and satisfaction.

A. "It is well established that a purported agreement with the United States is not binding unless the other party can show that the official with whom the agreement was made had authority to bind the Government." S.E.R., Jobs for Progress, Inc. v. United States, 759 F.2d 1, 4 (Fed.Cir.1985) (citations omitted). The oral agreement was a modification of the contract, since it increased the amount the government would pay for the work Mil-Spec had done. Only the contracting officer was authorized to bind the government to such a modification. Cf. 48 C.F.R. § 2.101 (1986) ("'Contracting officer' means a person with the authority to enter into, administer, and/or terminate contracts and make related determinations and findings.").

Mr. Barker, who negotiated the oral settlement with Mr. Barnes, was not the contracting officer but only a negotiator. As such, he had no authority to commit the government. As Mr. Barker himself recognized, only the contracting officer had that authority: Mr. Barker's notes of the negotiation and agreement stated that the "negotiated price of $6,367.00" was "accepted subject to approval of the Contracting Officer."

The contracting officer also recognized this fact, since he prepared and signed a form 30 contract modification document that embodied the oral settlement previously negotiated. Unless and until there was a binding modification to which both Mil-Spec and the contracting officer had agreed in writing, there could not be a binding modification of the contract. The oral agreement of September 27, 1983, could not and did not constitute a valid accord and satisfaction. The contracting officer's subsequent approval of the oral agreement, reflected in his signature of the written contract modification form he prepared, did not nunc pro tunc turn the prior oral agreement into a valid contractual commitment that bound the government.

B. The Federal Acquisition Regulations applicable to the contract in this case require that a modification of a contract be in writing and executed by both parties. Federal Acquisition Regulations System, 48 C.F.R. § 2.101 (1986), the Definitions section, states in pertinent part:

> "Contract" means a mutually binding legal relationship.... It includes all types of commitments that obligate the Government to an expenditure of appropriated funds and that, except as otherwise authorized, are in writing.... contracts include ... bilateral contract modifications.

Pertinent provisions of 48 C.F.R. provide as follows:

> § 43.101 (1986):

> "Contract modification" means any written change in the terms of a contract (see 43.103).

* * *

> "Supplemental agreement" means a contract modification that is accomplished by the mutual action of the parties.

> § 43.103 (1986):

> Contract modifications are of the following types:

> (a) Bilateral. A bilateral modification (supplemental agreement) is a contract modification that is signed by the contractor and the contracting officer....

> § 43.301 (1986):

> (a)(1) The Standard Form 30 (SF 30), Amendment of Solicitation/Modification of Contract, shall ... be used for —

* * *

> (v) Supplemental agreements (see 43.103);

Thus, any bilateral modification of a contract is a "supplemental agreement," which requires the execution of a written standard form 30.

Mr. Hooppaw, the contracting officer, recognized that the oral settlement agreement that Mr. Barker had negotiated with Mr. Barnes would not be effective until both the contracting officer and Mr. Barnes had signed a written modification agreement. After the oral settlement had been negotiated, Mr. Hooppaw prepared a written modification agreement, signed it, and sent it to Mr. Barnes to sign. If Mr. Hooppaw had believed that the oral settlement itself was a valid agreement that bound both parties to the contract, there would have been no need for him to prepare the form 30 contract modification agreement. All he need have done was to have written a simple letter to Mr. Barnes summarizing and confirming the oral agreement.

In SCM Corp. v. United States, 595 F.2d 595, 598 (1979), the Court of Claims held that where the pertinent regulations required that contract modifications be written, an oral modification that had not been reduced to writing and signed by both parties was ineffective. The situation in SCM was analogous to that in the present case.

In SCM the contractor sought an equitable adjustment of approximately $122,000. The contracting officer and the contractor by telephone agreed to settle the dispute for $55,000. Preparation of the written contract modification provision was delayed because the agency lacked funds to make the payment. When the contracting officer finally sent the written modification, the contractor refused to sign it on the ground that it did not properly reflect the oral agreement.

The contractor then filed suit for the $55,000, alleging a breach of the oral settlement agreement. The Court of Claims rejected the claim on the ground that the governing Armed Services Procurement Regulations, the pertinent provisions of which were similar to the Acquisition Regulations involved in this case, "require that settlements are written contracts to be executed on standard form 30." 595 F.2d at 598. . . .

C. The oral settlement agreement contemplated and provided that the $6,367 would be paid to Mr. Barnes. . . . Although the government may have acted within its legal authority in making payment to the IRS, such payment cannot be said to have been a term of the settlement to which Mr. Barnes agreed.

CONCLUSION

The decision of the Armed Services Board of Contract Appeals is reversed, and the case is remanded to the Board to consider the merits of Mil-Spec's claim.

REVERSED and REMANDED.

Notes and Questions

1. The court does not resolve this case by an absence of offer and acceptance, nor by a requirement of a writing under the Statute of Frauds. Both these rules apply, in appropriate circumstances, to government contracts. Evidently, the agreement between the government negotiator and the government contractor satisfies offer and acceptance and does not require a writing as a matter of basic contract law. Moreover, the court does not suggest that any stronger or higher principles of offer and acceptance, or any stronger or higher form of the Statute of Frauds, applies. What, then, are the issues?

2. Note the importance in the case of Standard Form 30, the classic embodiment of government contract modifications. Basic contract law discusses "formalities." The requirement of consideration and the Statute of Frauds exemplify such formalities: a seller's solemn oral commitment to offer a house for purchase to a buyer thirty days hence for just $100,000 is not binding; the same commitment, for which the buyer pays $100 and receives a written receipt with the key details on it, is binding. Yet, the importance in government contracting law of standard forms and standard clauses dwarfs the importance of formalities in basic contract law. Why? Is there something more than the service of bureaucratic order and convenience?

3. Meeting in this case the contracting officer's "negotiator" begins to suggest the cast of characters in the drama of government contracting. Soon, the cast will include many different kinds of contracting officers to handle different phases of major contracts: the Procuring Contracting Officer ("PCO"), the Administrative Contracting Officer ("ACO"), and, that dreaded creature, the Terminating Contracting Officer ("TCO") (perhaps known to colleagues as "The Terminator" and played in the movies by Arnold Schwarzenegger). A larger population consists of the many representatives and assistants, like the negotiator here, such as technical representatives, legal advisers, and accounting assistants. A recurring question consists of whether a contracting officer can delegate authority to these assistants when the contracting officer plainly expresses her wish to do so, particularly on matters calling for the assistants' specialized expertise and which the contracting officer fears, with reason, will only be hindered in execution by failure to delegate. Would this case have come out differently if the contracting officer gave the negotiator an SF 30 signed in blank? Suppose the contracting officer told both the negotiator and the contractor that the negotiator had full authority to reach agreement within a range of outcomes known to the officer, and the negotiator then did so?

Harbert/Lummus Agrifuels Projects, et al., Plaintiffs-Cross Appellants, v. The United States, Defendant-Appellant

Nos. 97-5047, 97-5052
United States Court of Appeals, Federal Circuit
142 F.3d 1429
April 21, 1998

Before SCHALL, Circuit Judge, FRIEDMAN, Senior Circuit Judge, and GAJARSA, Circuit Judge.

GAJARSA, Circuit Judge.

The United States seeks review of the decision of the United States Court of Federal Claims in Harbert/Lummus v. United States, 36 Fed. Cl. 494 (1996), holding that the United States entered into an oral, unilateral contract with Harbert/Lummus to continue guaranteeing future borrowing requests until completion of a construction project and awarding Harbert/Lummus damages for breach of this contract. Harbert/Lummus cross-appeals, seeking review of the trial court's method of calculating these damages and refusal to recognize the existence of a second contract to accelerate the construction and payment schedule. Because the contracting officer lacked the authority to enter into the oral, unilateral contract and did not ratify the contract, we reverse the decision of the trial court regarding the existence of a binding contract in which the Department of Energy ("DOE") promised not to suspend its guarantee and vacate the trial court's damages award.

BACKGROUND

The facts of this case have been set out in great detail in the trial court's decision and will be referred to in this opinion only to the extent necessary for an understanding of the issues that give rise to this appeal. During the oil crisis in the late 1970's, the federal government investigated alternative sources of energy. Congress passed the Biomass Energy and Alcohol Fuels Act of 1980 (the "Act"), which created the Alcohol Fuels Program (the "Program") to encourage private companies to design and build alternative fuel energy plants. The Act created the Office of Alcohol Fuels (the "Program Office") within DOE to administer the Program. Specifically, the Program Office was vested with the power to issue government loan guarantees for up to 90 percent of the cost of construction of ethanol and other alternative fuel plants. The Program Office had no independent contracting authority.

One of these loan guarantees was issued to Agrifuels Refining Corporation ("Agrifuels"), which in turn contracted with Harbert/Lummus to construct an ethanol plant. The funds that Agrifuels needed to construct the plant were provided by lending banks and guaranteed by DOE through a loan guarantee agreement and a loan servicing agreement. Harbert/Lummus was not a party to these contracts and was in contractual privity only with Agrifuels through the construction contract. This construction contract provided for a bonus for Harbert/Lummus for early completion and a penalty for late completion.

* * *

During construction of the plant, Harbert/Lummus stated at a meeting at which all the parties were present that it was not receiving timely payments and that it wanted the accelerated construction schedule to be adopted by the parties. The Deputy Director of the Program Office responded that "DOE was committed to funding the project to completion, and if the contractor completes the project, all the payments would work out in the end." Id. at 506. The Deputy Director did not have authority to bind the government. The trial court found that the CO was present at the same meeting, but did not question the offer and was silent after the offer was made. Id. The trial court found that the CO adopted the Deputy Director's statement by his silence and created a new, binding unilateral offer to Harbert/Lummus that the government would continue its role as guarantor of future borrowing requests by Agrifuels in exchange for Harbert/Lummus' continued work on the project. Id. at 513. When Harbert/Lummus continued work on the project, the trial court held that Harbert/Lummus had accepted DOE's offer, thereby creating a binding contract. Id. at 513–14.

Prior to completion of the plant, the ultimate parent companies of Agrifuels declared bankruptcy, triggering an event of default under the loan agreements between Agrifuels and DOE. DOE eventually decided to stop funding the project and Harbert/Lummus sued for damages for breach of DOE's promise to not withdraw its guarantee until completion of the project. The trial court awarded Harbert/Lummus $2,870,768 in damages for breach of this unilateral contract.

This appeal concerns the alleged formation of two oral contracts. The first contract regards the unilateral offer by the Deputy Director to continue guaranteeing Agrifuels' borrowing requests until completion of the project. The second contract regards the alleged acceptance by DOE of an accelerated construction and payment schedule. With regard to the unilateral contract to continue to guarantee funding, the government argues that the trial court erred in recognizing this contract as binding because (1) the Act and its implementing regulations do not authorize DOE to contract directly with construction contractors, (2) DOE could not enter into this oral contract because of restrictions imposed by statute and regulations, (3) the CO was not delegated the authority to enter into such a contract, and (4) the CO did not ratify the contract. In its cross-appeal, Harbert/Lummus argues that the trial court erred in calculating the damages with respect to DOE's breach of this oral agreement. We need only determine whether the CO had the authority to enter into the oral, unilateral contract and whether he ratified such contract....

DISCUSSION

In reviewing judgments of the Court of Federal Claims, we review conclusions of law de novo and findings of fact for clear error. See City of El Centro v. United States, 922 F.2d 816, 819 (Fed. Cir.1990). Because neither party challenges the trial court's findings of fact, we review the trial court's decision with regard to contract formation de novo. See Trauma Serv. Group v. United States, 104 F.3d 1321, 1325 (Fed.Cir.1997) ("In the absence of factual disputes, the question of contract formation is a question of law, reviewable de novo.").

A. The Alleged Contract to Continue Guaranteeing Funding of the Project

It is well established that the government is not bound by the acts of its agents beyond the scope of their actual authority. See Federal Crop Ins. Corp. v. Merrill, 332 U.S. 380, 384, 68 S. Ct. 1, 3, 92 L. Ed. 10 (1947); Trauma Serv. Group, 104 F.3d at 1325. Contractors dealing with the United States must inform themselves of a representative's authority and the limits of that authority. See Federal Crop Ins., 332 U.S. at 384, 68 S. Ct. at 3. Moreover, "anyone entering into an agreement with the Government takes the risk of accurately ascertaining the authority of the agents who purport to act for the Government, and this risk remains with the contractor even when the Government agents themselves may have been unaware of the limitations on their authority." Trauma Serv. Group, 104 F.3d at 1325.

The burden was on Harbert/Lummus to prove that the CO had the authority to enter into the oral, unilateral contract. See id. The fact that Harbert/Lummus may have believed that the CO had authority is irrelevant; Harbert/Lummus must prove that the CO had actual authority. Id. For the reasons set forth below, we hold that the CO did not have authority to enter into an oral contract to continue to guarantee funding of the project until its completion.

The CO's authority to commit and bind DOE contractually was specifically conditioned in his delegation of authority as follows:

> [The CO] is hereby delegated the authority, with respect to actions valued at $50 million or less, to approve, execute, enter into, modify, administer, closeout, terminate and take any other necessary and appropriate action (collectively, "Actions") with respect to Financial Incentive awards on behalf of the Department of Energy without the *prior written approval* of or further delegation being necessary from the Director, Office of Procurement Operations (or designee). However, a separate prior written approval of any such action must be given by or concurred in by [the CO] to accompany the action. At that dollar threshold, a specific delegation from the Director, Office of Procurement Operations (or designee) is not required. This delegation shall include the authority to make all required determinations and decisions, except those that are specifically to be made by other authority.

Thus, the CO's delegation of contracting authority contained a separate and independent provision which required that all actions entered into by him be accompanied by his prior, written approval. Harbert/Lummus directs us to nothing in the record that evidences any separate, prior written approval by the CO of the oral, unilateral contract. Accordingly, the CO was not authorized to bind the government in disregard of this explicit provision. Harbert/Lummus argues that the CO had implied authority to enter into the unilateral contract and that such a contract was "necessary and appropriate" with regard to his actions relating to the Financial Incentive awards. These arguments are unpersuasive in light of the express mandate in the delegation that the CO agree to any action by prior, written approval. Harbert/Lummus also argues that, because the government does not dispute the CO's authority to enter into a written contract with Harbert/Lummus to care for the plant after DOE ceased its guarantees, the CO must have had the authority to enter into the oral, unilateral contract because both contracts stemmed from the CO's authority to minimize DOE's expenses with regard to the project. Again, this argument is unpersuasive because it does not address the fact that the unilateral contract was oral and did not contain the required written approval.

As we have held before, agency procedures must be followed before a binding contract can be formed. See American Gen. Leasing, Inc. v. United States, 218 Ct. Cl. 367, 587 F.2d 54, 57–58 (1978) (holding that express oral agreement with government agent was not binding because, among other factors, applicable regulations required contract to be in writing); New Am. Shipbuilders, Inc. v. United States, 871 F.2d 1077, 1080 (Fed. Cir.1989) ("Oral assurances do not produce a contract implied-in-fact until all the steps have been taken that the agency procedure requires; until then, there is no intent to be bound. Thus, it is irrelevant if the oral assurances emanate from the very official who will have authority at the proper time, to sign the contract or grant."). It appears evident that, if Harbert/Lummus had examined the CO's delegation of authority, it could not have reasonably believed it had entered into a binding contract with the government in the absence of the required written approval by the CO. Because there is no evidence of such prior, written approval by the CO of the unilateral contract, we hold that the CO lacked the authority to enter into the oral contract and it is therefore not binding upon the government. See EWG Assocs., Ltd. v. United States, 231 Ct. Cl. 1028, 1030 (1982) (explaining that the government is not estopped from denying the existence of a contract where the acts upon which the contractor relies are unauthorized); see also OPM v. Richmond, 496 U.S. 414, 420–33, 110 S. Ct. 2465, 2469–76, 110 L.Ed.2d 387 (1990) (explaining that the government is not estopped by the unauthorized acts of its agents).

Even if the CO somehow possessed the authority to enter into the oral contract, we hold that he did not ratify it. The trial court found that the Deputy Director, who did not have any contracting authority, actually made the offer to enter into the unilateral contract. Agreements made by government agents without authority to bind the government may be subsequently ratified by those with authority if the ratifying officials have actual or constructive knowledge of the unauthorized acts. See United States v. Beebe, 180 U.S. 343, 354, 21 S.Ct. 371, 375, 45 L.Ed. 563 (1901). The Supreme Court has stated that:

> Where an agent has acted without authority and it is claimed that the principal has thereafter ratified his act, such ratification can only be based upon a full knowledge of all the facts upon which the unauthorized action was taken. This is as true in the case of the government as in that of an individual. Knowledge is necessary in any event.... If there be want of it, though such want arises from the neglect of the principal, no ratification can be based on any act of his. Knowledge of the facts is the essential element of ratification, and must be shown or such facts proved that its existence is a necessary inference from them.

Id. at 354, 21 S.Ct. at 375.

In our case, the trial court merely found that the CO was present when the Deputy Director made the offer and was silent after the offer was made. There was no finding that the CO even heard the statement. This is not sufficient evidence to support a finding of actual knowledge by the CO of the offer. In addition, the facts as found by the trial court do not support imputing to the CO constructive knowledge of the unilateral contract. The mere fact that Harbert/Lummus continued performing its construction activities would not have put the CO on notice of the existence of a new, unilateral contract because Harbert/Lummus had been performing its construction activities before the offer by the Deputy Director in accordance with its construction contract with Agrifuels. In the absence of either actual or constructive knowledge of the unilateral contract, the CO's silence cannot be a ratification of the unilateral contract. Moreover, ratification must also be based on a demonstrated acceptance of the contract. See EWG Assocs., Ltd., 231 Ct.Cl. at 1030. Silence in and of itself is not sufficient to establish a demonstrated acceptance of the contract by the CO. See id. The silence in this case by the CO was not an assent or acceptance of the oral, unilateral contract.

In addition, as previously discussed, the CO's delegation of authority expressly provided that even a ratification by the CO would have to be in writing. In the absence of such a writing, the CO could not have properly demonstrated his acceptance of the contract. Because we find that the government is not bound by this oral contract to guarantee funding of the project to completion, we reverse the decision of the trial court that there was such a contract and we vacate the trial court's damages award with respect to this alleged contract. We therefore need not reach Harbert/Lummus' argument that such damages were improperly calculated.

CONCLUSION

For the foregoing reasons, we reverse the judgment of the trial court with respect to its recognition of a binding oral, unilateral contract between the government and Harbert/Lummus and therefore we vacate the trial court's damages award for breach of this contract. We affirm the judgment of the trial court with respect to its finding that DOE was not contractually bound to an accelerated construction and payment schedule.

Notes and Questions

1. Like the *Mil-Spec* case, this case does not concern an action which the statutes or regulations place beyond any officials' authority, but only concerns who has the available authority to take that action and whether an official with the authority has exercised it through the authorized procedural mechanism. This time, since the CO did have delegated authority to take contracting steps like modifications, and the CO was the official who entered into the alleged oral, unilateral contract, the issue does not concern whether the official had authority but solely whether that official exercised it through the authorized procedures. The opinion discusses why an it considers the CO's action to be unauthorized insofar as the delegation of authority only authorized written actions. Conceptually or practically, does this differ from the Statute of Frauds? How?

This opinion cites a line of cases after American General Leasing, Inc. v. United States, 587 F.2d 54 (Ct. Cl. 1978), that have found various statutes or regulations barring the enforcement of a merely oral contract. The issue continues to get fought over. In a competing line of cases, courts have found that the government entered implied-in-fact contracts without written agreements. See, e.g., PacOrd, Inc. v. United States, 139 F.3d 1320 (9th Cir. 1998). This line of cases was criticized in Arnie Bruce Mason, Note, *Implied-in-Fact Contracts Under the Federal Acquisition Regulation: Why PacOrd Got It Wrong*, 41 Wm. & Mary L. Rev. 709 (2000).

2. The Alcohol Fuel Programs had contracted, as to a loan guarantee, directly with Agrifuels Refining Corporation. As the construction contractor for Agrifuels, Harbert/Lummus had the status of a subcontractor, as the opinion notes when stating that Harbert/Lummus was only in contractual privity with Agrifuels. The case begins to suggest the subtleties in the relationship between the government, and its subcontractors. As later chapters will discuss, on the one hand, the government keeps its distance from subcontractors on many issues, such as usually not (albeit with exceptions) allowing subcontractors to surmount that barrier of privity for purposes of pressing claims against the government. On the other hand, as this case itself illustrates, often the government has ardent desires regarding what subcontractors do. A subcontractor like Harbert/Lummus may view itself as having the worst of both worlds. Its prime contractor, Agrifuels, went bankrupt, as in the private sector, but then the ultimate party upon whom it depended, the government, invoked the special defenses of the public sector to escape its promises. Is it fair for the subcontractor to view itself as so unfortunate? What are the compensations to a subcontractor for that situation?

3. After the opinion determines that the CO did not have authority to enter this oral contract, the opinion then addresses separately the issue of whether the CO ratified the contract. The extremely high formal requirements for exercise of authority naturally lead to enhanced importance for the possibility, if they are not met, of ratification. Suppose Harbert/Lummus had written a memorandum of confirmation after the meeting, and the Deputy Director wrote back to it, truthfully, that the CO had read and orally agreed with the memorandum. Would that suffice for ratification?

4. For a discussion, see Christopher S. Pugsley, *The Game of "Who Can You Trust?"—Equitable Estoppel Against the Federal Government*, 31 Pub. Cont. L. J. 202 (2001).

Donald C. Winter, Secretary of the Navy, Appellant, v. Cath-dr/Balti Joint Venture, Appellee

No. 2006-1359

497 F.3d 1339

United States Court of Appeals, Federal Circuit

Aug. 17, 2007

Before LOURIE, PROST, and MOORE, Circuit Judges.

Opinion for the court filed by Circuit Judge MOORE. Opinion dissenting-in-part filed by Circuit Judge PROST.

MOORE, Circuit Judge.

The Secretary of the Navy (Navy) appeals the decision of the Armed Services Board of Contract Appeals (Board) finding in favor of Cath-dr/Balti Joint Venture (Cath) on 13 of 37 claims for an equitable adjustment in contract price. *Cath-dr/Balti Joint Venture*, ASBCA Nos. 53581, 54239, 05-2 BCA ¶ 33046 (Aug. 17, 2005)*(Board Opinion)*. The Navy asserts that the Board erred in concluding that a Resident Officer in Charge of Contracts (ROICC), who was also the Project Manager (PM) during the performance period, had the authority to commit the government to compensable contract changes. Because the contract explicitly reserved authority to modify the contract to the Contracting Officer (CO), the ROICC did not have actual express or implied authority to direct the contractor to perform compensable contract changes, and we reverse the Board's conclusion as to claims 2, 8, 13, 17, and 26/32.

BACKGROUND

I.

On September 29, 1998, Cath and the Navy entered into a fixed price contract for external renovation of a historic dental research facility at the Great Lakes Naval Training Center in Illinois. The contract incorporates by reference several standard government clauses including Federal Acquisition Regulation (FAR)§ 52.243-4 (Aug.1987) (Changes Clause), which provides that the CO may, at any time, make changes in the work within the general scope of the contract by written order designated as a change order. FAR§ 52.243-4 also provides that for any change affecting the contractor's cost or time of performance under the contract "whether or not changed by any such order, the [CO] shall make an equitable adjustment and modify the contract in writing." The contract also includes FAR§ 52.236-2 Differing Site Conditions (April 1984), which requires that a contractor give written notice to the CO of subsurface, latent, or unknown physical conditions at the site that differ materially from those indicated in the contracting documents. After such notice, the CO "shall" investigate the site conditions and if they do materially differ and cause an increase in the cost of or time required for completion of the contract "an equitable adjustment shall be made under this clause and the contract modified accordingly" by the CO. Additionally, the contract incorporates Naval Facilities Engineering Command (NAVFAC) Clause 5252.201-9300 Contracting Officer Authority (June 1994) and NAVFAC Clause 5252.242-9300 Government Representatives (June 1994). The Contracting Officer Authority clause reserves authority to the CO to bind the government to any "contract, modification, change order, letter or verbal direction to the contractor," and the Government Representatives clause indicates that while the Engineer in Charge (EIC) will be designated by the Contracting Officer as his authorized representative responsible for monitoring performance and technical management, in no event will any modification of the contract by anyone other than the CO bind the government.

II.

* * *

Cath began work under the dental facility contract on January 25, 1999. Soon thereafter, Cath received a letter from the Navy that reassigned the day-to-day administration of the contract to EIC Tim Meland and indicated that all correspondence regarding the contract should be sent to Meland's attention. In response to this letter, Cath submitted a RFI seeking "documentation of assignment of authority" and the "level of authority" of Meland, among others. The Navy responded to this RFI with respect to Meland as follows:

> Mr. Tim Meland. Project Manager: the Government Manager on all assigned projects. Responsible for construction management and contract administration on assigned projects while providing quality assurance and technical engineering construction advice. Provides technical and administrative direction to resolve problems encountered during construction. A project manager analyzes and Interprets contract drawings and specifications to determine the extent of Contractors' responsibility. Prepares and/or coordinates correspondence, submittal reviews, estimates, and contract modifications in support to ensure a satisfactory and timely completion of projects.

* * *

III.

After Cath's renovation work under the contract was deemed substantially complete, it submitted a cumulative request for a contract modification and several adjustments to the PM, in accordance with the procedure for equitable adjustment requests set forth in the preconstruction conference presentation.

* * *

A CO issued a 15 page Final Decision on July 27, 2001, detailing each claim and finding entitlement to an equitable adjustment for 12 claims. In this decision, the CO recommended that Cath and the ROICC office negotiate the amount Cath is entitled to for its meritorious claims and asked that Cath's request for a final decision on those claims be "held in abeyance subject to further discussions with the ROICC."

* * *

The Navy argued for the first time on appeal that the CO did not direct the work set forth in the claims for equitable adjustment and that under the contract only the CO has the authority to change the scope of work or authorize compensable changes. In an order dated August 17, 2005, the Board sustained in whole or in part 13 of Cath's 37 claims. *Board Opinion*, Op. at 81–83. With respect to all but one of the claims that the Navy has appealed to this court, the Board determined that the ROICC PM directed changes that resulted in costs beyond those required by the contract and that these changes were compensable because the delegation of authority clause in the contract gave him responsibility for construction management and contract administration. The Board concluded that Meland, as the PM, had "express actual authority" to resolve minor problems that arose during the project based on the Navy's RFI response, which indicated that he was responsible for construction management and contract administration and that he was authorized to provide "'technical and administrative direction to resolve problems encountered during construction.'" *Board Opinion*, Op. at 9 (quoting *Urban Pathfinders, Inc.*, ASBCA No. 23134 79-1 BCA ¶ 13,709 at 67,260 (1979)).

* * *

ANALYSIS

The Navy appeals the Board's equitable adjustment of the contract price with respect to claims 2, 7, 8, 13, 17, 26/32, 33, and 37. To demonstrate entitlement to an equitable adjustment, Cath must prove that the contract was modified by someone with actual authority. Where a party contracts with the government, apparent authority of the government's agent to modify the contract is not sufficient; an agent must have actual authority to bind the government. *See Trauma Serv. Group v. United States,* 104 F.3d 1321, 1325 (Fed.Cir.1997). Such actual authority may be express or implied from the authority granted to that agent. We must determine whether Meland had express or implied authority to bind the government to contract modifications he approved, or whether these changes were ratified by the CO.

I. Express Authority

With respect to contracts for supplies and services, the federal government has given the authority to enter into and modify contracts to only a limited class of government employees: contracting officers. *See* 48 C.F.R.§ 1.601(a) (vesting agency heads with authority to contract for supplies and services and mandating that "[c]ontracts may be entered into and signed on behalf of the Government only by contracting officers"); 48 C.F.R.§ 43.102 ("Only contracting officers acting within the scope of their authority are empowered to execute contract modifications on behalf of the Government."). In addition to possessing authority to enter into a contract on behalf of the government, contracting officers have the authority to, among other things, administer the contract and ensure the contractor's compliance with the contract terms. *See* 48 C.F.R. §§ 1.602-1, -2.

* * *

It is very clear, however, that the contracting officer's limited delegation of authority to the EIC did not include the authority to make contract modifications, nor could it have. For one thing, such a delegation was prohibited by a Department of Defense regulation, which states that "[a] contracting officer's representative (COR) ... [m]ay not be delegated authority to make any commitments or changes that affect price, quality, quantity, delivery, or other terms and conditions of the contract." 48 C.F.R.§ 201.602-2 (1998). Indeed, this express limitation on the COR's authority was incorporated into a clause of the contract itself, which, likewise, states that "[t]he COR is not authorized to make any commitments or changes that will affect price, quality, quantity, delivery, or any other term or condition of the contract." *See* 48 C.F.R.§ 252.201-7000.

Moreover two other clauses in the contract made it clear to Cath that the contracting officer was the only person with the authority to make changes to the contract. The same clause that designates the EIC as an authorized representative of the contracting officer provides that:

> [i]n no event, however, will any understanding or agreement, modification, change order, or other matter deviating from the terms of the contract between the contractor and any person other than the Contracting Officer be effective or binding upon the Government, unless formalized by proper contractual documents executed by the Contracting Officer prior to completion of this contract.

* * *

The contract is clear, only the CO had the authority to make modifications. Meland did not have the express authority to bind the government to contract modifications.

II. Implied Authority

The issue of implied authority is a much closer case. The government is not without blame for the confusion surrounding the contract in this case. For example, the contract required the CO to attend the preconstruction conference during which the Navy explained contract administration procedures. The CO did not attend. At that meeting the Navy presentation included a slide that stated

Contract Modifications

Modifications are *written* alterations to the contract which may change the work to be performed and/or the contract price and time. Oral modifications *will not* be used.

"Bilateral modification —the contractor and the ROICC have agreed upon an adjustment to the contract

"Unilateral modification—the ROICC can direct the contractor to take some action under the contract

No work is to be performed beyond the contract requirements without *written notification from the ROICC.*

Cath dutifully complied with the Navy's directions for day-to-day contract administration presented in the preconstruction conference through the entire process. The problem is that these Navy directives contradicted the clear language of the contract and it is the contract which governs. The law and the unambiguous contract terms compel the result that we reach.

Authority to bind the government may be implied when it is an integral part of the duties assigned to the particular government employee. *See H. Landau & Co. v. United States,* 886 F.2d 322, 324 (Fed.Cir.1989) (internal citations omitted). In *Landau,* we held that a government employee possessing both the authority to ensure that a contractor acquired the raw materials needed to fulfill a contract and the authority to draw checks on the government bank account may have also had the "implicit authority" to guarantee payment to the contractor's supplier of raw materials. *Id .Landau,* however, is inapposite to this case. Here, the ROICC could not have had the *implicit* authority to authorize contract modifications because the contract language and the government regulation it incorporates by reference *explicitly* state that only the contracting officer had the authority to modify the contract. Modifying the contract could not be "considered to be an integral part of [the ROICC project manager's] duties" when the contract explicitly and exclusively assigns this duty to the CO. *Id.* We cannot conclude that Meland had implied authority to direct changes in the contract in contravention of the unambiguous contract language.

III. Ratification

Cath argues that even if Meland did not have actual authority to bind the Navy to contract modifications, the changes directed by Meland were ultimately ratified and were therefore binding.

* * *

Ratification requires knowledge of material facts involving the unauthorized act and approval of the activity by one with authority. *Harbert/Lummus Agrifuels Projects v. United States,* 142 F.3d 1429, 1433–34 (Fed.Cir.1998). Whether a contract has been ratified involves questions of fact, which has not been addressed by the Board in the first instance. *See United States v. Beebe,* 180 U.S. 343, 354, 21 S.Ct. 371, 45 L.Ed. 563 (1901); *Brainard v.*

Am. Skandia Life Assurance Corp., 432 F.3d 655, 661 (6th Cir.2005). For example, the parties dispute whether the CO had full knowledge of all material facts at the time he issued the July 27, 2001 Final Decision finding entitlement. While it appears from the detailed fifteen-page decision that the CO did have full knowledge, the government contends he did not. Given the dispute over knowledge and the lack of Board findings on this point, we remand to the Board to consider this issue in the first instance.

* * *

CONCLUSION

For the foregoing reasons, the decision of the Board is

AFFIRMED IN PART, REVERSED IN PART, AND VACATED AND REMANDED IN PART.

COSTS

Each party shall bear its own costs.

PROST, Circuit Judge, dissenting-in-part.

I join the majority opinion except for Part III of the Analysis section, from which I respectfully dissent. In Part III, the majority concludes that it is necessary to remand this case so that the Board can determine whether the Contracting Officer's ("CO's") July 27, 2001 decision letter amounted to a "ratification" of certain changes directed by the Project Manager. I do not think a remand is necessary, and would hold that the CO's July 27, 2001 decision letter does not constitute a ratification of the Project Manager's unauthorized change orders.

* * *

For these reasons, I respectfully dissent.

2. Law in Statutes, Regulations, and Standard Clauses

In contrast to the common law background of basic (private) contract law, government contract law derives primarily from non-judicial public law sources. In theory, this consists of an evenly layered three-tier legal structure: statute, regulations, and contract clauses. In practice, the layers vary in extent; often Congressional statutes address only in general terms the issues that arise in particular contexts. Regulations, however, tend to be extensive, detailed, and comprehensive. The government contracts themselves can vary: some may be voluminous, resolving a multitude of issues and bringing the whole range of statutory and regulatory law to bear by cues relating to their sources in statutes and regulations. On the other hand, sometimes the government contracts do not contain the clauses that would expressly bring in that whole range of law. Then, the issue is posed of what is known, after a case involving the G.L. Christian company, as the "*Christian* doctrine." The case in this section, *Appeal of University of California, San Francisco*, deals with that doctrine.

It is also useful to get some overview at this point, historically, of the government contracting law statutes and regulations. Readings on this subject are included below. It would not be possible to lay these out completely, for to describe the whole of government contracting statutes and regulations would cram the entire book into this section. At this point, it helps to have a sense of the historic rise of government contracting law from the early 19th century statutes, through the World War I and II development, into the much more elaborate development as large-scale government procurement continued in the post-World War II era. Congressional action continued by a series of "reform" statutes of the 1980s and 1990s, principally the Competition in Contracting Act (1984), the Federal Acquisition Streamlining Act (1994), and the Federal Acquisition Reform Act (1996)

Meanwhile, elaborate sets of agency regulations had developed. From the origins in the regulations of individual military services and individual civilian departments came, in the post-World War II era, consolidation into comprehensive military procurement regulations (the Armed Services Procurement Regulations) and comprehensive civilian procurement regulations (the Federal Procurement Regulations). From these, the Federal Acquisition Regulation, the "FAR," came in 1983 as a comprehensive code of regulations operating throughout the government. It is no exaggeration to say that government contracting law today follows the FAR as much as "code" subjects in private contracting law follow the various articles of the Uniform Commercial Code.

In reading *Appeal of University of California, San Francisco*, do not try at this point to absorb the detailed law of required disclosure of cost and pricing data. We will return to this case in the section discussing that area of law. Rather, without getting into the details of that area of law, the question at this point is simply: is the contract controlled by that set of legal rules when the contract does not contain the clause usually used to indicate that the contract is under those rules (namely, the "Defective Pricing" clause)?

Regulations

From: Government Contract Guidebook Steven W. Feldman
(Thomson Reuters 4th ed. updated 10/2010))

Government procurement is essentially procurement by regulation. The informality that often accompanies the solicitation and award of a purely commercial contract is obviously inappropriate where public funds are being expended for public purposes.

Because of this, regulations play a key role in government contracts.

* * *

1. Federal Acquisition Regulation

The basic set of regulations relating to federal procurement is the FAR. The FAR, which went into effect on April 1, 1984 is the primary set of regulations for *all* federal executive agencies, unless otherwise excluded. It is prepared, issued, and maintained by the Secretary of Defense, the Administrator of General Services, and the Administrator of the National Aeronautics and Space Administration. Applicable provisions of the FAR are incorporated into every federal government procurement contract and have the same effect as if they were set forth in the contract itself. It has the force and effect of law, because it is published in the *Federal Register* and the *Code of Federal Regulations*.

Before the FAR's promulgation, two sets of regulations governed government contracts. One was the Defense Acquisition Regulation—the DAR. The DAR (which was at one time called the Armed Services Procurement Regulation—the ASPR) governed procurements by military agencies. The other pre-FAR set of regulations was called the Federal Procurement Regulations—the FPR—governing procurements by civilian agencies.

The FAR is a massive document. At its most basic level of organization, as found in Chapter 1 of Title 48 in the Code of Federal Regulations, it consists of eight "subchapters," which in turn are composed of 53 "parts." Figure 2-1 below lists the parts of the FAR, showing how they are arranged under each of the subchapters. A current copy of the FAR is available at http://www.arnet.gov/far.

The FAR establishes uniform policies and procedures for the procurement of supplies and services (including construction). It applies to all such purchases by and for the use of the federal government made within or outside the United States for procurements that obligate appropriated funds.

The FAR is by no means a static document. As already mentioned, it is subject to frequent revision through the coordinated action of the DAR Council and the CAA Council. Unless otherwise specified, the general rule is FAR changes apply to solicitations issued on or after the effective date of the change. Revision is accomplished through the issuance of Federal Acquisition Circulars (FACs). An interim FAR amendment establishes the Federal Procurement Data System to serve as the single authoritative source of all procurement data for a host of applications and reports.

Figure 2.1: FEDERAL ACQUISITION REGULATION STRUCTURE

Subchapter A: General
Part 1—Federal Acquisition Regulations System
Part 2—Definitions of Words and Terms
Part 3—Improper Business Practices and Personal Conflicts of Interest
Part 4—Administrative Matters

Subchapter B: Competition and Acquisition Planning
Part 5—Publicizing Contract Actions
Part 6—Competition Requirements
Part 7—Acquisition Planning
Part 8—Required Sources of Supplies and Services
Part 9—Contractor Qualifications
Part 10—Market Research
Part 11—Describing Agency Needs
Part 12—Acquisition of Commercial Items

Subchapter C: Contracting Methods and Contract Types
Part 13—Simplified Acquisition Procedures
Part 14—Sealed Bidding
Part 15—Contracting by Negotiation
Part 16—Types of Contracts
Part 17—Special Contracting Methods
Part 18—Emergency Acquisitions

Subchapter D: Socioeconomic Programs
Part 19—Small Business Programs
Part 20—[Reserved]
Part 21—[Reserved]
Part 22—Application of Labor Laws to Government Acquisitions
Part 23—Environment, Conservation, Occupational Safety, and Drug-Free Workplace
Part 24—Protection of Privacy and Freedom of Information
Part 25—Foreign Acquisition
Part 26—Other Socioeconomic Programs

Subchapter E: General Contracting Requirements
Part 27—Patents, Data, and Copyrights

Part 28—Bonds and Insurance
Part 29—Taxes
Part 30—Cost Accounting Standards Administration
Part 31—Contract Cost Principles and Procedures
Part 32—Contract Financing
Part 33—Protests, Disputes, and Appeals

Subchapter F: Special Categories of Contracting
Part 34—Major System Acquisition
Part 35—Research and Development Contracting
Part 36—Construction and Architect-Engineer Contracts
Part 37—Service Contracting
Part 38—Federal Supply Schedule Contracting
Part 39—Acquisition of Information Technology
Part 40—[Reserved]
Part 41—Acquisition of Utility Services

Subchapter G: Contract Management
Part 42—Contract Administration and Audit Services
Part 43—Contract Modifications
Part 44—Subcontracting Policies and Procedures
Part 45—Government Property
Part 46—Quality Assurance
Part 47—Transportation
Part 48—Value Engineering
Part 49—Termination of Contracts
Part 50—Extraordinary Contractual Actions
Part 51—Use of Government Sources by Contractors

Subchapter H: Clauses and Forms
Part 52—Solicitation Provisions and Contract Clauses
Part 53—Forms

2. Agency acquisition regulations

Agency acquisition regulations are limited to (a) those necessary to implement FAR policies and procedures within the agency and (b) additional policies, procedures, solicitation provisions, or contract clauses that supplement the FAR to satisfy the specific needs of the agency. Agency procurement regulations change almost as frequently as the FAR, and practitioners should carefully note these revisions as they research a particular issue. For example, in 2005, the Department of Transportation reissued the Transportation Acquisition Regulation, and in 2003, the Department of Homeland Security issued its Homeland Security Acquisition Regulation.

Although the various civilian agencies have each issued their own sets of regulations implementing the FAR, the most comprehensive set is the DFARS (the Defense FAR Supplement), which applies to all military and DOD agencies. It is organized to correspond to the 53 parts of the FAR and incorporates several appendices and supplements. DOD completely rewrote the DFARS in 1991 to (1) eliminate unnecessary text and clauses, (2) eliminate or modify thresholds, certifications, and other regulatory burdens on Contracting Officers and contractors, and (3) rephrase all remaining text and clauses in plain English. DOD periodically revisits the DFARS to transform the regulation by reducing, streamlining, and revising its content. Thus, in 2004, the DOD issued a companion resource to the DFARS, "Procedures, Guidance and Information," that contains mandatory and non-mandatory internal DOD procedures, non-mandatory guidance, and supplemental information.

As with the FAR, the DFARS is codified in the Code of Federal Regulations (designated as Chapter 2 of Title 48). Most of the other agency regulations implementing the FAR are also codified in Title 48. The Army Federal Acquisition Regulation Supplement and the Army Corps of Engineers' Engineer FAR Supplement are examples of regulations not published in the *Federal Register* or the *Code of Federal Regulations*. Nevertheless, it is an elemental principal of administrative law that agencies are bound to follow their own regulations.

The DFARS is supplemented from time to time by the issuance of Defense Acquisition Circulars (DACs) or Departmental Letters. A DAC may include—in addition to DFARS revisions—policies, directives, and informational items. These Circulars can be of significance to contractors. Unless otherwise stated in the DAC, any new provisions, policies, or directives are effective as of the date stated in the DAC.

3. Deviations

Deviations from the FAR are allowed only if they are (a) authorized and (b) approved by a designated official. The same holds true for deviations from the DFARS. Generally, deviations from the FAR consist of use of a contract clause containing language differing from the standard FAR language, use of forms other than prescribed forms, alteration of prescribed forms, or omission of a mandatory contract clause. Other types of deviations exist as well, such as the issuance of policies or procedures that govern the contracting process that are not properly incorporated into an agency acquisition regulation. A deviation will not be present, however, where an agency created clause merely prescribes terms in an area not addressed in the FAR.

Where the agency properly uses a deviation, the agency cannot be faulted for not using an otherwise mandatory provision or clause. A deviation contrary to the FAR will be unauthorized and unenforceable.

G. L. Christian and Associates v. The United States

Court of Claims
312 F.2d 418
No. 56–59
Jan. 11, 1963

DAVIS, Judge.

This case, which involves claims totaling $5,156,144.50, grew out of the deactivation of Fort Polk, Louisiana, by the Department of the Army in 1958. At the time when the decision to deactivate Fort Polk was made, a large housing project, which was to consist of 2,000 dwelling units for the use of military personnel at Fort Polk, was being constructed under a contract that had previously been made by the Corps of Engineers ... The housing contract was terminated by the Corps of Engineers on February 5, 1958, after which numerous claims for damages were submitted to the Government.

* * *

II

The Government concedes that the claimants are entitled to be made financially whole, at least with respect to all reasonable expenses that they incurred in preparing to perform work under the Fort Polk housing contract, in partially performing that contract from August 1957 to January 1958, and in meeting the situation that arose when the contract was formally terminated by the Government early in February 1958. The controversy revolves around the proper amounts of the claimants' unreimbursed expenses and the legal question whether the claimants are entitled to recover for anticipated profits. At the time work was suspended in January 1958, the project was only 2.036% complete and the work was substantially behind schedule.

The principal legal question is whether the claimants should be permitted to recover for anticipated profits. In this connection, it is settled that, when the Government enters into a contract, it has rights and it ordinarily incurs responsibilities similar to those of a private person who is a party to a contract ... and if the Government terminates a contract without justification, such termination is a breach of the contract and the Government becomes liable for all the damages resulting from the wrongful act....

The right to recover for anticipated profits arises, however, only if the termination of the contract by the Government is wrongful and constitutes a breach. If the Government has reserved the right to terminate a contract for its convenience and then does so, there is no breach and normally there can be no recovery for the profits....

In the present case, although the Fort Polk housing contract did not contain any provision expressly authorizing the Government to terminate the contract for its convenience, the Government contends that the contract should be read as if it did contain such a clause. This argument is largely based upon Section 8.703 of the Armed Services Procurement Regulations. Section 8.703 provided (with an exception which is not pertinent here) that 'the following standard clause shall be inserted in all fixed-price construction contracts amounting to more than $1,000,' and then proceeded to prescribe a detailed termination clause that began with the unequivocal declaration that 'the performance of work under this contract may be terminated by the Government in accordance with this clause in whole, or from time to time in part, whenever the Contracting Officer shall determine that such termination is in the best interest of the Government,' and included a formula which did not encompass anticipated profits. As the Armed Services Procurement Regulations were issued under statutory authority, those regulations, including Section 8.703, had the force and effect of law. See Williams v. Commissioner of Internal Revenue, 44 F.2d 467, 468 (C.A.8, 1930); Ex parte Sackett, 74 F.2d 922—923 (C.A.9, 1935). If they applied here, there was a legal requirement that the plaintiff's contract contain the standard termination clause and the contract must be read as if it did....

Despite the unusual character of the contract, we have little difficulty in reading the Procurement Regulations, especially the rule requiring the insertion of the standard termination clause, as applying to the present type of agreement....

We are not, and should not be, slow to find the standard termination article incorporated, as a matter of law, into plaintiff's contract if the Regulations can fairly be read as permitting that interpretation. The termination clause limits profit to work actually done, and prohibits the recovery of anticipated but unearned profits. That limitation is a deeply ingrained strand of public procurement policy. Regularly since World War I, it has been a major government principle, in times of stress or increased military procurement, to provide for the cancellation of defense contracts when they are no longer needed, as well as for the reimbursement of costs actually incurred before cancellation, plus a reasonable profit on that work—but not to allow anticipated profits.... Since World War II, the standard termination clauses promulgated by the Defense Department and its constituent agencies have taken the same tack. Literally thousands of defense contracts and subcontracts have been settled on that basis in the past decades.

This history shows, in our view, that the Defense Department and the Congress would be loath to sanction a large contract which did not provide for power to terminate and at the same time proscribe anticipated profits if termination did occur. Particularly in the field of military housing, tied as it is to changes and uncertainties in installations would it be necessary to take account of a possible termination in advance of completion, and to guard against a common law measure of recovery which had been disallowed for so many years in military procurement. The experienced contractor in this case, for its part, could not have been wholly unaware that there might be a termination for the convenience of the Government, which the defendant would not deem a breach. Although the housing contract does not contain such an express provision, there are at least four references in it (and the accompanying agreements) to a 'termination of the Housing Contract for the convenience of the Government' and to the Government's assumption of certain obligations in that event. These references must have had some meaning. For many years unearned profits have not been paid upon such terminations, and we think it probable, too, that Centex-Zachry knew of that general policy.

For all of these reasons, we believe that it is both fitting and legally sound to read the termination article required by the Procurement Regulations as necessarily applicable to the present contract and therefore as incorporated into it by operation of law.

It follows that Centex-Zachry and its subcontractors cannot recover unearned but anticipated profits....

Appeal of University of California, San Francisco
1996 WL 681971 (V.A.B.C.A.), 97-1 BCA 28,642, VABCA No. 4661
November 25, 1996

Opinion is in Chapter 17 on TINA and Defective Pricing

Notes and Questions

1. Just how fundamental is the *Christian* doctrine? The *Christian* doctrine, in a nutshell, puts the parties to a government contract as much under the control of standard, "mandatory" government contract clauses when those clauses have been left out of the contract document, as when they have been put in. The opinion in *Appeal of University of California, San Francisco* discusses a number of other cases, harkening back to the original *Christian* decision itself, regarding the reasons for the *Christian* doctrine. Just how fundamental is that doctrine? Consider the following two views, assessing which captures better the place of this doctrine.

On the one hand, the jurisprudence of government contract law could view the *Christian* doctrine as serving some of the same fundamental necessities of the public law sphere as the limited-authority doctrines discussed in *OPM v. Richmond* and *Mil-Spec*. In a government structured by the Constitution and the enactments under it, and controlled by the elected Congress and President, the law governing each government contract cannot be left to the individual discretion of the particular contracting officers involved in the contract's drafting. The power belongs to the Congress, the President, and the formal processes they supervise that produce implementing regulations, not to the individual government officials who draw up particular contracts. Hence, the *Christian* doctrine implements the public law nature of government contracting, by importing into every contract what those higher formally-acting authorities prescribe.

On the other hand, the *Christian* doctrine does not have nearly the historic pedigree, recited in *OPM v. Richmond*, of the rule barring estoppel of the government by the actions of government agents and the limited authority of those agents. The *Christian* doctrine only arose in the post-World War II era. Moreover, while there were, historically, agency regulations and standard government clauses, their comprehensive interaction became more significant in that same post-World War II era. In that sense, it could be argued that the *Christian* doctrine lacks the deep significance of the doctrine discussed in *OPM v. Richmond*, which was well understood by Supreme Court Chief Justice John Marshall and has roots in the text of the Constitution. Rather, the *Christian* doctrine represents a modern innovation, like many of those in administrative law, coordinating the more complex, regulation-dependent system of recent decades. Moreover, the *Christian* doctrine does not apply with the extensive completeness of the *OPM v. Richmond* doctrine. Rather, as the *UCSF* opinion reflects, only a regulation-by-regulation, clause-by-clause assessment will determine whether the *Christian* doctrine applies to particular regulations and clauses.

2. Consider the larger role and responsibility for government contract lawyers this case creates. In private sector contracting, the parties to the contract, and their lawyers, can more or less take care of their concerns by adjusting the drafting of the contractual instrument. By contrast, the private party to a government contract finds himself at the mercy of the entire body of federal regulations. She derives scant comfort from what the instrument itself says, and depends upon her lawyer to know what dangers lurk in the whole Federal Acquisition Regulation.

3. A related issue concerns the type of interpretation principles to apply—the ones for public law, or, the ones for contract clauses. See William E. Slade, A Question of Intent, 7 Fed. Cir. Bar J. 251 (Fall 1997).

4. *OPM v. Richmond* expressed a doctrine that applied regardless of how unfair it seemed to the individual, the retired welder, who had relied to his peril on the advice of a Navy specialist. In the *UCSF* case, the University of California might contend that it was unfair to penalize it for relying on the government officers' omission of a defective pricing clause. Does the University have as much of a fairness argument as the welder did in *OPM v. Richmond*? Does the court weigh fairness arguments in deciding this case? Considering the reasons for the *Christian* doctrine, should it?

3. Budgets

The law of government budgeting warrants a brief mention at this point. Like the other characteristic principles of government contracting in this chapter, it marks part of the network by which the Constitution and statutes, and the Congress and the President, control government contracting interactions. Moreover, budgeting has enormous practical influence in government contracting decisions. Contracting officers have one eye on all the rest of government contracting law as it empowers or constrains them, and the other eye on how much government money they have to spend as this independently empowers or constrains them.

Most government contracting expends appropriated funds in the narrow sense of "appropriation," that is, funds provided by Congress in annually enacted appropriation laws. For example, most of the money for defense procurement comes in the annual Department of Defense Appropriation law. (However, the government also spends large sums for entitlements, such as Medicare, in which the funds are promised by statutes that are not appropriation laws and that are not enacted annually.) Appropriations get decided in an annual budgeting cycle. For example, for the Army to get funds to buy laptop computers, its officials would put a request for those funds in their service's draft budget. The Office of Management and Budget, which is the President's budgeting arm, would approve inclusion of that request in the President's official budget request. Then, the House and Senate Appropriation Committees would consider the laptop request and include the money as they report appropriation bills to their chambers.

Once Congress enacted a Department of Defense appropriation law containing the money corresponding to that request, the money would then be passed out within the government, with the Office of Management and Budget "apportioning" the funds for the Army, and the Army "allotting" the funds to particular matters. Ultimately one of the Army's contracting officers would be formally notified of the availability of funds to be "obligated" by award of a contract. Upon the contractor's delivery and the Army's acceptance of the laptops, the Army would issue a Treasury check to the contractor, drawing down the Army's account in the Treasury, and "liquidating" the contractual obligation.

Many aspects of budgeting will receive attention later. Some particular items warrant mention now. In general, appropriation laws primarily contain bare provisions setting forth amounts of money and their tersely stated objects. Even these bare appropriation provisions contain a great deal of law governing the expenditure of funds. They tell how long the funds remain available, which may be one year, several years, or even longer. And they tell the object for the funds, which may be expressed very broadly, such as a general appropriation of billions of dollars for the Navy's operations and maintenance, or may be expressed very narrowly, such as specific appropriation of a few thousands dollars for a particular improvement in the Library of Congress. Broad appropriations carry non-binding but highly influential guidance in the form of the original detailed budget requests submitted to the Congress, and the committee reports and other legislative history of the appropriation bills within Congress.

Furthermore, appropriation laws can, and do, contain expressive language further governing the expenditure of those funds. Appropriation laws frequently contain limitations that preclude spending the funds for various purposes, from statutory clauses putting an end to a war by forbidding further military expenditures on it to statutory clauses imposing "Buy America" rules by forbidding expending the funds to make purchases from foreign sources. Such law enacted by inclusion in appropriation laws has as much force and effect as any other statute. In fact, a fair portion of the statutory background of government contract law entered the Statutes at Large aboard appropriation laws. For example, the entire Federal Acquisition Reform Act of 1996 got enacted by inclusion in an appropriation law.

A number of government offices serve fiscal and financial purposes, and these interact with the contracting officers and directly or indirectly with the contractors. Departments typically have elaborate financial offices tasked to formulate proposed budgets and to track the obligation and the ultimate expenditure of the enacted funding. A very important agency, the Government Accounting Office ("GAO") headed by the Comptroller General, performs a variety of functions including fiscal investigations. The GAO historically gives advisory opinions about the legality of expenditure of funds. From this general function of the GAO arose its specific function, of great importance in government contracting law, of deciding one particular type of issue regarding contracting, namely, the "bid protest" discussed in the chapters on sealed bidding and negotiated procurements.

Agencies have several types of offices to conduct financial investigations, particularly investigations of government contractors. These include the offices that conduct the large number of regular audits, such as the Defense Contract Audit Agency for military contracts. They also include the Inspector General offices, which look into possible overcharging, fraud, and other contractual abuses.

C. State Procurement

In one sense, no casebook can treat fully the law of procurement by state and local governments, even if the entire casebook focused on that law. Since state procurement law derives largely from statutes, regulations, and contract clauses, each state has written its own law. There is no unifying "common law" of state procurement law, and there is no uniform state procurement law adopted in fifty states like the Uniform Commercial Code. No one book could even reproduce, let alone discuss, the specifics of the procurement law in the fifty different state systems and the thousands of local systems.

However, in another sense, simply by dint of discussing federal procurement law a great deal of what would be needed to practice state procurement law will be discussed. There have always been unifying factors between federal and state procurement law. These factors have become increasingly important since the end of World War II and the rise of a uniform, regularized federal system centered upon the Federal Acquisition Regulation as a complete and orderly code. Both state government lawyers and the practitioners with which they deal have tended to bring the federal law that they master into their state contracting.

The two readings in this chapter do not seek to describe comprehensively state procurement law. Rather, they aim to illustrate the mix of carried-over federal law and the retained particularized law of the individual state, that make up the whole of state procurement law. In these readings, look for the following:

First, look at how the structure of state procurement law resembles the structure of federal procurement law. That is, in a way parallel to the sources of federal procurement law, the sources of state procurement law consists of state statutes, state regulations, and state standard contract clauses. Both of the readings discuss Maryland's adoption of a new statutory procurement code in 1980, the adoption of the state procurement regulations (in the "Code of Maryland Regulations" or "COMAR"), and the use of standard Maryland contract clauses. Similar authority limitations and appropriation mechanisms to the federal ones allow the state constitutions and laws, and the state elected legislatures and governors, to direct and control the actions of state officials, including state contracting officers.

Second, look at what makes up the mix of current state procurement law. Part of it consists of borrowings from federal law: the bid protest and contract dispute systems at the state level, for example, resemble the federal ones, as do substantive rules on many subjects from bid bonds to construction contract arrangements for unexpected costs (known as "differing site conditions"). Another part of it consists of modernized state systems codifying, unifying, centralizing, and organizing state procurement arrangements, such as the 1980 system established in Maryland. Modernized state procurement systems often draw on the American Bar Association's Model Procurement Code. A residual part of it consists of continuation of traditional state procurement arrangements, often tied to the particularized governing structure of that state or locality. For example, the Maryland system preserved a central role in the awarding of contracts for the Board of Public Works, a state body consisting of the Governor and a few other state officials. This is a classic state arrangement tying state procurement to the state governing structure, which varies from state to state and has no close federal analogue.

For further discussions of the issues in this section, see: Melissa J. Copeland, *State And Local Procurement Update: A Look At Recent Changes In Alabama, Georgia, Maryland, And South Carolina*, 45 Procmt. Law. 10 (Spring 2010); Kathryn E. Swisher, *Expanded Use Of GSA Schedules By State And Local Governments*, 42 Procrmt. Law. 20 (Spring 2007); Marshall J. Doke (Jr.), *State And Local Government Bidding Preferences*, 42 Procrmt. Law. 7 (Summer 2007); Constance Cushman, *The ABA Model Procurement Code: Implementation, Evolution, and Crisis of Survival*, 25 Pub. Cont. L.J. 173 (1996); Lewis J. Baker, *Procurement Disputes at the State and Local Level: A Hodgpodge of Remedies*, 25 Pub. Cont. L.J. 265 (1996); F. Trowbridge von Baur, *A Personal History of the Model Procurement Code*, 25 Pub. Cont. L.J. 4 (1976).

Kennedy Temporaries v. Comptroller of the Treasury

No. 484 Sept. Term 1983
Court of Special Appeals of Maryland
468 A.2d 1026
Jan. 4, 1984

Argued before MOYLAN, LISS and WILNER, JJ.

WILNER, Judge.

Appellant bid on a State contract. He was underbid by one of his competitors and therefore did not get the contract. Alleging that the low bidder should have been disqualified because of an insufficient bid bond, appellant eventually commenced a proceeding that has grown in complexity at each successive stage.... [W]e shall be obliged to discuss in some detail not only the factual and procedural history of the case but also the procurement law, the regulations issued under it, and some of the procedures mandated by the law and the regulations.

I. The Procurement Law

In 1980, after several years of study, the General Assembly enacted a new procurement code for the State. It took effect July 1, 1981, and is presently codified as Md.Code Ann. art. 21.

The heart of the law is § 2-201(a), which states simply that no State agency in the Executive Branch "may enter into a contract for supplies, services, or construction except in accordance with the provisions of this article and the regulations established pursuant to this article." The law then sets forth some basic rules governing the methods by which the State is to select and deal with its suppliers. In title 3, for example, it authorizes five types of source selection (§ 3-201(a)), establishes a preference for one of them—competitive sealed bidding (§ 3-201(b)), and requires that when that method is used, "[t]he contract shall be awarded to the responsive and responsible bidder whose bid is ... the lowest bid price...." Other sections in title 3 specify qualification standards for bidders (subtitle 4), bond requirements (subtitle 5), and restrictions on certain types of contracts (subtitle 7).

In title 7 (§ 7-201), the law establishes a specific four-step procedure for resolving disputes relating to both the formation of a contract (i.e., the award of a contract) and a contract already awarded. The first step is the agency procurement officer who, upon timely demand, and "consistent with … all applicable laws and regulations," is authorized to "negotiate and resolve" these disputes, including disputes "concerning the qualification of bidders … and the determination of the successful bidder.…" (§ 7-201(a)). The second step is review of the procurement officer's decision by the agency head, who may "approve or disapprove the procurement officer's decision" and whose determination "is deemed final action by the agency.…" (§ 7-201(c)). The third step is an appeal to the Board of Contract Appeals, an independent entity created by § 7-202. The decision of that Board, according to § 7-201(d), "is final only subject to judicial review." Judicial review, in accordance with the Administrative Procedure Act, is the fourth and final step. (§ 7-203).

Subject to these statutory criteria, the essential thrust of the law is to continue overall control over State procurement in the Board of Public Works, where it has resided for at least fifty years, but to permit the Board, by regulation, to delegate part of its control authority to four other State agencies having special procurement responsibilities—the University of Maryland and the Departments of Budget and Fiscal Planning, General Services, and Transportation. These five agencies—but primarily the Board of Public Works—are directed to develop the necessary implementing details and procedures by administrative regulation. We see this in § 2-101.

Section 2-101(a) places in the Board of Public Works "power and authority over the procurement, management, and control of all supplies, services, construction, and other items procured by the State." See also Md.Code Ann. art. 78A, §§ 1B and 10. To carry out the provisions of the statute, the Board "has authority to set policy and to adopt regulations which are consistent with this article," as well as to exercise any authority conferred on the other four specified agencies. Subsection (b) also deals with regulations. It states, in relevant part, that the Board "shall adopt regulations, consistent with this article, governing procedures for the review and approval of procurement contracts … [and] procedures for review of determinations.…" The Board is further directed to "ensure that the regulations of the procurement agencies provide for procedures which are consistent with this article and which are substantially the same among the agencies."

The four departmental procurement units derive their special authority from § 2-101(c). That section directs each of those agencies to adopt regulations "consistent with this article" concerning a number of things, including "[r]ejection of bids, consideration of alternate bids, and waiver of informalities in bids."

Regulations were, in fact, adopted by the Board and the four other agencies, effective July 1, 1981. They appear in COMAR, Title 21, and include, among other things, procedures and requirements relating to bid bonds (21.06.07), protests (21.10.02), the Board of Contract Appeals (21.02.02 and 21.10.06), and the waiver of minor irregularities and deficiencies in bids (21.05.02.12 and 21.06.02.03). Approval authority over certain types of procurement contracts was delegated to the other four agencies (21.02.01.03–07), but anything not delegated was reserved to the Board of Public Works. With respect to any such contracts (including service contracts exceeding $100,000), the agency procurement officer has no authority to award the contract. His decision, or, upon review, that of the agency head or the Board of Contract Appeals, is in the nature of a recommendation to the Board of Public Works, which alone can approve or reject.

When these various provisions governing the dispute-resolution process and the overall authority of the Board of Public Works are read together harmoniously, as they should be, the legislative intent seems clear that the dispute-resolution process set forth in § 7-201 should be completed before the Board of Public Works, as the final approval authority, acts on a disputed matter concerning contract formation, in order that the Board may then act in conformance with the decision reached through that process. That is what § 2-201(a) would seem to require; and only in that manner can the prerogatives of the Board under the law be clearly and neatly meshed with the more specific criteria and procedures mandated by the General Assembly.

II. Factual and Procedural Setting

At some point in the early fall of 1981, the Comptroller of the Treasury determined that he would need additional temporary personnel to assist in the processing of income tax returns expected to be received during the winter and spring of 1982. On October 1, 1981, through his procurement officer, John A. Clinton, the Comptroller issued an invitation to about twenty companies to bid on a contract to provide such personnel for the period January 1 — June 30, 1982. Enclosed with the invitation was a memorandum describing the bidding process. Paragraph P of that memorandum dealt with bid bonds. Reflecting the provisions of Md.Code Ann. art. 21, § 3-504 and COMAR 21.06.07.01 and .02, Paragraph P stated:

> Bids exceeding $25,000 in anticipated price must contain a Bid Bond in an amount equal to at least five percent (5%) of the total amount bid. The preferred bid security is a bond in form satisfactory to the State underwritten by a company licensed to issue bonds in Maryland. The bond shall be in substantially the form contained in Appendix (F). State procurement regulations permit other forms of bid securities. Contact the issuing officer to discuss any other form of bid security. Failure to provide an acceptable bid security with the bid when required shall result in the bid being rejected. (Emphasis in original.)

When the bids were opened on November 17, 1981, it appeared that the two lowest bidders were Bay Services, Inc. at $608,159, and Kennedy Temporaries at $621,502. Bay Services' bid was accompanied by a bid bond, in proper form, in the amount of $30,000, which was $407.95 short of five percent of its bid. Kennedy did not submit a bid bond. Its bid was accompanied by a letter from a branch officer of Maryland National Bank stating, in relevant part:

> As part of the above bid proposal, it is necessary to provide a $50,000.00 'Bid Proposal Bond.'

> Please be advised by this letter that Maryland National Bank guarantees to provide any collateral necessary to the State of Maryland to be held as collateral against performance; should Stephen G. Kennedy's bid be accepted by the State of Maryland.

Mr. Kennedy was in attendance when the bids were opened, and he asked if he could see the amount of the bid bond posted by Bay Services. The procurement officer initially rejected his request—"until we got everything sorted out"—but permitted such an inspection on November 23, 1981. Mr. Kennedy then noticed the shortfall and pointed it out to Ms. Mary Ann Porter, the personnel manager of the Comptroller's office, indicating that, as a result of the deficiency, the Bay Services bid should be rejected. The next day, Mr. Clinton, the procurement officer, called, and Kennedy iterated his complaint to him.

On November 25, 1981, Clinton wrote to Bay Services, pointing out the deficiency in the bid bond and advising that "a question has been raised" with respect to it. Clinton called attention to COMAR 21.05.02.12, permitting him to waive "technicalities or minor regulations [sic, irregularities] in bids," and COMAR 21.06.02.03, defining "minor irregularity" and empowering the procurement officer to "give the bidder ... an opportunity to cure any deficiency resulting from a minor informality or irregularity in a bid ... or waive the deficiency, whichever is to the advantage of the State."

Obviously regarding the shortage in the bid bond as "minor," Clinton purported to exercise his prerogative under the latter regulation and directed Bay Services to file an additional $500 in approved security by December 1, 1981. A copy of that letter was sent to Kennedy. Two days later—on November 27—Clinton sent another letter to Bay Services, again with a copy to Kennedy. In this letter he abandoned reliance on COMAR 21.05.02.12 and 21.06.02.03 and instead invoked his authority under COMAR 21.06.07.02B. That regulation provides, in relevant part:

> If a bid does not comply with the security requirements of this regulation, the bid shall be rejected as nonresponsive, unless the failure to comply is determined by the procurement officer to be nonsubstantial when:
>
> * * *
>
> (2) The amount of the bid security submitted, though less than the amount required by the invitation for bids, is equal to or greater than the difference in the price stated in the next higher acceptable bid....

Because the $30,000 bid bond filed by Bay Services was greater in amount than the $13,000 difference between its bid and that of Kennedy, Clinton concluded that the deficiency was "nonsubstantial" and would therefore be excused altogether. He ended the letter with the statement, "your bid bond is accepted without any need for further action."

... On December 2, 1981, the matter was taken up by the Board of Public Works which, as we have noted, retained under the law full approval authority over service contracts exceeding $100,000. The transcript of that meeting shows that both Mr. Clinton and Mr. Kennedy appeared and presented their respective views. No mention was made by Mr. Clinton (or by anyone else) of the lack of written protest; but neither did Mr. Kennedy give any indication that he intended to pursue the matter before the Board of Contract Appeals. Clinton maintained that the deficiency in the Bay Services bid bond was nonsubstantial and argued that "it just doesn't make sense to disqualify a low bidder for a $407 deficiency in a bond and cost the State $13,000." Kennedy, on the other hand, forcefully argued his case—that the statute was there, that it was clear, and that it ought to be applied uniformly—and he seemed clearly to understand that the final resolution of the matter was in the Board's hands. The Board was apparently unimpressed by Kennedy's argument, as it approved the contract with Bay Services that day, although it is not certain from the record when that decision was first communicated to Kennedy.

On December 7, 1981, Kennedy called and left a message for Clinton requesting "the final decision of the Procurement Office." ...

Clinton received [from Kennedy a] letter on December 30, and responded immediately. He stated first that his recommendation that the contract be awarded to Bay Services, which had been approved by the Board of Public Works, as indicated in his letter of December 9, was his "final recommendation." ... Nothing further happened until January 15, 1982, when, by letter of that date, Kennedy appealed to the Board of Contract Appeals....

In a decision rendered July 20, 1982—three weeks after the contract with Bay Services had been fully completed—the Board of Contract Appeals concluded that:

> ... In excusing the deficiency in Bay Services' bid bond, Clinton acted in conformance with COMAR 21.06.07.02B. The bond exceeded the difference between the two bids and thus the deficiency could, under the regulation, properly be regarded as "non-substantial." The statute, however, art. 21, § 3-504, was explicit. Subsection (b) requires the bid bond to be "in an amount equal to at least 5 percent of the amount of the bid," and subsection (c) states that, if the invitation re-

quires that a bid bond be provided, "a bidder ... that does not comply shall be rejected." To the extent that COMAR 21.06.07.02B permitted the waiver of "nonsubstantial" deficiencies in bid bonds, it was inconsistent with that clear legislative mandate and therefore was void.

In light of those conclusions, the Board "sustained" Kennedy's appeal....

Neither party was satisfied with the Board's decision and thus both appealed to the Circuit Court for Baltimore City....

The court, though agreeing with the Comptroller that the Board of Contract Appeals had no authority to declare COMAR 21.06.07.02B invalid, nonetheless effectively affirmed the Board's decision. The court itself declared the regulation to be "an improper extension of the administrative authority of the Procurement Officer" and thus to be "null and void." It also found, however, that Kennedy's claim for damages was "barred by the doctrine of sovereign immunity."

The court's decision brought no more solace to the parties than that of the Board of Contract Appeals, and we therefore again have cross-appeals....

III. Discussion

A. Precis

We think that the Comptroller's third argument is valid; Kennedy does not qualify as a "responsive" bidder, and thus has no legal status to challenge the award to Bay Services. We believe, in addition, that, even if Kennedy were to be regarded as having such status, by failing to pursue his administrative remedy in conformance with the requirements of § 7-201, he has waived his right to complain....

B. Kennedy's Standing As A Responsive Bidder

In Part II, above, we observed that Kennedy's bid was not accompanied by a bid bond. In place of such a bond, it submitted a letter from Maryland National Bank guaranteeing "to provide any collateral necessary to the State of Maryland to be held as collateral against performance," should Kennedy's bid be accepted.

Section 3-504(a), in stating the requirement of a bid bond, provides: "The bid bond shall be provided by a surety company authorized to do business in this State, or the equivalent in cash, or in a form satisfactory to the procurement officer." COMAR 21.06.07.01B expands upon that. It permits, as bid security, a surety bond, a bank check, or a "[p]ledge of securities backed by the full faith and credit of the United States government or bonds issued by the State of Maryland."

A bid bond is a very limited kind of performance bond. It is designed to assure only that a bidder, if successful, will, in fact, enter into the contract he has bid upon, and to provide a secure fund to compensate the State if he fails to do so. The condition of the bond is that the principal will "execute such further contractual documents, if any, and give such bond(s) as may be required by the terms of the bid...." COMAR 21.06.07.03 (Exhibit E). See Board of Education v. Allender, 206 Md. 466, 476, 112 A.2d 455 (1955); Harran Transportation Co. v. Board of Ed., 71 Misc.2d 143, 335 N.Y.S.2d 971 (1972). Its function and its legal effect end once a contract is signed, for at that point the condition of the bond has been satisfied. As the Comptroller points out, the loss accruing from the default by a successful bidder—i.e., his failure to enter into the contract in accordance with his bid—is normally the difference between what the State would have paid absent the default (usually the amount of the defaulter's bid) and what it actually has to pay as the result of the default (generally the next highest bid accepted by the State). That is what a bid bond is intended to secure; and indeed the guarantee of the surety is that, in the event of a default in executing a contract, "the Principal shall pay the State for any cost of procuring the work which exceeds the amount of its bid." COMAR 21.06.07.03 (Exhibit E).

The letter from Maryland National Bank does not, in our judgment, satisfy the bid bond requirement of the statute, the regulation, or the invitation to bid. In the first place, the pledge of collateral was against "performance" should Kennedy's bid be accepted, not specifically against loss occurring by virtue of a default in entering into the contract. Second, it is not clearly a pledge of securities backed by the full faith and credit of the United States or the State of Maryland. If, as Kennedy claims, Mr. Clinton was without authority to waive the $408 deficiency in Bay Services' bond, he surely was without authority to waive this type of deficiency.

C. Protest Requirements—Waiver

The statutory provisions governing the resolution of disputes arising under the procurement law are, as we have said, found in § 7-201.... The process is more sharply defined in COMAR 21.10.02, which requires, among other things, that a protest "shall be in writing and addressed to the respective procurement officer representing the State agency" (21.10.02.02) and that where the basis of the protest is not apparent before the bid opening, "bid protests shall be filed not later than 7 days after the basis for protest is known or should have been known, whichever is earlier." (21.10.02.03).

Kennedy discovered the basis of his protest on November 23, 1981; to comply strictly with the regulation Kennedy should therefore have filed a written protest with Mr. Clinton by November 30. That clearly was not done, and thus there can be no legitimate claim of compliance by Kennedy with the requirements of the regulation.

Kennedy's response is that, by taking cognizance of his complaint, Clinton effectively waived the seven-day-written-protest requirement, to which the Comptroller rejoins that Clinton had no legal authority to waive that requirement.

... We also would note that, even if regarded as merely procedural in nature, the regulation was not that of the Comptroller. It was adopted by the Department of Budget and Fiscal Planning, with the approval of the Governor and the Board of Public Works, and was imposed by those agencies upon the Comptroller's office in the latter's capacity as a procurement agency. Whatever the procurement officer's authority might be to waive a procedural regulation of the Comptroller, we find no authority in the law for him to waive a requirement externally imposed pursuant to clear statutory authority. Such a power would be inconsistent with the whole thrust and scheme of the law....

For all of these reasons, we conclude that Kennedy's appeal to the Board of Contract Appeals should have been dismissed. We shall remand the case to the Circuit Court for Baltimore City for entry of an order to that effect.

JUDGMENT VACATED

Notes and Questions

1. Parse the aspects of *Kennedy Temporaries* that have close federal analogues, and the aspects that are unique to state procurement or to this particular state. Start with the procedures. The issues in *Kennedy Temporaries* received consideration at each of the following levels: the contracting officer, the Board of Public Works, the Board of Contract Appeals, the Circuit Court, and the Court of Special Appeals. Which of these have federal analogues? What is the role of the others?

2. Now, consider the aspects which governed the decision of the appeal: the bid bond requirements, the bidder's "standing" to challenge the award, and the strictness of the timing rules that forbade their waiving by the Board of Contract Appeals. What aspects of this would be identical in a federal contract?

Fair Treatment for Contractors Doing Business with the State of Maryland

Scott A. Livingston, 15 Univ. of Baltimore L. Rev. 215 Winter, 1986

I. INTRODUCTION

In 1980, the Maryland General Assembly enacted the Procurement Article, which incorporates into Maryland law the policy of providing fair treatment for persons who deal with the state procurement system. Prior to the Article taking effect in 1981, Maryland did not have a comprehensive statute that regulated procurement of public works by state agencies.

The Article was enacted to provide for a comprehensive and impartial system of procurement. In the opinion of the General Assembly, persons who have a reasonable expectation of fair treatment from the state will compete more vigorously for state contracts. The Procurement Article contains provisions that were designed to implement the fair treatment policy. Specific provisions govern the manner in which the state awards contracts. Other provisions specify mandatory terms for inclusion in contracts and establish a method for resolution of disputes.

This article examines procurement methods used by various state agencies prior to 1981. The article explains the laws that govern state procurement of public works and evaluates the degree to which the Procurement Article has provided fair treatment for contractors working for the state. Section II describes the recent history of Maryland procurement with emphasis on the period immediately preceding 1981. Section II also discusses procurement of architectural and engineering services, use of procurement to achieve socio-economic policy, and development of dispute resolution procedures. Section III examines the methods used to award contracts and resolve disputes under the Procurement Article. In addition, section III discusses cases in which Maryland appellate courts reviewed disputes resolved by a board of contract appeals. In section IV, the author addresses the future of Maryland procurement and presents suggestions for modifying the system in a manner that advances the policies underlying the Procurement Article, especially the policy of promoting fair treatment of contractors doing business with the state.

II. PROCUREMENT PRIOR TO 1981

The history of Maryland is reflected in the history of public works, to borrow a phrase from Victor Hugo. Events of political history, fortunate and otherwise, have influenced legislation governing procurement of public works by the state.

A. How Contracts Were Awarded
1. General

Prior to 1981, the methods state agencies used to award contracts were dictated by the Board of Public Works and the General Assembly. The seminal powers of the Board of Public Works could be circumscribed by the General Assembly; however, the General Assembly did not enact a comprehensive procurement statute limiting the scope of the Board's powers until 1981. Approval by the Board of Public Works usually provided sufficient authorization for a state agency to award a contract.

Instead of enacting a comprehensive procurement statute, the General Assembly enacted legislation that created various executive branch agencies. The enabling legislation for these agencies usually contained provisions that mandated the manner in which the new agencies would conduct procurement....

B. Terms of the Procurement Contract
1. No Uniformity Prior to 1981

Prior to 1981, state law did not require the inclusion of uniform terms in state contracts for procurement of public works construction services. The contract terms differed from agency to agency. It is difficult to say whether the particular terms used reflected the diverse needs of each agency or merely the personal preferences of various procurement officers.

¥   ¥   ¥

In the early seventies, [Maryland Department of Transportation, or MDOT] conducted a study of the various clauses used by the modal administrations of MDOT. MDOT found that numerous, often conflicting clauses were contained in boilerplate procurement contracts. In 1976, after several years of study, MDOT adopted its 'General Provisions for Construction Contracts.'

The General Provisions were important for several reasons. First, the terms set out in the General Provisions fairly allocated the risks inherent in public works construction. Second, the General Provisions represented a major effort to coordinate the procurement practices of the agencies in MDOT, the department that enjoyed the largest public works budget in state government. Third, the provisions were modeled so closely on federal clauses that case law construing the federal clauses could be used to provide guidance under Maryland law for interpretation of the terms contained in the General Provisions. Previously, because of the doctrine of sovereign immunity, there had been a dearth of Maryland case law on contract claims against the government.

The sudden application of familiar federal clauses and case law encouraged national competition for state contracts, especially on the Baltimore Metro project. Only a limited number of contractors can procure the finances, equipment, and other resources needed to build subway stations and tunnels. These contractors usually are familiar with the provisions used in standard federal contracts. Familiarity with the provisions enables contractors to anticipate the costs of risks allocated under federal contracts and submit their bids accordingly. Prudent contractors tend to compete less vigorously for contracts that contain unfamiliar or unfair clauses.

2. Socio-Economic Policies

In Maryland, the process used to award procurement contracts for public works incorporates procedures designed to implement socio-economic policies identified by the General Assembly. Public funds are spent on projects in such a way as to encourage certain business practices that appear to be in the public interest. For example, Maryland has enacted legislation designed to encourage the purchase of American-made steel for state public works projects. Among the several socio-economic policies identified by the General Assembly, the one that most drastically affects traditional practices in public works procurement is the Minority Business Enterprise Program.

In order to understand how the Minority Business Enterprise (MBE) policies affected procurement, it is necessary to examine procurement practices prior to 1978. Traditionally, the state awarded public works contracts to the low bidder based on a formal advertisement for sealed bids. The party identified as the low bidder became the prime contractor pursuant to a contract with the state.

When a prime contractor elected to enter into subcontracts for performance of work on a project, the state generally was not involved in the selection of any subcontractor. The prime contractor was responsible for completing the project according to contract specifications; accordingly, he exercised virtually unlimited discretion in the selection of subcontractors.

Prime contractors usually did not subcontract with businesses owned and operated by black individuals. Instead, prime contractors subcontracted with firms that they had dealt with for years, a practice that civil rights advocates found operated to exclude minority firms. The traditional practice of subcontracting with firms that the prime contractor previously had done business with tended to exclude minority businesses from participating in public works projects.

* * *

During its 1978 session, the General Assembly enacted legislation designed to alter the traditional practice of subcontracting on public works projects. The legislation called for state agencies to intervene on behalf of minority businesses in the selection of subcontractors for major public works projects. As indicated in the preamble to the legislation, the General Assembly was 'concerned that minority businesses may experience the effect of past discrimination' in the award of subcontracts on state public works projects. The General Assembly directed MDOT to establish departmental procedures for procuring construction services that encourage minority business participation to the extent of ten percent of the dollar value of contracts exceeding $100,000.

Anticipating the passage of minority business legislation by the General Assembly, MDOT established an MBE Program. MDOT designed the MBE Program in a fashion that implemented the policy of encouraging participation by minority businesses in MDOT construction projects.

* * *

C. Resolution of Disputes

Parties to state public works contracts recognize that disputes commonly, if not invariably, arise regarding the interpretation of contract terms. Inclusion of a 'Disputes Clause,' which provides a procedure for fairly resolving contract disputes, helps prevent litigation concerning the interpretation of contract terms from impeding completion of public works projects. Prior to 1976, the Disputes Clause provided the principal means that a contractor could use to obtain appropriate compensation from the state in the event of dispute. An examination of the respective positions of the state and the contractor illustrates the manner in which the Disputes Clause functions in the public works construction process.

1. Disputes are Inherent

Disputes are inherent in the construction of public works projects. A tension exists between the state and the contractor who agrees to build a project. Each party is oriented to the contract price, which is a fixed amount reached on the basis of competitive sealed bidding. Not only is the contract price fixed, but it is fixed as the lowest amount offered by any responsible contractor who competitively bid for the project.

The rationale used to justify the practice of awarding the contract to the low bidder is that the practice promotes price competition among those seeking public works contracts. Although it may promote competition, the practice of awarding to the low bidder produces an anomalous effect. As a practical matter, awarding the contract to the lowest responsible bidder forces both the contractor and the state to search intensively for means to protect, if not improve, their positions once the contract price is fixed and performance is begun.

The parties' abilities to improve their respective positions largely depend upon the contractual language that allocates cost risks associated with performance. The contractor, who has underbid his competitors to win the contract, wants to minimize his performance costs. Thus, the contractor interprets the contract language in a manner that enables him to render the minimum performance — at the lowest cost — that complies with the terms of the contract. The state, however, like any owner who hires a contractor, is inclined to demand the maximum possible performance.

Contract price disputes occur because the contract price is fixed low and fixed early at the time of bid opening. At this point, both the contractor and the state estimate generally, but neither can estimate exactly, how much money it will cost to perform the contract. Hence, the contractor has no extra money in his bid to pay for unforeseen expenses that occur during performance. To maintain its profit position, the contractor is justified in requesting extra compensation when unforeseen expenses arise.

A public works contract generally allocates the construction risks and provides for a contractual means to deal with the risk that a dispute will arise. In the contract, the parties agree to make adjustments to the contract price upon the occurrence of certain events that affect cost or time of performance. For example, if the subsurface conditions at the project site differ materially from those indicated in the plans, the contract price will be adjusted to compensate for increased costs incurred as a result. A contractor who encounters subsurface conditions that differ materially from those indicated in the plans presents to the state a claim for an equitable adjustment. The term 'claim' is thus neutral insofar as it merely signifies the contractor's exercise of a right promised by the state.

The parties recognize in advance that there may be disputes over whether an equitable adjustment is justified. Although each party is oriented to the contract price, both view as advantageous the provision of a contractual procedure for resolving disputes regarding claims for equitable adjustments arising under the contract.

2. Resolution via a Disputes Clause

The procedure that governs the resolution of disputes is set forth in a Disputes Clause. The current Disputes Clause authorizes the state to decide initially the proper interpretation of contract requirements. Generally, the procedure contemplates a three-tiered process. First, a lower-level official in the agency that commissioned the project is authorized to interpret the contract terms. Second, a contractor who is dissatisfied with the interpretation can obtain upper-level administrative review within the agency. While the interpretation is under review, the contractor remains obligated to perform the disputed work. Third, the contractor can appeal the agency's final decision to an outside forum that reviews the agency's decision.

* * *

III. POST-1981 MARYLAND PROCUREMENT SYSTEM
A. Passage of the Procurement Article

The Procurement Article provides an equitable, modern system for the procurement of public works projects. Three important features distinguish the modern system from the procurement practices used by the state prior to 1981. First, the Procurement Article establishes uniform methods for the awarding of all state contracts. The preferred method for awarding contracts for construction of public works is competitive sealed bidding. By using the method of competitive sealed bidding, the state is obligated to award contracts for construction of public works to the lowest responsive and responsible bidder. Second, the Procurement Article establishes specific clauses that must be included in all state construction contracts. The clauses are contained in regulations that have been promulgated to implement the provisions of the Procurement Article. These mandatory clauses are designed to allocate fairly the risks inherent in the construction of public works projects. Third, the Procurement Article establishes the Maryland State Board of Contract Appeals (MSBCA).

* * *

Instead of merely having jurisdiction over disputes regarding contracts entered into by the Department of Transportation, as did MDOT BCA, MSBCA has jurisdiction over disputes relating to any contract entered into by the state. In addition, MSBCA has jurisdiction to hear and decide bid protests, which are disputes relating to the formation of state contracts. Prior to the establishment of MSBCA, bid protests were resolved summarily by the Board of Public Works. The practice of summary resolution of bid protests by the Board of Public Works was altered by the General Assembly because it left the state vulnerable to public criticism of political favoritism.

* * *

V. CONCLUSION

The modern era of Maryland procurement began in 1976 when the General Assembly passed legislation that provided for a partial waiver of the doctrine of sovereign immunity. Shortly thereafter, MDOT created a board of contract appeals, introduced standard clauses for inclusion in procurement contracts, and instituted responsible procedures for contract award. These three safeguards were designed to enhance MDOT's ability to insure fair treatment for contractors.

In 1981, with the passage of the Procurement Article by the General Assembly, the safeguards provided by MDOT became applicable to virtually all state contracts. The policy of fair treatment for contractors doing business with the State of Maryland was incorporated into law. In the future, the policy of providing fair treatment for contractors who do business with the state will continue to be a crucial aspect of Maryland procurement.

Notes and Questions

1. Clearly, state procurement in Maryland went through a major change in 1981. What drove it through that change? What aspects of the pre-1981 system persist?

2. From *Kennedy Temporaries* and this article, how much do you think a lawyer in Maryland who has regular work with the federal procurement system and occasional contact with the Maryland procurement system can handle Maryland state procurement matters? How much do you think a lawyer in California with the same regular work with the federal procurement system and occasional contact with non-Maryland procurement systems can handle Maryland state procurement matters?

3. How "neutral" are the trends in state procurement, such as greater parallelism to the federal system and to the system in other states, and greater codification and regularization? Focus on the aspect that some of these trends encourage non-local vendors to find it easier to compete for state contracts. Consider how these trends fit with powerful trends in the private commercial realm toward reducing other state barriers to a uniform national market (e.g., the shift from statewide banking to nationwide banking) and beyond that, to a global market. Sometimes the nationalization and globalization trends are con-

sidered to reduce the power of localities to run their own lives, as when locally-oriented businesses are replaced by national and multinational ones. When a state changes its procurement system to make it more open to non-local vendors, does it "gain" like consumers who get benefits from global vendor competition, or does it "lose" like sovereigns who surrender one of their great powers, the power to promote local values through locally-oriented procurement?

Chapter 2

Sealed Bids and Competitive Proposals

"It gives me great confidence to know that I am going into space aboard a shuttle that was built by the low-cost contractor." — Senator Jake Garn (R-UT)

The main line of the evolution of formal competition has run through two methods, sealed bids and competitive proposals. Sealed bids held sway during peacetime until after World War II. It still gets some use, both at the federal and state levels, although especially at the federal level much more of formal competition, by dollar volume, occurs by competitive proposals. Competitive proposals increasingly came to predominate as both defense and civilian procurement involved more complex goods and services. Sealed bids mainly deserves study because many of its concepts and procedures serve as a foundation for understanding all acquisition methods. This chapter starts with the aspects best illustrated in the context of sealed bids, before turning to competitive proposals.

By statute, a federal agency is to solicit sealed bids if: (1) there is sufficient time to solicit, receive, and evaluate the sealed bids; (2) award can be made based only on price and price-related factors; (3) it is not necessary to have discussions with the bidders about their bids; and (4) there is a reasonable expectation of receiving more than one sealed bid. Once, sealed bids were the favored method for protecting the integrity of the procurement system. Such protection was needed to avoid the type of cost overruns and insider deal making that made such popular congressional hearing fodder in the mid-1980s and that led to the wholesale change of procurement law and the enactment of the Competition in Contracting Act.

The problematic reality of trying to make good procurement decisions simply on the basis of price makes sealed bids no longer the most common procurement method, especially for large dollar procurements. In a choice between "sealed bids" and "competitive proposals," sealed bids can almost always be awarded in less time due to the almost rote decision of awarding to the low priced bidder. Similarly, the third factor that is to be considered when making the decision to use sealed bids, the need or lack thereof for discussions with potential contractors, is lessening as the government relies more on commercial items that are designed for general use and not specifically designed to meet specific government needs. Likewise, the fourth factor, the possibility of competition is not really a choice between sealed bids and competitive proposals, but more of a choice between contracting with a single source and use of either of the formal competitive methods.

It is the second factor, award based on price and price-related factors, that keeps sealed bidding from being the favored procurement methodology. As required by the mandates of the Competition in Contracting Act, government contracting officials are required, except in limited circumstances when less than full and open competition is permissible, to use competitive proposals when sealed bids are not appropriate. Competitive proposals are used when the government wants to evaluate offers based on non-price related factors such as the technical capability or the quality of the product being offered, in addition to the price.

In the 1990s, the federal procurement system was influenced by the new concept that almost any procurement decision based simply on price alone will result in less than the best deal for the government. Non-price related factors such as past performance have taken on greater importance in award decisions thus forcing government contracting officers to utilize the more discretionary procurement method of competitive proposals (RFPs).

For further discussion of the subjects of this chapter, see the cites in the specific subchapters, and see: *See generally* Steven Feldman, *Government Contract Awards—Negotiation and Sealed Bidding* (Thomson Reuters 2010–2011 ed.); Jessica Fickey, *Fraud In The Bidding Process: The Limited Remedies Available To Contractors*, 38 Pub. Cont. L.J. 913 (Summer 2009); Omar Dekel, *The Legal Theory Of Competitive Bidding For Government Contracts*, 37 Pub. Cont. L.J. 237 (Winter 2008); Lani A. Perlman, *Guarding The Government's Coffers: The Need For Competition Requirements To Safeguard Federal Government Procurement*, 75 Fordham L. Rev. 3187 (May 2007).

A. Sealed Bids

Sealed bidding, principally known by the initials "IFB" for "Invitation for Bids," but also known as "formal advertising," has been around since at least the time of the Civil War. It was at that time that government officials decided that collusion and bias among contractors and federal procurement officials could be lessened by attempting to create the ever-desirable "level playing field" and a system of almost mandatory fairness through equal competition.

The requirements of sealed bidding are quite simple. It starts with the government publicizing an invitation to bid to provide a very specific item (hence the term, formal advertising). In order to give each and every prospective bidder an opportunity to compete for the government's business, invitations for bids are to be widely and visibly publicized. This is done by posting on the government's web-based service, FedBizOpps.

After processing the bids, the government is to award a firm-fixed-price contract for goods or services to the "responsible" contractor submitting a "responsive" bid that will be most advantageous to the government. By doing business with only "responsible" contractors, the government avoids the false economy of awarding a contract to the lowest-priced, but less reliable bidder, only to incur additional costs associated with untimely deliveries, unsatisfactory performance, or ultimately, contract default. In order to be deemed responsible, a potential contractor (and its subcontractors) must: (1) have adequate financial resources to perform the contract; (2) be able to meet with the required delivery or performance schedule; (3) have a satisfactory performance record (although not having any performance record at all cannot disqualify a bidder); and (4) have a satisfactory record of integrity and business ethics. Potential contractors can run afoul of responsibility issues on grounds spanning all their bids by having committed a fraud or similar offense such as embezzlement, theft, forgery, bribery, falsification or destruction of records, tax evasion, or receiving stolen property and thereby having either the company, individuals within the company, or both, "debarred" from doing business with the government.

The concept of submitting a "responsive" bid goes to the heart of achieving fairness and a level playing field among potential contractors. Unlike the method of "competitive proposals" discussed in the next chapter, sealed bids or IFBs require the contractor's proposed bid to meet each and every mandatory and material requirement of the solicitation and specification of the product or service to be provided. By requiring the government to use specifications which do not include restrictive provisions or conditions except to the extent necessary to satisfy the needs of the government, each prospective contractor is able to determine exactly what it is the government wants, and can therefore compete fairly on price and price-related factors alone for the government's business. Governmental discretion to choose a particular brand name item (e.g. Coke or Pepsi) or a particular contractor is eliminated when the sealed bid solicitation states that the government wants to buy a cola soft drink. At the same time, the offer of 7-Up will disqualify a potential bid as not being responsive to the government solicitation requirements.

For further discussion of the subjects in this part, see: Susan L. Turley, *Wielding the Virtual Gavel — DOD Moves Forward With Reverse Auctions*, 173 Mil. L. Rev. 1 (2002); Steven L. Schooner, *Fear of Oversight: The Fundamental Failure of Businesslike* Government, 50 Am. U. L. Rev. 627 (2001); Girard R. Visconti, *Quiet Falls over Public Bid Protest*, 46 R.I. B.J. 13 (April, 1998); George M. Coburn, *Unfavorable Past Performance Determinations as De Facto Debarments*, Procurement Law., Summer 1996, at 26; Daniel I. Gordon, *Unbalanced Bids*, 24 Pub. Cont. L.J. 1 (1994); William P. Rudland, *Rationalizing the Bid Mistake Rules*, 16 Pub. Cont. L.J. 446 (1987); Colleen A. Preston, *Evaluating Bids Against Cost Limitations*, 15 Pub. Cont. L.J. 463 (1985); Alfred A. Gray, *Responsiveness Versus Responsibility: Policy and Practice in Government Contracts*, 7 Pub. Cont. L.J. 46 (1974).

1. Responsiveness

The issue of responsiveness in sealed bidding goes to the heart of the governmental policy of trying to establish a level playing field for all would-be government contractors. Where price is the only factor to be considered, all other elements of the procurement must be identical in order to give each competitor the very same chance of doing business with the government. This is true whether the government is buying items or, as the following case demonstrates, when the government is selling an item.

Maintaining the requirement that all bidders are on an equal footing also goes a long way in eliminating potential fraudulent activity on the part of either government officials, contractors, or both. Consider the consequences in the following case had one bidder been privately "advised" by a government official that the government would accept contract terms more favorable to the bidder than set forth in the solicitation. Similarly, consider the consequences if a bidder, unsure of the volatility of the marketplace, submitted a bid knowing that she could possibly disavow it simply by adding in a differing term, if the offered price was not consistent with marketplace pricing — in other words, if it turned out not to be a good deal for the contractor.

ECDC Environmental, L.C., Plaintiff, v. The United States, Defendant, and Great Lakes Dredge & Dock Co., Intervenor

No. 97-723C.
40 Fed.Cl. 236
Jan. 30, 1998

OPINION

FLUTEY, Judge.

This case is presently before the court on the parties' cross-motions for judgment upon the administrative record. Plaintiff, ECDC Environmental, initiated this pre-award bid protest action pursuant to 28 U.S.C. § 1491 (1994), *as amended by* Administrative Dispute Resolution Act of 1996, Pub.L. No. 104-320, 110 Stat. 3870, 3874–75 (1996). Plaintiff alleges that defendant, acting through the United States Department of the Army Corps of Engineers, New York District, improperly rejected plaintiff's bid as nonresponsive to the solicitation. Plaintiff therefore asks this court to order plaintiff's bid responsive and direct defendant to award the contract in accordance with the terms of the solicitation. Defendant maintains that it properly rejected plaintiff's bid and that defendant is entitled to judgment as a matter of law. Another offeror on the procurement, Great Lakes Dredge & Dock Co., has intervened in this matter on the side of defendant.

Factual Background

On March 4, 1997, defendant issued Solicitation No. DACW 51-97-B-0006 (the solicitation) for maintenance dredging and disposition of dredged materials, multiple channels project. Defendant conducted the solicitation pursuant to a two-step process, which included technical and price phases.

More specifically, step-one of the solicitation required offerors to submit technical proposals to defendant by April 25, 1997. Amendment No. 0001 to the solicitation attached a blank government standard form SF 1442 for offerors to complete and return as part of step-one of the procurement. Six offerors, including plaintiff and intervenor, submitted timely step-one technical proposals to defendant. As required by the solicitation, plaintiff submitted with its step-one technical proposal a completed SF 1442 (step-one SF 1442), which consisted of one double-sided page. Item 13A on the front-side of the step-one SF 1442 stated that "[s]ealed offers in original and 6 copies to perform the work required are due at the place specified in Item 8 by 5:00 pm (hour) local time 04/18/97 (date)." Item 13D on the front-side of the step-one SF 1442 notified offerors that "[o]ffers providing less than 90 calendar days for Government acceptance after the date offers are due will not be considered and will be rejected." The back-side of plaintiff's step-one SF 1442 was signed by Mr. Timothy L. Dunlap, Director of Business Development for plaintiff. Defendant determined that plaintiff's technical proposal was responsive to the solicitation and acceptable to defendant. Plaintiff therefore proceeded to step-two of the procurement, as did Great Lakes Dredge & Dock Co. (intervenor) and a third offeror, Consolidated Technologies, Inc. (CTI).

On July 15, 1997, defendant issued Amendment No. 0002 (amendment 2) to the solicitation, which stated that step-two of the solicitation, sealed bid opening, would occur on August 15, 1997. In addition, amendment 2 attached a new SF 1442 to be used in the step-two bidding process (step-two SF 1442). Item 13A on the front-side of the step-two SF 1442 indicated that [s]ealed offers in original and 1 copies to perform the work required are due at the place specified in Item 8 by 11[:]00[am] (hour) local time on 08/15/97 (date). Item 13D on the front-side of the step-two SF 1442 notified offerors that: [o]ffers providing less than 90 calendar days for Government acceptance after the date offers are due will not be considered and will be rejected. On the backside of the step-two SF 1442, an offeror was to acknowledge receipt of amendments to the solicitation. The backside of the step-two SF 1442 also made reference to Item 13D, which established the minimum bid acceptance period as ninety days. Specifically, Item 17, on the backside of the step-two SF 1442 stated that:

> [t]he offeror agrees to perform the work required at the prices specified below in strict accordance with the terms of this solicitation, if this offer is accepted by the Government in writing within ___ calendar days after the date offers are due. (Insert any number equal to or greater than the minimum requirement stated in Item 13D. Failure to insert any number means the offeror accepts the minimum in Item 13D.

Plaintiff submitted its step-two sealed bid to defendant on August 15, 1997. Also on that date, defendant opened the bids submitted by plaintiff, intervenor, and CTI. At bid opening, the apparent low bidder appeared to be plaintiff, with intervenor as the apparent second low-est bidder.[7] The parties stipulate that, at the time of bid opening, plaintiff's bid included a signed and executed back-side of the step-two SF 1442, but failed to include the front-side of the step-two SF 1442. Defendant said nothing about the omission at that time.

* * *

On October 15, 1997, defendant's contracting officer (CO), Ms. Ella D. Snell, informed plaintiff that its bid was nonresponsive and would be rejected by defendant. The CO in-dicated that her decision was based upon 48 C.F.R. § 14.301(a) (1997) (FAR 14.301), which requires that bids must comply in all material respects with the solicitation in order to be considered for award. According to the CO, plaintiff's bid did not comply in all material respects with the solicitation because the bid did not contain an unequivocal commit-ment that defendant had ninety days after bid opening to accept plaintiff's bid. The CO also explained that, because plaintiff submitted the back-side of the step-two SF 1442 with the front-side of the step-one SF 1442, it was reasonable to conclude that plaintiff did not commit to the required minimum bid acceptance period for step-two. Accordingly, defendant deemed plaintiff's bid nonresponsive to the solicitation.

* * *

On October 22, 1997, plaintiff filed its complaint in this court challenging defendant's determination that plaintiff's bid was nonresponsive. In its complaint, plaintiff asks that this court declare plaintiff's bid to be responsive to the solicitation and direct defendant to award the contract in accordance with the terms of the solicitation.

* * *

Discussion

As previously noted, plaintiff alleges that defendant improperly rejected plaintiff's bid as nonresponsive to the solicitation. In response, defendant asserts that plaintiff's failure to timely submit a complete bid rendered plaintiff's bid submission ambiguous as to the minimum bid acceptance period. Defendant therefore maintains that its decision to re-ject plaintiff's bid as nonresponsive was proper, rational, and in accordance with appli-cable laws and regulations. Intervenor concurs with defendant.

---

7. Plaintiff's bid was for $178,436,750, while the next lowest bid was for $185,902,000. *Id.*, tab 6, at 432.

* * *

Significantly, the parties in the present case do not dispute that, at the time of bid opening, plaintiff's step-two bid did not include a complete step-two SF 1442. Rather, plaintiff's bid included only a signed and executed back-side of the step-two SF 1442, which was made a part of the solicitation by amendment 2. As previously noted, the front-side of the step-two SF 1442 stated the minimum bid acceptance period (ninety days) that offerors were required to hold their bids open for defendant's acceptance. Defendant maintains that plaintiff, in failing to include the front-side of the step-two SF 1442 and thereby omitting this material information, created an ambiguity as to the precise length of time to which plaintiff had committed to keep its bid open for defendant's acceptance.

Defendant further argues that plaintiff created an even greater ambiguity by including with its step-two bid a newly signed and executed step-one SF 1442 specifying a different time-frame concerning the minimum bid acceptance period. In that regard, defendant argues that the inclusion of the step-one SF 1442 at this phase in the bidding process led the CO to reasonably conclude that the only time period to which plaintiff was committing itself was the span of time associated with the step-one phase of the procurement.

* * *

Pursuant to the procurement regulations governing competitive sealed bid procurements, defendant must make award to the responsible bidder who submits the lowest responsive bid. 48 C.F.R. § 14.103-2 (1997). Defendant makes its bid responsiveness determinations by reference to the bids when they are opened. *Toyo Menka Kaisha, Ltd. v. United States,* 220 Ct.Cl. 210, 597 F.2d 1371, 1377 (1979); *see also Honeywell, Inc. v. United States,* 870 F.2d 644, 648–49 (Fed.Cir.1989); *Firth Constr. Co. v. United States,* 36 Fed.Cl. 268, 274 (1996). Thus, a bid that is non[ ]responsive on opening may not be made responsive by subsequent submissions or communications. *Firth,* 36 Fed.Cl. at 274.

To be deemed responsive, a bid must comply in all material respects with the invitation for bids. FAR 14.301(a). Accordingly, defendant shall reject any bid that fails to conform to the essential requirements of the invitation for bids. 48 C.F.R. § 14.404-2(a) (1997). Material or essential requirements are those terms that go to the substance of the bid. *See Firth,* 36 Fed.Cl. at 272. In a case similar to the case at bar, the court recently held that, elements of the SF 1442, such as when performance will commence, when it will be completed, acknowledgement of the obligation to furnish bonds, and an agreement to hold the bid open for a specific period of time, are material [terms]. *Id.* at 273.

Moreover, the bid as submitted must obligate the offeror to perform exactly what is being called for in the solicitation. *Bean Dredging Corp. v. United States,* 22 Cl.Ct. 519, 522 (1991) (quoting *Wright Assocs., Inc.,* 90-1 CPD ¶ 549 (June 12, 1990)). Stated differently, a bid submission must obligate the bidder to perform in accordance with the material terms of the [invitation for bids]. There are two elements to the inquiry: "a clear intent to be bound, and sufficient terms so that acceptance of the offer forms a contract upon the basis of the [invitation for bids]." *Firth,* 36 Fed.Cl. at 273 (citations omitted). Here, as in *Firth,* the question presented is whether plaintiff's bid submission contained sufficient terms so that [defendant's] acceptance of the bid, without more, would have formed a contract binding [plaintiff] to the terms stated in the [solicitation]. *Id.* To answer that broad question, this court also must query whether the step-two bid submitted by plaintiff incorporates by reference the missing material terms on the front-side of the step-two SF 1442. *See id.* at 274.

* * *

Plaintiff does not read the court's decision in *Firth* as compelling the result urged by defendant. Rather plaintiff insists that the court took care in *Firth* to distinguish between the import of the front[-] and back [-side] of th[e SF 1442]. More particularly, plaintiff contends that the court in *Firth* focused upon the importance of the *back-side* of the SF 1442 and the effect of its omission on the enforceability of the offeror's bid, and simply adverted to the factual situation involved here, *i.e.,* an offeror's failure to submit the *front-side* of an SF 1442.

* * *

Unlike the offeror in *Firth,* however, plaintiff in the present case did submit a signed and executed back-side of the step-two SF 1442. Here, what plaintiff did not submit was the front-side of the step-two SF 1442. Nevertheless, plaintiff asserts that the terms contained on the front-side of the step-two SF 1442 were incorporated by reference into its bid through plaintiff's submission of the signed and executed back-side of the form, which refers to items included on the front-side of the form. As such, plaintiff argues that its bid was sufficient to bind plaintiff to all of the terms of the SF 1442, including those terms found on the front-side of the form. This court agrees.

In explaining the basis for its assent, this court initially notes an important difference between the terms found on the front-side of an SF 1442 and those included on the back-side of the form. Namely, the material elements contained on the front-side of the SF 1442 are inserted by defendant, while the material terms on the back-side of the form must be filled in by the offeror. It is axiomatic that, because defendant itself inserted the material terms on the front-side of the step-two SF 1442, defendant was aware of those terms. Moreover, plaintiff's assent to those terms properly may be inferred from the signed and executed back-side of the step-two SF 1442.

* * *

Importantly, plaintiff in the present case does not insert any alternative minimum bid acceptance period in item 17 on the back-side of the step-two SF 1442.[16] Accordingly, this court determines that plaintiff's agreement to the ninety-day default period contained in item 13D on the front-side of the step-two SF 1442 provided by defendant may be inferred from plaintiff's inclusion of the signed and executed back-side of the step-two SF 1442 with its bid. This conclusion is especially warranted in light of the fact that defendant itself inserted the ninety-day minimum bid acceptance period in item 13D on the front-side of the step-two SF 1442 and therefore was fully aware of the duration of the default period. Thus, plaintiff's step-two bid contained sufficient terms so that "[defendant's] acceptance of the bid, without more, would have formed a contract binding [plaintiff] to the terms stated in the [solicitation]." *Id.* at 273.

Moreover, printed on the back-side of the step-two SF 1442 submitted by plaintiff in the present case is the language: STANDARD FORM 1442 *BACK.* Thus, the back-side of the step-two SF 1442 submitted by plaintiff clearly identified the complete form as consisting of both a front- and back-side. It is clear to this court that the items contained on the front-side of the step-two SF 1442 were incorporated by specific reference on the back-side of the form, which was signed and executed by plaintiff. *See E. Gornell & Sons, Inc.,*

---

16. This detail also distinguishes the case at bar from the facts of the *Blount* case previously decided by this court. Specifically, plaintiff here simply inadvertently omitted a page from its step-two bid submission. By contrast, the plaintiff in *Blount* took exception to a solicitation requirement in its bid, thereby rendering the bid nonresponsive. *Blount,* 22 Cl.Ct. at 230.

B-170044, 1970 WL 4234, at *2 (C.G., Oct. 15, 1970) (finding a bid responsive despite the fact that the bid omitted pages containing material terms, because the bid identified the complete solicitation to which it responded and incorporated by reference the missing material terms).... This court therefore concludes that plaintiff unequivocally committed itself to the ninety-day minimum bid acceptance period. The CO's decision to the contrary is unreasonable.

* * *

Determining that plaintiff's bid is responsive, this court further decides that plaintiff should have been allowed to correct the mistake in its bid pursuant to the mistake-in-bid procedures set out in 48 C.F.R. § 14.407 (1997) (FAR 14.407). *Arguendo*, to the extent that plaintiff's bid contained an apparent mistake, the CO should have sought verification of plaintiff's bid in accordance with FAR 14.407-1, which provides that a contracting officer shall examine all bids after opening for mistakes and shall seek verification of an offeror's bid in cases of apparent mistakes or where the contracting officer has reason to believe a mistake may have been made. *Id.* In light of the severity of the effect caused to plaintiff by defendant's failure to verify plaintiff's bid, this court determines that the CO's actions constituted a clear and prejudicial violation of applicable ... regulations.

* * *

Conclusion

Based upon the foregoing discussion, this court concludes that plaintiff has demonstrated, by clear and convincing evidence, that defendant acted unreasonably and not in accordance with applicable law and regulations in finding plaintiff's bid nonresponsive to the solicitation. Accordingly, plaintiff's cross-motion for summary judgment upon the administrative record is granted and defendant's motion for summary judgment upon the administrative record is denied. The Clerk is directed to enter judgment in favor of plaintiff, declaring plaintiff's bid to be responsive and ordering defendant to proceed with contract award under the terms of Solicitation No. DACW 51-97-B-0006.

Notes and Questions

1. Is there real significance to what was missing? In general, is real significance required to satisfy the issue of responsiveness?

2. When the court says a bid "must comply with all material respects" is that standard broad or narrow?

3. The concept of responsiveness directly relates to trying to eliminate any prejudice against any particular bidder. The FAR speaks to bids complying in all "material respects" (FAR 14.301(a)) and "essential requirements" (FAR 14.404-2) of invitations for bids. Substantial deviations in proposed contract terms relating to price, quantity, or quality are considered to be the most likely to result in prejudice to other bidders. Is the variation of *any* contract term always going to result in prejudice to other bidders? For example, if one bidder proposes a different delivery date than the one called for in the solicitation, does that result in prejudice? Does it matter whether the delivery date is sooner or later than the solicitation proposed date?

4. Is the government willing to pay a premium in support of its policy of a level playing field? Is there ever an instance where a particular deal is so good that the government would be foolish to pass it up notwithstanding the fact that it violates procurement policies and requirements? Conversely, does fairness dictate that the government must always award a contract to the responsible bidder offering the lowest price? What should be the

result if the lowest offered price is unreasonably high? Who is responsible for making such a determination?

5. Unbalanced bids. An unbalanced bid consists, in essence, of a bid that seems deceptively low because its structure might let the bidder benefit from high charges on some items without the government ultimately benefitting from low charges on other items. Scrutiny of a possibly unbalanced bid may particularly occur for proposals involving high start-up costs for the government. While some of these may legitimately be line item expenses in the base term of the contract, others may simply be front-loading the profits of a multi-year contract, anticipating that subsequent years will not occur quite as predicted. The crux of the analysis in evaluating bids which include below-cost items is whether other line items are overpriced in relation to cost. If there are no such items, the bid cannot be deemed mathematically unbalanced.

In the event that a line item is found to be overpriced, the second step of the analysis is to determine whether "… there is a reasonable doubt that the bid will result in the lowest overall cost to the Government even though it may be the low evaluated bid, or if it is so unbalanced as to be tantamount to allowing an advance payment."(FAR§ 52.214-(10)(e)(1990)). For a more detailed discussion of this subject, see Daniel I. Gordon, *Unbalanced Bids*, 24 Pub. Con. L.J. 1 (1994); *Matter of General Atronics Corp.*, B-272685, 1996 WL 625079 (C.G.); *Wizards-Movers Elite, Inc.*, B-255753.2 (1994); *Matter of Atlantic Research Corp.*, B-247650 (1992)(protester must indicate overstated prices as basis for conclusion of mathematical unbalancing); *Matter of Earth Engineering and Sciences, Inc.*, B-248219 (1992) (protester must show reasonable doubt that mathematically unbalanced bid will result in lowest overall cost to Government).

2. Responsibility

Unlike commercial counterparts who are free to do business at their own risk and risking their own money with whomever they please, including scoundrels and the like, government contracting officers can do business only with contractors that are deemed to be responsible. Whereas responsiveness concerns *what* gets offered, responsibility concerns *who* offers it. The contracting officer must decide as to a potential awardee whether to make an affirmative determination of responsibility, or, a negative determinations of responsibility. In such a case, the party affected by such a determination clearly has standing and a direct economic interest in maintaining its capability to do business with the government. As a result, such negative determinations are likely to result in disputes and possible litigation. In contrast, it has sometimes been suggested that competitors cannot challenge an affirmative determination of responsibility. The following case shows otherwise.

Impresa Construzioni Geom. Domenico Garufi, Plaintiff-Appellant, v. United States, Defendant-Appellee

United States Court of Appeals, Federal Circuit
238 F.3d 1324
Jan. 3, 2001

Before NEWMAN, LINN, and DYK, Circuit Judges.

DYK, Circuit Judge.

… [W]e find that a substantial question has been raised concerning the rationality of the contracting officer's responsibility determination. We therefore reverse and remand the case to the Court of Federal Claims to allow a limited deposition of the contracting officer concerning the basis for the responsibility determination so that the Court of Federal Claims can properly review the responsibility determination....

I

This case involves a contract for maintenance, groundskeeping, janitorial, and other services, to be performed at the United States Naval Air Station in Sigonella, Italy. The appellant, Impresa Construzioni Geom. Domenico Garufi ("Garufi"), an unsuccessful bidder, challenged the award of the contract to Joint Venture Conserv ("JVC"). The background of this controversy is as follows:

On August 28, 1998, the Navy issued a Request for Proposals ("RFP") for the services contract at the Sigonella base. Four offerors responded to the solicitation, including Garufi and JVC. JVC is a joint venture composed of three companies: Lara Srl ("Lara"), Impredil Construzioni Srl ("Impredil"), and Coop. Bosco Etneo arl ("Bosco"). It appears that Lara and Impredil had previously performed similar contracts at the Sigonella base. Also, these two companies (Lara and Impredil), at least previously, were controlled by Carmelo La Mastra, while Bosco was controlled by Carmelo La Mastra's brother-in-law, Alfio Bosco.

In a 1997 proceeding, an Italian court, the Court of Catania Third Penal Division, found that Carmelo La Mastra had engaged in bid rigging and was involved in a Mafia organization in connection with previous contracts at the Sigonella base, apparently in the early 1990's. The Italian court found that Carmelo had been involved in intimidating a competitor into withdrawing from a bid for a contract at the Sigonella base, and that "probably in connection with that [same] bid the owner of another firm ... was killed." The Italian proceeding was also directed against Salvatore La Mastra and Alfio Bosco, the son and brother-in-law of Carmelo La Mastra. The court found that the seizure of property levied against Carmelo "La Mastra's children" and Bosco "appears to be legitimate" in light of "the free availability of immovable properties and societies registered fictitiously under the name of people close to him" and that such past and future transfers of property "may facilitate the consummation of other similar crimes or may make worse the consequences of the crimes already consummated." As a result of these findings the Court of Catania, in December 1997, placed Lara, Impredil, and Bosco under a receivership run by a legal administrator. The receivership papers gave the legal administrator authority to perform "all the necessary or opportune lawful acts for the management and administration" of the companies.

Shortly thereafter, also in December 1997, Lara and Impredil, with the approval of the legal administrator, conferred signatory power on Salvatore La Mastra, Carmelo La Mastra's son, to negotiate contract changes and sign modifications for various contracts at the Sigonella base.

Furthermore, in May 1998, also after the receivership had been established, Impredil filed registration papers at the Chamber of Commerce, Industry, Handicraft and Agriculture of Catania specifically listing Carmelo La Mastra as a "Company Officer" with the title of "Technical Manager appointed on 25 Jan. 1998" and as a "company signatory" of Impredil. The term "Technical Manager" is not defined in the document nor does the document disclose the job description or amount of control that a technical manager has over the company.

In June 1998, Carmelo La Mastra was indicted by the Anti Mafia District Office in Catania for his involvement in a "Mafia-type association" and for involvement in bid-rigging at the Sigonella base. The record does not disclose the outcome of that proceeding.

All of the events described in the preceding four paragraphs occurred before the 1998 RFP involved here. The RFP for the Sigonella contract, issued on August 28, 1998, stated that the contract would be awarded to the offeror who submitted the proposal that represented the best value to the government. On September 15, 1998, Lara, Impredil, and Bosco formed JVC as a temporary joint venture for the purpose of making a joint bid in response to the RFP....

Garufi and JVC submitted proposals, along with two other offerors....

Upon initial evaluation by a technical board and a price board, one of the competitors was eliminated from the competitive range by the contracting officer, leaving appellant Garufi, JVC, and one other bidder....

Under the Federal Acquisition Regulation ("FAR") the contract could not be awarded to JVC unless JVC was found to be "responsible," including a finding of "a satisfactory record of integrity and business ethics." 48 C.F.R. §9.104-1(d). On March 5, 1999, the contracting officer signed a responsibility determination, noting that JVC had "a satisfactory record of performance, integrity, and business ethics" and is "otherwise qualified and eligible to receive an award under applicable laws and regulations." The contracting officer therefore awarded the contract to JVC on March 5, 1999.

Garufi filed several protests with the General Accounting Office ("GAO"), challenging the Navy's elimination of Garufi from the competitive range and the grant of the contract to JVC. The GAO issued a final decision on June 17, 1999, denying Garufi's protests.

On June 28, 1999, Garufi filed a bid protest suit in the United States Court of Federal Claims pursuant to 28 U.S.C. § 1491(b)(1), which grants the Court of Federal Claims jurisdiction over bid protest actions against the government....

Garufi and the government then filed cross-motions for summary judgment. On July 30, 1999, the Court of Federal Claims denied Garufi's motion for summary judgment and granted the government's cross-motion. *Impresa Construzioni Geom. Domenico Garufi v. United States,* 44 Fed. Cl. 540 (1999)....

III

The history of the judicial review of government contracting procurement decisions is both long and complicated. In *Perkins v. Lukens Steel Co.,* 310 U.S. 113, 60 S.Ct. 869, 84 L.Ed. 1108 (1940), the Supreme Court held that private parties lacked standing to challenge a government contract award for violation of procurement law, concluding that Congress enacted procurement laws for the protection of the government, rather than for those contracting with the government....

However, following the 1946 enactment of the Administrative Procedure Act ("APA"), 5 U.S.C. §§ 551–559, 701–706, the District of Columbia Circuit in 1970 in *Scanwell Laboratories, Inc. v. Shaffer,* 424 F.2d 859 (D. C. Cir.1970), held that in the APA Congress had statutorily changed the rule of *Lukens Steel* and that APA review of the procurement decisions of government agencies and officials was available in district courts....

Bid protest cases were also brought in the Court of Federal Claims and its predecessor courts, but on a very different theory—that the government made an implied contract with prospective bidders to fairly assess their bids, and that the Court of Federal Claims had jurisdiction under the Tucker Act....

IV

In 1996, Congress passed the ADRA, thereby clarifying the Court of Federal Claims' bid protest jurisdiction. *See* Administrative Dispute Resolution Act of 1996, Pub. L. No. 104-320, § 12, 110 Stat. 3870, 3874–76. The ADRA provides that the Court of Federal Claims and district courts shall have concurrent jurisdiction over bid protest actions, and that the courts "shall review the agency's decision pursuant to the standards set forth in section 706 of title 5" of the APA. 28 U.S.C. § 1491(b)(1), (4). Pursuant to the ADRA, the district courts' jurisdiction over bid protests was to terminate on January 1, 2001, unless extended by Congress, and the Court of Federal Claims was to have exclusive jurisdiction over bid protest actions. *See* ADRA § 12(d).

The legislative history of the ADRA confirms what is obvious on the face of the statute— that the new legislation "applies the Administrative Procedure Act standard of review previously applied by the district courts (5 U.S.C. § 706) to all procurement protest cases in the Court of Federal Claims." H.R. Conf. Rep. No. 104-841, at 10 (1996). Under the ADRA, all bid protest actions under the APA are now reviewed under the standards applied in the *Scanwell* line of cases....

Under the APA standards that are applied in the *Scanwell* line of cases, a bid award may be set aside if either: (1) the procurement official's decision lacked a rational basis; or (2) the procurement procedure involved a violation of regulation or procedure....

What we have said so far is sufficient to dispose of the government's first argument, i.e., that "absent allegations of fraud or bad faith" by the contracting officer, the responsibility determination of the contracting officer is immune from judicial review. In this connection, the government relies primarily on our predecessor court's decisions in *Keco Indus., Inc. v. United States*, 203 Ct.Cl. 566, 492 F.2d 1200 (Ct.Cl.1974) and *Trilon Educational Corp. v. United States*, 217 Ct.Cl. 266, 578 F.2d 1356, 1358 (Ct.Cl.1978). The government has seriously misread these cases, which impose no such limits....

VI

We turn now to Garufi's claim that the contracting officer's responsibility determination concerning JVC's "record of integrity and business ethics" violated the APA. Under the Federal Acquisition Regulation, "[n]o purchase or award shall be made unless the contracting officer makes an affirmative determination of responsibility." 48 C.F.R. § 9.103(b). In making the responsibility determination, the contracting officer must determine that the contractor has "a satisfactory record of integrity and business ethics." 48 C.F.R. § 9.104-1(d). Furthermore, "[i]n the absence of information clearly indicating that the prospective contractor is responsible, the contracting officer shall make a determination of nonresponsibility." 48 C.F.R. § 9.103(b). FAR 9.105-2(b) requires that "[d]ocuments and reports supporting a determination of responsibility or nonresponsibility ... must be included in the contract file." However, the contracting officer is not required to explain the basis for his responsibility determination, and he has not done so here. Rather, the contracting officer signed the contract thereby making the required determination according to FAR 9.105-2(a) and in conclusory fashion determined that JVC had "a satisfactory record of performance, integrity, and business ethics."

Contracting officers are "generally given wide discretion" in making responsibility determinations and in determining the amount of information that is required to make a responsibility determination. *John C. Grimberg Co. v. United States*, 185 F.3d 1297, 1303 (Fed. Cir.1999). But this discretion is not absolute.

Unfortunately, the regulations concerning responsibility determinations are cryptic, but this court in *Trilon*, 578 F.2d at 1360, and the Comptroller General have recognized that we may look to the more extensive debarment regulations for guidance, at least on questions related to the "integrity and business ethics" requirement. *See, e.g., Steptoe & Johnson*, Comp. Gen. Dec. B-166118, 1969 WL 4287, at *5 (Mar. 28, 1969); *Secretary of the Army*, 39 Comp. Gen. 868, 872, 1960 WL 1741 (1960).

In this case, Garufi alleges that the contracting officer's responsibility determination is arbitrary because JVC does not fulfill the "satisfactory record of integrity and business ethics" requirement of FAR 9.104-1(d). This is said to be so because of the alleged involvement of Carmelo La Mastra and his relatives in JVC, and the findings of the Italian court in 1997 that Carmelo La Mastra engaged in criminal activities with respect to earlier contracts at the Sigonella base.

Two relevant propositions are established by earlier cases and supported by the debarment regulations. First, past criminal activities by a corporate officer do not automatically establish that the bidder fails the responsibility requirement.... The regulations make clear that "the existence of a cause for debarment, however, does not necessarily require that the contractor be debarred," and directs the agency official to balance the seriousness of the contractor's actions against the "remedial measures or mitigating factors" before making any debarment decision. 48 C.F.R. § 9.406-1(a).

The government urges that similarly, past improper actions by the former principal owner and head of two of JVC's components does not mandate a finding of non-responsibility of JVC. In view of the seriousness of the offenses found by the Italian court to have been committed by Carmelo La Mastra and his relatives, his and his relatives' central past role in the companies comprising JVC, and the direct relationship between these offenses and the predecessor government contracts at the Sigonella base, the government would be hard pressed to support a responsibility finding with respect to JVC save for the court-appointed Italian receivership. However, the debarment regulations specifically recognize that a "bona fide change in ownership or management" may result in a reduction in the scope or period of debarment, 48 C.F.R. § 9.406-4(c)(3), and the District of Columbia Circuit has similarly recognized that an effective receivership may make debarment inappropriate. *Robinson v. Cheney,* 876 F.2d 152, 160 (D. C. Cir.1989). The government here urges that the Italian receivership eliminated the control of Carmelo La Mastra and his relatives over JVC, making it appropriate to find JVC responsible.

This leads, however, to a second proposition: the creation of a receivership does not necessarily achieve a change in control or require a finding that the contractor in receivership is responsible.

Here the government points out that the administrator is empowered to "represent and run the joint venture without any limitations or exceptions." The government urges that Carmelo La Mastra and his relatives accordingly no longer control JVC, and therefore any misconduct by them should not be imputed to the company.

The appellant denies that the appointment of the legal administrator divested Carmelo La Mastra and his relatives of control over the company. Appellant notes that the record before the contracting officer showed that, after the appointment of the administrator, Carmelo's son Salvatore was given signatory power over the contracts previously held by Lara and Impredil at Sigonella, as well as the power to negotiate contract changes and modifications. The debarment regulations themselves recognize the relevance of family connections. 48 C.F.R. § 9.403. Furthermore, Carmelo himself was appointed technical manager of Impredil, one of the component companies of JVC, and was listed as a company signatory of Impredil.

The appellant relies on *Robinson,* 876 F.2d at 160–61, for the proposition that the appointment of a receivership, by itself, is not necessarily sufficient to establish a company's present responsibility and cleanse the company of the consequences of past improper conduct. In *Robinson,* the owner of a military clothing supply company, fearing debarment for bribing government officials, transferred his company to a trust (naming himself as beneficiary) in order to avoid his company being debarred by the government for his past actions, which allegedly included bid rigging. Despite the trust arrangement, the government initiated debarment proceedings against the supply company "based upon 'information ... indicating that [the supply company] lacks the business integrity and present responsibility to be a Government contractor.'" *Id.* at 155. The government then debarred the company, finding that the existence of the trust agreement failed to adequately screen the company from the former owner's (and now beneficiary's) acts of bid rigging, and that his actions therefore affected the company's responsibility. *See id.* at 157. The trustee challenged the debarment proceedings and the findings of non-responsibility in light of the trust agreement.

The court in *Robinson* sustained the debarment. The court acknowledged that the "ultimate inquiry as to 'present responsibility' relates directly to the contractor itself, not to the agent or former agent personally responsible for its past misdeeds. Thus, the contractor can meet the test of present responsibility by demonstrating that it has taken steps to ensure that the wrongful acts will not recur." *Id.* at 160. Although the trust agreement in *Robinson* gave ultimate decision-making authority to someone other than the wrongdoer, who was accused of bid rigging, the court nevertheless held that the trust agreement on its face was not sufficient to assure that the wrongdoer would "not continue to act improperly in [the company's] interest." *See id.* at 161. Particularly important was the absence in the trust agreement of specific terms barring the wrongdoer from acting on behalf of the company or participating in its management. *See id.* at 160. Furthermore, "nothing in either the trust agreement or in any other submission by the company gave the Government any assurance that [the wrongdoer] would not conduct illicit dealing on behalf of [the company] entirely outside company channels." *Id.*

This case is similar to *Robinson* in that the receivership agreement does not specifically bar Carmelo La Mastra from acting on behalf of or participating in the management of JVC. Indeed, as previously discussed, official papers filed by Impredil specifically list Carmelo La Mastra as a "technical manager" with signatory authority. It is noticeably unclear from the record what type of control or influence a "technical manager" has over a company. Furthermore, the record shows that prior to the award Carmelo La Mastra's son Salvatore La Mastra was given signatory authority to act on behalf of Impredil and Lara.

If this were a debarment proceeding involving government debarment of JVC, where the burden rests on the debarred company to show that it has taken steps to ensure that the wrongful acts will not recur, *see id.* at 160, we would follow *Robinson* and hold that the record does not establish the effectiveness of the receivership to insulate Carmelo La Mastra from control of JVC. But this is not a debarment proceeding, and the burden of establishing arbitrary and capricious action rests on the disappointed bidder. *See* 5 U.S.C. § 706. ...

This conundrum leads us into a most difficult and confusing area of administrative law, namely the circumstances under which an administrative agency will be compelled to provide an explanation for its decision. ...

Contracting officers are not obligated by the APA to provide written explanations for their actions. Decisions by contracting officers are not adjudicatory decisions to be made on the record after a hearing. *See John C. Grimberg Co. v. United States,* 185 F.3d at 1303. Nor are they formal rulemakings. As the government correctly points out, where the contracting officer makes a determination of responsibility, as opposed to the situation in which he makes a determination of non-responsibility, the regulations do not require the contracting officer to "make, sign and place in the contract file a determination of" responsibility which states the basis for the determination. 48 C.F.R. § 9.105-2(a).

However, under the APA even where an explanation or reason is not required, a reviewing court has power to require an explanation....

Based on the evidence of the Italian court proceedings, the Impredil filing at the Chamber of Commerce listing Carmelo La Mastra as a technical manager and company signatory, and the letters granting Salvatore La Mastra signatory authority of Lara and Impredil, which the parties agreed were all before the contracting officer, we conclude that this is one of those rare cases in which an explanation is required....

In ordering the deposition of the contracting officer, we wish to make clear that we are not ordering a deposition into the contracting officer's mental process, that is, the thought process by which he made his decision. Such inquiries are inappropriate. *See, e.g., United States v. Morgan*, 313 U.S. 409, 422, 61 S.Ct. 999, 85 L.Ed. 1429 (1941). The deposition is to be confined strictly to placing on the record the basis for the contracting officer's responsibility determination, that is, his grounds for concluding that JVC had a "satisfactory record of performance, integrity, and business ethics," including most particularly his assessment of the control issue. In order to answer the question of whether there was a lack of rational basis for the contracting officer's decision, we must know: (1) whether the contracting officer, as required by 48 C.F.R. § 9.105-1(a), possessed or obtained information sufficient to decide the integrity and business ethics issue, including the issue of control, before making a determination of responsibility; and (2) on what basis he made the responsibility determination....

This is a most unusual case. Upon remand, the scope of discovery and the review of the contracting decision are to be appropriately limited in scope.

CONCLUSION

For the reasons stated above, we affirm the Court of Federal Claims' decision in part, and reverse and remand in part.

AFFIRMED-IN-PART, REVERSED-IN-PART, AND REMANDED.

Notes and Questions

1. In *Garufi*, the responsibility issue arises in the unusual way that a competing offeror challenges the responsibility of the awardee. Why does the government object to judicial review of responsibility determinations, particularly in the context of competitor protests? What would make a contracting officer's responsibility determination differ from her other determinations such as regarding the responsiveness of a contractor's bid, or evaluating a proposal?

2. How is a finding of lack of responsibility for a single procurement different from a total debarment from doing business with the government in all instances? Note how the *Garufi* opinion distinguishes nonresponsibility from debarment in terms of the government's burden and the appropriate levels of requisite contracting officer explanation. Why? See Steven W. Feldman, *The* Impresa *Decision: Providing the Correct Standard of Review for Affirmative Responsibility Determinations*, The Procurement Lawyer, Winter 2001, at 5.

3. In *Garufi*, the offeror whose responsibility is in question is an enterprises in which an individual plays a role who personally has an unsatisfactory record. Much of the issue is whether the enterprise is run in a way that should relieve it from that individual's record. Consider this in forward business planning terms, as well as how it is presented in these cases, of subsequent litigation defense. How much can counsel for an enterprise that will seek government contracts deal with past bad records by purely formal steps, and how much must an enterprise actually and substantively purge itself of links to such past records?

4. The regulations on responsibility are found at FAR 9.104. These cover a diverse range of issues. For example, in recent years, the criterion of satisfactory past performance of previous government contracts has increased in importance as a component of determination of responsibility. Current regulations mandate a negative presumption regarding would-be awardees who have recently defaulted on other contracts, and direct contract officers to examine "[p]ast failure to apply sufficient tenacity and perseverance," which is specified as "strong evidence of nonresponsibility." See FAR 9.104(3)(b); *Matter of Information Resources Incorporated*, B-271767 (1996); *Matter of North American Construction Corp.*, B-270085 (1996)(contractor characterized as "change order artist" by one of its references.); *Matter of Shepard Printing*, B-260362 (1995).

5. Bankrupt offerors. The Government can find that a contractor lacks responsibility because of lack of financial ability to perform the contract (FAR 9.104-1(a)). However, ironically, the bankruptcy statutes preclude the use of this fact as the *sole* basis of a nonresponsibility determination. See, e.g., *Matter of: Harvard Interiors Manufacturing Co.*, B-247400 (1992).

3. Process

Carothers Construction Inc., Plaintiff, v. The United States, Defendant, Barron Construction Company, Intervenor

United States Claims Court.
18 Cl. Ct. 745
Nov. 29, 1989

FUTEY, Judge.

This pre-award contract action is before the court on defendant's motion for summary judgment and plaintiff's cross-motion for injunctive and declaratory relief. This action originally came before the court on plaintiff's motion filed on October 18, 1989, requesting that the Department of the Navy be enjoined from awarding a contract to Barron Construction Company to construct an Aviation Support Equipment Training Facility at the Naval Air Station in Millington, Tennessee. Before the contracting officer decided whether Barron's bid was responsive, plaintiff filed a protest with the General Accounting Office which alleged that Barron's bid was untimely submitted and therefore non-responsive. The General Accounting Office issued a recommendation which concluded that the bid was responsive and the Navy announced that it will adopt the General Accounting Office's recommendation. Plaintiff asserts, inter alia, that Barron's bid was not timely submitted and a determination to the contrary violates Federal procurement practices and the government's obligation to consider Carothers Construction Inc.'s bid fairly and honestly. For the reasons stated hereinafter, defendant's motion for summary judgment, which requests denial of plaintiff's claim for a permanent injunction of the award of the subject contract to Barron, is granted and plaintiff's cross-motion for injunctive and declaratory relief is denied and its complaint is dismissed.

Factual Background

On February 27, 1989, the Southern Division of the Naval Facilities Engineering Command (Navy) issued a solicitation, No. N62467-84-B-0153 (solicitation) for submission of sealed bids on the construction of an Aviation Support Equipment Training Facility at the Naval Air Station Memphis in Millington, Tennessee. Subsequently, several amendments to the solicitation changed the date and place of the bid opening, which was finally set for 2:00 p.m. on June 1, 1989, in Building S-236, room 116, Naval Air Station, Memphis, Tennessee.

The events at issue occurred in room 116 and principally involve three individuals: Dolores Quinton (Quinton), the bid opening officer for the solicitation, Luke Thoele (Thoele), a contracts specialist, and Allen Townsend (Townsend), a representative of Barron Construction Company (Barron), a contractor which bid on the solicitation. Sometime before 2:00 p.m. on June 1, 1989, Townsend submitted a bid on behalf of Barron (Barron's bid) then several minutes later he retrieved it from Quinton and left the room. Later, he resubmitted Barron's bid with a notation on the outside of the envelope which stated, "DEDUCT $40000 AL TOWNSEND 1:54 P.M." Quinton took Barron's bid to her immediate supervisor, Richard Johnson, who told her that the attempted modification was ineffective. After being told of this, Townsend again retrieved Barron's bid and immediately left the room. At approximately three minutes before 2:00 p.m., Townsend contacted O.P. Barron, president of Barron, and asked for instruction. O.P. Barron told Townsend to open Barron's bid envelope and deduct $40,000.00. With approximately two minutes to go before bid opening, Townsend removed documents from Barron's bid envelope and wrote on them. At five seconds before 2:00 p.m., Quinton instructed Townsend to "hand me something." Townsend handed Quinton a set of documents with a copy of Barron's bid on top. At 2:00 p.m., Quinton began announcing that the time for receipt of bids had passed. What happened next is contested by the parties. Defendant contends that simultaneously with Quinton's announcement, Townsend threw the rest of the Barron bid documents on the table in front of Quinton. After Quinton finished, Thoele took the documents from Quinton and collected the rest of Barron's bid documents from the table. In contrast, plaintiff avers that up to fifteen seconds after the commencement of Quinton's announcement, Townsend continued to place the remainder of Barron's bid documents in the possession of the government and did not relinquish control of all Barron's bid documents before the 2:00 p.m. bid deadline. The parties agree that nine bids were received and Barron's was found to have submitted the lowest bid, with a bid price of $9,680,000.00 while the second lowest bidder, Carothers Construction Inc. (Carothers) submitted a bid price of $9,822,045.00.

Plaintiff filed a pre-award protest by letter with the Navy contracting officer (CO) on June 5, 1989.... After contacting the CO on June 19, 1989, and learning that a decision had not yet been rendered,[1] plaintiff filed on that same day a protest by letter with the General Accounting Office (GAO) which realleged the contentions in the CO protest.

The Navy agency issued a report on July 26, 1989, which addressed plaintiff's arguments, as expressed in its letters to the CO and the GAO, and denied its protest.[3] In response, on August 9, 1989, plaintiff submitted comments on the agency report to the GAO and requested that its protest be sustained because Barron's bid "(i) was not submitted prior to the scheduled time of submission of bids, and/or (ii) failed to include the required bid bond."

The GAO issued a recommendation dated October 11, 1989, which determined that Barron's bid was not submitted late. Relying on the declarations of Quinton, Thoele and

---

1. There is no indication in the pleadings that there was a decision by the Contracting Officer (CO); however the parties stated during oral argument that there was a decision which, in essence, ratified Quinton's acceptance of Barron's bid.

3. The report noted that Barron's bid failure to enclose a bid in a sealed envelope as provided by the terms of the invitation is a technicality which can be waived by the CO. Matter of R. Bruce Hoffe, B-153288 (Mar. 19, 1964); see Central Mechanical Construction Inc., B-220594, 85-2 CPD 730 (Dec. 31, 1985); see also FAR § 14.405.

Dana Brignole (Brignole), an agency procurement clerk present at the bid opening, the GAO held that "while the manner of the submission of the bid ... was irregular, the evidence clearly shows that the Barron representative relinquished control of its bid (including all bid documents) simultaneously with ... [Quinton's] ... declaration that the time for receipt of bids had passed. Accordingly, we find that Barron's bid was not submitted late."

Plaintiff filed a "Complaint for Declaratory And Injunctive Relief" in this court on October 18, 1989, requesting that the Navy be enjoined from awarding the contract to Barron. The government represented to this court in a telephone conference held on October 19, 1989, that the Navy decided to abide by the recommendation of the GAO, but would not award the contract until November 9, 1989. In addition, on this date, Barron gave notice to the court that it would appear in this action and assert its interest.

On October 25, 1989, defendant filed a motion for summary judgment. On October 31, 1989, plaintiff filed a response to defendant's motion for summary judgment and a cross-motion for injunctive and declaratory relief. On November 6, 1989, Barron filed a motion to intervene. Oral argument was held on November 7, 1989.

In the present action, plaintiff asserts that Barron's bid was untimely submitted. Therefore, such an award would violate Federal procurement law, regulations and policies, and constitute a breach of the Navy's contractual obligation to consider plaintiff's bid fairly and honestly.

Discussion

Jurisdiction to review pre-award contract decisions of a government agency is conferred on this court pursuant to 28 U.S.C. § 1491(a)(3) (1982), of the Federal Courts Improvement Act of 1982. United States v. John C. Grimberg Co., 702 F.2d 1362, 1366–72 (Fed. Cir.1983). Section 1491(a)(3) provides:

> To afford complete relief on any contract claim brought before the contract is awarded, the court shall have exclusive jurisdiction to grant declaratory judgments and such equitable and extraordinary relief as it deems proper, including but not limited to injunctive relief. In exercising this jurisdiction, the court shall give due regard to the interests of national defense and national security.

Pre-award contract claims under this statute are founded upon an implied-in-fact contract which arises by virtue of the bid solicitation process which obligates the government to consider offers fairly and honestly. Keco Indus., Inc. v. United States, 192 Ct.Cl. 773, 784, 428 F.2d 1233, 1237 (1970); Heyer Pro. Co. v. United States, 135 Ct.Cl. 63, 69, 140 F. Supp. 409, 413 (1956); Paxson Elec. Co. v. United States, 14 Cl. Ct. 634, 638 (1988). Accordingly, plaintiff's suit is properly before this court.

* * *

The issue before the Claims Court is whether the Navy can justifiably follow the GAO's recommendation that Barron's bid was submitted timely and, therefore, was responsive to solicitation. The dispositive inquiry in deciding that question was a rational one. Honeywell v. United States, 870 F.2d 644, 647 (1989); Hayes Int'l Corp. V. United States, 7 Cl.Ct. 681, 684–85 (1985) (citations omitted); Caddell Const. Co. v. United States, 7 Cl.Ct. 236, 241 (1985) (citations omitted). As subsequently discussed, a rational basis existed.

Recommendations of the GAO are accorded "due weight and deference by this court given the GAO's long experience and special expertise in ... bid protest matters." Baird Corp. v. United States, 1 Cl.Ct. 662, 668 (1983) (citations omitted). Because the GAO has such an important role in resolving contested procurement matters, normally the agencies will follow its decisions. Honeywell, 870 F.2d at 647, 648. In addition, Congress intended that procurement agencies would follow the Comptroller General's recommendation, because an agency's failure to follow requires notice to the Comptroller General and an eventual report to Congress. Id. at 648.

* * *

Plaintiff also alleges that the GAO violated procurement statutes and regulations by concluding that Barron's bid was timely. Specifically, the GAO violated FAR § 14.304-1 which provides that bids "received in the office designated in the invitation for bids after the exact time set for opening are 'late bids.' " Plaintiff reads this in conjunction with the solicitation which states that "[a]ny bids submitted by hand after the time set for receipt will not be accepted" and argues that the GAO must reject Barron's bid because there is no evidence that it was submitted at 2:00 p.m., the exact time specified in the solicitation. In addition, plaintiff asserts that the evidence shows that Quinton's announcement was not commenced until after 2:00 p.m. and for that reason the bid was untimely, whether or not it was submitted simultaneously with the announcement.

This court notes that plaintiff's interpretation of FAR § 14.304-1 is unsupported by FAR § 14.402-1 and the GAO decisions which have interpreted both provisions. FAR § 14.402-1(a) provides that "[t]he bid opening officer shall decide when the time set for opening bids has arrived and shall inform those present of that decision." See K. L. Conwell, B-220561, 86-1 CPD ¶ 79 (Jan. 23, 1986). Consistent with that provision is the rule of law applied in the GAO's decision "[t]he bid opening officer's declaration of bid opening time is determinative of lateness unless it is shown to be unreasonable under the circumstances." Chattanooga Office Supply Co., B-228062, 87-2 CPD ¶ 221 (Sept. 3, 1987).

The record before the GAO shows that Quinton made several announcements of the bid opening time prior to the final announcement at 2:00 p.m. Therefore, the GAO concluded, the record shows that Quinton's announcement was reasonable and determinative of lateness. "The time when a bid is submitted is determined by the time that the bidder relinquishes control of the bid." Chestnut Hill Constr., Inc., B-216891, 85-1 CPD ¶ 443 (Apr. 18, 1985). The GAO interpreted this to mean that a bid is late if submitted after the time the contracting or bid opening officer announces that the time set for bid opening has arrived, citing Amfel Constr., Inc., B-233493.2, 89-1 CPD ¶ 477 (May 18, 1989). It was upon this basis that the Comptroller General framed the critical inquiry of when Barron relinquished control of its bid documents in relation to the bid opening officer's declaration that the time for receipt of bids had passed. In finding that the bid was relinquished simultaneously with Quinton's 2:00 p.m. announcement, the GAO also found that the bid was timely under Amfel, because the bid was not submitted after the time of the announcement. In light of the precedent cited and applied by the GAO, this court cannot hold that the GAO's decision was irrational.

The GAO's finding that Townsend relinquished control of Barron's bid (including all bid documents) simultaneously with Quinton's announcement that the time for receipt of bids had passed had ample support in the record. The GAO based its finding on the unsworn declarations of Quinton, Brignole and Thoele. The Comptroller General focused on the following: Quinton declared that she was watching the clock, and "when the second hand reached the 12 she began to announce that the time for receipt of bids had passed. At that time … [Townsend] threw the other copies of the bid (and other bid documents) on the table in front of her." Supporting this was the statement of Brignole that Townsend placed the other bid documents simultaneously with Quinton's announcement. Finally, the Comptroller General noted Thoele's declaration that he picked up the documents on the table. Based on these unsworn declarations, the court finds that a rational basis existed for the GAO's decision.

* * *

Conclusion

For all the above reasons, the court finds that the Comptroller General's decision that Barron's bid was not submitted late had a rational basis and, therefore, the decision to follow the recommendation by the CO was not arbitrary and capricious, and not contrary to the law.

Notes and Questions

1. Take this opinion as a vivid description of the bid opening, that formal peak of the bidding process. This seems to have been a particularly colorful opening. Throw in a few clerical errors and borderline nonresponsive specifications, and this could be a whole exam question. Does the highly structured and formal nature of this process derive from the formality in classic private offer and acceptance, e.g., the well-known formalities at auctions and the "mirror image" rule for acceptances? Or, does it derive from formality in public policy, such as the limits on authority of officials and the imperative to curb favoritism and corruption?

2. Fundamental to the sealed bidding and public opening of bids is the requirement that all bids be received by a date and time certain. Mountains of litigation have ensued from trying to decide acceptable reasons for considering a late bid. For example, is a bid sent by facsimile late when the first page is received prior to the time stated for receipt of bids but the last page is received just minutes afterwards? Or is a bid late when the courier delivering acts as a good Samaritan in an auto accident thereby saving a life but delaying the delivery of the bid beyond the stated time?

3. Why should the government deny itself the benefit of a late bid, especially where the late bid is the most advantageous bid for the government? FAR 14.304-1 provides for very limited circumstances whereby late bids can be considered—all relating to government (including U.S. Postal Service) mishandling of the bid. (See *Matter of C.R. Hipp Construction Co., Inc.*, B-274328, 1996 Wl 669947 (C.G.)(bid received from agency mailroom staff by opening officer after announcement that no more hand-carried bids would be accepted but prior to bid opening was timely); *Matter of Family Stress Clinics of America*, B-270993 (1996)(contract officer's oral amendment extending submission date over duration of government shutdown not communicated to one firm on RFP distribution list); FAR §§ 14.304-1(a)(1)–(4); 52.214-7). With respect to bid modifications, FAR § 52.214-7(2)(f) allows but does not compel consideration of " ... a late modification of an otherwise successful bid that makes its terms more favorable to the Government ..."

4. For a discussion, see Brian P. Waagner & Elizabeth D. Evans, *Agency Discretion in Bid Timeliness Protests: The Case for Consistency*, 29 Pub. Cont. L. J. 713 (2000).

McClure Electrical Constructors, Inc., Appellant, v. John H. Dalton, Secretary of the Navy, Appellee

United States Court of Appeals, Federal Circuit
132 F.3d 709
Dec. 17, 1997

Before NEWMAN, PLAGER, and RADER, Circuit Judges.

RADER, Circuit Judge.

McClure Electrical Constructors, Inc. (McClure Electrical) challenges denial of its claim for contract reformation. McClure Electrical sought contract reformation to correct its unilateral bid mistake. On September 26, 1996, the Armed Services Board of Contract Appeals (Board) affirmed the contracting officer's final decision not to reform the contract. See McClure Elec. Constructors, Inc., ASBCA No. 49,711, 96-2 BCA ¶ 28,593 (1996). Because the Board did not err in so deciding, this court affirms the Board's decision.

I.

McClure Electrical entered into a contract to build an electrical substation at a naval center in Louisville, Kentucky. Mr. McClure, the company's president, prepared three bid worksheets to determine the bid amount for this project. However, in preparing a recapitulation sheet, Mr. McClure did not transfer the amount from the third bid worksheet and instead twice transferred the amount from the first bid worksheet. Due to this error, McClure Electrical's bid was $16,530 lower than intended.

Due to this error, McClure Electrical's bid was the lowest of the eight entered bids by $28,000. When the contracting officer at the Department of the Navy reviewed the bids, she noticed the disparity between McClure Electrical's $145,000 bid and the Government estimate of $282,869. Suspecting a possible error and wishing to confirm the apparent low bid, the contracting officer sent a bid verification request to McClure Electrical. The letter did not state explicitly the contracting officer's suspicion of a possible error. In the relevant portion of that letter, the contracting officer wrote: "[a]s evidenced by the enclosed Abstract of Offers, you are the apparent low bidder. Please review your bid worksheets for possible errors or omissions." The contracting officer enclosed abstracts showing the amount of each bid and the amount of the Government estimate for the project. These amounts were appreciably higher than McClure Electrical's bid.

With the contracting officer's bid verification request and the amounts of each bid in his possession, Mr. McClure reviewed his company's bid and confirmed its accuracy in a letter to the contracting officer. After completion of the project, Mr. McClure's son, vice-president of McClure Electrical, reviewed the project to determine why McClure Electrical had lost money on the contract and discovered the error. McClure Electrical then sought reformation of the contract to increase its price by $19,000—the mistakenly omitted materials costs of $16,530, plus sales tax, overhead, profit, and bond costs. McClure Electrical argued that the Navy's bid verification request was inadequate because the contracting officer did not expressly state her suspicion that McClure Electrical had submitted an erroneous bid. The contracting officer denied relief, and the Board affirmed. McClure Electrical now appeals to this court.

II.

... The FAR set forth a process for handling suspected mistakes in bids. 48 C.F.R. §§ 14.406-1, 14.406-3(g) (1992). To determine adequacy of a bid verification request, this court examines de novo the Board's interpretation of the controlling FAR. "Notwithstanding this lack of deference on questions of law, [this court] accord[s] respect to the board's interpretation of regulations that are within its field of expertise: federal procurement law." Ingalls Shipbuilding, Inc. v. Dalton, 119 F.3d 972, 975 (Fed.Cir.1997); see also Erickson Air Crane Co. v. United States, 731 F.2d 810, 814 (Fed.Cir.1984) ("[L]egal interpretations by tribunals having expertise are helpful to us, even if not compelling.").

III.

In Solar Foam Insulation, ASBCA No. 46,921, 94-2 BCA ¶ 26,901 (1994), the Board set out its rules for allowing reformation of a contract due to a contractor's unilateral bid mistake. The contractor must show by clear and convincing evidence that:

(1) a mistake in fact occurred prior to contract award; (2) the mistake was a clear-cut, clerical or mathematical error or a misreading of the specifications and not a judgmental error; (3) prior to award the Government knew, or should have known, that a mistake had been made and, therefore, should have requested bid verification; (4) the Government did not request bid verification or its request for bid verification was inadequate; and (5) proof of the intended bid is established.

Id.

In this appeal, the parties do not dispute that the contractor has shown sufficient evidence to satisfy elements (1)—(3) and (5). Only element (4), the adequacy of the Government's request for bid verification, is at issue. In reviewing this appeal, this court examines the request for verification of a bid for adequacy.

The controlling regulations, 48 C.F.R. §§ 14.406-1 and 14.406-3(g) (1992), set forth a process for handling suspected bid mistakes:

> After the opening of bids, contracting officers shall examine all bids for mistakes. In cases of apparent mistakes and in cases where the contracting officer has reason to believe that a mistake may have been made, the contracting officer shall request from the bidder a verification of the bid, calling attention to the suspected mistake.

48 C.F.R. § 14.406-1 (1992). The regulations further provide that:

> [s]uspected or alleged mistakes in bids shall be processed as follows.... (1) The contracting officer shall immediately request the bidder to verify the bid. Action taken to verify bids must be sufficient to reasonably assure the contracting officer that the bid as confirmed is without error, or to elicit the allegation of a mistake by the bidder. To assure that the bidder will be put on notice of a mistake suspected by the contracting officer, the bidder should be advised as appropriate—(i) That its bid is so much lower than the other bids or the Government's estimate as to indicate a possibility of error ... or (iv) Of any other information, proper for disclosure, that leads the contracting officer to believe that there is a mistake in [the] bid.

48 C.F.R. § 14.406-3(g)(1) (1992).

Although the contracting officer did not expressly state that she suspected an error, she did reveal the amounts of all bids. With this information in hand, McClure Electrical could see that the next lowest bid was almost 20% higher than its bid. In other words, the next lowest bid was equal to McClure Electrical's bid plus 20% of McClure Electrical's bid. The disparity between McClure Electrical's bid and the Government estimate was even greater. The Government estimate was $282,869, or almost twice McClure Electrical's bid.

In a similar case, Klinger Constructors, Inc., ASBCA No. 41,006, 91-3 BCA ¶ 24,218 (1991), the contracting officer sent the low bidder a letter stating that its bid was "substantially lower than the Government estimate." Id. The bid verification request also disclosed the difference between the contractor's bid and the Government estimate. This discrepancy was the only information that could have formed a basis for the contracting officer's opinion that an error in the bid may have been made. In Klinger, the Board correctly determined that "the contracting officer's notification adequately alerted the contractor to the possibility of a mistake and the basis for the suspicion." Id.

McClure Electrical asserts that the record suggests that the Navy sends a bid verification request to low bidders as a matter of standard operating procedure. Thus, McClure

Electrical argues, its receipt of such a letter did not give adequate notice of a suspected error because a "bid verification" letter comes to every low bidder regardless of the presence of a suspected error. To the contrary, the contracting officer in this case testified the Navy sends these letters only if the contracting officer has a concern that there may be a bid error.

In requesting bid verification, the contracting officer, although not expressly so stating, informed McClure Electrical that its bid was considerably lower both than any other bid and the Government's estimate by providing the Abstract of Offers. With that information (i.e., the bid abstracts) in hand, McClure Electrical should have been able to infer that a possible error occurred in its bid calculations and thus, was on notice of the possibility of such an error.

The contracting officer did not, of course, have access to McClure Electrical's bid worksheets, which contained the error. The contracting officer only suspected an error due to the discrepancy between McClure Electrical's bid and other bids. Thus, by disclosing the other bids and the Government's estimate, the contracting officer called attention to all information on which she had based her suspicion of a mistake. Under the circumstances, this disclosure was fully adequate. The contracting officer had no way of knowing McClure Electrical had made an error on its worksheets. Because the bid verification request sent out by the contracting officer was adequate to put McClure Electrical on notice of a suspected bid mistake, this court affirms the decision of the Board.

IV.

The Navy's contracting officer provided McClure Electrical with an adequate request for bid verification. McClure Electrical had in its possession all of the information known to the contracting officer, information from which it was just as able as the contracting officer to infer the possibility of a mistake. Therefore, the bid verification request placed McClure Electrical on notice of a suspected error. The Board properly affirmed the contracting officer's denial of contract reformation.

AFFIRMED.

Notes and Questions

1. FAR 14.407-2 permits correction only after the bidder submits verification of the bid intended for clerical mistakes that are facially obvious, such as misplaced decimal points, obviously incorrect discounts, obvious mistakes in designation of unit, or similar typographical errors. See, e.g., *Matter of H. A. Sack Co., Inc.*, B-278359 (1998)(Awardee permitted to correct spreadsheet error after bid submission.); *Matter of Brazos Roofing, Inc.*, B-275319.2, 1997 WL 49033 (C.G.); William P. Rudland, *Rationalizing the Bid Mistake Rules,* 16 Pub. Cont. L.J. 446 (1987). What type of verification could be used to support the correction of such mistakes? Does allowing such correction serve the policy of promoting a level playing field?

2. Consider that the contractor satisfied four of the five elements for reformation of a contract due to a unilateral bid mistake mistake in fact, of a clerical nature, which the government should have known, and regarding which the contractor can prove its intended bid. Looking at the matter from the contractor's perspective, should not its right to reformation turn on the factors bearing on the nature of its mistake, which are the same regardless of what kind of bid verification form the Navy sends? Why make reformation turn on the adequacy of the government's request for bid verification?

3. Two-Step Sealed Bidding. Without going deeply into the topic of the chapter regarding negotiated proposals, brief mention may occur of a hybrid between sealed bids and negotiated proposals, namely, the hybrid method of Two-Step Sealed Bidding. This

is the preferred procurement method for acquisition of rapidly evolving technical items or services. The first step is the issuance of a Request for Technical Proposals (RFTP), which must include a description of the items or services sought, evaluative criteria to be employed, and due date, among other features (FAR 14.503-1). In response to proposals that are considered at least "reasonably susceptible of being made acceptable," the government may conduct discussions with offerors. (FAR 14-503-1(a)(8)(iii)).Step two is the usual sealed bidding process, except that participation is limited (via invitations for bids, or IFBs) to those firms which were determined to have submitted technically acceptable proposals in the first phase (FAR 14.503-2).

B. Competitive Negotiation

The method of requesting competitive proposals, principally known by the initials "RFP" for "Request for Proposals" and formerly known as "negotiated procurement," is by far the most common method by which the government purchases products and services with a value in excess of the simplified acquisition threshold of $100,000. It is the second principal leg of a triangle of procurement methods that includes sealed bids and sole source contracting. Whereas the prospective contractors in sealed bidding are generally known as "bidders" that submit "bids," with competitive proposals, prospective contractors are generally known as "offerors" that submit "offers" or "proposals." The very broad discretion given government contracting officials, based upon a mandatory impartial and comprehensive evaluation process, to select the offer representing the "best value" to the government makes the use of competitive proposals the favorite competitive procurement methodology for large dollar items and services.

An RFP contains, at a minimum, the: (1) government's requirements which include restrictive specifications only to the extent necessary to satisfy the needs of the agency; (2) anticipated terms and conditions of the contract; (3) information required to be in the offeror's proposal; and (4) factors and significant subfactors along with their relative importance to be used to evaluate the proposals received. After issuance of an RFP, there is a well-developed process in the government by which potential offerors can submit written questions and receive written answers to those questions, distributed to all interested offerors in the form of an amendment to the solicitation.

The RFP process differs from the sealed bids or IFBs in two critical ways. First, in comparison to sealed bids where price and price-related factors are the only evaluation factors, in competitive proposals, price or cost is not the only factor. Indeed, price or cost is often not even a principal factor (although by statute price or cost is always at least one of the factors.) An agency has broad discretion to include evaluation factors that represent the key areas of importance and emphasis to be considered in the contract award decision. The evaluation factors are to allow for a meaningful comparison and discrimination among proposals. There is no statutory or regulatory limit on the type or scope of non-price related evaluation factors that may be considered by an agency when reviewing proposals. Such factors most often include items such as: technical expertise; technical capability and management capability; personnel qualifications; offeror past performance; method of compliance with specific specifications; and delivery times. The only limit that exists, and it is one that is strictly enforced, is that all factors to be evaluated must be listed in the solicitation. A sure way for an agency to have a bid protest sustained against it is to make an award decision based on undisclosed evaluation factors.

In addition, the solicitation must disclose whether all evaluation factors other than cost or price, when combined, are significantly more important, equal to, or significantly less important than to the cost or price evaluation factor. Cost or price generally is a more important evaluation factor when the government requirement is clearly definable and risk of unsuccessful contract performance is slight. This is often the case for widely available commercial items and services being purchased by the government. Where the government requirement is less definitive, more development work is required, or the performance risk is higher, technical or past performance considerations may be more important than cost or price. Such is often the case for new weapon system development or complete government system overhauls.

The second critical way in which competitive proposals differ from the sealed bid process is the process that follows. In the typical sequence, a federal agency, after establishing a competitive range of the most initially highly ranked proposals, will hold discussions with the offerors in the competitive range prior to making an award decision. Thereby, offerors are given a chance to improve their proposals to be more consistent with the government requirements so that the government may make a best-value determination and contract award. During these discussions, the government identifies significant weaknesses, deficiencies, and other aspects of the offeror's proposal, e.g., cost, price, technical approach, past performance, and proposed contractual terms and conditions, for each offeror. The purpose of the discussions is to allow each offeror to revise its proposal based upon information discussed during the negotiations. Then, each offeror makes its "best and final offer" or "BAFOs."

While award may be made only to a "responsible" offeror, just as award may be made only to a responsible bidder under sealed bids, the concept of "responsiveness" critical in the sealed bid environment is not applicable in the competitive proposal environment. Offerors are free to propose alternative approaches to meeting the government needs — with the single caveat that an offer must meet the material requirements of the solicitation.

For further discussion of these subjects, see: Erin L. Craig, *Searching For Clarity: Completing The Unfinished FAR Part 15 Rewrite*, 39 Pub. Cont. L.J. 661 (Spring 2010); H. Jack Shearer, *How Could It Hurt To Ask? The Ability To Clarify Cost/Price Proposals Without Engaging In Discussions*, 39 Pub. Cont. L.J. 583 (Spring 2010); Anna Sturgis, *The Illusory Debriefing: A Need For Reform*, 38 Pub. Cont. L.J. 469 (Winter 2009); Shereen M. Marcus, Note, *Efficiency in Exchange: An Economic Analysis of Acquisition by* Negotiation, Note, 32 Pub. Cont. L.J. 659 (2003); David A. Whiteford, *Negotiated Procurements: Squandering the Benefit of the Bargain*, 32 Pub. Cont. L.J. 509 (2003); Nathanael Causey, Contractor Challenges To The Government's Evaluation Of Past Performance During The Source-Selection Process: "Thou Protesteth Too Much?," 2002 Army Law. 25 (Aug. 2002); Scott J. Kaplan, Trustworthiness In Public Contracting: Back To Boss Tweed? CF&I Steel v. Bay Area Rapid Transit District, 31 Pub. Cont. L.J. 237 (Winter 2002); David T. Douthwaite, *Why Procure Construction by Negotiation?* 25 Pub. Cont. L.J. 423 (1996).

1. Negotiation Process

The competitive proposal process is often considered superior to sealed bids by those directly involved with actual procurements because it allows the government and prospective contractors to discuss the solicitation requirements and the offeror's response to those requirements, prior to the government making an award decision. This early exchange of information and concerns can eliminate post-award confusion and problems that can result in costly and time-consuming litigation and delayed delivery. At the same time, however, in an environment that seeks to create a level playing field among all competitors, discussions offer a greater opportunity for one competitor to receive "extra" help or consideration by government officials not offered to others.

As previously noted, the competitive proposal process has an idealized sequence—RFP, proposals, competitive range, discussions, BAFO, award. However, it can have a number of variants. The contracting officer might decide, looking at the proposals, to pick the best and make an award without discussions, either on the initial proposals, or after some clarifications or other steps. As a result, the decision to hold discussions and the content thereof is a serious one. Before 1997, FAR part 15 imposed very rigid requirements on the duty to conduct discussions with all offerors once discussions were opened. While the concept existed of providing to some offerors mere clarifications without across-the-board discussions, it gave little room for meaningful exchange. Then, a signal "FAR Part 15 rewrite" occurred. One of the purposes of the FAR part 15 rewrite, in loosening the definitions triggering discussions with all offerors, was to lighten the burden on contracting officers faced with many offerors. *See, e.g.,* Computer Literacy World v. Department of the Air Force, GSBCA 134238-P (1995)(granting protest in which the Air Force received fifty-three proposals and disqualified forty-seven on minor grounds, including the six lowest-price ones, without any discussions). The next opinion reflects what the rewrite produced.

A few other terms deserve brief introduction before seeing them in action in the cases. The "evaluation factors" in the RFP play a key role in this process, providing the basis for deciding which proposals get into the competitive range, and later serving as the basis for discussions and for evaluating the BAFO for award. And, when proposals get eliminated, the rejected offeror can request and receive a "debriefing" as to the reason. The debriefing assists the offeror in deciding whether to protest.

Information Technology & Applications Corporation, Plaintiff-Appellant, v. United States, Defendant-Appellee

United States Court of Appeals, Federal Circuit
316 F.3d 1312
Jan. 10, 2003

Before NEWMAN, DYK and PROST, Circuit Judges.

DYK, Circuit Judge.

This case involves the distinction between "clarifications" and "discussions" under the 1997 revision to Subpart 15.3 of the Federal Acquisition Regulations. 48 C.F.R. §§ 15.300–08 (2002). Information Technology and Applications Corporation ("ITAC") appeals the decision of the United States Court of Federal Claims denying its bid protest and granting the United States motion for summary judgment on the administrative record. *Info. Tech. & Applications Corp. v. United States,* 51 Fed.Cl. 340 (Fed.Cl.2001).... [W]e affirm.

BACKGROUND

On March 19, 2001, the Air Force issued Solicitation and Request for Proposals No. FA2550-01-R-0001 ("RFP") to obtain a contract for professional services in support of its Space Warfare Center. The winning contractor was to examine, assess and develop means of integrating national intelligence assets with the Department of Defense space systems, in order to enhance combat and research and development capabilities at the Space Warfare Center. The Air Force intended to make an award to one lead contractor, which would perform overall program management and integration, operations support, systems engineering and analysis, and other work related to the Space Warfare Center. The term of performance was to be twelve months, beginning on October 1, 2001, with seven one-year options.

Under the RFP, the contract was to be awarded "to an offeror who gives the Government the greatest confidence that it will best meet [the] requirements affordably." RFP at 81. In accordance with 10 U.S.C. § 2305(a)(2)(A) and 41 U.S.C. § 253a(b)(1), the RFP also disclosed "all the significant factors and significant subfactors" that the agency "reasonably expect[ed] to consider," and their relative importance. 10 U.S.C. § 2305(a)(2)(A) (2000); 41 U.S.C. § 253a(b)(1) (2000); RFP at 81–85.

ITAC, [RS Information Systems, Inc. ("RSIS")] and a third offeror submitted timely proposals in response to the RFP. All three proposals anticipated that some of the work would be performed by subcontractors. RSIS's proposal relied heavily on the role of its subcontractors, which were to perform at least 75% of the work on the contract.

The Air Force sent various "evaluation notices" ("ENs") to all three offerors. These evaluation notices were brief letters to the offerors requesting additional information regarding their proposals. The Air Force sent three ENs to ITAC, five ENs to RSIS, and three ENs to the third offeror. At issue in this case are ENs Nos. 0001, 0002 and 0002a, which the Air Force sent to RSIS after the offerors had submitted "past performance" information, but before the due date for the other parts of the proposals. The ENs at issue sought "additional information ... to verify relevant past performance for [the] lead and support roles" of at least ten subcontractors that RSIS listed in its proposal. EN No. 0002. The Air Force sent ENs to the other bidders requesting additional information on their subcontractors as well. The disputed ENs were labeled "FAR 15.306(a) Clarification [s]" and included the notice, "Please note that this clarification does not constitute oral discussions with the offeror." EN 0002, referring to 48 C.F.R. § 15.306(a).

RSIS responded to the ENs on May 1, 2001, explaining which parts of the project each subcontractor would support and detailing the subcontractors' relevant experience with regard to those tasks. For example, in response to EN 0002, RSIS responded, "[subcontractor] Aerojet has developed and integrated the CTPP/ALERT and the JTAGS IR missile warning processing systems into the tactical missile warning C2 operational architecture, (Similarities to [contract] Requirements, V-57, and V-59)." (RSIS Response to Evaluation Notice.)

The Air Force gave both ITAC and RSIS an "overall exceptional rating" for their "past performance" experience. (Proposal Analysis Report for RFP # FA2550-01-R-0001, July 11, 2001). The Air Force determined that prior contracts of RSIS and its subcontractors were relevant to their ability to perform the Space Warfare Center contract.

The Air Force performed an independent "Most Probable Cost analysis" on the proposals submitted by RSIS and the third bidder. The "Most Probable Cost analysis" was an independent analysis of the bidder's estimated cost for "reasonableness" and "realism." RFP at 85. The Air Force "assess[ed] the compatibility of the overall proposed costs with the scope of effort to be performed." *Id.* The Air Force did not perform a "Most Probable Cost analysis" on ITAC's proposal, because its evaluation team found that ITAC's proposed hours were so minimal and unrealistic that it was infeasible to perform an adequate analysis. (Source Selection Decision Document at 4.) As a result of this independent analysis performed with respect to RSIS and the third bidder, the Air Force increased the estimated labor hours for RSIS and the third bidder, after determining "that additional hours were required in each labor category to successfully perform the effort." *Info. Tech. & Applications Corp. v. United States*, No. 01-637 C, slip op. at 9 n. 15 (Fed.Cl. Dec. 7, 2001).

There is no suggestion that these adjustments resulted from RSIS's responses to the disputed ENs.

On July 23, 2001, the Air Force announced its decision to award the contract to RSIS. In its Source Selection Decision Document, the Air Force explained that all three proposals were rated equally for "Program Management and Integration" and for "Past Performance" (which was the subject of the disputed ENs), and that these were not, therefore, "discriminating factors." (Source Selection Decision Document at 2.) The Air Force determined that although "[a]ll Offerors provided proposals which met minimum contract requirements," and "all proposals were fundamentally sound," "key discriminators were made in Mission Capability..., Proposal Risk, and Cost/Price." *Id.* at 1. RSIS performed higher than ITAC in the categories of "Mission Capability" and "Proposal Risk." *Id.* at 2–4. In the area of "Cost/Price," the Air Force found, "RSIS provided the lowest overall price for the written Task Order and provided the best overall price to the Government." *Id.* at 5. The Air Force concluded:

> In summary, RSIS offered an excellent proposal with lower risk and several innovative approaches to improve efficiency of SWC operations that were deemed to be beneficial to the Government. As a result, the RSIS proposal provided the overall best value to the Government. Based on my integrated assessment that the RSIS proposal provided a better technical and lower risk offer, I direct the award to RS Information Systems.

Id. Because "Cost/Price" was one of the categories in which RSIS scored higher than ITAC, the refusal of the Air Force to conduct a "Most Probable Cost analysis" of ITAC's proposal or make a similar adjustment to its labor hours to make them more realistic is alleged to have been a significant factor in ITAC's not winning the contract.

On August 6, 2001, ITAC filed a bid protest with the General Accounting Office ("GAO"). The GAO denied the bid protest and the Air Force awarded the contract to RSIS on November 7, 2001.

On November 13, 2001, ITAC filed this post-award bid protest in the Court of Federal Claims.... The theory was that if discussions had been opened, ITAC would have had the opportunity to cure the weaknesses in its proposal.

The ability of the contracting officer to conduct "discussions" is governed by both statute and regulation. Under 41 U.S.C. § 253b(d) and 10 U.S.C. § 2305(b)(4)(A), an agency may award a contract "after discussions with the offerors" or "based on proposals received and without discussions with the offerors." 41 U.S.C. § 253b(d) (2000); 10 U.S.C. § 2305(b)(4)(A) (2000). If the agency decides to hold discussions, however, it first must establish a "competitive range comprised of all the most highly rated proposals." 48 C.F.R. § 15.306(c)(1) (2002). In order to determine the competitive range, the agency may engage in "communications" with the offerors, which are defined as "exchanges, between the Government and offerors, after receipt of proposals, leading to establishment of the competitive range." 48 C.F.R. § 15.306(b) (2002).

If the agency decides to award the contract after holding discussions, it must hold discussions "with all responsible offerors who submit proposals within the competitive range." 41 U.S.C. § 253b(d)(1)(A) (2000); 10 U.S.C. § 2305(b)(4)(A)(i) (2000). However, the agency may hold "discussions conducted for the purpose of minor clarification" with one or more offerors. 41 U.S.C. § 253b(d)(1)(B) (2000); 10 U.S.C. § 2305(b)(4)(A)(ii) (2000). The procurement regulations define "clarifications" as "limited exchanges, between the Government and offerors, that may occur when award without discussions is contemplated." 48 C.F.R. § 15.306(a)(1) (2002).

On December 7, 2001, the Court of Federal Claims denied the bid protest, granting the government's motion for summary judgment on the administrative record....

DISCUSSION

* * *

The appellant's primary argument, and the only argument worthy of extended treatment, is that the Air Force violated the statute and regulations by holding "discussions" with RSIS and not with the appellant.

The statute provides, in part:

(1) An executive agency shall evaluate competitive proposals in accordance with subsection (a) of this section and may award a contract—

(A) after discussions with the offerors, provided that written or oral discussions have been conducted with all responsible offerors who submit proposals within the competitive range; or

(B) based on the proposals received and without discussions with the offerors (other than discussions conducted for the purpose of minor clarification)....

41 U.S.C. § 253b(d)(1) (2000). Substantively identical language appears in 10 U.S.C. § 2305(b)(4)(A). The purpose of the rule that the government may not hold discussions with only one bidder is "to prevent a bidder from gaining an unfair advantage over its competitors by making its bid more favorable to the government in a context where the other bidders have no opportunity to do so." *Data Gen. Corp. v. Johnson*, 78 F.3d 1556, 1561 (Fed.Cir.1996). The government contends that the ENs in question did not constitute discussions, but rather were "clarifications."

In order to construe the meaning of the terms "discussion" and "minor clarification" in the statute, we begin with an analysis of the language of the statute itself....

The relevant dictionary definitions are as follows.

"Discussion" is defined as, "consideration of a question in open usu. informal debate: argument for the sake of arriving at truth or clearing up difficulties." *Webster's 3d International Dictionary* 648 (1968) ("Webster's"). Webster's defines "to clarify" in the relevant sense alternatively as, "to free (the mind or understanding) of confusion, doubt, or uncertainty"; "to explain clearly: make understandable"; and "to make less complex or less ambiguous: put in order." *Id.* at 415. Webster's defines "minor" in the relevant sense alternatively as, "1 a: inferior in importance: comparatively unimportant: lower in standing or reputation than others of the same kind.... b: being the less important of two things." *Id.* at 1439.

Although these definitions make clear that "discussions" are more substantial communications than "minor clarifications," none of these various definitions serves to illuminate with any precision which specific exchanges of information constitute "discussions," and which exchanges constitute "minor clarifications." ...

We first note that the regulations were altered significantly in 1997. *Compare* 48 C.F.R. §§ 15.601, 15.607, 15.610 (1991), *with* 48 C.F.R. § 15.306 (2002). The preexisting regulations strictly limited the definition and purpose of clarifications....

Under the new regulation, 48 C.F.R. § 15.306, "clarifications" are defined as "limited exchanges, between the Government and offerors, that may occur when award without discussions is contemplated." 48 C.F.R. § 15.306(a) (2002). The regulation further provides examples of clarifications:

> If award will be made without conducting discussions, offerors may be given the opportunity to clarify certain aspects of proposals (*e.g., the relevance of an offeror's past performance information and adverse past performance information to which the offeror has not previously had an opportunity to respond*) or to resolve minor or clerical errors.

48 C.F.R. § 15.306(a)(2) (2002) (emphasis added).

In contrast, under the regulation, "discussions" involve "negotiations": "When negotiations are conducted in a competitive acquisition, they take place after establishment of the competitive range and are called discussions." 48 C.F.R. § 15.306(d) (2002) . Because discussions involve negotiations, they may include "bargaining," which "includes persuasion, alteration of assumptions and positions, give-and-take, and may apply to price, schedule, technical requirements, type of contract, or other terms of a proposed contract." *Id.* And unlike clarifications, discussions "are undertaken with the intent of allowing the offeror to revise its proposal." *Id.* Also unlike clarifications, discussions take place after the government has established a "competitive range" of the most highly rated proposals. 48 C.F.R. § 15.306(c) (2002). Discussions need only be held with each offeror within the competitive range. 48 C.F.R. § 15.306(d)(1) (2002).

The stated purpose of the 1997 amendments to section 15 of the regulations was to "provide for empowerment and flexibility" and "shift from rigid rules to guiding principles." 62 Fed. Reg. 51,225 (Sept. 30, 1997). Specifically, the new regulations were intended to "[s]upport[ ] more open exchanges between the Government and industry, allowing industry to better understand the requirement [sic] and the Government to better understand industry proposals." *Id.* at 51,224. The order adopting the new regulations stated that:

> We drafted the rule to allow as much free exchange of information between offerors and the Government as possible, while still permitting award without discussions and complying with applicable statutes. . . . This policy is expected to help offerors, especially small entities that may not be familiar with proposal preparation, by permitting easy clarification of limited aspects of their proposals.

Id. at 51,228–29. Thus, the definition of "clarifications" was significantly broadened. Rather than being "for the sole purpose of eliminating minor irregularities, informalities, or apparent clerical mistakes," clarifications now provide offerors "the opportunity to clarify certain aspects of proposals (e.g., the relevance of an offeror's past performance information and adverse past performance information to which the offeror has not previously had an opportunity to respond). . . ." *Compare* 48 C.F.R. § 15.601 (1991), *with* 48 C.F.R. § 15.306(a)(2) (2002). . . . Because the regulation's definitions represent a reasonable interpretation of the statutory terms, we defer to them and turn to the question of whether this regulation was properly applied to the facts of this case.

IV

The communications in question in this case, ENs 0001, 0002 and 0002a, were for the purpose of obtaining additional information about the subcontractors that RSIS had listed in its proposal. Specifically, the ENs asked RSIS to provide "additional relevant past performance information, to further describe the lead role for [the subcontractors]." EN 0002. In its response, RSIS explained which parts of the project each subcontractor would support and detailed their relevant experience with regard to those tasks. The government argues that these communications constituted clarifications, and not discussions. We agree for two reasons.

First, these communications were not discussions. As explained above, the new regulation contemplates discussions as occurring in the context of negotiations. 48 C.F.R. § 15.306(d) (2002). As such, when discussions are opened, bidders have the opportunity to revise their proposals, in order "to maximize the Government's ability to obtain the best value." *Id.* at § 15.306(d)(2). In this case, the government did not give RSIS the opportunity to revise its proposal, and RSIS did not change the terms of its proposal to make it more appealing to the government. Under these circumstances, it is clear that ENs 0001, 0002 and 0002a, and RSIS's response to them, did not constitute discussions.

Second, the Air Force's request was merely a request for clarification of the relevant experience of RSIS's subcontractors, as permitted by the regulation. The regulation provides that "offerors may be given the opportunity to clarify certain aspects of proposals." 48 C.F.R. § 15.306(a)(2) (2002). One example that the regulation provides of such a clarification is "the relevance of an offeror's past performance information. . . ." *Id.* We can discern no distinction between this clear example in the regulation and the Air Force's request for clarification of the subcontractors' relevant experience in this case. We therefore conclude that the challenged communications, ENs 0001, 0002 and 0002a, were merely requests for clarification.

We reject appellant's argument that the ENs could not be clarifications because they "requested additional information." Any meaningful clarification would require the provision of information, and the example of a clarification given in the regulation, "the relevance of an offeror's past performance information," requires the provision of information. *Id.* The appellant also contends that a clarification cannot call for new information if the information is "necessary to evaluate the proposal." There is no requirement in the regulation that a clarification not be essential for evaluation of the proposal. . . . Appellant's cramped conception of "clarification" is, moreover, not in harmony with the stated purpose of the 1997 amendments, which was to "[s]upport[ ] more open exchanges between the Government and industry, allowing industry to better understand the requirement [sic] and the Government to better understand industry proposals." 62 Fed. Reg. at 51,224. . . . For the foregoing reasons, the decision of the United States Court of Federal Claims is

AFFIRMED.

PAULINE NEWMAN, Circuit Judge, dissenting.

I agree with the panel majority that the 1997 amendment to section 15 of the Federal Acquisition Regulations was intended to liberalize the protocol governing exchanges between federal acquirers and bidders during the procurement process. Section 15 was designed to enhance convenience, but without diminution in fairness. The amended regulation does not exonerate the agency's unusual procedure in this case, however generously it may be construed. Whatever the distinction between "clarifications" and "discussions" in 48 C.F.R. § 15.306, the procedure by which the Air Force implemented its "independent cost evaluation" without informing ITAC of the agency's action when advised that the labor hours of all bids were too low, does not meet any reasonable definition of "clarification."

"Clarifications" are defined as "limited exchanges, between the Government and offerors, that may occur when award without discussions is contemplated." 48 C.F.R. § 15.306(a)(1) (2001). The agency's unilateral increase of the labor hours of two of the three offerors, without disclosure to the third of the agency's concern, cannot be rationalized as mere "clarification." It is surely not the type of individual interchange that was intended to be authorized by the amendment to section 15.

ITAC states that had it been told that its labor hours were too low, it would have explained the economies that it expected to achieve through certain new cost-saving technologies. ITAC was no stranger to this contract; it was the incumbent contractor and it must be assumed to have known, as well as anyone, the labor needed to perform the contract. ITAC was not offered the same opportunity of a revised proposal as were the other bidders. Instead, the Air Force simply refused to perform a "most probable cost analysis" on the ITAC proposal, thereby precluding the award to ITAC. While the labor hours of the other offerors were unilaterally increased by the evaluation team, by ten percent for one offeror and thirty percent for the other, ITAC was simply disqualified.

The purpose of the section 15 amendment was to "support[ ] more open exchanges between the government and industry, allowing industry to better understand the requirements and the government to better understand industry proposals." 62 Fed. Reg. at 51,224. It was not intended to authorize agencies to act without regard to fundamentals of fair procurement. From my colleagues' blanket ratification of a procurement that was seriously flawed, I respectfully dissent.

Notes and Questions

1. The court majority obviously gives the rewritten FAR Part 15 an expansive reading. Do you understand the dissent, particularly its observation that the protesting party is the incumbent contractor? Is it striking that the Air Force could, in effect, kick out the existing contractor and move in a new one without discussions that would give a warning as to what it was doing?

2. Was the Air Force avoiding burdensome discussions in this instance? Ordinarily, observers find it more suspicious when an agency pushes the rules to keep an incumbent contractor than when it displaces one. In this case, did the elimination of the safeguard of discussions mean that the incumbent could have been the favourite of the pre-2001 decisionmakers and the new contractor the favourite of the post-2001 ones?

3. As with other acquisition reform, the FAR Part 15 rewrite has received some critical scrutiny about whether it fosters competition or just works to the advantage of whatever contractors obtain awards. An Air Force contract attorney found in a scholarly study that the government has not gotten the benefit of the new bargaining flexibility. Among other reasons, the unchecked discretion of the contracting officers, coupled with the downsizing of the acquisition personnel workforce, has led contracting officers to use their freedom as they feel they must, merely to process acquisitions in the most minimal way to meet the larger per-person burdens, not to flexibly deploy resources in order to bargain hard when the government would benefit David A. Whiteford, *Negotiated Procurements: Squandering the Benefit of the Bargain*, 32 Pub. Cont. L. J. 509 (2003). For background, see Paul E. Van Maldeghem, *The FAR Part 15 Rewrite: Road to the Final Rule*, 33 Procurement Law., Summer 1998, at 3.

4. FAR provisions for award without discussion. By statute, defense agencies may invite proposals for award without discussions, provided that the solicitation states that proposals are intended to be evaluated and an award made without discussions unless they are determined to be necessary. 10 U.S.C. § 2305(b)(4)(A)(ii). The Defense FAR Supplement (DFARS) provides for an award without discussions for a solicitation for commercial items based on price and price-related factors, and specifically states that the government may accept other than the lowest offer. 48 C.F.R. § 252.211-7014 (1991). Conversely, another FAR provision permits an award on initial proposals without discussion only when full and open competition exits, or there is prior cost experience such that

award without discussion would result in the lowest overall cost to the government. 48 C.F.R. § 15.610 (a)(3) (1997).

5. Protests of awards without discussions. Protests of awards without discussion are common and yield a variety of results. In the *University of South Carolina (USC)*, the Comptroller General found that review and approval of personnel substitutions in a proposal prior to award constituted discussions, and, hence, required that discussions be conducted with other offerors in the competitive range. B-240208, 90-2 CPD ¶ 249 (1990). Awards to other than the lowest offer are commonly protested but found appropriate when the low offeror's proposal is non-conforming. *Sterling Machine Co.*, B-236585, 89-2 CPD ¶ 409 (1989). Protests are also not sustained where an urgency in procurement is demonstrated and justifies an award to other than the lowest offer. *Raytheon Co.*, B-240333, 90-2 CPD ¶ 384 (1990). For more information on the issue of awards without discussions, see Christopher A. Barnes, *New and Improved Awards Without Discussions or Foreign Competition*, 20 Pub. Cont. L.J. 532 (1991), and Michael A. Mark, *Contract Award on Initial Source Selection Proposal*, 19 Pub. Cont. L.J. 252 (1990).

6. One way agencies have of ensuring a fair procurement process while still taking advantage of discussions, if need be, is to issue a solicitation whereby award will be made to the lowest priced, technically acceptable offer. Using this procedure, the solicitation contains the evaluation factors and significant subfactors that will be used to establish whether a proposal is technically acceptable or not, with offers not being ranked, but merely evaluated as technically acceptable or unacceptable. Award is then made to the lowest priced, technically acceptable offeror. FAR 15.101-2. Discussions, if any, are only needed to assist certain offerors to cross the technically acceptable threshold, rather than improving their offer in comparison to others received. The competition is essentially based upon price, with the government reserving the ability to discuss potential problem areas with offerors prior to award.

W & D Ships Deck Works, Inc., Plaintiff, v. United States, Defendant
United States Court of Federal Claims
No. 97-308C
39 Fed. Cl. 638 (1997)

WEINSTEIN, Judge.

On April 30, 1997, plaintiff filed a complaint seeking to enjoin award of a federal government contract until plaintiff's proposal was reinstated in the negotiation process, together with a motion for a temporary restraining order (TRO). The government indicated it would take no further action on the contract until a hearing was held on May 5, 1997. At the hearing, after a full argument on the merits of plaintiff's complaint, the court denied the TRO motion and, sua sponte, granted judgment to the government on the pleadings, and dismissed the complaint. This opinion constitutes the court's written findings of fact and conclusions of law.

Facts

* * *

On December 11, 1996, the United States government, acting through the Military Sealift Command, Atlantic (MSCLANT), of the United States Navy, issued Solicitation No. N62381-97-R-0300 (the solicitation), requesting proposals on a negotiated fixed-price contract to: (1) paint the topsides of ships; (2) repaint the topsides of ships; (3) paint the decks of ships; (4) apply non- skid surfaces to the decks of ships; (5) paint interiors of ships;

and (6) clean the exterior painted surfaces of ships. Solicitation at 1, 8, 12, 16, 19, 23, 26. All the ships subject to the contract were located either in Norfolk, Virginia, or in Baltimore, Maryland. Id. at 28. The government designated the contract as a 100% set-aside for small businesses. Id. at 1. Plaintiff, W & D Ships Deck Works, Inc. (W & D), a small company located in Atlantic Beach, Florida, submitted a timely proposal. Compl. ¶¶ 1, 6.

Around March 21, 1997, the contracting officer ("CO") for the solicitation notified plaintiff that its proposal was determined to be outside the competitive range for negotiations due to unacceptable deficiencies in the technical proposal. Id. ¶ 7. Plaintiff's protest of this decision with MSCLANT was filed on March 28, 1997, and rejected by the CO, with a detailed explanation of the reasons, on April 22, 1997. Id. ¶¶ 8, 9; MSCLANT letter at 1 (Ex. D to Compl.)

Plaintiff's complaint seeking injunctive relief in this court, filed on April 30, 1997, alleges that there was "no major deviation in Plaintiff's proposal from any of the Solicitation's requirements," Compl. ¶ 11, and that any deviations were "minor irregularities," Id. ¶ 13, involving "post-bid responsibility matters or post-award contract administrative matters." Id. ¶ 11.

Discussion

At the hearing, the court denied plaintiff's motion for a TRO as unlikely to succeed on the merits and dismissed the complaint, sua sponte, pursuant to Rules of the United States Court of Federal Claims (RCFC) 12(b)(4), because there were no material facts in question and the government was clearly entitled to judgment.

* * *

III. Merits of Plaintiff's Complaint

In the case currently before the court, plaintiff does not object to the solicitation, nor to any award (since none has been made). Therefore, it may obtain review under § 1491(b)(1) based only on an objection to the proposed award or violation of a statute or regulation. Plaintiff's complaint does not identify any specific statute or regulation that MSCLANT officials allegedly violated to plaintiff's prejudice in reviewing the proposal. Rather, the complaint merely alleges generally that plaintiff's proposal is satisfactory and complete in respects MSCLANT found unsatisfactory and incomplete and implicitly contends that the CO abused his discretion in making the competitive range determination. Plaintiff's sole basis for objecting to the proposed award—to another—is that its own bid was not considered although it was within the competitive range.[1]

The competitive range is the group of proposals submitted in response to a government solicitation "that could be made competitive through negotiation." CACI, 719 F.2d at 1571. Under the federal regulation controlling evaluation for inclusion in the competitive range of negotiated bid proposals, a CO, after receiving all the proposals, must determine which proposals are in the competitive range for the purpose of conducting further negotiations. 48 C.F.R. § 15.609(a) (FAR § 15.609(a)). All proposals not in the competitive range are excluded from further negotiations and consideration.

The Federal Circuit has determined that COs have broad discretion in evaluating proposals and determining which, if any, fall into the competitive range. Birch & Davis Int'l, Inc. v. Christopher, 4 F.3d 970, 973 (Fed.Cir.1993). Contracting officers' statutory discretion even permits them to limit the competitive range to exclude some proposals that

---

1. At the hearing, defendant disclosed that plaintiff's bid was the lowest.

otherwise would be included if this will promote efficient competition by narrowing the field. See 10 U.S.C. § 2305(b)(4)(B); 41 U.S.C. § 253b(d)(2).

Proposals need not be included within the competitive range if they are "so technically inferior or out of line as to price, as to render discussions meaningless." Birch & Davis, 4 F.3d at 974 (quoting M.W. Kellogg Co./ Siciliana Appalti Constr., S.P.A. v. United States, 10 Cl.Ct. 17, 23 (1986)). By regulation, the CO is instructed to include only those proposals that have "a reasonable chance of being selected," excluding all others. FAR § 15.609(a). However, the FAR requires that the benefit of the doubt be given to those proposals that are on the borderline for inclusion. Id.

Courts may not overrule agency competitive range decisions except where the CO's actions are clearly unreasonable. Birch & Davis, 4 F.3d at 973. "Close scrutiny" is given only to decisions that result in a competitive range of only one bidder.[2] Id. at 974. GAO decisions uniformly hold that agency decisions establishing the competitive range are "primarily a matter of administrative discretion which will not be disturbed ... absent a clear showing that the determination lacked a reasonable basis." PRC Computer Center, Inc., 55 Comp. Gen. 60, 68 (1975); see also Talco, Inc., 89-2 CPD 171 (1989); Interaction Research Institute, Inc., 89-2 CPD 15 (1989). Although not binding, see e.g., National Forge Co. v. United States, 779 F.2d 665, 668 (Fed.Cir.1985) (citing Burroughs Corp. v. United States, 223 Ct.Cl. 53, 617 F.2d 590, 597 (1980)), GAO decisions on this topic are more numerous and detailed than decisions by this court or the Federal Circuit. Because the decisions are well reasoned, this court adopts the GAO's approach in these competitive range decisions.

The CO, by statute, is limited to evaluating proposals based on the factors identified in the solicitation. 10 U.S.C. § 2305(b)(1). The FAR too states that the competitive range determination is based on price and "other factors that were stated in the solicitation." FAR § 15.609(a). The CO informed plaintiff that it had been rejected because its technical proposal did not contain a substantial amount of information required by the solicitation. Plaintiff received unsatisfactory ratings on items within each of the four sections in the evaluation factor sequence.

Section L-16 of the solicitation ("Requirements for submission of Proposals") states that the "offeror's technical proposal must contain, but not necessarily be limited to, data set forth for the [enumerated] evaluation factors.... Failure to respond to any one of the evaluation factors may result in disqualification of the proposal." Id. at 82 (emphasis in original). It also states that "[d]ata previously submitted, or presumed to be known, ... cannot be considered unless they are physically incorporated in the proposal," and that "[a]ll information must be presented in sufficient depth to allow for the Government to make a fair and comprehensive evaluation of the offeror's understanding of the specification." Id. at 81. These statements make it clear that MSCLANT may disqualify an offeror if its technical proposal is deemed incomplete and that the technical proposals had to contain all of the information specifically requested.

Section M of the solicitation ("Evaluation Factors for Award"), notes that for proposals to be technically acceptable, "all categories [listed in section L] must be evaluated as technically acceptable." Id. at 85. Gaps in the following information led the CO to find plaintiff's proposal to be technically unacceptable and, as a result, outside of the competitive range.

---

2. While the plaintiff did not seek "close scrutiny" review, the court determined at the hearing that the CO's competitive range included three of the seven proposals submitted. Therefore, the heightened level of review would not apply to this protest.

First, in section 16.1.0, the solicitation required offerors to include in their technical proposals "a narrative which demonstrates an understanding of the overall scope of work." Id. at 82. The narrative also had to describe in detail how the contractor intended to perform the work. Id. There are six work items involved in the contract: (1) topside initial coating, id. at 8; (2) topside maintenance recoating, id. at 12; (3) exterior decks initial coating, id. at 16; (4) exterior deck non-skid coating, id. at 19; (5) interior painting, id. at 23; and (6) cleaning of exterior painted surfaces, id. at 26. Each item is described separately and in detail in section C of the solicitation.

Plaintiff's proposal discussed items three and four, regarding deck work only and thus, as the CO reasonably found, did not "demonstrate a satisfactory understanding of the overall scope of work required," which merited an unsatisfactory rating. MSCLANT letter at 1 (emphasis in original). Plaintiff failed even to mention any aspect of the contract not related to the deck work. Plaintiff's narrative provides only a cursory discussion, in fewer than twenty lines of text, of only one item — item four, the application of non-skid surface material. Proposal at 1.

Second, the solicitation in section 16.1.3 required offerors to provide information concerning five specific areas of material control. The CO reasonably found that the plaintiff's answers were "vague and brief," essentially failing to address any of the five areas in sufficient depth. MSCLANT letter at 1. Plaintiff's proposal mentions all five items, but in such cursory fashion as to be practically useless to evaluators. For example, with respect to item five, ripout material to be reinstalled, the proposal states: "Material which has been removed from the ship for reinstallation at a later dateis [sic] also kept segregated and inventoried separately." Proposal at 3. That is a conclusory statement, not a description of how it is done, including pertinent data, as is required. Similarly, in response to item three, environment protection for material stored (covered stowage and/or weather proofing) and size, location and type of material storage, the proposal states: "When received, the products are stored in an environmentally controlled warehouse." Id. The answer again contains less information than the question. The point of these questions is to provide the government evaluators with sufficient information to determine which offerors have the ability to perform the contract. Plaintiff's answers simply do not meet that need and it was reasonable for the agency to find them deficient.

Third, in section 16.2.0, the solicitation required offerors to submit a list of the capital equipment available to perform the contract and to provide a description of the facility. Plaintiff's proposal merely states that it "has all the necessary tools," "such as grinders, needle guns, descobraders, air tools, and air compressors." Proposal at 4 (emphasis added). Thus, it does not specify any, never mind all, the equipment it has. (A simple affirmation that plaintiff has the tools, accompanied by an illustrative listing premised with "such as" may be read to mean that plaintiff does not actually have any of those particular items). The proposal also states that plaintiff has a tentative agreement to lease 10,000 square feet from its subcontractor to use as its facility for this contract but does not further describe this facility. Clearly these disclosures do not permit the agency to make an informed selection among offerors and warrant the CO's rating of the solicitation as unsatisfactory on these points. MSCLANT letter at 2.

Fourth, in section 16.3.1, the solicitation required offerors to identify subcontractors and "explain the procedures to be utilized to control materials, quality assurance and inspections." Solicitation at 83. The CO reasonably rated plaintiff's response to this item to be unsatisfactory, MSCLANT letter at 2, because in response to this item, plaintiff merely identified the subcontractor (Surface Technologies) that would be used on the contract. Proposal at 5. Plaintiff did not even hint at the procedures that it intended to use to control materials used by the subcontractor and to perform quality assurance and inspections of the subcontractor's work, as specifically required by the solicitation. The proposal simply concludes that the subcontractor is "fully cognizant of the contract requirements and specifications for the performance of those requirements," id., but does not explain how the conclusion was reached, or how the contractor will ensure subcontractor compliance, as is specifically required by the solicitation.[3]

Fifth, in section 16.3.2, the solicitation required a detailed description of the quality control plan the contractor intended to implement, including providing the identity of the "individuals" who would perform quality control functions and discussing their other duties, as well as listing all NACE Certified Coating Inspectors who would be involved. Solicitation at 83. The CO reasonably rated plaintiffs reply to this section as unsatisfactory because plaintiff did not identify any specific individuals who would perform quality control functions and, perforce, did not list the other duties of those individuals. MSCLANT letter at 2. According to the agency, the plan also cited a calibration system standard that had been canceled several years earlier. Id. It is obvious to the court that information like the identity of the quality control officers and the extent of their other duties is essential to the government's analysis of a bid such as this. Without this information, the adequacy of plaintiff's proposal is purely speculative.

Sixth, in section 16.4.0, the solicitation required the offerors to discuss relevant past experience. The section listed seven specific items that the offerors "shall" address with respect to prior experience. Solicitation at 83–84. The CO reasonably rated plaintiff's response to this section as unacceptable because plaintiff cited only its previous experience with non-skid deck surface application (only one part of the contract) and because plaintiff failed to answer at least five of the seven specific requests for information concerning previous contract experience. MSCLANT letter at 2–3. (Plaintiff did not provide types of availability, man-days expended, required and actual completion dates, original and final contract prices, and percentages of growth. Id.) In response to this request, which obviously would provide exceptionally valuable information to government officials deciding to whom to award the contract, plaintiff's proposal lists several previous jobs, but provides only the ship name, the job location, and a contact name and phone number, and does not even identify the type of work done on these jobs. Again, for no reason apparent from the proposal, plaintiff withheld specifically requested information that appears to be essential to MSCLANT's decision-making process.

The GAO has soundly upheld agency exclusions of proposals from the competitive range for technical unacceptability when the proposal would require "major revisions" to become acceptable. See, e.g., Interaction Research, 89-2 CPD 15 (1989); PRC, 55 Comp. Gen. at 69 (citing other decisions). That would be the case in this instance. For plaintiff to make its proposal technically acceptable, it would have to revise, and substantially amplify, all but one section. Most of those revisions would entail significant changes or extensive additions, thus requiring a "major revision" of the original proposal.

The GAO has also properly concluded that if a proposal fails to provide information sufficient to determine if the offeror is technically acceptable, it is reasonable for the agency to exclude it from the competitive range, Talco, 89-2 CPD 171 (1989); that if an offeror

---

3. This complete nonresponsiveness on the part of plaintiff was deemed sufficient by plaintiff's counsel at the hearing because the agency knew the subcontractor. However, the proposal specifically states: "Data previously submitted, or presumed to be known ... cannot be considered unless they are physically incorporated in the proposal." Solicitation at 81. Confronted with this discrepancy, plaintiff's counsel had no further explanation.

fails to demonstrate in its proposal how it will perform the work required by the contract, as required by the solicitation, it is within the agency's discretion to exclude the proposal from the competitive range, Federal Services, Inc., 89-2 CPD 182 (1989); and that it is within an agency's discretion to exclude a technically unacceptable proposal from the competitive range even if it is from the low price bidder. Id. This court agrees with these standards, and each supports upholding the CO's decision in this case.

The GAO has outlined five factors that it considers in reviewing an agency decision to exclude a proposal from the competitive range. PRC, 55 Comp. Gen. at 69; see also Electrospace Systems, Inc., 58 Comp. Gen. 415 (1979). This court finds those factors well reasoned (and even self-evident) and adopts them for use in this case. Those factors are: (1) did the solicitation specifically call for the information that the agency found lacking; (2) do the informational deficiencies tend to show the offeror did not understand the contract's requirements; (3) does the offeror essentially have to rewrite the proposal to correct the deficiencies; (4) was only one offeror left in the competitive range; and (5) whether the proposal, if reasonably correctable, would provide a cost savings. Id.

Considering these five factors in turn, it is clear, first, that the solicitation specifically called for the information that the agency found lacking. Indeed, items 16.1.3 and 16.4.0 broke the specific information required down into enumerated subparts that plaintiff did not even attempt to address. This court finds that every item found lacking in plaintiff's proposal was specifically requested by the government in the solicitation.

Plaintiff did not provide any reasons why its proposal was deficient in so many respects. Except for an unconvincing explanation (in court) of why it was unable to provide the costs or man-days expended on earlier contracts in response to a specific request in the relevant experience section, Tr. 38–42, plaintiff contends that its proposal is as complete as it needs to be. The court disagrees. The proposal fails to demonstrate how plaintiff will perform the work required under the contract and is thus, as the CO found, grossly deficient.

Second, the informational deficiencies in the proposal tend to show that plaintiff did not understand the scope of the contract. Even at the outset, in the statement of work, plaintiff never mentioned at least four of the six major work components of the contract. Plaintiff provided a quality control plan that the agency determined did not apply to this contract. And finally, in the list of experience required by 16.4.0, plaintiff discussed only non-skid application experience, ignoring the other large components of the project.

At the hearing, plaintiff argued that there was no need for it to address the aspects of the contract it ignored because any firm that had the technical ability to apply the non-skid surface could also do all the other work. Even if it were true that plaintiff had the technical ability to perform the painting and cleaning aspects of the contract, and that all others capable of doing one type work could do it all, plaintiff nonetheless was required to demonstrate to MSCLANT that plaintiff had this ability and that it understood the scope of the contract, and it was required to do this in the proposal.

Third, plaintiff would have to rewrite most of its proposal in order to provide the missing information. The solicitation required that offerors' technical proposals provide information basically in nine areas. MSCLANT reasonably found plaintiff's proposal deficient in all but one of those areas. In order to correct these deficiencies, plaintiff would have to add so much additional information in most of the sections that the final product would be tantamount to a complete rewriting of the proposal. For example, in the statement of the work section, plaintiff would have to add information about at least four of the six work components of the contract. Or, in the experience section, plaintiff would have to add information concerning five of the seven specific requested items for every job listed. After such changes, the new proposal would necessarily be drastically different than the one submitted.

Fourth, plaintiff has not alleged that the CO approved only one offeror for the competitive range, so this factor does not apply in this case. See footnote 6, supra (discussing this point).

Fifth, because this court agrees with the agency's determination that plaintiff's proposal was not reasonably correctable, the cost savings factor does not apply in this case.

Each of the applicable factors weighs heavily in favor of upholding the agency's decision in this case. In light of the broad discretion accorded contract officers in making competitive range determinations by the Federal Circuit, Birch & Davis, 4 F.3d at 973, MSCLANT's evaluation of plaintiff's proposal was not "clearly unreasonable," id., but rather, manifestly reasonable.

* * *

Conclusion

If the government were required to give further consideration to proposals like that submitted by plaintiff, or allow further response, bidders would have no incentive to make their best (or even responsive) proposals early in the process. This would make the bidding process completely chaotic; bids and requests for proposals would become moving targets, never to be halted or hit. This court will not accept plaintiff's invitation to establish a contracting scheme that would be so contrary to the established rules governing bid proposals and their evaluation, particularly when the solicitation warned that it would not permit supplementation, or the cross-referencing envisioned by plaintiff.

For the reasons stated herein, plaintiff's motion for a TRO is denied and its complaint is dismissed, without prejudice. The Clerk is directed to enter judgment for defendant.

Notes and Questions

1. The court's decision not to require discussions with the offeror may legitimately defer to the contracting officer. However, is there any reason to fault the contracting officer for eliminating this offer. Without forgiving the errors and faults of the offeror, study the clues in this opinion as though you were a contracting officer with the time and energy, as well as the zeal, to foster competition and save the government money. The offeror is a low-budget, out-of-town (Florida) operation which threw in a sketchily documented but potentially promising bit of competition. By eliminating it, does the contracting officer signal to the local (Baltimore, Norfolk) contractors that they need not cut their prices to meet that kind of competition?

2. Note how the multi-stage operation of the competitive proposals system produces much more room for strategizing—and, hence, the need by the government to structure the situation so as not to be gamed—than with sealed bids. A bidder on an IFB dare not hold back her best offer for later because there will not be a "later"—the award goes to the lowest responsive and responsible bid. In contrast, an offeror on an RFP might hold back her best offer initially, figuring to make a better offer at the final stage, after using discussions and other clues provided later on to try to gauge the competition. If an offeror puts in too inferior an initial offer, what does this case show will happen? However, is that what happened in this case?

Key to the process of competitive proposals is the statutory requirement that the solicitation include all significant evaluation factors and subfactors and the relative importance of each. This requirement promotes the fundamental policy of establishing a level playing field so that each competitor will know what is expected rather than having to rely on best guesses or even worse, improperly obtained agency information. Such a policy also promotes the elimination of the unstated personal bias of government selection officials. This next case demonstrates how the courts enforce this requirement.

Isratex, Inc. v. United States

United States Claims Court.
25 Cl. Ct. 223
Feb. 6, 1992

NETTESHEIM, Judge.

On cross-motions for summary judgment after argument, this pre-award bid protest action questions whether the Government lawfully can exclude an offeror from participation in a negotiated procurement. The offeror's product demonstration model failed a mandatory test. The request for proposals, however, did not indicate the relative importance of the characteristics involved, nor did it advise offerors that automatic exclusion would follow from the test failure.

FACTS

The following facts are undisputed. On March 25, 1991, the Department of Defense, Defense Logistics Agency ("DLA"), Defense Personnel Support Center ("DPSC"), issued Solicitation DLA100-91-R-0120. DPSC is a supply center located in Philadelphia, Pennsylvania, that is maintained by DLA. The solicitation requested proposals for the manufacture of "792,408 EA Parka, Extended Cold Weather Clothing System (ECWS) Woodland Camouflage." Half of the quantity was set aside for small businesses. The solicitation requested that proposals be submitted by April 19, 1991.

On April 17, 1991, Amendment 0002 modified the solicitation; this amendment, inter alia, extended the closing date for proposals to May 21, 1991, and added a requirement that offerors submit a Product Demonstration Model (the "PDM"). Section L of the solicitation, entitled "INSTRUCTIONS, CONDITIONS AND NOTICE TO OFFERORS," stated, after modifications by Amendment 0002, that the proposal was to be submitted in three parts: PDM, Past Performance, Accelerated Delivery. Section L also stated that "[a] properly executed solicitation constitutes an acceptable pricing proposal." Section L required that each offeror submit two PDMs. With respect to the submission of the PDMs, Section L provided, in pertinent part, the following:

SUBMISSION OF PRODUCT DEMONSTRATION MODEL:

a. Models, as specified below, must be furnished as part of the offer and must be received by the time set forth for closing of offers. Models will be evaluated to determine compliance with all characteristics listed in the end item specification.

b. Failure of the models to conform to all such characteristics may result in rejection of the offer.

* * *

d. The PDM's shall be tested as follows:

1. One (1) complete garment shall be tested for hydrostatic resistance of the seams in accordance with para. 4.5.1 of MIL-P-44188B ["The parka shall be tested at four different locations.... Evidence of leakage in one or more seam locations shall be considered a test failure."].

2. The other complete garment shall be subjected to visual and dimensional examination in accordance with paras. 4.4.2 and 4.4.3 of MIL-P-44188B. [Paragraph 4.4.2 provides an extensive list of possible defects for which end items are to be examined. Defects include cuts, tears, holes, omitted items, incorrectly placed or attached items, and improper stitching. Paragraph 4.4.3 specifies dimensions to which the end items must conform.]

Section M, entitled "EVALUATION CRITERIA AND BASIS FOR AWARD," as modified by Amendment 0002, stated, in part, the following:

b. The technical quality of proposals shall be determined by assessment of the following technical evaluation factors. They are listed in descending order of importance:

1. Product Demonstration Model

2. Past Performance

3. Accelerated [D]elivery[.]

With respect to the requirement that offerors provide two PDMs, Section M provided the following:

EVALUATION OF THE PRODUCT DEMONSTRATION MODELS:

Product Demonstration Models must be submitted as part of the offer at no expense to the Government. Characteristics for which the models will be tested or evaluated are:

1. Quality of construction (including seam sealing)

2. Workmanship

3. Conformance to the dimensional and visual requirements of the end item specification.

4. Test requirements: One (1) complete garment shall be tested for hydrostatic resistance of the seams in accordance with para. 4.5.1 of MIL-P-44188B. The other complete garment shall be subjected to visual and dimensional examination in accordance with paras. 4.4.2 and 4.4.3 of MIL-P-44188B....

Jacqueline Pelullo, the contracting officer who drafted Amendment 0002, was tasked with buying the items required under the solicitation. She testified on deposition that the manner of listing these subfactors was not intended to show their order of importance. Specifically, she stated:

When I wrote this [the subfactors] up, I just listed them. They're — in my mind there was no separate weight for any of the items....

* * *

In my mind, they are not all even. I just wanted to say, the way they're listed here was not meant to show an order of importance. I don't believe that we indicated that.

In addition, Contracting Officer Pelullo stated that she knew the hydrostatic resistance test was "very important." Section M also provided an "ADJECTIVAL RATING SYM-

BOLOGY" that set forth three possible ratings: "Acceptable," "Marginally Acceptable," and "Unacceptable." The definition given for "Unacceptable" read, as follows:

> Unacceptable: Proposal fails to meet solicitation requirements. Offeror's record of past performance demonstrates a lack of commitment to customer satisfaction and timely delivery of quality goods. A rating of this magnitude indicates a product of unacceptable quality with no probability of successful performance. The technical proposal is unacceptable without substantial correction which would constitute a new proposal.

Amendment 0006 to the solicitation, issued on June 27, 1991, established the final quantity of parkas required by the solicitation and the final closing date for offers. The number of parkas was 672,888, 336,432 of which were set aside for small businesses. The closing date for offers was extended to July 15, 1991. DPSC received 20 offers by the closing date. Isratex, Inc. ("plaintiff"), was one of the offerors that submitted a timely proposal to DPSC. Two of DPSC's employees, along with two employees of the United States Army Natick Research, Development and Engineering Center ("Natick"), conducted the evaluations of plaintiff's and the other offerors' PDMs. Plaintiff's PDM failed the hydrostatic resistance test due to three leaks in the back neck hood seam. Three other offerors' PDMs also failed the hydrostatic resistance test. PDMs that failed the hydrostatic resistance test received automatically, i.e., regardless of any other factor, a rating of "Unacceptable." DPSC eliminated from further consideration proposals that received a rating of "Unacceptable" on the PDM. PDMs that passed the hydrostatic resistance test, but exhibited other specification deficiencies—either workmanship or dimensional deficiencies—received ratings of "Marginally Acceptable." DPSC directed some of the offerors that received a "Marginally Acceptable" rating on their PDMs to submit new PDMs.

On November 12, 1991, DPSC sent a letter to plaintiff and the other three offerors whose PDMs failed the hydrostatic resistance test, notifying them that their proposals would not receive further consideration. The letter to plaintiff stated, in part:

> [Y]ou are advised that your proposal submitted in response to subject solicitation was determined not to be within the competitive range determined for negotiation purposes. This determination was made after an integrated assessment of all evaluated factors, such as Production Demonstration Models, technical proposal, acceleration of delivery and price. Therefore, your proposal, as well as any further revisions, will not be considered.

Attached to the letter was an evaluation of plaintiff's PDM, rating the PDM as "Unacceptable" and noting the deficiencies with the PDM. With respect to the other factors that the solicitation stated would be evaluated, Ms. Pelullo testified in her deposition that plaintiff's past performance was rated "Marginally Acceptable," that plaintiff's accelerated delivery was rated as "Acceptable," and that plaintiff's price appeared to be in the competitive range.

On November 12, 1991, in addition to notifying those offerors that failed the hydrostatic resistance test that their proposals had been eliminated from further consideration, DPSC issued Amendment 0007 to the solicitation. Amendment 0007, in relevant part, modified the definition of "Unacceptable" to read:

> Unacceptable: The Production Demonstration Model fails to meet the stated technical features of the specification/solicitation requirements. Offeror's record of past performance demonstrates a lack of commitment to customer satisfaction and timely delivery of quality goods. A rating of this magnitude indicates a product of unacceptable quality with no probability of successful performance.

The Model is unacceptable as submitted and cannot be made acceptable without substantial correction which would constitute a new proposal.

Contracting Officer Pelullo explained that this modification was intended to expand the symbology in Amendment 0002, which originally had added the PDM requirement. Plaintiff's proposal was evaluated under the definition of "Unacceptable" as it was formulated in Amendment 0002, not as it appeared in Amendment 0007.

Subsequent to receiving notification that its proposal was no longer under consideration, plaintiff submitted two new PDMs to DPSC. DPSC advised plaintiff that these PDMs would not be evaluated. No offeror whose PDMs failed the hydrostatic resistance test was permitted to submit new PDMs.

Plaintiff filed a complaint and motion for a temporary restraining order pursuant to 28 U.S.C. § 1491(a)(3) (1988), seeking to enjoin DPSC from awarding the contract unless and until DPSC evaluates plaintiff's resubmitted PDMs. During briefing defendant reported that contract award was deferred until at least February 7, 1992. Plaintiff's request for permanent injunctive relief consequently proceeded to the merits without an interim order. At argument defendant advised the court that the earliest date for contract award had been extended to February 21, 1992. The parties agreed that disposition by summary judgment was appropriate.

DISCUSSION

1. Standards for injunctive relief

Pursuant to 28 U.S.C. § 1491(a)(3), the Claims Court may grant injunctive relief in a pre-award bid protest case where the Government has breached its implied duty to consider a bid honestly and fairly.

2. Evaluation of plaintiff's proposal

Plaintiff contends that DPSC's evaluation of plaintiff's proposal for Solicitation DLA100-91-R-0120 was not in accordance with the evaluation scheme set forth in the solicitation. Plaintiff relies, in part, on 10 U.S.C. § 2305 (1988 & Supp. II 1990), to support its position. 10 U.S.C. § 2305 provides, in pertinent part:

§ 2305. Contracts: planning, solicitation, evaluation, and award procedures

(a)(1)(A) In preparing for the procurement of property or services, the head of an agency shall—

(i) specify the agency's needs and solicit bids or proposals in a manner designed to achieve full and open competition for the procurement;

* * *

(2) In addition to the specifications described in paragraph (1), a solicitation for sealed bids or competitive proposals ... shall at a minimum include—

(A) a statement of—

(i) all significant factors (and significant subfactors) which the head of the agency reasonably expects to consider in evaluating sealed bids (including price) or competitive proposals ...

(ii) the relative importance assigned to each of those factors (and subfactors)....

Plaintiff's contention with respect to section 2305(a)(2) is that DPSC's solicitation did not state the relative importance of the subfactors relating to the PDM.

The solicitation listed four subfactors that would be evaluated with respect to the PDM. The solicitation numbered these subfactors, but did not state the relative importance of each of them. Contracting Officer Pelullo acknowledged that the order in which the subfactors were listed was not intended to represent their relative importance and that the solicitation did not state the relative importance of the subfactors. Nevertheless, the contracting officer stated that in her evaluation of the proposals she considered subfactor 4, the hydrostatic resistance test, as "very important;" that failure of the hydrostatic resistance test resulted in rejection of the PDM, regardless of any other factor; and that rejection of an offeror's PDM resulted in automatic rejection of the offeror's proposal.

Consequently, the issue for decision is whether there was a clear and prejudicial violation of an applicable procurement statute. Section 2305(a)(2) requires that a solicitation set forth the relative importance of subfactors. Solicitation DLA100-91-R-0120 did not state the relative importance of the four subfactors listed for the PDM. When no indication of relative importance is given, an offeror can assume that the subfactors will be equally weighted. Informatics, Inc., No. B-194734, 79-2 C.P.D. (Fed.Pub.) P 144, aff'd sub nom. Information Processing Servs. Div., Info. Servs. Group of Informatics, Inc. v. Harris, 26 C.C.F. (CCH) ¶83,698 (D.D.C.1979); Dikewood Servs. Co., No. B-186001, 76-2 C.P.D. (Fed.Pub.) ¶520. If the relative importance of all subfactors was not given because a solicitation contemplated that all subfactors were of equal importance, the solicitation would comport with section 2305. In that circumstance no relative importance would exist among the subfactors. That situation is not present in the case at bar.

In this case the contracting officer considered the hydrostatic resistance test as a "very important" subfactor, so important, in fact, that failure of the test caused offerors' proposals to be rejected. Deficiencies relating to workmanship or dimensional requirements of the PDM did not result in rejection of other offerors' proposals; indeed, DPSC directed those offerors to submit new corrected PDMs. Thus, the hydrostatic resistance test was accorded far greater weight than the other subfactors in evaluation of an offeror's PDM and proposal. Section 2305(a)(2) required that DPSC weigh equally the subfactors, in the absence of a statement of their relative importance. DPSC neither stated the relative importance of the subfactors nor equally weighed the subfactors. DPSC therefore violated 28 U.S.C. §2305(a)(2) when it gave predominant weight to the hydrostatic resistance test subfactor.

Having established the clear violation of an applicable procurement statute, the next question to be addressed is whether the violation was prejudicial. If defendant's contention were accepted—that the solicitation alerted offerors that a PDM's passing the hydrostatic resistance test was a sine qua non for staying in the competition—DPSC's violation of the statute would not have prejudiced plaintiff. In other words, if the solicitation put offerors on notice that passing the hydrostatic resistance test was a mandatory requirement of the solicitation, DPSC's violation of section 2305 would not be deemed prejudicial.

Amendment 0002 to the solicitation put plaintiff and the other offerors on notice that failure of the PDM "to conform to all such characteristics [all characteristics listed in the end-item specification] may result in rejection of the offer." This language, however, does not effect notice that passing the hydrostatic resistance test was a mandatory requirement. The language applies to all end-item specifications relating to the PDM. If the court were to construe the language as putting an offeror on notice that passing the hydrostatic resistance test was mandatory, the court effectively would be holding that satisfying all end-item specifications relating to the PDM was required or a PDM would be rejected. Such a construction would transmute the permissive "may" to a mandatory "shall." To the contrary, Contracting Officer Pelullo did not view the satisfaction of all end-item specifications as mandatory; acting pursuant to this standard, she decided not to reject some proposals with PDMs that exhibited deficiencies. If DPSC intended that passing the hydrostatic resistance test was a mandatory requirement, DPSC should have stated so in language typically used for such purposes. See Hughes Advanced Sys. Co., GSBCA No. 9601-P, 88-3 B.C.A. (CCH) ¶ 21,115, at 106,602 (citing International Business Machs. Corp., GSBCA No. 9293-P, 88-1 B.C.A. (CCH) ¶ 20,512, at 103,697 (RFP stated: "Proposals ... shall meet all the [G]overnment's requirements in Section C in order to be eligible for evaluation...."); Spectragraphics Corp., GSBCA No. 9194-P, 88-1 B.C.A. (CCH) ¶ 20,333, at 102,786 (RFP stated: "The Government shall not consider for award proposals that do not meet the mandatory requirements."); CPT Corp., GSBCA No. 8134-P-R, 86-1 B.C.A. (CCH) ¶ 18,727, at 94,206 (RFP stated: "In order to have an acceptable proposal, the offeror must meet all of the mandatory requirements set forth in Section C.2 of the Solicitation Document....")).

Had the solicitation given notice that the hydrostatic resistance test would be the deciding factor in an evaluation of an offeror's proposal, DPSC's violation of 28 U.S.C. § 2305(a)(2) would not have prejudiced plaintiff. Defendant argues unpersuasively that the solicitation gave such notice. Defendant contends that because a separate garment was required for the hydrostatic resistance test, because leakage in a seam caused failure of that test, and because the defining characteristic of the garment to be manufactured was its waterproof nature, an offeror was on notice that the hydrostatic resistance test was of predominant importance. The law does not support defendant's argument.

"[W]here one factor is to have predominant consideration over the other factors, this should be disclosed to the offerors." Sperry Rand Corp., Univac Div., No. B-179875, 74-2 C.P.D. (Fed.Pub.) ¶ 158, at 11. "As a matter of sound procurement policy, the fullest possible disclosure of all of the evaluation factors and their relative importance is to be preferred to reliance on the reasonableness of the offerors' judgment as to the relative significance of the various evaluation factors." BDM Servs. Co., No. B-180245, 74-1 C.P.D. (Fed.Pub.) ¶ 237, at 8. In the case at bar, offerors were not given notice that the hydrostatic resistance test would be a predominant factor in the evaluation of proposals. The solicitation stated that one garment was required for the hydrostatic resistance test and one garment was required for visual and dimensional examination. The solicitation listed the hydrostatic resistance test and the visual and dimensional examination together as one of the four subfactors relating to the PDM that would be evaluated. The solicitation did not specify that the hydrostatic resistance test would be of predominant importance.

The inference that defendant asks this court to draw is not unreasonable: An offeror could have been expected to discern that a waterproof PDM was an absolute requirement for award. See supra note 10. However, an offeror also could have been expected to discern that a PDM must be void of visual and dimensional defects, such as cuts, tears, holes, incorrectly attached components or improperly sized components. The offeror would have to have been clairvoyant to anticipate that failing the hydrostatic resistance test alone would automatically disqualify its proposal, while exhibiting other deficiencies would allow the offeror to be given a second chance at contract award.

Defendant's contentions that the solicitation gave notice that passing the hydrostatic resistance test would be a mandatory requirement or a predominant factor in evaluation of proposals do not provide a credible basis for holding that DPSC's violation of the statute was nonprejudicial to plaintiff. Because the solicitation did not state the relative importance of the subfactors, plaintiff could assume that the subfactors would be equally

weighed. When DPSC accorded predominant weight to the hydrostatic resistance test—
in effect making it a mandatory requirement—DPSC violated section 2305(a)(2).

Plaintiff was prejudiced thereby, since DPSC rejected its proposal while at the same
time not rejecting other proposals that exhibited deficiencies with respect to subfactors
that should have been accorded weight equal to that of the hydrostatic resistance test. The
evidence supports a finding that DPSC's violation of section 2305(a)(2) was both clear and
prejudicial.

Notes and Questions

1. The solicitation stated in this instance "[f]ailure of [the bid sample] to conform to
all such characteristics [specifications] *may result in rejection of the offer*." Emphasis
added. How does such language distinguish competitive proposals/RFPs from sealed
bids/IFBs? Had the agency used the IFB process with passing the waterproofing test a
mandatory specification requirement, would the protester still have been able file a successful protest?

2. The court made a finding not only of a violation of procurement law, but in order
to sustain the protest, also made a finding that the violation prejudiced the protestor. How
was prejudice established in this case? Do all violations of procurement law result in prejudice to the protester? What must a finding of prejudice include generally?

John H. Dalton, Secretary of the Navy, Appellant, v. Cessna Aircraft Company, Appellee

United States Court of Appeals, Federal Circuit
98 F.3d 1298
Oct. 22, 1996

Before NEWMAN, LOURIE, and SCHALL, Circuit Judges.

Opinion for the court filed by Circuit Judge SCHALL. Dissenting opinion filed by Circuit
Judge NEWMAN.

SCHALL, Circuit Judge.

This action arises under the Contract Disputes Act of 1978, as amended ("CDA"), 41
U.S.C. §601–613 (1994). The United States Navy ("Navy") appeals from part of the decision of the Armed Services Board of Contract Appeals ("Board") in CESSNA Aircraft
Co., ASBCA No. 48118, 95-1 BCA (CCH) ¶27,560, 1995 WL 113915 (March 6, 1995). In
its decision, the Board sustained the appeal of CESSNA Aircraft Company ("Cessna")
seeking an equitable adjustment under its contract with the Navy for flight training services. We reverse.

BACKGROUND
I.

Cessna was awarded Contract No. N00019-83-C-0090 ("the contract") by the Navy on
May 10, 1983. Cessna, 95-1 BCA at 137,344. The contract was a firm fixed-price services
contract titled "Undergraduate Naval Flight Officer/Training System Upgrade (UNFO/TSO)."
Id. Under the contract, Cessna was to provide services to assist in radar and navigation
training for undergraduate naval flight officers ("UNFOs"). Id. The procurement grew
out of the fact that the T-39 aircraft the Navy had been using in its UNFO training program were becoming obsolete. Id. at 137,345. In 1981, the Navy decided to enter into a

multi-year contract for training services under 10 U.S.C. § 2306(g) (1994),[1] rather than purchase its own equipment. Id.

The Navy issued a Request for Information ("RFI") on May 14, 1982, setting forth what it was contemplating in its procurement and inviting potential bidders to attend a presolicitation conference to be held on May 27, 1982. Cessna, 95-1 BCA at 137,345. In its RFI, the Navy stated: "Annual flight training systems will be designed to support a tactical [Naval Flight Officer] training rate of from 300–350 students per year. For planning purposes the estimated flying hours needed to conduct this training will range from 12,000–17,000 hours per year." The RFI did not specify any contemplated number of hours per graduated student. Id. at 137,346. The Navy also stated that the RFI "represents a reliable statement of the Navy requirement and possible procurement approaches for satisfying this requirement."

At the pre-solicitation conference, potential bidders asked questions about the procurement and had them answered. Cessna, 95-1 BCA at 137,345. On June 29, 1982, the Navy distributed to potential bidders, in written form, the questions and answers from the pre-solicitation conference. Id.

A number of questions at the conference addressed the issue of the rate of flight training services that the contractor would be required to provide. In response to all such questions, the Navy consistently referred potential bidders to the then-forthcoming Request for Quotations ("RFQ"). One question asked, "If [Navy] is going to modify the [training] syllabus where will they get their info and training?" The distributed answer read: "The Navy does not intend to modify the syllabus."

Cessna representatives met with the Navy's Wing Commander, Captain Thaubald, on September 9, 1982, and questioned him about the 17,000 hour provision. Cessna, 95-1 BCA at 137,346. Captain Thaubald testified before the Board that, at that meeting, he indicated to Cessna that "current usage projected 12,000 flying hours annually, but that if Congress approved a battle group increase the [Navy] would use 17,000 hours." Id.

On October 1, 1982, the Navy issued its RFQ. Cessna, 95-1 BCA at 137,345. The services that the contractor was to provide were described in Section C, titled "Description or Specifications." It stated that the contractor was to

> provide services to assist in Radar and Navigation training of Undergraduate Naval Flight Officers. These services shall consist of an annual rate of 17,000 airborne training service hours (approximately 58 airborne training hours per graduated student) on Contractor-furnished radar equipped aircraft of common configuration. Id. at 137,344. Because of a gradual phase-in of services, the contractor was to begin providing a total of 17,000 airborne training service hours in the third year of the contract (FY 1986). Id. The "Program Description and Objectives" section of the RFQ reiterated the language of Section C, stating that "[h]ands-on training on the radar within the aircraft, as well as the training instructor pilot services, will consist of airborne training services of 17,000 hours per year (approximately 58 hours per student)." Other parts of the contract recited the 17,000 airborne training service hours ("ATSH") provision unaccompanied by the 58-hour parenthetical. These clauses called for 17,000 hours of flight services to be provided in the third, fourth, and fifth program years and in the option years.

---

1. 10 U.S.C. § 2306(g) allows an agency to "enter into contracts for periods of not more than five years" for certain types of services, "for which funds would otherwise be available for obligation only within the fiscal year for which appropriated."

Attached to the RFQ were a Statement of Work ("SOW") and the training syllabus then used by the Navy in the UNFO program. Paragraph 3.1.2 of the SOW defined the scope of contractor support services:

> The Contractor shall furnish all equipment and services required to ensure the UNFO Training System is available for Navy use in accordance with the provisions of this SOW.... The Contractor shall provide sufficient aircraft to accomplish the annual UNFO training rate requirement and meet a 95% mission completion rate. The Government may or may not order flights on any given day, depending on the necessity of the work and suitability of flying conditions. The schedule of operations will be planned by the Government with the cooperation of the Contractor's Representative. Most flight operations will be conducted during daylight hours, however some night and overnight operations will be required. The current training syllabus requires three (3) overnight flights per week of one (1) or two (2) night's duration.

Attached to the SOW was the training syllabus or "curricula" then in use by the Navy. Paragraph 3.1.1 of the SOW stated, "For Contractor planning purposes, copies of the existing curricula currently used by the Chief of Naval Air Training for training student Naval Flight Officers are attached." There was no indication in the SOW as to whether or not the syllabus would be altered by the Navy. According to the syllabus appended to the SOW, the UNFO training program was to be conducted in five curricula grouped into three phases: basic (one curriculum), intermediate (one curriculum), and advanced (three curricula).

The basic flight training was conducted on Navy aircraft, not on Cessna's T-47 aircraft, and thus was not part of the 17,000 hour requirement. The intermediate curriculum required 12 hours of training for all UNFOs. After completing the intermediate phase, an UNFO would take one of the three curricula in the advanced phase. Each curriculum in the advanced phase had its own hourly training requirement. For example, UNFOs in the "Tactical Navigation" segment would receive 37.2 training flight hours; UNFOs in the "Overwater Jet Navigation" segment would receive 37.2 training flight hours; and UNFOs in the "Radar Intercept Officer" segment would receive 46.3 training flight hours. Therefore, UNFOs in the Radar Intercept Officer program would receive the most training flight hours. By adding the 12 flight hours in the intermediate curriculum to the 46.3 flight hours in the Radar Intercept Officer curriculum, a bidder could deduce that an UNFO would receive up to 58.3 hours of training.

After the RFQ was issued, a post-solicitation conference was held on October 18–19, 1982. Cessna, 95-1 BCA at 137,346. At the conference, potential bidders had a chance to ask questions and have them answered. On October 29, 1982, the Navy distributed the questions asked at the conference, along with answers to the questions. Id. Among the questions asked and answered were the following:Question: Would the annual rates for services remain constant over the life of the contract? If not, what factors could cause it to change? If an option to extend the contract is exercised, how would the rate change?

> Answer: The annual rate ... for services needed should be proposed by the contractor based on RFQ requirements.

> Question: What factors will be used to determine the annual rate for services?

> Answer: The contractor should propose the annual rate for services based on the RFQ.

On November 8, 1982, the Navy released the answers to additional questions that had been received. One question and its answer were as follows:

> Question: To enable each offeror to propose the most cost effective solution, will the government specify the following:

1) Fuel cost per gallon.

2) Escalation factor.

3) Expected flight hours (We understand that the 17,000 may be the maximum[)].

Answer: As previously stated, we cannot reveal the price of fuel to be used, nor can we reveal the other factors used to estimate fuel costs.

In its proposal, submitted in response to the RFQ on December 1, 1982, Cessna stated: "Personnel and aircraft requirements have been derived based on required training service levels and are based on current experience as modified to meet the levels established in the RFQ." Before the Board, James Lyle, Program Manager for Cessna, testified that Cessna relied upon the training syllabus attached to the SOW in preparing its bid.

In its April 4, 1983 best and final offer, which incorporated by reference its December 1, 1982 proposal and which was revised on April 25, 1983, Cessna offered fifteen radar equipped T-47 aircraft to replace the Navy's T-39 aircraft, rather than the twenty it had originally thought necessary. Cessna, 95-1 BCA at 137,347. Cessna also offered a lower price in its best and final offer than it had previously bid. Id. Cessna based its best and final offer upon the training syllabus that was attached to the RFQ, and upon the clause stating that approximately 58 flight hours per student would be required. Id. at 137,346–47. According to Cessna, it calculated that the Navy would use the full contingent of 17,000 hours contemplated in the specification only if the Navy increased the number of students it trained under the program. Id. at 137,347. The Board found that both Cessna and the Navy projected that if the Navy were to keep training students at the same rate as it had under the training syllabus, a maximum of only 12,000 flight hours would be utilized. Id. at 137,346. In its December 1, 1982 proposal, however, Cessna referred to the 17,000 ATSH provision without qualification. In describing radar and navigation training, Cessna stated that "[u]nder the prospective contract, Cessna is to provide services to assist in radar and navigation training of UNFOs consisting of an annual rate of 17,000 airborne training service hours in Cessna-furnished radar-equipped aircraft of common configuration." Referring to the "Full-Up Operational UNFO/TSU Services Phase" of the contract, Cessna stated: "During this phase, flying hour availability will be 17,000 hours per year."

II.

After entering into the contract and reaching the later years, the Navy realized that it was not utilizing 17,000 ATSH per year. Cessna, 95-1 BCA at 137,348. In order to use all of the ATSH for which it believed it had contracted, the Navy updated its training syllabus to increase the number of flight hours per UNFO to 78 hours. Id. at 137,349. The Navy also made operational changes to the scope of the services it was utilizing under the contract. Id. at 137,349–51. In terms of operational changes, the Navy began requiring Cessna to transport non-student passengers, such as Navy VIPs and Navy officers who needed to log flight hours in order to receive flight pay. Id. at 137,349–50. The Navy also required Cessna to perform rescue flights, and to make overnight flights above and beyond those specified in the contract. Id. at 137,350. In addition, the Navy used Cessna's aircraft to conduct target flights. Id. at 137,359–51.

Objecting to the use of the updated syllabus and to the operational changes, Cessna filed a certified claim for an equitable adjustment with the contracting officer on June 1, 1987. Cessna stated that it was seeking an equitable adjustment because the Navy had made constructive changes to the contract, such as (i) using Cessna's "services to fly nontraining missions as well as to fly missions outside the contract's training parameters," and (ii) changing "the UNFO training syllabus to increase the flight training requirements from those provided by the Navy for bidding purposes." Cessna and the Navy negotiated until October 4, 1988. On October 11, 1988, pursuant to the CDA, Cessna filed an appeal with the Board on the ground that the contracting officer had not issued a final decision within a reasonable time.

On February 2, 1989, the contracting officer issued his decision denying Cessna's request for an equitable adjustment. With respect to the issue of whether the updated syllabus constituted a change requiring an equitable adjustment under the changes clause of the contract, the contracting officer stated, "I find that the syllabus is irrelevant to the annual 17,000 hour requirement. I find that the contract clearly entitles the Navy to 17,000 hours of airborne training services each year." With respect to the operational changes, the contracting officer found that Cessna was not entitled to an equitable adjustment.

The Board rendered a 3–2 split decision in the appeal. . . .

DISCUSSION

I.

* * *

What the government does challenge on appeal is the Board's holding that Cessna is entitled to an equitable adjustment as a result of the syllabus change increasing the number of flight hours per UNFO to 78 hours. The government contends that the Board's holding is incorrect as a matter of law in two respects. First, the government argues, the Board erred in construing the phrase "annual rate of 17,000 airborne training service hours (approximately 58 airborne training hours per graduated student)" as calling for 17,000 ATSH, qualified by the provision of approximately 58 training hours per UNFO. As seen above, the Board determined that the 17,000 hour requirement set forth in Section C was merely a contingency that would depend upon an increased number of students, rather than a flat requirement of 17,000 hours of service annually. The government's interpretation is that the Navy contracted for an unqualified 17,000 ATSH and that the reference to 58 hours per student was merely an estimate. Under the government's interpretation, a change in the syllabus to increase the number of training hours per student could not give rise to a claim for an equitable adjustment so long as the Navy did not use more than 17,000 ATSH. Second, the government asserts that Cessna's interpretation of the contract necessarily gave rise to an ambiguity of which Cessna was aware. Under these circumstances, Cessna was under a duty to seek clarification before submitting its proposal, which it did not do. Accordingly, Cessna is barred from recovery. For its part, Cessna responds that the Board correctly interpreted the contract. Addressing the government's second argument, Cessna contends that any ambiguity in the contract was latent and that, accordingly, under the doctrine of contra proferentem, it was not required to seek clarification. For the reasons set forth below, we hold that Cessna is barred from seeking an equitable adjustment for the syllabus change because, in view of its interpretation of the contract, it was under a duty to seek clarification before submitting its proposal.

II.

It is undisputed that the contract was a firm fixed-price services contract. Such a contract provides for a price that is not subject to any adjustment on the basis of the contractor's cost experience in performing the contract. This contract type places upon the contractor maximum risk and full responsibility for all costs and resulting profit or loss. It provides maximum incentive for the contractor to control costs and perform effectively and imposes a minimum administrative burden upon the contracting parties.

48 C.F.R. § 16.202-1 (1995).

According to the Federal Acquisition Regulations ("FAR"), fixed-price contracts are "suitable for acquiring commercial items ... or for acquiring other supplies or services on the basis of reasonably definite functional or detailed specifications." Id. at § 16.202-2. The regulations suggest situations where this type of contract may be appropriate, such as when performance uncertainties can be identified and reasonably quantified. Id. at § 16.202-2(d). Because fixed-price contracts do not contain a method for varying the price of the contract in the event of unforeseen circumstances, they assign the risk to the contractor that the actual cost of performance will be higher than the price of the contract.

Contract interpretation is an issue of law. Interstate Gen. Gov't Contractors v. Stone, 980 F.2d 1433, 1434 (Fed.Cir.1992). Reading the 58-hour statement in the context of the entire contract, we conclude that it was reasonable for the Navy to interpret the statement as an estimate. First, given that this was a firm fixed-price contract that assured Cessna would be paid regardless of the number of airborne flight hours the Navy consumed,[6] it was reasonable for the Navy to take the position that the contract should not be interpreted as containing a provision potentially qualifying the manner in which the Navy used the full amount of the services procured. Put another way, in the setting of this contract, in the absence of language clearly and unambiguously placing a qualification on the manner in which the Navy could consume the services it was procuring, it was reasonable for the Navy to interpret the reference to 58 hours per graduated student as an estimate. This was especially so, we believe, in view of the fact that the 58-hour statement appeared in parentheses and was qualified by the word "approximately." In short, it can hardly be said that the statement was clothed in the garb of a binding contractual provision.

In addition, settled principles of contract interpretation lead us to the conclusion that it was reasonable for the Navy, when viewing the contract as a whole, to construe the 58-hour parenthetical as an estimate, rather than a binding provision. We read the language of a particular contractual provision in the context of the entire agreement, United States v. Johnson Controls, Inc., 713 F.2d 1541, 1555 (Fed.Cir.1983), and construe the contract so as not to render portions of it meaningless, Fortec Constructors v. United States, 760 F.2d 1288, 1292 (Fed.Cir.1985). Also, we apply the interpretation that accords a reasonable meaning to each of the provisions. Hol-Gar Mfg. Corp. v. United States, 169 Ct.Cl. 384, 351 F.2d 972, 979 (1965). Finally, where an agreement contains general and specific provisions which are in any respect inconsistent, "the provision directed to a particular matter controls over the provision which is general in its terms." Hills Materials Co. v. Rice, 982 F.2d 514, 517 (Fed.Cir.1992). Here, we are faced with separate provisions of a single contract, one set of provisions specific and one general. The specific provisions of the contract are the portions of the syllabus noted above that called for 17,000 hours of flight services for various work items for the third, fourth, and fifth program years and for the option years, without qualification as to the number of hours per student. The general provisions, of course, are the sections of the contract containing the "58 airborne training hours per graduated student" parenthetical. The Navy could reasonably take the position that the contract as a whole, including the more specific provisions, compelled the conclusion that the 58-hour parenthetical merely represented an estimate and therefore did not place a qualification on the extent of the services to which the Navy was entitled under the contract.

---

6. Before the Board, the contracting officer testified that the Navy intended to "pay for 17,000 [hours] whether [they] flew it or not."

The foregoing notwithstanding, we will assume for the purpose of deciding this appeal that it was reasonable for Cessna to construe the "annual rate of 17,000 airborne training service hours" provision as qualified by the "approximately 58 airborne training service hours" parenthetical. We hold as a matter of law, however, that, in view of the nature of the contract and the principles of contract interpretation noted above, this construction of the contract gave rise to a patent ambiguity. See Newsom v. United States, 230 Ct.Cl. 301, 676 F.2d 647, 649 (Cl.Ct.1982) ("The existence of a patent ambiguity is a question of contractual interpretation which must be decided de novo by the court."). We presume both Cessna and the government "to be endowed with at least a modicum of business acumen," Firestone Tire & Rubber Co. v. United States, 195 Ct.Cl. 21, 444 F.2d 547, 551 (1971), and we view Cessna as a knowledgeable bidder. Cessna should have recognized that its construction of the contract—based as it was upon a qualified parenthetical statement—was squarely in conflict with the construction of the contract that reasonably flowed from the basic nature of the contract (firm fixed-price) and its provisions. This patent ambiguity created an obligation on Cessna's part to seek clarification before submitting its proposal. Fortec Constructors, 760 F.2d at 1291 ("The existence of a patent ambiguity in the contract raises the duty of inquiry, regardless of the reasonableness of the contractor's interpretation."); S.O.G. of Arkansas v. United States, 212 Ct.Cl. 125, 546 F.2d 367, 369 (1976) ("The case presents another example of a contractor who, faced with a patent ambiguity in Government bid documents, did not meet his responsibility to have the ambiguity resolved before bidding.").

Faced with what it should have recognized as a patent ambiguity—in light of its interpretation of the firm fixed-price contract—Cessna did not meet its obligation of inquiry. It has never been asserted that Cessna sought clarification from the Navy with regard to its interpretation of the RFQ before submitting its proposal. At the same time, none of the questions and answers provided to prospective bidders by the Navy clarified the point. We have quoted above the questions and answers that are pertinent to this issue. These questions and answers either do not address the issue or are ambiguous. In any event, contrary to what the Board determined, it cannot be said that they provide a basis for concluding that the Navy shared Cessna's construction of the contract. Under these circumstances, Cessna did not meet its obligation of seeking clarification. See Community Heating & Plumbing Co., Inc. v. Kelso, 987 F.2d 1575, 1580 (Fed.Cir.1993) ("The Navy's response to the . . . letter expressly failed to address the issue of the conduit sleeves and thus provided a strong indication to Community that confusion still existed between the parties. Community was therefore obligated to request further clarification regarding the proper installation of the conduit sleeves."); Aviation Contractor Employees, Inc. v. United States, 945 F.2d 1568, 1571 (Fed.Cir.1991) (holding that a "somewhat evasive" response by the government to bidders' pre-bid questioning was sufficient to "clearly put bidders on notice" that the government intended to restrict option pricing). Having failed to seek clarification, Cessna was not entitled to rely upon its interpretation of the contract. Grumman Data Sys. Corp. v. Dalton, 88 F.3d 990, 998 (Fed.Cir.1996) ("If a solicitation contains contract language that is patently ambiguous, a protestor cannot argue, before the Board or before this court, that its interpretation is proper unless the protestor sought clarification of the language from the agency before the end of the procurement process.") The Board therefore erred in holding that Cessna was entitled to an equitable adjustment by reason of the syllabus change.

CONCLUSION

For the foregoing reasons, the part of the Board's decision that relates to the syllabus change is reversed.

COSTS

Each party shall bear its own costs.

REVERSED.

PAULINE NEWMAN, Circuit Judge, dissenting.

The Armed Services Board of Contract Appeals, resolving the several disputes arising from this contract, found that the Navy did not have unrestricted use of Cessna's aircraft and flight services up to 17,000 hours of flight time. The Board held that it was an incorrect interpretation of the contract to require Cessna to provide services beyond those explicitly set forth in the contract, up to the maximum of 17,000 hours. This is the ruling that the Navy appeals.

* * *

There was no unresolved, patent ambiguity at the time the contract was entered into.

The contract explicitly provided for "approximately 58 hours" of flight training per student. In evidence was the statement of the contracting officer that the Navy "does not intend to modify the syllabus." Section 3.1.1 of the Statement of Work provided that the curriculum for student training (the Syllabus) was attached for "Contractor planning purposes" and that its purpose was to "define the contractor effort necessary to support the training requirement of Undergraduate Naval Flight Officers." Although the panel majority chooses to find that there was a patent ambiguity concerning the obligation to provide 58 hours per student, in view of the ceiling of 17,000 hours, the Board, viewing the mutual understandings embodied in the contract, did not find such ambiguity. Indeed, the Navy did not state that it was entitled to 78, not 58, hours per student until three years into contract performance.

The Navy does not dispute, as indeed it can not, that the contract is explicit as to the "approximately 58 hours" of flight time per student. The Navy does not argue that 78 is approximately 58. The Board rejected the Navy's litigation-created position that it had unlimited call on the Cessna planes and personnel, and held that the Navy was bound by the provisions of the contract, including the provision of approximately 58 hours per student. Indeed, the Navy has taken the strange position of arguing that its own contract requirement is of no significance.

Evidence as to the representations during the bid process were before the Board. There was an inquiry as to the 17,000 figure, and witnesses for both sides testified that their understanding was that this figure was a maximum, "if Congress approved a battle group increase," in the words of the Navy wing Commander. The Navy represented explicitly that its training schedule was 58 hours per student, and included this figure in the contract. The contract states:

> SECTION C—DESCRIPTION OR SPECIFICATIONS ... These services shall consist of an annual rate of 17,000 airborne training service hours (approximately 58 airborne training service hours per graduated student)....

Cessna structured its low bid in accordance with these representations and requirements. See Sylvania Elec. Prods., Inc. v. United States, 198 Ct.Cl. 106, 458 F.2d 994, 1008 (1972) (if contractors can not rely on government representations "the amounts of the bids received would soon show the results").

The Board held that the Navy was bound by the representations in the Training Syllabus, the pre-bid explanations, and the contract itself. The panel majority, overruling the Board, holds that Cessna was properly required to provide 78 airborne training hours when the Navy so chose, three years into contract performance. The Board found that was not the agreement. Although Cessna took the risk of whether "Congress approved a battle group increase," the stated purpose of the 17,000 hour limit, that did not include a change of the 58 hour figure to 78 hours, any more than it included the Navy's other excursions beyond the contract provisions....

Notes and Questions

1. Using the opinion, reconstruct the process of negotiation, and specifically the back and forth over the contractor's obligations as to the quantity of airborne training hours. What did each of these stages signify, and what took place at that stage: the RFI; the pre-solicitation conference with its Q&A; Cessna's meeting with the "customer" (the Wing Commander); the various contents of the RFQ; the post-solicitation conference with its Q&A and the additional answers; Cessna's proposal; Cessna's BAFO; and, the awarded contract.

2. Imagine that you were a lawyer either in the role of counsel to Cessna's team seeking the contract, or in the role of counsel to the Navy team going through the negotiation process. Can you articulate the tension on each team: on Cessna's side, wanting to win the contract without an overgenerous proposal (and therefore craving clarity); on the Navy's side, wanting meaningful negotiations within the limits of what internal bureaucratic agreement could be obtained in advance (and therefore maintaining flexibility and ambiguity)?

3. As this opinion discuses, the courts impose a duty of inquiry and clarification where there is a patent ambiguity. *Sturm v. United States*, 421 F.2d 723 (Cl. Ct. 1970), *Community Heating & Plumbing Co. v. Kelso*, 987 F.2d 1575 (Fed. Cir. 1993). A term is patently ambiguous where it is "so glaring as to raise a duty to inquire." *Hills Materials Co. v. Rice*, 982 F.2d 514, 516 (Fed. Cir. 1992). Conversely, latent ambiguity is "not glaring, substantial, or patently obvious." *Grumman Data Sys. Corp. v. Dalton*, 88 F.3d 990, 997 (Fed. Cir. 1996).

4. Consider the opposite of the ambiguous provisions of this case's solicitation—the unduly restrictive provisions that, by excessively narrow constraints on what the government will take from offerors—for example, specifications that only allow a specific brand name of some product or component—inhibits full and open competition. The Competition in Contracting Act only speaks of allowing restrictive provisions in meeting the contracting agency's minimum needs. 10 U.S.C. § 2305(a)(1)(B). FAR 10.004(b) provides for the use of brand name specifications or its equivalent only in the absence of any other available specification. However, such specifications determined to further a federal policy have been held not to be unduly restrictive. *Marlen C. Robb & Son Boatyard & Marina, Inc.*, B-256316 (1994); *Accord Trilectron Indus*, B-248475 (1992).

2. Evaluation

Lockheed Missiles & Space Co., Inc., Appellant, v. Lloyd Bentsen, Secretary of the Treasury, Appellee, et al.

United States Court of Appeals, Federal Circuit
4 F.3d 995 (1993)

Before NIES, Chief Judge, BENNETT, Senior Circuit Judge, and NEWMAN, Circuit Judge.

BENNETT, Senior Circuit Judge.

DECISION

Appellant, Lockheed Missiles & Space Co., Inc. (Lockheed), appeals from the decision of the General Services Administration Board of Contract Appeals (board) denying Lockheed's bid protest in connection with the Treasury Multi-User Acquisition Contract (TMAC) awarded by appellee Department of the Treasury to intervenor AT & T Federal Systems (AT & T). We affirm the decision of the board.

BACKGROUND

On January 4, 1989, a Request for Proposals (RFP), Solicitation No. IRS-88-079, was issued in connection with TMAC, a contract for the procurement of office automation systems, software, and maintenance/support services for use by the IRS. The goods and services supplied by TMAC would directly affect approximately 130,000 IRS employees. Section M of the RFP stated that award would be made to the vendor whose proposal offers "the best overall value to the Government" as determined by "comparing differences in the value of technical features with difference in overall cost to the Government." Section M stressed technical factors over price but also indicated that the IRS would not award the contract at a significantly higher cost to achieve slightly superior technical features.

Section M.3 of the RFP divided the technical factor into two major features each worth 100 points. The features were in turn divided into subfactors of equal "point value" within their respective feature groups. Cost/price was assigned a value of zero points. Section M.4 of the RFP explained the technical evaluation methodology. To select the winning proposal, the IRS created a formal source selection structure. The structure contained the following entities: (1) a Source Selection Official (SSO) to make the source selection decision; (2) a Source Evaluation Board (SEB) to make recommendations to the SSO; (3) a Technical Evaluation Panel (TEP) to perform the technical evaluations of proposals; and (4) a Business Management Evaluation Panel (BMEP) to evaluate the price proposals.

In response to the IRS solicitation, proposals were submitted in confidence by various vendors including AT & T, Lockheed and International Business Machines Corporation (IBM). Each submitted proposal contained a recommended system/software/services package and its estimated cost to the government. The cost of the IBM proposal was approximately $700 million while the cost of the Lockheed proposal was about $900 million. In comparison, AT & T's proposal would cost the government approximately $1.4 billion. Nevertheless, AT & T was awarded the contract.

Thereafter, IBM and Lockheed protested the nonselection of their proposals. In a hearing before the board (TMAC I), both protestors asserted that the IRS: (1) conducted an improper price evaluation; (2) failed to follow the evaluation scheme stated in the RFP; and (3) misevaluated the protestors' proposals. In a decision dated September 25, 1991, the board granted the bid protests. In its opinion, the board stated that although the RFP placed technical factors above price, the IRS evaluation scheme had improperly "discount[ed] price as a factor almost entirely." Slip op. at 28. In support of its conclusion, the board noted that there was no analysis explaining why the government would receive benefits commensurate with the excessive price charged by AT & T.

The board's TMAC I decision was also critical of the RFP. "[N]othing in the RFP justified the overwhelming priority that the IRS accorded technical factors over price. The mere statement that technical was more important than cost in no way communicated the degree to which the IRS emphasized the former." Slip op. at 29. Accordingly, the board instructed the IRS as follows:

> If the agency believes a suitable price/technical tradeoff analysis can be prepared that would comply with the RFP, it may proceed to make one and either confirm the previous award or make a new selection determination as appropriate.

Alternatively, based on the award decision that the agency made, if it appears possible that the RFP, as written, will not permit an award in conformance with the Government's needs, respondent retains discretion to amend the RFP to provide a clear statement of its intention to emphasize technical over cost to the degree it believes necessary, and reopen negotiations or take other appropriate actions in accordance with statute and regulation.

Slip op. at 30.

After the board's decision in TMAC I, the IRS formed a "working group" to advise the SEB and the SSO on how best to proceed. The working group produced a report which concluded that: (1) a price/technical tradeoff could be performed in accordance with the RFP and (2) the tradeoff supported the award to AT & T. The working group report served as the basis for the decision to award AT & T the contract a second time. Once again, Lockheed and IBM protested, and the action was ultimately brought before the board.

In TMAC II, the board found that the selection of AT & T was consistent with the RFP solicitation and was the most advantageous choice for the government, price and other factors considered. The board noted that because no vendor had timely protested the RFP's evaluation provisions, the IRS was left with considerable discretion in conducting its analysis. Accordingly, the board denied the bid protests stating that the IRS decision was reasonable and not an abuse of discretion. Lockheed now appeals.

OPINION

The parties do not dispute the board's findings of fact. The decision of the board on any question of law is neither final nor conclusive and is reviewed de novo by this court. 41 U.S.C. § 609(b) (1988); Planning Research Corp. v. United States, 971 F.2d 736, 740 (Fed.Cir.1992).

As an initial matter, we note that in its arguments before this court, Lockheed did not protest alleged improprieties in the RFP. Moreover, because Lockheed failed to timely file a protest with the board based upon alleged improprieties in the RFP's proposal evaluation provisions, see GSBCA Rules of Practice 5(b)(3)(i), the board did not address that issue and it cannot be raised now on appeal. Broughton Lumber Co. v. Yeutter, 939 F.2d 1547, 1555 (Fed.Cir.1991); Finch v. Hughes Aircraft Co., 926 F.2d 1574, 1576 (Fed.Cir.1991).

Effective contracting demands broad discretion....

Lockheed argues that the IRS violated applicable statute and regulation by reducing price as a factor in its decision to award the TMAC contract to such an extent that price was effectively eliminated as a consideration. Price (or cost) must always be a "factor" in an agency's decision to award a contract. 10 U.S.C. § 2305(b)(4)(B); 41 U.S.C. § 253a(b)(1)(A) (1988); FAR § 15.605(b). Moreover, the importance of price in a price/technical tradeoff must not be discounted to such a degree that it effectively renders the price factor meaningless. See Grumman Data Sys. Corp., GSBCA No. 11635-P, 92-1 BCA CCH ¶ 24,700 at 123,721.

At first glance, Lockheed's argument appears persuasive. For example, Lockheed points out that the AT & T proposal costs 100% more than the IBM proposal and one-half billion dollars more than Lockheed's. Lockheed further notes that, despite the huge difference in price, the board found only two quantified technical subfactors representing less than 15% of all available technical points in which the higher priced AT & T proposal was technologically superior to the Lockheed proposal. Finally, Lockheed asserts that under the IRS's method of evaluation, Lockheed would not have been awarded the contract even if elements of its proposal were given away for free. Accordingly, Lockheed argues that the IRS would have paid almost any amount to acquire the most technically advantageous package.

In TMAC I, the board properly found that the price/technical tradeoff analysis presented by the IRS was deficient because it failed to indicate whether the government would receive benefits commensurate with the price premium it proposed to pay. Without that missing information, the board could not confirm that price had been a factor in the award decision. Similarly, we cannot determine whether the IRS effectively discounted price as a factor without first ascertaining whether the technical advantages of the AT & T proposal were worth their additional cost.

The board in TMAC II found, based upon the IRS's price/technical tradeoff analysis, that the AT & T technical advantages were worth the extra cost. For example, the board found that the Lockheed software would not increase productivity as much as the AT & T software because Lockheed's software required users to memorize various operating system commands. While such a small software advantage may have only resulted in a few extra points for the AT & T proposal in the overall evaluation, the board found that the actual dollar value of the software advantage to the IRS was significant. The total productivity value of the AT & T software solution was calculated to be $467 million as compared to $80 million for Lockheed.

In addition, the board found that AT & T's models 2 and 3 multi-user systems (MUSs) significantly outperformed their Lockheed counterparts during the "Functional Workload Demonstrations." The IRS quantified this advantage and calculated productivity values of $500,720,221 for the AT & T MUS models and $35,295,084 for the Lockheed devices. Finally, the board considered the impact of the nonquantified discriminators and found that the AT & T proposal offered substantially more value to the government than the other proposals.

Accordingly, the findings of the board indicate that the IRS, through its price/technical tradeoff analysis, neither disregarded price nor discounted it to such a degree that it was effectively rendered meaningless. . . .

Lockheed raises a second argument in its brief when it asserts that the IRS abused its discretion by skewing the importance of the two aforementioned technical subfactors, software and MUS productivity, beyond the limits established by the RFP. Lockheed argues that although the two subfactors represented less than 15% of all available technical points, those subfactors provided the IRS's main justification for spending millions of additional dollars for the AT & T proposal.

Section M.3 of the RFP identifies and assigns point values to the technical subfactors considered important by the IRS. The IRS used the assigned point values to evaluate and compare the technical strengths of the different proposals. Cost/price considerations did not enter into this part of the analysis since cost was assigned a value of zero points. After the AT & T proposal's technical strengths were determined, the IRS then went on to decide whether the value of those technical strengths was worth the higher price.

Neither the FAR nor the broad language of the RFP requires that evaluation points be proportional to cost. Accordingly, a proposal which is one point better than another but costs millions of dollars more may be selected if the agency can demonstrate within a reasonable certainty that the added value of the proposal is worth the higher price. Here, as we have already noted, the IRS tradeoff analysis revealed that the dollar value of the two technical subfactors together with the value of the nonquantified discriminators justified the additional price of the AT & T proposal. Thus, use of the IRS's evaluation method did not constitute an abuse of discretion because the method did not skew the importance of the two technical subfactors.

CONCLUSION

Government agencies are accorded a good deal of deference in awarding contracts. FAR § 15.605(b) (1992). Here, the IRS has sufficiently demonstrated that price was a factor in the final decision to award the TMAC contract. The decision of the board is therefore

AFFIRMED.

Notes and Questions

1. The court concluded that even a single point difference in technical scores can allow an agency to spend millions of additional tax dollars on the slightly higher rated proposal. What review standard will the courts employ to determine whether the correct decision was made? When is the court justified in overturning a procurement decision?

2. The court noted that the protestor's failure to timely protest the solicitation evaluation factors and procedures resulted in the agency having broad discretion as to their use. Such protests of asserted deficiencies in the solicitation must be filed prior to the date for receipt of initial proposals, i.e., a prospective offeror must sue its prospective customer while everyone is still in the starting gate, something that many companies are unwilling to do. However, the failure to resolve ambiguities or potentially unfair evaluation factors on a timely basis ensures broad discretion in the use of those evaluation procedures after proposals are received.

3. Note that the protestors alleged the agency: (1) failed to evaluate proposals in accordance with the solicitation criteria, i.e,. used factors not listed in the solicitation; and (2) failed to evaluate the protestor's proposal in accordance with the factors listed, i.e., the protestor's offer did not receive as high a rating as the protestor believed it should. These two protest grounds form the basis of many if not most protests involving competitive proposals.

Sheila Widnall, Secretary of the Air Force, Appellant, et al. v. B3H Corporation, Intervenor, et al.

United States Court of Appeals, Federal Circuit
75 F.3d 1577
Feb. 8, 1996

Before NEWMAN, LOURIE, and CLEVENGER, Circuit Judges.

CLEVENGER, Circuit Judge.

The Secretary of the Air Force (Air Force) and Logistics Techniques, Inc. (LOGTEC) appeal the July 8, 1994 decision of the General Services Administration Board of Contract Appeals (GSBCA or Board), B3H Corp. v. Department of Air Force, GSBCA No. 12813-P, 94-3 B.C.A. (CCH) P 27,068, 1994 WL 372020 (1994), granting the protest of B3H Corporation (B3H) in a best value procurement. B3H cross-appeals the GSBCA's dismissal of B3H's protest based on alleged improprieties involving Air Force personnel and LOGTEC. We reverse the Board's granting of B3H's protest on the best value issue and affirm the Board's denial of B3H's protest on the procurement impropriety issue.

I

On June 8, 1992 the Air Force solicited a contract on an indefinite delivery/indefinite quantity basis to provide technical support for the Air Force Material Command at Wright-Patterson Air Force Base. The solicitation stated that evaluation of the offerors would be based on technical, managerial, and cost factors in descending order of importance. At issue in this case are the portions of that solicitation reserved for small businesses. Section M-991 of the solicitation provided, in pertinent part, that "[t]he Government will award a contract resulting from this solicitation to the responsible offeror whose offer, conforming to the solicitation, will provide the best value to the Government.... The Government reserves the right to award to other than the lowest offeror."

The Source Selection Evaluation Board (SSEB) evaluated, among other companies, the proposals of LOGTEC, Aries Systems International, Inc. (Aries), and B3H. The SSEB determined that while the estimated cost of the LOGTEC offer was higher than B3H and Aries, LOGTEC and Aries were higher rated in the technical area. LOGTEC was also higher rated than Aries and B3H in the management area. After a working group performed a price/technical tradeoff analysis, on February 18, 1994 the Source Selection Authority (SSA) awarded the contracts at issue to LOGTEC and Aries determining that these offerors provided the best value to the Government.

B3H filed a protest in response to the SSA's findings on April 15, 1994.... [T]he GSBCA granted B3H's protest on the best value issue. The GSBCA held that the SSA did not adequately justify the higher cost of LOGTEC and Aries, even after the price/technical tradeoff analysis had been considered. Nor, in the Board's opinion, did the record as a whole demonstrate that the added value of the LOGTEC and Aries proposals were worth their higher price. Having granted B3H's best value protest, the GSBCA allowed the Air Force to continue its contracts with LOGTEC and Aries, but prohibited the Air Force from renewing the options on the contracts unless the awards were affirmed in a new source selection.

* * *

III

At issue in this case is a best value procurement authorized by 48 C.F.R. §15.605(c) (1994) ("[I]n certain acquisitions the Government may select the source whose proposal offers the greatest value to the Government in terms of performance and other factors.")....

In an early post-CICA decision, DALFI, Inc., GSBCA No. 8755-P, 87-1 B.C.A. (CCH) ¶19,552, 1986 WL 20777 (1986) (DALFI I), the Board upheld a protest of DALFI for a contract selection by the Naval Aviation Logistics Center (NALC). The NALC had chosen the lower rated $17 million proposal of SDI over the higher rated $20 million DALFI proposal. The GSBCA held that the NALC erred in part by taking SDI's assertion of a lower cost to the Government at face value and not conducting a price realism analysis that would assess the proposal's true cost. The Board stated that the procurement had been "converted ... from one for the highest technically rated proposal representing the best buy to the Government into one for the lowest price for a technically acceptable proposal." DALFI I, at 98,809. Nevertheless, the Board later accepted the agency's choice after the agency quantified the proposal's technical differences and determined that the technical superiority of DALFI was not worth its higher cost. DALFI, Inc., GSBCA No. 8975-P-R, 87-3 B.C.A. (CCH) ¶20,070, at 101,628, 1987 WL 41150 (1987) (DALFI II); cf. Pyramid Technology Corp., GSBCA No. 8743-P, 87-1 B.C.A. (CCH) ¶19,580, at 99,022–23, 1987 WL 46607 (1987) (contracting officer properly relied on lower price when the technical merits of the offerors were similar).

Once an agency has independently rated each proposal to determine its fulfillment of the requirements of the contract's solicitation, the agency typically performs a tradeoff analysis singling out and evaluating the differences between each of the qualifying proposals. These differences, often termed discriminators, may be either quantified or non-quantified for the Board does not require that each difference in a proposal be assigned an exact dollar value representing its worth to the Government. See TRW Inc., GSBCA No. 11309-P, 92-1 B.C.A. (CCH) ¶ 24,389, at 121,789, 1991 WL 175673 (1991).

* * *

Recently, this court has reviewed ... cases in which the Board initially refused to accept an agency's procurement decision based on the lack of a reasoned explanation for the selection.... [T]he Board and this court later upheld the agency selection after the agency reevaluated its decision and proffered reasonable explanations as to why its initial choice was correct. In International Business Machs. Corp. & Lockheed Missiles & Space Co., GSBCA Nos. 11359-P, 11362-P, 94-2 B.C.A. (CCH) ¶ 26,782, 1991 WL 542336 (1991) (Lockheed I), the Board granted IBM's and Lockheed's protests, rejecting the IRS' acceptance of AT & T's proposal to build its automation system. The IRS could not justify the increased cost of $500–700 million for the project simply by stating that AT & T's winning proposal was technically superior to the lower offers. Furthermore, AT & T's offer was only 15% more technically superior than the other proposals. The Board directed the IRS to justify its award to AT & T or initiate a new procurement for the contract. Lockheed I, at 133,201–03.

The IRS formed a working group to re-analyze the procurement, which performed a price/technical tradeoff analysis by identifying quantifiable and non-quantifiable discriminators between the various proposals. The group assigned dollar values to four quantifiable discriminators (price risk, software integration, system performance and training) in an attempt to determine the true cost to the Government of each proposal. The group also designated negative, positive or neutral ratings for ten non-quantifiable discriminators. Based on this analysis, the IRS concluded that the technical superiority of the AT & T proposal made it the best value to the Government despite its higher price. Lockheed Missiles & Space Co. v. Department of Treasury, GSBCA Nos. 11776-P, 11777-P, 93-1 B.C.A. (CCH) ¶ 25,401, at 126,499–501, 1992 WL 512122 (1992) (Lockheed II), aff'd, 4 F.3d 955 (Fed.Cir.1993)....

IV

This case involves a solicitation which stated that technical, managerial and cost factors would be evaluated in that order of precedence. The offers of LOGTEC and Aries were judged to be superior in the technical area. While LOGTEC was rated higher than Aries and B3H in the management area, total cost evaluations revealed that LOGTEC and Aries were respectively 15% and 8.8% more expensive than B3H's offer. The Air Force created a price/technical tradeoff working group (P/TTO Group) to further analyze the proposals. The P/TTO Group identified one quantified discriminator quantifying the estimated risk that an offeror would need to expend additional funds to provide trained personnel than the offeror originally calculated. This dollar value was added to the total evaluated cost of each offer to obtain a value adjusted cost. Although B3H's price risk was approximately four times higher than LOGTEC's and Aries', the value adjusted costs of LOGTEC and Aries were still respectively 16% and 4% higher than B3H.

The P/TTO Group also identified six non-quantified discriminators: (1) experience with the relevant Air Force software; (2) hardware maintenance experience; (3) hardware sizing experience; (4) data management experience; (5) whether the offeror already had offices near the Air Logistics Centers (ALC co-location); and (6) the offeror's subcontractor control plan. Each offeror was assigned a positive, neutral or negative evaluation for all six discriminators. The P/TTO Group gave LOGTEC a positive rating for the subcontractor control plan discriminator and assigned Aries and B3H neutral ratings for that category. While LOGTEC and Aries received a negative rating and B3H a neutral one for the hardware maintenance experience discriminator, the ratings of LOGTEC and Aries were superior to B3H's for all other non-quantified discriminators. With respect to those superior ratings, the P/TTO Group predicted that the proposal of B3H would result in completing the task order in a longer period of time and with a lower level of quality.

Relying upon the analysis of the P/TTO Group, the SSA in his written determination that LOGTEC's superior proposal was worth its extra cost stated: "I assess that the relative superiority of the [LOGTEC] proposal as indicated in the [excellent] rating in the Management Area will result in improved quality and cost control that represents value to the Government which mitigates the ... difference in cost." As to the award to Aries, the SSA similarly wrote: "B3H had more negative and fewer positive non-quantified discriminators than [Aries].... The technical superiority of [Aries] represents the Best Value to the Government considering the [small] difference in cost...."

At the B3H protest hearing, the SSA elaborated at length on the rationale for choosing LOGTEC and Aries. When B3H asked the SSA to explain in specific detail the basis for his decision, the SSA's response took up forty-three pages of testimony and covered all seven discriminators explaining how he considered them, evaluated their import, and why he did what he did. He had earlier given twenty-two pages of testimony on the same subject. In general, the SSA's testimony was that prior experience in the areas of the various non-quantifiable discriminators resulted in shorter start up times, quicker execution, a better quality product, shorter learning curves, and less staffing time, all of which would produce economic benefits to the Air Force. With respect to the issue of what justifies the higher estimated costs of the awards, the SSA testified:

> If specifically you mean what do we expect would occur through the execution of the contract with Aries and Logtec that would justify the increased price ... we can go back through the discriminators if you like and we can go back through the superior technical management proposal for characteristics. But in summary, what we would expect is that we would get a ... substantially higher quality product. We would expect that we would be in a better position to control and understand the cost that would be expended in the conduct of the individual task. That is that the costs that are identified in the initial response to the statement of work, would in fact be much closer to the cost that would be expected to be incurred through the conduct of that cost.

In essence, the SSA determined that the inferior management and lower non-quantified discriminator ratings of B3H meant that there was a likelihood that B3H's offer would produce unnecessary cost overruns and actually cost more than an estimated value adjusted cost, which was designed to factor in that risk. Thus, the SSA concluded the superior management and technical evaluations of LOGTEC and Aries justified incurring the increased value adjusted cost.

V

... Fulfilling its statutory duty under 41 U.S.C. § 607(e) (1988), the Board in this case reviewed the Air Force's procurement decision. The Board found that one non-quantified discriminator, the ALC co-location, did not have a rational basis. Except for this finding, the Board found no fault with the methodology of the SSA's decision. Just as in Computer Sciences Corp., the Board here did not reject the procurement on the basis of one suspect discriminator, but continued its analysis with the offending discriminator factored out of its inquiry.

Although the SSA gave a reasoned explanation as to why he chose LOGTEC and Aries, the GSBCA did not defer to his reasonable decision. For example, the Board found fault with the SSA's emphasis on LOGTEC's and Aries' superiority over B3H in the software experience and data management experience non-quantified discriminators. The Board held that the record does not support the SSA's decision to emphasize these two discriminators over the others. Yet, weighing which non-quantified discriminator to emphasize in an analysis is exactly the type of decision the SSA is entrusted to make. As the Board does not require that every discriminator be assigned an exact dollar value, TRW, it necessarily must rely on an agency's judgment in giving disparate weight to the various non-quantified discriminators in a best value determination.

The Board should have followed its clear line of precedent and deferred to the reasonable decision of the SSA in this case. The Air Force's P/TTO Group developed seven discriminators and assessed how each of the offeror's proposals fared under those chosen criteria. Using his independent judgment and consistent with the solicitation's stipulation that cost was the least important factor for this contract, the SSA relied on this analysis and reasonably determined that the technical and managerial superiority of LOGTEC's and Aries' proposals were worth the 15% and 8.8% higher cost. This case is no different from the many previous cases in which the GSBCA deferred to reasonable best value decisions made using substantially similar forms of analysis. Indeed, the SSA's concern that B3H's proposal might lead to excessive cost overruns seems no different from such recent explanations accepted by the Board in ATLIS (fear of cost overruns due to new technology) and Titan (fear of cost overruns due to subcontractor problems.) In reversing the GSBCA's grant of B3H's protest on the best value issue, we emphasize that the settled law remains settled.

Notes and Questions

1. *Numerical weights.* Under the FAR any RFP must clearly state all factors which are to be the major considerations in evaluation, and their relative importance and weight in comparison to the other criteria set forth in the proposal. 48 C.F.R. 315.406-5. The FAR further provides that any changes made to these evaluation factors for one offeror requires that the RFP be amended and re-submitted to all offerors. 48 C.F.R. § 15.606 (c). The GAO and the General Service Board of Contract Appeals hold consistently, however, that these FAR provisions do not require a government agency to disclose in an RFP the specific numerical weights being applied to each evaluation factor. See, e.g., *Network Solutions Incorporated (NSI)*, Comp. Gen. 89-1 CPD ¶ 459 (1989), *citing* 48 C.F.R. § 15.605 (e).

2. *Construing silence about factor importance.* Where a proposal fails to expressly state the relative importance of technical and price factors to each other, they are considered to be of equal importance. 48 C.F.R. § 315.406-5. The Comptroller General found this provision to be applicable in the *Johns Hopkins University*, when the University protested the award by the Agency for International Development to another offeror for the provision of a maternal and neonatal health and nutrition project in developing countries. Comp. Gen. 89-1 CPD ¶ 240 (1989). The protest was denied when no prejudice was found to have resulted from the solicitation's failure to indicate that the technical and price factors would be weighted equally in evaluation. *Id.*

Matter of: Environmental Tectonics Corporation
General Accounting Office
B-280573.2
December 1, 1998

Environmental Tectonics Corporation (ETC) protests the issuance of a purchase order to USA Models, Inc. under request for quotations (RFQ) No. N61339-98-Q-2010, issued by the Naval Air Warfare Center Training Systems Division (NAWCTSD), Department of the Navy, for acrylic replacement windows for hypobaric low pressure chambers.[1] ETC challenges the agency's evaluation of its past performance and the agency's decision to issue a purchase order to a higher-priced vendor.

We deny the protest.

The RFQ, issued in April 1998 as a combined synopsis/solicitation for commercial items, provided that the agency intended to issue a purchase order to the responsible vendor whose quotation was most advantageous to the government, price and other factors considered. The RFQ provided that the best value award factors, in descending order of importance, were pricing, delivery schedule, risk, and past performance. Combined synopsis/solicitation, Apr. 8, 1998; CO Statement at 1. The RFQ stated that simplified acquisition procedures applied to this procurement. See Federal Acquisition Regulation (FAR) Part 13.

Three firms, including ETC and USA Models, submitted quotations which were rated as follows:[2]

	ETC	USA Models
Delivery Schedule	Acceptable	Acceptable
Risk	Acceptable	Acceptable
Past Performance	High Risk	Low Risk

ETC's quotation was approximately 46 percent lower than the quotation from USA Models. SSD at 2.

With respect to past performance, for ETC, the agency checked the firm's performance under eight contracts for various training equipment. Three contracts were with the British government. The British references (a contracting director and a technical person) reported that ETC's performance under a contract for a fire service trainer had deficiencies which took the firm a long time to correct; ETC's performance under a contract for a maintenance trainer had delivery delays; and ETC's performance under a contract for a critical design review for a human-carrying centrifuge had delivery delays and, over the

---

1. The acrylic windows, which represent a safety upgrade, will replace existing glass windows which may implode into the chambers when internal pressures are lowered, causing injury or death to government personnel. The window replacement has been ranked a top priority modification for aviation physiology trainers. Contracting Officer's (CO) Statement at 1; Source Selection Decision (SSD), Sept. 4, 1998, at 1.

2. These ratings reflect the agency's assessment after taking corrective action in response to an earlier protest filed by ETC challenging, among other things, the agency's evaluation of the firm's past performance.

objections of the British government, ETC ordered long lead-time items prior to design approval. The British references further reported that [deleted]. Past Performance Questionnaire (PPQ), July 20, 1998. In addition, the British references reported [deleted]; the British references reported that they [deleted]. Id.; see also Memo to the File, July 20, 1998. Another contract (the one listed by ETC in its quotation as a past performance reference) was for two unique high altitude chambers for the Federal Aviation Administration (FAA). The FAA reference (the contracting officer), noting that "ETC had very good people and a very good product," reported that ETC had delayed delivery of the product and was "slow in delivering," but eventually had resolved technical and software problems. Memo to the File, Oct. 1, 1998; PPQ, July 21, 1998. Finally, NAWCTSD had a contract with ETC to provide a centrifuge-based flight environment trainer (CFET). The agency reported late, unacceptable delivery by ETC; agency acceptance of the trainer as nonconforming; and difficulty in engaging in discussions with ETC to settle a substantial monetary claim filed by the firm under the CFET contract. PPQ, Aug. 13, 1998.[3]

For USA Models, the agency checked the firm's performance under four contracts. The reference for a contract for a prototype of a smoke control model to be used as a teaching tool reported that USA Models was ahead of schedule and was an outstanding performer, delivering the highest quality product. PPQ, Aug. 5, 1998. The reference for an acrylic windows contract reported timely and very good performance by USA Models. PPQ, Aug. 5, 1998. The reference for a contract for plastic acrylic models of rockets and mines reported early delivery by USA Models, with the firm doing extra work under the contract. PPQ, Aug. 3, 1998. Finally, the reference for a contract for various trainers, including a cockpit simulator, reported on-schedule delivery and correction of a deficiency by USA Models. PPQ, Aug. 3, 1998.

The contracting officer, who served as the source selection authority, selected USA Models as the most advantageous vendor. In this regard, the contracting officer determined that ETC's low-priced quotation did not offset the unacceptably high risk of ETC not meeting the critical terms and conditions of the contract, based on ETC's past performance history showing that its corporate management had not committed to timely delivery of quality products, to correcting deficiencies, and to settling disputes. The contracting officer concluded that the performance risk associated with ETC outweighed the value to the agency of the firm's low-priced quotation. Therefore, given USA Models' record of superior past performance history and its minimal performance risk, the contracting officer determined that it was worth paying a price premium to that firm. Accordingly, the agency issued a purchase order to USA Models as the most advantageous vendor. SSD at 3–5.

ETC challenges the agency's evaluation of its past performance, objecting to the agency's consideration of its performance under the CFET contract and the British contracts, which were not listed in ETC's quotation for past performance references. ETC maintains that its performance under these contracts is not relevant because the deliverables were for sophisticated design/build, as opposed to commercial, items. ETC believes only the FAA contract (listed in its quotation for a past performance reference) and the China Lake contracts should have been considered by the agency in evaluating the firm's past performance.

---

3. The agency also checked references for an Air Force contract for centrifuge maintenance, PPQ, July 28, 1998, and two Navy contracts for environmental chambers at China Lake. PPQ, July 21, 1998. These references, which reported satisfactory performance by ETC, were also considered by the agency.

When using simplified acquisition procedures, an agency must conduct the procurement consistent with a concern for fair and equitable competition, and must evaluate quotations in accordance with the terms of the solicitation. M3 Corp., B-278906, Apr. 1, 1998, 98-1 CPD p 95 at 3. In reviewing protests against an allegedly improper evaluation, we will examine the record to determine whether the agency met this standard and reasonably exercised its discretion. Id.

Contrary to ETC's assertion, in evaluating quotations, an agency may properly consider evidence of a vendor's past performance from sources that are not listed in the vendor's quotation. See, e.g., TEAM Support Servs., Inc., B-279379.2, June 22, 1998, 98-1 CPD p 167 at 6. Here, the agency had direct knowledge of ETC's performance and associated problems under the Navy's CFET contract, and the agency sought specific information addressing ETC's performance under the British contracts. In response to ETC's primary contention, while the design/build technology for the deliverables under the Navy CFET and British contracts may have been distinguishable from the commercial item technology for the acrylic windows being procured under this RFQ, the record shows that for the most part, the negative past performance information conveyed to the agency by the various references related not so much to the technical aspects of ETC's performance, but to broader aspects of ETC's performance—ETC's corporate management's effectiveness in ensuring timely delivery of products and timely correction of deficiencies, and its receptiveness to engaging in claims settlement discussions. In fact, consistent with what was reported by the Navy and the British references, the FAA contracting officer also reported that ETC was slow to deliver. Because timeliness of delivery, timeliness of resolving deficiencies, and corporate attitude and responsiveness are considerations which are common to all contracts regardless of the technology involved, we believe the information reported concerning ETC's corporate management's working relationship with its customers is clearly relevant to the agency's evaluation of ETC's past performance. Id.; see also SDA Inc., B-256075, B-256206, May 2, 1994, 94-2 CPD p 71 at 6–7. Accordingly, based on reports of ETC's past performance and the agency's own experience with ETC, we believe the agency could reasonably conclude that ETC presented a high performance risk.

ETC also argues that the agency was required to conduct discussions with the firm regarding the referenced negative past performance information. However, ETC confuses the requirements applicable to negotiated procurements with those applicable to procurements using simplified acquisition procedures. Specifically, the provisions of FAR Part 15, see FAR s 15.306 (FAC 97-02), governing exchanges with offerors in a negotiated procurement about their past performance are not applicable in a procurement, like this one, conducted using simplified acquisition procedures. See M3 Corp., supra, at 4–5. While FAR Part 13, see FAR s 13.106-2(b)(1), affords an agency the discretion to use the provisions of FAR Part 15 in conducting a simplified acquisition procurement, the agency, here, exercised its discretion and chose not to conduct exchanges concerning vendors' past performance during the reevaluation of quotations.[5] We have no basis to object to the agency's action in this regard.

---

5. Although the agency held discussions with vendors, including ETC, prior to taking corrective action, during the reevaluation process, the agency did not conduct discussions. Since the reevaluation process superseded and mooted the initial evaluation process, consistent with the terms of the RFQ, the agency could properly issue the purchase order to USA Models on the basis of initial quotations without conducting discussions. See Combined synopsis/solicitation, supra.

Finally, ETC, the low-priced vendor, challenges the agency's best value determination resulting in the issuance of a purchase order to USA Models, a higher-priced vendor.

In a best value procurement, price is not necessarily controlling in determining the quotation that represents the best value to the government. Rather, that determination is made on the basis of whatever evaluation factors are set forth in the solicitation, with the source selection official often required to make a price/technical tradeoff to determine if one quotation's technical superiority is worth the higher price that may be associated with that quotation. In this regard, price/past performance tradeoffs are permitted when such tradeoffs are consistent with the solicitation's evaluation scheme. See Rotair Indus., Inc., B-276435.2, July 15, 1997, 97-2 CPD p 17 at 3. In this case, where the RFQ does not expressly specify that price will be the determinative factor for award, the agency retains the discretion to select a vendor with a higher-priced quotation and higher past performance rating, if doing so is in the government's best interest and is consistent with the solicitation's stated evaluation and source selection scheme. See University of Kansas Med. Ctr., B-278400, Jan. 26, 1998, 98-1 CPD p 120 at 6.

While ETC's quotation was approximately 46 percent lower than the quotation of USA Models, we conclude that the contracting officer reasonably determined that the performance risk associated with ETC, based on past performance information, outweighed the value to the agency of the firm's low price. More specifically, five of the eight past performance references for ETC reported poor timeliness and quality of performance and provided an overall negative past performance assessment. SSD at 3. The contracting officer noted that at the time of his selection decision, only the Navy CFET trainer and the British fire trainer had been delivered, inspected, and accepted; both of these contracts were delivered late and with major deficiencies. Id. The contracting officer noted that meeting the schedule under this RFQ is a critical factor, and based on ETC's past performance history, concluded that ETC's inability to timely deliver quality products made ETC an unacceptably high performance risk. Id. at 4. In addition, the contracting officer expressed a concern with ETC's lack of willingness to resolve disputes in a cooperative and businesslike manner, as evidenced by the Navy's experience with ETC in attempting to resolve the claim under the CFET contract. Id.

Therefore, based on this record, the contracting officer concluded there was an unacceptably high risk of ETC not performing in accordance with the terms of the RFQ because its corporate management failed to demonstrate on other contracts a firm commitment to timely delivery of acceptable products, to correcting deficiencies, and to settling disputes. Id. The contracting officer believed the performance risk associated with ETC outweighed any price savings associated with its low-priced quotation. Id.

In contrast, USA Models had a superior past performance history, delivering products on time or ahead of schedule, performing in a highly satisfactory manner, doing extra work, and correcting deficiencies. The contracting officer believed USA Models would satisfy the RFQ requirements in a timely manner, and that the firm's superior past performance history justified the payment of a price premium and outweighed the price differential between ETC and USA Models. Id. at 5.

Under these circumstances, we have no basis to question the reasonableness of the agency's price/past performance tradeoff and its decision to issue a purchase order to USA Models as the most advantageous vendor.

The protest is denied.[7]

---

7. Since we conclude that the agency's evaluation of ETC's past performance was reasonable, there is no credible basis to find that the agency acted in bad faith in performing this evaluation. Moreover,

Comptroller General of the United States

Notes and Questions

1. This GAO opinion reflects the greatly increased importance of past performance. Look at the case, first from the perspective of ETC, then from the perspective of the contracting officer. ETC must consider a price 46 percent lower than its competition as highly deserving of success. On the other hand, the contracting officer looked at ETC's poor past performance record as foreshadowing trouble both for the Navy "customer" and for the contracting officer herself.

2. The 1990s witnessed the rise of past performance as a criterion of proposal evaluation. This began in 1993 with Office of Federal Procurement Policy (OFPP) Policy Letter No. 92-5 encouraging that past performance be utilized as an evaluation factor for award in solicitations "expected to exceed $100,000." Section 1091 of the Federal Acquisition Act of 1994 (FASA) requires the OFPP to "establish policies and procedures concerning past performance." In 1995, the FAR Council promulgated Federal Acquisition Circular 90-26 on past performance information. In 1995, the OFPP issued an interim edition of "A Guide to Best Practices for Past Performance," intended as a non-mandatory guide for recording and using contractor past performance in the award selection process.

In 1997, the rewritten Part 15 of the FAR mandated that past performance be included as an evaluation factor in each competitively negotiated acquisition expected to exceed the $100,000 mark. FAR § 15.304. Other FAR Part 15 provisions afford the contractor the opportunity to identify all types of prior contracts that might have a bearing on their past performance record, while prohibiting agencies from making findings about a contractor's past performance where there is no available past performance information. Additionally, FAR § 42.15 addresses the rule and timetables for compiling past performance, while § 12.206 states that past performance is a relevant evaluation factor in all commercial item contract awards. In 1999, the Department of Defense issued its own guide on past performance information. For a fuller treatment, see Nathanael Causey, *Past Performance Information,* De facto *Debarments, and Due Process: Debunking the Myth of Pandora's Box,* 29 Pub. Cont. L. J. 638 (2000).

3. The GAO has held in favor of bidders protesting noncompliance by agencies with the FASA and FAR requirements of past performance as an evaluation criterion. *NavCom Defense Electronics, Inc.,* B-276163 (1997); *In the Matter of: Holiday Inn-Laurel-Protest and Request for Costs,* B-270860.3 (1993). Appellate courts have also held in favor of the protestor where an agency ignored the past performance evaluation factor altogether. *Latecoere International Inc. v. United States Department of the Navy,* 19 F.3d 1342 (11th Cir. 1994).

4. On the other hand, the GAO sustains protests by offerors claiming misevaluation of past performance where the record fails to support the agency conclusion. *The Real Estate Center-Cost,* B-274081 (1998); *Mechanical Contractors, S.A.,* B-277916 (1997); *Ogden Support Services, Inc.,* B-270012.3 (1996); and others. Such protests may be sustained by the GAO even when the agency decision is not unreasonable on its face.

---

contrary to ETC's assertion, the agency chose not to issue the purchase order to the firm as a result of the price/past performance tradeoff based on the underlying evaluation, not because the agency had de facto debarred the firm.

5. For a comprehensive discussion and potential concerns on the use of contractor past performance as an evaluation factor, see W.W. Goodrich, *Past Performance as an Evaluation Factor in Public Contract Source Selection*, 47 Am. U. L. Rev. 1539 (1998).

Bannum, Inc., Plaintiff-Appellant, v. United States, Defendant-Appellee

No. 04-5008.
United States Court of Appeals, Federal Circuit.
April 21, 2005.

Before MICHEL, Chief Judge, NEWMAN, and GAJARSA, Circuit Judges.

GAJARSA, Circuit Judge.

Bannum, Inc. appeals from the judgment of the United States Court of Federal Claims in favor of the United States, dismissing its post-award bid protest with prejudice. *Bannum, Inc. v. United States*, No. 03-1284 (Fed.Cl. Aug. 7, 2003) (final judgment incorporating bench ruling made during oral argument on August 6, 2003). Although it determined the government violated its regulation and the terms of a request for proposals in evaluating the bids at issue, the trial court ruled there was no significant prejudice to Bannum. We affirm.

I.

On February 24, 2002, the Department of Justice, Bureau of Prisons ("BOP") issued a request for proposals ("RFP") for a contract relating to Community Correction Center ("CCC") services in the Florence, South Carolina area. On April 24, 2002, Bannum, Inc. ("Bannum") bid on the contract. The Alston Wilkes Society ("Alston Wilkes") submitted its bid the next day. As the "incumbent" contractor, from 1998 to 2003 Bannum rendered the same services at issue in the RFP.

The RFP provided that the bid selection would turn on "best-value" procurement. Under this system the BOP evaluated bids under five factors, each assigned a different point value: (1) past performance (400 points); (2) community relations (350 points); (3) technical (250 points); (4) management (250 points); and (5) cost (250 points). Past performance on other government contracts was the most important criteria.

The BOP valued past performance by reviewing Contract Evaluation Forms ("CEFs") completed for other BOP contracts. The CEFs are "annual assessments" that grade contractors with "overall performance" scores. The BOP's CEF process is governed by 48 C.F.R. § 42.1503 (Federal Acquisition Regulation or "FAR" § 42.1503). Section 42.1503 provides, in relevant part:

> Agency evaluations of contractor performance prepared under this subpart *shall be provided to the contractor as soon as practicable after completion of the evaluation.* Contractors shall be given a minimum of 30 days to submit comments, rebutting statements, or additional information. *Agencies shall provide for review at a level above the contracting officer to consider disagreements between the parties regarding the evaluation.* The ultimate conclusion on the performance evaluation is a decision of the contracting agency. *Copies of the evaluation, contractor response, and review comments, if any, shall be retained as part of the evaluation.* These evaluations may be used to support future award decisions, and should therefore be marked "Source Selection Information."

FAR § 42.1503(b) (2004) (emphases added).

BOP procedures called for Management Center Administrators ("MCA"), under FAR § 42.1503, to review CEFs and contractor rebuttals. MCAs supervise "Correctional Management Centers" comprising two or more "community correction field offices." The MCA works "a level above CCC Oversight Specialists." It is undisputed that MCAs do not supervise BOP contracting officers.

The RFP required bidders to submit a list of all contracts completed in the preceding three years, or currently in progress. The RFP further cautioned "offerors would be well served to be aware of possible dissatisfied customers and address the issues in initial proposal submissions."

* * *

On October 9, 2002, the BOP scored Bannum's past performance based on 16 of Bannum's past contracts. The BOP determined Bannum's past performance warranted 74% of the possible 400 points, assigning 296 points for this portion of Bannum's bid. The BOP did not alter its CEF review process as Bannum had assumed it would.

On January 13, 2003, BOP awarded the contract to Alston Wilkes. BOP notified Bannum of the award on January 23, 2003.

In March 2003, in response to alternative dispute resolution in the Government Accountability Office ("GAO")—not involving this specific action—the BOP re-evaluated its recent Community Correction Center award decisions. For this bid a contracting officer re-scored Bannum's past performance on the basis of 15 contracts and awarded Bannum 312 points rather than the original 296. Nonetheless, Alston Wilkes still received higher points than Bannum in each factor.

This was not a *de novo* review and the record does not show that this contracting officer accounted for every Bannum rebuttal.

* * *

On May 28, 2003, Bannum filed this bid protest in the United States Court of Federal Claims, asking the court to set aside the contract award to Alston Wilkes and compel the BOP to re-evaluate Bannum's bid.

Bannum and the government filed cross-motions for judgment on the administrative record. On August 6, 2003, the trial court heard argument and granted judgment for the government. Although the court ruled the BOP had violated both FAR § 42.1503(b) and the terms of the RFP when assigning weights (based on the CEFs) to Bannum's past contract performance, it determined that Bannum was not sufficiently prejudiced by the violations to warrant setting aside the award to Alston Wilkes.

On August 7, 2003, the trial court entered judgment for the United States and dismissed the action. Bannum timely appealed, and this court has jurisdiction under 28 U.S.C. § 1295(a)(3).

II.
A.

A bid protest proceeds in two steps. First, as discussed below, the trial court determines whether the government acted without rational basis or contrary to law when evaluating the bids and awarding the contract. Second, as discussed further in Section III, if the trial court finds that the government's conduct fails the APA review under 5 U.S.C. § 706(2)(A), then it proceeds to determine, as a factual matter, if the bid protester was prejudiced by that conduct.

* * *

B.

As noted above the lower court ruled that the BOP's failure to comply with FAR § 42.1503(b), and the terms of the RFP, were violations of law under § 706(2)(A). Although the government argues the court was mistaken, we find no error in these rulings.

The trial court focused on the BOP's process by which the MCA, rather than someone "at a level above the contracting officer," reviewed CEFs and contractor rebuttals. The government, however, urges the court to adopt the reasoning expressed by another Court of Federal Claims decision, in a related case, holding that the same CEF review process applied by the BOP 'substantially' complies with FAR § 42.1503. *See Bannum, Inc. v. United States,* 60 Fed. Cl. 718, 729 (2004) ("Review by MCAs satisfies the requirement that '[a]gencies shall provide for review at a level above the contracting officer to consider disagreements between the parties regarding the evaluation,' because it provides for third party review. *See* FAR § 42.1503(b). The provision does not require that a supervisory contract officer perform the review. *See id.*"). We find this reasoning unpersuasive.

The FAR specifically required the BOP to "provide for review at a level above the contracting officer to consider disagreements between the parties regarding the evaluation." FAR § 42.1503(b). By its plain terms, a review "at a level above the contracting officer" contemplates review by a person with authority to direct the contracting officer's response. *See, e.g.,* Webster's Ninth New Collegiate Dictionary 45 (1985) (defining "above" as "superior to (as in rank, quality or degree)"). The fact that FAR § 42.1503(b) uses "above" instead of "independent" tends to support the view that "above" means someone with authority over the contracting officer.

The regulation explains that the review is provided "to consider disagreements between the parties regarding the evaluation." FAR § 42.1503(b). Since "[t]he ultimate conclusion on the performance evaluation is a decision of the contracting agency," the review plainly is intended to account for any bias or mistake in the contracting officer's review. *Id.* But since the agency's ultimate decision on any dispute necessarily involves evaluating the contracting officer's review of the contract, the reviewing authority should be someone familiar with the contract, the history of its implementation, and the particular concerns of both the contracting officer and the contractor in performing the contract. Someone in a supervisory or decision-making role in relation to the contracting officer complies with this regulatory requirement.

This understanding comports with guidance from the Office of Federal Procurement Policy ("OFPP") concerning the contractor's right to have performance evaluations reviewed. In language that mirrors FAR § 42.1503(b), a 1992 Policy Letter explains that if evaluation is done by a contracting officer, contractors have a right to discuss such evaluation "with the head of the contracting activity." OFFP Policy Letter 92-5 § 7(a)(3) (OFFP Dec. 30, 1992) (notification to contractors). This policy comports with a construction of FAR § 42.1503(b) that requires someone in a supervisory or decision-making capacity, in relation to the contract and contracting officer at issue, to review disputes regarding performance ratings. In other words, the regulation specifies a supervisory role at least inasmuch as the reviewer has authority to settle disputes between the contracting officer and the contractor.

* * *

The government also sees performance evaluation under 48 C.F.R. § 42.1503(b) as a tool for improving current performance on existing contracts, suggesting the evaluation must be done in view of the detailed factual context surrounding contract administration. Again, this comports with review by someone supervising a contracting officer. For example, on May 22, 2003, DOD, GSA, and NASA—through the Civilian Agency Acquisition Council and Defense Acquisition Regulations Council—adopted a final rule requiring evaluation of Federal Prison Industries contract performance. Responding to a comment that the evaluation was irrelevant in view of a mandatory source status, the government replied by citing the May 2000 OFPP guide "Best Practices for Collecting and Using Current and Past Performance Information." "[T]he active dialog that results from assessing a contractor's current performance results in better performance on the instant contract, and [ ] such assessments are a basic best practice for good contract administration." 68 Fed.Reg. 28095 (May 22, 2003). The FAR review, therefore, should be undertaken by someone with not only an understanding of the contracting requirements, but also the authority to direct the contracting officer.

For all these reasons the lower court's reasoning in the related case, which the government urges this court to adopt, is unpersuasive. Review by the MCA does not satisfy FAR § 42.1503(b) simply because the MCA is a "third party." The trial court in this action correctly applied the proper analysis to the BOP's use of these CEFs.

Bannum further argues that the BOP violated the FAR in failing to assess Bannum's rebuttals, on the prior contracts, when assessing its bid. The trial court rejected this argument, and we likewise find it unconvincing. As the Comptroller General decided in 2001, a bid protest is not the proper forum, under FAR § 42.1503(b), to litigate CEF disputes. *See In re Ocean Technical Servs., Inc.,* No. B-288,659, 2001 CPD P 193, 2001 WL 1505946, *3 (Comp.Gen. Nov.27, 2001) ("Our bid protest forum is not the place for a firm to first complain of not having received an assessment, nor do we serve as a forum for a firm to dispute the substance of an agency's assessment of the firm's work.").

III.

The trial court was required to determine whether these errors in the procurement process significantly prejudiced Bannum. *Alfa Laval Separation, Inc. v. United States,* 175 F.3d 1365, 1367 (Fed.Cir.1999); *Statistica, Inc. v. Christopher,* 102 F.3d 1577, 1581 (Fed.Cir.1996); *Data Gen. Corp. v. Johnson,* 78 F.3d 1556, 1562 (Fed.Cir.1996). Prejudice is a question of fact. *Advanced Data Concepts,* 216 F.3d at 1057. To establish "significant prejudice" Bannum must show that there was a "substantial chance" it would have received the contract award but for the errors in using its CEF scores on prior contracts. *Info. Tech.,* 316 F.3d at 1319; *Alfa Laval,* 175 F.3d at 1367.

* * *

B.

The trial court did not clearly err in finding that Bannum was not significantly prejudiced by the BOP's violations. To establish prejudice Bannum was required to show that there was a "substantial chance" it would have received the contract award but for the BOP's errors in the bid process. *Info. Tech.,* 316 F.3d at 1319; *Alfa Laval,* 175 F.3d at 1367; *Statistica,* 102 F.3d at 1582. This test is more lenient than showing actual causation, that is, showing that but for the errors Bannum would have won the contract. *Alfa Laval,* 175 F.3d at 1367; *Data Gen.,* 78 F.3d at 1562.

Bannum necessarily relies on the difference between the 104 points the BOP docked it based on the CEFs, and the 74.5 points by which Alston Wilkes won the bid. Had the BOP deducted fewer than 29.5 points for past performance, Bannum would have prevailed. But neither Bannum nor the record explains why Bannum had a substantial chance of scoring at least 74.5 points higher on past performance had the BOP reviewed the CEFs in accordance with the FAR. The independent review pursuant to the separate GAO proceeding increased Bannum's past performance award by 16 to 312 points, an amount insufficient to alter the award outcome. There is nothing besides Bannum's conjecture to support the contention that another review, comporting with the FAR, would provide it a substantial chance of prevailing in the bid. Bannum's argument rests on mere numerical possibility, not evidence. In sum, we find no clear error in the trial court's determination and will not disturb it. Accordingly, the judgment of the Court of Federal Claims is affirmed.

AFFIRMED

Notes and Questions

1. What is the theory of the contractor about past performance review? Does it make sense?

2. What is the role of the contractor's lawyer?

3. What kind of situations might occur in which a scoring of past performance was not quite as straightforward as in this case?

C. Modifications

Cardinal Maintenance Service, Inc., Plaintiff, v. The United States, Defendant, and Navales Enterprises, Inc., Defendant-Intervenor
United States Court of Federal Claims
63 Fed.Cl. 98
Nov. 22, 2004

FIRESTONE, Judge.

Pending before the court are the parties' cross-motions for judgment upon the administrative record pursuant to Rule 56.1 of the Rules of the United States Court of Federal Claims ("RCFC"). The plaintiff, Cardinal Maintenance Service, Inc. ("Cardinal"), challenges the award of a contract for custodial services at Hickam Air Force Base, Hawaii ("Hickam AFB") to the intervenor, Navales Enterprises, Inc. ("Navales"). Prior to the award of the contract in dispute, Cardinal had been the incumbent custodial service contractor at Hickam AFB. The subject contract was awarded by the defendant, the United States Air Force (the "Air Force" or "government") to Navales on February 20, 2003. Cardinal filed the present action nearly a year later on January 27, 2004. Cardinal challenges both the award of the contract to Navales and the Air Force's post-award administration of the contract. Cardinal charges that the Air Force violated the Competition in Contracting Act, Pub.L. No. 98-369, 98 Stat. 1175 (1984) ("CICA"), by authorizing contract modifications outside the scope of the original contract. For the reasons set forth below, Cardinal's motion for judgment upon the administrative record is **GRANTED**. The government's and Navales' cross-motions for judgment upon the administrative record are therefore **DENIED**.

I. Statement of the Facts

A. The Solicitation and Award

The following facts are set forth in the Administrative Record ("AR") and are not in dispute. On June 7, 2002, the Air Force issued Request for Proposal No. F64605-02-R-0026

("RFP") for custodial services at Hickam AFB. The solicitation combined Contract F64605-97-C-0004 for custodial services in Building 1102 for the Pacific Air Command ("PACAF") and contract F64605-97-C-0017 for custodial services for the 15th Air Base Wind buildings. In all, the RFP called for the performance of custodial services in approximately 92 buildings throughout Hickam AFB. The solicitation stated that the contract would be awarded for a base year with four one-year options, except for the PACAF headquarters building, which would have a six-month base period and four one-year options. Prior to issuing the RFP, the Air Force imposed a fifteen percent reduction in funding FY2003 contracts for custodial services, refuse collection, and grounds maintenance.

* * *

The Air Force received twenty-four proposals in response to the RFP.

* * *

The record reveals that the Air Force's Source Selection Authority performed a best value evaluation. The best value was determined by evaluating two factors: price and past performance. Because past performance was weighted nearly equal to price, the government reserved the right to select an offer other than the lowest price offer when the perceived benefits of the higher priced proposal merited the additional cost. The evaluations were conducted on an anonymous basis.

* * *

Navales' price proposal for the base and option years amounted to $4,066,463.95. Cardinal's price proposal amounted to $5,957,133.60 for the same services.

* * *

With respect to past performance, the Air Force assessed each offeror's past performance as a prime contractor on similar service contracts.

* * *

After the evaluation process Navales was given a Very Good/Significant past performance rating. Cardinal was given an Exceptional/High Confidence past performance rating. *Id.*

The Source Selection Evaluation Report ("SSER") sets forth in detail the basis for the Air Force's selection of Navales for award. After comparing Navales to the other offerors, the SSER concluded: "[Navales'] Very Good/Significant Confidence past performance rating, together with their strengths of providing strong top management, excellent administrative support and experienced project managers in previous contracts, and their lower price outweighs Offerors [Cardinal], X, A and D's Exceptional/High Confidence rating at a higher price. Therefore, I consider [Navales] to be the best value to the Government." AR at 34.

On February 27, 2003, the Air Force sent a letter to each unsuccessful bidder, including Cardinal, explaining why the contract was awarded to Navales. Cardinal filed a bid protest regarding the award with the General Accounting Office ("GAO") on March 14, 2003. Cardinal withdrew its protest before the GAO issued a decision. On July 1, 2003, Navales commenced performance.

B. Post-Award Modifications to the Navales Contract

The solicitation provided that the Air Force would have the right to expand or contract the quantity and type of custodial services to be provided by the winning bidder following the award. The proposal required offerors to complete and submit an "Add/Delete of Service Cost Sheet" immediately following award. Section 1.6 of the Solicitation stated:

1.6 *Additions/Deletions*: The contractor shall provide costs for adding or deleting services on Appendix D. Negotiations and final acceptance of the prices proposed in appendix D may be held prior to or immediately after award with the
intent to incorporate the prices as part of the contract. Appendix D will then be
utilized during the contract performance period to facilitate the incorporation
of additions and deletions of services.

AR at 435.

The Navales contract has been modified eight times following its initial award.

* * *

Modification P00003 also memorialized the parties' agreement to eliminate the "Add or
Delete Services Cost Sheet"

* * *

Modification P00004, dated August 15, 2003, increased the quantity of service required
for the men's and women's locker rooms. It also added cleaning of the spinning room
and lobby and weekend service at the base Gymnasium/Fitness Center, including the
Health and Wellness Center. This modification increased the total annual cost of the contract by $183,689.98. The Price Negotiation Memorandum for the Modification states, in
relevant part, as follows:

> Contract No. F64605-03-C-0003 was awarded on 27 February 2003 and was
> protested to the U.S. General Accounting Office on 14 March 2003.... a. Due to
> the short lead-time prior to contract performance, it is paramount that *the gov-
> ernment immediately begins requesting proposals from the contractor for incorpo-
> rating services that were initially omitted from the contract.* It was decided that a
> request would be issued for all areas that needed to be addressed and modifica-
> tions would be executed in order of priority and impact.

AR at 4871 (emphasis added). With respect to Modification P00003, the Price Negotiation Memorandum goes on to state:

> b. [Modification P00003] had been previously executed changing the base pe-
> riod of performance and eliminating a price sheet that was to be used for min-
> imal additions and deletions of service. It was determined in the best interest of
> parties, the government and the contractor, for this pricing structure to be
> deleted by modification and all future modifications to be accomplished through
> negotiation. This was found necessary due to the volume of square footage omit-
> ted from the contract statement of need. *Had the price sheet been used it would
> have resulted in extremely excessive costs bordering changes outside the scope of
> the contract.*

AR at 4871(emphasis added). Finally, the Price Negotiation Memorandum explains the
rationale for eliminating a portion of the Navales contract dealing with the Child Development Centers. This portion of the contract was later awarded to Choe Enterprises,
Inc. ("Choe"), another government contractor. The Price Negotiation Memorandum
stated:

> c. *Because the value of the proposed modifications was considerable in comparison
> to the awarded contract amount each individual requirement was reviewed to de-
> termine if it was possible to remove them from the [Navales contract] and award them
> separately.*

* * *

AR 4871-72 (emphasis added).

All told, the modifications for the first year included a decrease of $203,298 due to a start date delay and an increase of $255,689.98 for modifications P00002 and P00004. This resulted in a net increase of approximately $52,000 over the original contract price for the base year.

* * *

C. The Modifications to Navales' Contract and the Award to Choe were made in Violation of CICA

At the heart of Cardinal's case is its contention that the Air Force materially changed the Navales contract in violation of the requirements for competition set forth in CICA. CICA requires executive agencies procuring property or services to "obtain full and open competition through the use of competitive procedures." 41 U.S.C. § 253(a)(1)(A) (2004). Here, Cardinal contends that the government modified the Navales contract in contravention of CICA's competitive procedures. Cardinal asks that the Air Force be required to re-compete a contract for all of the custodial services required by the Air Force.

Whether the Air Force violated CICA's competitive procedures when it modified the Navales contract turns on whether the modifications materially changed the scope of the original contract. As the Federal Circuit explained in *AT & T Communications Inc., v. Wiltel, Inc.,* 1 F.3d 1201 (Fed.Cir.1993), "CICA ... does not prevent modification of a contract by requiring a new bid procedure for every change. Rather, only modifications outside the scope of the original competed contract fall under the statutory competition requirement." *Id.* at 1205.

Significantly, CICA does not contain a standard for determining whether a modification falls within the scope of the original competed contract. To address this problem, the Federal Circuit looked to the "cardinal change" doctrine by analogy. The cardinal change doctrine prohibits the government from forcing contractors to undertake tasks that were not within the scope of their original contract. In applying this concept to CICA, the Federal Circuit has held that the government cannot modify a contract to such an extent that the contract, as modified, is materially different from the contract that was originally competed. *Executive Bus. Media, Inc. v. United States Dep't. of Defense,* 3 F.3d 759, 764 (4th Cir.1993). According to the Federal Circuit, the question turns on whether the original contract, as modified, calls for "essentially the same performance." *Id.* at 763 n. 3.

Both this court and the GAO, in the exercise of its bid protest jurisdiction, have looked to a variety of factors to determine whether a contract, as modified, calls for "essentially the same performance." *Id.* Several cases have endorsed the factors identified by the Comptroller General in *Matter of: Neil R. Gross & Co., Inc.,* Comp. Gen. B-237,434, 1990 WL 269546 at *2: "In determining the materiality of a modification, we consider factors such as the extent of any changes in the type of work, performance period and costs between the contract as awarded and modified." (citing *Matter of the American Air Filter Co., Inc.,* Comp. Gen. B-188,408, 1978 WL 13375); *see also AT & T Communications,* 1 F.3d at 1205; *CESC Plaza Ltd. Partnership v. United States,* 52 Fed.Cl. 91, 93 (2002); *Northrop Grumman Corp. v. United States,* 50 Fed.Cl. 443, 466 (2001).

Most recently, in *CW Government Travel, Inc. v. United States,* 61 Fed.Cl. 559 (2004), the court found that the addition, by contract modification, of traditional travel services to a contract to provide military travel services using a paperless automated travel management system was a material change; thus the contracting agency's failure to issue a competitive solicitation for traditional travel services violated CICA. As the *CW Govern-*

ment Travel court explained, a "modification generally falls within the scope of the original procurement if potential bidders would have expected it to fall within the contract's changes clause." *Id.* at 574 (citing *AT & T Communications,* 1 F.3d at 1205).

Tested by the standards set forth in the above-cited cases, the court finds that the addition to, and deletion of work from, the Navales contract materially changed the original competed contract. The changes to the Navales contract were not changes of the type that were specifically authorized or even foreseen in the original contract. Rather, the modifications authorized substantial changes, which the contracting officer identified as "considerable" with costs that were potentially "extremely excessive." AR at 4871. The Navales contract contemplated "minimal additions and deletions of service" which would be accomplished through application of the Add/Delete of Service Cost Sheet, set forth in Section 1.6 of the solicitation. The modifications to the Navales contract were not, however, made through this provision. Instead, the contracting officer concluded that the Air Force needed to remove the Add/Delete of Service Cost Sheet from the Navales contract to make the changes the Air Force wanted. Specifically, the contracting officer explained:

> It was determined in the best interest of parties, the government and contractor, for this pricing structure [the Add/Delete of Service Cost Sheet] to be deleted by modification and all future modifications to be accomplished through negotiation.... *Had the price sheet been used it would have resulted in extremely excessive costs bordering changes outside the scope of the contract.*

AR at 4871 (emphasis added). In other words, the Air Force deleted the Add/Delete of Service Cost Sheet clause in the Navales contract, which authorized only minor changes, in order to make future major modifications. The Air Force feared that if it did not do this, then the excessive costs would "*border[on] changes outside the scope of the contract.*" AR at 4871 (emphasis added).[4]

In its briefs and at oral argument, the government relied on several cases for the conclusion that changes such as those made to Navales' contract were not cardinal changes. In *Northrop Grumman,* this court concluded that modifications made to a contract were not outside the scope of the contract, and as such, did not constitute a cardinal change. *Northrop Grumman,* 50 Fed.Cl. at 468. *Northrop Grumman* is not relevantly similar to the present case, however. In that case, following the award the contractor was not fulfilling the contract as it had promised in its original bid. As a consequence, modifications were made in order bring the contractor "up to the specifications of the solicitation and contract.... The reasonable bidder expects to be held to its promise to provide the government with the benefit of its bargain and to work with the government until that promise is fulfilled." *Id.* at 468. Because the post-award modifications were made to bring performance into line with what the contractor promised, the modifications were, almost by definition, within the scope of the original solicitation. *See id.*

In the present case, the modifications to Navales' contract were not made in order ensure that Navales performed in accordance with the original solicitation and contract. Rather, the modifications expressly changed performance from the solicitation and con-

---

4. At oral argument, the government introduced for the first time an alternate explanation of this language. The government alleged that this language referred to the fact that the original Navales bid suffered from a calculation defect which made the price unreasonably high, and that the final bid as accepted did not suffer from such a defect. As such, the government argues that this language is irrelevant to the cardinal change determination. However, the language of the administrative record does not support the government's explanation. Furthermore, the government could point to no document supporting its allegation. Therefore, the court finds the government's alternative argument unavailing.

tract on which Navales and the other contractors had bid. Therefore, modification of the Navales contract is distinguishable from the modifications in *Northrop Grumman. See id.*

In *PCL Constr. Serv., Inc. v. United States,* 47 Fed.Cl. 745, 806 (2000), this court considered whether a series of changes amounted to a cardinal change within the meaning of CICA. The court found that there was no cardinal change. However, contrary to the government's suggestion, *PCL* is not like the present case. In *PCL,* the plaintiff's construction manager admitted that "there was not a dramatic change" between the contract as promised to the plaintiff and the contract as modified. *PCL,* 47 Fed.Cl. at 805.

* * *

In addition, the court in *PCL* held that a series of modifications is a cardinal change when they "exceed[ ] the scope of the contract's changes clause." *PCL,* 47 Fed.Cl. at 804. Implicit in this rule is the understanding that the government does not have an unlimited right to modify the contract to eliminate the changes clause itself for the purpose of contravening the competitive nature of the contract. If, as the government maintains, the government can make changes outside the scope of the contract simply by changing the scope of the contract after award, then there would be no force to the cardinal change doctrine, and thus the purposes of CICA would be largely defeated. *See Krygoski Constr. Co., Inc. v. United States,* 94 F.3d 1537, 1543 (Fed.Cir.1996) (holding that the purpose underlying the contracting officer's discretion as to whether to terminate or recompete a contract is to "further full and open competition"). As noted, the contracting officer's decision to modify the Navales contract to eliminate the contract's Add/Delete of Service Cost Sheet had the result of defeating the full and open competition attempted during the original bidding process. For these reasons *PCL,* rather than supporting the government's proposition, belies it by highlighting this essential flaw in the government's elimination of the Add/Delete of Service Cost Sheet.

* * *

In view of the foregoing, the government's reliance on the Add/Delete of Service Cost Sheet provision in the solicitation to suggest that the modifications to the Navales contract were within the scope of the original contract is wholly misplaced. Def.'s Cross-Mot. for J. Admin. Record at 15. As explained above, the Air Force specifically modified Section 1.6 of the contract to avoid the limitations provided for in that section. As the contracting officer went on to explain, the proposed modifications to the Navales contract were "*considerable* in comparison to the awarded contract amount." AR at 4871 (emphasis added). It was for this reason that, "each additional requirement was reviewed to determine if it was possible to remove them from the [contract] and award them separately. For instance, in the case of the Child Development Center (CDC), it was mutually agreed … that this was possible…. Therefore, the CDC requirement will be removed and negotiated as a sole source 8a contract." AR at 4871–72. It is not disputed that the Air Force reduced Navales' contract by $31,000 to remove the CDC requirement and then provided Choe with a sole source 8a contract for over $250,000. Indeed, the government has increased the cost of the original contract by nearly eighty percent. Where, as here, the amount of additional work nearly doubles the price of the contract that was awarded, and the nature of the work was so substantially increased that the change provision of the contract had to be deleted to accomplish the modifications, the originally awarded contract has been materially changed. *See Neil R. Gross,* Comp. Gen. B-237,434, 1990 WL 269546.

* * *

The Air Force's decision to modify the Add/Delete of Service Cost Sheet of the original contract, in order to avoid changing the "scope of the contract" was not sufficient to overcome CICA's mandates. The government cannot circumvent CICA by modifying a contract to allow for modifications that were not originally within the scope of the contract. *Northrop Grumman,* 50 Fed.Cl. at 464. This would defeat the language and purpose of CICA. Accordingly, where, as here, the government modified the contract to allow for changes not contemplated in the original contract, the government cardinally changed the contract; by doing so without resoliciting the contract, and by instead eliminating the limitations on changes specifically set forth in the original contract, the government violated CICA. Because the government's procurement was not in accordance with law, the court is authorized to overturn this illegal action. *See* 5 U.S.C. §706(2)(A); 28 U.S.C. §1491(b)(4).

* * *

E. Conclusion

For the above-stated reasons, and on those bases alone, Cardinal's cross-motion for judgment upon the administrative record is **GRANTED**. The government's cross-motion for judgment upon the administrative record and Navales' cross-motion for judgment upon the administrative record are **DENIED**.

* * *

IT IS SO ORDERED

Notes and Questions:

1. This case revisits the issue of when a modification so materially changes the scope of a contract that CICA requires a new competition. This was first definitively addressed in the cited *AT&T Communications, Inc. v. Wiltel, Inc.,* 1 F.3d 1201 (Fed. Cir. 1993). *Wiltel* did not find the modification in question in that case so material as to require a new competition, even though it increased the contract by $100 million. Does this outcome seem a rare fluke, or does the protest of a modification seem a live and ready tool for the competitors over a type of government contract to maintain their competitive balance? See Mark G. Jackson, G. Matthew Koehl, Derek D. Crick, *Recognizing & Challenging Out-of-Scope Changes,* 03-13 Briefing Papers 1 (2003); J. Andrew Jackson & Steven A. Alerding, *Expanding Contracting Opportunities Without Competition,* 26 Pub. Cont. L.J. 205 (1997).

2. Conceptually, Judge Firestone's insightful opinion connects several areas of government contracts law. She brings together several different areas in which courts have implemented Congress's emphatic pro-competition mandate in CICA, such as in the seminal termination for convenience case of *Krygoski Constr. Co., Inc. v. United States,* 94 F.2d 1537 (Fed. Cir. 1996), in this book's chapter on termination. And, she employs the approach that issues arising during the pendency of a contract, such as a modification, ought be decided from the perspective of offerors during the time of the original competition. This we see also in cases about the necessity of adhering to the contract specifications, and the interpretation of a contract with a latent ambiguity, in the chapter on contract administration.

3. Government contract modifications involve many legal issues besides the one in this case. To take just one example, government attorneys must analyze the legality of funding of contract modifications, since it must be analyzed whether the appropriations that originally funded the contract can fund the modification. John D. Schminky, *Proper Funding of Contract Modifications Under the Antecedent Liability Rule,* 26 Pub. Cont. L.J. 221 (1997).

Chapter 3

Commercial, IDIQ, and MAS Contracting

The 2000s continued the rapid evolutions in contracting methods signified by commercial contracting, IDIQ contracting, and the GSA "multiple award schedules" (MAS). Broadly speaking, the classic methods of sealed bids and competitive proposals involved fostering of competition along formalized processes. These newer, evolving methods involved reducing the formalized aspects, and following the less formal procurement methods of the commercial market.

The chapter begins with the electronic gateway to federal contracting, FedBizOps. Technically, FedBizOps is the gateway to all contracting, both the tradition of sealed bids and competitive proposals, and the newer aspects of commercial and IDIQ contracting. However, as a web-based portal, FedBizOps belongs with the other newer phenomena.

Given the pace of developments in this context, the cases and materials in this section cannot be taken as describing enduring guides to the process that will be followed in coming years. Change happens too fast for that. Rather, these are intended as examples which would assist in understanding up-to-the-minute procedures.

For further discussion of the subjects in this chapter, see the cites for each specific subsection, and see: Steven Feldman, *Government Contract Guidebook*, §§ 4.30–4.31 (Thomson Reuters, 4th ed. 2010); Mason Alinger, *Recent Developments In Task And Delivery Order Contracting*, 39 Pub. Cont. L.J. 839 (Summer 2010); Robert J. Sherry, G. Matthew Koehl, Sheila A. Armstrong, *Competition Requirements In General Services Administration Schedule Contracts*, 37 Pub. Cont. L.J. 467 (Spring 2008); Stephen M. Daniels, *An Assessment of Today's Federal Procurement System*, 38 Procurement Lawyer, Fall 2002, at 1; Robert Mahealani M. Seto, *Basic Ordering Agreements: The Catch-22 Chameleon of Government Contract Law*, 55 SMU L. Rev. 427 (2002); Steven L. Schooner, *Fear of Oversight: The Fundamental Failure of Businesslike Government*, 50 Am. U. L. Rev. 627 (2001).

A. FedBizOpps

To increase competition and to assist small and disadvantaged business concerns in participating in government contracting, agencies must provide notice of proposed procurements and publicize solicitations. Most proposed procurements over $25,000 require advertising in digest form, called a "synopsis," In pre-Web days, Commerce Business Daily used to serve as the location of such publication, and, hence, the "portal" to federal government contracting. With the rise of the web, the Federal Business Opportunities — "FedBizOpps" — website has become the new "portal" to federal government contracting.

FedBusOpps carries the electronic publication of notices. It is searchable the way search engines work. Each synopsis requires a "procurement classification code" to be found readily. FedBusOpps has both notices, and "Justifications" — "J&As" — for other than full and open competition.

For a discussion of the history and operation of FedBizOpps, see Jennifer E. McCarthy, *Commerce Business Daily is Dead: Long Live FedBizOpps*, 31 Pub. Cont. L.J. 513 (2002).

The next case sheds light on its role.

TMI Management Systems, Inc.
B-401530, 2009 CPD P 191, 2009 WL 3108215 (Comp. Gen.)
September 28, 2009

DIGEST

Agency's misclassification of a procurement for facilities support services on the Federal Business Opportunities Internet website under a "miscellaneous" product classification code improperly deprived the protester of an opportunity to respond to the agency's solicitation and was not consistent with the agency's obligation to use reasonable methods to obtain full and open competition.

DECISION

TMI Management Systems, Inc. of Easton, Pennsylvania, protests request for proposals (RFP) No. HSFEHQ-09-R-0046, issued by the Department of Homeland Security, Federal Emergency Management Agency (FEMA), for facility support services. TMI argues that FEMA's misclassification of the procurement on the Federal Business Opportunities (FedBizOpps) website prevented the firm from submitting a proposal.[1]

We sustain the protest.

FEMA has a requirement for on-site facility support services for temporary housing units (THUs) located at temporary housing storage sites and staging areas. TMI currently holds a blanket purchase agreement (BPA) with FEMA under which the firm has received orders to provide nearly identical support services.

In February, 2009, FEMA posted a presolicitation notice, announcing the agency's intention to issue a solicitation for facilities support services for its temporary housing units, on the FedBizOpps website under procurement classification code 99, "Miscellaneous."[3] The notice also included North American Industry Classification System (NAICS) code 561210 (Facilities Support Services). Agency Report (AR), Tab 2, Presolicitation Notice, at 2. On April 10, FEMA posted a notice of the issuance of the RFP on the FedBizOpps website under the entry "Issuance of Final Solicitation," again under product classification code 99.

The RFP provided for award of a contract for THU services to supply the receipt, storage, preventative maintenance, transportation and disposition of housing units located at

---

1. The FedBizOpps website, *www.fbo.gov*, is the government-wide point of entry for the electronic publication of notices. Federal Acquisition Regulation (FAR) sections 2.101, 5.003, 5.101, 5.201.

3. Procurement classification codes are a system under which procurements are classified by product and service codes. FedBizOpps, Frequently Asked Questions. Services are classified under alphabetical letter-codes from B to Z, whereas products are classified under numerical codes from 10 to 99. The agency's use of the "99" code here thus indicated that it was acquiring goods, rather than services.

sites throughout the United States. Offerors were informed that the services would include administrative assistance; accountable property officer support; vehicle and equipment support; materiel handling support; THU operations support; transportation/equipment operation; and specialty support (such as providing electricians, welders, carpenters and mechanics to provide building maintenance and repair). RFP, Statement of Work (SOW), at C-2–C-5. All of the agency's presolicitation and solicitation notices were listed under product classification code 99 and included NAICS code 561210. The extended closing date for receipt of proposals was stated to be May 20.

TMI protested to our Office on June 26, after the closing date for receipt of proposals, that FEMA's classification of the RFP under a product (as opposed to service) code did not reasonably inform the protester or other firms of the procurement.[4] TMI argues that the RFP should have been classified under either code M, "Operation of Government-Owned Facility," or code R, "Professional, Administrative, and Management Support Services."[5] FEMA has suspended award of a contract pending our resolution of the protest.

The Competition in Contracting Act of 1984 (CICA) generally requires contracting agencies to obtain full and open competition through the use of competitive procedures, the dual purpose of which is to ensure that a procurement is open to all responsible sources and to provide the government with the opportunity to receive fair and reasonable prices. 41 U.S.C. sect. 253(a)(1)(A) (2006). In pursuit of these goals, a contracting agency must use reasonable methods to publicize its procurement needs and to timely disseminate solicitation documents to those entitled to receive them. *Kendall Healthcare Prods. Co.*, B-289381, Feb. 19, 2002, 2002 CPD para. 42 at 6. The official public medium for providing notice of contracting actions by federal agencies is the FedBizOpps website, which has been designated by statute and regulation as the government-wide point of entry. 15 U.S.C. sect. 637(e); 41 U.S.C. sect. 416; FAR sections 2.101, 5.101(a)(1), 5.201(d). An agency's notice must provide an "accurate description" of the property or services to be purchased and must be sufficient to allow a prospective contractor to make an informed business judgment as to whether to request a copy of the solicitation. *See* 15 U.S.C. sect. 637(f); *Jess Bruner Fire Suppression*, B-296533, Aug. 19, 2005, 2005 CPD para. 163 at 4. In this regard, the FAR requires agencies to use one of the procurement classification codes identified at the FedBizOpps website to identify services or supplies in its notices on FedBizOpps, *see* FAR sect. 5.207(e), and contracting officers must use the most appropriate classification category. *See Gourmet Distributors*, B-259083, Mar. 6, 1995, 95-1 CPD para. 130 at 2. We have found that an agency failed to effectively notify potential offerors of a procurement and to obtain full and open and competition under CICA, where the agency misclassified the procurement. *See Frank Thatcher Assocs., Inc.*, B-228744, Nov. 12, 1987, 87-2 CPD para. 480 at 2–3 (misclassification of procurement in the Commerce Business Daily, formerly the official public medium for identifying proposed contract actions and now replaced by FedBizOpps).

Here, FEMA classified this acquisition for support services under a miscellaneous code for products, rather than services. FEMA's contracting officer contends that none of the

---

4. A search can be conducted on the FedBizOpps website by selecting terms from drop-down menus and/or inserting terms into search boxes. Among the drop-down choices are product and service classification codes, NAICS codes, and set-aside designations. Other search parameters include, for example, active or archived status, dates, and key words. Once a product or service code (or codes) has been selected, the search is limited to procurements identified under that code or codes.

5. The TMI employee responsible for locating government solicitations stated during a telephone hearing conducted by the GAO attorney assigned to this protest that he generally searched for opportunities under classification code categories M and R.

service codes appeared applicable to the support services for THUs sought here. We find, however, as explained below, that although no service code was an exact match, a number of service codes include services such as those solicited here, and FEMA does not reasonably explain why one of these service codes would not have been more appropriate than a miscellaneous product code, which indicated that the agency was procuring goods.

The SOW listed a number of services categories, including clerical and office support, vehicle and equipment maintenance and repair, material handling, maintenance and placement of THUs, and maintenance of buildings and facilities. RFP, SOW, at C-2–C-5. A number of service codes appear to encompass similar services, such as codes J, "Maintenance, Repair & Rebuilding of Equipment," M, "Operation of Government-owned Facilities," and R, "Professional, Administrative, and Management Support Services."

FEMA's contracting officer acknowledges that facilities support services described by NAICS code 561210 are often posted under code M, but she states that she did not use this code because "sites on which the services will take place" are not owned by FEMA, but leased from commercial or public entities. *See* AR, Contracting Officer's Statement, at 1. The contracting officer also did not use codes J or R, because these codes included some services that were not solicited by the RFP. *Id.* at 2. Although we agree that none of the service codes is an exact match for the services solicited by the RFP, it is incumbent upon the agency to classify its procurement under the most appropriate category to promote competition. *Gourmet Distributors,* B-259083, *supra,* at 2–3. The agency has provided no reasonable explanation, and the record does not otherwise show, why code 99, a miscellaneous product code, is a better match than one of these service codes.[6] In this regard, we found from our own review of the FedBizOpps website that a number of procurements that include NAICS code 561210 were classified under either code J, M, or R, but no procurement with this NAICS code was classified under code 99. In short, we find no reasonable basis for FEMA's classification of this procurement under product code 99.

Notwithstanding the requirement to classify procurements accurately, FEMA argues that the availability of electronic search engines has "changed the issue of who is responsible for finding notice of an acquisition when it is misclassified." AR at 3. Specifically, FEMA argues, citing our decision in *Jess Bruner Fire Suppression,* B-296533, *supra.,* that "a prudent offeror would have found the announcement regardless of the product or service classification code because of the key words used in the FedBizOpps announcement." AR at 2. Our decision in *Jess Bruner* did not involve a solicitation posted on FedBizOpps under an improper classification code. Product and service codes are provided to make manageable searches of large numbers of procurements; that is, the classification codes allow potential offerors to narrow their searches in a meaningful way to find procurement opportunities. Misclassifying a procurement makes difficult, if not impossible, the task of locating procurement opportunities under other search terms. Here, because TMI reasonably relied in its search on the codes that most closely represented the types of services it could provide—M and R—as a means to narrow the search results, it could not have found this listing no matter what additional search terms it entered or selected. FEMA's argument that a prudent vendor could have used various available search

---

6. In this regard, the *Product and Service Codes Manual,* August 1998, maintained by the Federal Procurement Data System, General Services Administration, describes the kinds of products under classification code category 99 as including signs and advertising displays, jewelry, collectors and historical items, smoker's articles (*e.g.,* ashtrays, lighters), ecclesiastical equipment, cemetery and mortuary equipment, and "miscellaneous items," which the manual describes as including "[o]nly those items which cannot conceivably be classified in any existing classes." *See Product and Service Codes Manual,* Aug. 1998, at 136–37.

terms, such as the NAICS code, to locate the listing assumes the vendor would anticipate that the procuring agency might have misclassified the requirement and would therefore omit any product or service code from its search. We find this assumption unreasonable.

In conclusion, we find that FEMA's misclassification of this procurement deprived TMI of an opportunity to respond to the RFP and that FEMA therefore did not use reasonable methods to obtain full and open competition as required by CICA. *Frank Thatcher Assocs., Inc., supra,* at 2–3.

We recommend that FEMA reopen the competition and reissue it with a synopsis posted on FedBizOpps under an appropriate classification. We also recommend that the protester be reimbursed the costs of filing and pursuing the protest, including reasonable attorneys' fees. 4 C.F.R. sect. 21.8(d)(1) (2009). TMI should submit its certified claim for costs, detailing the time expended and cost incurred, directly to the contracting agency within 60 days after receipt of this decision. 4 C.F.R. sect. 21.8(f)(1).

The protest is sustained.

B. Commercial Contracting

Generally speaking, commercial contracting involves foregoing government-specific procurement formalities and following instead the analogy of commercial (private marketplace) methods. It also includes more government openness to purchasing items with characteristics, contract terms, and vendors, like those purchased by commercial (private) buyers.

To sketch polar opposites, before commercial contracting, a Defense Department purchase of a consignment of spare parts might, in theory, have occurred by soliciting sealed bids, using highly formal and rigid specifications, an elaborate government-specified set of terms, and a set of prospective vendors who sold only to the government because only these could and would deal with the government's procedures and requirements. In contrast, with commercial contracting, the same spare parts would get purchased from commercial vendors, on commercial terms, without formal or rigid specifications or processes, just by seeking a few price quotes and deciding among them.

The Federal Acquisition Streamlining Act (FASA), in 1994, established commercial acquisition. FAR Part 12 implements FASA by establishing commercial acquisition policies. It makes numerous laws inapplicable to commercial item purchasing. That includes both goods and services. Among important points, to oversimplify slightly, the government they shall only include clauses consistent with customary commercial practice; only acquires the technical data and rights in that data customarily provided to the public; and, acquires commercial computer software under licenses customarily provided to the public.

As for the key aspects for buying commercial items, price-wise, agencies may only used fixed price for acquisition of commercial items. The only appropriate evaluation factors are technical capability, price and past performance, and use of technical subfactors is discouraged.

For further discussion of the issues in this section, see: Neil S. Whiteman, *Charging Ahead: Has the Government Purchase Card Exceeded Its Limit?*, 30 Pub. Cont. L.J. 403 (2001); Carl J. Vacketta & Susan H. Pope, *Commercial Item Contracts: When Is a Government Contract Term or Condition Consistent with "Standard" or "Customary" Commercial Practice?*, 27 Pub. Cont. L.J. 291 (1998); Charles Tiefer & Ron Stroman, *Congressional Intent and Commercial Products*, Procurement Lawyer, Spring 1997, at 22.

Matter of: Access Logic, Inc.

January 3, 1997
B-274748.2

Access Logic, Inc. protests the award of a contract to EISI, Inc., under request for offers (RFO) No. 2-36632(CDT), issued by the National Aeronautics and Space Administration (NASA), for a 360-degree rear projection display system which will be used to simulate the outside view from an air traffic control tower.

We sustain the protest.

NASA conducted this procurement under the procedures set forth in Part 12 of the Federal Acquisition Regulation (FAR), "Acquisition of Commercial Items." Pursuant to FAR § 12.202 (Federal Acquisition Circular (FAC) 90-39), the agency conducted market research to determine which products would best meet its needs. After evaluating various projectors and screens during demonstrations held at vendor and customer sites and an industry convention, pursuant to the streamlined procedures set forth in FAR Subpart 12.6, and in particular FAR § 12.603, the agency issued the RFO as a combined synopsis/solicitation. The RFO incorporated FAR § 52.212-1 (FAC 90-39), "Instructions to Offerors—Commercial Items," which stated that offers must show, among other things, "[a] technical description of the items being offered in sufficient detail to evaluate compliance with the requirements of the solicitation. This may include product literature, or other documents, if necessary." The RFO also stated that award would be made to the responsible offeror which submitted the lowest-priced, technically acceptable offer responsive to the solicitation.

Among other items, the RFO specified the Electrohome Marquee 9501LC ACON brand name projection systems, or equal, and Optawave projection screens, or equal.[1] Although the RFO specified brand name or equal items, it did not include the standard "brand name or equal" clause which alerts offerors to include information in their offers sufficient to establish the equality of the products they are offering to the listed brand name. The RFO included a "Projection Display System Requirements Document," which apparently constituted the agency's salient characteristics, and included required specifications for the projectors and screens. That document also stated that the contractor is to provide all necessary design, engineering, installation labor, projector adjustments, project management, documentation, screens, equipment and materials, to furnish a complete and operational projection display system.

Six proposals were submitted. Instead of the brand name projection system, Access Logic proposed as an equal a BarcoGraphics 1209 rear projection display system; the firm also proposed Dia-Nippon ProScreen 180 degree viewing cone screens as equal to the brand name screens. Access Logic's proposal, which was priced at $665,901, was rejected as technically unacceptable for reasons which we will address in detail below. Award was made to EISI at a price of $773,168, as the lowest-priced, technically acceptable offeror.

Based on our review of the record, we conclude that NASA improperly found Access Logic's offer unacceptable for failing to meet requirements not set forth in the RFO. Once

---

1. The RFO in fact only stated that "or equal" offers would be considered for the projectors, and not the screens. Nonetheless, the solicitation included detailed technical requirements for the screens—suggesting that a brand name or equal method also was intended for the screens. More importantly, in its evaluation of proposals and its defense of this protest, NASA has treated the solicitation as a brand name or equal solicitation for both the projectors and the screens. Under these circumstances, we have reviewed the evaluation as if the RFO permitted offers of equal products for both items.

offerors are informed of the criteria against which proposals will be evaluated, the agency must adhere to them. Grey Advertising, Inc., 55 Comp. Gen. 1111 (1976), 76-1 CPD p 325. In a brand name or equal acquisition, the contracting agency has an obligation to inform offerors of the characteristics that are essential to the government's needs and a product offered as an "equal" one need not meet unstated features of the brand name product. Tri Tool, Inc., B-265649.2, Jan. 22, 1996, 96-1 CPD p 14. Similarly, in an acquisition of commercial items, the description of the agency's needs "must contain sufficient detail for potential offerors of commercial items to know which commercial products or services to offer." FAR § 12.202(b); Metfab Eng'g, Inc.; Mart Corp., B-265934; B-265934.2, Jan. 19, 1996, 96-1 CPD p 93.

Among the reasons for rejecting Access Logic's offer, NASA concluded that Access Logic's offer did not meet RFO requirements concerning the "gain" and "half gain" angle for the projection screens and took exception to an RFO requirement concerning vertical mullions between the screens. Concerning these requirements, the RFO stated that:

> "The [c]ontractor shall provide a 360 degree rear projection screen system, with minimum vertical mullions, ... Use only products which comply with the following requirements:
>
> 1. Custom fresnel/lenticular acrylic optical screens with 4.0 gain, ...
>
> . . . . .
>
> 3. Physical separation between the screens to be as small as possible so as to make it difficult to see the screen edge lines."

The only reference in Access Logic's proposal concerning the mullions was a statement that "[t]he screens will be installed as-close together as-possible, with minimal vertical mullions." NASA reports that Access Logic's proposal "did not provide any actual designs or other supporting information indicating an acceptable construction method. Thus, [Access Logic's] proposal was considered unclear and in need of clarification." NASA orally requested Access Logic to clarify the reference in its proposal to mullions. According to Access Logic, it responded to this inquiry by stating that, based on a post-award review of the site, including a seismic review, in the best case, it would fuse the screens together so there would be no mullions and, in the worst case, 3/4-inch wide mullions would be used to connect the screens.[2]

According to NASA, Access Logic's response to the agency's questions indicated the firm was uncertain as to how to satisfy the installation requirements and, absent more specific information about the fusing alternative, the agency was obligated to evaluate the 3/4-inch mullion alternative. NASA found the proposal's reference to mullions and Access Logic's explanation to be unacceptable because 3/4-inch mullions "would create a thick defined edge line between screens and significantly distract from images of aircraft and ground equipment moving across the screens." Also, according to NASA, Access Logic's apparent need for post-award input "cast doubt on whether [Access Logic] was capable of designing and installing the screens in a manner that would satisfy the Government's requirements." NASA also states that Access Logic's experience—which appears to involve

---

2. Access Logic explains that it informed the agency that it intended to perform an on-site engineering review, including a seismic review (given that the facility will be located in an earthquake zone) to determine the most effective installation to meet technical requirements and building codes, including seismic considerations. The firm also states that it explained that it expected the mullions to be barely visible with the screens fused together and that "at worst case we expected the mullions would be 3/4 of an inch, which would provide sufficient support from a seismic perspective."

mostly two-screen, co-planar installations rather than curved, seamless installations like that required by the solicitation—did not alleviate this concern.

The RFO did not require mullions of any specific width. The only requirements were for "minimum vertical mullions" and for "[p]hysical separation between the screens … as small as possible so as to make it difficult to see the screen edge lines." Nothing in Access Logic's proposal indicated that it would not meet these requirements in installing the system. On the contrary, the proposal statement that "[t]he screens will be installed as-close together as-possible, with minimal vertical mullions," is entirely consistent with the RFO requirements. Moreover, nothing in the market research submitted by NASA indicates there is a consensus in the industry that 3/4-inch mullions would not be "as small as possible" or that the screens could be attached with no visible line between them. In fact, NASA's market research report states the expectation that in NASA's planned facility "the screens will have a small but discernible line between them." In addition, NASA makes no effort to rebut Access Logic's belief that the 3/4-inch mullion size would be "as small as possible" depending upon the seismic protection need. Thus, it appears that NASA simply has its own view, one that would not be readily apparent to the commercial sector, as to the width of the mullions that it would be willing to accept. To the extent that NASA had such a specific requirement, it should have specified it in the RFO. Since it did not, a vendor's failure to meet the requirement cannot provide a basis for rejecting the vendor's proposal.[3] Industrial Storage Equip.-Pac., B-228123, Dec. 4, 1987, 87-2 CPD p 551. Under the circumstances, we conclude that NASA's determination that Access Logic's proposal took exception to an RFO requirement concerning the mullions was unreasonable.

* * *

In other words, while NASA's concern about the brightness consistency of the projection screens and its desire for projection screens with a high half gain angle are reasonable, these concerns were not reasonably conveyed to vendors. In this respect, the record does not show that the specification of a gain of 4.0—the only information in the RFO concerning brightness of the screens—should have conveyed to vendors in the commercial marketplace that high half gain angles were mandatory.

NASA also concluded that the projectors proposed by Access Logic failed to meet a requirement of the RFO for automatic convergence.… Automatic convergence is a function that automatically converges or focuses a picture on a screen for maximum clarity and avoids the need for manual focusing.

On its face, Access Logic's proposal stated that the proposed projectors have an automatic convergence feature and NASA does not question whether that feature would be provided. Rather, the agency explains that it considered Access Logic's proposal unacceptable because it did not include documentation demonstrating that the automatic convergence system proposed by the firm would work in the rear projection system required by the agency. In our view, however, since the proposal otherwise recognized the system would use rear projection and did not take exception to the requirement for automatic convergence in the rear projection format, the absence of a specific statement that the automatic convergence feature of the proposed equipment would work in the rear projection system

---

3. Although the agency also argues the proposal should have included design or other supporting information to show compliance with this requirement, the RFO had no such requirement. The RFO only required design information during performance of the contract.

provided no basis for concluding that the proposal was unacceptable.[4] See Inframetrics, Inc., B-257400, Sept. 30, 1994, 94-2 CPD p 138.

Finally, NASA found Access Logic's proposal unacceptable because it did not list the firm's key personnel or design and engineering staff that would install the projection system. As Access Logic points out, however, the RFO did not require the submission of information about key personnel or staff. Although the contractor is to provide all necessary design, engineering, installation labor, projector adjustments, project management, etc., to provide a complete and operational projection display system, there was no requirement for offerors to submit any information concerning staff. Under the circumstances, the absence of such information in Access Logic's proposal provided no basis for finding that proposal unacceptable. Grey Advertising, Inc., supra.[5]

Although the record indicates that EISI delivered the projectors and screens and related equipment to NASA before the contract was suspended as a result of this protest, the equipment has not yet been installed. Accordingly, we recommend that NASA terminate the contract and resolicit with an appropriate statement of the agency's needs.... *

The protest is sustained.[6]

Notes and Questions

1. The drive toward commercial acquisition encompasses many aspects, and this opinion reflects perhaps the most key one—having the contracting agency open itself to, and make a genuine choice among, commercially available items, rather than imposing over-elaborate specifications (especially insufficiently articulated ones) and making contractors thus provide, at higher-than-market price, what specifications demand. See the Winter 1998 issue of the Public Contract Law Journal, notably, Carl J. Vacketta & Susan H. Pope, *Commercial Item Contracts: When Is a Government Contract Term or Condition Consistent with "Standard" or "Customary" Commercial Practice?*, 27 Pub. Cont. L.J. 291 (1998). For a critical perspective on the uses being made of commercial contracting procedures, see Stephen M. Daniels, *An Assessment of Today's Federal Procurement System*, 38 Procurement Lawyer, Fall 2002, at 1.

---

4. Agency officials assert they orally asked Access Logic's president about the automatic convergence capability of the projectors proposed by the firm and the firm failed to provide information responsive to that question. While the record concerning the communications between NASA and Access Logic is unclear, Access Logic's president states that, when asked, he orally informed the agency that the firm's proposed projectors do provide automatic convergence for a rear screen projection format and that, had NASA asked, the firm would have submitted commercial literature specifically stating that it does. We note that Access Logic has submitted to this Office commercial literature that shows that its proposed automatic convergence unit will work in a rear projection screen system....

5. NASA also concluded that Access Logic's proposal was unacceptable because it did not include information concerning service personnel. As a matter of contract performance, the RFO required that "the Contractor shall have an office with full time service personnel located within 100 miles of the [NASA] site." Since the RFO did not require the submission of information about personnel or staff and NASA has referred to nothing in Access Logic's offer that suggests the firm would not meet this requirement, we conclude it was unreasonable to find the proposal unacceptable on this basis.

6. Access Logic filed a supplemental protest in which it argues (1) NASA illegally conducted this procurement as a "brand name only" procurement under the guise of a "brand name or equal" procurement without properly documenting the "brand name only" procurement, and (2) NASA was biased against Access Logic because agency officials were predisposed to award only to an offeror proposing the brand name products. Since we have sustained the protest and since it is not practicable for us to make a recommendation for corrective action, no useful purpose would be served by addressing these issues.

2. Notice that the RFO stated that award would be made to the lowest-priced, technically acceptable responsive offer. In other words, the agency did not say that it would trade off technical merit for price. To deny Access Logic the award, the agency had to find its offer not merely technically inferior, but technically unacceptable. Hence the piling-on of NASA criticisms of Access Logic, and the apparent conviction of the GAO that underneath all those NASA criticisms was a simple unwillingness by NASA to recognize that, by the RFO's stated criteria, Access Logic's offer was technically acceptable—whether imperfect or even inferior.

3. Did NASA try to use commercial item acquisition methods just to buy from a preferred vendor? Or did GAO decide the protest in a way that put the rigidity of classic contracting methods back into the commercial item acquisition process?

Matter of GIBBCO LLC
B-401890, 2009 CPD P 255, 2009 WL 4810593 (Comp.Gen.)
December 14, 2009

DIGEST

1. Protest that agency improperly issued a solicitation for housing units meeting certain air quality standards under Federal Acquisition Regulation (FAR) subpart 12.6 streamlined procedures for commercial items is denied, where the agency reasonably determined that the solicited units were commercial items.

2. In a procurement conducted under FAR subpart 12.6 streamlined procedures for commercial items, protest that agency required submission of proposals in less than 30 days is denied, where the agency was only required to provide offerors with a reasonable opportunity to respond.

DECISION

GIBBCO LLC of Prattville, Alabama, protests the terms of solicitation No. HSFEHQ-09-R-0105, issued as a commercial item acquisition by the Department of Homeland Security, Federal Emergency Management Agency (FEMA), for "alternative housing units" for disaster victims. GIBBCO contends that the solicited units are not commercial items and that the agency did not provide sufficient time for interested vendors to submit responses.

We deny the protest.

The solicitation, issued as a combined synopsis/solicitation on the FedBizOpps website on August 19, 2009, pursuant to the Federal Acquisition Regulation (FAR) subpart 12.6 streamlined procedures for evaluation and solicitation for commercial items, provided for multiple awards of fixed-price, indefinite-delivery/indefinite-quantity contracts for alternative housing units.[1] According to the solicitation's statement of work (SOW), this acquisition was "intended to expand FEMA's repertoire of available disaster housing with new units that address the most crucial issues facing FEMA today." SOW at C-1. Offerors were informed that the closing date for receipt of proposals was September 10. FebBizOpps Notice, Aug. 19, 2009.

---

1. Although the solicitation was posted as a combined synopsis/solicitation, a solicitation on standard form 33 was included with the FedBizOpps notice, even though the FAR does not contemplate that a separate solicitation will be issued in the acquisition of commercial items using steamlined procedures when a combined synopsis/solicitation is issued. *See* FAR sect. 12.603(c)(2)(i). This was not challenged by the protester.

Offerors were informed that the solicited housing units were for the purpose of providing temporary housing to disaster victims and would likely be subjected to extended road travel, multiple installations and deactivations, and various extreme weather conditions. In this regard, the SOW stated that the solicitation was open to all unit types, including "Factory Built Housing, Manufactured Housing (HUD-Code), Modular Housing, Panelized Housing, and other types of alternative units such as yurts, shipping containers, transportable multiple dwelling units, duplex units, and stackable units." SOW at C-1. The SOW identified a number of requirements that the housing units must meet, including compliance with air quality standards specified in the solicitation.

Gibbco protests that FEMA cannot use the FAR subpart 12.6 streamlined procedures to acquire these housing units, because the housing units, as specified in the SOW, are not commercial items. Protest at 2. The protester argues that the solicited housing units must be custom-made to meet the solicitation's air quality specifications and would be of much higher quality than the industry standard for a manufactured housing unit.

FEMA disagrees that the solicited housing units are not commercial items. The contracting officer states that he considered the extensive market research and field assessments performed by FEMA's Joint Housing Solutions Group (JGSG) (which considered more than 200 housing units and performed field assessments on nearly 50 units) and a commercial item acquisition conducted by FEMA in 2008 for housing units to conclude that the solicited housing units here were commercial items. With respect to the 2008 commercial item acquisition for housing units (solicitation No. HSFEHQ-08-R-0106), FEMA solicited proposals for similar housing units with the same formaldehyde levels and similar air quality testing requirements, receiving a number of proposals from which the agency made seven awards and pre-qualified a number of other commercial item vendors. AR at 7; Contracting Officer's Statement at 1. FEMA contends that any modifications that must be made to commercial housing units to satisfy the solicitation's air quality specifications are minor because these modifications do not alter the commercial nature, nongovernmental functions, or essential physical characteristics of the units. See AR at 7. In this regard, FEMA states that it received proposals from a large number of offerors in response to the solicitation here. Finally, FEMA states that the agency is aware that since Hurricane Katrina in 2005 and the public disclosure of the numerous claims made concerning air emissions and formaldehyde in alternative housing units that the alternative housing unit industry began making changes to limit formaldehyde emissions.

Determining whether a product is a commercial item is largely within the discretion of the contracting agency, and such a determination will not be disturbed by our Office unless it is shown to be unreasonable. See Aalco Forwarding, Inc., et al., B-277241 et al., Oct. 21, 1997, 97-2 CPD para. 110 at 8, (agency properly determined that services could be acquired as commercial item under FAR part 12 procedures notwithstanding inclusion of government-unique requirements in solicitation); see also Premier Eng'g & Mfg., Inc., B-283028, B-283028.2, Sept. 27, 1999, 99-2 CPD para. 65 at 5 (determination as to whether modifications to a commercial item are minor are within the agency's technical judgment that will be disturbed only where unreasonable).

The FAR defines a "commercial item," as relevant here, to be:

(1) Any item, other than real property, that is of a type customarily used by the general public or by non-governmental entities for purposes other than governmental purposes, and

(i) Has been sold, leased, or licensed to the general public; or

(ii) Has been offered for sale, lease, or license to the general public;

* * *

(3) Any item that would satisfy a criterion expressed in paragraphs (1) or (2) of this definition, but for

(i) Modifications of a type customarily available in the commercial marketplace; or

(ii) Minor modifications of a type not customarily available in the commercial marketplace made to meet Federal Government requirements. Minor modifications mean modifications that do not significantly alter the non-governmental function or essential physical characteristics of an item or component, or change the purpose of a process. Factors to be considered in determining whether a modification is minor include the value and size of the modification and the comparative value and size of the final product. Dollar values and percentages may be used as guideposts, but are not conclusive evidence that a modification is minor[.]

FAR sect. 2.101. The solicitation incorporated by reference FAR sect. 52.202-1, which in turn incorporates this FAR commercial item definition.

The record shows that FEMA reasonably determined that the housing units solicited here are commercial items. As noted by the agency, and not disputed by Gibbco, FEMA conducted an earlier commercial item acquisition for alternative housing units meeting air quality standards and testing specifications that are nearly identical to the solicitation at issue here and made several awards and pre-qualified a number of other vendors. Given this history, we find that the contracting officer could reasonably determine that FEMA could expect to receive commercial items in response to the solicitation here. With respect to Gibbco's complaint that, to satisfy the solicitation's emission and air quality testing requirements, it would have to use different materials and that the required testing would require the services of an "industrial hygienist" and would entail additional production time, this does not establish that any modifications that would have to be performed on commercial housing units to satisfy the solicitation's specifications were not minor. *See Canberra Indus., Inc.*, B-271016, June 5, 1996, 96-1 CPD para. 269 at 5 (solicited item within FAR definition of commercial item where regularly sold to public and modification does not alter item's function or physical characteristics). Accordingly, we find that Gibbco's arguments provide us with no basis to object to the agency's decision to issue the solicitation under FAR subpart 12.6 streamlined procedures for the acquisition of commercial items.

Gibbco also complains that the solicitation required the submission of proposals within 22 days of the date the solicitation was issued and that the agency should have provided at least a 30-day response time for receipt of bids or proposals as required by the FAR for the acquisition of non-commercial items.[3]

Part 12 of the FAR prescribes policies and procedures unique to the acquisition of commercial items, including streamlined procedures for evaluation and solicitation for commercial items. *See* FAR sections 12.000–12.603. Among other things, the streamlined procedures under FAR subpart 12.6 permit a contracting officer to reduce the time required to solicit and award contracts for commercial items. *See* FAR sect. 12.603(a). In this re-

---

3. FAR sect. 5.203(c) provides that "[e]xcept for the acquisition of commercial items (see 5.203(b)), agencies shall allow at least a 30-day response time for receipt of bids or proposals from the date of issuance of a solicitation, if the proposed contract action is expected to exceed the simplified acquisition threshold."

gard, FAR sect. 5.203(b) provides that, for the acquisition of commercial items in an amount estimated to be in excess of $25,000, an agency must provide potential offerors with a reasonable opportunity to respond to the solicitation.

Given our decision above that the contracting officer had a reasonable basis to issue the solicitation under the FAR subpart 12.6 streamlined procedures for the acquisition of commercial items, Gibbco's argument that the agency was required to provide at least a 30-day response time is without merit. Agencies need only establish a solicitation response time that will afford potential offerors a reasonable opportunity to respond to each proposed contract action for the acquisition of commercial items. *See American Artisan Prod.,* B-281409, Dec. 21, 1998, 98-2 CPD para. 155 at 3 (contracting officer's decision to allow 15-day response time for commercial item acquisition reasonable based on prior experience with previous procurement). Gibbco provides no information or arguments showing that the requirement for the submission of proposals within 22 days for this commercial item acquisition was unreasonable.

The protest is denied.

B. IDIQ and MAS Contracting

1. IDIQ Contracting

In 1994, as part of FASA, federal agencies first received statutory authority to utilize task and delivery orders under indefinite-delivery, indefinite quantity contracts (IDIQ). FAR Subpart 16.5 discusses IDIQ contracting involves the award of an overarching contract — usually to multiple awardees — and then the award, to particular awardees, of particular tasks and delivery orders.

For example, a military army might compete an IDIQ contract solicitation to supply it with logistical support services. Out of eight offerors, it might award the IDIQ contract to three of them. Then, each time it needs a reasonable amount of such services, it might compete that delivery order among the three awardees of the IDIQ contract. (Orders for goods are delivery orders; orders for services are task orders.) This competition for the task order would use simple, quick methods. The winner would receive the award of that specific task order. The next time the army needed logistical support services, it would again compete the task order among the three awardees of the IDIQ contract, and one of those three, by no means necessarily the same as the previous awardee, would win this task order.

The IDIQ innovation proved very effective. Its use spread in the years after FASA. However, initially, FASA did not impose procedural requirements on task and delivery order competition, and barred protests to GAO or to the Court of Federal Claims. This remained largely unchanged for well over a decade, until section 843, entitled "Enhanced Competition Requirements for Task and Delivery Order Contracts," of the FY 2008 defense authority amended FASA. Section 843 reacted against the excesses of the 2000s, which had seen levels of competition in procurement plummet in IDIQ contracting among other aspects.

Section 843 specified requirements, for task or delivery orders in excess of $5 million, for "fair opportunity" to be considered. The agency must provide to all contract holders (that is, all awardees of the base IDIQ contract) notice of the award, including a clear statement of the requirements; factors and subfactors for evaluating proposals; and debriefings and statements about the basis of the award.

For orders over $100 million, section 843 prohibited award to a single source unless the agency head determined in writing that such an award is based on one of the prescribed justifications.

Section 843 also lifted the prior ban on protests to GAO. Protests of task and delivery order awards could now go to GAO. However, the ban remained in place on protests to the Court of Federal Claims. *A & D Fire Protection, Inc. v. United States*, 72 Fed. Cl. 126, 133–36 (2006).

For further discussion of the issues of this subsection, see Mason Alinger, *Recent Developments In Task And Delivery Order Contracting*, 39 Pub. Cont. L.J. 839 (Summer 2010); Noah B. Bleicher, Wesley L. Dunn, Daniel I. Gordon, Jonathan L. Kang, *Accountability In Indefinite-Delivery/Indefinite-Quantity Contracting: The Work Of The U.S. Government Accountability Office*, 37 Pub. Cont. L.J. 375 (Spring 2008); Jennifer Ann Cukier, The *Networx Acquisition: Is The Last Mega-IDIQ Dinosaur Dying On The Plain?*, 36 Pub. Cont. L.J. 385 (Spring 2007); Kevin J. Wilkinson, *More Effective Federal Procurement Response To Disasters: Maximizing The Extraordinary Flexibilities Of IDIQ Contracting*, 59 A.F. L. Rev. 231 (2007); Annejanette Kloeb Heckman, *Challenges To Task And Delivery Order Awards Under Multiple Award Contracts: Recent Developments And Proposals For Change*, 42 Procrmt. Law. 1 (Winter 2007).

Decision Matter of: DynCorp International LLC

B-402349 (Comp.Gen.), 2010 CPD P 59 (Comp.Gen.), 2010 WL 893517
(Comp.Gen.)
COMPTROLLER GENERAL
March 15, 2010
DIGEST

Protest that task order requests for proposals (TORP) are outside the scope of multiple-award indefinite-delivery/indefinite-quantity (ID/IQ) contracts is sustained, where the ID/IQ contracts were limited to providing counter-narcoterrorism support services worldwide, and the TORPs sought mentoring, training, facilities, and logistics support services for the Ministry of the Interior and Afghan National Police in general law enforcement and counter-insurgency activities, which were not reasonably contemplated under the ID/IQ contracts.

DECISION

DynCorp International LLC, of Falls Church, Virginia, protests the issuance of task order requests for proposals (TORP) 150 for mentoring and training the Ministry of the Interior and Afghan National Police and TORP 166 for facility maintenance and logistics support for the Afghan National Police Development Program, by the Department of the Army under multiple-award indefinite-delivery/indefinite-quantity (ID/IQ) contracts to provide program and operations support for the Department of Defense Counter Narcoterrorism Technology Program Office. DynCorp contends that the TORPs are outside the scope of the ID/IQ contracts.

We sustain the protest.

BACKGROUND

On August 24, 2007, five ID/IQ contracts were awarded on the basis of full and open competition to Blackwater Lodge & Training Center, Inc. (now U.S. Training Center); Lockheed Martin Integrated Systems, Inc.; Northrop Grumman/TASC, Inc.; Raytheon

Technical Services Company; and ARINC Engineering Services, LLC. These contracts were awarded pursuant to request for proposals No. W9113M-06-R-0014, issued by the United States Army Space & Missile Defense Command/Army Forces Strategic Command for program and operations support for the Department of Defense Counter Narcoterrorism Technology Program Office.[1] The mission of the Counter Narcoterrorism Technology Program Office is to provide technology to the Department of Defense, other federal agencies, partner nations, and state and local authorities engaged in counter-drug and counter-narcoterrorism operations.

* * *

The scope of work for the ID/IQ contracts was limited to providing the "necessary goods and services required by the [Counter Narcoterrorism Technology Program Office] to support the counter-narcoterrorism mission" of the above listed agencies, nations, and authorities in three "program performance areas": technology development and application; training, operations, and logistics support; and program and executive support. AR, Tab 4e, ID/IQ Contract Performance Work Statement, at 6, 13. The performance work statement stated:

> These support services will support the technology development and application of new counterdrug technologies. Support for training, operations, and logistic[s] for military and civilian missions (including conveyances, weapons, security services, etc.), and professional and executive support for information operations and information technology (IT) deployment will also be provided under this acquisition.

Id. at 5. The performance work statement indicated that although these services would be provided worldwide, the current "primary countries of interest" were Colombia and Afghanistan. *Id.* at 6. The performance work statement also specifically noted, as examples, that the goods and services provided would outfit and support counter-narcoterrorism units such as the Counter Narcotics Police in Afghanistan and the Counter Narcotics Brigade in Columbia. *Id.* at 6.

With regard to training and security services specifically, the performance work statement stated that the services would be "in support of counter-narcoterrorism missions and objectives." *Id.* at 18, 19. The performance work statement also identified representative examples of the training and security services contemplated, including security force training for border police in Afghanistan, training of counter-narcoterrorism forces in Afghanistan, and protective services for counter-narcoterrorism activities in Afghanistan. *Id.*

In addition, the solicitation for these ID/IQ contracts included three sample task orders, each of which included a sample performance work statement to illustrate representative TORPs. The sample task orders were to: (1) develop high resolution short wave infrared cameras for surveillance and reconnaissance aircraft; (2) provide intelligence surveillance and reconnaissance support in the Trans-Sahara region of Africa; and (3) train Afghan Border Police to perform functions necessary to deny the flow of illegal persons, drugs, and weapons across borders. AR, Tabs 4b-e, Sample Task Orders.

The first of the two task order requests at issue here, TORP 150, seeks mentoring and training services for the Afghan Ministry of the Interior and Afghan National Police.[2] AR,

---

1. The contracts were for a base year and four 1-year options, and had a collective ceiling price of $15 billion. Agency Report (AR) at 14.

2. TORP 150 includes a base and two option years; the total government estimate for this work is $905,264,000. AR, Tab 5a, TORP Acquisition Strategy, at 9.

Tab 5c, TORP 150 Performance Work Statement, at 1. The Ministry of the Interior is responsible for nationwide law enforcement in Afghanistan and controls the Afghan National Police. The Afghan National Police consists of a variety of organizations, most of which are involved in general law enforcement, safety and security, and counter-insurgency activities.[4] Only two of these organizations—the Afghan Border Police and Counter-Narcotics element—have a mission directly involving counter-drug operations. Protest, exh. 6, Afghan National Police Fact Sheet, at 1; Comments at 24–25. Specifically, the Afghan Border Police are responsible for patrolling Afghanistan's borders, conducting counter-smuggling operations, and managing immigration; the Counter-Narcotics element is responsible for eliminating the production and trafficking of illicit drugs. Protest, exh. 6, Afghan National Police Fact Sheet, at 1; Comments at 25. Thus, the Ministry of the Interior and Afghan National Police are involved in counter-drug and counter-narcoterrorism activities, but these activities are not their primary functions.

The stated "objective" of TORP 150 is to "support the Afghanistan [Ministry of the Interior] and the [Afghan National Police] to increase their overall capabilities to provide a trained and professional police presence, enhance public security, and support the rule of law in Afghanistan." AR, Tab 5c, TORP 150 Performance Work Statement, at 1. In furtherance of this objective, the TORP requests 100 mentors to "provide for the administration and execution of the functions of the [Ministry of the Interior]," with approximately 30 of these mentors designated as key personnel. *Id.* at 2–4. One of the designated key personnel mentors is to provide training and support for the "Director [of] Afghan Border Police." *Id.* at 6. As noted above, the Afghan Border Police are involved in counter-narcoterrorism operations.

* * *

The second of the two task order requests at issue here, TORP 166, seeks facility maintenance and logistics support for TORP 150. Specifically, TORP 166 requires facility maintenance and logistics support services for the "Afghan National Police Development Program" in Camp Gibson, Afghanistan, and facility maintenance and logistics support for 14 other named camps.

* * *

DISCUSSION

DynCorp, which does not hold an ID/IQ contract with the Counter Narcoterrorism Technology Program Office, protests that TORPs 150 and 166 are outside the scope of the underlying ID/IQ contracts because the requested services are unrelated to counter-narcoterrorism.[8] The Army asserts that the ID/IQ contracts are written broadly so as to include the services requested here.

---

4. The Afghan National Police consists of the following organizations: Afghan Uniformed Police, Afghan Border Police, Afghan National Civil Order Police, and several "specialized elements" such as Counter-Narcotics, Counterterrorism, Fire Fighting, Major Crimes Task Force, and the Special Police Operations Unit. AR, Tab 5c, TORP 150 Performance Work Statement, at 1; AR, encl. 3, Counter Narcoterrorism Technology Program Office Memorandum (Dec. 4, 2009), at 1–2; Protest, exh. 6, Afghan National Police Fact Sheet, at 1. The Uniformed Police, which is the largest organization within the Afghan National Police, is responsible for general law enforcement, public safety, and internal security throughout Afghanistan. The National Civil Order Police is responsible for addressing civil disturbances in large urban areas. The remaining organizations are smaller and have specialized missions, primarily focused on a variety of criminal and counter-insurgency activities. Protest, exh. 6, Afghan National Police Fact Sheet, at 1; Comments at 24–25.

8. DynCorp previously provided training for the Ministry of the Interior and Afghan National Police under a task order with the Department of State that expired on January 31, 2010 (but was ex-

Under the Federal Acquisition and Streamlining Act of 1994 (FASA), as modified by the National Defense Authorization Act of Fiscal Year 2008, our Office is authorized to hear protests of task orders that are issued under multiple-award contracts (or protests of the solicitations for those task orders) where the task order is valued in excess of $10 million, or where the protester asserts that the task order increases the scope, period, or maximum value of the contract under which the order is issued. 10 U.S.C. sect. 2304c(d) (2006); 10 U.S.C.A sect. 2304c(e)(B) (2009); *Innovative Techs. Corp.*, B-401689 *et al.*, Nov. 9, 2009, 2009 CPD para. 235 at 6. Task orders that are outside the scope of the underlying multiple-award contract are subject to the statutory requirement for full and open competition set forth in the Competition in Contracting Act of 1984 (CICA), absent a valid determination that the work is appropriate for procurement on a sole-source basis or with limited competition. 41 U.S.C. sect. 253(A)(1)(A) (2006); *Anteon Corp.*, B-293523, B-293523.2, Mar. 29, 2004, 2004 CPD para. 51 at 4; *Erwin and Assocs., Inc.*, B-278850, Mar. 23, 1998, 98-1 CPD para. 89 at 7.

The analysis of whether a task order is outside the scope of a multiple-award contract is the same as the analysis of whether a contract modification is outside the scope of a single-award contract. *Anteon Corp., supra,* at 4–5. In addition, the law in this area is well-settled. In determining whether a task order is beyond the scope of the contract, GAO and the courts look to whether there is a material difference between the task order and that contract. *Id.* at 5; *MCI Telecomms. Corp.*, B-276659.2, Sept. 28, 1997, 97-2 CPD para. 90 at 7; *see also AT & T Commc'ns, Inc. v. Wiltel, Inc.*, 1 F.3d 1201, 1204 (1993); *CCL, Inc.*, 39 Fed. Cl. 180, 191–92 (1997). Evidence of such a material difference is found by reviewing the circumstances attending the procurement that was conducted; examining any changes in the type of work, performance period, and costs between the contract as awarded and as modified by the task order; and considering whether the original contract solicitation adequately advised offerors of the potential for the type of task order issued. *Anteon Corp., supra,* at 5; *Data Transformation Corp.*, B-274629, Dec. 19, 1996, 97-1 CPD para. 10 at 6. The overall inquiry is whether the task order is of a nature that potential offerors would reasonably have anticipated. *Anteon Corp.*, B-293523, B-293523.2, Mar. 29, 2004, 2004 CPD para. 51 at 5.

DynCorp argues that the services requested by the TORPs at issue here are outside the scope of the underlying ID/IQ contracts, because the requested services are broader than and only indirectly related to the underlying contracts' counter-narcoterrorism efforts. In DynCorp's view, these TORPs involve support services for counter-insurgency and other efforts unrelated to counter-narcoterrorism, and include support for organizations within the Ministry of the Interior and Afghan National Police that are not directly involved in counter-narcoterrorism operations. Protest at 20–26; Comments at 21–34.

The Army admits that the Ministry of the Interior and Afghan National Police are primarily involved in counter-insurgency activities. AR at 40. However, according to the

---

tended to March 31, 2010 to allow for transition). In the past, the Department of State maintained responsibility for training the Ministry and most of the organizations within the Afghan National Police, while the Counter Narcoterrorism Technology Program Office maintained responsibility for training for the Afghan Border Police, which, as noted above, is engaged in counter-narcoterrorism operations. Pursuant to an interagency decision, the Department of State and Department of Defense's Combined Security Transition Command-Afghanistan decided that the responsibility for training the Afghan National Police (including the Afghan Border Police) should be performed by the Department of Defense. The Department of Defense decided to procure the training for the Ministry of the Interior and the Afghan National Police through the Counter Narcoterrorism Technology Program Office ID/IQ contracts. AR at 14–15. The Army concedes that many of the services that are the subject of this protest were provided in the past by DynCorp under its task order with the Department of State. *Id.* at 21.

Army, there is a "nexus" between these counter-insurgency activities and counter-nar-coterrorism "because in Afghanistan the insurgency is funded by drug trafficking" and therefore "any organization or ministry conducting counter[-] insurgency operations in Afghanistan necessarily is involved in countering illegal drug trafficking." AR at 23, 34–38; Contracting Officer's Statement at 49–53 (explaining how drug trades support insurgency). Because of this funding "nexus," the Army contends that there is no difference between counter-insurgency and counter-narcoterrorism— "the two are the same." AR at 43. The Army also argues that the language of the underlying ID/IQ contracts (and sample tasks included within them) is broad enough to include training for all police and Ministry of the Interior activities and is not limited to counter-narcoterrorism. AR at 31–34, 43–49.

Based on our review of the record, we find that the underlying ID/IQ contracts do not contemplate providing the services requested by the TORPs here. As noted above, the underlying ID/IQ contracts advised that future task orders would be related to the counter-narcoterrorism mission of the Counter Narcoterrorism Technology Program Office. AR, Tab 4e, ID/IQ Contract Performance Work Statement, at 6, 18–19. Although the ID/IQ contracts were broadly written and included some training and logistics support, these contracts made clear that the activities had to be related to counter-nar-coterrorism operations.

Here, with regard to TORP 150, only a small portion of requested training services arguably relate to counter-narcoterrorism or support the counter-narcoterrorism mission of the Counter Narcoterrorism Technology Program Office. *See* Contracting Officer's Statement at 54. The vast majority of the TORPs' requested services involve training the Ministry of the Interior and Afghan National Police in activities that support their missions of providing general law enforcement and fighting the insurgency. These activities and missions are not mentioned anywhere in the ID/IQ contracts. The fact that there may be some small overlap in the services requested by the TORPs with those required under the ID/IQ contracts does not permit an agency to purchase other services under the ID/IQ contracts that were not reasonably contemplated when the ID/IQ contracts were issued. *Anteon Corp., supra,* at 5.

In addition, we find the disconnect between the underlying ID/IQ contracts and TORP 166 particularly striking. Although, as mentioned above, the ID/IQ contracts contemplated certain training and logistics support for counter-narcoterrorism activities, the performance work statement for TORP 0166 essentially identifies a logistics contract unrelated to these activities for the operation of 15 specific camps located throughout Afghanistan. For example, to support the operation of these camps, the task order anticipates providing dining facilities; maintaining water systems; providing heating, ventilation, and air conditioning services; maintaining the electrical system, a fleet of vehicles, and communications systems; and providing medical services, a laundry, and morale, welfare and recreation activities. AR, Tab 5e, TORP 166 Performance Work Statement, at 3–11.

* * *

In sum, we find that the TORPs for training and associated facilities and logistics support for the Ministry of the Interior and Afghan National Police are outside the scope of the ID/IQ contracts to support worldwide counter-narcoterrorism operations. We sustain the protest on this basis.

RECOMMENDATION

We sustain the protest and recommend that the Army cancel the TORPs and either conduct a full and open competition for these services, or prepare the appropriate justification required by CICA to limit the competition. We also recommend that the agency reimburse the protester the reasonable costs of filing and pursuing its protest, including attorneys fees. 4 C.F.R. sect. 21.8(d)(1). The protester must submit its certified claim for costs, detailing the time expended and the costs incurred, directly to the agency within 60 days after receipt of this decision. 4 C.F.R. sect. 21.8(f)(1).

The protest is sustained.

2. MAS Contracting

The General Services Administration (GSA) has a Federal Supply Schedule (FSS) program of Multiple Award Schedules (MAS). This program aims to provide federal agencies with a simplified procedure for buying commercial goods and services at competitive prices. It sets up a government-wide shopping catalog known as a schedule. In recent years the FSS program has had 100 different schedules offering 11 million commercial supplies and services. Small businesses do very well under the FSS program.

This FSS program uses contracts with the vendors called schedule contracts. The schedule contract works like an IDIQ contract—there may be several vendors with contracts for each significant schedule, and when an agency comes along, it makes an order that is like a task or delivery order.

Specifically, GSA, or another agency to which it delegates a part of the program like the Veterans Administration, issues a solicitation for a schedule. The solicitation stays open, so other vendors who come along later, after the initial ones, may obtain a schedule contract and be eligible for orders.

GSA's contracting officer must determine whether the prices offered by the would-be schedule contractor are "fair and reasonable." To make this determination, the contracting officer compares what this would-be schedule contractor offers, as prices or discounts to the government, with what the vendor offers to commercial customers. The vendor must disclose its "commercial sales, discounts and marketing practices," commonly referred to as commercial sales practice data, on a CSP-1 form. A vendor must justify why it does not offer the government a set of terms as good as it offers its commercial customers. FSS contracts require the vendor to select a tracking (commercial) customer to identify lower pricing offered to that customer.

This process of exchanges with the vendor about discounts, and proposed terms and conditions, constitutes negotiation, akin to what follows a regular RFP and proposal. GSA's Policy Statement on Multiple Award Schedule procurement establishes a goal of obtaining "most favored customer" (MFC) pricing. At the close of negotiations, the government will give the vendor a request for a "best and final offer" (BAFO) or a "final optional proposal revision" (FOPR). When that is in, the contracting officer either awards, or denies, a schedule contract. Generally, the GSA will award a MAS to any vendor that offers price discounts comparable to those offered by other vendors.

At some point, a MAS vendor may face an audit by the GSA Inspector General's Office of Audits. A contractor best prepares for this by compliance controls and records retention. Hanging over this is the FSS "price reduction clause." This requires that price reductions be given to the government as to the commercial customers, typically using the tracking customer as a guide.

Once a schedule is awarded, agencies throughout the government can place orders against it, pursuant to ordering procedures set forth in FAR Subpart 8.4. Orders placed against the GSA Schedule contracts using the procedures of FAR Subpart 8.4 are considered to be issued using full and open competition. Accordingly, ordering activities are not permitted to seek competition outside the MAS program for such orders and shall not synopsize the requirement.

For further discussion of the issues in this section, see: Jason N. Workmaster, *The GSA Schedules Program: To Be Or Not To Be (Commercial)?*, 45 Procrmt. Law. 16 (Winter 2010); Robert J. Sherry, G. Matthew Koehl, Sheila A. Armstrong, *Competition Requirements In General Services Administration Schedule Contracts*, 37 Pub. Cont. L.J. 467 (Spring 2008); Roger D. Waldron, *Back To The Future: Interagency Contracting Centralized And Managed Through GSA*, 43 Procrmt. Law. 1 (Summer 2008); Carl L. Vacketta, *Comprehensive Portrait of Multiple Award Schedule Now Available*, 32 Pub. Cont. L.J. 607 (2003)(reviewing John W. Chierichella & Jonathan S. Aronie, et al., *Multiple Award Schedule Contracting* (2002)).

———

When an agency places an order against at GSA Schedule, it may find that several MAS contractors would fill it, meaning that they are, to some extent, competitors. Even then, FAR Subpart 8.4. seems not to require great formality or a high level of competition for the award of the order to one of these contractors. Typically, for an order that does not require a Statement of Work, a non-Department of Defense agency need only "survey" three schedule contractors' offerings. For an order for services that requires a Statement of Work, the regulation only requires that agency to issue a "request for quotations" (RFQ) to three schedule contractors. The following case, *Matter of; REEP, Inc.*, involves an RFQ.

Although an ordering agency, when placing their GSA Schedule contract orders, need not make much formal effort to get a high level of price competition, the ordering agency may choose to seek additional discounts anyway. As a practical matter, and particularly in the information technology arena, "spot" discounting to the approved GSA Schedule pricing may be the norm, even for orders below the maximum order threshold.

Matter of: REEP, Inc.

General Accounting Office, 2002
B-290,665

REEP, Inc. protests the Department of the Army's issuance of delivery order Nos. DAKF23-02-F-5215 and DAKF23-02-F-5315 to Worldwide Language Resources, Inc. under that firm's Federal Supply Schedule (FSS) contract in connection with its acquisition of language training services for the 5th Special Forces Group (SFG). The protester maintains that the agency improperly issued these delivery orders on a sole-source basis to Worldwide, even though REEP could have provided the same services under its FSS contract at a lower price.

We sustain the protest.

The 5th SFG has an ongoing requirement for language training services and has been meeting its need through the award of delivery orders under the FSS. Worldwide had been performing these services under a prior 1-year delivery order awarded in March 2001 and due to expire on March 15, 2002. On March 4, 2002, the agency issued request for quotations (RFQ) No. DAKF-23-02-Q-0040 (RFQ 0040) in an effort to meet its requirement for language training services. REEP filed a protest in our Office in which it asserted that the RFQ's terms were unduly restrictive and that Worldwide had a conflict of interest that should preclude the firm from competing to provide language training services. In response to that protest, the agency advised our Office that it intended to cancel the RFQ, redraft the solicitation and evaluate REEP's conflict of interest allegation with a view to avoiding, neutralizing or mitigating any possible conflict on the part of Worldwide. Based on this proposed corrective action, we dismissed REEP's protest (B-290155, April 29, 2002). On May 24, the agency issued a new solicitation (RFQ No. DAKF23-02-Q-0059) for its language training services requirement. REEP has filed a protest in our Office challenging the terms of that RFQ, which we intend to address in a separate decision.

In order to meet its ongoing requirement for language training services during this same period, the agency issued two FSS delivery orders to Worldwide, the first on March 15 and the second on June 3. These delivery orders were executed without issuance of solicitations or receipt of competitive quotations. The delivery orders were awarded against Worldwide's contract under FSS No. 69; Worldwide is the only vendor with a language training contract under that schedule. In contrast, REEP, Worldwide and numerous other vendors hold language training contracts under FSS No. 738-II.

REEP maintains that it was improper for the agency to award the delivery orders to Worldwide without also considering vendors' prices under FSS No. 738-II. REEP states, and the agency does not dispute, that its prices under its FSS contract are lower than Worldwide's.

We agree with REEP. Agencies are not required to conduct competitive acquisitions when making purchases under the FSS; by statutory definition, the award of a delivery order under the FSS satisfies the requirement for full and open competition—so long as award is made to the vendor providing the best value to the government at "the lowest overall cost." 10 U.S.C. § 2302(2)(c) (2000); Federal Acquisition Regulation (FAR) § 8.404(a). Provided that agencies satisfy this statutory condition, they are not required to seek further competition, synopsize the requirement or make a separate determination of fair and reasonable pricing before awarding an FSS delivery order. FAR § 8.404. To ensure that it is meeting the statutory obligation to obtain the best value at the lowest overall cost to the government when placing orders under the FSS, an agency is required to consider reasonably available information, typically by reviewing the prices of at least three schedule vendors. FAR § 8.404(b)(2); Commercial Drapery Contractors, Inc., B-271222, B-271222.2, June 27, 1996, 96-1 CPD ¶ 290 at 3.

Here, the agency's only explanation for its actions is that it placed the delivery orders with Worldwide because it was the only vendor with a contract under FSS No. 69. However, the record shows that the agency had actual knowledge of numerous other vendors that offered the same language training services under FSS No. 738-II. The agency has not asserted that there is anything unique about the training offered by Worldwide under its FSS contract—for example, that it includes features not available from other vendors—that would provide a basis for paying a price premium for the services. Accordingly, we find that the agency failed to meet its obligation to consider reasonably available information, namely, the prices offered by other vendors under FSS No. 738-II, before placing its delivery orders with Worldwide. Had it done so, it would apparently have discovered that the same requirement could be met at a lower overall cost to the government. Under these circumstances, we sustain REEP's protest.

Since the agency continued (and has completed) performance under the delivery orders awarded to Worldwide, corrective action is not practicable. Accordingly, we recommend that REEP be reimbursed the costs of filing and pursuing its protest, including reasonable attorneys' fees. 4 C.F.R. § 21.8(d)(1) (2002). REEP's certified claim, detailing the time spent and the costs incurred, should be submitted to the agency within 60 days of receiving this decision. 4 C.F.R. § 21.8(f)(1).

The protest is sustained.

Notes and Questions

1. This opinion suggests the situation that the Special Forces Group strongly desires to continue purchasing its language training from Worldwide; REEP doggedly insists on some kind of competition; the Special Forces Group is trying to use the tools of commercial contracting to buy from its preferred vendor; and the GAO does not think too highly of that use of those tools. Is purchasing from a preferred vendor an improper goal for such tools?

2. See Michael J. Benjamin, *Multiple Award Task and Delivery Order Contracts: Expanding Protest Grounds and Other Heresies*, 31 Pub. Cont. L.J. 429 (2002).

As the basis for a schedule, GSA issues a solicitation. That solicitation uses as broad an item description as practicable. The solicitation is not supposed to use the kind of detailed specifications set forth in non-commercial buys. By following commercial practices, GSA makes the solicitation like what commercial sellers are used to providing to commercial buyers in buying what is available in the commercial marketplace.

This seeks to let a number of contractors, including commercially oriented contractors, offer a wide range of comparable items. The expectation is that this will let agency-customers choose what meets their particular needs. In determining what is "commercial," GSA may look to FASA.

Quantico Arms & Tactical Supply, Inc.
B-400391, 2008 CPD P 173, 2008 WL 4394896 (Comp.Gen.)
September 19, 2008

DIGEST

Protest arguing that a request for quotations issued to Federal Supply Schedule contract holders for flame-resistant long-sleeved base garments improperly fails to include detailed size measurements is denied where the record shows that the lack of size specifications will not prevent vendors from preparing quotations and competing on a common basis.

DECISION

Supply, Inc., a small business, protests the terms of a solicitation for long-sleeved flame-resistant shirts by the United States Marine Corps under request for quotations (RFQ) No. M67854-08 Q-3039.

We deny the protest.

BACKGROUND

This procurement involves long-sleeved shirts that are part of the Marine Corps's flame-resistant organizational gear (FROG). The Marine Corps posted the RFQ electronically as a small business set-aside using the General Services Administration (GSA) e-Buy system on July 2, 2008. The RFQ sought quotations from Federal Supply Schedule (FSS) vendors to supply an initial quantity of 120,000 long-sleeved mock-neck shirts made of a flame-resistant modacrylic fiber blend. The RFQ specified that the shirt fabric was required to pass a vertical flame test in accordance with a commercial testing standard (ASTM 6413-99). RFQ at 3. The RFQ also divided the 120,000 shirts into specific quantities of sizes small, medium, large, extra large and "XX large," and included an option for an additional lot of 120,000 shirts. RFQ at 4.

Among other things, the RFQ required each vendor to submit laboratory testing information to show that the shirts would meet a flame-resistance test, and submit two samples of its FROG shirt (both in size large). RFQ at 14. The RFQ provided that "[a]ward will be made to the responsible quoter offering the lowest price technically acceptable proposal." RFQ at 15.

The Marine Corps answered several questions about the sizes of the shirts, including the following:

> Q5. Why are no standards provided for the dimension of the shirts, especially in light of the potential for abuse of these subjective descriptions?

> A5. The Government does not expect any quoters to abuse the dimensions of the shirts that are to be provided. Each quoter is required to quote only products that are currently available on each quoter's respective GSA Federal Supply Schedules. Each quoter is also required to provide a sample of two "large" shirts which would expect to provide a sense of the dimensions in connection with the quoter's other sizes to be submitted on contract relative to the "large" size. The Government also expects that standard commercial practices for shirt sizing will be utilized when each quoter prepares and submits their quote. The Government has not experienced problems in the past with respect to reliance on such commercial standards for shirt sizing on various procurements of like items and believes such commercial standards provide reasonable expectations between any prospective quoter and the Government.

RFQ amend. 2.

This protest was filed before the due date for receipt of quotations. Shortly thereafter, the Marine Corps received quotations from several vendors, including Quantico. To date, no award has been made.

DISCUSSION

The protest essentially raises one issue—that the RFQ improperly fails to specify with precision what is meant by the size designations of small, medium, large, extra large, and XX large. In this there is no single industry standard for shirt sizes, and that a sample of only two large-sized shirts will not allow the Marine Corps to determine whether vendors are offering comparably-sized products.

In response, the Marine Corps argues that it has adequately stated its needs in the context of a purchase of commercial items. While the agency acknowledges that it uses size specifications for short- and long-sleeved T-shirts, it contends it is not required to do so here. The Marine Corps explains that in the case of short- and long-sleeved T-shirts, those shirts are part of the visible uniform, making a high degree of consistency important. The agency explained that it decided not to specify sizes in this procurement because it places a higher priority on the flame-resistant function, than on uniformity of sizes.

The Marine Corps summarizes its judgment as follows:

> In order to receive the best product available [the Marine Corps] in its best technical judgment, determined that inserting numeric size dimensions ... would unnecessarily limit a prospective offeror's ability to offer the best product to meet the Marine Corps requirement.

Agency Report at 2–3.

Protester argues that the Marine Corps will not obtain sufficient information from vendors to allow the agency to compare quotations, and notes that even retail stores resort to setting size standards for their products. Protester's Comments at 6–8. Protester's Comments at 10. For the reasons set forth below, we conclude that the agency was not required to include detailed size specifications in this solicitation.

The FSS program, directed and managed by the General Services Administration, gives federal agencies a simplified process for obtaining commonly used commercial supplies and services. Federal Acquisition Regulation (FAR) sect. 8.402(a). In preparing specifications for commercial item procurements, contracting officers are encouraged to "describe the type of product … and explain how the agency intends to use the product … in terms of function to be performed, performance requirement or essential physical characteristics." FAR sect. 12.202(b). A key element of efforts to increase purchases of commercial products is stating requirements in broad functional or performance terms, rather than using detailed military specifications. *Wincor Mgmt. Group, Inc.,* B-278925, Apr. 10, 1998, 98-1 CPD para. 106 at 2–3. While we will consider a protest that a solicitation lacks sufficient detail for vendors to compete intelligently, and on a common basis, for an order, the level of detail needed in a commercial item specification is a matter left largely to the judgment of agency contracting officials. *Adventure Tech, Inc.,* B-253520, Sept. 29, 1993, 93-2 CPD para. 202 at 5 (denying protest that IFB for rain jackets in sizes "large, medium, and small" was defective because sizes were not defined); *see also Adventure Tech, Inc.-Recons. & Entitlement to Costs,* B-253520.2, B-253520.3, Feb. 9, 1994, 94-1 CPD para. 105 at 3.

We recognize that the approach taken by the Marine Corps here generates some risk. By not specifying what it means by each of the stated sizes in this solicitation, the agency risks that some vendors might attempt to cut corners on shirt sizes to save money on fabric costs, and thus undercut their competition. There is also some risk that the agency might receive shirt sizes that do not meet its (unstated) expectations. On the other hand, we also recognize that this procurement is limited to companies that already hold FSS contracts, so that the Marine Corps might reasonably expect that it will receive quotations for products that are acceptable in the commercial marketplace.

In our view, the risk here is consistent with—and appropriate in light of—longstanding Congressional direction that agencies should take advantage of the commercial marketplace, and avoid creating detailed specifications for commercial goods. 10 U.S.C. sect. 2377 (2000); *see also* S. Rep. No. 103-258, at 5 (1994), *as reprinted in* 1994 U.S.C.C.A.N. 2561, 2566 ("The purchase of proven products such as commercial … items can … reduce the need for detailed design specifications or expensive product testing"). Here, there is an existing commercial market for these shirts, and the Marine Corps has experience in purchasing (directly or indirectly) almost 250,000 such shirts in the recent past without incident.

In short, we cannot conclude that the agency was required to impose size specifications on the vendors of these flame resistant has not established that the lack of size specifications in the RFQ impairs vendors from competing intelligently, and on a common basis, for this Marine Corps requirement. *See Adventure Tech, Inc.-Recons. & Entitlement to Costs, supra.*

The protest is denied.

———————

The next case, *Idea International, Inc. v. United States and ICATT,* is a high cost, highly sophisticated procurement for a MAS contract. Among its features, the protest itself goes to Court of Federal Claims, not the GAO. Earlier in the chapter, protests of IDIQ orders were discussed. These protests may go to GAO, but not to the Court of Federal Claims. In terms of mechanics, there may be definite resemblances between IDIQ contracts and their orders, and some MAS contracts and their orders. *IDEA International* discusses as a jurisdictional holding why protests of MAS order awards may go to the Court of Federal Claims.

Also, for MAS awards, two or more companies may form a "team arrangement." One way is for two or more companies to form a limited partnership or joint venture to act as the contractor. Another way is for a contractor to agree to team with another contractor and have it act as a subcontractor to pursue a specific government project. Either way, the contractors complement each other's capabilities to make a better offer than they could offer separately.

Teaming may offer a way for contractors to receive orders for which they would not independently qualify. Conversely, the ordering office may find that awarding the order to the team provides a total solution or better technical or more cost-effective solution. *Idea International* discusses such teaming arrangements. Although the rule is that all team members must have schedule contracts, that was not true in *Idea International.*

Additionally, some agency buys resemble traditional competitive procurements involving complexities of choice. They include requirements for technical proposals, set out evaluation factors, and provide for best value awards. *Idea International* involves such a procurement.

IDEA International, Inc., Plaintiff, v. The United States, Defendant, and ICATT Consulting, Inc., Defendant-Intervenor

United States Court of Federal Claims
74 Fed.Cl. 129
Nos. 06-652C, 06-717C.
Filed Under Seal Nov. 21, 2006.
Reissued for Publication Dec. 1, 2006.

WHEELER, Judge.

In this bid protest, Plaintiff, IDEA International, Inc. ("IDEA"), is challenging an August 7, 2006 contract award by the Department of Defense Education Activity ("DoDEA") to Defendant-intervenor, ICATT Consulting, Inc. ("ICATT"). The contract is for a Remote Location Home School Program for the dependents of DoD military and civilian personnel located overseas. After contract award, IDEA filed a bid protest at the Government Accountability Office ("GAO") alleging irregularities in the agency's evaluation of proposals and selection of ICATT. DoDEA, believing that IDEA was eligible for an automatic stay of performance following a timely bid protest, issued a Determination and Finding overriding the stay so that ICATT could perform the contract and provide the needed home schooling services. IDEA commenced this judicial action on September 14, 2006 as a challenge to the agency's override of the automatic stay provided in 31 U.S.C. § 3553(d)(3). On October 17, 2006, before the Court had decided the stay override issue, IDEA filed a new action bringing the merits of its GAO protest to this Court. The two actions have been consolidated, although the stay override challenge has been rendered moot by IDEA's election to bring the merits of its protest to the Court.

* * *

For the reasons stated below, the Court concludes that it has subject matter jurisdiction to review this protest relating to a task order under a GSA Federal Supply Schedule ("FSS") contract. On the merits, the Court finds that DoDEA's acquisition of home schooling services was less than a model procurement. The selected awardee, ICATT, did not have the capability itself to meet the agency's requirements, so it teamed with a subcontractor, WWIDEA, that did not hold a GSA Schedule contract. A procuring agency may not limit a solicitation to holders of GSA Schedule contracts, and then procure non-Schedule services through the awarded contract. Where, as here, teaming arrangements are made to respond to such a solicitation, all team members must hold GSA Schedule contracts. While the agency should have followed this basic tenet of FSS task order contracting, DoDEA's solicitation did not explicitly inform offerors of the consequences of proposing non-Schedule subcontractors. In a dispute between small businesses, the Court is reluctant to disqualify ICATT where fault most squarely lies with the agency for failing to inform offerors of the applicable rules.

* * *

Factual Background

On May 18, 2006, DoDEA issued its Remote Location Home School Program Solicitation No. HE1254-06-Q-0024 ("the Solicitation") to provide a comprehensive, secular home school program for the dependents of active duty military and DoD civilians located overseas. Administrative Record ("AR") 15–33. The program is available to dependents in grades K–12 who are residing in areas not served by a DoD dependents school or for whom a DoDEA school is not nearby. AR 20. The program was to serve up to 700 eligible students residing in specified locations outside the United States. *Id.* The contract was to run for 12 months from the date of award. AR 19, 20.

DoDEA restricted the procurement to holders of GSA Federal Supply Schedule ("FSS") 69 contracts, covering IT professional services. AR 15, 29. The Solicitation indicated that DoDEA would award a firm-fixed price contract by delivery order against the selected offeror's Schedule 69 contract.[6] AR 29. DoDEA placed the Solicitation as a request for quotations through the GSA's E-Buy website, a service that facilitates FSS purchases. See Federal Acquisition Regulation ("FAR") § 8.402(d); AR 34. DoDEA established a June 16, 2006 due date for the submission of offers. AR 15.

The Solicitation stated that proposals would be evaluated and a contract awarded "under the Best Value Continuum approach, to the responsible Offeror(s) whose offer is considered most advantageous to the Government, price and other factors considered." AR 29. The significant evaluation categories were Technical, Past Performance, and Price. *Id.* The Solicitation stated that "no proposal will receive the award unless the Price of that proposal has been determined to be fair and reasonable." *Id.*

Under the "Technical" evaluation factor, the two subfactors were: Instructional Program and Technical Support. The Technical subfactors were to be rated Exceptional, Acceptable, or Unacceptable. AR 29–31. Under the "Past Performance" evaluation factor, the four subfactors were: Quality of Product or Service, Customer Service, Program Effectiveness, and Overall Satisfaction. AR 30. The Past Performance subfactors were to be rated Satisfactory, Neutral, or Not Acceptable. AR 32. The Price was to be offered on a per student cost basis on a single contract line item ("CLIN") for "On-line Home School Program Services." AR 16, 33. The Solicitation indicated that invoices were to be submitted and paid based upon the number of enrolled students. AR 18.

* * *

---

6. The term "task order" would have been a better description for a contract to provide services. The term "delivery order" generally applies to contracts for the delivery of products.

IDEA and ICATT submitted proposals to DoDEA on the June 16, 2006 due date. AR 68, 185. IDEA had been the incumbent contractor for six years providing home schooling services for students in the Pacific Rim. AR 69. ICATT did not have any prior home schooling experience, but it teamed with a subcontractor, World Wide IDEA ("WWIDEA"), started in 2002 by former employees of IDEA. AR 194–96. As of the proposal date, WWIDEA had one five-year educational consulting contract with the Idaho Whitepines School District. AR 205.

ICATT holds a GSA Schedule 69 contract, and it lists Special Item Number ("SIN") 27-500, "Course Development; Administration," among its awarded items. AR 600. ICATT's GSA Price List for Course Development and Administration identifies prices per hour ranging from $31.00 to $141.30 for various consultant services, none of which include certified teachers. AR 56–57.

* * *

IDEA's GSA Schedule 69 contract and its GSA Price List contain prices per student with categories dependent upon the number of students to be enrolled in the program. AR 37, 662. For its Geographic Coverage, IDEA identifies "the 48 contiguous states, Alaska and Hawaii, the District of Columbia, the Commonwealth of Puerto Rico and International areas." *Id.*

ICATT proposed a price of $4,800 per student, or a total of $3,360,000 based upon 700 students. AR 268. IDEA proposed a price of $4,900 per student, as set forth in its GSA Schedule 69 contract, or a total of $3,430,000 based upon 700 students. AR 184. IDEA's price was 2.08% higher than ICATT's price.

* * *

On August 7, 2006, the agency's SSA determined that the award should be made to ICATT based upon its slightly lower price. AR 378–80. The SSA did not address the TEB's recommendation that award be made to IDEA, and did not weigh the technical and past performance evaluations against ICATT's slight price advantage. *Id.* The SSA recited that both offerors had received "Acceptable" technical evaluations, and "Satisfactory" past performance ratings. *Id.* DoDEA awarded a contract to ICATT that same day. AR 385–97.

History of Proceedings

On August 10, 2006, IDEA (an Alaska-based firm) learned of the contract award through an inquiry to the office of Alaska's Senator Lisa Murkowski. AR 437–40. By letter dated August 8, 2006, received by IDEA on August 14, 2006, DoDEA provided a formal notice to IDEA of the award to ICATT. AR 384. IDEA received a debriefing from DoDEA on August 22, 2006, and on August 28, 2006, IDEA filed a bid protest with the GAO. AR 419–40.

On October 10, 2006, ICATT's counsel filed a motion to dismiss IDEA's GAO protest. ICATT asserted that this procurement was conducted under FAR Subpart 8.4, "Federal Supply Schedules," that a debriefing is not required in such acquisitions, and that IDEA's bid protest filed more than ten days after IDEA knew or should have known the basis of its protest therefore was untimely. AR 479–82. In similar fashion, Defendant filed a motion to dismiss IDEA's judicial action, arguing that, since there was no requirement for a debriefing in a FAR Subpart 8.4 acquisition, IDEA was not entitled to a statutory stay of performance, and therefore the agency did not need to issue a determination overriding the stay. At that point, IDEA moved the merits of its protest from GAO to this Court.

* * *

Discussion

Defendant and intervenor ICATT have moved to dismiss Counts II and III of IDEA's Complaint for lack of subject matter jurisdiction, based upon a prohibition in the Federal Acquisition Streamlining Act of 1994 ("FASA") which provides that "[a] protest is not authorized in connection with the issuance of a task order or delivery order except for a protest on the ground that the order increases the scope, period, or maximum value of the contract under which the order is issued." 10 U.S.C. § 2304c(d). However, this provision is not intended to apply to protests relating to the placement of orders under GSA Federal Supply Schedule contracts.

FASA makes clear that "[t]his section [including the prohibition on bid protests] applies to task and delivery order contracts *entered into under sections 2304a and 2304b of this title.*" 10 U.S.C. § 2304c(f) (emphasis added). The ICATT and IDEA GSA Schedule contracts at issue here were not entered into under 10 U.S.C. §§ 2304a or 2304b, but pursuant to the authority for GSA's Federal Supply Schedule program that preexisted the enactment of FASA. *See* 41 U.S.C. § 259(b)(3). FASA itself recognizes that GSA's Federal Supply Schedule program is not affected by FASA, providing that "[n]othing in this section may be construed to limit or expand any authority of the head of an agency or the Administrator of General Services to enter into schedule, multiple award, or task or delivery order contracts under any other provision of law." 10 U.S.C. § 2304a(g). The Federal Supply Schedule program existed long before the passage of FASA in 1994, and the language of section 2304a(g) confirms that Congress intended for the FSS program to remain separate and distinct from the new FASA authority. The provisions of 10 U.S.C. § 2304a(g) demonstrate that Congress understood the difference between GSA Schedule contracts and task or delivery order contracts, but the prohibition on bid protests in 10 U.S.C. § 2304c(d) makes no mention of orders under "schedule contracts."

* * *

IV. *ICATT's GSA Schedule 69 Contract*

As required by DoDEA's Solicitation, ICATT holds a GSA Schedule 69 contract, listing three Special Item Numbers ("SINs") including SIN 27-500, "Course Development; Test Administration." AR 600. On its GSA Schedule price list, ICATT identifies seven labor categories: Principal Consultant, Senior Consultant, Consultant, Trainer/Instructional Designer, Project Manager, Business Analyst, and Research Analyst. AR 56. The prices per hour for these seven categories range from $67.50 to $141.30. *Id.* For each labor category, ICATT has provided a description of the services included, none of which includes teaching or home schooling. AR 56–57. Thus, while ICATT lacks experience in the schooling requirements of DoDEA's Statement of Work, it seemingly possesses the project oversight and management skills called for in the Solicitation.

To enhance its proposal with the necessary home schooling component, ICATT teamed with WWIDEA. AR 185. Although the precise breakdown of the work between ICATT and WWIDEA is not evident in their proposal, WWIDEA is prominently described as a team member with ICATT, and the proposal contains approximately equal components describing the skills, personnel, and experience for ICATT and WWIDEA. *Id.* The problem, however, is that WWIDEA does not possess a GSA Schedule 69 contract.

Although our Court has not addressed the precise issue of whether subcontractors in a Federal Supply Schedule procurement must possess GSA Schedule contracts, the GAO consistently has held that they must. *See Altos Fed. Group, Inc.,* B-294120, 2004 CPD ¶ 172 at 2, 2004 WL 1791349 (July 28, 2004) (By announcing intention to award to an existing FSS contractor, vendors were on notice from agency that all items were required to be within the scope of the vendor's or its subcontractors' FSS contracts); *Information Ventures, Inc.*, B-293743, 2004 CPD ¶ 97 at 2, 2004 WL 1146255 (May 20, 2004) (Non-FSS products and services may not be purchased using FSS procedures); *OMNIPLEX World Servs. Corp.*, B-291105, 2002 CPD ¶ 199 at 4, 2002 WL 31538212 (Nov. 6, 2002) (While a schedule contractor may be permitted to use subcontractors to provide services in its FSS contract, "it may not properly use subcontractors to offer services not included in either its own or those companies' FSS contracts, since this would mean that it was improperly including non-FSS goods or services in an FSS sale."); *Pyxis Corp.*, B-282469 *et al*, 99-2 CPD ¶ 18 at 4, 1999 WL 510244 (July 15, 1999) (Agency improperly included non-FSS items on delivery orders placed from Schedule contract).

ICATT's price proposal contained an all-inclusive price per enrolled student of $4,800, or a total price of $3,360,000 based upon 700 students. AR 268, 270. However, it is not possible to link this price per student to the hourly labor rates contained in ICATT's GSA Schedule contract. The Court, and the procuring agency, cannot tell how much of the services or the price are attributable to WWIDEA, or which types of ICATT's consultants are included in the price. The only real pricing benchmarks are provided by IDEA's competing GSA Schedule price of $4,900 per student, and by certain historical pricing from other agency contracts. AR 377. There is no evidence that DoDEA ever considered whether WWIDEA held a Schedule contract, or whether the services offered by ICATT and WWIDEA were covered by ICATT's Schedule contract. As Defendant's counsel candidly agreed during the hearing on the merits, ICATT would not have received the contract award without the participation of its home schooling subcontractor, WWIDEA. (Hearing, Nov. 14, 2006, Tr. 59).

Where an agency announces an intention to order from an existing GSA Schedule contractor, it means that "the agency intends to order all items using GSA FSS procedures and that all items are required to be within the scope of the vendor's FSS contract." *Tarheel Specialties, Inc.*, B-298197 *et al*, 2006 WL 2820577 at *3 (July 17, 2006). Non-FSS products or services may not be purchased using FSS procedures. Instead, the purchase of non-FSS services "requires compliance with the applicable procurement laws and regulations, including those requiring the use of competitive procedures." *Id.* (citing *OMNIPLEX World Servs. Corp., supra.*).

While DoDEA should have followed the above rules in purchasing services under the FSS, the Solicitation did not inform prospective offerors that all services including those of subcontractors must be available from a current GSA Schedule contract.

* * *

Without any clear guidance in the Solicitation that an offeror should propose only subcontractors with a GSA Schedule contract, the Court is reluctant to disqualify a small business offeror such as ICATT for WWIDEA's failure to have a Schedule contract. The procuring agency should have been aware of this requirement, and it should have included instructions in the Solicitation.

V. *The Agency's Evaluation and Award Process*

The Court is concerned that the agency's SSA did not weigh the benefits of IDEA's slightly superior technical proposal against ICATT's slightly lower price. The Administrative Record shows that the TEB evaluated IDEA and ICATT equally with "Acceptable" ratings for Instructional Program and Technical Support, and with "Satisfactory" ratings for Past Performance. AR 374. Overall, the TEB gave each offeror an "Acceptable" rating. *Id.* However, the TEB also stated that IDEA "clearly provided the most thorough description of services and gave strong evidence of an established program model focusing on the relationship between content standards and home based instruction." AR 376. The TEB concluded that "[e]ither offeror could perform the requirements of the project," but that IDEA "is the recommended source for this solicitation because they have a slightly stronger proposal." *Id.* The individual evaluator ratings included in the record support this conclusion. They show higher ratings for IDEA than for ICATT. AR 275–373.

* * *

In light of the Court's ultimate ruling in this case, it is not necessary to decide whether the SSA's decision meets the applicable "arbitrary and capricious" standard. It is sufficient to say that the decision lacks the full analysis that the Court would expect in a "best value" determination. The Court acknowledges that this award decision presented two proposals that were quite close both in the technical evaluation and in price, and that reasonable minds may differ on the best choice to be made. Nevertheless, the Administrative Record ought to contain greater detail supporting the "best value" determination.

* * *

IT IS SO ORDERED.

Notes and Questions

1. Should the Court of Federal Claims also have jurisdiction over protests of IDIQ contracts?

2. Can you articulate why the Court reiterates the general rule that all team members must hold schedule contracts, but does not let that rule govern this case?

3. Should a procurement this sophisticated be made off of the FSS, as opposed to being done by a published synopsis and a solicitation which receives any and all offers, that is, a full and open competition rather than an FSS buy? An agency may say it benefits from following fewer and simpler procedures by an FSS buy, such as limiting the number of competing offers it must evaluate.

Chapter 4

Contract Types, Costs, and Budgets

The previous chapters regarding sealed bidding, negotiated procurement, and other buying methods, start from a process familiar in basic (private) contract law, namely, offer and acceptance. In contrast, this chapter addresses topics with few analogies in private contract law, having to do with a group of unique constraints in government contracting arising from how the government pays for what it buys. These topics range from how the government funds its contracts and the variety of types of contracts including their variety as to the methods of contractor charging of the government, to the various controls devised by the government to constrain special charging methods.

Starting with the government's elaborate funding system, briefly touched upon in the first chapter, the principal interest is the government's unique constraints. These flow from appropriations and, particularly, the doctrines that limit how appropriations can be spent, including time and object limitations.

Then, the following section addresses the different types of contracts. Of course, the government, like private commercial buyers, may pay a fixed price for a well-determined amount of goods or services. However, the government's special needs induce it to purchase in other ways far different than a fixed price for a fixed quantity. Of particular importance for the rest of the chapter, the government frequently purchases on a "cost" basis, as when it funds development of a new high-technology fighter plane not by paying a fixed price, but by reimbursing the contractor for all the costs of research and includes a profit. Cost-based purchasing is invaluable when the risks and uncertainties are too great to sensibly shift from the government to the contractor, but the open-ended nature of cost-based purchasing requires the government to constrain the contractor's charges.

Finally, cost-based contracting requires constraints on just what categories of expenses the government will reimburse in the way of costs, i.e., what costs are "allowable." The FAR establishes categories of allowable and unallowable costs. Additionally, broad principles apply, referred to as reasonableness and allocability. And, an entire set of accounting standards, the Cost Accounting Standards, lets the government pay the costs of different contractors without too-wide differences in their internal accounting systems leading either to chaos or to playing games with the Treasury.

For further discussion of the subjects in this chapter, see the cites in each particular subchapter, and see: Thomas A. Lemmer, Philip R. Seckman, Taylor M. Menlove, *Maximizing Contractor Recovery Or IR&D Costs: Federal Circuit Affirms STK Thiokol*, 45 Procrmt. Law. 2 (Summer 2010); Robert G. Hanseman, Catherine Kidd, *Enforceability Of Teaming Agreements*, 46 Procrmt. Law. 18 (Fall 2010); Thomas A. Lemmer, Taylor M. Menlove, Tyson J. Bareis, *The New Rules: What The Federal Circuit's Tecom II Decision Means For Contractor Litigation Strategy And Recovery Of Legal Costs*, 45 Procrmt. Law. 10 (Fall 2009); James E. Durkee, *The Proper Obligation And Use Of Appropriated Funds In Interagency*

Contracting Under Non-Economy Act Authorities: Have We Got It Right Yet?, 38 Pub. Cont. L.J. 318 (Winter 2009); Fernanda Kellner de Oliveira Palermo, *Are Share-In-Savings Contracting And Public-Private Partnerships Capable Of Challenging Traditional Public Procurement Processes?*, 38 Pub. Cont. L.J. 633 (Spring 2009); Michael E. Sainsbury, *Seeking One Rule To Bind Them: Unifying The Interpretation & Treatment Of The "Title Vesting" Language Of The Progress Payment Clause*, 32 Pub. Cont. L.J. 327 (Winter 2003).

A. Funding

Judge Advocate General's School, Funding and Funding Limitations
Contract Attorneys Course Deskbook (2006)

FUNDING AND FUND LIMITATIONS

I. INTRODUCTION.

A. The Appropriations Process.

1. U.S. Constitution, Art. I, § 8, grants to Congress the power to "… lay and collect Taxes, Duties, Imports, and Excises, to pay the Debts and provide for the common Defense and general Welfare of the United States.…"

2. U.S. Constitution, Art. I, § 9, provides that "[N]o Money shall be drawn from the Treasury but in Consequence of an Appropriation made by Law.…"

B. Historical Perspective.

1. For many years after the adoption of the Constitution, executive departments exerted little fiscal control over the monies appropriated to them. During these years, departments commonly:

a. Obligated funds in advance of appropriations.

b. Commingled funds and used funds for purposes other than those for which they were appropriated.

c. Obligated or expended funds early in the fiscal year and then sought deficiency appropriations to continue operations.

2. Congress passed the Antideficiency Act (ADA), 31 U.S.C. §§ 1301, 1341, 1342, 1350, 1351, and 1511–1519, to curb the fiscal abuses by the executive departments which frequently created "coercive deficiencies" that required supplemental appropriations. The Act consists of several statutes that authorize administrative and criminal sanctions for the unlawful obligation and expenditure of appropriated funds.

II. KEY TERMINOLOGY.

A. Fiscal Year (FY). The Federal Government's fiscal year begins on 1 October and ends on 30 September.

B. Period of Availability. Most appropriations are available for obligation for a limited period of time, *e.g.*, one fiscal year for operation and maintenance appropriations. If activities do not obligate the funds during the period of availability, the funds expire and are generally unavailable for obligation thereafter.

C. Obligation. An obligation is any act that legally binds the government to make payment. Obligations may include orders placed, contracts awarded, services received, and similar transactions during an accounting period that will require payment during the same or a future period. DOD Financial Management Regulation 7000.14, vol. 1, p. xxi.

D. Budget Authority.

1. Congress finances federal programs and activities by granting "budget authority." Budget authority is also called obligational authority.

2. Budget authority means "… authority provided by law to enter into obligations which will result in immediate or future outlay involving government funds…." 2 U.S.C. § 622(2).

   a. Examples of "budget authority" include appropriations, borrowing authority, contract authority, and spending authority from offsetting collections. OMB Cir. A-34, § 11.2.

   b. "Contract authority," as noted above, is a limited form of "budget authority." Contract authority permits agencies to obligate funds in advance of appropriations but not to disburse those funds absent appropriations authority. See, e.g., 41 U.S.C. § 11 (Feed and Forage Act).

3. Agencies do not receive cash from appropriated funds to pay for services or supplies. Instead they receive the authority to obligate a specified amount.

E. Authorization Act.

1. An authorization act is a statute, passed annually by Congress, that authorizes the appropriation of funds for programs and activities.

2. An authorization act does not provide budget authority. That authority stems from the appropriations act.

3. Authorization acts frequently contain restrictions or limitations on the obligation of appropriated funds.

F. Appropriations Act.

1. An appropriations act is the most common form of budget authority.

2. An appropriation is a statutory authorization to "incur obligations and make payments out of the U.S. Treasury for specified purposes." The Army receives the bulk of its funds from two annual Appropriations Acts: (1) the Department of Defense Appropriations Act; and (2) the Military Construction Appropriations Act.

3. The making of an appropriation must be stated expressly. An appropriation may not be inferred or made by implication. Principles of Fed. Appropriations Law, vol. I, p. 2–13, GAO/OGC 91-5 (1991).

G. Comptroller General and General Accounting Office (GAO).

1. Investigative arm of Congress charged with examining all matters relating to the receipt and disbursement of public funds.

2. Established by the Budget and Accounting Act of 1921 (31 U.S.C. § 702) to audit government agencies.

3. Issues opinions and reports to federal agencies concerning the obligation and expenditure of appropriated funds.

III. ADMINISTRATIVE CONTROL OF APPROPRIATIONS.

A. Methods of Subdividing Funds.

1. Formal subdivisions. Appropriations are subdivided by the executive branch departments and agencies.

   a. These formal limits are referred to as apportionments, allocations, and allotments.

   b. Exceeding a formal subdivision of funds violates the ADA. 31 U.S.C. § 1517(a)(2); DFAS-IN Reg. 37-1, para. 7-5b.

2. Informal subdivisions. Agencies may subdivide funds at lower levels, *e.g.*, within an installation, without creating an absolute limitation on obligational authority. These subdivisions are considered funding targets. These limits are not formal subdivisions of funds.

   a. These targets also may be referred to as allowances.

   b. Incurring obligations in excess of a target is not necessarily an ADA violation. If a formal subdivision is breached, however, an ADA violation may occur, and the person responsible for exceeding the target may be held liable for the violation.

   c. Army policy allows formal subdivisions of funds at the Major Command (MACOM) level and above.

* * *

IV. LIMITATIONS ON THE USE OF APPROPRIATED FUNDS.

A. General Limitations.

1. The authority of executive agencies to spend appropriated funds is limited.

2. An agency may obligate and expend appropriations only for a proper **purpose**.

3. An agency may obligate only within the **time** limits applicable to the appropriation (e.g., O&M funds are available for obligation for one fiscal year).

4. An agency must obligate within the **amounts** appropriated by Congress and formally distributed to or by the agency.

B. Limitations Based Upon Purpose.

1. The "Purpose Statute," (31 U.S.C. § 1301(a)) provides that agencies shall apply appropriations only to the objects for which the appropriations were made, except as otherwise provided by law.

2. Three-Part Test for a Proper Purpose. Secretary of Interior, B-120676, 34 Comp. Gen. 195 (1954).

   a. Expenditure of appropriations must be for a specified purpose, or **necessary and incident** to the proper execution of the general purpose of the appropriation.

   b. The expenditure must not be prohibited by law.

   c. The expenditure must not be otherwise provided for, i.e., it must not fall within the scope of some other appropriation.

3. Appropriations Acts. DOD has nearly one hundred separate appropriations available to it for different purposes.

   a. Appropriations are differentiated by service (Army, Navy, etc.), component (Active, Reserve, etc.), and purpose (Procurement, Research and Development, etc.). The major DOD appropriations provided in the annual Appropriations Act are:

      (1)   Operation and Maintenance—used for the day-to-day expenses of training exercises, deployments, operating and maintaining installations, etc.;

(2)   Personnel — used for military pay and allowances, permanent change of station travel, etc.;

(3)   Research, Development, Test and Evaluation (RDT&E) — used for expenses necessary for basic and applied scientific research, development, test, and evaluation, including maintenance and operation of facilities and equipment; and

(4)   Procurement — used for production and modification of aircraft, missiles, weapons, tracked vehicles, ammunition, shipbuilding and conversion, and "other procurement."

b. DOD also receives smaller appropriations for other specific purposes (e.g., Overseas Humanitarian, Disaster, and Civic Aid (OHDACA), Chemical Agents and Munitions Destruction, etc.).

c. Congress appropriates funds separately for military construction.

4. Authorization Acts.

a. Annual authorization acts generally precede DOD's appropriations acts.

b. The authorization act may clarify the intended purposes of a specific appropriation, or contain restrictions on the use of the appropriated funds.

5. Legislative History.

a. Legislative history is the record of congressional deliberations that precede the passage of a statute. It is not legislation. Tennessee Valley Authority v. Hill, 437 U.S. 153 (1978).

b. The legislative history is not necessarily binding upon the Executive Branch. If Congress provides a lump sum appropriation without restricting what may be done with the funds, a clear inference is that it did not intend to impose legally binding restrictions. SeaBeam Instruments, Inc., B-247853.2, July 20, 1992, 92-2 CPD ¶ 30; LTV Aerospace Corp., B-183851, Oct. 1, 1975, 75-2 CPD ¶ 203.

6. The Necessary Expense Rule.

a. The Purpose Statute does not require Congress to specify every item of expenditure in an appropriation act, although it does specify the purpose of many expenditures. DOD has reasonable discretion to determine how to accomplish the purpose of an appropriation. Internal Revenue Serv. Fed. Credit Union — Provision of Automatic Teller Mach., B-226065, 66 Comp. Gen. 356 (1987).

b. The standard for measuring the propriety of a particular expenditure, if not specified in the statute, is:

(1) Whether it is reasonably necessary to carry out an authorized function; or

(2) Whether it will contribute materially to the effective accomplishment of that function.

c. A necessary expense does not have to be the only way, or even the best way, to accomplish the object of an appropriation. Secretary of the Interior, B-123514, 34 Comp. Gen. 599 (1955). A necessary expense, however, must be more than merely desirable. Utility Costs under Work-at-Home Programs, B-225159, 68 Comp. Gen. 505 (1989).

C. Limitations Based upon Time. 31 U.S.C. § 1502(a).

1. Appropriations are available for limited periods. An agency must incur a legal obligation to pay money within the period of availability. If an agency fails to obligate funds before they expire, they are no longer available for new obligations.

a. Expired funds retain their "fiscal year identity" for five years after the end of the period of availability. During this time, the funds are available to adjust existing obligations, or to liquidate prior valid obligations, but not to incur new obligations.

* * *

2. Appropriations are available only for the bona fide need of an appropriation's period of availability. 31 U.S.C. § 1502(a). See Magnavox—Use of Contract Underrun Funds, B-207453, Sept. 16, 1983, 83-2 CPD ¶ 401; To the Secretary of the Army, B-115736, 33 Comp. Gen. 57 (1953).

3. In analyzing the bona fide need for a given item or service, the following factors are appropriate for consideration:

   a. The required delivery date in the contract.

   b. The normal rate of consumption.

   c. When the government will make facilities, sites, or tools available.

   d. Whether the government controls when the contractor may begin the work.

   e. Normal weather conditions when planning for outdoor construction or renovation projects.

* * *

D. Limitations Based upon Amount.

1. The Antideficiency Act, 31 U.S.C. §§ 1341–44, 1511–17, prohibits any government officer or employee from:

   a. Making or authorizing an expenditure or obligation in excess of the amount available in an appropriation. 31 U.S.C. § 1341(a)(1)(A).

   b. Making or authorizing expenditures or incurring obligations in excess of formal subdivisions of funds; or in excess of amounts permitted by regulations prescribed under 31 U.S.C. § 1514(a). See 31 U.S.C. § 1517(a)(2).

   c. Incurring an obligation in advance of an appropriation, unless authorized by law. 31 U.S.C. § 1341(a)(1)(B).

   d. Accepting voluntary services, unless otherwise authorized by law. 31 U.S.C. § 1342.

* * *

Notes and Questions

1. Alexander Hamilton set up the federal funding system as the masterful first Secretary of the Treasury in the 1790s. If he came back, he would compare this section to the system he developed when the only office copiers were clerks with quill pens, when the only office calculators were those same clerks' ten fingers, and when rapid communication consisted of horseback riders carrying letters back and forth on bad roads over quite great distances. Would the system described in this section that is in use two centuries later, implemented by computers and electronic communications, strike him as new? Or does that system follow in large measure from the Anglo-American concept of legislatively- and legally-directed spending shaped by the struggles of medieval Parliaments and colonial legislatures in the centuries before the 1790s with kings and governors? In short, is the federal funding system part of modern sophisticated accounting, or part of classic democratic governance?

2. Why is it that a government contracting practitioner can function quite adequately knowing only what this section describes (and perhaps less), while his opposite number, a government official with a major function in contracting, would probably want to know much more than this section, particularly as regards the funding of her particular sphere of contracting?

3. A large part of pertinent funding law can be found in the General Accounting Office's (GAO's) opinions and other pronouncements. Most notably, GAO has a multivolume reference work, *Principles of Federal Appropriation Law*, that is not considered light reading but can answer many questions in this subject.

4. For further discussion of the subjects of this section, see: Major Timothy D. Matheny, *Go On, Take the Money and Run: Understanding the Miscellaneous Receipts Statute and its Exception*, 1997-SEP. Army Law. 31 (1997); Steven N. Tomanelli, *Fiscal Implications of Contract Disputes*, 31 Procurement Law., Summer 1996, at 1; Karen L. Manos, *The Antideficiency Act: Constitutional Control Gone Astray*, 11 Pub. Cont. L.J. 155 (1979).

Charles Tiefer, Controlling Federal Agencies by Claims on Their Appropriations? The Takings Bill and the Power of the Purse

13 Yale Journal on Regulation 501 (1995)

Principle of Lump-Sum Discretion: Executive Branch Authority Over Allotment of Lump-Sum Appropriations

When the Appropriations Clause declares that no money shall come from the Treasury except pursuant to "Appropriations made by Law," it leaves open the question of who will exercise, and how, the power to decide the specific objects of spending. As Professor Stith has observed, "[t]he Constitution does not require any particular degree of specificity in appropriations language." During the government's formative years, Jeffersonian philosophy, in contrast to Hamilton's views, limited the Executive role. Until well into the twentieth century, Congress followed the Jeffersonian lead in implementing the Appropriations Clause by drafting spending bills with numerous expressly detailed line items specifying the particular objects for which funds were available. In response, agencies would overspend their detailed line items, "coercing" Congress to appropriate more money to cover the "deficiency" in their funds, thereby engendering the passage of bills understandably known as "coercive deficiency appropriations."

Those maneuvers shaped today's system. With the expansion of the federal government in the early and mid-twentieth century, passage of a series of "framework" statutes for the fiscal constitution, notably, the Budget and Accounting Control Act of 1921 and the Anti-Deficiency Act, overhauled the old machinery and ended both detailed line itemization and coercive deficiency appropriations. These framework statutes created the Executive's "allotment" power for breaking the lump sum down into the specific objects for which funds are available. The principle of lump-sum discretion became the dominant organizing principle for Appropriations Clause implementation. Congress shifted to enacting far more general line items in the appropriation bills, each of which would "fund each broadly defined federal program or activity in one lump sum, termed a budget 'account.'" The President's annual proposed budget now includes a massive description of the various accounts, with Treasury identification numbers and object classifications. Once Congress enacts the lump-sum appropriation for an agency's operations, the agency head formally allots the lump sum. Each allotment is exclusively available for a particular object. As discussed below, during the fiscal year, an agency can change its allotments by another power known as "reprogramming."

It has become increasingly important that the Anti-Deficiency Act precludes not only obligations in excess of appropriations, but also obligations in excess of allotments. To avoid a situation in which an agency can either coerce a deficiency appropriation to cover the excess outflow or be required to curtail operations, agencies have the power and the duty to allot funds so as to limit how much of an appropriation can be drained for any object.

In 1993, the Supreme Court reinforced and elaborated the "lump-sum discretion" principle at the heart of this twentieth century system. In *Lincoln v. Vigil*, the Court rejected a suit challenging the Indian Health Service's decision to end the allotment from its lump-sum appropriation of funds for one particular object, a specific Indian health program. Despite numerous indications that Congress intended that the agency should continue to spend the appropriation on that program, the Court held that

> [t]he allocation of funds from a lump-sum appropriation is another administrative decision traditionally regarded as committed to agency discretion. After all, the very point of a lump-sum appropriation is to give an agency the capacity to adapt to changing circumstances and meet its statutory responsibilities in what it sees as the most effective or desirable way.

The Court quoted with approval the fuller discussion in a classic 1984 D.C. Circuit opinion by then-Judge Scalia, *UAW v. Donovan*, that "[a] lump-sum appropriation leaves it to the recipient agency (as a matter of law, at least) to distribute the funds among some or all of the permissible objects as it sees fit."

Limitation of Cost Clause

The government has a mechanism, even with cost-reimbursement contracts, of putting a limit on what it will pay. The Limitation of Cost Clause (LOCC) as provided in the FAR § 52.232-20, provides for contractors to notify the government as costs of contract performance exceed those estimated costs specified in the Schedule. The FAR sets forth the procedure by which contractors must notify the C.O. of any anticipated increase in costs for the performance of the contract. *See* John D. Schminky, *Proper Funding of Contract Modifications Under the Antecedent Liability Rule*, 26 Pub. Cont. L. J. 221 (1997). There will be no reimbursement for cost overruns in cost-reimbursement contracts where the contractor "knew or should have known" that costs would be excessive but did not notify the government. *Titan Corp. v. West*, 129 F.3d 1479 (Fed. Cir. 1997). It is a contractor's duty to monitor costs and to inform the government of probable overruns prior to their occurrence. *Advanced Materials, Inc. v. Perry*, 108 F.3d 307 (Fed. Cir. 1997).

Cherokee Nation of Oklahoma et al., Petitioners, v. Michael O. Leavitt, Respondent

Supreme Court of the United States
125 S.Ct. 1172
Argued Nov. 9, 2004
Decided March 1, 2005

* * *

Justice BREYER delivered the opinion of the Court.

The United States and two Indian Tribes have entered into agreements in which the Government promises to pay certain "contract support costs" that the Tribes incurred during fiscal years 1994 through 1997. The question before us is whether the Government's promises are legally binding. We conclude that they are.

I

The Indian Self-Determination and Education Assistance Act (Act), 88 Stat. 2203, as amended, 25 U.S.C. § 450 *et seq.*, authorizes the Government and Indian tribes to enter into contracts in which the tribes promise to supply federally funded services, for example tribal health services, that a Government agency would otherwise provide. See § 450f(a); see also § 450a(b). The Act specifies that the Government must pay a tribe's costs, including administrative expenses. See §§ 450j-1(a)(1) and (2). Administrative expenses include (1) the amount that the agency would have spent "for the operation of the progra[m]" had the agency itself managed the program, § 450j-1(a)(1), and (2) "contract support costs," the costs at issue here. § 450j-1(a)(2).

The Act defines "contract support costs" as other "reasonable costs" that a federal agency would not have incurred, but which nonetheless "a tribal organization" acting "as a contractor" would incur "to ensure compliance with the terms of the contract and prudent management." *Ibid.* "Contract support costs" can include indirect administrative costs, such as special auditing or other financial management costs, § 450j-1(a)(3)(A)(ii); they can include direct costs, such as workers' compensation insurance, § 450j-1(a)(3)(A)(i); and they can include certain startup costs, § 450j-1(a)(5). Most contract support costs are indirect costs "generally calculated by applying an 'indirect cost rate' to the amount of funds otherwise payable to the Tribe." Brief for Federal Parties 7; see 25 U.S.C. §§ 450b(f)-(g).

The first case before us concerns Shoshone-Pauite contracts for fiscal years 1996 and 1997 and a Cherokee Nation contract for 1997. The second case concerns Cherokee Nation contracts for fiscal years 1994, 1995, and 1996. In each contract, the Tribe agreed to supply health services that a Government agency, the Indian Health Service, would otherwise have provided. See, *e.g.,* App. 88–92 (Shoshone-Pauite Tribal Health Compact), 173–175 (Compact between the United States and the Cherokee Nation). Each contract included an "Annual Funding Agreement" with a Government promise to pay contract support costs. See, *e.g., id.,* at 104–128, 253–264. In each instance, the Government refused to pay the full amount promised because, the Government says, Congress did not appropriate sufficient funds.

Both cases began as administrative proceedings. In the first case, the Tribes submitted claims seeking payment under the Contract Disputes Act of 1978, 92 Stat. 2383, 41 U.S.C. § 601 *et seq.,* and the Act, 25 U.S.C. §§ 450m-1(a), (d), 458cc(h), from the Department of Interior (which manages the relevant appropriations). See, *e.g.,* App. 150–151, 201–203. The Department denied their claim; they then brought a breach-of-contract action in the Federal District Court for the Eastern District of Oklahoma seeking $3.5 million (Shoshone-Pauite) and $3.4 million (Cherokee Nation). See *Cherokee Nation of Okla. v. Thompson,* 311 F.3d 1054, 1059 (C.A.10 2002). The District Court found against the Tribes. *Cherokee Nation of Okla. v. United States,* 190 F.Supp.2d 1248 (E.D.Okla.2001). And the Court of Appeals for the Tenth Circuit affirmed. 311 F.3d 1054.

In the second case, the Cherokee Nation submitted claims to the Department of Interior. See App. 229–230. A contracting officer denied the claims; the Board of Contract Appeals reversed this ruling, ordering the Government to pay $8.5 million in damages. *Appeals of the Cherokee Nation of Okla.,* 99-2 B.C.A. ¶ 30,462, p. 150488, 1999 WL 440045 (1999); App. to Pet. for Cert. in No. 03-853, pp. 38a–40a. The Government sought judicial review in the Court of Appeals for the Federal Circuit. The Federal Circuit affirmed the Board's determination for the Tribe. *Thompson v. Cherokee Nation of Okla.,* 334 F.3d 1075 (C.A.Fed.2003).

In light of the identical nature of the claims in the two cases and the opposite results that the two Courts of Appeals have reached, we granted certiorari. We now affirm the Federal Circuit's judgment in favor of the Cherokee Nation, and we reverse the Tenth Circuit's judgment in favor of the Government.

II

The Government does not deny that it promised to pay the relevant contract support costs. Nor does it deny that it failed to pay. Its sole defense consists of the argument that it is legally bound by its promises if, and only if, Congress appropriated sufficient funds, and that, in this instance, Congress failed to do so.

The Government in effect concedes yet more. It does not deny that, *were these contracts ordinary procurement contracts,* its promises to pay would be legally binding. The Tribes point out that each year Congress appropriated far more than the amounts here at issue (between $1.277 billion and $1.419 billion) for the Indian Health Service "to carry out," *inter alia,* "the Indian Self-Determination Act." See 107 Stat. 1408 (1993); 108 Stat. 2527-2528 (1994); 110 Stat. 1321-189 (1996); *id.,* at 3009-212 to 3009-213 (1996). These appropriations Acts contained no relevant statutory restriction.

The Tribes (and their *amici*) add, first, that this Court has said that it is

> "a fundamental principle of appropriations law that where Congress merely appropriates lump-sum amounts without statutorily restricting what can be done with those funds, a clear inference arises that it does not intend to impose legally binding restrictions, and indicia in committee reports and other legislative history as to how the funds should or are expected to be spent do not establish any legal requirements on the agency." *Lincoln v. Vigil,* 508 U.S. 182, 192[, 113 S.Ct. 2024, 124 L.Ed.2d 101] (1993) (internal quotation marks omitted).

See also *International Union, United Auto., Aerospace & Agricultural Implement Workers of America v. Donovan,* 746 F.2d 855, 860–861 (C.A.D.C.1984) (Scalia, J.); *Blackhawk Heating & Plumbing Co. v. United States,* 224 Ct.Cl. 111, 135, and n. 9, 622 F.2d 539, 552, and n. 9 (1980).

The Tribes and their *amici* add, second, that as long as Congress has appropriated sufficient legally unrestricted funds to pay the contracts at issue, the Government normally cannot back out of a promise to pay on grounds of "insufficient appropriations," even if the contract uses language such as "subject to the availability of appropriations," and even if an agency's total lump-sum appropriation is insufficient to pay *all* the contracts the agency has made. See *Ferris v. United States,* 27 Ct.Cl. 542, 546 (1892) ("A contractor who is one of several persons to be paid out of an appropriation is not chargeable with knowledge of its administration, nor can his legal rights be affected or impaired by its maladministration or by its diversion, whether legal or illegal, to other objects"); see also *Blackhawk, supra,* at 135, and n. 9, 622 F.2d, at 552, and n. 9.

As we have said, the Government denies none of this. Thus, if it is nonetheless to demonstrate that its promises were not legally binding, it must show something special about the promises here at issue. That is precisely what the Government here tries, but fails, to do.

* * *

B

The Government next points to an Act proviso, which states:

> "Notwithstanding any other provision in this subchapter, the provision of funds under this subchapter is [1] *subject to the availability of appropriations* and the Secretary [2] is *not required to reduce funding for programs, projects, or activities serv-*

ing a tribe to make funds available to another tribe or tribal organization under the subchapter." 25 U.S.C. § 450j-1(b) (emphasis and bracketed numbers added).

The Government believes that the two italicized phrases, taken separately or together, render its promises nonbinding.

1

We begin with phrase (2). This phrase, says the Government, makes nonbinding a promise to pay one tribe's costs where doing so would require funds that the Government would otherwise devote to "programs, projects, or activities serving … another tribe," *ibid.* See Brief for Federal Parties 27–36. This argument is inadequate, however, for at the least it runs up against the fact—found by the Federal Circuit, see 334 F.3d, at 1093–1094, and nowhere here denied—that the relevant congressional appropriations contained *other* unrestricted funds, small in amount but sufficient to pay the claims at issue. And as we have said, *supra,* at 1177–1178, the Government itself tells us that, in the case of ordinary contracts, say, procurement contracts,

> "if the amount of an unrestricted appropriation is sufficient to fund the contract, the contractor is entitled to payment *even if the agency has allocated the funds to another purpose* or assumes other obligations that exhaust the funds." Brief for Federal Parties 23 (emphasis added).

See, *e.g., Lincoln,* 508 U.S., at 192, 113 S.Ct. 2024; *Blackhawk,* 224 Ct.Cl., at 135, and n. 9, 622 F.2d, at 552, and n. 9; *Ferris, supra,* at 546.

The Government argues that these other funds, though legally unrestricted (as far as the appropriations statutes' language is concerned) were nonetheless unavailable to pay "contract support costs" because the Government had to use those funds to satisfy a critically important need, namely, to pay the costs of "inherent federal functions," such as the cost of running the Indian Health Service's central Washington office. Brief for Federal Parties 9–10, 27–34. This argument cannot help the Government, however, for it amounts to no more than a claim that the agency has allocated the funds to another purpose, albeit potentially a very important purpose. If an important alternative need for funds cannot rescue the Government from the binding effect of its promises where ordinary procurement contracts are at issue, it cannot rescue the Government here, for we can find nothing special in the statute's language or in the contracts.

The Government's best effort to find something special in the statutory language is unpersuasive. The Government points to language that forbids the Government to enter into a contract with a tribe in which it promises to pay the tribe for performing federal functions. See 25 U.S.C. § 458aaa6-(c)(1)(A)(ii); see also §§ 450f(a)(2)(E), 450j-1(a)(1), 450l(c) (Model Agreement § 1(a)(2)). Language of this kind, however, which forbids the Government to contract for certain kinds of services, says nothing about the *source* of funds used to pay for the supply of contractually legitimate activities (and that is what is at issue here).

We recognize that agencies may sometimes find that they must spend unrestricted appropriated funds to satisfy needs they believe more important than fulfilling a contractual obligation. But the law normally expects the Government to avoid such situations, for example, by refraining from making less essential contractual commitments; or by asking Congress in advance to protect funds needed for more essential purposes with *statutory* earmarks; or by seeking added funding from Congress; or, if necessary, by using unrestricted funds for the more essential purpose while leaving the contractor free to pursue appropriate legal remedies arising because the Government broke its contractual promise. See *New York Airways, Inc. v. United States,* 177 Ct.Cl. 800, 808–811, 369 F.2d 743, 747–748 (1966); 31 U.S.C. §§ 1341(a)(1)(A) and (B) (Anti-Deficiency Act); 41 U.S.C. § 601 *et seq.* (Contract Disputes Act); 31 U.S.C. § 1304 (Judgment Fund); see generally 2 General Accounting Office, Principles of Federal Appropriations Law 6-17 to 6-19 (2d ed. 1992) (GAO Redbook). The Government, without denying that this is so as a general matter of procurement law, says nothing to convince us that a different legal rule should apply here.

2

Phrase (1) of the proviso says that the Government's provision of funds under the Act is "subject to the availability of appropriations." 25 U.S.C. § 450j-1(b). This language does not help the Government either. Language of this kind is often used with respect to Government contracts. See, *e.g.,* 22 U.S.C. § 2716(a)(1); 42 U.S.C. § 6249(b)(4); § 12206(d)(1). This kind of language normally makes clear that an agency and a contracting party can negotiate a contract prior to the beginning of a fiscal year but that the contract will not become binding unless and until Congress appropriates funds for that year. See, *e.g., Blackhawk, supra,* at 133–138, 622 F.2d, at 551–553; see generally 1 GAO Redbook 4-6 (3d ed.2004); 2 *id.,* at 6-6 to 6-8, 6-17 to 6-19 (2d ed.1992). It also makes clear that a Government contracting officer lacks any special statutory authority needed to bind the Government without regard to the availability of appropriations. See *Ferris,* 27 Ct.Cl., at 546; *New York Airways, supra,* at 808–811, 369 F.2d, at 748–749; *Dougherty v. United States,* 18 Ct.Cl. 496, 503 (1883); 31 U.S.C. §§ 1341(a)(1)(A) and (B) (providing that without some such special authority, a contracting officer cannot bind the Government in the absence of an appropriation). Since Congress appropriated adequate unrestricted funds here, phrase (1), if interpreted as ordinarily understood, would not help the Government.

The Government again argues for a special interpretation. It says the language amounts to "an affirmative *grant* of authority to the Secretary to adjust funding levels based on appropriations." Brief for Federal Parties 41 (emphasis in original). In so arguing, the Government in effect claims (on the basis of this language) to have the legal right to disregard its contractual promises if, for example, it reasonably finds other, more important uses for an otherwise adequate lump-sum appropriation.

In our view, however, the Government must again shoulder the burden of explaining why, in the context of Government contracts, we should not give this kind of statutory language its ordinary contract-related interpretation, at least in the absence of a showing that Congress meant the contrary. We believe it important to provide a uniform interpretation of similar language used in comparable statutes, lest legal uncertainty undermine contractors' confidence that they will be paid, and in turn increase the cost to the Government of purchasing goods and services. See, *e.g., Franconia Associates v. United States,* 536 U.S. 129, 142, 122 S.Ct. 1993, 153 L.Ed.2d 132 (2002); *United States v. Winstar Corp.,* 518 U.S. 839, 884–885, and n. 29, 116 S.Ct. 2432, 135 L.Ed.2d 964 (1996) (plurality opinion); *id.,* at 913, 116 S.Ct. 2432 (BREYER, J., concurring); *Lynch v. United States,* 292 U.S. 571, 580, 54 S.Ct. 840, 78 L.Ed. 1434 (1934). The Government, in our view, has provided no convincing argument for a special, rather than ordinary, interpretation here.

The Government refers to legislative history, see Brief for Federal Parties 41–42 (citing, *e.g.,* S.Rep. No. 100-274, at 48, 57), but that history shows only that Executive Branch officials would have liked to exercise discretionary authority to allocate a lump-sum appropriation too small to pay for all the contracts that the Government had entered into; the history does not show that Congress granted such authority. Nor can we find sufficient support in the other statutory provisions to which the Government points. See 25

U.S.C. §450j-1(c)(2) (requiring the Government to report underpayments of promised contract support costs); 107 Stat. 1408 (Appropriations Act for fiscal year (FY) 1994) (providing that $7.5 million for contract support costs in "initial and expanded" contracts "shall remain available" until expended); 108 Stat. 2528 (1994) (same for FY 1995); 110 Stat. 1321-189 (same for FY 1996); *id.,* at 3009-213 (same for FY 1997). We cannot adopt the Government's special interpretation of phrase (1) of the proviso.

* * *

For these reasons, we affirm the judgment of the Federal Circuit; we reverse the judgment of the Tenth Circuit; and we remand the cases for further proceedings consistent with this opinion.

It is so ordered.

* * *

Notes and Questions:

1. The opinion emphasizes the importance of appropriations law for government contracting. It is authored by Justice Breyer, who has emerged as the Court's leader on government contract law. Justice Breyer surveys familiarly a number of doctrines of appropriations law, taking several that had previously been articulated primarily at the level of the courts of appeals and elevating them to pronouncements of the High Court.

2. In the continuing legal struggle between contractors and the government, this case seems, at first glance, a big victory for the contractors. However, there is an unwritten rule that says, in cases involving Indians, the Court tries hard to rule for the Indians. Since in this case the Court notes that the Government "does not deny that, were these contracts ordinary procurement contracts its promises to pay would be legally binding," it is hard to see how this advances the contractors that far in ordinary procurement contracts situations where the government disputes that it has made legally binding promises to pay. Hence, contractors should not count their chickens about whether every close question will be decided in their favor. Rather, Justice Breyer's respectful tracing of the language about contracts "subject to the availability of appropriations" and his approving cite to *Lincoln v. Vigil* might just be used, in subsequent cases, to accept the government's use of its important power to divide appropriations into allotments, and insert clauses that subject contracts to the availability of appropriations — including to their allotment.

3. One important area for speculation is the tension between this case and the broad reach of the Anti-Deficiency Act. As the *Hercules, Inc. v. U.S.* case, in the casebook, reflects, the government can resist vague liabilities such as asserted indemnification of contractors by the combination of the absence of specific appropriations and the Anti-Deficiency Act. Suppose the Cherokee case involved ordinary procurement contractors (rather than Indian tribes) who ran into malpractice liability during contract performance, and came back the following year seeking indemnification. Would the Anti-Deficiency Act bar them or would the language in this case entitle them, assuming the next year's appropriation lacked relevant language either way?

2. Another important area for speculation is the tension between this case and the principles that have grown up regarding multi-year contracting. Contractors in multi-year programs, like stretched-out weapons procurement, typically have a strong clause about each year's orders being "subject to the availability of appropriations." This case belittles such language, in the particular context. Yet, for a multi-year program, it represents Congress's stern unwillingness to budget in early years for an excess amount in later

years—a budget prerogative deriving directly from the "No Appropriations" Clause and celebrated by other Court decisions. Suppose, in a multi-year contract for military services paid out of a large lump-sum appropriation, the Defense Department decided in the third year to cancel the program, and by not allotting it funds, declared it not only cancelled, but, specifically, cancelled for lack of appropriations. Could the contractor claim for amounts beyond its allotment, and answer the defense of lack of appropriations by saying, "there's always the Judgment Fund"?

B. Contract Types

Government contract types fall into two categories based on how the government pays: fixed price and cost-reimbursement. To illustrate, the government may want to buy ten more units of a type of computer it has bought before. It would likely issue an invitation for bids on a fixed-price contract, and award a contract to pay a fixed sum ($1,000, or $10,000, or $100,000) per computer. Fixed-price contracts shift the risks of production to the contractor. The contractor who must supply computers for $10,000, makes the most profit if the costs of production turn out the same or less than expected. However, if the costs of production go up, the contractor makes less profit or may even have to fulfill the contract at a loss.

In contrast, the government might want to hire a research and development firm to develop some new type of instrument specially adapted to its meteorological needs at unheated Arctic facilities. It would likely issue a request for proposals on a cost-reimbursement contract, and award a contract to pay the costs of a research and development firm to attempt to develop that instrument. The government would pay the firm's costs for the project—salaries and other personnel costs, materials, overhead—plus profit. In contrast, cost-reimbursement contracts shift the risks of production to the government. The research and development firm that takes on a cost-reimbursement contract to attempt to develop a new instrument will have its costs paid whether the project turns out doable in six months, nine months, or twelve months, or even if twelve months of effort turn out not enough to surmount the technical challenges involved.

For further discussion of the issues in this subchapter see: Lia A. Mandaglio, *Outcome-Based Award Fees: Incorporating Launch And Post-Launch Safety Mechanisms Into NASA's Contractual Incentive Structure*, 40 Pub. Cont. L.J. 187 (Fall 2010). Eric Aaserud, GSA Schedule Contracts: Opportunities & Obligations, 39 Procrmt. Law. 4 (Summer 2004); Stephen D. Knight, Federal Circuit Cost Decisions Bode Ill For Contractors, 39 Procrmt. Law. 1 (Winter 2004);Thomas F. Burke, C. Stanley Dees, The Impact Of Multiple Award Contracts On The Underlying Values Of The Federal Procurement System, 44 GC ¶ 431 (Nov. 6, 2002); Karen Daponte Thornton, Fine-Tuning Acquisition Reform's Favorite Procurement Vehicle, The Indefinite Delivery Contract, 31 Pub. Cont. L.J. 383 (Spring 2002).

Note on Contract Types

Federal procurement contracts fall into two main types—fixed-price and cost-reimbursement. These differ as to whether the government or the contractor bears the risk of rising production costs. They also differ as to whether the government simply pays the price without further ado, or, must scrutinize the details of the contractor's justifications of its costs. That means cost-reimbursement contracts have room for disputes over costs, and hence for lawyers to play a role, while fixed-price contracts do not fall prey to that kind of disputes

Contracting officers decide, in their discretion, whether to choose a fixed price or cost-reimbursement type. However, this general principle has caveats. Within the agency, for some important type of acquisition, the agency may develop an "acquisition strategy" as to which the choice of contract type might receive approval at a higher level. Conversely, when the agency does not cabin the contracting officer discretions, the contracting officer may negotiate with the potential awardees over the type of contract. Finally, a contracting officer who makes a poor choice of type of contract may get criticism from quarters such as the agency inspector general.

Fixed-price contracts

Looking specifically at fixed-price contracts, for these the government fixes the price at the time of contracting. This works best for acquiring either commercial items, for which the market sets the price, or for other goods and services with reasonably definite specifications and for which the government can set fair and reasonable prices. For example, bulk commodities or weapons of a long-established model warrant fixed-price contracts. Most construction projects, as to which the prices would resemble those for similar construction, warrant fixed price.

There are variations in which, among others, the contract has a fixed price but has an "economic price adjustment" (for inflation) or "prospective price redetermination" (for repricing in future periods). A fixed-price contract without such provisions is called "*firm fixed-price.*"

The fixed-price type has the advantage that the contractor, not the government, assumes the risk of increases in performance costs. Moreover, the contractor has a strong incentive to keep costs down and to perform economically, since cost savings add to the profit for the contractor. If some development causes production costs to rise, the contractor cannot just pass the new higher costs on to the government. Rather, the higher costs come out of the contractor's own profits, unless the contractor can meet the relatively high standard to obtain a change or equitable adjustment.

However, fixed price contracts do have their drawbacks for the government. The government may overpay. For a variety of reasons, the contractors seeking the contract may build a large premium into their proposals. The contractors do that to protect themselves against risks, or because lack of competition or their proposal's attractiveness allows them to build a high profit margin into their proposals. Eventually, the government may realize that the high price lets the contractors make very large profits, but the government cannot recover anything.

Cost-Reimbursement Contracts

Cost reimbursement contracts provide that the government reimburses the contractor for all incurred costs, so long as they are reasonable, allowable, and allocable to the contract. This type of contract works best when the government acquires something for which the government and the contractor cannot estimate the price in advance. Rather than make the contractor build a huge risk premium into their proposal, the government guarantees the contractor to reimburse its costs plus to pay a profit. The classic example consists of a research contract to create a new type of plane for the first time, say, a carrier-based stealth plane. Rather than make the firm performing the research build in a very high risk premium for its protection, the government uses a cost-reimbursement contract.

Conversely, the government, not the contractor, assumes the risk of increases in performance sots. The contractor has no strong incentive to keep costs down. Quite the opposite, the higher the (properly justified) costs, the higher the base to which the percentage profit figure gets applied to calculate the government's profit payment to the contractor.

Cost-type contracts impose extra administrative burdens. The government must ensure that the contractor's "business systems" are adequate. Business systems consist of accounting systems such as the estimating system (that estimates the costs in advance), the purchasing system (that insures the contractor completes its own acquisitions of goods and services), and the billing system (that bills the government for properly incurred costs). Government agencies conduct a kind of surveillance over the contractor to see that its systems function properly and that it does not overcharge the government.

Variations include the cost-plus-award fee contract. This provides for a base fee, which is a kind of definite profit, and an award amount judged by the government to represent an evaluation of contractor performance. For example, the contract for help with logistics in Iraq and Afghanistan, such as providing dining facilities, called "LOG-CAP," was of this type. It was a cost type to reflect that the contractor could not predict the changing expenses of the war zone, and had an award fee to reward good performance.

Other variations include fixed-price incentive contracts and cost-plus-incentive-fee contracts. The incentive fees derive from a formulaic adjustment of the base fee, such as the relationship between the price ceiling and a target cost.

Other contract types

In a time-and-materials contract, the government pays the contractor a fixed hourly rate for direct labor hours, at rates which include overhead, general and administrative expenses, and profit. The government pays for materials at cost plus materials-handling charges. A labor-hour contract is similar, except that the government supplies the materials. On the one hand, these seem similar to the way providers of services like legal transcription, or plumbing repairs, charge private customers. On the other hand, they may become a formula for contractors to bill more hours than a task really warrants. Accordingly, Subpart 12 of the FAR imposes requirements upon use of time-and-materials and labor-hours contracts to acquire commercial services.

Agencies use letter contracts when they have a need so pressing that the agency cannot wait for the execution of a formal (i.e., definitized) contract. They are written preliminary instruments that permit the contractor to commence performance immediately, pending definitization of the agreed-to contract. They should be as complete as possible, to include a price ceiling where appropriate. Typically the contractor submits a proposal which provides a basis for definitizing within 180 days or before completion of 40 percent of the work. In 2003–2004, the government used letter contracts for support for the war in Iraq, in order to obtain the support immediately without waiting to definitize. However, the delay in definitizing led to serious problems, such as whether the government should follow its regulations and withhold part of the payment for task orders still undefinitized after a period of time.

The basic ordering agreement is not a contract. Rather, it is a written instrument of understanding, negotiated between procuring activities and contractors, that contains terms applicable to future contracts or orders between the parties. It sets forth descriptions of the supplies and services, and the methods of pricing, issuing delivery orders, and making deliveries under the orders. They serve like accounts at department stores, making it simple to order substantial, but unknown at the start, quantities of goods or services.

Coyle's Pest Control, Inc., Appellant, v. Andrew Cuomo, Secretary of Housing and Urban Development, Appellee

United States Court of Appeals, Federal Circuit
154 F.3d 1302
Aug. 24, 1998

Before NEWMAN, PLAGER, and RADER, Circuit Judges.

RADER, Circuit Judge.

On summary judgment, the Department of Housing and Urban Development's Board of Contract Appeals (the Board) denied Coyle's Pest Control, Inc.'s (Coyle's) breach of contract claim for $1,525,170.74. See Coyle's Pest Control, Inc., HUD BCA No. 96-A-121-C10, 97-1 BCA ¶ 28,717 (Jan. 6, 1997). Because the Board correctly determined that the contract was invalid and unenforceable when interpreted as either a requirements or an indefinite quantity contract, this court affirms.

I

The Department of Housing and Urban Development (HUD), through the Small Business Administration, awarded Contract No. H06C94050400000 to Coyle for termite inspection and subterranean treatment of HUD-owned properties in thirty-four Texas counties. Section B.1 of the contract required Coyle "to furnish all labor, service, equipment, transportation, materials and supplies to provide subterranean termite control and related services on assigned properties owned by [HUD]." Clause C.2.D stated that properties would be "assigned on an as-needed basis." (emphasis added).

The contract, effective December 20, 1993, provided for a one-year term (the base year) as well as two one-year options. Section B.2 established a fixed price for inspection services and a two-tier, fixed price scheme for treatment services. This section set treatment prices at one of two levels depending on whether the range of properties assigned monthly was 0–170 or 171–240; the option years included modest increases for each of the two levels. The estimated value of the contract, including the base year and the two option years, was $1,930,000.

Section L.14 labeled the contract a "fixed unit rate-indefinite quantity contract." Nonetheless, the contract did not include two provisions typically present in indefinite quantity contracts: (1) a specified minimum number of properties to be assigned to Coyle; and (2) the indefinite quantity clause found in Federal Acquisition Regulation (FAR) 52.216-22 and then required by FAR 16.505(e). See 48 C.F.R §§ 52.216-22, 16.505(e) (1993). Also absent were two provisions generally associated with requirements contracts: (1) a clause requiring HUD to order all of its subterranean termite inspections and treatments from Coyle; and (2) the requirements clause found in FAR 52.216-21 (a mandatory feature of requirements contracts then under FAR 16.505(d)). See id §§ 52.216-21, 16.505(d).

In June 1995, during the first option year, HUD proposed Modification No. 4 to the contract. The proposed modification prevented Coyle from treating properties that HUD had already inspected and found free of termite infestation. Coyle rejected the modification. Thereafter, HUD informed Coyle that it would receive a "substantially lesser amount of properties" for termite services. At about the same time, in July 1995, HUD also altered its national policy for termite services and began to permit buyers of HUD properties to order their own termite inspections. Due to changes in the parties' relationship, ultimately, on September 25, 1995, they agreed to a revised version of Modification No. 4. As adopted, Modification No. 4 increased prices for both inspection and treatment services beyond that originally contemplated for the option years. More specifically, the parties changed the two-tiered pricing system for treatment services to a higher, single-rate system.

In sum, HUD assigned properties to Coyle from the beginning of the base year to slightly beyond the contract's first option year and paid to Coyle $694,228.04 for services during this period. On December 7, 1995, however, Coyle submitted a certified claim for $1,525,170.74—an amount equal to the difference between the estimated value of the contract ($1,930,000) and the amount HUD actually paid during the base year ($404,829.26). Coyle asserted that the contract was a firm fixed price agreement that entitled it to the estimated value of the contract. The contracting officer rejected Coyle's characterization of the contract and denied its claim. On appeal to the Board, Coyle asserted an alternative theory for recovery, that the contract was susceptible to interpretation as a valid and enforceable requirements contract. The Board rejected this characterization and denied Coyle's claim on January 6, 1997. Coyle appeals.

* * *

III

The Board, in a concise, well-reasoned opinion, held:

> The contract at issue in this appeal ... does not contain the necessary elements of an enforceable indefinite quantity contract, nor an enforceable requirements contract. The enforcement of such a contract would fail for lack of consideration in the absence of a clause stating a minimum quantity or a clause requiring [HUD] to purchase all of its requirements from [Coyle]. Because the contract is not enforceable for lack of consideration, [Coyle] is entitled to payment only for services ordered by [HUD] and performed by [Coyle]. It is undisputed that [Coyle] has been paid for all services performed. Consequently, we must conclude that [Coyle's] claim for an additional payment of $1,525,170.74 fails as a matter of law.

Coyle's Pest Control, 97-1 BCA ¶ 28,717 at 143,345. This court discerns no error in the Board's reasoning or conclusion.

In approving the Board's judgment, this court rejects the notion that Torncello v. United States, 231 Ct.Cl. 20, 681 F.2d 756 (1982) (en banc), requires it to save an otherwise unenforceable indefinite quantity contract by interpreting it as an "implied" requirements contract. See id. 681 F.2d at 761–62. Coyle extracts out of context from Torncello two inflexible rules for contract interpretation. First, "contract terms ... must fit into one of the three possible types of supply contracts: those for a definite quantity, those for an indefinite quantity and those for requirements." Id. at 761 (citing Mason v. United States, 222 Ct.Cl. 436, 615 F.2d 1343, 1347 (1980)). Second, a court must "assume that the parties intended that a binding contract be formed. Thus, any choice of alternative interpretations, with one interpretation saving the contract and the other voiding it, should be resolved in favor of the interpretation that saves the contract." Id. Applying its reading of Torncello to this case, Coyle argues that its contract with HUD qualifies as either an indefinite quantity contract or a requirements contract. Because it lacks a minimum quantity term, Coyle continues, the contract should be interpreted as a requirements contract.

* * *

This case, however, does not fit into any of the three neat categories Coyle extracts from Torncello. The record does not support the conclusion that the agreement was a requirements contract. Indeed the contract called itself an indefinite quantities contract (albeit without a minimum quantity clause) and lacked the terms of a requirement contract. Finally, Coyle does not maintain that the contract fits into the third category of definite quantities contracts.

IV

Setting aside Coyle's overreaching interpretation of Torncello renders analysis of this contract relatively straightforward. At the outset, neither party disputes the existence of a valid, binding agreement; the dispute here centers on the scope and nature of the agreement. Next, this court assesses the merits of interpreting this agreement as a requirements contract, as Coyle has asserted

> A requirements contract is formed when the seller has the exclusive right and legal obligation to fill all of the buyer's needs for the goods or services described in the contract.... [A]n essential element of a requirements contract is the promise by the buyer to purchase the subject matter of the contract exclusively from the seller.

Modern Sys. Tech. Corp. v. United States, 979 F.2d 200, 205 (Fed.Cir.1992) (citations omitted). As this passage suggests, a requirements contract necessarily obligates the Government to purchase exclusively from a single source. Because this agreement does not include the FAR requirements clause, it is more difficult to find the required exclusivity.

The contract does include terms that suggest exclusivity. For instance, the contract obligates Coyle "to furnish all labor, service, equipment, transportation, materials and supplies to provide subterranean termite control and related services on assigned properties by [HUD]." (emphasis added). While the contract states that Coyle will provide all labor and services for a given property, the clause does not require HUD to assign Coyle all properties in the region. Thus, this contract language falls short of the exclusivity language necessary for a requirements contract.

This court finds no reason to interpret this agreement as a requirements contract based on Coyle's affidavit evidence. Even assuming that these affidavits accurately reflect Coyle's beliefs, they cannot override or contradict the plain language of the contract, which does not require sufficient exclusivity for a requirements contract. See Gould, Inc. v. United States, 935 F.2d 1271, 1274 (Fed.Cir.1991). Moreover Coyle's affidavits do not reconcile Coyle's intent with the contrary intent of HUD. Cf. Crown Laundry & Dry Cleaners, Inc. v. United States, 29 Fed. Cl. 506, 518 (1993) (finding an implied requirements contract when testimony from both parties evinces a clear intent to form a requirements contract). This court therefore affirms the Board's determination that this agreement is not a requirements contract.

This court next analyzes the merits of interpreting this agreement as an indefinite quantity contract. While many factors are relevant, including the absence of the FAR-mandated "indefinite quantity" clause, this court cannot read this agreement as an indefinite quantity contract because it lacks a minimum quantity term. Regardless of whether the contract is susceptible to interpretation as an indefinite quantity contract, a contract lacking this term cannot be construed as a valid indefinite quantity contract. See Willard, Sutherland & Co. v. United States, 262 U.S. 489, 493, 43 S.Ct. 592, 67 L.Ed. 1086 (1923) ("[If t]here is nothing in the writing which required the Government to take ... any ascertainable quantity[, i]t must be held that, for lack of consideration and mutuality, the contract was not enforceable [as an indefinite quantity contract]."). Thus, this court affirms the Board's determination that the contract cannot be an enforceable indefinite quantity contract.

This contract neither required HUD to order from Coyle termite services for all its properties nor contained a minimum quantity term. Thus, the contract is not enforceable as either a requirements contract or as an indefinite quantity contract. As such, Coyle is entitled to payment only for services actually ordered by HUD and provided by Coyle. See Willard, 262 U.S. at 494, 43 S.Ct. 592 ("By the conduct and performance of the parties, the contract was made definite and binding as to the [quantity] ordered and delivered according to its terms."). In other words, this court has reached the same conclusion as and affirms the Board's decision.

AFFIRMED.

Notes and Questions

1. Various trends in recent years have led to increased use of contracting flexibility in matters such as quantity. The government contracting lawyer should understand how a proposed, or awarded, contract works in these regards because it affects judgments about other legal actions and issues from protesting to termination. This court looks through the contract for use of FAR clauses for indefinite quantity and requirements contracts (particularly the minimum quantity term). What does the court find, in looking for those clauses, and how does it reason from this? The following notes delve into the significant content of those FAR clauses.

2. ID/IQ Contracts

Under FAR 16.504, Indefinite-Quantity/Indefinite-Delivery contracts are described as those in which the government contracts for a quantity within a limited range of a defined minimum up to a defined maximum quantity, over a fixed period. The contracting agency schedules deliveries or performance through the issuance of task orders based on needs. Binding contracts require more than a nominal quantity be contracted for, and maximum quantity estimates should be based on records of prior requirements and consumption or the most current information available. Additionally, the FAR sets forth solicitation and contract requirements for indefinite-quantity contracts, and describes a multiple award preference in § 16.504(c). Where government agencies fail to order the minimum quantity estimated, the courts nevertheless have favored the agencies, finding that the termination for convenience clause provides adequate consideration to the contractor. *Appeal of Montana Refining Co.*, ASBCA No. 50515 (1999) *(distinguishing Maxima Corp. v. United States*, 847 F.2d 1549 (Fed. Cir. 1988)), and *PHP Healthcare Corp.*, ASBCA No. 39207 (termination for convenience cannot occur after the end of the contract term).

FAR 52.211-(16–18) sets forth the Variation in Estimated Quantity clause, providing for estimated quantities of unit-priced items in fixed-price contracts. This clause provides for equitable adjustment of the contract when the actual quantity of the items varies more than 15 percent above or below the estimated quantity. Re-pricing requests by the contractors, of items outside the 15 percent variation range are at the discretion of the Contracting Officer, and are not required. *Foley Co. v. United States*, 11 F.3d 1032 (Fed. Cir. 1993). When adjustments are made, they must be based on cost variations created by quantity variations. *Clement-Mtarri Cos.*, 92-3 BCA ¶ 25,192 (1992).

3. Requirement Contracts

Requirement contracts, as stated in the FAR § 16.503, provide that all actual purchase requirements by the contracting agency for supplies or services over a specified period be filled by the contractor. The agency schedules deliveries or performance with the contractor. The estimation of requirements is performed by the contracting officer and is based on records of previous requirements and consumption, and is *not* a representation that the quantity will be actually required or ordered. Such contracts are useful where the agency anticipates recurring requirements but can not state precise quantity needs during the defined period of the contract.

Challenges of breach of contract are upheld where the government purchases the same goods or services elsewhere. *Cleek Aviation v. United States,* 19 Cl. Ct. (1990). Where there is an issue of quantity miscalculation attributable to negligent estimates or mathematical error, the courts have likewise favored the contractor in recouping costs. *See Celeron Gathering Corp. v. United States,* 34 Fed. Cl. 745 (1996), and *Chemical Technology, Inc. v. United States,* 645 F.2d 934 (Ct Cl. 1981).

Textron Defense Systems, Appellant, v.
Sheila E. Widnall, Secretary of the Air Force, Appellee
United States Court of Appeals
Federal Circuit
143 F.3d 1465
No. 96-1535.May 7, 1998
Rehearing Denied; Suggestion for Rehearing In Banc Declined Aug. 25, 1998

Before NEWMAN, PLAGER, and SCHALL, Circuit Judges.

Opinion

PLAGER, Circuit Judge.

This case involves a research and development contract funded by the Strategic Defense Initiative Office ("SDIO") as part of the so-called 'Star Wars' anti-ballistic missile defense system. In a decision by the Armed Services Board of Contract Appeals ("the Board") dated May 2, 1996, ASBCA Nos. 47352 and 47950, the Board denied Textron's appeal for payment of additional costs and fees on a cost-plus-award-fee ("CPAF") contract. Because Textron received all that it was entitled to under the language of the contract, we affirm.

BACKGROUND

The United States Air Force (hereinafter "Government") awarded the CPAF contract to Textron's predecessor in interest, AVCO Everett Research Laboratory, Inc., on November 8, 1984, with an effective date of September 18, 1984. The subject of the contract was the research and development of an excimer laser device ("EMRLD") that could be used as part of the Star Wars program. The stated objective of the contract was "technology development and laser system design leading to the demonstration of a closed cycle repetitively pulsed electron beam pumped excimer laser."

The contract incorporated the DAR 7-402.2(c) Limitation of Funds ("LOF") (1966 OCT) clause, the DAR 7-203.10 Termination (1973 APR) clause, the DAR 7-105.3(c) Stop Work Order (1971 APR) clause, and a version of the AFSC DAR 7-150.3 Award Fee (1977 DEC) clause. The CPAF contract called for a zero base fee and an Award Fee not subject to the Termination or Disputes clauses as to the payment and amount of the award fee, respectively.

The original estimated cost of the contract, as awarded, was $53,144,000. This estimate was revised upwards as a result of a series of contract modifications to a final total of $132,618,264. The contract was incrementally funded. The contract schedule at award allotted only $3,457,992 to the contract. Subsequent adjustments brought the total allotted amount to $113,479,301. Each award fee allotment was made by a contract modification which stated that it was issued pursuant to the Award Fee clause of the contract. All other allotments were made pursuant either to the LOF clause or the Changes clause.

The contract created a series of award fees (i.e., profit) that Textron was eligible to receive at the end of each performance period based on its performance during that period. The decision as whether Textron would receive any such award, and if so, how much, was left to the discretion of a Fee Determining Official ("FDO") based on the FDO's assessment of Textron's performance in several specified areas. Initially, the contract specified four performance periods.

That award fee schedule was changed on August 3, 1988, pursuant to bilaterally executed Modification P00057. The Modification increased the number of performance periods from four to seven and 'back end-loaded' the award fees in order to create more incentives in the later stages of the program. The revised plan provided for the following:

Period	Maximum Award Fee
1	$1,000,000
2	$1,100,000
3	$1,200,000
4	$2,000,000
5	$4,000,000
6	$6,484,656
7	$1,000,000

Under the revised schedule, approximately $11.5 million of the possible $16.8 million was available in the last three periods (i.e., periods five through seven). Modification P00057 retained the discretionary award fee determination scheme of the original plan. Of the $5.3 million available for award fees in periods one through four, Textron was only awarded approximately $2.5 million, or less than 50% of the amount available.

Funding the program was a constant struggle. From the summer of 1985 through the end of 1987, Textron's expenditures under the contract exceeded the allocated funding. Textron did not stop work or request the contracting officer to terminate the contract when those overruns occurred, apparently under the assumption that further funding would be allocated. On several occasions those assumptions turned out correct. However, there were no assurances ever given by the contracting officer that future overruns would be covered.

Even before the contract was awarded, the contracting officer informed Textron that "SDI[O] might not continue funding" of EMRLD. In the same notice, the contracting officer urged Textron to "pay particularly close attention to the 'Limitation of Funding' clause." During the course of the contract, the contracting officer repeatedly reminded Textron that the LOF clause was in effect. On one occasion, after learning that Textron was operating in a cost-overrun situation, the contracting officer warned Textron that "*any work performed beyond the funding limit* is at *your* own *risk,* as there is a possibility that additional funds may not be made available."

The funding situation became even more tenuous in the fiscal years after 1987 because funding was no longer being provided by SDIO or the Air Force. Instead, the funds, if any, were to be congressionally directed. In an internal memorandum, Textron acknowledged the difficulty it faced obtaining future funding on "the Hill," unless it could "find a champion in the Air Force or SDIO."

Textron completed the fourth performance period on September 15, 1989 and began work on the fifth performance period. About that same time, Congress decided not to provide specific funding for EMRLD in fiscal year 1990. Accordingly, by letter dated September 29, 1989—a mere two weeks into the fifth performance period—the Government directed Textron to stop all work effective October 1, 1989. Textron was permitted to perform specific close-out work, which had been separately funded by a final allotment under the LOF clause by unilateral modification P00071. On December 28, 1990, the contracting officer terminated for the convenience of the Government all remaining work under the contract, with the exception of certain atmospheric tests that are not relevant here.

On December 19, 1990, Textron submitted a termination settlement proposal to the Government. That proposal requested $13,428,348 over and above the $113,479,301 paid to date under the contract. At that time, the total allowable costs incurred by Textron in performing the contract, including termination costs, were $112,190,867. When the parties were unable to agree on a settlement, Textron submitted a certified termination claim to the contracting officer in the amount of $10,225,925. That claim included $1,368,389 for unreimbursed costs and $8,857,536 in additional award fee. The award fee claim was arrived at by multiplying the percent of contract completion (77.4%) by the total award fee pool available for periods five through seven ($11.4 million). By final decision dated February 14, 1994, the contracting officer allowed Textron a total of $110,958,138 in costs and $2,251,163 in award fees, and denied its claim for any additional costs and fees.

Textron appealed the final decision to the Board. The Board affirmed the contracting officer's final decision with regard to both costs and award fees. *See Textron Defense Sys.*, ASBCA Nos. 47352 & 47950, 96-2 BCA ¶ 28,332. Textron now appeals that decision to this court.

DISCUSSION

Textron advances two principal arguments before this court, as it did before the Board. The first is that, under the contract's Termination clause, Textron is entitled to a pro-rata share of the award fee based on the percentage completion of the contract because the Government terminated the contract for convenience. The second is that it is entitled to recover additional costs under the LOF clause up to the total amount allotted to the contract including award fees. We have jurisdiction under 28 U.S.C. § 1295(a)(10) (1994). We consider each argument in turn.

I.

* * *

The Board concluded that Textron was not eligible for a further award fee as a matter of right upon termination for the convenience of the Government because the award fee clause of the contract was expressly made inapplicable to the termination clause. The relevant provision states:

> (j) *Payment of any Award Fee* to the contractor hereunder, as determined by the Fee Determining Official, *will not be subject to the clauses of this contract entitled* "Allowable Cost, Fixed Fee and Payment" and "*Termination.*"

(Emphasis added.) The plain language of the contract clearly exempts the Award Fee from the Termination clause of the contract. Textron would have us read this contract provision out of the contract. Such a reading is impermissible. *See Fortec Constructors v. United States*, 760 F.2d 1288, 1292 (Fed.Cir.1985).

Even if we were to assume that the Termination clause applied, Textron would not be entitled to a percentage of the total award fee because it had no reasonable expectation of ever receiving the total award fee. It is for this reason that Textron's reliance on authority involving cost-plus-fixed-fee ("CPFF") and cost-plus-incentive-fee ("CPIF") contracts is misplaced. In both CPFF and CPIF contracts, the contractor has a reasonable expectation of receiving at least a portion of the fee. For a CPFF contract the fixed-fee is determined at the beginning of the contract, and both parties know that if the contractor completes the contract then the contractor will receive the fixed fee. The same is true of the "target fee" in a CPIF contract. *See* 48 C.F.R. § 49.115(b)(2) (1996). Accordingly, upon termination for convenience the contractor has a reasonable expectation of receiving some portion of either the fixed fee or the target fee. The regulations and case law reflect this expectancy. *See id.; North Am. Rockwell Corp.,* ASBCA No. 14329, 72-1 BCA ¶ 9,207. A contractor has no such reasonable expectation in a CPAF contract.

Beyond that, the award fee in a CPAF contract is the functional equivalent of the "incentive fee" in a CPIF contract, rather than the "target fee," because both the award fee and the incentive fee are discretionary whereas the target fee is fixed. It is well established, both by regulation and by case law, that a contractor is not entitled to a portion of the incentive fee upon termination of a CPIF contract for convenience. *See* 48 C.F.R. § 49.115(b)(2) (1996); *Salsbury Indus. v. United States,* 905 F.2d 1518, 1522 (Fed.Cir.1990). Thus even under the Termination clause a contractor in a CPAF contract is not entitled to a specific share of an award fee.

* * *

II.

Textron also claims that it was deprived of $1,232,729 in additional costs. Both parties agree that as of December 28, 1989, the amount paid by the Government to Textron under the contract was a total of $113,479,301, of which $2,521,164 was paid to Textron as payment of award fees. Textron claims that the full $113,479,301 should be available to pay its costs under the LOF clause.

We again first consider the language of the contract. Because the language is sufficiently clear, our inquiry ends there as well. *See Craft Mach. Works, Inc. v. United States,* 926 F.2d 1110, 1113 (Fed.Cir.1991) ("In contract interpretation, the plain and unambiguous meaning of a written agreement controls."). The LOF clause puts a duty on the contractor to contain its costs below the amount allotted to the contract or risk bearing those costs itself:

> The Contractor agrees to perform or have performed work on this contract up to the point at which the total amount paid and payable by the Government pursuant to the terms of this contract approximates but does not exceed the total amount actually allotted to the contract.

The dispositive question then is what is the "total amount actually allotted to the contract." That answer is found within the four corners of the LOF clause: "It is contemplated that from time to time the additional funds will be allotted to this contract up to the *full estimated cost set forth in the schedule, exclusive of any fee.*" (Emphasis added.) We think it clear that the "total amount actually allotted to the contract" does not include "any fee," because the main purpose of the LOF clause is to prevent the contractors "costs" from exceeding the "amount allotted to the contract." In this case, the payment schedule specifically provided for an express allocation of fund allotment between costs and fees. Given this express allocation, Textron's argument that the money allocated for payment of fees should be available to pay costs is simply wrong.

* * *

CONCLUSION

Textron has not met its burden of proving that the Board's decision was fraudulent, arbitrary, capricious, grossly erroneous, unsupported by substantial evidence, or otherwise not in accordance with law. *See* 41 U.S.C. § 609(b) (1994). Accordingly, the decision of the Board is

AFFIRMED.

Notes and Questions

1. The case discusses three variants of cost-plus contracts, each with a different kind of fee: CPAF, CPIF, and CPFF. Can you tell the difference?

2. What is supposed to be the beneficial effect on the cost-plus contractor of an award fee clause?

3. Recall that the government cannot obligate itself to spend money that is not being appropriated. What does the Limitation of Costs clause accomplish that goes beyond what the appropriations limit does?

C. Cost Accounting and Auditing

When the government contracts to pay a contractor for its costs on some project like the research for a new aircraft, both sides then have recourse to a body of law regarding what counts as "costs." That body of law may sometimes apply even to fixed-price contracts, such as when the government changes the required work and must pay the contractor for this modification. FAR Subpart 31.2 summarizes that body of law.

In terms of practical interactions, the initial discussions about costs may occur between the contracting officer's representatives and the contractor. However, further stages may involve the government's audit personnel, who can review the costs submitted by the contractor to decide whether to accept them, to investigate further, or to reject them. In this section, the *Newport News* case involves a dispute between government auditors wanting broad access to contractor documents as part of an investigation of costs, and the contractor personnel. It provides a general review of costs and of disputes over costs, before moving into the particular subject of what auditors can subpoena.

As *Newport News* alludes to, and as the next subsection addresses, much of the body of law regarding "costs" concerns the criterion called "allowability." To take obvious extreme examples, contractors who speeded up their progress by assassinating anyone getting in their way would not recover from the government the costs of those assassinations. The government has taken a great distance the notion that it will define the kinds of costs it will reimburse. The other subsection of this section picks up several types of issues in the body of law about costs: allocability, reasonableness, and the Cost Accounting Standards. "Allocability" is the process of assigning costs to cost objectives. A contractor may build an electric generating plant to service some government contract and also some unrelated nongovernment contracts. That would make some of the plant's costs allocable to the government contract, and some not. The Cost Accounting Standards comprise a special area of law concerning costs, establishing some uniformity and consistency as the government resolves cost issues on different contracts. For example, a government contractor will have a pension plan for its employees. It takes an elaborate Cost Accounting Standard to decide what the government should pay into that pension plan as part of "costs," and all the related issues, such as what happens if the contractor tried to liquidate the pension plan.

That pension plan example shows that this subject can matter a great deal. Like issues of tax law bound up with tax accounting, lawyers take a larger interest in the disputed issues of government contract cost accounting when the sometimes-enormous scale of what is at stake gets noted. Defense contractor pension plans can contain $100 billion of assets, with the Cost Accounting Standards controlling what can be done with that money.

For further discussions of this section's subject, see Christopher C. Bouquet, *Defense Contract Audit Agency Shines Spotlight On Lobbying Costs*, 44 Procrmt. Law. 3 (Winter 2009); Richard B. O'Keefe (Jr.), *Compensation Is Not A Four-Letter Word: Coping With A DCAA Executive Compensation Review*, 45 Procrmt. Law. 1 (Fall 2009); Karen L. Manos, The Proposed Rule On Cost Accounting Standards Administration—"There You Go Again", 45 GC ¶ 302 (July 30, 2003); Karen L. Manos, *DDP's Guidance Paper On Changes In Cost Accounting Practice*, 44 GC ¶ 80 (Feb. 27, 2002); John D. Inazu, Boeing v. Roche & The Benefit Theory Of Allocability: Unlocking Lockheed Or Ignoring Northrop?, 32 Pub. Cont. L.J. 39 (Fall 2002); Rein Abel, Factors To Consider In Determining The Agency In Which The Cost Accounting Standards Board Should Reside, 35 Proc. Law. 7 (Winter 2000).

Note on the Defense Contract Audit Agency

The Defense Contract Audit Agency (DCAA) conducts most government contract audits. Although the Secretary of Defense appoints the DCAA Director, and the DCAA Director serves under the Under Secretary of Defense (Comptroller)/Chief Financial audit, DCAA also conducts audits for many civilian agencies as well.

DCAA does a variety of types of audits. Forward pricing audits are the largest category followed by incurred cost audits, CAS and defective pricing. Forward pricing audits means that, before negotiating contracts or contract modifications, contracting officers may request a field pricing report of cost or pricing data. Incurred cost audits mean that DCAA does postaward audits of reimbursement vouchers for incurred costs (money actually spent on subcontractors, materials, labor and so on). When the agency questions a voucher as unallowable, unallocable, or unreasonable, it may issue a DCAA Form 1, "Notice of Costs Suspended and/or Disapproved." A copy goes to the Contracting Officer, who usually, but not always, sustains the DCAA and disallows the cost. At that point, a contractor who wants payment must take a claim to the boards of contract appeals or the claims court.

DCAA also reviews the business systems of contractors, to see whether, for example, the contractor uses competitive-type methods when buying materials or hiring subcontractors. Almost all these audits concern cost-type contracts. There are limited types of audits for fixed-price contracts. For those contractors subject to TINA, DCAA defective pricing audits look at compliance with TINA and whether contracts are based on current, complete and accurate cost or pricing data.

DCAA's access rights, pursuant to contract clauses, to a contractor's books and records are fairly broad, although the *Newport News* case has set a kind of limit. Also, DCAA conducts "floor checks" and "detailed employee interviews" in which auditors interview individual employees.

The agency also puts out the DCAA Contract Audit Manual, the "DCAM," that prescribes policies and procedures for DCAA auditors. It lays down the government's position on many contract auditing issues. The DCAM has an online version, so practitioners can use it as a reference work. DCAA also publishes Memorandums for Regional Directors (MRDs) to change or supplement the DCAM, and these get incorporated into the semiannual updates of the DCAM.

DCAA hit a high point in value during the Afghanistan and Iraq wars of the 2000s. It opened field offices in both countries. The government paid most of the key contractors for services, from logistics to interpreters, on a cost-reimbursement basis, because the risks and uncertainties of the war zone made it difficult, especially at first, to obtain fixed-price contracting. So, DCAA's audits were the check on waste, fraud, and abuse in wartime. Its audits during the Iraq war, when Bill Reed and April Stephenson were directors, made headlines for exposing the abuses of the logistics contract with Halliburton/KBR.

United States of America, Plaintiff-Appellant, v. Newport News Shipbuilding and Dry Dock Company, Defendant-Appellee

No. 88-3520
United States Court of Appeals, Fourth Circuit
862 F.2d 464
Decided Dec. 5, 1988

Before MURNAGHAN, WILKINSON and WILKINS, Circuit Judges.

WILKINSON, Circuit Judge:

This case concerns the scope of the subpoena power of the Defense Contract Audit Agency. DCAA seeks to subpoena the federal income tax returns, financial statements, and supporting schedules of Newport News Shipbuilding and Dry Dock Company, a large defense contractor. Because the order of the district court denying enforcement of the subpoena unduly restricts DCAA's statutory subpoena power, we reverse the order and remand for further proceedings consistent with this opinion.

I.

Newport News Shipbuilding and Dry Dock Company (NNS) is a major defense contractor. A large percentage of NNS's work is performed for the United States government; its business includes the design, construction, repair, and overhaul of vessels for the United States Navy. Much of its work for the Navy is performed under "cost" or "cost-plus" contracts, in which the contract price is based on NNS's cost or its cost plus a fixed fee.

DCAA was established in 1965 as a separate agency in the Department of Defense. DCAA's function is to assist DOD with audits during the negotiation, administration, and settlement of defense contracts. DCAA also provides accounting and financial advisory services to DOD entities responsible for procurement and government contract administration.

DCAA audits defense contractors' books and records in order to establish what constitutes an allowable cost under a particular government contract and federal procurement regulations. See Federal Acquisition Regulation §§ 31.201-2, 31.201-3 & 31.201-4, 48 C.F.R. §§ 31.201-2, 31.201-3 & 31.201-4 (1987). A contractor's total reimbursable cost is the sum of its allowable "direct" and "indirect" costs. A direct cost is one that can be identified with a particular contract. Indirect costs, such as general and administrative overhead, are those that are identified with two or more contracts. The allocation of indirect costs to particular contracts is often a complex process involving sophisticated cost accounting techniques. DCAA performs detailed analyses of a contractor's claimed costs in order to verify their accuracy and to identify unallowable costs. To assist in its responsibilities, DCAA is authorized by statute to inspect the plant and subpoena the books and records of a defense contractor. It is the scope of DCAA's subpoena power that is at issue here.

On February 11, 1987, DCAA issued a subpoena duces tecum to NNS pursuant to 10 U.S.C. § 2313(d) demanding:

Trial balance, adjusting entries, segment financial workpapers, consolidating entries, formal consolidated balance sheet and income statement, Federal income tax return, Virginia income tax return and any other supporting schedules, documentation or correspondence related to preparation and issuance of financial statements or preparation or payments of any tax liabilities on a Federal, state or local level for the period 1 January 1983 to the present [.]

NNS furnished the requested state tax returns to DCAA but refused to provide the remainder of the subpoenaed materials. NNS instead filed a declaratory judgment action to have the subpoena declared unlawful and unenforceable. The government moved to dismiss NNS's suit and subsequently petitioned for summary enforcement of the DCAA subpoena. On December 23, 1987, the district court denied enforcement of the subpoena, holding that the subpoenaed materials were not related to cost or pricing data connected to a particular contract, and did not form the basis for costs claimed, or anticipated, in connection with particular contracts. According to the district court, DCAA did not need the subpoenaed materials in order to properly perform its auditing function. The government appeals from this ruling.

Subsequent to the district court's refusal to enforce DCAA's subpoena, this court announced its decision in United States v. Newport News Shipbuilding & Dry Dock Co., 837 F.2d 162 (4th Cir.1988) ("Newport News I "), another subpoena enforcement dispute involving these parties. In that case, DCAA subpoenaed audits conducted by NNS's internal audit department. We affirmed the district court's refusal to enforce the subpoena and held that DCAA's statutory subpoena power extends to objective cost information related to government contracts, but not to all corporate materials such as the internal, subjective evaluations at issue there.

II.

DCAA's statutory subpoena power is set forth in 10 U.S.C. § 2313(d)(1), which reads:

The Director of the Defense Contract Audit Agency (or any successor agency) may require by subpoena the production of books, documents, papers, or records of a contractor, access to which is provided to the Secretary of Defense by [§ 2313(a)] or by section 2306a of this title.

By its terms, § 2313(d)(1) authorizes DCAA to subpoena only materials to which it has access under 10 U.S.C. § 2313(a) or 10 U.S.C. § 2306a. Resolution of this case therefore depends on the construction of these two statutory provisions. See Newport News I, 837 F.2d at 166 n. 2.

Sections 2313(a) and 2306a provide in pertinent part:

§ 2313.

(a) An agency named in section 2303 of this title is entitled, through an authorized representative, to inspect the plant and audit the books and records of—

(1) a contractor performing a cost or cost-plus-a-fixed-fee contract made by that agency under this chapter; and

(2) a subcontractor performing any subcontract under a cost or cost-plus-a-fixed-fee contract made by that agency under this chapter.

§ 2306a(f).

(1) For the purpose of evaluating the accuracy, completeness, and currency of cost or pricing data required to be submitted by this section with respect to a contract

or subcontract, the head of the agency ... shall have the right to examine all records of the contractor or subcontractor related to —

(A) the proposal for the contract or subcontract;

(B) the discussions conducted on the proposal;

(C) pricing of the contract or subcontract; or

(D) performance of the contract or subcontract.

* * *

(3) In this subsection, the term "records" includes books, documents, and other data.

It is pursuant to these statutes that DCAA issued the subpoena giving rise to this dispute.[1]

III.

NNS asserts that DCAA may subpoena materials only if they are used as a basis for determining contract costs or are relied upon in the process of allocating costs to a specific contract. This argument suggests that only cost or pricing data used to calculate costs charged to the government are reviewable by DCAA. Based on our review of the relevant statutes, we reject such a narrow construction of DCAA's auditing function and subpoena authority. We hold that 10 U.S.C. § 2313(a) and 10 U.S.C. § 2306a(f) provide DCAA access to objective factual materials useful in verifying the actual costs, including general and administrative overhead costs, charged by companies performing cost-type contracts for the government.

The language of 10 U.S.C. § 2313(a) and 10 U.S.C. § 2306a(f) supports this construction of DCAA's statutory subpoena authority. Section 2313(a), for example, permits DCAA auditors to "inspect the plant and audit the books and records" of a company performing a cost-type contract for the government. A plain reading of the statute suggests that DCAA may review a contractor's financial and cost data. Similarly, § 2306a(f)(1) provides DCAA access to all "records" related to the negotiation, administration, or settlement of cost-type contracts where such records are necessary "[f]or the purpose of evaluating the accuracy, completeness, and currency of cost or pricing data" submitted to the government by a defense contractor. The term "records" is defined to include "books, documents, and other data," 10 U.S.C. § 2306a(f)(3), and it is plain from the face of the statute that DCAA enjoys access to objective factual information concerning contract costs. No language in the statute limits DCAA's subpoena authority to data actually submitted to the agency or actually relied upon by the contractor in determining contract costs. In fact, DCAA's statutory task of "evaluating the accuracy, completeness, and currency" of submitted data suggests that DCAA is not confined solely to that data in performing its auditing function.

The statutory language, however, is not so conclusive that we can forego an analysis of "the policies underlying the statutory provision to determine its proper scope." Bowsher v. Merck & Co., 460 U.S. 824, 831 n. 7, 103 S.Ct. 1587, 1592 n. 7, 75 L.Ed.2d 580 (1983). The legislative histories of §§ 2313(a) and 2306a(f) reveal Congress' intent to provide DCAA access to objective financial data to verify the actual costs incurred in the performance of cost-type contracts. Section 2313(a) was enacted as part of the Armed Services Procurement Act of 1947, which was a comprehensive revision and restatement of military procurement law....

---

1. 10 U.S.C. § 2306(f)(5) was the predecessor statute to 10 U.S.C. § 2306a(f). Congress recodified § 2306(f)(5) in 1986, but the statute's content remains unchanged.

The legislative history of § 2306a(f) reveals a similar congressional intent. What is now § 2306a(f) originally was enacted in 1968 as part of the Truth in Negotiations Act, Pub.L. No. 90-512, 82 Stat. 863 (September 25, 1968), reprinted in 1968 U.S. Code Cong. Serv. & Admin. News 1003. The Act gave the government the right to examine a defense contractor's records, documents, and other data in order to verify cost and pricing information submitted during the contracting process. See S.Rep. No. 1506, 90th Cong., 2d Sess. (1968), reprinted in 1968 U.S. Code Cong. & Admin. News 3589. Sponsors and supporters of the legislation believed that a "post-award" audit, based on actual contract performance, was the best means of verifying whether cost charges submitted by defense contractors were accurate, current, and complete. Senator Proxmire of Wisconsin, the Senate sponsor of the bill, stated that congressional action on this access-to-records provision made it "unmistakably clear that the Government has full authority to conduct postaudit investigations of a contractor's cost data" in order to verify costs charged to the government. 114 Cong.Rec. 26333 (1968)....

DOD regulations implementing §§ 2313(a) and 2306a(f) reinforce our construction of DCAA's statutory subpoena power. Federal Acquisition Regulation § 15.106-2, 48 C.F.R. § 15.106-2 (1987), which specifically implements 10 U.S.C. § 2313(a), requires that defense contracts contain a clause guaranteeing DCAA access to certain documents. This standard contract clause provides in relevant part that:

> representatives of the Contracting Officer shall have the right to examine and audit—books, records, documents, and other evidence and accounting procedures and practices, sufficient to reflect properly all costs claimed to have been incurred or anticipated to be incurred in performing this contract.

Federal Acquisition Regulation § 52.215-2(a), 48 C.F.R. § 52.215-2(a) (1987). Objective data "sufficient to reflect properly all costs claimed" are reviewable by the government, id., and are therefore within the scope of DCAA's statutory subpoena authority. In addition, if a defense contractor is required to submit cost or pricing data to the government, DCAA has the right:

> to examine and audit all books, records, documents, and other data of the Contractor (including computations and projections) related to negotiating, pricing, or performing the contract..., in order to evaluate the accuracy, completeness, and currency of the cost or pricing data.

Federal Acquisition Regulation § 52.215-2(b), 48 C.F.R. § 52.215-2(b) (1987). DCAA's right of examination is not limited to cost or pricing data alone; it extends "to all documents necessary to permit adequate evaluation" of cost or pricing data submitted to the government. Id. See also Federal Acquisition Regulation § 15.106-2, 48 C.F.R. § 15.106-2 (1987) (DOD regulation specifically implementing 10 U.S.C. § 2306a(f)).

In sum, the scope of DCAA's statutory subpoena authority is not limited in the manner NNS suggests. Nowhere in § 2313(a) or § 2306a is DCAA's access to corporate records and documents restricted to those materials actually submitted or relied upon by contractors in calculating their claimed costs. The singular purpose of both statutory grants of subpoena authority was to enable DCAA to evaluate and verify the costs claimed by defense contractors. That purpose is not served, in our judgment, by the most cramped and restrictive reading possible of the statutory text. DCAA may thus subpoena objective factual information for the purpose of verifying costs, including general and administrative overhead costs, associated with being audited by DCAA. The agency performs an important function in the defense procurement system: cost auditing for the purpose of assisting in the negotiation and administration of defense contracts. 32 C.F.R. § 357.2 (1987).

Cost verification data therefore is the proper subject of a DCAA subpoena. Sections 2313(a) and 2306a(f)(1) are intended to provide DCAA access to objective financial and cost information, contained in a defense contractor's books, records, and other documents, that reflects upon the accuracy of cost charges submitted to the government.

IV.

The scope of DCAA's statutory subpoena authority also must be read against a practical understanding of the defense procurement process and sound auditing practice. Reviewed in this light, we disagree with the district court's conclusion that NNS's federal income tax returns, financial statements, and supporting schedules must fall outside the scope of DCAA's subpoena power.

We have noted that DCAA enjoys access to materials needed for factual verification of general and administrative overhead costs. Newport News I, 837 F.2d at 166. These costs are "indirect" costs and, by definition, cannot be identified with a specific contract. Indirect costs are, however, an allowable component of a contractor's total cost, Federal Acquisition Regulation §§ 31.201-1 & 31.203, 48 C.F.R. §§ 31.201-1 & 31.203 (1987), and as such, a defense contractor may allocate them to particular contracts and claim reimbursement for them from the government. DCAA therefore may subpoena objective factual records that reflect upon the accuracy of overhead cost charges submitted to the government.

Federal procurement regulations, for example, allow reimbursement for the reasonable cost of renting or leasing real or personal property required for the performance of a government contract, such as a warehouse for storing contract materials. Federal Acquisition Regulation § 31.205-36, 48 C.F.R. § 31.205-36 (1987). A defense contractor, however, is entitled to reimbursement only for that part of the warehouse dedicated to the performance of that particular contract. If the defense contractor were to sublease a portion of its warehouse space to an entity unrelated to that particular contract, the overhead cost for the warehouse charged to the government must be offset by any rental income received by the contractor. By reviewing the contractor's financial statements, which should include entries for such rental income, DCAA is better able to verify whether the contractor has properly computed and allocated its overhead costs as required by the contract and federal procurement regulations. The contractor's financial statements afford DCAA a useful method of corroborating overhead cost information submitted to the government.

More generally, a defense contractor's federal tax returns, financial statements, and supporting schedules may be subpoenaed to the extent that they assist DCAA in verifying costs charged under cost-type contracts. It is an essential element of sound auditing practice to obtain sufficient corroborative information to satisfy the auditor that other information upon which he relies is accurate and complete. This principle is, as we have noted, recognized in 10 U.S.C. § 2306a(f)(1) which authorizes DCAA to subpoena books, documents, and other objective factual materials that can be used to evaluate the "accuracy, completeness, and currency of cost or pricing data" submitted by a defense contractor.

A defense contractor, for example, must identify and exclude from any claim for government reimbursement all unallowable costs, such as certain bad debt, interest, lobbying, entertainment, public relations, and advertising expenses. Federal Acquisition Regulation § 31.201-6, 48 C.F.R. § 31.201-6 (1987). See also Federal Acquisition Regulation § 31.205, 48 C.F.R. § 31.205 (1987) ("Selected Costs"). Federal procurement regulations provide DCAA access to corporate materials in order to verify whether defense contractors have complied with this obligation. Federal Acquisition Regulation § 52.230-3, 48 C.F.R. § 52.230-3 (1987). A contractor's corporate tax return, for example, would include an entry for advertising expenses because they may be deductible for federal tax purposes. The tax return therefore may be helpful in verifying whether the contractor has identified and excluded its unallowable advertising expenses.

Similarly, the profit realized from a contractor's purchase of materials from a division or subsidiary cannot ordinarily be included in the allowable costs charged the government. Federal Acquisition Regulation §31.205-26(e), 48 C.F.R. §31.205-26(e) (1987). The government contends that cost entries submitted to it may not reveal the amount of profit hidden in the purchase price or the relationship between the companies involved in the transaction. A contractor's tax return, on the other hand, may well disclose the relevant corporate affiliations.

In short, we disagree with the district court's conclusion that the subpoenaed materials are not necessary for DCAA to properly perform its statutory function. First, many of these financial statements are in a readily usable form. Second, some of these statements have a high degree of reliability because they are independently reviewed and the contractor is subject to serious sanctions for supplying incorrect information. See, e.g., 26 U.S.C. §§7201–07 (criminal and civil penalties for supplying incorrect or incomplete federal tax information). Third, a contractor's tax returns and financial statements bear upon the consistency of its costing methods and the reconcilability of costs claimed for tax purposes and costs claimed in contract billings to the government. Fourth, access to these materials may allow DCAA to verify the accuracy of cost information submitted by NNS; it may allow DCAA to corroborate NNS's computation and allocation of direct and indirect costs to particular government contracts. All of these factors are relevant to DCAA's auditing mission....

V.

NNS contends, finally, that the materials subpoenaed by DCAA contain proprietary and business-sensitive information which should remain confidential. To some extent, of course, every auditor seeks information which the subject of the audit regards as confidential, and the audits here are no exception. DCAA's statutory subpoena authority, however, does not confer a privilege of confidentiality with respect to objective financial and cost information. Like other private firms, defense contractors have an interest in maintaining the confidentiality of their corporate materials. Newport News I, 837 F.2d at 170. But a contractor's interest in maintaining the confidentiality of these materials cannot outweigh, in all instances, DCAA's interest in reviewing them. By claiming reimbursement for its contract costs, a defense contractor represents that the costs are reasonable and allocable to a particular contract. DCAA is granted access to defense contractors' books and records; it does not, however, disclose these materials publicly or to the defense contractors' competitors. See, e.g., 32 C.F.R. §§290.20–290.29 (1987) ("Availability of DCAA records"); 32 C.F.R. §286.13(a)(4) (1987) (DOD Freedom of Information Act exemptions).

NNS's claim of confidentiality was more persuasive on the facts of our earlier decision. There we held that the scope of DCAA's statutory subpoena authority did not extend to the subjective assessments of NNS's internal audit staff. Newport News I, 837 F.2d at 170. We recognized that internal audits may "rely for their effectiveness on the candor that confidentiality allows." Id. In contrast, the subpoena at issue here requests production of objective financial and cost data and summaries, not the subjective work product of NNS's internal auditors. To the extent that the materials subpoenaed here would assist DCAA in verifying and evaluating the cost claims of the contractor, they are within the contemplation of DCAA's statutory subpoena authority.

VI.

The district court took too restrictive a view of DCAA's access to defense contractor records. Its blanket refusal to enforce the subpoena impaired DCAA's statutory subpoena power. We are unable to examine each requested document in light of the relevant statutory purposes. We therefore reverse the judgment of the district court and remand for review of DCAA's individual requests in light of the general standards of agency subpoena power and the particular principles set forth herein.

The order of the district court denying enforcement of the subpoena is hereby

REVERSED AND REMANDED.

Notes and Questions

1. The court uses many potential cost accounting disputes to illustrate the need for broad subpoena power. How many disputes did you spot?

2. For a case that proceeds with a much different spirit, see *Bowsher v. Merck*, 460 U.S. 824 (1983). There, a subpoena for government contractor records was rejected. The contractor, a drug company, had a fixed-price negotiated contract with the government, and the auditing authority, the Comptroller General, had statutory authority to inspect records only "directly pertinent" to the contracts in question. How would you distinguish the two cases?

3. This case brings the DCAA into center focus. The DCAA has a large role in government contracting so little understood by outsiders that it has a full-length manual, the DCAA Manual (or "DCAM") which provides informal guidance in many areas of how government contract law operates in practice—much as an IRS audit manual would provide much informal guidance about tax law in practice. Can you explain the difference between "routine" auditing and investigation?

4. Is it hopelessly wasteful and needlessly adversarial to have government auditors and investigators tasked with thorough scrutiny of the details of cost reimbursement requests? On the other hand, is it an invitation to waste, fraud, and abuse not to give them that task?

5. Potential purveyors of commercial items continue to contend that the burdens associated with audit and investigative mechanisms deter them from selling to the government, while government auditors warn of the dangerous effects of depriving the government of its audit rights. Provisions of FASA merged and consolidated government audit powers, and FARA § 4201 abolished executive agency audit powers over contracts for commercial items. However, the General Services Administration Multiple Awards Schedule Program requires an audit clause in all its contracts. For a detailed discussion of the complex collision of commercial sales streamlining, and auditing, see Ron R. Hutchinson, *The Government's Audit and Investigative Powers Over Commercial Item Contracts and Subcontracts*, 27 Pub. Con. L.J. 263 (1998); Richard J. Wall & Christopher B. Pockney, *Revisiting Commercial Pricing Reform*, 27 Pub. Con L.J. 315 (1998).

1. Allowability

The FAR sets forth a number of detailed cost principles for specific contexts: the *Bill Strong Enterprises* case itself describes that there is a list in FAR Subpart 31.2 of 51 such cost principles. They deal with a number of particular issues, from alcoholic beverages (unallowable) to rental costs (allowable, except for sale-and-leaseback charges beyond the costs if the contractor retained title). These detailed cost principles generate a considerable need for legal advice, both for planning and in the event of investigation or disputes.

Bill Strong Enterprises illustrates the diverse historic sources of the cost principles. The opinion's discussion works its way from the regulations before World War II, through a number of successor regulations, to the FAR. Similarly, it works its way through case law and contract board decisions on these issues. Finally, it considers the statutory law, particularly in 1985. In other words, the FAR summarizes the law of allowability, but the law itself is far more complex than the few words in the FAR convey.

The particular cost principle at issue in the *Bill Strong Enterprises* case has its own intrinsic interest. This cost principle concerns disputes with the government, and which costs incurred in connection with them the government should pay. Since lawyers have large roles in the managing of disputes, they have reason to learn just what costs during disputes might ultimately be paid by the government to help them give sound advice about what to spend on a dispute.

Bill Strong Enterprises, Inc., Appellant, v. John Shannon, Acting Secretary of the Army, Appellee

No. 94-1013
United States Court of Appeals, Federal Circuit
49 F.3d 1541
March 2, 1995.

Before RICH, CLEVENGER, and SCHALL, Circuit Judges.

CLEVENGER, Circuit Judge.

Bill Strong Enterprises, Inc. (BSE) appeals from a decision of the Armed Services Board of Contract Appeals (ASBCA or Board) denying BSE's claim for recovery of consulting costs. Bill Strong Enters., Inc., ASBCA Nos. 42946, 43896, 93-3 BCA ¶ 25,961 (1993). Because the Board misconstrued the applicable regulation, we reverse and remand for further proceedings.

I

On June 18, 1987, the Department of the Army (Government) awarded BSE a fixed-price contract (Contract No. DACA27-87-C-0073) for the renovation of family housing units at Selfridge Air National Guard Base, Mt. Clemens, Michigan. By a letter dated May 26, 1988, BSE notified the Government that houses were being released to it out of sequence, resulting in increased costs of approximately "$300,000 to date" and an estimated $1,500,000 for the entire contract. In a letter to the contracting officer (CO), dated June 9, 1988, BSE requested a final decision regarding the out-of-sequence availability of houses, but the letter did not request monetary relief, nor was it certified. Subsequent letters from the CO to BSE requested itemization of BSE's increased costs and informed BSE that an audit would be necessary.

On May 24, 1989, BSE sent the Government a letter, entitled "Claim against Government." In this letter, BSE alleged that the Government's delay in making the housing units available to BSE increased BSE's cost of performance by $520,001. BSE also alleged that, by consistently releasing the housing units out of sequence, the Government increased BSE's cost of performing the contract by an additional $52,000. In a letter dated June 6, 1989, the Government requested BSE to submit cost and pricing data with a Standard Form 1141, in accordance with Clause 71 of the contract. On June 14, 1989, BSE supplied the Government with a completed Standard Form 1141. On June 16, 1989, the Government requested the Defense Contract Audit Agency (DCAA) to audit BSE's claims, specifically, the significant discrepancy between the Government's records of the number of houses made available to BSE and the number alleged by BSE. DCAA was also asked to examine BSE's basis for determining its costs due to the out-of-sequence availability of housing units.

Renovation of all housing was completed and accepted by the Government on July 31, 1989.

On September 14, 1989, in response to DCAA's requests for specific cost data and additional information, BSE hired Excell, Inc., a consulting firm, to revise its data for resubmission to the CO.

According to the contract between Excell and BSE, Excell's responsibilities were to review, analyze, and determine the technical and overall merit of issues, develop a specific proposal, and prepare a Request for an Equitable Adjustment (REA) for BSE. The contract further stated that the REA preparation effort was "undertaken with no view toward litigation.... [but was limited] to the pursuit of an administrative remedy." In a letter dated September 28, 1989, BSE notified the Government that BSE's claim needed modification and requested an "immediate abeyance" of its previously submitted May 24 claim, stating that BSE would revise its claim documents.

On November 30, 1989, BSE submitted a revised certified claim, entitled "Request for Equitable Adjustment," for a total amount of $995,568, which included the costs for delay, and included $122,336 (eventually amended to $190,248) in costs for Excell's work in preparing the submittal....

On December 14, 1989, the Government ordered DCAA to audit BSE's November 30, 1989 claim. The DCAA audit report noted that BSE had submitted the revised claim because of DCAA's questions in its preliminary review of the May 24, 1989 claim. DCAA found that, unlike BSE's initial calculation, the calculation by Excell was based upon actual costs and employee time card records. DCAA questioned $529,572 of BSE's alleged substantive cost increase, but did not question the claimed amount for Excell's costs.

On October 26, 1990, the parties reached a settlement in which the Government agreed to pay BSE $290,000 for the delay and out-of-sequence availability costs. The settlement agreement, memorialized in Modification P00019, explicitly excluded the preparation costs BSE paid to Excell. In a memorandum of understanding, the parties agreed that the CO would issue a final decision regarding the recoverability of Excell's fees. The administrative aspects of the contract thus concluded with Modification P00019, executed one year and a half after field work under the contract was completed.

In a March 1, 1991 decision, the CO denied the recovery of Excell's costs incurred in preparing the November 30, 1989 submission. The CO found that the Government had acknowledged the shortage of unit availability and had discussed with BSE "that it recognized partial merit for the issues of lack of available units and the issuance of houses out of the specified sequence." The CO emphasized, however, that the Excell claim preparation was performed after the completion of the contract work and was consequently "not incurred in connection with the actual performance of the work." BSE appealed this final decision to the Board.

II

* * *

In a 3–2 split decision, the Board affirmed the CO's decision. The majority of the Board found that, at the time of BSE's November 30, 1989 submission, the Government did dispute the amount claimed by BSE. The Board held that, under FAR 31.205-33(d), BSE's consultant costs were "unallowable" because they were "incurred in the 'prosecution of claims … against the Government.'"[1] …

… On October 10, 1993, BSE appealed the Board's decision to this court.

IV

* * *

A

The 1987 regulation at issue in this case resides in Part 31 of the FAR (48 C.F.R. §§ 31.000–.703 (1987)), which is entitled, "Contract Cost Principles and Procedures." FAR 31.204(a) states that "[c]osts shall be allowed to the extent they are reasonable, allocable, and determined to be allowable under 31.201, 31.202, 31.203, and 31.205." Section 31.205 is entitled "Selected costs" and contains fifty-one provisions governing the allowability of fifty-one different categories of costs. Section 31.205-33, entitled "Professional and consultant service costs," is the relevant regulation in this case. Section 31.205-33(a) states that costs of professional and consultant services are allowable, in general, subject to the exceptions in paragraphs (b), (c), (d), and (e). Section 31.205-33(d) provides that "[c]osts of legal, accounting, and consultant services … incurred in connection with … the prosecution of claims or appeals against the Government (see 33.201) are unallowable." The cross-referenced section 33.201 is in the "Disputes and Appeals" part of the FAR and defines a "claim" to mean

> [a] written demand or written assertion by one of the contracting parties seeking, as a matter of right, the payment of money in a sum certain, the adjustment or interpretation of contract terms, or other relief arising under or relating to the contract. A claim arising under a contract, unlike a claim relating to that contract, is a claim that can be resolved under a contract clause that provides for the relief sought by the claimant. However, a written demand or written assertion by the contractor seeking the payment of money exceeding $50,000 is not a claim under the Contract Disputes Act of 1978 until certified as required by the Act and 33.207. A voucher, invoice, or other routine request for payment that is not in dispute when submitted is not a claim. The submission may be converted to a claim, by written notice to the contracting officer … if it is disputed either as to liability or amount or is not acted upon in a reasonable time.

In order to advance the interpretation of these regulations, we pause to examine their historical roots. Prior to World War II, the Treasury, War, and Navy Departments promulgated regulations classifying expenses incident to and necessary for the performance of a government contract. One of those regulations stated:

> Among the items which shall not be included as a part of the cost of performing a contract or subcontract or considered in determining such cost, are the following: … legal and accounting fees in connection with … the prosecution of claims against the United States (including income tax matters);.…

T.D. 5000, 1940-2 C.B. 397, 407; see Robert Braucher & Covington Hardee, Cost-Reimbursement Contracts With the United States, 5 Stan.L.Rev. 4, 14–15 (1952). This regulation suggests an expansive scope of the phrase "claims against the United States." Then,

---

1. FAR 31.205-33(d) states in full: Costs of legal, accounting, and consultant services and directly associated costs incurred in connection with organization and reorganization (see also 31.205-27), defense of antitrust suits, defense against Government claims or appeals, or the prosecution of claims or appeals against the Government (see 33.201) are unallowable (but see 31.205-47).

in 1949, the Armed Services Procurement Regulations were promulgated and provided that legal, accounting, and consulting services were allowable costs except when "incurred in connection with … the prosecution of claims against the United States." See 14 Fed.Reg. 683, 684 (Feb. 16, 1949). From 1949 until 1983, the language of this regulation remained virtually unchanged. See 32 C.F.R. § 15.205-31 (1960); 32 C.F.R. § 15.205-31 (1983). In 1983, the Federal Acquisition Regulations were established, and these regulations adopted the same language concerning the allowability of costs of legal, accounting, and consulting services. See 48 Fed.Reg. 42,102, 42,322 (Sept. 19, 1983); 48 C.F.R. § 31.205-33 (1984). Also, the newly-established FAR defined, for the first time, the term "claim" as it is set out above. See 48 Fed.Reg. at 42,349; 48 C.F.R. § 33.001 (1984). The language in both of these regulations remained unchanged until new language was promulgated in 1986, and that language appeared in the 1987 version of the Code of Federal Regulations as FAR 31.205-33(d).

In applying the regulations of this period between 1949 and 1986, the ASBCA inconsistently interpreted the language concerning the allowability of legal, accounting, and consulting costs. On the one hand, several Board decisions denied recovery of such costs.… On the other hand, a number of Board decisions permitted recovery of legal or consulting costs.…

The Court of Claims also addressed the allowability of legal and consulting costs. In Singer Co. v. United States, 215 Ct.Cl. 281, 568 F.2d 695 (1977), the contractor sought recovery of attorney and technical consultant fees incurred in connection with the preparation and documentation of its claims for equitable adjustment that it presented to the CO. Id. 568 F.2d at 720. The court distinguished the Allied Materials decision by noting that, in Allied Materials, Government liability was not disputed and the REA occurred in the midstream of contract performance. Id. at 721. In denying recovery of the costs, the Singer court stated:

> [T]he claims for equitable adjustment were not presented to the contracting officer until all work had been completed, they addressed no situation in which Government liability was clear or apparent and, in content, they offered nothing that could reasonably be considered as benefiting the contract purpose. Judged both from the standpoint of the time of their submission and the purpose of their submission, [the contractor's] requests for equitable adjustment were not performance-related; they bore no beneficial nexus either to contract production or to contract administration.

Id.… [2]

It was within this context that Congress passed the Defense Procurement Improvement Act of 1985, Pub.L. No. 99-145, § 911, 99 Stat. 583, 682 (codified at 10 U.S.C. § 2324 (1988 & Supp. V 1993)). The Act specified that penalties would be assessed against a Government defense contractor that claimed an unallowable cost in a submitted proposal for settlement of indirect costs. 10 U.S.C. 2324(a)–(d). The Act also directed the Secretary of Defense to promulgate regulations prescribing specific categories of unallowable costs. Id. § 2324(e). Finally, the Act ordered the Secretary of Defense to clarify the FARs concerning the allowability and unallowability of a different set of categories of costs:

> The Secretary shall prescribe proposed regulations to amend those provisions of the Department of Defense Supplement to the Federal Acquisition Regulation

---

2. See Melvin Rishe, Government Contract Costs 20–16 (1st ed. 1983); 2 Nash & Cibinic Report ¶ 24, at 63 (Apr.1988); Richard J. Bednar, et al., Construction Contracting 781 (1991); John Cibinic, Jr. & Ralph C. Nash, Jr., Cost-Reimbursement Contracting 828 (2d ed. 1993).

dealing with the allowability of contractor costs. The amendments shall define in detail and in specific terms those costs which are unallowable, in whole or in part, under covered contracts. These regulations shall, at a minimum, clarify the costs principles applicable to contractor costs of the following:

* * *

(H) Professional and consulting services, including legal services.

Id. § 2324(f)(1) (emphasis added).

Although the Conference Report accompanying the Act does not elaborate on the requirement to clarify the cost principles of allowable and unallowable costs, see S.Rep. No. 118, 99th Cong., 1st Sess. 447–50 (1985), reprinted in 1985 U.S.C.C.A.N. 472, 601–04, a House Report accompanying an earlier version of the bill casts significant light on the subject. See H.R.Rep. No. 169, 99th Cong., 1st Sess. 11–13 (1985). That Report states:

Although the committee expects the department to review and revise all cost principles as appropriate, 14 specific cost principles which have been the subject of numerous disputes in the past must be clarified.

… In order to eliminate ambiguity and doubt, the revised regulations are to define unallowable costs in detail and in specific terms.

Id. at 11–12. Congress thus instructed the Department of Defense to clarify the unsettled and confused cost principles concerning the allowability of certain costs, including legal and consulting costs, and to define the specific categories of costs that are unallowable.

In response to this congressional mandate, the Department of Defense and the General Services Administration amended the FAR. See 50 Fed.Reg. 51,778, 51,778 (Dec. 19, 1985) (notice of proposed rule-making). The relevant portion of FAR 31.205-33 was changed to make unallowable the costs incurred in defense against Government claims or appeals and the costs incurred in the prosecution of appeals against the Government. See 51 Fed.Reg. 12,296, 12,298 (Apr. 9, 1986) (final rule). According to the agencies, this change would assure consistent treatment of the costs in FAR 31.205-33. 51 Fed.Reg. at 12,298. Also, the amendment to FAR 31.205-33 added, without comment, the cross-reference "(see 33.201)" after the phrase, "the prosecution of claims or appeals against the Government." See 51 Fed.Reg. at 12,301.

We hold that, by referring specifically to FAR 33.201, the amended cost principle of FAR 31.205-33 recognized the word "claim" as a term of art, the meaning of which is set forth in FAR 33.201. See, e.g., Bos'n Towing & Salvage Co., ASBCA No. 41357, 92-2 BCA ¶ 24,864, at 124,034 (1992). Thus, the revised regulation, in response to the congressional directive, provides for a specific, clear, bright-line test for unallowability: a legal, accounting, or consulting cost incurred in connection with the prosecution of a CDA claim or an appeal against the Government is per se unallowable.[3]

Our interpretation of the term "claim" in FAR 31.205-33 thus promotes uniformity and clarity in the FAR. Our conclusion is further supported by the fact that the revisions to FAR 31.205-33 included, for the first time, costs incurred in connection with appeals

---

3. We note that this holding does not pertain to consulting costs incurred in settlement of claims made when a contract is terminated for the convenience of the Government. Such situations are governed by a separate regulation and separate case law, under which such costs are generally allowable. See 48 C.F.R. § 31.205-42(g) (1987); Acme Process Equip. Co. v. United States, 171 Ct.Cl. 251, 347 F.2d 538, 544–45 (1965); Baifield Indus., ASBCA No. 20006, 76-2 BCA ¶ 12,096, at 58,102–04 (1976); see also Rishe, supra note 5, at 6-57, 20-10, 20-15.

against the Government, which can only be brought after a contractor has made a 33.201 "claim" against the Government. Accordingly, the alternative holding in the Board's majority decision, stating that the requirements for a "claim against the Government" under FAR 31.205-33 are different from the CDA requirements for a "claim" for jurisdictional purposes, is an incorrect interpretation of the regulations.

B

Our next step in analyzing FAR 31.201-33 is to interpret what is meant by "incurred in connection with the prosecution of a [CDA] claim against the Government." We note that there are at least three distinct categories of legal, accounting, and consultant costs in the contract cost principles: (1) costs incurred in connection with the work performance of a contract; (2) costs incurred in connection with the administration of a contract; and (3) costs incurred in connection with the prosecution of a CDA claim. Since Congress demanded that the regulations state specifically what costs are unallowable and since the regulations only make the third category of costs unallowable, costs that fall within the first and second categories are presumptively allowable if they are also reasonable and allocable. See 48 C.F.R. § 31.204(a) (1987). Moreover, costs incurred in connection with contract performance or contract administration should ordinarily be recoverable because they normally "benefit[ ] the contract purpose," see Singer, 568 F.2d at 721, and "reimbursement of [these costs is] in the best interest of the United States." See H.R.Rep. No. 169, supra, at 12. Benefit to the contract purpose, whether in its work performance or administration, is therefore a prerequisite for allowability.

To assess allowability of a cost, the particular cost must be classified into a particular category. Costs that are incidental to contract performance are easily discernable and usually pose no problem. However, the line between costs that are incidental to contract administration and costs that are incidental to prosecution of contract claims is rather indistinct, see 2 Nash & Cibinic Report, supra, ¶ 24, at 63, and in need of clarification.

In the practical environment of government contracts, the contractor and the CO usually enter a negotiation stage after the parties recognize a problem regarding the contract. The contractor and the CO labor to settle the problem and avoid litigation. Although there is sometimes an air of adversity in the relationship between the CO and the contractor, their efforts to resolve their differences amicably reflect a mutual desire to achieve a result acceptable to both. This negotiation process often involves requests for information by the CO or Government auditors or both, and, inevitably, this exchange of information involves costs for the contractor. These costs are contract administration costs, which should be allowable since this negotiation process benefits the Government, regardless of whether a settlement is finally reached or whether litigation eventually occurs because the availability of the process increases the likelihood of settlement without litigation. See 48 C.F.R. § 33.204 (1987) ("It is the Government's policy to try to resolve all contractual issues by mutual agreement at the contracting officer's level, without litigation.") Additionally, contractors would have a greater incentive to negotiate rather than litigate if these costs of contract administration were recoverable. See 7 Nash & Cibinic Report, supra, ¶ 48, at 134–35.

In classifying a particular cost as either a contract administration cost or a cost incidental to the prosecution of a claim, contracting officers, the Board, and courts should examine the objective reason why the contractor incurred the cost. See Singer, 568 F.2d at 721 (judging the "purpose" of the contractor's submission). If a contractor incurred the cost for the genuine purpose of materially furthering the negotiation process, such cost should normally be a contract administration cost allowable under FAR 31.205-33, even if negotiation eventually fails and a CDA claim is later submitted. See Armada, 84-3 BCA ¶ 17,694, at 88,242–43. On the other hand, if a contractor's underlying purpose for incurring a cost is to promote the prosecution of a CDA claim against the Government, then such cost is unallowable under FAR 31.205-33.

C

Applying the foregoing discussion to the issues in the present case, we find that the majority opinion of the Board is flawed. First, as discussed above, the Board erred by holding that the cost principle in FAR 31.205-33 does not involve the same requirements for a claim under the CDA as set forth in this court's decisions in Dawco and Transamerica. As we held above, the definition of a "claim" under FAR 31.205-33 is the same as the definition of a claim for purposes of establishing jurisdiction under the CDA.

Second, the Board majority also erred in concluding that BSE submitted a CDA claim. As the majority correctly states, the May 24, 1989 submission was not a formal CDA claim because the Government did not at that time dispute BSE's assertion of a right to increased compensation. Nor did the situation ever ripen into a dispute. The Government never challenged BSE's assertion of its right, and the Government had even recognized that there was "partial merit" to BSE's contention that the houses were being issued out of the specified sequence. In the time period between the May 24, 1989 submission and the November 30, 1989 submission, the parties were in a negotiation posture. The Government was conducting an audit and requested more information from BSE to help analyze BSE's request. This exchange of information is exactly what is encompassed in the concept of contract administration....

Third, the Board majority also erred by classifying BSE's consultant costs as costs incurred in connection with the prosecution of a CDA claim under FAR 31.205-33. Since a CDA claim did not arise before BSE incurred Excell's costs, there is a strong legal presumption that the costs incurred were not incurred in connection with the prosecution of such a claim against the Government. Since BSE and the Government were consistently in a negotiation posture and since the consultant costs were incurred as part of the exchange of information, the facts demonstrate that BSE hired Excell for the purpose of promoting contract administration and that BSE incurred Excell's costs in order to further a negotiation process that benefitted the Government. Thus, as discussed above, these costs are not unallowable under FAR 31.205-33.

Finally, under the factual circumstances of this case, the Board majority erred in holding that the consulting costs were unallowable because they were incurred after the contract work performance was completed. First, in delay cases such as this, the contractor cannot calculate the additional expenses caused by the Government's delay until completion of the contract work. Thus, BSE's calculations prepared with Excell's assistance understandably awaited completion of the contract work. In addition, contract administration may continue, as it did in this case, after completion of contract work.

We are not, however, able simply to reverse with instructions to award BSE the contested sum. Neither the CO nor the Board made a determination regarding the reasonableness and allocability of these costs. Consequently, we remand this case with instructions to find the consultant costs allowable to the extent those costs were reasonable and allocable.[4]

---

4. We note that at the time of the appeal to this court, BSE and Excell were engaged in litigation in state court concerning the reasonableness of Excell's fees.

V

For these reasons, the decision of the Board is reversed and the case is remanded with instructions.

REVERSED AND REMANDED.

Notes and Questions

1. If you were counsel to Bill Strong Enterprises all the way through this case, which of your legal bills would the government pay?

2. Note how the legal issue of the allowability of these costs took a turn when Congress passed the Defense Procurement Improvement Act of 1985 requiring clarification of the allowability of many categories of costs, including these. During the military buildup of the 1980s, massive spending was followed by charges of significant abuse. Audits provided such examples as charges to government contracts for babysitting, kennel fees, jewelry, country club fees, and even a case in which expenditures for bribery of procurement officials were submitted for reimbursement as part of the cost of securing the contract. Some criticized high costs assigned to particular contract items (e.g. a $44 light bulb; $7,622 for a coffee maker; and perhaps most memorably, $640 for a toilet seat cover). Among the legislative responses was the Defense Procurement Improvement Act of 1985, Title IX of the Defense Authorization Act for 1986, Pub. L. 99-145, 99 Stat 699 (1985). See generally *Sundstrand Corp. v. Commissioner*, 98 T.C. 518 (1992); *United States v. Sperry Corporation and UNISYS Corporation*, No. 91 Cr. 00355 (E.D. Va. 1991); Michael S. McGarry, *Winning the War on Procurement Fraud: Victory at What Price?*, 26 CLMJLSP 249 (1993); Richard R. Kaesar, *Major Defense Acquisition Programs: A Study of Congressional Control Over DoD Acquisitions*, 34 Fed. Bar. N.J. 430 (1987); Dennis L. Phillips and Raymond M. Saunders, *Multiyear Contracts for Major Systems*, 22 Pub. Con. L.J. 161 (1993); Remarks of Rep. Gonzalez, 133 Cong. Rec. H6152-04 (daily ed. July 9, 1987).

3. Note that costs incurred in resolving a termination for convenience are allowable, while costs incurred in resolving other types of claim are not. The opinion plays down the element that the government would not want to fund the costs of pumping up the expenditures on consultants and lawyers to fight it. Why would that be a significant interest?

4. The opinion says the line between costs for negotiation and costs for prosecuting a claim is "rather indistinct." Suppose a contractor uses alternative dispute resolution with his contracting officer: preparing for mediation, for example, to make the negotiation more effective, or hiring an independent-minded "special counsel" to sort out internally some of its own dubious contractor practices. Allowable?

5. For a discussion, see Stephanie M. Himel-Nelson, *Recovery of Legal Expenses as Costs of Government Contract Administration*, The Procurement Lawyer, Fall 2001, at 13.

2. Allocability and Reasonableness

Cost Principles: Reasonableness and Allocability
From: Steven W. Feldman, Government Contract Guidebook
(Thomson Reuters 4th ed. updated 10/2010)

Reasonableness

The criteria for determining whether a cost is "reasonable" are necessarily open-ended and subjective. The FAR provides that a "cost is reasonable if, in its nature and amount, it does not exceed that which would be incurred by a prudent person in the conduct of competitive business." In determining whether a cost is reasonable, a number of considerations will be reviewed, including the contractor's "responsibilities to the government, other customers, the owners of the business, employees, and the public at large." A contractor's incurred costs for FAR Part 31 covered contracts are not presumed to be reasonable; rather, "the burden of proof shall be upon the contractor to establish that such cost is reasonable." However, a contractor's decisions regarding its business affairs will be accorded some deference. As one board observed, "the government should not superimpose its determinations concerning business matters on those of a contractor."

Where it has been successful in challenging a cost's reasonableness, the government has usually been able to establish that a contractor abused its discretion, such as where a contractor retained a large, unproductive work force for longer than was prudent under the circumstances or where the contractor incurred excessive promotional costs in connection with preparing an unsolicited proposal.

A Contracting Officer may attempt to eliminate the need for reasonableness determinations by requiring advance approval before a contractor incurs a particular type of cost. Unless specifically called for by the contract, however, such prior approval is not required. Moreover, government attempts to control costs through this device generally have not been successful because the government must specify and justify the basis for refusing approval. By contrast, the regulations do recognize advance agreements on the allowability of costs. Thus, to avoid subsequent disallowances or disputes based on costs, the parties may agree on the treatment of special or unusual costs, although the absence of an advance agreement will not, by itself, affect the allowability of costs

Allocability

"Allocability" is the second of the five general factors listed in FAR Subpart 31.2 for determining allowability. Simply put, allocation of costs is the process of assigning costs to cost objectives. The FAR cost principles contain the following definition of allocability:

> A cost is allocable if it is assignable or chargeable to one or more cost objectives on the basis of relative benefits received or other equitable relationship. Subject to the foregoing, a cost is allocable to a government contract if it:
>
> (a) Is incurred specifically for the contract;
>
> (b) Benefits both the contract and other work, and can be distributed to them in reasonable proportion to the benefits received; or
>
> (c) Is necessary to the overall operation of the business, although a direct relationship to any particular cost objective cannot be shown.

In determining questions of allocability, it is necessary to assess whether a cost should be charged directly or indirectly. The FAR defines a direct cost as "any cost that can be identified specifically with a particular final cost objective." The provision goes on to say that costs "identified specifically with the contract are direct costs of the contract and are to be charged directly to the contract," and "[a]ll costs specifically identified with other final cost objectives of the contractor are direct costs of those cost objectives and are not to be charged to the contract directly or indirectly."

In accordance with this definition, costs incurred for materials, labor, or other purposes that are clearly necessary for performing a particular contract are direct costs of the contract. Even if an expenditure is eventually determined to have been unnecessary for contract performance, the cost will nonetheless be allocable as a direct charge if the contractor reasonably believed it was necessary when it decided to incur the cost. The legal test is sometimes referred to as the "but for" test (i.e., whether the cost would have been incurred but for the existence of the contract).

The FAR defines an indirect cost as one "not directly identified with a single, final cost objective, but identified with two or more final cost objectives or an intermediate cost objective." The provision requires that "[i]ndirect costs shall be accumulated by logical cost groupings with due consideration of the reasons for incurring such costs" Based on this definition, "[c]ommonly, manufacturing overhead, selling expenses, and general and administrative (G&A) expenses are separately grouped."

Apart from the basic distinctions between direct and indirect costs, cost allocation is largely, but not exclusively, a function of the contractor's own accounting system. In this regard, it is clear that selection of an accounting system is the prerogative of the contractor's management, as long as the system follows applicable laws, generally accepted accounting principles, and the CAS (if they apply). The government, accordingly, may not disturb a contractor's otherwise proper method of keeping its books solely to obtain a financial advantage. For the government to require a change in a contractor's accounting system, it must either direct the change prospectively, pursuant to a statute or regulation, or show that the contractor's system is clearly inequitable

* * *

3. Cost Accounting Standards

Cost Accounting Standards

From: Steven W. Feldman, Government Contract Guidebook
(Thomson Reuters 4th ed. updated 10/2010)

In 1970, Congress passed a statute directing the establishment of the Cost Accounting Standards Board (CAS Board). The statute directed the Board to promulgate cost accounting standards that would achieve uniformity and consistency in the cost accounting practices followed by prime contractors and subcontractors in estimating, accumulating, and reporting costs under negotiated defense prime contracts and subcontracts. In general, it was agreed that the Standards:

(a) Should not require the application of precisely prescribed methods of computing each different type of cost.

(b) Should not be limited to cost-reimbursement contracts, but rather, should apply to all types of negotiated prime and subcontracts.

(c) Should evolve from sound commercial cost accounting practices and should be compatible with generally accepted accounting principles.

(d) Should require contractors to maintain contract performance records in conformity with the standards and with the approved practices set forth in disclosure statements.

In addition, the CAS Board was directed to prepare regulations requiring contractors, as a condition of contracting with the government, to (1) disclose in writing their cost accounting practices and (2) agree to a contract price adjustment in the event of noncompliance with applicable CAS or failure to follow disclosed or established cost accounting practices.

The CAS Board carried out its mission with vigor, promulgating regulations that established a number of individual standards (which are collectively referred to as the Cost

Accounting Standards) as well as requirements for contractor disclosure statements and contract price adjustments. The Board also promulgated regulations covering its own operations. However, the first Board ceased to exist on September 30, 1980 after Congress failed to appropriate funds for the Board's FY 1981 operations.

In 1988, a new, independent CAS Board was created.

* * *

Contractor obligations

The "Cost Accounting Standards" clause must be inserted in contracts subject to full coverage under the Cost Accounting Standards. The clause requires contractors to do all of the following:

(1) Disclose in writing their cost accounting practices by completing a "Disclosure Statement."

(2) Follow their disclosed practices consistently in estimating, accumulating, and reporting costs.

(3) Comply with all of the individual CAS in effect on the contract award date.

(4) Agree to an adjustment of the contract price when the contractor fails to comply with existing Standards or its own disclosed practices.

The basic clause has companion clauses.

Besides implementing the substance of the CAS Board's enabling statute, the "Cost Accounting Standards" clause also establishes the contract price adjustment procedure to be followed whenever a contractor makes a cost accounting practice change.

* * *

Notes and Questions

1. Note the comprehensive, integrated system by which the government applies cost accounting standards. By statute, Congress created the cost accounting system. Regulations provide for CAS coverage and exemptions. Contractors must submit a CAS Disclosure Statement form describing the practices. Contracting Officers include CAS clauses in the contracts. What can a commercial contractor, which may make only a small fraction of its sales to the government on CAS-covered contracts, do to comply with CAS and yet not have to redo the whole company's accounting system?

2. Contractor desire to be rid of interference with their accounting has called the continuing existence of the Cost Accounting Standards Board into question from time to time. For an account of one such debate, see Charles Tiefer & Danielle Brian, "Grabbing for the Purse Strings: Defense Contractors Take Aim At a Critical Accounting Watchdog," *Legal Times of Washington*, August 10, 1998, at 19.

Chapter 5

Contract Administration

In the specialized field of government contracting, much public attention is, by necessity and design, focused on the solicitation and contract award process. The actual administration of the contract receives much less public attention. Nevertheless, one must not lose sight of the fact that the government spends all those billions of federal dollars annually on government contracts to produce tangible benefit to the government, which thus makes the administration of those contracts of considerable importance and value.

This chapter begins with a section on the government contracting officer's discretion and the related issue of interpretation of the contracts. The role of the government contracting officer in the contract administration process cannot be overestimated. At the same time, contractors can, and do, interpret contracts differently than contracting officers. Contract interpretation issues involve a number of considerations such as the application of *contra proferentum*, a canon of interpretation with particular applicability in government contracts because most of their language is drafted by the government.

Next, the chapter addresses the related topics of specifications, inspections and warranty. Typically, contract specifications describe the work that the contractor undertakes to do, thus having critical importance in the administration of the contract. Conversely, the contractor relies, and legitimately so, on some of what the government tells the contractor in the specifications, such as the implied feasibility of prescribed work procedures. As the contract goes forward and the contractor completes work, the government will inspect that work, and the duties and rights bound up with such government inspection have a major role in contract administration. So, too, do the warranties that the contractor provides the government regarding the work.

Another section of the chapter addresses the specialized topic of technical data and other intellectual property rights. Some contractor work involves patents, copyrights, technical data, and other intellectual property. In fact, the main point of some contracts, such as contracts to perform research, may involve the development of new intellectual property. The government has certain policies worth study regarding such matters as what rights the government and the contractor have regarding such property.

A last section deals with the complexly interrelated subjects of progress payments, prompt payment, and other government assistance. The government might wish to pay contractors only when work has been done, and indeed, some time later when bureaucratic procedures have been completed. Yet, contractors may need progress payments during the course of their work, and even when they only get payment when the work is done, they have a statutorily-protected interest in prompt payment as soon as they submit a proper invoice. The government also provides other assistance, such as types of property contractors may need for their work.

For further discussion of the issues in this chapter, see: Steven Feldman, *Government Contract Guidebook*, § 18 (Thomson Reuters, 4th ed. 2010); Karen Manos, *Government Contract Costs & Pricing*, §§ 85.9, 85.13 (Thomson Reuters 2nd ed. 2009). Cheryl L. Scott,

Top Sheet: Kiewit And Other Latent Defects Cases, 45 Procrmt. Law. 5 (Summer 2010); Jerald D. Stubbs, *The Federal Circuit And Contract Interpretation: May Extrinsic Evidence Ever Be Used To Show Unambiguous Language Is Ambiguous*, 39 Pub. Cont. L.J. 785 (Summer 2010); Mark Gleason, *In The Name Of Boyle: Congress's Overexpansion Of The Government Contractor Defense*, 36 Pub. Cont. L.J. 249 (Winter 2007).

A. Contracting Officer Discretion and Interpretation

As noted, the role of the government contracting officer in the contract administration process cannot be overestimated. Of course, the government contracting officer can receive assistance, comments, and recommendations from numerous other government officials interested in contract performance, such as program managers and technical representatives, auditors, budgeters, and attorneys. Nevertheless, it is the government contracting officer alone who is the focal point with the appropriate authority for addressing and resolving contract administration issues.

As is the case with contracts between private entities, there are numerous areas that are subject to possible dispute between the contractor performing the work and the entity intended to receive the benefit, in this instance, the government. As a result, interpreting the intent of the contracting parties is of critical importance in resolving any such disputes.

Of considerable aid in such conflict resolution is the fact that government contracts are most often reduced to writing with numerous and detailed contract clauses that govern many aspects of performance. Both standard government clauses found in the Federal Acquisition Regulation and its supplements as well as clauses drafted by individual agencies and buying offices responsible for particular specialized areas, (e.g., information technology acquisition or real property construction), create a focused body of law on the responsibility of each party during contract performance. However, given the very wide variety of goods, property, and services purchased by the government as well as the often unique needs of government customers, the courts must rely on many of the same contract interpretation rules used at common law for discerning the intent of the parties when a dispute arises.

Although the occasional clear and unambiguous breach by one party or the other will arise in government contracting, it is far more common for a dispute about contract performance to be centered on an ambiguous provision with each side espousing an interpretation favorable to its position. Where both interpretations are considered reasonable, the courts, relying on the rule of *contra proforentum,* will often interpret the provision against the drafter if the other party can demonstrate reliance on its reasonable interpretation. This rule most often works to the benefit of contractors due to the simple fact that the government is most often the source of contract specifications and clauses.

As a counter to the *contra proforentum* rule, the courts can also examine whether the ambiguity was the result of an obvious and patent defect in the wording thereby requiring the other party (most often the contractor) to seek clarification. The failure to seek timely clarification can shift the burden back to the contractor to perform in accordance with the government's interpretation. In support of this process, contractors are often given a specific time period during the solicitation process to submit written questions about contract requirements and receive written responses. Such an exchange of correspondence is often useful in examining whether a defect was so obvious that a reasonable person would consider it as such.

In addition to determining responsibility for a particular contract provision, the courts will attempt to harmonize all provisions of the contract together. In a sealed bid situation where the bidder's offer is a mirror image of the solicitation document, this process of harmonization is straightforward. However, the much more common use of competitive proposals whereby an offeror is free—and often required—to submit a considerable amount of verbiage in response to the government's solicitation presents greater difficulties in attempting to harmonize all contract provisions. This process is further complicated by the fact that contractors often take exception, although often not clearly, to one or more requirements or provisions listed in the government solicitation as well as the government's fondness for incorporating by reference or including as attachments numerous other documents that may only generally have applicability to the specific contract at hand.

As an aid to such contract interpretation problems, the government solicitation will often include an "Order of Precedence" clause that sets forth the order by which the different parts of a contract are to be given precedence should a dispute arise. For example, FAR 52.215-8 provides that inconsistencies in the contract are to be resolved by giving precedence to the following sections of the contract in the following order: First, the Schedule, including contract forms, the description of supplies or services and the prices, packaging and marking requirements, inspection and acceptance terms, delivery or performance requirements, contract administration data, and special contract requirements; Second, Representations and other instructions listed in the solicitation; Third, Contract clauses (most often written by the government); Fourth, other documents, exhibits and attachments; and Fifth, the specifications. Note that the probable source of most disputes, the actual contract specifications, are last in line for determining the intent of the parties.

Finally, trade usage, the parties' acts during actual contract performance, and prior experience are also factors that a decisionmaker will use to determine the intent of the parties when resolving a contract dispute.

TEG-Paradigm Environmental, Inc., Plaintiff-Appellant, v. United States, Defendant-Appellee

No. 06-5007
United States Court of Appeals, Federal Circuit
465 F.3d 1329
Sept. 29, 2006

Before MICHEL, Chief Judge, RADER, and SCHALL, Circuit Judges.

SCHALL, Circuit Judge.

TEG-Paradigm Environmental, Inc. ("TEG") entered into a contract with the United States Department of Housing and Urban Development ("HUD"). Pursuant to the contract, TEG agreed to perform asbestos abatement work at the Geneva Towers, an apartment complex, in San Francisco. After the contract work was completed, TEG submitted a claim to the contracting officer in which it sought an equitable adjustment in the contract price. In support of its claim, TEG asserted that it had been required to perform excessive cleaning and that it had been required to remove excessive quantities of asbestos. After the contracting officer denied the claim, TEG filed suit in the United States Court of Federal Claims under the Contract Disputes Act of 1978, 41 U.S.C. §§ 601–613 (2000).

* * *

In due course, the parties filed cross-motions for summary judgment. The court granted summary judgment for the government on Counts One and Two of the complaint and for TEG on Count Three of the complaint. *Teg-Paradigm Envtl., Inc. v. United States,* No. 00-507C, slip op. at 26 (Fed.Cl. Aug. 30, 2002). TEG now appeals from the court's decision granting the government's motion for summary judgment on its two claims of breach of contract. Finding no error in the Court of Federal Claims's decision, we affirm.

BACKGROUND
I.

The Geneva Towers were two high-rise apartment buildings in San Francisco. HUD acquired the buildings in 1991 and decided to implode them to make way for new development. *Id.,* slip op. at 2. However, the buildings contained asbestos, which had to be removed before implosion. *Id.* HUD solicited bids on a contract for asbestos abatement and TEG was awarded the contract on May 8, 1997, for a fixed price of $5,153,625.00. The contract required that the abatement be complete on or by December 31, 1997, and provided for liquidated damages of $5,000 per day of delay. After several extensions, the deadline for finishing the abatement was changed to February 15, 1998. *Id.,* slip op. at 7. However, TEG did not finish the abatement work until March 31, 1998, causing HUD to assess $220,000 in liquidated damages against it. *Id.,* slip op. at 8. This delay was purportedly caused at least in part by disagreements between TEG and HUD over contract requirements. Specifically, the parties disagreed as to (i) whether the contract required TEG to abate asbestos in the pores and cracks of the Geneva Towers' surfaces and (ii) whether TEG was required to comply with the contract specifications rather than TEG's work plan.

A.

We begin with the facts relevant to the first point of contention between the parties, which concerns the level of asbestos abatement required by the contract (Count Two of the complaint).

The original contract specifications provided two separate abatement standards, one for friable and one for non-friable asbestos-containing materials. Friable materials are capable, when dry, of being crumbled, pulverized, or reduced to powder by hand pressure. *Id.,* slip op. at 2. The original asbestos abatement standard was set forth at Section 2080, 4.3C of the contract, which provided as follows:

> Friable materials applied to concrete, masonry, wood and nonporous surfaces, including but not limited to, steel structural members (decks, beams and columns), pipes and tanks, shall be cleaned to a degree that no traces of debris or residue are visible. Nonfriable materials applied to concrete, masonry, [or] wood shall be cleaned until no residue is visible other than that which is embedded in the pores, cracks, or other small voids below the surface of the material.

Thus, the original specifications established a stringent visibility standard for friable materials and a less stringent standard, one which allowed the contractor to leave asbestos in the pores and cracks, for non-friable materials. The original Section 2080, 4.3C likely provided the stringent visibility standard for friable asbestos-containing materials because they are more likely to become airborne and thus pose a health risk.

In the course of the bidding process, prospective bidders, including TEG, raised questions about which standard applied to the concrete on the exterior of the buildings. During a conference call concerning the prospective contract, TEG's representative noted, "It's a significant difference, because on one it has to be clean to a degree there's no trace; on the other, it's clean to a degree that material can still be embedded in pores, cracks and voids."

In response to the questions raised during the bidding process about the original asbestos abatement standard, the government modified the standard. The revised section 2080, 4.3C set forth a single standard for all asbestos-containing materials and provided as follows:

> Asbestos-containing materials applied to concrete, masonry, wood and non-porous surfaces, including, but not limited to, steel structural members (decks, beams and columns), pipes and tanks, shall be cleaned to a degree that no traces of debris or residue are visible by the Observation Services Contractor.

Thus, the revised Section 2080, 4.3C abolished the old standard applicable for non-friable materials that stated that it was acceptable to leave asbestos-containing materials in pores and cracks. Instead, a standard requiring that there be no visible asbestos, similar to the original standard for friable asbestos-containing materials, was adopted for all asbestos-containing materials.

As noted by the Court of Federal Claims, trade practice and custom in the asbestos abatement field includes presuming that any "debris and residue" contains asbestos. *Id.,* slip op. at 13. The court based its finding on the American Society for Testing Material ("ASTM") standard for asbestos abatement, which provides, "Any residue, dust, or debris found during the inspections is *assumed* to contain asbestos...."*Id.*

B.

The parties' second disagreement concerns whether the contract's specifications or TEG's work plan controlled the terms of TEG's performance (Count One of the complaint).

Section C of the contract specifications states that the contractor will provide a work plan for approval. The relevant portion of Section C provides:

> Contractor[']s Work Plan: Submit for approval a detailed plan of engineering controls and the work procedures to be used in the removal, repair, clean-up or encapsulation of materials containing Asbestos.

* * *

Pursuant to this provision, HUD requested that TEG submit its work plan on April 21, 1997. On April 25, 1997, TEG submitted a first version of its work plan. In response to deficiencies pointed out by HUD and ATC Associates, Inc. ("ATC"), HUD's asbestos engineer and technical advisor for the contract, TEG revised the work plan several times in late April and early May of 1997. Two weeks after the initial submittal of the work plan, TEG was awarded the contract.

Disputes arose during contract performance as to whether the work plan or the contract specifications governed performance. TEG pointed out discrepancies between the two documents in a letter dated June 17, 1997. For example, TEG noted in the letter that it had not closed vertical pipe cavities, as required by the specifications, because the work plan required the cavities to remain open in order to complete the project. The discrepancies between the work plan and the contract specifications led to the issuance of a Stop Work Order. After over a month of disputes, HUD accepted a Value Engineering Change Proposal ("VECP")[3] from TEG that made changes to the contract specifications to bring it more in line with the work plan. Work then continued under the revised specifications.

---

3. A VECP is a contractor's proposal to make a cost-reducing change to a government contract. *See* 48 C.F.R. §§ 48-201, 52.248-1–.248-3 (2006); *see also* John Cibinic, Jr., Ralph C. Nash, Jr. & James F. Nagle, *Administration of Government Contracts* 409 (4th ed.2006).

* * *

II.

* * *

On appeal, TEG argues that the Court of Federal Claims erred in holding that HUD applied the proper cleaning standard for abatement under the contract. TEG argues that the contract at Section 2080, 4.3C required that asbestos-containing materials be cleaned from "surfaces" so that no traces of debris or residue were visible. TEG contends that "surfaces" are not defined in the contract, but that from common usage dictionaries it is apparent that that they include only "[t]he outer-face, outside, or exterior boundary of a thing; outermost or uppermost layer or area." Appellant's Br. at 21 (quoting a definition found in *Random House Webster's College Dictionary* 1314 (2d ed.1999)).

* * *

TEG also argues that the government interfered with its work plan, which was a part of the contract. In support of its argument, TEG points out that the work plan was physically attached by HUD to the contract. Further, TEG contends that under Federal Acquisition Regulation ("FAR") § 14.201-1(c), *see* 48 C.F.R. § 14.201-1(c) (2006), the work plan, which is a representation or a statement of a bidder, was incorporated into the contract. TEG also contends that it was required to proceed under the work plan under FAR § 1552.211-74, 48 C.F.R. § 1552.211-74 (2006), and that therefore the work plan was part of the contract.

* * *

III.

When interpreting a contract, "'the language of [the] contract must be given that meaning that would be derived from the contract by a reasonably intelligent person acquainted with the contemporaneous circumstances.'" *Metric Constructors, Inc. v. Nat'l Aeronautics & Space Admin.*, 169 F.3d 747, 752 (Fed.Cir.1999) (quoting *Hol-Gar Mfg. Corp. v. United States*, 169 Ct.Cl. 384, 351 F.2d 972, 975 (Ct.Cl.1965)). When deriving this meaning, we begin with the contract's language. *Coast Fed. Bank, FSB v. United States*, 323 F.3d 1035, 1038 (Fed.Cir.2003) (en banc). When the contract's language is unambiguous it must be given its "plain and ordinary" meaning and the court may not look to extrinsic evidence to interpret its provisions. *Id.* at 1040; *McAbee Constr.*, 97 F.3d at 1435. Although extrinsic evidence may not be used to interpret an unambiguous contract provision, we have looked to it to confirm that the parties intended for the term to have its plain and ordinary meaning. *See Coast Fed. Bank*, 323 F.3d at 1040 (looking to contemporaneous evidence of the parties' understanding and "not[ing] that much of it is consistent with the [contract's] plain meaning"). When a provision in a contract is susceptible to more than one reasonable interpretation, it is ambiguous, *Edward R. Marden Corp. v. United States*, 803 F.2d 701, 705 (Fed.Cir.1986), and we may then resort to extrinsic evidence to resolve the ambiguity, *see McAbee*, 97 F.3d at 1435. We utilize extrinsic evidence to derive a construction that effectuates the parties' intent at the time they executed the contract. *See Dureiko v. United States*, 209 F.3d 1345, 1356 (Fed.Cir.2000).

Even when a contract is unambiguous, it may be appropriate to turn to one common form of extrinsic evidence—evidence of trade practice and custom. *Hunt Constr. Group, Inc. v. United States*, 281 F.3d 1369, 1373 (Fed.Cir.2002). We have stated that "evidence of trade practice may be useful in interpreting a contract term having an accepted industry meaning different from its ordinary meaning—even where the contract otherwise appears unambiguous—because the "parties to a contract ... can be their own lexicographers and ... trade practice may serve that lexicographic function in some cases." *Id.* (quoting *Jowett, Inc.*

v. United States, 234 F.3d 1365, 1368 (Fed.Cir.2000)). Trade practice and custom may not be used, however, "to create an ambiguity where a contract was not reasonably susceptible of differing interpretations at the time of contracting." *Metric Constructors,* 169 F.3d at 752.

The parol evidence rule provides a further limitation on the use of extrinsic evidence in interpreting contracts. Under the parol evidence rule, extrinsic evidence pre-dating a written agreement may not be used "to add to or otherwise modify the terms of a written agreement in instances where the written agreement has been adopted by the parties as an expression of their final understanding." *Barron Bancshares,* 366 F.3d at 1375 (citation and quotation marks omitted). However, extrinsic evidence such as prior agreements and documents will be considered part of a contract when they are incorporated into the contract. *See S. Cal. Fed. Sav. & Loan Ass'n v. United States,* 422 F.3d 1319, 1330 (Fed.Cir.2005). One common way to incorporate extrinsic evidence is through an integration clause that expressly incorporates the extrinsic evidence. *Id.; McAbee Constr. v. United States,* 97 F.3d 1431, 1434 (Fed.Cir.1996). Although the parol evidence rule bars the use of extrinsic evidence to supplement or modify a written agreement, the rule does not bar the use of extrinsic evidence to interpret the terms of a contract when the plain and ordinary meaning is not clear from the contract itself. *See* Restatement (Second) Contracts § 215 cmt. b (1981); 6-26 *Corbin on Contracts* § 579 (2006); Cibinic, Nash & Nagle, *supra,* at 199. Armed with these rules, we turn to the issues TEG raises on appeal.

IV.

We consider first TEG's claim that the Court of Federal Claims erred in holding that it was required to clean debris and residue from pores and cracks of the Geneva Towers under the contract's abatement standard. As seen, the provision of the contract containing the abatement standard for the Geneva Towers project, Section 2080, 4.3C, provided:

> Asbestos-containing materials applied to concrete, masonry, wood and non-porous surfaces, including, but not limited to, steel structural members (decks, beams and columns), pipes and tanks, shall be cleaned to a degree that no traces of debris or residue are visible by the Observation Services Contractor.

The Court of Federal Claims correctly identified two issues raised by the abatement standard. First, we must determine whether this standard requires the removal of asbestos within pores and cracks. Second, we must determine what asbestos-containing "debris or residue" means.

Based upon the plain language of the abatement standard, we conclude that the Court of Federal Claims did not err in ruling that TEG was required to remove asbestos within pores and cracks. The plain language of the contract indicates that it requires abatement to the point that there is no "debris or residue ... visible."

* * *

As we did in *Coast Federal Bank,* we turn to extrinsic evidence, specifically, the course of dealing of the parties, to confirm that our interpretation of the plain and ordinary meaning was, in fact, the parties' understanding. *See Coast Fed. Bank,* 323 F.3d at 1040. The original specifications provided for two different abatement standards for friable and non-friable materials. As far as friable materials were concerned, the specifications expressly stated that materials must be cleaned "to a degree that no traces of debris or residue are visible." In contrast, the specifications provided that non-friable materials "shall be cleaned until no residue is visible other than that which is embedded in the pores, cracks, or other small voids below the surface of the material." Thus, the original specifications expressly allowed for the contractor to leave non-friable asbestos in pores and cracks. In a pre-bid conference call, TEG's representative stated that it was not clear which standard, friable or non-friable, would apply and that this was an important difference. TEG's representative noted, "It's a significant difference, because on one it has to be clean to a degree there's no trace; on the other, it's clean to a degree that material can still be embedded in pores, cracks and voids." In our view, the conference call demonstrates that TEG understood the visibility standard, which was eventually adopted for all asbestos abatement under the contract, to require that no asbestos remain in the pores and cracks.

We find unpersuasive TEG's argument that the Court of Federal Claims erred by failing to consider other pieces of evidence, including ATC's letter and Mr. Oberta's expert opinion. These documents could be considered evidence of trade practice and custom, which we have found appropriate to consider in some cases even when a contract is unambiguous. *See Hunt Constr.*, 281 F.3d at 1373. However, neither of these documents aids in the interpretation of a term of art in the asbestos abatement field. Rather each document offers an alternate explanation of the contract's abatement standard generally. Under *Hunt Construction*, it is not permissible to use these extrinsic sources to impart ambiguity into an otherwise unambiguous contract—they may only be used to interpret a term of art. *Id.* at 1369; *see also Metric Constructors*, 169 F.3d at 752. Given the clarity of the meaning from the language and the parties' pre-contractual negotiations, none of the extrinsic evidence cited by TEG carries weight.

*   *   *

Turning to the second issue relevant to TEG's abatement standard claim, the meaning of "debris or residue," we see no error in the Court of Federal Claims's holding that, under the contract, any dust or powder found on inspection was assumed to be asbestos-containing "debris or residue" that had to be abated. "Debris" and "residue" are not defined in the contract. As previously noted, evidence of trade custom may be used to interpret terms of art such as "debris" and "residue." *See Hunt Constr.*, 281 F.3d at 1373. The ASTM standard for asbestos abatement provides that debris and residue is "assumed" to contain asbestos. *TEG-Paradigm*, slip op. at 13. Therefore, we agree with the Court of Federal Claims that trade practice and custom demonstrates that in the asbestos abatement field any "debris and residue" found is assumed to contain asbestos. *Id.* Thus, we affirm the Court of Federal Claims's holding that the contract required TEG to clean all visible powder and dust found on inspection, including powder and dust in cracks and pores.

*   *   *

V.

Turning to the work plan issue, we hold that the Court of Federal Claims correctly determined that the contract specifications, rather than TEG's work plan, governed the terms of contract performance. The government required a work plan conforming to the contract specifications before it accepted TEG's bid. Therefore, the work plan comprises a piece of extrinsic evidence pre-dating the formation of the contract. HUD required that bidders submit a work plan stating the details of the bidder's engineering controls and work procedures. Nowhere does the contract state that the work plan is to be integrated into the contract and supersede the contract specifications. In contrast to the work plan, several sections of the FAR are incorporated by Section F of the specifications.[4] Addi-

---

4. For example, Section F incorporates FAR sections 52.252-2 ("Clauses Incorporated by Reference"), 52.242-15 ("Stop-Work Order"), 52.242-17 ("Government Delay of Work"), and 52.211-12 ("Liqui-

tionally, Sections I, J, and K to the contract list not only numerous sections of the FAR that are incorporated by reference, but also several other documents relating to payment bonds, performance bonds, and wage rates.

We also find that there is no exception to the parol evidence rule for work plans in government contracts. The Court of Federal Claims correctly characterized TEG's work plan not as part of the contract, but rather as a pre-award submission used to aid the government in assessing TEG's ability to perform the contract. *TEG-Paradigm,* slip op. at 21. Under FAR 9.103, the government must award contracts to "responsible prospective contractors only." 48 C.F.R. § 9.103(a) (2006); *see also* Cibinic & Nash, *Formation of Government Contracts, supra,* at 404–06. Thus, the government requires pre-award submissions to assess whether the contractor will be able to perform the contract. Pre-award submissions, such as a work plan, are not part of the contract unless the contract specifically provides that they are to be incorporated. Examination of the contract at issue confirms that TEG's work plan was a pre-award submission that did not override the contract specifications. Section C of the contract specifications requires that the contractor submit a "work plan" containing information such as the names and contact information of the key personnel who would perform the contract, a detailed description of pollution control methods, and various safety and contingency plans. Again, nowhere in the contract is it stated that the contract incorporates the work plan. Thus, the government is correct that TEG's work plan was not part of the contract, but rather a piece of information that was used by the government to assess TEG's ability to perform in the pre-award stage.

Contrary to TEG's arguments, FAR sections 14.201-1 and 1552.22-74 do not compel us to find that work plans are incorporated into government contracts. FAR 14.201-1 sets forth the uniform contract format that must be used "to the maximum practicable extent" for certain types of contracts. 48 C.F.R. § 14.201-1 (2006). Section 14.201-1(c) states that acceptance of a bid "incorporates Section K, Representations, certifications, and other statements of bidders, in the resultant contract even though not physically attached." Section K of the contract at issue incorporates several sections of the FAR that require particular submissions, e.g., taxpayer identification, FAR 52.204-3, whether or not the business is women-owned, FAR 52.204-5, and the type of business, FAR 52.214-2, *see* 48 C.F.R. §§ 52.204-3, 52.204-5, 52.214-2 (2006), respectively. However, the work plan is contained in Section C of the contract and is therefore not a Section K representation, certification, or statement. We find TEG's arguments under FAR 1552.211-74(c) equally unpersuasive. FAR 1552.211-74(c) sets forth procedures for stopping work when a work plan is not approved. It does not state that work plans are incorporated into government contracts.

Finally, our holding that work plans are not incorporated into government contracts is in accordance with the general principle that the government is entitled to strict compliance with contract specifications. *See Granite Constr. Co. v. United States,* 962 F.2d 998, 1006–07 (Fed.Cir.1992) ("[T]he government generally has the right to insist on performance in strict compliance with the contract specifications and may require a contractor to correct nonconforming work."). This principle prevents contractors from submitting low bids and then substituting less-expensive materials for those required by the specification. Cibinic, Nash & Nagle, *supra,* at 815.

---

dated Damages-Supplies, Services, or Research and Development"). *See* 48 C.F.R. §§ 52.252-2, 52.242-15, 52.242-17, 52.211-12.

CONCLUSION

For the foregoing reasons, we therefore affirm the decision of the Court of Federal Claims granting summary judgment in favor of the government on TEG's claims for breach of contract.

Propellex Corporation, Appellant, v.
Les Brownlee, Acting Secretary of the Army, Appellee
See Chapter 6

B. Specifications, Inspection and Acceptance

By statute, federal agencies are required to specify needs for goods and services that will promote full and open competition and include restrictive provisions only to the extent necessary to satisfy the needs of the agency. 10 U.S.C. § 2305(a)(1); 41 U.S.C. § 253a(a). In addition, to the maximum extent practicable, specifications are to be stated in terms of functions to be performed, performance required, or essential physical characteristics. When functional and performance specifications are not possible, the government relies on design specifications that mandate how the contractor is to perform the required work.

Inspection constitutes the process by which the government ensures contract performance in compliance with contract specifications. The government can choose to either (1) rely on a contractor's own internal quality controls and inspect the final product or service when delivered to the government or (2) mandate, as part of the contract requirements, the maintenance of a quality control program that meets specific government requirements and allows for government inspections during performance. Either way, the ultimate goal is a product that the government can accept. Inspection is thus the bridge between specifications and acceptance.

The determination as to whether a proffered good or service meets contract requirements rests with the government contracting officer and is generally evidenced by the execution of a formal acceptance certificate. The responsibility for acceptance can be transferred from the contracting officer to a cognizant contract administration office or to another agency. Acceptance can occur before delivery, at the time of delivery, or after delivery depending upon contract terms.

For more on this topic, refer to: Frank Baltz, *The* Spearin *Doctrine: How Far Does It Go?*, 33 Procure. Law., Summer 1998, at 11; Kacey Reed, *The Supreme Court's Rejection of Government Indemnification to Agent Orange from Manufacturers in Hercules, Inc. v. United States: Distinguishing the Forest from the Trees?* 31 U. Rich. L. Rev. 287 (1997); Kevin C. Golden & James W. Thomas, *The* Spearin *Doctrine: The False Dichotomy Between Design and Performance Specifications*, 25 Pub. Cont. L.J. 47 (1995); Paul A. D'Aloisio, *The Design Responsibility and Liability of Government Contractors*, 25 Pub. Cont. L.J. 47 (1995); William R. Medsger, *Weapon System Warranties: Unleashing the Genius in American Industry?* 127 Mil. L. Rev. 63 (1990); Saul Perloff & Hal Perloff, *Latent Defects in Government Contracts Law*, 27 Pub. Cont. L.J. 87 (1997); Thomas E. Shea, *The Magic Keys: Finality of Acceptance Under Government Contracts*, 86 Mil. L. Rev. 111 (1979); Neil G. Wolf, *Boyle v. United Technologies Corp.: A Reasonably Precise Immunity — Specifying the Defense Contractor's Shield*, 39 DePaul L. Rev. 825 (1990); Mark S. Jaeger, *Contractor Liability for Design Defects Under the Inspection Clause: Latent Design Defects — A Sleeping*

Giant?, 21 Pub. Cont. L.J. 331 (1992); Commander George E. Hurley, Jr., *Government Contractor Liability in Military Design Defect Cases: The Need for Judicial Intervention,* 117 Mil. L. Rev. 219 (1987).

1. Specifications

Specifications describing the work undertaken by the contractor have two implications, represented by the very different cases in this section. On the one hand, the specifications impose a duty on the contractor who must provide what the specifications require, even though the contractor finds this onerous in the course of performing the contract. The contractor may then dispute whether the contract really imposes what the specifications apparently require; the government may respond by insisting on literal compliance.

On the other hand, the contractor may rely upon the specifications, expecting that anything they require, particularly in terms of methods of performance, will prove feasible. Then, if the requirements prove impossible or impractical, the contractor may insist that the government "impliedly warranted" the feasibility of the specifications; the government may respond by pointing to clauses intended to shift responsibility to the contractor, such as "site inspection" clauses.

The contractor's reliance upon the government's contract takes on particular urgency when the contractor gets sued for impacts upon third parties. While the government has power to shield contractors from, or to indemnify them regarding, liability to third parties, the government also has considerable reluctance to be so generous. Determining the extent of such immunity or indemnification raises again the issues recurring throughout government contracts, concerning the extent to which the rigid requirements such as affirmative statutory authorization surround the providing of public powers, resources, or assistance to private parties, even those awarded government contracts.

J.L. Malone & Associates, Inc., Appellant, v. The United States, Appellee

United States Court of Appeals, Federal Circuit.,
No. 89-1056., 879 F.2d 841 July 13, 1989.

Before FRIEDMAN, NIES, and MAYER, Circuit Judges.

FRIEDMAN, Circuit Judge.

This is an appeal from a decision of the Veterans Administration Board of Contract Appeals rejecting a contractor's appeal from the contracting officer's decision denying the contractor an equitable adjustment under a contract. The contractor sought compensation for (1) the additional cost it incurred for expanding the capability of an existing computer, as the contract required, rather than substituting a different computer, as the contractor proposed, and (2) the delay damages it incurred because of the government's alleged unreasonable delay in considering the proposed substitute. The Board denied both of these claims. Appeal of J.L. Malone & Assoc., 88-3 B.C.A. ¶ 20,894 (VABCA 1988). We affirm.

I

The Veterans Administration (VA) planned to replace the outdated fire alarm system at its Medical Center in Lexington, Kentucky. The VA's design called for integrating the new fire alarm system with the Center's recently installed heating ventilation and air conditioning

(HVAC) system, which was operated by a JC-80 computer manufactured by Johnson Controls. Integration was to be accomplished by expanding the memory of the existing JC-80 computer so as to allow it also to operate the new fire alarm system.

The VA's Invitation for Bids described the work as follows:

> Services of contractor to furnish all labor and materials ... to remove existing fire alarm system including transmitter, signaling devices and control panels and replace with a frequency multiplexed system utilizing and expanding existing transmitters, panels and Johnson [Controls] JC-80 computer at the Veterans Administration Medical Center, ... per specifications and Drawings. [Emphasis added.]

The specification stated at section 800-1(E) that:

> E. The contractor shall furnish, install and place in operating condition a fire safety system as herein described. The fire safety system shall operate as an integral part of the existing computerized building automation system.... [Emphasis added.]

The specification further provided that the new central processing unit (C.P.U.) was to be provided with 64,000 words of memory and that "[t]he existing C.P.U. shall be provided with an additional 32 thousand words of memory."

The contract contained two so-called "or equal" clauses that permitted the contractor to use substitutes of equal quality for products the contract specified.

General Provision 9 provided in pertinent part:

> (a) ... Unless otherwise specifically provided in this contract, reference to any equipment, ... by trade name, make, or catalog number, shall be regarded as establishing a standard of quality and shall not be construed as limiting competition, and the Contractor may, at his option, use any equipment, ... which in the judgment of the Contracting Officer, is equal to that named.

The second "or equal" clause appears in section 8 of the specifications describing the fire alarm system:

> 800-5. Equipment Ratings And Approval Of Equal Equipment
>
> B. Prior to construction, written approval shall be obtained by the Contractor from the Contracting Officer for any equipment which differs from the requirements of the drawings and specifications.
>
> ....
>
> 3. Any other items required for the satisfactory installation of the equal equipment shall be furnished and installed at no additional cost to the Government. This includes but shall not be limited to changes to branch circuits, circuit protective devices, conduits, wire, feeders, controls, panels,....
>
> 800-10. Drawings and Specifications: The drawings and specifications indicate the requirements for the systems, equipment, materials, operation, quality, etc. They shall not be construed to mean limitation of competition to the products of specific manufacturers.

There were four bids on the contract. The appellant's bid of $1,456,502 was more than $120,000 lower than the second lowest bid.

In preparing its bid the appellant obtained price quotations for fire alarm systems from two subcontractors, Johnson Controls and Honeywell. The Honeywell system was $152,000 lower than the Johnson Controls system.

The appellant was awarded the contract on December 7, 1981.

On April 19, 1982, the appellant made its first fire alarm submittal, which proposed a Honeywell fire alarm system separate and independent from the Johnson Controls HVAC system. The agency rejected this system as not complying with the contract specifications.

The appellant's second submittal, dated May 7, 1982, again proposed a separate Honeywell system. The proposal stated that the Honeywell system "meets and or exceeds every requirement" of the specifications "with the single exception of operating as an integral part of the existing computerized building automation system." The submittal further stated that "[t]he specification requirements for utilizing and expanding the existing Johnson Control[s] JC-80 computer and supplying a new identical 64K memory computer that will function as a back-up to the existing JC-80 computer cannot be provided due to the obsolescence of the existing computer." The agency rejected the second proposal on June 1, 1982.

The appellant's third submittal, dated July 28, 1982, the submittal here at issue, proposed to remove the existing JC-80 computer and furnish a Honeywell computer that would be capable of operating both the new fire alarm system and the existing HVAC system.

The submittal was reviewed for the VA by the engineering firm of Watkins & Associates. It informed the VA that the "proposed Honeywell system is not an integral part of the existing [computerized building automation] system," as required by paragraph 808-1(E) of the specifications, "but a replacement of it," and, therefore, in Watkins' opinion, the proposal "is an exception to the specifications and should not be honored at this time because this option was not given to the other bidders." The memorandum noted that although the VA "would be getting all new equipment and wiring for both the fire alarm as well as the HVAC control," there were at least eight disadvantages of accepting the Honeywell system in lieu of expanding the existing JC-80 system, the foremost of which would be the involvement of the VA in "legal problems with the other bidders."

At a September 28, 1982 meeting between the appellant and the VA, the appellant pointed out that the third submittal work would be done at no additional cost to the government. The contracting officer requested that the appellant provide, among other things, a statement "address[ing] the company's interpretation of the legalities of accepting this proposal and avoiding potential litigation." The appellant's response was that other bidders were "on notice that [the] 'or equal' provision was included in the referenced contract ... and were free to let that fact [a]ffect their bid in any way they so chose."

At a meeting the contracting officer held on October 14, 1982 with officials of Johnson Controls, at their request, a Johnson Controls representative "implied that if the Honeywell submittal were approved and the Johnson [Controls] equipment removed, a protest would be lodged through one or all of the other bidders."

In response to a request from the contracting officer that the VA's Office of General Counsel provide a legal opinion concerning the acceptability of the appellant's third submittal, the Assistant Deputy Administrator for Procurement and Supply informed the Center's Director on November 19, 1982, that:

> Our recommendation, with the concurrence of General Counsel, is to enforce the requirements of the contract. The contractor must install a fire alarm system which will operate as an integral part of the existing computerized building automation system. If the contractor fails to provide a submittal which meets specifications, default action should be initiated.

The contracting officer so notified the appellant by letter on November 19, 1982:

The specifications state that "the fire safety system shall operate as an integral part of the existing computerized building automation system." The system is interpreted as meaning the JC80 computer which must, therefore, remain in place. Since your submittal would require replacing the JC80, it is considered not in conformance with the specifications.

The appellant performed the contract using the Johnson Controls equipment. It then filed a claim of $292,459.07, covering (1) the $152,000 difference between the price for the Johnson Controls equipment and the Honeywell equipment, (2) increased installation costs, (3) project delay costs for overhead of $76,839.27, and (4) markups for overhead and profit.

The contracting officer denied the claim for a price adjustment, and the appellant appealed that decision to the Veterans Administration Board of Contract Appeals (Board). The Board denied the appeal. It held that "the 'or equal' provisions of the contract do not permit a contractor to remove and replace existing items of equipment which have been specified to remain." The Board explained:

> Those cases [holding that a contractor is permitted under an "or equal" provision of a contract to substitute items from another source if they are equal to the items from the source designated in the contract] do not discuss a situation, such as here, where a contract requires that a new system to be installed must be integrated with an existing system, and that certain specific items of equipment which are part of that existing system are to remain, be utilized and expanded.

The Board further stated that "[although] the evidence indicates that [the Honeywell system] was more advanced than the older existing computer" and the government "would have received a more state-of-the art computer with no additional cost," the issue "is not whether the Government exercised good judgment in drawing up its contract, or whether it would have benefitted by allowing [the appellant] to replace its existing equipment"; rather "[t]he integrity of the Government's competitive procurement system is involved." The Board explained:

> What [the appellant] proposed was a major change in the contract, which no reasonable bidder, in our opinion, would have anticipated as permissible when preparing its bid. The requirement for integrating the new system with the existing system and retaining the JC-80 computer was clear. It would have been unfair to the other bidders to have permitted such a basic change in the contract after award....

> If [the appellant], or any other bidder, felt that the proposed contract was unduly restrictive of competition by requiring that the existing Johnson Controls computer be utilized and expanded, and that the new fire alarm system be integrated with the existing system, rather than permitting replacement of the existing system, it should have protested prior to award.

The Board also rejected the appellant's delay claim, ruling that the contracting officer had not unreasonably delayed her decision on the third submittal.

* * *

II

A. The appellant's principal contention is that under the "or equal" clauses of the contract, it had the right to substitute the Honeywell computer for the existing Johnson Controls computer because the former was equal in quality to the latter. This argument rests upon a misconstruction of the contract.

The contractual reference to the Johnson Controls computer was not intended to define quality or type of product to be used. Its purpose was to describe the work the contractor was to perform. As the contractual specification stated, that work was to "replace" the "existing fire alarm system" by utilizing and expanding the existing "Johnson JC-80 computer," so that the new fire alarm system would "operate as an integral part of the existing computerized building automation system." In other words, the new fire alarm system was to be integrated with the existing computerized building automation system by "utilizing and expanding" existing equipment, including the Johnson Controls computer.

As the contract specifically pointed out, an essential element of the new fire alarm system was its utilization and expansion of the existing computer. The specifications explained how that computer was to be utilized and expanded to make it an "integral part" of the "existing computerized building automation system." They required that "[t]he new [central processing unit] shall be provided with 64 thousand words of memory. The existing C.P.U. [central processing unit, which included the Johnson Controls computer] shall be provided with an additional 32 thousand words of memory."

There is nothing in the contract that authorized, or even suggested, that Malone could remove the existing Johnson Controls computer and substitute a Honeywell computer. As the Board correctly noted:

> What Malone proposed was a major change in the contract, which no reasonable bidder, in our opinion, would have anticipated as permissible when preparing its bid. The requirement for integrating the new system with the existing system and retaining the JC-80 computer was clear. It would have been unfair to the other bidders to have permitted such a basic change in the contract after award.

In at least its second submittal to the contracting officer, the appellant recognized that the existing Johnson Controls computer was to be utilized and expanded and that any other design was at variance with the contractual requirement. The appellant there acknowledged that although the existing JC-80 computer was to be utilized and expanded, that "cannot be provided due to the obsolescence of the existing computer." The submittal further recognized that the fire alarm system was to operate as an integral part of the existing building automation system but maintained that that requirement was "impossible."

There was a similar recognition of the requirement in the statement that "[t]he requirement for the existing C.P.U. to be provided with an additional 32 thousand words of memory could be accomplished by installing a 32K memory plane of the same type as the existing memory plane if one could be found."

"It is settled that the Government is entitled to obtain precisely what it contracts for as long as it does not mislead the contractor." American Elec. Contracting Corp. v. United States, 579 F.2d 602, 608, 217 Ct.Cl. 338 (1978). The VA made a design decision that the existing JC-80 computer would be utilized and expanded. The Board found that the VA's primary reason for doing so was that "the existing equipment had been in use for about a year and a half, had been debugged and would presumably be 'cost effective.' " We cannot say that that design decision was impermissible or that there was any reason why the government was not entitled to obtain exactly what its contract specified.

The Board found that the Honeywell computer that the appellant proposed to install in its third submittal was more advanced than the existing JC-80 computer that the contract specified was to be utilized and expanded. The government, however, was not required to alter the basic design requirements of the contract. The government carefully considered the appellant's third submittal and justifiably concluded that the major change the appellant proposed would be inappropriate for various reasons, including the likelihood of protests by unsuccessful bidders.

B. The appellant relies heavily on Jack Stone Co. v. United States, 344 F.2d 370, 170 Ct.Cl. 281 (1965). In that case, a contract for the renovation of an electric power and a fire alarm system provided that:

> The Contractor shall furnish all labor and materials necessary to install complete all additions and revisions to the existing Fire Alarm System as herein specified and as shown on Drawings.... The existing system is of Sperti Faraday manufacture. All new equipment and parts furnished shall be of the same manufacturer to insure full and satisfactory performance of the completed system.

344 F.2d at 372. The specifications contained sixteen separate references to Sperti Faraday items. The contract also contained the following "or equal" provision:

> Reference in the specifications to any article, device, product, materials, fixture, form or type of construction by name, make, or catalog number, shall be interpreted as establishing a standard of quality, and not as limiting competition. The Contractor may make substitutions equal to the items specified if approved in advance in writing by the Contracting Officer.

The Court of Claims, reversing the Board, held that the contract authorized the contractor to use components manufactured by another company that were the equal of the Sperti Faraday components. The court stated that the effect of the "or equal" provision of the contract was that "under this contract plaintiff was not required to furnish Sperti Faraday equipment alone, but could supply articles from another source if they were equal to Sperti Faraday and if the consent of the contracting officer was sought in advance." 344 F.2d at 376.

Jack Stone did not address the situation here of a contractor who proposes to remove an existing item of equipment, which the contract expressly required was to be "utilized and expanded," and replace that item with one manufactured by a different source. In Jack Stone, the contractor proposed merely to use a "different manufacturer's components in conjunction with the existing fire alarm [system]." 344 F.2d at 372. In Jack Stone, the reference to Sperti Faraday products, in light of the "or equal" clause, was a designation of the kind and quality of product to be used.

In the present case, on the other hand, the reference to the Johnson Controls computer was a description of the work the contractor was to perform, namely, the replacement of the existing fire alarm system with a new system that would utilize and expand the Johnson Controls computer. Unlike the contract in Jack Stone, here the "or equal" clause did not authorize the contractor to substitute another product, even if it was of equal quality, for the Johnson Controls computer that the contract required the contractor to utilize and expand. Indeed, the general "or equal" clause of this contract applied "[u]nless otherwise specifically provided in this contract." The "utilizing and expanding" and the "integral part" provisions of the contract "otherwise specifically provided."

C. The appellant further contends that if the contract is construed to require it to utilize the existing Johnson Controls computer, the contract would be a "sole source" procurement that would require compliance with the provisions governing such procurement, and would be inconsistent with the "or equal" provisions of the contract. Our conclusion that the contractual requirement to utilize the existing Johnson Controls computer described the work to be performed and not the product to be used in performing the contract undermines the basis for this argument. A contractual requirement that in performing the work the contractor must utilize an existing item of equipment, which is identified by its manufacturer, does not make the contract a sole source procurement.

* * *

CONCLUSION

The decision of the Veterans Administration Board of Contract Appeals denying the appellant an equitable adjustment is

AFFIRMED

Notes and Questions

1. Does the fact that the Veterans Administration issued the solicitation as an IFB rather than an RFP have an impact on the outcome of this case? What could the contractor have done prior to submission of bids that would have altered this case? Why would a prospective contractor not take action prior to submission of bids?

2. Of critical importance to the outcome of this case is the conclusion of the courts that "the Government is entitled to obtain precisely what it contracts for as long as it does not mislead the contractor." *American Elec. Contracting Corp. v. United States*, 579 F.2d 602, 608, 217 Ct.Cl. 338 (1978). What policies support such a conclusion? What responsibility does a contractor have to inform the government that a proposed solution may not be the most desirable or least expensive?

3. FAR 11.104 provides:

Agency requirements shall not be written so as to require a particular brand-name product, or a feature of a product, peculiar to one manufacturer, thereby precluding consideration of a product manufactured by another company, unless—

(a) The particular brand-name, product, or feature is essential to the Government's requirements, and market research indicates other companies' similar products, or products lacking the particular feature, do not meet, or cannot be modified to meet, the agency's minimum needs;

(b) The authority to contract without providing for full and open competition is supported by the required justifications and approvals....

What was the justification for specifying a particular brand in this instance?

United States v. Spearin

Supreme Court of the United States
248 U.S. 132
Argued Nov. 14 and 15, 1918; Decided Dec. 9, 1918.

Mr. Justice BRANDEIS delivered the opinion of the Court.

Spearin brought this suit in the Court of Claims demanding a balance alleged to be due for work done under a contract to construct a dry dock and also damages for its annulment. Judgment was entered for him in the sum of $141,180.86 (51 Ct. Cl. 155), and both parties appealed to this court. The government contends that Spearin is entitled to recover only $7,907.98. Spearin claims the additional sum of $63,658.70.

First. The decision to be made on the government's appeal depends upon whether or not it was entitled to annul the contract. The facts essential to a determination of the question are these:

Spearin contracted to build for $757,800 a dry dock at the Brooklyn Navy Yard in accordance with plans and specifications which had been prepared by the government. The site selected by it was intersected by a 6-foot brick sewer; and it was necessary to divert and relocate a section thereof before the work of constructing the dry dock could begin. The plans and specifications provided that the contractor should do the work and prescribed the dimensions, material and location of the section to be substituted. All the prescribed requirements were fully complied with by Spearin; and the substituted section was accepted by the government as satisfactory. It was located about 37 to 50 feet from the proposed excavation for the dry dock; but a large part of the new section was within the area set aside as space within which the contractor's operations were to be carried on. Both before and after the diversion of the 6-foot sewer, it connected, within the Navy Yard but outside the space reserved for work on the dry dock, with a 7-foot sewer which emptied into Wallabout Basin.

About a year after this relocation of the 6-foot sewer there occurred a sudden and heavy downpour of rain coincident with a high tide. This forced the water up the sewer for a considerable distance to a depth of 2 feet or more. Internal pressure broke the 6-foot sewer as so relocated, at several places; and the excavation of the dry dock was flooded. Upon investigation, it was discovered that there was a dam from 5 to 5 1/2 feet high in the 7-foot sewer; and that dam, by diverting to the 6-foot sewer the greater part of the water, had caused the internal pressure which broke it. Both sewers were a part of the city sewerage system; but the dam was not shown either on the city's plan, nor on the government's plans and blueprints, which were submitted to Spearin. On them the 7-foot sewer appeared as unobstructed. The government officials concerned with the letting of the contract and construction of the dry dock did not know of the existence of the dam. The site selected for the dry dock was low ground; and during some years prior to making the contract sued on, the sewers had, from time to time, overflowed to the knowledge of these government officials and others. But the fact had not been communicated to Spearin by any one. He had, before entering into the contract, made a superficial examination of the premises and sought from the civil engineer's office at the Navy Yard information concerning the conditions and probable cost of the work; but he had made no special examination of the sewers nor special inquiry into the possibility to the work being flooded thereby, and had no information on the subject.

Promptly after the breaking of the sewer Spearin notified the government that he considered the sewers under existing plans a menace to the work and that he would not resume operations unless the government either made good or assumed responsibility for the damage that had already occurred and either made such changes in the sewer system as would remove the danger or assumed responsibility for the damage which might thereafter be occasioned by the insufficient capacity and the location and design of the existing sewers. The estimated cost of restoring the sewer was $3,875. But it was unsafe to both Spearin and the government's property to proceed with the work with the 6-foot sewer in its then condition. The government insisted that the responsibility for remedying existing conditions rested with the contractor. After 15 months spent in investigation and fruitless correspondence, the Secretary of the Navy annulled the contract and took possession of the plant and materials on the site. Later the dry dock, under radically changed and enlarged plans, was completed by other contractors, the government having first discontinued the use of the 6-foot intersecting sewer and then reconstructed it by modifying size, shape and material so as to remove all danger of its breaking from internal pressure. Up to that time $210,939.18 had been expended by Spearin on the work; and he had received from the government on account thereof $129,758.32. The court found that if he had been allowed to complete the contract he would have earned a profit of $60,000 and its judgment included that sum.

The general rules of law applicable to these facts are well settled. Where one agrees to do, for a fixed sum, a thing possible to be performed, he will not be excused or become entitled to additional compensation, because unforeseen difficulties are encountered.... Thus one who undertakes to erect a structure upon a particular site, assumes ordinarily the risk of subsidence of the soil.... But if the contractor is bound to build according to plans and specifications prepared by the owner, the contractor will not be responsible for the consequences of defects in the plans and specifications.... This responsibility of the owner is not overcome by the usual clauses requiring builders to visit the site, to check the plans, and to inform themselves of the requirements of the work, as is shown by Christie v. United States, 237 U. S. 234, 35 Sup. Ct. 565, 59 L. Ed. 933; Hollerbach v. United States, 233 U. S. 165, 34 Sup. Ct. 553, 58 L. Ed. 898, and United States v. Stage Co., 199 U. S. 414, 424, 26 Sup. Ct. 69, 50 L. Ed. 251, where it was held that the contractor should be relieved, if he was misled by erroneous statements in the specifications.

In the case at bar, the sewer, as well as the other structures, was to be built in accordance with the plans and specifications furnished by the government. The construction of the sewer constituted as much an integral part of any part of the dry dock proper. It was as necessary as any other work in the preparation for the foundation. It involved no separate contract and no separate consideration. The contention of the government that the present case is to be distinguished ... on the ground that the contract with reference to the sewer is purely collateral is clearly without merit. The risk of the existing system proving adequate might have rested upon Spearin, if the contract for the dry dock had not contained the provision for relocation of the 6-foot sewer. But the insertion of the articles prescribing the character, dimensions and location of the sewer imported a warranty that if the specifications were complied with, the sewer would be adequate. This implied warranty is not overcome by the general clauses requiring the contractor to examine the site,[1] to check up the plans,[2] and to assume responsibility for the work until completion and acceptance.[3] The obligation to examine the site did not impose upon him the duty of making a diligent inquiry into the history of the locality with a view to determining, at his peril, whether the sewer specifically prescribed by the government would prove adequate. The duty to check plans did not impose the obligation to pass upon their adequacy to accomplish the purpose in view. And the provision concerning contractor's responsibility cannot be construed as abridging rights arising under specific provisions of the contract.

Neither section 3744 of the Revised Statutes (Comp. St. 1916, § 6895) which provides that contracts of the Navy Department shall be reduced to writing, nor the parol evidence rule, precludes reliance upon a warranty implied by law. See Kellogg Bridge Co. v. Hamilton, 110 U. S. 108, 3 Sup. Ct. 537, 28 L. Ed. 86. The breach of warranty, followed by the government's repudiation of all responsibility for the past and for making working conditions safe in the future, justified Spearin in refusing to resume the work. He was not

---

1. "27. Examination of Site. — Intending bidders are expected to examine the site of the proposed dry dock and inform themselves thoroughly of the actual conditions and requirements before submitting proposals."

2. "25. Checking Plans and Dimensions; Lines and Levels. — The contractor shall check all plans furnished him immediately upon their receipt and promptly notify the civil engineer in charge of any discrepancies discovered therein. *** The contractor will be held responsible for the lines and levels of his work, and he must combine all materials properly, so that the completed structure shall conform to the true intent and meaning of the plans and specifications."

3. "21. Contractor's Responsibility. — The contractor shall be responsible for the entire work and every part thereof, until completion and final acceptance by the Chief of Bureau of Yards and Docks, and for all tools, appliances, and property of every description used in connection therewith...."

obliged to restore the sewer and to proceed, at his peril, with the construction of the dry dock. When the government refused to assume the responsibility, he might have terminated the contract himself, Anvil Mining Co. v. Humble, 153 U. S. 540, 551, 552, 14 Sup. Ct. 876, 38 L. Ed. 814; but he did not. When the government annulled the contract without justification, it became liable for all damages resulting from its breach.

Second. Both the main and the cross appeal raise questions as to the amount recoverable.

The government contends that Spearin should, as requested, have repaired the sewer and proceeded with the work; and that having declined to do so, he should be denied all recovery except $7,907.98, which represents the proceeds of that part of the plant which the government sold plus the value of that retained by it. But Spearin was under no obligation to repair the sewer and proceed with the work, while the government denied responsibility for providing and refused to provide sewer conditions safe for the work. When it wrongfully annulled the contract, Spearin became entitled to compensation for all losses resulting from its breach.

Spearin insists that he should be allowed the additional sum of $63,658.70, because, as he alleges, the lower court awarded him (in addition to $60,000 for profits) not the difference between his proper expenditures and his receipts from the government, but the difference between such receipts and the value of the work, materials, and plant (as reported by a naval board appointed by the defendant). Language in the findings of fact concerning damages lends possibly some warrant for that contention; but the discussion of the subject in the opinion makes it clear that the rule enunciated in United States v. Behan, 110 U. S. 338, 4 Sup. Ct. 81, 28 L. Ed. 168, which claimant invokes, was adopted and correctly applied by the court.

The judgment of the Court of Claims is, therefore, affirmed.

Mr. Justice McREYNOLDS took no part in the consideration and decision of these cases.

Notes and Questions

1. Key to this case is the determination of which party had responsibility to disclose superior knowledge. The government attempted to avoid this responsibility by formal and broad contract clauses placing the burden of discovery of defects and potential problems directly and unambiguously on the contractor. Why did this attempt fail notwithstanding the contract language to the contrary?

2. Would the government have overcome the implied warranty associated with the government specifications if it had used functional and performance specifications rather than detailed design specifications?

3. Due to the government's breach of the contract, the contractor received full compensation for money expended during performance plus the estimated profit he would have received if allowed to complete the work. In addition, the contractor sought but was denied compensation for the actual value of the work performed rather than for money actually spent. Which remedy was the contractor seeking in that instance?

4. Contract officers, aware of the Spearin doctrine, may want to word their IFBs or RFPs to prevent government liability by clearly worded disclaimers of warranty, or exculpatory clauses. A classic discussion of this is in *Rixon Electronics, Inc. v. United States*, 536 F. 2d 1345, at 1351–52 (Ct. Cl.1976)

(T)he question boils down to this: is the disclaimer clear enough, alone or as aided by the warning to check the bid? You can engage a contractor to make snowmen in August, if you spell it out clearly, you are not warranting there will be any subfreezing weather in that month. But if you say ... that the bid will generate a loss, and the bidder doesn't, apparently, believe you, what more can you say, legitimately, that will be more persuasive? Will you, with reason, conclude that the bidder wants to lose money, or at least, wants to break into this market so badly that loss of money is accepted as a minor consideration?

Mere general exculpatory clauses disclaiming any liability for accuracy of data that contractors may use in proposal preparation do not invariably defeat implied warranties of specifications. Exculpatory clauses are narrowly construed, particularly where the government attempts to avoid a remedy under a contract relief clause by means of a disclaimer. See *Teledyne Lewisburg v. United States*, 699 F. 2d 1336 (Fed. Cir. 1983). Furthermore, where the government has knowledge that information it provided contains incorrect, misleading or dangerous components, it has a duty to disclose this to the contractor. *Black v. Fairchild Industries*, No. 84-C-29223 (E.D. N.Y. 1986). That duty cannot be defeated by inclusion of an exculpatory clause. *Appeal of V & Z Heating Corporation*, 1998 WL 331671, DOTCAB No. 2953; *Christy Corporation v. United States*, 198 Ct. Cl. 986 (1972).

5. On the other hand, to find an implied warranty of specifications, it does not suffice merely that the government has detailed some characteristics, but requires that the specifications tell the contractor "just how to do the job." See *Appeal of Reflectone, Inc.* ASBCA No. 42,363, 1998 WL 354206. Moreover, the contractor must demonstrate it could not reasonably discover the actual facts, and the flawed specifications were material in nature. Whether it would have been reasonable for the prospective bidder to conduct further testing or investigation depends on the particular facts of each procurement, such as the cost of tests relative to the size of the job and the time available to prepare the bid or proposal. See *Robert E. McKee, Inc. v. City of Atlanta*, 414 F. Supp. 957 (N.D. Ga 1976).

Delbert Boyle, Personal Representative et al. Petitioner, v. United Technologies Corporation

Supreme Court of the United States
487 U.S. 500
Argued Oct. 13, 1987
Reargued April 27, 1988
Decided June 27, 1988

Justice SCALIA delivered the opinion of the Court.

This case requires us to decide when a contractor providing military equipment to the Federal Government can be held liable under state tort law for injury caused by a design defect.

I

On April 27, 1983, David A. Boyle, a United States Marine helicopter copilot, was killed when the CH-53D helicopter in which he was flying crashed off the coast of Virginia Beach, Virginia, during a training exercise. Although Boyle survived the impact of the crash, he was unable to escape from the helicopter and drowned. Boyle's father, petitioner here, brought this diversity action in Federal District Court against the Sikorsky Division of United Technologies Corporation (Sikorsky), which built the helicopter for the United States.

At trial, petitioner presented two theories of liability under Virginia tort law that were submitted to the jury. First, petitioner alleged that Sikorsky had defectively repaired a device called the servo in the helicopter's automatic flight control system, which allegedly malfunctioned and caused the crash. Second, petitioner alleged that Sikorsky had defectively designed the copilot's emergency escape system: the escape hatch opened out instead of in (and was therefore ineffective in a submerged craft because of water pressure), and access to the escape hatch handle was obstructed by other equipment. The jury returned a general verdict in favor of petitioner and awarded him $725,000. The District Court denied Sikorsky's motion for judgment notwithstanding the verdict.

The Court of Appeals reversed and remanded with directions that judgment be entered for Sikorsky. 792 F.2d 413 (CA4 1986)…. It also found, as a matter of federal law, that Sikorsky could not be held liable for the allegedly defective design of the escape hatch because, on the evidence presented, it satisfied the requirements of the "military contractor defense," which the court had recognized the same day….

II

Petitioner's broadest contention is that, in the absence of legislation specifically immunizing Government contractors from liability for design defects, there is no basis for judicial recognition of such a defense. We disagree…. [W]e have held that a few areas, involving "uniquely federal interests," *Texas Industries, Inc. v. Radcliff Materials, Inc.,* 451 U.S. 630, 640, 101 S.Ct. 2061, 2067, 68 L.Ed.2d 500 (1981), are so committed by the Constitution and laws of the United States to federal control that state law is pre-empted and replaced, where necessary, by federal law of a content prescribed (absent explicit statutory directive) by the courts—so-called "federal common law." See, *e.g., United States v. Kimbell Foods, Inc.,* 440 U.S. 715, 726–729, 99 S.Ct. 1448, 1457–1459, 59 L.Ed.2d 711 (1979); *Banco Nacional v. Sabbatino,* 376 U.S. 398, 426–427, 84 S.Ct. 923, 939–940, 11 L.Ed.2d 804 (1964); *Howard v. Lyons,* 360 U.S. 593, 597, 79 S.Ct. 1331, 1333, 3 L.Ed.2d 1454 (1959); *Clearfield Trust Co. v. United States,* 318 U.S. 363, 366–367, 63 S.Ct. 573, 574–575, 87 L.Ed. 838 (1943); *D'Oench, Duhme & Co. v. FDIC,* 315 U.S. 447, 457–458, 62 S.Ct. 676, 679–680, 86 L.Ed. 956 (1942).

The dispute in the present case borders upon two areas that we have found to involve such "uniquely federal interests." We have held that obligations to and rights of the United States under its contracts are governed exclusively by federal law. See, *e.g., United States v. Little Lake Misere Land Co.,* 412 U.S. 580, 592–594, 93 S.Ct. 2389, 2396–2397, 37 L.Ed.2d 187 (1973); *Priebe & Sons, Inc. v. United States,* 332 U.S. 407, 411, 68 S.Ct. 123, 125, 92 L.Ed. 32 (1947); *National Metropolitan Bank v. United States,* 323 U.S. 454, 456, 65 S.Ct. 354, 355, 89 L.Ed. 383 (1945); *Clearfield Trust, supra.* The present case does not involve an obligation to the United States under its contract, but rather liability to third persons. That liability may be styled one in tort, but it arises out of performance of the contract—and traditionally has been regarded as sufficiently related to the contract that until 1962 Virginia would generally allow design defect suits only by the purchaser and those in privity with the seller. See *General Bronze Corp. v. Kostopulos,* 203 Va. 66, 69–70, 122 S.E.2d 548, 551 (1961); see also Va. Code § 8.2-318 (1965) (eliminating privity requirement).

Another area that we have found to be of peculiarly federal concern, warranting the displacement of state law, is the civil liability of federal officials for actions taken in the course of their duty. We have held in many contexts that the scope of that liability is controlled by federal law…. The present case involves an independent contractor performing its obligation under a procurement contract, rather than an official performing his duty as a federal employee, but there is obviously implicated the same interest in getting the Government's work done.[1]

---

1. Justice Brennan's dissent misreads our discussion here to "intimat[e] that the immunity [of federal officials] … might extend … [to] nongovernment employees" such as a Government con-

We think the reasons for considering these closely related areas to be of "uniquely federal" interest apply as well to the civil liabilities arising out of the performance of federal procurement contracts. We have come close to holding as much....

The imposition of liability on Government contractors will directly affect the terms of Government contracts: either the contractor will decline to manufacture the design specified by the Government, or it will raise its price. Either way, the interests of the United States will be directly affected.

That the procurement of equipment by the United States is an area of uniquely federal interest does not, however, end the inquiry. That merely establishes a necessary, not a sufficient, condition for the displacement of state law. Displacement will occur only where, as we have variously described, a "significant conflict" exists between an identifiable "federal policy or interest and the [operation] of state law," *Wallis, supra,* at 68, 86 S.Ct., at 1304, or the application of state law would "frustrate specific objectives" of federal legislation, *Kimbell Foods,* 440 U.S., at 728, 99 S.Ct., at 1458....

Here the state-imposed duty of care that is the asserted basis of the contractor's liability (specifically, the duty to equip helicopters with the sort of escape-hatch mechanism petitioner claims was necessary) is precisely contrary to the duty imposed by the Government contract (the duty to manufacture and deliver helicopters with the sort of escape-hatch mechanism shown by the specifications). Even in this sort of situation, it would be unreasonable to say that there is always a "significant conflict" between the state law and a federal policy or interest. If, for example, a federal procurement officer orders, by model number, a quantity of stock helicopters that happen to be equipped with escape hatches opening outward, it is impossible to say that the Government has a significant interest in that particular feature. That would be scarcely more reasonable than saying that a private individual who orders such a craft by model number cannot sue for the manufacturer's negligence because he got precisely what he ordered....

There is, however, a statutory provision that demonstrates the potential for, and suggests the outlines of, "significant conflict" between federal interests and state law in the context of Government procurement. In the FTCA, Congress authorized damages to be recovered against the United States for harm caused by the negligent or wrongful conduct of Government employees, to the extent that a private person would be liable under the law of the place where the conduct occurred. 28 U.S.C. § 1346(b). It excepted from this consent to suit, however,

> "[a]ny claim ... based upon the exercise or performance or the failure to exercise or perform a discretionary function or duty on the part of a federal agency or an employee of the Government, whether or not the discretion involved be abused." 28 U.S.C. § 2680(a).

We think that the selection of the appropriate design for military equipment to be used by our Armed Forces is assuredly a discretionary function within the meaning of this provision. It often involves not merely engineering analysis but judgment as to the balancing of many technical, military, and even social considerations, including specifically the trade-off between greater safety and greater combat effectiveness. And we are further of the view that permitting "second-guessing" of these judgments, see *United States v. Varig Airlines,* 467 U.S. 797, 814, 104 S.Ct. 2755, 2765, 81 L.Ed.2d 660 (1984), through state tort

---

tractor. *Post,* at 2524. But we do not address this issue, as it is not before us. We cite these cases merely to demonstrate that the liability of independent contractors performing work for the Federal Government, like the liability of federal officials, is an area of uniquely federal interest.

suits against contractors would produce the same effect sought to be avoided by the FTCA exemption. The financial burden of judgments against the contractors would ultimately be passed through, substantially if not totally, to the United States itself, since defense contractors will predictably raise their prices to cover, or to insure against, contingent liability for the Government-ordered designs. To put the point differently: It makes little sense to insulate the Government against financial liability for the judgment that a particular feature of military equipment is necessary when the Government produces the equipment itself, but not when it contracts for the production. In sum, we are of the view that state law which holds Government contractors liable for design defects in military equipment does in some circumstances present a "significant conflict" with federal policy and must be displaced.

We agree with the scope of displacement adopted by the Fourth Circuit here, which is also that adopted by the Ninth Circuit, see *McKay v. Rockwell Int'l Corp., supra,* at 451. Liability for design defects in military equipment cannot be imposed, pursuant to state law, when (1) the United States approved reasonably precise specifications; (2) the equipment conformed to those specifications; and (3) the supplier warned the United States about the dangers in the use of the equipment that were known to the supplier but not to the United States. The first two of these conditions assure that the suit is within the area where the policy of the "discretionary function" would be frustrated—*i.e.,* they assure that the design feature in question was considered by a Government officer, and not merely by the contractor itself. The third condition is necessary because, in its absence, the displacement of state tort law would create some incentive for the manufacturer to withhold knowledge of risks, since conveying that knowledge might disrupt the contract but withholding it would produce no liability. We adopt this provision lest our effort to protect discretionary functions perversely impede them by cutting off information highly relevant to the discretionary decision.

We have considered the alternative formulation of the Government contractor defense, urged upon us by petitioner, which was adopted by the Eleventh Circuit in *Shaw v. Grumman Aerospace Corp.,* 778 F.2d 736, 746 (1985), cert. pending, No. 85-1529. That would preclude suit only if (1) the contractor did not participate, or participated only minimally, in the design of the defective equipment; *or* (2) the contractor timely warned the Government of the risks of the design and notified it of alternative designs reasonably known by it, *and* the Government, although forewarned, clearly authorized the contractor to proceed with the dangerous design. While this formulation may represent a perfectly reasonable tort rule, it is not a rule designed to protect the federal interest embodied in the "discretionary function" exemption. The design ultimately selected may well reflect a significant policy judgment by Government officials whether or not the contractor rather than those officials developed the design. In addition, it does not seem to us sound policy to penalize, and thus deter, active contractor participation in the design process, placing the contractor at risk unless it identifies all design defects.

* * *

Accordingly, the judgment is vacated and the case is remanded.

So ordered.

Justice BRENNAN, with whom Justice MARSHALL and Justice BLACKMUN join, dissenting.

* * *

Our "uniquely federal interest" in the tort liability of affiliates of the Federal Government is equally narrow. The immunity we have recognized has extended no further than a subset of "officials of the Federal Government" and has covered only "discretionary" functions within the scope of their legal authority.... Never before have we so much as intimated that the immunity (or the "uniquely federal interest" that justifies it) might extend beyond that narrow class to cover also nongovernment employees whose authority to act is independent of any source of federal law and that are as far removed from the "functioning of the Federal Government" as is a Government contractor, *Howard, supra,* 360 U.S., at 597, 79 S.Ct., at 1334.

The historical narrowness of the federal interest and the immunity is hardly accidental. A federal officer exercises statutory authority, which not only provides the necessary basis for the immunity in positive law, but also permits us confidently to presume that interference with the exercise of discretion undermines congressional will. In contrast, a Government contractor acts independently of any congressional enactment. Thus, immunity for a contractor lacks both the positive law basis and the presumption that it furthers congressional will.

Moreover, even within the category of congressionally authorized tasks, we have deliberately restricted the scope of immunity to circumstances in which "the contributions of immunity to effective government in particular contexts outweigh the perhaps recurring harm to individual citizens," *Doe v. McMillan,* 412 U.S. 306, 320, 93 S.Ct. 2018, 2028, 36 L.Ed.2d 912 (1973); see *Barr, supra,* 360 U.S., at 572–573, 79 S.Ct., at 1340, because immunity "contravenes the basic tenet that individuals be held accountable for their wrongful conduct," *Westfall, supra,* 484 U.S., at 295, 108 S.Ct., at 583. The extension of immunity to Government contractors skews the balance we have historically struck. On the one hand, whatever marginal effect contractor immunity might have on the "effective administration of policies of government," its "harm to individual citizens" is more severe than in the Government-employee context. Our observation that "there are ... other sanctions than civil tort suits available to deter the executive official who may be prone to exercise his functions in an unworthy and irresponsible manner," *Barr,* 360 U.S., at 576, 79 S.Ct., at 1342; see also *id.,* at 571, 79 S.Ct., at 1339, offers little deterrence to the Government contractor. On the other hand, a grant of immunity to Government contractors could not advance "the fearless, vigorous, and effective administration of policies of government" nearly as much as does the current immunity for Government employees. *Ibid.* In the first place, the threat of a tort suit is less likely to influence the conduct of an industrial giant than that of a lone civil servant, particularly since the work of a civil servant is significantly less profitable, and significantly more likely to be the subject of a vindictive lawsuit. In fact, were we to take seriously the Court's assertion that contractors pass their costs—including presumably litigation costs—through, "substantially if not totally, to the United States," *ante,* at 2518, the threat of a tort suit should have only marginal impact on the conduct of Government contractors. More importantly, inhibition of the Government official who actually sets Government policy presents a greater threat to the "administration of policies of government," than does inhibition of a private contractor, whose role is devoted largely to assessing the technological feasibility and cost of satisfying the Government's predetermined needs. Similarly, unlike tort suits against Government officials, tort suits against Government contractors would rarely "consume time and energies" that "would otherwise be devoted to governmental service." 360 U.S., at 571, 79 S.Ct., at 1339.

In short, because the essential justifications for official immunity do not support an extension to the Government contractor, it is no surprise that we have never extended it that far.

I respectfully dissent.

Notes and Questions

1. The opinion begins with the interesting federal-vs.-state choice of law question that turns up most prominently in first-year law school in the line of cases applying the *Erie* decision in civil procedure. Note the somewhat offbeat positioning: Justice Scalia, who ordinarily opposes creation of federal common law, supports it here; his dissenting colleagues to the left, who ordinarily support creation of federal common law, oppose it here. Why? This choice of law issue returns in the chapter on subcontracting.

2. What are the premises of the decision to provide tort immunity to this contractor?

3. Justice Scalia and the dissent make a centerpiece of their discussion the law-and-economics debate over whether the cost of tort suits against a defense contractor will be passed along to the government. You are aware of the distinction between alternative pricing methods—fixed-price or cost-reimbursement—and how much they matter to government contract lawyers. Is Justice Scalia saying that this distinction does not matter to economists—and hence, to policy decisions about law?

4. How does this decision apply if the contractor produces under performance rather than design specifications? If the contractor produces for the commercial market rather than just for defense? If the contractor produces services—or construction, as in *Spearin*—rather than goods?

5. Reconcile this decision with the following one—*Hercules*. See Charles E. Cantu & Randy W. Young, *The Government Contractor Defense: Breaking the Boyle Barrier*, 62 Alb. L. Rev. 403 (1998); Ronald A. Cass & Clayton P. Gillette, *The Government Contractor Defense: Contractual Allocation of Public Risk*, 77 Va. L. Rev. 257 (1991).

Hercules Incorporated, et al., Petitioners, v. United States

Supreme Court of the United States, 516 U.S. 417
Argued Oct. 30, 1995, Decided March 4, 1996

On Writ of Certiorari to the United States Court of Appeals for the Federal Circuit.

Chief Justice REHNQUIST delivered the opinion of the Court.

Petitioners in this case incurred substantial costs defending and then settling third-party tort claims arising out of their performance of Government contracts. In this action under the Tucker Act, they sought to recover these costs from the Government on alternate theories of contractual indemnification or warranty of specifications provided by the Government. We hold that they may not do so.

When the United States had armed forces stationed in Southeast Asia in the 1960's, it asked several chemical manufacturers, including petitioners Hercules Incorporated (Hercules) and Wm. T. Thompson Company (Thompson), to manufacture and sell it a specific phenoxy herbicide, code-named Agent Orange. The Department of Defense wanted to spray the defoliant in high concentrations on tree and plant life in order to both eliminate the enemy's hiding places and destroy its food supplies. From 1964 to 1968, the Government, pursuant to the Defense Production Act of 1950 (DPA), 64 Stat. 798, as amended, 50 U.S.C.App. § 2061 et seq. (1988 ed. and Supp. V), entered into a series of fixed-price production contracts with petitioners. The military prescribed the formula and detailed specifications for manufacture. The contracts also instructed the suppliers to mark the drums containing the herbicide with a 3-inch orange band with "[n]o further identification as to content." Lodging 30. Petitioners fully complied.

In the late 1970's, Vietnam veterans and their families began filing lawsuits against nine manufacturers of Agent Orange, including petitioners. The plaintiffs alleged that the veterans' exposure to dioxin, a toxic by-product found in Agent Orange and believed by many to be hazardous, had caused various health problems. The lawsuits were consolidated in the Eastern District of New York and a class action was certified. In re "Agent Orange" Product Liability Litigation, 506 F.Supp. 762, 787–792 (1980).

* * *

In May 1984, hours before the start of trial, the parties settled. The defendants agreed to create a $180 million settlement fund with each manufacturer contributing on a market-share basis. Hercules' share was $18,772,568, Thompson's was $3,096,597. Petitioners also incurred costs defending these suits exceeding $9 million combined.

Petitioners want the United States to reimburse them for the costs of defending and settling this litigation. They attempted to recover first in District Court under tort theories of contribution and noncontractual indemnification. Having failed there, they each sued the Government in the United States Claims Court, invoking jurisdiction under 28 U.S.C. § 1491, and raising various claims sounding in contract. On the Government's motions, the Claims Court granted summary judgment against petitioners and dismissed both complaints. Hercules, Inc. v. United States, 25 Cl.Ct. 616 (1992); Wm. T. Thompson Co. v. United States, 26 Cl.Ct. 17 (1992).

The two cases were consolidated for appeal and a divided panel of the Court of Appeals for the Federal Circuit affirmed. 24 F.3d 188 (1994).... We granted certiorari, 514 U.S. —, 115 S.Ct. 1425, 131 L.Ed.2d 308 (1995), and now affirm the judgment below but on different grounds.

We begin by noting the limits of federal jurisdiction. "[T]he United States, as sovereign, 'is immune from suit save as it consents to be sued ... and the terms of its consent to be sued in any court define that court's jurisdiction to entertain the suit.' " United States v. Testan, 424 U.S. 392, 399, 96 S.Ct. 948, 953, 47 L.Ed.2d 114 (1976), quoting United States v. Sherwood, 312 U.S. 584, 586, 61 S.Ct. 767, 769–770, 85 L.Ed. 1058 (1941). Congress created the Claims Court to permit "a special and limited class of cases" to proceed against the United States, Tennessee v. Sneed, 96 U.S. 69, 75, 24 L.Ed. 610 (1878), and the court "can take cognizance only of those [claims] which by the terms of some act of Congress are committed to it," see Thurston v. United States, 232 U.S. 469, 476, 34 S.Ct. 394, 395, 58 L.Ed. 688 (1914); United States v. Sherwood, supra, at 586–589, 61 S.Ct., at 769–771. The Tucker Act confers upon the court jurisdiction to hear and determine, inter alia, claims against the United States founded upon any "express or implied" contract with the United States. 28 U.S.C. § 1491(a).

We have repeatedly held that this jurisdiction extends only to contracts either express or implied in fact, and not to claims on contracts implied in law.... Each material term or contractual obligation, as well as the contract as a whole, is subject to this jurisdictional limitation. See, e.g., Sutton, supra, at 580–581, 41 S.Ct., at 565–566 (refusing to recognize an implied agreement to pay the fair value of work performed because the term was not "express or implied in fact" in the Government contract for dredging services); Lopez v. A.C. & S., Inc., 858 F.2d 712, 714–715, 716 (C.A.Fed.1988) (a Spearin warranty within an asbestos contract must be implied in fact).

The distinction between "implied in fact" and "implied in law," and the consequent limitation, is well established in our cases. An agreement implied in fact is "founded upon a meeting of minds, which, although not embodied in an express contract, is inferred, as a fact, from conduct of the parties showing, in the light of the surrounding circumstances, their tacit understanding." Baltimore & Ohio R. Co. v. United States, 261 U.S. 592, 597, 43 S.Ct. 425, 426–427, 67 L.Ed. 816 (1923). See also Russell v. United States, 182 U.S. 516, 530, 21 S.Ct. 899, 904, 45 L.Ed. 1210 (1901) ("[T]o give the Court of Claims jurisdiction the demand sued on must be founded on a convention between the parties—'a coming together of minds'"). By contrast, an agreement implied in law is a "fiction of law" where "a promise is imputed to perform a legal duty, as to repay money obtained by fraud or duress." Baltimore & Ohio R. Co., supra, at 597, 43 S.Ct., at 426.

Petitioners do not contend that their contracts contain express warranty or indemnification provisions. Therefore, for them to prevail, they must establish that, based on the circumstances at the time of contracting, there was an implied agreement between the parties to provide the undertakings that petitioners allege. We consider petitioners' warranty-of-specifications and contractual-indemnification claims in turn.

The seminal case recognizing a cause of action for breach of contractual warranty of specifications is United States v. Spearin, 248 U.S. 132, 39 S.Ct. 59, 63 L.Ed. 166 (1918). In that case, Spearin had contracted to build a dry dock in accordance with the Government's plans which called for the relocation of a storm sewer. After Spearin had moved the sewer, but before he had completed the dry dock, the sewer broke and caused the site to flood. The United States refused to pay for the damages and annulled the contract. Spearin filed suit to recover the balance due on his work and lost profits. This Court held that "if the contractor is bound to build according to plans and specifications prepared by [the Government], the contractor will not be responsible for the consequences of defects in the plans and specifications." Id., at 136, 39 S.Ct., at 61. From this, petitioners contend the United States is responsible for costs incurred in defending and settling the third-party tort claims.Neither the warranty nor Spearin extends that far. When the Government provides specifications directing how a contract is to be performed, the Government warrants that the contractor will be able to perform the contract satisfactorily if it follows the specifications. The specifications will not frustrate performance or make it impossible. It is quite logical to infer from the circumstance of one party providing specifications for performance that that party warrants the capability of performance. But this circumstance alone does not support a further inference that would extend the warranty beyond performance to third-party claims against the contractor. In this case, for example, it would be strange to conclude that the United States, understanding the herbicide's military use, actually contemplated a warranty that would extend to sums a manufacturer paid to a third party to settle claims such as are involved in the present action. It seems more likely that the Government would avoid such an obligation, because reimbursement through contract would provide a contractor with what is denied to it through tort law. See Stencel Aero Engineering Co. v. United States, 431 U.S. 666, 97 S.Ct. 2054, 52 L.Ed.2d 665 (1977).

* * *

[The dissenting opinion of Justice Breyer is omitted.]

Notes and Questions

1. Would it have been improper for the contractor in this instance to purchase liability insurance and include the cost of such insurance as part of the fixed price contract for Agent Orange? Why would a contractor choose not to do so?

2. What is the impact of Congress' refusal to grant the Court of Federal Claims (formerly the Claims Court) jurisdiction over implied-in-law contracts? What is the policy basis for not doing so?

3. The Court discusses the *Spearin* decision, reaffirming it and distinguishing it in interesting ways. When the government awards a contract, it wants the contractor to fulfill the contract's specifications. This decision holds, to oversimplify the matter, that the government stands behind those specifications for contract law purposes but not for tort law purposes. Why? And, why would the statutory and administrative authorizations that suffice for the government to have to pay when its specifications result in contractual burdens on the contractor, not suffice to say that the government should pay tort liability burdens?

2. Inspection

Inspection is how the government determines whether the contractor has followed the specifications. As noted, the government may inspect for itself, direct the contractor to maintain a quality control system that does the inspection, or both. The decision as to which system to rely on often depends upon the type of product or service being acquired. Commercial items are generally purchased with no government inspections prior to delivery and reliance on the contractor's quality assurance program, if any. FAR 52.212-4(a). In contrast, contracts for government-unique, non-commercial items will almost always permit government, in-process inspection and may mandate a quality assurance program that meets specific government requirements. FAR 52.246-2. Under reasonable circumstances, the degree and amount of government inspection and mandating of quality assurance requirements will vary with the nature of the item or service being acquired. The more critical the item, the more detailed the requirements. Of note, the government inspection when conducted at the contractor's facility is performed at the contractor's expense.

Where a formal acceptance certificate is lacking, the exercise of control and possession of an item can lead to an implied acceptance by the government. Whether by formal document or implication, final acceptance, in the context of government contracting, means that the contractor has performed in compliance with contract specifications and requirements. In order to recover damages suffered as a result of an inappropriate acceptance, the government must prove the existence of a latent defect, fraud, or gross mistake amounting to fraud that could not have reasonably been discovered at time of acceptance. Without such latent defects or fraud, the government is estopped from later rejecting non-conforming supplies or services that it properly accepted.

When a contractor tenders non-conforming goods, the government can select from various options based upon the provisions of standard contract clauses. The government can simply reject the non-conforming goods or services and demand performance consistent with contract requirements and within the timeframe provided for in the contract. Failure to comply can result in a default termination with excess costs of reprocurement being assessed to the contractor. As an alternative, the government can require repair of non-conforming products or reperformance of non-conforming services at no additional cost to the government. In circumstances where the repair or reperformance cannot be accomplished within the time specified for performance, the government can insist upon additional consideration being received from the contractor, generally in the form of reduced prices.

In certain circumstances, the government can and will accept non-conforming goods and services. Such a discretionary determination is based upon such factors as urgency or financial considerations and the conclusion that the supplies or services will perform their intended services in a safe manner. In such situations the government can and will demand consideration for accepting non-conforming goods.

One particularly important type of contract is the "first-article contract." The government may want to see the contractor produce an example of the product—a prototype—and decide whether to approve it before exercising its purchase options. Thus, a critical phase of examination and testing of the prototype occurs before full-scale performance. Only after approval of the first article does the contractor produce and deliver substantial numbers of units.

First-article contracts suit situations where the contractor has to design and build a new or substantially modified product. In effect, the contractor sets off with just the government contract's "Statement of Work" to explore some terra incognita of production. A contractor faces a substantial risk of default termination if the government comes down hard on its deficiencies.

Inspection of Supplies Clause—Fixed-Price
(Aug 1996)

(a) Definition. "Supplies," as used in this clause, includes but is not limited to raw materials, components, intermediate assemblies, end products, and lots of supplies.

(b) The Contractor shall provide and maintain an inspection system acceptable to the Government covering supplies under this contract and shall tender to the Government for acceptance only supplies that have been inspected in accordance with the inspection system and have been found by the Contractor to be in conformity with contract requirements. As part of the system, the Contractor shall prepare records evidencing all inspections made under the system and the outcome. These records shall be kept complete and made available to the Government during contract performance and for as long afterwards as the contract requires. The Government may perform reviews and evaluations as reasonably necessary to ascertain compliance with this paragraph. These reviews and evaluations shall be conducted in a manner that will not unduly delay the contract work. The right of review, whether exercised or not, does not relieve the Contractor of the obligations under the contract.

(c) The Government has the right to inspect and test all supplies called for by the contract, to the extent practicable, at all places and times, including the period of manufacture, and in any event before acceptance. The Government shall perform inspections and tests in a manner that will not unduly delay the work. The Government assumes no contractual obligation to perform any inspection and test for the benefit of the Contractor unless specifically set forth elsewhere in this contract.

(d) If the Government performs inspection or test on the premises of the Contractor or a subcontractor, the Contractor shall furnish, and shall require subcontractors to furnish, at no increase in contract price, all reasonable facilities and assistance for the safe and convenient performance of these duties. Except as otherwise provided in the contract, the Government shall bear the expense of Government inspections or tests made at other than the Contractor's or subcontractor's premises; provided, that in case of rejection, the Government shall not be liable for any reduction in the value of inspection or test samples.

(e) (1) When supplies are not ready at the time specified by the Contractor for inspection or test, the Contracting Officer may charge to the Contractor the additional cost of inspection or test.

(2) The Contracting Officer may also charge the Contractor for any additional cost of inspection or test when prior rejection makes reinspection or retest necessary.

(f) The Government has the right either to reject or to require correction of nonconforming supplies. Supplies are nonconforming when they are defective in material or workmanship or are otherwise not in conformity with contract requirements. The Government may reject nonconforming supplies with or without disposition instructions.

(g) The Contractor shall remove supplies rejected or required to be corrected....

(h) If the Contractor fails to promptly remove, replace, or correct rejected supplies that are required to be removed or to be replaced or corrected, the Government may either

    (1) by contract or otherwise, remove, replace, or correct the supplies and charge the cost to the Contractor or

    (2) terminate the contract for default. Unless the Contractor corrects or replaces the supplies within the delivery schedule, the Contracting Officer may require their delivery and make an equitable price reduction. Failure to agree to a price reduction shall be a dispute.

(I) (1) If this contract provides for the performance of Government quality assurance at source, and if requested by the Government, the Contractor shall furnish advance notification of the time

        (i) when Contractor inspection or tests will be performed in accordance with the terms and conditions of the contract and

        (ii) when the supplies will be ready for Government inspection.

    (2) The Government's request shall specify the period and method of the advance notification and the Government representative to whom it shall be furnished. Requests shall not require more than 2 workdays of advance notification if the Government representative is in residence in the Contractor's plant, nor more than 7 workdays in other instances.

(j) The Government shall accept or reject supplies as promptly as practicable after delivery, unless otherwise provided in the contract. Government failure to inspect and accept or reject the supplies shall not relieve the Contractor from responsibility, nor impose liability on the Government, for nonconforming supplies.

(k) Inspections and tests by the Government do not relieve the Contractor of responsibility for defects or other failures to meet contract requirements discovered before acceptance. Acceptance shall be conclusive, except for latent defects, fraud, gross mistakes amounting to fraud, or as otherwise provided in the contract.

(l) If acceptance is not conclusive for any of the reasons in paragraph (k) hereof, the Government, in addition to any other rights and remedies provided by law, or under other provisions of this contract, shall have the right to require the Contractor

    (1) at no increase in contract price, to correct or replace the defective or nonconforming supplies at the original point of delivery or at the Contractor's plant at the Contracting Officer's election, and in accordance with a reasonable delivery schedule as may be agreed upon between the Contractor and the Contracting Officer; provided, that the Contracting Officer may require a reduction in contract price if the Contractor fails to meet such delivery schedule, or

(2) within a reasonable time after receipt by the Contractor of notice of defects or nonconformance, to repay such portion of the contract as is equitable under the circumstances if the Contracting Officer elects not to require correction or replacement. When supplies are returned to the Contractor, the Contractor shall bear the transportation cost from the original point of delivery to the Contractor's plant and return to the original point when that point is not the Contractor's plant. If the Contractor fails to perform or act as required in (1) or (2) above and does not cure such failure within a period of 10 days (or such longer period as the Contracting Officer may authorize in writing) after receipt of notice from the Contracting Officer specifying such failure, the Government shall have the right by contract or otherwise to replace or correct such supplies and charge to the Contractor the cost occasioned the Government thereby.

Appeal of Technical Ordnance, Inc.

1989 WL 48024 (A.S.B.C.A.), 89-2 BCA 21,818, ASBCA No. 34,748
April 4, 1989

OPINION BY ADMINISTRATIVE JUDGE LIPMAN

The Government terminated the contract for default due to appellant's failure to satisfy the contract's first article testing requirements. Appellant seeks conversion of the default termination to a termination for the convenience of the Government.

FINDINGS OF FACT

The Department of the Navy, Navy Ships Parts Control Center (the Government) awarded contract No. N00104-84-C-A079 to Technical Ordnance, Inc. (appellant) on 25 April 1984. The contract required appellant to provide 6247 explosive bolts for the MK46 torpedo exercise head at $62.50 each, or a fixed price of $390,437.50.

The explosive bolts fasten onto the exercise head of the MK46 missile. During fleet training, at a certain point in the missile's run the exercise head gives a signal to the bolt to explode. The bolt's explosion drops two lead weights. The release of the weights results in the missile achieving a positive buoyancy so that the Navy can recover the missile after the exercise run. If the explosive bolt fails to operate, the weapon may sink (and the Navy may lose an expensive weapon) or the weapon may float at an unknown level under the water (which could result in its recovery by someone other than the United States).

The contract contained the FIRST ARTICLE APPROVAL-GOVERNMENT TESTING, ASPR 1-1906(b) (1969 SEP) clause. This clause indicated that "if the Contracting Officer disapproves any first article, the Contractor shall be deemed to have failed to make delivery within the meaning of the 'Default' clause of this contract, and this contract shall be subject to termination for default...." The delivery schedule required appellant to provide 50 first article samples by 24 July 1984.

The contract incorporated by reference MILITARY SPECIFICATION CARTRIDGES, EXPLOSIVE BOLT (For Torpedoes MK 46 All Mods) MIL-C-81093A. MIL-C-81093A stated, in pertinent part:

> 4.3.1 First article sample.... Acceptance of the first article sample shall be based on no defects in the sample. Further production of the cartridge by the supplier prior to approval of the first article sample, shall be at the supplier's risk....

* * *

4.5.6.2 Firing Test. Each cartridge to be tested shall be mounted in the fracturable bolt accepted to Dwg 2132278 and tested under the test circuit of FIGURE 3 and the test configuration of FIGURE 4. The firing signal shall be 0.5 plus or minus 0.02 ampere, applied alternately to the AB and CD bridgewire circuits in any group of functional samples. The firing signal shall be monitored and the magnitude and the duration of the signal recorded.... Acceptance criteria for the firing test shall be as follows:

(a) A 15 millisecond maximum firing delay, as shown by the duration of the electrical signal.

(b) Detonation after ignition.

(c) Complete fracture of the bolt.

Appellant incorporated MIL-C-81093A paragraphs 4.5.1 and 4.5.6.2 into its inspection plan and used the inspection plan in administration of the contract.

Appellant's first two first article test submissions failed to gain the Government's acceptance. The first failure resulted from firing deficiencies. The second first article test failure resulted from leakage problems.

In a 14 January 1987 report, the Government summarized test results from appellant's third first article test—a preproduction test sample of 50 explosive bolts submitted by appellant on 6 November 1986. The report stated:

2. TEST RESULTS

* * *

b. Test U—Firing Test 0 degrees F

Two bolts failed to meet the 15 millisecond bolt separation requirement. ***

3. CONCLUSION

It is concluded that the explosive bolts ... manufactured by Technical Ordnance, Incorporated ... failed to meet the requirements of [MIL-C-81093A].

The report also noted that: (1) although certain serial numbers were illegible, this was a discrepancy, not a defect, and (2) although 10 of 44 bolts leaked, none failed the post fire leak test requirements.

A 15 December 1986 memorandum from the Naval Undersea Warfare Engineering Station to the Navy Ships Parts Control Center recommended termination of the contract due to (1) the 15.98 and 16.13 millisecond firing times and (2) the illegible serial numbers.

The Government's test engineer tested the explosive bolts, and he used the specifications and the unpublished Naval Undersea Warfare Engineering Station STANDARD EVALUATION PROCEDURE FOR PREPRODUCTION EVALUATION OF THE EXPLOSIVE BOLT, DWG 2539131, PROCEDURE NO. WCB-T-056....

The manner in which the Government tested the explosive bolts differed from the specifications in both equipment and procedure....

By letter of 23 February 1987, the contracting officer terminated the contract for default. The only test failure cited for the third first article submission was the failure of the two bolts to meet the 15 millisecond maximum bolt separation time.

Appellant filed a timely appeal....

DECISION

The contract for the production and supply of explosive bolts was terminated for default due to the alleged failure of two of 50 bolts in the first article submittal to meet specification requirements for bolt separation. Appellant seeks a conversion of the default termination into one for the convenience of the Government based upon the Government's testing procedures.

Appellant cites Bula Forge, Inc., PSBCA No. 1490, 87-3 BCA p 20,159, for the proposition that the Government bears the burden of proving that the Government properly rejected the first article submission. In Bula Forge, the Postal Board explained:

> To support the default termination or rejection of a product because of failure to meet contract requirements, Respondent has the burden of proving the contractor's default. Roosevelt Components, Inc., ASBCA No. 17970, 74-2 BCA p 10,661. If it makes a prima facie case, the burden of going forward with evidence then shifts to the Appellant. Rohr-Plessy Corp., PSBCA No. 36, 76-2 BCA p 11,995. However, the ultimate burden of persuasion to prove by a preponderance of evidence that the rejection or termination was proper remains with the Government. Cf. Harco Manufacturing Co., ASBCA No. 27567, 85-1 BCA p 17,926.

(87-3 BCA at 102,034) We focus, therefore, on whether the Government has met its burden of proving, by a preponderance of the evidence, that the failure of the first article submission and resulting termination for default were proper.

The Government concedes that its testing practices deviated from MIL-C-81093A. The Government added a Government designed and built pulse generator to the constant power source. The Government added a counter to test apparatus and read the test results from the counter in lieu of the specified oscilloscope. Finally, the Government failed to record the testing with a camera.

The Government cites Solar Laboratories, ASBCA No. 19269, 74-2 BCA p 10,897, for the proposition that a deviation from contractual test procedures does not invalidate the test results as a matter of law. In Solar Laboratories, where the Government substituted thermocouples for mercury thermometers, the Board found that testing not prescribed in the contract could be used as a basis for rejection of contract items, provided that the tests did not impose a more stringent standard than the contract or the testing method prescribed. The Board explained:

> If the contractor shows that the testing was not in accordance with the contract, the burden shifts back to the Government to show comparability of the testing with the contractually prescribed method....
>
> In this case, it is undisputed that the Government's testing found that appellant's first articles failed to meet contractual heating requirements. It is likewise undisputed that the Government's testing procedures departed from the contract in three respects. Hence, the threshold question for us is whether the Government has established the comparability of its testing with contractually required testing.

(74-2 BCA at 51,859–60) To the extent that the Board there found comparability between the thermometers and the thermocouples, we distinguish the holding in Solar Laboratories.

In Solar Laboratories, all thermocouples were calibrated against a National Bureau of Standards thermometer before and after the testing and between the third and fourth test cycles, 74-2 BCA at 51,858, the Government brought forth extensive expert testimony including comparability experimentation establishing that there was no material difference in the results, 74-2 BCA at 51,861, the Government curtailed the tests due to the contractor's excessive failures, 74-2 BCA at 51,862, and the Government choice to use thermocouples derived from the thermocouples' automatic recording device which resulted in considerable personnel time savings, 74-2 BCA at 51,861.

In the present appeal, the Government used a self-constructed pulse generator which lacked instruction or calibration manuals. In addition, although the Government's witnesses asserted a preference for counters over oscilloscopes, the Government presented no evidence of their comparability. Further, unlike the excessive temperature failures in Solar Laboratories, the present appeal presents deviations of less than 2 milliseconds on two out of fifty bolts. Finally, the Government here presented no evidence that savings in time or effort would result from (1) its failure to use the camera, (2) its addition of the pulse generator, or (3) the substitution of the counter for the oscilloscope.

The Government deviated from the contractually specified test procedures. Moreover, the Government failed to show that the results achieved are comparable to those under the contractually designed procedures. The contract required that the Government record, in a specific manner, the results, as obtained by specific equipment, of these destructive tests. We cannot find the Government's rejection of the first articles to be proper. See Mega Construction, Inc., ASBCA No. 32127, 88-1 BCA p 20,427; Solar Laboratories, supra.

We sustain appellant's appeal, and the default termination is converted to a termination for the convenience of the Government.

Notes and Questions

1. First article testing as a form of inspection and acceptance is appropriate in four circumstances. First, it is appropriate when a contractor has not previously furnished the product to the Government. Second, it is appropriate when the contractor has previously furnished the item, but there have been subsequent changes in processes or specifications, production has been discontinued for an extended period of time, or problems surfaced with products previously submitted and accepted. Third, it is appropriate where the product is described by a performance specification. Finally, it is appropriate where it is essential to have an approved first article to serve as a manufacturing standard. FAR 9.303. Which of the above cited reasons could have been used to justify the use of first article testing in *Technical Ordnance, Inc.*?

2. First article testing is generally not used for research and development contracts, products already on a qualified products list wherein the products have previously been tested, commercial products, and products built to detailed technical specifications FAR 9.304.

3. When the government imposes first article testing on contractors, the FAR mandates that the contractor must be apprised of the performance or other characteristics that the first article must meet for approval and the tests to which the first article will be subjected for approval. FAR 9.306. The failure by the government to abide by the stated tests can release the contractor from the consequences of a default termination. However, note the remedy sought in *Technical Ordnance, Inc.* — a conversion of a default termination to one for the convenience of the government. The failure of a contractor to provide the desired government product, even when the failure is due to unclear government direction, will most often result not in the contractor receiving the benefit of its bargain (i.e., its profit), but merely avoiding excess costs of reprocurement associated with a default termination.

4. Under certain circumstances a contractor may be able to use the standard of "reasonable" government inspections as a defense to government claims. For example, if the government interferes with the performance of a contract through excessive supervision, by making it difficult for the contractor's employees to complete their work, or conducting multiple inspections, the contractor may be able to recover the costs of delay as well and receive an extension of time for completing the contract schedule. In addition, a contractor may recover costs if the government changes the location of the inspection or the contractor could not have reasonably anticipated the inspection at the time of contracting. An equitable adjustment may be proper if the government imposes an inspection standard stricter than the industry custom.

Mann Chemical Laboratories, Inc., Plaintiff v. United States of America, Defendant

Civ. A. No. 57-300
United States District Court for the District of Massachusetts
182 F.Supp. 40
March 2, 1960

SWEENEY, Chief Judge.

This is an action brought under the authority of 28 U.S.C. § 1346(a)(2), and is alleged to arise out of an express contract between the parties. The contract was for the furnishing of certain bottles of water purification tablets on specified dates. These tablets were intended for the use of the Armed Forces.

The case comes before this Court after decision by the Armed Services Board of Contract Appeals, hereinafter referred to as the 'Board', and in accordance with the Court's Order of December 29, 1958, D.C. 174 F.Supp. 563, was tried on the record and not 'de novo'. The plaintiff was allowed to testify at length on the facts surrounding the rejection of the tablets because of their spotted appearance.

Findings of Fact

The plaintiff contracted to furnish the defendant on specified dates with a large number of bottles of water purification tablets. The delivery dates in question were May 5th, May 20th, and June 5th, all in the year 1951. The plaintiff's claim is divisible into two parts: (1) Damages for wrongful termination of the contract with relation to the plaintiff's inability to secure acceptable bottles, and (2) Damages caused to the plaintiff by reason of the government's failure to accept the tablets themselves when proffered.

Both claims were processed before the Contracting Officer and the Board, and were decided against the plaintiff. The Board specifically found on reconsideration of its prior decision that the bottle delay was not excusable in that 'the condition necessary for holding the default to have been excusable was not shown'. The record amply supports this finding, and in fact at the hearing before this Court the plaintiff limited its evidence and argument to the second phase of this case.

Next we are met with the question whether the government unreasonably delayed the acceptance of the proffered tablets to the damage of the plaintiff, thereby breaching the contract. This Court is limited in its adjudication to the question whether the administrative decision by the Board was supported by the evidence and was not capricious or arbitrary. A review of the record taken in conjunction with the evidence presented at the trial convinces the Court that the plaintiff is not entitled to be compensated for its expenses attendant upon the defendant's delay in immediately accepting the tablets delivered on the three dates in question.

Late in June or in early July the plaintiff anticipated that certain brown spots would appear on what should be white tablets, and communicated this fact to the defendant, advising it that the spots were the result of excess moisture due to high humidity, and that they were not impurities. The government, in spite of the representations by the plaintiff, refused to accept the tablets until after an independent analysis of the tablets had been made. As a result of this analysis, the government, in December of 1951, issued shipping instructions to the plaintiff, and accepted the tablets in question. Thereafter the plaintiff submitted claims against the government for the wrongful termination of and for breach of the contract by reason of its failure to accept the deliveries as and when proffered.

The tablets were for the purification of what might otherwise be contaminated water, and it could be reasonably assumed that they were to be used under extreme conditions attendant upon the military invasion of new territory, and were for the safety and well being of the invading troops. While the contract did not call for white tablets, nevertheless the appearance of brown spots was not common, and suggested the probable presence of a foreign material.

Actually, if the quality of the tablets was impaired by the brown spots, they were worthless for the purpose intended, and this Court feels that the government was quite right in the careful steps that it took to be sure that the tablets were in strict conformance with the specifications. They could hardly do less, having in mind the purpose for which the tablets were intended. I find that the failure to accept the tablets when first offered because of their appearance was reasonable. The methods of sampling and testing by the governments were normal under the circumstances, and fully supported the Board's decision.

Conclusions of Law

From the foregoing I find and rule that judgment should be entered for the defendant.

3. Acceptance

When the government "accepts," it takes ownership of supplies, or approves services, provided as performance of the contract. Acceptance matters because the government thereby gives up some, but not all, its remedies for defects. To put it differently, the government, by accepting, acknowledges that the supplies or services conform with contract requirements. The "Inspection of Supplies for defects clause provides that government acceptance of the contract work is conclusive "except for latent defects, fraud, gross mistakes amounting to fraud, or as otherwise provided in the contract."

Before the government accepts, typically either the contractor provides a certificate of conformance, or the government takes quality assurance action. The government may evidence by executing an acceptance certificate, an inspection or receiving report, or a commercial shipping document. The government also accepts construction projects. It may inspect and accept projects by phases or parts of the work

The government may also make implied acceptance. For goods, that means retention or use of the goods. By contrast, in construction, under the "Use and Possession Prior to Completion" clause, the government's possession or use is not acceptance.

Sometimes, the government catches the tender of nonconforming goods or services. Typically, contractors then get an opportunity to replace or correct such goods or services. This usually must occur without additional cost to the government. When the government accepts supplies and subsequently pays for them, with fully knowledge that it terminated for default because of the defect in those supplies. The government may lose the right to rescind its acceptance. Otherwise, the government may reject nonconforming supplies or services.

After acceptance, much of the legal focus in this subject concerns the government's rights (i.e., to revoke acceptance) with respect to its belated discovery of nonconformance "post-acceptance." One exception to acceptance consists of "latent" defects, which could not be discovered by a reasonable inspection. The government has a heavy burden to prove that a defect was latent. Expert testimony is typically crucial. And, the government must assert latent defect claims in a timely fashion.

The government has used the concept of a "gross mistake" amounting to fraud more frequently than it has used the fraud theory. A gross mistake consists of a mistake so serious or uncalled for as not to be reasonably expected or justifiable.

Also, the government may revoke acceptance for "fraud." A contractor would show fraud when it has intent to deceive the government, makes a statement or representation it knows to be untrue, and the government accepts the contract item in reliance on that misrepresentation. Ordinarily, in a case of fraud, the government has other and stronger remedies in the criminal and civil statutes. However, for revocation of acceptance, the government need only show a preponderance of the evidence, while the criminal and civil remedies have higher evidentiary burdens.

Notes and Questions

1. Testing methods and inspection standards are subject to a reasonableness standard. The actual intended use of the product or service and the usual quality of such products or services under similar conditions form the basis of a reasonableness test. How did the court apply the reasonableness test in *Mann Chemical Laboratories, Inc.*?

2. As noted, the government cannot reject what it has previously accepted absent certain matters, notably the existence of latent defects. A latent defect is one that existed at time of acceptance and could not be discovered by ordinary and reasonable care or by a reasonable inspection. It is the duty of the government to prove that the defect is latent. *See e.g.*, FAR 52.246-12 (Inspection of Construction clause); FAR 52.246-21 (Warranty of Construction clause); *Windsor Mount Joy Mutual Ins. Co., v. Giragosian*, 57 F.3d 50 (1st Cir. 1995) (holding that the district court's finding that a latent defect caused the boat to sink was not inconsistent with the insured being "on notice of the boat's unseaworthy condition before setting sail," when the insured was not aware of the defect.); Mark S. Jaeger, *Contractor Liability for Design Defects under the Inspection Clause: Latent Design Defects—a Sleeping Giant?* 21 Pub. L. J. 331 (1992); *Kaminer Constr. Corp. v. United States*, 203 Ct.Cl. 182 (1973) (while inspection would have revealed defect, requiring an inspection to locate sixteen bolts out of 12,000 bolts was unreasonable).

3. When can and will the government rely upon contractor inspection? Generally, the government relies on the contractor to complete all necessary inspections to determine if supplies and services conform to quality requirements. *See* FAR 46.202-2. However, subsection "b" of the same FAR provision allows the government to consider the nature of supplies and services, the potential for economic loss due to defect, the likelihood of contractor correction of any defects, and the cost of a government inspection when determining if the government is not to rely on a contractor inspection. *See* FAR 46.202-3 (standard inspection requirements for contractors); FAR 46.202-4 (quality requirements for inspections for complex contracts).

4. The contract should specify the terms of acceptance of contractor supplies. *See* FAR 46.503 (discussing the place of acceptance). When the contracting officer accepts supplies

either formally or impliedly from the contractor, the government is effectively acknowl-edging that the supplies comply with the terms of the contract. *See* FAR 46.501 (denot-ing usual method of acceptance is by a written certificate or report).

Appeal of Fischer Imaging Corporation
VABCA No. 6343
2002 WL 31424586
October 22, 2002

See Chapter 9.

In the Matter of Instruments for Industry, Inc., Debtor-Appellee, v. United States of America, Appellant

United States Court of Appeals, Second Circuit. 496 F.2d 1157
Argued March 12, 1974
Decided May 28, 1974

Before HAYS and MANSFIELD, Circuit Judges, and DAVIS, Judge.

DAVIS, Judge:

Instruments for Industry, Inc. ('IFI'), the appellee, entered into a contract in 1960 with the Bureau of Naval Weapons of the Navy Department for twenty units of electronic countermeasure equipment. The agreement contained a standard form 'Disputes' clause requiring initial administrative determination of disputes arising under the contract. The equipment was delivered and accepted by the Government. Under the contract terms in-spection was made, and acceptance finalized, at the contractor's plant. In 1965, within one year of delivery, the contracting officer notified IFI that the equipment had allegedly been defective upon delivery and acceptance, and that IFI owed more than three hun-dred ninety thousand dollars under the 'Guaranty' clause of the contract. However, no final contracting officer's decision to this effect was issued until July 1972.

* * *

In 1966 IFI filed for a Chapter XI arrangement under the Bankruptcy Act in the United States District Court for the Eastern District of New York. A few months later, the United States filed proof of claim in these proceedings for the amount said to be due because of the faulty equipment, as well as for an uncontested balance owing under another con-tract. IFI moved to delete the Navy's claim for the defects, arguing that final acceptance under the 'Inspection' clause prevented recovery, but the Bankruptcy Judge denied the motion and designated the Armed Services Board of Contract Appeals as a fact-finding body to liquidate the Navy's claim. On review, the District Court reversed this order. The court decided that the Navy's rights were cut short by the 'Inspection' clause, and ex-punged the claim. This appeal tests the correctness of that legal ruling.

This is another instance of the frequent tension in federal procurement between two form clauses, both bearing on the same general subject and both inserted into the same government contract without explicit reconciliation. The 'Guaranty' clause, under which the Navy makes its claim, provides in relevant part:

> The Contractor guaranties that at the time of delivery thereof, the supplies provided for under this contract will be free from any defects in material or work-manship and will conform to the requirements of the contract. Notice of any

such defect or nonconformance shall be given by the Government to the Contractor within one year of the delivery of the defective or nonconforming supplies. If required by the Government within a reasonable time after such notice, the Contractor shall with all possible speed correct or replace the defective or nonconforming supplies or part thereof.... If the Government does not require correction or replacement of defective or nonconforming supplies, the Contractor, if required by the Contracting Officer within a reasonable time after the notice of defect or nonconformance, shall repay such portion of the contract price of the supplies as is equitable in the circumstances.

This clause shall not limit any rights of the Government under the clause of this contract entitled 'Inspection.'

The section of the 'Inspection' clause relied upon by the contractor is:

(d) ... Except as otherwise provided in this contract, acceptance shall be conclusive except as regards latent defects, fraud, or such gross mistakes as amount to fraud.

At no time has the Government contended that the defects it claims to have discovered were latent, or that any fraud or gross mistakes amounting to fraud were in any way involved. Nor is it asserted that the defects surfaced or came into being after delivery. The only issue is whether the Navy's rights under the 'Guaranty' clause, with respect to pre-existing non-latent defects, survive acceptance under the 'Inspection' provision.

It is very difficult to harmonize the face of the two clauses which do not in words or by clear inference refer to each other. On the one hand, if the 'Guaranty' article preserves the Government's rights to order correction of or payment for non-latent defects for one year after delivery—as it seems to say—then the earlier acceptance is clearly not 'conclusive' as the 'Inspection' clause explicitly declares for non-latent deficiencies. On the other, if the 'Guaranty' clause in this contract is limited in application—because of the presence of the 'Inspection' provision—to latent defects, then its actual scope would be less than its literal terms. The 'Guaranty' article, thus restrictively read, would give the Government a flat right to correction of, or price adjustment for, latent defects for one full year after delivery, but with a co-existing further right, if the circumstances prove it reasonable, thereafter to revoke acceptance under the 'Inspection' clause with respect to latent defects.

It has been suggested (see Federal Pacific Electric Co., IBCA 334, 1964 BCA P4494) that full reconciliation of the literal terms of the two clauses can be attained through the prefatory phrase of the 'Inspection' article—'Except as otherwise provided in this contract.' This language, it is said, refers to the 'Guaranty' clause, and on the assumption the latter article 'provides otherwise' the 'Inspection' provision becomes wholly inoperative for non-latent defects.[7] The obvious vice of this suggested adjustment is that it subverts the clear import of the most important aspect of subpart (d) of the 'Inspection' article—'acceptance shall be conclusive except as regards latent defects, fraud or such gross mistakes as amount to fraud'—which affirmatively gives significant rights to the contractor in the absence of the stated exceptions.

* * *

---

7. Taken by itself, the 'Guaranty' provision seems to cover all types of defects, latent and non-latent, in its twin references to 'defects in materials and workmanship' and 'conform(ity) to the requirements of the contract.'

The upshot is that the combination of the two mismatched clauses in this one agreement, without adequate textual harmonization, makes them both ambiguous and evokes the familiar principle of contra proferentem — 'the general maxim that a contract should be construed most strongly against the drafter, which in this case was the United States.' United States v. Seckinger, 397 U.S. 203, 210, 90 S.Ct. 880, 884, 25 L.Ed.2d 224 (1970).... 'This oft-repeated and much-applied rule serves important purposes. It puts the risk of ambiguity, lack of clarity, and absence of proper warning on the drafting party which could have forestalled the controversy; it pushes the drafters toward improving contractual forms; and it saves contractors from hidden traps not of their own making.' Sturm v. United States, 421 F.2d 723, 727, 190 Ct.Cl. 691, 697 (1970).

There can be no doubt that the interpretation favoring the contractor is 'reasonable and practical.' See United States v. Seckinger, supra, 397 U.S. at 210–211. The express terms of the 'Inspection' clause are given full effect as to non-latent defects, and, absent an acceptance expressly and reasonably conditioned upon the Government's later inspection of the supplies and equipment, the one-year-after-delivery portion of the 'Guaranty' article is confined to latent defects. See notes 5 and 6, supra, and the pertinent text. That is not an unreasonable or unacceptable rationalization, in the absence of more precise guidelines. It is preferable to the opposite reading which would give full scope to the literal terms of the 'Guaranty' article, at the cost of obliterating the 'acceptance' portion of the 'Inspection' clause. There is a less drastic intrusion upon both the contract language and the reasonable expectations of the parties.

* * *

It follows that the Government has no proper claim and that the District Court was correct in expunging it.

Affirmed.

Notes and Questions

Instruments for Industry underlines the Inspection Clause's powerful policy of finality in government acceptance. It is a particularly striking policy because, in contrast to so many government contracting policies, it is a policy for protecting the contractor against the government, not vice versa. Is the source of the policy just a notion of fairness toward contractors in the form of repose? Or, does the policy work, in the long run, for the government's benefit as well, by such means as reducing the contractor's need to price into its bid a risk premium to cover post-acceptance government claims?

C. Government Assistance, Including Progress Payments and Prompt Payment, and Sureties

The government's system of payment, bonding, and other assistance such as furnishing property is a major, complex topic. The system seeks to resolve several competing tensions. On the one side, contractors for the government, like private contractors, need a system of payment, financing, and assistance that sustains them. On the other hand, the government has both its public fiscal constraints and its policy reasons, for caution about going too far in such sustaining of contractors. These tensions have produced a variety of mixed and compromised arrangements, some effectively combining legal strictness and practicality, some not.

As to payments, the first question concerns what comes first, contractor performance or government payment. This question arises in basic (private) contract law, as the issue of the order of performance, also known as "constructive conditions of performance." In each situation of exchanging performance for payment, either the exchange occurs simultaneously, or one precedes the other; at common law, usually performance precedes payment, but by contract, interim or advance payments may be arranged by explicit provision. For government contracting, the various possibilities get arranged by explicit choice of applicable FAR provisions and contract clauses.

In general, the government starts out with a strong preference for completion of the work before payment. That serves the public fiscal constraint that public funds be spent for Congressionally and administratively decided public purposes, namely, the work, which is most simply and directly assured if the work is completed before payment. That also avoids the practical risks, which the government prefers not to carry, of payments before completion. But for many kinds of contracts the government does provide partial or "progress" payments, paying as the work is done, before completion. Under limited circumstances, the government even makes "advance" payments, paying before the work is done, effectively loaning the contractor funding.

The second question regarding payments concerns the government making payments promptly once due. Given the government's elaborate fiscal controls and bureaucratic complexities, government agencies readily fall into the practice of paying contractors late. However, contractors need payments on time to meet their own responsibilities without undue burdens of financing. So, Congress passed the Prompt Payment Act, providing limited but definite rights to contractors to obtain their payments on time.

For the government's assurance of protection if contractors do not meet their obligations, the government requires the posting of various kinds of security. Most significantly, the government may require contractors to post performance bonds, especially contractors on construction-type projects who receive progress payments. Such performance bonds create a three-sided relationship involving the government, the contractor, and the surety that stands behind the performance bond. When the contractor may falter, the government contracting officer must balance between making payments to and expecting performance from the contractor, or, turning to the surety, expecting performance from the surety but also therefore giving notice and handling payments as the surety would want.

Another large area concerns other non-funding assistance the government provides to contractors, in terms of government-furnished property. The government can provide help to contractors ranging from limited special tools or equipment, all the way to entire facilities that the contractor merely operates. While common themes and tensions run through all these areas, in each distinct statutes, FAR provisions, clauses, and doctrines have produced whole separate bodies of law.

For further discussions of the issues in this section, see: Ronald A. May, Russell I. Marmor, R. Earl Welbaum & David D. Crane, *Annual Survey of Fidelity and Surety Law,* 62 Def. Couns. J. 434 (1995)(re: remedies for sureties); Keith Witten, *Current Developments in Bad Faith Litigation Involving the Performance and Payment Bond Surety,* 28 Tort & Ins. L.J. 611 (1993); Steven N. Tomanelli, *Rights and Obligations Concerning Government-Furnished Property,* 24 Pub. Cont. L.J. 413 (1995); Steven N. Tomanelli, *Competitive Advantage Arising from Contractor Possession of Government-Furnished Property,* 23 Pub. Cont. L.J. 243 (1994); Bank of Washington, N.A , *Bank's Claim to Defaulting Contractor's Money Slightly Better,* 11 No. 9 Andrews Gov't Cont. Litig. Rep. 7 (May 20, 1998).

1. Government-Furnished Property

The government may furnish property to help contractors. FAR 45.101 defines Government Furnished Property ("GFP") as "property in the possession of or directly acquired by the government and made available to the contractor." Such property may be real, personal, tangible, or intangible. The government may provide "material" (that gets incorporated into or expended in performance like supplies), motor vehicles (under quite restricted circumstances), "special tooling" and "special test equipment" (bearing on the particular supplies or services), and an umbrella term called "production and research property."

Among the subjects covered by the law regarding GFP, the government limits the advantage of bidders already in possession of GFP vis-a-vis others without it. Accordingly, under the FAR, the government has a duty to provide GFP under the terms of the contract, including related data and information, in a timely fashion and in a suitable manner for the intended use. *See* FAR 52.245(a). If the government does not provide GFP by the required time and this causes a delay, the contractor may receive an equitable adjustment. *See* FAR 52-245-2(a)(4). However, the government can furnish property "as is" or with disclaimers.

The FAR and standard clauses provide elaborate rules for the protection of the government's interest in all such government-furnished property. The government wants clear record-keeping, amounting to a written property control system. Also, the government wants allocation of responsibility for damage. For loss or damage to the GFP while it is in the contractor's possession, a contractor with a competitive fixed price contract will be held liable regardless of fault. In contrast, for a negotiated fixed price contract not based on competition or market prices, the contractor only bears a limited risk. When the contractor no longer needs the GFP, it must prepare a contractor inventory schedule.

Additionally, the government has provisions as to title that protect the government's interest against risks from contractor insolvency. Title to government-furnished property remains in the government.

For further discussion, see Steven N. Tomanelli, *Rights and Obligations Concerning Government-Furnished Property*, 24 Pub. Cont. L.J. 413 (1995); Steven N. Tomanelli, *Competitive Advantage Arising from Contractor Possession of Government-Furnished Property*, 23 Pub. Cont. L.J. 243 (1994).

Franklin Pavkov Construction Co., Appellant, v. James G. Roche, Secretary of the Air Force, Appellee

United States Court of Appeals, Federal Circuit
279 F.3d 989, No. 01-1010
Decided: Jan. 28, 2002

Before CLEVENGER, GAJARSA and DYK, Circuit Judges.

GAJARSA, Circuit Judge.

This is an appeal from the Armed Services Board of Contract Appeals (the "Board"). On appeal, Franklin Pavkov Construction Company ("FPC") seeks an equitable adjustment for claims arising from a fixed-price contract to install four sets of three-story stairs on two dormitory buildings at Shaw Air Force Base, South Carolina (the "Project"). FPC argued that it received defective specifications and defective government-furnished material, and that it was entitled to other adjustments. The Board denied all but one of FPC's claims. We affirm the Board's decision.

I. BACKGROUND

On October 26, 1995, the Twentieth Contracting Squadron at Shaw Air Force Base, South Carolina (the "Government") awarded the Project to FPC. The Project had been previously bid and contracted to a different contractor in 1991. The previous attempt to implement the project was unsuccessful.

* * *

On October 26, 1995, the Government awarded the Project to FPC as a fixed-price contract for $158,100. The completion date was scheduled for November 26, 1996.

* * *

The contract for the Project also included a short-form Government Furnished Property ("GFP") clause. This clause required the Government to supply GFP identified in the list. Federal Acquisition Regulations ("FAR") Government-Furnished Property (Short Form) § 52.245-4(a); 48 C.F.R. § 52.245-4(a) (2000). However, the contract did not explicitly obligate the government to provide shop drawings as part of the GFP.

Just before FPC started construction, the Government moved the purportedly listed GFP to a fence-enclosed but unlocked location 100 to 200 yards from the job site. The Government made two attempts to meet with Vince Pavkov in November 1995 to take an inventory of the GFP. Vince Pavkov cancelled the first planned meeting. At the second meeting in late November 1995, the parties met at the fenced location and began to take the inventory. However, before completing the inventory, Vince Pavkov had to leave. One of the items that the parties did not inventory were the "stair nosings," devices that prevent slipping on the steps. The GFP list indicated that the Government was to supply eighty-seven stair nosings, but when Vince Pavkov later went to retrieve them he found only ten in the fence-enclosed area. FPC advised the Government of the missing nosings on May 14, 1996, approximately six months after the GFP was delivered. Fabricating and procuring the missing stair nosings had a long lead-time. In order to avoid delaying the Project, FPC obtained permission from the Government to use a substitute aluminum channel.

FPC recognized another problem with the GFP. The configuration of some of the parts caused FPC to question whether all of the stairs were "typical" as shown on the 1995 drawings. After it discovered the D & H drawings, FPC determined that some stair directions were not typical as indicated. The direction of a set of stairs is the direction in which they rise or fall when viewing the side of the building. A note on the D & H drawings indicated that the stair parts may be matched to stairs running in specific directions. This knowledge made the work go more smoothly for FPC. However, for one of the buildings, FPC had to unexpectedly construct new concrete forms for stairs running in the opposite direction in order to use the GFP because some of the stair railings would only fit stairs running in the reverse direction. FPC did not bring the stair direction problem to the attention of the Government until the claim was filed. On March 21, 1997, the Government deemed all the work acceptable and formally accepted it as of that date.

On March 28, 1997, FPC submitted a certified claim to the contracting officer for additional costs and other adjustments, totaling $117,129, and resulting from, among other items, the allegedly defective specifications and the missing GFP. On June 17, 1997, the contracting officer denied FPC's claim. FPC appealed the contracting officer's decision to the Board.

The Board ruled against FPC for all but one count of its claim. *See Franklin Pavkov Constr. Co.*, 2000 ASBCA LEXIS 136, 00-2 B.C.A. (CCH) ¶ 31,100, 153,597, ASBCA No. 50828, 2000 WL 1279909 (Aug. 29, 2000).

* * *

With respect to the GFP, the Board held that delivery occurred when the Government and Vince Pavkov met in the fence-enclosed location near the job site to inventory the material in late November 1995, before commencement of the work. *Id.* at 153,609. The GFP clause in the contract required FPC to give written notice if the GFP is not suitable for its intended use. The Board reasoned that the notice must be timely and therefore that the contract implicitly required FPC to inventory the GFP even though the contract did not explicitly have a clause requiring the parties to conduct a joint inventory. FPC gave the Government notice of unsuitable GFP in May 1996, six months after the Government and Vince Pavkov first met in the fence-enclosed area. The Board found that this notice was not timely. *Id.* The Board denied FPC's requested relief except as to one count.

On appeal, FPC asserts that it is entitled to equitable adjustment for three reasons: ... (2) the GFP was inadequate and incomplete because it did not comply with the 1995 drawings and this caused FPC additional cost to build additional concrete forms; and (3) the Government never properly discharged its duty to deliver the GFP and is therefore responsible for the costs to replace the missing material. We have jurisdiction under 41 U.S.C. § 607. *See* 41 U.S.C. § 607(g)(1)(A) (1994).

* * *

III. DISCUSSION

* * *

FPC next argues that the Government never completed delivery of the GFP. Its logic is as follows. The contract did not state a time or location for delivery. Thus, a reasonable delivery is required. Only after delivery is accepted does the risk of loss shift to FPC. The GFP remained in the care, custody and control of the Government until FPC came to the fence-enclosed area and retrieved it piece by piece. Thus, FPC alleges error by the Board in its holding that delivery occurred when the Government and FPC met in the fence-enclosed area to inventory the GFP in November 1995, which was only a partial inventory due to Vince Pavkov leaving during the inventory process.

The Board decided the GFP issue against FPC on two bases. First, it found that the parties completed delivery and that the risk of loss shifted to FPC. Second, it found that FPC did not timely notify the Government that there were problems with the GFP.

Both bases go to the question of each parties' respective obligations for delivery of GFP. Although the Government is obligated to supply the GFP, delivery is not a one-sided affair. Delivery is the voluntary transfer of possession. *See* U.C.C. § 1-201(14).[3] A successful transfer requires each party to fulfill its role in conveying the physical possession or control of the GFP. The time, place and manner of delivery, if not specified in the contract or by subsequent agreement of the parties, should be a reasonable time, place and manner that enables the contractor to perform under the contract. *See Blaine Co. v. United States,* 157 Ct.Cl. 53, 57 (1962); U.C.C. § 2-503(1)(a). In other words, absent agreement otherwise, the Government must "put and hold [the GFP] at the [contractor's] disposi-

---

3. Although the Federal Acquisition Regulations are extensive and usually specify the meaning of terms in government contracts, in the past we have relied on the Uniform Commercial Code ("U.C.C.") in cases such as this where a gap needs to be filled or the meaning of a term requires supplementation. *See Texas Instruments Inc. v. United States,* 922 F.2d 810, 814 (Fed.Cir.1990) (citing U.C.C. § 2-209(2) to support the proposition that an integrated executory contract requires a signed writing for modification). Thus, the U.C.C. can inform the analysis of issues raised in government contracts.

tion and give the [contractor] any notification reasonably necessary to enable the [contractor] to take delivery." U.C.C. § 2-503(1)(a).

Concomitantly, absent agreement otherwise, the contractor has a duty to reasonably respond to such notification. It must promptly and properly receive the GFP to complete delivery. This includes inspecting and taking an inventory of the GFP within a reasonable time. *See* U.C.C. § 2-606(1)(a); *see also* FAR § 52.245-4(b) ("The Contractor shall maintain adequate property control records in accordance with sound industrial practice."). If the contractor does not so inspect and inventory the GFP and promptly notify the Government of any shortcomings, or reject the GFP, acceptance of delivery is deemed to occur. *See* FAR § 52.245-4(a)(1) (requiring a contractor to submit timely written notice to obtain equitable adjustment for ineffective delivery of GFP), *see also* U.C.C. § 2-606(1)(a). Rejection of the GFP is ineffective unless the contractor notifies the Government within a reasonable time. *See* FAR § 52.245-4(a)(1); *see also* U.C.C. § 2-602(2)(a). Timely notification of any deficiencies with the GFP provides the Government an opportunity to cure.

In *Blaine,* the contract obligated the government to supply cloth for the contractor to manufacture jackets for the Army under a delivery schedule spanning seven months in 1951. *Blaine,* 157 Ct.Cl. at 54. So that the contractor could complete another jacket-manufacturing contract, the parties agreed to delayed deliveries of cloth and jackets during the first few months of the schedule, with the entire contract to be completed by the final delivery. *Id.* at 55. The government made the cloth available at a government facility, but the contractor delayed in picking up the cloth because the contractor was unable to secure storage space. *Id.* The contractor was five days late for final delivery and sought to recover labor and overhead costs for these five days, alleging that the delay resulted from the government's failure to deliver sufficient quantities of cloth in time for the contractor to manufacture the jackets by the deadline. Our predecessor court, the Court of Claims, held that once the parties deviated from the original schedule, the government's duty was to "make sufficient cloth available at proper times to enable [the contractor] to perform under the contract—that is, to make reasonable shipments under the circumstances." *Id.* at 57.

As in *Blaine,* the Government here tendered delivery of the GFP in a time, place and manner that enabled FPC to perform the contract. Therefore, the Board had substantial evidence to conclude that any issues of delivery, or resulting problems with the GFP, are not a basis of recovery due to: (i) the risk of loss shifting to FPC because it did not inspect and inventory the GFP within a reasonable time; and (ii) FPC's failure to timely notify the Government of problems with the GFP.

The Board found that the GFP was available for use by FPC from the day the work began. *Pavkov,* at 153,608. The contract did not specify a time for delivery, thus the Government is "obligated to deliver the [GFP] in sufficient time for it to be installed in the ordinary and economical course of performance." *Pavkov,* at 153,608 (citing *Peter Kiewit Sons' Co. v. United States,* 138 Ct. Cl. 668, 674–75, 151 F. Supp. 726 (1957); *Oxwell, Inc.,* 86-2 B.C.A. (CCH) ¶ 18,967, 95,776, ASBCA No. 27523 (June 2, 1990)). FPC claims that the Government never completed delivery. However, FPC ignores its own duty in the delivery process. FPC was willing to meet the Government at the fence-enclosed location to undertake an inventory of the GFP. This indicates that the fence-enclosed location was of a time, place and manner for delivery acceptable to both parties. Given that the contract did not specify formalities of delivery, this meeting constituted a reasonable tender of delivery and notice to FPC that the Government had put the GFP at FPC's disposition for it to construct the Project. FPC should have promptly and properly "received" the GFP at that time by inspection and inventory. FPC removed material from the fence-enclosed location without complaint as to delivery by that method. FPC had the opportunity to inspect and inventory the GFP on the day of the meeting and every day thereafter. That it never did so is due to no fault of the Government. Because FPC failed to fully inspect and inventory the GFP within a reasonable time, the Board was justified in deeming delivery to occur at the initial meeting in the fence-enclosed location. With delivery deemed to have occurred at that time, it was not error for the Board to apply the contract's risk of loss provision against FPC.

The contract's GFP clause requires FPC to submit a timely written request to obtain an equitable adjustment for flawed or missing GFP. The Board reasoned that implicit in this written request provision is the requirement that FPC inspect and inventory the GFP upon receipt. *Pavkov* at 153,609 (citing *Logicon, Inc.,* 90-2 BCA ¶ 22,786, ASBCA No. 39683, 1990 WL 42074 (Apr. 3, 1990)). FPC never fully inspected or inventoried the GFP. As a result, FPC delivered notice of missing GFP to the Government on May 14, 1996, six months after the Government and FPC partially inventoried the GFP. This delay is almost half of the estimated contract length of one year. FPC did not provide timely notice to the Government of any problems arising with the GFP as delivered. This untimely notice did not give the Government an opportunity to cure any deficiency. The Board correctly concluded that FPC's notice was not timely and proper notification of defective or missing GFP was not issued within a reasonable time after the meeting at the fence-enclosed location.

In sum, in a case where the contract does not specify the formalities of delivery, the Government reasonably met its delivery obligations by making the GFP available to FPC in a reasonable time, place and manner. However, FPC failed to discharge its obligations in the delivery process, neglecting to inspect and inventory the GFP, thereby also failing in its duty to notify the Government of any deficiencies in the inventory, which would allow the Government the opportunity to cure any such deficiencies. Therefore, the Board's legal determinations concerning delivery are correct.

C. Suitability of the GFP

FPC also argues that the Government violated its contractual requirement that the GFP be suitable for its intended use. FPC contends that the GFP was not suitable because it did not conform to the 1995 drawings, resulting in additional cost for FPC. FPC complains that the Board never addressed this element of FPC's equitable adjustment claim and it argues that if the Government had provided it with a complete drawing set the problems would have been less costly. FPC's arguments are not persuasive. We have concluded that the Government had no obligation to supply the drawings. FPC therefore cannot recover alleged damages resulting from its unawareness of those drawings.

CONCLUSION

Because we hold that the Board's findings are supported by substantial evidence, and its legal conclusions are correct that FPC does not have a claim for recovery arising from the specifications and drawings, and did not timely notify the Government of the missing items of GFP, we affirm the Board's decision.

AFFIRMED.

Notes and Questions

1. It is said that the government has two obligations in providing GFP—timeliness and suitability. This case touches on both, although with greater emphasis on timeliness. Note how the court's reasoning resembles what would be applied in a U.C.C. case regarding

private sellers and buyers of goods. That is, the court sorts out which party carries the risk, and how the risk transfers from one party to another, by having this turn on obligations of notification and response to notification. Does it matter that this is a case of a contractor who filed a claim, belatedly and affirmatively, to be paid more? Would the contractor get a more sympathetic hearing if this were a case of the government seeking, belatedly, to impose penalties for late performance, and the contractor were merely raising, defensively, the ground of that the requisite government-furnished property had not been timely furnished?

2. This case emphasizes aspects of GFP not particularly government-unique, what might be called the "contract," as distinct from the "property," side of GFP. Consider how differently the reasoning in the case would proceed if the issues involved the difference in the legal nature of ownership of property between a private and a government owner. For example, the government may shift risks involving GFP to a contractor, but it never relinquishes title. This matters considerably if, say, the contractor goes bankrupt. As to property that the contractor itself acquires after entering into the contract with an expectation that this will become government property, the point at which title vests in the government can turn on the type of contract. In a fixed-price contract, title does not shift to the government until delivery; in a cost-reimbursement type of contract, title vests earlier.

2. Prompt Payment

The Prompt Payment Act aims to reduce the practice by government agencies of making late payments. It has broad, government-wide applicability. It applies if the government does not promptly pay undisputed invoices, if deliveries of supplies or performance are partial or periodic, or if a construction contract provides for progress payments. 31 USC 3903(a)(5)–(6). However, it applies only to payments for supplies or services accepted by the government, that is "invoice payments" rather than those made prior to acceptance of supplies or services. Its requirements for the government are triggered by invoices in proper form. Under the Prompt Payment Act, a payment is prompt upon receipt thirty days after the government receives a proper invoice for amount due. 31 U.S.C. § 3901; *see also* FAR 32.905(e)(list of what constitutes a proper invoice).

For late payments, the government incurs an interest penalty. Interest begins to accrue the day after the payment due date and ends when payment is made calculated by the date of the check. If the invoice is not proper, the government must notify the contractor within seven days. FAR 32.905(e). While Congress intended the act to expedite invoice payments, Congress did not intend to speed up the array of other kinds of payments. It only applies to government delay in paying undisputed invoices, not to disputed or questioned ones, to change orders or requests for equitable adjustments.

Northrop Worldwide Aircraft Services Inc., Appellant v. Department of the Treasury, Respondent

January 30, 1992
GSBCA No. 1162-TD

Before Board Judges SUCHANEK (Chief Judge), LaBELLA, and HYATT.

Board Judge LaBELLA.

This appeal concerns a dispute over the application of the Prompt Payment Act ("PPA" or "The Act"), 31 U.S.C. § 3901 et. seq., to payments made under cost reimbursement contracts between the Department of the Treasury ("Treasury") and Northrop World-wide Aircraft Services, Inc. ("Northrop"). Treasury contends that payments it rendered to Northrop for services performed pursuant to these contracts are exempted from PPA interest penalties under the proper interpretation of that Act. Northrop insists that the charges it invoiced and the payments it received were payments for services already rendered in partial fulfillment of its contracts, and, as such, were subject to PPA interest penalty provisions. We ... grant the appeals....

Findings of Fact

The contracts at issue, Tc-85-37, Tc-87-38 and Tc-90-059, obligated Northrop to provide transportation, maintenance, storage and auction functions for items seized by Treasury's Customs Service under the direction and supervision of Custom's employees. Joint Stipulations 79, 81, 82, 84, 85, 87, 89–94, 98–103, 105, 107, 112, 113, 114, 117. These services were either performed by Northrop directly or through subcontractors which Northrop paid directly. Joint Stipulation 121. Only after Northrop had performed or provided an individual service, be it flying a seized aircraft to storage, or auctioning seized property and depositing the proceeds in a Government account, did it invoice the items of expense and present those invoices to Treasury for payment. Joint Stipulations 60, 82, 91, 94.

All three contracts are explicitly made subject to the PPA in clauses that are incorporated by reference. At the same time, none of the three prohibit partial payments being made to recognize progress. Appeal File, Exhibits 5, 6, 9; Appellant's Supplement to Appeal File, Exhibits 10, 12, 14; Joint Stipulations 9, 27, 44. The payment terms of the contracts further provide for payment to be divided into cost reimbursement, base, and award fees. Joint Stipulations 14, 32. To initiate payment of these costs and fees, Northrop was required to submit vouchers detailing its expenditures. Joint Stipulations 13, 31, 43. Contracts Tc-85-37 and Tc-87-38 each contain a provision that authorizes the payment of base and award fees before the completion of the contract. Joint Stipulations 15, 16, 19, 33–37. Although this provision is not incorporated in contract Tc-90-059, this contract provides that:

> payment for goods and services is made after charges invoiced against the procurement authorization are validated by an Accounts Payable Clerk. In order to verify an invoice, the following criteria must be met:
>
> - Goods or services were properly authorized.
>
> - Goods or services have been received.
>
> - Invoiced amounts match those authorized by the purchase order or property services subcontract.
>
> Only invoiced amounts meeting these criteria will be approved for payment.

Joint Stipulation 45. All of the services performed by Northrop or its subcontractors were provided in response to a request by Customs. Although no formal procedure for acceptance of services was instituted, performance was monitored and evaluated by Customs personnel, who were generally pleased with Northrop's performance. Joint Stipulations 79–81, 83–122.

Northrop never requested contract financing on these contracts, nor did the contracting officer make the legally required determinations to extend contract financing to Northrop. Joint Stipulations 3, 24, 41, 51–53.

None of the payments made under these contracts were progress payments, advance payments or prepayments, nor were they made before the receipt of property or services by the Government. Joint Stipulations 60–63. However, all payments under these contracts were subject to later audit, and possible correction, until final payment had occurred. Joint Stipulations 20, 21, 38, 46.

During fiscal years 1988, 1989, and 1990, the Customs Service paid interest penalties on late payments to Northrop under contracts Tc-85-37 and Tc-87-38. Joint Stipulation 77. Customs has since determined that these interest penalties were not required by the PPA. Consequently, Customs has recouped prior interest payments and denied appellant's claims for PPA interest under the three contracts. The amounts claimed are $100,708.81 on contracts Tc-85-37 and Tc-87-38, and $8,221.81 on contract Tc-90-059. Joint stipulations 68, 72. These claims were properly submitted to the contracting officer, who denied them in their entirety, and are the subject of these timely appeals. Joint Stipulations 68–70, 72–74, 76.

Discussion

Treasury points to the 1989 revision of OMB circular 125-A, the OMB circular promulgated to assist in the appropriate implementation of the PPA, as a final clarification of the Act as it applies to all three contracts. This latest circular, which specifically includes interim payments under cost type contracts as contract financing exempt from the PPA, is merely a clarification of the law as it has always existed, and Treasury contends that even the two contracts entered into before its issuance should be construed pursuant to its definition of contract financing. Under Treasury's reading, the PPA exempts all payments made on a cost reimbursement contract, except the final payment, from interest penalties.

The payments made to Northrop under the contracts in question are unquestionably for services either performed by Northrop or performed by subcontractors and paid for by Northrop prior to the submission of invoices to Treasury for payment. Respondent has also stipulated that it monitored appellant Northrop's performance to ensure compliance with the contract requirements. Such monitoring included both announced and unannounced inspections, the submission by Northrop of monthly progress reports, quarterly evaluations, Customs' field organizations reports, and Northrop's submission of activity reports. Although Treasury emphasizes the fact that nothing in the contracts in issue sets out exact prices to be paid, or "establishes a unit price to cover one month's services," Respondent's Appeal Brief at 25, we are not persuaded that this precludes acceptance of work performed by Northrop on a monthly basis. Acceptance is defined in the 1989 final revision of OMB circular 125-A as "acknowledgement by the Government that property and services conform with the requirements of the contract." 54 Fed.Reg. 4700 (1989). It is clear from the stipulations that Treasury closely monitored the performance of Northrop to ensure that the services provided did conform to the contract. This kind of close scrutiny warrants a finding of acceptance of work not timely rejected as non-compliant.

The PPA was intended to "provide incentives for the Federal Government to pay its bills on time." H.R.Rep. No. 461, 97th Cong., 2nd Sess. 1, reprinted in 1982 U.S.Code Cong. & Admin.News 111. The incentive took the form of an interest penalty, to be borne by an agency which failed to pay duly submitted invoices within a commercially reasonable time. Prior to the passage of the Act, suppliers of goods and services to the Government had no choice but to bear the cost of any agency delay in payment. Consequently, some companies ceased competing for Government contracts, and others built estimated interest into their bids. Id. The PPA was passed to alleviate the inequity caused by allowing the Government to pay its bills late with impunity, and to give the contractors and companies doing business with the Government a method of redress.

The payment of interest on late payments is not always required under the PPA, however. In particular, it would be beyond the scope of the Act to require an interest penalty on advance payments or other contract financing provided by the Government. The Office of Management and Budget (OMB), the executive agency charged with implementing the PPA through the issuance of clarifying rules and regulations, recognized this fact, and so explicitly excluded payments made "solely for financing purposes" from incurring interest penalties in its regulations governing implementation of the PPA. OMB Circular A-125, 47 Fed.Reg. 37,321, at 37,322 (1982). This circular, which has been revised several times, remains the best expression of OMB's position regarding the implementation of the PPA. The circular recognizes that in some circumstances the Government may make payments in advance of receipt of goods and services, and that "these payments, or contract financing, are referred to as progress payments, advances, or prepayments." OMB Circular 125-A, 49 Fed.Reg. 28,140 (1984). This type of payment arrangement must be requested by the contractor and approved by the agency following established guidelines. Id.

Contract financing is defined as:

> a Government disbursement of monies to a contractor under a contract clause or other authorization prior to acceptance of supplies or services by the Government. Contract financing payments include advance payments, progress payments based on cost under the clause at 52.232-16, Progress Payments, progress payments based on a percentage or stage of completion (see 32.102(e)(1)) other than those made under the clause at 52.232-5, Payments Under Fixed-Price Construction Contracts or the clause at 52.232-10, Payments Under Fixed-Price Architect-Engineer Contracts, and interim payments on cost-type contracts. Contract financing payments do not include invoice payments or payments for partial deliveries.

48 CFR 32.902 (1990) (FAR 32.902). Contract financing is only provided at the request of a contractor with approval of the Government, and it is not the favored method of conducting Government procurements. OMB Circular 125-A, 52 Fed.Reg. 21,926, at 21,928 (1987).

The dispute in this case largely hinges on the factual determination of whether the payments made to Northrop by Treasury constitute contract financing. If they do, they are largely exempt from the PPA interest penalty provisions. The Department of the Treasury acknowledges that the payments in question are not true contract financing, but nonetheless contends that they should be considered financing for the purposes of PPA interest penalties. Respondent's Appeal Brief, at 21–22. Treasury readily concedes that no traditional contract financing was requested or received by Northrop. Instead Treasury argues that contracts awarded not on a fixed price, but rather on a cost reimbursement, basis carry no obligation to comply with PPA provisions, and incur no interest penalties on any late payments other than on the final contract payment. Id. Respondent bases this conclusion on its reading of the 1989 final version of OMB Circular 125-A and the inclusion of the phrase "interim payments on cost-type contracts," the circular's definition of contract financing which is republished in FAR 32.902. Treasury's reliance on this one phrase of the definition is misplaced because the phrase is merely one component of the definition of contract financing, not the only component. Treasury's reading of FAR 32.902 completely ignores the first and last sentences of the definition, which state: "Contract financing payments" are those made in "advance of acceptance of supplies or services," and "do not include invoice payments or payments for partial deliveries." FAR 32.902 (emphasis added).

OMB itself emphasized the distinction between cost reimbursements and contract financing in an Attachment to OMB Circular 125-A:

1. This Attachment establishes standards for assuring that appropriate payment terms are included in all Government contracts. It supplements the guidance provided in paragraph g, "Payment Standards," of the basic Circular.

2. Generally, payments for goods and services acquired by the Federal Government are made after receipt, inspection, and acceptance of the goods and services, or through reimbursements on cost type contracts.

3. In other cases, payment may be made before receipt of goods or services. These payments, or contract financing, are referred to as progress payments, advances, or prepayments.

49 Fed.Reg. 21,140, at 21,141 (1984). OMB's segregation of contract financing from cost reimbursement establishes its belief that the two methods of payment are not part of the same category. The use of the term cost type contract in the definition of contract financing cannot, therefore, be read to mean all cost type contracts, but only those that fit the remainder of the definition. Where invoices have been submitted for payment after actual performance and receipt of services it would be illogical to call the payments for those rendered services contract financing merely because the service was not rendered under a set price contract.

The June 1987 revision to Circular 125-A was intended to "close loopholes in the circular that allow agencies to pay their bills late without including the required interest penalty." 52 Fed.Reg. 21,926 (1987). Respondent would have us open a new loophole, exempting from the PPA all cost type contracts, based on one phrase in the 1989 revision to OMB circular 125-A. To do so would be inconsistent with the PPA, and our reading of the intent of the 1989 revised circular. The commentary preceding the final revision of OMB Circular 125-A states:

The proposed circular prohibited payment of late payment interest penalties on periodic payments under cost reimbursement contracts unless the contracts defined these payments as partial payments for property or services furnished. Three industry associations recommended that interest be paid on such late payments. The intent of the proposed restriction was to prohibit payment of interest on contract financing payments.

54 Fed.Reg. 52,700, at 52,701 (1989). This prohibition does not appear in the revised circular. From its omission we can only conclude that the OMB either never intended to prohibit interest on cost reimbursements, or changed its mind after objection by the industry groups.

The commentary goes on to state:

The 1988 amendments require that interest penalties be paid on late payments when a contractor makes a partial delivery of supplies or periodic performance of service, performance has been accepted, and a proper invoice submitted under a contract where periodic payments are not prohibited.

Id. The revised circular itself provides: "an agency shall pay for partial delivery of supplies or partial performance of services unless specifically prohibited by the contract." OMB Circular 125-A; 54 Fed.Reg. 52,709 (1989). When taken together these statements and revisions contradict respondent's assertion that OMB was trying to carve out an exception to PPA interest penalties for payments under cost reimbursement contracts. This Board would be remiss in presuming from the mere use of one undefined phrase that OMB intended to contradict its prior position and promulgate regulations which are very likely in conflict with the purposes of the PPA. This is especially the case when, as here, the evidence so overwhelmingly points to a contrary conclusion.

In conclusion, appellant performed services for and at the request of Customs and, under Customs' supervision, incurred and paid expenses on behalf of the Government. Appellant then submitted invoices to the proper authorities which were not timely paid. The nature of these services precluded a fixed price contract because Customs did not know from month to month what service it would require. Instead, it requested service as needed, and confirmed that service was provided prior to issuing payments on submitted vouchers. Respondent has not alleged that the tardy payments in question were late because of a dispute over the propriety of the invoiced expense or dissatisfaction with appellant's performance. In fact, the Joint Stipulations indicate that the work was satisfactory; the tardiness of the payments is simply unexplained.

Payments made after performance and acceptance of goods or services do not fit the definition of contract financing. As we conclude that the payments made to Northrop were made after the performance and acceptance of the corresponding services, these payments were not contract financing. Therefore, any payments not timely made were subject to PPA interest penalty provisions.

Decision: The appeals are GRANTED. Appellant is entitled to receive interest penalties on payments not timely made under the cost reimbursement contracts in issue, plus interest on its claim as provided by law.

Notes and Questions

1. Why did the government oppose applying the prompt payment act to payments under cost reimbursement contracts?

2. What might "periodic performance of service" mean in the diverse circumstances of cost reimbursement contracts? Suppose a research and development contractor provides quarterly progress reports, with invoices, even if no particular milestones in the research should be expected to be achieved in that kind of short-term intervals. Can its lawyer draft into the terms of the contract some language that would classify the reports, and the research they describe, as a "periodic performance of service"?

3. Regulations were promulgated at 5 C.F.R. part 1315 — not in the Federal Acquisition Regulation. Note the reference in the opinion to OMB Circular 125-A. What kinds of payment might the OMB Circular, or the Prompt Payment Act, cover, beyond those for contracting under the FAR?

3. Assignment as Security for Credit

Industrial Bank of Washington, Appellant, v. United States of America et al.

United States Court of Appeals, District of Columbia Circuit
424 F.2d 932 No. 22790
Argued Jan. 22, 1970
Decided March 9, 1970

Before FAHY, Senior Circuit Judge, and LEVENTHAL and MacKINNON, Circuit Judges.

PER CURIAM:

Appellant Industrial Bank of Washington (Bank), on March 1, 1966, loaned money to Art's Decorating and Cleaning Company (Contractor), on the security of the Contractor's assignment to the Bank of all moneys due or to become due from the Government under contract executed October 29, 1965, for rendering by Contractor of cleaning services at a General Services Administration (GSA) building. The Bank gave notice of its assignment to the GSA, and to appellee Reliance Insurance Company (Surety) which had, under date of November 3, 1965, executed a performance bond to protect the Government against loss occasioned by the failure of the Contractor to perform the contract. On May 14, 1966, the Contractor defaulted. GSA terminated the contract and entered into a replacement contract that resulted in a contract loss to the Government.

Payments due the Contractor under the contract for services performed amounted to $4685. The Bank claimed the money due it from the Contractor on the loan, some $3896, plus interest. The Government declined to pay this on the ground that the unpaid balance will be set off against the Contractor's indebtedness to the United States resulting from the termination and reprocurement from another source.

The Bank brought an action against the United States, joining the Surety as a defendant, basing jurisdiction on the Tucker Act, 28 U.S.C. § 1346. The Government contested jurisdiction, and in the alternative sought summary judgment. The Surety also sought summary judgment. So did plaintiff Bank. The District Court, assuming jurisdiction for purposes of decision, granted the motion of each defendant for summary judgment, and denied the Bank's motion. We affirm the dismissal of the Bank's action with prejudice.

1. The District Court had jurisdiction of the action under the Tucker Act, which gives the District Courts concurrent jurisdiction with the Court of Claims of any civil action against the United States, not exceeding $10,000 in amount, founded upon any contract with the United States. 28 U.S.C. § 1346 (1964). Plaintiff sues on its rights pursuant to an assignment, expressly authorized by the Assignment of Claims Act of 1940 as amended, from one who had a right founded on a contract with the United States.

* * *

2. Proceeding to the merits, the Surety rightly points out that it is established doctrine that the surety on a performance or payment bond has a right of subrogation, derived from the right to resort to the remedy the United States was capable of asserting against the contractor, resulting in priority of undisbursed contract funds.

The Bank relies on the wording of the Assignment of Claims Act of 1940, as amended, as establishing a higher right in the assignee bank. The 1940 statute removes a disability on the bank to enforce its assignment of a claim against the Government. The words of the act are not properly applied if, following a termination for default, they are construed to give the bank as assignee of the contractor a right to funds in the hands of the Government which are needed for completion of the contract. The surety, upon completion of the contract, or payment of the funds needed for completion of the contract becomes entitled to those funds as the subrogee of the Government; its equitable right of subrogation relates back to the time of the giving of the bond; and it has priority over the subsequent right obtained by the bank by virtue of the assignment which was taken with knowledge of and subject to the equity of the surety. This is the view of the Court of Claims, the leading case being Royal Indemnity v. United States, 93 F.Supp. 891, 117 Ct.Cl. 736 (1950), which was cited with approval in Pearlman v. Reliance Insurance Company, 371 U.S. 132, 141, 83 S.Ct. 232, 9 L.Ed.2d 190 (1962).

* * *

When a surety on a Government contractor's performance bond makes a payment thereunder to or for the United States, he is subrogated to the rights of the Government as to any funds due or to become due under the contract. This subrogation, sometimes called an 'equitable lien,' relates back to the date of the bond, and is therefore superior to any conflicting claim thereafter asserted by another.... This right is potential only until the contractor's default causes the surety to pay. It is a shadowy thing until it is given substance by the occurrence of a loss to the surety; theretofore a mere right to subrogation, it then becomes an actuality. And the law gives the surety the added advantage of having subrogation effective as of the date of his original undertaking.

This court, analyzing the provision of the 1940 law, held the Government precluded from recovering amounts already paid to the assignee bank even after default, in the absence of fraud, and that hence the surety's right of subrogation gave it no rights against the bank for such funds. But its reasoning establishes that a contrary result is applicable as to funds still in the hands of the Government, that the bank is not entitled to these funds if needed by the Government to complete the contract or pay for the work needed to complete the contract, and that the surety making such payments has a right of subrogation as to those funds. Our 1950 decision was accomplished by a careful review of the authorities, the pre-1940 pronouncements of the Supreme Court, the post-1940 decisions of the Court of Claims and other courts. The Fifth Circuit's analysis, which our 1950 case cited for another point, was not persuasive on this issue. We adhere to the reasoning already stated by our court.

We have no occasion to consider any questions that may arise concerning funds in the hands of the Government in excess of those required to complete the contract. The judgment dismissing the Bank's claim with prejudice will be

Affirmed

Notes and Questions

1. Historically, units of government not only resisted delegation of a performing party's duties under the government contract, but also resisted assignment of the performing party's right to receive payment. Local governments which attempt to do so today, discover that U.C.C. section 9-318(4) changed the law to bar them from doing so (absent special provision of state law). This section declares: "A term in any contract between an account debtor and an assignor which prohibits assignment of an account or contract right to which they are parties is ineffective." See, e.g., *American Bank of Commerce v. City of McAlester*, 555 P.2d 581 (Okl. 1976). But, did the U.C.C. similarly change federal government contract law?

2. At the federal level, Congress enacted the Assignment of Claims Act in 1862, which ostensibly prohibited all assignments of performance of government contracts. It had the narrower goal to deal with Civil War problems with noncontractor middlemen securing government contracts (by favoritism or worse) and then turning the contract over to others who gave sub-par performance. The courts created limits on the act, notably in *Thompson v. Commissioner*, 205 F.2d 73 (3d Cir. 1953). Ultimately, an important practical aspect consists of the FAR novation process, by which the government formally recognizes a contractor's assignee. For a fuller look, see David R. White, *To Dance with the One You Came with: Federal Government Regulation of Assignments of Contractual Performance* , 29 Pub. Cont. L. J. 601 (2000).

3. As this case indicates, Congress made room by a 1940 statute, not for assignments of contract rights in general, but just for assignments to financing institutions as security for contract financing. This is governed by the Assignment of Claims clause in the FAR, 32.805 and 52.232-23 (clause itself). In this case, the bank loses. Why is the surety's right superior to the bank's?

Chapter 6

Changes and Delays

Government contracting law arranges an important compromise differing from basic (private) contract law in the common situation that the contracting officer, or simply the work itself, calls for something more or different than the contract specifies. The law, particularly that key standard clause the Changes Clause, strikes a compromise between the government's need for operational flexibility to make more or different demands without contractor resistance, and the contractor's need, without the weapon of resistance, to secure fair payment.

Historically, the government always wanted the ability to impose new demands on contractors. Because public purposes, rather than profitmaking, drive government contracting, the expense of changes during contracting does not deter the government from requiring them. At the same time, the government cannot put itself in a situation where the only way to obtain changes is to pay whatever the contractor demands. So, the government must insist on changes, but without letting contractors resist.

Contractors, meanwhile, generally welcome changes. They enjoy additional work for additional compensation. Changes occur without the open competition of contract formation, so that the contractor, who had to keep its proposals low to get the contract, makes much more profit on the changes. However, the contractor finds that the government uses the concept of the "equitable adjustment," with a set of formulae and procedures, to put some limits on wide-open demands.

In basic contract law, recent scholarship has suggested the general concept of the "relational" contract. At common law, the model contract consisted of a one-time exchange, like a single purchase of a single lot of goods. However, in recent times, a large category of contract law consists of complex relationships, such as between long-term buyers and suppliers, or between businesses and employee unions. In the relational contract, the initial offer and acceptance merely start a long-term process in which what is to be provided changes over time. Many aspects of the government contract, and particularly the "Changes" aspect, fit this relational model.

In particular, a relational contract not only anticipates changes, it calls for processes to resolve issues on an ongoing basis without jeopardizing the contract by such blunt tactics as cancellation or refusal to perform. Commercial arbitration, or management-labor grievance procedures, provide such processes. The Changes Clause and the equitable adjustment provide that process for government contracts. What gives it such interest is that this process has a large role for law and lawyers, rather than market bargaining, to determine the payment for changes.

For further discussions of this chapter's overall subject, see the sources cited in each section, plus: Steven Feldman, *Government Contract Guidebook*, § 15 (Thomson Reuters, 4th ed. 2010); Omer Dekel, *Modification Of A Government Contract Awarded Following A Competitive Procedure*, 38 Pub. Cont. L.J. 401 (Winter 2009); John D. Schminky, *Proper Funding of Contract Modifications Under the Antecedent Liability Rule*, 26 Pub. Cont. L. J. 221

(1997); Hal J. Perloff, Comment, *The Economic-Waste Doctrine in Government Contract Litigation*, 43 DePaul L. Rev. 185 (1993).

A. The Changes Clause, Cardinal Changes, and Formal Changes

The text of the Changes Clause well repays a close reading. First, section (a) provides that the "Contracting Officer may at any time, by written order ... make changes within the general scope of the contract." This distinguishes between changes "within" the contract's scope, and something else, which would be changes outside the contract's scope. The latter are called "cardinal changes." A contracting officer has the right pursuant to the contract to order changes, but not cardinal changes. If the contracting officer orders cardinal changes, the government has breached the contract and the contractor is entitled to cancel the contract and obtain a generous measure of damages. This, however, is rare. The case below, *Boston Shipyards*, shows why.

Second, the section (a) confines formal changes to those by the "Contracting Officer ... by written order." Extensive case law over the years has concerned the authority and methods for such formal changes. A contractor frequently receives instructions from one of the many representatives, project officers, inspectors, technical assistants, and other working for, or with, the contracting officer, and the contractor often obeys these. They may or may not have the authority to make formal changes. Even if not, they may or may not be making a "constructive change."

If contractors obey their lawyers, then when someone other than the Contracting Officer ordered a change, the contractor would promptly inform the Contracting Officer before performing the work, or, if such notice were impractical, write the Contracting Officer describing the change, and advising that a formal claim will be filed. Often, however, contractors do not do so but contact their counsel only much later.

Third, section (e) of the clause provides that "Failure to agree to any adjustment shall be a dispute under the Disputes clause." Hence, the Changes and Disputes clauses together create an orderly mechanism for resolving the issue of how much to pay. Section (e) further states "However, nothing in this clause shall excuse the Contractor from proceeding with the contract as changed."

As discussed in the chapter on termination, government contract law does not embrace the doctrine in basic (private) contracting of "efficient breach"; it penalizes, often severely, the government contractor who does not proceed with the contract. What this clause indicates is how government contract law penalizes the contractor who fails to proceed even when the government has changed the contract by imposing new and different demands, and even when the contract is in dispute. A change might well seem to a contractor not efficient. For example, it might double the contractor's government workload at a time when the contractor could make more profit by increasing its non-government workload. In a basic (private) contract situation, the contractor might refuse to perform the change, pay the damages caused by the need for the buyer to find another contractor, and emerge with a net profit. That is not the choice government contracting law anticipates for contractors to make. Rather, an array of penalties await the contractor who does so, and while abandonment of government contracts certainly occurs, it is hard to view it as "efficient" for all involved.

For further discussions of this section's overall subject, see T. Scott Leo, B. Scott Douglass & Cathleen M. Jareczek, *The Obligee's Duties to Provide Plans and Specifications, Make Payment, and Process Change Orders*, 32 Tort & Ins. L.J. 961, 1997; George E. Powell, Jr., *The Cardinal Change Doctrine and Its Application to Government Construction Contracts*, 24 Pub. Cont. L.J. 377 (1995); F. Trowbridge vom Baur, *The Origin of the Changes Clause in Naval Procurement*, 8 Pub. Cont. L.J. 175 (1976).

Changes Clause—Fixed-Price
(Aug. 1987)

(a) The Contracting Officer may at any time, by written order, and without notice to the sureties, if any, make changes within the general scope of this contract in any one or more of the following:

    (1) Drawings, designs, or specifications when the supplies to be furnished are to be specially manufactured for the Government in accordance with the drawings, designs, or specifications.

    (2) Method of shipment or packing.

    (3) Place of delivery.

(b) If any such change causes an increase or decrease in the cost of, or the time required for, performance of any part of the work under this contract, whether or not changed by the order, the Contracting Officer shall make an equitable adjustment in the contract price, the delivery schedule, or both, and shall modify the contract.

(c) The Contractor must assert its right to an adjustment under this clause within 30 days from the date of receipt of the written order. However, if the Contracting Officer decides that the facts justify it, the Contracting Officer may receive and act upon a proposal submitted before final payment of the contract.

(d) If the Contractor's proposal includes the cost of property made obsolete or excess by the change, the Contracting Officer shall have the right to prescribe the manner of the disposition of the property.

(e) Failure to agree to any adjustment shall be a dispute under the Disputes clause. However, nothing in this clause shall excuse the Contractor from proceeding with the contract as changed.

In re Boston Shipyard Corp., Debtor.
Appeal of Boston Shipyard Corp.
No. 89-1144
United States Court of Appeals, First Circuit
886 F.2d 451
Heard June 7, 1989; Decided Sept. 27, 1989

Before CAMPBELL, Chief Judge, REINHARDT[1] and TORRUELLA, Circuit Judges.

TORRUELLA, Circuit Judge.

Boston Shipyard Corporation ("BSC") appeals from the decision of the district court, which affirmed the bankruptcy court's grant of summary judgment in favor of appellee, the United States Military Sealift Command ("MSC").

---

1. Of the Ninth Circuit, sitting by designation.

I. Background

BSC entered into a contract with MSC to overhaul the USNS Mississinewa. This contract was awarded even though BSC was in the midst of a Chapter 11 reorganization in the bankruptcy court. The original contract called for a 100 day performance period and for BSC to be paid $4,997,925.

As often happens, the contract proved to require much more time and expense than was originally anticipated. Each point that BSC realized a change in the contract specifications would be required, it filed a condition report or change order requesting authorization for the necessary changes so that the work could be done. Hundreds of these change orders were submitted and BSC claims that the delay in their resolution led to increased financial burdens on BSC, as well as to greatly hindered progress, causing the work to fall far behind schedule.

By the end of August 1985, BSC's financial condition had worsened and MSC payments were necessary for the company's continued ability to perform on the contract....

BSC curtailed its operations on the contract effective October 17, due, it claims, to the "effect of MSC's delays, disruption and failure to compensate BSC." Brief of Appellant at 24. A press release issued on that day stated that "[t]oday Boston Shipyard Corp. is forced to cease operations." On November 15, MSC terminated the contract because of this default by BSC.

The government filed a Proof of Claim in the United States Bankruptcy Court on February 25, 1986 seeking $9.2 million in reprocurement costs. BSC objected to the Proof of Claim and filed a counterclaim seeking to convert the default termination into a termination for the convenience of the government.

... Six months later, after full briefing and a hearing on the issues, the bankruptcy court entered summary judgment in favor of the government on the remainder of the case, based on its conclusion that BSC had inexcusably abandoned the contract. Upon appeal, the district court affirmed both summary judgment orders and BSC now appeals this decision.

* * *

IV. The Summary Judgment

BSC also challenges the district court's decision affirming the grant of summary judgment to MSC on the remainder of the claims. This decision is dependent upon whether BSC's termination of services constituted abandonment and breach of contract, thereby warranting the government's termination of the contract, or whether BSC's cessation of work could be justified by MSC's actions.

In granting MSC's motion, the bankruptcy court relied upon the Master Agreement for Repair and Alteration of Vessels (the "Master Agreement") as the controlling contract between the parties. Clause 13 of the Master Agreement consists of Federal Acquisition Regulation ("FAR") § 52.233-1, which states

> (h) The Contractor shall proceed diligently with performance of this contract, pending final resolution of any request for relief, claim, appeal, or action arising under the contract, and comply with any decision of the Contracting Officer.

The bankruptcy court held that under this provision BSC was obligated to continue work until its dispute with MSC was resolved and that therefore its cessation constituted wrongful abandonment of the contract. The court carefully examined the actions of MSC and concluded that BSC's breach was not justified by these actions. This decision was affirmed without significant discussion by the district court.

* * *

BSC bases the second part of this argument on MSC's alleged failure to make progress payments and other acts which led to BSC's weakened financial condition, which, it argues, justified abandonment of the contract. We agree with the decisions of the courts below.

Although Clause 13 is admittedly controlling, BSC argues that its work cessation was justified because MSC's actions had caused a cardinal change to the agreed-upon contract. See Air-A-Plane Corp. v. United States, 187 Ct.Cl. 269, 408 F.2d 1030 (1969). A cardinal change is considered a breach of the contract and therefore further work, even when a disputes clause exists, is not required. General Dynamics Corp. v. United States, 218 Ct.Cl. 40, 585 F.2d 457, 462 (1978); Allied Materials & Equipment Co. v. United States, 215 Ct.Cl. 406, 569 F.2d 562, 563 (1978). Change orders or other changes are considered to be cardinal changes if they greatly increase the burden of the contract, in effect changes that are outside the scope of the contract itself. General Dynamics, 585 F.2d at 462. A cardinal change is said to occur

> when the government effects an alteration in the work so drastic that it effectively requires the contractor to perform duties materially different from those originally bargained for. By definition, then, a cardinal change is so profound that it is not redressable under the contract, and thus renders the government in breach.

Allied Materials, 569 F.2d at 563–64 (emphasis added). In making this determination, the court is to look at all relevant circumstances, including, but certainly not limited to, the increase in cost of completing the contract and the number of changes made. See Air-A-Plane, 408 F.2d at 1033.

There were 86 post-August change orders, most of which were initiated by BSC through condition reports. The contract between the parties contained a change clause, providing for an effective and efficient procedure for dealing with changes that would arise in the course of the contract's performance. Thus, the parties clearly anticipated that changes would need to be made.

Moreover, the contract was an "open and inspect" contract calling for reconditioning work throughout the ship. In this type of contract the full amount of the work that will be necessary can not be known until the ship is opened up in dry dock and only then can the full extent of the contract be established. Moreover, the contract provided for a large number of so-called "B" items, which were not required by the contract, but which the government could, at its discretion, require BSC to perform. These factors also indicate that the need for change orders must have been anticipated by the parties from the contract's inception.

We cannot conclude that these change orders amounted to a cardinal change, putting the government in breach and justifying BSC's abandonment of the contract. Some delay and disruption must be expected in the performance of any contract. See Magoba Construction Co. v. United States, 99 Ct.Cl. 662, 690 (1943). Accepting all of BSC's allegations as true, the change orders that arose were predictable, due to the type of contract at issue in this case. Moreover, they were not of the magnitude or extent that would signify a cardinal change.

BSC also argues that its failure to perform due to its financial incapacity must be excused because its money problems had been caused by MSC's actions. Unfortunately, it concentrates this part of its argument on cases which hold that the government must make financial remuneration for change orders issued, a premise not disputed, it seems, by either party. Nevertheless, we will use what guidance the cases do give to properly focus this inquiry.

We start with the general premise that a contractor's default may be excused if the causes of the default were beyond the contractor's control. *Southeastern Airways Corp. v. United States*, 230 Ct.Cl. 47, 673 F.2d 368, 377–78 (1982). Financial incapacity, however, is generally not considered beyond the contractor's control. *Id.* 673 F.2d at 378. This rule is understandable, as a contractor who makes and then accepts a bid should have the financial ability to perform. But, as with most rules, there are always exceptions. Thus, if the financial problems are caused by factors beyond the contractor's control, or by the government's actions themselves, then the contractor's default may be justified. *Id.*; see also *National Eastern Corp. v. United States*, 201 Ct.Cl. 776, 477 F.2d 1347, 1356 (1973) (stating that a contractor's incapacity is "a fortiori" beyond the control of the contractor if caused by acts of the Government).

The period in question ranged from September 1 to October 15, when BSC stopped its operations. BSC argues that government delays resulted in non-payment of $218,907, plus $30,608 for contract modifications which went uncollected. Thus, BSC argues that a total of $249,515, delayed in payment over short periods of time, prevented it from working on a contract worth, by the termination date, over $6.5 million. We cannot agree. The evidence in the record indicates that BSC's "thin capitalization made it impossible for it to absorb even routine and foreseeable problems." *Southeastern Airways*, 673 F.2d at 378. It is clear that in this case BSC's financial problems were not caused by any delay or disruption by MSC. Rather, BSC's "[f]inancial incapacity predated commencement of performance." *Id.*

A different decision would make government contracts truly unworkable, allowing contractors to demand immediate reimbursement for cost overruns, even if the government disagrees with the claim. There would then be no meaning to default or dispute clauses that define procedures in case of disputes.

Affirmed.

Notes and Questions

1. In a basic (private) contract, what kinds of argument would a contractor like Boston Shipyards make that the buyer of its shipyard services ultimately sought from it more than it had bound itself to? How did the common law regard contracts like this "open and inspect" contract, that is, contracts that left key aspects for future determination? Would Boston Shipyards have a better chance than it had in this case? What is the difference?

2. The court says that the "change clause" provides "an effective and efficient procedure for dealing with changes." How so? Is that a happy coincidence, or if not, what is the tie between the change clause and the government getting what it wants in this case?

3. The court rejects the argument that a contractor's financial vulnerability can justify its demanding "immediate reimbursement for cost overruns." And, the court seeks to assure that there is "meaning to default or dispute clauses that define procedures in case of disputes." Surely the government knew who it was contracting with: the shipyard was in bankruptcy at the time of award, and the government presumably did a preaward survey to determine the contractor's responsibility. Is the government truly without a role in the

contractor's inability to perform? The doctrine of "efficient breach" might have suggested that when the government contracts with so vulnerable a contractor, the government should divert some of what it saved by taking the contractor's offer to buying insurance for itself (e.g., by a backup deal with another shipyard). That is not the route the government or the court take here. What in the nature of the public purposes behind government contracting necessitates the government's toughness, backed up by the court, in dealing with a contractor when the government might well have been the least cost avoider in this situation?

4. The opinion refers to a large number of formal change orders. Changes may be initiated by the government or proposed by the contractor. Often the process is something of a hybrid, where the contractor is encouraged to formulate a detailed proposal. In such cases, the contractor is generally deemed to be a volunteer, and therefore not eligible for compensation for the costs of preparing the proposal. See, e.g. *Appeal of BMT Services*, IBCA No. 3794A-97, 1998 WL 422560.

The following is a typical procurement regulation (this one for the Department of Agriculture) regarding how adjustments for change orders are to be priced:

7 C.F.R. § 3016.36 (f)(1):

Grantees and subgrantees must perform a cost or price analysis in connection with every procurement action including contract modifications. The method and degree of analysis is dependent on the facts surrounding the particular procurement situation, but as a starting point, grantees must make independent estimates before receiving bids or proposals. A cost analysis must be performed when the offeror is required to submit the elements of his estimated cost, e.g., under professional, consulting, and architectural engineering services contracts. A cost analysis will be necessary when adequate price competition is lacking, and for sole source procurements, including contract modifications or change orders, unless price reasonableness can be established on the basis of a catalog or market price or a commercial product sold in substantial quantities to the general public or based on prices set by law or regulation. A price analysis will be used in all other instances to determine the reasonableness of the proposed contract price.

5. Both the changes clause and the disputes clause require the contractor to perform the work, that is, the contractor has a duty to proceed. If the contractor asserts wrongly that the government breached the contract by ordering a cardinal change which the contractor refused to follow, then the contractor can get terminated for default. But, if the contractor asserts rightly that the government breached the contract by ordering a cardinal change, then the contractor receives damages.

For examples of cases of contractors held to have breached their duty to proceed pending outcome of dispute resolution processes, see *Appeals of Benju Corporation*, ASBCA No. 43,648, ASBCA No. 43,841, ASBCA No. 43,954, ASBCA No. 46,220, 1997 WL 593961; *Judiciary Square Ltd. Partnership v. S.E.C.*, GSBCA No. 12920-SEC, 1996 WL 559866; *William A. Hulett*, AGBCA No. 92-196-3 1992 WL 228400 (Ag. B.C.A.).

6. As to the complex issue of how to handle a government contractor's bankruptcy, see Samuel R. Maizel & Tracy J. Whitaker, *The Government's Contractual Rights and Bankruptcy's Automatic Stay* 752 PLI/Comm 603 (Practising Law Institute Commercial Law and Practice Course Handbook Series) PLI Order No. A4-4519 (April, 1997); David M. Pronchik, "What Do You Mean ... You Can't Terminate This Contract for Default?," Procurement Law., Winter 1995, at 11.

B. Equitable Adjustments and Constructive Changes

Equitable adjustments have an important history which has helped shape the contemporary rules of computation and proof. Tracking some of that history provides a useful introduction.

The equitable adjustment as its hallmark includes payment for increased costs and for profits on work performed, but not profits on work unperformed, so-called "unearned" profits. A classic image behind this doctrine consists of the hasty change, such as the end of World War I or World War II, which necessitates immediate ending of what had been an all-out production drive. To pay off what would have been the full measure of wartime profits to contractors who had done nothing yet to earn them would have seemed scandalous.

An elaborate line of legal evolution thereafter concerned "impact costs." When the government adds work, what about paying the contractor not just for the added work, but for the "impact" of the added work on the duration or cost of the work not changed? In *United States v. Rice*, 317 U.S. 61 (1942), the Supreme Court held that the contract made no provision for any increase in the cost of the work not changed. Subsequently, the government developed the Suspension of Work Clause to give a mechanism for government-imposed increase in the duration of work. As for government-imposed increase in costs, in the 1960s the changes clauses were amended for payment of impact costs. *Merritt-Chapman & Scott Corp. v. United States*, 192 Ct. Cl. 848, 429 F.2d 431 (1970).

What that history shows is the complex balance involved in the contemporary rules, both the rules about when the contractor can obtain an equitable adjustment and the rules of computation and proof. The equitable adjustment diverged long ago from the measure of damages in basic (private) contract law. At common law, there is no hesitation as a measure of contract damages to pay "unearned" profits; that is what the expectation interest is all about. Just why government contract law diverges so much merits consideration after some case reading. In any event, the story of the overruling of the *Rice* doctrine shows that the government has not simply redrafted its clause to squeeze contractors as tightly as possible. Government contracting law must strike a balance between the government's need for flexibility without paying scandalous unearned profits and the reasonable rewarding of contractors for compliance with changes.

1. Constructive Changes

The success of the disputes process and the equitable adjustment has caused their utilization in many government contracting situations besides formal changes. Hence, the concept of the "constructive change" has ballooned. It includes contract interpretations, government interferences with work, defective specifications, nondisclosure of vital information, and speeding up the work ("acceleration"). Several of these receive discussion in other chapters. In this chapter, the goal is not to expound rules for all the different types, but to illustrate some common elements.

Two cases here illustrate equitable adjustments in situations other than formal change orders. The *General Builders* case illustrates the connection between termination for convenience and the equitable adjustment formula. In *General Builders*, the contractor succeeded in showing that its termination for default was wrongful and it should receive treatment as though terminated for convenience. However, that just starts the process, which then turns to what the contractor should receive as an equitable adjustment.

In *Blinderman*, the contractor seeks an equitable adjustment under the "Suspension of Work" clause. It contends that the government did not cooperate enough, in effect delaying the work. Obviously, this differs from a formal change order, as the government got nothing more, and sought nothing more. Still, the flexible concepts of constructive change and equitable adjustment get stretched to apply.

General Builders Supply Co., Inc., on Behalf of Itself and for the Benefit of Hupp, Inc. v. The United States

No. 188-68
United States Court of Claims
409 F.2d 246
April 11, 1969

DAVIS, Judge.

General Builders Supply Co., Inc., the plaintiff, made a contract in 1964 with the General Services Administration to furnish 7,859 refrigerators, for use in Germany, at $119 each. General Builders then subcontracted to purchase these articles from the Gibson Refrigerator Division of the Hupp Corporation, at $116. Hupp built pre-production models and submitted them for inspection to the Government, which rejected them three times. The contract was then terminated for default on the ground that the pre-production models failed to meet the specifications. No production refrigerators were made or delivered.

On appeal, the Board of Contract Appeals of the General Services Administration determined that the work had been improperly terminated for default. The case was returned to the contracting officer for calculation of the recovery for the erroneous termination. General Builders made claim, not only for the costs actually incurred before termination, but also for the anticipated profits said to have been lost by plaintiff and by Hupp. These amounted, plaintiff said, to more than $23,500 for itself and slightly over $102,400 for the subcontractor. The contracting officer allowed recovery of $6,491.77, for the costs, but denied the demand for unearned but anticipated profits. Plaintiff was satisfied with the cost computation but appealed the rejection of the profit. The Board of Contract Appeals affirmed, holding that the default clause in the contract did not permit the award of anticipatory gain. The suit in this court attacks that conclusion. Both parties have moved for summary judgment and there is no factual controversy bearing on the legal question of the Government's liability for such profits.

The concept of an 'equitable adjustment' has had a long history in federal procurement, going back for about fifty years. See United States v. Callahan Walker Constr. Co., 317 U.S. 56, 63 S.Ct. 113, 87 L.Ed. 49 (1942); United States v. Rice, 317 U.S. 61, 63 S.Ct. 120, 87 L.Ed. 53 (1942); Ribakoff, Equitable Adjustments Under Government Contracts, in Government Contracts Program, The George Washington University, Changes and Changed Conditions 26, 27 (Gov't Contracts Monograph No. 3, 1962). First used in the standard 'changes' and 'changed conditions' articles, the term has been taken over for other clauses, such as the 'suspension of work' and 'government-furnished property' provisions. See J. Paul, United States Government Contracts and Subcontracts 430 (1964). The consistent practice appears to have been that an 'equitable adjustment,' as that phrase is used in these articles, can cover an allowance for a profit on work actually done, but does not encompass unearned but anticipated profits. See United States v. Callahan Walker Constr. Co., supra, 317 U.S. at 61, 63 S.Ct. 113; Bennett v. United States, 371 F.2d 859, 864, 178 Ct.Cl. 61, 69–70 (1967); cf. Bruce Constr. Corp. v. United States, 324 F.2d 516,

163 Ct.Cl. 97 (1963). This is far from an unnatural interpretation since, in these clauses, the 'equitable adjustment' is usually tied by express words to an increase or decrease in the contractor's costs.

The plaintiff, which impliedly concedes that this has been the practice under the other clauses, maintains that a different reading for 'equitably adjusted' is proper in the newer 'default' article. The contention is that the 'changes', 'changed conditions', and similar clauses dealt with a different problem, and the interpretation which was appropriate in that context does not fit as well into the present situation. There are, we think, two related answers to that argument. One is that 'equitable adjustment' has become a term of art (in federal contracts) with a commonly understood meaning in the aspect involved in this case (compare Ambrose-Augusterfer Corp. v. United States, 394 F.2d 536, 545, 184 Ct.Cl. 18, 33 (1968)), and that accepted content should be followed unless there are very strong counterbalancing reasons. Such a counterweight might be a marked alteration in context, but if the change is not significant and drastic it should not be sufficient to alter the established meaning of this specialized term. Here, the change in context — even if one accepts plaintiff's point that the context does in fact differ — is moderate, rather than severe. A concept hitherto applied to an ongoing agreement is now to be applied to one which is at its end, without any future. That change in context does not seem any greater than the transfer of the concept of an 'equitable adjustment' from the 'changes' article to the clause controlling 'government-furnished property' or allowing an award for 'suspension of work'.

The more basic reason for rejecting plaintiff's argument is that, at bottom, the context is not at all different in kind. With regard to amounts, a termination is essentially the same as a change under the 'changes' clause reducing the number of items to be furnished. In fact, a 'change' of that kind can often be characterized as a partial termination, and vice versa. Cf. Williamsburg Drapery Co. v. United States, 369 F.2d 729, 177 Ct.Cl. 776 (1966); Nesbitt v. United States, 345 F.2d 583, 170 Ct.Cl. 666 (1965), cert. denied, 383 U.S. 926, 86 S.Ct. 931, 15 L.Ed.2d 846 (1966); National Presto Indus., Inc. v. United States, 338 F.2d 99, 102, 167 Ct.Cl. 749, 753 (1964), cert. denied, 380 U.S. 962, 85 S.Ct. 1105, 14 L.Ed.2d 153 (1965). Whether the decrease be total or partial, and whether it be called a change or a termination, the focus will still be on the amount of money with which the contractor should be left as a result of the transaction. In that calculation, reasonable costs and a reasonable profit on work actually done will normally be important, regardless of whether one proceeds by subtracting from the original fixed-price or by adding from zero. In other words, the problem of the 'equitable adjustment' is entirely comparable whether the contractor is faced with a termination or with a change in quantity of work. There is therefore no reason for discarding the historical meaning that term has acquired under the 'changes' and like clauses.

It is possible that this particular plaintiff did not comprehend the impact of the meaningful words 'equitably adjusted' in the 'default' article of the contract, but nevertheless there was much to put it on notice. FPR Circular No. 25, supra, which spelled out the aim of the new clause, was available to government contractors and to the public. The Federal Procurement Regulations provided that, on termination of a fixed price contract, '(a)nticipatory profits and consequential damages shall not be allowed' (41 C.F.R. § 1-8.303 (a) (1968)), and said expressly that directives like the one just quoted could be used (in addition to computing the award on a convenience-termination) 'for guidance in negotiating a settlement agreement, or in making an equitable adjustment' (41 C.F.R. § 1-8.000(b) (1968) (emphasis added)). Moreover, the meaning of 'equitable adjustment' had become, so to speak, a 'trade usage' for those engaged in contracting with the Federal Government.

The knowledgeable federal contractor would understand it, and plaintiff, if it was not so knowledgeable, was charged with making itself aware of that usage. Cf. Uniform Commercial Code § 1-205. Since it was dealing with the Government, as to which a whole body of special contract provisions has developed, plaintiff could hardly take the naive stance that it had the right to read its contract as an unsophisticated layman might, without bothering to inquire into the established meaning and coverage of phrases and provisions which appear to be unusual or special to federal procurement. Cf. Beacon Constr. Co. of Mass. v. United States, 314 F.2d 501, 161 Ct.Cl. 1 (1963). In this instance, slight inquiry would have brought forth the information that 'equitably adjusted' was a term of art, and anticipatory profits would not be allowed.

Although plaintiff urges us, in effect, to strain to read the contract as permitting the recovery of such unearned gain—on the ground that the policy of the law has been to avoid allowing the defendant to escape payment of such profits where it has acted improperly—the fact is that the development of federal procurement has been to the contrary. It has long been held that, on cancellation of a contract under the power of eminent domain, just compensation does not include anticipatory profits. Russell Motor Car Co. v. United States, 261 U.S. 514, 523–24, 43 S.Ct. 428, 67 L.Ed. 778 (1923). A major reason for the initiation and increasing use of convenience-termination articles has been to allow the Government to avoid paying unearned profits. G. L. Christian & Assoc. v. United States, 312 F.2d 418, 426–427, 160 Ct.Cl. 1, 15–16, rehearing denied, 320 F.2d 345, 160 Ct.Cl. 58, cert. denied, 375 U.S. 954, 84 S.Ct. 444, 11 L.Ed.2d 314 (1963); Nolan Bros., Inc. v. United States, supra note 3, 405 F.2d, at 1256, 186 Ct.Cl at 607. As for default terminations, the clauses first recognized a breach if the invocation of the article was shown to be wrong or the default excusable (see J. D. Hedin Constr. Co. v. United States, supra, 408 F.2d 424, 187 Ct.Cl. —). They were then modified to reject such profits if the default for which the contractor was terminated turned out to be excusable, leaving untouched the situation where there was in fact no default (and the Government invoked the default article). After Klein v. United States, supra, 285 F.2d 778, 152 Ct.Cl. 8 (1961), granting unearned profits in such a case, the default articles were further amended, in general, to bar anticipated profits even in the instance in which it was found that there had been no default at all, and the contracting officer had acted erroneously. See Schlesinger v. United States, 390 F.2d 702, 710 n. 11, 182 Ct.Cl. 571, 585 n. 11 (1968). In 1967, GSA required convenience-termination clauses in contracts like the present one, so that from that time on the problem now before us is unlikely to arise. All in all, there appear today to be very few government contracts in which unearned gain can be granted if there is a termination (either for default or for convenience). The trend has been steadily adverse to the allowance of that component of common-law damages, and the policy of federal procurement law is no longer what plaintiff insists. See Nolan Bros., Inc. v. United States, supra, and cases cited.

The result is that plaintiff cannot recover on its claim for anticipatory profits, the demand it makes here....

Notes and Questions

1. The case makes clear that the equitable adjustment draws the line against paying "unearned" profits. That phrase has a kind of populist ring, like refusing to pay those who have not labored and sweated for their reward, but that has, of course, nothing to do with it. At common law, contractors receive their expectation interest in the event of breach. In the realm of private contracts, the argument might well be made that if a merchant put into a contract of adhesion with a non-merchant a clause denying the latter the ordinary measure of direct damages ("unearned" profits), the clause was unconscionable. Why can the government do this?

One argument in basic (private) contract law for paying the measure of expectation damages has been that there are reliance damages that would be hard to prove and would go uncompensated, thereby discouraging reliance in the future absent payment of expectation damages. Do government contractors, knowing that the public needs the freedom to cancel contracts in response to shifts in policy, have forewarning enough to make a judgment about reliance? Or is it that, just as the government cannot let its authority be curtailed by estoppel, the government cannot let its budget be mortgaged by reliance? Is it the ample measure of profit in government contracting when performed that allows the government to withhold profits when changes eliminate performance?

2. Computation and Proof of Equitable Adjustments

Computation and proof of equitable adjustment follow from the previously discussed considerations. The components of computation should keep the contractor whole, preserving the government's position as to what the change did not affect.

Looking at components, the adjustment process can be broken down into three component parts: work added, work deleted, and overhead and profit. When the contracting officer (or, on appeal, a tribunal) sets the adjustment, she prices the new work as the reasonable cost to the contractor. Ideally, pricing occurs before the costs are actually incurred, by estimating them from actual or historical costs. The adjustment thus relates to the contractor's costs, not the value to the government. When the change deletes work, the government gets a downward adjustment equal to the amount of cost the contractor would have incurred had the work been performed.

Figuring overhead and profit pose particular problems. Normally, direct costs can bear a standard amount of overhead. However, the parties may demonstrate that the change produces extra high overhead. Similarly, the CO can apply a standard profit percentage, but the changed work could warrant different profit by being more or less demanding or risky. The FAR provides direction for considering factors called the "weighted guidelines" method. FAR 15.902, 15.905.

As for proof, the tribunals prefer actual cost data; if the contractor offers estimates, they should be prepared with detailed substantiating data by experts who are knowledgeable, competent, and familiar with the facts. Of four methods, the "actual cost" method uses the actual costs relating to the change. The "total cost" method compares the total cost of the work performed, minus the original estimate of the work. A "modified total cost method" excludes from the total cost comparison amounts attributable to underbidding, contractor inefficiency, and unrelated contractor costs. Finally, the "jury verdict" method simply takes conflicting evidence and lets an approximation be made.

Propellex Corporation, Appellant, v.
Les Brownlee, Acting Secretary of the Army, Appellee

No. 02-1358
United States Court of Appeals, Federal Circuit
342 F.3d 1335
Decided: Sept. 9, 2003

Before MICHEL, RADER, and SCHALL, Cicuit Judges

SCHALL, Circuit Judge.

Propellex Corporation ("Propellex") appeals from the final decision of the Armed Services Board of Contract Appeals ("Board") that sustained the final decision of the contracting officer denying in part Propellex's claim for additional compensation under two contracts between Propellex and the Department of the Army's Armament, Munitions and Chemical Command ("Army") for the production and delivery of gun primers. *Propellex Corp.*, ASBCA No. 50,203, 02-1 B.C.A. (CCH) § 31,721, at 156,730–31, 2001 WL 1678757 (Dec. 27, 2001). Propellex sought recovery under a modified total cost method. The Board denied Propellex's appeal because it concluded, *inter alia,* that Propellex had failed to establish that it was impracticable for it to prove its actual losses directly, which is one of the requirements for recovery under the total cost method. *Id.* at 156,730. Because the decision of the Board is supported by substantial evidence and is free of legal error, we affirm.

BACKGROUND

I.

The Army awarded Propellex two fixed price contracts, contract no. DAAA09-88-C-0817 (the "817 contract") and contract no. DAAA09-90-C-0455 (the "455 contract"), for the production and delivery of a specified number of MK 45 primers. The 817 contract also called for the production and delivery of a specified number of MK 153 primers. A primer is a component of a gun shell. A shell generally includes a projectile and a propellant charge. The primer is an explosive device that ignites the propellant charge in the shell. The propellant charge in turn propels the projectile. A key component of a primer is black powder.

Under each contract, before the Army would accept a lot for delivery, Propellex was required to submit samples of the primers in the lot to the Naval Surface Warfare Center ("NSWC") in Indian Head, Maryland, for, *inter alia,* testing of the moisture content of the black powder contained in the primers. Under the contracts, the moisture content of the black powder in the primers could not exceed a certain level. To ensure compliance with this requirement, Propellex performed its own moisture analysis on the black powder before sending the primers to NSWC for testing.

In September of 1990, Propellex sent to NSWC for testing samples of primers from lot six of the 817 contract. Following testing, the Army determined that the sample primers did not comply with the requirements of the contract because the moisture content of their black powder exceeded what was allowed under the contract. As a result, the Army rejected the lot. The Army stated that the excess moisture in the primers was the fault of Propellex, and it directed Propellex to resolve the problem.

In response to the Army's rejection, Propellex conducted an investigation to determine the cause of the alleged moisture in the primers. Although primer production continued during the investigation, Propellex diverted a number of its production employees to investigate the moisture problem. Propellex kept records of the tests it performed. However, the records did not include the number of employees, labor hours, or amount of materials involved in the testing. During the investigation, which spanned a period of two years, the Army also rejected lots 1, 2, and 3 of the 455 contract for excess moisture and other defects.

On February 16, 1993, after Propellex had completed its investigation, it notified the Army that it had not found any evidence indicating that the moisture content of the black power in its primers was above the level specified as acceptable in the contracts. It suggested that the Army determine if there was a defect in its testing procedures.

On April 7, 1993, Propellex's consultant, Edward Williams, and the Defense Contract Management Agency's quality assurance engineer, Bryan Nussbaum, observed NSWC's testing of samples from lot five of the 455 contract. Over the next few months, they further observed and analyzed NSWC's testing procedures. As a result of their observations and analysis, they found defects in the procedures. Eventually, the Army accepted all of the primers that Propellex produced under the contracts.

On September 16, 1994, Propellex filed a claim with the contracting officer, seeking an equitable adjustment under the 817 and 455 contracts in the total amount of $1,790,065. The contracting officer determined that Propellex was entitled to a recovery in the amount of $77,325. However, she denied the balance of Propellex's claim:

> Based on a review of the Request for Equitable Adjustment, the supporting documentation available to the Contracting Officer and all other relevant facts, it is the Contracting Officer's decision that the Government was and is responsible for only a small portion of the claimed amounts. Based on insufficient data to further support damages claimed by Propellex, the Contracting Officer finds an Equitable Adjustment in the amount of $77,325.00 due to Propellex as a result of the Equitable Adjustment Claim under contracts DAAA09-88-C-0817 and DAAA09-90-C-0455.

Propellex timely appealed the contracting officer's final decision to the Board under the provisions of the Contract Disputes Act of 1978, 41 U.S.C. §§ 601–613 ("CDA").

II.

Following a hearing, the Board granted Propellex's appeal with respect to entitlement, finding that NSWC had not conducted the primer acceptance tests in accordance with contract testing requirements. *Propellex,* 02-1 B.C.A. at 156,729. As a result, the Board awarded Propellex $33,110, plus interest, for claim preparation costs and consulting expenses. *Id.* at 156,730. However, the Board denied in toto Propellex's claims for the cost of the moisture investigation and for unabsorbed overhead costs. *Id.*

In denying Propellex's claim for the cost of the moisture investigation, the Board observed that Propellex had advanced the claim using a modified total cost method. *Id.* at 156,729. The Board stated that to recover under the total cost method, a contractor must prove: (1) the impracticability of proving its actual losses directly; (2) the reasonableness of its bid; (3) the reasonableness of its actual costs; and (4) lack of responsibility for the added costs. *Id.* (citing *Servidone Constr. Corp. v. United States,* 931 F.2d 860, 861 (Fed.Cir.1991)). The Board noted that in using a modified total cost method to prove its claim, Propellex adjusted its bid for possible understatement and excluded some of the costs for which it admitted responsibility. *Id.* at 156,729–30. Nevertheless, the Board determined that Propellex had failed to establish the impracticability of proving its actual losses directly and the lack of responsibility for the added costs. *Id.* at 156,730. It therefore denied Propellex's claim for additional compensation for increased costs under the contracts. *Id.* Propellex has timely appealed the Board's decision. We have jurisdiction pursuant to 28 U.S.C.§ 1295(a)(10).

ANALYSIS

* * *

II.

We have stated that the preferred way for a contractor to prove increased costs is to submit actual cost data because such data "provides the court, or contracting officer, with documented underlying expenses, ensuring that the final amount of the equitable adjustment will be just that — equitable — and not a windfall for either the government or the contractor." *Dawco Constr., Inc. v. United States,* 930 F.2d 872, 882 (Fed.Cir.1991), *overruled on other grounds by Reflectone, Inc. v. Dalton,* 60 F.3d 1572 (Fed.Cir.1995). As noted, Propellex advanced its claim using the modified total cost method. The modified total cost method is a modification of the total cost method. Under the total cost method, the measure of damages is the difference between the actual cost of the contract and the contractor's bid. *See Raytheon Co. v. White,* 305 F.3d 1354, 1365 (Fed.Cir.2002). Before a contractor can obtain the benefit of the total cost method, it must prove: (1) the impracticability of proving its actual losses directly; (2) the reasonableness of its bid; (3) the reasonableness of its actual costs; and (4) lack of responsibility for the added costs. *Servidone,* 931 F.2d at 861. The modified total cost method is the total cost method adjusted for any deficiencies in the contractor's proof in satisfying the requirements of the total cost method. *Id.* at 861–62. In *Boyajian v. United States,* 191 Ct.Cl. 233, 423 F.2d 1231 (1970), the Court of Claims described the use of a modified total cost method:

> [T]he total cost method was used as "only a starting point" with such adjustments thereafter made in such computations as allowances for various factors as to convince the court that the ultimate, reduced, figure fairly represented the increased costs the contractor directly suffered from the particular action of defendant which was the subject of the complaint.

Id. at 1240 (citation omitted). Before the Board, Propellex sought recovery under a modified total cost method by adjusting its bid for possible understatement and by excluding from the computation of its claim some of the costs for which it admitted responsibility. *See Propellex,* 02-1 B.C.A. at 156,729–30. However, under its modified total cost method claim, Propellex still had the burden of proving the four requirements for a total cost recovery set forth above. The modified method simply was a way of easing that burden somewhat. *See Raytheon,* 305 F.3d at 1365; *Servidone,* 931 F.2d at 861–62.

In addressing the impracticability requirement, the Board noted that Propellex's witnesses testified, and its expert agreed, that Propellex did not segregate and record, and could not estimate, the labor hours and costs of the black powder moisture investigation. *Id.* The Board further noted that the hours and costs attributable to the moisture investigation were commingled with all labor hours and costs of contract performance, so that Propellex could not prove its costs directly. *Id.* Yet, the Board observed, Propellex's expert found no difficulty in approximating certain costs not attributable to the moisture investigation. *Id.* The Board also observed that, in connection with its case on entitlement, Propellex had documented its investigative efforts. *Id.* The Board concluded that "[s]uch evidence ... [did] not establish the impracticability of proving Propellex's claimed losses directly." *Id.* With respect to the fourth requirement for use of the modified total cost method, the Board stated that "[t]he most serious failure of Propellex's modified total cost proof ... [was] that it did not exclude from the claim amounts ... costs under both contracts 817 and 455 not attributable to black powder moisture investigation...." *Id.* The Board added that it had attempted to reconstruct from the record a reasonable approximation of those costs, but had found that the evidence did not permit such an approximation. *Id.* Accordingly, the Board concluded that Propellex's claim under a modified total cost method failed because Propellex had not established the impracticability of proving its actual losses directly and the lack of responsibility for the added costs. *Id.*

On appeal, Propellex challenges both of these rulings.

* * *

We agree with the government that substantial evidence supports the Board's finding that Propellex failed to demonstrate the impracticability of proving its actual losses directly. The evidence shows that Propellex could have set up its accounting system to track the costs of the moisture investigation and that it failed to do so.

* * *

In short, the evidence shows that Propellex could have set up its accounting system to track the costs of the moisture investigation, but that it failed to do so.

Although Propellex does not dispute that it could have set up its accounting system to track the costs of the moisture investigation, it argues that because it "reasonably believed that it was to blame [for the moisture problem], there was no reason [for it] to set up an account to track such costs." We are not persuaded by this argument. First, Propellex did record in detail every aspect of the testing related to the moisture problem, with the exception of costs. Second, assuming Propellex believed it was responsible for the moisture problem, it was all the more important for it to segregate costs relating to that problem from costs incurred under the contracts for which it was entitled to be paid by the Army. Where it is impractical for a contractor to prove its actual costs because it failed to keep accurate records, when such records could have been kept, and where the contractor does not provide a legitimate reason for its failure to keep the records, the total cost method of recovery is not available to the contractor.

* * *

In sum, substantial evidence supports the Board's conclusion that Propellex did not establish the impracticability of proving its actual losses directly and thus cannot recover under the modified total cost method.

We do not agree with Propellex that the Board erred as a matter of law when it contrasted Propellex's ability to estimate certain costs that were not related to the moisture investigation with its inability to directly prove the investigation's costs. Contrary to Propellex's view, under the Board's ruling, compliance with requirement four of the total cost method, i.e., removing the costs that were not related to the moisture investigation, does not make it impossible to establish the first requirement, i.e., the impracticability of proving the contractor's losses directly. That is so because a contractor can always show why a court should not rely on its ability to segregate and remove certain costs in determining whether the contractor established the first requirement. The four requirements of the total cost method are distinct requirements and a contractor must prove all of them before it can obtain the benefit of the total cost method. Accordingly, it was not error for the Board to rely on Propellex's ability to estimate the costs that were not related to the moisture investigation as undercutting Propellex's argument that it is impracticable for it to prove its losses directly.

CONCLUSION

Because substantial evidence supports the Board's conclusion that Propellex has not established the impracticability of proving its losses directly, as required under the total cost method, the decision of the Board is

AFFIRMED.

C. Delays

For further discussion of the subjects in this section, see: Thomas H. Gourlay (Jr.), *Constructive Acceleration And Concurrent Delay: Is There A "Middle Ground"?*, 39 Pub. Cont. L.J. 231 (Winter 2010); Thomas J. Kelleher (Jr.), Eric L. Nelson, Garrett E. Miller, *The Resurrection Of Rice? The Evolution (And De-Evolution) Of The Ability Of Contractors To Recover Delay Damages On Federal Government Construction Contracts*, 39 Pub. Cont. L.J. 305 (Winter 2010); W. Stephen Dale, Kathryn T. Muldoon, *A Government Windfall: ASBCA's Attack On Concurrent Delays As A Basis For Constructive Acceleration*, 44 Procrmt. Law. 4 (Summer 2009).

Blinderman Construction Co., Inc., Appellant, v. The United States, Appellee

Appeal No. 53-82
United States Court of Appeals, Federal Circuit
695 F.2d 552
Dec. 10, 1982

COWEN, Senior Circuit Judge.

Pursuant to the Contract Disputes Act of 1978, 41 U.S.C. §§ 601, et seq., the appellant (contractor) appeals from a decision of the Armed Services Board of Contract Appeals (Board) which denied, in part, the contractor's claim in the amount of $45,312, and its request for a time extension of 13 days for the completion of the contract. The case is before us on cross-motions for summary judgment filed in the United States Court of Claims prior to October 1, 1982, and thereafter transferred to this court.

The claim grows out of a contract entered into between the contractor and the Department of the Navy (Navy) for installation of permanent improvements in multifamily housing at the Great Lakes, Illinois Naval Base (Base).

The claim of $45,312, includes three separate items.

* * *

The third and largest item is for damages sought for what the Board refers to as a claim for "access delays," and a time extension of 13 days. The contractor contends that the additional expense and delay were incurred by reason of the Navy's failure to discharge its contractual obligation to provide access to apartments occupied by Naval personnel. A summary of the claim of $45,312 shows that it includes an item of $11,579 for "delay costs," and $33,733 claimed on the ground that the impact of the delays was to extend the completion of the project by 9 working days.

The claim for access delays involves an interpretation of the provisions of the contract, and for the reasons to be set forth, we disagree with the Board's interpretation and re-

verse its decision on this question of law. However, in view of its holding, the Board did
not decide whether or to what extent the Navy's delay was unreasonable. Also, at oral argument, Government counsel stated that if we disagreed with the Board, the case should
be remanded because of concurrent delays attributable to the contractor and its subcontractor. We agree, and therefore we deny both motions for summary judgment, except as
stated above, and remand the case to the Board for further proceedings in accordance
with this opinion.

I. Factual Background and Prior Proceedings.

By contract dated March 31, 1978, the contractor was required to furnish and install
electrical meters, gas meters, hot water meters, hot water heating meters and condensate
meters in the apartments housing Naval personnel at the Base. The contract was to have
been completed by September 12, 1978, but the completion date was extended by a change
order to October 3, 1978. The contract was let in conformity with the national policy to
conserve energy by metering energy usage in military housing. About 139 buildings and
656 individual apartments were involved in the work to be performed.

The contractor was required to provide a quality control inspection system to insure
compliance with the contract plans and specifications. The contract contained the standard clauses for construction contracts including "Changes," "Suspension of Work," and
"Liquidated Damages". Since the work was not completed until October 20, 1978, the
contractor was charged by the Navy with liquidated damages of $2,975 for 17 days of in-
excusable delays. On other claims not in issue, the Board found that the contractor was
entitled to a time extension of 6 days and remission of liquidated damages in the amount
of $1,050; thus the contractor was charged with net liquidated damages of $1,925 for 11
days of inexcusable delays.

Following the adverse decision of the contracting officer, the contractor elected to proceed under the Contract Disputes Act of 1978 and appealed the decision to the Board.
The Board denied the claim before us in an initial opinion of November 14, 1980, and then,
in an opinion on motion for reconsideration, on February 25, 1981. The cross-motions
for summary judgment on the contractor's appeal from the Board's decision were thereafter filed in the United States Court of Claims.

* * *

III. The Claim for Delays in Obtaining Access to the Apartments.

This claim presents the only difficult issue in this appeal, because its resolution involves an interpretation of the following provisions of the contract:

> SCHEDULING OF WORK: Work shall be scheduled to issue [sic] minimum de-
> scription [sic] of service to the housing units. The contractor shall notify the oc-
> cupants of the housing unit[1] at least 3 days prior to commencing any work in a
> housing unit. The contractor shall perform his work between the hours of 8:00
> A.M. and 5:00 P.M. and having once started work in a housing unit shall work
> to completion in consecutive work days....
>
> In no case shall a unit be left overnight without a completed meter installation,
> including testing and resumption of gas service.

---

1. An amendment to the IFB changed 'contracting officer' to 'occupants of the housing unit.'

PROGRESS CHARTS: The Contractor shall, within 15 days after receipt of notice of award, prepare and submit to the Contracting Officer for approval, a practicable construction schedule in accordance with Clause entitled 'Progress Charts and Requirements for Overtime Work' of the General Provisions except as modified herein. Progress chart shall clearly indicate when the contractor will require access to individual buildings and shall further indicate the anticipated durations of all utility outages.

METHODS AND SCHEDULES OF PROCEDURES: The work shall be executed in a manner and at such times that will cause the least practicable disturbance to the occupants of the buildings and normal activities of the station. Before starting any work, the sequence of operations and the methods of conducting the work shall have been approved by the Contracting Officer.

The facts as found by the Board or which are otherwise established by undisputed evidence, show that the contractor experienced considerable difficulty and delays in gaining access to approximately 60 apartments. After the contractor had prepared and delivered to the Navy a progress chart showing when the contractor required access to the buildings, the contractor's quality control manager (CQC) had the responsibility for notifying the occupants of the time when the work in their apartments was to be performed. The specifications required that this notice be given 3 days before work was to be commenced, and the CQC attempted to notify them personally at least 3 but usually 7 days before the work was to begin.

Notices to the occupants were given in the morning, during the noon-hour, or in the afternoon. If CQC could not reach the occupants during the day, he tried to see them in the evening. If all of these efforts failed, the CQC would, in accordance with a suggestion made by the Navy's project manager, leave a yellow card on the doorknob of the apartment, indicating when the work in that unit would begin. The Navy had, at the site of the work, a project manager who represented the contracting officer in the administration of the contract, and most of the contractor's dealings were with this project manager. In some instances, the occupants refused to permit the contractor's workmen to enter their apartments, even after notice was received by them. At times, the contractor was unable to serve personal notice because the occupants were on military leave for periods for as long as 2 weeks. In other instances, the occupants would go out during the lunch hour while the work was being performed, leaving their doors locked with the tools of the workmen inside. On most of the occasions complained of by the contractor, the occupants were not at home when the work was scheduled despite notice given to them in person or by a card left on the doorknob.

Whenever the contractor or the subcontractors were unable to gain access to an apartment for any of the reasons mentioned above, they would call on the project manager to provide the access they needed. If the occupants could be contacted by telephone, the project manager would ask them to return home and permit entry into their apartments. If the occupants were absent from the apartment on vacation, the project manager first telephoned them to get permission to enter their apartments. Then he would obtain keys from the Housing Section at the Base to admit the workmen. Thus on occasion, access by the workmen could not be obtained until several days after the scheduled date for commencing work. The workmen were carpenters, plumbers, pipefitters, electricians, and laborers, and their work had to be coordinated and performed in a planned sequence. Because of the delays, they would have to leave buildings with work unfinished in several apartments and work in another building. To complete the contract, they would have to backtrack to those apartments which they were unable to enter during the time previously scheduled for the work.

Shortly after experiencing delays for lack of access to the apartments, the contractor notified the project manager that the contractor's responsibilities ended after it had notified the occupants in the manner described above; that a record would be kept of the delays, and that a claim would be submitted later for the increased costs incurred as a result of such delays.

As previously stated, the contractor gave the project manager notice that claims would be submitted for the increased costs due to the delays in getting access to the apartments. On December 1, 1978, after the contract had been completed, the contractor submitted to the project manager the claim in issue. Attached thereto was an itemized breakdown of the dates and extent of the delays. . . .

At the contractor's request, the claim was submitted to the contracting officer, who agreed with the project manager and denied the claim by written "final decision."

* * *

On appeal, the contractor argued before the Board that the 150-day completion schedule, the provision for liquidated damages, the specification limiting work hours, and the requirement for the contracting officer's approval of the construction schedule and sequence of the work, implied a duty on the part of the Navy to make the apartments in the buildings available in accordance with the schedule and sequence of work which had been approved by the project manager.

In its opinion, the Board noted that the invitation for bids had originally provided that the contractor would notify the contracting officer at least 3 days prior to commencing work in any unit, but that this requirement was amended to state that the notification was required to be given by the contractor to the occupants of the housing units. The Board concluded that the necessary implication of this change was that "the contractor, and not the Navy, was obliged to make arrangements with each tenant as to the specific time work would start and any necessary preparations by the tenants in each apartment." Thus, the Board essentially adopted the project manager's view that the specifications required the contractor, not only to give notice to the occupants, but also to obtain in each case, an agreement permitting entry into the individual apartments, specifying the time for the work, and covering necessary preparations by the occupants.

The Board's holding on this crucial issue is a decision on a question of law, which is not final or conclusive on judicial review. 41 U.S.C. §609(b). It is with this conclusion of law that we disagree.

The Government has correctly observed that this is not a case in which the Government expressly contracted to provide access to the premises to perform the contract work, as in Delta Equipment & Constr. Co. v. United States, 104 F.Supp. 549, 122 Ct.Cl. 340 (1952). Nor is it a case like Broome Constr., Inc. v. United States, 492 F.2d 829 (Ct.Cl.1974), and similar cases where the courts have held that the contractor is not entitled to an adjustment under the "Suspension of Work" clause where the claimed delays were due to the acts of another contractor or to bad weather.

The answer to the question is not free of doubt. However, after considering the language of the specifications and other pertinent facts and circumstances, we conclude that there should be applied here the rule enunciated in Worthington Pump & Machinery Corp. v. United States, 66 Ct.Cl. 230, 240 (1928) and Edward E. Gillen Co. v. United States, 88 Ct.Cl. 347, 368 (1939). Therefore, we hold that the contractor complied with the "Scheduling of Work" provision by giving as much notice as was reasonably required by that provision. After the contractor notified the project manager that the contractor's reasonable efforts had not resulted in gaining entry to certain apartments, the Navy was under an implied obligation to provide such access so that the contractor could complete the contract within the time required by its terms. Consequently, if any part of the contractor's work was thereafter delayed for an unreasonable period of time because of the Navy's failure to provide access to the apartments, the contractor is, under the "Suspension of Work" clause,[2] entitled to an increase in the cost of performing the contract. Chaney and James Constr. Co. v. United States, 421 F.2d 728, 190 Ct.Cl. 699 (1970). We have reached this conclusion on several grounds.

We find that if their ordinary meaning is attributed to the words used in the "Scheduling of Work" provision, there is simply nothing in that specification or elsewhere which states that the contractor is required to make an arrangement with or obtain an agreement from each apartment occupant as the Board decided.

It was reasonable for the contractor to interpret this provision of the specifications to relieve it of further responsibility to notify the occupants after reasonable efforts to give the notice had been exhausted. If the Government had intended the specifications to convey an intent to require the contractor to make an agreement covering the matters found by the Board with each of the 656 occupants, the drafters of the specifications wholly failed to convey this meaning. Therefore, the provision must be construed against the Government. Troup Bros., Inc. v. United States, 643 F.2d 719, 224 Ct.Cl. 594 (1980); Singer-General Precision, Inc. v. United States, 427 F.2d 1187, 192 Ct.Cl. 435 (1970); Jefferson Constr. Co. v. United States, 151 Ct.Cl. 75 (1960).

The conduct of both parties during construction and before the contractor's claim was submitted to the project manager provides persuasive evidence that the contract should be construed as urged by the contractor....

We do not hold that the contractor was justified in believing that it would encounter no difficulty in notifying the occupants when the work would begin. However, the evidence shows that in view of the contractor's previous experience on the same base, it believed the Navy would provide access to the apartments when such difficulties arose.

IV. The Contractor's Right to Recover Damages.

Our holding with respect to the Government's liability should not be construed as a decision that the contractor is entitled to recover the increased costs it claims were incurred because of lack of access to the apartments. In view of its interpretation of the contract, the Board made no finding on the extent of the Government's unreasonable delay or on the issue of damages. As previously stated, Government counsel at oral argument contended

---

2. SUSPENSION OF WORK (1968 FEB)
   (b) If the performance of all or any part of the work is, for an unreasonable period of time, suspended, delayed, or interrupted by an act of the Contracting Officer in the administration of this contract, or by his failure to act within the time specified in this contract (or if no time is specified, within a reasonable time) an adjustment shall be made for any increase in the cost of performance of this contract (excluding profit) necessarily caused by such unreasonable suspension, delay, or interruption and the contract modified in writing accordingly. However, no adjustment shall be made under this clause for any suspension, delay, or interruption to the extent (1) that performance would have been so suspended, delayed, or interrupted by any other cause, including the fault or negligence of the Contractor or (2) for which an equitable adjustment is provided for or excluded under any other provision of this contract.

that if we disagreed with the Board on the access claim, the case should be remanded because of concurrent delays attributable to the contractor and its subcontractor.

The Board found that:

> The mechanical subcontractor needed 20 workers to do the mechanical work required in the time allowed. It was never able to hire that many workers. That labor shortage, in part, caused the subcontractor to fall behind schedule and required it to hire Hans Jensen to do some of the mechanical work.

This finding is supported by substantial evidence.

Where both parties contribute to the delay "neither can recover damage, unless there is in the proof a clear apportionment of the delay and the expense attributable to each party." Coath & Goss, Inc. v. United States, 101 Ct.Cl. 702, 714–15 (1944); Commerce International Co. v. United States, 338 F.2d 81, 90, 167 Ct.Cl. 529 (1964).

* * *

V. Conclusion.

For the reasons stated, the Board's decision involving the power outage of August 18, 1978, is affirmed, but its decision on the access claim is reversed. With these exceptions, both motions for summary judgment are denied and the case is remanded to the Board to make such findings of fact and conclusions of law as will enable it to determine: (1) whether and to what extent any part of the contractor's work was unreasonably delayed by the Navy's failure to provide access to the apartments; (2) whether any unreasonable delays caused by the Navy were concurrent with or separate from delays due to the subcontractor's shortage of labor or other delays chargeable to the contractor, and (3) whether the contractor is entitled to a time extension and/or a recovery of damages and if so, how much.

AFFIRMED IN PART, REVERSED IN PART, AND REMANDED.

Notes and Questions

1. One way into this case is to recognize how strong the government's argument is. Did the CO grant the contractor's claim? No. Did the ASBCA? No. And did the Court of Claims come close to not granting it? It said, "The answer to the question is not free of doubt." Why? Consider this short formulation of the argument against the contractor: This contractor bid on an IFB. If the contractor was not willing to deal with the problems, it should have put in a higher bid, and let the next highest bidder, if willing, take the contract. What interpretive question did the board of contract appeals resolve to find against the contractor?

2. On the other hand, can you describe the delicate situation faced by the contractor? How do you suppose those in the military housing greeted contractor employees showing up to install energy charging meters? One hopes the heavy armament had not been brought home back to the military housing when the meter-installers rang the doorbell. It seems as though the military housing occupants viewed this as an exercise for practicing a cross between nonviolent protest and guerrilla warfare. What interpretive rule did this court apply to find for the contractor?

3. Is the Suspension of Work clause a general "excusable delay" clause? A prior version of it was called the "Stop Work Order" clause, signifying how extreme the government interference had to be to justify relief for the contractor. What happens if the delay is the result of the "acts of another contractor or bad weather," to quote the case? Did the government itself affirmatively act in this case to delay the contractor?

Suspension of Work Clause
(Apr. 1984)

(a) The Contracting Officer may order the Contractor, in writing, to suspend, delay, or interrupt all or any part of the work of this contract for the period of time that the Contracting Officer determines appropriate for the convenience of the Government.

(b) If the performance of all or any part of the work is, for an unreasonable period of time, suspended, delayed, or interrupted

    (1) by an act of the Contracting Officer in the administration of this contract, or

    (2) by the Contracting Officer's failure to act within the time specified in this contract (or within a reasonable time if not specified), an adjustment shall be made for any increase in the cost of performance of this contract (excluding profit) necessarily caused by the unreasonable suspension, delay, or interruption, and the contract modified in writing accordingly. However, no adjustment shall be made under this clause for any suspension, delay, or interruption to the extent that performance would have been so suspended, delayed, or interrupted by any other cause, including the fault or negligence of the Contractor, or for which an equitable adjustment is provided for or excluded under any other term or condition of this contract.

(c) A claim under this clause shall not be allowed

    (1) for any costs incurred more than 20 days before the Contractor shall have notified the Contracting Officer in writing of the act or failure to act involved …

    (2) unless the claim, in an amount stated, is asserted in writing as soon as practicable after the termination of the suspension, delay, or interruption, but not later than the date of final payment under the contract.

Note on Delays — Compensable and Excusable

Delays matter a great deal in government contracting law, especially in construction contracts. A contractor is responsible for both the time and cost of delays that it causes or that are within its control — that is, the *unexcused delays*. For example, a contractor should have planned and prepared to handle the ordinary bad weather or ordinary subcontractor delays that may come its way. A contractor with an unexcused delay may face liquidated damages (i.e., damages calculated by a formula in the contract) and even, in an extreme case, termination for default. *General Injectables & Vaccines, Inc. v. Gates*, 527 F.2d 1375 (Fed. Cir. 2008).

Normally, the government excuses the contractor for events beyond the contractor's control, that is, the *excusable delays*. For example, a supplier or other subcontractor may inflict delays beyond the contractor's control, and, not involving negligence by either the contractor or the subcontractor. A contractor with such an excusable delay does not face the paying of damages.

Finally, for a limited number of delays — delays by the government itself — the government agrees to pay compensation. These are *compensable delays*. For example, the government may issue a "stop work order" when continued work by the contractor would get in the government's way. Then, the government may owe the contractor damages.

It is commonly said that excusable delays entitle the contractor to "days, not dollars" and compensable delays entitles the contractor to "both days and dollars."

Excusable delays

The purpose of the Excusable Delays clause is to remove uncertainty and needless litigation by defining delays with more particularity and to protect the contractor from the unforeseeable. Contractors thus know they are not to be penalized for unexpected impediments to prompt performance. Since their bids can be based on the foreseeable and probable, rather than possible, hindrances, the government gets lower bids.

There are similar clauses about excusable delays both in construction contracts and in supply contracts, although the issue matters most in construction contracts. Moreover, there is language in the Default Clause for excusing failure to perform that is similar to the langue in the Excusable Delays clause itself.

The Excusable Delays clause provides that, except for defaults of subcontractors at any tier, the contractor shall not be in default for any failure to perform the contract if the failure arises from causes beyond the control and without the fault or negligence of the contractor. Examples of such causes include acts of God or of the public enemy, acts of the government in either its sovereign or its contractual capacity, fires, floods, epidemics, quarantine restrictions, stakes, freight embargoes, and unusually severe weather. See FAR § 52.249-14.

As to performance failures of subcontractors at any tier, the contractor shall not be in default if the cause of the failure was beyond the control and without the fault or negligence of either the prime contractor or the subcontractors. The delay is not excusable as to the prime contractor if the contracted supplies or services were obtainable from another source, or if the Contracting Officer ordered the contractor to obtain the supplies or services from another source and the contractor failed to comply reasonably with that order.

In order to avail himself of the Excusable Delays article, the contractor is required to request a time extension of the Contracting Officer, setting forth the facts and extent of the failure. If the Contracting Officer determines that the delay is in fact excusable, the delivery schedule is to be revised.

To illustrate briefly with a few of the different types of excusable delay:

Weather: A prudent contractor considers ordinary weather. The term "unusually severe weather" in the Excusable Delays clause does not include any and all weather that prevents work under the contract. Rather, it only means weather surpassing in severity the weather usually encountered or reasonably to be expected in the particular locality and during the same time of year involved in the contract. 14 Comp. Gen. 431 (1934).

Strikes: A contractor will not be automatically excused from performance merely because he establishes the existence of a strike. It must also be shown that the delay caused by the strike was beyond the control and without the fault or negligence of the contractor, *Sun Constr. Co.,* IBCA No. 208, 61-1 BCA 2926.

Compensable Delays

Compensable delays make the contractor whole when the delay is caused by government action. Such delays include the government's orders and acts, and, differing site conditions and other contingencies for which the contract assigns the risk to the government. An example is when the government orders a contractor to finish earlier, which the contractor does but only by incurring additional costs. When the government expressly orders this, it is called acceleration. When the government does not expressly order it, but it creates a situation in which the contractor must speed up in this way, it is called *constructive acceleration.*

Concurrent Delays

A complex issue over the years has concerned concurrent delays, when both the government and the contractor contribute to the delay. It is said, as a rule of thumb rather than a legal doctrine, that when the issue is excusable delay, the government tends to allow the excuse and not to "battle" the contractor over the delay.

There has been murkiness about the issue of apportionment of delays. On the one hand, it is argued that if the proof makes a clear apportionment of the delay and the expense attributable to each party, then damages can be assessed. On the other hand, it is argued that the government cannot assess damages even if the delays may be apportioned. There has been complex case law on this. See *Sauer Inc. v. Danzig,* 224 F.3d 1340, 1347 (Fed. Cir. 2000)*; PCL Const. Services, Inc. v. U.S.,* 53 F.3d 479 (2002). For sophisticated treatment in the commentary, including discussion of more recent cases in the ASBCA, see Thomas H. Gourlay Jr., *Constructive Acceleration and Concurrent Delay: Is There a "Middle Ground"?,* 39 Pub. OInct. L.J. 231 (2010); W. Stephen Dale & Robert M. d'Onofrio, *Reconciling Concurrency in Schedule Delay and Constructive Acceleration,* 39 Pub. Cont. L.J. 161 (2010); W. Stephen Dlay & Kathryn T. Muldoon, *A Government Windfall: ASBCA's Attack on Concurrent Delays as a Basis for Constructive Acceleration,* 44-SUM Procurement Law. 4 (2009);

In the past, there had been a judicially-created presumption that the government is at fault for any delay in construction coupled with an extension of a period of performance. The Federal Circuit overturned this presumption in *England v. Sherman R. Smooth Corp.,* 388 F.3d 844 (Fed. Cir. 2004).

Notes and Questions

1. Closely akin to the contractor's rights when the government causes "unreasonable delays" are the contractor's rights when the government violates its implied duty to cooperate and to prevent interference with the contractor's performance. Interference claims arise when the government's inexcusable conduct precludes or increases the cost of performance by the contractor. This includes the government's excessive inspection, incompetence, and physical interference attributable to the government. See *WRB Corp. v. United States,* 183 Cl.Ct. 409 (1968)(government must act reasonably in inspection of contractor's work); *Harvey C. Jones, Inc.,* IBCA No. 2070, 90-2 BCA ¶ 22, 762 (incompetence by government is interference); *C.M. Lowther, Jr.,* ASBCA No. 38407, 91-3 BCA ¶ 24,296 (water seepage from the government's malfunctioning sump pump is interference)). Additionally, the case of *R.B. Bewachungsgessellschaft mbH,* ASBCA No. 42213, 91-3 BCA ¶ 24,310 held that it was interference when the government conducted disruptive criminal investigations in its contractual capacity.

2. When the contractor invokes its right to cooperation, the government may raise the interesting defense that interference is the result of a sovereign act, for it is well established that the government cannot be held liable for costs of interference resulting form sovereign acts. *Hills Materials Co.,* ASBCA No. 42410, 92-1 BCA ¶ 24.636 (*citing Deming v. United States,* 1 Ct.Cl. 190 (1865)). The doctrine may apply to an act by Congress that is out of the control of the contracting agency, while not applying where an agency retains discretion in allocating and distributing funds under an existing contract. *Appeal of Contract Management,* ASBCA No. 44885, 95-2 BCA ¶ 27,886. The sovereign acts doctrine is an affirmative defense for which the government bears the burden of proof. *Appeal of Dyncorp,* ASBCA No. 49714, 97-2 BCA ¶ 29,233.

3. Another related ground upon which contractors may seek an equitable adjustment consists of additional effort or cost as a result of the government's failure to disclose vital

information. There are several circumstances that all must exist in order for the government's duty to arise. First, the procuring agency must possess important, relevant information that was available at the time of procurement activity. *Bethlehem Corp. v. United States*, 462 F.2d 1400 (Ct.Cl. 1972) (knowledge by non-procuring agency having no connection to procuring agency does not make government liable for non-disclosure). Next, the information must not be that which the contractor could reasonably be expected and able to seek elsewhere. *H. N. Bailey & Assocs. v. United States*, 499 F.2d 376 (Ct.Cl. 1971) (information that is general industry knowledge is not required to be disclosed by the government); *Maitland Bros. Co.*, ENG BCA No. 5782, 94-1 BCA ¶ 26,473). Finally, the government must know that the contractor lacks the information. *Hardeman-Monier-Hutcherson v. United States*, 458 F.2d 1364 (Ct.Cl. 1972); *Max Jordan Bauunternehmung v. United States*, 820 F.2d 1208 (Fed. Cir. 1987). The issue of superior government knowledge can arise in cases regarding surprises on construction sites; see *Covco Hawaii* and its notes in this chapter's section on differing site conditions.

4. Yet another related issue regarding equitable adjustments consists of constructive acceleration, which occurs when a contractor, faced with an excusable delay, is ordered to complete performance in accordance with the original contract schedule. One type of action leading to a finding of constructive acceleration occurs when the contractor encounters threats of termination in the presence of an excusable delay. *Intersea Research Corp.*, IBCA No. 1675, 85-2 BCA ¶ 18.058. In *Norair Engineering Corp. v. United States*, the court found the government's refusal to grant a delay for an excusable delay, and subsequent threats of liquidated damages constituted a constructive acceleration (666 F.2d 546 (Ct.Cl. 1981)). Delay in governmental approval for a requested time extension by the contractor has also been found to be constructive acceleration by the agency (*Fishbach & Moore Int'l Corp.*, ASBCA No. 18146, 77-1 BCA ¶ 12,300, *aff'd*, 617 F.2d 223 (Ct.Cl. 1980).

Chapter 7

Intellectual Property

Government agencies and contractors may clash over intellectual property. Agencies must promote full and open competition, which can lead to lower prices and lower expenditures of tax dollars. In order to accomplish those goals, the government agencies must be able to supply all potential contractors with the intellectual property, or data, necessary to produce the desired product or service.

Contractors, on the other hand, view intellectual property or data as the crown jewels of their corporation, the exclusive use of which leads to higher profits and fewer corporate dollars spent competing for business. The entity that controls the data necessary for the manufacture of a product or the provision of a service can often control the price and the terms under which it is sold. Congressional focus on the high prices paid by the government for spare parts for weapon systems and other government-needed items has generated considerable interest in this area. Careful attention to the potential for conflict prior to entering into a contract will serve both the government purchaser and the government contractor well.

The issue of intellectual property rights in data is traditionally divided into three areas: patents, copyrights, and technical data. *See* FAR Part 27. Software has emergent as important as each of the rest. Those first and second areas are not the most controversial with standard, well-developed FAR clauses clearly delineating the rights of both the government and contractor. The area of technical data, however, has been the subject of intense scrutiny, debate, and statutory enactment, with the issue of restrictive markings taking on special importance. With the promulgation in 1995 of regulations for Department of Defense acquisitions, some semi-permanent order was brought to this area. Still, civilian agencies and the Department of Defense have separate and specific regulations.

For further discussion, see the cites in specific subchapters, and see: Ralph C. Nash Jr. & Leonard Rawicz, Intellectual Property in Government Contracts (6th ed. 2008); Leon E. Trakman, *The Boundaries Of Contract Law In Cyberspace*, 38 Pub. Cont. L.J. 187 (Fall 2008); Michael S Mireles, *Adoption Of The Bayh-Dole Act In Developed Countries: Added Pressure For A Broad Research Exemption In The United States*, 59 Me. L. Rev. 259 (2007); Elizabeth A. Rowe, *The Experimental Use Exception To Patent Infringement: Do Universities Deserve Special Treatment?*, 59 Me. L. Rev. 283 (2007).

A. Patents and Copyrights

Note on Patents

Government contracting imposes a discrete set of issues on the ordinary patent law applicable to the private sector. Here are two of the biggest.

First, sometimes, a government contractor, during the performance of a government contract, develops an invention. That is particularly possible if it is a contract for research, design, or development. Historically, government agencies took title to such inventions. However, this set back development and commercialization of promising technology. Congress passed the Bayh-Dole Act, and, the FAR has regulations in Part 27 to advamce those goals.

Accordingly, in recent years, government policy with regard to patents encourages the maximum practical commercial use of inventions made during the course of a contractor performing a federally funded research and development contract. Since 1983 by Presidential Memoranda, all contractors have been extended the right to retain title in inventions made while performing government contracts. This patent policy is based on the assumption the best incentive for a contractor to further develop inventions made while performing a government contract is to allow the contractor to retain the patent rights.

A party's rights turn on whether there was a "subject invention" developed during the contract performance. Contractors must disclose these and elect to retain title. Specifically, with very limited exceptions, contractors may elect to retain title to the patent by following specifically prescribed procedures that include disclosure to the government.

In exchange for obtaining patent rights, the contractor grants to the government a nonexclusive, nontransferable, irrevocable, paid-up license to practice, or have practiced on its behalf, any subject invention throughout the world. The government also retains the right to "march in" and require the contractor to grant to the government a license for the use of the invention if the contractor has not taken effective steps to achieve its practical application, or if it is necessary for public health or safety needs.

Restrictions to patent rights are placed on contractors when: (1) the contractor is not located or does not have a place of business in the United States or if the contractor is subject to the control of a foreign government; (2) the government determines in exceptional circumstances that it would be in the public interest for the government to retain title; (3) the government determines that the patent is necessary to protect the security of foreign intelligence or counterintelligence activities; or (4) the contract involves a Department of Energy government-owned, contractor-operated facility dedicated to naval nuclear propulsion or weapons-related programs.

Central to the patent policy in government contracting are the definitions of the terms "invention" and "subject invention." The term *invention* means "any invention or discovery which is or may be patentable or otherwise protectable under title 35 of the United States Code...." FAR 52.227-11(a)(1). The term *subject invention* means "any invention of the contractor conceived or first actually reduced to practice in the performance of work ..." under a contract. FAR 52.227-11(a)(6). The use of the word *or* in the definition of "subject invention" ensures that inventions "conceived" of prior to a contract but reduced to practice during the performance of a contract are covered by the government's patent policies. Similarly, if an invention is "conceived" of during contract performance, but reduced to practice after the contract is ended, the invention is still covered by the policy and most importantly, by the requirements for notification and filing for patent protection and the granting to the government of license rights.

Second, a contractor performing a government contract might be sued by a third party for infringing their patent. This is the issue in *Sevenson.* Furthermore, the government encourages the use of inventions in performing contracts and will even, by appropriate contract clause, authorize and consent to such use while indemnifying the contractor against possible infringement claims. However, when purchasing commercial items, the government generally seeks indemnification from patent infringement claims by the contractor in the production of the necessary items.

28 U.S.C. sec. 1498 avoids the problem of a suit by a third party stopping performance. The provision imposes a two-part test. The invention has to be used "for the government" and "with the authorization or consent of the government."

When the use of an invention passes both parts of the test, exclusive jurisdiction lies in the Court of Federal Claims. The patent owner sues the United States, not the contractor, with the remedy being money damages but no injunctive relief.

If the patent holder insists on suing the infringing contractor in district court, the contractor has an affirmative defense to the suit. The *Sevenson* case is about a government contractor, sued by a patent holder for infringement, invoking this affirmative defense.

For further discussion, see Matthew A. Williams, Emily C. Lamb, *Patent Reform And Its Effect On University Technology Transfer*, 55 Fed. Law. 12 (Sept. 2008); Heather Petruzzi, *The Missing Link: The Need For Patent Protection In The Development Of Biodefense Vaccines*, 37 Pub. Cont. L.J. 71 (Fall 2007); Michael Kenneth Greene, *Patent Law In Government Contracts: Does It Best Serve The Department Of Defense's Mission?*, 36 Pub. Cont. L.J. 331 (Spring 2007); W. Jay DeVecchio, Patent Rights Under Government Contracts, Briefing Papers, June 2007, at 1.

Sevenson Environmental Services, Inc., Plaintiff-Appellant, v. Shaw Environmental, Inc., Defendant-Cross Appellant

United States Court of Appeals, Federal Circuit
Nos. 2006-1391, 2006-1408
Feb. 21, 2007

Before Linn and Dyk, Circuit Judges.

Opinion by Linn, Circuit Judge.

This is a patent infringement case in which the United States District Court for the Western District of New York concluded at summary judgment that suit against a hazardous waste remediation contractor was barred by government contractor immunity under 28 U.S.C. § 1498. Because we agree with the district court that the contractor's use of the accused method was "for the Government and with the authorization and consent of the Government," *see* § 1498(a), we affirm.

I. BACKGROUND

This appeal relates to the cleanup of a lead-contaminated parcel of land near Colonie, New York ("the Colonie site") that is owned by the United States and managed by the U.S. Army Corps of Engineers. The defendant, Shaw Environmental, Inc. ("Shaw"), is a hazardous waste remediation firm that in 2002 contracted with the Corps of Engineers to engage in cleanup and remediation work at the Colonie site.[2] The plaintiff, Sevenson

---

2. Shaw is the third contractor at the Colonie site. The original contract was with ICF Kaiser.

It was ICF Kaiser's subcontractor, Kiber Environmental Services, that first performed a treatability study at the Colonie site and recommended the use of the accused phosphoric acid method.

In early 1999, the ICF Kaiser contract was acquired by IT Group, Inc., and IT Corporation (collectively, "IT"). In 2002, after IT declared bankruptcy, Shaw obtained the remediation contract. The instant infringement action followed.

Environmental Services, Inc. ("Sevenson"), is a corporation that holds several U.S. patents regarding hazardous waste remediation, including some that claim methods for treating hazardous waste by applying phosphoric acid: U.S. Patent Nos. 5,527,982; 5,732,367; 5,916,123; 5,994,608; and 6,139,485. Sevenson alleges that Shaw's work at the Colonie site infringes these patents.

Shaw's relationship with the Government is defined by two separate contracts, the "Total Environmental Restoration Contract" ("TERC") and the "Pre-placed Remedial Action Contract" ("PRAC"). (The PRAC replaced the TERC because of funding issues.) Both the TERC and PRAC require Shaw to perform hazardous waste remediation at a number of government-owned waste sites, including the Colonie site. Both contracts contain the same authorization and consent clause:

> The Government authorizes and consents to all use and manufacture, in performing this contract or any subcontract at any tier, of any invention described in and covered by a United States patent ... used in machinery, tools, or methods whose use necessarily results from compliance by the Contractor or subcontractor with (i) specifications or written provisions forming a part of this contract or (ii) specific written instructions given by the Contracting Officer directing the manner of performance.

Report & Recommendation, slip op. at 3.

Both contracts also require development of a Work Plan that contains a detailed specification of the work that is to be performed. In particular, the TERC provides:

> WORK PLAN (WP). For each TERC Delivery Order, the Contractor is required to submit a WP. The WP, which is written by the Contractor, describes the Contractor's detailed approach for the performance of this Delivery Order. The WP is based upon the Government's statement of work, which is a general description of work that the Contractor is required to perform. The WP describes the activities that will be performed in the field or office by the Contractor as outlined in individual Delivery Orders.

* * *

> 3.3 WP ACCEPTANCE. Except as otherwise provided in individual Delivery Orders, approval of the WP is required prior to the start of field activities. No change in the approved plan shall be implemented without written concurrence of the Contracting Officer.

Sevenson filed the instant patent infringement suit against Shaw in the United States District Court for the Western District of New York on July 23, 2002. Complaint, *Sevenson Envtl. Servs., Inc. v. Shaw Envtl., Inc.,* No. 02-CV-527 (W.D.N.Y. July 23, 2002). Shaw moved for summary judgment on the ground that pursuant to its contracts with the government and to 28 U.S.C. § 1498(a), the United States was the proper defendant, and that the suit should therefore be dismissed. The district court, adopting the report and recommendation of the magistrate judge, agreed and entered judgment in favor of Shaw. *Sevenson Envtl. Servs. v. Shaw Envtl., Inc.,* No. 02-CV-527 (W.D.N.Y. Mar.22, 2006). The district court also denied as moot Shaw's motion to dismiss the case or otherwise sanction Sevenson for alleged discovery violations. *Id.*

Sevenson appeals. Shaw cross-appeals, asserting that the district court erred (1) when it denied Shaw's motion to dismiss for discovery violations and (2) when it denied Shaw's motion to amend its answer to include declaratory judgment counterclaims against Sevenson as to additional unasserted patents.

We have jurisdiction pursuant to 28 U.S.C. § 1295(a)(1).

II. DISCUSSION

* * *

B. Section 1498(a)

The relevant statutory provision reads as follows:

> (a) Whenever an invention described in and covered by a patent of the United States is used or manufactured by or for the United States without license of the owner thereof or lawful right to use or manufacture the same, the owner's remedy shall be by action against the United States in the United States Court of Federal Claims for the recovery of his reasonable and entire compensation for such use and manufacture.

* * *

> For the purposes of this section, the use or manufacture of an invention described in and covered by a patent of the United States by a contractor, a subcontractor, or any person, firm, or corporation for the Government and with the authorization or consent of the Government, shall be construed as use or manufacture for the United States.

28 U.S.C. § 1498(a). Because Shaw is a contractor, its use of the patented method qualifies as "use ... for the United States," and it is thus immune from suit except "by action against the United States in the United States Court of Federal Claims," if two criteria are met: (1) the use is "for the Government"; and (2) the use is "with the authorization and consent of the Government." *Id.; see Hughes Aircraft Co. v. United States,* 209 Ct.Cl. 446, 534 F.2d 889, 897–98 (1976). Sevenson argues that Shaw's use of phosphoric acid does not meet either criterion.

1. Use "for the Government"

Sevenson's first argument is that the phrase "for the Government," as used in § 1498(a), "refers to the 'primary purpose of the contract' between the private party and the government." Appellant's Br. at 33. We disagree. The text of the statute contains an awkward circularity: use "for the United States" is defined as use that is both "for the Government" *and* "with the authorization and consent of the Government." In context, the "for the Government" prong of the definition appears to impose only a requirement that the use or manufacture of a patented method or apparatus occur pursuant to a contract with the government and for the benefit of the government. The statute imposes no additional "primary purpose" condition.

The cases that Sevenson cites are not to the contrary. For example, in *Riles v. Amerada Hess Corp.,* a district court concluded that where an offshore oil drilling operation leased drilling rights from the government for a 12.5% royalty and was required to get government approval for its drilling platform installation methods, the infringement of a patent on those methods was not part of a use "for the Government." 999 F.Supp. 938, 940 (S.D.Tex.1998). The government received some benefit from the infringement, to be sure, but the drilling was not a "governmental function" that the government had sought or required the driller to carry out. *Id. Riles* noted that "[c]learly, Defendant did not agree to drill for the Government simply because the Government receives some monetary benefit as a byproduct of the activity." *Id.* Similarly, in *Larson v. United States,* the United States Claims Court held that use of infringing medical devices by Medicare and Medicaid providers did not fall within § 1498 because the use of those particular devices, though funded by the government, was not required by it, nor were the providers under the government's control. 26 Cl.Ct. 365, 369–70 (1992).

Here, in contrast, Shaw's use of the accused method has been in its capacity as a government contractor and pursuant to its contract for the benefit of the government. In similar cases, where infringing activity has been performed by a government contractor pursuant to a government contract and for the benefit of the government, courts have all but bypassed a separate inquiry into whether infringing activity was performed "for the Government." Instead, the inquiry has reduced to the "very simple question" of whether the plaintiffs "establish that the government authorized or consented to the ... infringement ..., if such infringement in fact occurred." *Auerbach v. Sverdrup Corp.*, 829 F.2d 175, 180–81 (D.C.Cir.1987) (applying the parallel copyright infringement provisions of 28 U.S.C. § 1498(b)); *see also Carrier Corp. v. United States*, 208 Ct.Cl. 678, 534 F.2d 244, 247 (1976) (proceeding, after a determination that infringing use of a patented device was not directly "by the Government," to an analysis of whether the government authorized and consented to the infringing use).

Sevenson's specific factual arguments on the "for the Government" question also fail. It is irrelevant whether the TERC or PRAC encompassed a range of other tasks besides remediation at the Colonie site; whether Shaw (or its predecessor) or the Government selected the allegedly infringing method; whether the risk of an injunction (one purpose of § 1498) was mitigated by the existence of noninfringing alternative treatment methods; and whether Shaw agreed to defend against Sevenson's patent claims (an issue between Shaw and the government in which Sevenson has no stake). It is also irrelevant whether Shaw reaped the benefits of choosing phosphoric acid rather than another remediation method. The question is not whether the choice of remediation method was made "for the Government," but whether the infringing method was practiced "for the Government," and that question is answered in the affirmative by the observation that the government sought and received hazardous waste remediation services at the Colonie site. Any dispute about whether another method would have benefited the government equally without infringing Sevenson's patent rights goes to whether the government "authoriz [ed] and consent[ed]" to this particular use.

2. Use "with the Authorization and Consent of the Government"

Where, as here, a government contract contains an explicit authorization and consent clause (and the parties have alleged no alternative source for government authorization and consent), the scope of the government's authorization and consent to liability naturally hinges on the language of that clause. Contrary to Sevenson's characterizations of this appeal as an implied authorization and consent case, the issue here is whether the government, through the TERC and PRAC, expressly authorized and consented to the use of the accused method.

Sevenson characterizes the authorization and consent clause as "narrow"—as did our predecessor court, describing an almost identical clause, in *Carrier*. 534 F.2d at 247. In this case, however, the authorization language of the contract is broad enough. Both the TERC and the PRAC grant government authorization and consent "to all use and manufacture, in performing this contract ... of any invention described in and covered by a United States patent ... used in machinery, tools, or methods whose use necessarily results from compliance by the Contractor or subcontractor with (i) specifications or written provisions forming a part of this contract." Notably, this language explicitly encompasses "specifications" that are a part of the contract, as well as the base language of the contract itself. As both the government's contracts specialist and Sevenson's Rule 30(b)(6) designee acknowledged, Shaw's Work Plan is such a specification. Because it requires that Shaw use the accused method at the Colonie site, the accused use "necessarily results from compliance" with the contract's "specifications," and the government has authorized and consented to the use.

Carrier, the only on-point, binding precedent that the parties have cited to us, is thus factually distinguishable. In *Carrier,* a garbage company entered into a contract to remove refuse at Andrews Air Force Base. 534 F.2d at 246. It was sued for infringement of a patent on certain types of rubbish compactors and containers. *Id.* at 246. Interpreting § 1498(a) in light of a similar authorization and consent clause, and notwithstanding a requirement that "[a]ll equipment ... shall become operative only after inspection and acceptance by the Contracting Officer or the Technical Representative," the Court of Claims held that the use of infringing equipment was not "necessary" to the contract because "neither the contract specifications nor any specific written instructions ... required [the contractor] to use any particular type of equipment" and "containers were available in the open market which could have been purchased and used, and which would not have infringed plaintiff's patent." *Id.* at 247–48. Here, in contrast, the government did more than an "inspection and acceptance"; it required in the contracts the development of a detailed written Work Plan, and that Work Plan required the use of the infringing method. Unlike the contractor in *Carrier,* Shaw's use of a noninfringing alternative to the accused method would put it in breach of its contracts. Thus, Shaw's use of the accused method was "necessar[y]" in a way that use of patented devices in *Carrier* was not.

Accordingly, Shaw's use of the accused method was both "for the Government" and "with the authorization and consent of the Government," and Shaw is entitled to immunity from suit under § 1498(a).

III. CONCLUSION

For the foregoing reasons, we conclude that the district court properly granted summary judgment in favor of Shaw. Because we also discern no error in the rulings of the district court relevant to Shaw's cross-appeal on the issue of sanctions, we affirm.

Copyrights

With the written permission of a government contracting officer, a contractor may copyright data first produced in the performance of a contract. When such a claim is made, the contractor must affix the applicable copyright notice and acknowledgment of government sponsorship and contract number. The latter requirements help ensure that the government and others acting on its behalf can take advantage of the paid-up, nonexclusive, irrevocable worldwide license that the contractor must grant to the government to reproduce, prepare derivative works, distribute copies to the public, and perform publicly and display publicly the copyrighted data.

When copyrighted data not first produced in the performance of a contract is incorporated into data delivered under a contract, the contractor must first obtain approval of the contracting officer to do so and must grant the government the same type of paid-up, nonexclusive, irrevocable worldwide license to use the data. In exchange, the government agrees not to remove any copyright notices and to include such notices on all reproductions of the data.

For further discussion, see Robyn A. Littman, *Lessons From The Procurement World: Understanding Why The Government Denies Its Employees Recovery After Infringing Their*

Copyrighted Works, 39 Pub. Cont. L.J. 879 (Summer 2010); W. Jay DeVecchio, Copyright Protection Under Government Contracts, Briefing Papers, May 2005, at 1; David A. Vogel, *Does the FAR Violate the Copyright Law?*, 33 Procurement Law., Summer 1998, at 12.

C. Technical Data

Note on Rights in Technical Data

The term *data* is simply defined as "recorded information, regardless of form or the media on which it may be recorded." FAR 27.401. The term *technical data* is defined as "data other than computer software, which are of a scientific or technical nature." *Id.* As stated above, the allocation of rights in and use of technical data generate considerable controversy in government contracting. On the one hand, the government seeks to acquire or obtain access to technical data in order to: (1) obtain competition among contractors; (2) fulfill governmental responsibilities for disseminating the results of tax dollar sponsored activities; (3) ensure the appropriate utilization of research and development so that additional technological development is encouraged; (4) meet the specialized needs of military activities; and (5) ensure the capability of supplying the needs of military activities. On the other hand, contractors seek to protect their proprietary and economic interests in technical data in order to avoid jeopardizing their commercial position in the marketplace and the economic investment spent on developing the data into a useful property interest.

As a result of these conflicting policy demands, federal statute and regulation have developed an approach to the rights in technical data that attempts to serve the interest of both parties to a contract. Although actual ownership of data is generally vested in the contractor, the allocation of the actual rights to use that data is set forth in a stair step approach for levels of use.

The first step and goal of any government agency is to obtain "unlimited rights" in technical data. Such rights allow the government to use, disclose, reproduce, prepare derivative works, distribute copies to the public, and perform publicly and display publicly, in any manner and for any purpose, and to have or permit others to do so. In essence, with unlimited rights in technical data, the government can achieve each of the policy purposes cited above including allowing all interested contractors to use the data in order to compete for government contracts. The *FN Manufacturing* case discusses the competition aspect.

A contractor grants civilian agencies of the government "unlimited rights" in: (1) data first produced in the performance of a contract; (2) form, fit, and function data delivered pursuant to a contract; (3) data delivered under the contract in the form of manuals or instructional and training material for installation, operation, or routine maintenance and repair of items, components, or processes delivered or furnished for use under the contract; and (4) all other data delivered under a contract unless otherwise protected by the contractor. Similarly, a contractor grants an agency of the Department of Defense "unlimited rights" in: (1) data which has been or will be developed exclusively with government funds; (2) studies, analyses, or test data required as an element of performance under the contract; (3) data created exclusively with government funds; (4) form, fit, and function data; (5) data necessary for installation, operation, maintenance, or training purposes; (6) corrections or changes to technical data furnished to the contractor by the government; (7) data that is publicly available without restrictions; (8) data in which the government obtained unlimited rights pursuant to another contract or pursuant to negotiations; or (9) data previously furnished with "government purpose rights" and those rights have expired.

A second level or step toward data rights is "government purpose rights" wherein the government has the rights to: (1) use, modify, reproduce, release, perform, display, or disclose technical data within the government without restriction; and (2) release or disclose technical data outside the government and authorize persons to whom release or disclosure has been made to use, modify, reproduce, release, perform, display, or disclose that data for US government purposes that includes any activity in which the government is a party including competitive procurements. An agency obtains "government purpose rights" in data that was developed with mixed funding, i.e., both the contractor and the government contributed funds toward the development of the data. Although the term *government purpose rights* is only found in the regulations applicable to the Department of Defense, a similar concept is used with civilian agencies where the development of the data is funded by both parties and the agency and the contractor are permitted to agree to limiting the use of the data by the government to governmental purposes.

The third level or step is actually divided into two terms: (1) "limited rights" for data other than software; and (2) "restricted rights" for software. With limited rights, the government may not disclose the data outside the government nor use the data for purposes of manufacturing. The government may, however, identify specific purposes for which the limited rights data may be used including: (1) use by support service contractors; (2) evaluation by nongovernmental evaluators; (3) use by other contractors in the same program; (4) emergency or repair work; or (5) release to a foreign government for information or evaluation or emergency repair or overhaul work. A contractor can grant the government "limited rights" in data that was developed exclusively with private funds. In order to protect such data, a contractor is required to mark the data with a "limited rights" notice. Failure to mark the data will result in the government receiving unlimited rights in that data.

For software, the regulations speak in terms of "restricted rights" which mean that the software may only be: (1) used or copied for use on the computer for which it was acquired; (2) used or copied for a backup computer if the original computer is inoperative; (3) reproduced for safekeeping or backup purposes; (4) modified or adapted for use with other restricted rights software; (5) disclosed to service contractors for any of the first four uses; and (6) used on a replacement computer. Software receives the protection of "restricted rights" when it is: (1) developed at private expense and is a trade secret; (2) commercial or financial and is confidential or privileged; or (3) is published copyrighted computer software. As is the case with limited rights data, the contractor must mark the software with a "restricted rights" notice in order to protect it. Failure by the contractor to do so will give the government unlimited rights in that software.

For both civilian and defense agencies, the key factor is whether the data were developed with government funds or private funds—a determination that is not as easy at it may seem, especially for contractors that regularly do business with the government. For data relating to noncommercial items, the government may challenge the "limited rights" or "restricted rights" notice placed on data by a contractor. If the markings are challenged, the contractor must present evidence so as to justify the marking, i.e., the source of funding for development of the data.

Since 1995, the acquisition of rights in technical data for commercial items and commercial computer software has been substantially simplified. In essence, unless otherwise negotiated with the contractor, for commercial items the government gets the very same rights in technical data that a commercial customer would receive and the government receives the very same license rights for commercial computer software that a commercial customer receives. Furthermore, the burden of proof as to the source of funding for the technical data is shifted from the contractor to the government. In other words, if the government wants to challenge the status of the technical data, it must prove that the data were developed at government expense rather than having the contractor prove the data were developed at private expense.

Ultimately, because of the complexity of the statutes and regulations involving data rights, it is to the benefit of the contractor and government alike to determine with certainty the rights in the data that will be delivered under a contract prior to the contract being executed. The failure to delineate those rights ahead of time can only lead to disputes as the government seeks to use the data for reprocurement or other purposes and the contractor seeks to protect its crown jewels.

For further discussion of the subjects in this section, Taylor M. Norton, *Protecting Subcontractors' Intellectual Property In Government Contracts: Trades Secrets And Proprietary Data*, 57 Fed. Law. 38 (Oct. 2010); Eli Mazour, *If You Fix It, They Will Come: Drawing Lessons Learned From Patent For Dealing With Rights In Technical Data*, 38 Pub. Cont. L.J. 667 (Spring 2009); Brendan Lill, *Restrictive Legends in Federal Procurement: Is he Risk of Losing Data Rights Too Great?*, 38 Pub. Cont. L.J. 895 (2009); W. Jay DeVecchio, Technical Data & Computer Software After *Night Vision*: Marking, Delivery & Reverse Engineering, Briefing Papers, April 2006, at 1; Christine C. Trend, *Killing the Goose that Laid the Golden Egg: Data Rights Law and Policy in Department of Defense Contracts*, 34 Pub. Cont. L.J. 287 (2005);

FN Manufacturing, Inc., Plaintiff, v. The United States, Defendant, and Colt's Manufacturing Company, Inc., Intervenor

United States Court of Federal Claims
No. 98-447 C., 42 Fed.Cl. 87
Oct. 28, 1998
REDACTED

WIESE, Judge.

RULING ON LAW

This is a suit for declaratory and injunctive relief. Plaintiff, FN Manufacturing, Inc. (FNMI), the domestic subsidiary of a European arms manufacturer, is asking the court to declare illegal, and to enjoin the Government from continuing with performance under, a sole-source contract awarded to Colt's Manufacturing Company, Inc. (Colt's), the intervenor here, on May 5, 1998. The challenged award involves the manufacture of a quantity of M4/M4A1 carbines—the successor weapon to the M16 rifle currently in use by the United States Army and North Atlantic Treaty Organization ground forces. FNMI is one of the Government's principal manufacturing supply sources for the M16 rifle.

This is the third time this case has come before the court.…

We turn now to the issue of current concern. In the interest of seeking an expeditious resolution of this controversy, the parties have asked the court to rule on the following question: whether the Government, in the settlement of a contract dispute, is free to relinquish rights in technical data, if by doing so, it disables itself from competitively conducting future procurements involving the use and application of the relinquished data. Put another way, does a contracting agency have the authority to agree to a contract settlement that establishes a contractor's exclusive ownership of technical data, thereby restricting all future procurements involving the data to sole-source purchases?

Facts

On June 30, 1967, Colt's entered into a technical data and patent license agreement with the Government, affording the Army limited rights to the M16 rifle and the XM177 submachine gun. Under the terms of this license, the Army was permitted to release the technical data package (TDP) for use in competitive procurements involving the acquisition of the M16 and its component parts, subject to the limitation that the manufacture be carried out in the United States.

Subsequent to the signing of the M16 licensing agreement, Colt's developed the M4 and M4A1 carbines, weapons derived from, and sharing a majority of their parts with, the M16 rifle. While the parties do not agree to what extent—if at all—the Government contributed financially to the development of the M4 and M4A1, it is clear that Colt's committed its own funds to the project. In a letter dated March 5, 1985, Colt's informed the Army that, based on the fact that the M4 and M4A1 were derived from the M16, Colt's considered the M4 and M4A1 to be covered by the 1967 Licensing Agreement. The Government did not challenge that assertion.

In January 1996, an Army engineer authorized the release of the M4A1 TDP to the Navy. The Navy, unaware of the terms of the 1967 Licensing Agreement, used the TDP in conjunction with an advertised solicitation for M4A1 adapters,[1] thereby improperly disclosing the TDP to some 21 contractors, including FNMI. This disclosure was improper for several reasons, including the fact that it did not relate to an authorized use (the solicitation at issue did not involve the procurement of a weapon or a weapon component) and the information was disseminated without obtaining required non-disclosure statements from the participating contractors. Upon learning of the solicitation, Colt's notified the Government on December 26, 1996, that it had violated the 1967 Licensing Agreement by failing adequately to protect Colt's proprietary data. And, because it believed the breach to be material, Colt's further advised the Government that the licensing agreement was terminated and that the Government would no longer be permitted to use the data in the procurement or manufacture of the M16, M16A1, XM177, XM177E2, M4 or M4A1.

The Government responded to Colt's letter on February 14, 1997. In its reply, the Government acknowledged that Colt's might in fact be entitled to damages because of the unauthorized release, but disputed that the licensing agreement had been materially breached. Relying on Article XX of the licensing agreement, the Government asserted that a breach would arise—and termination would be appropriate—only in the event that the Government failed to use its best efforts to remedy the violation. Because it had presumably corrected its error by recovering all copies of the TDP from the Navy and by securing non-disclosure statements from 19 of the 20 contractors (with FNMI, the lone hold-out, providing a letter attesting that it had not improperly used the data), the Government maintained that it had met its obligation under the licensing agreement, and that the 1967 Licensing Agreement therefore remained intact.

An investigation of the incident by the Inspector General—prompted by congressional inquiry—concluded that both the release of the data to the Navy, and the Navy's distri-

---

1. M4A1 adapter kits permit modification of the M4A1 to allow the weapon to allow the weapon to fire during training exercises.

bution to contractors, were improper. In its June 17, 1997, audit report, the Inspector General recommended that procedures be implemented to better safeguard Colt's proprietary data.

In a July 29, 1997, letter to the Army, Colt's estimated the damages arising from the improper release of Colt's technical data at between 43.5 and 70 million dollars. At Colt's request, a series of meetings were held during the late summer and early fall of 1997 to discuss the M16 licensing issue and also—at Colt's insistence—ownership of the technical data rights relating to the M4 carbine. Although Colt's had previously characterized the M4 as subject to the 1967 Licensing Agreement, the company now sought the Army's confirmation that the M4 Carbine was not covered by the licensing agreement. In support of that contention, Colt's offered evidence that * * of the M4's parts had been developed, tested and refined solely at Colt's expense.

Colt's and the Army conducted settlement discussions in September 1997. Despite the Army's earlier representation to Colt's that the disclosure did not constitute a breach of the licensing agreement, the Army nonetheless possessed, in the words of an Army attorney involved in the settlement negotiations, a "great concern" that a resort to litigation in the absence of a settlement might jeopardize the Army's right to use Colt's proprietary technical data in the manufacture of the M16.

A final agreement, referred to as the "M4 Addendum," was reached on December 24, 1997. Described by the participants as a "global settlement," the addendum and an earlier-executed Memorandum of Understanding were designed to address the entire range of issues then existing between Colt's and the Government, including clarification of a military use restriction in the 1967 Licensing Agreement, that, according to Colt's, barred the Government from selling surplus weapons to state and local police authorities. The M4 Addendum itself was comprised of two parts: first, a characterization of the Army's rights in the M4 technical data; second, a clarification of the status of the M16 licensing agreement.

With regard to the M16 rights, the Addendum reaffirmed the status quo set forth in the 1967 Licensing Agreement, thus constituting, by its terms, the complete satisfaction of all claims arising from the improper disclosure (meaning that the terms of the 1967 license essentially would remain in place with Colt's neither pursuing its multi-million dollar damage claim nor maintaining its position that the license was terminated in light of the alleged breach). As to the M4 data rights, the Addendum granted the Government a non-exclusive, non-transferable limited rights license in M4 data that precluded the Government from using the M4's technical data package in competitive procurements until the year 2011. Edward L. Stolarun, a patent attorney employed by the U.S. Army Material Command Headquarters and a participant in the negotiations, later characterized the Addendum's resolution of the M4 data issue as an acknowledgment by the Government, reached after careful review of Colt's documentation, that Colt's indeed possessed proprietary rights in the M4 technical data.

On May 5, 1998, the Army awarded a sole-source contract for M4 carbines to Colt's, citing as its justification for the sole-source award the Army's lack of technical data rights in certain components of the M4. In response, FNMI filed a protest in this court, challenging the justification on the ground that the Army had improperly relinquished data rights in the M4 that it already possessed, and in doing so had impermissibly created the very circumstance—the absence of data rights—on which it then relied to support its sole-source decision. While the question of whether the Government *relinquished* data rights already in its possession or merely *acknowledged* data rights belonging to Colt's is central to the resolution of this case, we need not reach that issue in order to present the following Ruling on Law.

Analysis

FNMI's argument against the legitimacy of the Government's actions is twofold. It contends, first, that the Government, in relinquishing technical data rights in the M4, violated the terms of 10 U.S.C. § 2320 (1994) by failing to retain rights sufficient to allow for competitive procurement, and, second, that the M4 addendum to the M16 licensing agreement impermissibly inhibited competition in contravention of the Competition in Contracting Act (CICA), 10 U.S.C. § 2304 (1994). We address these arguments in turn.

The Addendum as a Violation of 10 U.S.C. § 2320

Plaintiff's first challenge to the sole-source award arises from its assertion that the Government unlawfully relinquished rights in technical data to which it was otherwise entitled. Leaving aside the issue of whether the Government in fact possessed any such rights—an assertion we accept as true only for purposes of this Ruling on Law—we turn to the question of what limits, if any, 10 U.S.C. § 2320 imposes on the Government's authority to relinquish technical data rights.

The subsection of the statute on which plaintiff relies, 10 U.S.C. § 2320(a)(2)(G)(ii), reads as follows:

(G) The Secretary of Defense may—

* * *

(ii) agree to restrict rights in technical data otherwise accorded to the United States under this section if the United States receives a royalty-free license to use, release, or disclose the data for purposes of the United States (including purposes of competitive procurement).

... We cannot accept the argument that the Government, in relinquishing a right to use the M4 technical data for proposes of competitive procurement, thereby violated 10 U.S.C. § 2320(a)(2)(G)(ii) because the limitations imposed by that subsection have no application where—as here—the data at issue was developed either wholly or partially at private expense. That conclusion derives both from the specific language of the referenced subsection—it applies only to those rights "specifically *accorded* to the United States" (italics supplied) under the provisions of 10 U.S.C. § 2320—and from the remainder of the statutory framework, in particular § 2320(a)(2)(E), which authorizes the Government, in situations where a developmental effort involves both federal and private funding, to negotiate the particular rights it will receive. We explain further.

Under 10 U.S.C. § 2320, the United States is "accorded" rights in technical data in one instance only, *i.e.,* where Government money represents the *exclusive* funding source in the development of the item or process in question. In that circumstance alone, the statute gives to the United States a right, described as an "unlimited" right. . . .

Conversely, in the situation where an item or process is developed by a contractor or subcontractor exclusively at private expense, the contractor or subcontractor "may restrict the right of the United States to release or disclose technical data pertaining to the item or process to persons outside the Government, or permit the use of the technical data by such persons." 10 U.S.C. § 2320(a)(2)(B).

In contrast to the exclusive funding situations identified above, the statute does not specify any minimum rights that the Government or the contractor must receive where the development of an item has been achieved through the use of *both* Government funds and private funds. Rather, in such instances, the statute specifies that "the respective rights of the United States and of the contractor ... in technical data pertaining to such item or process shall be established as early in the acquisition process as practicable ... and shall be based upon negotiations between the United States and the contractor taking into account:

* * *

(ii) The interest of the United States in increasing competition and lowering costs by developing and locating alternative sources of supply and manufacture.

(iii) The interest of the United States in encouraging contractors to develop at private expense items for use by the Government

(iv) Such other factors as the Secretary of Defense may prescribe.

10 U.S.C. § 2320(a)(2)(E).

Two conclusions are evident from the statutory framework set forth in 10 U.S.C. § 2320. First, rights which result from negotiations between contractor and Government cannot be said—in contrast to the unlimited rights specifically conferred by section 2320(a)(1)(A) in the case of exclusive Government funding—to have been *accorded* under the statute. Rather, they are rights sanctioned by the statute. Hence, in mixed funding situations, the limitations of section 2320(a)(2)(G)(ii) do not, by their terms, apply.

Second, the negotiation process prescribed for the mixed funding situation imposes no minimum requirement as to the level of rights in technical data that the Government must obtain. Rather, what is called for is an evaluative process in which the Government's interests in securing broad rights in technical data are weighed against the economic incentive to the private sector that the acceptance of more limited Government rights might help secure. Were we to interpret the limitations set forth in § 2320(a)(1)(G)(ii) as applying to a mixed funding situation, the Government would be required to *retain* a higher level of rights in technical data in subsequent negotiations (meaning, the settlement negotiations) than it would have been required to *obtain* during initial negotiations. Since 10 U.S.C. § 2320 imposes no minimum requirement on rights the Government must negotiate in the mixed funding context, we see no reason to preclude it from relinquishing rights it had no obligation to obtain in the first instance. Contrary to plaintiff's argument, we see nothing within the statutory language of 10 U.S.C. § 2320 to change that result.

To the extent, then, that it is correct to view this case as one in which the development of the M4 was achieved through both public and private sources, the Government clearly had the right to relinquish any rights it may otherwise have negotiated.

The Addendum as a Violation of the Competition in Contracting Act (CICA)

Our holding that the Government has the right to relinquish its interest in technical data does not, however, immunize the Addendum from challenge on the grounds that it violated the Competition in Contracting Act's mandate for full and open competition in Government procurements. 10 U.S.C. § 2304. Plaintiff argues that the practical effect of the M4 Addendum—the limiting of competition until 2011—runs afoul of CICA, and must, as a consequence, be struck down as contrary to law. While we agree that certain relinquishments of technical data rights could in fact represent impermissible violations of CICA, we refuse to go so far as to conclude that *any* relinquishment of data rights which serves to limit or eliminate competition must necessarily be found unlawful.

If the Government relinquishes data rights as a bargaining tool to satisfy or extinguish an unrelated claim, it comes into conflict with the Competition in Contracting Act and its actions must be voided. *Executive Business Media v. United States Department of Defense*, 3 F.3d 759 (4th Cir.1993) and *Earth Property Servs., Inc.*, B-237742, March 13, 1990, 90-1 CPD ¶ 273, the primary cases on which plaintiff relies, illustrate that principle. The Government may not simply "give away" data rights which are not at stake if, in doing so, it subverts the goals of CICA.

If instead, however, the Government relinquishes data rights that are themselves in dispute, its actions cannot be said impermissibly to contravene CICA. This is so because the range of settlement possibilities available to the Government as a litigant seeking to establish its data rights cannot be narrower than the range of possible outcomes litigation of the matter could produce. Put differently, we do not read CICA as preventing the Government from achieving, through settlement, a result with regard to data rights that a court, faced with the identical dispute, could itself reach as an adjudicated outcome.

Applying that rationale to the case before us, we conclude that the Government's relinquishment of its rights in the M4 technical data would run afoul of CICA if the Government's rights could not, under any reasonable assessment of the litigation risks, have been construed as being in jeopardy. More specifically, if neither the alleged breach of the M16 Licensing Agreement nor Colt's independent claim that the M4 had been developed at private expense reasonably held out the possibility that the Government's rights in the M4 would be compromised or lost through litigation of those issues, then the terms of the settlement must be deemed illegal. The Government's relinquishment of rights that were not legitimately in dispute would amount to an impermissible give-away—an action prompted not by a bonafide assessment of the risks facing it in litigation nor by the factors enumerated in § 2320(a)(2)(E), but rather by an interest in ridding itself of the burden of a lawsuit at the price of granting the contractor exclusive control over important technical data, thereby subverting the aims of the Competition in Contracting Act. That, as discussed above, is something the Government may not do.

Conclusion

To the extent that the M4 was not developed solely at public expense, the Government was free, under 10 U.S.C. § 2320, to relinquish rights in technical data without retaining the authority competitively to procure the items dependent on that data. The relinquishment may nonetheless represent an impermissible violation of CICA, however, if the settlement reached with respect to the technical data rights at issue adopted a position not realistically within the outcome risks posed either by the threatened breach of contract action or by Colt's separate claim of ownership of the M4. We leave open for further inquiry the factual issues this Ruling poses: specifically, whether the M4 rights belonged to the Government in the first instance, and if so, whether the loss of those rights could reasonably be interpreted as within the litigation risks the Government faced.

Notes and Questions

1. There are relatively few recent judicial opinions illuminating some of the interface of government contracting and intellectual property rights, because most issues are resolved in negotiations, not by litigation. The *FN* opinion itself includes a thirty-year chronology of such issues resolved between Colt and the government. What was worked out at each stage? What kinds of documentation do lawyers—for Colt and for the government—create at each stage?

2. *FN* and other cases make the rights in technical data a function of where the money came from for development. What is a short statement of the rules that emerge from this opinion?

3. Does the government's position reflect weakness vis-a-vis Colt? How? Why?

C. Restrictive Markings and Software

Note on Restricted Rights and Markings

A contractor may deliver to the government technical data developed exclusively with private funds, and not lose all rights to the government, if the contractor takes the necessary measures to protect those rights. If the contractor does take the necessary measures, the government only receives "limited rights." A similar process occurs with software for civilian use under the FAR, with the different term that what the government receives is "restricted rights."

The admonition for this situation is "Mark it or lose it." In a series of cases, the courts have denied contractors' claims that they only intended to provide the government with limited or restricted rights, when the contractors failed in any respect to mark properly. In *Xerxe Group, Inc. v. United States,* 278 F.3d 1357 (Fed. Cir. 2002), *Block v. United States,* 66 Fed. Cl. 68 (2005), *Night Vision Corp v. United States,* 68 Fed. Cl. 368 (2005), and *General* Atrionics, ASSBCA No. 49196, 02-1 BCA para. 31,798, at 157,067, the courts told the contractors they would all lose on an issue of rights in technical data or software if their marking were flawed.

The requirements on the contractor start with the responsibility to notify the government of its intent to deliver data with less than unlimited rights. And, it must mark these data with prescribed proprietary legends. For competitive negotiations to seek a contract award, for example, the FAR specifies language that must be included in a notice on the proposal's title page and further specifies that every page of the proposal must contain a reference to the notice on the title page.

This requirement applies to computer software as well. Documentary materials as well as the actual software itself require marking. There is a slight difference between the DFARS for defense procurement and the FAR for civilian procurement. The DFARS requires that the restrictive rights legend by embedded in the electronic version of the software if the software can be transmitted from one computer to another. Commonly, the contractor embeds the legends so as to appear in the "boot" screens, screens displayed during installation, and the "help" menus.

Under the FAR for civilian agencies, marking software is simpler. Unlike the DFARS, there are no explicit requirements in the FAR for placing the legend, nor a requirement to embed the legend electronically. There is a short form "Restricted Rights Notice." The FAR says that "If delivery of such computer software is so required, the contractor may affix the following 'Restricted Rights Notice' to the computer software…." Also unlike the DFARS, the FAR does not afford the government unlimited rights in manuals and other software documentation that must be delivered under the contract. The FAR expressly excludes such items from the allocation of unlimited rights.

Some of the rules tempt the contractor who does not want to surrender rights in intellectual property, simply not to deliver data and software at all. Rather, the contractor might withhold limited rights technical data and restricted rights software and instead deliver only form, fit, and function data. Of course, it is one thing to withhold data and software when preparing unsolicited proposals. It is quite another thing, when dealing with a competition for a contract award, to persuade the government to be content without the prospect of getting the technical data or software.

Dowty Decoto, Inc., Plaintiff-Appellee, v.
Department of the Navy et al. Defendants-Appellants

No. 88-3732
United States Court of Appeals, Ninth Circuit
883 F.2d 774
Argued and Submitted June 6, 1989, Decided Aug. 23, 1989

Before SCHROEDER, BEEZER and BRUNETTI, Circuit Judges.

SCHROEDER, Circuit Judge:

The Navy appeals from a district court's permanent injunction prohibiting disclosure of a subcontractor's technical data. We affirm the injunction, holding that under any applicable regulations, the subcontractor never surrendered disclosure rights to the Navy.

The challenged injunction was obtained by the appellee Dowty Decoto, a manufacturer of aeronautical equipment. Since 1971 Dowty Decoto has supplied the Navy with "repeatable holdback bars" used in launching F-14 Tomcat fighter planes from aircraft carrier decks. Decoto has supplied the bars pursuant to a subcontract with Grumman Aerospace Corp., the prime contractor supplying the Navy with F-14s. Decoto also sells the bars directly to the Navy on a purchase order basis for use as spares. In addition to the F-14, Decoto also supplies holdback bars for the F-18 Hornet and T-45A trainer aircraft.

On all drawings and data Decoto supplied pursuant to the subcontract, Decoto placed a restrictive legend stating that the data was proprietary and subject only to limited disclosure rights under the contract. It is not disputed that the form of the legend was appropriate for reserving limited disclosure rights in Decoto.

In 1983 the Navy wrote to Decoto asking Decoto voluntarily to remove the restrictive legends from data it had furnished the Navy. Decoto refused, stating that the Navy had never obtained disclosure rights from Decoto. Three years later, the Navy requested Decoto to substantiate its position that the government had acquired only limited rights in the data. After an informal administrative review of Decoto's submissions, and some informal discussions, the Navy handed down an administrative decision in a letter dated April 27, 1987, advising that Decoto had failed to substantiate its use of restrictive rights legends. It advised that it would obliterate or ignore the legends on the data, and would disclose the data to third parties for the purpose of obtaining competitive bids. Decoto then filed this suit for a permanent injunction in district court, pursuant to the Administrative Procedure Act ("APA"), 5 U.S.C. § 706 (1982), to prohibit the Navy from disclosing the data. The district court granted the injunction.

There is no dispute that unless the Navy has a right to Decoto's data and drawings, they otherwise represent trade secrets of Decoto. The Trade Secrets Act forbids government agents from disclosing confidential information "in any manner or to any extent not authorized by law." 18 U.S.C. § 1905 (1982). If the Navy has no authority to disclose the holdback bar data, its disclosure of Decoto's trade secret would violate section 1905, and "any disclosure that violates § 1905 is 'not in accordance with law' within the meaning of 5 U.S.C. § 706(2)(A)." Chrysler Corp. v. Brown, 441 U.S. 281, 318, 99 S.Ct. 1705, 1726, 60 L.Ed.2d 208 (1979). Thus, the APA authorizes this injunction preventing the Navy from disclosing Decoto's data, provided that such disclosure violates the Trade Secrets Act. Id. at 316–17, 99 S.Ct. at 1724–25; Conax Florida Corp. v. United States, 824 F.2d 1124, 1128 (D.C.Cir.1987).

Our determination of whether the Navy's action was properly enjoined as a violation of the Trade Secrets Act is in turn guided by regulations governing the Navy's authority to disclose the data in the absence of Decoto's acquiescence. The contentions of the parties center on a particular provision of the Armed Services Procurement Regulations (ASPR), regulations promulgated by the Department of Defense governing the acquisition of items for military use, which were in effect when the contract between Decoto and Grumman was signed.[1]

The provision at issue is contained in ASPR §§ 9-202 & 9-203, 32 C.F.R. §§ 9-202 & 9-203 (1965),[2] which deal with rights in technical data. Section 9-202.2 declares the governmental policy of granting to the government unlimited rights to disclose data concerning any item developed at government expense. The policy restricts governmental disclosure of data only where an item was developed at private expense, and where the contractor takes care to mark all data and drawings with a legend prescribed by the regulations setting forth the proprietary nature of the data and the contract under which the data was furnished. Section 9-203(a) implements the policy by requiring that the text of section 9-203(b), which takes the form of a contract clause, be inserted into all government contracts. The language of section 9-203(b) carries out the apportionment of data rights anticipated by the ASPR.[3]

Throughout the administrative and district court proceedings, as well as in this appeal, the dispute between Decoto and the Navy has centered on two issues, one legal and one factual. The legal issue concerns whether ASPR § 9-203 applies at all between Decoto and the Navy, since the form clause language anticipated by the regulations was never inserted into the Decoto-Grumman subcontract and the Navy was not a party to that con-

---

1. The ASPR have since been integrated into the new Federal Acquisition Regulations System. See 48 Fed.Reg. 42,103 (1983). The old regulations were amended as necessary and recodified into C.F.R. Title 48.

2. Congress later enacted a specific statute regarding rights in technical data, 10 U.S.C. § 2320 (Supp. V 1987), directing the Secretary of Defense to prescribe regulations defining the interests and rights of the government, contractors, and subcontractors in technical data. The statute to a great degree merely codifies the then-existing ASPR regulations. H.R.Rep. No. 690, 98th Cong. 2d Sess. 15, reprinted in 1984 U.S.Code Cong. and Admin.News 4237, 4246. Section 2320 and the regulations promulgated under it, 48 C.F.R. Ch. 2, Sbpt. 227.4, carry forward generally unchanged the provisions of ASPR §§ 9-202 & 9-203.

3. Section 9-203(b) provides in pertinent part:
(b) Basic Data Clause.
RIGHTS IN TECHNICAL DATA (FEB.1965)
(a) Definitions.
* * *
(b) Government Rights.
   (1) The Governmental shall have unlimited rights in:
      (i) technical data resulting directly from performance of experimental, developmental or research work which was specified as an element of performance in this or any other Government contract or subcontract;
      * * *
   (2) The Government shall have limited rights in:
      * * *
      (ii) technical data pertaining to items, components or processes developed at private expense, other than such data as may be included in the data referred to in (b)(1)(i), (iii), (iv), (v), and (vi);
provided that each piece of data to which limited rights are to be asserted pursuant to (2)(i) and (ii) above is marked with the [proper] legend in which is inserted the number of the prime contract under which the technical data is to be delivered and the name of the Contractor or subcontractor by whom the technical data was generated.

tract. The factual issue concerns whether, assuming that the regulations do apply, the holdback bar was "developed" at private expense within the meaning of the regulations.

* * *

While we recognize the significance of the legal issues presented in this regard, we find it unnecessary in this case to resolve them, for the decision of the district court must be affirmed on its alternative, factual grounding. Even if the ASPR regulations were read into the subcontract and superseded its express terms, Decoto nevertheless retained its rights to the technical data because the holdback bar was developed at private expense. See ASPR §§ 9.202.2(c) & 9-203(b) clause (b)(2)(ii).

Under the APA, we may overturn the contracting officer's decision that the Navy was authorized to disclose Decoto's data only if the decision was arbitrary, capricious, an abuse of discretion, or otherwise not in accordance with law. See 5 U.S.C. § 706(2)(A). After reviewing the record, we conclude that it compelled the district court's holding that the bar was developed at private and not government expense. The Navy contracting officer's decision was arbitrary, and its implementation was therefore properly enjoined by the district court.

The contracting officer's decision relied in part upon language of the Decoto-Grumman subcontract, which the Navy contends created unlimited data rights in the government under the ASPR. The subcontract language relied upon recited that design and development were within the subcontract's scope. The subcontract language calls for Decoto to "design, develop, manufacture, test and deliver all items as required."

The Navy, however, is mistaken in its belief that the recitals of a contract alone can determine whether an item was actually developed at private expense. ASPR § 9-203(b) clause (b)(1)(i) purports to grant unlimited rights in the government to "technical data resulting directly from performance of experimental, developmental, or research work which was specified as an element of performance in this or any other Government contract or subcontract" (emphasis added). The regulation requires actual development and work, not merely contract recitals. Procurement authorities use a test based on physical and economic reality, not language, to determine which party actually "develops" an item within the meaning of the statutes and regulations. This test has now been codified within the new Federal Acquisition Regulations System (FARS). See 48 C.F.R. § 227.471 (1987).

The leading administrative decision in this area, from which the current regulation is derived, is In re Bell Helicopter Textron, 85-3 B.C.A. (CCH) ¶ 18,415 (A.S.B.C.A.1985). It concerned a defense research project that had gone through various phases of funding alternately provided by the government and the private contractor. The Armed Services Board of Contract Appeals there recognized that the crucial factor in determining who "developed" an item concerned who took the risk of investing money to transform the item from a speculative idea into a workable item that would probably succeed in its intended use. The Board defined the term "developed" accordingly:

> In order to be "developed," an item or component must be in being, that is, at least a prototype must have been fabricated ... ; and practicability, workability, and functionality (largely synonymous concepts) must be shown through sufficient analysis and/or test to demonstrate to reasonable persons skilled in the applicable art that there is a high probability the item or component will work as intended. All "development" of the item or component need not be 100 percent complete, and the item or component need not be brought to the point where it could be sold or offered for sale. An invention which has been "actually reduced to practice" under patent law has been "developed," but the converse is not necessarily true in every case.

85-3 B.C.A. (CCH) at 92,434.

The Department of Defense adopted this "workability" definition in a regulation it implemented in 1987 for defining the term "developed" in this context:

> "Developed", as used in this subpart, means that the item, component or process exists and is workable. Thus, the item or component must have been constructed or the process practiced. Workability is generally established when the item, component, or process has been analyzed or tested sufficiently to demonstrate to reasonable people skilled in the applicable art that there is a high probability that it will operate as intended.... To be considered "developed," the item, component or process need not be at the stage where it could be offered for sale or sold on the commercial market, nor must [it] be actually reduced to practice within the meaning of [the patent law].

48 C.F.R. § 227.471. The Navy points to no authority adopting a different definition for the term "developed," nor does it argue that the definition has changed since the time when the holdback bars were developed.

Under this standard, our review of the record must focus on the realities of who invested the money that transformed the holdback bar from an uncertain idea into a workable device for its intended application. The record overwhelmingly shows that Decoto's money, and not the Navy's, played this role.

The record reflects that Decoto clearly had the technology in place and had developed the bar to the point of workability even before Decoto entered into the contract with Grumman. By the time Decoto originally approached the Navy with the design for the bar, Decoto already had two patents in place on the "high energy release locking actuator ring," which forms the heart of the bar's design. The Navy apparently believed in the feasibility of Decoto's existing design, inasmuch as the Navy itself referred Decoto to Grumman for further funding. In negotiating the contract with Grumman, Decoto never quoted or asked for any funds for design effort or production tooling. The contract calls for the production of first units of the bar within a very short time; four preproduction units were to be delivered within three and a half months, and six production models were to follow within approximately three more months. Decoto's technology was sufficiently developed to allow Decoto successfully to meet these commitments.

The entire framework of the Decoto-Grumman subcontract operates as a straight parts procurement agreement rather than one for research and development. The contract calls for Decoto to supply holdback bars to the Navy as finished products. It contains no expenditure category for research and development work. The total price paid to Decoto under the contract represents simply the aggregate of individual payments for manufactured bars and supporting documentation. The contract is of the "fixed-price" type, promising payment of a specific price for each unit delivered, rather than a "cost-type" contract, which would reimburse the contractor for whatever expenses it incurred plus adding percentage for the contractor's profit. Fixed-price contracts like Decoto's have not normally been used for projects requiring research and development. See Bell Helicopter Textron, 85-3 B.C.A. (CCH) at 92,401.

The contracting officer's decision pointed to changes occurring in the bar's design during the course of performance of the subcontract to support the conclusion that the Navy indirectly financed design and development of the bar through payments by Grumman. The only evidence in the record that supports the position that the Navy actually financed any of the bar's development is a "Subcontractor Change Proposal" (SCP) that Decoto sent to Grumman during the term of the contract. The original preproduction contract, dated December 1970, carried a price of $72,344.88. Roughly two years later, in November 1972, Decoto sent six SCPs to Grumman in response to Grumman's request that the bars withstand 2,000 successful launch cycles rather than the 700 cycles demonstrated by the preproduction units. The proposals sought increases in the contract price, all of which were to be passed through to the Navy, requesting a total of $141,875.20 in additional payments to Decoto. Five of the six SCPs concerned small specific changes in the bar's design, and were approved by Grumman for the full amounts requested. The sixth request, upon which the Navy here relies, was characterized by Grumman as a "change in scope." It was the largest and most general in nature, and requested $106,724.22, of which Grumman approved only $53,000. As a result, the SCPs added only $88,158.98, bringing the total government expenditures for the bars from $151,721.94 to $239,880.92 as of that time.

The justification provided by Decoto in the sixth SCP for seeking reimbursement of nearly $107,000 refers to a "completely new design" that had been developed by Decoto in response to Grumman's demands that the bars last longer. The contracting officer's decision held, and the Navy argues on appeal, that this demonstrates that the Navy paid for development of the bar, the payment flowing through Grumman during the term of the contract.

Despite Decoto's assertions at the time that $107,000 was necessary, there exists no evidence in the record to show that the money actually paid by the Navy through the SCP "developed" the bar to workability within the definition established by Bell Helicopter Textron and 48 C.F.R. § 227.471. The record contains nothing to suggest that prior to this SCP the holdback bar had a low probability of success in its intended application, or that the bar obtained a high probability of success only as a result of the funding provided by the SCP. Indeed, since the government provided less than half of the development costs requested in 1972, and in effect provided only partial reimbursement for development that had already taken place, the SCP does not support the government's position that the Navy financed the crucial research and development.

* * *

Other evidence in the record suggests that the bars had achieved workability before any government money was paid to Decoto, and that the changes that the government helped finance during the course of the contract were aimed at increasing performance rather than achieving workability. When the original Decoto-Grumman contract was amended to reflect the increase in contract price, the additional payment was not placed under a research and development category, but was accounted for under a new heading of "qualification test."

The Navy itself recognized that the bars manufactured without the design changes covered by the SCP were workable. This is most clearly evidenced by the fact that, although the Navy was aware of the changes wrought by the SCPs, it nevertheless approved the ordering and use of forty-two pre-change design bars for use in launching F-14s from aircraft carriers. The Navy merely assigned a different part number to these pre-change units to keep track of their shorter life span. There is nothing in the record to suggest that any of these pre-change bars ever failed to operate properly. The record does contain evidence that in over 250,000 deck launches using the bar only one possible operational failure has ever been noted.

The government directs us to language in Bell Helicopter Textron, 85-3 B.C.A. (CCH) at 92,423, suggesting that if a contractor receives even partial reimbursement for development costs previously voluntarily expended, the government may receive unlimited data rights. We do not believe such a rule, even if appropriate in some cases, should apply in a situation like this where the contractor could not reasonably have been aware that an application for reimbursement could later lead to total forfeiture of data rights which the contractor had in good faith sought to retain by appropriate legends. Here the government did not give Decoto any notice of its intent to claim data rights until ten years after the SCP was submitted.

The Navy contracting officer's findings that the key research and development, as defined under the standard of Bell Helicopter Textron and 48 C.F.R. § 227.471, occurred after the contract had begun and was financed by the government were arbitrary and unsupported by the record, and are therefore insufficient under the APA to support a holding that the holdback bars were developed other than at private expense. Because Decoto's holdback bar was privately developed and its technical data contained the proper restrictive legend, ASPR §§ 9-202 & 9-203 granted only restricted data rights in the bar to the Navy. These regulations do not authorize the Navy to disclose Decoto's technical data. Such disclosure would violate the Trade Secrets Act, and is therefore properly enjoinable under the APA.

The district court's entry of injunction against the Navy was proper and is AFFIRMED.

Notes and Questions

1. Government-funded research and development ("R&D") leads to many patents, with the perennial issue being whether the government should receive full title to the patents or just a license for their use. The government has made policy on this by the 1980 "Bayh-Dole" Act, Patent and Trademark Amendments of 1980, P.L. 96-517, 94 Stat. 3019, 35 USC § 200 et seq., and by a 1983 executive branch memorandum, President's Memorandum to the Heads of Executive Departments and Agencies, "Government Patent Policy" (Feb. 18, 1983). These are reflected in the FAR and the various FAR "Patent Rights" clauses. FAR patent rights clauses mandate contractors to disclose to the government any "subject invention" which is "any invention of the contractor conceived or first actually reduced to practice in the performance of work under this contract." FAR 52.227-12(a). Once disclosed, a contractor has the option to retain title to the invention. FAR 27.302(b).

However, the FAR also allows agencies to provide otherwise if: "(1) ... the contractor is not located in the United States or is subject to control of foreign government, (2) when the contract is for operation of certain government-owned contractor-operated Department of Energy facilities, (3) in 'exceptional circumstances' when a restriction on contractor title rights will better serve FAR policy objectives, and (4) when granting title in an invention would endanger national security." If a contractor retains title to the patent, the government receives a license which permits other contractors to sell products to the government even if they are in direct competition. *See* FAR 52.227-11(b); FAR 52.227-12(b). For a general discussion, see William L. Geary, Jr., *Protecting the Patent Rights of Small Businesses: Does the Bayh-Dole Act Live Up to Its Promise?*, 22 Pub. Cont. L.J. 101 (1992)).

For discussions of developments regarding what the government and the contractor receive in terms of rights in discoveries, see Jack E. Kerrigan & Christopher J. Brasco, *The Technology Transfer Revolution: Legislative History and Future Proposals*, 31 Pub. Cont. L. J. 277 (2002); Diane M. Sidebottom, *Updating the Bayh-Dole Act: Keeping the Federal Government on the Cutting Edge*, 30 Pub. Cont. L. J. 225 (2001); Richard N. Kuyath, *Barriers to Federal Procurement: Patent Rights*, The Procurement Lawyer, Fall 2000, at 1.

2. Technical Data. FAR 27.403 provides that: "all contracts that require data to be produced, furnished, acquired or specifically used in meeting contract performance re-

quirements, must contain terms that delineate the respective rights and obligations of the government and the contractor regarding the use, duplication, and disclosure of such data …"

The government can acquire unlimited rights for "data first produced in the performance of a contract … ; form, fit and function data … ; data that constitutes manuals or instructional and training material …" and data that is not limited rights data or restricted data for computer software. FAR 27.404(a). Limited rights data concerns trade secrets, commercial, financial, confidential or privileged information, or items developed by private funding. *See* FAR 27.404(b); *see also* FAR 52.227-14(definitions of terms); Jeff E. Schwartz, *The Acquisition of Technical Data Rights by the Government*, 23 Pub. Con. L. J. 513 (1994).

Note on Government Licensing of Commercial Software

In recent years, commercial software has come to play a special role beyond that of other intellectual property, as key (or more so) for the government as for the rest of society. Yet, the licensing to the government of commercial software involves major problems as to the terms and conditions of contracts and the rest of the limits of rights and use. Although some of the problems derive from the inherent complexity of the rapidly evolved intellectual property scheme for this suddenly blossomed subject, other problems derive from the continuing lack, despite Congressional enactments creating a special regime for commercial software contracts, of the absence of an updated licensing policy in the FAR, particularly considering the differential rules for military and civilian agencies.

Since World War II, the military, which was very much in the business of buying or developing cutting-edge computer and electronics technology, had gone through an elaborate evolution of data rights. See *Bell Helicopter Textron*, ASBCA No. 21192, 85-3 BCA para. 18,415 at 92,418. When the FAR, particularly after the addition of subpart 27.4 in 1987, brought military and civilian procurement regulations together, a unified system for the government might have ensued. However, the military resumed maintaining a separate system in the Defense Federal Acquisition Regulation Supplement (DFARS). During a period of extremely rapid evolution in computer software, symbolized by Microsoft licensing its operating systems, the DFARS also evolved until it incorporated in 1995 an important treatment of the newly emerging subject. Meanwhile, Congress had its own series of enactments, with FASA in 1994 and the Clinger-Cohen Act in 1996 encouraging recognition of "commercial" purchases in general and commercial computer software in particular.

Pursuant to the rules laid down by these enactments and promulgations, whether the software supplied to the Government will be treated as commercial software at all, and whether a vendor's standard commercial license will apply, depends on whether the purchaser is a military or civilian agency. On the military side, the 1995 revision of the DFARS did specifically address the process for licensing commercial software. The DFARS specifies that vendors may use their standard commercial software agreements when contracting with the military agencies, greatly strengthening the vendors' rights.

On the civilian side, the general FAR provisions have not changed along with the military DFARS; the FAR does not specify the use of a commercial contractor's license, and there are no regulations for civilian agencies comparable to the rest of the DFARS provisions. The result is that civilian agencies are not limited to the restrictions on rights provided by commercial software licenses, and the ultimate terms of the contract with the civilian agency are often dependent upon negotiation.

Turning to data rights, the basic DFARS data rights clause expressly provides a definition for commercial software and software acquired by a military agency that falls within that definition is purchased under a "standard" commercial license. All of the standard licensing terms and conditions under the commercial contract will apply. Under the DFARS

> Commercial computer software means software developed or regularly used for nongovernmental purposes which — (i) has been sold, leased, or licensed to the public; (iii) Has not been offered, sold, leased or licensed to the public, but will be available for commercial sale, lease or license in time to satisfy the delivery requirements of this contract, (iv) satisfies a criterion of paragraph ... (1)(i), (ii), or (iii) of this clause and would require only minor modification to meet the requirements of the contract.

DFARS 252.227-7014. If software is sold to a military agency and falls within the definition of "commercial software," the government is restricted by the terms of the standard commercial software license customarily provided to the public, unless the license is inconsistent with federal procurement law. DFARS 227.7202-1(a).

In contrast, the general FAR data rights clause does not define "commercial software." So, with civilian agencies, often the rights granted to the government by the FAR go beyond the terms of the standard commercial contract and the vendor's standard contract terms will be dependent upon negotiation.

Contractors' preservation of rights in commercial software depends upon identifying and marking it. An important case before the Armed Services Board of Contract Appeals, *General Atrionics Corp.*, ASBCA No. 49196, 02-1 BCA para. 31,798, at 157,067, nailed this down. The contractor had marked its proposal, but it had not marked the delivered software, and its claim for license fees was denied. In contrast, the contractor won in *Ship Analytics*, ASBCA No. 50914, 01-1 BCA para. 31,253, at 154,353. Computer software provided to the Navy for training, pursuant to carefully protected licensor rights, was given to other contractors to compete for an upgrade contract, and the board upheld the licensor's claim for wrongful release.

For the civilian agencies not under the DFARS, FAR Part 12 does specify the minimum that a government agency is supposed to abide by the specific terms and conditions of the contractor's standard commercial license, unless a term specifically conflicts with statutory requirements of the FAR. However, under FAR 2.101 "Computer software" is defined as "computer programs, computer data bases, and related documentation." The FAR does not specifically define "commercial computer software" and does not distinguish between software and documentation. In addition, the FAR does not contemplate the difference between commercial software, or any other software specifically developed for the government at private expense. Standard commercial software agreements are therefore treated the same as any other commercial license and are subject to the restricted rights clause of the FAR 52.227-19. Where the terms of the standard commercial license conflict with or are inconsistent with the restricted rights clause provided by the FAR, the government does not have to specifically abide by those terms and they are often dependent upon negotiation.

One such example is that under the FAR, the rights of use of the commercial software are restricted to a computer, rather than to the number of users, which is standard for a commercial contract. Thus, restrictions on use of the software may not be limited to a single individual user. In addition, most standard commercial licenses prohibit "modifying, adapting, or combining" rights, which is however, specifically allowed to the government under the "restricted rights" provisions.

A fundamental difference between military and civilian procurement concerns items developed with mixed private as well as government funding. Under the DFARS, for such an item the government obtains government purpose rights and the agency's rights are limited to the use for which the item was purchased. Under the FAR, however, if an item is developed with mixed funding, the government may still retain unlimited rights.

For more information on this subject, see: C. Peter Dungan, *Less Is More: Encouraging Greater Competition In Computer Software Procurement By Simplifying The DFARS Licensing Scheme*, 39 Pub. Cont. L.J. 465 (Spring 2010); David A. Kessler, *Protection And Protectionism: The Practicalities Of Offshore Software Development In Government Procurement*, 38 Pub. Cont. L.J. 1 (Fall 2008); Christine C. Trend, *Killing the Goose That Laid the Golden Egg: Data Rights Law and Policy in Department of Defense Contracts*, 34 Pub. Cont. L. J. 287 (2005); W. Jay DeVecchio, *Licensing Commercial Computer Software*, 04-03 Briefing Papers 1 (Feb. 2004).

Data Enterprises of the Northwest, Appellant, v. General Services Administration, Respondent

04-1 BCA P 32,539, GSBCA No. 15,607
General Services Board of Contract Appeals
February 17, 2004

Before Board Judges DANIELS (Chairman), HYATT, and GOODMAN.

GOODMAN, Board Judge.

This appeal was filed by Data Enterprises of the Northwest (DEN or appellant), on June 8, 2001, from the General Services Administration's (GSA or respondent) contracting officer's final decision dated May 18, 2001, denying appellant's certified claim dated December 15, 2000.[1]

* * *

Summary of Events Leading to Appellant's Claim

Appellant's software, ATICTS [Automated Tool Inventory Control and Tracking System], is used for tool inventory management. Appellant has developed, continuously improved, and licensed its software to commercial and Government customers since 1970. ATICTS is a COTS product and was originally DOS-based software. In 1995, appellant negotiated and was awarded by GSA a Multiple Award Schedule (MAS) contract, pursuant to which federal agencies could enter into a license to use ATICTS software and also receive support and training. The contracting officer's memorandum of negotiation and award emphasizes that the basis of negotiation was the terms of DEN's commercial license.

As will be discussed in this decision, by purchasing a license to use ATICTS software, Government agencies gain restricted rights to use the software. The license to use ATICTS allows the Government agency to use the software for its intended purpose, to track tools, and does not include the right to use ATICTS as a basis for developing tool management software which would compete with ATICTS in the public and private marketplace. The Government breached its contract with DEN by using DEN's proprietary information to develop competing tool management software, by allowing a third-party contractor to analyze DEN's proprietary information for the purposes of disclosing same to a third-party developer, and disclosing this information to a third-party developer.

---

1. To shorten the opinion, the entire section for Findings of Facts is omitted, and several opinion sections which were in the text have been moved into footnotes.

In the years prior to 1998, appellant spent approximately two million dollars to enhance the DOS-based version of ATICTS by creating ATICTS 2000, the Windows-based version of its software. The primary documentation for ATICTS 2000 is the ATICTS Workbook, which is approximately 250 pages in length and contains a legend stating that it is copyrighted and contains proprietary information. The ATICTS Workbook contains a detailed description of the functions performed by ATICTS 2000, including representations of computer screens and step-by-step direction for the user. An integral part of ATICTS 2000 is its data dictionary, which is resident on the CD-ROM media of the software and contains the structure of every element of the ATICTS 2000 database application. The ATICTS Workbook is only available to licensed users of ATICTS.

Since 1998, the Naval Systems Support Group (NSSG) has been responsible for the Department of Defense's management of tool management applications. In early 1999, NSSG issued a purchase order for a four-user license for ATICTS 2000 to upgrade the current license for ATICTS at the Norfolk Naval Shipyard (NNSY).

At that time, NSSG had two separate systems to track tools and equipment. The Tool Inventory Management Application (TIMA) system, using ATICTS, was used to track tools. ATICTS and ATICTS 2000 both operated using a database management system known as Pick (D3). The Facility Equipment Management (FEM) system, using software by the name of MAXIMO, developed by Anteon, was used to track equipment. MAXIMO uses Oracle as a database management system.

The Government made a determination that it would benefit from the development of software that would manage both equipment and tools. Generally, the Government or any private entity is not prohibited from developing software that has functionality similar to or even the same as existing software. The Government was certainly free to develop tool tracking software to replace ATICTS without violating its contract with appellant. Various Government personnel testified during the hearing in this appeal that the Government's goal was to have a third party determine if the development of such software was feasible, and if it was, to develop such software by determining the needs of the Government end users, without using ATICTS-related information, since tool inventory management was a business function whose processes were not specific to particular software. Internal Government correspondence indicates that the Government was aware that by attempting to develop such software NSSG became a direct competitor to appellant. There was nothing wrong with this approach, had the Government actually followed it and not used appellant's proprietary information.

Instead, it is clear that the Government embarked on a different route. In early 2000, AMS, NSSG's support contractor for tool management, issued a written proposal to NSSG known as the Proposed Approach. This proposal suggested that NSSG, through AMS, should analyze the functionality of ATICTS 2000 by creating a document known as a Software Requirements Specification (SRS), which would then be used by a third-party developer, Anteon, to determine the feasibility of incorporating the functionality of tool management into Anteon's MAXIMO software. If incorporation of ATICTS' functionality into MAXIMO was determined to be feasible, Anteon would then enhance MAXIMO so that it could be used to track both tools and equipment. NSSG would experience cost savings and efficiency by using only one software program which operated using Oracle as a database management system.

It is clear from the record in this appeal that the Government, based upon AMS's Proposed Approach, allowed AMS to analyze appellant's software, ATICTS 2000, for the purpose of providing information directly to Anteon. Anteon was then tasked under a separate contract with the Government to develop tool management software to replace ATICTS 2000 at Government facilities. Anteon did this by enhancing MAXIMO, and the enhanced portion of MAXIMO came to be known as FEM TM.

... AMS, at the direction of the Government, transmitted appellant's proprietary and copyrighted information—the entire ATICTS Workbook and portions of the ATICTS Workbook in the document known as the SRS—to Anteon's senior information engineer, Kenneth Linna, to use in Anteon's feasibility study. AMS later transmitted additional proprietary information—various versions of the ATICTS 2000 data dictionary—to Mr. Linna, who used them in the development of the Anteon product FEM TM.

* * *

The second disclosure of appellant's proprietary information occurred when Anteon received the SRS prepared by AMS....

In July 2000, NSSG notified DEN that it was developing software that it would use for tool tracking to replace ATICTS 2000. When appellant complained to the Government that it believed the Government had wrongfully disclosed its proprietary information to third parties, the Government investigated and was informed by Anteon that it had received the SRS and the ATICTS Workbook. In fact, Anteon had informed the Government that it had used the ATICTS Workbook as the primary source of the Anteon Analysis. Responding to appellant's concerns, the contracting officer revealed to appellant that Anteon had "reviewed" the ATICTS Workbook. The contracting officer then directed Anteon to return the ATICTS Workbook to the Government at the Government's request.

At about the same time that the Government directed Anteon to return the ATICTS Workbook, AMS made a third disclosure of DEN's proprietary information to Anteon. Anteon's Kenneth Linna, the same person who relied heavily upon the ATICTS Workbook to perform the feasibility study, requested and received from AMS various versions of the ATICTS 2000 data dictionary, which he used during the development phase of FEM TM.

* * *

The Government cautioned its users before the first user conference that incorporation of tool management into its FEM system as the result of Anteon's enhancing MAXIMO with tool management functionality was to be accomplished without using any ATICTS-related information. By that time, Anteon had already received the ATICTS Workbook, the SRS, and the ATICTS data dictionaries....

Appellant filed a claim with the contracting officer alleging breach of contract, copyright infringement, and a taking of its property without just compensation pursuant to Fifth Amendment to the United States Constitution....

The Contract Between Appellant and Respondent Contains Negotiated Rights

This dispute arises from the parties' differing views of the Government's right to use appellant's proprietary information, the ATICTS Workbook and the ATICTS 2000 data dictionaries. The Government asserts that pursuant to its contract with appellant it acquired unlimited rights, which included the right to use appellant's proprietary information for development of competing software and to disclose the ATICTS Workbook and the ATICTS data dictionaries to anyone, including a third-party software developer who would use this information to develop software with the same functionality as ATICTS. In denying appellant's claim, the contracting officer states that "the [ATICTS Workbook] was given to a contractor (Anteon), reviewed, and returned to the Navy." The contracting officer characterized the Workbook as "data," and concluded that the Government acquired unlimited rights to such data under FAR clause 52.227-14, Rights in Data, and that such rights include the right to reproduce the data and a paid up, nonexclusive, irrevocable worldwide license in any copyrighted data.

* * *

In order to understand the rights acquired by the Government with respect to the AT-ICTS Workbook, the information contained in the Workbook which was included in the SRS, and ATICTS data dictionaries, we must first review the applicable regulatory structure and contract language.

The contract between GSA and DEN was a Federal Supply Schedule, Multiple Award Schedule contract applicable to all departments or independent agencies of the executive branch of the Federal Government. 48 CFR 8.401 (a), 8.403-2 (1994). The contract was for the acquisition of licenses to use existing commercial software which was not developed at Government expense.

Generally, when computer software has been designed, developed, or generated under a Government contract, the Government has "unlimited rights" to the delivered software and may use the software for any purpose. 48 CFR 27.404(a). On the other hand, when the Government enters into a contract to acquire a license to use computer software developed at private expense, the Government enters into an agreement with the contractor that restricts the use of the software to specific purposes. This software is referred to as "restricted software," and the Government acquires a license to use such software with "restricted rights." 48 CFR 27.405(b)(2). If the Government uses restricted software for any purpose that is not permitted by the contract, the Government has breached the contract.

ATICTS 2000 was developed at private expense and is therefore restricted software. When existing commercial software such as ATICTS 2000 is acquired under the MAS, the FAR does not mandate the use of any specific contract clause, but, rather, allows negotiation of rights. 48 CFR 27.405(b)(2), 27.409(k). Specific rights were negotiated and included in the contract, commensurate with DEN's commercial license, which was used as the basis of negotiation and award, and these rights were expressly set forth in the clause of the contract entitled "Utilization Limitations."

As discussed below, the Utilizations Limitations clause did not give the Government unlimited rights to the software. In that clause, the Government clearly promised not to copy or otherwise disclose the software and the documentation and restricted the use of the software consistent with DEN's commercial license. The provisions of two additional clauses incorporated by reference into the contract, FAR clause 52.227-14, "Rights in Data" (June 1987), and FAR clause 52.227-19, "Commercial Computer Software—Restricted Rights" (June 1987), as applied to DEN's software, do not conflict with the rights in the Utilization Limitations clause or DEN's commercial license....

* * *

The Scope of the Solicitation and the Contract

The solicitation stated that the procurement was for "software products" and further stated that "for purposes of the solicitation, software products are defined to be licenses (including upgrades), documentation, and media." The term "license" was defined in the contract's glossary, whose purpose was "to provide offerors and GSA with common ground to facilitate negotiations."[2]

2.

　　SOFTWARE-LICENSE AGREEMENT—A contract between the software vendor (licensor)
　　and the software user (licensee) granting the licensee permission to use a given software
　　product subject to certain conditions and obligations. Synonym: License Agreement.

The Utilization Limitations Clause of the Contract Set Forth Conditions of the License Acquired by the Government

The Utilization Limitations clause of the contract, contained in a section of the contract entitled "Terms and Conditions Applicable to Perpetual Software License (Special Item 132-33)[SIN 132-33] and Maintenance (Special Item 132-34) of General Purpose Commercial Information Technology Software," established the conditions under which the Government as licensee could use the software which it licensed under the contract, and it placed restrictions on the use of the documentation and media. This clause reads:

> ... The government also agrees to comply with the following:
>
> * * *
>
> c. FAR clauses 52.227-14 RIGHTS IN DATA—GENERAL (JUN 1987) and 52.227-19 COMMERCIAL COMPUTER SOFTWARE—RESTRICTED RIGHTS (JUN 1987) are incorporated by reference as part of this pricelist.

It should be noted that the Utilization Limitations clause refers to SIN 132-33, which originally was SIN 132-31, which, according to the price schedule, contained the license, documentation, and media. The clause references license, documentation, and media (disks) and clearly does not grant the Government unlimited rights to any of these. Rather, the Government must refrain from changing or removing any insignia or lettering from the software or documentation, cannot produce copies of the documentation or the media, and the title and ownership of the software and documentation remain with the contractor. Use of the documentation is limited to the facility for which the software is acquired. There is nothing in this clause, or in DEN's commercial license, that would allow the Government as licensee to use the software to develop competing software or disclose proprietary information to a third party to use to develop competing software. The license grants to the licensee the right only to use the software for its intended purpose—to track tools.

* * *

The Government Did Not Acquire Unlimited Rights to the ATICTS Workbook Dictionary of the ATICTS 2000 Data Dictionary Pursuant to FAR Clause 52.227-14, Rights in Data

The contracting officer asserts in his final decision that the Government acquired unlimited rights to the ATICTS Workbook pursuant to the FAR clause 52.227-14, Rights in Data—General (JUN 1987). The regulatory requirements for the use of the Rights in Data clause and language of the clause itself do not support the contracting officer's conclusion.

FAR subpart 27.4 explains the use of the Rights in Data clause and contains the following definitions:

> Computer software, as used in this subpart, means computer programs, computer data bases, and documentation thereof.
>
> Data, as used in this subpart, means recorded information, regardless of form or the media on which it may be recorded. The term includes technical data and

---

DEN's commercial software license agreement that was applicable to ATICTS 2000 and the basis of negotiation of the contract reads in pertinent part:

> Customer acknowledges that the license granted hereunder is limited to the Use of Licensed Programs as provided herein and that the Use thereof by an entity other than Customer is prohibited. Customer shall have no right to assign or sub-license any of the Licensed Programs or the Use thereof.

* * *

computer software. The term does not include information incidental to contract administration, such as financial, administrative, cost or pricing or management information.

Restricted computer software, as used in this subpart, means computer software developed at private expense and that is a trade secret; is commercial or financial and confidential or privileged; or is published copyrighted computer software; including minor modifications of such computer software. 48 CFR 27.401.

ATICTS 2000 is restricted computer software based on the above definition — it was developed at private expense, is commercial, contains explicitly marked proprietary information, and is published and copyrighted. The ATICTS Workbook is "documentation" under the contractually supplied definition of "documentation." Documentation is included in the definition of "computer software," and computer software is also included in the definition of "data." The ATICTS Workbook is therefore "data" included in restricted computer software. The Government does not acquire unlimited rights to such data that is included in restricted commercial software, pursuant to FAR 27.404(a) set forth below:

(a) Unlimited Rights Data. Under the clause at 52.227-14, Rights in Data-General, the Government acquires unlimited rights in the following data (except as provided in paragraph (f) of this section for copyrighted data): ...

(3) data (except as may be included with restricted computer software) that constitute manuals or instructional and training material for installation, operation, or routine maintenance and repair of items, components, or processes delivered or furnished for use under a contract.

48 CFR 27.404(a)(emphasis added) states that the ATICTS Workbook was a deliverable under the delivery order when training was ordered. The fact that the Workbook may have been received during training does not change the fact that the Workbook is 1) proprietary information and "documentation" as defined in the contract, 2) included electronically with the software itself and in hard copy, and 3) therefore data included with restrictive software to which the Government does not acquire unlimited rights.

The ATICTS 2000 data dictionary is also data included in restricted software and does not come within any category of data to which the Government acquires unlimited rights under the Rights in Data clause. [3]

The Government Did Not Acquire Unlimited Rights to the ATICTS Workbook or the ATICTS 2000 Data Dictionary Pursuant to FAR Clause 52.227-19. Commercial Computer Software—Restricted Rights

The FAR clause entitled "Commercial Computer Software—Restricted Rights (JUNE 1987)," which was incorporated into the contract, does not support the Government's position that it gained unlimited rights to the ATICTS Workbook. [4]

---

3. It is not data first produced in the performance of the contract; form, fit, and function data delivered under the contract; or data delivered under the contract that constitute manuals or instructional and training material for installation, operation, or routine maintenance and repair of items, components, or processes delivered or furnished for use under this contract.

4. The clause begins with the following definition:
(a) As used in this clause, restricted computer software means any computer program, computer data base, or documentation thereof, that has been developed at private expense and either is a trade secret, is commercial or financial and confidential or — privileged, or is published and copyrighted. 48 CFR 52.227-19(a)

ATICTS 2000 is restricted computer software based on the above definition—it was developed at private expense, is commercial, contains explicitly marked proprietary information, and is published and copyrighted. The ATICTS 2000 data dictionary is an integral part of the restricted software. The ATICTS Workbook is also "documentation" under the contractually supplied definition of "documentation." Documentation is included in the definition of "restricted computer software."

* * *

The ATICTS Workbook, because it is included with restricted computer software, comes within the above exception in FAR 27.404(a)(3) and in Rights in Data clause subparagraph (b)(iii).[5] The Government's argument as to the ATICTS Workbook ignores this exception, and is based on the theory that because the Workbook is used in training end users, it is data pursuant to subparagraph (b)(iii) above. . . .

The rights afforded to the Government under the Commercial Computer Software clause do not supersede or expand those that the Government has by virtue of the Utilization Limitations clause.

Paragraph (c)(3) of the Commercial Computer Software clause states further:

> (3) If the restricted computer software delivered under this purchase order/contract is published and copyrighted, it is licensed to the Government, without disclosure prohibitions, with the rights set forth in paragraph (c)(2) of this clause unless expressly stated otherwise in this purchase order/contract.

48 CFR 52.227-19(c)(3).

This provision does not give the Government the right to disclose appellant's software for the purpose of software development. Even though the software is published and copyrighted, the specific prohibitions in the contract in the Utilization Limitations clause previously discussed are clear expressions that the Government does not receive the software without disclosure prohibitions. Accordingly, the Commercial Computer Software clause defers to the Utilization Limitations clause in this instance.

Finally, paragraph (d) of the Commercial Computer Software clause affords the contractor further rights to assure protection of disclosure of its material if that material is copyrighted. [6]

The appellant complied with this provision by placing the following legend conspicuously and directly below its copyright statement in the ATICTS Workbook:

---

5. GSBCA 15607 59. The Rights in Data clause itself reads in pertinent part:
   (b) Allocation of rights. (1) Except as provided in paragraph (c) of this clause regarding copyright, the Government shall have unlimited rights in—
       (i) Data first produced in the performance of this contract;
       (ii) Form, fit, and function data delivered under this contract;
       (iii) Data delivered under this contract (except for restricted computer software) that constitute manuals or instructional and training material for installation, operation, or routine maintenance and repair of items, components, or processes delivered or furnished for use under this contract. 48 CFR 52.227-14(b).
6. This provision reads:
   If any restricted computer software is delivered under this contract with the copyright notice of 17 U.S.C. 401, it will be presumed to be published and copyrighted and licensed to the Government in accordance with subparagraph (c)(3) of this clause, unless a statement substantially as follows accompanies such copyright notice: Unpublished—rights reserved under the copyright laws of the United States.

GSBCA 15607 6348 CFR 52.227-19(d).

Copyright, 1998, Data Enterprises of the Northwest, Inc. Workbook Version 11/06/99.

These materials contain confidential and proprietary information and may not be used, reproduced, distributed or disclosed except as specifically authorized under prior written agreement with Data Enterprises of the Northwest, Inc.

The fact that the Government distributed copies of the ATICTS Workbook without this copyright statement and proprietary language is itself a breach of the Utilization Limitations clause and both incorporated clauses.

* * *

Decision

The appeal is GRANTED IN PART and DISMISSED FOR LACK OF JURISDICTION IN PART. Appellant is awarded damages for breach of contract as stated herein.

Notes and Questions

1. Suppose a civilian agency like the GSA, rather than the Navy, had obtained the ATICTS 2000 license, and suppose that agency had awarded by a contract which contained only very general restrictions that the software and accompanying data and documentation would be used for governmental purposes. (a) If the agency did what the Navy did in this case, what would the agency argue to defeat DEN's claim? (b) Further suppose that DEN was casual about markings and put them only in its software. Would DEN lose?

2. The DEN opinion protects the licensor's rights as to the software itself; the Workbook as documentation, and therefore data included with restricted computer software; and the data dictionary as data included with restricted computer software. However, technical data comes in many types, of which the kind included with restricted computer software is only one. What would other kinds be? What might be the nine types that the DFARS provides are to be delivered to the government with unlimited rights? See Christine C. Trend, *Killing the Goose That Laid the Golden Egg: Data Rights Law and Policy in Department of Defense Contracts,* 34 Pub. Cont. L. J. 287, 306–314 (2005).

3. Is it better to have custom licensing tailored to the balance of government and contractor needs in each particular situation? Or does this involve too much expense and strain both for the acquisition workforce and the contractor's contracting personnel? Which produces more uncertainty and litigation: using an all-purpose license for a situation it does not fit, or drafting up an idiosyncratically worded license that does not conform to any well-understood models or precedents?

D. Information Technology

Information technology has become a big part of what government purchases, from weapons control systems for the military, to accounting systems for the civilian agencies, to hardware and software for students at the state and local government level. To some extent, the federal government has sought to make special provision for information technology procurement, hoping perhaps that some higher-level coordination and direction would keep the government's information systems compatible, or at least prevent such nightmares as widespread government obsolescence or total inability for different government agencies to communicate. In particular, Congress enacted the Information Technology Management Reform Act (ITMRA) of 1996. *See, e.g.*, John A. Howell, *Governmentwide Agency Contracts: Vehicle Overcrowding on the Procurement Highway*, 27 Pub. Cont. L.J. 395 (1998).

However, in many respects, information technology procurement draws upon provisions available in government contracting generally, just adapting them to the particular context. Given the very rapid pace of private sector innovation as to hardware and software, the government may try more to keep up with that pace by procurement from the commercial sector, rather than trying to sponsor government-unique efforts. For example, in the *L.A. Systems* case, the contracting officer resorted to simplified acquisition procedures, available for information technology and other procurement alike, to speed along a computer purchase.

L.A. Systems, Protester, v. Department of the Army, and Defense Information Systems Agency, Respondents

GRANTED: February 12, 1996
GSBCA No. 13472-P

Before Board Judges PARKER, WILLIAMS, and GOODMAN.

GOODMAN, Board Judge.

On November 9, 1995, protester, L.A. Systems, filed the instant protest challenging an alleged improper sole-source acquisition of central processing units (CPUs) from Amdahl Corporation (Amdahl). The procurement was by the Rock Island Arsenal defense megacenter (Rock Island DMC) through the delegated procurement authority of the Defense Information Systems Agency (DISA). The protest alleges that respondents have impermissibly evaded full and open competition as required by the Competition in Contracting Act (CICA), 10 U.S.C. s 2304(a)(1) (1994), by dividing a requirement for the CPUs into a number of smaller acquisitions in order to use the simplified acquisition procedures of Federal Acquisition Regulation (FAR) Part 13 and thereby avoid the requirements for full and open competition in FAR Part 6.... We grant the protest.

Findings of Fact

Amdahl proposal

1. In July 1995, Amdahl presented a proposal (Amdahl proposal) to the DISA WESTHEM Configuration Control Board (CCB) to upgrade, through leasing, approximately twenty Amdahl 5890-600E (600E) CPUs in use at six defense megacenters with either 1100A or 1400A CPUs. Protester's Exhibit 2.

2. On August 1, 1995, the CCB reviewed the Amdahl proposal. The minutes of the CCB meeting of that date read, in relevant part:

> Amdahl has made an offer to DISA WESTHEM to replace all 5890-600E's with 5995-1100s for $49.9K each....

> Since the capital funding is below $50,000, the DMC may exercise this option using their own funds without prior CCB approval....

Rock Island DMC decides to upgrade

3. The Director of Rock Island DMC (the Director) made a decision to upgrade the DMC's 600E CPUs. This decision was confirmed in an e-mail message dated August 11, 1995, to staff members, which read, in relevant part:

[The Amdahl] offer was approved in concept by the CCB on 1 Aug 95. It is open to any DISA WESTHEM megacenter with 600E machines. The megacenter must provide $49.9K and can make the decision to exercise this option on a case by case basis. Upgrading the 1100A to a 1400A requires approximately $300,000 in additional capital, and CCB and CRC approval for the additional capital funding.

* * *

Procurement of CPUs

4. In mid and late August 1995, Rock Island DMC prepared requirements packages supporting the two CPU upgrades which are the subject of this protest. The requirements package which accompanied each purchase request included a mission needs statement, a statement of urgency, and an AMC Form 2110, Purchase Request and Commitment. Transcript at 92–93.

5. On August 21, 1995, the Director signed the mission needs statement for the first CPU upgrade and obtained concurrence.

* * *

6. The mission needs statement listed the "Amdahl 59995[sic]-1400A" as the item which needed to be acquired. Protester's Exhibit 25.

7. A statement of urgency was prepared to support the procurement. The statement read as follows:

> Defense Megacenter Rock Island is currently utilizing an Amdahl 5890-600E in support of a large Army Material [sic] Command workload. it is installed as two 300Es to provide more domain capacity than a single 600E permits. It is fully utilized and incapable of providing additional support for growing customer requirements or new workload.

> The CPU has a MVS/XA operating systems [sic] installed. IBM has announced it will discontinue support for this operating level soon....

> Amdahl has announced that it will shortly discontinue support of the 600E series hardware.

> In order to continue servicing current customer base at an acceptable level during fiscal year end, to have resources to service their growth requirements and to support any new requirements, this machine must be upgraded.

* * *

8. The contracting officer received the documentation supporting the procurement of the first CPU in early September 1995. Protester's Exhibit 27.

9. The contracting officer decided not to synopsize the procurement of the first Amdahl CPU in the Commerce Business Daily (CBD) based on her evaluation of the urgency statement. She confirmed this decision in a memorandum dated September 11, 1995. Protester's Exhibit 22. The contracting officer testified that she used the urgency statement solely for the purpose of avoiding synopsizing the requirements in the CBD. Transcript at 40, 98....

11. On September 13, 1995, the contracting officer conducted what she characterized as "an informal market survey" with regard to an Amdahl 1400A. She solicited an oral quote from Amdahl and reviewed commercial literature from another potential supplier and the General Services Administration (GSA) schedule contract of at least one other firm for

additional quotes. This process took less than one hour. The contracting officer determined that Amdahl offered the lowest price. Transcript at 53–56; Protester's Exhibit 23.

12. On September 13, 1995, the contracting officer telephoned a representative of Amdahl and placed an oral order for an Amdahl 1400A with 512 mb of main memory, 0 mb of expanded storage, and 128 parallel channels. Transcript at 28, 416. The contracting officer issued purchase order number DAAA08-95-M-4632 on September 13, 1995, to confirm her oral order. Transcript at 29; Protester's Exhibit 9.

13. On September 14, 1995, the contracting officer received a purchase request from Rock island DMC to procure a second CPU upgrade. When she received this request, the contracting officer had already awarded the first CPU upgrade. The contracting officer testified:

A: The first CPU, [purchase order DAAA08-95-M-] 4632, was complete and off my desk the time I did the second one.

Q: Any reason why you didn't do the two of them together?

A: One was already done. I didn't get the other requirement until afterwards.

Transcript at 77–78.

14. The requirements packages for both CPU upgrades were identical except for the dates documents were prepared and approved....

15. The contracting officer handled this procurement in the same manner as she had the earlier one. She decided not to synopsize the procurement in the CBD based upon the statement of urgency, and she used the market information she had already gathered....

Procurement of expanded memory ...

[Two purchase orders were issued for expanded memory, without synopsizing, based on the statement of urgency.]

Alleged justification for urgency and four separate purchase orders

32. According to the Director, the requirement for additional computing power (and therefore to upgrade the CPUs) and for additional expanded memory had existed in January 1995. The fact that the acquisition had not been made by August 1995 now made the requirement urgent as "[t]he longer the requirement goes, the more urgent it becomes." Transcript at 294....

34. The Director said there were four separate purchase orders for the two CPUs and the two expanded memory units because he did not have the funds all at once. Transcript at 319. As the funds became available for each purchase order, the requirements packages were issued. Id. at 321. The Director did not want to let the total amount of funds accumulate before issuing the purchase orders, as he was afraid that the CCB would "get [the] money." Id. at 320.

35. When the Director executed the mission needs statements for the CPUs and the expanded memory units, he knew the funds to acquire these items were available. Transcript at 314. Based on the signatures on the mission needs statements, funds were available for the CPUs on August 21 and 29, 1995, and for the expanded memory units on August 30 and September 13, 1995. Id. at 319.

36. The Director testified that a factor contributing to the perceived urgency was the desire "to spend ... year-end '95 dollars to reduce ... costs in '96." Transcript at 307....

Discussion

The Competition in Contracting Act (CICA) requires that contracting officers shall promote and provide for full and open competition in soliciting offers and awarding government contracts. Federal Acquisition Regulation (FAR) Part 6 contains policies and procedures designed to promote full and open competition.

The requirements for full and open competition set forth in FAR Part 6 need not be utilized for "contracts awarded using the simplified acquisition procedures of [FAR] Part 13." 48 CFR 6.001 (1995) (FAR 6.001). According to FAR Part 13, "Simplified acquisition procedures shall be used to the maximum extent practicable for all purchases of supplies or services not exceeding the simplified acquisition threshold...." FAR 13.103(a).[8]

The threshold for determining when the simplified acquisition procedures are applicable to a given procurement requires that the aggregate purchase fall under $100,000. FAR 13.101. However, if the contracting officer wants to use the simplified acquisition procedures for a purchase over $50,000, he/she must use the Federal Acquisition Computer Network (FACNET), which is the preferred means for soliciting simplified acquisitions. FAR 13.103(b), 13.106-1(a)(2).

FAR 13.103(c) contains the following prohibition:

> Requirements aggregating more than the simplified acquisition threshold shall not be broken down into several purchases that are less than the threshold merely to permit use, of simplified acquisition procedures.

Additionally, FAR 6.302-2, sets forth circumstances in which full and open competition need not be provided:

6.302-2 Unusual and compelling urgency.

(a) Authority. (1) Citations: 10 U.S.C. 2304(c)(2) or 41 U.S.C. 253(c)(2).

(2) When the agency's need for the supplies or services is of such an unusual and compelling urgency that the Government would be seriously injured unless the agency is permitted to limit the number of sources from which it solicits bids or proposals, full and open competition need not be provided for.

(b) Application. This authority applies in those situations where (1) an unusual and compelling urgency precludes full and open competition, and (2) delay in award of a contract would result in serious injury, financial or other, to the Government....

(c) Limitations....

(2) This statutory authority requires that agencies shall request offers from as many potential sources as is practicable under the circumstances.

* * *

FAR 5.201(b)(1) requires procurements to be synopsized in the Commerce Business Daily (CBD) unless one of the exceptions in FAR 5.202 apply. FAR 5.201(b)(1) reads as follows:

> (b) For acquisitions of supplies and services other than those covered by the exceptions in 5.202, and special situations in 5.205, the contracting officer shall transmit a notice to the CBD (synopsis)(see 5.207) for each proposed—

---

8. FAR 13.101 defines "simplified acquisition procedures" as "the methods prescribed in [FAR Part 13] for making purchases of supplies or services using imprest funds, purchase orders, blanket purchase agreements, Government-wide commercial purchase cards, or any other appropriate authorized method."

(1) contract actions meeting the thresholds in 5.101(a)(1);

FAR 5.101(a)(1) reads as follows:

(a) As required by the Small Business Act (15 U.S.C. 637(e)) and the Office of Federal Procurement Policy Act (41 U.S.C. 416), contracting officers shall disseminate information on proposed contract actions as follows:

(1) For proposed contract actions expected to exceed $25,000, by synopsizing in the Commerce Business Daily (CBD) (see 5.201);

FAR 5.202(a)(2) provides that the Government need not synopsize a proposed contract action in the CBD if the contracting officer determines, that:

(2) The contract action is made under the conditions described in 6.302-2 and the Government would be seriously injured if the agency complies with the time periods specified in 5.203;

Protester's grounds of protest allege violations of the above statutes and regulations.

* * *

Respondent's use of the simplified acquisition procedures and decision not to synopsize

In the procurements which are the subject of the instant protest, respondents used the simplified acquisition procedures, and did not synopsize the requirement in the CBD based upon the statements of urgency.

Improper fragmentation to avoid simplified acquisition procedures

The first ground of protest addressed by protester is:

The Respondents improperly fragmented the requirement for two Amdahl 5995 1400A's, each including 512 MB's of memory, to avoid the $100,000 simplified acquisition threshold in violation of FAR 13.000 and FAR 13.103(c). Each of the four purchase orders had a value of $49,900 so the aggregate of the four purchase orders equalled $199,600, which exceeded the $100,000 simplified acquisition threshold. Accordingly, pursuant to FAR 6.001, the Respondents had to comply with the competition requirements of FAR Part 6. The Respondents failed to comply with FAR Part 6. The Respondents did not obtain full and open competition as required by FAR 6.101.

Protester's Post-Hearing Brief at 45–46

Respondents respond to this ground by arguing that:

Protester has introduced no evidence indicating that Rock Island deliberately manipulated its requirements in order to use the Simplified Acquisition procedures. After the CCB approved the CPU upgrades, [the Director] established an internal priority list for his office identifying the acquisition of two CPU upgrades and two segments of expanded memory as the megacenter's top priority. When Rock Island collected sufficient year-end funds from its customers, the megacenter initiated the purchase of these items. Documentary evidence introduced at the hearing reveals that funding became available on August 21 and 29, 1995, for the two CPU upgrades, and on August 30 and September 13, 1995, for the expanded memory segments. Although Protester may argue that the Contracting Officer intentionally divided these requirements in order to avoid the simplified acquisition threshold the record does not support such a conclusion. The contracting officer processed and completed these procurements on an individual basis because that is how she received them from the megacenter. There is no ev-

idence that the had any advance knowledge of the megacenter's total requirements, i.e, 2 CPUs and 2 purchases of expanded memory, before receiving them.

Clearly, if circumstances permitted, Respondent would have preferred to conduct these acquisitions in a consolidated fashion that allowed for separate awards
for the CPUs and the expanded memory. In fact, this conclusion is supported
by [the Director] who indicated, but for an insufficient quantity of funds, these
procurements would have been combined.

Respondent's Post-Hearing Brief at 13–14 (citations omitted).

That the contracting officer had no "advance knowledge of the megacenter's total requirements" is not dispositive of the issue. The prohibition in FAR 13.103(c) against
breaking down requirements into several purchases that are less than the simplified acquisition threshold does not excuse fragmentation merely because the contracting officer is unaware that a series of orders is actually one requirement. To read the regulation
as respondent suggests would allow a contracting officer to receive orders for a fragmented
requirement and circumvent the regulation as long as the contracting officer is not told
of the true nature of the requirement by individuals who had such knowledge.

In this instance, the Director did have knowledge that the two CPUs and the two expanded memory units were to be purchased, and the determination that these items were
required was made at the same time. Findings 33–34. When the CPUs were purchased, the
expanded memory was configured on the two upgraded CPUs. Finding 28. Respondent
alleges that these purchases could not have been made in a consolidated fashion because
of a lack of available funding. The Director testified as to his belief that to allow funds to
accumulate in sufficient quantity to purchase the two CPUs and two expanded memory
units would result in a loss of funds. Finding 34. However, sufficient funds were approved
for all four purchase orders before the first of the four purchase orders was issued. Finding 35. All of these circumstances demonstrate that the acquisition of the two CPUs and
two expanded memory units were not four separate events, but in fact: were components
of one requirement. Fragmentation of the requirement was a violation of FAR 13.103(c).
See, e.g., Digital Services Group, GSBCA 8735-P, 87-1 BCA p 19,555, 1987 BPD p 6.

Failure to comply with FAR 6.302-2 and to synopsize the procurement in the CBD

Protester's second ground of protest is as follows:

FAR 5.201(b)(1) required the Respondents to synopsize because each $49,900
purchase order exceeded the $25,000 threshold in FAR 5.101(a)(1). The Re-
spondents improperly claimed an urgency exception under FAR 5. 202(a)(2),
which authorizes the Contracting Officer not to synopsize [the contract action
in the CBD] only if (1) the contract actions were made under the conditions described in FAR 6.302-2, and (2) the Respondents would have been "seriously injured" if synopsis occurred. According to the Contracting Officer, the purchase
orders were not issued subject to FAR 6.302-2. The Urgency Statements and the
memoranda of record justifying the avoidance of synopsizing the requirements
did not establish urgency or the possibility of the Respondents being "seriously
injured" if synopsis occurred.

Protester's Post-Hearing Brief at 47.

Respondents have alleged that the procurements were in accordance with FAR 6.302-
2, which permits less than full and open competition under certain circumstances, including situations of urgent need. Finding 10. However, the record does not support
respondents, alleged compliance with this regulation.... The only alleged urgency factor
which was time related was the attempt to spend funds before the CCB took the funds away

from the megacenter and to spend year-end funds in 1995 to reduce costs in 1996. Findings 34, 36. Such a circumstance is not considered urgent to justify less than full and open competition. Computer Literacy World v. Department of the Air Force, GSBCA 13438-P, 1995 BPD p 231 (Dec. 11, 1995).

Additionally, even though respondents contend that the procurements were meant to comply with FAR 6.302-2, the justifications and approvals for awarding a contract without full and open competition as required by FAR 6.303-1, 6.303-2, and 6.304 were not provided. Finding 37.

Since the procurements were not in compliance with FAR 6.302-2, they are not encompassed by the exception in FAR 5.202(a)(2) to avoid synopsizing in the CBD. The failure to synopsize was a violation of FAR 5.101(a)(1).

Alleged failure to solicit a reasonable number of sources

Protester's third ground of protest is as follows:

> 10 U.S.C. § 2304 provides that except in certain situations, "the head of an agency in conducting a procurement for property or services shall obtain full and open competition through the use of competitive procedures in accordance with the requirements of this chapter and the Federal Acquisition Regulation." 10 U.S.C. § 2304(a)(1). Full and open competition means that "all responsible sources are permitted to submit sealed bids or competitive proposals on the procurement." 10 U.S.C. § 2302(3)(D) and 41 U.S.C. § 403(6).
>
> * * *
>
> Respondent asserts that the two "informal market surveys" conducted by the contracting officer for the CPUs and expanded memory units, which took less than an hour, Findings 11, 21, were sufficient. Additionally, respondent argues, "Agencies may use informal market surveys in lieu of formal solicitation mailing lists when conducting small purchase acquisitions."

Respondent's Post-Hearing Brief at 19.

As we have found that the simplified acquisition procedures were not applicable this procurement should not have been conducted as a small purchase acquisition. There were other suppliers of comparable and compatible equipment who were not provided an opportunity to compete. Finding 38. Respondent's "informal market surveys" combined with its failure to synopsize the contract action in the CBD were insufficient to provide full and open competition.

Relief

The Amdahl 600Es that were replaced with Amdahl 1100As remain at Rock Island DMC and are kept in storage. Finding 27. The upgraded CPUs and expanded memory are currently being used by Rock Island DMC, but acceptance has been suspended pending the resolution of this protest. Finding 39. It would be wasteful and inconvenient to have respondent revert to using the previously dismantled 600Es.... Accordingly, respondent should conduct a competitive procurement in accordance with law and regulation, and replace the upgraded CPUs and expanded memory if another offeror is successful in that procurement.

Decision

The protest is GRANTED. The suspension order remains in effect until the procurement is concluded.

ALLAN H. GOODMAN
Board Judge

Notes and Questions

1. The case depicts a tension for the contracting officer between conducting "full and open competition," which involves procedures that take time and effort, and instead resorting to alternatives that bring faster results. Does information technology procurement present this tension no differently than in any other context? Note that although some aspects of the urgency here are both dubious and nonspecific to information technology, both IBM and Amdahl were relentlessly phasing out old products. Does the pace at which new products emerge from the high technology sector to replace old ones in information technology, and the need to move more promptly through the procurement process than with mere commodities or with items procured for a stockpile, create a greater need for the faster, simpler, more commercial procurement methods?

2. Use the time-labeled events of August and September 1995 in this case as a revealing roadmap of information technology procurement. In sum, Amdahl made a proposal in 1995. An information technology control board analyzed and approved the offer, the director of the agency customer decided to upgrade, staff prepared a documentation "package," the Director approved the package, and it went to the contracting officer; then, the contracting officer decided how to procure, conducted an informal market survey, telephoned a purchase order, and issued a written purchase order, then went through a second cycle for the next purchase request.

How much does the seller in Amdahl's position likely understand of all this? Note that it would not at all be astonishing for some of the documentation for a government contracting purchase to be drafted by the potential seller, though that is not suggested in this case. If you were Amdahl's counsel, could you assist government contracting personnel to prepare the documentation needed for an agency to make a rapid purchase, either the (unsuccessful) way in this case, or the (more complete) way that the Board requires? Could you at least discuss knowledgeably with them what they were doing? If you were counsel for the protester, could you have picked apart the procurement so well?

Information Systems and Networks Corporation, Plaintiff, v. The United States, Defendant

No. 91-1643C

34 Fed. Cl. 457

United States Court of Federal Claims

Nov. 21, 1995

See Opinion in the Chapter on Termination

Chapter 8

Small Business and Subcontractors

While government contract law focuses principally on government dealings with prime contractors, subcontractors do play a vital role in the government contracting process. And although the very largest of federal contracts with amounts in the hundreds of millions of dollars or more, and the headlines to match, go to large companies, the fact of the matter is that the vast majority of federal contracts, by sheer number, are small dollar purchases including a large portion from small businesses. Even the contractors on the very largest of prime contracts generally perform through a series of subcontracts with suppliers, manufacturers, and service providers of various sizes, and with varying sophistication about the complex set of applicable legal rules. Add to that mix the political importance of supporting "small businesses" by those elected to Congress and the White House, with the resulting orientation toward small business in legislation and regulations, and it becomes apparent why a whole separate area of law concerns subcontractors and small businesses.

For further discussion of the issues in this chapter, the cites in the subchapters, and see: Christina Clemm, *The Small Business Administration's Affiliation Rules: A Trap For The Unwary*, 57 Fed. Law. 52 (Oct. 2010); Kathryn E. Swisher, *Third Time's A Charm? Size Determination Appeal Decisions Provide Necessary Guidance, But Unresolved Issues Remain*, 45 Procrmt. Law. 12 (Summer 2010); Damien C. Specht, *Recent SBIR Extension Debate Reveals Venture Capital Influence*, 45 Procrmt. Law. 2 (Spring 2010); Reginald M. Jones, Douglas P. Hibshman, *Limitations On Teaming Arrangements In Small Business Set-Asides*, 45 Procrmt. Law. 3 (Spring 2010); Helaman S. Hancock, *America's War On Tribal Economies: Federal Attacks On Native Contracting In The SBA 8(A) Business Development Program*, 49 Washburn L.J. 717 (Spring 2010).

A. Privity and Subcontractors

Privity of contract and the lack thereof is one legal phrase that every subcontractor on a federal contract learns at some point, particularly when a dispute or claim arises as a result of government action or inaction. Due to lack of privity of contract between the government and a subcontractor, the courts have consistently barred subcontractors from direct access to the various Boards of Contract Appeals and the federal courts in actions against the government. Only a very limited exception occurs when the prime contractor acts as a purchasing agent for the government. Any uncertainty about the longstanding law in this regard ended with the enactment of the Contract Dispute Act of 1978, Pub. Law 95-563, by which only contractors, not subcontractors, may pursue claims against the government, and the term "contractor" is clearly defined as "a party to a Government contract other than the Government." 41 U.S.C. § 601(4). To make the matter even clearer, the FAR prohibits a government contracting officer from consenting to a subcontract that obligates the contracting officer to deal directly with a subcontractor or that makes the results of arbitration, judicial determination, or voluntary settlement between the prime contractor and subcontractor binding on the government. FAR 44.203(b).

Lack of privity and the resulting barrier to direct claims does not, however, mean that no way whatsoever exists for a subcontractor's claim to be heard. The regulations permit, and the astute government subcontractor will ensure, that its subcontract with the federal prime contractor will provide for "sponsorship" of a subcontractor's claim. Sponsorship is the practice whereby the prime contractor nominally prosecutes what in fact is the subcontractor's claim against the government. The appeal of the claim is brought in the name of prime contractor even though the subcontractor is the real party in interest. FAR 44.203(c) states:

> Contracting officers should not refuse consent to a subcontract merely because it contains a clause giving the subcontractor the right of indirect appeal to an agency board of contract appeals if the subcontractor is affected by a dispute between the Government and the prime contractor. Indirect appeal means assertion by the subcontractor of the prime contractor's right to appeal or the prosecution of an appeal by the prime contractor on the subcontractor's behalf. The clause may also provide that the prime contractor and subcontractor shall be equally bound by the contracting officer's or board's decision. The clause may not attempt to obligate the contracting officer or the appeals board to decide questions that do not arise between the Government and the prime contractor or that are not cognizable under the clause at 52.233-1, Disputes.

Payment for such indirect appeal is generally the responsibility of the subcontractor.

Cases in this section illustrate the application of the classic barrier of privity. The *Merritt* case provides one of those rare but blessed occasions of a relevant Supreme Court opinion by Justice Brandeis which describes what is still good government contracting law, regarding the essential impact of the privity barrier. Then, the *Navcom* case shows the interaction of the privity barrier between government and subcontractor, and, what forum resolves issues between subcontactor and prime contractor.

For further discussion of the subject of this section, see: Robert T. Ebert, Joseph W.C. Warren, & Kris D. Meade, *The Impact of Procurement Reform Legislation on Subcontracting for Commercial Items: Easing But Not Eliminating the Burdens*, 27 Pub. Cont. L.J. 343 (1998); John J. Thrasher, *Subcontractor Dispute Remedies: Asserting Subcontractor Claims against the Federal Government*, 23 Pub. Cont. L.J. 39 (1993); Robert G. Bugge, *A User's Guide to the ABA's Model Fixed-Price Supply Subcontract*, 15 Pub. Cont. L.J. 502 (1985).

Merritt v. United States

Supreme Court of the United States
267 U.S. 338
Decided March 2, 1925

Mr. Justice BRANDEIS delivered the opinion of the Court.

In July, 1918, or earlier, the United States contracted with the Panama Knitting Mills for a quantity of khaki at $3.20 a yard. In June, 1919, this contract was canceled by a new agreement between the government and the mills, made pursuant to the Dent Act, March 2, 1919, c. 94, 40 Stat. 1272 (Comp. St. Ann. Supp. 1919, §§ 3115 14/15 a-3115 14/15 e). Under the cancellation agreement the government adjusted its liability by accepting delivery of half of the khaki originally contracted for, paying the contract rate together with the carrying charges. The mills had a subcontract with the plaintiff for the supply of the khaki. By falsely representing that the government compelled settlement on the basis of $2.50 a yard plus the carrying charges, the mills induced the plaintiff to release it, on that basis, from the subcontract. When the government learned of the fraud thus perpetrated, it exacted from the mills a repayment of $5,210.02 — the difference between the amount actually paid by the government and what would have been paid if settlement had been made on the basis of $2.50 a yard. This suit was brought in March, 1923, to recover from the United States the sum so repaid. The Court of Claims dismissed the petition on demurrer for failure to state a cause of action. The case is here on appeal under section 242 of the Judicial Code (Comp. St. § 1219).

Plaintiff cannot recover under the Dent Act. There are three obstacles. It does not appear, as required by section 1 (Comp. St. § 3115 14/15 a), that, prior to November 12, 1918, an agreement with the plaintiff, express or implied, was entered into by the Secretary of War, or 'by any officer or agent acting under his authority, direction, or instruction, or that of the President.' Baltimore & Ohio R. R. Co. v. United States, 261 U. S. 385, 43 S. Ct. 384, 67 L. Ed. 711; Baltimore & Ohio R. R. Co. v. United States, 261 U. S. 592, 43 S. Ct. 425, 67 L. Ed. 816. It does not appear, as required by section 1, that any such agreement had been 'performed, ... or expenditures ... made or obligations incurred upon the faith of the same ... prior to' November 12, 1918. Price Fire & Water Proofing Co. v. United States, 261 U. S. 179, 183, 43 S. Ct. 299, 67 L. Ed. 602. It does not appear, as required by section 1, that the claim sued on was presented before June 30, 1919. The Dent Act affords relief, although there is no agreement 'executed in the manner prescribed by law,' but only under the conditions stated. The plaintiff is not helped by section 4 (Comp. St. § 3115 14/15 d), which deals with subcontracts; among other reasons, because it does not appear, as therein prescribed, that, before the payment made by the government to the prime contractor, the plaintiff had 'made expenditures, incurred obligations, rendered service, or furnished material, equipment, or supplies to such prime contractor, with the knowledge and approval of any agent of the Secretary of War duly authorized thereunto.'

Plaintiff cannot recover under the Tucker Act (Judicial Code, § 145, 24 Stat. 505 [Comp. St. § 1136]). The petition does not allege any contract, express or implied in fact, by the government with the plaintiff to pay the latter for the khaki on any basis. Nor does it set forth facts from which such a contract will be implied. The pleader may have intended to sue for money had and received. But no facts are alleged which afford any basis for a claim that the repayment made by the mills was exacted by the government for the benefit of the plaintiff. The Tucker Act does not give a right of action against the United States in those cases where, if the transaction were between private parties, recovery could be had upon a contract implied in law. Tempel v. United States, 248 U. S. 121, 39 S. Ct. 56, 63 L. Ed. 162; Sutton v. United States, 256 U. S. 575, 581, 41 S. Ct. 563, 65 L. Ed. 1099, 19 A. L. R. 403. For aught that appears repayment was compelled solely for the benefit of the government, under the proviso in section 1 of the Dent Act, which authorizes recovery of money paid under a settlement, if it has been defrauded.

The practice of the Court of Claims, while liberal, does not allow a general statement of claim in analogy to the common counts. It requires a plain, concise statement of the facts relied upon. See rule 15, Court of Claims. The petition may not be so general as to leave the defendant in doubt as to what must be met. Schierling v. United States, 23 Ct. Cl. 361; The Atlantic Works v. United States, 46 Ct. Cl. 57, 61; New Jersey Foundry & Machine Co. v. United States, 49 Ct. Cl. 235; United States v. Stratton, 88 F. 54, 59, 31 C. C. A. 384.

Affirmed.

Notes and Questions

1. The Court in *Merritt* distinguishes between the authority of the Court of Claims to hear cases involving contracts "implied in fact" and the lack of such authority to take jurisdiction over claims of contracts "implied in law." What is the difference and why would Congress want to limit jurisdiction to just those implied in fact contracts?

2. In *Merritt*, the prime contractor was, under current terminology, terminated for the convenience of the government. The prime contractor had not, however, protected itself against such an occurrence in its contract with its subcontractor Merritt. This failure was the apparent basis for the fraud allegedly perpetrated against Merritt. How can a prime contractor protect itself against such terminations without having to resort to fraudulent activity?

3. Note the choice-of-law and procedural implications of *Merritt*. It sharply distinguishes between claims by the prime contractor which occur against the United States under federal statutes and other federal law in a federal forum, and the claims of the subcontractor which cannot occur directly against the United States. The subcontractor may or may not have a claim against the prime contractor, but if it does, what body of law governs that claim, federal law or basic contract law (today, the Uniform Commercial Code or the common law of contracts, both matters of state rather than federal law)? What forum does such a claim get litigated in, federal court or state court?

W.G. Yates & Sons Construction Co., Inc., Appellant, v. Louis Caldera, Secretary of the Army, Appellee

United States Court of Appeals, Federal Circuit
No. 98-1529
192 F.3d 987 (1999)
Decided Sept. 23, 1999

Before MICHEL, RADER, and GAJARSA, Circuit Judges.

GAJARSA, Circuit Judge.

DECISION

W.G. Yates & Sons Construction Co., Inc. ("Yates") appeals the final decision of the Armed Services Board of Contract Appeals ("ASBCA"), ASBCA No. 47213, Contract No. DAHA22-92-C-0002. The ASBCA held that (1) Yates remained conditionally liable to its subcontractor, Industrial Door Co. ("IDC"), and therefore Yates had standing to bring a claim of its subcontractor against the Army; (2) the Army did not violate 10 U.S.C. § 2319 regarding qualification requirements for subcontractors; ... and (4) IDC did not satisfy the requirement of the solicitation regarding the installation of at least ten "similar" doors. We affirm the Board's conclusion that Yates remained liable to IDC but reverse the Board's conclusion that the Army did not violate 10 U.S.C. § 2319....

* * *

For the reasons set forth below, we affirm-in-part, reverse-in-part, and remand.

BACKGROUND

On November 19, 1991, the Army issued a solicitation for the construction of support facilities and a composite maintenance hangar to house two tanker aircraft at the Mississippi Air National Guard Base at Key Field, Meridian, Mississippi. Section 08375 of the solicitation, entitled "HANGAR DOORS," required the design, manufacture, and installation of "motor operated steel hangar doors," approximately 306 feet wide and 67 feet high, for a total area of about 20,500 square feet.

This section also contained the two provisions that are at issue before us — paragraphs 1.4.B Qualifications and 1.4.C Standard of Quality:

> B. Qualifications: 1.... [T]he manufacturer must support with written evidence that they have designed, manufactured, and installed a minimum of 10 similar door systems *which have been in satisfactory operation for a minimum of five years,* with a minimum of five installations that are equal to or in excess of 60'-0"....
>
> * * *
>
> C. Standard of Quality: ... 2. *Other manufacturers requesting approval as an equal to the companies named must submit their request in writing with the information as detailed in paragraph 1.4B of these specifications. Requests for approval shall be made at least three weeks prior to bid date to permit checking of references and qualifications by the [CO].* Hangar doors will not be approved by the [CO] except by those manufacturers who have so qualified and been approved in writing as having the required experience in the type and size of doors required for this project.

(Emphasis added.)

In a telephone conversation with a representative of IDC on January 13, 1992, less than three weeks prior to the date for opening bids, the contracting officer ("CO") informed IDC that it would waive the pre-bid qualification requirement of paragraph 1.4.C.2 if IDC could meet the remaining requirements at the time of submittal of bids. After the conversation, the CO deleted *only* the requirement of paragraph 1.4.C.2 necessitating a three-week pre-bid qualification for any non-listed manufacturer, thereby permitting qualification after prime contract award but prior to approval of subcontractor.

On January 30, 1992, Yates bid $10,118,000, which included $500,000 for the hangar doors based on its subcontractor IDC's $490,000 proposal. The Army awarded Yates the contract. Yates entered into a subcontract with IDC as manufacturer of hangar doors for $455,000. IDC submitted a list of 45 hangar door projects to support its qualification under paragraph 1.4. The Army disapproved of IDC as not meeting the requirements of paragraph 1.4, noting that only four of the hangar door projects submitted (Nos. 5 (two doors), 9, and 16) met the "similarity" requirement.

* * *

After a series of communications between Yates and the Army in which the parties disagreed as to what "similar" meant, the CO continued to reject IDC, and Yates eventually contracted with and submitted ASC as its subcontractor for the hangar doors. The subcontract between Yates and ASC was for a fixed-price of $614,371, which was $159,371 greater than the proposal from IDC. The Army subsequently approved ASC, which was listed as a "prequalified manufacturer" under paragraph 1.4.C, in one day.

On July 8, 1993, Yates, IDC, and IDC's surety entered into a "Liquidation and Consolidated Claim Agreement" ("LCCA"). The agreement provided, inter alia, that IDC had a claim of $113,000 (presumably for damages and costs due to the government's improper rejection), that Yates had a $159,371 claim for excess reprocurement costs, and that Yates would sponsor IDC's claims in Yates' name, and if denied by the CO, to appeal IDC's and Yates' claims to the ASBCA. Further, the agreement provided that if the government's rejection of IDC was improper, "*Yates is liable to IDC for its damages and costs* but only as, when, and to the extent Yates receives payment from the Government for IDC's damages and costs." (Emphasis added.)

* * *

DISCUSSION

* * *

B. Severin Doctrine

As a general rule, subcontractors under government contracts do not have standing to sue the government. *See Severin v. United States,* 99 Ct.Cl. 435, 442 (1943). This is because such subcontractors lack privity with the government, and the government has not consented to be sued by those with whom it is not in privity. *See id.* However, if the prime contractor is liable to the subcontractor for damages sustained by the subcontractor, that prime contractor can bring an action against the government for the subcontractor's damages. *See id.* at 443. In this circumstance, the prime contractor itself is injured by the acts of the government and, therefore, has standing to sue the government in a pass-through suit on behalf of its subcontractor. *See E.R. Mitchell Const. Co. v. Danzig,* 175 F.3d 1369, 1370 (Fed.Cir.1999). There is privity between the parties because the prime contractor, and not the subcontractor, is suing the government. Finally, if the government seeks dismissal of the prime contractor's pass-through suit, the government bears the burden of proof, and must show that the prime contractor is not responsible for the costs incurred by the subcontractor. *See id.* These rules are commonly known as the *Severin doctrine.*

In its brief to this court, the Army argues for dismissal of Yates' claim under the Severin Doctrine, asserting that Yates bears no real liability to IDC for IDC's damages. In fact, the Army contends that the subcontract made between Yates and IDC on April 1, 1992, "absolved Yates of all liability." We find no language in the subcontract or the LCCA to support this position and, therefore, the Army has not met its required burden.

The original subcontract under section (f) of the Contractor's (Yates') obligations states: "Should the Owner [the Army] fail to pay the Contractor for the work performed by the Subcontractor, then the Contractor shall have no obligation to pay the Subcontractor *unless and until such time as the Owner pays the Contractor.*" (Emphasis added.)

Moreover, the LCCA between Yates and IDC provides:

> 4. ... Yates agrees to reimburse IDC for damages or extra costs recovered from the Government but only as contemplated in the Subcontract and as provided for in this Agreement and, as a condition precedent to Yates' liability to IDC, only to the extent Yates receives payment from the Government for IDC's Claim.

> 10. ... Yates and IDC stipulate that if the Government's rejection of IDC was improper, to the extent IDC suffered damages and costs as a result, *Yates is liable to IDC for its damages and costs but only as, when, and to the extent Yates receives payment from the Government for IDC's damages and costs.*

(Emphasis added.)

Following the Severin Doctrine, our predecessor court held in *J.L. Simmons Co. v. United States,* 158 Ct.Cl. 393, 304 F.2d 886 (Ct.Cl.1962), that this specific type of conditional liability that Yates and IDC established through the subcontract and the LCCA, in which the prime contractor remains conditionally liable to the subcontractor "only as and when the former receives payment for [damages] from the Government ... do[es] not preclude suit by the prime contractor in behalf of its subcontractor." *Id.* at 889; *see also Kentucky Bridge & Dam, Inc. v. United States,* 42 Fed. Cl. 501, 527 (1998) (holding that conditional liability on the part of the prime contractor to the subcontractor based on future payment by the government to the prime contractor is "considered sufficient liability to avoid application of the Severin Doctrine"). Given the specific language of the subcontract and the LCCA, Yates clearly remained conditionally liable to IDC.

* * *

Therefore, Yates cannot avoid liability if it receives payment from the government for its damages, and Yates is "subject to liability on these claims and will continue to be so until liability is extinguished in accord with the method agreed to" by Yates and IDC in the subcontract and the LCCA. *See Simmons,* 304 F.2d at 890. Because Yates remains liable to its subcontractor, the ASBCA correctly held that Yates has standing to bring a suit against the government on behalf of IDC for IDC's damages and expenses.

* * *

D. Qualification Requirements

10 U.S.C. § 2305(a)(1)(A)(i) & (B)(ii) (emphasis added). This provision addresses specifications, and not qualification requirements. Specifications are the requirements of the particular project for which the bids are sought, such as design requirements, functional requirements, or performance requirements. *See* 10 U.S.C. § 2305(a)(1)(C). The specifications for this project would include the size of the doors, structural steel requirements, ability to withstand wind loads, and the like. Qualification requirements, on the other hand, are activities which establish the experience and abilities of the bidder to assure the government that the bidder has the ability to carry out and complete the contract. They are defined as "requirement[s] for testing or quality assurance demonstration[s] that must be completed before the award of a contract." 10 U.S.C. § 2319(a). The requirement at issue here relates to successful completion of other, similar hangar door projects. This is not a "specification" because it relates to other projects. As discussed above, this is a qualification requirement, and thus is governed by § 2319. Therefore, the Army's contention that § 2305(a)(1)(B)(ii) applies in this case is without merit.

* * *

Because the requirement in paragraph 1.4.B meets the definition of "qualification requirement" as set forth in§ 2319, the Army was obligated to follow the provisions as established in that statute, including subsections (b)(1) through (b)(6), that list the actions that the head of an agency must take when establishing a qualification requirement. The record establishes that the Army did not follow the statutory and regulatory requirements, thereby rendering the qualification requirement invalid and unenforceable. See 10 U.S.C. § 2319(b) (1994); 48 C.F.R. § 9.206-1(a) (1998). Therefore, IDC was not obligated to meet the qualification requirement regarding the design, manufacture, and installation of at least ten similar door systems for five years prior to award date, making the Army's disqualification of IDC contrary to its statutory and regulatory mandates. Under the LCCA, because IDC was wrongfully disqualified, Yates is liable to IDC for IDC's damages and costs. Therefore the government is liable to Yates for these damages and costs. Furthermore, the government is also liable to Yates for the excess reprocurement costs, and under the LCCA, this amount must be paid over to IDC when it is received.

CONCLUSION

For these reasons, we affirm the Board's conclusions that Yates remained liable to IDC but reverse the Board's conclusion that the Army did not violate 10 U.S.C. § 2319. Because we find that the Army did violate § 2319, thereby rendering the purported qualification requirement invalid, we do not need to reach the issues of the alleged conflict of interest violation in the promulgation of the requirement or whether IDC satisfied the "similarity" requirement.

Thus, we *AFFIRM-IN-PART, REVERSE-IN-PART,* and *REMAND.*

Questions:

1.   Is the Severin Doctrine a broad exception to the Rule of "Privity" that subcontractors cannot sue the government?

2.   What is the difference between specifications and qualifications? Doesn't each compare the current contractor with other contractors in the past?

NavCom Defense Electronics, Inc., Plaintiff-Appellee, v. Ball Corporation, Defendant-Appellant

No. 94-56396
United States Court of Appeals, Ninth Circuit
92 F.3d 877
Decided Aug. 8, 1996

Before BROWNING, WALLACE, and FARRIS, Circuit Judges.

PER CURIAM:

This is an appeal from the district court's order granting summary judgment for NavCom and enjoining Ball from submitting its contract dispute with NavCom to arbitration. For the reasons set out below, we affirm the district court's denial of Ball's motion to dismiss, reverse the court's grant of summary judgment, vacate the order prohibiting arbitration, and remand for entry of an order consistent with this opinion.

I.

The Air Force awarded NavCom a contract to produce a radar altimeter system. NavCom subcontracted with Ball to design and manufacture antennas to be used as part of the system. The Air Force required that the antennas meet certain pass/fail criteria, including the "MIL-STD-810" salt fog test. NavCom developed the NavCom Salt Fog Test Procedure to ensure that its antennas met Air Force specifications, and the Air Force approved the test. The subcontract required Ball's antennas to pass the NavCom Salt Fog Test.

Ball asserted that NavCom's test procedures were more rigorous than those required by the Air Force, but eventually performed the test according to NavCom's procedure. NavCom claimed that the antennas failed, while Ball insisted that the antennas passed the Air Force's criteria. NavCom directed Ball to redesign the antennas.

Ball asked NavCom to pay an equitable adjustment for redesign costs in the amount of $1,467,949. Ball claimed its prototype antenna could meet Air Force pass/fail criteria and failed only because of the more stringent NavCom testing procedure. Ball also claimed NavCom required a redesign option that was more costly than other options.

The central question is whether the dispute between NavCom and Ball should have been submitted to an Air Force contracting officer or to arbitration. The Ball/NavCom contract required that the decision of a contracting officer about the prime contract would be binding on the two parties in disputes about the subcontract.[2] In the same paragraph

---

2. "All Disputes between [NavCom] and [Ball] under this Purchase Order shall be resolved in the courts of competent jurisdiction provided, however, that if the face of this Purchase Order refers to a contract with the United States Government, then and in that event, any decision of the Contracting

the contract provided that any dispute not settled by agreement of the parties would be submitted to arbitration.[3]

NavCom informed Ball that it planned to submit a claim to the contracting officer as specified in the contract. The claim submitted by NavCom described the dispute between NavCom and Ball and then argued, ostensibly on behalf of Ball, that the Air Force should be liable for increased costs because the Air Force's pass/fail criteria were ambiguous. Although Ball cooperated to at least some degree in drafting the claim (as required under the contract), Ball objected throughout the process to submission of the claim to the contracting officer. For instance, in a letter commenting on a draft version of the claim NavCom planned to submit, Ball wrote:

> Ball wishes to be on record that it has no claim against the Air Force and therefore does not endorse NavCom's statements in the draft letter that NavCom is "sponsoring" a claim "on behalf of Ball" pursuant to a "contractual obligation".... [I]f Ball was being sponsored, the effort was noticeably lacking in fervor; two, NavCom seems more intent on sidestepping or evading its liability to Ball by attempting to divert Ball's claims to the Air Force.

The Contracting Officer eventually denied the claim, finding that "Ball's argument that the MIL-STD-810 failure criteria are ambiguous is unfounded" and that the antennas had failed the test.

Just prior to the Contracting Officer's decision, Ball filed a demand for arbitration under the contract's arbitration provision. After initially participating, objecting to locale and choosing acceptable arbitrators, NavCom filed this suit in state court seeking to enjoin the arbitration. Ball removed the suit to federal court.

NavCom moved for a preliminary injunction prohibiting arbitration, and for partial summary judgment prohibiting arbitration and determining the subcontract required the disputed claim be resolved in the Court of Federal Claims where appeal of the contracting officer's decision was pending. Ball moved to dismiss for failure to state a claim.

The district court summarily granted NavCom's motion for a preliminary injunction and partial summary judgment and denied Ball's motion to dismiss....

Ball appeals ... arguing that its claim against NavCom was not and could not be resolved by the contracting officer and that its dispute with NavCom was arbitrable under the contract.

II.

The Contract Disputes Act of 1978, 41 U.S.C. §§ 601—613 ("CDA"), provides the statutory framework for resolving disputes between government contractors and the government. Section 605(a) provides that "[a]ll claims by a contractor against the government relating to a contract ... shall be submitted to the contracting officer for a decision," and § 601(a)(4) defines a "contractor" as "a party to a Government contract other than the Government." Under the CDA, contracting officers have jurisdiction only over claims by *contractors* against the government, not over claims brought directly by subcontractors.

Officer under a Government prime contract, which relates to this Purchase Order shall be conclusive and binding upon [NavCom] and [Ball]."

3. "Any dispute arising under this Purchase Order which is not settled by agreement of the parties shall be subjected to arbitration in accordance with the rules of the American Arbitration Association, and judgment of the award rendered by the arbitrator(s) may be entered into any court having jurisdiction thereof."

Erickson Air Crane Co. v. United States, 731 F.2d 810, 813 (Fed.Cir.1984)("hornbook rule" that subcontractors have no standing to enforce claims under CDA); *United States v. Johnson Controls, Inc.,* 713 F.2d 1541, 1548–49 (Fed.Cir.1983); *Clean Giant, Inc. v. United States,* 19 Cl.Ct. 390, 392 (1990); *see also* Senate Report No. 1118, 95th Cong., 2d Sess. 16–17, *reprinted in* 1978 U.S.Code Cong. & Ad.News 5235, 5250–51 (discussing exclusion of claims brought by subcontractors).

A subcontractor may assert a claim against the government only by having the prime contractor "sponsor" and certify the subcontractor's claim. *Erickson Air Crane,* 731 F.2d at 813; *See* Federal Acquisition Regulation 44.203(c); Major John J. Thrasher, "Subcontractor Dispute Remedies: Asserting Subcontractor Disputes against the Federal Government," 23 Pub. Cont. L.J. 39, 82–99 (1993). The contracting officer has no jurisdiction to resolve disputes between a subcontractor and the prime contractor. *U.S. West Communications Servs. v. United States,* 940 F.2d 622, 627 (Fed.Cir.1991)("A government contractor's dispute with its subcontractor was by definition specifically excluded from CDA coverage.").

III.

Whether Ball's claims could be submitted to the contracting officer depends upon whether they are claims against NavCom or against the Air Force. Ball has consistently alleged that Nav-Com, and not the Air Force, was responsible for the increased costs: Ball has contended that the NavCom Salt Fog Test procedure was too rigorous and the results were therefore invalid, and that the redesign of the antennas directed by NavCom was more expensive than other alternatives. These claims do not challenge Air Force conduct or suggest the Air Force was responsible for increased costs. They are claims by a subcontractor against a contractor, and the contracting officer therefore had no jurisdiction to resolve the dispute under the CDA.

NavCom's arguments to the contrary are unpersuasive. NavCom asserts that it did, in fact, submit Ball's claims to the contracting officer. However, Ball's allegations were neither presented to nor decided by the contracting officer. NavCom's claim did note that "[t]he language of MIL-STD-810 is overly restrictive," but Ball did not challenge the government's MIL-STD-810 pass/fail criteria but NavCom's test procedure. NavCom argued only that Ball and NavCom had arrived at different and reasonable interpretations of the Air Force's test criteria, and that because the redesign costs stemmed from ambiguity in the criteria which was attributable to the Air Force, the Air Force should pay the equitable adjustment. Nav-Com's claim that the pass/fail criteria were ambiguous simply did not address or include Ball's claims that NavCom's testing procedures were too rigorous or that NavCom demanded that Ball redesign the antenna in too costly a fashion. Nor did the contracting officer rule on Ball's claims; he found only that the "argument that the MIL-STD-810 failure criteria are ambiguous"—the theory advanced by NavCom, not Ball—was "unfounded."

Citing no authority, NavCom contends Ball's claims were claims against the government which NavCom could properly bring before the contracting officer if the claims could "be flowed up to the government so that ultimate financial responsibility will rest with that entity." This formulation begs the question it purports to answer—whether the claims allege government liability. In essence, NavCom contends that if it can transform Ball's claims into a claim against the government, no matter how distorted or unrelated to Ball's original claims, review by the contracting officer is Ball's sole avenue for relief and Ball is precluded from asserting its claims in any other forum. Neither the statute nor the contract contemplates that result.

NavCom points out that the subcontract provides that "if the face of this Purchase Order refers to a contract with the United States Government then ... any decision of the Contracting Officer under a Government prime contract, which relates to this Purchase

Order shall be conclusive and binding," and argues that because the subcontract does refer to a government contract and the contracting officer's decision relates to the subcontract, Ball is bound by that decision and barred from arbitrating its claims.

This argument fails. The parties cannot by contract expand the contracting officer's jurisdiction beyond that granted by the CDA. As we have said, contracting officers have no jurisdiction over claims on disputes between the contractor and subcontractor. Moreover, the contracting officer decided only whether the Air Force was liable; that determination cannot bind the parties on the question of whether NavCom is liable to Ball. The extent to which Ball may be bound by the contracting officer's holdings on the issues he did decide—that the MIL-STD-810 was not ambiguous and that the antennas failed the MIL-STD-810 requirements—and the impact the contracting officer's findings may have on Ball's claims, can be determined in arbitration.

NavCom argues that the Court can supply missing words in the contract to carry out the intent of the parties, *Heidlebaugh v. Miller,* 126 Cal.App.2d 35, 38, 271 P.2d 557 (1954), and submitted evidence that but for a drafting error, the arbitration clause would have provided that "[a]ny dispute arising under this Purchase Order *which is not covered by [the Contracting Officer provision], and which is not settled by agreement of the parties shall be decided by arbitration.*" This added language cuts against NavCom's position rather than supporting it—since the dispute between NavCom and Ball cannot be submitted to a contracting officer under the CDA, it is arbitrable under the contract.

NavCom goes on to argue that the Court should give effect to the mutual intent of the parties, Cal. Civ. Code §§ 1636, and that the "main purpose" of the contract was to safeguard NavCom from inconsistent judgments. Even if NavCom had presented some evidence to support this theory, Ball could still arbitrate its claims against NavCom; were the arbitrator to find NavCom liable, there would be no inconsistency between findings that the Air Force is not liable but NavCom is because NavCom alone caused the additional costs.

We conclude that Ball's claims against NavCom are arbitrable under the contract.

Notes and Questions

1. The Navcom opinion weaves together two analytically distinct questions: the boundary limits of the system for disputes between the government and prime, and the a contest over the forum for disputes between prime and subcontractor. Even recognizing that most disputes involving the subcontractor do not overlap with the limited jurisdiction of the system under the CDA for resolving disputes between the government and the prime contactor, still, sometimes there can be some overlap. Suppose the contracting officer had decided, in the course of reviewing NavCom's claim, that (1) that the Air Force had indeed changed (i.e., tightened) the contractual requirements in relation to NavCom's test procedures; (2) that NavCom's redesign option was what the Air Force wanted and indeed insisted upon; and (3) that the government owed a $500,000 equitable adjustment to NavCom which NavCom then tendered to Ball. (Assume that the ambivalence described in the opinion had not existed—that NavCom had fought tooth-and-nail to obtain this nice set of rulings for Ball.) Should those determinations now allow NavCom to bar an arbitration by Ball? If not, should they at least be treated by the arbitrator as binding? Who is making the relevant distinctions here between arbitrable and non-arbitrable issues: Congress, the courts, the contracting officer, or the private parties?

2. Note the discussion of how the Contract Disputes Act of 1978, by confining the uses of the disputes system rather narrowly, shaped this case. The CDA, and the privity doctrine discussed in *Merritt*, function similarly. In the wake of the privity doctrine and the

CDA, case law developed which defines the limited number of exceptions to the general rule that a subcontractor cannot bring a direct dispute or appeal against the government. One of them, discussed in *United States v. Johnson Controls, Inc.*, 713 F.2d 1541 (Fed. Cir. 1983), concerns when the government has used a contractor as a mere agent to place contracts for performance, in which case these contracts are then directly between the government and the performing businesses even though these businesses may get the label "subcontractor" stuck to them.

For example, in the construction context, the government might hire one contractor to find and to contract with various specialized ones, contemplating that the government itself will deal directly with those specialized ones. (Note, as a side-problem, that, the Federal Acquisition Regulation, 48 C.F.R. 44.203(b)(3), precludes contracting officers from consenting to direct disputes by subcontractors.) Conversely, when the government puts in an "ABC" clause, both in its prime contract and in the agreements between the prime and the subcontractors, unequivocally stating that no contractual relationship shall exist between the government ("A") and the "subcontractors" ("C"), but only between each of them and the prime ("B" — hence, "ABC clause"), that is an important factor suggesting no direct relationship does, in fact, exist between government and subcontractor.

Note on Flowdown, and Other, Terms for Subcontractors

1. Generally, in pursuing claims against the government, subcontractors are required to either secure consent to proceed in the name of the prime or to have their appeals prosecuted by the prime (FAR § 44.203(c)). Under a sponsorship arrangement, the words and concerns of the subcontractor are mouthed by the prime, which must certify the good-faith basis for claims over $100,000. (FAR § 52.233-1; Contract Disputes Act of 1978, 41 U.S.C.§ 601 et seq.).

Where they do not enjoy such a cooperative relationship, subcontractors, lacking privity with the government necessary to make claims in their own right, have been seeking a serviceable substitute for decades. Three theories of subcontractor standing are agency (as was unsuccessfully alleged in *Johnson Controls*); contract implied-in-fact (as claimed to no avail in *National Micrographics v. United States,* 38 Fed. Cl. 46 (1997)); and third-party beneficiary status, which found the court's favor in *D & H Distributing Co. v. United States,* 102 F.3d 542 (Fed. Cir. 1996). For a more detailed examination of this topic, see Major David A. Wallace et al., *Contract Law Developments of 1997—The Year in Review,* 1998-JAN ARMLAW 3; Stephen G. Lee, *Hiring the Cheapest Piper: Arbitration of Subcontractor Disputes by Boards of Contract Appeals,* 23 Pub. Con. L.J. 105 (1993).

2. Traditionally, notwithstanding the privity barrier, many requirements have been placed on subcontracts, from disclosure of cost and pricing data to compliance with labor standards. In 1994, Congress enacted the Federal Acquisition Streamlining Act allowing prime contractors greater freedom to subcontract commercially. Specifically, FASA's pertinent provision, codified at 41 U.S.C. § 427, removed most barriers between prime contractors seeking commercial items or components, and prospective subcontractors, who were previously deterred by cost and pricing documentation requirements. Additionally, FAR § 12.50 ends the applicability of 18 varied restrictions on subcontractors, including the Walsh-Healey Act (41 U.S.C. § 43), the Service Contract Act (41 U.S.C. § 351), the Tariff Act of 1930 (19 U.S.C. § 1202), and the Drug-Free Workplace Act of 1988 (41 U.S.C.§ 701, et seq.), and modifies the applicability of CAS (41 U.S.C.§ 422) and TINA (41 U.S.C.§ 254(d) and 10 U.S.C.§ 2306(a)) requirements. FAR 13.006 makes numerous part 52 provisions inapplicable to contracts and subcontracts at or below the simplified acquisition threshold. For an examination of this subject, see Robert T. Ebert,

Joseph W.C. Warren and Kris D. Meade, *The Impact of Procurement Reform Legislation on Subcontracting for Commercial Items: Easing But Not Eliminating the Burdens*, 27 Pub. Cont. L.J. 343 (1998).

3. Perhaps the legally most interesting requirement placed on subcontracts consists of "flow-down" clauses. "Flow-down" clauses are prime contract provisions that become part of a subcontract by one of four mechanisms. First, a prime contract clause may be expressly written as mandatory flow-down clause. Second, a prime contract may require that the substance of a clause "flow-down" to any subcontract. Third, as a matter of an operation of law, e.g., a provision in the FAR, a clause may be required to flow from the prime to the subcontract. Finally, absent a required "flow-down, a clause may still do so if the duties imposed on the prime contractor by the clause make the contract incapable of being effectively fulfilled unless that duty also flows to a subcontractor.

4. Examples of "flow-down" clauses are numerous. "Inspection" clauses, "Termination" clauses, and "Disputes" clauses are all clauses that, while not mandatory as "flow-down" clauses to a subcontract, are recommended for inclusion by the prime contractor where there is reliance on subcontractor performance and cooperation. "Changes" clauses, "Limitation of Liability," "Cost and Pricing Data," and "Warranty" clauses are examples of provisions that require "flow-down" by their substance, to subcontracts when they are present in the prime contract. Some examples of mandatory clauses include "Subcontracts (Fixed-Price Contract)" clauses, "Examination of Records by the Comptroller General" clause, and "Insurance" clauses (where the subcontractor is working on a government installation). Additionally, there are clauses that may have a substance requirement for flow-down in some instances, but are expressly mandatory to particular subcontract types.

5. There is a detailed "ABA Model for Fixed-Price Supply Subcontract Terms and Condition." This form sets forth the terms and conditions of the subcontract inclusive of applicable clauses. See Robert G. Bugge, *A User's Guide to the ABA's Model Fixed-Price Supply Subcontract*, 15 Pub. Cont. L.J. 502 (1985). A 1996 revision of this model introduced significant changes in the form, most significantly removing the "optional clauses" previously supplied in the prior form, but including specific "flow-down" clauses for defense contracts, both short and full versions of the applicable clauses, and a user's guide. For a discussion of the issue of mandatory flowdown into subcontracts, see Frank J. Baltz & J. Russell Morrissey, *Do You Know If You Are a Government Contractor: FAR Clauses Incorporated Into Subcontracts Without Reference*, 34 Procurement Lawyer, Summer 1999, at 36.

Empire Healthchoice Assurance, Inc.
dba Empire Blue Cross Blue Shield, Petitioner, v.
Denise F. McVeigh as Administratrix of the Estate of
Joseph E. McVeigh
547 U.S. 677
Decided June 15, 2006

GINSBURG, J., delivered the opinion of the Court, in which ROBERTS, C. J., and STEVENS, SCALIA, and THOMAS, JJ., joined. BREYER, J., filed a dissenting opinion, in which KENNEDY, SOUTER, and ALITO, JJ., joined.

Justice GINSBURG delivered the opinion of the Court.

The Federal Employees Health Benefits Act of 1959 (FEHBA), 5 U.S.C.§ 8901*et seq.* (2000 ed. and Supp. III), establishes a comprehensive program of health insurance for federal employees. The Act authorizes the Office of Personnel Management (OPM) to contract with private carriers to offer federal employees an array of health-care plans. See§ 8902(a) (2000 ed.). Largest of the plans for which OPM has contracted, annually since 1960, is the Blue Cross Blue Shield Service Benefit Plan (plan), administered by local Blue Cross Blue Shield companies. This case concerns the proper forum for reimbursement claims when a plan beneficiary, injured in an accident, whose medical bills have been paid by the plan administrator, recovers damages (unaided by the carrier-administrator) in a state-court tort action against a third party alleged to have caused the accident.

* * *

The instant case originated when the administrator of a Plan beneficiary's estate pursued tort litigation in state court against parties alleged to have caused the beneficiary's injuries. The carrier had notice of the state-court action, but took no part in it. When the tort action terminated in a settlement, the carrier filed suit in federal court seeking reimbursement of the full amount it had paid for the beneficiary's medical care. The question presented is whether 28 U.S.C.§ 1331 (authorizing jurisdiction over "civil actions arising under the ... laws ... of the United States") encompasses the carrier's action. We hold it does not.

FEHBA itself provides for federal-court jurisdiction only in actions against the United States. Congress could decide and provide that reimbursement claims of the kind here involved warrant the exercise of federal-court jurisdiction. But claims of this genre, seeking recovery from the proceeds of state-court litigation, are the sort ordinarily resolved in state courts. Federal courts should await a clear signal from Congress before treating such auxiliary claims as "arising under" the laws of the United States.

I

EHBA assigns to OPM responsibility for negotiating and regulating health benefits plans for federal employees. See 5 U.S.C. § 8902 (a). OPM contracts with carriers, FEHBA instructs, "shall contain a detailed statement of benefits offered and shall include such maximums, limitations, exclusions, and other definitions of benefits as [OPM] considers necessary or desirable." § 8902(d). Pursuant to FEHBA, OPM entered into a contract in 1960 with the BCBSA to establish a nationwide fee-for-service health plan, the terms of which are renegotiated annually. As FEHBA prescribes, the Federal Government pays about 75% of the premiums; the enrollee pays the rest. § 8906 (b) (2000 ed.). Premiums thus shared are deposited in a special Treasury Fund, the Federal Employees Health Benefits Fund, § 8909(a). Carriers draw against the Fund to pay for covered health-care benefits. *Ibid.*; see also 48 CFR § 1632.170(b) (2005).

The contract between OPM and the BCBSA provides: "By enrolling or accepting services under this contract, [enrollees and their eligible dependents] are obligated to all terms, conditions, and provisions of this contract." App. 90. An appended brochure sets out the benefits the carrier shall provide, see *id.,* at 89, and the carrier's subrogation and recovery rights, see *id.,* at 100. Each enrollee, as FEHBA directs, receives a statement of benefits conveying information about the Plan's coverage and conditions. 5 U.S.C. § 8907(b). Concerning reimbursement and subrogation, matters FEHBA itself does not address, the BCBSA Plan's statement of benefits reads in part:

"If another person or entity ... causes you to suffer an injury or illness, and if we pay benefits for that injury or illness, you must agree to the following:

"All recoveries you obtain (whether by lawsuit, settlement, or otherwise), no matter how described or designated, must be used to reimburse us in full for benefits we paid. Our share of any recovery extends only to the amount of benefits we have paid or will pay to you or, if applicable, to your heirs, administrators, successors, or assignees."

* * *

FEHBA contains a preemption provision, which originally provided:

The provisions of any contract under this chapter which relate to the nature or extent of coverage or benefits (including payments with respect to benefits) shall supersede and preempt any State or local law, or any regulation issued thereunder, which relates to health insurance or plans to the extent that such law or regulation is inconsistent with such contractual provisions." 5 U.S.C.§ 8902(m)(1) (1994 ed.).

To ensure uniform coverage and benefits under plans OPM negotiates for federal employees, see H.R.Rep. No. 95-282, p. 1 (1977),§ 8902(m)(1) preempted "State laws or regulations which specify types of medical care, providers of care, extent of benefits, coverage of family members, age limits for family members, or other matters relating to health benefits or coverage,"*id.*, at 4–5 (noting that some States mandated coverage for services not included in federal plans, for example, chiropractic services). In 1998, Congress amended§ 8902(m)(1) by deleting the words "to the extent that such law or regulation is inconsistent with such contractual provisions." Thus, under§ 8902(m)(1) as it now reads, state law—whether consistent or inconsistent with federal plan provisions—is displaced on matters of "coverage or benefits."

* * *

II

Petitioner Empire Healthchoice Assurance, Inc., doing business as Empire Blue Cross Blue Shield (Empire), is the entity that administers the BCBSA Plan as it applies to federal employees in New York State. Respondent Denise Finn McVeigh (McVeigh) is the administrator of the estate of Joseph E. McVeigh (Decedent), a former enrollee in the Plan. The Decedent was injured in an accident in 1997. Plan payments for the medical care he received between 1997 and his death in 2001 amounted to $157,309. McVeigh, on behalf of herself, the Decedent, and a minor child, commenced tort litigation in state court against parties alleged to have caused Decedent's injuries. On learning that the parties to the state-court litigation had agreed to settle the tort claims, Empire sought to recover the $157,309 it had paid out for the Decedent's medical care. Of the $3,175,000 for which the settlement provided, McVeigh, in response to Empire's asserted reimbursement right, agreed to place $100,000 in escrow.

* * *

… The District Court rejected both arguments and granted McVeigh's motion to dismiss for want of subject-matter jurisdiction. *Ibid.*

A divided panel of the Court of Appeals for the Second Circuit affirmed, holding that "Empire's clai[m] arise[s] under state law." *Id.*, at 150.

* * *

III

Title 28 U.S.C.§ 1331 vests in federal district courts "original jurisdiction" over "all civil actions arising under the Constitution, laws, or treaties of the United States." A case "aris[es] under" federal law within the meaning of§ 1331, this Court has said, if "a well-pleaded complaint establishes either that federal law creates the cause of action or that the plaintiff's right to relief necessarily depends on resolution of a substantial question of federal law." *Franchise Tax Bd. of Cal. v. Construction Laborers Vacation Trust for Southern Cal.,* 463 U.S. 1, 27–28, 103 S.Ct. 2841, 77 L.Ed.2d 420 (1983).

* * *

A

Clearfield is indeed a pathmarking precedent on the authority of federal courts to fashion uniform federal common law on issues of national concern. See Friendly, In Praise of *Erie—And of the New Federal Common Law,* 39 N.Y.U.L.Rev. 383, 409–410 (1964).

* * *

In post-*Clearfield* decisions, and with the benefit of enlightened commentary, see, *e.g.,* Friendly, *supra,* at 410, the Court has "made clear that uniform federal law need not be applied to all questions in federal government litigation, even in cases involving government contracts," R. Fallon, D. Meltzer, & D. Shapiro, Hart and Wechsler's The Federal Courts and the Federal System 700 (5th ed.2003) (hereinafter Hart and Wechsler).[3] "[T]he prudent course," we have recognized, is often "to adopt the readymade body of state law as the federal rule of decision until Congress strikes a different accommodation." *United States v. Kimbell Foods, Inc.,* 440 U.S. 715, 740, 99 S.Ct. 1448, 59 L.Ed.2d 711 (1979).

Later, in *Boyle,* the Court telescoped the appropriate inquiry, focusing it on the straightforward question whether the relevant federal interest warrants displacement of state law. See 487 U.S., at 507, n. 3, 108 S.Ct. 2510. Referring simply to "the displacement of state law," the Court recognized that prior cases had treated discretely (1) the competence of federal courts to formulate a federal rule of decision, and (2) the appropriateness of declaring a federal rule rather than borrowing, incorporating, or adopting state law in point. The Court preferred "the more modest terminology," questioning whether "the distinction between displacement of state law and displacement of federal law's incorporation of state law ever makes a practical difference." *Ibid. Boyle* made two further observations here significant. First, *Boyle* explained, the involvement of "an area of uniquely federal interest ... establishes a necessary, not a sufficient, condition for the displacement of state law." *Id.,* at 507, 108 S.Ct. 2510. Second, in some cases, an "entire body of state law" may conflict with the federal interest and therefore require replacement. *Id.,* at 508, 108 S.Ct. 2510. But in others, the conflict is confined, and "only particular elements of state law are superseded." *Ibid*

* * *

For the reasons stated, the judgment of the Court of Appeals for the Second Circuit is *Affirmed.*

Justice BREYER, with whom Justice KENNEDY, Justice SOUTER, and Justice ALITO join, dissenting.

This case involves a dispute about the meaning of terms in a federal health insurance contract. The contract, between a federal agency and a private carrier, sets forth the details of

---

3. The United States, in accord with the dissent in this regard, see *post,* at 2142, several times cites *United States v. County of Allegheny,* 322 U.S. 174, 64 S.Ct. 908, 88 L.Ed. 1209 (1944), see, *e.g.,* Brief as *Amicus Curiae* 10, 15, 26, maintaining that the construction of a federal contract "necessarily present[s] questions of "federal law not controlled by the law of any State," "*id.,* at 26 (quoting 322 U.S., at 183, 64 S.Ct. 908). *Allegheny* does not stretch as widely as the United States suggests. That case concerned whether certain property belonged to the United States and, if so, whether the incidence of a state tax was on the United States or on a Government contractor. See *id.,* at 181–183, 186–189, 64 S.Ct. 908. Neither the United States nor any United States agency is a party to this case, and the auxiliary matter here involved scarcely resembles the controversy in *Allegheny.*

a federal health insurance program created by federal statute and covering 8 million federal employees. In all this the Court cannot find a basis for federal jurisdiction. I believe I can. See *Clearfield Trust Co. v. United States,* 318 U.S. 363, 63 S.Ct. 573, 87 L.Ed. 838 (1943).

I

* * *

In sum, the statute is federal, the program it creates is federal, the program's beneficiaries are federal employees working throughout the country, the Federal Government pays all relevant costs, and the Federal Government receives all relevant payments. The private carrier's only role in this scheme is to administer the health benefits plan for the federal agency in exchange for a fixed service charge.

* * *

This Court has applied this principle, the principle embodied in *Clearfield Trust,* to Government contracts of all sorts. See, *e.g., West Virginia v. United States,* 479 U.S. 305, 308–309, 107 S.Ct. 702, 93 L.Ed.2d 639 (1987) (contract regarding federal disaster relief efforts); *United States v. Kimbell Foods, Inc.,* 440 U.S. 715, 726, 99 S.Ct. 1448, 59 L.Ed.2d 711 (1979) (contractual liens arising from federal loan programs); *United States v. Little Lake Misere Land Co.,* 412 U.S. 580, 592, 93 S.Ct. 2389, 37 L.Ed.2d 187 (1973) (agreements to acquire land under federal conservation program); *United States v. Seckinger,* 397 U.S. 203, 209, 90 S.Ct. 880, 25 L.Ed.2d 224 (1970) (Government construction contracts); *United States v. County of Allegheny,* 322 U.S. 174, 183, 64 S.Ct. 908, 88 L.Ed. 1209 (1944) (Government procurement contracts).

* * *

With respect, I dissent.

Notes and Questions:

1. Suppose OPM wants to get its recovery from what the lawsuit has provided to the victim of the accident off the "top," without taking any account of what the victim owes to lawyers and other creditors. And suppose, that state law supports the victim in their position. In that situation, who does one expect to win: the carrier backed by the law, or, the victim backed by the state law respected by the state's own law?

2. Is the court discussing just this particular statute, or, is it making general law for other statutes as well?

3. Does this case have a meaning for the relationship between the federal government, federal contractors, and subcontractors?

Arthur S. Lujan, Labor Commissioner of California, et al., v. G & G Fire Sprinklers, Inc.

Supreme Court of the United States
532 U.S. 189 No. 00-152
Argued Feb. 26, 2001, Decided April 17, 2001

Chief Justice REHNQUIST delivered the opinion of the Court.

The California Labor Code (Code or Labor Code) authorizes the State to order withholding of payments due a contractor on a public works project if a subcontractor on the project fails to comply with certain Code requirements. The Code permits the contractor, in turn, to withhold similar sums from the subcontractor. The Court of Appeals for the Ninth Circuit held that the relevant Code provisions violate the Due Process Clause of the Fourteenth Amendment because the statutory scheme does not afford the subcontractor a hearing before or after such action is taken. We granted certiorari, 531 U.S. 924, 121 S.Ct. 297, 148 L.Ed.2d 239 (2000), and we reverse.

Petitioners are the California Division of Labor Standards Enforcement (DLSE), the California Department of Industrial Relations, and several state officials in their official capacities. Respondent G & G Fire Sprinklers, Inc. (G & G) is a fire-protection company that installs fire sprinkler systems. G & G served as a subcontractor on several California public works projects. "Public works" include construction work done under contract and paid for in whole or part by public funds. Cal. Lab. Code Ann. § 1720 (West Supp.2001). The department, board, authority, officer, or agent awarding a contract for public work is called the "awarding body." § 1722 (West 1989). The California Labor Code requires that contractors and subcontractors on such projects pay their workers a prevailing wage that is determined by the State. §§ 1771, 1772, 1773 (West 1989 and Supp.2001). At the time relevant here, if workers were not paid the prevailing wage, the contractor was required to pay each worker the difference between the prevailing wage and the wages paid, in addition to forfeiting a penalty to the State. § 1775(West Supp. 2001). The awarding body was required to include a clause in the contract so stipulating. *Ibid.*

The Labor Code provides that "[b]efore making payments to the contractor of money due under a contract for public work, the awarding body shall withhold and retain therefrom all wages and penalties which have been forfeited pursuant to any stipulation in a contract for public work, and the terms of this chapter." § 1727 (West Supp.2001). If money is withheld from a contractor because of a subcontractor's failure to comply with the Code's provisions, "[i]t shall be lawful for [the] contractor to withhold from [the] subcontractor under him sufficient sums to cover any penalties withheld." § 1729 (West 1989).

The Labor Code permits the contractor, or his assignee, to bring suit against the awarding body "on the contract for alleged breach thereof in not making ... payment" to recover the wages or penalties withheld. §§ 1731, 1732 (West Supp.2001). The suit must be brought within 90 days of completion of the contract and acceptance of the job. § 1730. Such a suit "is the exclusive remedy of the contractor or his or her assignees." § 1732. The awarding body retains the wages and penalties "pending the outcome of the suit." § 1731.

In 1995, DLSE determined that G & G, as a subcontractor on three public works projects, had violated the Labor Code by failing to pay the prevailing wage and failing to keep and/or furnish payroll records upon request. DLSE issued notices to the awarding bodies on those projects, directing them to withhold from the contractors an amount equal to the wages and penalties forfeited due to G & G's violations. The awarding bodies withheld payment from the contractors, who in turn withheld payment from G & G. The total withheld, according to respondent, exceeded $135,000. App. 68.

G & G sued petitioners in the District Court for the Central District of California. G & G sought declaratory and injunctive relief pursuant to Rev. Stat. § 1979, 42 U.S.C. § 1983, claiming that the issuance of withholding notices without a hearing constituted a deprivation of property without due process of law in violation of the Fourteenth Amendment. The District Court granted respondent's motion for summary judgment, declared §§ 1727, 1730–1733, 1775, 1776(g), and 1813 of the Labor Code unconstitutional, and enjoined the State from enforcing these provisions against respondent. App. to Pet. for Cert. A85–A87. Petitioners appealed.

A divided panel of the Court of Appeals for the Ninth Circuit affirmed. *G & G Fire Sprinklers, Inc. v. Bradshaw*, 156 F.3d 893, 898 (C.A.9 1998) *(Bradshaw I)*. The court concluded that G & G "has a property interest in being paid in full for the construction work it has completed," *id.*, at 901, and found that G & G was deprived of that interest "as a result of the state's action," *id.*, at 903. It decided that because subcontractors were "afforded neither a pre- nor post-deprivation hearing when payments [were] withheld," the statutory scheme violated the Due Process Clause of the Fourteenth Amendment. *Id.*, at 904.

* * *

Where a state law such as this is challenged on due process grounds, we inquire whether the State has deprived the claimant of a protected property interest, and whether the State's procedures comport with due process. *Sullivan, supra,* at 59, 119 S.Ct. 977. We assume, without deciding, that the withholding of money due respondent under its contracts occurred under color of state law, and that, as the Court of Appeals concluded, respondent has a property interest of the kind we considered in *Logan v. Zimmerman Brush Co.,* 455 U.S. 422, 102 S.Ct. 1148, 71 L.Ed.2d 265 (1982), in its claim for payment under its contracts. 204 F.3d, at 943–944. Because we believe that California law affords respondent sufficient opportunity to pursue that claim in state court, we conclude that the California statutory scheme does not deprive G & G of its claim for payment without due process of law. See *Logan, supra,* at 433, 102 S.Ct. 1148 ("[T]he Due Process Clause grants the aggrieved party the opportunity to present his case and have its merits fairly judged").

* * *

In *Cafeteria & Restaurant Workers v. McElroy,* 367 U.S. 886, 895, 81 S.Ct. 1743, 6 L.Ed.2d 1230 (1961) (citations omitted), we said:

> "The very nature of due process negates any concept of inflexible procedures universally applicable to every imaginable situation. "'[D]ue process,' unlike some legal rules, is not a technical conception with a fixed content unrelated to time, place and circumstances.' It is 'compounded of history, reason, the past course of decisions....'"

We hold that if California makes ordinary judicial process available to respondent for resolving its contractual dispute, that process is due process.

The California Labor Code provides that "the contractor or his or her assignee" may sue the awarding body "on the contract for alleged breach thereof" for "the recovery of wages or penalties." §§ 1731, 1732 (West Supp.2001). There is no basis here to conclude that the contractor would refuse to assign the right of suit to its subcontractor. In fact, respondent stated at oral argument that it has sued awarding bodies in state superior court pursuant to §§ 1731–1733 of the Labor Code to recover payments withheld on previous projects where it served as a subcontractor. See Tr. of Oral Arg. 27, 40–41, 49–50. Presumably, respondent brought suit as an assignee of the contractors on those projects, as the Code requires. § 1732 (West Supp.2001). Thus, the Labor Code, by allowing assignment, provides a means by which a subcontractor may bring a claim for breach of contract to recover wages and penalties withheld.

Respondent complains that a suit under the Labor Code is inadequate because the awarding body retains the wages and penalties "pending the outcome of the suit," § 1731, which may last several years. Tr. of Oral Arg. 51. A lawsuit of that duration, while undoubtedly something of a hardship, cannot be said to deprive respondent of its claim for payment under the contract. Lawsuits are not known for expeditiously resolving claims, and the standard practice in breach-of-contract suits is to award damages, if appropriate, only at the conclusion of the case.

Even if respondent could not obtain assignment of the right to sue the awarding body under the contract, it appears that a suit for breach of contract against the contractor remains available under California common law. See 1 B. Witkin, Summary of California Law §§ 791, 797 (9th ed.1987) (defining breach as the "unjustified or unexcused failure to perform a contract" and describing the remedies available under state law). To be sure, § 1732 of the Labor Code provides that suit on the contract against the awarding body is the "exclusive remedy of the contractor or his or her assignees" with respect to recovery of withheld wages and penalties. § 1732 (West Supp.2001). But the remedy is exclusive only with respect to the contractor and his assignees, and thus by its terms not the exclusive remedy for a subcontractor who does not receive assignment. See, *e.g., J & K Painting Co., Inc. v. Bradshaw,* 45 Cal.App.4th 1394, 1402, 53 Cal.Rptr.2d 496, 501 (1996) (allowing subcontractor to challenge Labor Commissioner's action by petition for a writ of the mandate).

In *J & K Painting,* the California Court of Appeal rejected the argument that § 1732 requires a subcontractor to obtain an assignment and that failure to do so is "fatal to any other attempt to secure relief." *Id.,* at 1401, n. 7, 53 Cal.Rptr.2d, at 501, n. 7. The Labor Code does not expressly impose such a requirement, and that court declined to infer an intent to "create remedial exclusivity" in this context. *Ibid.* It thus appears that subcontractors like respondent may pursue their claims for payment by bringing a standard breach-of-contract suit against the contractor under California law.... We therefore conclude that the relevant provisions of the California Labor Code do not deprive respondent of property without due process of law. Accordingly, the judgment of the Court of Appeals is reversed.

Notes and Questions

1. This Supreme Court case makes a point about privity, but several other government contract issues make cameo appearances: labor rules, subcontractor rights, and constitutional due process.

2. Note how the privity barrier creates the issue in this case. The due process problem is much less acute when the government mulcts its direct general contractor for violation of a labor standard, without any subcontractor being in the picture. In that situation, the direct contractor has any normal remedy it wishes to pursue. Here, however, the privity barrier puts the subcontractor in some doubt where it can find its forum to contest the government's determination.

Why would a subcontractor like G & G consider its general contractor insufficiently interested in proceeding? Review the chapter on labor standards. Note that the main effect of an adverse public decision may be to brand violators as outlaws and, hence, to deny them future contracts. A general contractor might well be indifferent to the subcontractor receiving that branding, and, indeed, might consider passing on to the subcontractor, or even absorbing itself, some relatively limited monetary penalties as a small price to pay for showing the government that it had neither any role in, nor tolerance of, the subcontractor's alleged transgressions. Chief Justice Rehnquist goes through all the ways privity allows the subcontractor to proceed in the face of the privity barrier and the general contractor's indifference. If you were G & G and you feared potentially disastrous future exclusion from subcontracts, would you be reassured? Observe that G & G fought this from the case's start in 1995 until the decision in 2001.

B. Small Business Programs and Affirmative Action Issues

1. Note on Small Business Programs

Congress passed the Small Business Act in 1953 to help small businesses get federal contracts. It reaffirmed and refined its commitment in the Small Business Jobs Act of 2010 (together "the Act"). See 15 U.S.C.§637. The Act created the Small Business Administration (SBA), which supervises several programs, each of which has government-wide goals for prime contracts. These are 23% for Small Businesses (SBs); 5% for Small Disadvantaged Businesses (SDBs); 5% for Women-Owned Small Businesses (WOSBs); 3% for Historically Underutilized Business Zone (HUBZone); and 3% for the Service-Disabled Veteran-Owned Small Business Concerns (SDVO SBCs).

The main method for agencies to meet these goals consists of "set-asides," in which competition on particular procurements gets restricted to a category of contractors, such as SBs or SDBs. Purchases under the simplified acquisition threshold, for most contracts $150,000, are set aside. (These set-asides do not include purchases below the micro-purchase threshold, for most contracts $300.) Purchases above the simplified acquisition threshold can be set aside when the agency expects proposals from at least two small businesses and award will be at a fair market price, the "rule of 2." The rule of 2 extends to task and delivery order competitions.

Determination of what constitutes a "fair market price" is left to the contracting officer who can exercise very broad authority. Small business "fair market prices" can be considerably higher than what a large business would charge the government for a similar product or service. In essence, contracting officers may pay premium prices for products and services offered by small business concerns in support of congressional policy of assisting and ensuring the continued viability of small business concerns through the procurement process.

SBs must self-certify their status and size, and re-certify after events like mergers. A firm's status can be challenged by the filing of a size protest—either by a contracting officer or by a business competitor. This challenge goes to an SBA official and can be appealed further to the SBA's Office of Hearings and Appeals (OHA).

For a contractor to be "small" enough to get this help depends upon the "size standards" for the contractor's "North American Industrial Classification" (NAIC). Congress requires the SBA to review and update one third of the size standards every 18 months.

The SBA may find a concern small under two standards. One, the revenue size, applies if the concern's average annual receipts over the past three completed fiscal years is at or below the dollar figure assigned to a particular NAICS code. The SBA generally reviews a concern's tax returns. The other, the employee or "head count," means that a concern is small if the average number of individuals employed by the concern for the preceding 12 months is at or below the number of employees reflected in the applicable size standard.

In addition to looking at either the number of employees or annual revenues, SBA has fairly strict regulations concerning permissible and non-permissible business "affiliates" of a small business concern. Such regulations are intended, in part, to eliminate business that act as "fronts" for large business concerns in order to take advantage of the procurement opportunities reserved for small business concerns. The SBA will examine factors such as stock ownership, common management, common facilities, key employees, and contractual relationships in making a determination as to the affiliation between two businesses. Should two businesses be "affiliated," they must count either the total number of employees of both or the total annual receipts of both to determine their eligibility as a small business concern.

SBs must meet minimums, usually 50%, of the performance of a contract's work by themselves (rather than others), as reflecting in the "Limitations on Subcontracting" Clause (FAR 52-219-14). Also, under the Certificate of Competency (COC) program, contracting officers must refer SB nonresponsibility determinations to the SBA. If the SBA issues a COC, it effectively establishes the SB's responsibility.

Among other areas affected by the SB body of law, prime contracts must adopt a "subcontracting plan" for SBs and to firms in the other programs. Agencies have limits, under the 2010 Act, in their "contract bundling," which would consolidate previously smaller contracts in ways that might limit small business competition. Under certain conditions, awards of sole-source contracts are proper to SBs and to firms in the other programs.

2. Minority Small Disadvantaged Businesses

For further discussion of the subjects in this subchapter, see: Trent Taylor, *The End Of An Era? How Affirmative Action In Government Contracting Can Survive After Rothe*, 39 Pub. Cont. L.J. 853 (Summer 2010).; Christopher R. Noon, *The Use Of Racial Preferences In Public Procurement For Social Stability*, 38 Pub. Cont. L.J. 611 (Spring 2009).

As part of the Small Business Act, Congress established aid for small disadvantaged businesses (SDBs). To qualify as an SDB, a firm must meet the definition of a "small business," be at least 51% owned or controlled by disadvantaged individuals, and be under such individuals' daily management. "Disadvantaged" has two aspects. It involves economic disadvantage, addressed by a ceiling of $750,000 net worth (not counting home or the SDB itself). And, it involves social disadvantage, which is mainly being in a minority such as racial and ethnic categories that qualify include Black Americans, Hispanic Americans, Native Americans, Asian-Pacific Americans, Subcontinent Asian Americans and other minorities as well as Indian Tribes and Native Hawaiian Organizations.

There are fairly strict regulatory requirements as to the business concerns that qualify for procurement assistance from the 8(a) Business Development Program. *See* 13 C.F.R. Part 124. The concern must be a small business and unconditionally owned (51%) by one or more qualified socially and economically disadvantaged individuals. Also, the concern cannot be controlled by non-qualified companies and must have a detailed business plan and have a potential for success in order to be admitted to the program. Once in the program, contracting opportunities, with the assistance of the SBA, are set aside for the exclusive participation of qualified 8(a) firms, either on a sole source basis or a limited competition basis where more than one such qualified firm is able to compete for and provide the required products or perform the necessary services.

The selected contract is awarded to the SBA which in turn awards a subcontract to the qualified small disadvantaged concern. In other words, technically SBA is the prime, and the 8(a) firm has a subcontract from SBA.

Prior to the court challenge (see below), the program had several ways to help SDBs. It gave SDBs a price evaluation adjustment (PEA) in FAR Part 19.11, such as adding 10% to the bid of competing non-SDB firms. However, Congress suspended the PEA for a number of years because the SDB program met its goal without the PEA. And, in FAR Subpart 19.12, it provided an evaluation factor. This may help in offers by teams in which the SDB is just one of the participants, making it desirable to primes seeking an award to have an SDB with them. Also, the program provides an incentive for subcontracting with SDBs.

For further discussion of the issues in this section, see Denise Benjamin Sirmons, *Federal Contracting With Women-Owned Businesses: An Analysis Of Existing Challenges & Potential Opportunities*, 33 Pub. Cont. L.J. 725 (Summer 2004); Deirdre Roney, *HUBZones: The Class-Based Idea*, 32 Pub. Cont. L.J. 933 (Summer 2003); Paul D. Hancq, Karen S. White, *A Preference For Native American Contractors*, 2002 Army Law. 39 (Sept. 2002); Eric D. Phelps, *The Cunning Of Clever Bureaucrats: Why The Small Business Regulatory Enforcement Fairness Act Isn't Working*, 31 Pub. Cont. L.J. 123 (Fall 2001); Katherine R. Boyce, *Incentive Payment Program Expands Federal Subcontracting Opportunities For Indian Country*, 48 Fed. Law. 38 (Mar./Apr. 2001); Gilbert J. Ginsburg and Janine S. Benton, *One Year Later: Affirmative Action in Federal Government Contracting After Adarand* 45 Am. U. L. Rev. 1903, (1996); Steven K. DiLiberto, Comment: *Setting Aside Set Asides: The New Standard for Affirmative Action Programs in the Construction Industry*, 42 Vill. L. Rev. 2039 (1997); Laura M. Padilla, *Intersectionality and Positionality: Situating Women of Color in the Affirmative Action Dialogue* 66 Ford. L. Rev. 843 (1997); Mary K. O'Melveny, *Playing the "Gender" Card : Affirmative Action and Working Women*, 84 Ky. L.J. 863 (1995–1996).

San Antonio General Maintenance, Inc., et al., Plaintiffs, v. James Abnor, et al., Defendants

Civ. A. No. 87-1861
United States District Court, District of Columbia
691 F. Supp. 1462
Decided Nov 16, 1987

JOYCE HENS GREEN, District Judge.

Most litigation involving federal programs produces predictable arguments on both sides: the government attempts to withdraw benefits and the individual asserts continued eligibility and entitlement. This case, however, presents an interesting twist on that familiar scenario. Plaintiffs San Antonio General Maintenance, Inc. (SAGM) and Pedro G. Molina, Jr., brought this action for declaratory and injunctive relief against defendants James Abdnor, Administrator of the Small Business Administration (SBA), and Edward C. Aldridge, Jr., Secretary of the Air Force. SAGM, which currently holds a contract to provide custodial services at Kelly Air Force Base in San Antonio, Texas, seeks to require defendants to permit competitive bidding on their next awarding of the contract; the SBA and the Air Force, however, have determined to retain the contract under a special program for socially and economically disadvantaged small business concerns. Simultaneously with the filing of its complaint, SAGM moved for a temporary restraining order and for a preliminary injunction, and defendants responded with a motion to dismiss or, in the alternative, for summary judgment. These matters were considered at a final hearing held in September 1987. For the reasons set forth below, plaintiffs' requests for injunctive and declaratory relief will be denied and defendants' motion for summary judgment will be granted.

I. Background

Section 2[8](a) of the Small Business Act of 1958, 15 U.S.C. § 637(a), established a special program designed to benefit "socially and economically disadvantaged" small business concerns.[1] In order to "foster business ownership" and "promote the competitive viability" of these firms, 15 U.S.C. §631(e)(2), the Act authorizes the SBA to enter into procurement and construction contracts with any federal agency. The SBA then subcontracts with qualifying small businesses, which actually provide the services directly to the federal agency. See 15 U.S.C. §637(a)(1). Contracts designated for the 2[8](a) program are therefore effectively withdrawn from the customary competitive bidding procedures generally applicable to federal procurements. Id. §§631(e)(1)(C) and 637(a)(5) & (6).

Participation in the 2[8](a) program is not eternal, however. Mindful that "these contracts be a means to fostering competitive viability ... and not an end in themselves," S.Rep. No. 974, 96th Cong., 2d Sess. 3 (1980), U.S.Code Cong. & Admin.News 1980, pp. 4953, 4954, Congress amended the Act in 1980 and directed the SBA to establish a fixed period of time within which each 2[8](a) participant could remain within the program. See 15 U.S.C. §636(j)(10)(A)(i). After reaching the end of its fixed term the disadvantaged concern is "graduated" from the 2[8](a) program and expected to compete for government contracts on an equal footing with other non-disadvantaged firms. Plaintiff SAGM, a Texas corporation, and its president, plaintiff Pedro Molina, Jr., were accepted into the 2[8](a) program in 1976 and 1972, respectively, and were graduated in June 1985. In 1984, however, SBA awarded SAGM a one-year 2[8](a) contract, with two one-year extensions, to provide custodial services at the Kelly Air Force Base in San Antonio, Texas. Having graduated from the 2[8](a) program and with its contract due to expire on September 30, 1987, SAGM initiated discussions with SBA representatives in early 1987 in order to assure that SAGM would be permitted to bid on the Kelly contract when it was released into the competitive procurement process. In June 1987, however, the SBA and the Air Force decided that the Kelly contract would remain within the 2[8](a) program and be awarded to another disadvantaged small business, Rite-Way Services, Inc.

SAGM filed this action on July 9, 1987. In its complaint, it contends that the SBA maintained a general policy and practice allowing a graduating 2[8](a) firm to competitively bid on the next contract awarded for the same services after the 2[8](a) participant's fixed term had expired. Plaintiffs claim that the SBA's actions (1) violated the Administrative Procedure Act, 5 U.S.C. §§701 et seq., because the agency arbitrarily departed from its established practices without prior notice or an adequate explanation; and (2) contravened several SBA regulations governing the 2[8](a) procurement program.

* * *

IV. The Merits
A. SBA Decision

Before considering whether the SBA's decision to award the Kelly contract to Rite-Way was an arbitrary and capricious departure from existing agency policy regulations, the Court must resolve issues strenuously disputed by the parties: exactly what was the existing agency policy and what are the regulations that govern this action? Plaintiffs contend that SBA's decision to retain the Kelly contract within the 2[8](a) program violated three agency regulations applicable to this case. The complaint first alleges that the SBA's actions contravened 13 C.F.R. §124.301(b)(8)(iii) and (b)(8)(iv)(B), which re-

---

1. The Act defines these concerns by means of a numerical formula, see 15 U.S.C. §637(a)(4), and specifically identifies certain minorities—such as blacks, Hispanics and Indians—that qualify for the program.

quired the SBA to make a number of findings with respect to the adverse impact upon SAGM before retaining the contract within the 2[8](a) program. The plain language of these regulations, however, demonstrates the futility of plaintiffs' reliance upon them. Section 124.301(b)(8) states: "SBA will not accept for 8(a) award proposed procurements not previously in the section 8(a) program if any of the following circumstances exist ..." (emphasis added). The highlighted language clearly indicates that these regulations are designed to serve as guidance to SBA officials considering the addition of new contracts to the 2[8](a) program; the regulation nowhere mentions graduation from the program or the fixed program participation term. These regulations do not, therefore, apply to this case.

SAGM also vigorously asserts that the SBA's "past policy and practice" permitted graduating 2[8](a) firms to bid competitively on the next contract to be awarded for the same services once the 2[8](a) participant's eligibility for the program had expired, Complaint P 11, and, to support its view, offers two pieces of evidence: (1) plaintiff Molina's assertion that, at a February 26, 1987, meeting in San Antonio, he was informed by two local SBA officials that SBA policy "had always been" to allow graduating firms to bid competitively on the 2[8](a) contracts that they had just relinquished, see Molina Affidavit at 4–5; and (2) the fact that six former 2[8](a) contractors have indicated that their contracts were competitively bid after completion of their program eligibility. Fiorino Affidavit, Exh. P-3 to Plaintiffs' Supplemental Filing at 4–6.

Defendants steadfastly oppose this view. First, they assert that the SBA prefers to keep contracts within the 2[8](a) program whenever possible, thus preventing a graduating 2[8](a) firm from "taking his contract" with him after graduation. Memorandum in Support of Motion to Dismiss at 14; Luna Dep. at 30–31. In certain selected instances, however, the SBA does allow 2[8](a) contracts to be released for competitive bids on a case-by-case basis in accordance with the factors set forth in paragraph 46(e) of SOP 80-05. Thus, defendants contend that paragraph 46(e) constitutes the agency policy governing graduating firms. Second, defendants contest plaintiffs' factual claims regarding the former 2[8](a) firms that were allowed to bid after expiration of their program eligibility. See Luna Declaration, Exh. G to Memorandum in Support of Motion to Dismiss.

* * *

The SBA's decision to retain the Kelly contract within the 2[8](a) program was made by Joseph Luna, the Assistant Regional Administrator in SBA's Dallas office, and is memorialized in a June 26, 1987, memorandum. See Exh. B to Motion to Dismiss....

Although far from a model of clarity, the Luna memorandum establishes that SBA did not act in an arbitrary or capricious manner in deciding to forego competitive bidding on the Kelly contract. The memorandum discloses that the agency considered the relevant factors and articulated its reasons for reaching the decision that it did. Only one of these factors supported SAGM's desire to engage in competitive bidding, and the other factors all militated in favor of retaining the Kelly contract in the 2[8](a) program. Given that the SBA's general policy was to retain 2[8](a) contracts within the program whenever possible and to release these contracts only in the limited circumstances specified in paragraph 46(e), given that Mr. Luna addressed these factors and concluded that the Kelly contract should remain as an 2[8](a) procurement, and given the deferential review accorded to federal agencies in procurement matters, the Court concludes that plaintiffs have failed to carry their burden of demonstrating that the SBA's actions were arbitrary and capricious.

B. The Air Force Decision

Section 1207(a) of the National Defense Authorization Act of 1987, Pub.L. No. 99-661, 100 Stat. 3816, 3973, establishes "a goal of 5 percent" of all Defense Department contracts be awarded to small, disadvantaged businesses (SDBs), black colleges, and other minority institutions. Plaintiffs claim that the Air Force's decision to retain the Kelly contract as an 2[8](a) contract, rather than as an SDB set-aside, violates section 1207 and two of its implementing regulations.[2] The rather unusual chain of events leading up to the Air Force's conclusion that the Kelly contract should be kept within the 2[8](a) program is recounted in the Declaration of Stephanie Apple, the Kelly contracting officer at the time. See Exh. C to Motion to Dismiss. In February 1987, Apple approved the award of the Kelly contract to the SBA under the 2[8](a) program. In April 1987, however, Apple learned that the procuring unit at Kelly was dissatisfied with the qualifications of Rite-Way (which had been chosen by the SBA under the 2[8](a) program); she therefore decided to utilize the SDB set-aside route in filling the contract. After the SBA appealed this decision to the Secretary of the Air Force, after a congressional inquiry into the matter, and after SBA assured the Air Force that Rite-Way would receive the technical assistance it needed to perform the contract,[3] Apple reconsidered her position and decided, in June 1987, to keep the contract within the 2[8](a) framework.

Plaintiffs do not attack the Air Force's decisional process as arbitrary and capricious under section 706(2)(A), see Complaint PP 22–24, nor do they seriously dispute Apple's version of these facts. Rather, the complaint first asserts (P 22) that the Air Force failed to comply with section 1207 when it made the determination to maintain the contract in 2[8](a) status. This claim is completely without merit and must be rejected as a matter of law. First, the very language of section 1207(a) states that the 5% contract figure is merely a "goal" that the Defense Department should seek to attain. But — above and beyond that — section 1207(e)(3) plainly authorizes the use of 2[8](a) awards to reach the 5% contracting goal ("the Secretary of Defense may enter into contracts using less than full and open competitive procedures (including awards under section 8(a) of the Small Business Act)"). Plaintiffs' contention based on the language of section 1207 must fail.

On May 7, 1987, the Department of Defense issued interim regulations interpreting section 1207. See 52 Fed. Reg. 16,263–67. Plaintiffs assert that the Air Force's actions violated two provisions of these interim regulations that require it to publish a synopsis of the Kelly contract and to make certain findings when setting-aside a contract for SDB treatment. See 48 C.F.R. § 205.207(d) and 219.502-72(a) (52 Fed. Reg. at 16,264, 16,266). Plaintiffs' argument puts the cart before the horse, however. In accordance with the language of section 1207, the interim regulations make clear that Department of Defense agencies have discretion in determining whether to proceed by way of an SDB set-aside or through the 2[8](a) program. See 48 C.F.R. § 219.201(a) (52 Fed. Reg. at 16,265). Moreover, the regulations stress that the 2[8](a) program, rather than the set-aside procedure, is the preferred path. See 48 C.F.R. § 219.801 ("The Department of Defense, to the greatest extent possible, will award contracts to the SBA under the authority of section 8(a) of the Small Business Act and will actually identify requirements to support the business plans of 8(a) concerns") (emphasis added) (52 Fed. Reg. at 16,267). Because they do not challenge the Air Force's exercise of its discretionary authority to award the contract by

---

2. There is no dispute that SAGM would qualify as an SDB if the Air Force had chosen to go that route.

3. Ironically, one of the consultants being considered by the SBA to provide technical assistance to Rite-Way is plaintiff Molina. See Tr. 26–29.

means of an 2[8](a) award, plaintiffs cannot be heard to complain that the agency failed to apply proper set-aside procedures.

V. Conclusion

The defendants' motion for summary judgment will be granted. The applicability of SBA and Air Force regulations and the interpretation of relevant statutory provisions are questions of law appropriate for resolution on a motion for summary judgment. And the only issue that is not a pure question of law — whether the SBA acted in an arbitrary and capricious fashion under paragraph 46(e) of SOP 80-05 — presents no genuine issues of material fact that would preclude summary judgment. Because the defendants did not violate applicable laws, rules or regulations, plaintiffs' request for declaratory and injunctive relief will accordingly be denied.

Notes and Questions

1. Initially, the 8(a) program did not require qualified firms to leave the program, i.e., "graduate." This "eternal" preference led to abuses whereby certain firms carefully remained qualified in order to focus solely on federal contracts with little or no effort being expended to be successful in the commercial marketplace. Congress finally amended the Small Business Act by requiring a set term for graduation. The current term for participation in the program is nine years. 13 CFR § 124.2.

2. The requirement of possessing the "potential for success" is intended to ensure that only truly capable firms receive benefits from the 8(a) program. Currently, a firm must be in business in its primary industry classification for at least two full years immediately prior to the date of its 8(a) application unless a waiver is obtained. 13 CFR § 124.107 The two year requirement helps weed out those firms established for the sole reason of taking advantage of the program by individuals that would normally not qualify.

3. As is the case with small business set asides, the award to an 8(a) qualified firm must be made at a "fair market price." FAR 19.806. In estimating the fair market price for an acquisition, the contracting officer is to use cost or price analysis and consider commercial prices for similar products and services, available in-house cost estimates, data obtained from the SBA or the proposed contractor, or data obtained from other government agencies. The contracting officer is granted broad authority in making the determination of what is a fair market price and such decisions can be successfully challenged only if proven to be arbitrary and capricious.

4. A less often used procurement preference statute is the Buy Indian Act, 25 U.S.C. § 47. The Act requires the government to contract for the use of American Indian labor to the extent practicable and authorizes discretionary purchases of the products of Indian industry in the open market. Contracts can be but are not required to be set aside for exclusive participation by Indian firms. As a result, the number of such set asides is limited.

3. Affirmative Action Challenges

The federal government's efforts to aid minorities connect this chapter of government contracting law with one of the most controversial issues of our time. To the practically-minded, this controversy simply makes this a fast-changing and uncertain subject. To those interested in larger issues, this controversy makes what would otherwise seem the relatively humdrum subject of small business contracting a matter of special interest and excitement.

Adarand Constructors, Inc., Petitioner v.
Federico Pena, Secretary of Transportation, et al.

Supreme Court
515 U.S. 200
Decided June 12, 1995

Justice O'CONNOR announced the judgment of the Court ...

Petitioner Adarand Constructors, Inc., claims that the Federal Government's practice of giving general contractors on Government projects a financial incentive to hire subcontractors controlled by "socially and economically disadvantaged individuals," and in particular, the Government's use of race-based presumptions in identifying such individuals, violates the equal protection component of the Fifth Amendment's Due Process Clause....

I

In 1989, the Central Federal Lands Highway Division (CFLHD), which is part of the United States Department of Transportation (DOT), awarded the prime contract for a highway construction project in Colorado to Mountain Gravel & Construction Company. Mountain Gravel then solicited bids from subcontractors for the guardrail portion of the contract. Adarand, a Colorado-based highway construction company specializing in guardrail work, submitted the low bid. Gonzales Construction Company also submitted a bid.

The prime contract's terms provide that Mountain Gravel would receive additional compensation if it hired subcontractors certified as small businesses controlled by "socially and economically disadvantaged individuals," App. 24. Gonzales is certified as such a business; Adarand is not. Mountain Gravel awarded the subcontract to Gonzales, despite Adarand's low bid, and Mountain Gravel's Chief Estimator has submitted an affidavit stating that Mountain Gravel would have accepted Adarand's bid, had it not been for the additional payment it received by hiring Gonzales instead. *Id.,* at 28–31. Federal law requires that a subcontracting clause similar to the one used here must appear in most federal agency contracts....

These fairly straightforward facts implicate a complex scheme of federal statutes and regulations, to which we now turn. The Small Business Act (Act), 72 Stat. 384, as amended, 15 U.S.C. §631 *et seq.,* declares it to be "the policy of the United States that small business concerns, [and] small business concerns owned and controlled by socially and economically disadvantaged individuals, ... shall have the maximum practicable opportunity to participate in the performance of contracts let by any Federal agency." §8(d)(1), 15 U.S.C. §637(d)(1).....

In furtherance of the policy stated in §8(d)(1), the Act establishes "[t]he Government-wide goal for participation by small business concerns owned and controlled by socially and economically disadvantaged individuals" at "not less than 5 percent of the total value of all prime contract and subcontract awards for each fiscal year." 15 U.S.C. §644(g)(1). It also requires the head of each federal agency to set agency-specific goals for participation by businesses controlled by socially and economically disadvantaged individuals. *Ibid.*

The Small Business Administration (SBA) has implemented these statutory directives in a variety of ways, two of which are relevant here. One is the "8(a) program," which is available to small businesses controlled by socially and economically disadvantaged individuals as the SBA has defined those terms. The 8(a) program confers a wide range of benefits on participating businesses, see, *e.g.,* 13 CFR §§ 124.303–124.311, 124.403 (1994); 48 CFR subpt. 19.8 (1994), one of which is automatic eligibility for subcontractor compensation provisions of the kind at issue in this case, 15 U.S.C. § 637(d)(3)(C) (conferring presumptive eligibility on anyone "found to be disadvantaged ... pursuant to section 8(a) of the Small Business Act"). To participate in the 8(a) program, a business must be "small," as defined in 13 CFR § 124.102 (1994); and it must be 51% owned by individuals who qualify as "socially and economically disadvantaged," § 124.103....

The other SBA program relevant to this case is the "8(d) subcontracting program," which unlike the 8(a) program is limited to eligibility for subcontracting provisions like the one at issue here....

The contract giving rise to the dispute in this case came about as a result of the Surface Transportation and Uniform Relocation Assistance Act of 1987, Pub.L. 100-17, 101 Stat. 132 (STURAA), a DOT appropriations measure. Section 106(c)(1) of STURAA provides that "not less than 10 percent" of the appropriated funds "shall be expended with small business concerns owned and controlled by socially and economically disadvantaged individuals." 101 Stat. 145. STURAA adopts the Small Business Act's definition of "socially and economically disadvantaged individual," including the applicable race-based presumptions, and adds that "women shall be presumed to be socially and economically disadvantaged individuals for purposes of this subsection." § 106(c)(2)(B), 101 Stat. 146....

The operative clause in the contract in this case reads as follows:

"*Subcontracting.* This subsection is supplemented to include a Disadvantaged Business Enterprise (DBE) Development and Subcontracting Provision as follows:

"Monetary compensation is offered for awarding subcontracts to small business concerns owned and controlled by socially and economically disadvantaged individuals....

"A small business concern will be considered a DBE after it has been certified as such by the U.S. Small Business Administration or any State Highway Agency....

* * *

"The Contractor will be paid an amount computed as follows:

"1. If a subcontract is awarded to one DBE, 10 percent of the final amount of the approved DBE subcontract, not to exceed 1.5 percent of the original contract amount.

"2. If subcontracts are awarded to two or more DBEs, 10 percent of the final amount of the approved DBE subcontracts, not to exceed 2 percent of the original contract amount." App. 24–26.

To benefit from this clause, Mountain Gravel had to hire a subcontractor who had been certified as a small disadvantaged business.... The record does not reveal how Gonzales obtained its certification as a small disadvantaged business.

After losing the guardrail subcontract to Gonzales, Adarand filed suit.... The District Court granted the Government's motion for summary judgment. *Adarand Constructors, Inc. v. Skinner,* 790 F.Supp. 240 (1992). The Court of Appeals for the Tenth Circuit affirmed. 16 F.3d 1537 (1994)....

* * *

III

... Respondents concede ... that "the race-based rebuttable presumption used in some certification determinations under the Subcontracting Compensation Clause" is subject to some heightened level of scrutiny. *Id.,* at 27. The parties disagree as to what that level should be....

The Court resolved the issue, at least in part, in 1989..*Richmond v. J.A. Croson Co.,*, 588 U.S. 469 (1989), concerned a city's determination that 30% of its contracting work should go to minority-owned businesses. A majority of the Court in *Croson* held that "the standard of review under the Equal Protection Clause is not dependent on the race of those burdened or benefited by a particular classification," and that the single standard of review for racial classifications should be "strict scrutiny."

* * *

A year later, however, the Court took a surprising turn. *Metro Broadcasting, Inc. v. FCC,* involved a Fifth Amendment challenge to two race-based policies of the Federal Communications Commission (FCC).... [It held] that "benign" federal racial classifications need only satisfy intermediate scrutiny, even though *Croson* had recently concluded that such classifications enacted by a State must satisfy strict scrutiny. "[B]enign" federal racial classifications, the Court said, "—even if those measures are not 'remedial' in the sense of being designed to compensate victims of past governmental or societal discrimination—are constitutionally permissible to the extent that they serve *important* governmental objectives within the power of Congress and are *substantially related* to achievement of those objectives." ...

[W]e hold today that all racial classifications, imposed by whatever federal, state, or local governmental actor, must be analyzed by a reviewing court under strict scrutiny. In other words, such classifications are constitutional only if they are narrowly tailored measures that further compelling governmental interests. To the extent that *Metro Broadcasting* is inconsistent with that holding, it is overruled.

* * *

IV

Because our decision today alters the playing field in some important respects, we think it best to remand the case to the lower courts for further consideration in light of the principles we have announced. The Court of Appeals, following *Metro Broadcasting* ... the case in terms of intermediate scrutiny. It upheld the challenged statutes and regulations because it found them to be "narrowly tailored to achieve [their] *significant governmental purpose* of providing subcontracting opportunities for small disadvantaged business enterprises." 16 F.3d, at 1547 (emphasis added). The Court of Appeals did not decide the question whether the interests served by the use of subcontractor compensation clauses are properly described as "compelling." It also did not address the question of narrow tailoring in terms of our strict scrutiny cases, by asking, for example, whether there was "any consideration of the use of race-neutral means to increase minority business participation" in government contracting, *Croson, supra,* at 507, 109 S.Ct., at 729, or whether the program was appropriately limited such that it "will not last longer than the discriminatory effects it is designed to eliminate[.]".....

Moreover, unresolved questions remain concerning the details of the complex regulatory regimes implicated by the use of subcontractor compensation clauses.... The question whether any of the ways in which the Government uses subcontractor compensation clauses can survive strict scrutiny, and any relevance distinctions such as these may have to that question, should be addressed in the first instance by the lower courts.

Accordingly, the judgment of the Court of Appeals is vacated, and the case is remanded for further proceedings consistent with this opinion.

It is so ordered.

[Concurring and dissenting opinions omitted]

Notes and Questions

1. The SBA still has its 8(a) program, it still is being used to help minority businesses, and although it remains controversial, the program seems to survive despite all, as do the other major such programs. See Danielle Conway-Jones & Christopher Leon Jones, Jr., *Department of Defense Procurement Practices After* Adarand: *What Lies Ahead for the Largest Purchaser of Goods and Services and its Base of Small Disadvantaged Business Contractors,* 1 How. L.J. 391 (1995).

2. Even the Supreme Court decision in Adarand did not have the immediate terminating effect on federal government contracting affirmative action programs that some anticipated. The Justice Department continued to justify and to defend such programs. On remand, the Eleventh Circuit sustained the program, citing new Congressional actions as well as that Justice Department defense. The Supreme Court again granted certiorari, which surely must have made observers wonder whether the program had finally used up all its nine lives, but after oral argument, the Court decided to dismiss the case on procedural grounds, apparently taking its cue from the suggestions of the Justice Department.

3. In a very important development after *Adarand* for government contracting law, the Federal Circuit considered a challenge to several aspects of the SDB program in Rothe Development Co. v. United States, 545 F.3d 1023 (Fed. Cir. 2008). It applied strict scrutiny to the program pursuant to *Adarand,* closely scrutinized the studies and other support supporting the program, and found they were insufficient. So, the court found section 1207 unconstitutional on its face. On the other hand, it did confine its decision to the particular case, saying that if Congress enacted a new version, as it had often done, the support for that would receive a fresh look. The decision had special significance coming from the Federal Circuit because of its jurisdiction over government contracting issues.

4. Veterans Programs

Knowledge Connections, Inc., Plaintiff, v. United States, Defendant, and Catapult Technology, Ltd., Intervening Defendant

No. 06-786C
United States Court of Federal Claims
76 Fed.Cl. 6
Reissued: April 3, 2007

OPINION AND ORDER

Plaintiff Knowledge Connections, Inc. ("KCI") lodged this bid protest involving an information-technology set-aside procurement for service-disabled, veteran-owned small businesses. The General Services Administration ("GSA") administered the procurement, known as the Veterans Technology Services Government-wide Acquisition Contract

("VETS GWAC"), under an "executive agent" designation bestowed on GSA by the Office of Management and Budget ("OMB"), the overseer of all federal procurement of information technology. VETS GWAC was part of an effort to implement Executive Order 13360, by which Order the President sought to effectuate two federal statutes that (1) set a government-wide goal of not less than three percent for the participation in federal procurement contracts of small businesses owned and controlled by service-disabled veterans and (2) permit certain set-aside and restricted-competition procurements for service-disabled, veteran-owned businesses. *See* Exec. Order No. 13360, 69 Fed.Reg. 62,549, 62,549 (Oct. 26, 2004); *see also* 15 U.S.C. §§ 644(g)(1), 657f. Conceptually, by way of the VETS GWAC, GSA endeavored to select a pool of pre-qualified, service-disabled, veteran-owned small businesses that then would compete for information technology "task orders" from individual agencies across the federal government.

KCI filed its complaint on November 22, 2006, amending it on November 29, 2006. KCI initially claimed a variety of errors in the procurement process, Am. Compl. ¶¶ 15–23, but it ultimately focused on its allegations that GSA (1) arbitrarily limited the number of awardees, (2) violated a condition of OMB's "executive agent" designation that prohibited GSA from taking into account an offeror's lack of government contracting experience, and (3) arbitrarily employed a tiering arrangement for evaluation of past experience based on monetary values of previous contracts offerors had performed, thus in effect excluding from consideration for an award KCI and others who did not have a broad range of prior work. Pl.'s Mot. for Judgment on the Administrative Record ("Pl.'s Mot.") at 7; Pl.'s Resp. to Def.'s Supplemental Brief at 1–2. On November 29, 2006, Catapult Technology, Ltd., an offeror identified at the time as a potential awardee, was granted leave to intervene in this matter.

FACTS
A.Statutory Background

In 1999, Congress amended Section 15(g)(1) of the Small Business Act to require the President to establish a government-wide goal of not less than three percent for the participation in federal procurement contracts of small businesses owned and controlled by service-disabled veterans. *See* Veterans Entrepreneurship and Small Business Development Act of 1999 (the "1999 Act"), Pub.L. No. 106-50, § 502(a)(2), 113 Stat. 233, 247 (codified at 15 U.S.C. § 644(g)(1)). In responding to public comments on proposed amendments to the Federal Acquisition Regulation ("FAR") pursuant to the 1999 Act, the Civilian Agency Acquisition Council and the Defense Acquisition Regulations Council ("Councils") specifically rejected a request that the FAR refer to the three percent goal:

The FAR does not specify the statutory Government[-]wide goals for any small business category because they have no regulatory purpose for agencies. Statutory goals for small businesses are established on a Government[-]wide basis. Within these Government[-]wide goals, SBA negotiates separate annual goals for each small business category with each agency. The individual agency goals attempt to reflect the agency mission and its contracting requirements, and these individual agency goals may be higher or lower than the Government [-]wide goal. SBA then tracks cumulative agency achievements against the Government[-]wide goal. Accordingly, specifying the 3 percent service-disabled veteran-owned small business goals in the FAR is inappropriate in that only the goal negotiated with SBA is relevant to that agency.

Federal Acquisition Regulation; Veterans Entrepreneurship and Small Business Development Act of 1999, 66 Fed.Reg. 53,492, 53,492 (Oct. 22, 2001). A further amendment of the Small Business Act was enacted in 2003, when Congress added Section 36 to give federal agency contracting officers discretion to set aside certain procurements for service-disabled, veteran-owned small businesses through the use of sole-source contracts and contracts in which competition was restricted to such businesses. *See* Veterans Benefits Act of 2003 ("2003 Act"), Pub.L. No. 108-183, § 308, 117 Stat. 2651, 2662 (codified at 15 U.S.C. § 657f). In issuing a final rule amending the FAR to include regulations for the sole-source and set-aside provisions of the 2003 Act, the Councils rejected a public comment that requested altering the language from "may set-aside" to "shall set aside." *See* Federal Acquisition Regulation; Procurement Program for Service-Disabled Veteran-Owned Small Business Concerns, 70 Fed.Reg. 14,950, 14,953 (March 23, 2005); 48 C.F.R. § 19.1405(a) (2004). The Councils explained that by using the words "may award" the Veterans Benefits Act of 2003 "established a discretionary, not mandatory, set-aside authority for [service-disabled, veteran-owned small businesses]." 70 Fed.Reg. at 14,953; *see* 15 U.S.C. § 657f(a) ("contracting officer may award a sole source contract"); 15 U.S.C. § 657f(b) ("contract officer may award contracts on the basis of competition restricted to small businesses owned and controlled by service-disabled veterans"); 48 C.F.R. §§ 19.1405(a) ("may set aside acquisitions"), 19.1406(a) ("may award contracts").

B. Executive Order 13360 and OMB's "Executive Agent" Authority

On October 20, 2004, President Bush issued Executive Order 13360, the objective of which was to accomplish "more effective[ ] implement[ation]" of Sections 15(g) and 36 of the Small Business Act, *i.e.,* 15 U.S.C. §§ 644(g)(1), 657(f). 69 Fed.Reg. at 62,549. The Executive Order required that agency heads develop a strategy for implementation of these statutory provisions and specifically directed the Administrator of GSA, subject to applicable legal and fiscal constraints, to "establish a Government-wide Acquisition Contract [GWAC] reserved for participation by service-disabled veteran businesses." *Id.* at 62,550.

In February 2005, responding to the president's direction, GSA sent OMB a proposal to establish the VETS GWAC, which GSA described as a "streamlined acquisition vehicle" through which GSA would "offer a pre-qualified group of [service-disabled, veteran-owned small business] information technology firms the opportunity to compete for government [information technology] services orders from [government agencies]." AR 18–19 (GSA, VETS (Veterans Technology Services) Business Case For a Service-Disabled Veteran-Owned Small Business (SDVOSB) Government-wide Acquisition Contract (GWAC), Feb. 3, 2005) ("Business Case"). GSA indicated that "[e]valuation criteria [would], at a minimum, focus on technical expertise, successful past performance and price" and also highlighted the flexibility that the VETS GWAC would afford governmental agencies ("clients"):

* * *

AR 18, 21, 32 (Business Case).

OMB, which is charged with overseeing the federal government's acquisition of information technology, reviewed GSA's Business Case and granted GSA the designation of "executive agent" for the VETS GWAC. AR 85 (Letter from Joshua B. Bolten, Director, OMB, to Stephen A. Perry, Administrator, GSA (July 5, 2005)).

C. GSA's Procurement Actions

* * *

On March 31, 2005, GSA issued VETS GWAC under Solicitation 6FG2005MTV00001, and it amended the solicitation on seven occasions through July 2005. AR 144–45. GSA described the VETS GWAC as a multiple-award indefinite delivery, indefinite quantity contract limited to service-disabled, veteran-owned vendors and designed to provide "a wide range of information technology support services, while providing the greatest amount of flexibility possible to efficiently and effectively support agency daily operations, protection of infrastructure, the fight against terrorism, and the development and marketing of information technologies." AR 178 (Solicitation §§ C.2). As the "executive agent" for the VETS GWAC, GSA was charged with selecting a pool of eligible awardees who would then compete for task orders issued by individual federal agencies. AR 18 (Business Case), 151, 178, 994 (Solicitation §§ B.1, C.1, C.4). The solicitation indicated that GSA anticipated awarding 20 contracts in each of two separate and distinct functional areas: Functional Area 1 (Systems Operations and Maintenance) and Functional Area 2 (Information Systems Engineering). AR 182–83, 263 (Solicitation §§ C.11.1–C.11.2, L.9). The VETS GWAC proposed a base period of five years and one additional five-year optional period. AR 151 (Solicitation § B.1). Although awardees were guaranteed task orders of at least $2,500, the solicitation warned that "GSA [did] not have projects designated/earmarked for this Contract program and they are not guaranteed to be forthcoming." AR 151–52 (Solicitation §§ B.2–B.3).

GSA first eliminated offers that were incomplete, did not adhere to the solicitation instructions, or included unreasonable pricing. AR 266 (Solicitation §§ M.2–M.3). For offers passing these rudimentary tests, GSA then conducted a trade-off process based on (1) non-price technical merit and (2) price. AR 266 (Solicitation §§ M.3–M.4). GSA evaluated technical merit on the basis of "examples of past performance" by the offerors, plus each offeror's "contract performance plan." *Id.* (Solicitation § M.4). GSA graded an offeror's past performance on a pass-fail basis by reviewing a Dun & Bradstreet evaluation of the offeror's performance of at least six contracts within three years of the original deadline for receipt of offers, June 3, 2005. AR 150 (Solicitation § A), AR 1006–07 (Solicitation § L.2.d.). Each offeror's submitted "contract performance plan" was to explain (1) how the offeror could perform the breadth of the work in each of the numerous listed "work-scope elements" associated with the Functional Area for which the offeror was bidding ("CPP1"), (2) the offeror's depth of experience in each of those "work scope elements" ("CPP2"), and (3) how the offeror could properly manage the limitations on subcontracting requirements ("CPP3"). AR 1008–11 (Solicitation § L.2.e.), 1246 (Executive Summary of VETS GWAC Source Selection (undated)).

* * *

On June 28, 2005, KCI submitted a proposal for Functional Area 1 and another for Functional Area 2. AR 1042–1141 (KCI's Proposal, Functional Area 1), 1143–1244 (KCI's Proposal, Functional Area 2).

* * *

After evaluating 148 proposals for Functional Area 1 and 126 proposals for Functional Area 2, AR 1329 (Trade-off Analysis Documentation, Functional Area 1), 2115 (Trade-off Analysis Documentation, Functional Area 2), GSA selected 43 potential awardees for Functional Area 1 and 36 potential awardees for Functional Area 2. AR 2114 (Trade-off Analysis Documentation, Functional Area 1), 2716 (Trade-off Analysis Documentation, Functional Area 2). The 79 potential awards for both functional areas were projected to go to 45 vendors. AR 2717–22 (Letter from Babcock to Offerors (Aug. 25, 2006)). By letter of August 25, 2006, GSA provided offerors a list of the "apparently successful offerors," which list did not include KCI. *Id.*

* * *

ANALYSIS

* * *

C. OMB's Requirement that GSA not Exclude Offerors for Lack of Government Contract Experience

KCI also alleges that GSA contravened the conditions on the authority OMB granted the agency under its "executive agent" designation by excluding KCI based on its lack of government contract experience. Pl.'s Mot. at 7; *see* AR 93 (Letter from Bolten to Perry, Encl. B (July 5, 2005)). The government denies KCI's allegation, citing the absence of such a restriction in the solicitation and evidence in the administrative record of offerors receiving credit for non-government contract experience. Def.'s Cross-Mot. at 32–36.

* * *

KCI's non-selection was not based on its lack of government contract experience, but rather on its overall lack of breadth of experience as measured under CPP2. KCI was not precluded from citing its experience as a commercial contractor, and KCI and other offerors in fact received credit for such experience. Thus, GSA did not eliminate KCI based on a lack of government contract experience in contravention of OMB's grant of the "executive agent" designation. AR 93 (Letter from Bolten to Perry, Encl. B (July 5, 2005)).

D. CPP2's Monetary Tiering Evaluation Scheme

KCI also argues that the monetary tiering arrangement of CPP2 violated the conditions on OMB's grant of the "executive agent" designation. Pl.'s Resp. to Def.'s Supplemental Br. at 1–2. KCI alleges that KCI and other offerors were excluded because of a lack of "experience in Tiers 1 and 2," the two lower-monetary-value tiers. *Id.* at 2.

CPP2's monetary tiers as applied to each of the numerous work-scope elements raise questions about whether CPP2's evaluation scheme was consistent with Executive Order 13360 and OMB's "executive agent" designation. Executive Order 13360 declared that agencies "shall more effectively implement" certain statutory provisions that set a government-wide goal of three percent for the participation in federal procurement contracts of service-disabled, veteran-owned small businesses and permitted certain set-aside and restricted-competition procurements for such businesses. 69 Fed.Reg. at 62,549; 15 U.S.C. §§ 644(g)(1), 657f. In seeking to implement the executive order, OMB's grant to GSA of the "executive agent" designation provided that awardees be "the most highly qualified service-disabled veteran owned small businesses." AR 93 (Letter from Bolten to Perry, Encl. B (July 5, 2005)).

* * *

CPP2's tiering arrangement coupled with the numerous work-scope elements operated as a significant constraint on the solicitation. Offerors that could have been "the most highly qualified" in some of the work-scope elements, but not in most or all of them, fared less well then those with broad experience. *See* AR 1009–11 (Solicitation § L.2.e.), 1246 (Executive Summary of VETS GWAC Source Selection (undated)). The breadth of experience CPP2 required suggests that GSA preferred offerors that were a mile wide and an inch deep in terms of experience, such that the awardees were simply "qualified" firms across a broad spectrum of information technology areas, rather than a pool of "the most highly qualified" offerors in a narrower class of work-scope elements, as seemingly contemplated by OMB. In short, GSA ostensibly emphasized breadth of experience at the expense of "the most highly qualified" criterion that OMB mandated. In addition, the breadth of experience required by CPP2's high number of work-scope elements—and the likely resulting reduction in the number of awardees—seems inconsistent with the command of Executive Order 13360 that agencies attempt to meet the government-wide goal of three percent for the participation in federal contracts of service-disabled, veteran-owned small businesses. 69 Fed.Reg. at 62,549; 15 U.S.C. § 644(g)(1).

* * *

Certain sections of the solicitation stressed that the VETS GWAC's objective was to provide government agencies with the ability to obtain a broad range of information technology services. *See* AR 152 (Solicitation § B.3) ("requirements may range from simple to highly complex"), 178 (Solicitation § C.2) (VETS GWAC intended "to provide civilian agencies and the Department of Defense (DoD) the ability to obtain a broad range of [c]omprehensive IT support services"), 179 (Solicitation § C.4) ("The anticipated services require a diversity of skills suitable to a multitude of information technology environments in support of a variety of IT support areas."); *see also* AR 142 (Frequently Asked Questions, Question 29) (rigorous evaluation methodology necessary to ensure well-qualified awardees who could perform "the breadth of the work"). The government points to these sections as justification for CPP2's criteria. Def.'s Supplemental Br. at 1–2. However, the solicitation does not tie the objective of selecting broadly qualified awardees to the over-reaching goal of the VETS GWAC and OMB's executive designation. The lack of such linkage in the administrative record precludes this court from determining whether CPP2's focus on experience in multiple monetary tiers for each of the numerous work scope elements was consistent with Executive Order 13360 and OMB's "executive agent" designation.

Remedy

* * *

B. Terms of Remand

* * *

This case accordingly is remanded to GSA to determine whether the large number of work-scope elements and the tiering arrangement specified in CPP2 limited the number of awardees in a way that was inconsistent with Executive Order 13360 or OMB's "executive agent" designation. In making this determination, GSA should address (1) the requirement in Executive Order 13360 that agencies "more effectively implement" Sections 644(g)(1) and 657f of Title 15, which set a government-wide goal of three percent for the participation in federal procurement contracts of service-disabled, veteran-owned small businesses and permitted agencies to establish certain set-aside and restricted-competition procurements for such businesses, 69 Fed.Reg. at 62,549; 15 U.S.C. §§ 644(g)(1), 657f, and (2) the condition that OMB placed on its grant to GSA of the "executive agent" designation for the VETS GWAC: that GSA must select "the most highly qualified service-disabled veteran owned small businesses." AR 93 (Letter from Bolten to Perry, Encl. B (July 5, 2005)).

5. HUBZone

Matter of: Mission Critical Solutions

B-401057, 2009 CPD P 93, 2009 WL 1231855 (Comp.Gen.)
COMPTROLLER GENERAL
May 4, 2009

DIGEST

Protest is sustained where contracting agency did not consider whether two or more qualified Historically Underutilized Business Zone (HUBZone) small businesses could be expected to submit offers and whether award could be made at a fair market price, as required by the HUBZone statute, 15 U.S.C. sect. 657a, prior to deciding to award contract to an Alaska Native Corporation on a sole-source basis.

* * *

BACKGROUND

The agency reports that prior to January 2008, the IT support services at issue here were provided by a large business. In December 2007, the Army notified the Small Business Administration (SBA) that the effort was appropriate for set-aside under SBA's 8(a) program and that it intended to award a sole-source contract to MCS (the protester). SBA accepted the requirement into the 8(a) program and authorized the Army to negotiate directly with MCS. On January 31, 2008, the Army awarded MCS a 1–year contract for approximately $3.45 million.

Near the conclusion of the 1–year period of performance, the Army determined that it would structure the follow-on contract for the services to include a base and 2 option years. Because this raised the anticipated value of the contract to an amount in excess of $3.5 million, a sole-source award to the incumbent contractor was precluded by Federal Acquisition Regulation (FAR) sect. 19.805–1; as relevant here, that provision states that, unless SBA accepts the requirement on behalf of a concern owned by an Indian tribe or an Alaska Native Corporation, an acquisition offered to SBA under the 8(a) program must be awarded on the basis of competition limited to eligible 8(a) firms if (1) there is a reasonable expectation that at least two eligible and responsible 8(a) firms will submit offers and that award can be made at a fair market price, and (2) the anticipated total value of the contract, including options, will exceed $3.5 million (for non-manufacturing acquisitions). The Army then determined that an 8(a) Alaska Native Corporation firm, Copper River Information Technology, LLC, was capable of performing the requirement. On December 17, 2008, the Army notified SBA that, if SBA concurred, it intended to award a contract to Copper River. On December 23, SBA accepted the requirement on behalf of Copper River. The Army awarded a contract to Copper River on January 13, 2009. The protester learned of the award on January 22 and protested to our Office on January 29.

DISCUSSION

The protester challenges the agency's decision to make award on a sole-source basis to Copper River, arguing that the HUBZone statute, 15 U.S.C. sect. 657a (2006), requires that the procurement be set aside for competition among HUBZone small businesses. As explained below, we conclude that it was improper for the agency to proceed with a sole-source award to Copper River without considering whether a set-aside for HUBZone concerns was required.

The HUBZone Program was established by Title VI of the Small Business Reauthorization Act of 1997, Pub. L. No. 105–135, to provide federal contracting assistance to qualified small business concerns located in historically underutilized business zones in an effort to increase employment opportunities, investment, and economic development in those areas. *See* FAR sect. 19.1301(b). Section 602(b)(1)(B) of the Act, 15 U.S.C. sect. 657a, provides that, "notwithstanding any other provision of law," "a contract opportunity *shall* be awarded pursuant to this section on the basis of competition restricted to qualified HUBZone small business concerns if the contracting officer has a reasonable expectation that not less than 2 qualified HUBZone small business concerns will submit offers and that the award can be made at a fair market price." (Emphasis added.) We have interpreted this language to mean that a HUBZone set-aside is mandatory where the enumerated conditions are met. *International Program Group, Inc.,* B–400278, B–400308, Sept. 19, 2008, 2008 CPD para. 172 at ___.

The statutory language authorizing the 8(a) program differs from the language authorizing the HUBZone program in that it gives the contracting agency the discretion to decide whether to offer a contracting opportunity to SBA for the 8(a) program. In this connection, the statute provides in relevant part as follows:

> In any case in which [SBA] certifies to any officer of the Government having procurement powers that [SBA] is competent and responsible to perform any specific Government procurement contract to be let by any such officer, such officer shall be authorized in his discretion to let such procurement contract to [SBA] upon such terms and conditions as may be agreed upon between [SBA] and the procurement officer.

15 U.S.C. sect. 637(a)(1)(A) (2006).

In a case regarding the HUBZone program, the Ninth Circuit distinguished the mandatory language of the HUBZone statute from the discretionary language of the 8(a) statute as follows:

> [A]s the district court noted, "Congress has used the term 'shall' to mandate that certain contracting opportunities be set aside for competition restricted to HUBZone small businesses. With regard to the 8(a) program ... Congress has ... le[ft] to agency discretion the initial offer and acceptance of contracts into the 8(a) Program." [Citation omitted.] The text of the Section 8(a) Program is materially different from that of the HUBZone Program. Accordingly, the discretionary nature of the Section 8(a) Program cannot be imported into the HUBZone Program thereby eliminating the mandatory aspect of the HUBZone Program.

Contract Mgmt. Indus., Inc. v. Rumsfeld, 434 F.3d 1145, 1149 (9th Cir. 2006).[3] Similarly, our Office concluded in *International Program Group, Inc., supra,* that the discretion granted a contracting officer under a program that permits, but does not require, the setting aside of an acquisition for a particular subgroup of small businesses (in that case, the service-disabled veteran-owned (SDVO) small business program) does not supersede the mandatory nature of the HUBZone set-aside program.[4] In view of the mandatory nature of the language in the HUBZone statute, and the discretionary nature of the statutory language authorizing the 8(a) program, we conclude that it was improper for the agency to proceed

---

3. This decision (and the underlying District Court decision discussed in 6, *infra*) concerned a challenge to an agency's decision to set aside a procurement for HUBZone small business concerns rather than small businesses.

4. In its comments on the protest here, SBA argued that "the contracting officer has discretion not necessarily in using the 8(a) program, since that is an initial determination made by the SBA, but in deciding whether the 8(a) participant to be utilized by the SBA is capable of performing," and that "[t]he ultimate discretion as to whether a requirement should be placed in the 8(a) program rests with the Administrator of the SBA[;][t]he Administrator will place a requirement into the 8(a) program when he or she decides it is necessary or appropriate." SBA Comments, Mar. 3, 2009, at 10. We understand SBA to be arguing that the cited excerpt from 15 U.S.C. sect. 637(a)(1)(A) does not give the contracting officer the discretion to decline to place in the 8(a) program a contract that SBA has determined appropriate for performance under the program, and that the only discretion conferred upon the contracting agency by the 8(a) statute is the discretion to reject SBA's nomination of a specific contractor for performance. We do not agree with SBA that the only discretion conferred upon the contracting agency by the 8(a) statute is the discretion to reject SBA's nomination of a particular contractor for performance. In fact, this construction of the statute is at odds with SBA's own regulations, which give SBA the right to appeal to the head of the procuring agency—implying that the ultimate authority rests with the latter official—"[a] contracting officer's decision not to make a particular procurement available for award as an 8(a) contract." 13 C.F.R. sect. 124.505(a)(1). Moreover, even assuming that the ultimate discretion as to whether a requirement should be placed in the 8(a) program rests with the Administrator of SBA, that does not mean that the SBA's discretionary authority under the 8(a) statute supersedes the mandatory aspect of the HUBZone program.

with a sole-source award to Copper River without considering whether a set-aside for HUBZone concerns was required.

We recognize that our conclusion that an agency must make reasonable efforts to determine whether it will receive offers from two or more HUBZone small businesses, and if so, set the acquisition aside for HUBZone firms, even where a prior contract for the requirement has previously been performed by an 8(a) contractor, is inconsistent with the views of SBA, as argued in connection with this protest and as implemented through its regulations. Those regulations essentially provide that HUBZone set-asides are not required even where the criteria specified in 15 U.S.C. sect. 657a(b)(2)(B) are satisfied if the requirement has previously been performed by an 8(a) contractor or the contracting officer has chosen to offer the requirement to the 8(a) program. *See* 13 C.F.R. sections 126.605, 126.606, and 126.607.

* * *

Contrary to the position taken by SBA in its comments on the protest, the contracting agency concedes that "before it recommends a requirement for SBA consideration as a candidate eligible for the 8(a) Program, it must first follow the HUBZone set-aside prescriptive set out in 15 U.S.C. sect. 657a(b)(2)," Agency Report at 7; that is, it must make reasonable efforts to ascertain whether it will receive offers from at least two HUBZone small business concerns. *See International Program Group, Inc., supra,* at 7; *Global Solutions Network, Inc.,* B–292568, Oct. 3, 2003, 2003 CPD para. 174 at 3. The Army asserts, however, that the point at which it was required to investigate whether HUBZone firms could be expected to compete was when the requirement was originally offered to SBA under the 8(a) program (*i.e.,* December 2007), and that any objection by the protester to the agency's failure to investigate therefore should have been raised at that time and is now untimely.

We disagree. The HUBZone statute requires that a "contract opportunity" be awarded on the basis of competition restricted to HUBZone small business concerns when the enumerated conditions are met, and, in our view, a separate "contract opportunity" arises every time an agency prepares to award a new contract. Our view is supported by SBA's regulations, which define a "contract opportunity" as a situation in which "a requirement for a procurement exists." 13 C.F.R. sect. 126.103. Moreover, the SBA regulations governing the award of 8(a) contracts clearly anticipate a reevaluation of the potential for competition, and a decision whether the requirement should continue under the 8(a) program, every time the award of a follow-on contract is contemplated. *See* 13 C.F.R. sect. 124.503(f). Accordingly, given that MCS protested to our Office within 10 days after learning that the contract opportunity at issue here had been awarded to Copper River, we think that its protest is timely.

In sum, because the Army did not consider whether two or more qualified HUBZone small businesses could be expected to submit offers and whether award could be made at a fair market price, as required by the HUBZone statute, prior to deciding to award to Copper River on a sole-source basis, we sustain MCS's protest. We recommend that the agency undertake reasonable efforts to determine whether two or more qualified HUBZone small business concerns will submit offers and whether award can be made at a reasonable price if the contract opportunity is set aside for competition among HUBZone firms. If there is such an expectation, we recommend that the Army terminate the contract awarded to Copper River and resolicit the requirement on the basis of competition restricted to HUBZone small business concerns.

* * *

The protest is sustained.

Chapter 9

Health Care

For pertinent purposes, federal health care contracting law starts with the enactment in 1964 of Medicare, to pay for health care for seniors, and Medicaid, to pay for health care for the poor. As both the role of health care purchasing in the economy has grown, and the role of the government in health care purchasing has grown, federal health care contracting law has come to encompass Medicare, Medicaid, Tricare for military families, VA care for veterans, and other programs.

Congress did not model Medicare and Medicaid on the systems for regular government procurement, but rather on a combination of the income security entitlement systems in the Social Security Act of 1935 and the private-sector mechanisms for health care insurance. Accordingly, the discussion of Medicare and Medicaid below must begin with some fundamental descriptions of these quite different payment systems.

To this day, much of Medicare and Medicaid practice remains a part of health care law without connection to government contracting law generally. However, certain similarities and trends have brought these areas together. At the start in 1964, health care providers contract primarily with individual beneficiaries themselves, provide their services directly to the beneficiaries, and then the beneficiaries submit claims for payment to the government. To the extent that the providers billed the government directly, they did so as assignees of the beneficiaries, not as direct contractors of the government billing the government for what they had provided to the government. This "insurance model" contrasts with regular government contractors who contract with, and provide goods and services directly to, the government, before then submitting claims for payment to the government.

However, over time, more of health care providing takes on a character akin to regular government contractors, with the government paying providers directly, and sometimes contracting with them directly. Moreover, both health care providers and regular government contractors are making claims that the government pays. The dynamic development of False Claims Act law since the 1986 Amendments, by making that Act an important part of both health care contracting law and regular government contracting law, has brought together the law of the two types of "claims" on the government. Since the False Claims Act applies equivalently to fraud by health care providers and regular government contractors, it spawns a uniform law of federal procurement fraud applicable to both.

And, Medicare and Medicaid originally began as systems for reimbursement of privately set fees. However, as health care costs soared from 1965 to the 1990s, health care contracting law developed mechanisms for government administrators to restrict prices. This meant more intense administrative review of provider claims. In this way, the health care claims-processing system developed limited, but important, resemblances to classic government contract administration.

For further discussion of the issues of this chapter, see the citations for the particular subchapters, and see: James W. Kim, *The Past, Present And Future Of Government Contracting*

In Healthcare, 19 Annals Health L. 141 (2010); Julie Kristen Lappas, *Changing Horses In The Middle Of The Stream: The Medicare Part D Bidding Process And It Effect On The Stability Of Dual-Eligible Beneficiaries*, 38 Pub. Cont. L.J. 487 (Winter 2009); Devin S. Schindler, *Pay for Performance, Quality of Care and the Revitalization of the False Claims Act*, 19 Health Matrix 387 (2009); John T. Brennan, Jr. & Michael W. Paddock, *Limitations on the Use of the False Claims Act to Enforce Quality of Care Standards*, 2 J. Health & Life Sci. L. 37 (2008); John M. Degnan & Sally A. Scoggin, *Avoiding Health Care Qui Tam Actions*, 74 DEF. COUNS. J. 385 (2007); Leon Aussprung, *Fraud and Abuse: Federal Civil Health Care Litigation and Settlement*, 19 J. Legal Med. 1 (1998); John R. Munich, *The Medicaid Anti-Fraud Amendments of 1994: Attorney General's Newest Weapon in the Fight Against White Collar Crime*, 52 J. Mo. B. 26 (1996); Pamela H. Bucy, *Crimes by Health Care Providers*, 1996 U. Ill. L. Rev. 589 (1996); Cathy L. Naugle, *How to Recognize a Health Care Fraud Case Before They Serve the Search Warrant!* 40-FEB Advocate (Idaho) 15 (1997).

A. Medicare: Physician (Including Prescriptions)

To describe in a highly simplified way, Congress established the Medicare program by Title XVIII of the Social Security Act, enacted in 1965 and codified at 42 U.S.C. sec. 1395 et seq. Medicare pays for health care for seniors by its two distinct parts: Part A for inpatient hospital care and Part B for physician care. For this book's purposes, we may disregard the eligibility, coverage, benefits, financing, and numerous other aspects of Medicare, and focus on its payment of provider claims. For fuller treatment of Medicare subjects generally, see Barry R. Furrow, Thomas L. Greaney, Sandra H. Johnson, Timothy Jost, & Robert L. Schwartz, Health Law (1995); Rand E. Rosenblatt, Sylvia S. Law, Sara Rosenbaum, Law and the American Health System (1997); Charles Tiefer, *Treatment for Medicare's Budget: Quick Operation or Long-Term Care?*, 16 St. Louis U. Pub. L. Rev. 27 (1996).

The Health Care Finance Administration ("HCFA") of the Department of Health and Human Services administers the Medicare program. HCFA promulgates extensive regulations, codified at 42 C.F.R. Parts 405–424, and 482–498, and also issues key manuals and instructions. The most important of the manuals are the Provider Reimbursement Manual, the Intermediary Manual, and the Carriers Manual. As the Supreme Court's *Guernsey* opinion below makes clear, when Medicare claims issues reach the courts, the courts analyze these regulations and manuals much as, in regular government contract claims cases, they analyze the regulations and manuals of the contracting departments.

Given the enormous scale of the program, HCFA could not process the claims itself. Rather, it delegates the processing and paying of claims to Medicare Part A "fiscal intermediaries" and Medicare Part B "carriers." These are private entities, often Blue Cross or Blue Shield associations, under contract with the Secretary of HHS. For Part A providers to receive payment, they must meet conditions of participation and enter into a contract called a provider agreement. Part B providers must meet conditions of coverage. As with regular government contracting law, a large part of the legally significant contract interaction between claimants and the government consists of submissions of the basis for the claim on government-prescribed forms. The forms serve as the government-directed embodiment of the government contracting law in statutes and regulations and, for Medicare, of the conditions of participation or coverage.

Physicians commonly submit their claims on HCFA form, "HCFA 1500." The *Krizek* case brings together some of the essentials linking and differentiating claims payment under government contract law, and under health care contracting law: the unifying law of the False Claims Act; the centrality of legal analysis of the fundamental unit, the "claim"; and the respective roles assigned by Medicare's mechanism for claims payment to HCFA, the carrier, and the provider.

For further discussions of health care contracting, particularly the recent emerging law of health care fraud, see: Edward Vishnevetsky & John Browning, *How Durable a Program? A Look at the Past, Present, and Future of Competitive Bidding and Durable Medical Equipment*, 22 Health Law, April 2010, at 14; Joan H. Krause, *"Promises to Keep": Health Care Providers and the Civil False Claims Act*," 23 Cardozo L. Rev. 1363 (2002); Joan H. Krause, *Health Care Providers and the Public Fisc: Paradigms of Government Harm Under the Civil False Claims Act*, 36 Ga. L. Rev. 121 (2001); Charles Tiefer & Heather Akehurst-Krause, *Risky Business: Medicare's Vulnerability to Selection Games of Managed Care Providers*, 28 U. Balt. L. Rev. 319 (1999); Aaron M. Altschuler, Sarah Henley Kanwit, Theodore L. Radway, *Health Care Fraud*, 35 Am. Crim. L. Rev. 841 (1998). Jeffrey A. Lovitky, *Medicare/Medicaid Fraud: A Growing Area of Concern for Health Care Providers*, 76 Mich. B.J. 308 (1997). Kaz Kikkawa, Note, *Medicare Fraud and Abuse and Qui Tam: The Dynamic Duo or the Odd Couple?* 8 Health Matrix 83 (1998).

United States of America, Appellant/Cross-Appellee v. George O. Krizek, M.D., et al., Appellees/Cross-Appellants

Nos. 96-5045, 96-5046
United States Court of Appeals, District of Columbia Circuit
111 F.2d 934
Decided May 2, 1997

Before: SILBERMAN, GINSBURG and SENTELLE, Circuit Judges. Opinion for the court filed by Circuit Judge SENTELLE.

SENTELLE, Circuit Judge.

This appeal arises from a civil suit brought by the government against a psychiatrist and his wife under the civil False Claims Act ("FCA"), 31 U.S.C. §§ 3729–3731, and under the common law. The District Court found defendants liable for knowingly submitting false claims and entered judgment against defendants for $168,105.39. The government appealed, and the defendants filed a cross-appeal. We hold that the District Court erred and remand for further proceedings.

I.

The government filed suit against George and Blanka Krizek for, inter alia, violations of the civil FCA, 31 U.S.C. §§ 3729–3731. Dr. George Krizek is a psychiatrist who practiced medicine in the District of Columbia. His wife, Blanka Krizek, worked in Dr. Krizek's practice and maintained his billing records. At issue are reimbursement forms submitted by the Krizeks to Pennsylvania Blue Shield ("PBS") in connection with Dr. Krizek's treatment of Medicare and Medicaid patients. The government's complaint alleged that between January 1986 and March 1992 Dr. Krizek submitted 8,002 false or unlawful requests for reimbursement in an amount exceeding $245,392. The complaint alleged two different types of false claims: first, some of the services provided by Dr. Krizek were medically unnecessary; and second, the Krizeks "upcoded" the reimbursement requests, that is billed the government for more extensive treatments than were, in fact, rendered.

A doctor providing services to a Medicare or Medicaid recipient submits a claim for reimbursement to a Medicare carrier, in this case PBS, on a form known as the "HCFA 1500." The HCFA 1500 requires the doctor to provide his identification number, the patient's information, and a five-digit code identifying the services for which reimbursement is sought. . . .

Procedures Terminology Manual ("CPT"). For instance, the Manual notes that the CPT code "90844" is used to request reimbursement for an individual medical psychotherapy session lasting approximately 45 to 50 minutes. The CPT code "90843" indicates individual medical psychotherapy for 20 to 30 minutes. An HCFA 1500 lists those services provided to a single patient, and may include a number of CPT codes when the patient has been treated over several days or weeks.

Before the District Court, the government argued that the amount of time specified by the CPT for each reimbursement code indicates the amount of time spent "face-to-face" with the patient. The government focused on the Krizeks' extensive use of the 90844 code. According to the government, this code should be used only when the doctor spends 45 to 50 minutes with the patient, not including time spent on the phone in consultation with other doctors or time spent discussing the patient with a nurse. The government argued that the Krizeks had used the 90844 code when they should have been billing for shorter, less-involved treatments.

Based on its claims of unnecessary treatment and up-coding the government sought an extraordinary $81 million in damages. This amount included $245,392 in actual damages and civil penalties of $10,000 for each of 8,002 separate CPT codes. During a three-week bench trial, the District Court determined that the case would initially be tried on the basis of seven patients which the government described as representative of the Krizeks' improper coding and treatment practices. United States v. Krizek, No. 93-0054 (D.D.C. March 9, 1994) (Protective Order). The determination of liability would then "be equally applicable to all other claims." Id. On July 19, 1994, the District Court issued a Memorandum Opinion, United States v. Krizek, 859 F.Supp. 5, 8 (D.D.C.1994) [hereinafter Krizek I], holding that the government had not established that the Krizeks submitted claims for unnecessary services. The Court noted that the government's witness failed to interview the patients or any doctors or nurses. Id. The District Court also rejected the government's theory that the Krizeks were liable for requesting reimbursement when some of the billed time was spent out of the presence of the patient. Id. at 10. The Court found that it was common and proper practice among psychiatrists to bill for time spent reviewing files, speaking with consulting physicians, etc. Id.

Despite having rejected the government's arguments on these claims, the Court determined that the Krizeks knowingly made false claims in violation of the FCA. Id. at 13. The Court found that because of a "seriously deficient" system of recordkeeping the Krizeks "submitted bills for 45–50 minute psychotherapy sessions . . . when Dr. Krizek could not have spent the requisite time providing services, face-to-face, or otherwise." Id. at 11, 12. For instance, on some occasions within the seven-patient sample, Dr. Krizek submitted claims for over 21 hours of patient treatment within a 24-hour period. Id. at 12. The Court stated, "While Dr. Krizek may have been a tireless worker, it is difficult for the Court to comprehend how he could have spent more than even ten hours in a single day serving patients." Id. The Court stated that these false statements were not "mistakes" nor merely negligent conduct. Under the statutory definition of "knowing" conduct the Court is compelled to conclude that the defendants acted with reckless disregard as to the truth or falsity of the submissions. As such, they will be deemed to have violated the False Claims Act. Id. at 13–14.

Having found the Krizeks liable within the seven-patient sample, the Court attempted to craft a device for applying the determination of liability to the entire universe of claims. Here, the District Court relied on the testimony of a defense witness that he could not recall submitting more than twelve 90844 codes—nine hours worth of patient treatment—for a single day. Id. at 12. Based on this testimony, the District Court stated that nine hours per day was "a fair and reasonably accurate assessment of the time Dr. Krizek actually spent providing patient services." Id. The Court, accordingly, determined that the Krizeks would be liable under the FCA on every day in which claims were submitted in excess of the equivalent of twelve (12) 90844 claims (nine patient-treatment hours) in a single day and where the defendants cannot establish that Dr. Krizek legitimately devoted the claimed amount of time to patient care on the day in question. Id. at 14. On April 6, 1995, the District Court, with the consent of the parties, referred the matter to a Special Master with instructions to investigate the 8,002 challenged CPT codes and, applying the nine-hour presumption, to determine 1) the single damages owed by the Krizeks; 2) the amount of the single damages trebled; 3) the number of false claims submitted by defendants; and 4) the number of false claims multiplied by $5000. United States v. Krizek, No. 93-0054 (D.D.C. April 6, 1995) (Order of Reference). After considering evidence submitted by the parties, the Special Master determined that the defendants requested reimbursement for more than nine hours per day of patient treatment on 264 days. United States v. Krizek, No. 93-0054, at 15 (D.D.C. June 6, 1995) (Special Master Report). The Special Master found single damages of $47,105.39, which when trebled totaled $141,316.17. He then determined to treat each of the 1,149 false code entries as a separate claim, even where several codes were entered on the same HCFA 1500. Multiplied by $5000 per false claim, this approach produced civil penalties of $5,745,000. After considering motions by the parties, the District Court issued a second opinion, United States v. Krizek, 909 F.Supp. 32 (D.D.C.1995) [hereinafter Krizek II], which modified its earlier decision. The Court stated that it accepted the Special Master's factual findings, id. at 33, but was applying a different approach in calculating damages. First, the Court awarded damages of $47,105.38 to the government for unjust enrichment based on the nine-hour presumption. Id. at 33. The Court then stated:

> While the Court set a nine hour benchmark to determine which claims were improper, the Court will now set an even higher benchmark for classifying claims that fall under the False Claims Act so that there can be no question as to the falsity of the claims. The Court has determined that the False Claims Act has been violated where claims have been made totaling in excess of twenty-four hours within a single twenty-four hour period and where defendants have provided no explanation for justifying claims made for services rendered virtually around the clock.

Id. at 34. Claims in excess of twenty-four hours of patient treatment per day had been made eleven times in the six-year period. Id. The Court assessed fines of $10,000 for each of the eleven false claims, which, combined with single damages of $47,105.39, totaled $157,105.39. Id. The Court also assessed Special Master's fees against the Krizeks in the amount of $11,000. Id. The government appealed, and the Krizeks cross-appealed. We first turn to the government's appeal.

* * *

III.

The Krizeks cross-appeal on the grounds that the District Court erroneously treated each CPT code as a separate "claim" for purposes of computing civil penalties. The Krizeks assert that the claim, in this context, is the HCFA 1500 even when the form contains a number of CPT codes.

The FCA defines "claim" to

> include any request or demand, whether under a contract or otherwise, for money or property which is made to a contractor, grantee, or other recipient if the United States Government provides any portion of the money or property which is requested or demanded, or if the Government will reimburse such contractor, grantee, or other recipient for any portion of the money or property which is requested or demanded.

31 U.S.C. § 3729(c). Whether a defendant has made one false claim or many is a fact-bound inquiry that focuses on the specific conduct of the defendant. In United States v. Bornstein, 423 U.S. 303, 307, 96 S.Ct. 523, 527, 46 L.Ed.2d 514 (1976), for instance, the Supreme Court considered the liability of a subcontractor who delivered 21 boxes of falsely labeled electron tubes to the prime contractor in three separate shipments. The prime contractor, in turn, delivered 397 of these tubes to the government and billed the government using 35 invoices. The trial court awarded 35 statutory forfeitures against the subcontractor, one for each invoice. The Court of Appeals reversed, holding that there was only one forfeiture because there had been only one contract. The Supreme Court disagreed with both positions and held that there had been three false claims by the subcontractor, one for each shipment of falsely labeled tubes. Id. at 313, 96 S.Ct. at 529–30. The Court stated, "[T]he focus in each case [must] be upon the specific conduct of the person from whom the Government seeks to collect the statutory forfeitures." Id. Because the subcontractor committed three separate causative acts—dispatching each shipment of the falsely marked tubes—it would be liable for three separate forfeitures. Id.; see also United States ex rel. Marcus v. Hess, 317 U.S. 537, 552, 63 S.Ct. 379, 388, 87 L.Ed. 443 (1943) (holding that the government was entitled to a forfeiture for each project for which a collusive bid was entered even though the bids included additional false forms); United States v. Grannis, 172 F.2d 507, 515 (4th Cir.) (assessing ten forfeitures against defendant for each of ten fraudulent vouchers even though the vouchers listed 130 items), cert. denied, 337 U.S. 918, 69 S.Ct. 1160, 93 L.Ed. 1727 (1949).

* * *

The gravamen of these cases is that the focus is on the conduct of the defendant. The Courts asks, "With what act did the defendant submit his demand or request and how many such acts were there?" In this case, the Special Master adopted a position that is inconsistent with this approach. He stated,

> The CPT code, not the HCFA 1500 form, is the source used to permit federal authorities to verify and account for discrete units of medical service provided, billed and paid for. In sum, the government has demanded a specific accounting unit to identify and verify the services provided, payments requested and amounts paid under the Medicare/Medicaid program. The CPT code, not the HCFA 1500 form, is that basic accounting unit.

United States v. Krizek, No. 93-0054, at 21 (D.D.C. June 6, 1995) (Special Master Report). The Special Master concluded that because the government used the CPT code in processing the claims, the CPT code, and not the HCFA 1500 in its entirety, must be the claim. This conclusion, which was later adopted by the District Court, misses the point. The question turns, not on how the government chooses to process the claim, but on how many times the defendants made a "request or demand." 31 U.S.C. s 3729(c). In this case, the Krizeks made a request or demand every time they submitted an HCFA 1500. Our conclusion that the claim in this context is the HCFA 1500 form is supported by the structure of the form itself. The medical provider is asked to supply, along with the CPT codes, the date and place of service, a description of the procedures, a diagnosis code, and the charges. The charges are then totaled to produce one request or demand—line 27 asks for total charges, line 28 for amount paid, and line 29 for balance due. The CPT codes function in this context as a type of invoice used to explain how the defendant computed his request or demand. The government contends that fairness or uniformity concerns support treating each CPT code as a separate claim, arguing that "[t]o count woodenly the number of HCFA 1500 forms submitted by the Krizeks would cede to medical practitioners full authority to control exposure to [FCA] simply by structuring their billings in a particular manner." Precisely so. It is conduct of the medical practitioner, not the disposition of the claims by the government, that creates FCA liability. See Alsco-Harvard Fraud Litigation, 523 F.Supp. 790, 811 (D.D.C.1981) (remanding for determination whether invoices were presented for payment at one time or individually submitted as separate demands for payment). Moreover, even if we considered fairness to be a relevant consideration in statutory construction, we would note that the government's definition of claim permitted it to seek an astronomical $81 million worth of damages for alleged actual damages of $245,392. We therefore remand for recalculation of the civil penalty.

* * *

Having determined that liability was properly determined by the seven-patient sample, we turn now to the question whether, in considering the sample, the District Court applied the appropriate level of scienter. The FCA imposes liability on an individual who "knowingly presents" a "false or fraudulent claim." 31 U.S.C. § 3729(a). A person acts "knowingly" if he: (1) has actual knowledge of the information; (2) acts in deliberate ignorance of the truth or falsity of the information; or (3) acts in reckless disregard of the truth or falsity of the information, and no proof of specific intent to defraud is required. 31 U.S.C. § 3729(b). The Krizeks assert that the District Court impermissibly applied the FCA by permitting an aggravated form of gross negligence, "gross negligence-plus," to satisfy the Act's scienter requirement. In Saba v. Compagnie Nationale Air France, 78 F.3d 664 (D.C.Cir.1996), we considered whether reckless disregard was the equivalent of willful misconduct for purposes of the Warsaw Convention. We noted that reckless disregard lies on a continuum between gross negligence and intentional harm. Id. at 668. In some cases, recklessness serves as a proxy for forbidden intent. Id. (citing SEC v. Steadman, 967 F.2d 636, 641 (D.C.Cir.1992)). Such cases require a showing that the defendant engaged in an act known to cause or likely to cause the injury. Id. at 669. Use of reckless disregard as a substitute for the forbidden intent prevents the defendant from "deliberately blind[ing] himself to the consequences of his tortious action." Id. at 668. In another category of cases, we noted, reckless disregard is "simply a linear extension of gross negligence, a palpable failure to meet the appropriate standard of care." Id. In Saba, we determined that in the context of the Warsaw Convention, a showing of willful misconduct might be made by establishing reckless disregard such that the subjective intent of the defendant could be inferred. Id. at 669.

The question, therefore, is whether "reckless disregard" in this context is properly equated with willful misconduct or with aggravated gross negligence. In determining that gross negligence-plus was sufficient, the District Court cited legislative history equating reckless disregard with gross negligence. A sponsor of the 1986 amendments to the FCA stated,

> Subsection 3 of Section 3729(c) uses the term "reckless disregard of the truth or falsity of the information" which is no different than and has the same meaning

as a gross negligence standard that has been applied in other cases. While the Act was not intended to apply to mere negligence, it is intended to apply in situations that could be considered gross negligence where the submitted claims to the Government are prepared in such a sloppy or unsupervised fashion that resulted in overcharges to the Government. The Act is also intended not to permit artful defense counsel to require some form of intent as an essential ingredient of proof. This section is intended to reach the "ostrich-with-his-head-in-the-sand" problem where government contractors hide behind the fact they were not personally aware that such overcharges may have occurred. This is not a new standard but clarifies what has always been the standard of knowledge required.

132 Cong. Rec. H9382-03 (daily ed. Oct. 7, 1986) (statement of Rep. Berman). While we are not inclined to view isolated statements in the legislative history as dispositive, we agree with the thrust of this statement that the best reading of the Act defines reckless disregard as an extension of gross negligence. Section 3729(b)(2) of the Act provides liability for false statements made with deliberate ignorance. If the reckless disregard standard of section 3729(b)(3) served merely as a substitute for willful misconduct — to prevent the defendant from "deliberately blind[ing] himself to the consequences of his tortious action" — section (b)(3) would be redundant since section (b)(2) already covers such struthious conduct. See Kungys v. United States, 485 U.S. 759, 778, 108 S.Ct. 1537, 1550, 99 L.Ed.2d 839 (1988) (citing the "cardinal rule of statutory interpretation that no provision should be construed to be entirely redundant"). Moreover, as the statute explicitly states that specific intent is not required, it is logical to conclude that reckless disregard in this context is not a "lesser form of intent," see Steadman, 967 F.2d at 641–42, but an extreme version of ordinary negligence.

* * *

We are also unpersuaded by the Krizeks' argument that their conduct did not rise to the level of reckless disregard. The District Court cited a number of factors supporting its conclusion: Mrs. Krizek completed the submissions with little or no factual basis; she made no effort to establish how much time Dr. Krizek spent with any particular patient; and Dr. Krizek "failed utterly" to review bills submitted on his behalf. Krizek I, 859 F.Supp. at 13. Most tellingly, there were a number of days within the seven-patient sample when even the shoddiest recordkeeping would have revealed that false submissions were being made — those days on which the Krizeks' billing approached twenty-four hours in a single day. On August 31, 1985, for instance, the Krizeks requested reimbursement for patient treatment using the 90844 code thirty times and the 90843 code once, indicating patient treatment of over 22 hours. Id. at 12. Outside the seven-patient sample the Krizeks billed for more than twenty-four hours in a single day on three separate occasions. Krizek II, 909 F.Supp. at 34. These factors amply support the District Court's determination that the Krizeks acted with reckless disregard. Finally, we note that Dr. Krizek is no less liable than his wife for these false submissions. As noted, an FCA violation may be established without reference to the subjective intent of the defendant. Dr. Krizek delegated to his wife authority to submit claims on his behalf. In failing "utterly" to review the false submissions, he acted with reckless disregard.

Notes and Questions

1. The reader may find some of *Krizek* a challenge when reading it apart from the chapter on the False Claims Act. When reading the case just for its place in this chapter (rather than as another False Claims Act case), simply note the common applicability of the False Claims Act to (1) the health care services rendered by Dr. Krizek to Medicare

and Medicaid patients, and to (2) regular government contracting. This serves to create a unifying bond between those two systems of government payment of "claims" for contractually-provided services. Of course, the text of the False Claims Act applies to both types of "claims." Note, in addition, that the case law for each type of "claim" applies to the other. For example, the *Krizek* opinion relies upon such classic Supreme Court opinions applying the False Claims Act to regular government contracting as United States ex rel. Marcus v. Hess, 317 U.S. 537 (1943), and United States v. Bornstein, 423 U.S. 303 (1976).

What does this unifying bond of the nature of the "claim" and the protections of the Treasury against fraud tell about the deep structure of government contract law? If you were to describe to a interested layperson (assuming there were such a person) the fundamentals of government contracting, would you start with how "claims" are submitted and paid, or would you start elsewhere: with how the contracting officer supervises the systems for competitive acquisition, contract administration, disputes and termination? There is a law of the federal fisc even more fundamental than the law of what contracting officers do. Think back to where Chapter 1 of this casebook started: with the essential doctrines unique to (public) government contract law and differentiating it from basic (private) contract law, such as the lack of estoppel against the government and the limited authority of government agents. Those fundamental doctrines arise from the limitations under the Constitution and its implementing statutory system on payments out of the Treasury with no meaningful parallel in basic (private) contracting. The law of "claims" and fraud similarly arises from that fundamental law of the federal fisc. It is that special public law regarding controls on payments out of the public Treasury that unifies regular government contracting law and health care contracting law.

2. What do you think of the defenses argued by Dr. Krizek, who readers of this opinion have nicknamed the "24 hour doctor"? Does his talk of leaving the billing to someone else (in this case, his wife) seem to you fanciful? Defense arguments look one way when viewed with a focus on the extreme case of the physician who bills for more than 24 hours in a day. However, the law established in this case applies to the non-extreme cases, namely, the countless health care providers who would vastly prefer to devote their time, skill, and attention to health care rather than to government contracting law. Do we really expect to obtain maximum compliance with the rules of health care contracting by the brute-force method of threatening them with $10,000 statutory penalties for miscoding?

In regular government contracting, most of control on the contractor comes not from fraud law, but from contracting officer supervision as the contractors do their work and make their deliveries. However, the government does not come into the health care picture until after the work is done and "delivered," at the late stage of claims payment. Can fraud case law substitute as a control for the entire regular government contracting apparatus of contracting officer supervision?

3. How many different arguments on each side regarding the "$81 million question," whether the claim is the item of coded medical service, or the entire HCFA 1500 form can you tease apart?

4. How many different argument on each side can you tease apart about the scienter level for which the statute says the standard is "reckless disregard?"

5. For a discussion of Medicare contracting with another set of contractors to ferret out fraud and abuse, see Richard J. Webber, *Medicare Integrity Program: Health Care Financing Administration Readies Its First Competitive Solicitation*, 33 Procurement Lawyer, Spring 1998, at 3.

Incident to services

Medicare allows the services of non-physicians (example: nurse practitioners and physicians assistants) to be billed incident to the services of a physician. This means that non-physicians services are billed as if a physician performed the service. The physician must perform an initial service for the patient. After the initial service sufficient subsequent services must be performed to reflect the doctor's active participation in the course of treatment.

For a service to be incident to the service of a physician the service must: (1) an integral, although incidental, part of the physician's professional services; (2) commonly rendered without charge or included in the physician's bill; (3) commonly performed in the physician's offices or clinics; and (4) furnished under the physician's direct supervision.

The direct supervision requirement of Medicare has been defined not to require a physician's presence in the same room that treatment has been rendered. Direct supervision does require that a physician is in the office suite and is immediately available.

For a further discussion of Medicare's incident to services see: Claudia Brett Goldin & Wallis S. Stromberg, *Who is Helping the Doctor: Physicians' Delegation of Medical Services*, 32-DEC CoLo. LAW. 81 (2003); Georgette Gustin, *Allied Health Professionals Should Provide Only Those Services That are Within Their Scope of Practice*, 9 No. 3 J. HEALTH CARE COMPLIANCE 23 (2007); Susan Corcoran, *To Become a Midwife: Reducing Legal Barriers to Entry into The Midwifery Profession*, 80 Wash. U. L. Q. 649 (2002); Thomas A. Scully, *ABA Health Law Section Comments to Stark II, Phase I*, 2001 HEALTH LAW. 3 (2001).

United States, ex rel., Plaintiff, Karyn L. Walker, a.k.a. Karyn L. Denk-Walker, Plaintiff-Appellant Cross-Appellee, v. R&F Properties of Lake County, Inc., A Florida Professional Association, Defendant-Appellee Cross-Appellant

United States Court of Appeals, Eleventh Circuit
433 F.3d 1349 (2005)

COX, Circuit Judge:

Plaintiff Karyn L. Walker is a qui tam relator , seeking recovery on behalf of the United States pursuant to the False Claims Act, 31 U.S.C. § 3729. Walker appeals a summary judgment granted to Defendant R&F Properties of Lake County, Inc., formerly known as Leesburg Family Medicine, (LFM)....

We conclude that the district court erred in holding that Walker had not produced sufficient evidence of the falsity of the claims submitted by LFM to resist summary judgment....

I. BACKGROUND & PROCEDURAL HISTORY

The Medicare Program is a system of health insurance administered by the United States Department of Health and Human Services, through the Center for Medicare and Medicaid Services (CMS). CMS was formerly known as the Health Care Financing Administration (HCFA). Medicare Part B is a federally subsidized, voluntary health insurance program that pays a portion of the costs of certain health services, including the costs of clinic visits to healthcare providers (among them, physicians, physician assistants, and nurse practitioners). Reimbursement for Medicare Part B claims is made through CMS, which contracts with private insurance carriers throughout the United States to administer and pay claims within their regions from the Medicare Trust Fund. These insurance carriers are known as Fiscal Intermediaries, or FIs. In general, when a healthcare service is rendered to a patient covered by Medicare Part B, the healthcare provider bills Medicare/CMS through the FI. The FI reviews the bill and pays the healthcare provider. CMS publishes a series of manuals that provide billing and payment instructions to the Medicare community. Among these manuals are the Medicare Carrier's Manual, directed to the FIs, and the Provider Reimbursement Manual, directed to healthcare providers.

... Many, if not most, of LFM's patients are covered by Medicare Part B. LFM submits claims for Medicare reimbursement for healthcare services rendered by physicians, physician assistants and nurse practitioners to its FI, Blue Cross Blue Shield of Florida, pursuant to a contract between LFM and Blue Cross Blue Shield....

* * *

Healthcare providers may bill Medicare Part B for the services of physician assistants and nurse practitioners in one of two ways; the amount of reimbursement the providers receive is dependent on the billing method. Physician assistant or nurse practitioner services may be billed as services "incident to the service of a physician." 42 CFR §§ 410.10, 410.26. To be correctly billed in this manner, the physician assistant or nurse practitioner services must have been provided under certain circumstances. When physician assistant or nurse practitioner services are billed as "incident to the service of a physician," the physician's Unique Provider Identification Number (UPIN) is used on the bill submitted to the FI. Alternatively, a provider may bill Medicare for physician assistant and nurse practitioner services under the physician assistant's or nurse practitioner's own UPIN. Billing Medicare in this second way indicates that the physician assistant or nurse practitioner has performed the service under some level of supervision by a physician, but the requirements of 42 CFR § 410.26 have not necessarily been met. For services billed under a physician assistant's or nurse practitioner's UPIN, the FI pays 85% of what it would pay for the same services billed under a physician's UPIN.

* * *

Effective January 1, 2002, 42 CFR § 410.26 was amended to read, in relevant part:(b) Medicare Part B pays for services and supplies incident to the service of a physician (or other practitioner).... (5) Services and supplies must be furnished under the direct supervision of the physician (or other practitioner)....

* * *

Walker worked for LFM from February 1997 until May 1999 as a nurse practitioner. During that time, there were many occasions when she saw patients independently without physician supervision. Physicians were not always physically present in the LFM clinic while Walker and other nurse practitioners and physician assistants saw patients, but physicians were always available for consultation by pager and telephone.

* * *

V. DISCUSSION

* * *

A. The Grant of Summary Judgment

In this case, the district court granted summary judgment for LFM because it found that, as a matter of law, Walker's complaint and evidence did not present the possibility of a false or fraudulent claim. As stated above, the district court found that the regulatory language that Walker claimed was violated when LFM submitted its claims was ambiguous and therefore could not, as a matter of law, serve as the predicate for a false claims action. We find error in the district court's reasoning.

First, we note that the district court granted LFM summary judgment on Walker's entire complaint even though a subset of the claims alleged by Walker were allegedly submitted after the Medicare regulation had been amended and clarified. See supra n. 1. As of January 1, 2002 (four months before Walker filed her original complaint in this case), the regulation providing conditions for coverage of services rendered "incident to the service of a physician" was clear about the meaning of that phrase. As of that date, all services billed as "incident to the services of a physician" must have been rendered under a physician's "direct supervision." 42 CFR § 410.26(b)(5) (2002). In order to satisfy this "direct supervision" requirement, "the physician must [have been] present in the office suite and immediately available to furnish assistance and direction throughout the performance of the procedure." 42 CFR § 410.26(a)(2) (2002), 410.32(b)(3)(ii) (2002). This regulatory language unambiguously requires that a physician be present in the office....

Medicare claims may be false if they claim reimbursement for services or costs that either are not reimbursable or were not rendered as claimed.... Given the clear definition of services rendered "incident to the service of a physician" that became effective January 1, 2002, Walker should be permitted to present evidence to a fact-finder supporting her allegations that any Medicare claims LFM submitted from January 1, 2002 until the date of her complaint for services of nurse practitioners or physician assistants "incident to the service of a physician," were not, in fact, rendered in compliance with the applicable Medicare regulation and, therefore, were false. An issue of fact also exists as to whether LFM physician certifications on the HCFA 1500 forms submitted from January 1, 2002 until the date of Walker's complaint were false.

Additionally, the district court erred by holding that any ambiguity in the earlier version of 42 CFR § 410.26 and the HCFA 1500 certification necessarily forecloses, as a matter of law, the falsity of claims submitted by LFM prior to January 1, 2002. We agree that the regulatory language in effect until January 1, 2002 was ambiguous. But we disagree as to the legal significance of that ambiguity. In opposition to LFM's motion for summary judgment, Walker submitted provisions from the Medicare Carrier's Manual, Medicare bulletins, seminar programs, and expert testimony regarding proper billing "incident to the service of a physician," as used in 42 CFR § 410.26. She also presented two notes written by LFM's employee that paraphrase a billing consultant's advice. All of these sources were offered to show the meaning of the language in the regulation and on the HCFA 1500 form and the reasonableness of LFM's claimed understanding of that language. At least some of these sources would support a finding that, in the Medicare community, the language was understood to mean that a physician had to be physically present in the office suite and otherwise more involved in a patient's course of care than the LFM physicians were. The district court considered this evidence irrelevant and held that, because none of it held the force of law, it could not be the basis for a false claim.

As the district court recognized, the Supreme Court has stated that agency interpretations contained in policy statements, manuals, and enforcement guidelines are not entitled to the force of law.... For that reason, we agree with the district court that evidence of a defendant's failure to comply with an administrative guideline does not necessarily establish that the defendant presented legally false claims—claims in violation of a statute or regulation—to the United States. But that is not the issue here. What is at issue is whether any evidence outside the language of a Medicare regulation (including guidance issued by the governmental agency charged with administering the regulatory scheme) can be consulted to understand the meaning of that regulation. We hold that it can.

The Supreme Court has held that agency interpretations are "entitled to respect ... to the extent that those interpretations have the power to persuade." ... Indeed, we have followed this rule in the context of Medicare false claims cases. In affirming a criminal false claims conviction, this court looked to a manual published by HCFA to determine the meaning of a Medicare regulation and establish the falsity of the defendant's claims for Medicare reimbursement.... The fact that the Medicare Carrier's Manual was not issued to Defendants does not negate its probative value regarding the meaning of a Medicare regulation....

In a case remarkably similar to this one, the Eighth Circuit recently held, "If a statement alleged to be false is ambiguous, the government (or here, the relator) must establish the defendant's knowledge of the falsity of the statement, which it can do by introducing evidence of how the statement would have been understood in context." Minnesota Assoc. of Nurse Anesthetists v. Allina Health System Corp., 276 F.3d 1032, 1053 (8th Cir.2002) (emphasis added). In the Minnesota case, the relator alleged that anesthesiologists billed Medicare as if they had "personally performed" an entire anesthesia case or were "continuously involved" in the performance of that case when, in fact, they were not continuously present during the case and were instead simultaneously engaged in other activities. Id. at 1037, 1038. A district court granted the defendants summary judgment because the court considered the Medicare regulation's phrases "personally performed" and "continuously involved" to be ambiguous. Id. at 1052–1053. The Eighth Circuit reversed, stating, "If the [relator] shows the defendants certified compliance with the regulation knowing that the HCFA interpreted the regulations in a certain way and that their actions did not satisfy the requirements of the regulation as the HCFA interpreted it, any possible ambiguity of the regulations is water under the bridge." Id. at 1053. The Eighth Circuit found that evidence presented by the relator (including the defendants' attorney's advice, HCFA memoranda, a bulletin published by the FI, and an American Society of Anesthesiologists newsletter) was relevant to a determination of the Medicare regulation's meaning and that there was a question of fact as to the defendants' understanding of the meaning of the regulatory language. Id. at 1053–54.

In opposition to LFM's motion for summary judgment, Walker presented provisions from the Medicare Carrier's Manual in use during the relevant time period,[3] bulletins published by the FI (and received and maintained by LFM) that provide guidance on proper "incident to the service of a physician" billing, programs for seminars attended by LFM personnel that reviewed information on proper "incident to the service of a physician" billing, and copies of notes handwritten by LFM personnel documenting conversations between LFM administrative personnel and a billing consultant regarding the need for UPINs for physician assistants and nurse practitioners. Each of these pieces of evidence is relevant to the meaning of the Medicare regulation at issue and LFM's understanding of that meaning.... Taken together, they are sufficient to support findings that the Medicare regulation required that a physician be physically present in the office suite and otherwise more involved in a patient's course of care than the LFM physicians were and that LFM knew of these requirements. Thus, they raise an issue of fact as to the falsity of LFM's

---

3. The parties agree that, throughout the time period relevant to this lawsuit (whatever that might be), the Medicare Carrier's Manual set forth five criteria for a service to be covered as "incident to the services of a physician." To be covered, a service must: ... (4) be furnished under the direct personal supervision of a physician; ... The parties also agree that, since at least 1992, the MCM has defined "direct personal supervision in the office setting" to require that "the physician must be present in the office suite and immediately available to provide assistance and direction throughout the time the aide is performing services." MCM, § 2050.1.B. at 2-20....

billing for nurse practitioner and physician assistant services "incident to the service of a physician." Summary judgment was inappropriate.

* * *

VI. CONCLUSION

For the reasons stated above, we reverse the grant of summary judgment in favor of R&F Properties of Lake County, Inc., formerly known as Leesburg Family Medicine. We find no error in the district court's denial of R&F Properties of Lake County, Inc.'s motion to dismiss the Amended Complaint. Finally, we conclude that the district court erred in limiting the temporal scope of discovery and remand for further proceedings consistent with this opinion.

REVERSED AND REMANDED.

* * *

Notes and Questions

1. The direct supervision requirement varies based on state law. Virginia requires that the physician be in the same room that the procedure is performed. Georgette Gustin, *Allied Health Professionals Should Provide Only Those Services That are Within Their Scope of Practice*, 9 No. 3 J. Health Care Compliance 23 (2007).

2. "Medicare allows an exception to this supervision standard for physician-directed clinics, which are clinics or group associations where: (1) at least one physician is present at the clinic to perform medical services at all times the clinic is open; (2) each patient is under the care of a clinic physician; and (3) non-physician services are under the medical supervision of a clinic physician. Such a clinic can be an office of a group practice that meets the three criteria." Claudia Brett Goldin & Wallis S. Stromberg, *Who is Helping the Doctor: Physicians' Delegation of Medical Services*, 32-DEC Colo. Law. 81 (2003).

3. If one physician authorizes the incident to services and a different physician supervises the services, will the services be billable as incident to services? Thomas A. Scully, *ABA Health Law Section Comments to Stark II, Phase I*, 2001 Health Law. 3 (2001).

4. The incident to services can be a barrier to some skilled medical professions. Some scholars argue that midwives are hit particularly hard by the incident to billing scheme. For a discussion of this potential problem *see* Susan Corcoran, *To Become a Midwife: Reducing Legal Barriers to Entry into The Midwifery Profession*, 80 Wash. U. L. Q. 649 (2002).

Note on Medicare Part D

The Medicare Prescription Drug Improvement and Modernization Act of 2003 established the federal government's first prescription drug benefit plan, Medicare Part D. Medicare Part D beneficiaries are required to pay a monthly premium. Private insurers offer prescription drug benefits to Medicare beneficiaries under Medicare Part D.

Medicare Part D beneficiaries choose a prescription drug provider, from a list of authorized providers. Medicare Part D is approved by Medicare but sold and administered by private insurance companies. These plans are not administered by the government, and are still considered part of the Medicare program. The federal government must approve companies who sell the prescription drugs. However, aside from the federal governments approval, Medicare Part D is administered entirely by private businesses.

The providers must provide coverage for drugs listed under the Medicare formulary. These providers may include additional drugs that exceed Medicare requirements in their plans. Providers may cease coverage of these non-formulary medications without warning the beneficiaries.

For a further discussion of The Medicare Prescription Drug Improvement and Modernization Act of 2003 and Medicare Part D, see: Rick D. Hogan et al., *The Public's Health and the Law in the 21st Century: Fifth Annual Partnership Conference*, 35J.L., MED. & ETHICS 17 (2007); Eleanor Bhat Sorresso, *A Philosophy of Privatization: Rationing Health Care Through the Medicare Modernization Act of 2003*, 21 J.L. & HEALTH 29 (2008); Elizabeth C. Borer, *Modernizing Medicare: Protecting America's Most Vulnerable Patients From Predatory Healthcare Marketing Through Accessible Legal Remedies*, 92 MINN. L. REV. 1165 (2008); Catherine M. Boerner, *Zone Program Integrity Contracts to be Awarded in Support of CMS Efforts*, 10 No. 1 J. HEALTH CARE COMPLIANCE 31 (2008); Allison Dabbs Garrett & Robert Garis, *Leveling the Playing Field in the Pharmacy Benefit Management Industry*, 42 VAL. U. L. REV. 33 (2007); Kelly Barnes, *Are You Ready for New and Upcoming Prescription Drug Legislation?*, 10 No. 2 J. HEALTH CARE COMPLIANCE 35 (2008); Pi-Yi Mayo, *Medicare Part D*, 43 JUN HOUSTON LAW . 22 (2006).

Cigna Government Services, LLC, Plaintiff, v. United States of America, Defendant, and Noridian Administrative Services, LLC, Intervenor, and Palmetto GBA, LLC, Intervenor

No. 06-108C
United States Court of Federal Claims
70 Fed. Cl. 100
Filed Under Seal March 3, 2006
Reissued March 10, 2006

* * *

OPINION AND ORDER GRANTING A DECLARATORY JUDGMENT

WILLIAMS, Judge.

In this post-award bid protest, Plaintiff CIGNA Government Services, LLC (Cigna), challenges an override decision issued by the Department of Health and Human Services Centers for Medicare and Medicaid Services (CMS) in a pending protest at the Government Accountability Office (GAO). This action arises out of CMS' procurement for Medicare claims administration services covering durable medical equipment, prosthetics, orthotics, and supplies (DMEPOS) — the first in a series of procurements conducted under the Medicare Prescription Drug Improvement Modernization Act of 2003, Pub.L. 108-173 (MMA) requiring competitive contracting procedures and compliance with the Federal Acquisition Regulation (FAR) to replace existing contracts which had not been subject to the requirements of full and open competition. The solicited services include processing and paying DMEPOS claims, handling first-level appeals of denied claims, and serving as the primary contact with CMS for providers. The solicitation included four separate geographic jurisdictions for award designated as A, B, C and D. At issue here are the awards in Jurisdictions C and D.

Under the Competition in Contracting Act (CICA), Cigna's timely protest to GAO of contract awards to Noridian Administrative Services, LLC (Noridian) and Palmetto

GBA, LLC (Palmetto) triggered an automatic stay of these awards for 100 days to enable GAO to resolve the protest and provide meaningful relief in the event the protest is sustained. The agency decision challenged here overrode the stay on the ground that continued performance is in the best interests of the United States—immediately enabling the awardees to begin performing the contracts. Such performance is ongoing. This matter comes before the Court on Plaintiff's request for a declaratory judgment invalidating the override and motion for a permanent injunction—both of which would effectively reinstate the stay.

The essence of the override decision is that the stay would delay CMS' scheduled implementation of a newer and better Medicare claims processing system—a massive undertaking—preventing the Government from reaping the cost savings and enhanced performance under the new contracts. The problem with this delay-based justification is that CMS, in a report to Congress in February 2005, asserted that it had "flexibility" in its procurement schedule which could accommodate "any unforseen changes in the marketplace or legislative environment" and still enable CMS to meet the Congressionally-mandated implementation date of 2011 for the new contracts. CMS' asserted need to maintain its "tight schedule" which underlies this override directly contradicts its self-proclaimed schedule flexibility in its report to Congress.

* * *

CMS' override decision determined that proceeding with the awards until GAO decides the protest would not take work away from Cigna. However, potential loss of work is not the only harm to Cigna here—the override ignores the competitive advantage that awardees could gain in the event of a recompetition by performing the new contract now. Cigna's proposal had received [ ] in both Jurisdictions C and D, and one technical evaluation factor for award in the Solicitation, the most important, "capability," assesses an offeror's "understanding of requirements." Clearly, there is a risk that a contractor would gain an "understanding of requirements" by performing them. In addition, the transition from Cigna to Noridian in Jurisdiction D involves a transfer of Cigna's processes and methodologies to Noridian now, which, in the absence of a stay, poses a risk of an unfair competitive advantage to Noridian should GAO order a recompetition.

* * *

Findings of Fact

* * *

Cigna is a Part B Medicare Carrier for Idaho, North Carolina and Tennessee, and the incumbent DME Regional Contractor (DMERC) for CMS Region D. Cigna has served as the incumbent Jurisdiction D DMERC contractor for the past 13 years. Cigna and the other three DMERCs currently process DMEPOS claims for the Medicare program and will continue to do so until the transition under the challenged procurement is completed.

* * *

Noridian, the contract awardee for the Jurisdiction D DME MAC contract, is headquartered in Fargo, North Dakota, is not an incumbent DMERC, and has not processed DMEPOS claims previously. Palmetto, the contract awardee for the Jurisdiction C DME MAC contract, is headquartered in Columbia, South Carolina and currently serves as the DMERC for the majority of the states in Jurisdiction C except for Virginia and West Virginia, which AdminaStar Federal, Inc., another DMERC, currently services....

* * *

The Solicitation

On April 15, 2005, CMS issued the DME MAC Solicitation on a full-and-open competition basis. The DME MAC procurement was the first procurement by CMS applying the FAR competition and other requirements. Pl.'s TRO Ex. 2. The Solicitation generally sought proposals for DME MACs to replace the DMERCs and to provide specified FFS health insurance benefit administrative services, including Medicare claims processing and payment services, for DMEPOS in each of the four DME jurisdictions. SOW at 13; Pl.'s TRO Ex. 1.

... Each contract covered one of the four DME jurisdictions....

The SOW required the DME MAC to receive and control Medicare claims (both electronic and paper) from DMEPOS suppliers and beneficiaries within its jurisdiction, as well as to determine whether the claims are complete and should be paid. Pl.'s TRO Ex. 1, at 14, 62–78. The SOW also required the contractor to calculate Medicare payment amounts and remit the payments to the appropriate party. *Id.* The contractor was required to develop relationships with the DMEPOS suppliers and provide a variety of supplier services, *e.g.*, answering written inquires and educating the suppliers on Medicare rules, regulations, and billing procedures. *Id.* at 13–14. Finally, the Solicitation required the contractor to conduct re-determinations on appeals of claims and respond to complex beneficiary inquires referred from the Beneficiary Contact Centers. *Id.* at 14, 78–88, 88–104.

Section L of the Solicitation set out the instructions for the technical proposal as follows:

> The offeror shall provide a clear and concise description of its understanding of the requirements of the tasks provided in the statement of work. The offeror shall provide a description of their [sic] operational methodology to accomplish each of the requirements in the statement of work.

Solicitation § L. 15. The proposals were to be judged on a series of factors with "all evaluation factors other than cost/price when combined" being "significantly more important than cost/price." *Id.* § M.2. The Solicitation stated that "the Government is more concerned with obtaining superior technical/management features than with making an award on the lowest overall cost to the Government." *Id.* An offeror's capability was most important to the procurement. *Id.* § M.4. Within capability the offeror's understanding of the requirements was the most important factor, with project management second in weight. *Id.* When judging a proposal's project management section, "[t]he offeror's overall approach for managing the ongoing operations of the DME MAC contract" would be evaluated. *Id.* In terms of the Project Management Plan, the offeror would be evaluated on:

> the degree to which its project management plan and work breakdown structure demonstrate[d] its ability to accomplish the requirements. The offeror [would] also be evaluated on its knowledge of the difficulties, uncertainties, and risk associated with successful ongoing operations, and the degree to which the offeror has identified any potential risks to ongoing operations and its strategies to respond to risks.

Id. The Solicitation provided for award by jurisdiction to the offeror whose proposal offered the best overall value to the Government. Solicitation § M.2.a.

The Awards

On January 6, 2006, CMS awarded the DME MAC contract for Jurisdiction C to Palmetto and the contract for Jurisdiction D to Noridian. Pl.'s. TRO Ex. 2 at 1, 4. CMS notified Cigna of these award determinations the same day by telephone. On January 9, 2006, Cigna timely requested a postaward debriefing, which CMS held on January 20, 2006. Cigna filed a protest with GAO on January 24, 2006, within five days of the debriefing.

Cigna's Protest

* * *

Because Cigna timely filed its protest pursuant to CICA's protest and stay provisions and GAO timely provided CMS with notice of the protest, CMS stayed performance of the protested contracts pending GAO's resolution of the protest, in accordance with CICA. 31 U.S.C. § 3553(d)(3) (2005); 48 C.F.R. § 33.104(c)(1) (2005). GAO is to decide the protest within one hundred days from the date Cigna filed the protest, *i.e.,* on or before May 4, 2006. 31 U.S.C. § 3554(a)(1) (2005); 4 C.F.R. § 21.9(a) (2005).

The Override

On February 10, 2006, CMS issued an override of the CICA stay and directed Noridian and Palmetto to commence performance of the challenged contracts. CMS concluded that GAO is to issue its decision on Cigna's protest by May 4, 2006 and that continued performance of activities for both Jurisdiction C and D contracts until that time would be in the best interests of the Government.

In concluding that the override was in the best interests of the United States, the override decision listed a number of determinations:

- Proceeding with the transfer implementation activities will thus not take work away from the current contractors until the time of the cutover. In this instance the cutover is planned for July 1, 2006;

- Delaying transfer-implementation activities until after May 4 ... would make timely completion of this cutover impossible ... The result would be increased costs of benefit administration under the old contracts for this workload, increased costs because of non-simultaneous cutovers in the four DME MAC jurisdictions, and poorer service for the program and its beneficiaries for an extended period. In addition, the delay in this implementation would result in a backup of administrative capacity of the agency, resulting in delays in further workload transfers for the claims under Parts A and B of the Medicare Program, with further (and larger) forgone savings and failure to achieve anticipated improvements in service on a timely basis.

* * *

- The implementation of the new DME MAC contract will result in enhancements to the services provided to Medicare beneficiaries through improved contractor performance and more effective management of Medicare data and information providing the Government with the ability to better manage the billions of dollars in DME program expenditures estimated in [FY] 2006.... The new DME MAC contracts include explicit performance expectations for the contractors to improve the assurance that the right claims are paid timely and correctly.... Delays in implementation ... are likely to result in higher payment errors that create an unnecessary and unacceptable risk of financial harm to the Medicare trust funds.

* * *

Discussion
Jurisdiction and Standard of Review

The Court has jurisdiction to review an agency's best interests override of a CICA stay. 28 U.S.C. § 1491(b)(1);.... In reviewing an agency's override, the Court reviews the defendant's action under the standards in the Administrative Procedure Act (APA), 5 U.S.C. § 706; 28 U.S.C. § 1491(b)(4);.... The APA directs a reviewing court to overturn agency actions that are arbitrary, capricious, an abuse of discretion or otherwise not in accordance with law. 5 U.S.C. § 706(2)(A). In order to prevail, the protestor must show by a preponderance of the evidence that the agency's actions were either without a reasonable basis or in violation of applicable procurement law. *Gentex Corp. v. United States,* 58 Fed.Cl. 634, 648 (Fed.Cl.2003)....

The Supreme Court has identified four circumstances which constitute arbitrary and capricious agency action: if the agency has relied on factors which Congress has not intended it to consider, entirely failed to consider an important aspect of the problem, offered an explanation of its decision that runs counter to the evidence before the agency, or is so implausible that it could not be ascribed to a difference in view or the product of agency expertise. *Motor Vehicle Mfrs. Ass'n of the United States, Inc. v. State Farm Mut. Auto. Ins. Co.,* 463 U.S. 29, 43, 103 S.Ct. 2856, 77 L.Ed.2d 443 (1983); ...

CICA's Automatic Stay and Override Provisions

CICA automatically stays contract performance when an agency timely receives notice of a GAO protest. Specifically, 31 U.S.C. § 3553(d)(3)(A)(iii) requires the agency to "direct the contractor to cease performance under the contract and to suspend any related activities that may result in additional obligations being incurred by the United States under the contract." The statute further provides that performance may not be resumed while the protest is pending. 31 U.S.C. § 3553(d)(3)(B).

CICA provides for an override of the automatic stay only where the head of the contracting agency determines that "(i) performance of the contract is in the best interests of the United States; or (ii) urgent and compelling circumstances that significantly affect interests of the United States will not permit waiting for the decision of the Comptroller General concerning the protest." 31 U.S.C. § 3553(d)(3)(c). In the event of an override on "best interests" grounds, CICA specifies that if the protest is subsequently sustained, the GAO is to recommend a remedy "without regard to any cost or disruption from terminating, recompeting or reawarding the contract." 31 U.S.C. § 3554(b)(2).

CMS' Override Decision Contradicted its Own Assertions About the Schedule, Failed to Consider Relevant Factors, and Was Based Upon An Inaccurate Estimate of Cost Savings

On February 10, 2006, seventeen days after Cigna filed its protest and sixteen days after the stay issued, CMS issued an override decision at GAO, determining that continued performance of the implementation activities of the challenged DME MAC contracts would be in the best interests of the United States. The agency's rationale for overriding the statutory stay in this complex, costly procurement for Medicare claims processing was contained in a three and one-half page memorandum with little explanation and generalized conclusions. The override decision was not signed by the head of the contracting activity (HCA) as required by regulation. CMS essentially bases its override determination on the following:

* * *

- CMS' plan for Medicare Contracting Reform involves an "extremely tight" schedule and any delays to that schedule will strain the administrative capacity of CMS and add significant risks to CMS' implementation plan;

* * *

- the potential harm to the Medicare program in delaying implementation of the DME MAC contracts outweighs the risk that GAO will require corrective action as a result of the Cigna protest.

CMS' Assertion That Delay Will Compromise Its "Extremely Tight" Schedule Is Inconsistent With Its Representation to Congress That Its Schedule Is Flexible

CMS' override is largely premised on the costs and risks associated with delay to its schedule. However, CMS' claim of its "extremely tight" schedule directly contradicts CMS' statement to Congress that its accelerated 2009 schedule—the very same overall schedule CMS claims it must meet here—had built-in flexibility of two years. CMS represented to Congress that: "The schedule published in the 2005 report to Congress ... with a 2009 completion date, provides CMS the flexibility to adjust in response to any unforeseen changes in the marketplace or legislative environment and still meet the statutory implementation date." AR, Tab 1 at 55.

Although GAO's caution that CMS not rush was directed at later phases of the procurement than the start-up phase at issue here, both CMS' own words to Congress and the schedule itself demonstrate that its claim that an "extremely tight" schedule leaves no room for delay in this procurement is totally unfounded. It is apparent that a 70-day delay in transition activities will not prevent CMS from meeting its statutory deadline, given the two years of slippage CMS has built into its schedule.

It is unreasonable for CMS to represent to Congress that its schedule permits "flexibility" to adjust to unforeseen changes of its choosing—changes in the marketplace or legislative environment—but then to eschew any notion of flexibility and insist upon an "extremely tight schedule" to dislodge CICA's automatic stay. Because the schedule clearly has two years of flexibility, CMS' refusal to avail itself of that flexibility to abide by a 70-day statutory stay is arbitrary and capricious.

* * *

The Override Decision Did Not Articulate or Evaluate the Risks to the Agency or the Bidders If GAO Sustains Cigna's Protest

Neither CMS' written finding nor its administrative record contains any assessment of the potential risks to the agency if GAO were to grant Cigna's protest and direct a recompetition, as Cigna is urging. CMS did not evaluate the ramifications of Cigna prevailing on its protest at all—even in the most cursory fashion. Nor did CMS attempt to quantify the costs of recompeting these contracts and redoing the activities it is now conducting with potentially different vendors in the event a GAO-ordered reevaluation were to change the results.

CMS' Override Determination and alleged costs savings analysis reflect no consideration of the termination and transition costs involved if the contract awardees continue performance but GAO sustains Cigna's protest....

* * *

The statutory mandate of ensuring competition was not adequately considered in the override decision....

* * *

The whole point of the CICA stay provision is to ensure that the statutory mandate for competition is enforced....

* * *

The override decision's conclusion that Cigna will continue performing services implying that Cigna will not be harmed, ignores the realities of the competitive federal procurement arena. Cigna will be harmed if GAO grants its protest and orders a reprocurement because its competitors will be gaining an understanding of the requirements of the Solicitation by performing the new, restructured, consolidated work....

Declaratory Relief

Given that the override decision is inconsistent with CMS' own report to Congress, unsupported by the AR and arbitrary and capricious, the Court grant's Plaintiff's request for a declaratory judgment, declaring the override decision invalid, resulting in a reinstatement of the stay. Because the declaratory judgment will reinstate the stay and vacate the override, having the same effect as an injunction, the Court does not reach the issue of injunctive relief. In so ruling, the Court has taken into account the necessity of resolving this matter expeditiously recognizing that each day that passes prolongs the time when the stay is not in effect.

Conclusion

1. The Court grants Plaintiff's request for a declaratory judgment.

2. The override decision issued by CMS on February 10, 2006, is hereby declared to be arbitrary and capricious and invalid. The override decision is set aside, and the automatic stay in Cigna's GAO protest is reinstated *de jure.*

Notes and Questions

1. The Centers for Medicare and Medicaid Services impose marketing restrictions on companies that participate in Medicare Part D. These restrictions do not include a prohibition on cold calling and selling unrelated products. Because of this many Medicare providers have pressured senior citizens into purchasing plans that they can not afford, and sold a variety of unrelated products in the process (life insurance, funeral plans, etc.). Elizabeth C. Borer, *Modernizing Medicare: Protecting America's Most Vulnerable Patients From Predatory Healthcare Marketing Through Accessible Legal Remedies*, 92 Minn. L. Rev. 1165 (2008).

2. Much of Medicare Part D is based upon the efficiency of private companies. If private companies are truly better suited to providing the general population with their healthcare needs why does there need to be a special set-aside for underserved rural areas? Pi-Yi Mayo, *Medicare Part D*, 43-JUN Houston Law. 22 (2006).

3. Private business policing private business

Is a private business or a governmental oversight body a more reliable way of policing Medicare? Catherine M. Boerner, *Zone Program Integrity Contracts to be Awarded in Support of CMS Efforts*, 10 No. 1 J. Health Care Compliance 31 (2008).

4. There is a sizable hole in Medicare part D coverage. Drug expenditures that fall between $2,000 and $4,850, are not covered by this plan at all. Rick D. Hogan et al., *The Public's Health and the Law in the 21st Century: Fifth Annual Partnership Conference*, 35 J.L., Med. & Ethics 17 (2007).

B. Medicare: Hospital

The evolution of Medicare pricing has brought Medicare hospital payment to sophistication of a kind resembling regular government procurement. In brief, Medicare Part A requires providers like hospitals to enter into a contract with Medicare called a provider agreement. Provider agreements impose elaborate conditions of participation. 42 U.S.C. § 1395cc. Providers receive payment under a complex system derived from the 1960s and 1970s when pricing was simple—Medicare virtually paid what the hospitals charged—that has adapted only somewhat to the new pricing system after the 1980s, when HCFA controls pricing.

To understand Medicare hospital payment, start with the evolution in the pricing systems, as summarized in the following segment:

Payment and Delivery Systems

Charles Tiefer, "Budgetized" Health Entitlements and the Fiscal Constitution,
33 Harv. J. Legis. 411, 449–451 (1996)

The current provider payment system, which constitutes the core of modern federal health insurance finance, arose and developed almost wholly through provisions in budget reconciliation bills. Medicare and Medicaid initially employed retrospective payment systems, uder which the government reimbursed providers retrospectively for their actual costs. This funding system contributed to the explosion of health care costs since it gave providers incentives to charge more, to control costs little, and to increase their incomes and profits. . . .

During the 1980s and early 1990s, Congress authorized the change from retrospective to prospective payment systems for several programs. Under the Boren Amendment to reconciliation bills in 1980 and 1981, Congress allowed states to operate their Medicaid programs under prospective payment systems, in which states could decide prospectively what rates to pay providers for particular kinds of services. Pursuant to the 1983 Social Security legislation, Medicare hospital reimbursement switched to a prospective payment system, known generally as Diagnosis Related Groups ("DRGs"). Through reconciliation bills during the late 1980s, Medicare doctror reimbursement switched to a prospective payment system known as the Medicare Fee System, or MFS.

Prospective payment has been considered a successful health care cost control policy. It discourages providers from running up consts by reimbursing at prospectively set rates. The existing prospective rate-setting system allows Congress to make savings simply by legislating rate reductions.

Claims Payment

Although the pricing system changed greatly after the 1980s, the system for payment of claims, which is the focus of legal practice interest, has adapted only somewhat. Hospitals' claims get submitted, processed, and paid in what could be summarized as three stages: claims for DRG services, annual cost reports, and audits. Take, for example, a brief inpatient hospitalization of a Medicare beneficiary for an operation. The prospective payment system (PPS) for DRGs allows hospitals to submit claims soon after they render the services. Thus, a hospital would submit the bill for the operation, priced according to the DRG system, to its fiscal intermediary soon after the operation and the fiscal intermediary would process and pay it.

At the end of a year, the hospital submits an enormous form, its annual "cost report." This summarizes the services for which it has already billed under the DRG system. It also provides information on various costs which HCFA still reimburses apart from the DRG pricing system. The Supreme Court's *Guernsey* opinion below treats one of these types of costs, namely, certain kinds of capital costs. Other elements paid on this annual basis include hospital units excluded from PPS, like psychiatric and rehabilitation units, and other types of costs not handled through DRGs, such as the costs of graduate medical education which Medicare agrees to pay. Again, the fiscal intermediary processes and pays the net balance owed by the Medicare system to the hospital.

Ultimately, an audit occurs of the cost report. That audit may disallow some of the claims submitted by the hospital. The *Consumer Health Services* case illustrates one of the kinds of legal conundrums that arise during this multi-stage claims process: what is the status of the amounts already paid by the fiscal intermediary to the hospital if hospital bankruptcy intervenes?

Another kind of legal conundrum arises from the system of hospital claims payment, illuminated by the *Columbia Health Care* case. Health care law imposes many conditions and duties on providers, much as government contract law imposes many conditions and duties on contractors. Does the provider lose the right to payment by failing to meet some of those conditions and duties? The conditions at issue in that case have particular interest for lawyers for they do not concern some esoteric medical standard, but the "Stark laws," a set of conflict-of-interest rules imposed by Congress on health care providers. Government contract lawyers will recognize the *Columbia* case as part of questions that have often arisen with regular government contracting, namely, what is the impact upon the right to payment of transgressions of ethics rules regarding conflicts-of-interest, self-dealing, kickbacks, and the like.

Donna E. Shalala, Secretary of Health and Human Services v. Guernsey Memorial Hospital
No. 93-1251
Supreme Court of the United States
514 U.S. 87
Decided March 6, 1995

Justice KENNEDY delivered the opinion of the Court.

In this case a health care provider challenges a Medicare reimbursement determination by the Secretary of Health and Human Services. What begins as a rather conventional accounting problem raises significant questions respecting the interpretation of the Secretary's regulations and her authority to resolve certain reimbursement issues by adjudication and interpretive rules, rather than by regulations that address all accounting questions in precise detail.

The particular dispute concerns whether the Medicare regulations require reimbursement according to generally accepted accounting principles (GAAP)....

I

Respondent Guernsey Memorial Hospital issued bonds in 1972 and 1982 to fund capital improvements. In 1985, the Hospital refinanced its bonded debt by issuing new bonds. Although the refinancing will result in an estimated $12 million saving in debt service costs, the transaction did result in an accounting loss, sometimes referred to as an advance refunding or defeasance loss, of $672,581. The Hospital determined that it was entitled to Medicare reimbursement for about $314,000 of the loss. The total allowable amount of the loss is not in issue, but its timing is. The Hospital contends it is entitled to full reimbursement in one year, the year of the refinancing; the Secretary contends the loss must be amortized over the life of the old bonds.

The Secretary's position is in accord with an informal Medicare reimbursement guideline. See U.S.Dept. of Health and Human Services, Medicare Provider Reimbursement Manual § 233 (Mar. 1993) (PRM). PRM § 233 does not purport to be a regulation and has not been adopted pursuant to the notice-and-comment procedures of the Administrative Procedure Act. The fiscal intermediary relied on § 233 and determined that the loss had to be amortized. The Provider Reimbursement Review Board disagreed, see App.

to Pet. for Cert. 54a, but the Administrator of the Health Care Financing Administration reversed the Board's decision, see id., at 40a. In the District Court the Secretary's position was sustained, see Guernsey Memorial Hospital v. Sullivan, 796 F.Supp. 283 (SD Ohio 1992), but the Court of Appeals reversed, see Guernsey Memorial Hospital v. Secretary of HHS, 996 F.2d 830 (CA6 1993)....

We granted certiorari, 511 U.S. 1016, 114 S.Ct. 1395, 128 L.Ed.2d 69 (1994), and now reverse.

II

Under the Medicare reimbursement scheme at issue here, participating hospitals furnish services to program beneficiaries and are reimbursed by the Secretary through fiscal intermediaries. See 42 U.S.C. §§ 1395g and 1395h (1988 and Supp. V). Hospitals are reimbursed for "reasonable costs," defined by the statute as "the cost actually incurred, excluding therefrom any part of incurred cost found to be unnecessary in the efficient delivery of needed health services." § 1395x(v)(1)(A). The Medicare statute authorizes the Secretary to promulgate regulations "establishing the method or methods to be used" for determining reasonable costs, directing her in the process to "consider, among other things, the principles generally applied by national organizations or established prepayment organizations (which have developed such principles) in computing" reimbursement amounts. Ibid.

The Secretary has promulgated, and updated on an annual basis, regulations establishing the methods for determining reasonable cost reimbursement. See Good Samaritan Hospital v. Shalala, 508 U.S. 402, — —, 113 S.Ct. 2151, 2155, 124 L.Ed.2d 368 (1993). The relevant provisions can be found within 42 CFR pt. 413 (1993). Respondent contends that two of these regulations, §§ 413.20(a) and 413.24, mandate reimbursement according to GAAP, and the Secretary counters that neither does.

A

Section 413.20(a) provides as follows:

> "The principles of cost reimbursement require that providers maintain sufficient financial records and statistical data for proper determination of costs payable under the program. Standardized definitions, accounting, statistics, and reporting practices that are widely accepted in the hospital and related fields are followed. Changes in these practices and systems will not be required in order to determine costs payable under the principles of reimbursement. Essentially the methods of determining costs payable under Medicare involve making use of data available from the institution's basis accounts, as usually maintained, to arrive at equitable and proper payment for services to beneficiaries."

Assuming, arguendo, that the "[s]tandardized definitions, accounting, statistics, and reporting practices" referred to by the regulation refer to GAAP, that nevertheless is just the beginning, not the end, of the inquiry. The decisive question still remains: Who is it that "follow[s]" GAAP, and for what purposes? The Secretary's view is that § 413.20(a) ensures the existence of adequate provider records but does not dictate her own reimbursement determinations. We are persuaded that the Secretary's reading is correct.

Section 413.20(a) sets forth its directives in an ordered progression. The first sentence directs that providers must maintain records that are sufficient for proper determination of costs. It does not say the records are conclusive of the entire reimbursement process. The second sentence makes it clear to providers that standardized accounting practices are followed. The third sentence reassures providers that changes in their recordkeeping practices and systems are not required in order to determine what costs the provider can recover when principles of reimbursement are applied to the provider's raw cost data. That sentence makes a distinction between recordkeeping practices and systems on one hand and principles of reimbursement on the other. The last sentence confirms the distinction, for it contemplates that a provider's basic financial information is organized according to GAAP as a beginning point from which the Secretary "arrive[s] at equitable and proper payment for services." This is far different from saying that GAAP is by definition an equitable and proper measure of reimbursement.

* * *

The regulations' description of the fiscal intermediary's role underscores this interpretation. The regulations direct the intermediary to consult and assist providers in interpreting and applying the principles of Medicare reimbursement to generate claims for reimbursable costs, §413.20(b), suggesting that a provider's own determination of its claims involves more than handing over its existing cost reports. The regulations permit initial acceptance of reimbursable cost claims, unless there are obvious errors or inconsistencies, in order to expedite payment. §413.64(f)(2). When a subsequent, more thorough audit follows, it may establish that adjustments are necessary. Ibid.; see also §§421.100(a), (c). This sequence as well is consistent with the Secretary's view that a provider's cost accounting systems are only the first step in the ultimate determination of reimbursable costs.

* * *

B

The Secretary's reading of her regulations is consistent with the Medicare statute. Rather than requiring adherence to GAAP, the statute merely instructs the Secretary, in establishing the methods for determining reimbursable costs, to "consider, among other things, the principles generally applied by national organizations or established prepayment organizations (which have developed such principles) in computing the amount of payment ... to providers of services." 42 U.S.C. §1395x(v)(1)(A).

... The regulations are comprehensive and intricate in detail, addressing matters such as limits on cost reimbursement, apportioning costs to Medicare services, and the specific treatment of numerous particular costs. As of 1993, these regulations consumed some 620 pages of the Code of Federal Regulations.

As to particular reimbursement details not addressed by her regulations, the Secretary relies upon an elaborate adjudicative structure which includes the right to review by the Provider Reimbursement Review Board, and, in some instances, the Secretary, as well as judicial review in federal district court of final agency action. 42 U.S.C. §1395oo(f)(1); see Bethesda Hospital Assn. v. Bowen, 485 U.S. 399, 400–401, 108 S.Ct. 1255, 1256–1257, 99 L.Ed.2d 460 (1988)....

III

We also believe it was proper for the Secretary to issue a guideline or interpretive rule in determining that defeasance losses should be amortized....

Although one-time recognition in the initial year might be the better approach where the question is how best to portray a loss so that investors can appreciate in full a company's financial position, see APB Opinion 26, ¶¶4–5, reprinted at App. 64, the Secretary has determined in PRM §233 that amortization is appropriate to ensure that Medicare only reimburse its fair share. The Secretary must calculate how much of a provider's total allowable costs are attributable to Medicare services, see 42 CFR §§413.5(a), 413.9(a) and (c)(3) (1993), which entails calculating what proportion of the provider's services were delivered to Medicare patients, §§ 413.50 and 413.53. This ratio is referred to as the provider's "Medicare utilization." App. to Pet. for Cert. 49a. In allocating a provider's total allowable costs to Medicare, the Secretary must guard against various contingencies. The percentage of a hospital's patients covered by Medicare may change from year to year; or the provider may drop from the Medicare program altogether. Either will cause the hospital's Medicare utilization to fluctuate.

Given the undoubted fact that Medicare utilization will not be an annual constant, the Secretary must strive to assure that costs associated with patient services provided over time be spread, to avoid distortions in reimbursement. As the provider's yearly Medicare utilization becomes ascertainable, the Secretary is able to allocate costs with accuracy and the program can bear its proportionate share. Proper reimbursement requires proper timing. Should the Secretary reimburse in one year costs in fact attributable to a span of years, the reimbursement will be determined by the provider's Medicare utilization for that one year, not for later years. This leads to distortion. If the provider's utilization rate changes or if the provider drops from the program altogether the Secretary will have reimbursed up front an amount other than that attributable to Medicare services. The result would be cross-subsidization, id., at 50a, which the Act forbids. 42 U.S.C. § 1395x(v)(1)(A)(I).

* * *

[The dissenting opinion is omitted.]

Notes and Questions

1. Note the general structure of policy implementation and dispute resolution for Medicare hospital payment issues indicated in the opinion. HCFA issues both regulations—which, the opinion casually notes, fill up 620 pages in the Code of Federal Regulations, suggesting an impressive quantity of material for lawyers to work on—and other forms of guidance, namely, the HCFA Manuals. Hospitals submit their claims to their fiscal intermediary. If disputes arise, in certain circumstances the hospitals can take them to the Prover Reimbursement Review Board, and, ultimately, to the courts. The PRRB had far more work under the pre-DRG system in which all payments to hospitals consisted of cost reimbursements, than under the DRG system in which most (but not all) issues of pricing get resolved by uniform national rate-setting mechanisms.

2. Also note how much the *Guernsey* case turns on accounting issues. Recall the chapter on cost issues and its criteria of allowability, reasonableness, allocability, and Cost Accounting Standards (CAS). The issue raised in this case is the sufficiency of GAAP (generally accepted accounting principles), as argued by claimants, versus the necessity of accounting methods more focused on assuring that payments from the Treasury only go for what Congress has agreed, as argued by the government. This same issue arises in regular government contracting, as to the sufficiency of GAAP, as argued by contractors, versus the necessity of CAS. Four justices dissented in this case. Can you imagine their reasoning?

3. What is the division of labor on such issues between lawyers and accountants? Should accountants brief and argue Supreme Court cases? Should lawyers pore over hospital cost reports deciding how to allocate administrative costs between different hospital units?

4. Also note the importance in the opinion of recordkeeping requirements, reminiscent of the discussion in the chapter on cost issues of the importance there of government investigator access to a broad range of contractor records. Cost-reimbursement systems, whether in regular government contracting or in health care contracting, call for massive recordkeeping and massive government (or fiscal intermediary) review of those records.

The "form" for a hospital's annual cost report today covers several reams of papers when printed out, and it must be distributed, filled out, and returned in electronically-readable format for the system to cope.

Would doing away totally with massive recordkeeping and record-review produce the improved efficiencies that resulted from the successful deregulations of the 1980s such as those of transportation and energy rate regulation? Or, would doing away with such mechanisms of supervision of claims drawn out of the Treasury produce the scandalous waste, abuse, and fraud that resulted from the unsuccessful deregulation of the 1980s, namely, the effective deregulation of the savings and loan industry? One answer is that the shift to date, away from retroactive reimbursement of "reasonable" hospital charges and toward forward and fixed-pricing through DRGs, has been a great success story, taming what loomed as a monster of paperwork, disputation, and zooming charges.

United States of America, Appellant, v.
Consumer Health Services of America, Inc. et al., Appellees

No. 96-5148
United States Court of Appeals, District of Columbia Circuit
108 F.3d 390
Decided March 18, 1997

Before: SILBERMAN, SENTELLE, and RANDOLPH, Circuit Judges. Opinion for the Court filed by Circuit Judge SILBERMAN. Concurring opinion filed by Circuit Judge SENTELLE.

SILBERMAN, Circuit Judge:

The United States appeals the district court's affirmance of the bankruptcy court's denial of its motion to deduct prior Medicare overpayments from reimbursement otherwise due the appellees. We reverse.

Consumer Health Services of America was a provider of home health care services. In 1976, it signed a Medicare provider agreement that qualified it to participate in Medicare Part A, which compensates providers of certain health care services for the elderly in accordance with regulations promulgated by the Secretary of Health and Human Services. To ensure that Medicare service providers such as Consumer are paid promptly, the Medicare statute provides for periodic payments for services on an estimated basis prior to a determination of the exact amount of reimbursement due for those services. These interim payments, to be made not less often than monthly, are calculated and made by a "fiscal intermediary" designated by the Secretary. At the end of each "reporting period" (the length of which is currently set at one year), the intermediary audits the provider to determine whether the provider has been over or underpaid, and by how much. While the provider is obliged to submit its "cost report" to the intermediary within five months of the close of a cost period, the intermediary must only complete the audit within a reasonable time.

When the audit is completed, the service provider is subject to a "retroactive adjustment." If the provider has been underpaid, it receives a "final adjustment" amounting to the difference between "the reimbursement due" and "the payments made." If the provider has been overpaid, it need not necessarily remit the balance of the overpayment immediately. Although the intermediary may suspend a provider's authorization to participate in Medicare if the provider's account is out of balance, the regulations also provide for an arrangement by which the intermediary and the provider may "enter[ ] into an agreement ... for liquidation of the overpayment." The agreement envisaged by this regulation is quite simple: the provider will keep performing Medicare services, and the intermediary will deduct from its periodic payments amounts to be applied to liquidation of the prior overpayment. In determining how much to deduct, the intermediary balances two objectives: it wants to liquidate the debt, but it also wants to ensure that the provider has sufficient incentive to continue performing needed services.

In 1984, Consumer's fiscal intermediary concluded its audit for 1981–82 and determined that it had overpaid Consumer by approximately $81,000. Pursuant to an "agreement … for liquidation of the overpayment," the intermediary began deducting from Consumer's periodic payments amounts necessary to recover the excess. In 1987, Consumer petitioned to reorganize its business under Chapter 11 of the Bankruptcy Code. At that time, Consumer still owed over $32,000 on the 1981–82 overpayments. Operating under Chapter 11, Consumer continued to provide Medicare services and to receive periodic payments. Its intermediary did not, however, continue to deduct the amounts attributable to the 1981–82 overpayment, because it was uncertain concerning the legal issue in this case—whether such deductions would violate the Bankruptcy Code's automatic stay of actions to recover pre-petition debts. After a little more than a year of operation under Chapter 11, Consumer converted its bankruptcy case into a liquidation proceeding under Chapter 7, and it submitted claims for reimbursement for Medicare services performed during the period it was operating under Chapter 11. Assuming no deduction for the 1981–82 overpayments, the intermediary estimated that these claims amounted to about $15,000. The government then brought a motion in the bankruptcy court requesting "that the court affirm [its] right to reduce payments due to account for prior overpayments."

For reasons not apparent from the record, the matter was pending before the bankruptcy court for six years, and then, after the Third Circuit decided a virtually identical case, see In re University Medical Center, 973 F.2d 1065 (3d Cir.1992), the bankruptcy court denied the government's motion. The court assumed the Bankruptcy Code's automatic stay applied to the government's claim for the pre-petition overpayments, and so it saw the issue as whether the government was entitled "to make recoupment" on the provider agreement between Consumer and the Secretary. The court characterized the agreement as an "executory contract," i.e., a contract on which performance is due from both parties, and it recognized that if Consumer could be said to have "assumed" the contract, "the contract would be enforceable … and the Secretary's withholding of payments would merely be the exercise of a contractual right." The court rejected, however, the argument that Consumer's post-petition provision of Medicare services constituted assumption of the contract. It relied on the prevailing view that a debtor operating under Chapter 11 cannot "assume" an executory contract without formal approval by the bankruptcy court, which the parties agreed had been neither sought nor received. The court also rejected the government's claim for "equitable recoupment," under which a creditor may deduct a pre-petition debt from payments for post-petition services, if (and only if) the debt and the services are part of a single "transaction." According to the court, under the Medicare statute and regulations, "the amount due the provider for one year [i.e., the pre-petition debt] stems from services completely unrelated to those provided in later years [i.e., the post-petition services]." It thus concluded that the government's claim for overpayments made in 1981–82 and calculated in 1984 was not part of the same transaction as Consumer's claim for compensation for services performed in 1987–88. Finally, relying on NLRB v. Bildisco & Bildisco, 465 U.S. 513, 104 S.Ct. 1188, 79 L.Ed.2d 482 (1984), the bankruptcy court determined that even though performance under the provider agreement did not amount to assumption of it, Consumer was still entitled to the "reasonable value" of the Medicare services it provided while operating under Chapter 11.

The government appealed to the district court, which affirmed in a one-sentence order embracing the reasoning of the bankruptcy court. This appeal followed.

II.

The government's primary contention is that the bankruptcy court failed to recognize that the amount of Medicare's substantive liability for any services rendered (including those rendered by a debtor operating under Chapter 11) must by statute take into account prior overpayments. In the alternative, the government argues that it should be able to deduct the overpayments under the doctrine of equitable recoupment, since those overpayments and the post-petition services were part of a single transaction. We see these two arguments not as true "alternatives" but rather as closely related.

The Medicare statute provides that the amount due for Medicare services be calculated as follows:

> The Secretary shall periodically determine the amount which should be paid under this part to each provider of services with respect to the services furnished by it, and the provider of services shall be paid, at such time or times as the Secretary believes appropriate (but not less often than monthly) and prior to audit or settlement ... the amounts so determined, with necessary adjustments on account of previously made overpayments or underpayments. 42 U.S.C. § 1395g(a) (emphases added).

The statute quite clearly says that the government is liable for particular Medicare services only in the amount that "shall be paid," and that amount consists of what the Secretary has determined "should be paid" for those services, less adjustments for prior overpayments. The bankruptcy court's decision, which did not focus on the statute's actual language, had the effect of eliminating from the statute the words "with necessary adjustments on account of previously made overpayments" when a provider seeks the protection of the bankruptcy law.

* * *

We think the Third Circuit, and the bankruptcy court below, overlooked the importance of the language of the substantive Medicare statute. Those courts assumed that the amount due on post-petition services was to be determined by the regulations detailing how much a provider normally gets for the services rendered. Only then, after that determination, did the courts inquire into whether the prior overpayments could be deducted from the amount due. And in completing that inquiry, the courts looked to principles governing pre-assumption performance of executory contracts by debtors operating under Chapter 11. As we have explained, we disagree with the premise that the "amount due" should be calculated with reference to the fee schedule set out in the regulations. That fee schedule only determines what "should be paid"; the amount actually due under the statute is the amount which "shall be paid"—which includes "necessary adjustments for prior overpayments." In this case, then, the amount due is the approximately $15,000 Consumer "should be paid" for post-petition services rendered, less the "necessary" adjustment for the as-yet-unremitted overpayments. To conclude otherwise, we think, would allow the Bankruptcy Code to modify an explicit statutory scheme defining liability for particular services. Neither the trustee, the bankruptcy court, nor the Third Circuit in In re University Medical Center has offered authority for the proposition that the Bankruptcy Code can act to override an explicit statutory limitation on what the government owes for a particular service. That the limitation in question is defined by the amount the government has previously (over)paid to the provider does not, in our view, alter the analysis.

Nor does our analysis differ significantly under the doctrine of equitable recoupment, which exempts a debt from the automatic stay when the debt is inextricably tied up in the post-petition claim. See generally In re B&L Oil, 782 F.2d 155, 156 (10th Cir.1986); Howard C. Bushman III, Benefits and Burdens: Post-Petition Performance of Unassumed Executory Contracts, 5 BANKR.DEV. J. 341, 352–53 (1988).

Whether the recoupment exception applies in a particular case turns on whether the creditor's and debtor's respective claims arise out of the same "transaction," and what exactly constitutes a "transaction" is not readily apparent from the caselaw. In In re University Medical Center, the court rejected an "open-ended" definition of "transaction" in favor of a "stricter" requirement that "both debts ... arise out of a single integrated transaction so that it would be inequitable for the debtor to enjoy the benefits of that transaction without also meeting its obligations." 973 F.2d at 1080–81. The court concluded that the annual account reconciliation process described above defined the scope of any single transaction under Medicare Part A. The Third Circuit thought that since the provider's account was reconciled each year, any particular pre-petition monthly payment should be thought to apply to the services rendered that month and any prior overpayment that had given rise to a "retroactive adjustment." The payment could not be construed as an "advance payment[ ]" for future services. Thus, the provider's "post-petition services were the beginning of transactions that would stretch into the future, but they were not part of the [pre-petition] transactions." 973 F.2d at 1081–82.

Even under the Third Circuit's stricter standard, we believe that Consumer's claim for post-petition services and the pre-petition overpayments qualify. Unlike the Third Circuit, we do not think the frequency of the audit appropriately defines the "transaction." The audit is simply the mechanism by which the intermediary determines whether and by how much it ought to adjust subsequent periodic payments to a particular provider. Its frequency is determined by the Secretary, presumably in the interests of an efficient reimbursement scheme; it would seem to have little to do with how one conceptualizes the relation between past overpayments and current compensation due. It is the statute and regulations which dictate the effect of the audit on the provider's participation in Medicare. An audit is nothing more than a snapshot in time — whether it is monthly, annual, or decennial is, in our view, irrelevant.

In determining whether the pre-petition and post-petition services should be thought of as one transaction, the key to us is the Medicare statute. Since it requires the Secretary to take into account pre-petition overpayments in order to calculate a post-petition claim — as we have described above — Congress rather clearly indicated that it wanted a provider's stream of services to be considered one transaction for purposes of any claim the government would have against the provider. The Third Circuit said that "[t]he [pre-petition] overpayments ... cannot be deemed advance payments for [the provider's subsequent] services." Id. at 1081. That observation, in our view, is contrary to manifest congressional intent. In sum, it does not matter whether we consider the government's claim in terms of its statutory substantive liability or in terms of the equitable recoupment doctrine. Under either analysis, the automatic stay is of no consequence. Accord In re Harmon, 188 B.R. 421, 425 (9th Cir. BAP 1995).

* * *

III.

As is apparent, our analysis is driven by the explicit statutory directive that, in compensation for its services rendered post-petition, Consumer "shall be paid" the amount the Secretary has determined it "should be paid," "with necessary adjustments on account of previously made overpayments." 42 U.S.C. § 1395g(a). The amount Consumer "should be paid" is approximately $15,000. What it "shall be paid," then, turns on what adjustments are "necessary."

The government would have us decide that the "necessary" adjustment in this case is the entire outstanding balance on the 1981–82 overpayments, $32,000. Such a deduction would leave the trustee owing approximately $17,000, a debt which would presumably be treated as a run-of-the-mill pre-petition claim. The statute itself does not really mandate the government's reading, however. It is not entirely clear what Congress meant by "necessary," or, to put it another way, what is necessary in any given case may involve drawing a balance between what would be the quickest repayment to the government, and what would give the provider sufficient incentive to continue providing services. As Congress has not "spoken unambiguously to the precise issue at hand," we turn to "the agency's action under 'Step Two' of Chevron, and defer to the agency's interpretation if it represents a 'permissible construction' of the statute." Consumer Fed'n of America and Public Citizen v. U.S. Dep't of Health and Human Servs., 83 F.3d 1497, 1503 (D.C.Cir.1996) (quoting Chevron U.S.A. Inc. v. Natural Resources Defense Council, Inc., 467 U.S. 837, 842–43, 104 S.Ct. 2778, 2781–82, 81 L.Ed.2d 694 (1984)).

The Secretary's regulation permits the intermediary, in an overpayment situation, either to seek to recover the full extent of prior overpayments — threatening to suspend a provider's participation in Medicare if it does not pay — or to enter into an agreement with the provider (which is what occurred here) whereby the provider continues its services with appropriate deductions for the past overpayments. See 42 C.F.R. § 405.373(a)(2). To be sure, the latter alternative forms an executory contract, but it is not to be treated as would the post-petition performance of an ordinary executory contract under bankruptcy law; it is the statute which sets forth the extent of the government's obligation — the contract only implements the timing and pace of the payment of that obligation. If we were to conclude otherwise, the Secretary might be forced to insist on a provider's immediate repayment of the full amount once the intermediary determined the government overpaid — which could jeopardize the operation of the program. We do not think that comports with the statute, which sought to protect the taxpayer's interest yet provide the Secretary with the flexibility necessary to operate the program.

On the record before us, we cannot say what the "necessary" deduction is, for the parties have not included in the record documentation explaining exactly how much the intermediary was deducting from Consumer's periodic payments to account for the 1981–82 overpayments at the time Consumer petitioned for Chapter 11. On remand, the bankruptcy court will be able to calculate the amount Consumer "shall be paid," since the intermediary can clarify what it has determined "should be paid," and the parties can supplement the record to allow the court to determine what deductions are "necessary."

* * *

The district court decision is reversed, and the case is remanded to the bankruptcy court for proceedings consistent with this opinion.

So ordered.

SENTELLE, Circuit Judge, concurring:

I concur with the majority's result and join in much of its reasoning. However, I would base the result solely on the majority's statutory rationale. That is, although I do not think the question free from doubt, I agree that the bankruptcy court in this case and the Third Circuit in In re University Medical Center, 973 F.2d 1065 (3rd Cir.1992), concluded without adequate authority that the bankruptcy code modifies the Medicare statute's explicit scheme for defining the government's liability to service providers. While any act of the bankruptcy court under the code is in a sense in breach of the source of law that gives rise to the obligation that the bankruptcy court reduces or extinguishes, this does not imply

that the bankruptcy court is empowered by the code to depart from the statutory definition of the obligation in the first instance. To that extent, I think the bankruptcy court has
overreached, and I concur in the reversal.

As I think the first rationale is sufficient, I do not join the majority in deciding the second question as to what constitutes a single "transaction." While I am not convinced that
the majority is incorrect, neither am I convinced that it is necessary to create a precedent
on that question which might arise in some other context. With that one reservation, I join
the majority's opinion and result.

Notes and Questions

1. This is a 1997 remand, anticipating more proceedings to come, of a case regarding
1981–82 overpayments. How does that strike you?

2. The case alludes to "periodic estimated payments," a system of less significance in recent years as Medicare pricing and payment has evolved. Apart from that, this case illustrates the special workings of the Medicare claims payment system that continues: early
submission to, and processing and payment of claims by, a fiscal intermediary; years later,
audit and "necessary adjustment." How does this compare with the system in regular government contracting, for certain types of work, of early submission of requests for progress
payments for processing and payment; years later, upon final delivery or completion of
the work, acceptance and final payment?

3. There are two issues: (1) whether the government can deduct as an "adjustment" from
later (post-petition) payments its prior overpayments; and, (2) what counts as a "necessary"
adjustment. On that first issue, the court finds a great deal of guidance in the wording of the
Medicare statute, 42 U.S.C. § 1395g(a). What would the counter-argument be? Do the words
of this provision, or anything else for that matter, suggest that Congress wrote the section
to give guidance about bankruptcy? On that second issue, the court does not find so much
guidance in the statute's wording and so it defers to HCFA's flexible approach. Who gets
power under the court's approach to decide the division of losses between the government
and the bankrupt's creditors? Did Congress, which was not specifically talking about bankruptcy, make that power allocation, or does the court decide for itself on policy grounds?

4. The case is a foray into the sub-specialty of government contracting law, namely, dealing with bankruptcy. To some extent, Congress and the procuring agencies can, and do,
take precautions to safeguard the government's special interests against the vicissitudes of
contractor bankruptcy. To some extent, the government has to cope with contractor bankruptcy much like private contractual parties do. What does the court identify as the government's
special interest regarding bankrupt, but still-functioning health care providers? Like the
sub-specialty of government contracting law dealing with intellectual property, this sub-
specialty can hardly be appreciated without grounding in the other area of law at issue.

C. Medicaid

Besides Medicare, the federal government funds Medicaid which pays for health care
for the poor. Medicaid is a joint federal-state program, operating through individual programs managed by each of the fifty states. To some extent, like Medicare, it is a system by
which Treasury payments flow to provider-claimants; to some extent it is, like numerous
other programs of grants by the federal government to the states, a system run by states

belonging to the realm of state rather than federal law. The *Krizek* opinion above deals with a health care provider for both the Medicare and Medicaid programs. For discussion of Medicaid law, see Furrow, Greaney, et al., HEALTH LAW, *supra*, chapter 14; Rosenblatt, Law & Rosenbaum, LAW AND THE AMERICAN HEALTH CARE SYSTEM, *supra*, chapter 2, section H.

Medicaid is a federally funded health care program for the poor. Under this system the federal government gives money to each state. Each state is then responsible for administering it's own Medicaid program, and disbursing these funds to the health care providers. Medicaid may require individual patients to provide a co-pay in certain situations. The state's administration of Medicaid programs must comply with federal law.

Individual states are required to develop their own plans for administering Medicaid. This plan must state the methods used to calculate payments for each service that Medicaid provides. The states payments for services must be consistent with efficiency, economy and quality of care. The Medicaid agency is obligated to perform an audit, if the payment is based upon costs.

For a further discussion of Medicaid contracting issues see: 2 Am. Jur. 2d Admin. Law § 508 (2008); 15 Am. Jur. 2d Civil Rights § 68 (2008); Mark E. REAGAN & Mark A. Johnson, *Taming the Medicaid Beast: The Federal Government's Ambitious Attempt to Combat Medicaid Fraud, Waste, and Abuse*, 3 J. Health & Life Sci L. 1 (July, 2010); Richard G. Frank & Sherry A. Glied, *Better But Not Well: Mental Health Policy in the United States Since 1950*, 33 J. Health Pol. Pol'y & L. 135 (2008); Harry M. Feder, *Qios Support Value Driven Health Care Initiative*, 10 No. 1 J. Health Care Compliance 39 (2008); Melinda S. Stegman, *Standards of Ethical Coding: Why Everyone Should be Aware of Them*, 10 No. 1 J. Health Care Compliance 59 (2008); Sean Reilly, *Finding Silver Linings*, 68 La. L. Rev. 331 (2008); Kim Van Winkle, *States Target Medicaid Fraud in the Pharmaceutical Industry: The Texas Experience*, 20 No. 2 Health Lawyer 10 (2007); Frank J. Thompson, *Executive Federalism and Medicaid Demonstration Waivers: Implications for Policy and Democratic Process*, 32 J. Health Pol. Pol'y & L. 971 (2007); Lawrence Scheinert, *Hewlett-Packard's Spy Games and the "Duty of Caremark": How Inconsistent Standards Governing a Director's Duty of Care Disgraced a Company*, 18 U. Fla. J.L. & Pub. Pol'y 447 (2007); Michael A. Igel, *A Perfect 10 The Deficit Reduction Act of 2005 Provides Incentive for Florida to Amend its Own False Claims Act Litigation*, 81-Nov Fla. Bar J. 23 (2007); Harold L. Kaplan & Timothy R. Casey, *Recoupment in Health Care Bankruptcies: A Shrinking Issue?*, 26-OCT Am. Bankr. Inst. J. 16 (2007); Liesa L. Richter, *Corporate Salvation or Damnation? Proposed New Federal Legislation on Selective Waiver*, 76 Fordham L. Rev. 129 (2007).

Orthopaedic Hospital and the California Association of Hospitals and Health Systems, Plaintiffs-Appellants, v. Kimberly Belshe, Director of the State Department of Health Services, State of California, Defendant-Appellee

United States Court of Appeals for the Ninth Circuit
103 F.3d 1491
August 9, 1996, Argued, Submitted, Pasadena, California
January 9, 1997, Filed

FLETCHER, Circuit Judge:

Plaintiffs-Appellants Orthopaedic Hospital and the California Association of Hospitals and Health Systems claim that Defendant-Appellee Director of the California Department of Health Services violated section 1396a(a)(30)(A) of the federal Medicaid Act, 42 U.S.C. §§ 1396a–1396v (West 1992 & Supp. 1996) by setting reimbursement rates for hospital providers of outpatient services without proper consideration of the effect of hospital costs on the relevant statutory factors: efficiency, economy, quality of care, and access. The district court granted summary judgment in favor of the Director. We reverse and remand with direction.

FACTUAL BACKGROUND & PROCEDURAL HISTORY

I. The Medi-Cal Program

Title XIX of the Social Security Act, 42 U.S.C. §§ 1396a–1396v (the "Medicaid Act"), authorizes federal grants to states for medical assistance to low income persons who are aged, blind, disabled, or members of families with dependent children. The program is jointly financed by the federal and state governments and administered by the states. The states, in accordance with federal law, decide eligible beneficiary groups, types and ranges of service, payment levels for services, and administrative and operating procedures. Payment for services is made directly by the states to the individuals or entities that furnish the services. 42 C.F.R. § 430.0. To receive matching federal financial participation for such services, states must agree to comply with the applicable federal Medicaid law.

Among the health care services that must be provided by states participating in Medicaid are the medical services at issue in this case—hospital outpatient services. 42 U.S.C. §§ 1396a(a)(10)(A), 1396d(a)(2)(A). Hospital outpatient services are preventive, diagnostic, therapeutic, rehabilitative, or palliative services that are furnished to outpatients by an institution that is licensed as a hospital. 42 C.F.R. § 440.20(a).

* * *

Some of the services provided by hospital outpatient departments could be provided more economically by non-hospital providers such as freestanding clinics or doctors' offices because those providers have lower fixed costs than do hospitals. However, hospital outpatient departments are more widely available to Medi-Cal beneficiaries. Hospitals that accept any Medicare payments and operate emergency departments are required by law to examine and (if an emergency medical condition exists) to treat any patient who presents him or herself, regardless of the patient's ability to pay. 42 U.S.C. § 1395dd. In contrast, other outpatient service providers are free to deny care to Medi-Cal recipients and others who are unable to pay for care. With no incentive to use the most economical provider, Medi-Cal beneficiaries frequently choose the more accessible and convenient hospital outpatient departments over less costly facilities, some of which may be entirely unavailable or less available to them.

The Defendant-Appellee's agency, the Department of Health Services of the State of California, is the state agency responsible for the administration of California's version of Medicaid, the Medi-Cal program. Medi-Cal has a prospective reimbursement system that sets reimbursement rates for specific services, regardless of where those services are performed (e.g., in hospitals, doctors' offices, or freestanding outpatient clinics). Cal. Code Regs. tit. 22, §§ 51501–51557.

Hospital outpatient departments receive an additional reimbursement for room charges, not received by non-hospital providers. Cal. Code Regs. tit. 22, § 51509(g). However, this additional payment is offset by a 20% reduction in the reimbursement rate for physician services furnished in hospital outpatient departments. Cal. Code Regs. tit. 22, § 51503(i). All other outpatient reimbursement rates are the same as those applicable to non-hospital providers. Cal Code Regs. tit. 22, § 51509.

Hospitals which serve a disproportionate share of Medi-Cal beneficiaries and small and rural hospitals are eligible for additional reimbursement from Medi-Cal. However, there are relatively few funds available for these additional payments: $14 million annually. 3 A.R. at 242. In 1991, the total payments for outpatient services were approximately $355 million. 3 A.R. at 436.

Hospitals that serve a disproportionately large share of Medi-Cal outpatients as compared to other hospitals receive additional funds. This is calculated annually based on a prescribed formula. *See* Cal. Welfare and Institutions Code § 14105.98 (West. Supp. 1996).

The Medicaid Act requires a participating state to develop a state plan which describes the policy and methods to be used to set payment rates for each type of service included in the program. 42 C.F.R. § 447.201(b). California's state plan requires the Department to develop an evidentiary base or rate study, have a public hearing on the proposed rates, determine final rates based on the evidentiary base including public input, and adopt final rates through regulations. However, the state plan also allows the legislature to adjust the rates so long as the requirements of 42 C.F.R. Part 447 are met. Before any rate changes are made, the Department must consult with representatives of concerned provider groups.

In 1982 the California legislature reduced the outpatient reimbursement rates by 10%, and the rates for laboratory services by 25%. In 1984 and 1985 the Department made across the board rate increases resulting in a net increase of 2% over the rates in effect prior to the 1982 reduction. Since 1985 the Department has modified the rates for certain services and has provided additional reimbursement for disproportionate share and small and rural hospitals.

II. Prior Litigation

The Hospitals challenge the adequacy of certain of the reimbursement rates the State of California has set for hospitals that provide outpatient services to Medi-Cal beneficiaries. The reimbursement rates currently in effect were set by the Director upon the district court's remand in *Orthopaedic Hosp. and the Cal. Ass'n of Hosp. and Health Sys. v. Kenneth Kizer, M.D., Director of the Cal. Dep't of Health Serv.*, No. CV 90-4209 SVW (JRx), 1992 WL 345652 (C.D. Cal.) *("Orthopaedic I")*....

* * *

III. The Remand

Upon remand, the Department conducted a rate study as required by the decision in *Orthopaedic I....* The Department also issued a Statement of Administrative Decision in which it stated that the Department "does not feel that it is necessary to change Medi-Cal reimbursement for hospital outpatient services from current levels. Having considered efficiency, economy, quality of care and access, the Department has therefore decided to readopt the [existing] reimbursement levels...."

* * *

In April 1994 the Department issued its final administrative decision readopting the hospital outpatient reimbursement rates without change.

IV. District Court Review of Readopted Rates

The Hospitals alleging that the Department's readoption of its original rates did not satisfy 42 U.S.C. § 1396a(a)(30)(A) or the mandate of the court in *Orthopedic I*, returned to court filing two actions, Case Nos. 94-4764 and 94-4825 *("Orthopaedic II/III")*. They were consolidated by the district court.

* * *

DISCUSSION

This appeal turns upon the proper interpretation of 42 U.S.C. § 1396a(a)(30)(A) which states that under the Medicaid Act, a state plan for medical assistance must:

> provide such methods and procedures relating to the utilization of, and the payment for, care and services available under the plan ... as may be necessary to safeguard against unnecessary utilization of such care and services and to assure that payments are consistent with efficiency, economy, and quality of care and are sufficient to enlist enough providers so that care and services are available under the plan at least to the extent that such care and services are available to the general population in the geographic area. 42 U.S.C. § 1396a(a)(30)(A).

Whether the statute requires the Department to consider the costs hospitals incur in delivering services when setting specific payment rates under § 1396a(a)(30)(A) is the issue. We conclude that the Director must set hospital outpatient reimbursement rates that bear a reasonable relationship to efficient and economical hospitals' costs of providing quality services, unless the Department shows some justification for rates that substantially deviate from such costs. To do this, the Department must rely on responsible cost studies, its own or others', that provide reliable data as a basis for its rate setting.

The statute provides that payments for services must be consistent with efficiency, economy, and quality of care, and that those *payments* must be sufficient to enlist enough providers to provide access to Medicaid recipients. The Department cannot know that it is setting rates that are consistent with efficiency, economy, quality of care and access without considering the costs of providing such services. It stands to reason that the *payments* for hospital outpatient services must bear a reasonable relationship to the costs of providing quality care incurred by efficiently and economically operated hospitals.

The Department argues that the payments must be *sufficient* (i.e. high enough) to ensure access, but they only need to be *consistent* with efficiency, economy, and quality of care.

> It is true that "consistent," not "sufficient," modifies the terms, efficiency, economy, and quality of care. But even "consistency" would appear to require that the Department consider the costs of providing the services for which it is reimbursing.... For payments to be consistent with efficiency, economy and quality of care, they must approximate the cost of quality care provided efficiently and economically. The Department cannot set rates consistent with efficiency and economy in the health care system without considering the costs to the hospitals that provide most of the services. Judgments can be made as to the efficiency of the providers, the economies they practice and the quality of the services they deliver, but costs are an integral part of the consideration.

The district court found that it would be inefficient and uneconomical to set rates that compensated hospitals for their costs since hospitals are the most expensive providers of outpatient services. The district court reasoned that states should be able to provide incentives for one type of care over another. We agree, but undercompensating hospitals gives no incentives to Medi-Cal beneficiaries to use more economical providers unless it results in a cessation of the delivery of emergency services by hospitals. Non-hospital providers are not nearly as available to Medi-Cal beneficiaries as are hospitals. And no lack of economic incentive excuses a hospital that serves Medicare patients from its legal obligation to provide emergency care to all comers if it operates an emergency department. Until the Department provides incentives to non-hospital providers to furnish more services to Medi-Cal beneficiaries, and requires Medi-Cal beneficiaries to utilize non-hospital providers whenever possible, undercompensating hospital outpatient departments does nothing to shift users to more efficient and economical delivery of care outside the hospital setting.

Since the payments themselves must also be consistent with quality of care, the Department must consider the costs of providing quality care. The Department argues that the payments do not independently have to support quality care because quality is assured by other regulations. Essentially, the Department's position is that it doesn't have to pay the costs of quality care because hospitals are contractually obligated to provide quality care once they agree to take Medicaid patients, and because hospitals' licensing requirements require them to provide quality care. We disagree. The Department, itself, must satisfy the requirement that the payments themselves be consistent with quality care.

* * *

> The Committee believes the removal of the ceiling on physician payments based on medicare will not result in an increase in expenditures for physician services under medicaid. The States all face clear cost pressures in their medical programs. Therefore, the Committee expects this provision will be used by the States to improve the administration of their medicaid programs and to try innovative approaches to physician payment rather than merely to raise physician fees above medicare levels.

H.R. Rep. No. 97-158, vol. II, at 312 (1981).

By removing the reasonable charges limitation, Congress wanted to simplify the administrative burden, and allow states more flexibility in devising ways to make services available, while at the same time containing costs. But states still must comply with the efficiency, economy, quality of care, and access standards. It appears that Congress intended payments to be flexible within a range; payments should be no higher than what is required to provide efficient and economical care, but still high enough to provide for quality care and to ensure access to services.

The Budget Committee also noted that states should now "be free to design their reimbursement systems to provide incentives for provision of primary care over specialty care or to reduce the urban-rural differential in payment levels." *Id.* at 313. The Department argues that if reimbursement levels were related to costs, it would be impossible to achieve these goals. But undercompensating hospitals cannot achieve these goals. Incentives to non-hospital providers to treat Medicaid outpatients and encouragement of Medicaid patients to utilize alternate services is required. The Department argued, as an example, that their 1989 reduction in reimbursement for cesarean sections, that was intended to discourage unnecessary cesarean sections, would not have been allowed if the Department had to reimburse at a level that related to the cost of services. But the Department forgets that it is still free to discourage unnecessary procedures through utilization controls without violating § 1396a(a)(30)(A). If a reimbursement rate provides an incentive to use an inappropriate service, then it is not consistent with efficiency, economy, and quality of care.

The equal access to care provision of § 1396a(a)(30)(A) was added by amendment in 1989, although it had been implemented prior to 1989 through federal regulation. 42 C.F.R. § 447.204. In its Rate Study, the Department admitted that the access requirement serves to mandate a minimum payment standard. 1 A.R. at 13. However, the Department contends that in the absence of a de facto access problem, any payment rate would meet this minimum standard.

De facto access, produced by factors totally unrelated to reimbursement levels, does not satisfy the requirement of § 1396a(a)(30)(A) that payments must be sufficient to enlist enough providers. Currently, access appears to be driven to a degree by factors independent of costs of the services. Hospitals that accept any Medicare payments and that operate emergency departments are legally required to treat emergency patients regardless of their ability to pay. 42 U.S.C. 1395dd. Emergency room services represent more than 50 percent of all Medi-Cal payments for hospital outpatient services. 2 A.R. at 60–69; 3 A.R. at 166. Hospitals have a legal obligation to provide those services regardless of the level of Medi-Cal reimbursement rates. Some hospitals also serve patients with non-emergency conditions regardless of their ability to pay because those hospitals have a mission to serve everyone. A hospital's only option to avoid accepting insufficient Medicaid reimbursements is to close their emergency departments or stop accepting any federal funds through Medicare.

In this case there has been no assertion of a provider participation problem. However, as discussed above, any hospital that accepts any Medicare payments and operates an emergency department, cannot opt out of providing emergency care for Medicaid patients, regardless of the reimbursement rates. 42 U.S.C. § 1395dd. Since most hospitals accept Medicare patients and operate emergency departments, and many hospitals have public service missions to provide care regardless of patients' ability to pay, currently provider participation by such institutions is assured.

The compelling "other" reasons for provider participation by such institutions has allowed the Department to ignore the relationship of reimbursement levels to provider costs when determining whether payments are sufficient to ensure access to quality services. The result is that the Department has not sought to shift services to entities that could provide them more economically and efficiently but rather to force hospitals to provide the service and to shift the cost to other patients. This technique of underpayment for services received is not economic, efficient or attentive to adequate access. It is neither economical nor efficient for the system as a whole. The Department need not follow a rigid formula of payments equal to an efficiently and economically operated hospital's costs regardless of other factors such as incentives and utilization controls. But the Department must undertake to determine what it costs an efficient hospital economically to provide quality care. Absent some justification from the Department, the reimbursement rates must ultimately bear a reasonable relationship to those costs.

The Department argues that such an interpretation of § 1396a(a)(30)(A) effectively applies the rate-setting statute for inpatient services, § 1396a(a)(13)(A) (the "Boren Amendment"), to outpatient services. The Boren Amendment requires states to set reimbursement rates based on the costs that must be incurred by efficiently and economically operated hospitals. The Department argues that the lack of such explicit language in § 1396a(a)(30)(A) indicates that Congress did not intend provider costs to be a factor in outpatient rates. The Department further argues that requiring the Department to consider costs when setting outpatient reimbursement rates would render the Boren Amendment superfluous.

We disagree. The Boren Amendment requires the Department to make assurances to the Secretary of Health and Human Services that rates are reasonable and adequate to meet the hospitals' costs, and requires periodic cost reports from hospitals subject to audit by the Department. These requirements are not part of § 1396a(a)(30)(A). The requirements of § 1396a(a)(30)(A) are more flexible than the Boren Amendment, but not so flexible as to allow the Department to ignore the costs of providing services. For payment rates to be consistent with efficiency, economy, quality of care and access, they must bear a reasonable relationship to provider costs, unless there is some justification for rates that do not substantially reimburse providers their costs.[3]

I. Department's Readoption of Existing Reimbursement Rates

Because the Department must consider hospitals' costs based on reliable information when setting reimbursement rates, we conclude that the Department's readoption of the existing Medi-Cal rates violated § 1396a(a)(30)(A).

Since the Director maintains that the payments themselves do not have to bear any relationship to hospitals' costs, she does not even argue that the Department considered them. The department's initial reevaluation of its rates consisted of:

> (1) a contrast of program expenses to the statutory Medi-Care ceiling; (2) Departmental and federal utilization controls that assure that the payments are consistent with sound medical policy regarding medical necessity and quality of care; and (3) independent analyses of substitute providers' efficiency, costs and charges and of various other components of the reimbursement system.

Appellee's Brief at 29.

The analysis of substitute providers involved an inquiry into whether non-hospital providers could deliver outpatient services more efficiently than hospital providers. Upon determining that non-hospital providers were more efficient, the Department concluded that "absent an access problem, 'it is not appropriate to pay additional reimbursement to a provider type that (1) is not as cost efficient as other providers in providing the services, or (2) charges the program more than other providers do for the same services.'" Appellee's Brief at 32.

The Department's analysis fails to consider that the majority of outpatient services are in fact provided in hospitals, and that the majority of hospital outpatient services are in the emergency room. The Department contends that it shouldn't have to compensate hospitals for their costs because emergency rooms are overused and are often used for non-urgent conditions. True as this may be, emergency rooms are overused precisely because they are the only accessible providers of primary care for many people, particularly Medicaid recipients. The Department cannot ensure access by relying on regulations requiring hospitals to treat patients in the emergency room, and then refuse to pay the cost of such treatment because theoretically it could have been provided more efficiently elsewhere. Nowhere does it appear that the Department inquired whether Medi-Cal beneficiaries had adequate access to outpatient services in non-hospital settings.

In concluding that the existing payment rates were consistent with quality of care, the Department relied solely upon the fact that hospitals are forced to provide quality care because of other legal and contractual obligations which have nothing to do with the payment rates. Clearly this conclusion was not based on any consideration of the costs of providing quality care.

The Department's initial Rate Study did not include any analysis of the relationship of reimbursement rates to provider costs. Instead, the Rate Study devoted its analysis to sup-

---

3. It is not justifiable for the Department to reimburse providers substantially less than their costs for purely budgetary reasons. *See Beno v. Shalala*, 30 F.3d 1057, 1069 (9th Cir. 1994) (rejecting budget cutting as a legitimate justification for the approval of a waiver from federal AFDC requirements)....

porting the conclusion that "the failure of existing rates to fully compensate providers based upon a cost or charge criterion is not relevant to whether the rates are consistent with efficiency or economy."

After publishing its Rate Study and hearing public comments, the Department did commission a study by Peterson Consulting to evaluate the relationship of reimbursement rates to provider costs. The Peterson study came to conclusions that were markedly different from those in Dr. Zaretsky's analysis for the Hospitals. The main difference in methodology between the two studies is that the Peterson study looked at total Medi-Cal payments to hospitals including inpatient, outpatient and disproportionate share payments, while the Zaretsky analysis looked specifically at outpatient payments.

... Since the Department did not consider hospitals' costs when reevaluating its rates, it has not appropriately applied § 1396a(a)(30)(A).... Therefore, the Department's actions in readopting the original reimbursement rates were arbitrary and capricious, and contrary to law.

CONCLUSION

* * *

Upon remand, the Department should undertake responsible cost studies that will provide reliable data as to the hospitals' costs in providing outpatient services to the end that it determine the cost to an efficient hospital economically providing quality care. The state must then set rates that have some reasonable relation to such costs, the state bearing the burden of justifying any rate that substantially deviates from such determined costs.

REVERSED and REMANDED.

Notes and Questions

1. If a health care provider does not voluntarily disclose evidence of Medicaid fraud, this is used as a factor in denying further participation in Medicaid programs. Because of this policy many health car providers fully disclose their records to the federal government. What privacy interests and or privileges could be violated by this full disclosure? Liesa L. Richter, *Corporate Salvation or Damnation? Proposed New Federal Legislation on Selective Waiver*, 76 FORDHAM L. REV. 129 (2007).

2. What would happen if Medicaid reimbursed mental health facilities at a much lower rate than other residential treatment centers? Would mental health patients flock to Nursing homes and other equivalent care facilities? What would the consequences of this shift be? Richard G. Frank & Sherry A. Glied, *Better But Not Well: Mental Health Policy in the United States Since 1950*, 33 J. HEALTH POL. POL'Y & L. 135 (2008).

3. Anyone who brings a successful qui tam action against a Medicaid provider is entitled to up to thirty percent of the amount recovered. This is undoubtedly a strong tool to combat Medicaid fraud. However, do the risks associated with frivolous claims outweigh the effectiveness of this fraud deterrent? John M. Degnan & Sally A. Scoggin, *Avoiding Health Care Qui Tam Actions*, 74 DEF. COUNS. J. 385 (2007).

4. The government is allowed to recoup overpayments to health care providers that are involved in bankruptcy proceedings. However, this is a discretionary act. What type of abuses could this discretion cause? Harold L. Kaplan & Timothy R. Casey, *Recoupment in Health Care Bankruptcies: A Shrinking Issue?*, 26-OCT AM. BANKR. INST. J. 16 (2007).

D. TRICARE, VA Healthcare, and Other

Note on Tricare

Congress set up the TRICARE healthcare system for military families largely in response to the high costs associated with the former program, Civilian Health and Medical Program of the Uniformed Services (CHAMPUS). The CHAMPUS program provided cost reimbursement to families of military service members, and retirees and their eligible family members, when treatment at Military Treatment Facilities (MTFs) was unavailable. When these beneficiaries could not obtain treatment at MTFs they obtained treatment from civilian doctors. CHAMPUS reimbursed the costs that the beneficiaries incurred from the civilian doctors. This cost reimbursement plan under CHAMPUS incurred enormous costs for the federal government.

In response to these costs the Department of Defense (DOD) launched the TRICARE program. Under TRICARE beneficiaries that cannot obtain treatment through MTFs have three options. TRICARE Prime is basically an HMO program. Under TRICARE Prime, beneficiaries must first go to their primary care providers and receive referrals to specialists. In return for this inconvenience, those that use TRICARE Prime incur very low co-payments and deductibles.

TRICARE Extra essentially works as a preferred provider network. This gives beneficiaries a good amount of discretion to choose their health care providers. That discretion comes at the cost of higher co-payments and deductibles. TRICARE Standard is very similar to the original CHAMPUS program. TRICARE Standard allows for fee-for-service coverage, the downside being higher co-payments and deductibles. The plan that covers beneficiaries eligible for Medicare. So, TRICARE is named TRICARE for Life and that coverage was added in 2002.

TRICARE Management Activity (TMA), formerly the Office of CHAMPUS, administers these TRICARE Programs within the DOD. TMA is responsible for awarding contracts to civilian companies, and these companies are contracted to administer various aspects of TRICARE. These contracts are called regional support contracts.

TRICARE issues a request for proposals (RFP) for the three TRICARE regions. This is a competitive bid, where any contractor could submit a proposal for any and all of the three regions. However, any single contractor would only be awarded one region. The contractors under this proposal received a fixed administrative cost per claim. Additionally, the contracts gave incentives for performance and for moving beneficiaries treatment to MFTs.

For further discussions of TRICARE contracting issues see: Fed. Pub. LLC (2007), DP GLASS-CLE 173 (Westlaw); David W. Burgett et al., *2006 Government Contract Decisions of the Federal Circuit*, 52 Am. U. L. Rev., 1073, 1112 (2007); John H. Cawley & Andrew B. Whitford, *Improving the Design of Competetive Bidding in Medicare Advantage*, 32 J. Health Pol. Pol'y & L. 317, 331 (2007); Robert E. Korroch, et al., *2004 Year-In-Review: Analysis of Significant Federal Circuit Government Contracts Decisions*, 34 Pub. Cont. L.J. 573 (2005); Major Steven Patoir, *Contract and Fiscal Law Development of 2004 — The Year in Review*, 2005-Jan Army Law 82, (2005); Kimberly D. Baker & Arissa M. Peterson, *Post-Caremark Implications for Health Care Organization Boards of* Directors, 3 Seattle J. for Soc. Just. 387 (2004); Major Mary E. Harney, et al., *Contract and Fiscal Law Developments of 1999 — The Year in Review*, 2000-JAN Army Law. 1, 123 (2000); Major Kathyrn R. Sommerkamp, et al., *Developments of 1996 — The Year in Review*, 1997-Jan Army Law. 3, 102 (1997); Captain Bryant S. Banes, *Ruminations on "Public Interests": Government use of Minimum Experience Requirements in Medical Service Contracts*, 1996-Jul Army Law. 29 (1996); *Contract Performance*, 2002-FEB Army Law. 56 (2002).

Total Medical Management, Inc., Plaintiff-Appellee, v. The United States, Defendant-Appellant

See Chapter 1

PGBA, LLC, Plaintiff, v. United States, Defendant, Wisconsin Physicians Service Insurance Corporation, Intervening Defendant

United States Court of Federal Claims
No. 03-2773-C.
Filed Under Seal March 31, 2004
Reissued April 22, 2004

LETTOW, Judge.

... Plaintiff, PGBA, LLC ("PGBA"), filed this case to challenge the government's award of a contract for the processing of certain beneficiaries' claims under TRICARE, a military health care benefits program, to Wisconsin Physicians Service Insurance Corporation ("WPS"), the intervening-defendant.... For the reasons set forth below, the Court finds that the government committed errors that materially affected the bidding process adversely to PGBA. Applying 28 U.S.C. § 1491(b)(2), the Court declines to order injunctive or declaratory relief against the contractual award, but it concludes that PGBA is entitled to recover its reasonable costs incurred in bid preparation and proposal.

BACKGROUND

A. The Contract Solicitation

TRICARE is the government health care system that provides benefits to dependents of active duty service members as well as retired service members and their dependents. TMA [TRICARE Management Activity] administers TRICARE within the Department of Defense. TMA contracts with civilian companies to implement various aspects of the program....

* * *

In October 2000 Congress passed "TRICARE for Life" legislation, Pub.L. 106-398, Div. A, Title VII, § 712, 114 Stat. 1654A-176 (Oct. 30, 2000) (codified at 10 U.S.C. § 1086(d) and 42 U.S.C. § 1395ggg). Def.'s Counter-Stmt. of Facts at 3. Prior to the enactment of this statute, when an individual who was eligible for TRICARE benefits became eligible for coverage under Medicare due to age or health, such an individual would lose his or her eligibility for TRICARE benefits. Compl. ¶ 7. However, pursuant to the TRICARE for Life law, individuals eligible for Medicare coverage now remain eligible for TRICARE benefits, with Medicare typically serving as the primary payer and TRICARE as secondary payer, reimbursing only those portions of a claim not covered by Medicare. Def.'s Counter-Stmt. of Facts at 3–4.[2] Upon passage of TRICARE for Life, TMA added the processing of dual-eligible beneficiaries' claims to the existing MCS [Managed Care Support] contracts

---

2. In some instances, TRICARE covers categories of costs that Medicare does not, and in those instances TRICARE serves as the primary payer. *See* Hr'g Tr. at 50–52, 81.

by way of modifications to those contracts. Compl. ¶ 8. The MCS prime contractors, in turn, modified their subcontracts to incorporate processing of this new class of claims. *Id.* Accordingly, PGBA, as a subcontractor, took responsibility for processing approximately 82% of the dual-eligible beneficiaries' claims, and WPS took on work regarding the remaining 18%. *See* Def.'s Counter-Stmt. of Facts at 4–5.

In 2002, TMA announced plans to reorganize the MCS system by consolidating the contracts and geographic coverage to three contracts covering three regions. Compl. ¶ 9. The new system of contracts is known as "TRICARE Next Generation" or "T-Nex." The T-Nex adjustments to the TRICARE system also incorporate a revision of the claim processing system for dual-eligible beneficiaries, replacing the existing sub-contracting scheme with one stand-alone contract. This new contract will consolidate all claims processing for dual-eligible beneficiaries, without regard to the regional specifications related to the more comprehensive T-Nex contracts. TMA issued a Request for Proposals ("RFP") for the new contract, labeled the "TRICARE Dual Eligible Fiscal Intermediary Contract" or "TDEFIC," under Solicitation Number MDA906-02-R-007 on September 6, 2002. Compl. ¶ 12. The TDEFIC was intended to provide claims-processing and associated customer-support services for approximately 1.7 million dual-eligible TRICARE beneficiaries. *Id.* The provision of services under the TDEFIC is scheduled to begin on April 1, 2004. AR B. 15, T. 68.

* * *

The solicitation also described evaluation factors and subfactors that would be considered by TMA in making its decision:

Factor 1		-Technical Merit (includes proposal risk)
	Subfactor 1	-Claims Processing
	Subfactor 2	-Beneficiary and Provider Satisfaction
	Subfactor 3	-Effective Management Approach
	Subfactor 4	-Transition In
	Subfactor 5	-Data Access
Factor 2		-Past Performance
Factor 3		-Price

AR B. 8, T. 52 at 493. The RFP stated that each of the three evaluation factors would be weighted equally and that each of the subfactors under the "Technical Merit" factor would be weighted equally. AR B. 15, T. 100 at 307, ¶ M-4.1. All evaluation factors other than price, when combined, would be considered significantly more important than price alone. *Id.* If all competing proposals were approximately equal in terms of non-price factors, then TMA could award the contract to the offeror of the lowest price. *Id.* ¶ M-4.2.

* * *

On February 12, 2003, PGBA, WPS, and Unisys Corporation ("Unisys") each submitted a proposal for TDEFIC. Compl. ¶ 16. Each offeror also made an oral presentation to TMA, Compl. ¶ 16; AR Vids., and TMA held discussions with each of the offerors. Compl. ¶ 16; *see infra,* at 201. After the discussions, the offerors were given the opportunity to revise or amend their proposals, and all three submitted "Final Proposal Revisions" on April 28, 2003. Compl. ¶ 16.

B. TMA's Consideration of the Proposals and Award to WPS

TMA employed a multiple-stage process in analyzing the three proposals, with responsibility for evaluating the proposals divided among various individuals and groups: a Contracting Officer, a Source Selection Authority ("SSA"), a Legal Advisor, and a Source Selection Evaluation Board ("SSEB") consisting of a Chair, a Source Selection Evaluation Team ("SSET"), a Performance Risk Assessment Group ("PRAG"), and a Price/Cost Team ("P/CT"). AR B. 15, T. 99 at 265–68.

* * *

C. Post-Award Proceedings

Both Unisys and PGBA filed post-award protests with GAO.... Under a provision of the Competition in Contracting Act of 1984, Pub.L. No. 98-369, Div. B, Title VII, § 2741(a), 98 Stat. 1200 (July 18, 1984) (codified, as amended, at 31 U.S.C. § 3553), an automatic stay of the award was engendered by these protests....

ANALYSIS

* * *

B. TMA's Evaluation of the Technical-Merit Factor

The main thrust of PGBA's challenge to TMA's award of the TDEFIC to WPS concerns the technical merit of the offerors' proposals. Four separate aspects of TMA's consideration are in dispute: (1) data access, (2) "transition in," (3) claims processing, and (4) customer satisfaction.

1. The data-access subfactor.

In the RFP, TMA indicated that "data access" (subfactor 5) was important because it wished to insure that "Government designated individuals" had "ready access" to "contractor maintained data to support DoD's financial planning, health systems planning, medical resource management, clinical management, clinical research, and contract administration activities." ...

... [T]he "Data Access" section of PGBA's original proposal merely provided a description of PGBA's two software packages, *id.* at 354–63, coupled with the simple assertion that "PGBA commits to meeting the government's data requirements." *Id.* at 353, 364.

... PGBA alleges that during the ensuing discussions, the Chair of the SSET criticized PGBA's proposal on the "data access" subfactor for its lack of specificity in terms of the number of government employees who would be given access to beneficiary claim processing data.

* * *

PGBA avers that as a result of this exchange, when it submitted its final revisions to its proposal, PGBA added specificity to the "Data Access" portion of its proposal and this specificity was then held against PGBA by the SSEB. It contrasts the adverse treatment it received with the uncritical evaluation accorded WPS. *See* Pl.'s Mot. at 25–28; Pl.'s Reply at 11. PGBA provided a written response to the question that was discussed with the SSEB, stating "PGBA will initially support access for up to 200 users of Execu-DASH, with 50 of those users having access to raw data through Business Objects." AR B. 11, T. 61 at 58.

* * *

The record supports PGBA's assertion that TMA erred both in the lack of clarity in the RFP respecting data access and in the SSEB's irregularity and inconsistency in evaluating this technical subfactor. As the SSA noted, the RFP was not adequate to demand the degree of specificity apparently sought by the SSEB Chair. Moreover, there was no basis for the SSEB to demand both clairvoyance and specificity on the part of PGBA but not of the other offerors. Such uneven treatment goes against the standard of equality and fair-play that is a necessary underpinning of the federal government's procurement process and amounts to an abuse of the agency's discretion. *See Doty v. United States,* 53 F.3d 1244, 1251 (Fed.Cir.1995) ("When procedural violations committed by the agency are egregiously removed from fairness, this constitutes an abuse of the agency's administrative discretion.") ...

A full assessment of prejudice turns on an evaluation of this fault along with an analysis of PGBA's other claims. However, PGBA's proposal was fully within the zone of consideration for a contractual award, and the SSA's and SSEB's handling of the data-access element shows an unequal and unfair treatment of PGBA in an area where the RFP concededly lacked clarity and the offerors had to rely on TMA to rectify the resulting ambiguity. That the SSEB affirmatively misled PGBA's representatives rather than curing the ambiguity goes a long way toward showing prejudice.

* * *

3. The claims-processing subfactor.

PGBA and WPS each received a Blue/Exceptional rating for the claim-processing subfactor. PGBA challenges several of the "discriminators" that the SSA and the SSEB applied in rating WPS as Blue and in justifying payment of WPS's higher cost. In this connection, PGBA alleges that the SSA misunderstood WPS's proposal as well as the applicable law and regulations that apply to the interaction between Medicare intermediaries and TRICARE claims processors. Pl.'s Mot. at 34.

First, PGBA argues that TMA incorrectly believed that WPS would be able to recover certain "cross-over" fees paid by TRICARE to Medicare intermediaries.

* * *

(a.) Cross-over fees.

After a dual-eligible beneficiary or his or her health care provider submits a claim to Medicare, a Medicare fiscal intermediary will process the claim, pay the portion covered by Medicare, and determine whether the beneficiary appears eligible for TRICARE benefits. AR B. 5, T. 41 at 204–205. The Medicare intermediary responsible for that claim will then transmit the claim payment information to a TRICARE claims processor (*i.e.,* PGBA or WPS under the existing sub-contractor scheme or the TDEFIC contractor in the future) for payment of the remaining portion. *Id.* Such a claim is referred to as a "cross-over claim." *Id.;* AR B. 15, T. 69 at 13 ("A cross-over claim is a claim that is paid by Medicare and then sent to TRICARE to pay the beneficiary's remaining out-of-pocket expenses."). When the TRICARE claims processor receives such information, that processor is charged a "cross-over fee." Def.'s Counter-Stmt. of Facts at 37, ¶ 73. This fee is assessed whenever information is exchanged between TRICARE claims processors and a Medicare intermediary, even in instances when a claim was submitted erroneously, *e.g.,* when a claim is sent to TRICARE for someone who is not eligible for a TRICARE benefit or when it is sent to TRICARE prior to Medicare's paying its portion. AR B. 5, T. 41 at 204–205....

PGBA argues that the SSA incorrectly believed that WPS would be able to recoup mistakenly paid benefit payments when she noted as a strength that WPS would utilize its position as a Medicare processor to "[g]et back money from Medicare Fiscal Intermediaries/Carriers for claims that shouldn't have crossed over." Pl.'s Mot. at 31 (quoting AR B. 15, T. 69 at 19).

* * *

The Court finds that the record supports PGBA's assertion that the SSA was mistaken regarding what money WPS would "get back" in relation to erroneously paid cross-over claims.... Although this apparent error relates only to one of the "discriminators" used by TMA to determine WPS's blue rating, the Court finds that it was nonetheless potentially prejudicial to PGBA given that (1) TMA assigned importance to it as part of the justification for making an award to the high bidder, (2) the error also reflected a misunderstanding of the cope of WPS's commitment to negotiate favorable Trading Partner Agreements, *see infra,* and (3) PGBA was admittedly competitive in the solicitation and very "close" to WPS.

* * *

E. PGBA's Request for Equitable Relief

* * *

Balancing the hardships between the government and WPS on the one hand and PGBA on the other, the Court determines that adequate justification does not exist to set aside the contract and require a new round of solicitation. This procurement has already lasted nearly one and one half years, from the issuance of the RFP in September 2002 to the anticipated work commencement date of April 1, 2004, and WPS avers that it has expended significant resources preparing for implementation. Interv.-Def.'s Opp. at 63; Interv.-Def.'s Reply at 24. Revoking the contract and requiring a new solicitation would likely engender an additional delay of at least the same length. In light of these considerations, the Court determines that the balance of hardships weighs in favor of denying PGBA's request for declaratory relief.

* * *

CONCLUSION

For the reasons set forth above, PGBA's motion for judgment upon the administrative record is denied in part and granted in part. The government's cross-motion for judgment upon the administrative record is denied in part and granted in part. WPS's cross-motion for judgment upon the administrative record is granted. PGBA is denied declaratory relief, but it may recover its reasonable bid preparation and proposal costs in an amount to be determined after further proceedings in this action. PGBA also is awarded costs pursuant to 28 U.S.C. § 2412(a).

* * *

Notes and Questions

1. The regional support contracts have been found to perform primarily administrative functions and are therefore exempt from the Truth in Negotiating Act ("TINA"). This means that when one of the three regional contractors submits cost or pricing data to the government this data does not need to be certified. Do you think that this is a problem? Fed. Pub. LLC (2007), DP GLASS-CLE 173 (Westlaw).

2. In Captain Bryant S. Banes article he opines that ridding TRICARE of all small business set-asides is the appropriate course of action. Captain Banes goes on to state that even something such as custodial services should be exempt from small business set asides. The justification stated for this is that beneficiaries of TRICARE deserve the best possible care available. Captain Bryant S. Banes, *Ruminations on "Public Interests": Government Use of Minimum Experience Requirements in Medical Service Contracts,* 1996-Jul Army

Law. 29 (1996). Do mandatory small business set asides necessarily reduce the quality of services received by beneficiaries of TRICARE?

3. When TRICARE contracts are awarded, many times the company that is awarded the contract employ former government officials that were responsible for awarding TRI-CARE contracts. The General Accounting office has found that absent some other impropriety this type of situation is proper. Major Kathyrn R. Sommerkamp, et al., *Developments of 1996—The Year in Review*, 1997-Jan Army Law. 3, 102 (1997).

4. One aspect of the TRICARE program is the pharmaceutical reimbursement plan. Under this TRICARE beneficiaries purchase drugs from retail pharmacies and the Department of Defense reimburses the pharmacies for the beneficiaries purchases.

Prior to 2004 the Department of Defense reimbursed the pharmacies and pharmaceutical companies based on the wholesale price. In 2004 the Veterans Administration (VA) sent a letter to the manufacturers stating that the VA would no longer pay wholesale prices for the drugs, rather the VA would now pay the Federal Ceiling Price for these drugs. This new pricing scheme was struck down because it did not comply with the notice-and-comment requirement for a substantive rule. David W. Burgett et al., *2006 Government Contract Decisions of the Federal Circuit*, 52 Am. U. L. Rev., 1073, 1112 (2007).

5. A determination of best interest is reviewable, when it is used to override a stay. There is a severe consequence to allowing this determination to be unreviewable, as the government sought in *PGBA*. This would essentially allow an agency to ignore an automatic stay with no reason. If a decision cannot be reviewed no reason needs to be given because there is no enforcement mechanisms to ensure that it is actually in the governments best interest to override the stay. Young Cho, *Judicial Review of "The Best Interest Of the United States" Justification for CICA Overrides: Overstepping Boundaries or Giving the Bite Back?*, 34 Pub. Cont. L.J. 337 (2005).

Note on VA Healthcare

The Veterans Administration makes most of its purchases through the Federal Supply Schedule. That Federal Supply Schedule allows the Veterans Administration to make purchases from several different contractors. Each purchase is individually negotiated between the contractor and the Veterans Administration National Acquisition Center. The Veterans Administration does not have to enter into contracts in any specific time period; the Veterans Administration may enter into contracts on an ongoing basis.

The Veterans administration makes purchases from the following Federal Supply Schedules: Medical Supplies, Dental Equipment and Supplies, Pharmaceuticals, Invitro Diagnostics and Reagents, Medical Equipment, Pacemakers, Antibacterial Soap, Wheelchairs, Cost-per-test Laboratory, Subsistence, New Item Introductory Schedule, and X-ray Equipment and Supplies.

Contractors that are awarded a Veterans Administration contract through the Federal Supply Schedule may also enter into a Blanket Purchase Agreement with the Veterans Administration. A Blanket Purchase Agreement is a simplified method of filling anticipated repetitive needs for supplies or services by establishing 'charge accounts' with qualified sources of supply. Blanket Purchase agreements are generally used to make purchases when the Veterans Administration does not know what the specifics of an order will be on a regular basis.

The Veterans Administration has sought to further reduce its procurement costs through the use of national formularies. National formularies allow the Veterans Administration to purchase a specific item through one contractor and use that product nationally.

Also, the Veterans Administration administers a Prime Vendor Program. Through this program the Veterans Administration awards a contract to distribute the various items that the Veterans Administration purchases and distribute the items to customers throughout a specified region.

For a further discussion of Veterans Administration contracting issues see: William B. Weeks et al., *Does the VA Offer Good Health Care Value*, 35 No. 4 J. Health Care Fin. (Summer, 2009); Austin B. Frakt, Steven D. Pizer & Ann M. Hendricks, *Controlling Prescription Drug Costs: Regulation and the Role of Interest Groups in Medicare and the Veterans Health Administration*, 33 J. Health Pol. Pol'y & L. 1079 (2008); Donna Lee Yesner, Stephen Ruscus, *Selling Medical Supplies And Services Through The Department Of Veterans Affairs Federal Supply Schedule Program*, 37 Pub. Cont. L.J. 489 (Spring 2008); Adam Oliver, *The Veterans Health Administration: An American Success Story?* Mil. Q., Vol. 85 No. 1 (2007).

Appeal of Fischer Imaging Corporation
VABCA No. 6343
2002 WL 31424586
October 22, 2002

OPINION BY ADMINISTRATIVE JUDGE KREMPASKY

* * *

FINDINGS OF FACT

... The Contract includes the standard Federal Acquisition Regulation ("FAR"), 48 C.F.R. Chapter 1, prescribed for ID/IQ contracts for commercial items, including the following clauses relevant to these appeals:

CONTRACT TERMS AND CONDITIONS-COMMERCIAL ITEMS, FAR

* * *

The relevant part of FAR 52.212-4 is subsection (a) INSPECTION/ACCEPTANCE which states:

> The contractor shall only tender for acceptance those items that conform to the requirements of this contract. The Government reserves the right to inspect or test any supplies or services that have been tendered for acceptance. The Government may require repair or replacement of nonconforming supplies or reperformance of nonconforming services at no increase in contract price. The Government must exercise its post acceptance rights (1) within a reasonable time after the defect was discovered or should have been discovered; and (2) before any substantial change occurs in the condition of the item, unless the change is due to the defect in the item.

* * *

(R4, tabs 2, 38) On September 20, 1996, VANAC awarded Delivery Order (DO) 797160814 to FIC for the "Epic 32 Single Plane Electrophysiology System and associated peripheral equipment (EP32) for delivery to VAMC LA for a price of $405,218....

Mr. Kris Kirwan, a SAMS inspector, inspected the EP32 on September 14–18, 1998. By memorandum of September 22, 1998 to the CO, Mr. Kirwan recommended rejection of the EP32.... FIC did not address one of the performance discrepancies listed by the VA, kvp fluoroscopic response time, in its October 25 letter. In a November 14, 1998 internal assessment, FIC acknowledged that the kvp response time problem could not be addressed with field forces. (R4, tabs 5, 27)

Mr. Bense requested that VAMC LA reinspect the EP 32 by "local verification" in a November 18, 1998 memorandum. The inspection/local verification was performed by VAMC LA and signed by Dr. Phillip Sager, Staff Physician in the VAMC LA Electrophysiology Lab on December 23, 1998.... Dr. Sager's report to the CO represented that most of the SAMS identified discrepancies had not been corrected. In addition, Dr. Sager complained that the EP32 fluoroscopic image was poor and that the "table [EP32] frequently breaks." Dr. Sager's response to the CO ended with the following statement:

> My staff and myself have spent many hours with Fischer trying to get the system's deficiencies fixed to no avail. The response has been terrible and if was possible to have the system removed and replaced by one from another vendor, that would be my choice. The vendor should definitely not be paid.

* * *

On February 17, 2000, Mr. Bense issued a CURE NOTICE to FIC citing that the EP32 did not function fully as ordered and that FIC had not ensured the proper functioning of the EP32. Mr. Bense gave FIC until March 1, 2000 to correct the EP32 "failures", including those noted in the February 16, 2000 inspection report, and to insure the compliance of the system with the OPERATIONAL UPTIME Contract clause....

* * *

(R4, tab 13) FIC responded to Mr. Bense's CO's February 16, 2000 inspection letter by a letter of March 3, 2000 wherein it represented that 12 of the 13 discrepancies listed in the VA's February 16 letter had been satisfactorily resolved and that FIC was taking steps to resolve the 13th listed discrepancy, kvp response time, with a "software/firmware" fix. ***

* * *

In the Termination for Cause, Mr. Bense also directed FIC to remove the EP32 from VAMC LA and informed FIC that the VA would be procuring replacement equipment and that FIC would be liable for any costs of the replacement equipment over the DO price. The Termination for Cause was accompanied by a unilateral modification terminating the DO for cause and reducing the DO to $0 and a Collection Voucher demanding FIC's immediate re-payment of the 80% of the DO price ($324,174) previously paid by the VA. Mr. Bense, on March 15, 2000, also sent a memorandum to VAMC LA directing it to cease using the EP32 and providing instructions concerning FIC's forthcoming removal of the system. FIC removed the EP32 from VAMC LA on May 18, 2000. (R4, tabs 16, 17, 29)

* * *

DISCUSSION

We have had recent occasion to address an appeal from a termination for cause under another delivery order placed under the Contract in *Fischer Imaging Corporation*, VABCA-6125–6127, 2002 WL 31057467 (September 10, 2002), which we will designate as *Fischer I*. *Fischer I* involved the VA's termination for cause of another delivery order under the Contract for an FIC electrophysiology system similar to the EP32. The positions of the parties in this case essentially mirror those taken in *Fischer I* and, since * the identical Contract provisions apply, the same result will obtain.

* * *

Notwithstanding its failure to complete its inspection of the EP32 until 53 days after it received FIC's request for inspection, the VA asserts its "deemed acceptance" is essentially without Contractual significance and it is permitted to act as if it never accepted the EP32. As we explained in *Fischer I*, adoption of the VA's position would require us to read the "deemed acceptance" provisions of the ACCEPTANCE PROCEDURES out of the Contract, contrary to the accepted rules of contract interpretation, which require that we try to reconcile the clear language of the Contract in order to impart meaning to all its terms.

Moreover, it would seem the position the VA takes in its BRIEF asserting that the deemed acceptance provisions of the Contract do not impact the VA's absolute right to unilaterally determine when it accepted the EP32, is contrary to the CO's understanding of the Contract terms. The CO, when requesting the initial SAMS inspection, asked that it be completed within the 30-day window provided in the Contract indicating that he understood the Contract terms regarding acceptance. *Hercules, Inc. v. United States*, 292 F.3rd 1378 (Fed. Cir. 2002); *Brant Construction Management, Inc.*, VABCA No. 5391, 98-2 BCA ¶ 30, 073.

As addenda to FAR 52.212-4(a), the Contract ACCEPTANCE PROCEDURES must be read in conjunction with the FAR clause and reconciled with those provisions. The FAR and VA acceptance terms can be reconciled by reading Paragraph (d) of the ACCEPT-ANCE PROCEDURES as an implementation of the FAR 52.212-4(a) instructions concerning post-acceptance rights.... Thus, the VA's failure to inspect within 30 days of the request for inspection is an "acceptance" of the EPX under the terms of the Contract.

Since the VA accepted the EP32, the termination of the DO for cause is an attempt by the VA to revoke that acceptance. In other words, we look to the parameters of the VA's post-acceptance rights to determine if the termination was proper. The Contract, in the clause at 52.212-4(a), in the factual situation here, provides for the VA to exercise its post-acceptance rights "within a reasonable time" after discovery of a deficiency in the EP32. Thus, we must ascertain, in the absence of a Contract definition of "reasonable", whether the VA's properly revoked its acceptance by the termination for cause in March 2000, 597 days after the VA accepted the EP32 and 540 days after the CO was first informed of the EP32 deficiencies forming the basis for the termination. As we did in *Fischer I*, we look to the Uniform Commercial Code (UCC) to provide us guidance on the effectiveness of the VA's revocation of acceptance....

The CO's knowledge of the EP32's deficiencies ostensibly making it unacceptable on September 22, 1998 and the VA's continuous productive use of the EP32 for medical procedures for well over one year prior to the attempted revocation speak for themselves. UCC § 2-608 states, in relevant part:

> (1) The buyer may revoke his acceptance of a lot or commercial unit whose non-conformity substantially impairs its value to him if he has accepted it
>
> (a) on the reasonable assumption that its nonconformity would be cured and it has not been seasonably cured....
>
> * * *
>
> (2) Revocation of acceptance must occur within a reasonable time after the buyer discovers or should have discovered the ground for it and before any substantial change in condition of the goods which is not caused by their own defects. It is not effective until the buyer notifies the seller of it.

As we explained in *Fischer I*, the VA could validly revoke its acceptance of the EP32 if the deficiencies "substantially" impaired the value of the EP32 to the VA and its acceptance of the EP32 was based on a reasonable expectation that FIC would cure the deficiencies.... The VA used the EP32 continually for approximately 18 months after it was aware of the response time deficiency; this fact indicates that the response time problem did not substantially impair the value of the EP32 to the VA.

* * *

Finally, the reasonableness of the CO's termination decision is called into question by the facts presented here. In December 1999, the CO solicited VAMC LA for evidence of the EP32's deficiencies necessary to effectuate removal of the system, a purpose he related to VAMC LA personnel who had already expressed "buyer's remorse" about its selection of the EP32 and complained to the CO. The response to this solicitation for damaging evidence is surprising only in the fact that VAMC LA could provide only generalized complaints and evidence that, in the course of over a year, a small number of service calls were required to support the EP32.

Mr. Bense issued the Cure Notice one day after sending FIC the results of the second SAMS inspection inviting FIC to resolve the deficiencies identified in the inspection and to schedule a re-inspection. By his own memoranda and actions, Mr. Bense documents his apparent cavalier disregard of FIC's representations that it had resolved all discrepancies. In the first place, his only attempt to verify FIC's representations was by way of a cursory inquiry to someone at VAMC LA with little or no knowledge of the system. Secondly, he essentially ignores FIC's claim that all discrepancies had been resolved because he received their letter two days after the March 1 date set forth in the Cure Notice. This suggests that the decision to terminate was made in January 2002 and that Mr Bense had no intent to consider any response FIC may make to the inspection or Cure Notice. In the same way that we found the CO's failure to adequately investigate how long it would take a contractor to complete work before terminating that contract for default to be arbitrary in *Jamco Constructors, Inc.*, VABCA Nos. 3271, 3516T, 94-1 BCA ¶ 26,405, Mr. Bense's failure to fairly and adequately consider whether FIC had cured the deficiencies on which the termination is based appears to be arbitrary which would make the termination for cause improper.

Since the VA's acceptance of the EP32 was not properly revoked, the termination of the DO for cause cannot stand. By operation of the Contract clause at FAR 52.212-4 (m), the termination of the DO for cause is converted to a termination for the Government's convenience within the terms of the clause at FAR 52.212-4 (1).

* * *

DECISION

... The termination of Delivery Order V797160814 for cause is converted to a termination for the Government's convenience.... Fischer Imaging Corporation is entitled to a judgment in the amount of $9,600 in the appeal in VABCA-6460 plus interest pursuant to the CONTRACT DISPUTES ACT from September 11, 2000, the date of the Contracting Officer's receipt of the claim.

Notes and Questions

1. It has been established that due to a Contract Doctors training and exercise of independent judgment they are not employees for the purpose of tort claims. Contract Nurses on the other hand are considered employee for the purpose of tort claims. What about Physician Assistants? Physician Assistants receive more training than nurse and less training than doctors. Physician assistants exercise independent judgment quite regularly.

Should Physician Assistants be considered employees for the purposes of tort claims? *Tort Claims Note*, 2000-DEC Army Law. 25 (2000).

2. Black's Law Dictionary defines reformation as "[a]n equitable remedy by which a court will modify a written agreement to reflect the actual intent of the parties." Is it fair to apply this remedy to Veterans Administration contracts that are competitively awarded based on exact written terms? Robert E. Corroch, *2000 Year in Review: Analysis of Significant Federal Circuit Government Contracts Decisions*, 30 Pub. Cont. L.J. 315 (2001).

3. A treatment program was set up to treat Veterans with posttraumatic stress syndrome. This program was set up separately form the Veterans Administration due to the fact that the Veterans distrusted the Veterans Administration. Because of the separation the Veterans administration was not liable for any tort claims relating to this program. *Liability/ Professional Issues*, 25 Mental & Physical Disability L. Rep. 861 (2001).

Empire Healthchoice Assurance, Inc. dba Empire Blue Cross Blue Shield, Petitioner, v. Denise F. McVeigh as Administratrix of the Estate of Joseph E. McVeigh

547 U.S. 677
Decided June 15, 2006
See decision in Chapter 8.

Chapter 10

Construction

The distinctions between construction contracts and "supply" (goods) in government contracting law arise partly from considerations present in basic (private) contract law as well. Government construction contracts have much in common with government supply (goods) contracts. This is why the rest of the chapters in this book apply to both. These similarities include contract awarding by competitive proposals or other methods; authority of government officials and rules of contract administration. Procedures for termination, protests and disputes; and, so on.

However, atop these considerations, a whole additional layer of government contract law especially for construction contracts gets added, that is, a large accumulation for construction contracts of additional statutes, regulations, clauses, and doctrines. The biggest differences concern performance. The "differing site conditions" clause anchors an entire system for dealing with the common complaint that construction contractors encounter conditions on the site during construction that come as a nasty surprise. Furthermore, the government accords financial protection to contractors who receive "defective specifications," i.e., misdrawn plans for their work.

Since the government will not tolerate mechanics liens on its buildings, Congress passed a bond-mandating statute, the Miller Act, to provide a substitute. The government's inability to abide delay has elicited an elaborate evolution of clauses meant to balance penalties for the construction contractor with relief when the government itself causes the delay, referred to as the "suspension of work" clauses. Construction work occurs on a government-owned worksite, leading to contract rules about the work-site. Because the government considers an important secondary goal of its public works projects to be providing decent jobs, statutes establish elaborate labor standards.

The other breach and remedies have their own doctrines as well. Elaborate rules disentangle the different causes of delay and the remedies for these. Moreover, the government owes contractors, when it keeps them waiting, for the cost of overhead. For lawyers, this doctrine, the *Eichleay* doctrine, represents a very complex evolution of consequential damages accounting; for construction firms, it represents a response to the major question of paying for overhead.

The first reading in this section starts with a survey of the many special aspects of government construction contracting. The *DeKonty* case which follows gives a pithy account of the rules of progress payments and project abandonment. Then the *Wickham* case lays out the *Eichleay* doctrine for factoring overhead into delay damages After that comes the discussion of progress payments, sureties, and Miller Act bonds. Finally, the chapter treats differing site conditions.

For further discussions of the general subject of government construction contracting, see: American Bar Association (Forum on the Construction Industry), Federal Government Construction Contracts (2d ed. 2010); W. Stephen Dale, Robert M. D'Onofrio, *Reconciling Concurrency In Schedule Delay And Constructive Accelerations*, 39 Pub. Cont.

L.J. 161 (Winter 2010); Nathan S. Page, *LEEDing The Charge: Using Green Builder Set-Asides To Expand Sustainable Construction And Design*, 39 Pub. Cont. L.J. 373 (Winter 2010); W. Stephen Dale, Kathryn T. Muldoon, *A Government Windfall: ASBCA's Attack On Concurrent Delays As A Basis For Constructive Acceleration*, 44 Procrmt. Law. 4 (Summer 2009); Jeff H. Eckland, Dave S. Laidig, *Lessons Learned From The Collapse And Rebuilding Of The I-35W Bridge: Would The Model Code For Public Infrastructure Have Made a Difference?*, 44 Procrmt. Law. 6 (Winter 2009); Aaron Silberman, *Green Buildings: Federal, State. And Local Governments LEED The Way*, 43 Procrmt. Law. 7 (Spring 2008); Mark E. Hanson, Edmund M. Amorosi, *Overseas Construction Under USAID Regulations: Not Business As Usual*, 43 Procrmt. Law. 7 (Fall 2007); Mark E. Hanson, Aspects Of Construction Scheduling, 41 Procrmt. Law. 3 (Fall 2006).

A. Construction in General

For further discussions of the general subject of government construction contracting and the specific subjects of this section, see: Xavier A. Fanco, *A Comparative Look At A Contractor's Right To Recover Direct Costs Versus Unabsorbed Home Office Overhead In The Event Of Frustrated Early Completion*, 43 Procrmt. Law. 16 (Winter 2008); Peter M. Kutil, Andrew D. Ness, *Concurrent Delay: The Challenge to Unravel Competing Causes of Delay*, 17-OCT Construction Law. 18 (1997); Linda L. Shapiro & Margaret M. Worthington, *Use of the Eichleay Formula to Calculate Unabsorbed Overhead for Government-Caused Delay Under Manufacturing Contracts*, 25 Pub. Cont. L.J. 513 (1996).

Construction Contracts vs. Supply Contracts
From: Government Contract Guidebook Steven W. Feldman
(Thomson Reuters 4th ed. updated 10/2010)

Similarities

The basic principles of government contracting are the same whether a contract is for supplies or construction (although supply contracts involve more varied procedures and contract types than construction contracts). Thus, the policy favoring open competition, the preferences for small businesses and other groups, the rules limiting the authority of government agents, the government's duty of fairness and noninterference with contractors, policies regarding patents and data, and the other fundamental policies and procedures reviewed in earlier chapters in this book with regard to supply contracts apply with equal force to construction contracts.

For example, if a contract is awarded through sealed bidding, the rules governing that method of contracting are generally the same whether the contract is for supplies or construction. Similarly, rules governing fixed-price contracting are the same for supply and construction contracts. In addition, although there are differences between supply and construction contract clauses and circumstances, similar rights and obligations attach in connection with termination for default or termination for convenience of the government, furnishing of government property, contract changes, equitable adjustments, payment, inspections and warranties, and disputes and remedies.

Differences

The differences between supply and construction contracts are primarily traceable to the different physical environments in which they are performed and to the differences in the nature of the contract work.

Differences—Government control

Whereas supply contracts are typically performed in a production facility owned or leased by the contractor and generally under its control, a construction contract is performed on government property. The construction contractor, even when it is responsible for quality control, is subject to a great deal more surveillance and control by government inspectors and other government representatives than the supply contractor.

A burdensome feature of construction contracts is the number of reports the contractor is required to file with the government. Daily reports of work accomplished are often required, as well as reports involving (a) quality control activities, (b) safety procedures, (c) labor disputes, (d) construction or completion schedules, and (e) descriptions—even samples—of materials the contractor proposes to use.

Another aspect of government control is the elaborate performance evaluations that are given to construction contractors....

Differences—Work site

The fact that the contract is performed on a government-owned site or in a government-controlled facility also poses problems of *access* to the work site by the contractor's employees, subcontractors, and material suppliers. Other difficulties faced by the construction contractor are *interference* from concurrent government activities conducted while work is being performed and from the activities of other government contractors, as well as the possible damage or loss of equipment and materials after work hours. The contractor is also responsible for maintaining a safe and clean site. Moreover, even though the work is done on federal property, the construction contractor is responsible for properly disposing of hazardous substances.

Differences—Contract clauses

Construction contractors must also comply with the standard clauses used only in construction contracts. For example, the standard "Permits and Responsibilities" clause makes the contractor "responsible for all damages to persons or property that occur as a result of [its] fault or negligence." That clause also makes the contractor responsible for all materials delivered and work performed "until completion and acceptance of the entire work, except for any completed unit of work, which may have been accepted under the contract." Similarly, the "Payments under Fixed-Price Construction Contracts" clause provides that at the time of each progress payment, the work shall become the sole property of the government (but the contractor remains liable for the repair of any damaged work). Thus, a contractor could be required to bear the cost of work and material damaged, stolen or otherwise removed from the contract site. The "Permits and Responsibilities" clause also requires the contractor to obtain "any necessary licenses and permits" and comply with federal, state, and local safety standards.

Another important standard clause in construction contracts is the "Material and Workmanship" clause. This clause requires that (1) equipment, material, and articles incorporated into the work be "new and of the most suitable grade for the purpose intended" and (2) the work be performed in "a skillful and workmanlike manner."

The "Performance of Work by the Contractor" clause is intended to assure adequate interest in and supervision of all work involved in larger projects—those exceeding $1 million (with some qualifications, such as under small business set asides)—by requiring the general contractor to perform a significant part of the contract work (set forth in the contract in terms of a percentage that reflects the minimum amount of work that must be so performed) with its own forces. For purposes of this clause, "work" includes both labor and materials.

Examples of other standard clauses typically found in government construction contracts (besides the "Specifications and Drawings" clause ...) include the "Accident Prevention" clause, the "Differing Site Conditions" clause, the "Other Contracts" clause requiring the contractor to cooperate with other contractors and government employees working at or near the work site, the "Use and Possession Prior to Completion" clause permitting the government to take possession of or use any completed or partially completed part of the project without legally "accepting" the contract work, and the "Cleaning Up" clause

Differences—Bonds

Construction contractors must also comply with statutory bonding requirements designed to protect both the government and subcontractors. The Miller Act requires construction contractors, for projects exceeding $100,000 that are to be performed in the United States, to furnish payment and performance bonds. For contracts between $30,000 and $100,000, the Contracting Officer selects two or more payment protections from a selection of five alternatives, giving "particular consideration" to inclusion of an irrevocable letter of credit as one of the selected alternatives. If a payment bond is required or selected it must be for the total amount payable under the contract unless the Contracting Officer finds such amount is impractical (but in no case can the amount be less than the performance bond)....

Differences—Labor standards

Construction contractors are subject to stringent statutory requirements regarding the treatment and payment of laborers....

Differences—Changes and delays

One of the most notable features of construction contracts is the number of contract modifications that may be necessary in performing the contract. Construction contracts are virtually always changed during performance as to some aspect of the work. These modifications take the form of ordered changes under the "Changes" clause or constructive changes (see Chapter 15). Such changes to the contract work frequently disrupt the project's schedule and increase its costs. Suspensions of work under a construction contract's "Suspension of Work" clause also frequently form the basis for contractor claims under construction contracts. (The subject of work suspensions is discussed in greater detail in Chapter 29.)

The Federal Circuit has overturned a judicially-created presumption that the government will be at fault for any delay coupled with an extension of a period of performance. In another decision, the court held that concurrent delay caused by the contractor and the government will prevent recovery of the contractor's unabsorbed home office overhead

Differences—Default termination

As mentioned in Chapter 19, terminations for default are less frequent in construction than in supply contracts. In construction contracts, the imposition of liquidated damages for delayed completion of work is more common. The government may collect liquidated damages until the time reasonably required to complete the work. Forgoing its right to terminate a contract for default does not waive the government's right to assess liquidated damages for late completion of the contract.

The "Default" clause for construction contracts varies from the supply contract "Default" clause in some respects. For example, the construction contract "Default" clause renders the *surety* liable for any damage to the government due to the contractor's failure to complete the work within the specified time. The clause also does not require that the government issue a cure notice to the contractor before terminating a contract for default. In addition, the clause requires the contractor to notify the government in writing of the causes of any excusable delay (such as fires, floods, strikes, etc.).

A major advantage for construction contractors is that they are entitled to payment for the value of work they have performed at the time of a termination for default, whereas supply contractors may get nothing for the work they have completed but not delivered. Because the surety company that has guaranteed performance by issuing a performance bond usually completes defaulted construction contracts, disputes concerning repurchase actions and excess costs of completion are relatively rare after termination of a construction contract for default. However, if the surety company is unwilling or unable to complete performance, or if a performance bond has not been furnished (as is the case in most contracts performed outside the United States), or if there is an urgent need to complete the work, the government may complete the project with its own forces and charge the surety and the defaulted contractor the excess costs of completing performance. In another approach, it may award a contract to an alternate contractor to finish the project and assess the defaulted contractor and surety any excess costs

The United States, Appellant, v. Dekonty Corporation, Appellee

No. 90-1356
United States Court of Appeals, Federal Circuit
922 F.2d 826
Decided Jan. 4, 1991

Before RICH, MAYER, and RADER, Circuit Judges.

RADER, Circuit Judge.

The United States (Government) appeals from the judgment of the Armed Services Board of Contract Appeals (Board). DeKonty Corp., 90-2 BCA (CCH) ¶ 22,645, at 113,584 (ASBCA 1990). The Board found that the Government breached its contract with the DeKonty Corporation (DeKonty) by expressing an intent to withhold a scheduled progress payment. The Government appeals. This court reverses.

BACKGROUND

The United States Navy (Navy) contracted with DeKonty for the construction of a child care facility at the Los Angeles Air Force Station. On several occasions during DeKonty's performance, the Resident Officer in Charge of Construction (ROICC) warned DeKonty that the Navy might terminate the contract for default. On July 5, 1985, the ROICC finally recommended a default termination. When informing DeKonty of the recommendation, the ROICC noted that "only a fraction of Termination for Default recommendations are ultimately approved and issued."

DeKonty stopped working at the site on July 16, 1985. On July 19, 1985, the Assistant ROICC wrote a memorandum to the Commanding Officer of the Western Division Naval Facilities Engineering Command (NAVFACENGCOM):

1. The Contractor, DeKonty Corporation, is currently being processed for default. WESTDIV has recommended default: the default package has been forwarded to NAVFACENGCOM for the final decision of the Contracting Officer.

2. Please process partial payment # 5.

3. Prior to issuing partial payment # 5, please check with Bobette Hill [the Termination Contracting Officer], Code 022, X7253, to determine 1) status of contract and 2) whether funds should be released at the time.

Six days later, Mr. DeKonty called the payment office to inquire about the status of progress payment # 5, due on August 8, 1985. He spoke with an unidentified individual who stated that the payment was on hold. Mr. DeKonty made notes of the conversation:

10:00 a.m. Called San Bruno about our June pay request, they informed us that of the $87,590.20 we applied for, approximately $9,000 was approved and they have this on hold until advised by Contracting Div. The Government/U.S. Navy has refused to comply with its contractual obligations.

On July 22, 1985, the ROICC told DeKonty to keep working. Nonetheless, on August 1, 1985, DeKonty formally abandoned performance. DeKonty alleged that the Navy had breached the contract by refusing to make the scheduled progress payment. The Navy later terminated the contract for default. DeKonty appealed to the Board which determined that the Navy committed an anticipatory breach before DeKonty abandoned performance. The Board stated that the Navy breached by expressing a clear intent not to make the August 8, 1985 progress payment. The Board awarded common law breach of contract damages.

DISCUSSION

Under 41 U.S.C. § 609(b) (1987), this court reviews de novo the Board's conclusions of law and defers to its findings of fact unless unsupported by substantial evidence. This court determines that the Board erred.

The Supreme Court set forth the standard for anticipatory breaches:

When one party to [a] ... contract absolutely refuses to perform his contract, and before the time arrives for performance distinctly and unqualifiedly communicates that refusal to the other party, that other party can, if he choose, treat that refusal as a breach and commence an action at once therefor.

Dingley v. Oler, 117 U.S. 490, 499–500, 6 S.Ct. 850, 853, 29 L.Ed. 984 (1886). Dingley further adopted the language of an earlier case which stated:

[A] mere assertion that the party will be unable, or will refuse to perform his contract, is not sufficient; it must be a distinct and unequivocal absolute refusal to perform the promise, and must be treated and acted upon as such by the party to whom the promise was made....

Id. at 503, 6 S.Ct. at 854 (quoting In re Smoot, 82 U.S. 36, 21 L.Ed. 107 (1872)). This court followed that standard in Cascade Pacific Int'l v. United States, 773 F.2d 287 (Fed.Cir.1985). Cascade held that a contracting officer may terminate a contract for anticipatory breach in the event of a

positive, definite, unconditional, and unequivocal manifestation of intent ... on the part of the contractor ... not to render the promised performance when the time fixed ... by the contract shall arrive....

Cascade, 773 F.2d at 293.

The Board relied on two events to support its anticipatory breach determination. The Board found positive and unequivocal intent to breach in the July 19 memorandum. The Board also found an intent to breach in the July 25 statement by the unidentified individual at the payment office. These two events, however, considered individually or collectively, do not show a "positive, definite, unconditional and unequivocal" intent to refuse timely performance of a contract obligation. Rather the record contains substantial evidence showing that the Navy did not express any intent to breach.

The July 19, 1985 Memorandum

The only portion of the July 19, 1985 memorandum which might be germane to DeKonty's allegation of breach is paragraph 3. In that paragraph, the Assistant ROICC asks the contracting officer to check the contract status before releasing payment. This paragraph is not an express refusal to pay DeKonty before the August 8 payment deadline. Rather the Assistant ROICC simply advised NAVFACENGCOM to check to see if the contract was still in effect before payment.

The circumstances justified the caution exhibited in the July 19 memorandum. DeKonty stopped performance at the job site on July 16. Default seemed imminent. Therefore, the Assistant ROICC correctly recommended that the Commanding Officer check the status of the contract before releasing funds. The July 19 memo is not "positive, definite, unconditional and unequivocal [evidence] of intent" to breach, but merely appropriate contract administration.

The July 25, 1985 Conversation

Even assuming that the unidentified person who answered the telephone at the payment office had authority to speak for the Navy, the July 25 conversation did not supply evidence of an anticipatory breach. DeKonty contends that this conversation confirmed suspicions raised by the July 19 memorandum. As stated earlier, the July 19 memorandum did not express an intent to refuse contract performance. Similarly, putting a payment "on hold" does not mean that it is not going to be paid on time. The payment was not due until August 8, 1985.

Moreover, after the July 19 memorandum, the Navy encouraged continued performance on the contract. On July 22, 1985, the ROICC, Commander Niece, and the Assistant ROICC, Lt. Com. Dampier, recommended that DeKonty "proceed with diligence in the execution of construction on this project." At that time, DeKonty remained under an obligation to perform. The Navy's efforts to encourage DeKonty's performance show that the Navy had not earlier expressed an unequivocal intent to breach.

The Navy also processed and approved DeKonty's sixth payment request. As the ROICC explained at a hearing before the Board, this action showed that the Navy considered the contract active. The Navy approved the sixth payment—dated July 31, 1985—on August 9, 1985. This evidence shows that the Navy intended to make timely payments.

In sum, the Navy's actions as a whole fall far short of communicating an intent not to perform in a "positive, definite, unconditional and unequivocal" manner. The July 19 memorandum and the July 25 telephone conversation do not satisfy the Cascade standard for an anticipatory breach.

CONCLUSION

The Board's decision was erroneous. In the absence of an anticipatory breach on this record, we need not reach the issue of damages.

REVERSED.

Notes and Questions

1. What are the multiple roles of progress payments? What does the ability to obtain them mean for a contractor? What does the ability to defer their payment mean for a contracting officer? This is a case that has two sides. What are the best arguments for each side? Can you tell the "story" of the case, at it seemed to the ASBCA? And the "story" as it seems to the Federal Circuit? Note how the Federal Circuit deems irrelevant most of the background, namely, that the government was processing a termination for default of the contractor. Shall we take a postmodern view and respect each story-narrative as true on its own terms? Or, does the opinion analyze the combination of the July 19th memorandum and the July 25th conversation to the point that, like a completed exam answer, it lays out a determinate series of criteria for the law of progress payments and project abandonment?

2. Generally speaking, under the Federal Acquisition Regulations (FAR), firm-fixed-price contracts in construction may be priced on a lump-sum or unit-price basis or by a combination of these. 48 C.F.R. § 36.207 (1998). Lump-sum pricing is when a lump sum is paid for defined parts of or the total work; unit pricing is payment for a specified quantity of work units. Id. Lump-sum pricing is preferable under specific circumstances set forth in FAR 36.207, and an economic price adjustment provision may be included in defined instances as well. Id.

"Repricing" of a unit-priced contract may occur. Under the Variation in Estimated Quantity (VEQ) clause, when a variation exists between the estimated and the actual quantity of the unit-priced item of more than 15 percent above or below the estimated quantity, an equitable adjustment in the contract price may be made. 48 C.F.R. § 52.212-11 (1992). In *Foley Co. v. United States*, 11 F.3d 1032 (Fed. Cir. 1993), the Court of Appeals held that the government was not entitled to equitable adjustment under the VEQ clause when the contractor actually removed greater than 115% of the estimated volume of sludge; the government failed to prove that Foley experienced a cost savings due solely to the increased volume removed. (The government unsuccessfully attempted to distinguish that case from the 1975 controlling case in which the Court of Claims found no basis for replacing a negotiated unit price with a repricing based on actual costs plus a reasonable profit. *Victory Construction Co. v. United States*, 510 F.2d 1379, 206 Ct. Cl. 274 (1975).) For more information on the evolution of the judicial treatment of this issue, see *Government Contracts Cases Before the United States Court of Appeals for the Federal Circuit*, 43 Am. U. L. Rev. 1417, 1475 (1994).

Wickham Contracting Co., Inc., Appellant, v. Dennis J. Fischer, Acting Administrator, General Services Administration, Appellee

No. 93-1146. United States Court of Appeals, Federal Circuit
12 F.3d 1574
Decided Jan. 6, 1994

Before RICH, MICHEL and CLEVENGER, Circuit Judges.

MICHEL, Circuit Judge.

Wickham Contracting Company appeals from a decision of the General Services Administration Board of Contract Appeals (Board), denying Wickham's claim for an equitable adjustment for overhead expenses incurred under a contract with the General Services Administration (GSA) as a result of GSA-imposed delays.... Regarding the Eichleay formula, we hold it is the only proper method of calculating unabsorbed home office overhead. No other formula may be used.

I. BACKGROUND

On July 28, 1977, Wickham entered into a contract with GSA to renovate the Federal Post Office and Courthouse in Albany, New York, for the sum of $2,968,000. The contract allowed 365 days from the notice to proceed to perform the work which was due to be completed on August 15, 1978. Early in the renovation process, GSA became concerned about structural problems with the building and ordered many delays in the work. The parties agree that, due to GSA-imposed delays, the work was not substantially complete until April 10, 1981, 969 days after the contracted date. Many of Wickham's claims against the government for additional costs due to such delays have been settled. However, certain costs associated with home office overhead have not.

Wickham's home office staff during the renovation work consisted of the president, a construction engineer, the project manager, and three secretaries. In addition to the Albany project, Wickham performed only two other major contracts during the same time frame—the West Point project and the Foley Square project. Both of these projects were managed mainly on site while the Albany project was managed mainly from the home office.

In June 1986, the contracting officer awarded Wickham an additional $333,084 on its claim for unabsorbed home office overhead due to the delay, based on the Eichleay formula.[1] Before the Board, Wickham argued that, for three reasons, it was due a larger amount for the unabsorbed home office overhead. Wickham complained that the percentage of the home office overhead pool allocated to the Albany contract based on the Eichleay formula, approximately 34%, was too low and did not fairly compensate Wickham for its overhead expenses. The contractor argued that it was entitled to be reimbursed for 80% of its overhead expenses incurred during the delay period because 80% of its home office activity and, therefore, 80% of its home office overhead expense was devoted to the Albany contract during that time frame. Wickham made the argument first to the contracting officer, then to the Board.

On appeal to us, Wickham repeatedly states that the 80% figure is undisputed. However, the government points out that Wickham did not keep current books or records which could document the 80% figure and that Wickham did not develop that figure until January 1985. The record supports the government's assertions. Therefore, we conclude the figure is disputed.

The Board did not make a clear finding as to whether Wickham actually proved that 80% of its home office activity was devoted to the Albany contract. Instead, the Board rejected Wickham's theory of recovery on the basis that unabsorbed overhead is always calculated according to the Eichleay formula when a contractor meets the Eichleay requirements after government-imposed delay. The Board applied the Eichleay formula based on the notion that it is a theoretical construct of the amount of unabsorbed overhead caused by the contract delay and, therefore, the actual amount of overhead allegedly caused by the contract was not relevant.

The parties agree on many of the components of the overhead pool. The components of the overhead pool to which the Board applied the Eichleay formula are general and

---

1. Wickham had already been partially compensated for overhead costs because the original contract price included a markup for overhead. In addition, when GSA issued change orders to pay Wickham for additional work, almost all of the orders included a markup of 10% for overhead.

administrative salaries, rent, insurance, depreciation, hospitalization and medical costs, dues and subscriptions, office expenses, auto and truck maintenance, utilities, plans and specifications, cleaning, protection, taxes and licenses, and officer's salaries. 92-3 BCA ¶ 25,040 at 124,818–19.

Before the Board, however, Wickham also argued that the contracting officer wrongly excluded several specific field costs from the overhead pool. The field costs are for travel and business meetings, telephones, professional fees, union welfare benefits, payroll taxes and equipment rental. Their inclusion would increase the amount paid to Wickham under either the Eichleay formula or Wickham's allocation figure of 80%. The Board, however, found that as direct, not overhead costs, they may not be included in the overhead pool.

* * *

Wickham appealed to this court pursuant to the Contract Disputes Act of 1978 (CDA), 41 U.S.C. § 607(g)(1) (1988). Our jurisdiction rests on that Act and 28 U.S.C. § 1295(a)(10) (1988).

* * *

III. ANALYSIS

A. The Eichleay Formula is Exclusive

1. Federal Circuit Law on Eichleay

The Board used the Eichleay formula[2] to calculate the amount of home office overhead costs for which Wickham would be reimbursed due to the GSA-imposed delay. Application of the Eichleay formula requires "that compensable delay occurred, and that the contractor could not have taken on any other jobs during the contract period."[3] C.B.C. Enters., Inc. v. United States, 978 F.2d 669, 673–74 (Fed.Cir.1992). Government contractors may use the Eichleay formula to calculate unabsorbed home office overhead when disruption, delay or suspension caused by the government has made uncertain the length of the performance period of the contract. Id. 978 F.2d at 672. The uncertainty often precludes additional jobs.

Suspension or delay of contract performance results in interruption or reduction of the contractor's stream of income from payments for direct costs incurred. This in turn causes an interruption or reduction in payments for overhead, derived as a percentage of direct costs, which is set by the contract. Home office overhead costs continue to accrue during such periods, however, regardless of direct contract activity. Consequently, this decrease in payments for direct costs creates unabsorbed overhead, unless home office workers are laid off or given additional work during such suspension or delay periods. When the period of delay is uncertain and the contractor is required by the government to remain ready to resume performance on short notice (referred to as "standby"), the contractor is effectively prohibited from making reductions in home office staff or facilities or by

---

2. The Eichleay formula requires three steps: 1) to find allocable contract overhead, multiply the total overhead cost incurred during the contract period times the ratio of billings from the delayed contract to total billings of the firm during the contract period; 2) to get the daily contract overhead rate, divide allocable contract overhead by days of contract performance; and 3) to get the amount recoverable, multiply the daily contract overhead rate times days of government-caused delay. Capital Elec. Co. v. United States, 729 F.2d 743, 747 (Fed.Cir.1984).

3. The parties stipulated that the government caused delay and disruption in Wickham's performance of the GSA contract such that Wickham satisfies the requirements for application of the Eichleay formula. GSA admitted to the Board that GSA had caused compensable delay of 969 days. Wickham's witness testified that because of the disruption, it was unable to commit to any additional contract work during the delay and GSA did not dispute this testimony.

taking on additional work. See Capital Elec. Co. v. United States, 729 F.2d 743, 748 (Fed.Cir.1984) (Friedman, J., concurring) ("[I]t is, ordinarily, not practicable to lay off main office employees during a short and indefinite period of delay."). Other reasons such as exhaustion of bonding capacity may also preclude additional contracts. Interstate Gen. Gov't Contractors, Inc., 12 F.3d 1053 (Fed.Cir.1993).

For the purpose of compensating Wickham for the effects of a project delay on home office overhead, the Board properly defined overhead as "those costs which are expended for the benefit of the business as a whole and which usually accrue over time." 92-3 BCA ¶ 25,040 at 124,818. The pool to which the Eichleay formula is applied must contain only such indirect costs. Home office costs, by their nature, cannot be traced to any particular contract. Thus, they are properly categorized as overhead costs and, assuming their allowability, included in the Eichleay pool. Were it possible to trace a cost to a particular contract, it would be a direct cost of the contract. C.B.C. Enters., 978 F.2d at 672.

The Armed Services Board of Contract Appeals devised the Eichleay formula to provide a fair method for allocating home office overhead costs, otherwise inallocable, to specific contracts. Eichleay Corp., ASBCA No. 5183, 60-2 BCA ¶ 2688, 1960 WL 538 (July 29, 1960), aff'd on reconsid., 61-1 BCA ¶ 2894, 1960 WL 684 (1960). The Eichleay board found it necessary to allocate overhead costs pro-rata because they "cannot ordinarily be charged to a particular contract. They represent the cost of general facilities and administration necessary to the performance of all contracts." 60-2 BCA ¶ 2688 at 13,574, 1960 WL 538. Thus, the Eichleay formula seeks to equitably determine allocation of unabsorbed overhead to allow fair compensation of a contractor for government delay. Id. at 13,573, 1960 WL 538. Allocation based on a pro-rata share is necessary because overhead cannot be traced to any particular contract since overhead consists of expenses which benefit and are necessary to every contract. Id.

2. Wickham's Arguments

In this case the ratio of billings from the delayed contract to total billings is about 34%. Thus, under the Eichleay formula, 34% of Wickham's overhead expense, incurred during the contract period, is allocable to the contract. However, Wickham claims that approximately 80% of its home office activity and, therefore, 80% of its home office overhead expense was devoted to the Albany contract during the delay period.[4] Thus, Wickham seeks compensation for 80% of the home office overhead costs actually incurred during the delay because, according to Wickham, they are directly attributable to the Albany contract. Wickham argues the Eichleay calculation is unfair because it is less than the actual percentage of overhead devoted to the delayed project. Therefore, per Wickham, the Eichleay formula should be used only when overhead costs cannot otherwise be accurately determined. In short, Wickham seeks to completely avoid the Eichleay formula.

Wickham's argument fails for a fundamental reason — Wickham confuses direct and overhead costs. As the Board noted, overhead costs benefit and are caused by the business as a whole, not any one project. Thus, overhead costs are never attributable to or caused by any one contract. Wickham's claim to "directly attributable" home office overhead is a non sequitur. If a cost is directly attributable to a contract, then it is a direct cost, not an overhead cost.

Wickham attempts to blur the distinction between overhead and direct costs simply to avoid the clear rule that the Eichleay formula governs the calculation of unabsorbed overhead. A contractor who wishes reimbursement for a cost directly attributable to a contract

---

4. This is because Wickham's other two contracts were managed mainly on site while the Albany project was managed from the home office.

must submit it as a direct cost. In a case such as this, where a contractor and the government have already consistently treated a cost as overhead, we will not upset their agreement by ourselves treating that cost as a direct cost and ordering reimbursement as such. In any event, we would lack jurisdiction under the CDA to do so because there were no contracting officer and board decisions denying such costs as direct costs. Therefore, there is no fact finding or ruling for us to review; and, of course, as an appellate court we may not make fact findings or initial rulings, generally or in the circumstances of this case.

Responding to Wickham's argument, the Board said, "[i]t makes no difference what the actual overhead effort was. We are here dealing with theoretics which produce approximations because more precise results cannot be obtained." 92-3 BCA ¶ 25,040 at 124, 818, 1992 WL 88326. In this statement the Board refers to the concept that the Eichleay formula calculates the unabsorbed overhead by a pro-rata share out of necessity. The Eichleay pool contains only overhead costs, those which cannot be attributed to a particular contract and which benefit and are caused by the business as a whole. To accurately determine how much unabsorbed overhead was caused by any one contract is impossible, even though Wickham claims to have done so.

Unlike direct costs which are incurred only because of a particular contract, overhead costs are incurred even if the contractor had not undertaken a particular project. Ordinarily, all home office expenses fall into the overhead category because the contractor must operate a home office in order to seek work and administer contracts whether or not he is performing a particular contract. For instance, a contractor must provide for the home office space, pay for utilities pertaining to that space, pay licensing fees and officer's salaries even when the contractor has no current contracts and is merely seeking work.

Given this established definition of overhead costs, the very premise of Wickham's argument is incorrect. Wickham contends that because 80% of its home office activity related to the Albany contract, 80% of its home office costs is directly attributable to that contract. Wickham fails to recognize that a cost is directly attributable to a contract only when the cost is caused by the contract. The Albany project did not cause 80% of Wickham's home office costs because Wickham would have incurred the individual cost components of the home office overhead whether or not it ever undertook the Albany project. For instance, the Albany project did not cause 80% of Wickham's home office rent even if 80% of the activity in that office related to the Albany project. Because Wickham would have incurred the same or similar rental expense in any event, no portion of the rent is directly attributable to the Albany project.

* * *

The Board's decision is therefore, in all respects,

AFFIRMED.

Notes and Questions

1. The opinion provides a mini-course in cost accounting. Can you explain and illustrate each of these concepts: cost "pools"; direct vs. overhead expenses; allocability? Note that these cost accounting concepts apply even though the underlying contract may be firm-fixed-price because cost accounting governs the figuring of equitable adjustments. What do you suppose happens if a commercial contractor, which does not keep its books in a way that makes cost accounting easy, runs into a situation like this case where it has to make an *Eichleay* claim based on elaborate cost figures? What's the sense of the requirement that the contractor be idle during the delay period? See *Satellite Electric Co. v. John H. Dalton*, 105 F.2d 1418 (Fed. Cir. 1997).

2. How does this way of figuring damages relate to basic (private) contract damages? Could you imagine similar arrangements to these between a private developer and its construction company? About this case, see John S. Pachter & Carl T. Hahn, *Jumping On (of Off) the* Eichleay *Bandwagon: Do We Have a Sticky* Wickham?, 31 Procurement Law., Summer 1996, at 3.

3. Liquidated damages are estimated when actual damages are difficult to calculate or estimate. ACC Alderman Construction Co., ASBCA 43958, 96-1 BCA ¶ 28046 (1995). Before a reasonable estimate of damages can be determined, the government first must clearly defined what the agency need is and which commercial products or services are suitable to meet the need. Federal Acquisition Regulation (FAR) 12.202 addresses this market research and description of need, and contains a description of the type of product or service, how the agency intends its use, and any performance requirement or essential physical characteristics. 48 C.F.R. § 12.202 (1997). FAR 36.206 designates the determination of the need for liquidated damages in a construction contract to the contracting officer. 48 C.F.R. § 36.202 (1995) .

In J.H. Strain and Sons, Inc., ASBCA 34432, 90-2 BCA ¶ 22770 (1990), the Administrative Judge held that the formula used in determining liquidated damages was appropriate and the assessment of them justified, stating "whether actual damages did or did not occur or was not proved to have occurred does not prevent recovery" (Martin J. Simko Construction, Inc v. United States, 11 Cl. Ct. 257, 271 (1986), quoting United States v. J. D. Street & Co., 151 F. Supp. 469, 472 (E. D. Mo. 1957)). This, however, is not the case when there has been substantial performance, as in *Sauer Incorporated*, ASBCA 39605 (1998), in which liquidated damages were reduced to 80% of the contract amount based on the Navy's acceptance and use as substantially complete of 20% of a facility contracted for.

B. Progress Payments and Sureties

For further readings on the subject of this section, see: Donavan Bezer, *The Inadequacy Of Surety Bid Bonds In Public Construction Contracting*, 40 Pub. Cont. L.J. 87 (Fall 2010); Edward G. Gallagher, Mark H. McCallum, *The Importance Of Surety Bond Verification*, 39 Pub. Cont. L.J. 269 (Winter 2010); Steven J. Koprince, *The Slow Erosion Of Suretyship Principles: An Uncertain Future For "Pay-When-Paid" And "Pay-If-Paid" Clauses In Public Construction Subcontracts*, 38 Pub. Cont. L.J. 47 (Fall 2008); Michael E. Sainsbury, *Seeking One Rule To Bind Them: Unifying The Interpretation & Treatment Of The "Title Vesting" Language Of The Progress Payment Clause*, 32 Pub. Cont. L.J. 327 (Winter 2003).

National American Insurance Company, Plaintiff-Appellee, v. United States, Defendant-Appellant

No. 2007-5016

United States Court of Appeals, Federal Circuit

498 F.3d 1301

Aug. 23, 2007

Before LINN, Circuit Judge, CLEVENGER, Senior Circuit Judge, and PROST, Circuit Judge.

PROST, Circuit Judge.

The United States appeals a September 6, 2006, decision by the United States Court of Federal Claims granting summary judgment that the government violated its duty as stakeholder in a Miller Act payment bond case by making final payment to a government contractor after being notified by the payment bond surety, National American Insurance Company ("NAICO"), that it was asserting a right to contract funds after having fully discharged the debt of the contractor. *Nat'l Am. Ins. Co. v. United States,* 72 Fed.Cl. 451 (2006). Because the Court of Federal Claims correctly held that NAICO was equitably subrogated to the rights of the contractor whose debt it discharged, we affirm.

I. BACKGROUND

On June 11, 1996, Innovative PBX Services, Inc. ("IPBX") contracted with the United States Small Business Administration to replace the telephone system at the Department of Veterans Affairs Medical Center in Palo Alto, California. IPBX subcontracted part of this work to Nortel Communications Systems, Inc., which was succeeded by Wiltel Communications, LLC ("Wiltel"). As required by the Miller Act, 40 U.S.C. § 3131(b), IPBX executed payment and performance bonds in favor of the United States, with NAICO as the surety.[1] After completion of its contract work, Wiltel notified NAICO that it was owed approximately $675,000 for labor and materials that IPBX had failed to pay. Wiltel then asserted a Miller Act claim under the payment bond issued to NAICO. NAICO settled Wiltel's claim, notified the government that no additional payments were to be made to IPBX due to the Miller Act claim, and requested that all remaining contract funds be held for NAICO's benefit. The government, however, did not follow NAICO's request and made its final contract payment to IPBX. As a result, NAICO filed a complaint in the Court of Federal Claims seeking damages of approximately $280,000 from the government. The Court of Federal Claims granted summary judgment in favor of NAICO, holding that: (1) NAICO, as a surety that had made payments on a payment bond and satisfied all outstanding claims, was equitably subrogated to the rights of IPBX; (2) the Tucker Act's waiver of sovereign immunity extended to NAICO as an equitable subrogee of IPBX; and (3) the government violated its duty as stakeholder in the payment bond by making final payment to IPBX after being notified by NAICO that it was asserting a right to contract funds. The United States appeals to this court. We have jurisdiction pursuant to 28 U.S.C. § 1295(a)(3).

II. DISCUSSION

* * *

B. Payment Bond Surety Subrogation Rights

On appeal, the United States asserts that NAICO can only stand in the shoes of the subcontractor whom it paid, and since the subcontractor has no privity with the United States, there can be no Tucker Act waiver of sovereign immunity. If we disagree, the United States does not contest its liability to NAICO on the facts of this case. Thus, this case involves only the subrogation rights of a payment bond surety. Generally, "[a] surety bond creates a three-party relationship, in which the surety becomes liable for the principal's

---

1. Pursuant to the Miller Act, a contractor awarded a contract of more than $100,000 with the United States is required to furnish two bonds: a performance bond "for the protection of the Government," and a payment bond "for the protection of all persons supplying labor and material in carrying out the work." 40 U.S.C. § 3131(b). The payment bond provision was designed to provide an alternative remedy to the mechanics' liens ordinarily available on private construction projects. *F.D. Rich Co. v. United States ex rel. Indus. Lumber Co.,* 417 U.S. 116, 122, 94 S.Ct. 2157, 40 L.Ed.2d 703 (1974). Because "a lien cannot attach to Government property," persons supplying labor or materials on a federal construction project were to be protected by the payment bond instead. *Id.* at 121–22, 94 S.Ct. 2157.

debt or duty to the third party obligee (here, the government)." *Ins. Co. of the W. v. United States,* 243 F.3d 1367, 1370 (Fed.Cir.2001) (*"ICW"*) (citing *Balboa Ins. Co. v. United States,* 775 F.2d 1158, 1160 (Fed.Cir.1985)). If a surety is unable to rely on privity of contract as the jurisdictional basis for a claim against the government, the surety may be able to invoke the doctrine of equitable subrogation to step into the shoes of the contractor for the purpose of satisfying the jurisdictional requirements of the Tucker Act, 28 U.S.C. § 1491(a). *See ICW,* 243 F.3d at 1373 (stating that the Tucker Act is not limited to claims asserted by the original claimant).

* * *

In 1896, the Supreme Court held that a surety could apply the doctrine of equitable subrogation in seeking retained funds from the government for completing performance of a government contract under a performance bond. *Prairie State Nat'l Bank v. United States,* 164 U.S. 227, 240, 32 Ct.Cl. 614, 17 S.Ct. 142, 41 L.Ed. 412 (1896). The Court extended its holding to a payment bond surety in *Henningsen v. United States Fidelity & Guaranty Co.,* 208 U.S. 404, 411, 28 S.Ct. 389, 52 L.Ed. 547 (1908).

In *United States v. Munsey Trust Co.,* 332 U.S. 234, 108 Ct.Cl. 765, 67 S.Ct. 1599, 91 L.Ed. 2022 (1947), the Supreme Court revisited the rights of sureties under the doctrine of equitable subrogation. In that case, the government, prior to releasing retained funds due a payment bond surety, deducted a portion of the amount that the contractor owed the government for failing to complete the contract. *Id.* at 238, 67 S.Ct. 1599. In an attempt to prevent the government from setting-off a portion of the retained funds, the payment bond surety argued that it was subrogated either to the rights of the laborers and materialmen whom it had paid or to the rights of the government itself. *Id.* at 240–44., 67 S.Ct. 1599.... [T]he Court held "that the government properly used its right to set off its independent claim" against the contractor. *Id.* at 244, 67 S.Ct. 1599; *see also Sec. Ins. Co. v. United States,* 428 F.2d 838, 841–43 (1970) (applying the holding in *Munsey Trust* and distinguishing between a performance bond surety's claim and a payment bond surety's claim with respect to the government's right to set off).

Fifteen years later, the Supreme Court again addressed the rights of sureties to recover funds retained by the government in *Pearlman v. Reliance Insurance Co.,* 371 U.S. 132, 83 S.Ct. 232, 9 L.Ed.2d 190 (1962). In *Pearlman,* the Court revisited *Prairie State* and *Henningsen* and affirmed that "[t]hese two cases..., together with other cases that have followed them, establish the surety's right to subrogation in [a retained] fund whether its bond be for performance or payment." *Id.* at 139, 83 S.Ct. 232. The Court also rejected the argument that *Munsey Trust* overruled the holdings in *Prairie State* and *Henningsen. Id.* at 140–41 (*"Munsey* left the rule in *Prairie State* and *Henningsen* undisturbed."). According to the Court: (1) the government had a right to use the retained fund to pay laborers and materialmen; (2) the laborers and materialmen had a right to be paid out of the fund; (3) the contractor, had he completed the contract and paid his laborers and materialmen, would have been entitled to the fund; and (4) the surety, having paid the laborers and materialmen, was entitled to the *benefit of all these rights* to the extent necessary to reimburse it. *Id.* at 141, 83 S.Ct. 232.

Subsequently, our predecessor court, the Court of Claims, analyzed the holdings of *Munsey Trust* and *Pearlman* in *United States Fidelity & Guaranty Co. v. United States,* 201 Ct.Cl. 1, 475 F.2d 1377 (1973), and distinguished the rights of a performance bond surety from those of a payment bond surety with respect to the government's priority to retained funds. According to the Court of Claims, the "most apparent" manner in which to reconcile any supposed differences between *Munsey Trust* and *Pearlman* was to conclude "that the surety was entitled to the benefit of *all* the rights of the laborers and material-men whose claims it paid *and* those of the contractor whose debts it paid." *Id.* at 1381–82 (emphases added). "The surety [was then] subrogated to the rights of the contractor who could sue the Government since it was in privity of contract with the United States.... [and] subrogated to the rights of the laborers and materialmen who might have superior equitable rights to the retainage but no right to sue the [United States]." *Id.* The Court of Claims then applied *Munsey Trust*'s priority rule in light of these legal conclusions to hold that "[a] surety that pays on a performance bond ... has priority over the United States to the retainages in its hands[, but that a] surety that pays on its payment bond ... does not." *Id.* at 1383.

Subsequent opinions of the Court of Claims and this court have reaffirmed, either explicitly or implicitly, the decision in *United States Fidelity & Guaranty. See Dependable Ins. Co. v. United States,* 846 F.2d 65, 67 (Fed.Cir.1988); *Balboa,* 775 F.2d at 1161; *United Elec. Corp. v. United States,* 227 Ct.Cl. 236, 647 F.2d 1082, 1083–86 (1981); *Great Am. Ins. Co. v. United States,* 203 Ct.Cl. 592, 492 F.2d 821, 828 (1974). In particular, in *Balboa,* under facts similar to the present case, we held that a payment bond surety could sue the United States for damages occasioned when the government made progress payments to a contractor, despite having been notified by the surety that it had made payments to subcontractors and materialmen and that payment should not be made without the surety's consent. 775 F.2d at 1163 ("[W]e hold that both the Claims Court and this court have jurisdiction to hear the claim of a Miller Act [payment bond] surety against the United States for funds allegedly improperly disbursed to a contractor."). Accordingly, it has been well-established that a payment bond surety that discharges a contractor's obligation to pay a subcontractor is equitably subrogated to the rights of both the contractor and subcontractor.

* * *

As discussed above, *Munsey Trust* involved a surety that claimed it was equitably subrogated to either the rights of the subcontractor whom it had paid or the rights of the government. 332 U.S. at 240–44, 67 S.Ct. 1599. Although the Supreme Court rejected the surety's claim that it was equitably subrogated to the rights of the government, the Court agreed that the surety was equitably subrogated to the rights of the subcontractor. *Id.* at 241–43, 67 S.Ct. 1599. Unfortunately for the surety, the subcontractor had no rights it could enforce against the United States. *Id.* at 242, 67 S.Ct. 1599. In that context, it is correct to state that the surety was subrogated only to the rights of the subcontractor and had no enforceable rights against the government.... [O]ur binding precedent clearly holds that a payment bond surety that discharges a contractor's obligation to pay a subcontractor is equitably subrogated to the rights of both the contractor and the subcontractor, as demonstrated by the preceding discussion.

Nonetheless, the government argues that *Department of the Army v. Blue Fox, Inc.,* 525 U.S. 255, 119 S.Ct. 687, 142 L.Ed.2d 718 (1999), represents a change in the law and precludes NAICO from bringing suit against the government.... Simply put, *Munsey Trust, Blue Fox,* and *ICW* did not change the established precedent that a *payment bond surety* that discharges a contractor's obligation to pay a subcontractor *may be equitably subrogated to the rights of the contractor.*

III. CONCLUSION

Because the Court of Federal Claims correctly held that NAICO was equitably subrogated to the rights of the contractor whose debt it discharged, we affirm.

AFFIRMED

Notes and Questions:

1. Why does it matter so much if there are suretyship rights? Do these situations occur, or threaten to occur, often?

2. What are some of the rights of a surety to make payments on behalf of subcontractors and others who are not being paid by the contractor itself?

3. What is the difference between a payment bond surety and a performance bond surety?

C. Miller Act

The lack of privity prevents subcontractors from seeking compensation directly from the government when the prime contractor has failed to pay the subcontractor for goods or services delivered to the government. Moreover, subcontractors cannot file mechanics liens against federal building projects or otherwise encumber federal work in order to secure payment. However, Congress has not forgotten subcontractors entirely. Performance and payment bonds are an available tool to be mandated by the government for the protection of itself and of subcontractors. This is particularly true for subcontractors, laborers, and materialmen on federal construction projects where the Miller Act, 40 U.S.C. § 270, requires the prime contractor to obtain performance and payment bonds on all contracts for the construction, alteration, or repair of any public building or public work of the United States exceeding $100,000. The Miller Act still does not give a right of action by a subcontractor against the government. But, it does offer the subcontractor protection in the form of providing security that subcontractors with valid claims under their subcontracts for materials delivered and services performed can obtain payment of those claims regardless of a prime contractor's insolvency or similar problems.

A performance bond is a written instrument executed by the prime contractor (the "principal") and a second party (the "surety" or "sureties"), to assure fulfillment of the contractor's obligations to a third party identified in the bond, generally the government. A performance bond secures performance and fulfillment of the contractor's obligations under the contract. A payment bond assures payments as required by law to all persons supplying labor or material in the prosecution of the work provided for in the contract. Each bond has a penal sum or penal amount which is the amount of money specified in a bond as the maximum payment for which the surety is obligated.

The penal amount on a Miller Act performance bond is 100% of the original contract price, unless the contracting officer determines that a lesser amount would protect the government's interests. When amendments to the contract increase the contract price, the amount of the performance bond can be increased. The penal amount on a Miller Act payment bond equals: (1) 50% of the contract price on contracts under $1 million; (2) 40% of the contract price on contracts under $5 million; or (3) $2 million if the contract price is more than $5 million. Payment bond amounts are also adjusted as the contract price is adjusted by amendment.

A contractor's failure to obtain the required performance and payments bonds is considered a breach of contract and grounds for a default termination of the prime contractor by the government. In addition to the statutory rights granted to subcontractors to proceed against sureties on Miller Act payment bonds, the subcontractor has the right to file a breach of contract action against the prime contractor when payment for goods or labor is not made.

It is of much importance, as the *MacEvoy* opinion discusses, which contractors can seek payment from Miller Act bonds. Although the Miller Act is considered remedial in nature and therefore has been construed liberally by the courts, the right to seek payment from the surety is still limited to persons who have furnished labor or material under a contractual relationship with the prime contractor or a subcontractor. The courts have taken great pain to ensure that a "subcontract" relationship exists before permitting invocation of the Miller Act. A "substantiality of the relationship" test is used to determine which party is an actual subcontractor on the theory that a prime contractor (and its surety) can protect itself by requiring performance and payment bonds from the few subcontractors with which the prime contractor has a substantial relationship in performing the prime contract.

The distinctions in this regard refer to subcontractors by "tiers," in the sense that a subcontractor who deals directly with a contractor is "1st tier," a subcontractor to a subcontractor is "2nd tier," and so on. A subcontractor to a subcontractor (2nd tier subcontractor) can be protected by the Miller Act if it provides notice of the claim to the prime contractor, but the employees or laborers of the 2nd tier subcontractor are not protected because they lack privity of contract with a subcontractor (that is, with a 1st tier subcontractor). Furthermore, where a "subcontractor" is considered to be merely a supplier with no substantial relationship to the prime, 2nd tier subcontractors to that supplier are similarly not protected by the Miller Act.

Recovery under the Miller Act is limited to payment for labor and materials used in the performance of a federal public building construction project. The labor and materials need not actually be used in the construction itself, but only need be used in the performance of the contract. This includes payment for rented equipment used during construction and equipment repairs.

In order to obtain protection under the Miller Act, the subcontractor must provide the prime contractor written notice of the claim after the last of the labor or material has been provided for which payment has not been received. Notice need not be given for each separate item furnished, thus allowing for timely notice to be made within 90 days after the final shipment of materials or items. There is no particular form required of the written notice of the claim, but it must sufficiently inform the prime contractor that a claim is being made. A letter advising the prime contractor of an outstanding balance due is generally considered insufficient notice.

Once written notice has been provided to the prime contractor, the claimant must file a claim within one year of the last delivery of supplies or performance of labor, in the name of the United States, in the federal district court in which the contract is being performed and executed regardless of the amount in controversy or diversity of jurisdiction. The Federal Rules of Civil Procedure will generally apply to issues relating to third party interveners, counterclaims, setoffs, and the like.

Many states have enacted state statutes for state contracts similar to the Miller Act for federal contracts, sometimes called "little Miller Acts." These state statutes have particular importance because the Miller Act has its chief application for public works construction contracts, and a large percentage of state contracts are for public works construction. Accordingly, the opinion below which illustrates much of the practical workings of the Miller Act, the *Allied Building* opinion, arises under a state equivalent of the Miller Act.

For further discussion of the subject of this section, see: Patricia H. Wittie, *Unpaid Ship Repair Subcontractors And Miller Act Waivers: Time For A Change?*, 42 Procrmt. Law.

9 (Spring 2007); David C. Farmer, *Hawaii's Amended Little Miller Act: A Catch 22 for Gap Claimants?* 1996-Nov. Haw. B.J. 37 (1996).

Clifford F. MacEvoy Co. et al. v.
United States, for Use and Benefit of Calvin Tomkins Co.
Supreme Court of the United States
322 U.S. 102
No. 483.
Argued March 7, 1944, Decided April 24, 1944

The United States entered into a contract with the petitioner Clifford F. MacEvoy Company whereby the latter agreed to furnish the materials and to perform the work necessary for the construction of dwelling units of a Defense Housing Project near Linden, New Jersey, on a cost-plus-fixed-fee basis. Pursuant to the Miller Act, MacEvoy as principal and the petitioner Aetna Casualty and Surety Company as surety executed a payment bond in the amount of $1,000,000, conditioned on the prompt payment by MacEvoy 'to all persons supplying labor and material in the prosecution of the work provided for in said contract.' The bond was duly accepted by the United States.

MacEvoy thereupon purchased from James H. Miller & Company certain building materials for use in the prosecution of the work provided for in MacEvoy's contract with the Government. Miller in turn purchased these materials from the respondent, Calvin Tomkins Company. Miller failed to pay Tomkins a balance of $12,033.49. There is no allegation that Miller agreed to perform or did perform any part of the work on the construction project. Nor is it disputed that MacEvoy paid Miller in full for the materials.

Within ninety days from the date on which Tomkins furnished the last of the materials to Miller, Tomkins gave written notice to MacEvoy and the surety of the existence and amount of Tomkins' claim for materials furnished to Miller. Tomkins as use-plaintiff then instituted this action against MacEvoy and the surety on the payment bond. The District Court granted petitioners' motion to dismiss the complaint for failure to state a claim against them. 49 F.Supp. 81. The Circuit Court of Appeals reversed the judgment. 137 F.2d 565. We granted certiorari because of a novel and important question presented under the Miller Act. 320 U.S. 733, 64 S.Ct. 267.

Specifically the issue is whether under the Miller Act a person supplying materials to a materialman of a Government contractor and to whom an unpaid balance is due from the materialman can recover on the payment bond executed by the contractor. We hold that he cannot.

The Heard Act, which was the predecessor of the Miller Act, required Government contractors to execute penal bonds for the benefit of 'all persons supplying him or them with labor and materials in the prosecution of the work provided for in such contract.' We consistently applied a liberal construction to that statute, noting that it was remedial in nature and that it clearly evidenced 'the intention of Congress to protect those whose labor or material has contributed to the prosecution of the work.' United States, for Use of Hill, v. American Surety Co., 200 U.S. 197, 204, 26 S.Ct. 168, 170, 50 L.Ed. 437. See also Mankin v. United States to Use of Ludowici-Celadon Co., 215 U.S. 533, 30 S.Ct. 174, 54 L.Ed. 315; United States Fidelity & Guaranty Co. v. United States for Benefit of Bartlett, 231 U.S. 237, 34 S.Ct. 88, 58 L.Ed. 200; Brogan v. National Surety Co., 246 U.S. 257, 38 S.Ct. 250, 62 L.Ed. 703, L.R.A.1918D, 776; Fleishmann Construction Co. v. United States to Use of Forsberg, 270 U.S. 349, 46 S.Ct. 284, 70 L.Ed. 624; Standard Accident Insurance Co. v.

United States for Use and Benefit of Powell, 302 U.S. 442, 58 S.Ct. 314, 82 L.Ed. 350. We accordingly held that the phrase 'all persons supplying (the contractor) ... with labor and materials' included not only those furnishing labor and materials directly to the prime contractor but also covered those who contributed labor and materials to subcontractors. United States, for Use of Hill, v. American Surety Co., supra, 200 U.S. 204, 26 S.Ct. 170, 50 L.Ed. 437; Mankin v. United States for Use of Ludowici-Celadon Co., supra, 215 U.S. 539, 30 S.Ct. 176, 54 L.Ed. 315; Illinois Surety Co. v. John Davis Co., 244 U.S. 376, 380, 37 S.Ct. 614, 616, 61 L.Ed. 1206. We had no occasion, however, to determine under that Act whether those who merely sold materials to materialmen, who in turn sold them to the prime contractors, were included within the phrase and hence entitled to recover on the penal bond.

The Miller Act, while it repealed the Heard Act, reinstated its basic provisions and was designed primarily to eliminate certain procedural limitations on its beneficiaries. There was no expressed purpose in the legislative history to restrict in any way the coverage of the Heard Act; the intent rather was to remove the procedural difficulties found to exist under the earlier measure and thereby make it easier for unpaid creditors to realize the benefits of the bond. Section 1(a)(2) of the Miller Act requires every Government contractor, where the amount of the contract exceeds $2,000, to furnish to the United States a payment bond with a surety 'for the protection of all persons supplying labor and material in the prosecution of the work provided for in said contract for the use of each such person.' Section 2(a) further provides that 'every person who has furnished labor or material in the prosecution of the work provided for in such contract' and who has not been paid in full therefor within ninety days after the last labor was performed or material supplied may bring suit on the payment bond for the unpaid balance. A proviso then states:

> 'Provided, however, That any person having direct contractual relationship with a subcontractor but no contractual relationship express or implied with the contractor furnishing said payment bond shall have a right of action upon the said payment bond upon giving written notice to said contractor within ninety days from the date on which such person did or performed the last of the labor or furnished or supplied the last of the material for which such claim is made....'

The Miller Act, like the Heard Act, is highly remedial in nature. It is entitled to a liberal construction and application in order properly to effectuate the Congressional intent to protect those whose labor and materials go into public projects. Fleisher Engineering & Construction Co. v. United States, for Use and Benefit of Hallenbeck, 311 U.S. 15, 17, 18, 61 S.Ct. 81, 82, 83, 85 L.Ed. 12; cf. United States to Use of Noland Co., Inc., v. Irwin, 316 U.S. 23, 29, 30, 62 S.Ct. 899, 902, 86 L.Ed. 1241. But such a salutary policy does not justify ignoring plain words of limitation and imposing wholesale liability on payment bonds. Ostensibly the payment bond is for the protection of 'all persons supplying labor and material in the prosecution of the work' and 'every person who has furnished labor or material in the prosecution of the work' is given the right to sue on such payment bond. Whether this statutory language is broad enough to include persons supplying material to materialmen as well as those in more remote relationships we need not decide. Even if it did include such persons we cannot disregard the limitations on liability which Congress intended to impose and did impose in the proviso of Section 2(a). However inclusive may be the general language of a statute, it 'will not be held to apply to a matter specifically dealt with in another part of the same enactment.... Specific terms prevail over the general in the same or another statute which otherwise might be controlling.' Ginsberg & Sons v. Popkin, 285 U.S. 204, 208, 52 S.Ct. 322, 323, 76 L.Ed. 704.

The proviso of Section 2(a), which had no counterpart in the Heard Act, makes clear that the right to bring suit on a payment bond is limited to (1) those materialmen, laborers and subcontractors who deal directly with the prime contractor and (2) those materialmen, laborers and sub-contractors who, lacking express or implied contractual relationship with the prime contractor, have direct contractual relationship with a subcontractor and who give the statutory notice of their claims to the prime contractor. To allow those in more remote relationships to recover on the bond would be contrary to the clear language of the proviso and to the expressed will of the framers of the Act.[1] Moreover, it would lead to the absurd result of requiring notice from persons in direct contractual relationship with a subcontractor but not from more remote claimants.

The ultimate question in this case, therefore, is whether Miller, the materialman to whom Tomkins sold the goods and who in turn supplied them to MacEvoy, was a subcontractor within the meaning of the proviso. If he was, Tomkins' direct contractual relationship with him enables Tomkins to recover on MacEvoy's payment bond. If Miller was not a subcontractor, Tomkins stands in too remote a relationship to secure the benefits of the bond.

The Miller Act itself makes no attempt to define the word 'subcontractor.'[2] We are thus forced to utilize ordinary judicial tools of definition. Whether the word includes laborers and materialmen is not subject to easy solution, for the word has no single, exact meaning. In a broad, generic sense a subcontractor includes anyone who has a contract to furnish labor or material to the prime contractor. In that sense Miller was a subcontractor. But under the more technical meaning, as established by usage in the building trades, a subcontractor is one who performs for and takes from the prime contractor a specific part of the labor or material requirements of the original contract, thus excluding ordinary laborers and materialmen. To determine which meaning Congress attached to the word in the Miller Act, we must look to the Congressional history of the statute as well as to the practical considerations underlying the Act.

It is apparent from the hearings before the subcommittee of the House Committee on the Judiciary leading to the adoption of the Miller Act that the participants had in mind a clear distinction between subcontractors and materialmen. In opening the hearings, Representative Miller, the sponsor of the bill that became the Miller Act, stated in connection with the various proposed bills that 'we would like to have the reaction and opinion of members in reference to those bills that deal with the general subject of requiring a bond for the benefit of laborers and materialmen who deal with subcontractors on public works.' And the authoritative committee report made numerous references to and distinguished among 'laborers, materialmen and subcontractors.' Similar uncontradicted statements were made in both houses of Congress when the Act was pending before them. The fact that subcontractors were so consistently distinguished from materialmen and laborers in the course of the formation of the Act is persuasive evidence that the word 'subcontractor' was used in the proviso of Section 2(a) in its technical sense so as to exclude materialmen and laborers.

---

1. 'A sub-subcontractor may avail himself of the protection of the bond by giving written notice to the contractor, but that is as far as the bill goes. It is not felt that more remote relationships ought to come within the purview of the bond.' H. Rep. No. 1263 (74th Cong., 1st Sess.), p. 3.

2. In analogous situations, state and lower federal courts have expressed divergent opinions as to whether the word 'subcontractor' includes laborers and materialmen. See annotation in 141 A.L.R. 321 for a summary of the conflicting cases. We have not heretofore had occasion to define the word in this connection. Any loose, interchangeable use of 'subcontractor' and 'materialman' in any prior decision of ours is without significance.

Practical considerations underlying the Act likewise support this conclusion. Congress cannot be presumed, in the absence of express statutory language, to have intended to impose liability on the payment bond in situations where it is difficult or impossible for the prime contractor to protect himself. The relatively few subcontractors who perform part of the original contract represent in a sense the prime contractor and are well known to him. It is easy for the prime contractor to secure himself against loss by requiring the subcontractors to give security by bond, or otherwise, for the payment of those who contract directly with the subcontractors. United States, for Use of Hill, v. American Surety Co., supra, 200 U.S. 204, 26 S.Ct. 168, 50 L.Ed. 437; Mankin v. United States for Use of Ludowici-Celadon Co., supra, 215 U.S. 540, 30 S.Ct. 177, 54 L.Ed. 315. But this method of protection is generally inadequate to cope with remote and undeterminable liabilities incurred by an ordinary materialman, who may be a manufacturer, a wholesaler or a retailer. Many such materialmen are usually involved in large projects; they deal in turn with innumerable sub-materialmen and laborers. To impose unlimited liability under the payment bond to those sub-materialmen and laborers is to create a precarious and perilous risk on the prime contractor and his surety. To sanction such a risk requires clear language in the statute and in the bond so as to leave no alternative. Here the proviso of Section 2(a) of the Act forbids the imposition of such a risk, thereby foreclosing Tomkins' right to use on the payment bond.

The judgment of the court below is reversed.

Allied Building Products Corporation v. United Pacific Insurance Company
No. 279, Sept. Term, 1988
Court of Special Appeals of Maryland
Nov. 10, 1988

Argued Before GILBERT, C.J., and ROSALYN B. BELL and FISCHER, JJ.

ROSALYN B. BELL, Judge.

Allied Building Products Corporation (Allied) appeals from a decision of the Circuit Court for Baltimore City granting cross-summary judgment for United Pacific Insurance Company (United Pacific). Allied is a large supplier of roofing and other building materials. United Pacific was the surety of a payment bond posted by Triangle General Contractors, Inc. (Triangle), guaranteeing payment for labor and materials on a State building project. Allied filed suit against United Pacific on August 20, 1987, alleging that it was entitled to relief from United Pacific due to the nonpayment of a subcontractor, Sain & Son Contractors, Inc. (S & S).

We are presented with two issues in this appeal:

… Was Triangle's affidavit, alleging that Allied had billed it for more roofing materials than actually delivered, sufficient to withstand Allied's summary judgment motion?

We reverse and remand.

The relevant facts are as follows. Triangle was the general contractor on a State project to construct the Francis Scott Key Elementary-Middle School in Baltimore City. United Pacific, appellee, was the surety for Triangle in accordance with Triangle's obligations to provide a payment bond pursuant to § 13-501(a)(2) of the Little Miller Act, Md. State Fin. & Proc. Code Ann. (1985). Briefly stated, this section requires a general contractor to post a payment bond in any construction contract awarded by the State which exceeds $50,000 in order to make certain that persons providing building materials are paid. By providing the payment bond, United Pacific guaranteed payment to all persons supplying materials for the school building project undertaken by Triangle. S & S, a construction subcontractor for Triangle, used roofing and other building materials supplied by Allied, which Allied delivered to the job site.

After the project was underway, Allied became concerned about receiving its payments on an open account it had provided to S & S. Consequently, Allied, S & S, and Triangle entered into a joint check agreement in November of 1985, pursuant to which Triangle agreed to pay S & S with joint checks made payable to S & S and Allied, thus ensuring that Allied would be paid for the building materials it had supplied to S & S. The agreement provided that Triangle assumed no liability for any materials purchased in excess of $100,000. Nevertheless, Triangle paid out a total of $123,846.74 to Allied under the joint check agreement.[1] When S & S did not meet its obligations, Allied gave notice and filed suit on the payment bond underwritten by United Pacific, claiming an unpaid balance of $75,889.18 for building materials delivered to the job site.

The trial court granted Allied's summary judgment motion on November 10, 1987, and United Pacific filed a motion to vacate the judgment, a motion in opposition of the summary judgment, and a cross-motion for summary judgment on November 20, 1987. These motions were heard in an unrecorded hearing in chambers on January 5, 1988. Judgment was entered in favor of United Pacific on both motions. Because the hearing was unrecorded, we can only assume that the trial court entered judgment for United Pacific based on its pleadings, which asserted, in essence, that the joint check agreement limiting Triangle's liability to $100,000 operated as a waiver of Allied's rights under the Little Miller Act.

The effect of the joint check agreement is thus the primary issue in this case. We hold that the lack of a specific waiver was fatal to United Pacific's cross-motion. The second question involves Allied's own motion, and for that answer we revisit the problem of the adequacy of an affidavit opposing summary judgment. We hold that United Pacific's affidavit was sufficient to raise a material factual issue regarding delivery, and as a result, Allied was not entitled to summary judgment. We begin our explanation with a brief history of the Little Miller Act and what it was intended to accomplish.

HISTORY

Construction projects such as office buildings and factories have increased dramatically. These projects typically involve large amounts of money; hence, if the contractor's business failed, suppliers who had extended credit could suffer substantial losses. Since suppliers had no recourse at common law, statutes providing for mechanics' liens were enacted to address this problem. See Cahn, Contractors' Payment Bonds in Maryland, 32 Md.L.Rev. 226 (1972).

Public projects such as schools, highways and public hospitals were typically exempt from mechanics' liens, however, and suppliers on State public projects in Maryland had no remedy until 1918, when Maryland adopted its version of a federal law known as the Heard Act, which required contractors to post bonds for State projects. 1918 Md.Laws ch. 127. In 1959, Maryland replaced this law with a new statute requiring contractors to post payment bonds on State construction projects. This new statute was patterned on a federal act known as the Miller Act.

---

1. Although the record extract does not specify, we assume Allied did furnish at least $100,000 in materials and was paid for them out of the $123,846.74 as no issue is raised in this regard.

Although nothing in the legislative history of the Maryland Act explicitly states that it was based on the federal Miller Act, the legislative history does show parallel development and, except for minor variations, the language of the two statutes is essentially the same.

* * *

The purpose of the Little Miller Act is remedial. The Act is intended to protect suppliers on State and other public projects where they would otherwise have no lien as a result of sovereign immunity. Hamilton & Spiegel, Inc. v. Board of Educ. of Montgomery County, 233 Md. 196, 200, 195 A.2d 710 (1963). The Act is to be liberally construed to effectuate this public purpose. Montgomery County Bd. of Educ. v. Glassman Constr. Co., 245 Md. 192, 201, 225 A.2d 448 (1967).

Under the Miller Act,

> "[t]he liability of the surety is measured by that of the prime contractor for the bond. The liability of the prime contractor to a project supplier of a subcontractor is governed by the subcontractor's obligation."

D & L Constr. Co. v. Triangle Elec. Supply Co., 332 F.2d 1009, 1013 (8th Cir.1964). The obligation is one, not of contract, but of statute, and therefore privity is not required. The liabilities of lower tier subcontractors to their suppliers are passed up the ladder to the surety. For example, in the instant case, it is S & S's liability to Allied that becomes the benchmark in determining Allied's damages as against Triangle, and ultimately United Pacific.

What is significant about both the federal and the state acts is that, although there have been amendments to both statutes, the basic coverage, purpose and procedures remain substantially the same. Generally, this Court will look to federal decisions construing the Miller Act to provide guidance in interpreting the Little Miller Act.

EFFECT OF THE JOINT CHECK AGREEMENT

On appeal, Allied contends that the trial court erred in granting judgment for United Pacific, asserting that at no time did it waive its right to the protection of the Little Miller Act. On the other hand, United Pacific asserts that it had no obligation to Allied because Triangle fulfilled its obligations under the joint check agreement. Since Triangle had no further liability to Allied, United Pacific claims it follows that it had no liability as Triangle's surety. We disagree with United Pacific's position, and explain.

Whether the cross motion for summary judgment was properly granted to appellee rests on the claim that Triangle's liability to appellant under the Little Miller Act was limited to $100,000. The joint check agreement was in the form of a letter from Triangle to S & S dated November 25, 1985. The letter stated in pertinent part:

> "You have asked us to make checks in payment for your work, under the above referenced contract, payable jointly to you and to Allied Roofers Supply Corporation. We are willing to do this, and will do so, subject to the following conditions:

* * *

> "2 We assume no liability for any materials purchased in excess of the total purchase of One Hundred Thousand Dollars and no/cents. Tax Included, ($100,000.00). Also we assume no liability for any materials not delivered to the job site and signed for by Triangle General Contractor's job superintendent for verification."

> "3. We will require a partial Release of Liens, and a Release of rights against our Payment Bond, from both you and your supplier as a condition of each payment to you.

"4. Also it is agreed, that all joint check payments will be applied by the Supplier to only S & S Drywall Contractor's account for the Francis Scott Key Middle School and no other accounts."

The letter was accepted by Triangle, S & S and Allied.

The Court of Appeals held in N.S. Stavrou, Inc. and Reliance Insurance Co. v. Beacon Supply Co., 249 Md. 451, 458–59, 240 A.2d 278 (1968), that the joint check agreement was not intended to guarantee payment in lieu of the contractor's bond obligation. The joint check agreement in Stavrou imposed a duty on the contractor to pay the supplier for materials not to exceed $20,000. The Court held that the contractor's conduct had the effect of exceeding this obligation. Stavrou, 249 Md. at 451, 240 A.2d 278. The Court pointed out that the contractor could have protected himself by requiring (in addition to the joint check agreement) the supplier to execute a bond waiver, but this was not done. The Court noted that in order to prevail the contractor "would had to have shown by a fair preponderance of the evidence an express or implied waiver on the part of [the supplier]...." Stavrou, 249 Md. at 458, 240 A.2d 278. Thus, the Court implicitly would have required language additional to or more specific than that of the joint check agreement in Stavrou in order to find a bond right waiver. The Stavrou Court, however, did not elaborate on what sort of language could constitute an express or implied waiver.

* * *

In United States ex rel. Koppers Co. v. Five Boro Construction Corp., 310 F.2d 701, 703 (4th Cir.1962), the Court held that a supplier had not waived its Miller Act rights by entering into a joint check agreement with the contractor and subcontractor. The agreement, reached by letter, was entered into after the supplier became apprehensive concerning the subcontractor's ability to pay for railroad materials delivered for a Navy building project. The Court found nothing in the joint check agreement which indicated that the supplier intended to waive its rights, observing that the supplier had three options when the subcontractor's ability to pay became questionable. The supplier could have (1) continued supplying materials until the job was completed and then file against the payment bond pursuant to the Miller Act, (2) refused to deliver any more materials, or (3), as happened in Koppers, agreed to deliver supplies pursuant to a joint check agreement. The Court stated:

"This insured payment to [the supplier] as the work progressed instead of delay in payment until completion of the job, but a request for and the acceptance of additional security does not indicate an intention to waive the right to that already in hand."

Koppers, 310 F.2d at 703.

United States ex rel. Clark-Fontana Paint Co. v. Glassman Construction Co., 397 F.2d 8 (4th Cir. 1968), involved a factual situation similar to that in the instant case. In Clark-Fontana, a paint supplier agreed to supply materials to a subcontractor, but requested the general contractor to make its checks jointly payable to the paint supplier and the subcontractor. Each check contained a notation that the subcontractor and supplier "waived and released to the extent of the full face value hereof any right any of them may have" to assert a claim under "any bond" given by the contractor. Clark-Fontana, 397 F.2d at 9. The supplier then allowed the subcontractor to keep most of the proceeds of these checks because the subcontractor was having trouble meeting his payroll. This subcontractor eventually went bankrupt, and the supplier filed suit under the Miller Act to recover the unpaid balance. The defendants (contractor, insurance company and subcontractor) claimed that the language on the checks constituted a waiver of the supplier's right to recover under the Miller Act. Clark-Fontana, 397 F.2d at 10.

The Court held that the notation was not a waiver because its language did not explicitly "say that the materialman [supplier] was obligated to deduct his current due from each check at the peril of losing his statutory rights." Clark-Fontana, 397 F.2d at 10. The Court stated:

> "[W]e do not hold that protection of laborers and materialmen may never be accomplished by other means so as to avoid the general contractor's statutory obligation. But where that result is attempted by means of express waiver, we think that congressional purpose requires that waiver be clear and explicit.... Absent the clear language of an express waiver, we think that none is to be implied; as we have held in the past, requesting and accepting additional security does not indicate an intention to waive the right to that already in hand."

Clark-Fontana, 397 F.2d at 10–11 (citation omitted).

Clark-Fontana illustrates the approach taken by the federal courts—while it is possible for a supplier to waive his rights under the Act, see, e.g., United States ex rel. B's Co. v. Cleveland Electric Co., 373 F.2d 585, 588 (4th Cir.1967), "the federal courts have been uniform in their insistence that a waiver be clear and explicit." United States ex rel. Youngstown Welding & Eng'g Co. v. Traveler's Indem. Co., 802 F.2d 1164, 1166 (1986). We adopt the federal position, holding that only a clear and express waiver will terminate a supplier's rights under a Little Miller Act payment bond, and that the taking of additional security by itself does not constitute a waiver of a bond claim. In the instant case, the joint check agreement did not waive Allied's rights under the Little Miller Act.

The joint check agreement itself, and the circumstances prompting its creation, indicates that it was intended to create additional security for Allied—not to narrow the security Allied already possessed under the Little Miller Act. The agreement came into being because Allied was concerned that S & S was a poor credit risk.[1] It was obviously Allied's reluctance to give S & S materials on credit which induced S & S to ask for this arrangement, as evidenced by the letter creating the joint check agreement, sent by Triangle to S & S, which began: "You have asked us to make checks in payment for your work ... payable jointly to you and to Allied...." Simply put, Allied would not have given S & S roofing materials unless it had some additional assurance of payment. Since paragraph 2 of the Joint Check Agreement limits the liability that Triangle would "assume," it is expressly indicative of the parties' intention that they were creating rights in Allied as against Triangle, not limiting ones that already existed, so that Allied would continue to supply the project.

As in Koppers, Allied as a supplier could have continued supplying materials to the job site and then filed (after proper notice) under the payment bond or it could have simply refused to supply any more materials on credit. It opted instead to work matters out via an agreement which was nothing more than a joint check agreement.

Joint check agreements are a commonly used payment method in the construction industry.

---

1. Allied's concern about S & S's credit is evidenced by the fact that it used S & S's credit application as an exhibit in its bond action. The credit application showed that S & S had been in existence for just two-and-one-half years, was a father-son operation, and had never done business with Allied before.

"In order to induce a supplier to deal with a subcontractor whose credit is questionable, the general contractor may agree to pay the subcontractor with checks payable to the joint order of the subcontractor and the supplier."

Cahn, Contractors' Payment Bonds in Maryland at 259. The subcontractor endorses the checks and turns them over to the supplier. The supplier then deducts the amount owed for materials, and returns the balance. Id., at 259. Triangle and United Pacific could have had Allied execute a waiver of its bond rights, but did not. The situation in the instant case is thus similar to Stavrou, where the Court declined to find a waiver in the joint check agreement. As held in Koppers, a joint check agreement, standing alone, will not constitute a waiver.

Moreover, the language in this agreement is far less specific than that contained in Clark-Fontana, which the Court held not specific enough to constitute a waiver. Additionally, paragraph 3 of the joint check agreement specified that Triangle "will require … a [r]elease of rights against our [p]ayment [b]ond from both you and your supplier as a condition of each payment to you." "Will require" clearly indicates future action, and by drafting this provision Triangle clearly contemplated obtaining separate signed releases for each payment at some future date. This provision would have no meaning if the paragraph immediately before it, paragraph 2, was intended by the parties to be a complete waiver.

Finally, United Pacific argues that, by paying Allied in excess of the stated $100,000.00 contract limit, Triangle fully satisfied its contractual obligation and hence no waiver is involved. We think that any distinction to be made here between a liability cap and a waiver is academic at best. Following Union Pacific's line of reasoning to its logical end, prior to the execution of the joint check agreement Allied possessed the right to sue under the Little Miller Act without limitation as to amount. Yet, Union Pacific contents that, immediately after the joint check agreement was executed, Allied's right to sue under the Miller Act for sums in excess of $100,000 suddenly disappeared. How would this be possible except by virtue of waiver? Since the joint check agreement did not constitute a waiver, we hold the trial court erred in granting the cross-summary judgment to United Pacific.

JUDGMENT VACATED AND CASE REMANDED FOR FURTHER PROCEEDINGS CONSISTENT WITH THIS OPINION.

Notes and Questions

1. In *Clifford F. MacEvoy Co.*, the court limited coverage of the Miller Act to subcontractors which perform part of the original contract on the theory that the prime contractor cannot be asked to be responsible for "unlimited liability" from the myriad number of materialmen and suppliers that might supply product or laborers during the course of a construction project. Yet, on fixed-price construction contracts, the total "liability" for materials and labor should be relatively well-known and not an "unlimited liability." What is another reason for the courts to limit the coverage of the Miller Act and the amount of bonds required?

2. Why have the courts gone to the great lengths reflected in the *Allied Building* case to protect subcontractors from contentions that they have waived their protections regarding Miller Act bonds? Are those protections creatures of the statute or of the subcontract?

3. Pursuant to Section 4104(b)(2) of the Federal Acquisition Streamlining Act of 1994 (Public Law 103-355), for construction contracts greater than $25,000 (the prior Miller Act applicability amount) and less than $100,000 (the new Miller Act applicability amount), a contracting officer is to select two or more of the following payment protections as a means of protecting the interests of the government: (1) A payment bond; (2) An irrevocable letter of credit; (3) A tripartite escrow agreement; (4) Certificates of deposit; or (5) U.S. Bonds, certified or cashier's check, bank draft, Post Office money order, or currency. The

contractor is permitted to select one of the various forms of payment protection. FAR 28.102-1(b). What is the policy basis behind allowing for different forms of payment protection on smaller dollar construction contracts?

4. The one year statute of limitations for filing a claim under the Miller Act is not a jurisdictional requirement, so that a contractor's assurances that a bill would be paid can act as an estoppel against the contractor asserting the statute of limitations.

D. Differing Site Conditions

A lot of litigation occurs over the issue of differing site conditions, which is what makes so narrow an issue matter so much. In other changes cases, the government changes its mind about what it wants; in differing site conditions, the government changes nothing, but the construction contractor discovers something different than it expected. If government contracting law put all the risk of such discoveries on the contractor, there would be little need for all that litigation.

However, government contracting law instead lifts a good deal of risk off of contractors and puts it on the government. The reason is simple. Between the government and the contractors the government can carry the risk better. If the government put the risk on the contractors, they would have to inflate their bids to match the risk, plus a premium for their difficulty in self-insuring against the risk. So, instead, the government effectively sets up a system by which it insures the contractors against two types of bad conditions. As the Court of Claims has stated, this means that contractors "will have no windfalls and no disasters." *Foster Constr. Co. v. United States*, 435 F.2d 873 (Ct. Cl. 1970). Considering the amount of litigation lawyers who handle these matters, though, may have no disasters and quite a few windfalls.

The FAR's standard "Differing Site Conditions" clause names the type of conditions that will justify an equitable adjustment. A contractor who encounters these "shall promptly, and before the conditions are disturbed, give a written notice of the Contracting Officer." Thereupon, "The Contracting Officer shall investigate...." If the claim checks out and the conditions "cause an increase or decrease in the Contractor's cost of, or the time required for, performing any part of the work ..." then "an equitable adjustment shall be made under this clause ..."

Two types of "Differing Site Conditions," naturally called Type I and Type II, get mentioned in the clause and stay quite separate as theories or litigation. They have in common a material difference between what the contractor reasonably expected and what it actually encountered; what differentiates them is the nature of that difference. In Type I conditions, the conditions differ from those represented in the contract. So, the focus concerns contractual representations. In Type II conditions, the conditions differ from the conditions that would usually be encountered.

In each of the two cases in this section, there is a preliminary jurisdictional issue. In *COVCO*, a federal case, it concerns the nonappropriated funds status of the project. In *Harmans*, a state case, it concerns whether a complex sale-and-leaseback counts as construction. Because the states do so much construction contracting, many differing site condition cases occurs at the state level and often closely follow the federal law.

The issue of differing site conditions tends to involve other important standard, and nonstandard government contract clause language besides the differing site conditions clause itself. As to standard language, contracts usually contain a standard "site inspection" clause, and the ability of a contractor to assert reimbursable surprise often depends upon what a site inspection would have found. As to nonstandard language, the government shapes future differing site condition cases by what it says in the contract about what the contractor must handle, and government's language in the contract can foreshadow that a project will be either a cakewalk or a hard struggle.

For further discussions of this section's overall subject, see: Contractor Did Not Show Differing Site Condition, COFC Finds, Gov't Cont., Decisions ¶ 387, November 23, 2010; J. Michael Littlejohn & Hal J. Peroff, *The Aftermath of Hurricane Katrina: Will Legal Issues Wash Away Contractors?*, 41WTR Procrmt. Law., at 3 (2006); ASBCA Sustains Appeal Of Type II Differing Site Condition Claim, Gov't Cont., Decisions ¶ 99, March 15, 2006; Hazel Glenn Beh, *Allocating the Risk of the Unforeseen, Subsurface and Latent Conditions in Construction Contracts: Is There Room for the Common Law?* 46 U. Kan. L. Rev. 115 (1997); Frank Baltz, *Does the Government Really Accept the Risk for Differing Site Conditions?*, 31 Procurement Law., Spring 1996, at 9; Leslie A. Sherman, *Recent Decision: Sovereign Immunity-Government Contractor Defense-Implied Warranty of Specifications…*, 35 Duq. L. Rev. 1045 (1997); Steven C. Sanders, *Unanticipated Environmental Costs in Construction Contracts: The Differing Site Conditions Clause as a Risk Allocation Tool*, 10 J. Nat. Resources & Envtl. L. 53 (1995).

Differing Site Conditions
(Apr 1984)

(a) The Contractor shall promptly, and before the conditions are disturbed, give a written notice to the Contracting Officer of

  (1) subsurface or latent physical conditions at the site which differ materially from those indicated in this contract, or

  (2) unknown physical conditions at the site, of an unusual nature, which differ materially from those ordinarily encountered and generally recognized as inhering in work of the character provided for in the contract.

(b) The Contracting Officer shall investigate the site conditions promptly after receiving the notice. If the conditions do materially so differ and cause an increase or decrease in the Contractor's cost of, or the time required for, performing any part of the work under this contract, whether or not changed as a result of the conditions, an equitable adjustment shall be made under this clause and the contract modified in writing accordingly.

(c) No request by the Contractor for an equitable adjustment to the contract under this clause shall be allowed, unless the Contractor has given the written notice required; provided, that the time prescribed in paragraph (a) of this clause for giving written notice may be extended by the Contracting Officer.

(d) No request by the Contractor for an equitable adjustment to the contract for differing site conditions shall be allowed if made after final payment under this contract.

Appeal of—Covco Hawaii Corporation
83-2 BCA ¶ 16,554
May 13, 1983

OPINION BY ADMINISTRATIVE JUDGE TING

* * *

We first consider whether the Contract Disputes Act of 1978 (CDA), 41 U.S.C. 601 et seq., is applicable to this appeal. Section 3 of the CDA provides that it 'applies to any express or implied contract (including those of the nonappropriated fund activities described in sections 1346 and 1491 of Title 28, United States Code) entered into by an executive agency....' Since sections 1346 and 1491 of Title 28 describe only the exchange activities of the various military services, we conclude that the Act does not apply to the United States Army Support Command, Hawaii Installation Club System, a nonappropriated fund instrumentality of the Department of the Army (finding 1). See, e.g., Commercial Offset Printers, Inc., 81-1 BCA p14,900; Potomac Company, Inc., ASBCA No. 25371, 81-1 BCA p14,950. There are precedents for Board jurisdiction over disputes involving nonappropriated fund contracts of the United States however, where such contracts contain a 'Disputes' clause. Rainbow Valley Corporation, ASBCA No. 11691, 68-1 BCA p6840, 68-2 BCA p7195; Beigh and Peck, ASBCA No. 7711, 1963 BCA p3740. Here, the 'Disputes' clause prescribed by Army Regulation 230-1 was included in appellant's contract (finding 23). We therefore have jurisdiction over the dispute.

Appellant seeks an equitable adjustment under the 'Differing Site Condition' clause. It contends that the profiles on the 'Profiles & Details' drawing (Drawing No. 31-02-01, Sheet No. 4, Ring No. 5) misled it into believing that 'earth' rather than 'rock' would be encountered (finding 28). Appellant's president says in an affidavit that during this site visit, large trees and thick vegetation were noted around the general area of Fort Ruger but he 'saw nothing which indicated that this area contained a ledge of solid lava rock.' (Finding 13) Appellant also alleges that since the Government had previously excavated the area and built a swimming pool, it must have known about the presence of rock (Finding 30). It alleges that the Government concealed this vital information (App. br. at 5). Finally, appellant says that although the Hawaiian Islands were formed by 'volcanic processes ... solid lava rock ledges of the kind encountered ... are not normally found when excavating to this depth....' (Finding 13)

The 'Differing Site Conditions' clause provides for two different types of conditions. Type I involves the discovery of subsurface or latent physical conditions at the site differing materially from those indicated in the contract. Type II provides for unknown physical conditions at the site of an unusual nature, differing materially from those ordinarily encountered.

As to what the contract documents indicate, we do not accept appellant's position that the term 'EXST. GROUND' on the Profiles & Details drawing (Drawing No. 31-02-01, Sheet No. 4, Ring No. 5) could be taken to mean that 'earth' or 'soil' would be encountered upon excavation. The broken lines designated as 'EXST. GROUND' merely show the elevation of then existing ground levels for grading purposes. The profiles make no representations as to the nature of the substance that a contractor would be expected to encounter. Indeed, appellant's interpretation would be in direct conflict with other provisions of the contract. For example, Note 6 of the Site & Utility Plan (Drawing No. 31-02-01, Sheet No. 1, Ring No. 2) cautioned appellant that 'no foundation investigation was performed ... rock excavation for installation and construction of access path ramp including retaining wall will be on an unclassified basis.' (Finding 6) Section 2A, Division 2, paragraph 6 of the Technical Provisions of the contract required '[t]he contractor [to] perform excavation of every type of material encountered including rock....' (Finding 25) The interpretation appellant urged upon us would violate the well-settled principle that an interpretation which gives a reasonable meaning to all parts of an instrument will be preferred to one which leaves a portion of it meaningless, and that a provision should not be construed as being in conflict with another unless no other reasonable interpretation is possible. Hol-Gar Mfg. Corp. v. United States, 169 Ct. Cl. 384, 351 F.d 972 (1965). Furthermore, the contract drawings clearly warned appellant that rock excavation would be on an 'unclassified basis.' (Finding 6) In Lang-Miller Development Co., AGBCA No. 81-129-3, 81-2 BCA p15,433, the Board there held that the Government's use of the term 'unclassified' in the contract documents does not imply a particular material or the absence of rock. The Government's case is far stronger here—appellant was told to expect rock; only the type of rock was not specified. Based upon the foregoing, we conclude that the contract documents did not misrepresent the subsurface physical conditions at the site. And since we have also found that the presence of lava rock could be ascertained by a reasonable pre-bid site investigation (findings 14–17), we conclude that no latent physical conditions existed. Hence, appellant is not entitled to recover under Type I conditions of the 'Differing Site Conditions' clause.

We now turn to appellant's Type II 'Differing Site Conditions' claim. In proving such a claim, a contractor must carry 'a relatively heavy burden of proof' in demonstrating that it has encountered a condition 'materially different from the 'known' and the 'usual.'' Charles T. Parker Construction Co. v. United States, 193 Ct. Cl. 320, 333, 433 F.2d 771, 778 (1970). In order to prevail, a contractor must also show that the condition could not have been reasonably anticipated or discovered prior to its bid. Perini Corporation v. United States, 180 Ct. Cl. 768, 381 F.2d 403 (1967); James E. McFadden, Inc., ASBCA No. 19921, 76-2 BCA p11,983; Kasmet Electrical, Inc., ASBCA Nos. 23473, 23474, 80-1 BCA p14,310. In connection with its Type II claim, appellant does not appear to be saying that the lava rock found at the site differed materially from the 'known' and 'usual' conditions prevalent in the Hawaiian Islands. Goolsby and Slavens' affidavits both state 'the Hawaiian Islands were formed in their entirety by volcanic processes, yet solid lava rock ledges of the kind encountered in this excavation are not normally found when excavating to this depth in Hawaiian soil.' (Aff. Warren H. Goolsby, III, p6; Aff. Donald M. Slavens, p11) The record evidence does not show the nature of the 'solid lava rock ledges' appellant allegedly encountered. Nor does the record evidence show the depth to which appellant excavated when it allegedly encountered the solid lava rock ledges. Without such evidence, we are unable to conclude that appellant encountered an unknown physical condition of an unusual nature. As we have already noted, the presence of lava rock could have been discovered by appellant prior to its bid (findings 14–16). Furthermore, appellant was required by paragraph 6, Section 2A, Division 2 of the Technical Provisions of the contract to '[excavate] ... every type of material ... including rock ... to the lines, grades and elevations indicated and as specified....' (Finding 25)

Nor has appellant made out a case of Government superior knowledge. The evidence show that the swimming pool was built by military personnel with Army and Navy materials in 1943 (finding 8). The Government has researched its records; no records describing the surface or subsurface conditions of the site before or during excavation for the pool have been found (finding 9). To make out a case of superior knowledge, a contractor must show that the Government possesses knowledge which is vital to the successful completion of the contract, and that it is unreasonable to expect the contractor to obtain that vital information from any other accessible source. H.N. Bailey & Associates v. United States, 196 Ct. Cl. 156, 499 F.2d 376 (1971). Here, appellant has alleged but has failed to prove that the Government possessed any vital information which it had not already made known to appellant in the pre-bid and contract documents. Accordingly we find no merit to this allegation.

As the Government correctly points out in its partial motion to dismiss filed on 25 April 1983, the Court of Appeals for the Federal Circuit has held in Fidelity Construction Company v. United States, USCC (18 February 1983), 1 FPD p68, Petition for re-hearing en banc denied, 17 March 1983, that the Equal Access To Justice Act, Pub. L. No. 96-481, 94 Stat 2325, 28 U.S.C. s 2412 (Supp. V 1981), does not authorize boards of con-tract appeals to award attorney fees and expenses against the United States. In any event the matter is moot in view of the disposition of the appeal on the merits.

This appeal is denied.

Notes and Questions

1. The case begins with a discussion of how a club, although not operating with ap-propriated funds, follows government contracting law. This points off into the great di-versity and variety of systems operating in the grey zone surrounding the federal government, from the United States Postal Service to Medicaid.

2. The contractor's first theory is Type I. This turns on what the contract actually spec-ified. What was that? Many other items besides the written specifications can count as the contract, from test borings to soil reports to government representations. In addition, the contractor's Type I theory turns on whether the subsurface problem was "latent." Why was this not latent? Interestingly, "subsurface" has not been considered to require that the problem be underground. For example, the clause applies to the situation of inability to obtain expected access to a work site because of who owns the trail. *E.R. McKee Const. Co. v. United States*, 500 F.2d 525 (Ct. Cl. 1974).

Observe the close relation of this issue to the issue of defective specifications, from the *Spearin* case in the chapter on contract administration.

3. The contractor's Type II theory turns, as the opinion states, on whether what the contractor encounters differs "materially different from the known and the usual." A con-tractor faces a heavy burden in proving this, which is less frequently alleged and more difficult to prove than the Type I conditions. Why did this theory fail? The contractor did have expert affidavits to support it. Perhaps experts are easier to line up when their duty involves an expenses-paid sojourn to the Hawaiian Islands.

4. The contractor's other theory concerns superior government knowledge. If Type II differing site conditions bear a resemblance to the basic (private) contract law issue of impracticability, this issue bears a resemblance to theories of fraud or misrepresentation; the government owes the contractor because of the wrong it did in withholding knowl-edge. Look at the sleuthing job done by the contractor's attorneys in this case trying to find such withheld knowledge.

Department of General Services v. Harmans Associates Limited Partnership
No. 491, Sept. Term, 1993
Court of Special Appeals of Maryland
633 A.2d 939
Dec. 8, 1993

Argued before WILNER, C.J., and BISHOP and FISCHER, JJ.

WILNER, Chief Judge.

The State Department of General Services (DGS) appeals from a judgment of the Cir-cuit Court for Baltimore City affirming, with one modification, a decision of the Board of Contract Appeals (BCA) awarding $163,719 in extra compensation to appellee, Harmans Associates Limited Partnership.... We shall deny the motion to dismiss, affirm the judgment in part, and reverse it in part.

Underlying Facts

The State owned a tract of unimproved land in Anne Arundel County on which it desired to have constructed a headquarters facility for the State Highway Administration. The facility was to consist of three buildings and related storage and parking areas. Normally, the State would have proceeded to procure the services of an architect/engineer to design the facility and then, through competitive bidding, select a contractor to build it in accordance with the plans and specifications prepared by the architect/engineer. It would have financed the construction through the sale of State general obligation bonds. See, in general, Md.Code, State Fin. & Proc. art., §§ 13-102, 8-114.

In this instance, the State chose a different method of achieving the result, one that involved a form of "creative financing." The principal objective, we are informed, was to avoid the creation of a State "debt"—i.e., a pledge of the full faith and credit of the State— to finance the construction and yet have the interest paid on the private financing remain tax-exempt.

Through a number of agreements entered into in March and April, 1988, including a ground lease, a conditional purchase agreement, and a facility agreement, the deal was structured in the following manner. Subject to certain contingencies, the State leased the unimproved land to Harmans for a 16-year period at a rental of $1/year. Harmans designed and constructed a facility "substantially in accordance with the Conceptual Plans and Technical Specifications" that were included with the State's request for proposals. When the facility was completed, Harmans subleased the ground to the State for the remaining term of the ground lease and sold the improvements to the State in accordance with the conditional purchase agreement. At the end of the 16-year period, the ground lease (and the sublease) will end, and the State will own both the land and the improvements free of any encumbrances.

The $10.9 million cost of construction was financed through a private sale of certificates of participation. The proceeds were deposited with a trustee and were used to pay Harmans as construction proceeded. To secure the certificates, Harmans mortgaged to the trustee its interest in the land and in the contracts with the State. The State, as "purchaser" of the facility, is required to make semi-annual payments to the trustee in amounts sufficient to pay the principal and interest on the certificates over the term of the ground lease. The State retains the right, however, to terminate its obligation to make these payments at any time, in which event the trustee has the right to take possession of the land and improvements and either to sell or operate them in order to discharge its obligations to Harmans and the certificate holders.

In November, 1989, Harmans filed with DGS two formal claims for an equitable adjustment in the contract price, each claim having several sub-parts. One claim sought $186,860 for unexpected site conditions, including excessive amounts of topsoil.... When, on May 24, 1990, the procurement officer denied those claims, Harmans appealed to BCA. In November, 1990, BCA, in a Memorandum Decision, concluded that it had no jurisdiction and, for that reason, dismissed the appeals. BCA viewed the transaction from which the claims arose as a lease of real property rather than as a construction contract, and Md.Code, State Fin. & Proc. art., § 15-211(a)(2) excepts from BCA's jurisdiction contract claims relating to a lease of real property. Harmans sought judicial review of that decision, and, in an order entered in April, 1991, the Circuit Court for Baltimore County concluded, as a matter of law, that the claims were not contract claims relating to a lease of real property.

It therefore reversed the dismissals by BCA and remanded the case to that Board for further proceedings.

Upon the remand, BCA heard evidence bearing on what remained of the two claims. In a decision filed on May 7, 1992, BCA directed a total equitable adjustment of $163,719, consisting principally of $113,329 for the soil conditions....

* * *

Jurisdiction Of BCA

The issue here, as we indicated, is whether the arrangement between DGS and Harmans, from which Harmans' claims arose, constitutes a lease or sale of real property. Through a combination of the definition of "procurement" in SFP, § 11-101(1), the definition of "contract claim" in § 15-215(b) of that article, and the stated jurisdiction of BCA in § 15-211, it is clear that BCA has jurisdiction to decide a claim that relates to a procurement contract, including a contract for construction, but that it does not have jurisdiction to decide claims arising from the sale or leasing of real property.

DGS's position, as stated in its brief, is that "[t]he essence of the transaction was the creation and transfer of interests in real property, not the mere construction of a building." This position is based principally on the ground lease and sublease used to implement the arrangement. A fair consideration of the overall transaction, especially in light of the State's own request for proposals, establishes exactly the contrary, however. The "essence of the transaction" was not the creation and transfer of interests in real property but the construction of the State Highway Administration facility. The State's request for proposals (RFP) stated explicitly:

> "The solicitation is based on the following concept:
>
> (1) The offeror shall design, construct and finance the facilities on property owned by the State.
>
> (2) The entire improved property shall be leased to the State Highway Administration under a lease/purchase agreement, or other creative financing mechanism as may be proposed by the offeror."

The acquisition by the State of a completed facility was the sole objective of the transaction. Neither the State nor Harmans had any business interest in leasing and subleasing unimproved land. The State needed a building and Harmans, as a developer, was willing to build it; that was the heart and soul of the agreements between them. The fact that this complex arrangement, designed to avoid the creation of a State "debt," utilized a lease and sublease cannot and does not change the true nature of the arrangement.

Even if we were to give some higher regard to the property instruments, the fact would remain that at least part of the transaction involved the construction of the facility. That is what the State was paying $10.9 million for, and, more important, that is the source of Harmans' claims. The claims for unexpected site conditions and smoke vents did not arise from any lease or sublease but solely from the construction work.

For these reasons, we find that the disputes were within the statutory jurisdiction of BCA.

Site Conditions

Harmans' claim for an equitable adjustment based on differing site conditions is based on a clause that should have been in the contract; DGS's defense is based on clauses that were in the contract. The simple question is which prevails.

As we indicated earlier, the traditional process for construction projects is for the State to select an architect/engineer to prepare detailed plans and specifications and then to select a contractor to build the facility in accordance with those plans and specifications. In requesting proposals from contractors, the State will normally provide information, taken from test borings, regarding soil conditions. In that regard, SFP, § 13-218(b) requires that "a procurement contract for construction shall include a clause providing for contract modification if the condition of a site differs from the condition described in the specifications." The particular clause that is mandated is set forth in the procurement regulations adopted by the Board of Public Works, COMAR 21.07.02.05. It requires (1) the contractor to notify the procurement officer promptly of subsurface conditions "differing materially from those indicated in this contract," (2) the procurement officer to investigate the conditions, and (3) if the procurement officer finds that such conditions do materially so differ and cause an increase or decrease in the contractor's cost of performance, "an equitable adjustment shall be made and the contract modified in writing accordingly."

The very next regulation, COMAR 21.07.02.06, requires construction contracts also to contain a clause in which the contractor acknowledges that he has "satisfied himself as to the character, quality and quantity of surface and subsurface materials or obstacles to be encountered insofar as this information is reasonably ascertainable from an inspection of the site, including all exploratory work done by the State, as well as from information presented by the drawings and specifications made a part of this contract."

Notwithstanding that both of these clauses are required by State procurement regulations to be included in every State construction contract, only the second one was included; the first was not.

Before soliciting proposals for this project, the State employed Greiner Engineering Services, Inc. to develop Conceptual Plans and Specifications, which were included with the RFP. Indeed, the Special Conditions, also made part of the RFP, required the contractor to construct the facilities "substantially in accordance with the Conceptual Plans and Technical Specifications enclosed as Exhibits I and II." Included in the drawings prepared by Greiner were 48 foundation boring logs. The bidders were informed that actual copies of the test boring logs and information regarding tests conducted on soil samples were available for examination.

Having provided this information and having required that construction be in substantial accord with the Conceptual Design and Specifications, the RFP then backed away from making any warranties as to subsurface soil conditions. In the Special Conditions attached as Schedule C to the RFP, the State said that the inclusion of the Conceptual Design and Specifications was for "informational purposes only," and that they were not to be taken as "construction documents and specifications" or as a representation as to the "technical sufficiency, or adequacy or safety of ... the subsoil conditions involved in the project." In the section of the Special Provisions attached to Greiner's drawings dealing with subsurface exploration, reference was made to the 48 test borings, but that reference was immediately followed by the disclaimer:

> "While the Owner believes the results of the test borings accurately indicate the existing soil conditions below the surface at points and planes indicated, the Owner assumes no responsibility for the actual conditions which may be encountered in the execution of the Contract. Offerors are advised to make their own subsurface investigations."

This, in turn, was followed by other statements to the effect that, if the offeror relies on the accuracy or completeness of the test borings, he does so "at his own risk," and that the information available as to underlying earth strata "must be used by the offeror at his discretion, and is not guaranteed as factual."

DGS's position is that the arrangement is not a construction contract, that, as a result, SFP, § 13-218(b) and COMAR 21.07.02.05 are irrelevant, that the provisions just noted make clear that no representations were made as to soil conditions, and that, accordingly, there is no basis for an equitable adjustment. We have, of course, rejected the major premise of that argument by concluding that the arrangement was a procurement contract for construction. Still, DGS contends, even if that is the case, the specific disclaimers, which were approved by the Board of Public Works as part of its approval of the lease, conditional purchase agreement, and facilities agreement, override the differing site clause required by the statute and the regulation. That is the issue upon which we need to focus.

It is not uncommon for procurement statutes or regulations to require a site condition clause similar to that at issue here, for the perception is that such a clause serves the interest of both the government and the contractor. As noted in Foster Const. C.A. & Williams Bros. Co. v. United States, 435 F.2d 873, 887, 193 Ct.Cl. 587 (1970), the clause is designed to ameliorate the risk to contractors from unknowable subsurface conditions. When dependable information on such conditions is unavailable, bidders will either have to make their own test borings or include in their bids a contingency element to cover the risk, either of which inflates the cost to the government. By providing test borings and an equitable adjustment clause, the government can avoid that inflation. 435 F.2d at 887, the Court explained:

> "The purpose of the changed conditions clause is thus to take at least some of the gamble on subsurface conditions out of bidding. Bidders need not weigh the cost and ease of making their own borings against the risk of encountering an adverse subsurface, and they need not consider how large a contingency should be added to the bid to cover the risk. They will have no windfalls and no disasters. The Government benefits from more accurate bidding, without inflation for risks which may not eventuate. It pays for difficult subsurface work only when it is encountered and was not indicated in the logs."

See also Stock & Grove, Inc. v. United States, 493 F.2d 629, 204 Ct.Cl. 103 (1974); Spirit Leveling Contractors v. U.S., 19 Cl.Ct. 84 (1989). BCA has adopted that same line of reasoning with respect to the Maryland requirement. See Appeal of Hardaway Constructors, Inc., MSBCA 1249, 3 MSBCA ¶ 227, p. 42 (MICPEL, 1989).

Maryland has adopted the general rule that contracts are made with reference to existing law and that laws affecting particular contracts are incorporated by implication in them. Denice v. Spotswood I. Quinby, Inc., 248 Md. 428, 237 A.2d 4 (1968). See also 17A Am.Jur.2d Contracts § 381. In a series of cases beginning with G.L. Christian & Assoc. v. United States, 312 F.2d 418, 160 Ct.Cl. 1 (1963), the Federal courts have adopted the more specific rule that, where procurement regulations adopted pursuant to statutory authority require that a contract contain a particular clause, the contract must be read as though it contained that clause, whether or not the clause was actually written in the contract. See S.J. Amoroso Const. Co., Inc. v. U.S., 26 Cl.Ct. 759 (1992); SCM Corp. v. United States, 645 F.2d 893, 227 Ct.Cl. 12 (1981); DeMatteo Const. Co. v. United States, 600 F.2d 1384, 220 Ct.Cl. 579 (1979).

This approach is not only consistent with Denice, supra, but is necessary for a proper implementation of the State procurement laws. The General Assembly has, by law, required a site condition clause to be included in every State construction contract, presumably for the reasons noted in the Foster Const. case. Although the Board of Public

Works has the authority, through its regulations, to draft the specific language of the clause, which it has done, neither the Board nor DGS is empowered to dispense with the clause altogether where the contract in question is a construction contract. To hold otherwise would be to permit Executive agencies to ignore the clear legislative mandate. Because we have concluded that this arrangement was a construction contract, we conclude further that the site condition clause set forth in COMAR 21.07.02.05 is effectively a part of the Harmans contract.

Normally, when examining a claim for equitable adjustment due to differing site conditions, two questions need to be addressed: (1) whether the site conditions were, in fact, different from what the contractor was led to expect; and (2) whether it was reasonable for the contractor to rely on the information supplied by the government. There is no real dispute here as to the first question. BCA found that the 48 soil boring logs indicated approximately 3–6 inches of topsoil when, in fact, Harmans encountered 1.5 to 2 feet, resulting in an excess of 12,000 cubic yards of topsoil that had to be moved. That was nearly double the 13,000 cubic yards estimated in the drawings. BCA found that this "unexpected condition was dramatically different from what any of the parties expected, requiring the removal of the unsuitable material and importation of borrow to complete construction." DGS does not contest BCA's finding that this was a material difference; its argument is that, in light of the various disclaimers, Harmans was not justified in relying on the Greiner conceptual plans and specifications.

BCA found that reliance by Harmans was reasonable. It quoted with approval statements by the U.S. Court of Claims and the Armed Services Board of Contract Appeals that soil borings "are the most specific and usually the most reliable indications of subsurface conditions," that, while those borings show the conditions only in the bored hole, it is simply not practical "to drill every square inch of a proposed construction site to determine subsurface conditions," and that "[t]his fact of life has to be taken into consideration in determining what use prospective bidders can make of the boring log information furnished to them."

On this basis, BCA observed:

> "The [Greiner] plans included soil boring samples which clearly indicated topsoil a contractor would reasonably expect to encounter. Based upon these borings bids resulted. The small percentage of work done to the plans by the contractor's architect in no way affected the representations by the State in providing the boring samples. Harmans had nothing to do with the preparation of the boring samples. The State offered this information in the RFP and bidders reasonably relied upon them in making their bids."

The reasonableness of Harmans' reliance on the test borings is a question of fact, to be determined from all of the circumstances, including, but not limited to, the provisions in the RFP and the various agreements. Applying normal rules of administrative law, BCA's findings of fact are entitled to deference if they are supported by substantial evidence. Here, they are.

The State's reliance, almost exclusively, on the various disclaimers noted misses two important points. The first is, if DGS really had no intention of allowing bidders to rely on those borings, why did it bother to have them made and to include them in the RFP? If prospective bidders were not permitted to rely on them in preparing their bids, what conceivable purpose did they serve? The State has informed us of no other purpose for including the boring logs in the RFP, and so we cannot conclude that BCA was clearly erroneous in finding that they amounted to representations upon which bidders reasonably could rely. Indeed, the inclusion of the clause required by COMAR 21.07.02.06 confirms the importance of the information supplied by the State. Supporting this as well is the illogic of the converse. As we indicated, the Legislature has required every State construction contract to contain a differing site condition clause. Representations with respect to site conditions are necessary to give that clause meaning. If, through its RFP, the State can disavow such representations, it can, in effect, thwart the legislative mandate.

In summary, it is apparent to us that, in using this scheme of "creative financing" to avoid the creation of a State debt, DGS has wittingly or unwittingly trampled upon some basic procurement requirements. BCA did not err in redressing that situation.

* * *

Notes and Questions

1. This is a state case illustrating the common occurrence of differing site conditions cases at state as well as federal levels. Would the opinion be any different if composed wholly from federal law? How does the court decide the jurisdictional question? Of course, ordinarily real estate acquisition differs from competitive bidding, with the government deciding what land it wants and then acquiring that by negotiated purchase or condemnation. If the government acquired land by competitive bidding, where would roads go? Exactly in the opposite direction than they should. The land offered for the lowest price would be in the direction away from people and business, and so roads would head straight for where roads are not needed.

2. This is a Type I case, concerning the asserted inclusion in the RFP of the information from soil borings and how the site differed from expectations. Someone has to bear the risk that soil borings will not forecast fully the subsurface conditions. Should the government recover from the Greiner firm?

3. The case turns partly on the important issue of the contractor's duty to investigate the site. The RFP included a standard "site investigation" clause, like FAR 52.236-3. As quoted here, the contractor must have "satisfied himself as to the character ... of surface and subsurface materials ... insofar as this information is reasonably ascertainable from an inspection of the site...." The clause limits the contractor to knowing what is "reasonably" ascertainable. A contractor who fails to inspect the site may be assuming the risk of what the investigation would have discovered.

4. The case also turns partly on the important issue of the nature of the government's disclaimers in the RFP. In this RFP, the government did not effectively disclaim responsibility for the inadequacy of the soil borings. By contrast, in the *COVCO* case the government escaped liability in part from having warned that the contractor might have to deal with rock. Contrast ineffective general disclaimers, such as in this case, *Fehlhaber Corp. v. United States*, 138 Ct. Cl. 571, *cert. denied*, 355 U.S. 877 (1957), with effective specific warnings, such as in the *COVCO* case, *Jefferson Construction v. United States*, 364 F.2d 420 (Ct. Cl.), *cert. denied*, 386 U.S. 914 (1966).

Chapter 11

International Procurement and Afghanistan and Iraq Wars

Government contracting has many diverse international aspects. No single framework treats them all. Rather, each aspect has its own framework, and, accordingly, this chapter consists of separate and diverse subchapters on different international aspects. It starts with the Buy America act, by which American procurement deals with the buying of foreign products. Then, it pulls together several aspects of foreign purchases or sales: the supremacy of federal policy about boycotts of a nation's products, foreign military sales, and European Union purchasing. The third subsection treats special aspects of procurement in the Afghanistan and Iraq wars.

A. The Buy American Act

The "Buy American Act" signifies an array of statutory and regulatory rules that give limited preferences to domestic products. In practice, these often involve determinations and calculations of various kinds that may be disputed legally about the application and scale of the preference. If parts from Country A are assembled in Country B and then used as materials in a proposal by a United States construction firm, how much of a preference should be given to a competing proposal by another United States construction firm with other parts from Country D assembled in Country E? Detailed answers may be found to some extent in the FAR and in agency-specific regulations, but in approaching these regulations it helps to have a general understanding.

The application of these preferences has been considerably affected by the network of international trade agreements joined by the United States. Obviously, for example, by joining the North American Free Trade Agreement ("NAFTA") with Canada and Mexico, the United States committed itself to opening its markets, including its government contracting market, to contractors in those countries. More broadly, by joining the GATT Agreement on Government Procurement which now operates through the World Trade Organization ("WTO"), the United States committed itself to opening its government contracting market to contractors in countries around the world. In fact, the GATT Agreement on Government Procurement involved a further commitment not only for the federal government contracting market, but also the state and local contracting markets to open — somewhat.

Accordingly, the first discussion in this subchapter is a brief general introduction to the Buy American Act. The second piece is the *John C. Grimberg* case, which illustrates how the statutes and regulations actually get applied in a dispute. That case includes a vigorous dissent which reflects the disagreements lurking here amidst the technical rules. Another discussion is an analysis of what the GATT Agreement on Government Procurement means for state and local government procurement, again reflecting the debated perspectives. Then comes the Supreme Court's opinion in *Crosby v. National Foreign Trade Council*, about pre-emption of state procurement-conditioning international policies, with background about the applicable international trade law.

Viewed one way, the Buy American Act and related preferences are a barrier to world free trade and an uneconomical means by which the costs of goods and services bought by the taxpayers gets inflated for the benefit of inefficient domestic producers and labor. Viewed another way, the trade agreements and the efforts of sharp lawyers to get government contracts for foreign products are a method by which the American industrial base and American jobs are exported abroad to countries that find ways to subsidize and protect their own home market. With rising globalization of production trade, these issues become increasingly important.

For further discussion of the subject of this section, see: Thomas D. Blanford, *Navigating The Recovery Act's Buy American Rule In State And Local Government Construction*, 46 Procrmt. Law. 3 (Fall 2010); Jeffrey A. Belkin, Donald G. Brown, *The Buy American Act Information Technology Exception: Should It Apply To The Trade Agreement Act-Covered Contracts?*, 24 No. 6 Westlaw J. Gov't Cont. 3 (July 26, 2010); John A. Howell, Article, *The Trade Agreements Act of 1979 versus The Buy American Act: The Irresistible Force Meets the Immovable Object*, 35 Pub. Cont. L.J. 495 (2006); Victor Mosoti, *The WTO Agreement On Government Procurement: A Necessary Evil In The Legal Strategy For Development In The Poor World?*, 25 U. Pa. J. Int'l Econ. L. 593 (Summer 2004); John Chiefichella, Jonathan Aronie & Andrew Skowronek, *Domestic & Foreign Product Preferences*, 00-13 Briefing Papers 1 (Dec. 2000).

Note on The Buy American Act

Congress enacted the Buy American Act (BAA) during the Great Depression in 1933 to give preferential treatment to U.S. producers and manufacturers. On many procurements, it means that that a foreign bid must beat the domestic bids by more than 6% if the domestic one is from a large business concern or by more than 12% if the domestic one is from a small business. The BAA also applies to construction. A construction contractor must use domestic, not foreign, materials, or win the award after factoring in the BAA differential.

The act applies to "end products." Contractors must fill out a Buy American Act certificate that each "end product" (except those separately listed) is a domestic end product. The separately listed items are foreign end products. The certificate heightens the risk for noncomplying with the BAA. For a contractor who knowingly noncomplies, the government, or a qui tam relator, may use the False Claims Act for false certifications.

Products from many countries get exempted, including European Union members, and, Canada and Mexico under NAFTA. Contractors get into trouble reselling with the large wave of products from China.

Many technical issues arise about where an end product is manufactured. The BAA regulations do not exempt resellers of products who merely perform assembly of components in the United States. Rather, domestic manufacturing operations must alter the "essential nature" of a component. The modern regulations made the source of origin matter not only for each component but for each subcomponent.

An inaccurate certification also exposes a bidder to a protest. However, once an award has been made, a protester must show that after proper reevaluation under the BAA, the defective bid was no longer lowest. Also, after award (as well as before) a contractor may seek a waiver of the applicable BAA requirements. If the awardee seeks the waiver because of an increase in cost, that increase must be a result of some unforeseen circumstance.

The BAA interacts in a complex way with the Trade Agreements Act (TAA). In response to trade agreements, that act lets the President waive discriminatory laws, such as the BAA, for "designated countries."

John C. Grimberg Company, Inc., Appellant, v. The United States, Appellee

No. 88-1378
869 F.2d 1475
United States Court of Appeals, Federal Circuit
Decided March 15, 1989

Before RICH and BISSELL, Circuit Judges, and BENNETT, Senior Circuit Judge.

BISSELL, Circuit Judge.

The decision of the Armed Services Board of Contract Appeals (ASBCA), John C. Grimberg, Co., ASBCA No. 32288, 88-1 BCA ¶ 20,346 (1987) [1987 WL 46574], reconsideration denied, 88-2 BCA ¶ 20,713 (1988) [1988 WL 44422], affirming the contracting officer's denial of the equitable price adjustment claim of John C. Grimberg Company, Inc. (Grimberg), is reversed and remanded.

BACKGROUND

On December 9, 1983, the United States Navy issued an invitation for bids on construction work at the Bethesda, Maryland Naval Center. The $3,330,000 fixed price contract included fabrication and installation of exterior precast concrete wall panels. Prior to bidding, Grimberg solicited precast panel quotations from several domestic subcontractors but received only one. Arban & Carosi (A & C) quoted a price of $245,000 — $165,500 for fabrication and $79,500 for erection, caulking and cleaning. The Navy awarded Grimberg the contract on March 15, 1984. Shortly thereafter, Grimberg unsuccessfully attempted to contact A & C to consummate the subcontract. After failing to reach A & C, Grimberg resolicited the domestic vendors previously contacted and received two quotations of $205,000 and $200,918 covering only the precast panel fabrication. Grimberg, however, subcontracted the fabrication and erection to a Canadian firm, Beer Precast Concrete, Ltd., for $237,000 — $120,000 for fabrication and delivery and $117,000 for erection and other miscellaneous work.

The Navy rejected the submittal of panel drawings because use of the Canadian fabricator violated the Buy American Act, 41 U.S.C. §§ 10a–10d (1982) (BAA). Grimberg requested a waiver of the BAA but the Navy refused. Faced with construction deadlines, Grimberg chose to obtain the precast panels from a domestic subcontractor and incurred costs of $200,000 for fabrication, $59,000 for erection, and approximately $23,000 for miscellaneous work.

Pursuant to the contract's disputes clause, Grimberg submitted an equitable adjustment claim for $53,847. The Navy denied the claim, determining that a post-award BAA waiver was not warranted. The ASBCA denied Grimberg's appeal, Grimberg, 88-1 BCA at 102,895, and subsequent motion for reconsideration, Grimberg, 88-2 BCA at 104,664.

ISSUE

Whether the ASBCA erred as a matter of law by failing to apply the criteria for determining unreasonable price differentials under the BAA and thereby abused its discretion by not granting an equitable adjustment.

OPINION

I.

Grimberg's claim is based on the Navy's failure to grant a post-award exception to the BAA. Without a waiver, Grimberg was prohibited from using the lower priced Canadian fabricated panels. The BAA requires that only domestic materials be used for public works contracts unless the head of an agency determines that such use is inconsistent with the public interest or the cost is unreasonable. 41 U.S.C. § 10d. The BAA primarily provides a competitive preference to domestic materials in awarding government contracts. Watkins, Effects of the Buy American Act on Federal Procurement, 31 Fed. Bar J. 191, 194 (1972); see also John T. Brady & Co. v. United States, 693 F.2d 1380 (Fed.Cir.1982) (stating that the BAA "is directed primarily to the period prior to the award").

The BAA is implemented by an Executive Order that provides in pertinent part:

[Section 2.](b) For the purposes of ... this order, the bid or offered price of materials of domestic origin shall be deemed to be unreasonable ... if the bid or offered price thereof exceeds the sum of the bid or offered price of like materials of foreign origin and a differential computed as provided in subsection (c) of this section.

[Section 2.](c) The executive agency concerned shall in each instance determine the amount of the differential referred to in subsection (b) of this section on the basis of one of the following-described formulas ... :

(1) The sum determined by computing six percentum of the bid or offered price of materials of foreign origin.

....

[Section 5.] ... In any case in which the head of an executive agency proposing to purchase domestic materials determines that a greater differential than that provided in this order between the cost of such materials of domestic origin and materials of foreign origin is not unreasonable ... this order shall not apply.

Exec. Order No. 10,582, 3 C.F.R. 230 (1954–58), reprinted in 41 U.S.C. § 10d app. at 1042 (1982) (hereinafter Executive Order No. 10,582).

II.

The ASBCA's interpretation of the BAA is a conclusion of law freely reviewable by this court. See United States v. Lockheed Corp., 817 F.2d 1565, 1567 (Fed.Cir.1987). The ASBCA denied Grimberg's appeal because it determined that the cost of domestic panels was not unreasonable in light of "the flexibility afforded procuring departments and agencies by Section 5 of the Executive Order [No. 10,582], and in light of the Brady guidelines." Grimberg, 88-1 BCA at 102,895. With regard to post-award equitable adjustments, we conclude that the ASBCA erred as a matter of law in interpreting the BAA and Brady.

The ASBCA erroneously construed section 5 of Executive Order No. 10,582 and disregarded the flexibility it affords the agencies in determining BAA waivers. The fact that the head of an agency is empowered to establish greater price differentials under section 5 does not mean that one should be established. Section 5 does not dictate greater price differentials, but rather represents an available option. If the agency head chooses not to exercise that option, the price differentials of section 2 become mandatory for determining what is unreasonable under the BAA. See L.G. Lefler, Inc. v. United States, 6 Cl.Ct. 514, 519 & n. 5 (1984) (holding that a waiver must be granted when the price differential standards are met and that the same standards used pre-award should apply post-award); Keuffel & Esser Co., 42 Comp.Gen. 608, 612 (1963) (explaining that the "Executive order fixes the differentials which shall be considered in determining unreasonable cost, unless the agency head determines," under section 5, that a greater price differential is not unreasonable); see generally Watkins, 31 Fed.Bar J. 191.

The plain language of Executive Order No. 10,582 supports this conclusion. Section 2(b) provides that the price of domestic materials "shall be deemed to be unreasonable" if it exceeds the price of like foreign materials plus a section 2(c) differential. Section 2(c) requires the executive agency to determine the price differential of section 2(b) based on one of the formulas set forth in section 2(c)(1) and (2). Therefore, in evaluating unreasonableness under the BAA, the formulas of section 2 become mandatory unless the head of the agency determines that a greater price differential should be applied.

In this case the fabrication price differential between the Canadian firm and the domestic firm is more than three times the differential established by section 2(c)(1), and the agency head has never determined that an alternative differential should be applied. Therefore, the ASBCA erred in not applying the prescribed formulas.

In post-award situations, however, that does not end the inquiry. Post-award, an exception to the BAA is granted under the contract's changes clause only where warranted by the circumstances. Brady, 693 F.2d at 1385–86. If all existing BAA criteria are met, the decision to grant a change is discretionary. See John T. Brady & Co., VABCA No. 1300, 84-1 BCA ¶ 16,925, at 84,196 (1983) [1983 WL 13698] (interpreting the Federal Circuit's instructions on remand). The ASBCA misconstrued Brady, by reading that decision as establishing a narrow range of circumstances for granting post-award exceptions. Grimberg, 88-2 BCA at 104,664. Brady merely holds that the BAA does not preclude post-award waivers and that additional factors may be considered in determining whether or not to grant an equitable adjustment.[2] See Brady, 693 F.2d at 1385–86.

In granting an equitable adjustment in the Brady remand, the Veterans Administration Contract Appeals Board (VABCA) recognized that "the request for an exception would have resulted in no increase in cost to the Government, in fact there may have been sufficient basis for a credit to the Government." Brady, 84-1 BCA at 84,196–97. The VACAB also realized the severe consequences to the contractor that the additional cost would bring and stated: "[i]t is certainly in the public interest to grant legally permissible exceptions where there is no resulting expense to the Government, and where to grant such an exception serves to increase the public's perception of its Government as one which deals fairly with its contractors." Id., at 84,197.

Here, Grimberg originally bid the panel fabrication at $165,500. After being awarded the contract, Grimberg found that it could not obtain the panels domestically at that price. Grimberg solicited a foreign bid of $120,000 and the Navy improperly denied a BAA waiver. Grimberg, ultimately obtained the panels from a domestic source for $200,000. Had the Navy granted the waiver, no increase in cost would have been incurred and the government may have been entitled to a credit. Instead, Grimberg was saddled with an additional fabrication cost of $34,500 beyond that which it had originally quoted.[3]

---

2. The dissent's conclusion sets forth a bright line test for permitting post-award exceptions to the BAA. Such a test is unwarranted; the granting of an equitable adjustment is discretionary and should not be so limited.

3. Footnote two of the dissent misreads the function served by the calculation delineated in Allis-Chalmers Corp. v. Friedkin, 481 F.Supp. 1256, 1266–68 (M.D.Pa.), aff'd, 635 F.2d 248 (3d Cir.1980). That calculation is for ascertaining the lowest bidder after the BAA surcharges have been properly

The failure to grant the requested waiver was an abuse of discretion. The Navy's actions constituted a constructive change and Grimberg is entitled to an equitable adjustment as prescribed by the contract. Accordingly, we reverse and remand to the ASBCA for a determination of the quantum due Grimberg.

COSTS

Each party is to bear its own costs.

REVERSED AND REMANDED.

BENNETT, Senior Circuit Judge, dissenting.

The issue set forth in the majority opinion is correct. Stated another way, the issue before us is whether the Armed Services Board of Contract Appeals (Board) erred in its determination that Grimberg (plaintiff/appellant) was not entitled to an equitable adjustment under the Changes clause on the grounds Grimberg was not entitled to an exception to the Buy American Act (BAA). 41 U.S.C. § 10a–b, 10d, and Executive Order No. 10,582 (1954), as amended by Executive Order No. 11,051 (1962). I dissent from the conclusion that the Board was in error.

OPINION

The majority opinion asserts this court's decision in John T. Brady & Co. v. United States, 693 F.2d 1380 (Fed.Cir.1982), is precedent for its position. I think not. First, with regard to the express holding of Brady, the issue decided was "whether the Board erroneously held that exceptions to the Buy American Act [could not] be granted after the contract [had] been awarded." Id. at 1384. In affirming the Claims Court's decision to remand to the Board in that case, this court reasoned that "it may be impossible for the contractor in some instances to make a pre-award request for the exemption." Id. at 1386 (emphasis added).

The fact situation in Brady was such a case. That is, a case where it was impossible for the contractor to make a pre-award request for a BAA exemption. The contractor could not enter a contract with the aluminum supplier since the Veteran's Administration (VA), the contracting agency, had not yet supplied the contractor with specific aluminum sheet sizes. A binding contract cannot be formed without sufficient specificity of the subject matter. It was on these facts that this court in Brady decided a post-award exemption to the BAA can in some instances be granted. The facts in the instant appeal, as discussed below, are very different from those in Brady and do not merit the same result as was reached in Brady.

Second, in addition to there being no express holding in Brady for the proposition that pre- and post-awards are treated equally, the rationale expressed in Brady also does not support any inferential rule that a post-award exemption should have been granted on the facts of the instant appeal. The cases discussed and relied upon by the court in Brady show that the Brady decision cannot support the granting of a post-award exemption (or an equitable adjustment in lieu thereof) except under extraordinary circumstances.

The BCA and Comptroller General (CG) decisions reviewed in the analysis section of Brady all demonstrate some of the extraordinary circumstances which would merit a post-award exemption.

---

added to the foreign bid, not for determining the propriety of granting a waiver to the BAA. The dissent's calculations are misleading.

* * *

Nor is there any harshness in requiring the contractor to bear the additional material costs. In Brady, harshness would have resulted since the difference in the actual cost of aluminum versus the expected cost was $50,806 which was 35.71% higher than expected.[1] In the instant appeal the difference between the expected domestic cost and the foreign cost was only $800 which was 0.33% higher than the domestic cost.[2] It is the A & C bid of $245,000 and not the actual cost claimed by the contractor of $282,000 that should be used in considering harshness. That was the amount on which the contractor based its original bid and that was the amount for which it would have obtained the materials had the contractor done what was reasonably necessary to finalize the contract with A & C. No written communication with A & C was ever attempted by Grimberg, only telephone calls. Board opinion at 2 (finding of fact No. 5). While it might be considered harsh to require the contractor to bear a 35.71% higher actual cost, a 0.33% increase does not even approach being harsh.

The majority opinion's reference to language in the BCA's discussion of Brady on remand is inapposite. The Board applied this court's instructions and found "[i]t is the opinion of the Board that the price escalation of the domestic aluminum meets all existing criteria for granting an exception to the "Buy American' provisions." Brady, 84-1 BCA at 84,196. The fact that granting the exemption would not have resulted in a cost increase to the government is not a rationale which supports the finding that the exemption should have been granted. If obtaining the lowest cost to the government was the predominant policy consideration in issue, all foreign materials would be allowed whenever they cost any amount less than domestic materials, and Congress never would have enacted the Buy American Act. See 48 C.F.R. § 14.404-1(a)(1) (1987) (requiring contracts to be awarded to lowest bidder, absent compelling contrary reasons).[3] Instead the general policy of reducing costs to the government must be balanced with the underlying policy of the Buy American Act to give a preference to domestic materials and thereby protect American workers and industry. See Watkins, Effects of the Buy American Act on Federal Procurement, 31 Fed.Bar J. 191, 191 (1972). In regard to the policy of increasing "the public's perception of its Government as one which deals fairly with its contractors," 84-1 BCA at 84,197,

---

1. [($190,000.87 (actual cost)—$140,000 (expected cost)) / $140,000 (expected cost)] x 100% = 35.71%.

2. $120,000 (foreign materials portion) x 1.06 (the 6% differential) + $117,000 (nonmaterial costs) = $244,200 (total foreign cost when adjusted with 6% differential). Percentage difference = [($245,000 (domestic price with A & C) – $244,200) / $244,200] x 100% = 0.33%. The proper application of the differential requires it only be applied to the materials portion of the foreign item. See, e.g., Allis-Chalmers Corp. v. Friedkin, 481 F.Supp. 1256, 1266–68 (M.D.Pa.1980). Then the nonmaterial portion of the foreign item is added back before comparing the foreign goods with the domestic goods. Id.

Footnote three of the majority contends these calculations are misleading. The majority does not, however, propose a different method of applying the differential. It is true that Allis-Chalmers was a protest by a domestic bidder of a contract award to a foreign bidder. The proper application of the differential is the same, however, whether it is for the purpose of determining the lowest bidder or the propriety of granting a BAA exemption. Both the statute and the executive order speak in terms of "materials" and not of labor, thus supporting the interpretation by the district court in Allis-Chalmers that the differential is only applied to the foreign materials.

3. But cf. Watkins, Effects of the Buy American Act on Federal Procurement, 31 Fed.Bar J. 191, 204–05 (1972) (discussing hidden costs to the government inherent with the use of foreign materials, e.g., increased unemployment compensation, welfare, and loss of personal and corporate income tax revenue).

Brady is substantially distinguishable from the facts of the instant appeal. As previously discussed, it was the government's delay in providing the exact dimensions for the aluminum sheets that prevented the contractor in Brady from entering a firm contract with ALCOA. Thus, holding for the contractor in Brady merely was in accordance with the rule that the government is liable for any additional cost caused by its own delay. Chalender, 127 Ct.Cl. at 563–64, 119 F.Supp. at 190. In contrast, in the instant appeal it was not the fault of the government that caused the failure of the contractor to firm up the subcontract on which it based its bid. Therefore the government should not be liable for the additional cost. WRB, 183 Ct.Cl. at 511–12.

* * *

CONCLUSION

Post-award exemptions are only granted in very limited circumstances. They have been granted where it was impossible for the contractor to request a pre-award exemption or where the material in issue was unavailable domestically. Neither of these circumstances nor any other circumstances requiring equity exists in the present appeal. Thus, the decision of the Board denying an equitable adjustment should be affirmed.

Notes and Questions

1. Start with the mechanics. Where does the 6% differential discussed in both the Massengale excerpt, and the *Grimberg* opinion come from? What does it apply to, i.e., what are the "rules of origin" that determine what is a foreign product? How is it determined what countries the Act's restrictions apply to? (For example: would *Grimberg* be analyzed differently as a result of the subsequent free trade agreements with Canada?) How does an agency head exercise discretion as to pre-award situations, compared to post-award situations?

2. Elsewhere in government contracts are many other situations deemed "constructive changes" warranting "equitable adjustments." How does the *Grimberg* possible foreign supplier situation resemble or contrast with those?

3. Distinguish two different, though complementary, debates about introducing Buy American Act substantive and procedural complexities into government contracting.

One debate occurs on economic grounds throughout trade questions. Should trade be completely "free" or are there policy reasons for preferences? For the tension between NAFTA and the Buy American Act, see Laura Eyster, NAFTA and the Barriers to Federal Procurement Opportunities in the United States, 31 Pub. Cont. L.J. 695 (2002).

A second debate is special to government contracting. How appropriate are government contracting procedures and personnel for managing a domestic preference? The "purist" view of government contracts sees the intrusion of Buy American as sheer interference with the straightforward goals of obtaining best value for the government with the lowest transactional costs. Yet, government contracting has devised an elaborate machinery of statutes, regulations, Executive orders, agency policies, contracting officer procedures, and administrative and adjudicative appeals for Buy American considerations. Is that machinery alien to the rest of government contracting? Note that unlike labor standards, where the government contracting agencies must share jurisdiction with an external specialized agency (the Department of Labor), the government contracting agencies administer Buy American themselves, without having recourse to external specialized trade-managing agencies like the United States Trade Representative or the Departments of Commerce and State.

The GATT Agreement on Government Procurement in Theory and Practice

Charles Tiefer, 26 U. Balt. L. Rev. 31 Summer, 1997

The Uruguay Round GATT Agreement on Government Procurement (AGP), which became effective January 1, 1997, appeared at first glance to end the preference barriers against foreign suppliers in procurement by American state and local governments. Such preference barriers are widespread. The United States' main international trading partners objected to these trade barriers in the Uruguay Round of GATT trade negotiations. They refused to open up protected procurement sectors of their own, while the American state government procurement sector remained discriminatory toward them. To bring the Uruguay Round to fruition, American negotiators had to, and did, match foreign concessions with the AGP's bar against in-state procurement preferences. In implementing the AGP, Congress had to, and did, approve this.

Accordingly, as described in this Article's next section, the AGP does extend GATT's principle of "non-discrimination" against foreign enterprise to the sector of state and local procurement. However, as the section further discusses, a closer look at the compromises made in the AGP negotiation and implementation processes at least begins raising questions about just how strongly the AGP acts.

As discussed in the Article's third section, the AGP explicitly limits its own scope of coverage: it only applies to thirty-seven states, and even to those, does not reach excepted sectors; moreover, the AGP creates ambiguity in implementation because it does not render in-state preferences invalid on their face or as applied to out-of-state domestic suppliers, only purporting to except selected foreign suppliers from their application. Most important, Congress's implementation of the AGP limits the remedying of state preferential decisions in major, if unobvious, ways. Congress has precluded, in the GATT implementation act, any private federal judicial remedy under the AGP.

Thus, procedurally, the AGP offers the foreign supplier considerably less than a smooth procedural route to American state contracts....

State Preferences

For obvious reasons, state and local government procurement often favors domestic suppliers, through a patchwork of formal and informal preferences that work against foreign suppliers. Congress has led the way in having a formal national "Buy America" preference in federal procurement, so, naturally, a number of the states have a similar one in their state procurement. The Congressionally enacted "Buy America" preference primarily serves a national goal to reduce domestic unemployment. It is implemented in each particular procurement by the federal contracting officer adding to each foreign proposal a "Buy America" factor, typically a six percent differential. Additionally, that central "Buy America" preference, and certain other formal "Buy America" preferences like a fifty percent differential for defense purchases, serve particular purposes in particular procurement sectors, such as the national security purpose of building up our domestic defense supply industry.

The federal "Buy America" regulations embody provisions for exceptions for foreign suppliers whose countries have joined the United States in reciprocal efforts at free trade, generally referred to as "qualified" countries. These exception regulations are implemented in each procurement by the contracting officer deciding whether a particular foreign supplier falls under an exception to the application of the differential and becomes a "BAA qualified" supplier. As a prime example, the federal government implemented GATT's

AGP, negotiation of which is discussed below, at the level of federal procurement by regulatory exceptions for suppliers in the GATT nations.

Those federal exception regulations teach an important lesson: it makes a difference how Congress implements international trade arrangements. Congress did not repeal the Buy America Act in favor of free trade. It did not even create some separate procedural system for implementing the GATT AGP. Rather, Congress kept the Buy America Act in effect, with a system for accommodations to free trade agreements on a procurement-by-procurement basis. This substantive and procedural arrangement for making exception decisions in individual procurements reflects how the balance of political forces in this context does not accord completely with either the vision of the purist free trade supporter, who might prefer an outright repeal of the Buy America Act, or that of domestic preference supporters, who regret any incursion into the Buy America Act's operation. Rather, the system reflects Congress's delicate political balance between a willingness to match foreign trade concessions and a desire to continue favoring domestic employment.

A second formal state rule has no matching federal counterpart. Many of the states have formal in-state preferences, that favor the state's own suppliers over out-of-state ones, both domestic and foreign. Some particular state legislatures simply declare that the state's procurement officers should favor suppliers of that state. Alternatively, some state legislatures specify particular differentials favoring suppliers within that state over outsiders. Often the preference concerns particular sectors, like western states with in-state preferences for their own beef. Given the small fraction of commerce in America that comes from overseas, such in-state preferences presumably operate primarily against other domestic suppliers rather than foreign ones.

States may also discriminate in favor of in-state suppliers by informal means. It stands to reason that the same political factors leading to the many "Buy America" and in-state preferences enacted formally as state legislation also lead to informal preferences by state administrators. Like state legislators, the state governors and their administrations are accountable to their state's public and their state's particular interest groups. Just as the local political support for favoring local suppliers influences state legislators, it may influence state administrations.

Both formal and informal in-state preferences can have two types of goals, just like the national "Buy America" goals: general favoring of state employment, and some particular interest regarding a particular procurement sector. At the state level, the particular interest would not be national defense, of course, or relief of some special political concern regarding that particular sector, much like a subsidy program meant to draw or to retain particular business for that state.

* * *

CONCLUSION

On its surface, the AGP appears to promise as a matter of substantive principle the opening of American state procurement on an equal basis to foreign suppliers. Its substantive coverage rules and, more important, the mechanisms of its remedies actually limit considerably its effect. In particular, in those states and at those times that the population strongly desires to favor its own firms in state procurement, the state government has ways of doing so. Correspondingly, foreign suppliers will find it difficult to engage in any kind of across-the-board campaign to pry open all the American state markets.

However this seems as economics, it makes good sense as politics. When the issues concern sensitive questions of federalism, the goals of free trade should not be considered matters of ironclad principle. Evolving politics forces and processes, rather than predetermined inflexible legal rules, will determine the pace and avenue of the opening to the world of the American state procurement sector.

At times this may prove an international embarrassment or an economic loss. It may create battle-points in future trade disputes. Yet, one of the main benefits of the American dual sovereignty system is its array of political mechanisms for adjustments between an overall set of national interests and the intense resistance of particular local populations on particular points. The AGP makes wise use of that flexibility to put future conflicts into political channels.

Notes and Questions

1. As the reading indicates, governments throughout the world have moved towards opening their government procurement to foreign providers, albeit with some resistance. Many governments have had to do much more than the United States, having virtually to establish a transparent government purchasing system for the first time. For details, see James J. Myers, *The New Uncitral Model Law on Procurement*, 23 Pub. Cont. L.J. 267 (1994).

B. International

Another aspect of the international aspects of government contract law concerns legal issues regarding selling to governments abroad. An issue of particular legal interest is selling to the foreign equivalent of the Department of Defense, that is, arms sales abroad. While a detailed treatment of this topic belongs to courses in international business transactions, government contracting law appropriately discusses a topic which, after all, involves "government" in contracting at both ends, because not only is the buyer a foreign country, but the United States government regulates such transactions on the seller's side too. Foreign governments obtain U.S. military items and services in two major ways: government-to-government sales under the foreign military sales (FMS) program, and direct commercial sales to the foreign governments.

Another example of the intricacies of this subject is discussed in Robert A. Borich Jr., *Globalization of the U.S. Defense Industrial Base: Developing Procurement Sources Abroad Through Exporting Advanced Military Technology*, 31 Pub. Cont. L.J. 623 (2002). This traces the impact on procurement of export control laws applicable to transfers of military technology. An example of the intricacies of this subject — offsets — is discussed in *U.S. Defense Exports: Update on Offsets*, the Procurement Lawyer, Summer 1998, at 23, by William H. Carroll.

Stephen P. Crosby, Secretary of Administration and Finance of Massachusetts, et al., Petitioners, v. National Foreign Trade Council

No. 99-474
Supreme Court of the United States
Argued March 22, 2000, Decided June 19, 2000

Justice SOUTER delivered the opinion of the Court.

The issue is whether the Burma law of the Commonwealth of Massachusetts, restricting the authority of its agencies to purchase goods or services from companies doing business with Burma, is invalid under the Supremacy Clause of the National Constitution owing to its threat of frustrating federal statutory objectives. We hold that it is.

I

In June 1996, Massachusetts adopted "An Act Regulating State Contracts with Companies Doing Business with or in Burma (Myanmar)," 1996 Mass. Acts 239, ch. 130 (codified at Mass. Gen. Laws §§ 7:22G-7:22M. The statute generally bars state entities from buying goods or services from any person (defined to include a business organization) identified on a "restricted purchase list" of those doing business with Burma. §§ 7:22H(a), 7:22J.... There are three exceptions to the ban: (1) if the procurement is essential ...; (2) if the procurement is of medical supplies, § 7:22I; and (3) if the procurement efforts elicit no "comparable low bid or offer" by a person not doing business with Burma, § 7:22H(d), meaning an offer that is no more than 10 percent greater than the restricted bid, § 7:22G....

In September 1996, three months after the Massachusetts law was enacted, Congress passed a statute imposing a set of mandatory and conditional sanctions on Burma....

II

Respondent National Foreign Trade Council (Council) is a nonprofit corporation representing companies engaged in foreign commerce; 34 of its members were on the Massachusetts restricted purchase list in 1998. *National Foreign Trade Council v. Natsios,* 181 F.3d 38, 48 (C.A.1 1999). Three withdrew from Burma after the passage of the state Act, and one member had its bid for a procurement contract increased by 10 percent under the provision of the state law allowing acceptance of a low bid from a listed bidder only if the next-to-lowest bid is more than 10 percent higher. *Ibid.*

In April 1998, the Council filed suit.... After detailed stipulations, briefing, and argument, the District Court permanently enjoined enforcement of the state Act.... The United States Court of Appeals for the First Circuit affirmed on three independent grounds.... The State's petition for certiorari challenged the decision on all three grounds and asserted interests said to be shared by other state and local governments with similar measures....[5]

III

A fundamental principle of the Constitution is that Congress has the power to preempt state law....

Applying this standard, we see the state Burma law as an obstacle to the accomplishment of Congress's full objectives under the federal Act....[7]

* * *

---

5. "At least nineteen municipal governments have enacted analogous laws restricting purchases from companies that do business in Burma."...

7. The State concedes, as it must, that in addressing the subject of the federal Act, Congress has the power to preempt the state statute. See Reply Brief for Petitioners 2; Tr. of Oral Arg. 5–6. We add that we have already rejected the argument that a State's "statutory scheme ... escapes pre-emption because it is an exercise of the State's spending power rather than its regulatory power." *Wisconsin Dept. of Industry v. Gould, Inc.,* 475 U.S. 282, 287, 106 S.Ct. 1057, 89 L.Ed.2d 223 (1986). In *Gould,* we found that a Wisconsin statute debarring repeat violators of the National Labor Relations Act, 29 U.S.C. § 151 *et seq.,* from contracting with the State was preempted because the state statute's additional enforcement mechanism conflicted with the federal Act. 475 U.S., at 288–289, 106 S.Ct. 1057. The fact that the State "ha[d] chosen to use its spending power rather than its police power" did not reduce the potential for conflict with the federal statute. *Ibid.*

B

Congress manifestly intended to limit economic pressure against the Burmese Government to a specific range....

The State has set a different course, and its statute conflicts with federal law at a number of points by penalizing individuals and conduct that Congress has explicitly exempted or excluded from sanctions. While the state Act differs from the federal in relying entirely on indirect economic leverage through third parties with Burmese connections, it otherwise stands in clear contrast to the congressional scheme in the scope of subject matter addressed. It restricts all contracts between the State and companies doing business in Burma, §7:22H(a), except when purchasing medical supplies and other essentials (or when short of comparable bids), §7:22I. It is specific in targeting contracts to provide financial services, §7:22G(b), and general goods and services, §7:22G(d), to the Government of Burma, and thus prohibits contracts between the State and United States persons for goods, services, or technology, even though those transactions are explicitly exempted from the ambit of new investment prohibition when the President exercises his discretionary authority to impose sanctions under the federal Act. §570(f)(2).As with the subject of business meant to be affected, so with the class of companies doing it: the state Act's generality stands at odds with the federal discreteness. The Massachusetts law directly and indirectly imposes costs on all companies that do any business in Burma, §7:22G, save for those reporting news or providing international telecommunications goods or services, or medical supplies, §§7:22H(e), 7:22I. It sanctions companies promoting the importation of natural resources controlled by the Government of Burma, or having any operations or affiliates in Burma. §7:22G. The state Act thus penalizes companies with pre-existing affiliates or investments, all of which lie beyond the reach of the federal Act's restrictions on "new investment" in Burmese economic development. §§570(b), 570(f)(2). The state Act, moreover, imposes restrictions on foreign companies as well as domestic, whereas the federal Act limits its reach to United States persons....

C

* * *

Second, the EU and Japan have gone a step further in lodging formal complaints against the United States in the World Trade Organization (WTO), claiming that the state Act violates certain provisions of the Agreement on Government Procurement,[19] H.R. Doc. No. 103-316, p. 1719 (1994), and the consequence has been to embroil the National Government for some time now in international dispute proceedings under the auspices of the WTO. In their brief before this Court, EU officials point to the WTO dispute as threatening relations with the United States, Brief for European Communities et al. as *Amici Curiae* 7, and n. 7, and note that the state Act has become the topic of "intensive discus-

---

19. Although the WTO dispute proceedings were suspended at the request of Japan and the EU in light of the District Court's ruling below, Letter of Ole Lundby, Chairman of the Panel, to Ambassadors from the European Union, Japan, and the United States (Feb. 10, 1999), and have since automatically lapsed, Understanding on Rules and Procedures Governing the Settlement of Disputes, 33 International Legal Materials 1125, 1234 (1994), neither of those parties is barred from reinstating WTO procedures to challenge the state Act in the future. In fact, the EU, as *amicus* before us, specifically represents that it intends to begin new WTO proceedings should the current injunction on the law be lifted. Brief for European Communities et al. as *Amici Curiae* 7. We express no opinion on the merits of these proceedings.

sions" with officials of the United States at the highest levels, those discussions including exchanges at the twice yearly EU-U.S. Summit.

IV

The State's remaining argument is unavailing. It contends that the failure of Congress to preempt the state Act demonstrates implicit permission. The State points out that Congress has repeatedly declined to enact express preemption provisions aimed at state and local sanctions, and it calls our attention to the large number of such measures passed against South Africa in the 1980's, which various authorities cited have thought were not preempted....[25]

The judgment of the Court of Appeals for the First Circuit is affirmed.

It is so ordered.

(Concurring opinion omitted)

Notes and Questions

The Supreme Court decided the case based on preemption, but the opinion's interest for this book concerns the special window it opens into the international dimensions of government contract law. Part of the opinion discusses the mechanics of how Massachusetts proceeded, such as the exception if a potential contractor doing business with Burma makes a bid ten percent better than all other bids. How do these mechanics compare with the mechanics of federal or state "Buy America Acts"?

The opinion discusses the contention the complaints that the state law violated the Agreement on Government Procurement (AGP), and the remedy for those who allege such a violation. The European Union and Japan did not, and could not, bring an AGP suit in federal court against the state, nor could the plaintiff in this case put an AGP count in this suit. Instead, the EU and Japan must lodge a complaint against the United States in the WTO, which then convened a WTO panel to resolve the dispute. Moreover, even if the EU and Japan won, that would not have the effect, under domestic law, of invalidating the Massachusetts statute. Rather, it would then become the federal government's problem either to do something about Massachusetts, or, to deal with the EU and Japan as they either impose some kind of sanction or seek some arrangement. The AGP's lack of a direct federal judicial remedy for violation of international government contracting law is no accident, but was part of getting the states not to oppose Congressional approval of the AGP. See Charles Tiefer, Free Trade Agreements and the New Federalism, 7 Minn. J. Glob. Trade 45 (1998). If a foreign business came to you as a client complaining about their bids being rejected in violation of the AGP, what would you advise? What might happen if they simply used the ordinary protest machinery?

---

25. See, e.g., *Board of Trustees v. Mayor and City Council of Baltimore,* 317 Md. 72, 79–98, 562 A.2d 720, 744–749 (1989) (holding local divestment ordinance not preempted by Comprehensive Anti-Apartheid Act of 1986 (CAAA)), cert. denied sub nom. *Lubman v. Mayor and City Council of Baltimore,* 493 U.S. 1093, 110 S.Ct. 1167, 107 L.Ed.2d 1069 (1990); Constitutionality of South African Divestment Statutes Enacted by State and Local Governments, 10 Op. Off. Legal Counsel 49, 64–66, 1986 WL 213238 (state and local divestment and selective purchasing laws not preempted by pre-CAAA federal law); H.R. Res. Nos. 99-548, 99-549 (1986) (denying preemptive intent of CAAA); 132 Cong. Rec. 23119–23129 (1986) (House debate on resolutions); id., at 23292 (Sen. Kennedy, quoting testimony of Laurence H. Tribe)....

Foreign Military Sales

Through the Foreign Military Sales (FMS) program, the U.S Government sells or leases equipment, services, and training from defense contractors to eligible friendly foreign governments and international organizations. The Arms Export Control Act (AECA) and the Foreign Assistance Act (FAA) authorize the Department of Defense (DOD) to participate in the FMS program. Through this program, the Department of Defense serves as an intermediary for the contractor, handling procurement, logistics and delivery and often providing product support and training. FMS should therefore be distinguished from the statutory Direct Commercial Sales (DCS) program which oversees direct sales between foreign governments and private U.S. defense contractors.

Either way, besides their foreign policy rationales, foreign sales contribute to the U.S. economy by improving U.S. balance of trade position, sustaining highly skilled jobs in the defense industrial base, expanding production lines, and lowering costs per unit for key weapons systems. On the other hand, there have been criticisms of such sales, both for their effects in adding to the world arms trade, and for the ways the terms for such trades, such as co-production agreements, may ultimately undermine the role of the United States government and contractors.

The AECA regulations and related statutes are implemented through the Security Assistance Management Manual (SAMM) and Volume 15 of the DOD Financial Management Regulation (FMR). These regulations outline the methods by which the DOD is authorized to enter into contracts for the procurement of defense articles or services for specifically enumerated purposes. The Secretary of Defense, in conjunction with the Secretary of State, is granted the power under the AECA to establish military requirements and implement the programs by which defense articles and services are transferred to foreign governments and international organizations. Authority to carry out the security assistance responsibilities under the AECA has been delegated to the Defense Security Assistance Agency (DSAA). The DSAA serves as the DOD focal point for security assistance budgetary and legislative matters. Additionally, the DSAA is responsible for keeping the DOD informed about the status of security actions, and presides over the international logistics and sales negotiations with foreign nations.

One characteristic which distinguishes FMS from other types of procurement is that the purchaser does not deal directly with the contractor, at least in certain phases. Eligible friendly governments request the purchase of defense articles and services through a Letter of Request (LOR) submitted to the DOD, which must specify the purchase request in sufficient detail to provide a firm basis for estimating cost. The AECA requires that the U.S. government recover all costs of performing FMS. Foreign governments participating in foreign military sales must therefore be eligible to pay the full cost for a defense article or service, and must be prepared to pay an additional charge for any administrative services, in addition to research and development for the equipment.

The DOD submits the LOR to the DSAA and if accepted, the U.S. government submits a Letter of Offer or Acceptance (LOA) outlining the terms and conditions of use for the defense articles by the foreign government. Congress must be notified of U.S. government intent before certain LOA's are issued, including offers to sell defense articles or services for $50 million or more, design and construction service of $200 million or more, and any major defense equipment that costs $14 million or more. For these big ticket items, the certification must divulge whether any gift, commission, or fee was paid by the foreign government to secure the LOA, and must fully describe the level of sensitivity of the technology, complete with justification necessitating the sale. Congress may, within a specific period of time, enact a joint resolution prohibiting the sale. The President may, however, waive Congressional review in times of national emergency, in which event the certification must describe the emergency as well as the national security interests involved.

United States of America ex rel. Russell HAYES, Plaintiff/Relator, v. CMC Electronics Inc., Defendant

United States District Court, D. New Jersey
297 F.Supp.2d 734
Dec. 1, 2003

OPINION

HOCHBERG, District Judge.

* * *

Introduction

This matter comes before the Court on Defendant CMC Electronic's ("CMCE") Partial Motion to Dismiss Counts I and II of the Complaint pursuant to Fed.R.Civ.P. 12(b)(6). In the alternative, Defendant has brought a Motion for Partial Summary Judgment pursuant to Fed.R.Civ.P. 56(c). The Defendant contends that the Plaintiffs do not have a cause of action under the False Claims Act, 31 U.S.C. § 3729 et seq. ("FCA") because the Government was precluded from sustaining losses or damages in the contracts at issue. In the alternative, the Defendant argues that this Court should grant partial summary judgment declaring that the Government's maximum recovery is limited to the FCA's statutory penalties. Assuming all the allegations of the Complaint to be true, this Court finds that CMCE's alleged false or fraudulent claims are covered by the FCA and that a question of fact exists as to the damages suffered by the Government. Therefore, the Defendant's Partial Motion to Dismiss and its alternative Motion for Partial Summary Judgment are denied.

Factual Background:

The relator, Russell Hayes ("Hayes"), brought a *qui tam* action under the False Claims Act for the alleged fraud committed by his former employer, Canadian Marconi Corporation (which changed its name to CMC Electronics Inc. and is hereafter referred to as "CMCE"). The United States intervened. Hayes was a former project manager for the company, responsible for ensuring that production of radios designed by CMCE pursuant to current contracts was completed within budget and on time.

CMCE designed and manufactured a secure radio communications system known as AN/GRC 103(v) Radio Set ("radio set"). CMCE sold most of these radio sets to the U.S. Department of Defense. According to the Plaintiff, CMCE began to purchase surplus and used equipment to fulfill its orders after a surplus of military equipment, including radio sets, emerged in the market during the 1980s and early 1990s.

Throughout the 1990s, the United States Government entered contracts to sell to Saudi Arabia various types of military hardware, including the radio sets. These contracts were entered pursuant to the Arms Export Control Act which is part of the Foreign Military Sales ("FMS") program designed by Congress to address the need for international defense cooperation. The Arms Export Control Act, 22 U.S.C. § 2751 et. seq. authorizes the President of the United States to sell defense articles and services to eligible allies from two sources of supply: 1) sales from the stocks of the Department of Defense, 22 U.S.C. § 2761 and 2) sales of procured items, 22 U.S.C. § 2762. 22 U.S.C. § 2762 provides that when procurement contracts are entered by the United States, the foreign country or organization to which the items will be sold must cover the entire cost of the procurement contract. The written agreement for these sales are called Letters of Offer and Acceptance (LOA).

Pursuant to 22 U.S.C. § 2762(a), on September 29, 1993, the United States Army Communications-Electronics Command ("CECOM") contracted with AEC Electronics ("AEC") for the purchase of 97 radio sets. The Government then resold these radio sets to the Saudi Government pursuant to an LOA with Saudi Arabia. On September 30, 1993, to fulfill its contract with the U.S., AEC entered a subcontract with CMCE for the sale of the radio sets to the U.S. CMCE agreed that "all the Equipment it provides under this Contract will be newly manufactured and that no used, reconditioned or overhauled Equipment will be provided."

According to the Plaintiffs, CMCE violated this provision by filling the contract with radio sets and multiplexers built with parts and components that were either previously used or obtained from the government surplus market. Thus, according to Hayes and the U.S., CMCE significantly overstated the cost of producing the contract for the production of the radio sets for the Saudi Arabian Patriot Program because it charged for new radios while supplying used radios.

Analysis

I. Defendant's Partial Motion to Dismiss:

* * *

B. *The False Claims Act:*

In this case, Hayes has alleged that CMCE presented fraudulent invoices to the U.S. Government. This is sufficient to state a claim for relief under the FCA.

* * *

In order to bring a cause of action under the FCA, the alleged false or fraudulent claim must be made for payment by the U.S. Government. *See, e.g., U.S. v. Neifert-White Co.,* 390 U.S. 228, 232–233, 88 S.Ct. 959, 19 L.Ed.2d 1061 (1968); *Hutchins v. Wilentz, Goldman & Spitzer,* 253 F.3d 176, 184 (3d Cir.2001). In this case, CMCE submitted a claim to the U.S. Government for payment at an inflated rate. The fact that the U.S. used funds obtained from Saudi Arabia to pay for the radios does not mean that the Defendant's false or fraudulent claim was not a demand for payment from U.S. funds.

Recently, the District Court for the Middle District of Florida considered a case almost identical to this one. In *U.S. v. Lockheed Martin Corp.,* the U.S. Government and its relator alleged that Lockheed Martin had double-billed the Government and submitted false invoices in connection with several LANTIRN [3] pods contracts. *Lockheed Martin,* 282 F.Supp.2d 1324, 1327 (M.D.Fla.2003). The U.S. Government purchased LANTIRN pods from Lockheed, and resold them to Saudi Arabia, Greece, and Bahrain, pursuant to LOAs. Lockheed Martin argued that the FCA did not apply because the pods were paid for by foreign funds which were required to cover the cost of the procurement contract pursuant to 22 U.S.C. § 2751 et seq. *Lockheed Martin,* 282 F.Supp.2d 1324, 1338–41. The Court rejected these contentions, holding that the submission of false invoices for payment by the U.S. Government was covered by the FCA regardless of whether the Government would resell the articles to a foreign government. Viewing the procurement contract and

---

3. LANTIRN stands for Low Altitude Navigation and Targeting Infrared for Night.

the contract with the foreign government as separate transactions, the Court explained that the foreign funds belong to the U.S. Government and that the application of the FCA to the false or fraudulent claim does not depend on when the U.S. Government received payment from the foreign government. *Lockheed Martin,* 282 F.Supp.2d 1324, at 1338–39.

This Court agrees with the reasoning of *Lockheed Martin.* CMCE argues that its Motion to Dismiss must be granted because the U.S. Government cannot sustain a loss because the Arms Export Control Act requires the foreign government to cover the cost of the procurement contract.[4] This argument is rejected. The "no loss" provision in the Arms Export Control Act does not insulate CMCE from liability for the submission of false claims to the government. *Lockheed Martin,* 282 F.Supp.2d 1324, 1340–41; *see also, U.S. ex rel. Marcus v. Hess,* 317 U.S. 537, 544, 63 S.Ct. 379, 87 L.Ed. 443 (1943)(explaining that the FCA does not make the extent of the safeguard of Government money dependent on bookkeeping devices used for the distribution of Government funds). Moreover, even if the U.S. Government were unable to prove actual monetary damages, the false claims are still actionable under the FCA.

Assuming the allegations in the Complaint to be true, the Government sustained monetary losses due to CMCE's false invoices. First, the Government paid more money than it otherwise would have paid if CMCE had disclosed that the radios contained used parts. The fact that the Saudi Government provided the funds that the U.S. used to purchase the radios cannot obviate the fact that the U.S. Government overpaid for the radios by reason of the false invoices. *Lockheed Martin,* 282 F.Supp.2d 1324, 1338–39; *U.S. v. Neifert-White Co.,* 390 U.S. 228, 233, 88 S.Ct. 959, 19 L.Ed.2d 1061 (1968)(holding that fraudulent invoices used as a basis to apply for a loan from the Commodity Credit Corporation is a claim covered by the FCA). Second, the U.S. government is likely to be required to reimburse the Saudi government for the loss sustained by the Saudi government. Third, the Government suffered damage to the integrity of the contracting process as Saudi Arabia received used radio sets despite paying for new ones. Finally, it is possible that Saudi Arabia will have less money to spend on other defense needs, thereby forcing the U.S. to increase its expenditures by a like amount to obtain the same level of global security.

Even if the false claim had thus far resulted in only the potential for loss to the U.S. Government, this would be sufficient for a cause of action under the FCA. The FCA applies to any person who makes a false or fraudulent statement "with the purpose and effect of inducing the Government to immediately part with money." *Neifert-White,* 390 U.S. at 232, 88 S.Ct. 959. There is no question that false or fraudulent invoices overcharging the Government for radios that the Government will resell to Saudi Arabia have the purpose and effect of inducing the U.S. Government to part with money.

* * *

… CMCE's claim was made for funds in the United States Treasury.[6] Thus, CMCE's alleged fraudulent or false statements are within the category contemplated in *Hutchins* as

---

4. 22 U.S.C. § 2762(a) provides that the President may enter contracts for the: procurement of defense articles or defense services for sale for United States dollars to any foreign country or international organization if such country or international organization provides the United States Government with a dependable undertaking (1) to pay the full amount of such contract which will assure the United States Government against any loss on the contract, and (2) to make funds available in such amounts and at such times as may be required to meet the payments required by the contract, and any damages and costs that may accrue from the cancellation of such contract, in advance of the time such payments, damages, or costs are due.

6. Funds used to pay for equipment that will be sold to foreign governments pursuant to a contract under the Arms Export Control Act are funds of the United States, regardless of whether pay-

actionable under the FCA. *See also, Lockheed Martin,* 282 F.Supp.2d 1324, 1339–40 (distinguishing *Hutchins* on the grounds that the Defendant in *Hutchins* made no claim for Government money or property).

* * *

Conclusion:

CMCE's alleged fraudulent claims had the purpose and effect of causing the United States to pay money it was not obligated to pay. Therefore, the Defendant's Partial Motion to Dismiss is denied. Because an issue of fact exists as to the actual damages suffered by the Government, Defendant's Motion for Partial Summary Judgment limiting the Government's recovery to the statutory penalty is also denied. An appropriate order will issue.

Notes and Questions:

1. Note the considerable complexity about the extent to which FMS is a federal government program involving contracting. As with the False Claims Act cases concerning Medicare, this case shows that the False Claims Act applies even when the "real" contract (the purchase by Saudi Arabia of radio sets) is not under the FAR and bears little relation to a standard government supply contract. As with Medicare, there is a triangular relation of the supplier or provider, the "beneficiary" (the recipient of medical care, or, the foreign recipient of military assistance), and the government agency. For marketing purposes, the supplier or provider "sells" to the "beneficiary." But, for legal purposes, the government polices the practices of the supplier. If CECOM itself, rather than a qui tam relator, decided that CMC Electronics (or AEC Electronics) committed a simple breach of its subcontract (or contract) to sell the 97 radio sets to CECOM, could CECOM invoke familiar contract clauses and remedies?

2. Conversely, suppose the deal involved not just radio sets, but, state-of-the-art advanced fighter planes, plus the services of maintenance and training. How much would the contract with the vendor look like a familiar government contract? What would have to be added so that the government kept the level of involvement and control appropriate to the national security complexities?

3. Some foreign governments insist on "offset" terms that give them some role in dealing with the cost of the purchase through their own activity, all the way up to a co-production agreement that may enable them to begin themselves selling parts or the whole of the defense items. It can sometimes be a nice challenge for the contractor to provide enough of such terms to entice the foreign government, without going so far as to destroy its own market or to elicit a rejection of the deal from the U.S. government. How might that be done?

Government Procurement in the European Union

The European Union, established in 1992, is an intergovernmental and supranational union of 25 European countries or independent member states. These countries united principally to establish a common market and to encourage the free movement of goods

---

ment from the foreign government is deposited into the FMS Trust Fund before or after the U.S. pays for the equipment. *Lockheed Martin,* 282 F.Supp.2d 1324, 1338–39; *Soboleski v. C.I.R.,* 88 T.C. 1024, 1987 WL 49312 (1987), *aff'd,* 842 F.2d 1292 (4th Cir.1988)(holding that money paid by Saudi Arabia into the FMS Trust Account for payment to certain Army Corps employees are appropriated funds and vested in the U.S. Government).

and services across the union. Key components of the EU are a customs union, a single currency, and a common trade policy which prohibits any import or export quantitative restrictions between member states. As for government procurement, the EU developed three Directives that apply when public authorities, defined as state, regional or local governments, seek to acquire goods and services, civil engineering or building works.

Unlike the FAR in the United States, the Directives are neither a statute nor regulation creating rights and obligations of the member states. Rather, the Directives define the legal framework for contract award within which each Member State may enact its own national requirements for contracts. To make a rough analogy, the Directives resembles United States programs which define a legal framework within which each state enacts its own system, such as state Medicaid or state National Guard programs. Thus, the Directives specifically address the formation of public procurement contracts, including the publicity, type of procedures, specifications, solicitation, selection, and award criteria. Yet, it remains within the authority of each national government to implement the specific provisions applicable to the performance of awarded contracts.

Though vastly different, the EU and US public procurement systems have the same basic ideals of open competition, equity and transparency. Open competition within the EU means that public procurement must be open to all competitors throughout the European Union. The Regulations implemented by each country set out detailed criteria to avoid discrimination on grounds of origin of a particular member state, and to ensure that all suppliers or contractors established in countries covered by the rules are treated on equal terms. Open competition and equal treatment of competitors requires widespread and effective publicity of procurement opportunities. Transparency is crucial in the selection among, and award of, tender offers. Before an award is made, all of the Directives require European-wide publication of procurement notices with the Official Journal of the EU (OJEU). In addition, the Directives require the use of several different means of publicity to ensure optimal dissemination of the information.

Standard procedures have been developed so that national authorities may tender the offer to the candidate vendor with the best legal, financial and technical capacities to perform the particular contract. Three procedures are provided by which responses may be made. The open procedure permits all contractors to openly respond to the advertisement in the OJEU. The restricted procedure sets forth specific selection requirements in the advertisement and thereby permits a purchaser to restrict the number of candidate vendors to whom they provide a tender offer for the contract. Finally the negotiated procedure, permitted in only limited circumstances pursuant to a countries' regulations, allows a purchaser to select one or more contractors with whom to pursue contract negotiations.

In the event of a breach of Regulations, the principal means of enforcement in Europe's legal system is either through an action brought by an individual contractor against the national authority in the nation's High Court, or by means of a contractor filing a complaint with the European Commission who may then bring an action against the member state in the European Court of Justice (ECJ). Either way, the result may be the suspension or setting aside of an incomplete contract award procedure.

A nation's High Court has the power to award damages and where a contract has already been entered into, an award of damages is the only remedy a High Court can provide. Under appropriate circumstances exist however, the ECJ has demonstrated that it may be prepared to overturn a contract award. A characteristic of European companies is that vendors tend to prefer merely to alert the European Commission rather than themselves challenging the public authority before a national court. By not directly contesting the procurement procedure, vendors avoid endangering the relationship with their client.

For further discussion of these issues, see: Marc Gabriel, Katherina Weiner, *The European Defence Procurement Directive: Toward Liberalization And Harmonization Of The European Defense Market*, 45 Procrmt. Law. 1 (Winter 2010); Martin Trybus, *Improving The Efficiency Of Public Procurement Systems In The Context Of The European Union Enlargement Process*, 35 Pub. Cont. L.J. 409 (Spring 2006); Yves Allain, *The New European Directives On Public Procurement: Change Or Continuity*, 35 Pub. Cont. L.J. 517 (Spring 2006); Katharina Summann, *Winds Of Change: European Influences On German Procurement Law*, 35 Pub. Cont. L.J. 563 (Spring 2006); Christopher H. Bovis, *Public Procurement in the European Union: Lessons From the Past and Insights to the Future*, 12 Colum. J. Eur. L. 53 (Winter 2005/2006); Servet Alyanak, *The Public Procurement System Of Turkey In Comparison To European Community Procurement Legislation*, 36 Pub. Cont. L.J. 203 (Winter 2007); Jean-Jacques Verdeaux, Public Procurement In The European Union & In The United States: A Comparative Study, 32 Pub. Cont. L.J. 713 (Summer 2003).

C. Afghanistan and Iraq Wars

The Afghanistan and Iraq wars and the continuing involvement of the United States have raised a number of complex procurement issues. There is a large literature on this subject. Much of it is about various defenses to suit: Thomas Gray, *Government-Contractor Immunity—I'm Just Following Orders: A Fair Standard Of Immunity For Military Service Contractors*, 32 W. New Eng. L. Rev. 373 (2010); Efrain Staino, *Suing Private Military Contractors For Torture: How To Use The Alien Tort Statute Without Granting Sovereign-Immunity Related Defenses*, 50 Santa Clara L. Rev. 1277 (2010); Michael R. Kelly, *Revisiting And Revising The Political Question Doctrine: Lane v. Halliburton And The Need To Adopt A Case-Specific Political Question Analysis For Private Military Contractor Cases*, 29 Miss. C. L. Rev. 219 (2010); Chris Jenks, *Square Peg In A Round Hole: Government Contractor Battlefield Tort Liability And The Political Question Doctrine*, 28 Berkeley J. Int'l L. 178 (2010); Andres Healy, *The Constitutionality Of Amended 10 U.S.C. § 802(a)(10): Does The Military Need A Formal Invitation To Reign In "Cowboy" Civilian Contractors?*, 62 Fla. L. Rev. 519 (Apr. 2010); Scott M. Sullivan, *Private Force/Public Goods*, 42 Conn. L. Rev. 853 (Feb. 2010); Charles Tiefer, *No More Nisour Squares: Legal Control Of Private Security Contractors In Iraq And After*, 88 Or. L. Rev. 745 (2009); Charles T. Kirchmaier, *Command Authority Over Contractors Serving With Or Accompanying The Force*, 2009 Army Law. 35 (Dec. 2009); Jenny S. Lam, *Accountability For Private Military Contractors Under The Alien Tort Statute*, 97 Cal. L. Rev. 1459 (Oct. 2009); Aaron J. Fickes, *Private Warriors And Political Questions: A Critical Analysis Of The Political Question Doctrine's Application To Suits Against Private Military Contractors*, 82 Temple L. Rev. 525 (Summer 2009); Christopher E. Martin, *Sovereignty, Meet Globalization: Using Public-Private Partnerships To Promote The Rule Of Law In A Complex World*, 202 Mil. L. Rev. 91 (Winter 2009). Andrew Finkelman, *Suing The Hired Guns: An Analysis Of Two Federal Defenses To Tort Lawsuits Against Military Contractors*, 34 Brook. J. Int'l L. 395 (2009); Aaron L. Jackson, *Civilian Soldiers: Expanding The Government Contractor Defense To Reflect The New Corporate Role In Warfare*, 63 A.F. L. Rev. 211 (2009); Chad C. Carte, *Halliburton Hears A Who? Political Question Doctrine Developments In The Global War On Terror And Their Impact On Government Contingency Contracting*, 201 Mil. L. Rev. 86 (Fall 2009); Kenneth Basco, *Don't Worry, We'll*

Take Care Of You: Immigration Of Local Nationals Assisting The United States In Overseas Contingency Operations, 2009 Army Law. 38 (Oct. 2009); Michael J. Davidson, *Court-Martialing Civilians Who Accompany The Armed Forces,* 56 Fed. Law. 43 (Sept. 2009); Steven Paul Cullen, *Out Of Reach: Improving The System To Deter And Address Criminal Acts Committed By Contractor Employees Accompanying Armed Forces Overseas,* 38 Pub. Cont. L.J. 509 (Spring 2009); Samuel P. Cheadle, *Private Military Contractor Liability Under The Worldwide Personal Protective Services II Contract,* 38 Pub. Cont. L.J. 689 (Spring 2009); Abigail Clark, *Reclaiming The Moral High Ground: U.S. Accountability For Contractor Abuses As A Means To Win Back Hearts And Minds,* 38 Pub. Cont. L.J. 709 (Spring 2009); Trevor A. Rush, *Don't Call It A SOFA! An Overview Of The U.S.-Iraq Security Agreement,* 2009 Army Law. 34 (May 2009); Robert W. Wood, *Independent Contractor vs. Employee And Blackwater,* 70 Mont. L. Rev. 95 (Winter 2009); Jennifer S. Martin, *Adapting U.C.C. § 2-615 Excuse For Civilian-Military Contractors In Wartime,* 61 Fla. L. Rev. 99 (Jan. 2009); John P. Figura, *You're In The Army Now: Borrowed Servants, Dual Servants, And Torts Committed By Contractors' Employees In The Theaters Of U.S. Military Operations,* 58 Emory L.J. 513 (2008); Trevor Wilson, *Operation Contractor Shield: Extending The Government Contractor Defense In Recognition Of Modern Warfare Realities,* 83 Tul. L. Rev. 255 (Nov. 2008).

The following case concerns sole-source contracting for wartime procurement:

Matter of: WorldWide Language Resources, Inc.; SOS International Ltd.

November 14, 2005
2005 WL 3143870

WorldWide Language Resources, Inc. and SOS International, Ltd. (SOSi) protest the Department of the Air Force's award of two sole-source contracts (Nos. FA7012-05-C-0003 and FA7012-05-C-0020) to Russian and Eastern European Partnership, Inc. (REEP) d/b/a Operational Support Services (OSS), for individuals performing services as bilingual-bicultural advisor/subject matter experts (BBA-SME) in Iraq....

We sustain the protests.

BACKGROUND

The protests concern two sole-source contracts, contract No. FA7012-05-C-0003 (with an estimated value of $10.7 million) and No. FA7012-05-C-0020 (with an estimated value of $35.5 million), awarded to OSS on December 3, 2004 and on July 29, 2005, respectively, both of which were to support the mission of the Multinational Forces-Iraq (MNF-I), particularly the Civil Affairs Command (CAC). The December contract required OSS to provide 50–75 bilingual-bicultural advisor-subject matter experts (BBA-SME), who were described as follows:

> Western oriented individuals of Iraqi background who speak both English and Iraqi-dialect Arabic or Kurdish and who are committed to a democratic Iraq to act as advisors to Iraqi units of government and non-government organizations....

The period of contract performance was 1 year, ending on December 2, 2005.

The July contract effectively increased to 200 the total number of BBA-SMEs that OSS was required to provide through December 2005 and also extended the period of performance through July 2006....

The BBA-SME requirement had its genesis in a program established by the Office of the Secretary of Defense (OSD) in 2003, known as the Iraqi Reconstruction and Development Council (IRDC). The IRDC was composed of approximately 150 individuals of Iraqi heritage from the world-wide exile community who provided assistance to the Coalition Provisional Authority with stabilizing and maintaining a civil government in Iraq. Agency Report (AR), Tab 15, Declaration of Victor A.D. Rostow, Special Assistant to the Under Secretary of Defense for Policy, Sept. 12, 2005, at 2. Some members of the IRDC were selected for their professional experience (*i.e.,* lawyers, physicians, engineers, information technology specialists), while others were selected for family and/or social contacts with ethnic and tribal groups. The services provided by these individuals were obtained through a contract awarded to the firm Science Applications International Corporation (SAIC).

When the Coalition Provisional Authority dissolved in June 2004, the IRDC program also came to an end. In the timeframe between June and July, however, the Deputy Secretary of Defense "determined that the success of the United States war effort required the services of experts in reconstruction and governance in the period leading up to the establishment of a constitutional Iraqi government," AR, Tab 15, *supra,* at 1, and sought a way to "support some 50–75 of [the IRDC] individuals who can operate independently throughout Iraq in support of MNF-I/CAC activities." AR, Tab 16h, e-mail from Victor A.D. Rostow, Subject: Iraqi Contractor Help, Nov. 18, 2004. As a consequence, the Deputy Secretary of Defense tasked Mr. Victor Rostow, Special Assistant to the Under Secretary of Defense for Policy, who had organized and managed the IRDC program, with establishing a program to hire Iraqis of Western orientation who were capable of assisting the Civil Affairs Command. AR, Tab 15, *supra,* at 1.

In a hearing held by our Office concerning the issues in this case, Mr. Rostow explained that the program "was to be in place and functioning when the Iraqi elections occurred in January [2005]." Hearing Transcript (Tr.) at 135. While the immediate need was to address the elections, the program's underlying purpose was to address the needs of the Iraqi community (*e.g.,* their medical, energy, and agricultural needs) and thereby create "a nudge toward democracy." Tr. at 136....

In mid-August 2004, Mr. Rostow began working on a statement of work for the program and contacted the Air Force with the requirement sometime between mid-August and mid-September. The Air Force's Center for Environmental Excellence (AFCEE) initially took responsibility for the BBA-SME acquisition. Tr. at 133, 140. After speaking with Mr. Rostow and receiving the scope of work for the BBA-SME requirement, the AFCEE decided to compete the BBA-SME requirement among the multiple contract holders of AFCEE's global engineering, integration, and technical assistance (GEITA) contract....

On October 27, 2004, AFCEE issued a solicitation for the BBA-SME requirement to the holders of the GEITA contract. AR, Tab 14, Declaration of Chief of Acquisition for the Air Force District of Washington, at 3. However, in early November, the BBA-SME solicitation and the plan to place the BBA-SME requirement under the GEITA contract were canceled after the director of contracting for AFCEE, with the concurrence of the Office of the Secretary of the Air Force, determined that the BBE-SME requirement was not within the scope of the GEITA contract....

Experiencing what it perceived to be significant pressure from OSD to quickly satisfy the BBA-SME requirement [...] the contracting activity decided to pursue a sole-source contract for the BBA-SME requirement "[b]ecause there was no way to competitively go out and get that effort done in a way that probably wouldn't result in a minimum four to six month slip of the schedule, maybe longer...." Tr. at 27. When the contracting activity sought a potential contractor for its expected sole-source award, it focused exclusively on OSS. After initial inquiries regarding OSS's capabilities and a November 18 meeting between OSS, OSD, and the Air Force, it was determined that the BBA-SME requirement should be awarded on a sole-source basis to OSS.

In early December, the Air Force executed a justification and approval (J & A) for other than full and open competition in support of the initial award to OSS. The December J & A, which cites 10 U.S.C. sect. 2304(c)(2) (2000) and Federal Acquisition Regulation (FAR) sect. 6.302-2 (unusual and compelling urgency) as the authority for the award to OSS, states that "OSS is the only known contractor who is in the position to provide deployed BBAs to Iraq in time to support the Iraqi national elections in January 2005." AR, Tab 1b.2, J & A, December 1, 2004, at para. 5. Describing OSS's "unique qualifications," the J & A noted that OSS is the largest provider of foreign language immersion training to the U.S. government; the firm's staff features former military specialists; OSS maintained a database of ... linguists, trainers, translators, and interpreters; and OSS had staff in Iraq. *Id.*

Under the heading "Market Survey," the J & A stated that "OSD could not locate an existing contract vehicle to support [the BBA-SME] requirement" and that because the AFCEE contracting option was cancelled, "there was not sufficient time to compete the requirement and meet the ... 1 December 2004 deadline for contract award...." *Id.* at para. 9. Moreover, the J & A highlighted the fact that OSS's cost of beginning operations in Iraq was reduced[.] ... The J & A further provided that the requirement was expected to last for only 12 months and that a follow-on procurement was not anticipated, but that if similar requirements arose in the future, market research would be performed and the effort would be competed. *Id.* at para. 11. On December 3, 2004, the Air Force awarded contract No. FA7012-05-C-0003 to OSS.

In late January or early February 2005, after OSS had begun performance, the MNF-I identified a requirement for approximately 275 BBA-SMEs and conveyed this information to OSD. Tr. at 170–71....

On July 11, 2005, the Air Force approved a J & A for other than full and open competition in support of the award of a contract to OSS with a 1-year performance period, plus one 3-month option, for expansion of the BBA-SME program. While initial discussions between OSD and the Air Force concerned justifying a sole-source award to OSS under FAR sect. 6.302-1 (only one responsible source and no other supplies or services will satisfy agency requirements), the July J & A, like the prior one, cited 10 U.S.C. sect. 2304(c)(2) and FAR sect. 6.302-2 (unusual and compelling urgency) as the authority for the sole-source award to OSS. The J & A explained that the BBA-SME requirement was critical for the Civil Affairs Command and that without the BBA-SME program "numerous CAC missions cannot be performed." AR, Tab 1.b.1, J & A, July 11, 2005, at para. 5. It stated that "OSS is the only contractor who is capable of meeting the government's requirement in the unusual and compelling timeframe required." *Id.* at para. 2. According to the J & A, the "critical need date" for the expanded BBA-SME requirement was July 1, 2005, and the national security interests of the government would be "seriously harmed" unless the agency was permitted to proceed with a sole-source award of the requirement. *Id.* at paras. 4 and 5. The J & A further stated that OSS was the only provider of subject matter experts with the requisite cultural competences and linguist skills. While there are a number of other providers of linguists (Titan Corp.) and linguists with security clearances, none of these providers have mined the Iraqi heritage community with a view to finding and deploying individuals with skills required by the MNF-I CAC.... They are the only provider that can perform the contract without significant additional start-up costs and recruitment delays. *Id.* at para. 5.

The J & A also indicated that the requirement was expected to last for only 15 months and that a follow-on contract was not expected. *Id.* at para. 11. On July 29, 2005, the Air Force awarded contract No. FA7012-05-C-0020 to OSS.

ANALYSIS

* * *

We next consider the protesters' arguments that the December 2004 and July 2005 sole-source awards to OSS were improper. The protesters argue that to the extent the awards to OSS were justified based on urgency, the urgent circumstances were the result of the Air Force's lack of advance planning. They argue that the J & As prepared in connection with the awards are not adequately justified and that the Air Force failed to request offers from as many potential sources as practicable.

The Competition in Contracting Act (CICA) requires agencies to conduct their procurements using "full and open competition." 10 U.S.C. sect. 2304(a)(1)(A). CICA, however, permits noncompetitive acquisitions in specified circumstances, such as when the agency's need for the services is of unusual and compelling urgency. 10 U.S.C. sect. 2304(c)(2). Specifically, the exception provides as follows:

> The head of an agency may use procedures other than competitive procedures only when ... (2) the agency's need for the property or services is of such an unusual and compelling urgency that the United States would be seriously injured unless the agency is permitted to limit the number of sources from which it solicits bids or proposals.

Id.; see also FAR sect. 6.302-2(a)(2).

This exception only allows an agency to "limit the number of sources"; an agency may not simply ignore the potential for competition. The mandate for agencies to effect some modicum of competition is reiterated in 10 U.S.C. sect. 2304(e), which provides that when an agency utilizes other than competitive procedures based on unusual and compelling urgency, the agency "shall request offers from as many potential sources as is practicable under the circumstance." *See also* FAR sect. 6.302-2(c)(2). In addition, CICA provides that under no circumstances may noncompetitive procedures be used due to a lack of advance planning by contracting officials or concerns related to the amount of funds available to the agency. 10 U.S.C. sect. 2304(f)(5); *see also* FAR sect. 6.301(c).

With regard to the requirement for advance planning, our Office has recognized that such planning need not be entirely error-free or successful. *See, e.g., HEROS, Inc.,* B-292043, June 9, 2003, 2003 CPD para. 111 at 6; *New Breed Leasing Corp.,* B-274201, B-274202, Nov. 26, 1996, 96-2 CPD para. 202 at 6; *Sprint Communications Co., L.P.,* B-262003.2, Jan. 25, 1996, 96-1 CPD para. 24 at 9. As with all actions taken by an agency, however, the advance planning required under 10 U.S.C. sect. 2304, must be reasonable. In enacting CICA, Congress explained: "Effective competition is predicated on advance procurement planning and an understanding of the marketplace." S. Rep. No. 50, 98th Cong., 2d Sess. 18 (1984), *reprinted in* 1984 U.S.C.C.A.N. 2191....

Based on this legal framework we sustain the protesters' challenges to each of the two sole-source awards to OSS for BBA-SME services, albeit on separate and distinct grounds.

December 2004 Sole-Source Award

Based on the factual context presented with regard to the December 2004 award to OSS, it is evident that the agency's efforts—as described and explained by the agency itself—were so fundamentally flawed as to indicate an unreasonable level of advance planning, which directly resulted in the sole-source award to OSS. In responding to the pro-testers' challenges to the December sole-source award, the Air Force suggests that its ac-tions and the justification underpinning the sole-source determination should be evaluated based on the circumstances faced by the contracting activity in November 2004 when it received the requirement and took steps to expeditiously procure the required BBE-SME services. For example, the Air Force highlights the fact that when the J & A was prepared in support of the award to OSS, the government was faced with the dilemma of needing BBA-SME services in place to support the January 2005 elections in Iraq—then only 2 months away—and it did not have a contractor to provide the services. AR, Tab 13, Sup-plemental Legal Memorandum at 15; AR, Tab 1.b.2, J & A para. 3.

We recognize the abbreviated contracting schedule faced by the contracting activity in its efforts to obtain a contract vehicle for the BBA-SME requirement—a schedule driven by expectations and mandates from higher echelons within the Department of Defense. The record, however, clearly reflects the fact that this narrow procurement window was the direct result of unreasonable actions and acquisition planning by the Air Force and the Department of Defense, to the extent these entities engaged in any acquisition plan-ning at all.

Specifically, 2–3 months were lost as a result of the initial plan to place the BBA-SME requirement under the GEITA contract—even though the requirement was clearly out-side the scope of the GEITA contract. As noted above, the GEITA contract was for advi-sory and assistance services in support of AFCEE's "continued excellence in the world environmental stewardship market," including support for AFCEE's programs involving environmental restoration, compliance, pollution prevention, conservation and planning, fuel facility engineering, base realignment and closure activities, and military family hous-ing initiatives, to include privatization and outsourcing activities. AR, Tab 17, GEITA Con-tract, Statement of Work, at 3, 4–5. The BBA-SME requirement, however, was for Western-oriented individuals of Iraqi background, who were committed to a democratic Iraq, and who would provide services in Iraq such as advising government ministers, plan-ning for and implementing elections, drafting constitutional documents, advising neigh-borhood, municipal, and national councils, and training security forces and details. The plan to use the GEITA contract was unreasonable on its face, given how widely it diverged from the BBA-SME requirement. In fact, as indicated above, a senior member within the Air Force, responsible for acquisition, characterized the plan as requiring a "sanity check" and indicated that it was the result of individuals "leaning way forward in the saddle" in an effort to support a customer because they were "not in the habit of saying no to any-one." AR, Tab 16.ss., E-mail, Subject: RE: GEITA Services for Bilingual-Bicultural Sup-port to Iraq, Nov. 10, 2004.

It was this gross error that directly resulted in the Air Force's determination to pursue a sole-source award for the BBA-SME requirement. "After the Air Force cancelled the GEITA plan, it initiated discussions with OSD regarding the option of making a sole-source award based on urgency. *See* AR, Tab 16.kk., E-mail, Subject: Iraqi Contracting Debacle, Nov. 12, 2004 (stating "[the Air Force] has assured me that [it] should have a contracting solution by COB today or Monday ... specifically mentioned 'sole-sourcing' and 'urgent and compelling' as options on any new contract").

July 2005 Sole-Source Award

Turning to the July 2005 sole-source award to OSS for expansion of the BBA-SME re-quirement, we find that the agency's J & A in support of the sole-source award to OSS was flawed because it was premised on the unsupported conclusion that OSS was the only contractor capable of meeting the BBA-SME requirement in a timely and cost-effective manner. We therefore sustain the protesters' challenge to this second sole-source award as well.

The July 2005 J & A, which nominally cited "unusual and compelling urgency" as the justification for the sole-source award to OSS, was in fact prepared based on the exception to full and open competition set forth in 10 U.S.C. sect. 2304(c)(1), which applies when the agency concludes that required services are only available from one responsible source. Specifically, the contracting officer testified with regard to the July J & A as follows: "I wrote this J & A, believing that I was going to use one responsible source.... I think the situation in Iraq is urgent, but it was written for ['only] one responsible source." Tr. at 277. Moreover, the reasoning set forth in the J & A is consistent with the "only one responsible source" exception....

The record further reflects that the contracting officer sought support from OSD in preparing the J & A for "only one responsible source," pursuant to 10 U.S.C. sect. 2304(c)(1) and FAR sect. 6.302-1, and expressly informed OSD that it would be required to conduct market research certifying that OSS was the only responsible source capable of providing the BBA-SME requirement without significant duplication of cost and loss of schedule. AR, Tab 12.b., E-mail, Subject: OSS-BBA Extension 4-22-05, Apr. 22, 2005. In support of this contention the contracting officer maintained that OSD conducted market research, considered the capabilities of other firms, and certified that OSS was the only capable source....

Contrary to this testimony of the contracting officer, Mr. Rostow testified that he had *not* considered the capabilities of other contractors and he did *not* know whether the Air Force had considered other contractors. Tr. at 178–79....

We conclude from this inconsistency that, contrary to the understanding of the contracting officer, firms other than OSS and their capabilities were simply not meaningfully considered. This was a critical error given that the J & A was premised on the notion that the capabilities of other firms had in fact been considered, and, as a consequence, we believe that the J & A's conclusions supporting the sole-source decision in this regard were unreasonable.

Moreover, the actions associated with the J & A were inconsistent with the requirements of the "unusual and compelling urgency" justification ultimately relied upon by the agency as the basis for the sole-source award to OSS. When relying on the urgency justification, as noted above, an agency is required to obtain competition to the maximum extent practicable. However, as a consequence of the agency's focus on the capabilities of OSS to the exclusion of all others, the agency failed to take any steps to obtain any competition for the expanded BBA-SME requirement. For example, in testimony before our Office regarding the consideration of other contractors, the Air Force indicated that due to the short time frame to fulfill the requirement, transition issues, and because OSS was "performing admirably," the Air Force determined that OSS "was uniquely qualified to be the source on this follow-on." Tr. at 65. The record shows that the expanded BBA-SME requirement was formally approved by the Under Secretary of Defense on May 2, 2005 and OSS's sole-source contract was ultimately awarded in late July — but during that entire period no effort was apparently made to identify other firms, consider their capabilities or provide for any degree of competition, even on a limited basis. In addition, while it may be the case that OSS's customers in Iraq were pleased with OSS's performance, their satisfaction did not provide a basis for disregarding the requirement to seek competition to the maximum extent practicable. *See TeQcom, Inc.,* B-224664, Dec. 22, 1986, 86-2 CPD para. 700 at 5 (agency's satisfaction with performance of incumbent contractor did not justify the use of non-competitive procedures). As a consequence, we sustain the protesters' challenge to the second sole-source award to OSS.

RECOMMENDATION

In crafting our recommendation in this case, we are sensitive to the pressing needs associated with the military's mission in Iraq. In view of the fact that OSS's initial sole-source contract is now substantially complete, and recognizing the agency's asserted need for the services at issue, we do not recommend termination of this contract. With regard to the second sole-source award, however, we recommend that the agency promptly obtain competition for the requirement, or prepare a properly documented and supported J & A in support of the expanded BBA-SME requirement, and, if necessary, promptly obtain competition to the maximum extent practicable. If, as a result of any recompetition, an offeror other than OSS is in line for award, we recommend that the agency terminate OSS's contract. We also recommend that the agency reimburse the protesters' reasonable costs of filing and pursuing the protests, including reasonable attorneys' fees. 4 C.F.R. sect. 21.8(d)(1). The protesters should submit their certified claim for costs, detailing the time expended and costs incurred, directly to the contracting agency within 60 days after the receipt of this decision. 4 C.F.R. sect. 21.8(f)(1).

The protests are sustained.

Notes and Questions

1. The Competition in Contracting Act [hereinafter "CICA"] provides seven general exceptions to the "full and open competition" requirement, two of which the Air Force considered as possible justifications to sole-source its contract to OSS. 41 U.S.C.A. § 253(a). How easy is it for government agencies to sidestep CICA's procurement requirement of "full and open competition" and instead justify sole-sourcing through one of these exceptions?

2. *See* Lani A. Perlman, *Guarding the Government's Coffers: The Need for Competition Requirements to Safeguard Federal Government Procurement*, 75 Fordham L. Rev. 3187 (2007) (examining CICA's history and current impact on government procurement law, and discussing the waste and abuses in government contracting under the Department of Homeland Security, which has a special exemption from the "full and open competition" requirement).

LOGCAP

See: Rebecca Rafferty Vernon, *Battlefield Contractors: Facing the Tough Issues*, 33 Pub Cont. L.J. 369 (2004). This addresses issues presented by external theater support contractors such as the Army's key "LOGCAP" program—issues such as command and control as to private contractor employees, and, the international law of armed conflicts. This updates the fine work by Michael J. Davidson, *Ruck Up: An Introduction to the Legal Issues Associated with Civilian Contractors on the Battlefield*, 29 Pub. Cont. L.J. 233 (2000).

Contracting Abuses in Abu Ghraib

The scandal of prisoner abuse at the Abu Ghraib Detention Facility in Iraq revealed highly problematic contracting practices. That scandal prompted an Army investigation headed by MG George R. Fay. Fay was to determine the extent of Army involvement in the abuse, and investigate whether Army personnel followed established interrogation procedures and comported with international law. The following excerpt presents Fay's findings on how Army outsourcing affected prison operations and contributed to detainee abuse.

AR 15-6 Investigation of the Abu Ghraib Detention Facility and 205th Military Intelligence Brigade

GEORGE R. FAY

INVESTIGATING OFFICER

* * *

g. Contract Interrogators and Linguists

(1) Contracting-related issues contributed to the problems at Abu Ghraib prison. Several of the alleged perpetrators of the abuse of detainees were employees of government contractors. Two contractual arrangements were involved:…

(a) Linguist contract-Titan, Inc.—Contract DASC01-99-D-0001.

* * *

… INSCOM awarded Contract DASC01-99-D-0001 to Titan, in March 1999. The contract called for Titan initially to develop a plan to provide and manage linguists throughout the world, and later, implement the plan as required. The contract called for three levels of linguists—some were required to obtain security clearances and some were not. The linguist candidates were subject to some level of background investigations, based on individual requirements for security clearances. Since the award of the contract, hundreds of linguists have been provided, with generally positive results. It is noted that the contract calls for translation services only, and makes no mention of contractor employees actually conducting interrogations. Since the statement of work is limited to translation services, the linguists apparently were not required to review and sign the IROE at Abu Ghraib. A recent review of the contract indicated that the current contract ceiling is approximately $650 Million. Other agencies can order linguist services under this contract. For the most part, the ordering activity also provides the funds for these delivery orders. The contract contains a clause that allows the Contracting Officer to direct the contractor to remove linguists from the theater in which they are performing. This clause has been invoked on occasion for misconduct.

(b) Interrogator contract-CACI, Inc.

[1] The second contractual arrangement is a series of Delivery Orders awarded to CACI, in August 2003[.]…

[2] These Delivery Orders were awarded under a Blanket Purchase Agreement (BPA) (NBCHA01-0005) with the National Business Center (NBC), a fee for service activity of the Interior Department. The BPA between CACI and NBC set out the ground rules for ordering from the General Services Administration (GSA) pursuant to GSA Schedule Contract GS-35F-5872H, which is for various Information Technology (IT) Professional Services. Approximately eleven Delivery Orders were related to services in Iraq. While CJTF-7 is the requiring and funding activity for the Delivery Orders in question, it is not clear who, if anyone, in Army contracting or legal channels approved the use of the BPA, or why it was used.

[3] There is another problem with the CACI contract. A CACI employee, Thomas Howard, participated with the COR, LTC Brady, in writing the Statement of Work (SOW) prior to the award of the contract (Reference Annex B, Appendix 1, BOLTZ). This situation may violate the provisions of Federal Acquisition Regulation (FAR) 9. 505-2 (b) (1).

[4] On 13 May 2004, the Deputy General Counsel (Acquisition) of the Army issued an opinion that all Delivery Orders for Interrogator Services should be cancelled immediately as they were beyond the scope of the GSA Schedule contract.

(2) Although intelligence activities and related services, which encompass interrogation services, should be performed by military or government civilian personnel wherever feasible, it is recognized that contracts for such services may be required in urgent or emergency situations. The general policy of not contracting for intelligence functions and services was designed in part to avoid many of the problems that eventually developed at Abu Ghraib, i.e., lack of oversight to insure that intelligence operations continued to fall within the law and the authorized chain of command, as well as the government's ability to oversee contract operations.

(3) Performing the interrogation function in-house with government employees has several tangible benefits for the Army. It enables the Army more readily to manage the function if all personnel are directly and clearly subject to the chain of command, and other administrative and/or criminal sanctions, and it allows the function to be directly accessible by the commander/supervisor without going through a Contracting Officer Representative (COR). In addition, performing the function in-house enables Army Commanders to maintain a consistent approach to training (See Paragraph 3.b.(3)) and a reliable measure of the qualifications of the people performing the function.

* * *

(5) Some of the employees at Abu Ghraib were not DoD contractor employees. Contractor employees under non-DoD contracts may not be subject to the Military Extraterritorial Jurisdiction Act (18 US Code 3261–3267). The Act allows DoD contractor employees who are "accompanying the Armed Forces outside the United States" to be subject to criminal prosecution if they engage in conduct that would constitute an offense punishable by imprisonment for more than one year if the conduct had occurred within the jurisdiction of the United States.

* * *

(7) The Army needs to improve on-site contract monitoring by government employees (using CORs) to insure that the Army's basic interests are protected. The inadequacy of the onsite contract management at Abu Ghraib is best understood by reviewing the statement of CPT Wood (Reference Annex B, Appendix 1, WOOD), the Interrogation OIC, who indicated she never received any parameters or guidance as to how the CACI personnel were to be utilized. She also indicates that her primary point of contact (POC) on matters involving the CACI Delivery Orders was the CACI on-site manager. There is no mention of a COR. Another indication of the inadequacy of the contract management is reflected in the statement of SOLDIER14 (Reference Annex B, Appendix 1, SOLDIER-14), who indicated he was never informed that the Government could reject unsatisfactory CACI employees. It would appear that no effort to familiarize the ultimate user of the contracted services of the contract's terms and procedures was ever made. In order to improve this situation, training is required to ensure that the COR is thoroughly familiar with the contract and gains some level of familiarity with the Geneva Conventions standards. It needs to be made clear that contractor employees are bound by the requirements of the Geneva Conventions.

* * *

(9) Emerging results from a DA Inspector General (DAIG) Investigation indicate that approximately 35% of the contract interrogators lacked formal military training as interrogators. While there are specific technical requirements in the linguist contract, the technical requirements for the interrogator contract were not adequate. It appears that the only mention of qualifications in the contract stated merely that the contractor employee needs to have met the requirements of one of two MOS, 97E or 351E, or "equivalent".

Any solicitation/contract for these services needs to list specific training, if possible, not just point to an MOS.... The necessity for some sort of standard training and/or experience is made evident by the statements of both contractor employees and military personnel. CIVILIAN-21 (CACI) seemingly had little or no interrogator experience prior to coming to Abu Ghraib (Reference Annex B, Appendix 1, CIVILIAN-21, ADAMS), even though he was a Navy Reserve Intelligence Specialist. Likewise, numerous statements indicated that little, if any, training on Geneva Conventions was presented to contractor employees (Reference Annex B, Appendix 1, SOLDIER-25, CIVILIAN-10, CIVILIAN-21 and CIVILIAN-11).... If the solicitation/contract allows "equivalent" training and experience, the Contracting Officer, with the assistance of technical personnel, must evaluate and assess the offerors'/contractor's proposal/written rationale as to why it believes that the employee has "equivalent" training. It appears that under the CACI contract, no one was monitoring the contractor's decisions as to what was considered "equivalent."

(10) In addition, if functions such as these are being contracted, MI personnel need to have at least a basic level of contract training so they can protect the Army's interests. Another indication of the apparent inadequacy of on-site contract management and lack of contract training is the apparent lack of understanding of the appropriate relationship between contractor personnel, government civilian employees, and military personnel. Several people indicated in their statements that contractor personnel were "supervising" government personnel or *vice versa*....

* * *

(12)... Meaningful contract administration and monitoring will not be possible if a small number of CORs are asked to monitor the performance of one or more contractors who may have 100 or more employees in the theater, and in some cases, perhaps in several locations (which seems to have been the situation at Abu Ghraib)....

(13) Proper oversight did not occur at Abu Ghraib due to a lack of training and inadequate contract management and monitoring. Failure to assign an adequate number of CORs to the area of contract performance puts the Army at risk of being unable to control poor performance or become aware of possible misconduct by contractor personnel. This lack of monitoring was a contributing factor to the problems that were experienced with the performance of the contractors at Abu Ghraib. The Army needs to take a much more aggressive approach to contract administration and management if interrogator services are to be contracted. Some amount of advance planning should be utilized to learn from the mistakes made at Abu Ghraib.

Notes and Questions

1. The Fay Report acknowledged that the law was unclear as to whether these government contractors were subject to the Military Extraterritorial Jurisdiction Act [hereinafter, "MEJA"] because they were not Department of Defense contractors. The MEJA imposes overseas jurisdiction over members of the Armed Forces and persons employed by the Armed Forces who, while outside of the United States, engage in behavior that would be punishable by imprisonment for more than one year if committed within the United States. *See* MEJA, 18 U.S.C. §§ 3261–3267 (2000 & Supp. IV 2004). Following the Fay Report, the MEJA was amended in 2004 to make clear that the provisions apply to non-Department of Defense contractors working in support of the Department's mission overseas. *See* Anthony E. Giardino, *Using Extraterritorial Jurisdiction to Prosecute Violations of the Law of War: Looking Beyond the War Crimes Act*, 48 B.C. L. Rev. 699, 716–17 (2007). For more information on the unique jurisdictional position of contractor "civilian-soldiers,"

see Katherine Jackson, *Not Quite a Civilian, Not Quite a Soldier: How Five Words Could Subject Civilian Contractors in Iraq and Afghanistan to Military Jurisdiction*, 27 J. Nat'l Ass'n Admin. L. Judiciary 255 (2007).

2. Steve L. Schooner, *Contractor Atrocities at Abu Ghraib: Compromised Accountability in a Streamlined, Outsourced Government*, 16 Stan. L. & Pol'y Rev. 549 (245). This addresses how inadequate contract administration, the use of contractors for augmentation of government employees, and the use of interagency acquisition instruments in the hands of fee-based government contracting offices, played a role on the path to the contractor participation in atrocities.

3. Parallel to, but going beyond, the Afghanistan and Iraq conflicts, a legal literature has developed around the international (and sometimes domestic) law issues of private military contracting. See Lucas Hanback, *The Contingency Contracting Corps In Counterinsurgency Operations: Using Money To Effectively Fight Insurgents*, 40 Pub. Cont. L.J. 171 (Fall 2010); Won Kidane, *The Status Of Private Military Contractors Under International Humanitarian Law*, 38 Denv. J. Int'l & Pol'y L. 361 (Summer 2010); Lyndsey M.D. Olson, *Herding Cats I: Disposal Of DOD Real Property And Contractor Inventory In Contingency Operations*, 2010 Army Law. 5 (Apr. 2010); Laura A. Dickinson, *Government for Hire: Privatizing Foreign Affairs and the Problem of Accountability Under International Law*, 47 Wm. & Mary L. Rev. 135 (2005); Deven R. Deswai, Article, *Have Your Cake and Eat It Too: A Proposal for a Layered Approach to Regulating Private Military Companies*, 39 U.S.F.L. Rev. 825 (2005); Clive Walker, David Whyte, *Contracting Out War?: Private Military Companies, Law and Regulation in the United Kingdom*, 54 I.C.L.Q. 651 (2005); Jon D. Michaels, *Beyond Accountability: The Constitutional, Democratic, and Strategic Problems With Privatizing War*, 82 Wash. U. L.Q. 1001 (2004); Ellen L. Frye, Note, *Private Military Firms in the New World Order: How Redefining "Mercenary" Can Tame the "Dogs of War,"* 73 Fordham L. Rev. 2607 (2005).

The following GAO protest decision concerns an important procurement in the Afghanistan war.

Decision Matter of: DynCorp International LLC

B-402349 (Comp.Gen.), 2010 CPD P 59 (Comp.Gen.),
2010 WL 893517 (Comp.Gen.)
COMPTROLLER GENERAL

For Opinion see Chapter 3.

Notes and Questions

1. The background is glimpsed in the opinion, and deserves teasing out. In both Iraq and Afghanistan, the United States employed contractors to train police. Given the conditions in Afghanistan, the police were not the police of peaceful towns in America, but were a part of the Afghan armed forces that took a higher casualty rate than the Afghan army itself. Initially, the Department of State awarded and managed the training contract. However, the responsibility got shifted to the Department of Defense. It looked for an IDIQ vehicle to award the contract off, and decided that the worldwide counternarcotics training IDIQ would serve.

2. Is it material that the incumbent contractor on the police training contract, DynCorp, could not bid on the counternarcotics IDIQ? Following the GAO ruling, the Department of Defense conducted full and open competition, and DynCorps won. Does that vindicate the GAO opinion?

3. More broadly, what does it say about war today that this is handled by a government contracting vehicle at all? On the one hand, is it extraordinary that so martial a task as training the local armed forces is done by a contractor? On the other hand, does it amount to having "judges on the battlefield" for a protest to come around the world, so to speak, from Kabul to the GAO about the awarding of that contract?

Chapter 12

Government and Contractor Labor Force

The government establishes an elaborate set of rules concerning the labor force of contractors which directly affect contracting, plus rules concerning the government's own labor force which may indirectly affect contracting. This chapter's first section addresses contracting-out, the process by which the government lets contractors compete with its own employees to see whether work should be contracted out. The next section touches lightly on the large subject of labor standards, such as "prevailing wage" standards, for employees of contractors working on government projects. A third section addresses labor policy for contractors—whether the government may use its leverage on contractors to promote specific labor policies. Last, a section takes a quick glance at the law governing the government's own labor force.

For further discussion of the subjects in this chapter, see the cites for each specific subchapter, and see David W. Gaffey, *Outsourcing Infrastructure: Expanding The Use Of Public-Private Partnerships In The United States*, 39 Pub. Cont. L.J. 351 (Winter 2010); George G. Booker, Dawn L. Seraphine, *Helping Your Client Transition From Commercial To Federal Government Contract Work*, 57 Fed. Law. 32 (Oct. 2010); Tishisa L. Braziel, *Contracting Out Contracting*, 38 Pub. Cont. L.J. 857 (Summer 2009); Janna J. Hansen, Note, *Limits of Competition: Accountability in Government Contracting*, 112 Yale L.J. 2465 (2003); Mary E. Harney, *The Quiet Revolution: Downsizing, Outsourcing, and Best Value*, 158 Mil. L. Rev. 48 (1998); Gregory E. Lang, *Best Value Source Selection in the A-76 Process*, 43 A.F.L. Rev. 239 (1997).

A. Contracting-Out: Public-Private Competition

For further discussion of the subjects in this section, see: Steven W. Feldman, Government Contract Awards: Negotiation and Sealed Bidding §§ 3:17–3:19 (available in Westlaw); Stiens & Turley, *Uncontracting: The Move Back to Performing In-house*, 65 A.F.L. Rev. 145 (2010); Katherine Southard, *U.S. Electric Utilities: The First Public-Private Partnerships*, 39 Pub. Cont. L.J. 395 (Winter 2010); Lucas Anderson, *Kicking The National Habit: The Legal And Policy Arguments For Abolishing Private Prison Contracts*, 39 Pub. Cont. L.J. 113 (Fall 2009); Kerry A. Carlson, *Most Efficient Organization (MEO) Protest Rights: Due Process Without* Purpose, 35 Pub. Cont. L.J. 221 (2006).

Note on A-76

All previous discussion in the chapters on sealed bids and competitive negotiation have concerned procurements in which the government had decided to buy from the private sector and the competition occurred between private offerors. In contrast, the government sometimes decides whether to provide something internally, that is, by the work of government employees, or to contract the work out. In order to make this decision, the government may use the formal process of a public-private competition. This process, which goes back in time to the Eisenhower Administration, makes the decision about whether to buy from the private sector by a competition between an internal government mode of performance, on the one hand, and one or more potential private contractors, on the other.

In the federal government, an elaborate mechanism has evolved to govern such public-private competitions. This is known as the "A-76" process, because its principal and most detailed guidance comes from Circular No. A-76 of the Office of Management and Budget and its Revised Supplemental Handbook promulgated in 1996. Since the A-76 process can end in protests, the GAO and the courts have written many opinions about the A-76 process.

The *Space Mark* judicial opinion, which describes the process of a public-private competition and the subsequent reviews and protest, is provided. Subsequently, in 2003, OMB substantially revised A-76 directive. The revised A-76 sought to merge the previously very separate processes of public-private competition, and private-private competition, into one "standard" competition. Many of the previous steps and safeguards were eliminated. Also, for limited-scale work, a "streamlined" form of the competition could occur. See Charles Tiefer, "OMB's New A-76: Tilting the Contracting-out Process," Federal Bar Association Government Contracts Section Newsletter, Spring 2003, at 6.

Conversely, in the late 2000s, the pendulum swung back the other way. Congress gave a boost to an in-sourcing process. Congress requires the Department of Defense to consider using its civilian employees to perform new functions and functions that are performed by contractors. 10 U.S.C. sec. 2463. And, Congress applied an existing DoD requirement, to the entire government—a requirement to conduct public-private competitions before contracting out functions performed by ten or more civilians.

Congress enacted provisions which made it less easy for the A-76 process to contract out government work. In particular, it enacted appropriation provisions about what costs had to be considered. For example, the process excludes consideration of the firm's health care and retirement costs if the firm contributes less towards its employee benefits than what the federal government contributes.

The A-76 process has the following steps. Before any competitions, the government inventories all its activities under the Federal Activities Inventory Reform (FAIR) act. The inventories can be reviewed with an eye toward what to consider contracting out. An agency's managers prepare a Performance Work Statement (PWS) for an activity. This becomes incorporated into a solicitation as the government's Statement of Work. Along with the creation of the PWS, the agency conducts a management study to establish the government's Most Efficient Organization (MEO). Knowing this will compete with private firms, agency employees may provide surprising input, even suggesting ways that the MEO could perform the work with fewer government employees—so that the savings will fend off privatization.

Using the MEO, agency personnel develop an in-house cost estimate. A cost comparison then occurs between the in-house cost estimate, and, the costs of the best offer by a private firm. Each agency is required to establish an appeals procedure for informal administrative review of the cost comparison results. Usually, agencies will appoint officials from other installations so as to preserve independence and impartiality. Both the private firm, and, the federal employees, have a right to protest to the GAO.

It is said that the contracting community sometimes believes that government officials conducting the A-76 procurement are biased in favor of in-house performance. Conversely, in the 2000s during the Bush Administration, employees and their unions felt the opposite—that the Administration pressured its manager to favor outsourcing.

In contemporary government contracting, the A-76 process has special importance. This is an era in which, due to political and economic developments, much argument is being made in other countries and in the United States to privatize activity which had previously been performed by the government. In other countries, this takes the more dramatic form of proposals to privatize whole sectors of production that had been nationalized, such as utility systems like telephone services. By contrast, for the federal government, the proposals are usually more modest in their individual scope, often being proposals to contract out services of a particular kind at a particular facility, such as clerical or information technology services at a particular civilian or defense center.

Even so, the aggregate of all such proposals amounts to a substantial potential change in public operations. An Administration may set goals, and seek to adjust procedures, to extensively contract out. A-76 competitions may simply seem a nuts-and-bolts variant on other competitive processes, with disputes that concern discrete, concrete, and specific accounting details. However, A-76 competitions reflect major philosophical issues about where the boundaries ought to be in society between public and private activity. It is a measure of the sophistication of government contract law that it can and does deal with such issues.

Space Mark, Inc., Plaintiff, v. The United States, Defendant

United States Court of Federal Claims
45 Fed. Cl. 267
Nov. 9, 1999

FIRESTONE, Judge.

This case arises from a solicitation issued by the Air Force for a Communications and Information Management contract at Los Angeles Air Force Base. The solicitation was part of a two step process aimed at determining whether the services described in the solicitation could be performed more economically by a private contractor when compared to the costs of the Air Force's in-house personnel performing the same work.[1]

In this action brought pursuant to 28 U.S.C. § 1491(b)(1) (1994 & Supp. III 1997), plaintiff, Space Mark, Inc. ("SMI"), the contractor that won the private competition challenges the Air Force's final cost comparison, which concluded that the Air Force's in-house organization could perform the work more economically than SMI. SMI contends that the Air Force's cost comparison was flawed procedurally and contains mistakes in violation of the relevant sections of OMB Circular A-76 and its Supplements, as well as 10 U.S.C. §§ 2304, 2462, 2468 and 32 C.F.R. Parts 169 and 169a.

FACTUAL BACKGROUND

The facts are set forth in the Administrative Record filed with the court on September 27, 1999. On November 25, 1998, the United States Air Force, acting through the Los An-

---

1. A variety of statutes and regulations govern how the Department of Defense is to compare the cost of private contractors providing supplies and services with the cost of the government providing those same goods or services. *See* 10 U.S.C. § 2462(b) (1994); Office of Management and Budget ("OMB") Circular A-76 and its Supplement. This action centers on the Air Force's compliance with those statutes and regulations.

geles Air Force Base Space and Missile Systems Center ("Air Force"), issued Solicitation No. F04693-98-R-0006 ("Solicitation") seeking proposals for the performance of communications and information management services at the base for a five-year term. The performance requirements were set forth in a Performance Work Statement ("PWS") accompanying the Solicitation.

The Air Force issued the Solicitation in support of a cost comparison study it was conducting under OMB Circular No. A-76, which states that it is the general policy of the federal government to rely upon commercial sources to provide the products and services the government needs. *See* 48 Fed. Reg. 37,110, 37,114 (1983). OMB Circular No. A-76 also provides that in-house performance of a commercial activity is authorized if a "cost comparison" demonstrates that the federal agency is operating *or* can operate the activity at a lower estimated cost than a qualified commercial source. *See id.* at 37.115.

The Air Force designed the subject cost comparison study to determine whether the services described in the PWS could be performed more economically by the Air Force's "most efficient, cost effective organization" or "MEO"[2] capable of performing the services, or if a commercial source could perform the services more economically. The Solicitation indicated that the competition would be divided into two stages. First, there would be a competition among commercial sources to select the lowest-priced, technically acceptable proposal. Second, the prevailing commercial source's proposal would be evaluated against the MEO's proposal. The Solicitation, as amended, set February 25, 1999, as the due date for proposals from both the private contractors and the MEO.

On December 9, 1998, the Air Force conducted a pre-proposal conference with potential contractors, including SMI. At the conference the Air Force gave the attendees information about the competition and the cost comparison procedures set forth in OMB Circular No. A-76; the Circular No. A-76 Revised Supplemental Handbook (March 1996) ("A-76 Supplemental Handbook"); Department of Defense Instruction ("DODI") 4100.33; Air Force Pamphlet ("AFP") 26-12; Supplemental Guidance to AFP 26-12 issued September 6, 1996; and Air Force Manual ("AFM") 64-108.

In accordance with the above-noted requirements, SMI submitted a timely proposal prior to the February 25, 1999 deadline. The Air Force also submitted their MEO proposal by February 25, 1999. The Air Force, however, revised the MEO proposal on April 22, 1999. It was the April 22, 1999 revised MEO proposal that the Air Force used to compare costs.

During March 1999, the Air Force's Source Selection Team performed an evaluation of proposals submitted by commercial sources in response to the solicitation. Following its evaluation, the Source Selection team determined that SMI's proposal was the only technically acceptable proposal. The Source Selection Team asked SMI to submit a final proposal for a cost comparison with the MEO's in-house cost proposal, which was to take place on April 23, 1999. On or about April 21, 1999, SMI submitted its final revised proposal.

On April 23, 1999, the Air Force's Contracting Officer ("CO") conducted the cost comparison and in accordance with the regulations publicly announced the results. SMI at-

---

2. The MEO is not the existing in-house organization, but the organization the agency would establish if it were competing for the work. In other words, the existing organization is allowed to make itself more efficient in order to compete. The A-76 Supplemental Handbook provides that "[a]gencies may consider existing management reinvention, consolidation, re-engineering, personnel classification, market and other analyses in the identification and development of the MEO." OFFICE OF MANAGEMENT AND BUDGET, CIRCULAR NO. A-76, REVISED SUPPLEMENTAL HANDBOOK 11 (1996) [hereinafter A-76 SUPPLEMENTAL HANDBOOK].

tended the public announcement. The CO first opened SMI's final revised proposal, which reflected a total price of $15,324,374. The CO then opened the Air Force's revised MEO cost comparison worksheet, which indicated that the MEO's final in-house cost estimate was $18,208,353. Because adjustments must be made to do a final comparison, the CO entered SMI's price information on the requisite OMB cost comparison worksheet. The data on the cost comparison worksheet was then entered into OMB's "COMPARE" computer program. The program generated a new worksheet indicating that in-house performance was more economical than contractor performance by $274,232. Based on these results, the CO announced the Air Force's tentative cost comparison decision in favor of the MEO. The decision would not become final, however, until SMI exhausted its administrative appeals.

In accordance with the Air Force's rules governing the cost comparison process, SMI received a copy of the tentative cost decision on May 3, 1999. The Air Force contends that it also sent SMI a copy of all of its supporting documentation, including a copy of the February 1999 initial proposal and the explanation of the changes to the April 1999 proposal. Under the Air Force's regulations, the February 1999 proposals and the change sheet should have been disclosed at the April 23 public announcement. It is not disputed that the Air Force did not publicly disclose that it had amended the February 1999 MEO proposal at the April public announcement, as required by the Air Force's procurement regulations. In addition, SMI contends that it never received a copy of these documents in the May package.

On May 12, 1999, SMI submitted a timely appeal of the Air Force's tentative cost comparison decision to the CO, based on the limited information it claims it had received. In its appeal SMI challenged the tentative cost comparison decision on two grounds. First, SMI asserted that the Air Force had violated OMB Circular No. A-76 and the A-76 Supplemental Handbook by adding the cost of three quality assurance evaluators ("QAE"), at a pay grade of GS-12, to SMI's proposed contract administration costs. Second, SMI challenged the Air Force's decision to add the relocation costs of 13 employees to SMI's proposed costs.

In accordance with AFP 26-12, the Los Angeles Air Force Base Cost Comparison Review Team heard SMI's appeal. The Review Team was made up of independent evaluators who did not participate in the cost comparison or evaluation of the April proposals. The Review Team denied SMI's appeal on May 30, 1999.

Thereafter, on June 2, 1999, SMI filed a protest with the General Accounting Office ("GAO") contesting the Air Force's cost comparison decision. After the protest was filed, the Air Force and SMI entered into a settlement agreement in which SMI agreed to withdraw its GAO protest and pursue its final administrative appeal to the major command under Section 15-2 of AFP 26-12. *See* AFP 26-12, *supra*, at 74. Pursuant to the terms of the settlement agreement, SMI submitted a major command-level appeal of the Air Force's cost competition decision to the Air Force Materiel Command ("AFMC"), on June 7, 1999.

* * *

By memorandum dated September 3, 1999, AFMC notified SMI that the final decision of the Air Force was to uphold the CO_s cost comparison decision and to proceed with implementation of the MEO. By memorandum dated September 8, 1999, the AFMC instructed SMC to cancel the Solicitation and take appropriate action to implement the MEO.

On September 17, 1999, SMI filed its complaint and motion for a temporary restraining order in this court, challenging the September 3, 1999 AFMC decision and seeking to enjoin the Air Force from implementing the MEO. On September 21, 1999, the Air Force agreed to wait 60 days before taking any action adverse to SMI. The matter was briefed, and the court heard oral argument on November 3, 1999.

DISCUSSION

* * *

II. The Inclusion of Quality Assurance in Contract Administration Costs

SMI challenges as arbitrary and unreasonable the Air Force's decision to include in its cost comparison the costs of three quality assurance evaluators at the GS-12 and GS-11 level to oversee the private contractor's performance. In SMI's view, quality assurance costs are common to both the government and a private contractor and should not have been considered as an added cost to SMI's proposal. SMI further states that, in any event, the inclusion of three QAEs at such high GS levels is unsupportable when examined against the contract administration requirements of the solicitation.

The AFMC determined that these three positions were created for the purpose of assuring contractor compliance with contract terms and conditions and were therefore properly included as contract administration costs under the OMB Circular A-76 Revised Supplemental Handbook, which states that contract administration costs "includes the cost of reviewing compliance with the terms of the contract...." *See* A-76 SUPPLEMENTAL HANDBOOK, *supra,* at 25. Additionally, the AFMC determined that the QAE duties are not common to both contract and Government performance, as required by the OMB Handbook. *See RTS Travel Services,* B-283055, 1999 WL 754536, at *3 (September 23, 1999). The AFMC determined that Air Force regulations support a ratio of 3 contract administrators for a 51-person commercial operation. In addition, the AFMC noted that a review of the QAE Core Personnel Documents ("CPD") reveals that these three positions are intended to provide contract administration for each of three areas of performance; namely, Visual Information Services, Communications and Computer Systems, and Records Management. The AFMC concluded that these positions would not be needed if the work were not contracted out.

The court finds that the inclusion of three QAEs was rational and consistent with the applicable regulations. As a review of the CPDs reveals, the QAEs are required to perform contract administration functions including: certifying invoices, verifying claims, approving contract payments, and interfacing with the CO on negotiating contract changes. These tasks are clearly identified as contract administration functions in the A-76 Supplemental Handbook and AFP 26-12.[12] The fact that these same employees also are tasked to perform certain quality assurance functions does not disqualify them as contract administrators. *See RTS Travel Services,* 1999 WL 754536 at *3. Where quality assurance functions are performed in the context of other contract administration functions, they properly may be included as contract administration costs. *See id.* Accordingly, the Air Force's decision

---

12. Under A-76 guidelines, "contract administration" includes "the cost of reviewing compliance with the terms of the contract, processing payments, negotiating change orders, and monitoring the closeout of contract operations [but] does not include inspection and other administrative requirements that would be common to contract and Government performance to assure acceptable performance." A-76 SUPPLEMENTAL HANDBOOK, *supra,* at 25. Similarly, Air Force guidance provides that contract administration costs include "the cost of reviewing contractor performance for compliance with the terms of the contract (quality assurance surveillance), processing contract payments, negotiating contract changes, and monitoring the closeout of contract operations." AFP 26-12, *supra,* at 55.

to include these positions as contract administration costs is not arbitrary, capricious, or otherwise not in accordance with law.

III. The Inclusion of Relocation Costs for 12 Employees

SMI argues that the administrative record does not support the AFMC's conclusion that privatizing the PWS would result in 12 relocations. SMI contends that data on the existing work force shows that only 5 existing employees would need to be relocated and that after applying the Air Force Command's general 10.11% "right of first refusal" statistic to the 5 employees, SMI should be responsible for only 4 relocations. SMI suggests that the data it relies upon is more realistic.

As discussed above, the AFMC addressed this argument in its decision, explaining that SMI was wrong to rely on data about the existing organization when SMI argued previously that only 5 existing employees would need to be relocated. As the AFMC stated: "The only position data relevant to the placement of employees is position data from the MEO, and not the original organization."

* * *

V. CONCLUSION

For all of the above-noted reasons, the court concludes that the Air Force's procurement decision was not arbitrary, capricious, or otherwise not in accordance with law. Accordingly, judgment for plaintiff on the administrative record and request for a permanent injunction is DENIED and judgment for defendant is GRANTED. The clerk is directed to enter judgment accordingly. Each party shall bear their own costs.

Notes and Questions

1. Space Mark presents a chronology of the procedural steps packed into less than a year from the issuance of the solicitation to the judicial decision on the protest. Can you identify each one and its significance? How do they match, or differ from, the steps in a regular, non-A-76, "private-private" competition? As noted earlier, in 2003 OMB issued a revised A-76, which changed the process significantly from that described in this opinion. See Charles Tiefer, "OMB's New A-76: Tilting the Contracting-out Process," Federal Bar Association Government Contracts Section Newsletter, Spring 2003, at 6.

2. The two substantive issues are quality assurance costs and employee relocation costs. Are these mundane accounting disputes? How might they reflect the deeper questions of whether to transform public into private activity?

3. Note the interesting concept of what is the public side of the competition, the "Most Efficient Organization." It "is not the costs of the existing in-house organization, but the organization the agency would establish ... to make itself more efficient in order to compete." Fn. 2. Opponents of the concept may complain that it presents potential private offerors with a "moving target" that is difficult to beat and that they may consider unfairly advantaged. Supporters of the concept may respond that the MEO is no less concrete than a private organization's projected plan for how it will perform, and that the MEO means that even if the work is not contracted out, the A-76 process forces the government to figure out how to be more efficient.

4. Procedurally, current government employees, particularly those organized in a public employees union, often provide their own input in the development of an MEO, and take advantage of their A-76 rights to participate in the internal reviews of the A-76 competition. In the early years, public employee unions could not file protests, a barrier which

was controversial. For a discussion of this controversy, see Charles Tiefer & Jennifer Ferragut, *Letting Federal Unions Protest Improper Contracting Out*, Cornell J.L. & Pub. Pol. (2001).

B. Labor Standards

Starting in the 1930s, Congress established an elaborate system to require government contractors not to afford substandard wage rates or working conditions to their employees. Two of these statutes, the Davis-Bacon Act and the Contract Work Hours and Safety Standards Act ("CWHSSA"), tightly control government construction work. The Services Contract Act applies, naturally enough, to services contracts. After regulatory elaboration in the decades after enactment, they have largely withstood efforts in the 1980s and 1990s by contractors to obtain deregulation, although some limited changes were made by the Federal Acquisition Reform Act ("FARA") of 1994. In effect, these statutes represent organized labor's effort to cement labor protections through government rules against efforts at release by government contractors.

Thus, the labor standards represent a stronghold that has withstood the trends toward globalization, deregulation, outsourcing, downsizing, and other techniques by which employers in the 1980s and 1990s freed themselves from bargained-for labor protections in non-government contexts. On the one hand, opponents may deride them as imposing expenses on the government that these trends have reduced elsewhere, and as creating "entry barriers" against efficient competition. On the other hand, supporters may defend them as necessary for a fair division of taxpayer expenditures on contracting between labor and management. In their absence, the competitive bidding system might become an engine for shifting government work away from employers of organized or otherwise decently-treated labor.

Strikingly, the Department of Labor, not contracting agencies, administers these labor standards. The case in this section, *Janik Paving*, demonstrates this in action, with a proceeding involving Department of Labor investigators, hearings, administrative law judges, and appeal boards An array of determinations, waivers, appeals, and so forth is made by the Department of Labor. Presumably, the labor supporters of these standards doubt that they would be administered with equivalent understanding of their goals by departments other than the Department of Labor.

The *Janik Paving* case deals with a contractor violating a key portion of the CWHSSA, regarding required overtime payment. It reflects the "tough" side of labor standard enforcement. On one side, the contractor allegedly not only failed to pay its employees the mandated rates for their overtime on a government-funded project, but falsified records to cover this up. On the other side, the Department of Labor hits back, not only by requiring the contractor to make compensatory payments, but by debarring it for two years. While the standards operate in a government contracts context, they also bring the harshness of management-labor clashes.

The Department of Labor and the contracting agencies have a complex division of their efforts. Not only does the Department of Labor handle the enforcement and adjudications discussed in *Janik Paving*, it also does such decisions as "wage determinations," setting the prevailing wage rates throughout the country to which some labor standards are pegged. Hence, government contractors may well find themselves dealing with the

Department of Labor. On the other hand, contracting officers still have a large role, as they supervise and pay the contractor

Janik Paving & Construction, Inc., et al., Plaintiffs-Appellants, v. William E. Brock, III, as Secretary of the United States Department of Labor, et al., Defendants-Appellees

No. 1322, Docket 87-6113
United States Court of Appeals, Second Circuit
828 F.2d 84
Decided Sept. 9, 1987

Before FEINBERG, Chief Judge, and LUMBARD and MINER, Circuit Judges.

LUMBARD, Circuit Judge:

On this appeal, we are primarily asked to decide whether the Secretary of Labor has the statutory authority to "debar" a contractor which has violated overtime hours and pay provisions of the Contract Work Hours and Safety Standards Act ("CWHSSA"), 40 U.S.C. ss 327–333, from working on any contract or subcontract receiving federal funding under numerous specified statutes, for a period of up to three years. Appellants, Janik Paving and Construction, Inc. and William J. Janik, its president, appeal from an order of the district court for the Western District (Elfvin, J.), which dismissed their action. They challenge the Secretary's authority to debar them from such work, as well as the sufficiency of the evidence which the Department of Labor amassed in support of the debarment order. We affirm.

Janik Paving has been primarily engaged in the highway paving and construction business since 1979. Most of its business, according to appellants, involves work on highway paving and construction projects which receive federal funding. This appeal arises from Janik's performance on two such contracts.

In 1980, Janik was awarded the prime contract by the Town of West Seneca, New York for the construction of certain sidewalks, curbs, and drains ("the Edson Street contract"); the work was to be financed under the Housing and Community Development Act of 1974. That same year, Janik was also awarded the prime contract by the New York State Department of Transportation for the installation of concrete and asphalt pavement in Holland, New York ("the Route 16 contract"), with financing to be provided under the Federal-Aid Highway Act of 1956.

Both of these federal financing statutes contained "Davis-Bacon" provisions, which obligated Janik, as contractor, to pay the laborers and mechanics it employed on these contracts the wages prevailing for similar construction in the same localities. See Davis-Bacon Act, 40 U.S.C. ss 276a–276a-5 (1931); Federal-Aid Highway Act of 1956, as amended, 23 U.S.C. s 113(a); Housing and Community Development Act of 1974, 42 U.S.C. ss 5310, 1440(g). Because both contracts involved federal assistance under statutes prescribing wage standards, Janik also was required to comply with the provisions of CWHSSA, which, in pertinent part, required contractors on federally-funded construction projects to pay their laborers and mechanics "time and one-half" for hours worked in excess of eight hours in one day or forty hours in one week. 40 U.S.C. ss 328, 329.[1]

---

1. The CWHSSA has since been amended to require contractors to pay overtime rates only for hours worked in excess of a forty-hour work week. 99 Stat. 583, 734 (1985).

Under the statute then and now, a contractor found in violation of overtime pay and hour requirements may be held liable to its affected employees for failure to pay the required amounts and to the government for liquidated damages in the sum of $10 for each calendar day on which these employees were underpaid. 40 U.S.C. s 328. A contracting governmental agency may withhold and pay directly to the affected workers any amounts in contract monies necessary to satisfy the contractor's overtime obligations. Id. at s 330(a). Criminal penalties may also be assessed. 40 U.S.C. s 332.

Enforcement of the CWHSSA is also subject to a regulatory regime which applies to sixty statutes prescribing labor standards for federal or federally-assisted contracts. See 29 C.F.R. s 5.1 (1983) (listing the statutes, collectively referred to as "Davis-Bacon Related Acts"). As pertains here, the regulations provide that, Whenever any contractor or subcontractor is found by the Secretary of Labor to be in aggravated or willful violation of [overtime hours and pay requirements of the CWHSSA or] the labor standards of any of the [other Davis-Bacon Related Acts], such contractor or subcontractor or any firm, corporation, partnership, or association in which such contractor or subcontractor has a substantial interest shall be ineligible for a period not to exceed 3 years ... to receive any contracts or subcontracts subject to any of the statutes listed in s 5.1. 29 C.F.R. s 5.12(a)(1) (the "debarment regulations").

Between February and June, 1981, the Department of Labor, through the Wage and Hour Division of its Employment Standards Administration, investigated Janik's performance of the Edson Street and Route 16 contracts. A Division investigator, Patrick Rafter, inspected payroll records and employee time cards which Janik kept for the two contracts. Rafter also interviewed, directly or through questionnaires, approximately 35 past and present Janik employees, 12 or 13 of whom complained about the insufficient overtime wages they had received on the Route 16 and Edson jobs. Based on Rafter's findings, the Division concluded that certain of Janik's employees had not been paid at overtime rates for all such hours worked and that certain of Janik's payroll records had been falsified. On May 9, 1983, the Wage and Hour Division notified Janik Paving and William Janik of its finding and advised them that they would be debarred from future federally-sponsored work. On May 25, 1983, appellants challenged these findings and requested an administrative hearing. See 29 C.F.R. ss 5.11(b), 5.12(b).

More than two years later, on June 12 and 13, 1985, an evidentiary hearing was held before Administrative Law Judge ("ALJ") Edward J. Murty, Jr. The Division's case consisted of the testimony of six of Janik's former employees who had worked on the Edson Street project during the period in question, 1980, as well as the testimony of Rafter, the Division's investigator.[2]

The former employees testified that they had consistently noticed that the hours which they recorded on the employee timecards submitted to the company were greater than those reflected on their pay stubs. All were aided in testifying by contemporaneous personal records which they kept of the hours they reported. Only two of the employees produced their records for the hearing, however, and only the records of one, Timothy Hart, were received in evidence.

Four of the employees further testified that they had consistently logged their hours on Janik's employee timecards in one-half hour increments. Janik's certified payroll records,

---

2. The Wage and Hour Division's allegations with respect to the Route 16 contract were settled prior to the hearing. Janik agreed to pay the affected workers $13,000 in back overtime pay. The Division agreed that Janik's settlement of these charges would not constitute evidence or admission of wrongdoing. Evidence pertaining to Janik's performance on the Route 16 contract was nonetheless received, as it pertained to the debarment issue.

however, showed that payments for overtime hours were made to the nearest quarter-hour....

Rafter testified he had concluded, from interviews with Janik's employees, that in 1980 Janik had a practice "of falsifying its payroll and reducing the hours and overtime situations so that when overtime was paid on reduced hours, straight time pay would result." He explained that many of the 20 to 22 workers who indicated no problems with their overtime pay had not worked for Janik during the period in question or had worked in capacities not subjecting their wages to the CWHSSA. He further testified the difference in time increments used by Janik and its employees in recording hours worked indicated improper recordkeeping. In his experience, Rafter stated, the use of quarter-hour increments could indicate that reported overtime hours were being manipulated to achieve straight time pay rates.

Janik presented three rebuttal witnesses. William Janik denied that his company had a policy of reducing overtime hours but avoided categorically denying that Janik had not reduced overtime hours....

By decision dated May 1, 1986, ALJ Murty found that the evidence conclusively established that Janik had "willfully paid employees straight time for overtime hours worked and willfully falsified their certified payrolls to conceal this practice," agreeing with the Division's charge that Janik had manipulated overtime pay rates by reducing overtime hours by one-third. The ALJ credited the testimony of the Division's six employee witnesses. He compared Timothy Hart's personal records with his pay stubs and found a pattern of reduction of overtime hours which corroborated the others' testimony. The ALJ found that Janik's witnesses "unconvincingly answered" the questions raised.

ALJ Murty ordered Janik to pay a total of $1,123.72 in back wages to nine specified employees. Finding Janik's violations to be willful, he also ordered that the company and its president be debarred. Since there was no evidence that Janik or William Janik had previously violated wage and hour laws, and since Janik had cooperated in settling the Route 16 charges, however, ALJ Murty prescribed a two year debarment period, instead of the maximum three years permitted by regulation.

Following unsuccessful appeals to the Department of Labor's Wage Appeals Board, appellants, on February 5, 1987, commenced this action to enjoin preliminarily the Secretary of Labor, other Department of Labor officials, and the Comptroller General from implementing the debarment order and to annul the debarment on the grounds that it was unsupported by substantial evidence. Judge Elfvin merged the motion for preliminary injunction with an expedited consideration of the merits of appellants' action. Appellees, in turn, withheld appellants' names from the Comptroller General's list of ineligible contractors pending the district court's determination.

On April 16, 1987, Judge Elfvin dismissed the action.... This appeal followed.

In assessing appellants' challenge to the Secretary of Labor's authority to debar violators of the CWHSSA's overtime provisions, we begin with the language of the statute. While expressly setting forth certain civil and criminal consequences attending a violation of overtime pay requirements, described above, the statute nowhere mentions debarment. The CWHSSA does, however, contain two provisions delegating rulemaking authority to the Secretary, only one of which is germane.

Section 330(d) of the CWHSSA states:

Reorganization Plan Numbered 14 of 1950 ... shall be applicable with respect to the provisions of this subchapter, and section 276c of this title, shall be applicable with respect to those contracts and subcontractors referred to therein who are engaged in the performance of contracts subject to the provisions of this subchapter.

Section 276c, adopted as part of the Copeland Anti-Kickback Act, 18 U.S.C. s 876 empowers the Secretary to "make reasonable regulations for contractors and subcontractors" engaged in federally-financed public work projects, 40 U.S.C.§ 276c (1964). Reorganization Plan No. 14 of 1950, 5 U.S.C. Appendix IX, p. 242, in pertinent part states:

> In order to assure coordination of administration and consistency of enforcement of the labor standards of each of the following Acts by the Federal agencies responsible for the administration thereof, the Secretary of Labor shall prescribe appropriate standards, regulations, and procedures, which shall be observed by these agencies, and cause to be made by the Department of Labor such investigations, with respect to compliance with and enforcement of such labor standards, as he deems desirable ...

One of the statutes which the plan initially covered was the Eight Hours Laws, 37 Stat. 137 (1912), as amended, 40 U.S.C. §§ 324–26 (1958), the CWHSSA's predecessor. Like the CWHSSA, this act specifically provided civil and criminal sanctions for violations of overtime work requirements but failed to mention debarment.

* * *

Based on the failure of the statute and legislative history to refer to debarment, appellants conclude that Congress did not mean to allow the Secretary of Labor such power. They argue that debarment constitutes a penalty, which, under well-established law, can be authorized only by specific statutory language. We disagree.

The debarment regulation at issue has been in effect since 1951 and has been relied upon since then by the Secretary in enforcing, not only the provisions of the CWHSSA, but also scores of other Davis-Bacon related acts which do not include their own enforcement mechanisms. While "the mere fact that the [regulation] is of long standing does not relieve us of our responsibility to determine its validity, see SEC v. Sloan, 436 U.S. 103, 98 S.Ct. 1702, 56 L.Ed.2d 148 (1978), it is noteworthy that no court has ever held that the [regulation] is invalid." Touche, Ross & Co. v. S.E.C., 609 F.2d 570, 578 (2d Cir.1979). Indeed, prior to the appellants' challenge to the validity of the Secretary's debarment regulation, the only such reported challenge was in Copper Plumbing & Heating Co. v. Campbell, 290 F.2d 368 (D.C.Cir.1961), where it was rejected.

In Copper Plumbing, the court had before it a challenge to the Secretary of Labor's debarment authority under the Eight Hours Laws. Relying on the Supreme Court's reasoning in Steuart & Bro. v. Bowles, 322 U.S. 398, 64 S.Ct. 1097, 88 L.Ed. 1350 (1944), the Court first determined that debarment was not a penal sanction.

* * *

We agree with the reasoning of Copper Plumbing and believe that it applies with equal force to the Secretary's authority under the current statute, the CWHSSA.

The effective enforcement of a statute often requires the use of coercive means. That a measure, such as debarment, may incidentally punish while it deters a statutory violation does not transform it into a purely punitive sanction. Consequently, we are not persuaded by the appellants' contention that debarment is a penalty and therefore is available as a sanction only when the statute specifically authorizes it.

We understand Steuart & Bro. to teach that if the sanction serves to compel compliance with the statute's substantive goals, then it should not be deemed a "penalty". That test is clearly satisfied here. Debarment of contractors found in willful violation of overtime requirements is as essential to the enforcement of labor standards in federal contracting as suspension was to wartime rationing; both serve to protect the integrity of their respective statutory schemes. Indeed, debarment may be the only realistic means of deterring contractors from engaging in willful overtime pay violations based on a cold weighing of the costs and benefits of noncompliance.

Moreover, the debarment prescribed by regulation is subject to modification. After six months, a debarred contractor may petition the Department of Labor to be removed from the Comptroller General's list of ineligible contractors. In deciding whether to remove the debarred contractor, the Department considers whether there has been a showing of "current responsibility to comply with the [the relevant] labor standards provisions." 29 C.F.R. § 5.12(c). These aspects of the debarment regulation make clear that it was promulgated primarily to enforce the statute, not to administer punishment.

* * *

Appellants further contend that the district court erred in applying an "arbitrary and capricious" rather than the "substantial evidence" standard to review the Secretary's debarment order. They alternatively argue that the order is not supported by substantial evidence. As it is clear to us that there was substantial evidence justifying appellants' debarment, we find it unnecessary to discuss the appropriate scope of judicial review.

"Substantial evidence", according to well-worn definition, is "such relevant evidence as a reasonable mind might accept as adequate to support a conclusion." See, e.g., Local One, Amalgamated Lithographers v. N.L.R.B., 729 F.2d 172, 175 (2d Cir.1984) (quoting Consolidated Edison Co. v. N.L.R.B., 305 U.S. 197, 229, 59 S.Ct. 206, 217, 83 L.Ed. 126 (1938)).

Here, the employee testimony—together with the personal time records of one of them, Timothy Hart, and the expert opinion of investigator Rafter—adequately supported ALJ Murty's conclusion that the Department of Labor had presented a prima facie case that not all of Janik's employees had been properly paid for overtime hours on the contracts in question.

All of the employee-witnesses testified that the overtime hours for which they were paid were consistently lower than those they actually reported. They came to this conclusion, their testimony makes clear, not as the result of an amorphous feeling, but based on contemporaneous records. ALJ Murty expressly found their testimony credible. We see no reason to differ with the ALJ's credibility determinations. The ALJ's credibility determinations were not so "hopelessly incredible" or "flatly contradicted" either by the "law of nature" or "undisputed documentary testimony" as to require being overturned. N.L.R.B. v. American Geri-Care, Inc., 697 F.2d 56, 60 (2d Cir.1982), cert. denied, 461 U.S. 906, 103 S.Ct. 1876, 76 L.Ed.2d 807 (1983).

It is not unusual, given the five year hiatus between appellants' alleged wage violations and the administrative hearing, that the employees' testimony lacked sharpness concerning the specific circumstances under which they worked undercompensated overtime hours or that some of the employees had made prior inconsistent statements concerning whether, or when, they had complained to the company about their pay. Nor, for similar reasons, is it surprising to find that many of the employees could no longer find or produce the original wage and hour records they kept of five year old jobs. Indeed, the Supreme Court, in articulating the burden of proof to which the Department and employees were generally subject in wage-standard violations noted that "[e]mployees seldom keep records themselves" and "even [when] they do, the records may be and frequently are untrustworthy." Anderson v. Mt. Clemens Pottery Co., 328 U.S. 680, 687, 66 S.Ct. 1187, 1192, 90 L.Ed. 1515 (1946).

* * *

In sum, we find no basis for disturbing ALJ Murty's decision to credit the testimony of the Department's witnesses. The former employees' testimony, which is corroborated by personal time records, sufficiently demonstrated the fact of underpayment for overtime hours. Janik's unjustified use of quarter-hour increments in recording overtime sufficed to give rise to a presumption of concealment, adequate, under the Department's regulations, to show a willful violation of overtime requirements necessary for debarment.

Affirmed.

Notes and Questions

1. A skeptic might ask just what this opinion has to do with government contracting. Procedurally, it involved the investigators of the Labor Department's Wages and Hours Division, a Labor Department Administrative Law Judge, the Labor Department Wage Appeals Board, and an appeal to the district court and to the 2d Circuit. That sounds like procedures for employment law. Moreover, the contracts were awarded by state and local authorities. How much does it signify that (1) the Davis-Bacon Acts, including CWHSSA, get implemented through government contract clauses; (2) Janik Paving mainly works on federal construction projects; (3) the contracts are financed federally; and, (4) the remedy is debarment from government contracting?

2. It is often argued that the labor standards statutes impose not only substantive burdens (higher labor costs) on federal contractors but also, unnecessary procedural burdens such as interference in payroll arrangements and added paperwork. What do the facts of this case suggest regarding such arguments?

3. How must Janik Paving's counsel have analyzed the situation in deciding upon settling the Route 16 contract allegations by paying the workers $13,000 in back overtime pay, asking for a hearing on the Edson Street allegations that ended with an order to pay the employees $1,123 in back wages, and litigating the case, including the debarment decision, up to the 2d Circuit? How did the procedural and legal expenditures on both sides compare with the wage remedy? What do contractors think of the sanction of debarment for labor standards violations? In the next reading, the many occasions for contractors to seek waivers, determinations, modifications, and other anticipatory, proper rulings on disputed matters will be indicated. How does a decision like Janik Paving affect contractors' willingness to employ counsel to help go through such procedures?

United States of America, ex rel. Plumbers and Steamfitters Local Union No. 38 et al., v. C. W. Roen Construction co., et al.

No. 97-17204
United States Court of Appeals, Ninth Circuit
183 F.3d 1088
Filed July 13, 1999

Before: SCHROEDER, REINHARDT, and SILVERMAN, Circuit Judges.

Opinion by Judge REINHARDT; Dissent by Judge SILVERMAN.

REINHARDT, Circuit Judge:

In this qui tam action, Plumbers and Steamfitters Local No. 38 alleges that C. W. Roen Construction Company and its president and office manager violated the False Claims Act (FCA), 31 U.S.C. §§ 3729–33, by certifying falsely that the Company had paid the applicable prevailing wage as required by the Davis-Bacon Act and related federal laws, when in fact it had paid its employees at a lower rate. The district court found that because the Department of Labor had not conducted an area practice survey for the area in question, and because the Department's other efforts to establish the prevailing wage were "uncertain," no reasonable juror could find that the defendants acted with the scienter necessary to violate the FCA. The court then granted summary judgment for the defendants. We conclude, however, that an area practice survey is not necessary in all cases to establish the prevailing wage, and that the status of the Department of Labor's determinations did not compel the conclusion that the plaintiffs could under no circumstances prove that the defendants acted with the requisite scienter. Given these determinations, and the presence of complex legal and factual issues that are not resolvable on the current state of the record, we hold that the district court erred in granting summary judgment to the defendants. We therefore reverse and remand for further proceedings.

Background

On September 1, 1994, C.W. Roen Construction Company entered into a construction contract with the City of Santa Rosa, California, to make improvements to the Laguna Wastewater Treatment Plant. (ER 158). The Laguna Plant was a federally funded project, and hence subject to the prevailing wage and reporting requirements set forth in the Davis-Bacon Act, 40 U.S.C. §§ 276a, et seq., and the Copeland Anti-Kickback Act, 40 U.S.C. § 276c. These statutes required Roen to pay its workers prevailing wages, and to submit weekly statements reflecting the wages it paid. See 40 U.S.C. § 276a & 276c. Under federal law, Roen was also required to certify its payments of the applicable wage rates. Under the relevant regulations:

> Each payroll submitted [to the Department of Labor] shall be accompanied by a "Statement of Compliance," signed by the contractor or subcontractor or his or her agent who pays or supervises the payment of persons employed under the contract and shall certify the following:
>
> ...
>
> (3) That each laborer or mechanic has been paid not less than the applicable wage rates....

29 CFR § 5.5(a)(3)(ii)(B). The regulations also dictate that:

> (D) The falsification of any of the above certifications may subject the contractor or subcontractor to civil or criminal prosecution under ... section 231 of title 31 of the United States Code [The False Claims Act].

29 C.F.R. § 5.5(a)(3)(ii)(D). It is undisputed that Roen did submit the certifications as required by federal law. The plaintiffs allege, however, that Roen's certifications amounted to false statements because the Company paid employees performing certain types of work less than the prevailing wage rate.

At issue in this case is the classification and payment of workers who performed certain types of piping work on the Laguna project (namely "mechanical, pressure, process, soil, waste, vent, potable, and non-potable water piping" (Complaint ¶ 14, ER 4)) between August 15, 1994 and February 1997. Roen classified workers who performed this piping work as Laborers, and paid them at the Laborer wage rate. It then certified that it was paying these workers the appropriate wage rates under Davis-Bacon. The plaintiffs claim that Roen thereby misclassified these workers; according to the plaintiffs, all workers who perform this type of piping work on wastewater treatment plants in Northern California must, under Davis-Bacon, be classified as Plumbers & Steamfitters and paid at the higher

Plumbers & Steamfitters wage rate. The plaintiffs argue that as a result of misclassifying and underpaying the workers, Roen violated the FCA.

The plaintiffs point out that in May 1992, the United Association of Journeymen and Apprentices of the Plumbing and Pipe Fitting Industry, AFL-CIO, Pipe Trades District Council No. 51(UA) and the Northern California District Council of Laborers signed a jurisdictional agreement (1992 Agreement) that resolved the classification of piping workers on Northern California water treatment plant projects. According to the 1992 Agreement:

> [i]n the construction of water treatment plants, wastewater (i.e., sewage) treatment plants, water reclamation plants, and all pumping facilities related to such plants, for work performed both inside and outside of buildings, the prevailing rate of per diem wages established for Plumber-Steamfitter-Pipefitter is paid to those employees who perform all piping work of every description and material (except as noted in paragraph 2), including but not limited to ... all process piping, soil, waste, vent, ... domestic and process water piping, ... all mechanical process equipment.

(ER 4). Paragraph 2 of the 1992 Agreement states that "[t]he prevailing rate of per diem wages established for Laborers is paid to those employees who, on the facilities described above, perform the installation of non-pressurized surface and storm drain piping...." (ER 40). That is, according to the 1992 Agreement, the workers who performed the piping work at issue in this case (again, "mechanical, pressure, process, soil, waste, vent, potable, and non-potable water piping" (Complaint ¶ 14, ER 4)) were classified as Plumber-Steamfitter-Pipefitters.

In January 1994, the District Director of the U.S. Department of Labor's Wage and Hour Division, Frank Conte, determined that the 1992 Agreement between the Plumbers and the Laborers established the appropriate classifications and wages for work done on water treatment plants in Northern California. In a letter to John Davis, counsel for the Plumbers and Steamfitters Local 38, the District Director wrote that:

> As of September, 1992, the agreement [between Northern California District Council of Laborers and Pipe Trades District Council No. 51] establishes the prevailing practice in Northern California for the construction of water treatment plants, wastewater treatment plants, water reclamation plants and all pumping facilities related to such plants in Northern California. For contracts for the construction of such plants awarded after September, 1992 and subject to Davis-Bacon and Related Acts the Wage and Hour Division will require the payment of prevailing wages in accordance with the agreement. (ER 39). In July 1994, plaintiff sent a copy of the District Director's 1994 letter to Roen Construction, putting Roen on notice of the Wage and Hour Division's determination that the relevant wage rate and job classifications would be derived from the 1992 Agreement. (ER 36–40).

In June 1994, the business manager of the Laborers District Council sent a letter to the UA purporting to terminate the 1992 Agreement that formed the basis of the original Conte letter. (ER 43). The UA, however, refused to accept the termination of the Agreement, and as far as the rather sparse record before us reflects, the Laborers took no further action to validate its position. In any event, in March 1996, nearly two years after the purported termination of the Agreement, Conte, along with Richard Cheung, a Labor Department Regional Wage Specialist, again wrote to Mr. Davis and reconfirmed the Department's earlier conclusion that the relevant wage classifications were those set forth in the Agreement. In this letter, the District Director stated:

The Wage and Hour Division has determined that the Agreement between Northern California District Council of Laborers and Pipe Trades District Council No. 51 … reflects a longstanding prevailing practice. The Department of Labor will therefore accept this Agreement as reflecting the prevailing practice.

Accordingly, for contracts for the construction of such plants awarded after September, 1992 and subject to the Davis-Bacon and Related Acts, the Wage and Hour Division will require the payment of prevailing wages in accordance with the Agreement.

(ER 24). It does not appear that the Labor Department's 1996 letter was ever sent to Roen.

In March 1997, following the time period charged in the plaintiffs' False Claims Act complaint, the Labor Department sent Davis another letter. In this letter, signed by John Fraser, the Acting Administrator of the Wage and Hour Division, the Department stated that it had "reexamined [its] position regarding Wage and Hour Division's ability to enforce the 1992 jurisdictional agreement." (ER 27). The letter concluded that the Department was unable to enforce that agreement because "there are indications that the written agreement was not followed." (ER 27). In such circumstances, the letter stated, an area practice survey is required to determine the actual practice before classifications may be enforced. It is undisputed that no such area practice survey has been completed, and the record suggests that the Department of Labor has now decided not to conduct such a survey.

Analysis

We first address a threshold question. In granting the defendants' motion for summary judgment, the district court relied on the sole ground that "no reasonable juror could find that defendants' scienter rose to the level required by the False Claims Act." (ER 229). The court appears to have assumed, without deciding, that the FCA extends to false claims that an employer has paid the prevailing wage required by the Davis-Bacon Act. The district judge did comment, however, that "[o]ther courts have been hesitant to hear FCA claims based on the alleged misclassification of workers because of the Davis-Bacon Act's regulatory scheme," suggesting that the FCA might, in fact, not cover claims such as the one before us today. (ER 229; citing United States ex rel. I.B.E.W., AFL-CIO, Local 217 v. G.E. Chen Construction, Inc., 954 F.Supp. 195 (N.D. Cal.1997); United States ex rel. Plumbers and Steamfitters Local Union 342 v. Dan Caputo Co., 1996 WL 400967 (N.D.Cal.1996); United States ex rel. Windsor v. DynCorp. Inc., 895 F.Supp. 844 (E.D. Va.1995)). Contrary to such suggestion, the FCA does indeed extend to false statements regarding the payment of prevailing wages.

As we noted in United States ex rel. Hopper v. Anton, 91 F.3d 1261, 1266 (9th Cir.1996), "the archetypal qui tam FCA action is filed by an insider at a private company who discovers his employer has overcharged under a government contract." It is also true, however, that FCA actions may be sustained under different theories of liability, including "false certification." See id. (citing United States v. Gibbs, 568 F.2d 347 (3d Cir.1977)). As we held in Anton, "[i]t is the false certification of compliance which creates liability when certification is a prerequisite to obtaining a government benefit." Id. (emphasis in original).

As shown above, in order to qualify for federal construction projects subject to Davis-Bacon and related Acts, contractors must "certify" that "each laborer or mechanic has been paid not less than the applicable wage rates." 29 CFR § 5.5(a)(3)(B)(3). Under Anton, therefore, if a contractor submits a false certification pursuant to this requirement he may be liable under the FCA. Moreover, the regulations governing federal construction contracts make this perfectly clear. Those regulations state explicitly that "[t]he falsification of any [such] certification[ ] may subject the contractor to civil … prosecution under …

section 231 of title 31 of the United States Code [The False Claims Act]." 29 CFR § 5.5(a)(3)(D).

We have no doubt, therefore, that a false certification that workers have been paid at the legally required wage rate may give rise to liability under the FCA. If, as the Plumbers allege, Roen and its president and office manager submitted such false certifications, it may be liable under the False Claims Act. See Anton, 91 F.3d at 1266.

We turn now to the question of scienter. The False Claims Act imposes liability only on those who "knowingly" present a "false or fraudulent claim" to the government. See 31 U.S.C. § 3729(a)(1). Mere negligence and "innocent mistakes]" are not sufficient to establish liability under the FCA. United States ex rel. Hochman v. Nackman, 145 F.3d 1069, 1073 (9th Cir.1998). While some of our cases may contain extraneous comments that might be read out of context to suggest that the FCA requires an intentional lie to trigger liability, those cases almost invariably reiterate the controlling statutory language that is determinative of their outcome. As the FCA provides, to rise to the level of "knowing" presentation, all that is required is that the party:

(1) has actual knowledge of the information;

(2) acts in deliberate ignorance of the truth or falsity of the information; or

(3) acts in reckless disregard of the truth or falsity of the information,

and no proof of specific intent to defraud is required.

31 U.S.C. § 3729(b). We have repeatedly emphasized this statutory language when describing the scienter requirement under the FCA. See, e.g., Hagood v. Sonoma County Water Agency, 81 F.3d 1465, 1478 (9th Cir.1996); Wang v. FMC Corp., 975 F.2d 1412, 1420 (9th Cir.1992); United States ex rel. Hagood v. Sonoma County Water Agency, 929 F.2d 1416, 1421 (9th Cir.1991). Thus, in order to be liable for an FCA violation, Roen's conduct need only qualify under one of the alternative statutory standards, such as "deliberate ignorance" or "reckless disregard".

The district court granted summary judgment to the defendants for two reasons. As the district court held:

> [The plaintiffs' claim] fails due to the FCA's scienter requirement: plaintiffs are unable to show that defendants knew of an intentional misclassification in their payroll records. This failure is inevitable given the uncertainty surrounding the Department of Labor's efforts to establish the classification relevant to this case and the undisputed fact that the Wage and Hour Division of the Department of Labor has not yet performed an area practice survey in Sonoma County to determine the actual classification practices there.

(ER 228). That is, the district court found summary judgment to be appropriate because (1) the Department of Labor had not conducted an area practice survey, and (2) the Department's other efforts to establish the prevailing wage were "uncertain." We disagree as to both reasons.

Under Davis-Bacon, employers are required to pay prevailing wages to all employees on covered federal construction projects. The wage rate an employer must pay is determined in two steps: first, the employer must ascertain an employee's proper job classification; second, the employer must ascertain the prevailing wage rate for that job classification. By matching the rate to the classification, the appropriate wage is derived. Although area practice surveys are one way in which wage classifications may be established, they are not the only way. Over twenty years ago, the Labor Department's Wage Appeals Board decided Matter of Fry Bros. Corp., 123 WAB No. 76-6, 1977 CCH Wages-Hours Administrative Rulings ¶ 31,113 at 42,757 (June 14, 1977). In Fry Brothers, the Department of Labor withheld funds from the contractor for underpayment of prevailing wages based on the misclassification of carpenters as laborers. Id. at 42,758. The Assistant Secretary of the Employment Standards Administration upheld the withholding of funds. Because the prevailing wage determinations that had been issued by the Department of Labor reflected union negotiated rates, the Secretary concluded that job classifications for the disputed project would be based correspondingly on the union negotiated agreements. The contractor objected to this method of establishing prevailing job classifications, and thus the wage rate applicable to its employees. The Wage Appeals Board, however, affirmed the Secretary's decision. The Board held that where the Department determines that the prevailing wage rate for an area derives from a collectively bargaining agreement, then the job classifications for that area must also be derived from that agreement. As the Board wrote:

> When the Department of Labor determines that the prevailing wage for a particular craft derives from experience under negotiated agreements, the Labor Department has to see to it that the wage determinations carry along with them as fairly and fully as may be practicable, the classifications of work according to job content upon which the wage rates are based.

Id. at 42,762.

There are two elements of the Fry Brothers decision relevant to the case before us. First, the Wage Appeals Board made clear that prevailing wage rates may be derived from collective bargaining agreements, not just from an area practice survey conducted by the Labor Department. Second, where the Department determines that prevailing wages are established by a collectively bargained agreement, the job classifications for the project or area at issue are also established by that agreement. We find both elements of two-decades old rule of Fry Brothers to be eminently reasonable. As the Wage Appeals Board explained:

> If a construction contractor who is not bound by classifications of work at which the majority of employees in the area are working is free to classify or reclassify, grade or subgrade traditional craft work as he wishes, such a contractor can, with respect to wage rates, take almost any job away from the group of contractors and the employees who work for them who have established the locality wage standard. There will be little left to the Davis-Bacon Act.

Fry Brothers at 42,762. In order to ensure that this evisceration of Davis-Bacon does not occur whenever the Department of Labor decides not to conduct an area practice survey, we adopt the rule of Fry Brothers here. Accordingly, we hold that an area practice survey is not a prerequisite to the determination of prevailing wage rates or job classifications.

Second, contrary to the district court's conclusion, there was nothing uncertain about the Department's efforts to establish the relevant wage classifications, at least during the period of time that Roen was making its wage certifications. The District Director of the Labor Department's Wage and Hour Division, in both his 1994 and 1996 letters to Plumber's counsel, made explicit that the 1992 Agreement established the prevailing practices for water treatment plants in Northern California. (ER 39). The letters could not have been clearer. The 1994 letter, for example, stated that "As of September, 1992, the agreement establishes the prevailing practice for Northern California for the construction of water treatment plants.... For contracts for the construction of such plants awarded after September 1992 and subject to Davis-Bacon and Related Acts the Wage and Hour Division will require the payment of prevailing wages in accordance with the [1992] agreement." (ER 39). The 1996 letter simply reconfirmed the 1994 letter. Moreover, although the letters were clear enough in themselves, the District Director also attached to his letters copies of the paragraphs of the 1992 Agreement that specified the relevant job classifications for piping work on water treatment facilities. The inclusion of these attachments enunciated the point that, according to the Wage and Hour Division, the relevant job classifications were established by the 1992 Agreement.

* * *

If Roen believed that the Laborers' attempted recission of the Agreement affected the Department's classifications during the period covered by the complaint, it could have sought clarification. Yet Roen, without making any effort to obtain such clarification, certified that the Laborer's rate was the prevailing wage and that it had paid that wage. Roen does not explain the theory under which it certified that the Laborer's rate constituted the prevailing wage rate—even Roen acknowledges that the Department of Labor is the sole authority responsible for determining prevailing wages, (Appellee's Brief at 25), and the DOL's letter had adopted a different and higher rate. This suggests that Roen's certification may well have risen at least to the level of "deliberate ignorance" or "reckless disregard."

We express no view on any other ground on which summary judgment might be based, or rejected. We may reverse an order granting summary judgment where the district court record " 'has not been sufficiently developed to allow the court to make a fully informed decision on particularly difficult and far reaching issues.' " Anderson v. Hodel, 899 F.2d 766, 770 (9th Cir.1990) (quoting William Schwarzer, Summary Judgment Under the Federal Rules: Defining Genuine Issues of Material Fact, 99 F.R.D. 465, 475 (1984)). We have held, moreover, that in certain cases "summary judgment may be inapposite because the legal issue is so complex, difficult, or insufficiently highlighted that further factual elucidation is essential for its prudently considered resolution." Eby v. Reb Realty, Inc., 495 F.2d 646, 649 (9th Cir.1974); see also Tovar v. United States Postal Serv., 3 F.3d 1271, 1278–79 (9th Cir.1993). The case before us fits this bill. Questions regarding the precise manner in which the Department may or must determine prevailing wage rates and job classifications, the effect of the Department's post-hoc repudiation of earlier wage-rate determinations on the question of the falsity of previously submitted wage-rate certifications, the extent to which contractors may be deemed to have knowledge of the Department's actions, the type of certification that is appropriate if the contractor contends that no prevailing wage exists or that the classification issue remains unresolved, and the various other questions the resolution of which may be required before this case can be finally resolved are both difficult and insufficiently developed on the current record to allow for summary judgment. To this point, neither the district court nor the parties have devoted sufficient attention to the elucidation and resolution of these issues to permit us to deem a grant of summary judgment appropriate.

The district court erred in concluding that because no area survey had been conducted and because the Department's other efforts to establish the relevant classifications were uncertain, summary judgment was proper. (ER 229). Further, development of numerous legal and factual issues is necessary before this case may be decided. We therefore reverse the district court's grant of summary judgment and remand for further proceedings not inconsistent with this opinion.

REVERSED AND REMANDED.

SILVERMAN, Circuit Judge, dissenting:

The majority's discourse on labor law is interesting, scholarly, probably correct, but largely beside the point. This is a False Claims Act case. The point is not whether an area practice survey is the only way to establish prevailing wages. The point is that the undisputed facts did not show that Roen's certifications, even if incorrect, were made with an intent to deceive as required by the FCA.

"For a qui tam action to survive summary judgment, the relator must produce sufficient evidence to support an inference of *knowing fraud*." United States ex rel. Hopper v. Anton, 91 F.3d 1261, 1267 (emphasis added) (quoting United States ex rel. Anderson v. Northern Telecom, Inc., 52 F.3d 810, 815 (9th Cir.1995)). As we said in Wang v. FMC Corp., 975 F.2d 1412, 1421 (9th Cir.1992):

> The weakest account of the act's "requisite intent" is the "knowing presentation of what is known to be false." Citing Hagood, supra, 929 F.2d at 1421. The phrase "known to be false" in that sentence does not mean "scientifically untrue"; it means "a lie."

This is especially true in a False Claims Act case premised on a false certification. In Hopper, we specifically held, "For a certified statement to be 'false' under the Act, it must be an intentional, palpable lie." Hopper, 91 F.3d at 1267. The majority argues that these principles are "extraneous comments" that have been "read out of context to suggest that the FCA requires an intentional lie to trigger liability, ..." With all due respect, if anything is out of context, it is the attempt to apply the False Claims Act to the resolution of a jurisdictional dispute between two unions, especially when one of the unions is not even a party to the lawsuit.

It is undisputed that at the time Roen submitted its first certification, both the Laborers and the Plumbers claimed jurisdiction over the piping work at the Laguna project. Two years earlier, prior to the commencement of the job, the Plumbers and the Laborers had a jurisdictional agreement regarding the type of work in issue. The two unions had agreed that it was Plumbers' work. It is undisputed that before Roen ever filed its first allegedly fraudulent certification, the Laborers rescinded the agreement and claimed the work as their own. The majority makes much of the 1994 letter from the Department of Labor. The problem with the letter is that it is specifically premised on the existence of the Plumbers-Laborers agreement, the very agreement that the Laborers rescinded before the Laguna job began.

Perhaps the Laborers' attempted recission of the agreement was ineffective. Perhaps Roen could have sought a clarification. Perhaps Roen was governed by the Department of Labor's letter regardless of the status of the jurisdictional dispute between the Plumbers and the Laborers. Perhaps an area practice survey is not a prerequisite to the determination of prevailing wages. Perhaps, in other words, Roen's certifications were mistaken. All that may be true, but in a False Claims Act case, that's not enough. To survive Roen's summary judgment motion, the Plumbers also had to show that Roen acted with an intent to deceive. In my view, Judge Illston got it exactly right when she held that in light of the then-existing jurisdictional war between the two unions, "[The Plumbers] are unable to show that [Roen] knew of an intentional misclassification in their payroll records." I would affirm.

Notes and Questions

1. Under the Davis-Bacon Act, laborers under a domestic construction contract receive no less than the minimum wage determined by the Secretary of Labor to be the prevailing wage rate for their particular category. 29 C.F.R. §1.3 provides that the Secretary may base these rates on information submitted voluntarily, field surveys, or formal hearings. Prevailing wages are based on the type of construction and the specific geographi-

cal area where performed. (FAR 22.404-1(a)). The wage determination also includes classification of laborers by the work they perform.

An aid to this process is the concept of "area practice". Wage rates for workers performing the same type of work on a similar project within a close geographic region are considered the "area practice" rates, and are to be used in determining wages in a contract. Where a geographic region surrounding the site of a government construction contract lacks a similar project for comparison, then "area practice" is absent and should not be substituted by extending the geographic area to include such a project. Comp. Gen. B-153051, 1964 CPD ¶ 8, 43 Comp. Gen. 623 (Contracting Officer erred in using a distant project in determining wage rates for ironworkers for a bridge construction contract).

Cases and contract appeals have generally found the Secretary's determination to be non-reviewable. *U. S. v. Binghamton Const.* Co., 347 U.S. 171 (1954); *Jack Picoult*, GSBCA 2923, 69-2 BCA ¶ 7845; *American Fed'n. of Labor-Congress of Indus. Org., Bldg., and Const. Trades Dept.*, B-211189, Apr. 12,1983, 83-1 CPD § 386; *Woodington Corp.*, ASBCA No. 34053, 87-3 BCA ¶ 19,957. However, there is jurisdiction by the contract appeals boards to review a wage rate determination where it may have an effect on the contractual rights of the party. *Inter-Con Security Sys., Inc.*, ASBCA No. 46251, 95-1 BCA ¶ 27,424). Further information on these issues can be found in the casebook excerpt from the Judge Advocate General's deskbook section on Selected Labor Standards.

2. Does applying the False Claims Act increase or decrease the significance of the Department of Labor's regulatory system? It does make the tribunal a federal court, rather than an administrative adjudicator within the Department. On the other hand, ratcheting up the penalties makes it that much more important for contractors to have the defense handy that they have made efforts to stay in compliance—such as by working with the Department of Labor's regulatory system.

3. The *Janik Paving* case used the contractor's falsification of records as a reason for debarment. This case uses the contractor's false certification as a reason for False Claims Act liability. Such intensification of penalties by targeting not just the contractor's (arguably good faith) noncompliance but the contractor's falsifications is controversial. On the one hand, market pressures might well lead to a crumbling of the whole labor standard system in the absence of intensified penalties for falsification, since the worst contractor practices, by allowing the lowest bids, would drive out any better ones. On the other hand, contractors argue that labor standards are collateral (if not opposed) to the primary goal of government contracting anyway, the obtaining by the government of goods and services of adequate quality at low price, so contractors should not be penalized so heavily when they accomplish the primary goal and fall short only on collateral ones.

4. Why have labor standard statutes and regulations largely endured since the 1930s despite contractor criticism, which from the 1980s on has taken the form of intense lobbying in Congress to create exceptions to the Davis-Bacon Act for defense contracting? Keep in mind the delicate regional balance involved in the original enactment of labor standards in the 1930s and not so obsolete. Regions and even local areas differ, in how unionized they are, and in their wage levels. Labor standard defenders argue that these statutes keep the federal government from becoming an anti-union force (for immobile work, locally; for movable work, nationally) by transferring work from unionized, high-wage workforces to non-unionized low-wage ones. Does the debate on this issue basically follow the debate on such issues as whether to raise national minimum wages, or are there special aspects having to do with government contracting?

C. Labor Policy for Contractors

Presidents have considerable power to promote general policies by making these a condition on government contracting. Policies may apply, not merely to the work specifically on government contracts, but to the firms that do any government contracting, even a small part of their overall business activity. In other words, the policies reach most of the economy. In this way, Presidents can act on a policy subject before Congress is ready to, or go beyond what Congress would do.

A diverse set of such policies have received Presidential implementation over the years, ranging from anti-discrimination to inflation control. In recent decades, the most important policies have concerned labor. For example, President Bush promulgated a rule requiring contractors and subcontractors to use the E-Verify system to check their employees are eligible to work in the United States. Earlier, President Bush promulgated an Executive Order requiring federal contractors to notify employees that they were not required to join a union to keep their jobs. The D.C. Circuit upheld the executive Order. *UAW-Labor Employment and Training Corp. v. Chao*, 325 F.3d 360 (D.C. Cir. 2003). However, Presidents cannot do whatever they want, as shown by the case of *Chamber of Commerce v. Reich*.

For further discussions of the subject of this subchapter, see: Lindsay L. Chichester, Gregory P. Adams, *The State Of E-Verify: What Every Employer Should Know*, 56 Fed. Law. 50 (July 2009); Michael H. LeRoy, *Presidential Regulation of Private Employment: Constitutionality of Executive Order 12,954 Debarment of Contractors Who Hire Permanent Striker Replacements*, 37 B.C. L. Rev. 229 (1996); Charles Thomas Kimmett, Note, *Permanent Replacements, Presidential Power, and Politics: Judicial Overreaching in Chamber of Commerce v. Reich*, 106 Yale L.J. 811 (1996); Gordon M. Clay, Comment, *Executive (Ab)Use of the Procurement Power: Chamber of Commerce v. Reich*, 84 Geo. L.J. 2573 (1996).

Chamber of Commerce of the United States, et al., Appellants, v. Robert B. Reich, Secretary, United States Department of Labor, Appellee

No. 95-5242. United States Court of Appeals, District of Columbia Circuit
74 F.3d 1322. Decided Feb. 2, 1996

Before: SILBERMAN, SENTELLE, and RANDOLPH, Circuit Judges. Opinion for the Court filed by Circuit Judge SILBERMAN.

SILBERMAN, Circuit Judge:

Appellants challenge President Clinton's Executive Order barring the federal government from contracting with employers who hire permanent replacements during a lawful strike. The district court determined that appellants' challenge is not judicially reviewable and, in any event, the Order is legal. We conclude that judicial review is available and that the Order conflicts with the National Labor Relations Act, and therefore we reverse.

I.

President Clinton issued Executive Order No. 12,954, 60 Fed.Reg. 13,023 (1995), on March 8, 1995, pursuant to his authority under the Federal Property and Administrative Services Act, 40 U.S.C. § 471 et seq. (the Procurement Act), which declares:

It is the policy of the executive branch in procuring goods and services that, to ensure the economical and efficient administration and completion of Federal Government contracts, contracting agencies shall not contract with employers that permanently replace lawfully striking employees.

Order at 13,023, § 1. The Order applies to all government contracts over $100,000. In 1994, federal procurement exceeded $400 billion and constituted approximately 6.5% of the gross domestic product. See STATISTICAL ABSTRACT OF THE UNITED STATES 451 (115th ed. 1995). As of 1993, approximately 26 million workers, 22% of the labor force, were employed by federal contractors and subcontractors. GENERAL ACCOUNTING OFFICE, REPORT TO SENATOR PAUL SIMON, WORKER PROTECTION: FEDERAL CONTRACTORS AND VIOLATIONS OF LABOR LAW (Oct. 1995) (GAO REPORT).

The Order explains that the "balance" between allowing businesses to operate during a strike and preserving worker rights is disrupted when an employer hires permanent replacements during a strike. "It has been found" that the hiring of permanent replacements results in longer strikes, can change a "limited dispute into a broader, more contentious struggle," and results in the loss to the employer of the "accumulated knowledge, experience, skill, and expertise" of the striking workers. These consequences adversely affect federal contractors' ability to supply high quality and reliable goods and services.

The Secretary of Labor is charged with implementing and enforcing the Order. If the Secretary finds that a contractor has permanently replaced lawfully striking workers, the Secretary "may make a finding that it is appropriate to terminate the contract for convenience" unless the head of the contracting agency objects. The Secretary is also to debar contractors that have permanently replaced striking workers from future government contracts unless the "labor dispute precipitating the permanent replacement of lawfully striking workers has been resolved, as determined by the Secretary" or the head of the agency determines that there is a compelling reason to lift the debarment. A debarment "normally will be limited to those organizational units of a Federal contractor that the Secretary finds to have permanently replaced lawfully striking workers."

On May 25, Secretary Reich issued final implementing regulations. See Permanent Replacement of Lawfully Striking Employees by Federal Contractors, 60 Fed.Reg. 27,856 (1995)....

Prior to the President's Executive Order, there were numerous legislative attempts to restrict the use of permanent replacements. In 1993 the Workplace Fairness Act was introduced in the Senate, see S. 55, 103d Cong., 1st Sess., which would have made the use of permanent replacements an unfair labor practice. Supporters similarly argued that the use of permanent replacements upsets the "balance" between labor and management and leads to lower productivity. See S.REP. NO. 110, 103d Cong., 1st Sess. 20–25 (1993). It failed to pass.

Appellants, the Chamber of Commerce, American Trucking Associations, Inc., Labor Policy Association, National Association of Manufacturers, Bridgestone/Firestone, Inc., and Mosler Inc., filed suit on March 15, prior to the Secretary's promulgation of the regulations, seeking declaratory and injunctive relief against the Secretary of Labor's enforcement of the Executive Order. They alleged that the Order is contrary to the National Labor Relations Act, 29 U.S.C. § 151 et seq. (NLRA), the Procurement Act and the Constitution. On expedited appeal we reversed the district court's determination that appellants' claims were not ripe. See Chamber of Commerce v. Reich, 57 F.3d 1099 (D.C.Cir.1995). The district court, on remand, again ruled in favor of the government. It held that appellants' statutory claim that the Executive Order violated the NLRA is not judicially reviewable since the Procurement Act vests broad discretionary authority in the President just as did the statute at issue in Dalton v. Specter, 511 U.S. 462, 114 S.Ct. 1719, 128 L.Ed.2d 497 (1994), in which the Supreme Court refused to review a claim that the President had abused his statutory discretion. Appellants' constitutional claim similarly was held to be unreviewable as nothing more than an argument that the President abused his statutory powers. The district court, in the alternative, rejected appellants' statutory claim on the merits, reasoning that under the Executive Order the government was acting in a proprietary capacity and, therefore, NLRA pre-emption was inapplicable. The court stressed that the President's interpretation of the Procurement Act as authorizing the Order was entitled to Chevron-like deference and was reasonable because it furthered the statutory values of "economy" and "efficiency" (the government does not attempt to defend on appeal the court's deference to the President's interpretation). The court also noted that the government was merely exercising an option "available" to a private contractor.

* * *

III.

Appellants' most powerful argument on the merits, it strikes us, is their claim that the Executive Order is in conflict with the NLRA. If that is so, it is unnecessary to decide whether, in the absence of the NLRA, the President would be authorized (with or without appropriate findings) under the Procurement Act and the Constitution to issue the Executive Order. It is, in that regard, undisputed that the NLRA preserves to employers the right to permanently replace economic strikers as an offset to the employees' right to strike. Almost 60 years ago, the Supreme Court explained that an employer retained the right "to protect and continue his business by supplying places left vacant by strikers. And he is not bound to discharge those hired to fill the places of strikers, upon the election of the latter to resume their employment, in order to create places for them." NLRB v. Mackay Radio & Tel. Co., 304 U.S. 333, 345–46, 58 S.Ct. 904, 910–11, 82 L.Ed. 1381 (1938). The Court has repeatedly approved and reaffirmed Mackay Radio....

The government would have us look at the case somewhat differently. Although nothing in the Procurement Act, passed in 1949 long after the original version of the NLRA, addresses labor relations — let alone the specific issue of replacement of strikers — the government, as we have noted, emphasizes the broad discretion that statute bestows on the President to set procurement policy for the entire government. Presidents have sought to affect, inter alia, the private employment practices of government contractors under that authority by issuing Executive Orders designed to ensure equal employment opportunities, see E.O. 11,246, 3 C.F.R. 339 (1964–65 Compilation) (1965); E.O. 11,141, 3 C.F.R. 179 (1964–65 Compilation), reprinted in 5 U.S.C. § 3301 Note (1976); E.O. 11,114, 3 C.F.R. 774 (1959–63 Compilation) (1963); E.O. 10,925, 3 C.F.R. 448 (1959–63 Compilation) (1961); E.O. 10,557, 3 C.F.R. 203 (1954–58 Compilation) (1954); E.O. 10,479, 3 C.F.R. 961 (1949–53 Compilation) (1953), and to limit the size of wage increases, see E.O. 12,092, 43 Fed.Reg. 51,375 (1978). These Orders were sustained in courts of appeals against attacks that asserted, inter alia, that the President exceeded his authority under the Procurement Act. See Contractors Ass'n of Eastern Pennsylvania v. Secretary of Labor, 442 F.2d 159 (3d Cir.), cert. denied sub nom. Contractors Ass'n of Eastern Pennsylvania v. Hodgson, 404 U.S. 854, 92 S.Ct. 98, 30 L.Ed.2d 95 (1971); Kahn, 618 F.2d 784. The government calls our attention to two Executive Orders issued by President Bush that actually dealt with matters covered by the NLRA. One of those barred government contractors from signing pre-hire agreements expressly permitted under the construction industry proviso to § 8(e) of the NLRA, see E.O. 12,818, 57 Fed.Reg. 48,713 (1992), and another required gov-

ernment contractors to post notices informing their employees that they could not be required to join or remain a member of a union, see E.O. 12,800, 57 Fed.Reg. 12,985 (1992).
(Neither of these orders provoked litigation so no court passed on their legality.)

Accordingly, the government suggests that if the authority to issue the Executive Order
can be found in the broad reaches of the Procurement Act—the later statute—that is the
end of the matter. The government explains "[t]here can be no conflict between the President's legitimate exercise of authority under the Procurement Act and [the NLRA rights]
relied on by appellants." The implication of this argument, if we understand it correctly,
is that if there is tension, or perhaps even conflict, between the two statutes, the Procurement Act trumps the NLRA. But the government's argument runs against the canon of
statutory construction: "[t]he cardinal rule ... that repeals by implication are not favored."
Traynor v. Turnage, 485 U.S. 535, 547, 108 S.Ct. 1372, 1381, 99 L.Ed.2d 618 (1988) (quoting Morton v. Mancari, 417 U.S. 535, 549–50, 94 S.Ct. 2474, 2482, 41 L.Ed.2d 290 (1974)).
The later statute displaces the first only when the statute "expressly contradict[s] the original act" or if such a construction "is absolutely necessary ... in order that [the] words [of
the later statute] shall have any meaning at all." Id. at 548, 94 S.Ct. at 2481 (quoting
Radzanower v. Touche Ross & Co., 426 U.S. 148, 153, 96 S.Ct. 1989, 1992, 48 L.Ed.2d 540
(1976)); see also Wood v. United States, 41 U.S. (16 Pet.) 342, 363, 10 L.Ed. 987 (1842)
(there should be a "manifest and total repugnancy in the provisions, to lead to the conclusion
that the [more recent laws] abrogated, and were designed to abrogate the [prior laws].").
Furthermore, the Supreme Court has emphasized that "[w]here there is no clear intention otherwise, a specific statute will not be controlled or nullified by a general one...."
Crawford Fitting Co. v. J.T. Gibbons, Inc., 482 U.S. 437, 445, 107 S.Ct. 2494, 2499, 96 L.Ed.2d
385 (1987) (quoting Radzanower, 426 U.S. at 153, 96 S.Ct. at 1992) (emphasis added in Crawford Fitting); see also Green v. Bock Laundry Mach. Co., 490 U.S. 504, 524, 109 S.Ct. 1981,
1992, 104 L.Ed.2d 557 (1989). The Procurement Act was designed to address broad concerns quite different from the more focused question of the appropriate balance of power
between management and labor in collective bargaining. The text of the Procurement Act
and its legislative history indicate that Congress was troubled by the absence of central
management that could coordinate the entire government's procurement activities in an
efficient and economical manner. The legislative history is replete with references for the
need to have an "efficient, businesslike system of property management." S.REP. NO. 475,
81st Cong., 1st Sess. 1 (1949); see also H.R.REP. NO. 670, 81st Cong. 1st Sess. 2 (1949).

The President's authority to pursue "efficient and economic" procurement, see 40 U.S.C.
§ 486(a), to be sure, has been interpreted to permit such broad ranging Executive Orders
as 11,246 and 12,092, respectively guaranteeing equal employment opportunities, and restricting wage increases on the part of government contractors—measures which certainly reach beyond any narrow concept of efficiency and economy in procurement. But
in those cases, the Third Circuit and this court did not perceive any conflict with another
federal statute. Here, undeniably there is some tension between the President's Executive
Order and the NLRA. To determine whether that tension constitutes unacceptable conflict we look to the extensive body of Supreme Court cases that mark out the boundaries
of the field occupied by the NLRA. Since the progenitors of these cases originally arose
in the context of state actions that were thought to interfere with the federal statute, they
are referred to collectively as establishing the NLRA "pre-emption doctrine." The principles developed, however, have been applied equally to federal governmental behavior that
is thought similarly to encroach into the NLRA's regulatory territory.

The Supreme Court has crafted two different types of NLRA pre-emption. Metropolitan Life Ins. Co. v. Massachusetts, 471 U.S. 724, 748, 105 S.Ct. 2380, 2393, 85 L.Ed.2d 728

(1985). Garmon pre-emption "forbids state and local regulation of activities that are 'protected by §7 of the [NLRA], or constitute an unfair labor practice under §8.' " Building & Constr. Trades Council v. Associated Builders & Contractors of Massachusetts/Rhode Island, 507 U.S. 218, 224, 113 S.Ct. 1190, 1194, 122 L.Ed.2d 565 (1993) (Boston Harbor)....

Machinists pre-emption, on the other hand, prohibits regulation of areas that Congress intended to be left "unregulated and to be controlled by the free play of economic forces." Lodge 76, International Ass'n of Machinists & Aerospace Workers v. Wisconsin Employment Relations Comm'n, 427 U.S. 132, 144, 96 S.Ct. 2548, 2555, 49 L.Ed.2d 396 (1976) (holding that a Wisconsin employment relations board could not find a refusal to work overtime, an action that did not violate the NLRA, an unfair labor practice). The underlying rationale is that union and management "proceed from contrary and to an extent antagonistic viewpoints and concepts of self-interest.... The presence of economic weapons in reserve, and their actual exercise on occasion by the parties, is part and parcel of the system that the Wagner and Taft-Hartley Acts have recognized." NLRB v. Insurance Agents' Int'l Union, 361 U.S. 477, 488–89, 80 S.Ct. 419, 426–27, 4 L.Ed.2d 454 (1960). In fact, Machinists itself refers to the "hiring of permanent replacements" as an economic weapon available to an employer. 427 U.S. at 153, 96 S.Ct. at 2559.

Nor, as we have noted, is there any doubt that Machinists "pre-emption" applies to federal as well as state action.

* * *

The Court held that since the union's activities were economic weapons preserved by the NLRA, the Board (which has the "primary responsibility for developing and applying national labor policy," Curtin Matheson, 494 U.S. at 786, 110 S.Ct. at 1549) lacked the power to conclude that the activities constituted a NLRA violation. The Court has described Machinists pre-emption as creating a "free zone from which all regulation, 'whether federal or State,' is excluded." Golden State Transit Corp. v. Los Angeles, 493 U.S. 103, 111, 110 S.Ct. 444, 451, 107 L.Ed.2d 420 (1989).

* * *

When the government acts as a purchaser of goods and services NLRA pre-emption is still relevant. In Wisconsin Dep't of Indus. v. Gould Inc., 475 U.S. 282, 106 S.Ct. 1057, 89 L.Ed.2d 223 (1986), the state of Wisconsin had passed a statute debarring persons or firms that had violated the NLRA three times within a five year period from selling products to the state. The Supreme Court rejected Wisconsin's argument that its scheme escaped NLRA pre-emption because it was "an exercise of the State's spending power rather than its regulatory power." Id. at 287, 106 S.Ct. at 1061. The Court determined that, despite the form, "[t]he manifest purpose and inevitable effect of the debarment rule is to enforce the requirements of the NLRA." Id. at 291, 106 S.Ct. at 1063.

The latest Supreme Court opinion on the subject, on which the government heavily relies, is Boston Harbor. In that case, an independent agency of the Massachusetts government, The Massachusetts Water Resources Authority (MWRA), faced with a federal court order directing it to clean up Boston Harbor, selected Kaiser Engineers, Inc. as its project manager with responsibility to advise MWRA as to work site labor-relations policy. Kaiser suggested, and MWRA agreed, that Kaiser be permitted to enter into a collective bargaining agreement with the Building and Construction Trades Council (BCTC). The agreement provided that all employees hired were obliged to become union members within seven days of their employment whether they were employed by the general contractor or any subcontractor. The bid specifications required that all bidding subcontractors agree to abide by the agreement. Such a "pre-hire" agreement in the construction industry is a legal option under § 8(f) of the NLRA as an exception to the general prohibition under § 8(e) against "hot cargo" agreements. Non-union construction contractors sued, asserting that the actions of the MWRA were pre-empted by the NLRA because the state agency was intruding into the collective bargaining process by forcing subcontractors to exercise the § 8(f) option. The First Circuit agreed over a dissent by then-Chief Judge Breyer and the Supreme Court reversed, determining that the bid specification was "not government regulation and that it is therefore subject to neither Garmon nor Machinists preemption." Boston Harbor, 507 U.S. at 232, 113 S.Ct. at 1199.

Of course, appellants argue that the case before us is controlled by Gould and distinguished from Boston Harbor; the government urges the opposite. The government points out that in Gould, Wisconsin conceded that its purpose was to deter labor law violations, see 475 U.S. at 287, 106 S.Ct. at 1061, so the Court was easily able to determine that the state sought to address conduct that was "unrelated to the employer's performance of contractual obligations to the State ..." Boston Harbor, 507 U.S. at 229, 113 S.Ct. at 1197. Echoing its arguments on reviewability, the government insists that the Executive Order is premised on the President's economic judgment that a government contractor's use of permanent replacements will cause longer, more contentious strikes and the loss of the accumulated skill of the strikers with correspondingly less efficient and economical performance by that contractor. That judgment, we are told, is certainly an economically rational one, and it is not up to a court to question either the President's motivation or the quality of his reasoning here any more than was done in Contractors Ass'n, 442 F.2d 159, or Kahn, 618 F.2d 784. Appellants, without directly challenging the President's economic analysis, observe that a struck company's use of permanent replacements is a good deal more efficient than temporary replacements; the Executive Order irrationally bars the former but not the latter.

We are similarly quite reluctant to consider the President's motivation in issuing the Executive Order. Chief Judge Breyer's dissent in Boston Harbor, on which the Supreme Court heavily relied, put the issue as follows: "In the case before us, the record makes clear that the MWRA is participating in a market place as a general contractor, like a private buyer of services. Its role as buyer is not, in any sense, a sham designed to conceal an effort to regulate." Associated Builders & Contractors of Massachusetts/Rhode Island v. Massachusetts Water Resources Auth., 935 F.2d 345, 366 (1st Cir.1991) (en banc) (Breyer, C.J., dissenting) (emphasis added). We do not think we are bound to that dichotomy, however—particularly when considering the President's Executive Order. It is not necessary for us to question the President's motivation in order to determine whether the Order is a regulation that is pre-empted by Machinists.

The Supreme Court in Boston Harbor, quoting Chief Judge Breyer, explained, "when the MWRA, acting in the role of purchaser of construction services, acts just like a private contractor would act, and conditions its purchasing upon the very sort of labor agreement that Congress explicitly authorized and expected frequently to find, it does not 'regulate' the workings of the market forces that Congress expected to find; it exemplifies them." 507 U.S. at 233, 113 S.Ct. at 1199 (quoting Associated Builders, 935 F.2d at 361 (Breyer, C.J., dissenting))....

We do not think it is necessary to resolve this doctrinal dispute in this case. We would be surprised if private contractors were to care whether a struck supplier hired permanent or temporary replacements, so long as the goods or services contracted for were provided in a timely fashion and met quality standards. There may well be, however, some companies who, for political or philosophic reasons—what the Supreme Court referred to as a "labor policy concern," Boston Harbor, 507 U.S. at 229, 113 S.Ct. at 1197—would not wish to do business with a struck company that hired permanent replacements. But even if that behavior were a good deal more common than we suppose, we would still regard the Executive Order as regulatory in character.

In Boston Harbor, the Court's analysis of the behavior of MWRA was based on the premise, stated after its summary of its precedent, that:

> When the State acts as regulator, it performs a role that is characteristically a governmental rather than a private role, boycotts notwithstanding. Moreover, as regulator of private conduct, the State is more powerful than private parties. These distinctions are far less significant when the State acts as a market participant with no interest in setting policy.... We left open [in Gould] the question whether a State may act without offending the pre-emption principles of the NLRA when it acts as a proprietor and its acts therefore are not "tantamount to regulation," or policy-making.

Id. at 229, 113 S.Ct. at 1197 (emphases added). The premise on which the Court's further analysis rested, then, was that the Massachusetts governmental entity, MWRA, was not seeking to set general policy in the Commonwealth; it was just trying to operate as if it were an ordinary general contractor whose actions were "specifically tailored to one particular job, the Boston Harbor clean-up project." Id. at 232, 113 S.Ct. at 1198. Surely, the result would have been entirely different, given the Court's reasoning, if Massachusetts had passed a general law or the Governor had issued an Executive Order requiring all construction contractors doing business with the state to enter into collective bargaining agreements with the BCTC or its Massachusetts-wide counterpart containing § 8(e) pre-hire agreements. Accordingly, we very much doubt the legality of President Bush's Executive Order 12,818—since revoked, but upon which the government relies—that banned government contractors from entering into pre-hire agreements under § 8(f).[2]

It does not seem to us possible to deny that the President's Executive Order seeks to set a broad policy governing the behavior of thousands of American companies and affecting millions of American workers. The President has, of course, acted to set procurement policy rather than labor policy. But the former is quite explicitly based—and would have to be based—on his views of the latter. For the premise of the Executive Order is the proposition that the permanent replacement of strikers unduly prolongs and widens strikes and disrupts the proper "balance" between employers and employees. Whether that proposition is correct, or whether the prospect of permanent replacements deters strikes, and therefore an employer's right to permanently replace strikers is simply one element in the relative bargaining power of management and organized labor, is beside the point. Whatever one's views on the issue, it surely goes to the heart of United States labor relations policy. It cannot be equated to the ad hoc contracting decision made by MWRA in seeking to clean up Boston Harbor.

That is not to say that the President, in implementing the Procurement Act, may not draw upon any secondary policy views that deal with government contractors' employment practices—policy views that are directed beyond the immediate quality and price of goods and services purchased. In Kahn, we recognized that the imposition of wage and price controls as a condition of eligibility for government contractors could result in the

---

2. We also are dubious that President Bush's Executive Order 12,800, which required government contractors to post notices informing their employees that they could not be required to join or remain a member of a union, was legal. It may well have run afoul of Garmon pre-emption which reserves to NLRB jurisdiction arguably protected or prohibited conduct.

government actually paying more for individual government contracts than might be so otherwise. 618 F.2d at 793. We thought, however, the President's judgment that the over-all impact of those controls would reduce government procurement costs was entitled to deference. Id. And, in Contractors Ass'n, the Third Circuit's opinion contained only the briefest discussion of the impact on cost of the Executive Order's requirement of an affirmative action covenant in federally assisted construction contracts. The court merely noted that this requirement would increase the pool of qualified labor and thereby reduce costs. 442 F.2d at 171. But labor relations policy is different because of the NLRA and its broad field of pre-emption. No state or federal official or government entity can alter the delicate balance of bargaining and economic power that the NLRA establishes, whatever his or its purpose may be.

If the government were correct, it follows, as the government apparently conceded, that another President could not only revoke the Executive Order, but could issue a new order that actually required government contractors to permanently replace strikers, premised on a finding that this would minimize unions' bargaining power and thereby reduce procurement costs. Perhaps even more confusing, under the government's theory, the states would be permitted to adopt procurement laws or regulations that in effect choose sides on this issue, which would result in a further balkanization of federal labor policy.

… We do not think the scope of the President's intervention into and adjustment of labor relations policy is determinative, but despite the government's protestations, the impact of the Executive Order is quite far-reaching. It applies to all contracts over $100,000, and federal government purchases totaled $437 billion in 1994, constituting approximately 6.5% of the gross domestic product. STATISTICAL ABSTRACT OF THE UNITED STATES 451 (1995). Federal contractors and subcontractors employ 26 million workers, 22% of the labor force. GAO REPORT. The Executive Order's sanctions for hiring permanent replacements, contract debarment and termination, applies to the organizational unit of the federal contractor who has hired permanent replacements. The organizational unit includes "[a]ny other affiliate of the person that could provide the goods or services required to be provided under the contract." 60 Fed.Reg. at 27,861 (emphasis added). If a local unit of Exxon had a contract to deliver $100,001 worth of gas to a federal agency, the organizational unit would include all the other affiliates of Exxon that could have provided the gas; no doubt a significant portion of the Exxon corporation. The broad definition of "organizational unit" will have the effect of forcing corporations wishing to do business with the federal government not to hire permanent replacements even if the strikers are not the employees who provide the goods or services to the government. Indeed, corporations who even hope to obtain a government contract will think twice before hiring permanent replacements during a strike. It will be recalled that in Kahn, 618 F.2d at 792–93, the government itself asserted that controls imposed on government contractors—given the size of that portion of the economy—would alter the behavior of non-government contractors.

* * *

We, therefore, conclude that the Executive Order is regulatory in nature and is preempted by the NLRA which guarantees the right to hire permanent replacements. The district court is hereby

Reversed.

Notes and Questions

1. In contrast to the labor standards and Buy American rules, the rule against striker replacement at issue in *Chamber of Commerce* did not derive from focused Congressional

enactments directing such a rule, but from Presidential invocation of generic authority in the 1949 act. Even with that distinction, *Chamber of Commerce* breaks with a number of previous occasions, some of which it grudgingly acknowledges, when the courts had upheld procurement-implemented policies based on a President's invocation of such generic authority. In particular, *Contractors Ass'n of Eastern Pennsylvania v. Secretary of Labor*, 442 F.2d 159 (3d Cir.), *cert. denied*, 494 U.S. 854 (1971), upheld President Nixon's order imposing affirmative action on government contractors; *AFL v. Kahn*, 618 F.2d 784 (D.C. Cir.), *cert. denied*, 443 U.S. 915 (1979), upheld President Carter's order imposing wage and price standards on government contractors.

The Court of Appeals distinguished these precedents by the asserted clarity with which the National Labor Relations Act leaves the field open for employer striker replacement. What were the counterarguments? By the same logic, could it have been said that Congress's silence equally clearly left the field open for companies not to engage in affirmative action or not to keep wages and prices down? So why did the courts uphold the affirmative action and price control executive orders?

2. How much does the President's ability to promulgate policies through government contracting depend on the few broad and vague words, little discussed on the floor of Congress, of the 1949 Federal Property and Administrative Services Act (this opinion calls it the "Procurement Act")? Presidents invoking FPASA make what is a thinly disguised claim of inherent Presidential power, albeit one which does not require them to challenge Congress, merely to act without any more sign of Congressional support than a noncontroversial statute enacted fifty years earlier without the slightest anticipation of how it would be used. Is such a Presidential assertion of power at odds with the Constitution's investiture of all legislative power in the democratically-elected Congress? Or is procurement an activity that mixes Presidential and Congressional prerogatives?

Another set of policies consists of statutorily-required drug-free workplace rules. See FAR subpart 23.5. The legal superstructure consists of Congressional enactments, implementing regulations, and a contract clause requiring contractors to make a "Certification Regarding a Drug-Free Workplace."

D. Government Workforce Issues

The federal government has an elaborate set of civil service and federal employee union statutes and rules that may affect those on the government side who work with contractors. These statutes and rules are too elaborate to delve deeply into. A contemporary example which provides a general sense about them concerns to what extent the Administration could limit the normal federal employee labor rights of employees in the Department of Homeland Security.

For further discussions of the issues in this section, see Miyuki Oshima, *The Continuing Uncertainty of Collective Bargaining for Department of Homeland Security Employees*, 40 U. Tol. L. Rev. 247 (2008); Ruben J. Garcia, Labor's Fragile Freedom of Association Post-9/11, 8 U. Pa. J. Lab. & Emp. L. 283 (2006); Charles Tiefer & Jennifer Ferragut, *Letting Federal Unions Protest Improper Contracting Out*, 10 Cornell J.L. & Pub. Pol. 581 (2001); Robert H. Shriver, *No Seat at the Table: Flawed Contracting Out Process Unfairly Limits Front-Line Federal Employee Participation*, 30 Pub. Cont. L. J. 613 (2001).

National Treasury Employees Union, et al., Appellees/Cross-Appellants v. Michael Chertoff, Secretary, United States Department of Homeland Security

United States Court of Appeals, District of Columbia Circuit
452 F.3d 839
Decided June 27, 2006

Before: RANDOLPH and GRIFFITH, Circuit Judges, and EDWARDS, Senior Circuit Judge.

Opinion for the Court filed by Senior Circuit Judge EDWARDS.

EDWARDS, Senior Circuit Judge.

When Congress enacted the Homeland Security Act of 2002 ("HSA" or the "Act") and established the Department of Homeland Security ("DHS" or the "Department"), it provided that "the Secretary of Homeland Security may, in regulations prescribed jointly with the Director of the Office of Personnel Management, establish, and from time to time adjust, a human resources management system." 5 U.S.C. § 9701(a) (Supp. II 2002).

* * *

In February 2005, the Department and Office of Personnel Management ("OPM") issued regulations establishing a human resources management system. *See* Department of Homeland Security Human Resources Management System, 70 Fed. Reg. 5272 (Feb. 1, 2005) (codified at 5 C.F.R. Chapter XCVII and Part 9701) ("Final Rule" or "HR system"). The Final Rule, *inter alia,* defines the scope and process of collective bargaining for affected DHS employees, channels certain disputes through the Federal Labor Relations Authority ("FLRA" or the "Authority"), creates an in-house Homeland Security Labor Relations Board ("HSLRB"), and assigns an appellate role to the Merit Systems Protection Board ("MSPB") in cases involving penalties imposed on DHS employees.

Unions representing many DHS employees (the "Unions") filed a complaint in District Court raising a cause of action under the Administrative Procedure Act, 5 U.S.C. § 701*et seq.,* to challenge aspects of the Final Rule. In a detailed and thoughtful opinion, *Nat'l Treasury Employees Union v. Chertoff,* 385 F.Supp.2d 1 (D.D.C.2005) ("*Chertoff I* "), the District Court found that the regulations would not ensure collective bargaining, would fundamentally and impermissibly alter FLRA jurisdiction, and would create an appeal process at MSPB that is not fair. Based on these rulings, the District Court enjoined DHS from implementing § 9701.706(k)(6) and all of Subpart E (§ 9701.501 *et seq.*) of the regulations.

* * *

The case is now before this court on appeal by the Government and cross-appeal by the Unions. We affirm in part and reverse in part.

We hold that the regulations fail in two important respects to "ensure that employees may ... bargain collectively," as the HSA requires. First, we agree with the District Court that the Department's attempt to reserve to itself the right to unilaterally abrogate lawfully negotiated and executed agreements is plainly unlawful. If the Department could unilaterally abrogate lawful contracts, this would nullify the Act's specific guarantee of collective bargaining rights, because the agency cannot "ensure" collective bargaining without affording employees the right to negotiate binding agreements.

Second, we hold that the Final Rule violates the Act insofar as it limits the scope of bargaining to employee-specific personnel matters. The regulations effectively eliminate all meaningful bargaining over fundamental working conditions (including even negotiations over procedural protections), thereby committing the bulk of decisions concerning conditions of employment to the Department's exclusive discretion. In no sense can such a limited scope of bargaining be viewed as consistent with the Act's mandate that DHS "ensure" collective bargaining rights for its employees.

* * *

I. BACKGROUND

A. The Homeland Security Act

The Homeland Security Act, Pub.L. No. 107-296, 116 Stat. 2135 (2002), was enacted in November 2002. It established the Department, a cabinet-level agency whose mission is to "prevent and deter terrorist attacks[,] protect against and respond to threats and hazards to the nation[,] ... ensure safe and secure borders, welcome lawful immigrants and visitors, and promote the free-flow of commerce." Final Rule, 70 Fed.Reg. at 5273 (internal quotation marks omitted). The Act merged 22 existing agencies from across the federal government, integrating 170,000 employees, 17 unions, 7 payroll systems, 77 collective bargaining units, and 80 personnel systems. See Chertoff I, 385 F.Supp.2d at 6 n. 1 (quoting 148 CONG. REC. S11017 (Statement of Sen. Thompson) (Nov. 14, 2002)).

As noted above, HSA authorizes the Secretary of Homeland Security, with the Director of the Office of Personnel Management, to promulgate regulations establishing a HR system. See 5 U.S.C. § 9701 (Supp. II 2002).

* * *

B. The Final Rule Adopting the HR System

On February 1, 2005, DHS and OPM promulgated the Final Rule establishing the new HR system. See Final Rule, 70 Fed.Reg. 5272. Although the HR system was established by DHS and OPM, we will refer only to "DHS" or the "Department" as the author of the regulations.

* * *

1.Collective Bargaining

As the District Court noted, the Final Rule "contain[s] an expansive management rights provision and severely restrict[s] collective bargaining to issues that affect individual employees." Chertoff I, 385 F.Supp.2d at 9. Collective bargaining under the new HR system is defined to mean "the performance of the mutual obligation of a management representative of the Department and an exclusive representative of employees ... to meet at reasonable times and to consult and bargain in a good faith effort to reach agreement with respect to the conditions of employment affecting such employees." 5 C.F.R. § 9701.504 (2006). Most "conditions of employment," however, are placed off-limits for bargaining.

* * *

In analyzing the provisions of 5 C.F.R. § 9701.511, the District Court wryly commented:

> Translated into English, this Regulation would give management full discretion over all aspects of the Department except those that might be seen as personal employee grievances.

Chertoff I, 385 F.Supp.2d at 10.

The new HR system also authorizes the Department to unilaterally abrogate lawfully negotiated and executed collective bargaining agreements. In addition to securing DHS's authority to override agreements that are in existence when the HR system takes effect, *see* 5 C.F.R. § 9701.506(a) (2006), the Final Rule purports to authorize the Department to unilaterally set aside provisions in agreements that are negotiated and executed under the new HR system. An agreement may be invalidated by DHS's Secretary (or a designee) within 30 days of being executed if found to be inconsistent with Departmental rules or regulations. *Id.* § 9701.515(d)(1)–(2).

* * *

2. The Roles of the Homeland Security Labor Relations Board and the Federal Labor Relations Authority

* * *

The Final Rule establishes the Homeland Security Labor Relations Board, composed of a rotating board of members—appointed by the Secretary of Homeland Security—who "must be independent, distinguished citizens of the United States who are well known for their integrity and impartiality" and have "expertise in labor relations, law enforcement, or national/homeland or other related security matters." 5 C.F.R. § 9701.508(a)(2) (2006).

* * *

The Role of the Merit Systems Protection Board

Normally, Chapter 77 allows federal employees to appeal adverse actions to the MSPB. As noted above, the HSA states that DHS employees must receive due process in pursuing their appeals, and that any modification of Chapter 77 by DHS must be crafted in consultation with MSPB. 5 U.S.C. § 9701(f) (Supp. II 2002). The Act also states that regulations "which relate to any matters within the purview of chapter 77 ... shall modify procedures under chapter 77 only insofar as such modifications are designed to further the fair, efficient, and expeditious resolution of matters involving the employees of the Department." *Id.* § 9701(f)(2)(C).

* * *

II. ANALYSIS

***

C. The Duty to Ensure Collective Bargaining

In a vain effort to defend the Final Rule's construction of a purported structure for collective bargaining, the Government points to § 9701(a), which says that the Department is authorized to promulgate a HR system "[n]otwithstanding any other provision of this part," and § 9701(b)(3), which says that any such system "shall— ... (3) not waive, modify, or otherwise affect [certain existing statutory provisions relating to, *inter alia,* merit hiring, equal pay, whistleblowing, and prohibited personnel practices]." The Government appears to argue that, read together, these two provisions authorize DHS to waive any provision relating to employee relations, save those specifically listed in § 9701(b)(3), and then to do entirely as it pleases in establishing a HR system. This argument is completely unconvincing.

* * *

Most importantly, at least with respect to the issues in this case, when Congress added the substantive requirement in the HSA guaranteeing DHS employees the right to bargain collectively, it obviously intended for this requirement to be construed reasonably and applied fully.

Although the HSA requires the Department to "ensure" that their employees may bargain collectively, the Act does not define collective bargaining. Fortunately, this is not a term without meaning. Indeed, "collective bargaining" is a term of art in the federal sector that has been defined by Congress in the FSLMS:

* * *

1. *DHS's Asserted Power to Unilaterally Abrogate Collective Bargaining Agreements*

The most extraordinary feature of the Final Rule is that it reserves to the Department the right to unilaterally abrogate lawfully negotiated and executed agreements. This is plainly impermissible under the HSA. If the Department could unilaterally abrogate lawful contracts, this would nullify the statute's specific guarantee of collective bargaining rights, because DHS cannot "ensure" collective bargaining without affording employees the right to negotiate binding agreements. The District Court's decision on this point is exactly right:

* * *

2. *The Scope of Bargaining*

The right to negotiate collective bargaining agreements that are equally binding on both parties is of little moment if the parties have virtually nothing to negotiate over. That is the result of the Final Rule adopted by DHS. The scope of bargaining under the HR system is virtually nil, especially when measured against the meaning of collective bargaining under Chapter 71. And this is saying a lot, because the scope of bargaining under Chapter 71 is extraordinarily narrow. This was made clear in *NTEU v. FLRA*, 910 F.2d 964 (D.C.Cir.1990) (en banc), where we pointed out the unique structure of the federal sector labor relations statute, which, because of "the special requirements and needs of the Government," 5 U.S.C. § 7101(b), excludes from negotiations a host of subjects that employers would be obliged to bargain about in the private sector. For instance, section 7106(a), the "management rights" provision of the statute, ensures that agencies need not bargain over the number of employees, their hiring, assignment, and discharge, the right to contract out work, and the authority "to take whatever actions may be necessary to carry out the agency mission during emergencies." 5 U.S.C. § 7106(a).

* * *

It is readily apparent that the Final Rule reflects a flagrant departure from the norms of "collective bargaining" underlying Chapter 71. In fact, the Government acknowledges the striking disparity between the FSLMS framework and the system established for DHS. *See* DHS's Reply Br. at 13. Even a quick glance at the Final Rule confirms what the Government acknowledges, *i.e.*, that the HR system shrinks the scope of bargaining well below what Chapter 71 provides. For example, "permissive" areas of bargaining under Chapter 71 are off limits for negotiation at DHS. *Compare* 5 U.S.C. § 7106(b)(1) (2000), *with* 5 C.F.R. § 9701.511(a)(2) & (b) (2006). This distinction is critical. Procedures for exercising rights affecting issues like work assignments and deployments are negotiable under Chapter 71, but not under the HR system. And, under the HR system, when management exercises one of its rights, it need not provide notice to labor representatives in advance. 5 C.F.R. § 9701.511(d) (2006). Moreover, the proposed HR system gives DHS broad new authority "to take whatever other actions may be necessary to carry out the Department's mission." *Id.* § 9701.511(a)(2) (2006). Presumably, this provision empowers DHS to take any matter off the bargaining table at any time, regardless of what concessions have already been made by union representatives. No analogous power exists anywhere in Chapter 71. Most strikingly, DHS management is prohibited from negotiating over the "procedures it will observe in exercising" the authority laid out in subsections (a)(1) and (a)(2) of the management rights provision. *Id.* § 9701.511(b). Instead, management must merely "confer" with labor representatives about the procedures it will use. *Id.* § 9701.511(c). These provisions stand in sharp contrast to Chapter 71's obligation to bargain over the procedures used to exercise management rights. 5 U.S.C. § 7106(b)(2) (2000).

* * *

III. CONCLUSION

The allowance of unilateral contract abrogation and the limited scope of bargaining under DHS's Final Rule plainly violate the statutory command in the HSA that the Department "ensure" collective bargaining for its employees. We therefore vacate any provisions of the Final Rule that betray this command. DHS's attempt to co-opt FLRA's administrative machinery constitutes an exercise of power far outside the Department's statutory authority. We therefore affirm the District Court's decision to vacate the provisions of the Final Rule that encroach on the Authority. We reverse the District Court's holding that MSPB's standard of review in penalty modification cases represents a failure to provide "fair" appellate procedures, because that issue is not yet ripe for review. And we express no view on the role of the HSLRB, because the matter cannot be addressed until DHS revises the Final Rule. Finally, we decline to amend the injunction.

The judgments of the District Court are affirmed in part and reversed in part, and the case is hereby remanded for further proceedings consistent with this opinion.

Notes and Questions:

1. What arguments are there in favor of the rules? Why are these losing arguments?

2. What are some of the subjects that can, or cannot, be the subject of bargaining?

Chapter 13

Termination for Convenience

The chapter discusses one mechanism for termination: termination for convenience. Although this mechanism terminates the contractor, it has more contrasts than similarities to termination for default. It does not have the normative overtones. An exemplary contractor, a veritable paragon of contracting virtue, may well undergo termination for convenience simply because the government no longer requires what it had engaged the contractor to do. The government deals generously with the contractor terminated for convenience, although it does not allow that contractor to receive unearned profits.

For example, at the end of a war, the government may terminate for convenience its most honored and treasured defense contractors, simply because the government no longer needs their weapons. Termination for convenience represents a kind of government remedy not found in typical basic (private) contracts, because the government reserves for itself this extraordinary discretion to bring a contract to an end, without the other party having the ability either to contest this effectively or to recover its anticipated profits. This section explores the bases, the mechanisms, and the scope of recovery, in termination for convenience.

Contracting officers may have other reasons for wishing to cancel, quite without any contractor default. The funding expected from the budget process may not be there. Something better may have come along. Or, the agency may be dissatisfied with the contractor, but for reasons insufficient to terminate for default. In each government contract, the government includes a clause to let it cancel in such situations: the termination for convenience clause.

The materials here treat termination for convenience in two stages. In a termination for default, the government merely pays for the value of what it got, which may be very little. In a termination for convenience, the government agrees to make the contractor whole. That may give the contractor's lawyer an opportunity to do well by her client, for there is considerable room for discussion and for the exercise of discretion in settling such a termination. Moreover, the termination clause itself anticipates that the contractor will play a large role in settlement.

For further discussion of the subject of this chapter, see the citations in each particular subchapter, and see: Steven Feldman, *Government Contract Guidebook*, § 20 (Thomson Reuters, 4th ed. 2010); Karen Manos, *Government Contract Costs & Pricing*, §§ 88.2–88.11 (Thomson Reuters 2nd ed. 2009); Bruce D. Page (Jr.), *When Reliance Is Detrimental: Economic, Moral, And Policy Arguments For Expectation Damages In Contracts Terminated For The Convenience Of The Government*, 61 A.F. L. Rev. 1 (2008); Charles Tiefer, *Forfeiture by Cancellation or Termination*, 54 Mercer Law Review 1031 (2003); Artie McConnell, *Bad Faith As A Limitation On Terminations For Convenience: As Bad As They Say Or Not So Bad?*, 32 Pub. Cont. L.J. 411 (Winter 2003); Marc A. Pederson, *Rethinking The Termination For Convenience Clause In Federal Contracts*, 31 Pub. Cont. L.J. 83 (Fall 2001).

A. Operation

The ordinary operation of termination for convenience deserves examination. The clause itself explains with unusual lucidity how the termination process works. From the government's perspective, the process involves an orderly wind-up of the contract, dealing with such matters as the announcement of the termination, handling work in progress and government property, and settling with subcontractors. From the contractor's perspective, the process's best part consists of the level of payment to which the government agrees, which is much more generous than in termination for default. For further discussion of the subjects of this section, see: Graeme S. Henderson, *Terminations for Convenience and the Termination Costs Clause*, 53 A.F.L. Rev. 103 (2002); Harris J. Handrews, Jr. & Robert T. Peacock, *Terminations: An Outline of the Parties' Rights and Remedies*, 11 Pub. Cont. L.J. 269 (1980); Joseph D. West, *Practical Advice Concerning the Federal Government's Termination for Convenience Clause*, 17-OCT Construction Law. 26 (1997); William H. Murphy, *Applying G&A Costs to Termination Settlement Expenses and Subcontract Settlements*, 33 Procurement Law., Spring 1998, at 13; Eric R. Fish, *Note: When a Termination for Convenience Settlement Proposal Constitutes a Claim Under the Contract Disputes Act*, 26 Pub. Cont. L.J. 423 (1997).

Given the unusual clarity of the Termination for Convenience Clause, one way to describe the termination process is simply to go through the clause, provision by provision. Accordingly, it is suggested that this discussion be read simultaneously with looking at the text of the clause, which follows it. First, this discussion goes through the whole process, from notice (provision (a)) to records retention (provision (n)). Then, the discussion zeroes in on the part of greatest interest, the formula for what the government pays the terminated contractor (provisions (f) and (g)).

Termination begins with the Contracting Officer "delivering to the Contractor a Notice of Termination specifying the extent of termination and the effective date" (provision (a)). This contrasts starkly with Termination for Default: there is no ten day "show cause" period, and no required explanation of "why." The procedures that follow do not exist for explaining or disputing reasons, only for giving the directions for an orderly wind-up. That might seem Kafkaesque in its unexplained nature, and, no doubt, contractors may often have strong reactions of baffled dismay. However, the government's lack of necessity to explain, or to provide procedural due process, springs from the normatively colorless nature of the action. The government is simply exercising its reserved rights. It makes no judgment about the contractor, and what it does should not affect a contractor's record and good standing. When the Notice specifies "the extent of termination," it alludes to the distinction between total and partial terminations. The government may terminate less than a whole contract, while at the same time reducing the work more than by a mere "change." A reduction that would not warrant treatment as a partial termination is called a "deductive change."

Upon receiving the notice, the terminated contractor has a series of winding up obligations laid out in numbered subparts of provision (b). The wind-up obligation list must deal with the range of very different scenarios for termination for convenience. Imagine three different scenarios, each of which makes different aspects of winding-up matter more. Start with a scenario in which (1) the government simply no longer needs the work, like the prime contract to develop a new aircraft, still at the initial stages of hiring subcontractors for research on component systems, for which the funds did not materialize as expected. That requires a quick, hopefully inexpensive wind-up. Then, imagine (2) a general contractor deep in working on a government project when rumors of its insolvency come in. The government decides to terminate the contract partially, shifting what it can to a definitely solvent contractor and having the potentially bankrupt one stay with the part that is hard to shift. Finally, imagine (3) a contractor that is doing something vital, like supplying a key component for an important new missile, and the military service just decides to switch the work to another, bigger contractor. The Contracting Officer's chief concern is full speed continuation, just at another company, and all other considerations do not matter.

Provision (b) tells the terminated-for-convenience contractor to "stop work" ((b)(1)) and "Place no further subcontracts or orders" ((b)(2)). The contractor must wind-up with subcontractors, including "Terminate all subcontracts" ((b)(3)), "Assign to the Government ... all right ... under the subcontracts terminated" ((b)(4)), and "settle" what will be "arising from the termination of subcontracts" ((b))(5)). Recalling the imaginary scenarios just listed, the steps in these provisions ((b)(1) to (5)) might be most of what the terminated aircraft prime contract scenario principally involves: an orderly shutting down of what the prime contractor had done in terms of starting subcontracts.

The terminated contractor has to "transfer ... and deliver to the Government" the work in progress and completed work ((b)(6)). If the Contracting Officer so directs, the contractor may "Sell ... any property of the types referred to in subparagraph (6) above" ((b)(7)). In the third scenario, the urgent missile component, the government may care the most about the step of getting the work in progress transferred to the new contractor.

If the termination is only partial, the contractor must "Complete performance of the work not terminated" ((b)(7)). The contractor must also protect the government as to "the property related to this contract ... in which the Government has or may acquire an interest" ((b)(8)). The scenario of the partial termination of the near-insolvent contractor may turn on these provisions. Not only must the contractor complete the work not terminated, the contractor must not prejudice the government's property interests. If the contractor is responding to other creditors' pressures to give up property interests, as when a near-insolvent contractor pledges its remaining assets in some of which the government has an interest, as security for credit from suppliers, this clause can lead to serious jockeying between the government and the private creditors.

While the terminated contractor juggles these various generalized governmental interests, the termination clause gives it a series of concrete steps to follow. It may "submit to the Contracting Officer a list, certified as to quantity and quality, of termination inventory" (provisions (c) and (d)), with various steps to follow regarding such inventory. This accords with the caution inherent generally regarding property in which the government has an interest.

As for how much the government will pay the contractor, the following provisions discuss two methods of deciding this: settlement (provisions (e) and (f)) by dint of a contractor settlement proposal, or a figure determined by the Contracting Officer (provision (g)). The task that may well engage much of terminated contractors' lawyers' attention consists here of developing and processing a settlement proposal.

The determinations by these clauses of what the terminated contractor gets is subject to the Disputes Clause (j). The government may make partial payments to the contractor (m). Finally, the contractor "shall maintain all records and documents relating to the terminated protion of this contractor for three years after final settlement," for governmental review (n).

On occasion, the parties may execute what is called a "no-cost settlement agreement." Effectively, the parties stipulate the contractor has no costs for which the government owes it and no credits owing to the government, so they might as well just walk away from the contract. This may occur either because there are, in fact, no costs or credits, or as the very simplest way to walk away from a dispute when both sides want out. It is a handy tool for government contract lawyers.

Termination for Convenience Clause (Fixed-Price)
(Sep 1996)

(a) The Government may terminate performance of work under this contract in whole or, from time to time, in part if the Contracting Officer determines that a termination is in the Government's interest. The Contracting Officer shall terminate by delivering to the Contractor a Notice of Termination specifying the extent of termination and the effective date.

(b) After receipt of a Notice of Termination, and except as directed by the Contracting Officer, the Contractor shall immediately proceed with the following obligations, regardless of any delay in determining or adjusting any amounts due under this clause:

(1) Stop work as specified in the notice.

(2) Place no further subcontracts or orders ...

(3) Terminate all subcontracts to the extent they relate to the work terminated.

(4) Assign to the Government, as directed by the Contracting Officer, all right, title, and interest of the Contractor under the subcontracts terminated, in which case the Government shall have the right to settle or to pay any termination settlement proposal arising out of those terminations.

(5) With approval or ratification to the extent required by the Contracting Officer, settle all outstanding liabilities and termination settlement proposals arising from the termination of subcontracts ...

(6) As directed by the Contracting Officer, transfer title and deliver to the Government

(i)   the fabricated or unfabricated parts, work in process, completed work, supplies, and other material produced or acquired for the work terminated, and

(ii) the completed or partially completed plans, drawings, information, and other property that, if the contract had been completed, would be required to be furnished to the Government.

(7) Complete performance of the work not terminated.

(8) Take any action that may be necessary, or that the Contracting Officer may direct, for the protection and preservation of the property related to this contract that is in the possession of the Contractor and in which the Government has or may acquire an interest.

(9) Use its best efforts to sell, as directed or authorized by the Contracting Officer, any property of the types referred to in subparagraph (b)(6) of this clause ...

(c) The Contractor shall submit complete termination inventory schedules....

(d) After expiration of the plant clearance period as defined in Subpart 45.6 of the Federal Acquisition Regulation, the Contractor may submit to the Contracting Officer a list, certified as to quantity and quality, of termination inventory....

(e) After termination, the Contractor shall submit a final termination settlement proposal to the Contracting Officer in the form and with the certification prescribed by the

Contracting Officer. The Contractor shall submit the proposal promptly, but no later than 1 year from the effective date of termination, unless extended in writing by the Contracting Officer upon written request of the Contractor within this 1-year period. However, if the Contracting Officer determines that the facts justify it, a termination settlement proposal may be received and acted on after 1 year or any extension. If the Contractor fails to submit the proposal within the time allowed, the Contracting Officer may determine, on the basis of information available, the amount, if any, due the Contractor because of the termination and shall pay the amount determined.

(f) Subject to paragraph (e) of this clause, the Contractor and the Contracting Officer may agree upon the whole or any part of the amount to be paid or remaining to be paid because of the termination. The amount may include a reasonable allowance for profit on work done. However, the agreed amount, whether under this paragraph (f) or paragraph (g) of this clause, exclusive of costs shown in subparagraph (g)(3) of this clause, may not exceed the total contract price as reduced by

(1) the amount of payments previously made and

(2) the contract price of work not terminated. The contract shall be modified, and the Contractor paid the agreed amount. Paragraph (g) of this clause shall not limit, restrict, or affect the amount that may be agreed upon to be paid under this paragraph.

(g) If the Contractor and the Contracting Officer fail to agree on the whole amount to be paid because of the termination of work, the Contracting Officer shall pay the Contractor the amounts determined by the Contracting Officer as follows, but without duplication of any amounts agreed on under paragraph (f) of this clause:

(1) The contract price for completed supplies or services accepted by the Government (or sold or acquired under subparagraph (b)(9) of this clause) not previously paid for, adjusted for any saving of freight and other charges.

(2) The total of—

(i) The costs incurred in the performance of the work terminated, including initial costs and preparatory expense allocable thereto, but excluding any costs attributable to supplies or services paid or to be paid under subparagraph (g)(1) of this clause;

(ii) The cost of settling and paying termination settlement proposals under terminated subcontracts that are properly chargeable to the terminated portion of the contract if not included in subdivision (g)(2)(i) of this clause; and

(iii) A sum, as profit on subdivision (g)(2)(i) of this clause, determined by the Contracting Officer under 49.202 of the Federal Acquisition Regulation, in effect on the date of this contract, to be fair and reasonable; however, if it appears that the Contractor would have sustained a loss on the entire contract had it been completed, the Contracting Officer shall allow no profit under this subdivision (iii) and shall reduce the settlement to reflect the indicated rate of loss.

(3) The reasonable costs of settlement of the work terminated, including—

(i) Accounting, legal, clerical, and other expenses reasonably necessary for the preparation of termination settlement proposals and supporting data;

(ii) The termination and settlement of subcontracts (excluding the amounts of such settlements); and

(iii) Storage, transportation, and other costs incurred, reasonably necessary for the preservation, protection, or disposition of the termination inventory.

(h) ... [T]he Contracting Officer shall exclude from the amounts payable to the Contractor under paragraph (g) of this clause, the fair value, as determined by the Contracting Officer, of property that is destroyed, lost, stolen, or damaged....

(i) The cost principles and procedures of Part 31 of the Federal Acquisition Regulation ... shall govern all costs claimed, agreed to, or determined under this clause.

(j) The Contractor shall have the right of appeal, under the Disputes clause, from any determination made by the Contracting Officer under paragraph (e), (g), or (l) of this clause, except that if the Contractor failed to submit the termination settlement proposal or request for equitable adjustment within the time provided in paragraph (e) or (l), respectively, and failed to request a time extension, there is no right of appeal.

(k) In arriving at the amount due the Contractor under this clause, there shall be deducted—

> (1) All unliquidated advance or other payments to the Contractor under the terminated portion of this contract;

> (2) Any claim which the Government has against the Contractor under this contract; and

> (3) The agreed price for, or the proceeds of sale of, materials, supplies, or other things acquired by the Contractor or sold under the provisions of this clause and not recovered by or credited to the Government.

(l) If the termination is partial, the Contractor may file a proposal with the Contracting Officer for an equitable adjustment of the price(s) of the continued portion of the contract. The Contracting Officer shall make any equitable adjustment agreed upon. Any proposal by the Contractor for an equitable adjustment under this clause shall be requested within 90 days from the effective date of termination unless extended in writing by the Contracting Officer.

(m) (1) The Government may, under the terms and conditions it prescribes, make partial payments and payments against costs incurred by the Contractor for the terminated portion of the contract, if the Contracting Officer believes the total of these payments will not exceed the amount to which the Contractor will be entitled.

> (2) If the total payments exceed the amount finally determined to be due, the Contractor shall repay the excess to the Government upon demand....

(n) Unless otherwise provided in this contract or by statute, the Contractor shall maintain all records and documents relating to the terminated portion of this contract for 3 years after final settlement.... The Contractor shall make these records and documents available to the Government, at the Contractor's office, at all reasonable times, without any direct charge....

The issues regarding what the government owes the terminated contractor deserve attention. Note how the termination clause's provision (h) makes cost principles apply. These have been discussed in another chapter. Normally, government contracts are either fixed price—no cost principles—or cost reimbursement. What the termination clause does is make cost principles apply universally, regardless of whether the contract originally involved them in pricing. The saying is that Termination for Convenience converts a fixed price contract into a cost reimbursement contract for the work performed.

Termination clause section (f) creates wide-open flexibility for the terminated contractor and the contracting officer to agree upon a settlement figure, in contrast to the greater precision and restriction of section (g) when the contracting officer determines a figure. Still, section (e) gives some guidance. The settlement "may include a reasonable allowance for profit on work done." However, "the agreed amount, whether under this paragraph (f) or paragraph (g) below … may not exceed the total contract price" with two reductions: "payments previously made," and "the contract price of work not done." Leaving aside payments made, an agreed figure between the contracting officer and the contractor can follow a basic formula: Contract Price (total) minus Contract Price (for work not done).

Moreover, the termination clause indicates several ways of raising that figure. It exempts a category of costs in subsection (g)(3), namely, the settlement costs of the termination. These include "Accounting, legal, clerical, and other expenses reasonably necessary for the preparation of termination settlement proposals and supporting data" ((g)(3)(i)). In other words, the government contracts lawyer billing for work reasonably necessary for preparing settlement proposals can get the contractor reimbursed by the government for her bills, a factor helping the lawyer to persuade the contractor to place some of the burdens of working on the settlement proposal onto the lawyer. Also, in a partial termination, the contractor can seek an equitable adjustment for the price of the "continued portion of the contract" (provision (l)).

Both sides must consider what happens without an agreement, namely, the contracting officer reaching a determination pursuant to provision (g). This is the part that gets fought about. In contrast with the previously noted ceiling, which starts with the total contract price and subtracts from it, the calculations pursuant to provision (g) start with the "contract price for completed supplies or services accepted by the Government" ((g)(1)), and adds to that. Usually, this formula will come well below the ceiling that starts with the total contract price, unless the unusual situation is present that the government terminates a contract in which a comparatively large portion of what there was to purchase has been produced and accepted.

To the price for completed supplies or services, the determination process adds, on the termination portion, the costs already incurred, such as start-up costs on the contract or the costs of materials ordered and not returnable without some expenditure ((g)(2)(i)). It also includes the cost of terminated subcontractor settlements ((g)(2)(ii)), and a figure for profit on the costs incurred. The clause takes special note to warn that if the "contractor would have sustained a loss on the entire contract had it been completed," then no profit gets allowed and the contracting officer "shall reduce the settlement to reflect the indicated rate of loss (g)(2)(iii). This may not be all that common, but it can happen, when contractors bid low seeking the work for various reasons, and some of those reasons may vanish as a result of termination by convenience (for example, the expectation of profiting by follow-on contracts like spare parts).

James M. Ellett Construction Company, Inc., Plaintiff-Appellant, v. The United States, Defendant-Appellee

No. 94-5161
United States Court of Appeals, Federal Circuit
93 F.3d 1537
Aug. 26, 1996

Before MAYER, MICHEL and BRYSON, Circuit Judges.

MAYER, Circuit Judge.

James M. Ellett Construction Company, Inc. appeals the judgment of the United States Court of Federal Claims, No. 90-641 C (July 29, 1994), dismissing its suit challenging a contracting officer's final decision for want of subject matter jurisdiction because Ellett had not submitted a "claim" that complied with the requirements of the Contract Disputes Act. Subsequent to the court's dismissal, this court clarified the definition of a claim, overruling the cases upon which the trial court had relied in dismissing Ellett's complaint. Reflectone, Inc. v. Dalton, 60 F.3d 1572 (Fed.Cir.1995) (in banc). Because Ellett submitted both a "claim" as that term is explained in Reflectone, and a termination settlement proposal that ripened into a claim which the contracting officer settled by determination, there was jurisdiction. Therefore, we reverse and remand for further proceedings.

Background

In July 1988, the Forest Service of the United States Department of Agriculture (agency) awarded Ellett a contract to construct a 2.7 mile logging road in the Siskiyou National Forest, Oregon. The contract contained the April 1984 version of the Federal Acquisition Regulation (FAR) clause authorizing the government to terminate the contract for its convenience, 48 C.F.R. § 52.249-2 (Alternate I), which states, in pertinent part:

(d) After termination, the Contractor shall submit a final termination settlement proposal to the Contracting Officer in the form and with the certification prescribed by the Contracting Officer....

(e) Subject to paragraph (d) above, the Contractor and the Contracting Officer may agree upon the whole or any part of the amount to be paid because of the termination....

(f) If the Contractor and the Contracting Officer fail to agree on the whole amount to be paid the Contractor because of the termination of work, the Contracting Officer shall pay the Contractor the amounts determined as follows, but without duplication of any amounts agreed upon under paragraph (e)....

* * *

(i) The Contractor shall have the right of appeal, under the Disputes clause, from any determination made by the Contracting Officer under paragraph (d) [or] (f).... If the Contracting Officer has made a determination of the amount due under paragraph (d) [or] (f)..., the Government shall pay the Contractor (1) the amount determined by the Contracting Officer ... if no timely appeal has been taken, or (2) the amount finally determined on appeal.

On July 28, 1988, the agency issued Ellett a partial notice to proceed, which authorized the construction of just 4,000 feet of the road, because of pending legislation to limit entry into the area. The agency then terminated the remainder of the contract for convenience on September 30, 1988.

By letter dated November 17, 1988, the stated purpose of which was "to file formal notice of claim pursuant to the Contract Disputes Act of 1978 [(CDA)]," Ellett sought to recover $545,157.19 from the agency. Specifically, the company claimed: (1) a $136,964.81 equitable adjustment for government-ordered changes; (2) $32,036.50 for "unforeseen and unexpected security costs" that were "not disclosed in the prospectus"; and (3) $376,155.88 in lost profits. Although not submitted on the forms the FAR requires for settlement proposals, see 48 C.F.R. § 49.206-1(c) (1995) ("Settlement proposals must be on the forms prescribed in 49.602...."), Ellett says this letter, like a termination settlement proposal, was intended to recover all money due under the contract. The contracting officer responded by letter of December 2, 1988, that FAR Part 49 governs "the settlement of termination proposals and requests for contract modification." The letter said Ellett needed to submit a settlement proposal on Standard Forms (SF) 1436 (Settlement Proposal (Total Cost Basis)) and 1439 (Schedule of Accounting Information), which were enclosed.

On March 3, 1989, Ellett submitted a settlement proposal on the required forms, requesting a net payment of $494,826. It admits that the amount sought in this request was largely duplicative of its November 17, 1988 submission, although different in some respects because of the requirements of the forms and unspecified intervening events. The parties then began to negotiate a mutually agreeable settlement.

In a January 12, 1990 letter to the contracting officer, Ellett observed that it had been "nearly 14 months" since the November 17, 1988 CDA "claim" and one year since the settlement proposal. Consequently, it said that unless the "outstanding claim" were resolved satisfactorily within thirty days, it would file suit in the United States Court of Federal Claims. The agency responded with a settlement offer of $120,649, which Ellett rejected in a March 31, 1990 letter, which also said that unless the agency agreed to a settlement of $250,000 within two weeks, it would file suit.

The government rejected the $250,000 settlement offer, and the contracting officer prepared a document styled "Contracting Officer's Findings and Determination," dated June 25, 1990. There he evaluated the termination settlement proposal and concluded that Ellett was entitled to termination costs of $416,144.01, less progress payments the agency had already made, for a net of $22,779.01.

On July 13, 1990, Ellett filed a complaint in the Court of Federal Claims, seeking $451,084 plus interest, costs, and attorneys fees. The government moved to dismiss … because the November 17, 1988 letter … was not properly certified. The court agreed that the letter was not properly certified and dismissed the suit. James M. Ellett Constr. Co. v. United States, No. 90-641 C (Cl.Ct. Feb. 6, 1991). We reversed. James M. Ellett Constr. Co. v. United States, No. 91-5071, 1992 WL 82447 (Fed.Cir. Apr. 24, 1992).

On remand, the government renewed its motion to dismiss, arguing that Ellett had not yet submitted a claim to the contracting officer for purposes of the CDA.… The court held that because there was not an existing dispute on November 17, 1988, Ellett's letter of that date was not a "claim"; it was a "unilateral cost (i.e. settlement) proposal." Slip op. at 11. The court also said that the November 17, 1988 letter did not request a final determination by the contracting officer, but was only an invitation to enter negotiations. It concluded that Ellett's March 3, 1989 termination settlement proposal was not a claim because it did not seek a final decision from the contracting officer. This appeal followed.

Discussion

* * *

A. The Termination Settlement Proposal

Ellett does not contend that its March 1989 settlement proposal was a CDA claim. Rather, it argues simply that once the contracting officer reviewed the proposal and unilaterally determined that it was due a net termination settlement of $22,779.01, it was entitled, under the terms of its contract and the FAR, to appeal that determination directly to the court.

This argument is not enough, however, for us to conclude that the court had jurisdiction.… Under the FAR, there are three requirements a nonroutine submission must meet to be a "claim." It must be: (1) a written demand or assertion, (2) seeking as a matter of right, (3) the payment of money in a sum certain. 48 C.F.R. § 33.201 (1995); Reflectone,

60 F.3d at 1575. Ellett's contract required nothing more. A routine request for payment, on the other hand, must also be "in dispute" when submitted to meet the definition of a "claim." 48 C.F.R. § 33.201; Reflectone, 60 F.3d at 1576.

Our threshold inquiry, therefore, is whether Ellett's termination settlement proposal was a routine submission. See Reflectone, 60 F.3d at 1577 ("[T]he critical distinction in identifying a 'claim' is ... between routine and non-routine submissions."). In that regard, a "demand for compensation for unforeseen or unintended circumstances cannot be characterized as 'routine.'" Id. (request for an equitable adjustment is "anything but a 'routine request for payment'"). On the other hand, vouchers, invoices, and similar requests for payment are "submitted for work done or equipment delivered by the contractor in accordance with the expected or scheduled progression of contract performance." Id.

Using these beacons as guides, it is difficult to conceive of a less routine demand for payment than one which is submitted when the government terminates a contract for its convenience. Such a demand, which occurs only in a fraction of government contracts is certainly less routine than a request for an equitable adjustment, several of which a contractor might submit on any one contract. Indeed, in concluding that a request for an equitable adjustment is not routine in Reflectone, we pointed to Supreme Court precedent equating a request for an equitable adjustment with an assertion of a breach of contract. That analogue is even more appropriate here, where, but for the convenience termination clause, the government's action would be a breach of contract, and it would be liable for resulting damages. See G. L. Christian and Assocs. v. United States, 160 Ct.Cl. 1, 312 F.2d 418, 423 (1963). A request for payment submitted after the government has terminated the contract during its performance is a far cry from a request submitted in accordance with the expected or scheduled progression of contract performance.

It is beyond serious dispute that the parties intended that Ellett construct the entire 2.7 mile logging road. Because of the unforeseen legislation, however, the government decided to invoke its right to terminate the contract. Ellett's demand for compensation arising from such circumstances can hardly be considered routine. If it were routine, like a voucher or invoice, there would be no need to negotiate. However, the FAR contemplates that only after the amount a contractor is owed because of a convenience termination is determined, whether by agreement, determination, or appeal, shall a contractor submit a voucher or invoice for that amount. 48 C.F.R. § 49.112-2(a)–(b) (1995).

Relying on a dictionary, the government argues that a termination settlement proposal is a routine request for payment because the FAR and the contract establish procedures for submitting one.... Once the government terminates for convenience, the procedures used to determine a contractor's recovery could be perceived as routine, in the sense that the same ones are followed each time. However, that does not make them routine in the overall scheme of the contract and the parties' expectations.... So, as a written assertion seeking, as a matter of right under the termination for convenience clause, the payment of $451,084 plus interest, costs, and attorneys fees, it met the FAR's requirements of a valid claim.

As we said in Reflectone, however, not every nonroutine submission constitutes a CDA claim. See 60 F.3d at 1577 n. 7. Besides meeting the FAR definition of a claim, the CDA also requires that all claims be submitted to the contracting officer for a decision. 41 U.S.C. § 605(a) (1994); see also 48 C.F.R. § 33.206; ... When a contractor submits a termination settlement proposal, it is for the purpose of negotiation, not for a contracting officer's decision. A settlement proposal is just that: a proposal. See 48 C.F.R. § 49.001 (1995) ("a proposal for effecting settlement of a contract terminated in whole or in part, submitted by a contractor or subcontractor in the form, and supported by the data, required by this part"). Indeed, it is a proposal that Ellett contractually agreed to submit in the event of a convenience termination. The parties agreed that they would try to reach a mutually agreeable settlement. If they were unable to do so, however, it was agreed, consonant with the FAR's requirements, that the contracting officer would issue a final decision, see id. §§ 52.249-2(f) (Alternate I), 49.103, 49.105(a)(4), which Ellett could appeal to the court or to the Department of Agriculture Board of Contract Appeals, id. § 52.249-2(i). Consequently, while Ellett's termination settlement proposal met the FAR's definition of a claim, at the time of submission it was not a claim because it was not submitted to the contracting officer for a decision.

Once negotiations reached an impasse, the proposal, by the terms of the FAR and the contract, was submitted for decision; it became a claim. In other words, in accordance with the contract's prescribed method of compensating Ellett for a convenience termination, a request that the contracting officer issue a decision in the event the parties were unable to agree on a settlement was implicit in Ellett's proposal. After ten months of fruitless negotiations, Ellett explicitly requested that the contracting officer settle its claim. This demand is tantamount to an express request for a contracting officer's decision. Hence, after the subsequent exchange of offers and counteroffers, the contracting officer settled Ellett's proposal by determination and Ellett filed suit.

That the termination settlement proposal would ripen into a claim requiring the contracting officer to issue a unilateral settlement determination was contemplated by the contract and the FAR. They provide explicitly that Ellett had the right to appeal the contracting officer's decision on its proposal. 48 C.F.R. § 52.249-2(i); see also id. § 49.109-7(d) (a contracting officer's settlement determination "shall advise the contractor that the determination is a final decision from which the contractor may appeal under the Disputes clause"). The FAR implicitly includes termination settlement proposals within the operative definition of a claim to the extent they are not favorably resolved by a contracting officer's decision. The government responds that Ellett's termination settlement proposal was not an appealable claim for three reasons: (1) once negotiations reached an impasse, Ellett was required to submit a new claim or convert its termination settlement proposal into a claim, detailing what issues were in dispute, an act it failed to perform; (2) because the FAR prohibits the payment of interest on a settlement agreement or a settlement by determination, a settlement proposal cannot be a CDA claim; and (3) Ellett's certification was defective because it had to be but was not made after the parties' negotiations stalled.

On the first argument, after negotiations reached an impasse, the contracting officer issued a unilateral decision on the settlement proposal pursuant to paragraph (f) of the termination for convenience clause. 48 C.F.R. § 52.249-2(f) (Alternate I); see also id. § 49.109-7 (governing settlements by determination). Ellett points out that under section (i) of that clause, "[t]he contractor shall have the right of appeal, under the Disputes clause, from any determination made by the Contracting Officer under paragraph (d) [or] (f)...." Id. § 52.249-2(i).

The right of appeal in the Disputes clause provides that "[t]he Contracting Officer's decision [on a claim] shall be final unless the Contractor appeals or files a suit as provided in the Act." Id. § 52.233-1(f). Under "the Act," a contractor may appeal a contracting officer's final decision to the appropriate agency board of contract appeals, 41 U.S.C. §§ 606–607 (1994), or to the Court of Federal Claims, id. § 609(a)(1). Indeed, the FAR grants contractors a right to appeal "from" a contracting officer's determination on a settlement proposal. 48 C.F.R. § 52.249-2(i). It does not speak of appealing that decision back "to" the contracting officer by submitting a new claim, a futile act.... Nor is there a requirement that the settlement proposal be converted into a claim. To the contrary, the FAR envisions a direct appeal of the contracting officer's determination. In the cover letter the contracting officer identified the settlement determination as the "final decision of the Contracting Officer," and provided the notice of appeal rights required by the FAR to be included in a contracting officer's final decision on a claim. 48 C.F.R. § 33.211(a)(4)(v) (1995). As further evidence of Ellett's appeal rights, 48 C.F.R. § 49.109-7(g) ("Decision on the contractor's appeal " (emphasis added)) instructs the contracting officer to "give effect to a decision of the [Court of Federal Claims] or a board of contract appeals, when necessary, by an appropriate modification to the contract."

* * *

B. The November 17, 1988 Submission

Ellett also argues that it was entitled to submit its November 17, 1988 "claim" independently of its termination settlement proposal. If this is correct, then it would be entitled to extra interest under the CDA. 41 U.S.C. § 611.

We need not strain to conclude that the November 17, 1988 submission, which we have already held was properly certified, met the requirements of a valid, nonroutine claim under Reflectone. The claim included requests for equitable adjustments for government-ordered changes in the work performed and for a constructive change because of the government's failure to disclose its superior knowledge. See Petrochem Servs., Inc. v. United States, 837 F.2d 1076, 1078–79 (Fed.Cir.1988). Requests for an equitable adjustment submitted in response to contract changes, like these, are precisely the type of claims we held were nonroutine in Reflectone. It is without question a written demand pursuant to the CDA; it seeks a sum certain of $545,157.19; and it does so as a matter of right under the Changes clause of the contract.

We disagree that Ellett's submission, which was identified as a claim under the CDA, failed because it closed with the remark that Ellett would be happy to meet with the government to discuss the adjustment of the claim.... The government argues that when it terminates a contract for convenience, all claims a contractor might have, including equitable adjustments, are subsumed within the termination settlement proposal. Ellett, on the other hand, argues that there is no authority in the CDA or the FAR "for simply eliminating valid contractor claims by terminating the contract." We agree with Ellett.... Our conclusion is buttressed by the FAR. If a contract is completely terminated, the termination contracting officer is required to settle all "related unsettled contract changes" as part of the final settlement. 48 C.F.R. § 49.114(a) (1995). An unsettled contract change is "any contract change or contract term for which a definitive modification is required but has not been executed." Id. § 49.001. On the other hand, if "a part, but not all, of the work that has not been completed and accepted under a contract" is terminated, id. § 49.001, the prime contractor must perform the continued portion of the contract and promptly submit any request for an equitable adjustment of price for that portion. Id. § 49.104(d). The contracting officer is required to address these claims unless that responsibility is delegated to the termination contracting officer. Id. § 49.114(b); see also id. § 49.208(b) (requiring termination contracting officers to ensure that no portion of costs included in an equitable adjustment made after partial termination are included in the termination settlement).

It is unclear from our record whether all of the work Ellett had completed at the time of termination had been accepted. Thus, we are unable to determine whether the termination was partial or complete. Regardless, the regulations anticipate the submission of claims independently of the termination settlement proposal.

Therefore, Ellett was entitled to submit a claim for the increased costs it incurred due to contract changes the government made on the work it performed, notwithstanding its termination settlement proposal. It submitted a claim for such costs, which was either constructively denied in the contracting officer's settlement determination or deemed denied because the contracting officer did not directly address the merits. Either way, the trial court had jurisdiction.

Conclusion

Accordingly, the judgment of the United States Court of Federal Claims is reversed, and the case is remanded for further proceedings consistent with this opinion.

Notes and Questions

1. The opinion illustrates that the contractor's inability to contest whether the government will terminate for convenience only begins, not ends, the lawyering role in such a termination. In effect, by seeking equitable adjustments as part of a termination settlement proposal, the contractor and the contractor's lawyer take the offensive against the government. They can, and do, contend that the government has engaged in what would have been called, a century ago, a breach of contract, and that therefore the terminated contractor deserves a large measure of damage relief.

2. Procedurally, the termination settlement proposal itself comes across as a combination of a contested proceeding, and a negotiation. The FAR offers separate guidance— for negotiated termination settlements, and for termination settlements imposed by the contracting officer to which the contractor may contest. Is this like an early form of alternative dispute resolution, in which the government and the contractor simply treat negotiation as a possible way to resolve their difference without litigating? Or, given the great variety of termination situations, should it be expected that in many types of situation, a comparatively amicable settlement can occur, and only occasionally need there by a contested proceeding about the size of the payment?

3. The goal after Termination for Convenience remains fair compensation to the contractor, and the FAR provides that business judgment be used in negotiating a settlement agreement—as opposed to rigid measures of cost and accounting data, which should be no more than a guide in reaching an agreement. FAR 49.201 (a). Nonetheless, the FAR provides for specific limitations to costs that may be claimed for settlement by the contractor. Logically, all FAR sections prohibit payment of termination costs that would exceed the total contract price. Then, the FAR addresses allowable and prohibited costs based on the type of contract and the nature of termination (by default or for convenience).

Generally, costs categorized as overhead may not be included in a settlement. For example, when a contract for commercial items is terminated for convenience, the settlement cannot include costs associated with unabsorbed overhead (FAR 252.211-7000). Allocable portions of costs attributed to facilities acquired for the work in a multi-year contract may be claimed, so long as the costs have not been charged to the contract through overhead (FAR 52.217-2). Settlement costs may include charges associated with the "storage, transportation, and other costs incurred ... for the preservation, protection, or disposition of the termination inventory" (FAR 52.249-2), but undelivered items in the contractor's stock which are readily marketable cannot be claimed (FAR 252.211-7000).

Jacobs Engineering Group, Inc., Plaintiff-Appellant,

v.

United States, Defendant-Appellee

No. 05-5052

434 F.3d 1378

United States Court of Appeals, Federal Circuit.

Jan. 19, 2006

Before MAYER, Circuit Judge, FRIEDMAN, Senior Circuit Judge, and BRYSON, Circuit Judge.

FRIEDMAN, Senior Circuit Judge.

A development and construction contract required the government to reimburse the contractor for 80 percent of its cost of performing the contract. The contract's termination-for-the-convenience-of-the-government clause ("termination clause") required the government upon such termination to pay the contractor "[a]ll costs reimbursable" under the contract. *See*48 C.F.R.§ 52.249-6(g); *Jacobs Eng'g Group, Inc. v. United States,* 63 Fed.Cl. 451, 455 (2005) (trial court decision). The question is whether, when the government so terminated the contract, it was required to reimburse the contractor for all of the costs the contractor incurred up to that point or only for 80 percent of them. Reversing the United States Court of Federal Claims, we hold that the contractor may recover all of its cost, rather than 80 percent.

I

The government entered into a contract with Jacobs Engineering Group, Inc. ("Jacobs")' predecessor (whose contract Jacobs took over when it acquired the predecessor) to develop, design, fabricate, construct, and install a gasification improvement facility. No fee was payable to the contractor, but the contract contained the following cost sharing provision covering the "total estimated cost for the work" of $28,750,375:

Cost Sharing. The Contractor and the Government agree to share the cost of the effort for Phase I and Phase II as follows:

	Government (80%)	Contractor (20%)	Total (100%)
Phase I	$19,850,784	$4,962,696	$24,813,480
Phase II	$ 3,149,515	$ 787,379	$ 3,936,894
Total	$23,000,299	$5,750,075	$28,750,370

The contract further provided that if the contracting officer approved a cost overrun, the contractor's share would be 20 percent.

The contract also contained a standard termination for convenience clause, Federal Acquisition Regulation ("FAR")§ 52.249-6 (May 1986), which authorized the government to "terminate performance of work [if][t]he Contracting Officer determines that a termination is in the Government's interest." If that occurred, the government was required to pay the contractor "[a]ll costs reimbursable under this contract, not previously paid, for the performance of this contract before the effective date of the termination, and part of those costs that may continue for a reasonable time with the approval of or as directed by the Contracting Officer." FAR§ 52.249-6(g)(1) (May 1986).

The contract also authorized the contractor to discontinue the project after Phase I was completed unless it received what it deemed "adequate cost sharing and ... an advanced patent waiver. "If the contractor did so, it would "be liable for 20% of the costs incurred during the performance period.""

During performance, the government terminated the contract for its convenience (because it did not have funds to complete performance). Jacobs submitted a termination settlement proposal which sought reimbursement of 100 percent of its costs, which the government rejected. The contracting officer then rejected Jacobs' claim for recovery of all of its costs, limiting recovery to 80 percent. Jacobs challenged that decision in the United States Court of Federal Claims.

On cross-motion for summary judgment, the court granted the government's motion and entered a judgment on its behalf. 63 Fed.Cl. at 459. The court stated:

> The termination clause does not invalidate the cost-sharing provision of the Contract. Rather, it clearly seeks to fashion a remedy for the contractor *in conjunction with* the cost-sharing provisions. Thus, only those costs that would be reimbursed under the Contract will be paid to the contractor in the event of a termination for convenience. Here 80 percent of Jacobs's costs were reimbursable under the cost-sharing provision and therefore, under the termination for convenience clause, Jacobs is entitled to only 80 percent of its costs not previously paid.

Id. at 457 (emphasis in original) (citations omitted).

II

The termination clause required the government, upon terminating the contract, to pay the contractor "[a]ll costs reimbursable under this contract." The government contends, as the Court of Federal Claims held, that since the contract required it to reimburse the contractor for only 80 percent of the costs, its payment under the termination clause is limited to 80 percent of the costs. We conclude, however, that the term "all costs reimbursable" defines the type or kind of costs for which the contract provides reimbursement and not the amount of such costs.

The contract specifies a substantial number of costs that are reimbursable and some that are not. Reimbursable costs include "fabricated or unfabricated, parts, work in process, completed work, supplies, and other materials procured or acquired for the work terminated, ... completed or partially completed plans, drawings, information, and other property that ... would be required to be furnished to the Government, ... and the jigs, dies, fixtures, and other special tools and tooling acquired or manufactured for this contract." FAR§ 52.249-6(c)(6) (May 1986). They also include costs allowable under FAR§ 31.2 (*see* FAR§ 52.249-6(h) (May 2004)), such as labor relations costs (FAR§ 31.205-21), plant protection costs (FAR§ 31.205 29), and help-wanted advertising costs for jobs specific to the project (FAR§ 31.205-34(a)(1)). On the other hand, entertainment costs (FAR§ 31.205-14), fines and penalties (FAR§ 31.205-15), and general help-wanted advertisement costs (FAR§ 31.205-34(b)) are not reimbursable. The termination clause's reference to "all costs reimbursable" under the contract appears designed to incorporate the contract's division between reimbursable and non-reimbursable costs.

Throughout the contract, when the parties intended the 80 percent-20 percent division of costs to cover particular situations, they explicitly so provided. The table shown above specified the amount of the costs for each phase of the contract that each party would bear. If the contractor terminated performance after Phase I was completed, it would "be liable for 20% of the costs incurred during the performance period." If there was an approved cost overrun, the contractor was required to absorb 20 percent of it.

In these circumstances, it seems most unlikely that if the parties had intended the termination clause to limit the contractor to 80 percent of the termination costs, they would not have said so instead of providing that the government would pay "[a]ll costs reimbursable" under the contract. We cannot read the latter phrase covering "all" reimbursable costs to mean 80 percent of such costs. In any event, to the extent there is an ambiguity on the point, it must be resolved in favor of Jacobs, the non-drafter of the contract.

Our conclusion also accords with the basic financial situation underlying the contract. FAR§ 16.303(b) states that "[a] cost-sharing contract may be used when the contractor agrees to absorb a portion of the costs, in the expectation of substantial compensating benefits." If the contract had been completely performed at an estimated cost of more than $28 million, the government's reimbursement of only 80 percent of that amount presumably would have resulted in a substantial loss to the contractor. Jacobs tells us in its brief that the reason the contractor entered into such a seemingly unattractive venture was the anticipation that as a result of its performance, it would obtain valuable patent rights, to which the contract referred.

As a result of the government's termination of the contract, Jacobs was denied the opportunity to obtain such patent rights. In these circumstances, it seems unfair to Jacobs to deny it full reimbursement for the costs of its performance up to the government's contract termination, which thwarted its possibility of obtaining the patent rights. "A contractor is not supposed to suffer as the result of a termination for convenience of the Government, nor to underwrite the Government's decision to terminate. If he has actually incurred costs…, it is proper that he be reimbursed those costs when the Government terminates for convenience and thereby custs [sic] off his ability to amortize those costs completely." *In re Kasler Elec. Co.,* DOTCAB 1425, 84-2 BCA 0 17374 (May 21, 1984).

CONCLUSION

The judgment of the Court of Federal Claims is reversed and the case is remanded to that court to award damages.

Notes and Questions

Partial terminations. The FAR provides the government with mechanisms by which to delete work from a fixed-price contract when the contracting officer determines it to be in the government's best interest. Under the "termination for convenience" clause the contracting officer may partially terminate the contract and the contractor maintains specific obligations in such instances. 48 C.F.R. § 52.249-2. The FAR also authorizes the contracting officer to enter into a settlement agreement with the contractor when termination occurs. 48 C.F.R. § 49.101.

Partial terminations compensate the contractor for additional costs incurred for work not terminated resulting from the work terminated, while placing some limits: contractors still do not obtain profits beyond what would have occurred with contract completion, nor do they reverse losses occurring had the contract been completed. 48 C.F.R. § 52.249-2. In the *Appeal of Power Generators, Inc.* the ASBCA held that the contractor providing a generator that became defective was entitled to costs incurred from attempts to repair it prior to subsequent partial termination, but proportionate to losses that would have been incurred had the contract been unchanged. ASBCA No. 7607, 1962 BCA ¶ 3358.

The other means by which work can be deleted is under the "Changes" clause, and equitable adjustment follows a different rule. 48 C.F.R. § 52.243-1.

Note on Termination for Convenience Settlements

1. Process

The contractor may have a year to develop a termination for convenience settlement proposal, or more, or less (e). Then, the contractor and the Contracting Officer try to reach agreement on the settlement proposal (f).

That proposal consists of a number of standard government forms, such as a settlement proposal certified by the contractor, inventory schedules, accounting information, and subcontractor proposals. The termination settlement proposal goes to the Defense Contract Audit Agency (DCAA) for an audit, generating an audit report. When the DCAA auditors want to advise the contracting officer against the allowability of particular costs, their audit report will "question" those costs. An agency contracts attorney may also review legal issues posed by the settlement proposal

A contracting officer may prepare use the audit report, a legal memo, and other so-called "field work" to generate a prenegotiation position. Once settlement negotiations end, if there is agreement, the contractor and the contracting officer prepare a settlement agreement. The agency prepares a Settlement Negotiation Memorandum for its internal review.

The issues regarding what the government owes the terminated contractor deserve attention. Note how the termination clause's provision (h) makes cost principles apply. These have been discussed in another chapter. Normally, government contracts are either fixed price — no cost principles — or cost reimbursement. What the termination clause does is make cost principles apply universally, regardless of whether the contract originally involved them in pricing. The saying is that Termination for Convenience converts a fixed price contract into a cost reimbursement contract for the work performed.

Termination clause section (f) creates wide-open flexibility for the terminated contractor and the contracting officer to agree upon a settlement figure, in contrast to the greater precision and restriction of section (g) when the contracting officer determines a figure. In fact, the parties may reach a "lump sum" agreement, in which they agree on the amount of the settlement even though they may reach the figure in different ways.

2. Guidance for Settlement

Section (e) does give some guidance for deriving a settlement figure. The settlement "may include a reasonable allowance for profit on work done." However, "the agreed amount, whether under this paragraph (f) or paragraph (g) below ... may not exceed the total contract price" with two reductions: "payments previously made," and "the contract price of work not done." Leaving aside payments already made, an agreed figure between the contracting officer and the contractor can follow a basic formula: Contract Price (total) minus Contract Price (for work not done).

Moreover, the termination clause indicates several ways of raising that figure. It exempts a category of costs in subsection (g)(3), namely, the settlement costs of the termination. These include "Accounting, legal, clerical, and other expenses reasonably necessary for the preparation of termination settlement proposals and supporting data" ((g)(3)(i)). In other words, the government contracts lawyer billing for work reasonably necessary for preparing settlement proposals can get the contractor reimbursed by the government for her bills, a factor helping the lawyer to persuade the contractor to place some of the burdens of working on the settlement proposal onto the lawyer. Also, in a partial termination, the contractor can seek an equitable adjustment for the price of the "continued portion of the contract" (provision (l)).

3. Determination When There Is No Settlement

Both sides must consider what happens without an agreement, namely, the contracting officer reaching a determination pursuant to provision (g). This is the part that gets fought about. In contrast with the previously noted ceiling, which starts with the total contract price and subtracts from it, the calculations pursuant to provision (g) start with the "contract price for completed supplies or services accepted by the Government" ((g)(1)), and adds to that. Usually, this formula will come well below the ceiling that starts with the total contract price, unless the unusual situation is present that the government terminates a contract in which a comparatively large portion of what there was to purchase has been produced and accepted.

To the price for completed supplies or services, the determination process adds, on the termination portion, the costs already incurred, such as start-up costs on the contract or the costs of materials ordered and not returnable without some expenditure ((g)(2)(i)). It also includes the cost of terminated subcontractor settlements ((g)(2)(ii)), and a figure for profit on the costs incurred. The clause takes special note to warn that if the "contractor would have sustained a loss on the entire contract had it been completed," then no profit gets allowed and the contracting officer "shall reduce the settlement to reflect the indicated rate of loss (g)(2)(iii). This may not be all that common, but it can happen, when contractors bid low seeking the work for various reasons, and some of those reasons may vanish as a result of termination by convenience (for example, the expectation of profiting by follow-on contracts like spare parts).

If they fail, the Contracting Officer determines a figure based on specified factors (g). That figure excludes "property that is destroyed, lost, stolen or damaged" (h) and follows the "cost principles and procedures" (i), much like an equitable adjustment. The figuring deducts payments to the contractor or government claims against the contractor (k). In a partial termination, the contractor can also propose equitable adjustments of the prices "of the continued portion of the contract."

When the contractor and the Contracting Officer disagree, this produces a "dispute" to resolve pursuant to the Disputes Clause. Namely, the contractor takes the dispute either to the applicable board of contract appeals (ASBCA or CBCA), or to the Court of Federal Claims.

For further treatment of these issues see Graeme S. Henderson, *Germinations for Convenience and the Termination Costs Clause*, 53 Air Force L. Rev. 103 (2002); Neil H. O'Donnell & Patricia A. Meagher, "Negotiating the Settlement Proposal," in Terminations of Government Contracts (2007)(available in Westlaw); Paul J. Seidman & David J. Seidman, *Maximizing Termination for Convenience Settlements / Edition II — Parts I & II*, 08-3 Briefing Papers 1, Feb. & April 2008.

B. Defense

The grounds for contesting a termination for convenience, encapsulated in the *Krygoski* opinion, deserve some notice. The issue of the grounds for contesting a termination for convenience is not nearly of the practical value of the issue of the grounds for contesting a termination for default. Contractors contest few terminations for convenience, and succeed in even fewer such contests. Rather, this examination gets at what termination for convenience illuminates about some of the fundamentals of government contracting. Convenience termination represents a major difference between basic (private) contracting, where the parties would generally have no such unilateral power to cancel and to resolve the damage issues in such a way, and government contracting. Does convenience termination exist as a demonstration of absolute sovereign will by which the government has simply decided to make sure that it always holds a trump card over the contractor, regardless of whether this makes either economic sense or accords with fairness? Or does convenience termination have more limited purposes and, if so, accompanying checks? As in many other contexts of government power in government contracting, a tradeoff has to be made between the desirability of encouraging government officers to make contracting decisions to effectuate government policy without undue hindrance, and the drive, by private parties, to interest courts and boards in establishing checks on economic inefficiency or on alleged misuse of official power.

While the contract boards and courts rarely invalidate a termination for convenience, they do discuss in a highly sophisticated and illuminating way what they consider the standard to be. This gives the distinct impression that the standard has changed over time, something which the *Krygoski* opinion both describes, as to prior opinions, and exemplifies, as to how its own statement of the standard varies from prior ones.

Each of the two types of standard discussed in *Krygoski* warrant separate consideration. First, as *Krygoski* describes, the contracting officer cannot properly terminate in bad faith or as an abuse of discretion. This reflects the role of reviewing tribunals in checking abuses of official power. The deferential standard applied, that contractors have a heavy burden of proof to show bad faith, reflects that the system contemplates a broad grant of power to terminate for convenience.

Second, a more unclear standard has applied to whether and when a contracting officer can terminate for reasons that, at the time of contracting, were anticipated, or knowable, rather than for an unforeseen later change in circumstances. This reflects, in part, the contrast between government contracting and basic (private) contracting. On purely economic grounds, a private contractor who possessed the power to cancel unilaterally, without needing any cause, would take simple advantage of shifts in the market of a kind fully anticipated at the time of contracting. For example, a buyer who contracted to buy widgets for delivery six months hence, with a power to cancel unilaterally without needing any cause, would cancel if the market price of widgets went down and not if the price went up. Such concerns underlie the serious question, at common law, whether a contract with such a power to cancel unilaterally without cause would be deemed no contract at all, an "illusory" contract without valid consideration because of the buyer's having a "free way out." The *Torncello* opinion, which has been discussed, interpreted, and reinterpreted in all the subsequent contested termination for convenience opinions, including *Krygoski*, reflects this fundamental concern.

For further discussion of the subjects in this subsection, see: Frederick W. Claybrook, Jr., *Good Faith in the Termination and Formation of Federal Contracts*, 56 Md. L. Rev. 555 (1997); Michael D. Garson, Krygoski *and the Termination for Convenience: Have Circumstances Really Changed?*, 27 Pub. Cont. L.J. 117 (1997).

G. L. Christian and Associates v. The United States

Court of Claims
312 F.2d 418
No. 56–59
Jan. 11, 1963

Opinion is in Chapter 1.

Notes and Questions

1. Observe how the G. L. Christian opinion refers back to the history of the power of termination for convenience as justification for the government's ability to provide a limited remedy. Why did government contract law diverge early from contract law in this regard? Why has the divergence continued?

2. In previous parts of this subchapter, the detailed wording of the termination for convenience clause has mattered greatly, sometimes for the government's benefit, sometimes for the contractor's benefit. Why is the court able, for purposes of this case, to get past the absence of that clause from the text of the contract?

Forfeiture by Cancellation or Termination

Charles Tiefer, 54 Mercer Law Review 1031 (2003)

Termination for convenience by the government provides a valuable field in which to study the doctrines of termination powers, for it allows a look back at almost a century and a half of readily examined development. During that time, vigorous debate has occurred between two positions: the position that public policy warrants the government terminating its contracts by paying for the contractors' reliance interest but not full expectation damages, and the opposition position of contractors, often backed by sympathetic commentators, that such termination transgresses their legitimate contract rights to full expectation damages....

Federal government termination of contracts for convenience doctrine dates back to seminal Supreme Court cases following the Civil War. During World War I, Congress provided legislatively for government termination for convenience, producing two signal Supreme Court rulings. In the first, the Court reasoned that, given the prospect of government termination of contracts at war's end, "[t]he possible loss of profits [from this] must be regarded as within the contemplation of the parties," and the remedy for the canceled contractor could just compensate the reliance interest without also compensating for the contractor's lost anticipated profits. Second, in *College Point*, the Court created the doctrine of constructive termination for convenience, allowing the government to compensate just for the reliance interest in diverse situations.[1]

The concept of termination for convenience received extensive use during and after World War II. In 1982, the Court of Claims, hearing a major case en banc, heeded criticisms by commentators in an important ruling that produced extensive debate over the following fourteen years: *Torncello v. United States.* An opinion for three of the six judges of the en banc court traced the history of termination for convenience in detail, suggested that without greater protection for contractors the government contract would be illusory, and concluded that the refusal to allow expectation damages could not be so generally justified.

---

1. The government could limits its compensation to the reliance interest even in situations where it had not considered itself to be, or notified that it was, terminating for convenience. As Justice Brandeis contrasted in one of his classic analyses of government contracting, in an ordinary contract, "the ordinary liability of one who, having contracted ... without cause, gives notice that he will not accept delivery ... [is] for the prospective profits." However, since the government's "right to cancel.... [was a] continuing right of cancellation, which was asserted later.... Prospective profits were not recoverable." ...

During the following decade and a half, *Torncello* drew extensive attention in subsequent cases[2] and commentary. The Federal Circuit, the newly-created successor court to the Court of Claims, although generally adhering to Claims Court precedents, began visibly undermining *Torncello* in 1990, and sent a second major signal in 1995. The Federal Circuit delivered the coup de grace against *Torncello* in 1996 in *Krygoski Construction Co. v. United States. Krygoski* culminated in what might be called a public policy analysis of how government officials could be trusted not to abuse a termination power....

Krygoski Construction Company, Inc., Plaintiff-Appellee, v. The United States, Defendant-Appellant

No. 95-5136
United States Court of Appeals, Federal Circuit
94 F.3d 1537
Aug. 1, 1996

Before RICH, RADER, and BRYSON, Circuit Judges.

RADER, Circuit Judge.

The United States Court of Federal Claims determined that the United States Army Corps of Engineers (Corps) had no justification for terminating a demolition contract with Krygoski Construction Company, Inc. (Krygoski) for the Government's convenience. Krygoski Constr. Co. v. United States, No. 214-89C (Fed.Cl. March 2, 1993). To remedy the breach, the trial court awarded Krygoski $1,456,851.10 in damages plus interest pending payment. Krygoski Constr. Co. v. United States, No. 214-89C (Fed.Cl. May 19, 1995). Because the trial court incorrectly relied on Torncello v. United States, 231 Ct.Cl. 20, 681 F.2d 756 (1982), this court reverses and remands.

BACKGROUND

In 1985, the Corps undertook demolition of an abandoned U.S. Air Force airfield and missile site near Raco, Michigan. During surveys of the site, the Corps found asbestos contamination. Based on blueprints and its survey, the Corps estimated that two buildings at the site contained asbestos contamination in 1600 linear feet of pipe insulation and 650 square feet of tank and duct insulation. The survey also revealed that extensive vandalism may have spread asbestos debris on the floors of the buildings.

On August 12, 1985, the Corps issued an invitation for bids on the demolition project. The solicitation noted that bids should range between $500,000 and $1,000,000. Eight bidders bid on the contract. Krygoski won the contract with the low bid of $414,696. On or about September 30, 1985, Krygoski and the United States through the Detroit District of the Army Corps of Engineers entered into Contract No. DACA35-85-C-0001. This contract required removal and disposal of the asbestos during restoration of the site.

* * *

The contract contained a Variations in Estimated Quantities (VEQ) Clause for items 1, 2, 4, and 5 above:

> Variation from the estimated quantity in the actual work performed under any second or subsequent sub-item ... will not be the basis for an adjustment in contract unit price.

---

2. By 1996, "Torncello has been cited for various legal propositions in 90 board of contract appeals decisions, 46 Claims Court and Court of Federal Claims decisions, and 12 Federal Circuit decisions." ...

This VEQ Clause anticipated variations in asbestos quantities for these four items at the Raco site. The VEQ Clause, however, did not contemplate quantity variations for asbestos removal in other areas.

Krygoski conducted a predemolition survey. Just ten days after Krygoski acknowledged receipt of the notice to proceed with the contract, Mr. Phillips, Krygoski's counsel, informed the Corps of asbestos in the vinyl flooring and roof insulation of the Raco buildings. Krygoski proposed to remove the tile for a unit price of $8.78 per square foot—the cost of removing additional duct insulation under item 2 of the VEQ Clause. The Corps requested Thermo Analytical, Inc. to take samples at potential new locations of asbestos contamination. The tests showed asbestos in the tile and the flashing at the Composite building, but not in the roof insulation.

From examining the drawings, the Corps' Area Office estimated asbestos removal needs at 36,340 square feet. At Krygoski's removal price of $8.78 per square foot, this amount of removal yielded an additional cost of about $320,000 for the floor tile. The Corps did not, however, actually test each tile. The Corps derived its estimate from the drawings.

The contracting officer, Lieutenant Colonel Phillip Johnson (LTC Johnson), considered a price increase of this dimension a cardinal change in the contract. LTC Johnson reached this conclusion because this increase exceeds 33% of the total contract cost. For a change of this magnitude, the Corps followed a general policy of terminating the contract for the convenience of the Government and reprocuring the work competitively under the Competition in Contracting Act. LTC Johnson also considered that Krygoski had not started work on the contract. In fact, Krygoski had done little beyond transporting four pieces of equipment to the Raco site. In light of these circumstances, the Corps terminated the contract for the convenience of the Government on September 5, 1986.

Following the termination, the Corps resolicited bids for the Raco site demolition. The Corps revised its specifications to reflect the additional asbestos removal work as well as other changes. The Corps received eight offers on this new solicitation, DACA35-87-B-001. Krygoski was the sixth lowest bidder at $1,200,000. Anderson Excavating & Wrecking Co. (Anderson) won the bidding at $443,200. Due to modifications to the contract, the Corps eventually paid Anderson a total of $542,861.60 to complete the contract.

Krygoski sued in the Court of Federal Claims alleging that the Corps breached its original contract. Relying on Torncello, 681 F.2d at 772 (reading the termination for convenience clause to require some change in the circumstances of the bargain or in the expectations of the parties), the trial court found the Government improperly terminated Krygoski's contract. In the alternative, the trial court found the Government abused its discretion in terminating the contract under the Kalvar standard. Kalvar Corp. v. United States, 211 Ct.Cl. 192, 543 F.2d 1298, 1301–02 (1976), cert. denied, 434 U.S. 830, 98 S.Ct. 112, 54 L.Ed.2d 89 (1977). Accordingly, the trial court awarded Krygoski $1,456,851.20 in damages plus interest. This amount included anticipatory lost profits. The Government appeals.

DISCUSSION

This court reviews Court of Federal Claims decisions for errors of law and clearly erroneous findings of fact. Cooper v. United States, 827 F.2d 762, 763 (Fed.Cir.1987) (citing Milmark Servs., Inc. v. United States, 731 F.2d 855, 857 (Fed.Cir.1984)).

The trial court thoroughly analyzed the factual circumstances and legal principles of this case. Its careful work properly framed the issues for this appeal. As the trial court perceived, the case law governing the decision to terminate a contract for convenience has not always set a clear, unambiguous standard. See Torncello, 681 F.2d at 764–72 (recounting history of terminations for convenience). An examination of termination for convenience law from several decades ago discloses mixed signals about limiting terminations under the bad faith/abuse of discretion standard in Kalvar, 543 F.2d at 1301–06, or the change of circumstances test in Torncello, 681 F.2d at 772. A full review of more recent case law, coupled with recent enactments, however, discloses a clear signal for implementation of termination for convenience clauses.

I.

At the outset, this court traces some of the history leading up to articulation of two tests for convenience terminations. The Government always possessed the power to terminate its contracts; such action, however, constituted a contract breach.... Terminations for the Government's convenience developed as a tool to avoid enormous procurements upon completion of a war effort. Because public policy counselled against proceeding with wartime contracts after an end to hostilities, the Government, under certain circumstances, began to terminate contracts and settle with the contractor for partial performance. In 1863, the Army, for example, promulgated Rule 1179 in the Army Regulations concerning contracting for subsistence stores. Rule 1179 expressly "provide[d] for [subsistence contract] termination at such time as the Commissary-General may direct." United States v. Speed, 75 U.S. (8 Wall.) 77, 78, 19 L.Ed. 449 (1868). The Supreme Court has acknowledged the Government's authority to settle breach claims after a convenience termination. Cf. United States v. Corliss-Steam Engine Co., 91 U.S. 321, 323, 23 L.Ed. 397 (1875) (finding the Navy Department had authority to suspend work under a contract and enter into a breach settlement for partial performance); see also Cibinic & Nash, at 1073–74.

After World War I, the Government terminated contracts in large numbers. New statutory authority provided for settlement of the claims from those terminations. See Dent Act, 40 Stat. 1272 (1919). When World War II started, the Contract Settlement Act of 1944, 58 Stat. 649, provided further statutory and regulatory provisions for contract termination. See Cibinic & Nash, at 1074.

In 1964, the first edition of the Federal Procurement Regulation (FPR) included optional termination for convenience clauses. FPR 1-8.700-2. By 1967, the FPR required termination for convenience clauses in most procurement contracts. 32 Fed.Reg. 9683 (1967). Thus, termination for convenience — initially developed for war contracts — evolved into a principle for Government contracts of far-ranging varieties, both civilian and military. See 48 C.F.R. § 49.502 (1995). The exigencies of war no longer limited the Government's ability to terminate a contract for convenience. Although wartime situations no longer limit use of the practice, the Government's authority to invoke a termination for convenience has, nonetheless, retained limits. A contracting officer may not terminate for convenience in bad faith, for example, simply to acquire a better bargain from another source. Torncello, 681 F.2d at 772. When tainted by bad faith or an abuse of contracting discretion, a termination for convenience causes a contract breach. See Allied Materials & Equip. Co. v. United States, 215 Ct.Cl. 902, 905–06, 1977 WL 9596 (1977); National Factors, Inc. v. United States, 204 Ct.Cl. 98, 492 F.2d 1383, 1385 (1974); Keco Indus., Inc. v. United States, 203 Ct.Cl. 566, 492 F.2d 1200, 1203–04 (1974); John Reiner & Co. v. United States, 163 Ct.Cl. 381, 325 F.2d 438, 442 (1963), cert. denied, 377 U.S. 931, 84 S.Ct. 1332, 12 L.Ed.2d 295 (1964).

The contractor's burden to prove the Government acted in bad faith, however, is very weighty. Kalvar, 543 F.2d at 1301 ("Any analysis of a question of Governmental bad faith must begin with the presumption that public officials act 'conscientiously in the discharge of their duties.'" (quoting Librach v. United States, 147 Ct.Cl. 605, 612 (1959))). Due to this heavy burden of proof, contractors have rarely succeeded in demonstrating the Government's bad faith. See Cibinic & Nash, at 1078; Kalvar, 543 F.2d at 1301; Librach, 147 Ct.Cl. at 612.

II.

In 1982, this court's predecessor articulated in dicta another test for the sufficiency of convenience terminations. Torncello, 681 F.2d at 758. In Torncello, the Navy awarded a requirements contract, but then purchased some work covered by the contract from a competing bidder at a lower price. Id. In an earlier case, Colonial Metals Co. v. United States, 204 Ct.Cl. 320, 494 F.2d 1355 (1974), the Court of Claims had allowed a termination for convenience under these circumstances. In Colonial Metals, the Navy terminated a contract for copper ingot solely to obtain a better price. In fact, the Navy knew of the better price at the time of contract award. The Court of Claims permitted this termination because "such a motive [contracting for a lower price elsewhere] is not improper." 494 F.2d at 1359.

Torncello offered the opportunity to revisit and overrule the Colonial Metals case. Indeed Colonial Metals was inconsistent with the Kalvar bad faith limit on terminations for convenience. Even factoring in Kalvar's presumption of good faith actions by public officials, 543 F.2d at 1301, the Navy in Colonial Metals contracted in bad faith. At the time of award, the Navy knew of the better price it later terminated the contract to obtain.

In Torncello, the Navy—knowing it could acquire the same services at a lower price from another contractor—again contracted with Torncello and Soledad Enterprises in an exclusive requirements contract. The Navy then began satisfying its requirements from that cheaper source. Torncello claimed the Navy breached the requirements contract. The Armed Services Board of Contract Appeals found the contract constructively terminated for the Government's convenience, disallowing Torncello contract breach damages. This court's predecessor overruled Colonial Metals because the Navy used the termination for convenience clause to escape a promise it never had an intention to keep. Torncello, 681 F.2d at 772. Indeed, then Chief Judge Friedman concurred with that narrow understanding of the court's action:

> As I understand the court's opinion, the court holds only that when the government enters into a requirements contract, knowing that it can obtain an item the contract covers for less than the contract price and intending to do so, there cannot be a constructive termination for convenience of the government when the government follows that course. On that basis, I join in the opinion.

Id. at 773;[1] see also Salsbury Indus. v. United States, 905 F.2d 1518, 1521 (Fed.Cir.1990), cert. denied, 498 U.S. 1024, 111 S. Ct. 671, 112 L.Ed.2d 664 (1991) (construing the Torncello holding).

Despite the adequate justification to overrule Colonial Metals under the existing Kalvar test, a plurality of judges in Torncello proceeded to articulate in dicta a broader test for gauging the sufficiency of a convenience termination. The plurality stated that the Navy

---

1. Six judges participated in the en banc Torncello opinion. A plurality of three judges joined the reasoning that postulated a broad alternative "change of circumstances" test for convenience terminations. The remaining three judges, then Chief Judge Friedman and Circuit Judges Davis and Nichols, each concurred separately under much narrower reasoning. Judge Davis stated: "I do not agree that 'abuse of discretion' is an inadequate or unsatisfactory general standard for gauging the contracting officer's use of the termination clause." Torncello, 681 F.2d at 773....

could not invoke a convenience termination unless some change in circumstances between the time of award of the contract and the time of termination justified the action. Torncello, 681 F.2d at 772. As in this case, trial courts and boards have occasionally vacillated between applying the long-standing Kalvar test or the Torncello test.

III.

Recent enactments, however, have underscored rules of Government contracting which render the plurality's dicta in Torncello inapplicable to the present regime of contract administration. Recent statutes fully address the concerns of the Torncello plurality regarding the Government's shopping for lower prices after contract award. The Competition in Contracting Act (CICA), Pub.L. No. 98-369, 98 Stat. 1175 (codified as amended in scattered sections of 10, 31 and 41 U.S.C.), compels the promulgation of regulations and procedures to ensure full and open competition. See 41 U.S.C. §§ 401, 405(a) and 416 (1994).

In 1984, CICA articulated significant factors addressing a contracting officer's decision to terminate a contract for the Government's convenience. CICA requires executive agencies, when procuring property or services, to "obtain full and open competition through use of competitive procedures." 41 U.S.C. § 253(a)(1)(A) (1994). Thus, CICA ensures that contracting officers receive bids at competitively low prices. For each solicitation, a contracting officer must maintain full and open competition in the procurement process, unless one of the limited exceptions applies. See 10 U.S.C. § 2304 (1994). CICA mandates impartial, fair, and equitable treatment for each contractor. See 10 U.S.C. §§ 2304 and 2305 (1994).

This competitive fairness requirement, with its bid protest remedies, restrains a contracting officer's contract administration. If, for instance, a contracting officer discovers that the bid specifications inadequately describe the contract work, regulations promulgated under CICA may compel a new bid. See 10 U.S.C. § 2305; 48 C.F.R. § 1.602-2. Thus, to accommodate CICA's fairness requirements, the contracting officer may need to terminate a contract for the Government's convenience to further full and open competition. 48 C.F.R. §§ 1.602-2(b); see 41 U.S.C. § 414 (1994). Thus, to further its full competition objective, CICA permits a lenient convenience termination standard.

Not every necessary alteration of the contract scope, however, requires a new bid procedure. See 41 U.S.C. §§ 423(e)(1), 423(e)(2) (1994) (providing procedures for certifications before a contract modification or extension). Only "modifications outside the scope of the original competed contract fall under the statutory competition requirement." AT & T Communications, Inc. v. WilTel, Inc., 1 F.3d 1201, 1205 (Fed.Cir.1993). CICA does not fully define a "standard for determining when modification of an existing contract requires new competition or falls within the scope of the original competitive procurement." Id. This court, nonetheless, has stated that a "cardinal change" is a drastic modification beyond the scope of the contract:

> Under established case law, a cardinal change is a breach. It occurs when the government effects an alteration in the work so drastic that it effectively requires the contractor to perform duties materially different from those originally bargained for. By definition, then a cardinal change is so profound that it is not redressable under the contract, and thus renders the government in breach.

Id. (citing Allied Materials & Equip. Co. v. United States, 215 Ct. Cl. 406, 569 F.2d 562, 563–64 (1978)); see also Air-A-Plane Corp. v. United States, 187 Ct. Cl. 269, 408 F.2d 1030, 1032–33 (1969). In WilTel, the question was not whether the Government modifications breached a contract, but was "whether Government modifications changed the contract enough to circumvent the statutory requirement of competition." 1 F.3d at 1205. In other words, the court inquired whether the modification was within the scope of the competition for the original contract. Id.

IV.

In the wake of CICA, with its protections for competition, this court has revisited the dicta in the Torncello plurality opinion. Salsbury, 905 F.2d at 1518. . . .

Again, more recently, this court has confronted an invitation to apply the reasoning and test of the Torncello plurality. Caldwell & Santmyer, Inc. v. Glickman, 55 F.3d 1578 (Fed.Cir.1995). . . .

In sum, on two recent occasions after enactment of CICA, this court has expressly repeated the narrow applicability of Torncello. Id. at 1582; Salsbury, 905 F.2d at 1521. Indeed this court's recent pronouncements are fully consistent with the policy goals of CICA and other Government procurement statutes. Under these policies, contracting officers have no incentive to terminate a contract for convenience except to maintain full and open competition under CICA. With an adequate contractor in place, the contracting officer has no interest to reprocure. Moreover, where an officer must choose between modifying or terminating a contract, ease of administration usually imparts a bias in favour of modification. Thus Salsbury and Caldwell suggest that this court will avoid a finding of abused discretion when the facts support a reasonable inference that the contracting officer terminated for convenience in furtherance of statutory requirements for full and open competition.

V.

Turning now to this case, the termination for convenience clause of the contract provided:

> The Government may terminate performance of work under this contract in whole or, from time to time, in part if the Contracting Officer determines that a termination is in the Government's interest.

See 48 C.F.R. § 52.249-2 (1995). This contract language governs the legal relations of the parties. Under the discretion conferred by this contract language, Contracting Officer LTC Johnson decided to terminate the contract with Krygoski because removing the asbestos-containing vinyl tile would constitute a cardinal change from the originally competed contract. The contracting officer felt that a change increasing the total contract price between 25% and 33% warranted resolicitation. The trial court stated that LTC Johnson cited "no authority for his definition of cardinal change." Because the Government ultimately removed only 9,000 square feet of tile, not 36,000 square feet, the trial court concluded that the Corps arbitrarily and capriciously miscalculated the scope of asbestos abatement. To the contrary, the contracting officer had a reasonable basis for terminating the contract for the Government's convenience. Asbestos removal was originally estimated to cost about $40,000 out of an estimated $415,000 demolition contract. Thus asbestos removal accounted for about 10% of the total cost of the contract. At that point, the contracting officer's experts increased the cost of asbestos removal by about $320,000. After this change, the total asbestos removal cost was about $360,000 on a contract near $775,000 — just under 50% of the total contract. Asbestos removal, originally about 10%, became about 50% of the contract work.

Under these circumstances, the contracting officer had ample justification for conducting a reprocurement competitively under CICA. With this change in the scope of contract work, different bidders, like asbestos removal firms, may have entered the competition on the contract. See 48 C.F.R. §§ 14.203-1, 14.203-2 (1995) (enumerating the methods of soliciting bids where invitations for bids or presolicitation notices are mailed to prospective bidders or are displayed in public places, like trade journals).

In determining whether a modification falls within CICA's competition requirement, this court in WilTel examined whether the contract as modified materially departs from the scope of the original procurement. WilTel, 1 F.3d at 1205. In this case, the contracting officer, LTC Johnson, determined that the removal of the asbestos-contaminated floor tile amounted to a cardinal change, a modification outside the scope of the original competed contract. The contract has no provision to increase the cost of the contract under the VEQ Clause for removal of asbestos-contaminated floor tile. In fact, if the removal of floor tile was within the scope of the contract, Krygoski may have the obligation to remove the tile without increasing the contract price. The contracting officer, recognizing the equities of this situation, terminated the contract for convenience to comply with CICA.

The trial court erred by invoking and relying upon the Torncello plurality test. The trial court improperly found no change of circumstances sufficient to justify terminating the contract for the Government's convenience. Although arguably the Government's circumstances had sufficiently changed to meet even the Torncello plurality standard, this court declines to reach this issue because Torncello applies only when the Government enters a contract with no intention of fulfilling its promises. Salsbury, 905 F.2d at 1521.

LTC Johnson's decision to terminate is analogous to that made in Caldwell. LTC Johnson terminated the contract to preserve full and open competition. He decided to avoid any prospect of prejudice to other bidders. Unlike the Torncello situation, this record shows no evidence that the Corps intended from the outset to void its promises. Thus, Torncello does not apply. Accordingly, this court finds that LTC Johnson did not abuse his discretion, act arbitrarily or capriciously or in bad faith in terminating the contract for the Government's convenience.

This court reverses and remands for termination for convenience damages which are to include costs of performance prior to termination, profits on that performance and termination costs. No anticipatory profits are to be awarded. Reversed and remanded to calculate these costs.

COSTS

Each party shall bear its own costs.

REVERSED AND REMANDED.

Notes and Questions

1. *Krygoski* gives a glimpse back into the historic mists of termination for convenience, including the unusual spectacle of a current clause's origin in Army Regulations of the Civil War. Congress enacted fresh statutory authority in connection with World War I and World War II. What is so fundamental about termination for convenience that it arose so early and has been important so long? See Joseph J. Petrillo & William E. Conner, From Torncello to Krygoski: 25 Years of the Government's Termination for Convenience Power, 7 Fed. Circuit B.J. 337 (1997).

2. This opinion also combines with the issue of termination for convenience another venerable concept, the difference between modifications within the scope of the original competed contract and cardinal changes. That distinction has been discussed elsewhere, in connection with equitable adjustments. What is the conceptual link among these various matters?

3. The opinion makes strong use of CICA to explain its downgrading of the Torncello opinion. Is this simply the instinct of a court, seeking to overcome a troublesome but high-profile precedent, to emphasize whatever basis it has to say that legal circumstances,

specifically legislation, changed after that precedent? Or, did CICA in fact seek to transform the role of the contracting officer into more active promoter of competitive contracting, significantly affecting the tools such an officer can use, like termination of previously awarded contracts to allow their recompetition?

4. In the facts of this case, who set whom up here? Could the contractor Krygoski fairly complain that the government had set it up to take the loss if its bid had turned out to be a good deal for the government, but for the government to withhold the gain when its bid turned out to be a good deal for the contractor? Or could the government fairly complain that it had correctly estimated the cost of performance as high, and the contractor set it up by bidding low and then demanding a high figure?

Chapter 14

Termination for Default

The first section of the chapter starts with the bases and defenses for a termination for default. The second section continues with the process for default, particularly the extent to which the contractor may challenge the government's exercise of its discretion to perform a termination for default. Then, the third section discusses the government's additional remedies, notably recovering excess costs of reprocurement.

For further discussion of the subject of this chapter, see Steven Feldman, *Government Contract Guidebook*, § 19 (Thomson Reuters, 4th ed. 2010); Karen Manos, *Government Contract Costs & Pricing*, §§ 88.12–88.14 (Thomson Reuters 2nd ed. 2009); Harris J. Handrews, Jr. & Robert T. Peacock, *Terminations: An Outline of the Parties' Rights and Remedies*, 11 Pub. Cont. L.J. 269 (1980).

Note on Termination for Default

Termination for default warrants full treatment, because of its potent impact on the contractor and the large role given to government contracting lawyers in its handling. We can usefully contrast termination for default with contract formation by bids or proposals. Contract formation warrants full treatment because all government contracts go through it, so the scale of activity is large. However, the contract formation process often has only a limited impact upon contractors, who may bid for many contracts in the course of obtaining a few. Moreover, government contract lawyers often have a limited role in contract formation, as nonlegal personnel do most of the work of formulating and processing IFBs, RFPs, bids and proposals, with lawyers getting deeply involved especially when protests occur.

In contrast, any single termination for default has an intense impact on that contractor. Partly this occurs in basic (private) contract law as well. A private buyer may cancel a contract on asserted grounds of the other party's breach (for simple comparison, let us speak only of seller/performer breach, not payor breach), or of the failure for a condition of payment to be fulfilled. Unless the seller successfully contests, this puts an end to the seller's performance and precludes the seller from profiting. The seller's breach exposes the seller to liability for damages. Similarly, when the government terminates a government contractor for default, unless the contractor successfully contests, this puts an end to its performance, precludes it from profiting, and exposes it to liability for damages.

However, basic (private) contract law avoids, for important reasons, too intense an impact on the contractor cancelled for breach. In private contracting, the concept of "efficient breach" reflects a school of contracting law analysis backed up by economic theory, that under some circumstances it may be efficient, and thus not something to be excessively discouraged, for a party (let us say, for simplicity, a seller) to breach and thereby to elicit cancellation. The "efficient breach" concept reflects that a seller may discover, after entering the contract, other better opportunities compared to fulfilling the contract.

For example, the market may be willing to pay the seller much more for taking some other deal, or the seller may have special reasons that it would experience an unexpectedly large loss in performing. Suppose it will cost the seller $1,000 to perform, but if the seller breaches someone else can perform for $1100, and, meanwhile, the seller can take another deal for $2000. Breach would be "efficient" if the seller pays the damages, namely, pays for the other performer to perform for $1100, takes the other deal for $2000, and divides up the added profit as a result of all this in some way between itself and the buyer. Basic (private) contract law keeps the measure of damages limited so as not to excessively discourage such efficient breaches; for example, almost never, in an ordinary breach without tortious or fraudulent aspects, does the recovery include punitive damages.

In contrast, government contracting law subscribes much less to the concept of "efficient breach." The implementation of public policy, including the implementation of the decisions of the elected Congress and President and the smooth functioning of the government agencies, gets set back by contractor defaults. That set back is only imperfectly compensated by damages. An extreme example consists of wartime supply, where contractor breach, in situations where the market for many reasons cannot function perfectly, sets back the national security. Even in peacetime, and even in situations where there is an operative market where the government can find alternative suppliers, the delay, disruption, and distraction of making up for the breach create a setback for the government.

An analogy from other government "contracting" activity consists of recalling what happens when government employees in responsible positions fail to appear at their posts or to perform there. The government does not simply extract damages from them, such as docking their pay, as a private employer of temporary help might in an efficient market. For military officers, the government may court-martial the absent soldier for going AWOL ("away without leave"). Even for civilian employees, the government may respond to absence or to failure to perform by conducting a suspension or termination proceeding, in which, for due process purposes, the government makes a civil determination of employee misconduct.

Termination for default thus amounts to more than a proceeding for the government to make an efficient distribution of the losses from the substitution of an alternative supplier. Rather, it amounts to a decision—an official judgment by the sovereign—of unexcused nonfeasance or misfeasance. It stamps the contractor with a civil judgment against it that it is guilty in its relations with the state of an unexcused failure to perform the duty to its country that it solemnly, voluntarily, and formally undertook.

This has both normative and practical significance. Normatively, the government declares that the contractor terminated for default is an unexcused failure. Even if no practical consequences followed, both the government and the contractor would have their lawyers pay major attention to such a declaration. While it is a civil matter, as a normative labeling it has overtones like other government-generated civil adjudications of failure to live up to norms. The government may consider it necessary to terminate for default in order to vindicate the norms of government contracting, to uphold the symbolic authority of the state, and to deter other contractors from similar unexcused failures.

On its part, the contractor may consider it necessary to contest the termination for default in order to defend its standing in its economic community, as it is viewed by the government, the public, its peer businesses, and its own stockholders and employees. Indeed, the culpable officers in the business might well contest the termination for default, if for no other reason than for their sense of personal honor, much as they might contest a charge against them by the government in any other context from their view of themselves as individuals fulfilling all their other civic obligations.

Practically, the government has the ability by a termination for default to impose penalties. These start with the ordinary measure of damages. In addition, as discussed below, the government will also sometimes impose on the contractor an added measure called "excess costs of reprocurement." Finally, the termination amounts to a negative entry on the contractor's record that could factor into either difficulty in obtaining future contract awards, or even into a formal suspension or debarment.

A. Bases and Defenses

One of the most important standard clauses in government contracts, the Default Clause, directs the bases and defenses for termination for default. The Clause's text provides an excellent introduction to termination for default. One general type of Default Clause applies to supply and service contracts, while another applies to construction contracts, but the similarities justify treating them all at once.

The Default Clause lists separate bases for termination for default. Each of these bases has gathered a considerable amount of doctrine and case law around it. First and foremost, the clause lists the ground of "failure to deliver or perform." This can involve either the fault of lateness, that is, failure to deliver or perform by the contractually required date, or the fault of flawed performance, that is, failure to meet the specifications. The fault of lateness raises the issue that the government insists in most circumstances that "time is of the essence" in its contracts. With respect to flawed performance, the great variety of government contracts comes into play. Packing boxes for government archives have to achieve a low level of match with the specifications; missiles that will carry nuclear warheads have to achieve a higher level.

Second, the clause lists the ground of "failure to make progress so as to endanger performance." This clause represents an important change from the common law, in which a buyer had to show before cancelling a contract with a seller prior to the date of performance that it was impossible for the seller to perform. The government need not show such impossibility, just a reasonable belief that the contractor cannot perform the entire contract within the time remaining for performance. Still, this ground provides something of a level battlefield for the government and the contractor to argue. After all, a contractor who is trying hard to perform can argue, if the government is simply nervous, the government should just terminate for convenience and go hire someone else. By terminating for default, the government penalizes contractors in advance of their actually failing to perform. So, the contractor can hope to enlist the tribunal's sympathies by showing that it was trying hard, in fact, with a likelihood of fulfilling its obligations.

Third, the clause lists the ground of failure to perform other provisions of the contract. Courts and boards will not sustain a default termination unless that "other provision" of the contract is a "material" or "significant" requirement. *Stone Forest Indus. v. United States*, 973 F.2d 1548 (Fed. Cir. 1992). Considering the large number of requirements in government contracts, this ground creates quite a lot of room for debate. Note also that although the default clause does not mention it explicitly, both the government and the contractor retain their common law right to terminate upon actual or anticipatory repudiation by the other party. The *DeKonty v. U.S.* opinion, in the chapter on specialized contracting's section on construction contracts, provides the classic definition of anticipatory repudiation.

For further discussion of the subject of this section, see: Paul J. Seidman & Robert D. Banfield, *How to Avoid & Overturn Terminations for* Default, 98-12 Briefing Papers 1 (1998); Brad Fagg, *Default Terminations for Failure to Make Progress*, 25 Pub. Cont. L.J. 113 (1995); Glenn T. Carberry and Phillip M. Johnstone, *Waiver of the Governments Right to Terminate for Default in Government Defense Contracts,* 17 Pub. Cont. L. J. 470 (1988).

Default Clause (Fixed-Price Supply and Service)
(Apr 1984)

(a) (1) The Government may, subject to paragraphs (c) and (d) of this clause, by written notice of default to the Contractor, terminate this contract in whole or in part if the Contractor fails to —

> (i) Deliver the supplies or to perform the services within the time specified in this contract or any extension;

> (ii) Make progress, so as to endanger performance of this contract (but see subparagraph (a)(2) of this clause); or

> (iii) Perform any of the other provisions of this contract (but see subparagraph (a)(2) below).

> (2) The Government's right to terminate this contract under subdivisions (a)(1)(ii) and (1)(iii) of this clause, may be exercised if the Contractor does not cure such failure within 10 days (or more if authorized in writing by the Contracting Officer) after receipt of the notice from the Contracting Officer specifying the failure.

(b) If the Government terminates this contract in whole or in part, it may acquire, under the terms and in the manner the Contracting Officer considers appropriate, supplies or services similar to those terminated, and the Contractor will be liable to the Government for any excess costs for those supplies or services. However, the Contractor shall continue the work not terminated.

(c) Except for defaults of subcontractors at any tier, the Contractor shall not be liable for any excess costs if the failure to perform the contract arises from causes beyond the control and without the fault or negligence of the Contractor. Examples of such causes include

> (1) acts of God or of the public enemy, (2) acts of the Government in either its sovereign or contractual capacity, (3) fires, (4) floods, (5) epidemics, (6) quarantine restrictions, (7)strikes, (8) freight embargoes, and (9) unusually severe weather. In each instance the failure to perform must be beyond the control and without the fault or negligence of the Contractor.

(d) If the failure to perform is caused by the default of a subcontractor at any tier, and if the cause of the default is beyond the control of both the Contractor and subcontractor, and without the fault or negligence of either, the Contractor shall not be liable for any excess costs for failure to perform, unless the subcontracted supplies or services were obtainable from other sources in sufficient time for the Contractor to meet the required delivery schedule.

(e) If this contract is terminated for default, the Government may require the Contractor to transfer title and deliver to the Government, as directed by the Contracting Officer, any

> (1) completed supplies, and (2) manufacturing materials ... [T]he Contractor shall also protect and preserve property ... in which the Government has an interest.

(f) The Government shall pay contract price for completed supplies delivered and accepted. The Contractor and Contracting Officer shall agree on the amount of payment for manufacturing materials delivered and accepted and for the protection and preservation of the property. Failure to agree will be a dispute under the Disputes clause....

(g) If, after termination, it is determined that the Contractor was not in default, or that the default was excusable, the rights and obligations of the parties shall be the same as if the termination had been issued for the convenience of the Government.

(h) The rights and remedies of the Government in this clause are in addition to any other rights and remedies provided by law or under this contract.

Information Systems and Networks Corporation, Plaintiff, v. The United States, Defendant
No. 91-1643C
34 Fed. Cl. 457
United States Court of Federal Claims
Nov. 21, 1995

MOODY R. TIDWELL, III, Judge:

This case is before the court on plaintiff's motion for partial summary judgment, filed pursuant to RCFC 56(c). Plaintiff seeks summary judgment only on the basis of liability, with, presumably, quantum to be determined later. For the reasons set forth below, the court denies plaintiff's motion.

FACTS

This case stems from contract No. F49642-88-D-0054, which the Department of Air Force, Air Force District of Washington ("Air Force" or "government") awarded to the Small Business Administration ("SBA") on September 22, 1988. The SBA then subcontracted with Information Systems and Networks Corporation ("ISN") for performance of the contract. Under the contract, ISN was required to provide the Air Force with labor services for developing a computer system that would support automatic data processing activities at the 7th Communications Group in Washington, D.C.

As part of the contract, a government Statement of Work ("SOW") required ISN to convert the PFORMS data base from the Air Force's leased Honeywell computer to a new IBM mainframe computer.[1] The SOW called for ISN to use VSAM software as the operating system while converting the data base. The crux of the dispute arises out of ISN's untimely delivery of, and certain alleged defects found in the converted PFORMS data base. The delivery of this particular system is referred to as Delivery Order 5004.

On July 3, 1990, ISN delivered the PFORMS project to the Air Force, but the system failed to allow multiple users as required in the specifications. In response to a July 9, 1990 request from the contracting officer, ISN submitted several suggestions to the Air Force on how the problems with the system could be corrected. ISN's July 19, 1990 response suggested a target delivery date of August 16, 1990 for the corrected system. ISN failed to meet the target date, allegedly because its subcontractor "walked off the job" after ISN was unable to make payment as a result of the government's withholding payment to ISN. Consequently, the contracting officer established two delivery dates of September 15, 1990

---

1. PFORMS is an automatic data processing system used in preparing budgets and comparing budget figures with actual expenditures from certain Air Force programs.

and October 1, 1990 whereby portions of the project needed to be finalized. Displeased with the work ISN submitted on these two dates, the government sent ISN a Show Cause Notice on October 3, 1990, giving it an opportunity to present any facts that may bear on the question of a possible default. ISN responded to the Notice on October 12, 1990, through counsel, attempting to establish its position on the delays and setbacks surrounding the previous months. The parties communicated minimally during the months that followed, and ISN submitted a claim to the contracting officer under the Contract Disputes Act ("CDA"), 41 U.S.C. _ 605 (1988 & Supp. V 1993), on March 25, 1991. On May 21, 1991, seven months after the government issued its Show Cause Notice, the Air Force terminated ISN for default. The "effective date" of the termination was March 19, 1991 — six days before ISN submitted its CDA claim.

ISN claims that the government neither specifically acknowledged nor answered ISN's response to the Show Cause Notice. The government refutes that claim by pointing to language in the termination, which stated that ISN's response was insufficient. Beyond these general facts explaining the basic outline of the contract and the schedule of events surrounding delivery of the converted database, the parties' respective descriptions and characterization of this dispute differ substantially.

In the termination notice, the Air Force alleged several deficiencies in ISN's attempted satisfaction of Delivery Order 5004. First, the Air Force alleged that contrary to the specifications, the system failed to support multiple users. The Air Force attributes this multi-user failure to ISN allegedly suggesting that it use the VSAM software in the TSO/ISPF environment, an environment not capable of supporting multiple users.[3] Although the Air Force made the final decision to use TSO/ISPF, the government argues that it relied on ISN's expert opinion to use that environment. However, ISN alleges that it used the TSO/ISPF environment at the government's direction, and because the government directed it to use TSO/ISPF, ISN cannot be terminated for default for following the government's instructions. Next, in support of terminating ISN for default, the Air Force alleged that ISN missed several deadlines, and when the program was finally submitted, ISN misrepresented the system's capabilities. Even after granting ISN an extension of time, the Air Force claimed that the system was "totally inoperable."

On November 27, 1991, ISN filed this action alleging breach of contract, requesting that the termination for default be converted to a termination for convenience, and claiming $458,184.99 still owed by the Air Force for services rendered.

As a result of ISN's delays and the alleged deficiencies in the submitted system, the Air Force filed a $52,892 counterclaim against ISN. This counterclaim represents the government's alleged cost of bringing the defective system into compliance with the specifications.

DISCUSSION

* * *

Plaintiff asks the court to grant summary judgment on four issues: (1) that the Air Force constructively changed the contract by requiring additional work; (2) that the Air Force breached its contract with ISN; (3) that the Air Force improperly terminated the contract with ISN, and thus, the termination for default should be converted to a termination for convenience; and (4) that ISN is not liable under the government's counterclaim.

---

3. TSO/ISPF is a commercial IBM software package which allows users to communicate with a mainframe computer.

A comprehensive analysis of the parties' memoranda leads the court to conclude that several genuine issues of material fact preclude summary judgment in this case.

At the heart of this dispute lies the question of whether Delivery Order 5004 was governed primarily by design or performance specifications. The difference between these two specifications is well settled. Design specifications "describe in precise detail the materials to be employed and the manner in which the work is to be performed." *Blake Constr. Co. v. United States,* 987 F.2d 743, 745 (Fed.Cir.1993), *cert. denied,*510 U.S. 963, 114 S.Ct. 438, 126 L.Ed.2d 372 (1993). Design specifications afford no discretion to the contractor, who is "required to follow them as one would a road map." *Id.* (quoting *J.L. Simmons Co. v. United States,* 188 Ct.Cl. 684, 689, 412 F.2d 1360 (1969)). Performance specifications, on the other hand, "set forth an objective or standard to be achieved, and the successful bidder is expected to exercise his ingenuity in achieving that objective or standard of performance, selecting the means and assuming a corresponding responsibility for that selection." *Id.* In essence, plaintiff argues that the specifications strictly instruct how the conversion process should take place, beginning with the alleged mandate to use the TSO/ISPF software. ISN claims that this mandate was an impossible specification, thus causing the government to breach the contract. The government claims that ISN made the decision to use TSO/ISPF, a system which does not allow multiple users to operate the system at the same time. Whichever party was responsible for deciding to use the TSO/ISPF software could provide substantial insight into which party is responsible for the multi-user failure. This dispute clearly represents a genuine issue of material fact which cannot be disposed of on summary judgment.

Plaintiff further argues that the Air Force breached the contract by failing to cooperate with ISN. ISN claims that the government failed to provide ISN with certain test results relating to the multi-user failure. If the Air Force would have notified ISN of the problems associated with the system earlier on, which the Air Force knew about, ISN argues, the defects could have been corrected in time for delivery. Moreover, ISN accuses the government of refusing to communicate, which too was a failure to cooperate. Plaintiff cites numerous cases standing for the proposition that the government has an implied duty to cooperate with its contractors. That the parties have a duty to cooperate with each other is not disputed. *See Malone v. United States,* 849 F.2d 1441, 1445 (Fed.Cir.1988). Rather, the issue at dispute here is whether the government breached that duty to cooperate. In fact, both parties have submitted contradicting, sworn affidavits in support of their respective positions.

* * *

Delivery Order 5004 was originally scheduled for completion on July 3, 1990. It was near this time when the submitted system failed the multi-user test, causing the contracting officer to demand that ISN fix any deficiencies. The parties thereupon agreed on a subsequent schedule outlining new delivery dates. ISN agreed to adhere to those dates in a letter dated September 11, 1990, making it clear that it did so at the government's direction. The Air Force maintains that this extension of the delivery date was a reasonable extension of time, not constituting a waiver of schedule. ISN, however, argues that the extension of time "proved to be unreasonable," and resulted in a waiver of the original delivery date. The court notes that when ISN agreed to adhere to the new schedule, it did not express a concern, at that time, of unreasonableness. Nonetheless, whether the extension of time constituted a waiver of schedule is a question of law which cannot be determined by the facts now before the court. Hence, another issue of material fact concerns the circumstances surrounding the extension of time and whether that extension was reasonable. Both parties agree that the delivery schedule was indeed extended, yet their characterization of the extension is quite different. "Reasonableness is a question of fact," and as such cannot be decided on summary judgment. *Engle Investors v. United States,* 21 Cl.Ct. 543, 550 (1989).

ISN further contends that because the government waited so long, until May 21, 1991, to terminate for default, it waived its right to do so. Both parties cite *DeVito v. United States,* 188 Ct.Cl. 979, 413 F.2d 1147 (1969), in support of their respective positions. *DeVito* outlines a two-part test to determine whether the government has waived a schedule:

> The necessary elements of an election by the non-defaulting party to waive default in delivery under a contract are (1) failure to terminate within a *reasonable time* after the default under circumstances indicating forbearance, and (2) *reliance* by the contractor on the failure to terminate and continued performance by him under the contract, with the Government's knowledge and implied or express consent.

Id. at 990–91, 413 F.2d 1147 (emphasis added).

Just after setting forth this two-part analysis, the court acknowledged that "[w]hat is a reasonable time for the Government to terminate a contract after default depends on the circumstances of each case." *Id.* at 991, 413 F.2d 1147. *DeVito* was a case involving "undisputed facts," *id.* at 994, allowing the court to determine whether the fact-sensitive, two-part test had been satisfied. As discussed above, in order for this court to analyze the *DeVito* test, it would be necessary to determine whether the time in which the government failed to terminate ISN was *reasonable*—clearly a genuine issue of material fact demonstrated by the conflicting evidence. "Whether the government has acted within a reasonable time after default is a question of fact." *International Fidelity Ins. Co. v. United States,* 25 Cl.Ct. 469, 480 (1992).

Similarly, deciding whether ISN relied on the government's failure to terminate would require the court to decide another genuine issue of material fact. Reliance is a question of fact, and because the parties have supplied conflicting evidence on the question of reliance, summary judgment is inappropriate. ISN provided the affidavit of Dana Palmer which states that ISN continued to work on the project even after the extended deadlines had passed, thus relying on the government's forbearance. However, the government points to the October 3, 1990 Show Cause Notice sent to ISN by the Air Force as a lack of forbearance on ISN's failure to meet the schedule. The government also turns the court's attention to a letter from Karen Hendricks, ISN's contracts administration manager, dated October 29, 1990, which states that "ISN has performed all work and delivered all data required under [Delivery Order 5004]," by the specified due dates. If ISN performed and delivered all necessary work on the Delivery Order by the due dates, the government argues, then ISN had no need to continue working on the project in reliance on the Air Force's failure to terminate. Summary judgment is not the appropriate method to analyze the credibility of this evidence, nor to try and reconcile these obvious factual inconsistencies.

* * *

CONCLUSION

Based on the foregoing discussion, plaintiff's motion for partial summary judgment on the issue of liability is denied. The parties are to confer and report back to the court within two weeks from the date of this order with a proposed trial schedule.

IT IS SO ORDERED.

Richard J. Danzig, Secretary of the Navy, Appellant, v. AEC Corporation, Appellee

United States Court of Appeals, Federal Circuit
No. 99-1343
224 F.3d 1333
Sept. 25, 2000

Before MICHEL, BRYSON, and GAJARSA, Circuit Judges.

BRYSON, Circuit Judge.

The dispute in this case arose when the government terminated its contract with AEC Corporation for default. The Armed Services Board of Contract Appeals ruled that the default termination was improper, and the government has appealed from that ruling. We reverse and remand for further proceedings.

I

In May 1989, the Navy awarded AEC a contract to complete the construction of a Naval and Marine Corps Reserve Training Center in Miami, Florida. The contract called for AEC to finish the work by October 14, 1990. By late 1990, it was apparent that AEC was behind schedule. AEC was having financial difficulties with its surety, and those problems were delaying the progress of the work. A cure notice issued by the Navy in December 1990 led to a meeting between the Navy and AEC on January 23, 1991. At that meeting, AEC provided a schedule with a projected completion date of April 16, 1991 [later extended to April 27]. The Navy agreed not to terminate the contract for default if AEC continued to make progress according to that schedule....

In late February 1991, AEC's surety froze the project's bank account, and the number of workers doing productive work on the project began to decline. At a meeting on March 5, 1991, the Navy asked why the project was progressing so slowly. AEC advised the Navy that it was unable to make progress on the project because the surety would not release funds from the project's bank account. The Navy responded by stating that AEC was close to being terminated for default.

On March 20, 1991, the Navy sent AEC a letter containing a cure notice. In the letter, the Navy stated that its agreement at the January 23 meeting not to pursue termination for default was contingent upon AEC's diligently pursuing completion of the contract by April 27, 1991. Since the January 23 meeting, the Navy charged, "work in place continues to progress at a dangerously low pace." Based on the decreasing number of man-hours being devoted to the job, the Navy expressed concern that AEC would not be able to complete the project by April 27. The Navy therefore stated that it considered AEC's "failure to diligently pursue completion a condition that is endangering performance of the contract" and advised that unless that condition was cured within 10 days, the Navy would consider terminating the contract for default.

AEC responded to the cure notice with a letter dated April 3, 1991. In the letter AEC explained that while it had previously appeared possible to complete the project by April 27, 1991, "numerous factors have prevented [the project's] scheduled progress." First, AEC claimed that "the many changes and delays caused by the Government have made an April completion impossible." Second, AEC complained that since January 1991 the surety had interfered with AEC and hampered its progress on the job by blocking the release of funds sufficient to enable AEC to pay its subcontractors and meet other project expenses. The "financial strangulation" by the surety, AEC stated, has progressed to the point of not only preventing AEC from meeting its April 27, 1991 completion date, it has made it impossible for AEC to predict an ultimate completion date at this time. As a matter of fact, unless [the surety and its affiliate] restrain [sic] from their present conduct and release the funds currently in [the project's] bank account, it is doubtful that AEC will ever be able to complete the project.

The Navy responded by letter the next day, stating that it could not evaluate AEC's response because AEC's contentions that burdensome changes and government-caused delays had made an April 27 completion impossible were vague and unsubstantiated. The Navy directed AEC to provide a detailed response to substantiate its allegations. The Navy added that the March 20 cure notice required AEC to cure the dangerously slow work pace within 10 days, and it "strongly encourage[d]" AEC to address the cure issue.

On April 5, AEC answered by stating that it "cannot cure the deficiency stated in your Cure Notice due to the restrictions that [the surety and its affiliate] have imposed on the disbursement of funds from the joint escrow account. Consequently we cannot give you any assurance as to when the project will be completed." AEC added that "[t]he financial strain of this action has been aggravated by costs incurred as a result of delays and additional work caused by the government." ... AEC advised the Navy that it had reduced its work force at the job site to two supervisory employees because of the financial restrictions imposed by the surety.

The Navy called a meeting at the site on April 9, 1991, at which it gave AEC an unsigned letter directing AEC to "show cause" why the contract should not be terminated for default. The letter directed AEC to respond within ten days. AEC received a signed copy of the letter on April 11. During the following 10 days, AEC did not respond to the Navy's "show cause" letter, and throughout that period AEC had only a handful of workers on the job site.

On April 22, 1991, the Navy terminated the contract for default. The termination notice stated that the contract was being terminated "due to failure to make progress in the work and for default in performance." AEC responded by letter the same day, expressing surprise that the Navy had terminated the contract without waiting for AEC's response to the show cause letter.

AEC appealed the termination. After the contracting officer denied the appeal, AEC appealed to the Armed Services Board of Contract Appeals, which held the termination invalid.

*　*　*

We agree with the government.... In response to the Navy's March 20, 1991, cure notice, AEC failed to give the Navy adequate assurances that it could complete the contract on a timely basis or even that it could continue to make progress toward completion. That failure, the government argues, justified the Navy's decision to terminate the contract for default. Because we agree with the government on that issue, we reverse the Board's decision and hold that the default termination was valid.

When the government has reasonable grounds to believe that the contractor may not be able to perform the contract on a timely basis, the government may issue a cure notice as a precursor to a possible termination of the contract for default. *See Discount Co. v. United States*, 213 Ct.Cl. 567, 554 F.2d 435, 438–39 (1977) (government issued a cure notice when the contractor had done no substantial work during the construction season). When the government justifiably issues a cure notice, the contractor has an obligation to take steps to demonstrate or give assurances that progress is being made toward a timely completion of the contract, or to explain that the reasons for any prospective delay in completion of the contract are not the responsibility of the contractor. *See Tubular Aircraft Prods., Inc. v. United States,* 213 Ct.Cl. 749, 750, 566 F.2d 1190 (1977) ("Plaintiff's minimal performance efforts coupled with its perilous financial situation warranted the issuance of a cure notice.

Thereafter, plaintiff's failure to advise the Government that corrective action would be taken in order to make performance at levels reasonably commensurate with contract requirements financially possible, justified the default termination."); *Composite Laminates, Inc. v. United States,* 27 Fed.Cl. 310, 323–24 (1992) ("When the government issues a cure notice, in order for a contractor to avoid default, a contractor must be able to provide adequate assurances to the government that it can complete contract requirements on time."); *International Verbatim Reporters, Inc. v. United States,* 9 Cl.Ct. 710, 723 (1986) (once the cure notice was issued to the contractor, "its failure to correct, explain or communicate with [the government] during the period what corrective action that would be taken, justified a termination for default")....

The law applicable to a contractor's failure to provide assurances of timely completion is a branch of the law of anticipatory repudiation. *See, e.g., Discount Co.,* 554 F.2d at 441 (when the government was not assured of timely completion, the court could properly "rely upon cases involving abandoned or repudiated contracts"). At common law, anticipatory repudiation of a contract required an unambiguous and unequivocal statement that the obligor would not or could not perform the contract. *See Dingley v. Oler,* 117 U.S. 490, 503, 6 S.Ct. 850, 29 L.Ed. 984 (1886); *Cascade Pac. Int'l v. United States,* 773 F.2d 287, 293 (Fed.Cir.1985). As the Restatement of Contracts has recognized, however, modern decisions do not limit anticipatory repudiation to cases of express and unequivocal repudiation of a contract. Instead, anticipatory repudiation includes cases in which reasonable grounds support the obligee's belief that the obligor will breach the contract. In that setting, the obligee "may demand adequate assurance of due performance" and if the obligor does not give such assurances, the obligee may treat the failure to do so as a repudiation of the contract. *Restatement (Second) of Contracts* § 251 (1981). The Uniform Commercial Code has adopted a similar rule for contracts involving the sale of goods. *See* U.C.C. § 2-609.

The law of government contracts has adopted that doctrine, expressing it as a requirement that the contractor give reasonable assurances of performance in response to a validly issued cure notice.... That rule, as the Restatement explains, rests "on the principle that the parties to a contract look to actual performance 'and that a continuing sense of reliance and security that the promised performance will be forthcoming when due, is an important feature of the bargain.'" *Restatement (Second) of Contracts* § 251 cmt. a (quoting U.C.C. § 2-609 cmt. 1).

* * *

Based on AEC's performance during February and March 1991, the Navy had a reasonable basis for concern that the contract would not be completed by April 27, 1991, the completion date that AEC had projected on February 5 and presented to the Navy to avoid default termination at that time. The Navy was therefore entitled to issue a cure notice demanding a correction of the slow pace of the work or a satisfactory explanation of how AEC planned to complete the work on a timely basis. The issuance of a cure notice was justified under the circumstances, even if the circumstances did not, at that point, justify a termination for default. *See National Union Fire Ins.,* 90-1 B.C.A. (CCH) at 111,855 (noting that the "right to demand assurance need not spring merely from a performance or progress failure, but may be asserted whenever reasonable grounds exist to believe a breach will be committed").

AEC's response to the cure notice did not satisfy its obligation to provide assurances to the Navy that it could timely complete the contract. AEC did not dispute the Navy's assertion in its cure notice that at its current pace it would not be able to complete the contract by April 27. In fact, AEC's April 3 letter stated that "the financial strangulation" of AEC by its surety had prevented AEC "from meeting its April 27, 1991 completion date" and had "made it impossible for AEC to predict an ultimate completion date at this time." Moreover, AEC stated that unless the surety and its affiliate released funds in the project's bank account, "it is doubtful that AEC will ever be able to complete the project." When the Navy asked for a more specific response, AEC responded on April 5 with a letter in which it reiterated that "due to the restrictions that [the surety and its affiliate] have imposed on the disbursement of funds from the joint escrow account ... we cannot give you any assurances as to when the project will be completed." Clearly, the April 3 and April 5 letters offered nothing to allay the Navy's concerns about AEC's ability to complete the contract on a timely basis.

At about the time of the April 3 and April 5 letters, AEC removed the contract files and office equipment from the work site and disconnected the telephone at the work-site office. At the same time, AEC advised the Navy that it had been forced to reduce its work force at the facility to two persons and that it could not "continue to incur costs on this project given the financial restrictions being imposed on us by [the surety and its affiliate]." Finally, at the meeting between representatives of the Navy and AEC on April 9, AEC was given a notice to show cause within 10 days why the contract should not be terminated for default, and AEC failed to respond within the 10-day period.

AEC's conduct, like its responses to the cure notice, clearly failed to provide the requisite assurances that AEC would complete the project on a timely basis. Rather than providing an assurance of timely completion, AEC told the Navy, through both its words and its conduct, that the contract was not likely to be completed until AEC was able to work out its financial difficulties with its surety. AEC offered the Navy no reason to believe that those difficulties would be resolved any time in the near future. Moreover, although AEC makes some effort to suggest that its financial difficulties were the fault of the government, there is no finding by the Board to that effect and no evidence supporting that suggestion. Thus, there is no reason in this case to depart from the normal rule that the contractor's financial difficulties are not a legitimate excuse for its failure to make progress....

AEC's assertions of government-caused delay similarly did not respond adequately to the Navy's request for assurances. Although AEC referred to government-caused delays in both the April 3 and April 5 letters, it was not specific as to what changes had caused delay or how much delay it considered the government to have caused, nor did it represent that it could complete the contract within the additional time to which it believed it was entitled.... AEC's responses to the cure notice thus did not adequately explain how its slow progress was the product of delay caused by the government or was otherwise excusable.

Under these circumstances, we conclude as a matter of law that AEC failed to respond adequately to the Navy's reasonable request for assurances of timely performance. The Navy was therefore entitled to regard AEC's failure to provide such assurances as a breach of the contract justifying termination of the contract for default. On remand, the Board shall address the remaining issues of liability based on our holding that the default termination was valid.

REVERSED and REMANDED.

Notes and Questions

1. This case reinforces the importance of the cure notice, particularly when the termination for default is going to be grounded, as here, in "endangering performance" (due later) rather than in failure to fulfill (measured by past delivery or past due dates). Note how the issues occur in two steps: the (pre-notice) reasonableness of the government's grounds for concern, and the (post-notice) adequacy of the contractor's response. Note, also, how closely this corresponds to the similar pattern in the basic general law of contracts and particularly under the Article Two of the U.C.C. The modern general law, and U.C.C. provision, have their two steps of the existence of a reasonable basis for demanding assurances, and, afterwards, whether adequate assurances are provided. How is government contract law similar to, and different from, basic general contract law in this regard?

2. The government meets its burden as to termination on the basis of endangering performance by showing various indicators of basis for concern. What were they in this case?

DCX, Inc., Appellant, v.
William J. Perry, Secretary of Defense, Appellee
No. 94-1385
United States Court of Appeals, Federal Circuit
79 F.3d 132
March 11, 1996
Appealed from Armed Services Board of Contract Appeals

Before MAYER, MICHEL, and BRYSON, Circuit Judges.

BRYSON, Circuit Judge.

DCX, Inc., appeals a decision of the Armed Services Board of Contract Appeals upholding the government's termination of a contract for default. We affirm.

I.

On April 1, 1988, the Defense Logistics Agency awarded a contract to DCX for light sets to be used in medical tents. The contract required DCX to perform a series of tests on the first light set that DCX manufactured under the contract and to supply the government with a First Article Test Report. The test report was due on June 30, 1988, and delivery of the light sets was required to begin by July 18, 1988. The contract provided that if DCX failed to deliver the test report on time, it "shall be deemed to have failed to make delivery within the meaning of the Default clause of this contract."

Because it did not have the facilities to perform the first article tests, DCX subcontracted the testing to Ball Brothers Aerospace Systems. Under the subcontract, the tests were to begin on May 19. Ball, however, did not begin DCX's tests until June 17. On that date, DCX advised the government that the testing process would not be completed until July 11 and that the government therefore would not receive the First Article Test Report until July 12. DCX blamed Ball's delay on the government's Defense Priorities and Allocations System (DPAS), which it asserted required Ball to postpone the DCX tests in favor of higher priority government contracts. On July 1, the day after the test report was due under the contract, the contracting officer advised DCX that it was in default, but she agreed to forbear termination until July 12, thus effectively granting DCX the additional time requested in its June 17 letter. When DCX failed to deliver the test report on the extended due date, however, the contracting officer referred the contract to the termination contracting officer who terminated the contract for default.

DCX appealed to the Armed Services Board of Contract Appeals, alleging that its failure to deliver the First Article Test Report was excusable because it was caused by the operation of the DPAS, and that the termination contracting officer had acted arbitrarily and capriciously in terminating the contract. DCX asked that the termination for default be converted into a termination for the convenience of the government.

The Board upheld the termination for default, finding that the delay was the fault of DCX and its subcontractor, Ball. The Board focused in particular on DCX's failure to guarantee timely performance by obtaining either a backup subcontractor or a binding time commitment from Ball to complete the tests by a date certain. With respect to DCX's proffered excuse for its failure to produce the test report by the extended deadline, the Board concluded that there was insufficient evidence that the operation of the DPAS caused the delay. The Board further found that the termination contracting officer adhered to the contract terms and the applicable procurement regulations, and that his termination decision was thus not arbitrary or capricious.

II.

On appeal, DCX makes [two] arguments: that the operation of the DPAS, not the negligence of DCX or its subcontractor, caused the delay in the delivery of the First Article Test Report; [and] that the contracting officer abused his discretion when he terminated the contract for default....

A.

The Board found that the government met its burden of proving that DCX did not perform in a timely fashion, and that DCX failed to meet its burden of proving that its nonperformance was excusable. See Lisbon Contractors, Inc. v. United States, 828 F.2d 759, 764 (Fed.Cir.1987); Switlik Parachute Co. v. United States, 216 Ct.Cl. 362, 573 F.2d 1228, 1234 (1978). DCX contends that the evidence conclusively showed that its failure to submit the First Article Test Report in a timely fashion was not attributable to any fault of DCX or Ball, but was caused by the government through the operation of the DPAS regulations, which require contractors to give precedence to higher priority government contracts. After reviewing the record, we agree with the Board that DCX failed to meet its burden of showing that the DPAS regulations excused its failure to fulfill the testing requirements of the contract.

The default clause in the contract excused any default caused by certain enumerated actions, including "acts of the Government." The default clause added, however, that "the failure to perform must be beyond the control and without the fault or negligence of the Contractor" or (in the case of a subcontract) "beyond the control of both the Contractor and subcontractor, and without the fault or negligence of either." Although the operation of the DPAS may give rise to excusable delay in an appropriate case, the DPAS regulations require performance of a lower priority contract to be deferred only if "required delivery dates [for the higher rated contract] cannot otherwise be met." 15 C.F.R. § 700.14(a). As the Board pointed out, DCX's witness, who admitted having only limited acquaintance with the government contract priority system, testified that Ball deferred DCX's tests in favor of higher priority government contracts, but he did not testify that the displacement of DCX's tests was necessary in order to meet the required delivery dates of the higher priority contracts.

Moreover, as the Board noted, DCX did not take steps to protect against the possibility of delay in the testing process. DCX did not obtain its subcontract with Ball until May

11, 1988, some six weeks after the award of the contract to DCX, and the subcontract with Ball contained no firm commitment as to the date on which the testing would be completed. In addition, the Board pointed out, DCX "had no backup arrangements or commitments from any other party, that were available, to perform the tests needed in the event Ball delayed or for any reason was unable to meet DCX's time of delivery requirements." The Board was thus warranted in finding that DCX's failure to perform was attributable to its own negligence and that of its subcontractor, rather than to the operation of the DPAS.

DCX next argues that the termination contracting officer acted arbitrarily and capriciously in terminating the DCX contract for default because he failed to follow certain provisions of the Federal Acquisition Regulation before he terminated the contract. The Board found that the termination contracting officer adhered to both the terms of the contract and the requirements of the applicable procedural regulations. Once again, we uphold the Board's findings as supported by the evidence before it.

The first regulatory provision that DCX complains was not followed is 48 C.F.R. § 49.402-3(a), which requires the contracting officer to obtain legal review before terminating a contract. The termination contracting officer testified that he obtained the required legal review before terminating the contract, although he was not able to state with certainty which attorney reviewed the proposed termination action. DCX argues that the termination contracting officer's testimony was incredible, but that contention is baseless. The witness was firm in asserting that a legal review was conducted, and in light of the large number of contracts he handled over a several-year period, it is hardly surprising that he could not recall all the details of the legal review.

The second regulatory provision on which DCX relies, 48 C.F.R. § 49.402-3(f), requires a contracting officer to consider various factors before exercising his discretion to terminate a contract when the contractor is in default. In this case, the termination contracting officer's contemporaneous memorandum and hearing testimony demonstrate that he addressed the pertinent regulatory factors and found that they did not counsel against termination under the circumstances of this case. Moreover, the factors in section 49.402-3(f) that contracting officers are directed to consider before terminating contracts are not prerequisites to a valid termination. Although compliance or noncompliance with section 49.402-3(f) may aid a Board of Contract Appeals or a court in determining whether a contracting officer has abused his discretion in terminating a contract for default, see Darwin Constr. Co. v. United States, 811 F.2d 593, 598 (Fed.Cir.1987); Fairfield Scientific Corp. v. United States, 222 Ct.Cl. 167, 611 F.2d 854, 862 (1979), the regulation does not confer rights on a defaulting contractor. A contracting officer's failure to consider one or more of the section 49.402-3(f) factors therefore does not require that a default termination be converted into a termination for the convenience of the government....

DCX argues that the termination contracting officer acted rashly by terminating the contract on July 13 without considering the reasons for the delay. As the officer testified, however, the government had already given DCX an extension of time within which to produce the First Article Test Report. The contracting officer agreed to forbear termination until July 12, as requested by DCX. When July 13 arrived, the contracting officer had not received either the report or a request for a further extension of time. Having been given no explanation for the further delay, the termination contracting officer was not required to assume that DCX had a valid excuse for the further delay or to seek out further information about the status of the DCX's efforts. We therefore find nothing in the record to persuade us that the termination contracting officer acted arbitrarily or capriciously in terminating the contract when he did.

Notes and Questions

1. How many different issues are argued, and can you describe the arguments for both sides? Try this chart:

Issue	DCX argument	Gov't/Fed Circuit response
Default Clause excuses if caused by "acts of the gov't"	Subcontractor said "gov't had higher priorities"	not definitely "necessary" no firm commitments nor backups so, subcontractor's (and DCX's) fault
FAR: TCO should get legal review	TCO can't recall what att'y reviewed it	busy TCO, needn't recall
FAR: TCO should consider factors	abuse of discretion?	Doesn't confer rights on defaulting contractor

2. Both *Radiation Technology* and this case involve the government's elaborate testing and inspection requirements. Can you explain how a "First Article" system works?

3. In this case, the contractor offers the defense of "excusable delay." Generally, excusable delays are those which the contracting firm can prove were unforeseeable, beyond its control, and not the result of the contractor's own acts or omissions (e.g. labor strikes, weather, and certain subcontractor delays). Other excusable delays include those caused by acts or omissions of the government itself, such as an agency's failure to make timely payments; failure either to accept or to reject goods within a reasonable period; defects in specifications or drawings; delayed award of the contract that deprives the awardee of sufficient start-up time; ordered or constructive suspensions of work; or, constructive changes to the scope of the contract itself . For a more complete treatment, see James P. Wiezel, *Refining the Concept of Concurrent Delay*, 21 Pub. Cont. L.J. 161 (1991); Michael R. Finke, *The Burden of Proof in Government Contract Schedule Delay Claims*, 22 Pub. Cont. L.J. 125 (1992); *Wilner v. United States*, 24 F.3d 1397 (Fed. Cir. 1994); *Tyger Construction Co. v. United States*, 31 Fed. Cl. 177 (1994).

4. In this case, the contracting officer said she would forebear for a period of time. Suppose the contracting officer did that several more times: would she waive the government's right to terminate for default? But, then, can the contracting officer reinstate the contractor's delivery duties by unilaterally imposing a reasonable new schedule? Where a due date has passed without termination for default and the contractor relies on that forebearance, there is an implied election to waive the strict deadline for performance and the courts infer that time is no longer of the essence. The courts deem this waiver to continue so long as the contractor continues to perform, until the issuance of a notice under the default clause indicating a "reasonable and specific" new time for performance, which reflects the contractor's ability to perform at the time notice is given (*Darwin Construction Co.*, GSBCA No. 10193, 1990 WL 157087). Such conduct would effectively reinstate a new performance date, as well as the "time is of the essence" element. See generally *I.T.T. Corp. v. United States*, 598 F. 2d 541 (Ct. Cl. 1975); *DeVito v. United States*, 413 F.2d 1147 (Ct.Cl. 1969); *Precision Dynamics, Inc.*, ASBCA 41360 (1997).

Lisbon Contractors, Inc., Appellee, v. The United States, Appellant

Appeal No. 86-1461
United States Court of Appeals, Federal Circuit
828 F.2d 759
Decided Sept. 9, 1987

Before NIES, BISSELL, and ARCHER, Circuit Judges.

NIES, Circuit Judge.

The United States appeals from the judgment of the United States Claims Court, No. 288-81C, awarding $95,748.15 to Lisbon Contractors, Inc. as termination for convenience costs under a construction contract. The Claims Court held that the United States wrongfully terminated Lisbon for default thereby converting the termination to one for convenience of the government. We affirm-in-part, reverse-in-part, vacate-in-part, and remand for entry of a reduced damage award.

I.

On August 8, 1979, Lisbon and the United States Soil Conservation Service (SCS) entered into Contract No. 50-3A75-9-35 for construction of a reinforced concrete flood control channel and a bridge. With extensions of time, the completion date was December 20, 1980. Work began in the fall of 1979 on the bridge portion of the contract. As is frequent in construction projects, Lisbon encountered difficulties. Lisbon's concrete subcontractor, Versatile Constructors, was a major source of Lisbon's problems. The government attributed that difficulty to poor supervision by Lisbon.

In the succeeding months the parties exchanged numerous letters discussing Lisbon's progress on the project. On several occasions the contracting officer's representative threatened to terminate Lisbon's right to proceed unless Lisbon took immediate action to correct specific problems. SCS was concerned about the following items: (1) Versatile Constructors' performance as the concrete subcontractor, (2) Anthony Rebimbas' performance as Lisbon's construction superintendent, (3) the quality of the concrete work, and (4) Lisbon's progress on the work. Typically Lisbon responded by taking some action to correct the problems, which did not fully satisfy SCS, whereupon negotiations would continue. In January, 1980, for example, the contracting officer required Lisbon to submit a revised construction schedule with information on additional work forces and equipment. Lisbon submitted a revised schedule with some details, but the contracting officer requested more.

To meet SCS's objections, Lisbon designated its vice president, Peter Campellone, as acting superintendent (with the government's approval) until it could find a replacement, and it terminated Versatile as the concrete subcontractor once the bridge was completed. It remedied specific complaints on work item deficiencies identified by SCS. SCS inspected and paid for the work. On April 7, 1980, Lisbon requested a meeting between the contracting officer and Lisbon's president, Anthony Marques, to resolve the items still at issue, namely, the construction schedule and the superintendent issues. Also Lisbon had requested a change in the specifications to allow it to remove concrete forms more quickly (the "sleeper joint" issue).

The parties met on April 30, 1980. Lisbon renewed its request for a modification of the contracting officer's interpretation of the sleeper joint issue which would enable Lisbon to perform the work more efficiently and expeditiously. Mr. Marques became incensed because SCS never made the analysis it had promised with respect to the requested change. At the meeting, SCS adamantly refused to approve the change, and tempers flared. Following the heated altercation on this issue, during which Mr. Marques had indicated he needed the change to complete the work on time, the SCS representatives reiterated their displeasure with various aspects of Lisbon's performance. The SCS representatives then left the meeting to caucus because, per the contracting officer, everybody was going in different directions. After discussing the matter among themselves for approximately twenty minutes, they returned and the contracting officer announced that, in his opinion, Lisbon could not complete the job satisfactorily within the time limitations set in the contract, and he was terminating the contract for default.

Mr. Marques promptly withdrew his "demand" for a change and offered to do everything necessary to complete the work on time, even at a loss, in accordance with the contract. The contracting officer refused to discuss Lisbon's further performance under the contract. Thus, the matter of the superintendent and the details of the revised schedule Lisbon had submitted, which did not depend on the proposed change, were never taken up. A telegram subsequently confirmed the termination. SCS rebid the contract and engaged a follow-on contractor to complete the project. The project was eventually completed on December 10, 1981.

The action of the contracting officer in terminating Lisbon for default was taken pursuant to General Provision 5 of the contract at issue here, which contains the following standard language:

> If the Contractor refuses or fails to prosecute the work, or any separable part thereof, with such diligence as will insure its completion within the time specified in this contract, or any extension thereof, or fails to complete said work within such time, the Government may, by written notice to the Contractor, terminate his right to proceed with the work or such part of the work as to which there has been delay.

* * *

> If, after notice of termination of the Contractor's right to proceed under the provisions of this clause, it is determined for any reason that the Contractor was not in default under the provisions of this clause, or that the delay was excusable under the provisions of this clause, the rights and obligations of the parties shall, if the contract contains a clause providing for termination for convenience of the Government, be the same as if the notice of termination had been issued pursuant to such clause.

The contract contains a standard termination for convenience clause. On December 19, 1980, Lisbon submitted a certified claim to the contracting officer, asserting that the government's termination for default was not justified and claiming a right to certain costs under the termination for convenience clause of the contract. The contracting officer responded by referring to the default termination decision, thereby rejecting the claim, and Lisbon timely filed a direct access action in the Court of Claims pursuant to the Contract Disputes Act (CDA), 41 U.S.C. §609(a) (1982).

* * *

In this case, the government bore the burden on the issue of default raised by the contractor's complaint.

B. Standard for Default for Failure to Prosecute with Diligence

With respect to the government's challenge to the standard imposed by the Claims Court to establish the contractor's default here, we do not agree that the Claims Court ultimately required the government to prove that the contractor could not possibly complete the work before the date fixed in the contract. To make this argument, the government relies on isolated statements of the court read out of context. On this issue, the court unequivocally held:

> The standard default clause does not require a finding that completion within the contract time is impossible. Termination for default is appropriate if a demonstrated lack of diligence indicates that [the government] could not be assured of timely completion. Case law that involves abandoned or repudiated contracts, and terminations that involve a failure to make progress, applies.

Discount Co. v. United States, 554 F.2d 435, 441 [213 Ct.Cl. 567] (1977); Universal Fiberglass Corp. v. United States, 537 F.2d at 398. Slip op. at 14.

We agree that the contractual language found in General Provision 5 does not require absolute impossibility of performance by the contractor before the government may declare the contract in default. See Discount Co. v. United States, 554 F.2d 435, 441, 213 Ct.Cl. 567, cert. denied, 434 U.S. 938, 98 S.Ct. 428, 54 L.Ed.2d 298 (1977). Nor does it permit default termination merely on the ground that performance is less than absolutely certain. Rather, we construe the contract, as did the Claims Court, to require a reasonable belief on the part of the contracting officer that there was "no reasonable likelihood that the [contractor] could perform the entire contract effort within the time remaining for contract performance." RFI Shield-Rooms, ASBCA Nos. 17374, 17991, 77-2 BCA (CCH) ¶ 12,714, 61,735 (Aug. 11, 1977); see also Discount, 554 F.2d at 441 (justifiable insecurity about the contract's timely completion required). Although the government argues strenuously to the contrary, the Claims Court placed upon the government no greater burden of proving default than that described in Discount.

C. The Evidence of Default

The sole basis here for termination for default was Lisbon's failure, under General Provision 5 of the contract, "to prosecute the work ... with such diligence as will insure its completion within the time specified in th[e] contract." At trial, the government did not offer direct testimony or any other direct evidence on the time which it estimated it would take Lisbon to complete the contract. Indeed, the contracting officer acknowledged that the government did not undertake a study to determine whether Lisbon could complete the work within the required time, or determine how long it would take a follow-on contractor to do the work. Such a comparison is mandated by the relevant procurement regulations. 41 C.F.R. § 1-18.803-5(a)(3).

The government argues that it was, nevertheless, justified in terminating for failure to make progress because Lisbon (1) did not sufficiently support its revised construction schedule to show the manner in which it would regain time to achieve the due date and (2) failed to designate an acceptable, full-time superintendent. Thus, per the government, the contracting officer had reasonable doubts concerning Lisbon's ability to complete the job in a timely fashion. Under the Discount decision, the government argues, the default for untimely progress was justified, the contractor being required in Discount to reasonably assure the contracting officer that he could complete the job on time.

The Claims Court made the following findings:

> 26. At the start of the April 30, 1980, meeting, the matters [the government] had complained about were in the following status:
>
> (1) Versatile's subcontract had been terminated.
>
> (2) [Lisbon] had a full-time superintendent.

(3) All previous complaints on various work item deficiencies had been remedied; the work had been inspected; and [Lisbon] had been paid for the work.

(4) Lisbon had submitted a revised schedule which showed the work could be completed timely, using procedures that accorded with [the government's] interpretation of the specifications on the sleeper joint issue.

Slip op. at 39.

To give any viability to the government's justification argument, the government must persuade us that findings (2) and (4) above are clearly erroneous. A finding of fact is clearly erroneous when "'although there is evidence to support it, the reviewing court on the entire evidence is left with the definite and firm conviction that a mistake has been committed.'" Milmark Servs., Inc. v. United States, 731 F.2d 855, 857 (Fed.Cir.1984) (quoting United States v. United States Gypsum Co., 333 U.S. 364, 395, 68 S.Ct. 525, 542, 92 L.Ed. 746 (1948)).

The record before us indicates that the parties arranged the April 30, 1980 meeting between Lisbon's president and the contracting officer to resolve their differences so they could pursue completion of the project. The superintendent and revised construction schedule problems were matters the parties sought to resolve at the meeting.

Whether Mr. Campellone, Lisbon's vice president, was a full-time superintendent on April 30, 1980, was disputed. The government maintains his health was too poor to permit him to work full time. He had been accepted by the government in January when there was minimal construction activity and it was intended he would serve only temporarily until the superintendent dispute was resolved. There is no dispute that Lisbon was prepared to discuss superintendence at the meeting, and that the meeting broke up before that issue was reached. On the record before us, we are not persuaded that the Claims Court's finding of fact (2) above is clearly erroneous.

The government maintains that the Claims Court erred in finding that Lisbon had submitted a revised schedule of work at the time of termination. Per the government, the schedule was not acceptable because Lisbon did not supply the details of the additional work forces and equipment necessary to complete the job under the contract. The government asked, for example, for the names of specific laborers Lisbon would commit to the job and for copies of sub-contracts. Per the government, these deficiencies, viewed in the context of past poor performance, were a sufficient basis for concluding that the contractor could not finish on time. The government also urges that Lisbon's president admitted at the meeting that Lisbon could not complete the work without a change in the contract specifications.

One purpose of the meeting was to work out problems of the work schedule. There was conflicting evidence concerning what occurred at the meeting, and the trial court found the testimony of Lisbon's witnesses more persuasive, a decision to which we must defer. Also the Claims Court took into consideration the circumstances surrounding Mr. Marques' alleged admission and discounted its importance. We agree it does not outweigh the other evidence. Per the Claims Court, the submitted revised schedule did not depend on obtaining a change in specifications and would have been taken up had the government not ended the negotiations following the altercation. The Claims Court also held, and we agree, that the contractor's failure to give all the requested details on the revised schedule was not in itself evidence of failure to make progress on the work which would justify the default termination.

In sum, we hold that on the basis of the entire record, the Claims Court did not err in determining that the government improperly terminated Lisbon for default. The Claims

Court properly converted the termination for default to a termination for convenience of the government as provided by General Provision 5 of the contract.

* * *

Notes and Questions

1. *Lisbon Contractors* concerns the second prong of the Default Clause, "failure to make progress." Note how this occurs prior to the date for delivery or completion. This corresponds in basic (private) contract law to implied repudiation. However, at common law, the contractor would have to bollix or delay matters so badly that it was impossible for performance to occur, to constitute implied repudiation and thereby to justify cancellation. What standard does the government set for when it can terminate for failure to perform, prior to the date of delivery? Which of the several factors that differentiate government termination from private cancellation justify the government's terminating, not because performance is impossible, but on an easier showing?

2. Even though the government has an easier showing to terminate for failure to make progress than is required at common law, it does not succeed in this case. Did the CO have much reason to doubt progress? How many different aspects of the arguments on both sides can you separate out? Try this chart:

CO's arguments	Contractor's arguments
health too poor	full time superintendant
no lists of laborers, names of subs	revised schedule of work
concrete sub had not done well	Versatile had been terminated
Lisbon had asked for change in specs	Lisbon had withdrawn that demand
("sleeper joint")	

3. For basic (private) contract law, the Uniform Commercial Code meets the need for parties to be able to check whether performance is endangered by giving those parties the ability to request assurances. UCC 2-609; Restatement (Second) of Contracts sec. 251. What is there about modern contracting that has led both government and private contracting to fill in this gap in the common law, which largely required contractors to await the day of performance to end the suspense about whether the other party would perform? Increases in the complexity of contracting parties' interdependence and organized production interconnection?

4. The third prong of the Default Clause allows termination for "failure to perform other contract provisions." In what are called "(a)(1)(iii) cases," terminations for default have been upheld on grounds unrelated to whether the product was completed as promised. For instance, in *Kirk Brothers Mechanical Contractors, Inc. v. Kelso*, 16 F. 3d 1173, 40 Cont. Cas. Fed.(CCH) 76,889 (1994), Kirk was "removed" for failure to promptly provide a refrigeration system, and upon the Navy's discovery of defective workmanship, was ultimately subjected to termination for default. Because the contract had no completion date and Kirk had no opportunity to cure the ASBCA converted the default into a termination for convenience. On appeal, however, the Navy prevailed on alternative

grounds, specifically that Kirk Bros. had violated the Davis-Bacon Act (40 U.S.C. § 276 et seq.) by destroying rather than retaining employee time cards. See FAR 52-249-8 (a)(1)(iii).

5. As far as appropriate bases for termination for default, an interesting question has concerned whether a contracting officer's termination can be justified on grounds of contractor fraud. Ordinarily, issues of fraud are not for a contracting officer or for a board of contract appeals, but for a federal court. 41 U.S.C. sec. 605(a); FAR 33.210. It has been argued that a contracting officer cannot justify termination for default on grounds of contractor fraud. However, the Federal Circuit has upheld a termination for default where the government raised the issue of fraud, by holding that the validity of the CO's final decision was not diminished by the assertion of fraud as an additional basis for termination. *Daff v. United States*, 78 F.3d 1566 (F.3d Cir. 1996).

B. Process

Note on Process for Termination for Default

The issues of "process" in termination for default operate at different levels: what ordinarily happens when a contracting officer invokes the default clause and what may happen when a contractor challenges the contracting officer's discretion in invoking the default clause.

Ordinary Process

At one level, the process concerns what happens when a contracting officer invokes the default clause and goes through regular procedures with a contractor. Partly, this concerns notice requirements. Ordinarily, two distinct types of notice apply. The Default Clause does not require that the government notify the contractor in writing of the possibility of the termination. However, this kind of notice, referred to in the FAR (49.607) as a "show cause" notice, ordinarily is provided, and the courts and boards may sometimes require it. *Udis v. United States*, 7 Cl. Ct. 379 (1985). Moreover, a careful contracting officer, knowing what follows from termination for default, will want all the information obtainable by such a show cause notice.

As previously discussed, the "failure to make progress" and "failure to perform any other provision" prongs include explicit requirements of a ten day opportunity to cure the failure. And while the contracting officer has the power to summarily terminate for failure to deliver or perform, a contracting officer may well decide, under the power to forebear, effectively to give the contractor under this prong the same type of opportunity to cure.

Once the contracting officer renders a final decision to terminate for default, the contractor may appeal that through the disputes process. A final decision gives the contractor notice of this. The disputes process is discussed in the chapter on remedies. Among the issues that arise about termination for default is that of the proper timing for appeal, including the effect, usually not considered to be major, of deficiencies in the notification of the right to appeal. *See Decker & Co. v. West*, 76 F.3d 1573 (Fed. Cir. 1996); *State of Florida, Department of Insurance v. United States*, 81 F.3d 1093 (Fed. Cir. 1996).

Challenging the Contracting Officer's Exercise of Discretion

At the other level of the process issue, contracting officers have broad discretion over whether, if grounds to terminate are present, to do so. The issue of "process" concerns, not whether the termination for default has sufficient justification, but how the contracting officers have exercised their discretion. Contracting officers do not operate in a vacuum. They work in an agency context with several hierarchies. One involves their "clients," so to speak, namely, those in the agency needing the goods or services being procured. Another involves the budget for contracting. Yet another involves the agencies' relations with the ultimate elected officials, the President and the Congress. A contracting officer may well make the decision to terminate for default, as opposed to simply tolerating or working out the contractor's problems, in light of the attitudes of these various hierarchies.

A powerful ambivalence runs through the termination process on this element, making this the meeting-ground of major strains in the public law of government contracting. The competing considerations resemble those concerning what checks should exist on the government firing or suspending its own employees: checking arbitary power vs. clogging the effective operation of government.

On the one hand, as noted, termination for default resembles other normative civil adjudications. The government does more than simply implement its policy: it takes a step that brands the contractor for unexcused failure. Furthermore, it penalizes the contractor. To a limited extent, the statutory and regulatory assignment of authority to make the termination decision to the contracting officer vests in that officer, and that officer alone, the discretion to brand and to penalize the contractor, so that the power to visit such sanctions will not be at large in the government. Any other system, where a contractor could be penalized by unseen and unknown forces for unstated reasons, would be Kafkaesque.

On the other hand, a termination for default ordinarily must stand or fall on whether the contractor defaulted. If the contractor defaulted then the government must be able to terminate the contractor without endless procedures of second-guessing and resistance. Otherwise the effective operation of government gets clogged and paralyzed. A contractor who should be terminated instead would seek to put the government's own decisionmaking process on trial. Instead of deterring future contractors from defaults, such a procedure deters future contracting officers from using the vital tools for managing contractors.

In the overwhelming majority of terminations for default, the tribunal declines to take an interest in putting the contracting officer on trial. However, it is appropriate to look at two cases which did reverse terminations for default, based on the process that led to the termination. Partly this owes to the importance of the issue. Also, though, these cases provide a much more complete picture of how termination works than gets provided in the vast majority of cases where the inquiry is confined to whether the contractor defaulted. Lawyers who may participate on either side of terminations for defaults, or who may give advice in situations where such termination could occur, can find much to analyze in the fuller picture that these opinions paint about what precedes a termination for default.

The first case on that issue, *Darwin*, introduces the basic concepts of the tension between the government's desire to confine the issues to the contractor's performance and the contractor's desire to broaden them to the government's arbitrariness. Then, the next case, *McDonnell Douglas*, involves a billion-dollar public issue, the termination of a major airplane development contract. It reveals the interaction of the Defense Department's planning, budgeting, and decision-making system, on the one hand, with the adjudication of terminations for default on the other.

For further discussion of the subject of this section, see: Bruce W. McLaughlin, *The Evolution of Darwin: A Contracting Officer's Primer for Default Terminations*, 19 Pub. Cont. L.J. 191 (1990).

Darwin Construction Co., Inc., Appellant, v. United States, Appellee

Appeal No. 86-1370
United States Court of Appeals, Federal Circuit
811 F.2d 593
Feb. 12, 1987

Before NIES, Circuit Judge, COWEN, Senior Circuit Judge, and NEWMAN, Circuit Judge.

COWEN, Senior Circuit Judge.

Appellant (Darwin) appeals from a reconsidered decision of the Armed Services Board of Contract Appeals (ASBCA or Board) which had reversed its earlier holding. The Board initially converted a termination for default into a termination for the convenience of the Government. Upon Government's motion for reconsideration, the Board reversed its earlier decision and upheld the termination for default. We reverse the Board's amended decision and remand with instructions for the Board to convert the termination for default into a termination for the convenience of the Government in accordance with the Board's initial decision.

BACKGROUND

Darwin was awarded a fixed price construction contract on June 3, 1983, for certain improvements to the Propellant Machinery Facility (PMF) at the Naval Ordnance Station (NOS) in Maryland. Contract work was to be completed within 150 calendar days, by November 15, 1983.

The contract provided that the contractor would be allowed access to the construction site only during two 14 calendar day periods which were to be separated by another period of at least 14 calendar days during which time normal Naval production operations at the facility would take place. Based upon the schedule agreed upon between the parties, the last day for construction was to have been November 7, 1983. At the conclusion of this second 14-day work period, Darwin had completed approximately 65 percent of the required contract work.

In response to a "show cause" letter Darwin noted that the late delivery of necessary equipment made it impossible for the contract to be completed by November 7. Darwin, nevertheless, asserted that it was physically and financially ready to complete the remaining contract work within a two week period beginning on December 17, 1983. Nevertheless, on February 13, 1984, the Navy terminated the contract for default, claiming that Darwin had not diligently performed during the two 14-day periods when it had access to the site. The Navy alleged that a 2-week shutdown of the facility during December was not possible in order to permit Darwin to complete the contract.

On appeal to the ASBCA, the Board found that "on the record ... no excusable cause for delay has been proven by the appellant. Therefore, as of 15 November, the date of completion for the performance of the captioned contract, Darwin was in default." Darwin Constr. Co., ASBCA No. 29340, 84-3 BCA ¶ 17,673 at 88,149 (1984).

Despite its finding of default, the Board held that the termination for default "must be converted to one for convenience of the Government." The decision stated that "the Board finds that this termination for default was arbitrary and capricious because it is evident to the Board that the default action was taken solely to rid the Navy of having to further deal with Darwin." (Emphasis supplied).

The Board's conclusion regarding the arbitrary action of the contracting officer was based, among others, on the following findings of fact made by the Board:

The only reason Darwin was unable to complete the work in time was that the material needed for the unfinished portion was not delivered in the second 2-week period for performing the contract. On November 15, 1983, the Navy knew that Darwin had performed 65 percent of the work in an acceptable manner, and there was no evidence to suggest that the contractor was financially unable to complete the remainder of the work.

The Navy knew that renewed performance could not begin at the very earliest until August 1984, and therefore, the Navy had no basis for concluding that Darwin's late performance in November 1983 would still be a viable cause for delay in August 1984—9 months later.

The failure of Darwin to complete the work on time did not interfere with the Navy's use of the building, which was still used for the production of explosives since Darwin had restored the building into usable condition. Darwin contemplated working from December 27 through December 31, 1983, having estimated that the remaining work could be completed in 4 days. There was no urgency associated with the contract.

When the contract was terminated on February 3, 1984, the Navy estimated the next available date when the remaining work could be completed as August 1984, but by the date of the hearing, this hoped-for completion date had regressed to January 1985.

At the time Darwin was performing work on the contract, many other construction contracts were being performed at the same ordnance station, and the Navy was content to collect liquidated damages for those contracts in which performance had been delayed.

Although needed material was delivered by October 4, 1983, Darwin did not receive Navy approval of the material until October 19, 1983. At that time, Darwin submitted a written request for a time extension on account of that delay. The Board found that there was no evidence in the record that the contracting officer had acted on that request as required by General Provision 5 of the contract, entitled "Termination for Default—Damages for Delay—Time Extension." With respect to the default termination, the Board observed that "this termination for default exudes an odor piscatorial," citing Alinco Life Insurance Co. v. United States, 373 F.2d 336, 341, 178 Ct.Cl. 813 (1967).

Accordingly, the Board converted the default termination into one for the convenience of the Government.

On the basis of the Government's motion for reconsideration, the Board reversed its initial decision and upheld the termination for default. Darwin Constr. Co., ASBCA No. 29340, 86-2 BCA ¶ 18,959 (1986).

In reversing its decision on reconsideration, the Board, at the Government's urging, noted that the Board should recognize and follow the decision in Kalvar Corp. v. United States, 543 F.2d 1298, 211 Ct.Cl. 192 (1976), cert. denied, 434 U.S. 830, 98 S.Ct. 112, 54 L.Ed.2d 89 (1977), in which the court held that "well-nigh irrefragable proof" is required to induce the court to abandon the presumption of good faith dealing by public officials.

* * *

DISCUSSION
I.

Darwin accepts all of the findings of fact made by the Board in its initial decision. However, Darwin contends that the Board erred as a matter of law in holding that it could not inquire into the motives or judgment of the contracting officer in electing to terminate the contract for default, once the Government determined that the contractor was in technical default. We agree that this rule of administrative restraint is legally erroneous and contrary to long-established judicial precedent as hereinafter set forth. Moreover, the Board's holding is a ruling on a question of law, which is neither final nor binding on the court. Zinger Construction Co. v. United States, 807 F.2d 979, 981 (Fed.Cir.1986), citing American Electronic Laboratories, Inc. v. United States, 774 F.2d 1110, 1112 (Fed.Cir.1985).

II.

As stated above, the Board found that the termination for default was "arbitrary and capricious because it was evident to the Board that the default action was taken solely to rid the Navy of having to deal with Darwin." On the basis of that finding we hold that the Board's decision on reconsideration is squarely in conflict with Schlesinger v. United States, 390 F.2d 702, 709, 182 Ct.Cl. 571 (1968).

The Board's finding that the contracting officer abused his discretion provides the legal predicate for converting the termination for default into one for the convenience of the Government. As the court pointed out in Schlesinger, the default article of the contract does not require the Government to terminate on a finding of default, but merely gives the procuring agency the discretion to do so, and that discretion must be reasonably exercised. Id. at 709, 182 Ct.Cl. 571. The facts of the case before us are almost identical to the salient facts in Schlesinger, where it was found that the contractor's status of technical default served only "as a useful pretext for taking the action found necessary on other grounds unrelated to the plaintiff's performance or to the propriety of the extension of time." Id. Because of the remarkable similarity in the facts, we quote the following from Schlesinger:

> As in John A. Johnson Contracting Corp. [v. United States], supra, the Navy used the termination article as a "device" and never made a "judgment as to the merits of the case". 132 F.Supp. [698] at 705, 132 Ct.Cl. [645] at 659–660 [1955]. Such abdication of responsibility we have always refused to sanction where there is administrative discretion under a contract. New York Shipbuilding Corp. v. United States, 385 F.2d 427, 435, 436–437, 180 Ct.Cl. 446, 460 (June 1967), and cases cited. This protective rule should have special application for a default-termination which has the drastic consequence of leaving the contractor without any further compensation. See Acme Process Equip. Co. v. United States, 347 F.2d 509, 527, 528, 171 Ct.Cl. 324, 355 (1965) rev'd on other grounds, 385 U.S. 138, 87 S.Ct. 350, 17 L.Ed.2d 249 (1966).

Id.

In a recent decision, Quality Environment Systems v. United States, 7 Cl.Ct. 428, 432 (1985), the Claims Court relied on the Schlesinger decision. The court held that if it was determined that a default decision represented an abuse of discretion, the contractual remedy would be to convert the termination into one for the convenience of the Government.

Accordingly, we hold as the court held in Schlesinger that the Board's decision on reconsideration must be reversed and the case remanded with instructions for the Board to reinstate its initial decision in which the default termination was converted into one for the convenience of the Government.

III.

The Government has made only one argument as the basis for affirmance of the Board's decision. The Government asserts that since Darwin failed to demonstrate with "well-nigh irrefragable proof" that the Navy's default termination of the contract was exercised in bad faith, the termination was proper. In support of its contention, the Government cites Kalvar Corp. v. United States, 543 F.2d 1298, 1301–02, 211 Ct.Cl. 192 (1976), cert. denied, 434 U.S. 830, 98 S.Ct. 112, 54 L.Ed.2d 89 (1977), and Knotts v. United States, 121 F.Supp. 630, 636, 128 Ct.Cl. 489 (1954).

In view of the Board's unequivocal finding that the contracting officer's default decision was arbitrary and capricious, we reject the Government's argument on several grounds.

* * *

Thus, these decisions of the Court of Claims and the Claims Court make it abundantly clear that when a contractor persuades a court to find that the contracting officer's default decision was arbitrary or capricious, or that it represents an abuse of his discretion, the decision will be set aside. There is nothing in these decisions to support the Government's contention that the aggrieved contractor must add another layer of proof by demonstrating that the decision was also made in bad faith.

IV.

Although neither party has referred to them, we find that the Armed Services Procurement Regulations (ASPR) in effect at the time the contract was terminated are pertinent here and lend further support to our decision. ASPR 18-618, entitled "Termination of Fixed-Price Construction Contracts for Default," 32 C.F.R., Parts 1 to 39, Volume III, revised as of July 1, 1983, provided as follows:

18-618.4 Procedure in Case of Default.

(a) The contracting officer shall consider the following factors in determining whether to terminate a contract for default:

(i) the provisions of the contract and applicable laws and regulations;

(ii) the specific failure of the contractor and excuses, if any, made by the contractor for such failure;

(iii) the period of time which would be required for the Government or another contractor to complete the work as compared to the time required for completion by the delinquent contractor;

(iv) the effect of a termination for default on the ability of the contractor to liquidate guaranteed loans, progress payments, or advance payments; and

(v) any other pertinent facts and circumstances.

It is clear from the findings made in the Board's initial decision that the contracting officer failed to comply with the provisions of 18-618.4(a)(iii), because the Board, in its initial decision, made the following findings of fact:

As for the material delay, the Board is convinced that by 19 December, the material delay had ceased; by 3 February, we are morally certain there was no shortage and by August 1984 the Board is persuaded that the Navy would concede that the contractor could have had all the material needed to complete this contract. Therefore, the Navy, knowing that renewed performance could only begin at the earliest in August 1984, had no basis for concluding that the delay causing Darwin's late performance in November would still be a viable cause of delay in August, nine months later.

84-3 BCA at 88,150.

This and other Board findings set forth in the BACKGROUND portion of this opinion show that when the contract was terminated on February 13, 1984, the Navy knew that if another contractor were selected, it could not begin work until August of 1984 at the earliest, and that if Darwin had been allowed to do so, it could have completed the work in August 1984, at least as soon as and probably much sooner than a successor contractor could have performed the unfinished work.

Notes and Questions

1. On first reading, this seems like an easy case, with the contractor completely right and the government completely wrong. After all, how many times does a court say that government action gives out an "odor piscatorial"? However, it is worth understanding the government's side. Note that the government won in the ASBCA on rehearing. The very fact that the government so forcefully sought rehearing shows the level of its interests at stake. Putting aside why the Navy did what it did, did Darwin commit a failure of performance sufficient for it to lose a trial as to termination for default? Did Darwin have a sufficient excuse to win a trial as to termination for default? So, who does the case put on trial?

2. Look at other sanctioning cases brought by the government; for example, can criminal defendants put the police or the prosecutors on trial for their exercise of discretion in proceeding against them when they committed the offense charged and have no adequate excuse? In a civil proceeding regarding taxpayers who fail to pay their taxes without excuse, can they put the IRS on trial? For all the satisfaction it gives to see citizens vindicated, what would happen to the enforcement of the criminal and tax codes if the defendants could put the government on trial? And if the government stops functioning, does that benefit anyone, even the contractors?

3. Something else the case illustrates: how contractors see termination for default. Look at what Darwin was willing to do to avoid it: work intensely the week between Christmas and New Year's.

4. Note how the government fights tenaciously to maintain the standard that assailing the exercise of discretion requires proof of bad faith, and that such proof must be "well nigh irrefragible." How different is the standard set forth in this case? Does it matter much what the standard is? First imagine that as a contractor's attorney, you have the awesome burden of proving government bad faith. It seems hard, with the government officers who conspired to injure your client presumably being clever enough to leave no evidence around. Then imagine that as a government official, when you terminate for default you must face Freedom of Information Act document demands, subpoenas, depositions, and comparisons with other cases to get at you any way the contractor can. The contractor might have large financial resources for this fight, while your own short-staffed office expects you to get on with the rest of your work. Now who feels the awesome burden? Both sides feel much is at stake in these cases.

McDonnell Douglas Corporation, Plaintiff-Cross Appellant, et al., v. United States, Defendant-Appellant

Nos. 98-5096, 98-5122, 98-5123
United States Court of Appeals, Federal Circuit.
182 F.3d 1319
July 1, 1999

Before MAYER, Chief Judge, MICHEL and CLEVENGER, Circuit Judges.

CLEVENGER, Circuit Judge.

This dispute arises out of the government's default termination of a contract between the United States Navy and defense contractors McDonnell Douglas Corporation and General Dynamics Corporation ("Contractors") to develop a carrier-based, low-observable "stealth" aircraft known as the A-12 Avenger. After several years of litigation, the United States Court of Federal Claims held that the government's termination of the contract for default could not be sustained because the government did not exercise the requisite discretion before entering a default termination, see McDonnell Douglas Corp. v. United States, 35 Fed. Cl. 358, 368–71 (1996) (hereinafter McDonnell Douglas IV), and converted the termination for default into a termination for convenience, awarding Contractors costs totaling $3,877,767,376. See McDonnell Douglas Corp. v. United States, 40 Fed. Cl. 529, 555–56 (1998) (hereinafter McDonnell Douglas IX). We hold that, because the termination for default was predicated on contract-related issues, it was within the discretion of the government. Accordingly, the Court of Federal Claims' conversion of the termination for default into a termination for convenience was in error. We reverse the trial court's judgment and remand the case to the trial court for a determination of whether the government's default termination was justified, an issue upon which we express or intimate no view.

I

A

In 1984, the Department of the Navy introduced the Advanced Tactical Aircraft Program, known as the A-12 program, to develop a carrier-based stealth aircraft for the Navy. In January 1988, Contractors entered into a Full Scale Engineering Development contract (the "A-12 FSD Contract") with the government to produce eight FSD aircraft at a target price of $4,379,219,436. See McDonnell Douglas IV, 35 Fed. Cl. at 361. The contract was structured as an incrementally funded, fixed-price incentive contract with a ceiling price of $4,777,330,294, and recited a schedule of installment payments over the five-year term of the contract. The first aircraft was originally scheduled to be delivered in June 1990, and subsequent aircraft were to be delivered each month through January 1991. See id. at 361–62.

From the outset, Contractors encountered difficulties in performing the contract. Particular problems included meeting the contract schedule and keeping the aircraft weight within specifications. . . .

In June 1990, Contractors informed the Navy that they could not meet the contract schedule, that the cost of completing the contract would substantially exceed the ceiling price, and that Contractors could not absorb the loss that would result from the contract. Contractors asserted that a fundamental problem with the FSD contract was its structure as a fixed-price contract and proposed that the contract be modified. Thereafter, Contractors submitted a proposal to change the contract schedule, but the Navy and Contractors failed to reach an agreement on that issue. Instead, on August 17, 1990, the Navy unilaterally issued a contract modification that changed the delivery schedule for the aircraft. Under this modification, the delivery date of the first aircraft was delayed until December 1991, and the remaining aircraft became due periodically between February 1992 and February 1993. See Contract Modification P00046 ¶ 1(b), Joint Appendix at 15,657.

In November 1990, Contractors submitted a formal request to the Navy to restructure the contract as a cost-reimbursement type contract....

During the Secretary's briefing to the President of the United States in early December 1990, the Secretary indicated his disappointment with the Navy's handling of the A-12 program and promised to take appropriate actions. On December 3, the Secretary directed the Deputy Secretary of Defense to review and report on the status of the A-12 program within ten days. This resulted in several meetings by the Defense Acquisition Board and Defense Procurement Review Boards. In addition, on December 12, the Secretary of the Navy responded to Secretary Cheney's December 3 request with a memorandum that expressed concern about Contractors' ability and willingness to perform under the contract, and which noted in particular Contractors' belief that the government should assume responsibility for failure to meet goals under the contract, and that the government should restructure the contract. The memorandum concluded with a statement that the Navy would examine whether the contract should be terminated for default, and would make a recommendation to the Secretary by January 5, 1991. See id.

On Friday, December 14, Secretary Cheney directed the Secretary of Navy to show cause by January 4, 1991 why the A-12 program should not be terminated. The following Monday, December 17, the Navy issued a cure notice to Contractors stating that unless they were able to meet contract specifications by January 2, 1991, the government might choose to terminate the contract for default. In particular, the cure letter stated that, inter alia, Contractors had "failed to fabricate parts sufficient to permit final assembly in time to meet the schedule for delivery," and had "fail[ed] to meet specification requirements." Joint Appendix at 16,524. The letter asserted that "[t]hese conditions are endangering performance of [the] contract." Id.

High-level meetings between the responsible government personnel, including the contracting officer and the general counsels of the Department of Defense and of the Navy, and Contractors, including the Chief Executive Officers of McDonnell Douglas and General Dynamics, occurred on December 18 and 21. During these meetings, Contractors asserted that they "[c]an't get there if we don't change contract," id. at 16,533, and "[i]t has got to get reformed to a cost type contract or we cannot do it." Id. at 16,549. When asked by the government on December 21 "can you correct deficiencies to provide an aircraft that meets the requirements," Contractors replied "[a]ll deficiencies cannot be corrected. Can we deliver a satisfactory aircraft for the Navy? Mother nature won't allow correction of all defects. We'll do the best we can and the Navy has to decide if that's good enough." Id. at 16,548–49.

Contractors responded to the cure notice on January 2 by admitting that they "[would] not meet delivery schedules or certain specifications of the original contract, or the revised FSD delivery schedule." Id. at 18,175. Contractors did not contest that they had failed to fabricate parts in time to meet the delivery schedule for the FSD aircraft. Nonetheless, Contractors asserted that they were not in default because, in their view, the delivery schedules were invalid or unenforceable. See id. at 18,175–78. As suggested cure, Contractors submitted a proposal to restructure the contract, pursuant to which Contractors would absorb a $1.5 billion fixed loss on the cost overrun from the contract, the contract would be restructured to a cost reimbursement contract, and Contractors would waive their claims for equitable adjustment. Contractors proposed to restructure the contract pursuant to Pub. L. No. 85-804, which gives the President of the United States the power to authorize departments or agencies connected with national defense to grant extraordinary relief under contracts if such an action facilitates the national defense. See 50 U.S.C. § 1431 (1994).

On Saturday, January 5, Secretary Cheney met with Undersecretary of Defense for Acquisition Yockey, the Secretary of the Navy, and the Chairman of the Joint Chiefs of Staff to discuss the budget and the A-12 program. At the meeting, Secretary Cheney noted that a scheduled payment of $553 million—one of the largest installment payments under the A-12 contract—was due on Monday, January 7. Later that day, Secretary Cheney, acting under authority pursuant to Pub. L. No. 85-804, decided not to grant relief. On Sunday, January 6, Undersecretary Yockey informed Rear Admiral William R. Morris, who at this time was acting as contracting officer over the A-12 contract, that Secretary Cheney had denied 85-804 relief and that no further funds would be obligated under the A-12 program. The next day, Admiral Morris issued the termination letter to Contractors stating that the government was terminating the A-12 contract due to Contractors' default.

B

On February 5, 1991, the Navy sent a letter to Contractors demanding the return of approximately $1.35 billion in unliquidated progress payments under the terminated contract. On June 7, Contractors filed suit in the United States Court of Federal Claims under the Contract Disputes Act, 41 U.S.C. § 609(a) (1994), requesting that the court: (1) grant their equitable adjustment claims dated December 31, 1990, (2) convert the government's termination for default into a termination for convenience, (3) deny the government's demand for return of progress payments, (4) award Contractors costs and a reasonable profit under the contract, (5) award them settlement expenses, and (6) award damages for breach of contract. See McDonnell Douglas Corp. v. United States, 25 Cl.Ct. 342, 346 (1992).

After several years of litigation in the Court of Federal Claims, that court ruled, in a decision dated April 8, 1996, that the government's default termination was invalid according to Schlesinger v. United States, 182 Ct.Cl. 571, 390 F.2d 702 (Cl.Ct.1968). See McDonnell Douglas IV, 35 Fed. Cl. at 368–71. The trial court held that under Schlesinger, the government is required to exercise "reasoned discretion" before terminating a contract for default, and that the government failed to meet this requirement because the Secretary of Defense's actions effectively forced the Navy to terminate the A-12 contract for default. See id. at 369–71. Therefore, the trial court vacated the government's termination for default and converted it into a termination for convenience. See id. at 361....

II

The level of discretion that must be exercised by the government before terminating a contract for default is a question of law, which we review de novo. See Darwin Constr. Co. v. United States, 811 F.2d 593, 596 (Fed.Cir.1987); Barseback Kraft AB v. United States, 121 F.3d 1475, 1479 (Fed.Cir.1997). We will upset the trial court's factual findings, however, only if they are clearly erroneous. See, e.g., Bass Enters. Prod. Co. v. United States, 133 F.3d 893, 895 (Fed.Cir.1998).

A

The trial court held that the government's termination of the A-12 contract did not comport with the rule laid down in Schlesinger by the United States Court of Claims, our predecessor court, for a proper default termination. Schlesinger involved a cap manufacturer who won a contract to supply the Navy with 50,000 service caps for enlisted men. The contract required the manufacturer to submit pre-production samples of component materials, as well as two samples of the completed cap, to the government for approval prior to production. In addition, the contract included a delivery schedule which set forth delivery dates for five separate installments of the completed caps. See Schlesinger, 390 F.2d at 703–04. Schlesinger did not submit the two sample caps and certain thread for pre-production approval, perhaps because he had fulfilled a contract for 240,000 identical Navy caps the previous year. Schlesinger also failed to deliver the first installment of caps as specified in the delivery schedule. See id. At the time, Schlesinger was also a prime suspect in an ongoing United States Senate subcommittee investigation regarding textile procurement irregularities within the military. Indeed, Schlesinger testified before the subcommittee during the pendency of his supply contract; shortly after his testimony, the chairman of the subcommittee sent a letter to the Navy implying that Schlesinger's contract should be terminated. This information was communicated to the contracting officer, who promptly terminated Schlesinger's contract. See id. at 705–06.

The Court of Claims held that the default termination of Schlesinger's contract was illegal. In doing so, the court first found that Schlesinger was indeed technically in default under the terms of the contract. See id. at 706–07. However, the court determined that neither the contracting officer nor anyone else in the Navy exercised independent judgment in terminating the contract for default. See id. at 707–08 (citing John A. Johnson Contracting Corp. v. United States, 132 Ct.Cl. 645, 132 F.Supp. 698, 704–05 (1955)). Thus, the court found that the contractor's "bare" or "technical" default "served only as a useful pretext for the taking of action felt to be necessary on other grounds unrelated to the [contractor's] performance…." Id. at 709.

The illegality in Schlesinger stemmed from the Navy's reliance on contractor default as a pretext to terminate its relationship with the contractor, independent of the state of actual performance under the contract. The court characterized Schlesinger's performance shortcomings as merely a "technical default" or "bare default," id. at 707, 708, and emphasized the Navy's total failure to consider the level of performance once it found a means for terminating by default. See, e.g., id. at 708 ("[T]he Navy acted as if it had no option but to terminate for default … once the mere fact of non-delivery was found."). In Schlesinger, it was improper for the Navy to terminate the contractor for default due solely to pressure from a congressional oversight committee because this ground for termination was totally unrelated to contract performance.

In short, Schlesinger bars only a termination for default in which there is no considered nexus between the default termination and the contractor's performance under the contract.…

A third case cited to us by Contractors, Darwin Construction Co. v. United States, 811 F.2d 593 (Fed.Cir.1987), further confirms the rule identified above. In Darwin, we adopted the Armed Services Board of Contract Appeals's finding that "the default action was taken solely to rid the Navy of having to deal with Darwin." Id. at 596 (internal quotation marks omitted). Thus, we held that the government used Darwin's technical default as a mere pretext for terminating the contract on grounds unrelated to performance. See id. Furthermore, Darwin clarifies what is meant by the "reasonable discretion" test used in Schlesinger and Johnson. In Darwin, we stated that, although a contracting officer has discretion with respect to contract termination, a termination for default will be set aside if it is arbitrary or capricious, or constitutes an abuse of the contracting officer's discretion. See id. at 598. When there is no nexus between the decision to terminate for default and contract performance, as was true in Darwin, Schlesinger, and Johnson, the termination for default may be arbitrary and capricious and set aside in favor of a termination for convenience.

Properly understood, then, Schlesinger and its progeny merely stand for the proposition that a termination for default that is unrelated to contract performance is arbitrary and capricious, and thus an abuse of the contracting officer's discretion. This proposition itself is but part of the well established law governing abuse of discretion by a contracting official. See, e.g., United States Fidelity & Guaranty Co. v. United States, 230 Ct.Cl. 355, 676 F.2d 622, 630 (1982) (listing four factors to be used in determining if conduct by a government official is arbitrary and capricious: (1) evidence of subjective bad faith on the part of the government official, (2) whether there is a reasonable, contract-related basis for the official's decision, (3) the amount of discretion given to the official, and (4) whether the official violated an applicable statute or regulation).

B

The record shows that the government's default termination was not pretextual or unrelated to Contractors' alleged inability to fulfill their obligations under the contract. Therefore, unlike the cases cited above, the government's decision to terminate the A-12 FSD Contract for default was related to contract performance, and the Court of Federal Claims erred by converting the termination into one for convenience without first addressing the question of breach.

* * *

More importantly, however, the record demonstrates that the government properly terminated the A-12 program for reasons related to contract performance. Admiral Morris, the contracting officer, testified at length about his decisional process that led to the termination for alleged default. He thought that he had three choices: to terminate for convenience, to terminate for default, or to do nothing. He rejected the latter as "irresponsible," thus focusing his attention on the other two choices. He eliminated the termination for convenience first, because he believed Contractors to be in material breach of the contract. This was so, in his words, because, as conceded in Contractors' response to the cure notice:

> They were in default because they acknowledged they would not be able to achieve the contract specifications and the contract requirements. Two, they had indicated that they would not be able to meet the delivery schedule that was currently in the contract. And three, they would not be able to perform the contract without extraordinary relief or additional funding for the contract. So they basically said they can't perform under the contract and they were in default of it.

Joint Appendix at 3,898–99. In further elaboration of his decision, again in the context of Contractors' response to the cure notice, Admiral Morris testified as to why he thought Contractors' default was material:

> They had failed to fabricate parts so as to endanger performance of the contract, and in my judgment, as would relate to the production options, failed to make progress, and it was clear to me that is where they stood on the 7th of January when I terminated the contract for default.

Id. at 3,917. As to why a termination for convenience was inappropriate, Admiral Morris stated that:

> [B]ecause I felt very strongly that as a result of the contractors' default, it would be nothing short of unconscionable for me to put the burden of the contractors' failure to make progress and the contractors' failure to fabricate parts, so as to en-

danger performance of the contract, put that burden on the government and the taxpayer to reimburse all costs and to pay the contractors a profit for their failures.

Id. at 3,920. Therefore, Admiral Morris terminated the contract for failure to make progress and for failure to meet contract requirements.

Failure to meet contract specifications and inability to meet the contract delivery schedule are of course relevant considerations to whether a contractor is in default....

The trial court also found that Secretary Cheney denied extraordinary relief, which led to the termination, because of concerns about the A-12 program's "cost and schedule." McDonnell Douglas IV, 35 Fed. Cl. at 372. The cost to complete a contract—more particularly, the inability of a contractor to perform a contract at the specified contract price—and the ability to meet a contract schedule are both fundamental elements of government contracts and are related to contract performance; as such, they are highly relevant to the question of default.

The government had specific concerns about when—and if—the A-12 aircraft would ever be delivered and how much it would cost. Secretary Cheney stated in testimony before Congress that the A-12 program was terminated because "no one could tell me how much the program was going to cost even just through the full-scale development phase or when it would be available. Data that had been presented at one point a few months ago turned out to be invalid and inaccurate." Hearings on National Defense Authorization Act for Fiscal Years 1992 and 1993—H.R. 2100 and Oversight of Previously Authorized Programs Before the House Comm. on Armed Servs., 102nd Cong. 60 (1991) (statement of Richard Cheney, Secretary of Defense). The evidence in the record demonstrates that the Secretary of Defense denied relief under Pub. L. 85-804, and Admiral Morris chose to terminate the contract for default, for reasons related to Contractors' state of performance of the contract. The trial court emphasized that although Contractors failed to meet the aircraft weight limit, the Navy essentially waived this requirement because the overweight aircraft would still meet all operational requirements. See McDonnell Douglas IV, 35 Fed. Cl. at 363, 376. However, although that finding is relevant to the ultimate determination of whether Contractors were in breach, or whether a breach was excused, it is insufficient to show, in light of all the other evidence in the record, that the government terminated the contract for reasons wholly unrelated to contract performance.

We think it clear beyond any doubt that Admiral Morris, unlike the contracting officer in Schlesinger, or in other cases that have upset terminations for default for lack of nexus to contract performance behavior, made his choice for reasons related to contract performance. Admiral Morris certainly knew that Contractors took another view of events transpiring during contract performance: although they admitted that they could not perform the contract according to its terms, they felt that the fault for their failure should be laid at the government's feet. Admiral Morris meant not to take away the right of Contractors to assert their defenses to termination for default, he instead only meant to assert the government's right to allege material breach on the record of contract performance that had been laid before him by Contractors themselves. Given the reasons stated for the action taken by the contracting officer in this case, it was legal error for the trial court to see these facts as commanding conversion of the termination for default into one for the convenience of the government.

To summarize, the government may not use default as a pretext for terminating a contract for reasons unrelated to performance; instead, there must be a nexus between the government's decision to terminate for default and the contractor's performance. The record and the facts found by the trial court establish that the government denied additional funding for the A-12 program and terminated the contract for default because of concerns about contract specifications, contract schedule, and price—factors that are fundamental elements of contract performance. Therefore, the trial court erred by vacating the termination for default without first determining whether a default existed. On remand, if the government can establish that Contractors were in default, then the termination for default would be valid. See Lisbon Contractors, Inc. v. United States, 828 F.2d 759, 765 (Fed.Cir.1987) (holding that the government bears the burden of proof with respect to the issue of whether termination for default was justified). Conversely, if the government is not able to make this showing, then the default termination was invalid and Contractors would be entitled to a suitable recovery, presumably under a termination for convenience theory.

CONCLUSION

We reverse the trial court's ruling that the government's default termination of the A-12 FSD Contract must be converted into a termination for convenience because the government did not exercise the necessary discretion. Of course, we do not hold today that the government's default termination is justified. As Contractors correctly point out, they have never been found to be in default of the contract. Because the trial court focused on the legitimacy of the government's default termination decision, rather than on whether Contractors were in fact in default, the parties have not yet been afforded the opportunity to fully litigate default. See McDonnell Douglas Corp. and General Dynamics Corp. v. United States, No. 91-1204C, slip op. at 2 (Fed. Cl. June 17, 1993). If the government fails to establish at trial that Contractors were in default under the contract, then the government's default termination would be improper and Contractors could rightfully recover damages under the theory of a termination for convenience....

Notes and Questions

1. There will be further detailed discussion of the procedure for termination for default in the section on "Disputes" in the chapter on Disputes and Other Remedies.

2. The *McDonnell Douglas* opinion reviews the key cases regarding pressure to terminate—*Schlesinger, Johnson*, and *Darwin*. It establishes as a standard that the decision to terminate for default need only have a "nexus" to or be "predicated on" contract-related issues for validity, as contrasted with being "pretextual" or "wholly unrelated" to the contract. Assume that frequently there will be considerable pressure to terminate for default for a variety of reasons, some of which, like agency budgets, or another contractor's superior connections, are not contract- or performance-related. Does this opinion establish as a standard that unless the decision to terminate is wholly the result of pressure and is completely pretextual, that decision is valid?

3. This opinion notes tersely that on Sunday, January 6, the contracting officer, Rear Admiral Morris, found out that the A-12 program would have no further funds, and the next day, he issued the termination letter. The trial court opinion, based on extensive deposition testimony by the officials, described that sequence more fully, under the heading "Monday Morning Rush." Morris told his Navy counsel on Sunday to prepare the termination memorandum the next day, which she did, editing a termination memorandum for another aircraft, but adding little regarding the A-12 because she had little information at her disposal. She did not even consult with Morris, nor with key others, about the basis for termination. This was part of why the trial court had considered the long-standing defaults, as mere excuses.

Does it shock you to hear that the role of a government contracts attorney consists of revising a model in this way? Would you look forward to being deposed about how you prepare documents?

4. For an important analysis of this issue, see Joshua I. Schwartz, *Administrative Law Lessons Regarding the Role of Politically Appointed Officials in Default Terminations*, 30 Pub. Cont. L. J. 144 (2001). Professor Schwartz extensively contrasts the different concepts applied to significant decisions (like default terminations) in administrative and procurement law. He suggests that in some cases, rather than having the agency head only informally (if potently) involved as was Secretary Cheney, the agency head should formally displace the contracting officer and unambiguously take on the responsibility for the determination. Intriguingly, he also proposes that sometimes the remedy when a reviewing tribunal sets aside a default termination, for failure to consider the proper factors, should only be a remand to the agency for reconsideration rather than outright conversion to a (much more contractor friendly) termination for convenience. What do you think of what Professor Schwartz himself acknowledges might seem "radical proposals" but which reflect a half-century of rich administrative law precedent? Do the differences between administrative and procurement law reflect a deep structure of different policy or merely the accidents of their separate historical paths?

5. Now that the appellate court has established that the termination is valid unless pretextual, will the government be able to fend off intrusive discovery about the procedure followed? Or do terminated contractors get to pursue their claim of pretextuality all the way up the chain of command to the level of Cabinet Secretary?

6. The opinion tiptoes around the alternative models for a contracting officer. A contracting officer exercises discretion about termination for default, which can be an extraordinarily significant and sometimes highly stigmatizing decision. Is the contracting officer like a judge, for whom it is abhorrent to imagine command pressure or political influence? Or is the contracting officer part of a system that resolves not merely administrative but also political issues, and should be left to do so? A criminal defendant, or a civil defendant in a suit brought by the government, cannot raise as a defense the politics of the decision to indict or to file suit. Must a terminated contractor be able to do so?

C. Excess Reprocurement and Other Remedies

In basic (private) contract law, one of the developments of interest in recent years has been the interaction between contract clauses regarding remedies and statutory or other constraints on such clauses. For example, extensive case law has developed concerning warranties that limit the remedy for breach to "repair or replacement," or that exclude consequential damages. In government contracting law, the questions concerning intriguing remedies for breach involve the "excess costs of reprocurement." Pursuant to the FAR clause, FAR 52.249-8(b), after termination for default contracting officers may acquire supplies or services substituting for what the defaulted contractor failed to provide. Then, in appropriate circumstances, they assess the defaulting contractor for the excess costs.

Seemingly, this is a reasonable remedy. The government does not universally invoke it, even in proper terminations for default, but only in appropriate circumstances. Moreover, the contractor can challenge the excess cost reprocurement by appealing the assessment. The appeal tests several factors that constrain the government.

In fact, the remedy can be potent. A conscientious contracting officer focuses on getting the goods or services needed by the agency, and accomplishing the "mission" for the agency. If that requires paying costs that are high, or higher, or even higher, then depending on the urgency of reprocurement, the contracting officer may have to pay them. Beyond that, the contracting officer may experience multiple temptations to pay such a high price. There is no love lost between a contracting officer and a defaulting contractor. Moreover, the agency may benefit from reprocuring higher rather than lower quality, particularly if the defaulted contractor, not the agency, pays the bill. As the saying goes, contracting officers go shopping with the defaulted contractors' charge cards in their pockets.

This may seem to resemble remedies in basic (private) contracts, namely, the remedy of "cover," or buying substitute goods. However, even under the best of circumstances, government contracting occurs in situations very far from a market. Reprocurement, occurring after delays and with many transitional distractions in difficult situations, is even further from a market. Accordingly, a separate set of issues concern the appropriate relation of the excess reprocurement costs to the original bids on the original IFB or RFP.

Notes and Questions

1. Imagine the contractor and the contracting officer here engage in contracting and termination as an intimate business game. Is the contractor a sleazy bluffer bent on dodging penalties for losing gambles, and the contracting officer a vigilant guardian of the taxpayers' money? Or is the contractor an enterprising market-oriented entrepreneur, and the contracting officer a hidebound bureaucratic disciplinarian relentlessly applying pain?

2. What is the relevance of the "price analysis"? Recall that in *Arrowhead Starr* case, the board of contract appeals cut back the excess costs of reprocurement for lack of competition in the reprocurement award. This opinion includes a string-cite of cases like that one. How can the government show reasonableness in an instance where it reprocures by contacting a sole source? Are you impressed by the procedures followed by the contracting officer to reprocure here?

Cascade Pacific International, Appellant, v. The United States, Appellee

Appeal No. 85-618
United States Court of Appeals, Federal Circuit
773 F.2d 287
Sept. 16, 1985

Before BALDWIN and KASHIWA, Circuit Judges, and MILLER, Senior Circuit Judge.

JACK R. MILLER, Senior Circuit Judge.

This is an appeal by Cascade Pacific International ("CPI"), from a decision of the General Services Administration Board of Contract Appeals under the Contract Disputes Act of 1978, 41 U.S.C. ss 601–613 (1982) ("CDA"), upholding the Contracting Officer's decisions to default terminate the subject contract and to grant in part the Government's claim for breach of contract damages. We affirm.

* * *

BACKGROUND

CPI entered into a one-year fixed-price supply requirements contract with the General Services Administration ("GSA") for builders' hardware (GS-04S-23598) ("'598"), including full surface and half surface spring hinges, on July 1, 1980. The contract prices per pair of full surface spring hinges ranged from $2.125 to $2.585, and those for half surface spring hinges ranged from $2.485 to $2.545. The specification indicated that the spring hinges were required to conform to Federal Specification FF-H-116E, which mandated, inter alia, that the spring hinges be plated and have a US10 finish, that the thickness of the metal be 0.082 +/– 0.005 inches, and that the spring hinges have button tips.

II. Assessment of Damages

Under provision 11.(b) of the General Provisions of the contract (pursuant to 41 C.F.R. § 1-8.707), when a contractor defaults, the Government "may procure, upon such terms and in such manner as the Contracting Officer may deem appropriate, supplies … [the same or] similar to those so terminated, and the Contractor shall be liable to the Government for any excess costs for such similar supplies." See also 41 C.F.R. § 1-8.602-6, FPR 1-8.602-6, to the same effect. Section 11.(f) can reasonably be read to permit the Government to proceed against a Contractor under other than specific contractual remedies, including the common law cause of action for breach of contract damages (hereafter "damages"). Rumley, 285 F.2d at 777; see supra note 5. This is not contested by CPI.

CPI contends, however, that excess reprocurement costs were improperly assessed by GSA and that the sua sponte imposition of damages rather than excess costs requested by the Government violates CPI's procedural due process right to sufficient notice of the charges, under either the CDA or the Federal Claims Collection Act of 1966 ("FCCA").

To uphold the board's decision to impose a monetary assessment against CPI, we must conclude that CPI received adequate notice of the possibility of the imposition of damages from the proceedings before the board and that the board correctly imposed damages; or, alternatively, that even though the board erroneously imposed damages, the Government adequately demonstrated its entitlement to excess reprocurement costs.

A. Excess Costs or Damages

The measure of damages is the reasonable reprocurement price less the original contract price. Marley v. United States, 423 F.2d 324, 333 (Ct.Cl.1970); Rumley, 285 F.2d at 777; J. Calimari and J. Perillo, Contracts 547 (2d ed. 1977). In contrast, excess reprocurement costs may be imposed only when the Government meets its burden of persuasion that the following conditions (factual determinations) are met: (1) the reprocured supplies are the same as or similar to those involved in the termination; (2) the Government actually incurred excess costs; and (3) the Government acted reasonably to minimize the excess costs resulting from the default. 41 C.F.R. s 1-8.602-6(a), FPR 1-8.602-6(a); Astro-Space Laboratories, Inc. v. United States, 470 F.2d 1003, 1018 (Ct.Cl.1972); Environmental Tectonics Corp. v. United States, 78-1 BCA P 12,986 (ASBCA 1978); Solar Laboratories, Inc. v. United States, 76-2 BCA P 12,115 (ASBCA 1976). The first condition is demonstrated by comparing the item reprocured with the item specified in the original contract. Environmental Tectonics Corp., 78-1 BCA at 63,308. The second condition requires the Government to show what it spent in reprocurement. Fairfield Scientific Corp. v. United States, 611 F.2d 854, 863–66 (Ct.Cl.1979). The third condition requires that the Government act within a reasonable time of the default, use the most efficient method of reprocurement, obtain a reasonable price, and mitigate its losses. Astro-Space Laboratories, Inc., 470 F.2d at 1018; Environmental Tectonics Corp., 78-1 BCA at 63,308, 63,309–10; Solar Laboratories, Inc., 76-2 BCA at 58,195–96.

The board concluded that condition (2) was not met by GSA because it failed to introduce the reprocurement contract with Mallin, and states that there was inadequate information on condition (3). Also, CPI argues that the Mallin spring hinges failed to satisfy condition (1). It asserts that since the Mallin spring hinges did not perform under testing equal to or better than its spring hinges, reprocurement of Mallin spring hinges would not fulfill the condition that the reprocured spring hinges meet the requirements of the contract. We considered this argument earlier and deem it meritless because Mallin spring hinges offered to GSA were plated and otherwise met the requirements of the specifications.

We disagree with the board that GSA failed to meet condition (2), but we agree that without introduction of the follow-on contract, the board did not have sufficient evidence to make a finding on condition (3). Therefore, the board was correct in declining to assess excess costs of reprocurement against CPI.

With respect to the assessment of damages, we are persuaded that the board's conclusion that "[t]here is ample evidence in this record from which we may conclude that the price of the substituted performance, as measured by the prices the Government would have paid under Mallin's successor requirements contract, was reasonable." 84-2 BCA at 86,483. The evidence includes a Lawrence Brothers catalogue cut showing a spring hinge (not necessarily possessing a US10 finish), six competitors' bids, including that of Mallin for its plated spring hinges, and CPI's own bid prices, which were more than its original bid by an average of about $1.25 per pair. The board correctly reduced the Government's claim to reflect the true number of pairs of spring hinges reprocured.

Notes and Questions

1. What are the specific standards for excess reprocurement costs? What is the reason for each? Why would the government not introduce the follow-on contract? As in *Darwin* and *McDonnell Douglas*, so, too, in the excess reprocurement cases, the defaulted contractor would much rather be critiquing the government that having to defend its own conduct.

2. What is the difference between excess reprocurement costs and assessment of damages? Recall the difference in the basic (private) contract law between the general measure of damages for breach by seller (market price minus contract price), and the "cover" measure of damages (cover price paid by buyer minus contract price).

3. Whether the contracting officer must entertain offers from the defaulted contractor on a repurchase contract has been much litigated. Hiring the defaulted contractor often does not appeal to the contracting officer, who has already been put through procedural paces to rid the procuring agency of the former awardee and now must accomplish the original contract task. While sometimes defaulted contractors cannot perform the job or lose interest in it altogether, often they consider themselves, perhaps rightly, all set to do the job, and would vastly prefer to do it than have the government pay someone else and charge that competitor's excess costs to them. Also, the defaulted contractor has tactical familiarity in bidding, from knowledge of the contract in general, and cost and pricing information in particular.

The government's duty to mitigate by limiting costs of reprocurement somewhat constrains the contracting officer's ability to exclude the defaulted contractor from a reprocurement process. A defaulting contractor's strong incentive and ability to come in with a low proposal means its participation may well limit the reprocurement's costs. So, the decisions have struck the balance that while automatic exclusion of a defaulting contractor would be an improperly automatic determination of non-responsibility, neither are such firms automatically entitled to resolicitation. (See ATA Defense Industries, Inc., B-275303 (1997), Montage, Inc., B-0277923 (1997), A.R.E. Manufacturing, B-246161 (1992), Shelf-Stable Foods, B-218067 (1985), Jim Challinor B-218809 (1985), Introl Corp., B-210321 (1983), Ikard Manufacturing Co., B-192316 (1978), Ikard Manufacuring Co.58 Comp. Gen. 54 (1978), PRB Uniforms, Inc., 56 Comp. Gen 976 (1977)).

Chapter 15

Bid Protest

The protest remedy provides the crucial procedural machinery for many of the previously discussed myriad of statutes and regulations applicable to the government's acquiring of goods and services. Those statutes and regulations, numbering in the thousands of pages, set forth how government personnel are to spend the hundreds of billions of tax dollars with which they are entrusted for both Department of Defense and civilian agency acquisitions. The statutes and regulations are intended to ensure that federal procurements are conducted fairly by both mandating certain activity (e.g., providing for full and open competition whenever possible) and prohibiting other activity (e.g., the disclosure of contractor proprietary information prior to award).

There is no doubt that the federal procurement system benefits from the active participation of firms and businesses in a competitive marketplace. Furthermore, Congress views the fair opportunity for their constituents to compete for government contracts as an overall positive aspect of government spending. As a result, Congress and the courts have ensured that bidders or others interested in government procurements have forums in which to raise concerns about contracts that have been or are about to be awarded improperly or illegally or to respond to complaints that a particular entity has been unfairly denied the opportunity to compete for the government's business.

Unfortunately (or some may say fortunately) for the government contractor and the government contract practitioner, the number of different forums in which "bid protests" may be raised include: (1) the actual Contracting Agency; (2) the General Accounting Office; and (3) the Court of Federal Claims. While having multiple different forums in which to pursue a bid protest provides the government contractor with the opportunity to do a bit of forum shopping, it also presents the practitioner with the need to be familiar with the various jurisdictional and procedural requirements of each. What follows is a brief description of each such forum.

For further discussions of the subject of this chapter, see: J. Andrew Howard, Katherine L. Miller, *The Bid Protest: A Primer*, 24 No. 7 Westlaw J. Gov't Cont. 3 (Aug. 9, 2010); Steven W. Feldman, Raymond Fioravanti, *Contract Dispute Or Bid Protest? The Delex Systems Dilemma*, 39 Pub. Cont. L.J. 483 (Spring 2010); William J Cea, Mark J. Stempler, *Fighting For Public Dollars: Pitfalls Of Protesting Government Bid Awards*, 84 Fla. B.J. 45 (Apr. 2010); Steven J. Koprince, *As Agencies' Use Of IDIQ Contracts Expands, Will Increased Contractor Protests Rights Follow*, 44 Procrmt. Law. 12 (Spring 2009); Richard J. Webber, *Bid Protests: Different Outcomes In The Court Of Federal Claims And The Government Accountability Office In 2008*, 44 Procrmt. Law.1 (Spring 2009); Michael J. Schaengold, T. Michael Guiffre & Elizabeth M. Gill, *Choice of Forum for Federal Government Contract Bid Protests*, 18 Fed. Circuit B.J. 243 (2009); Paul E. Pompeo, *Establishing Trends in Override Case Law*, 49 No. 9 Gov't Cont. para. 87; Phillip E. Santerre, *The GAO Bid Protest: The First Thirty Days — A Procedural Guide for the Local Counsel*, Army Law. (April 2009), at 55; Steven WS. Feldman, *Hearings in GAO Protests: Legal & Practical Considerations,*

09-10 Briefing Papers 1; Michael J. Benjamin, Multiple Award Task & Delivery Order Contracts: Expanding Protest Grounds & Other Heresies? 31 Pub. Cont. L.J. 429 (Spring 2002); Richard D. Lieberman, *Bid Protests at the Court of Federal Claims and the General Accounting Office: A Comparison*, 67 Fed. Cont. Rep. (BNA) 382 (Mar. 31, 1997); George M. Coburn, *Enlarged Bid Protest Jurisdiction of the United States Court of Federal Claims*, 33 Procurement Law., Fall 1997, at 16; William E. Kovacic, *Procurement Reform and the Choice of Forum in Bid Protest Disputes*, 9 Admin. L.J. 461 (1995).

A. The Contracting Agency

Although many agencies have had very informal procedures for resolving contractor disputes about the manner in which their contracts were awarded since 1991, the FAR has set forth slightly more formalized procedures for pursuing agency level protests. *See* FAR 33.103. Agency level protests received a further boost in 1995, when President Clinton issued Executive Order 12979 for the purpose of ensuring "effective and efficient expenditures of public funds and fair and expeditious resolution of protests to the award of Federal procurement contracts...." The order mandated that each agency prescribe administrative procedures for the resolution of protests as an alternative to the various other available forums.

The procedures required by the Executive Order are to:

(a) emphasize that whenever conduct of a procurement is contested, all parties should use their best efforts to resolve the matter with agency contracting officers;

(b) to the maximum extent practicable, provide for inexpensive, informal, procedurally simple, and expeditious resolution of protests, including, where appropriate and as permitted by law, the use of alternative dispute resolution techniques, third party neutrals, and another agency's personnel;

(c) allow actual or prospective bidders or offerors whose direct economic interests would be affected by the award or failure to award the contract to request a review, at a level above the contracting officer, of any decision by a contracting officer that is alleged to have violated a statute or regulation and, thereby, caused prejudice to the protester; and

(d) except where immediate contract award or performance is justified for urgent and compelling reasons or is determined to be in the best interest of the United States, prohibit award or performance of the contract while a timely filed protest is pending before the agency. To allow for the withholding of a contract award or performance, the agency must have received notice of the protest within either 10 calendar days after the contract award or 5 calendar days after the bidder or offeror who is protesting the contract award was given the opportunity to be debriefed by the agency, whichever date is later.

The FAR guidance for agency level protests now includes the procedures mandated by the Executive Order as well as additional details. FAR 33.103. In order to ensure that alleged disputes are dealt with and resolved on a timely basis, protests based on alleged improprieties in a solicitation must be filed before bid opening or the closing date for receipt of proposals. In all other cases, protests must be filed no later than ten days after the basis of protest is known or should have been known, whichever is earlier. Protests that do not meet these time deadlines for filing will almost always be rejected no matter how meritorious their grounds of protest, although the agency is allowed to consider an untimely protest for "good cause shown" or if it raises issues significant to the agency's acquisition system.

There is no particular form or style for preparing a protest. The regulatory guidance provides that protests shall be concise and logically presented to facilitate review by the agency. The protest document, filed either directly with the government contracting officer or other designated agency official must include the following:

(1) Name, address, and fax and telephone numbers of the protester.

(2) Solicitation or contract number.

(3) Detailed statement of the legal and factual grounds for the protest, to include a description of resulting prejudice to the protester.

(4) Copies of relevant documents.

(5) Request for a ruling by the agency.

(6) Statement as to the form of relief requested.

(7) All information establishing that the protester is an interested party for the purpose of filing a protest.

(8) All information establishing the timeliness of the protest.

As part of the protest, the protester may request an independent review of the protest at a level above the contracting officer. That official should be someone that has not had previous personal involvement in the particular procurement at issue.

Agencies are to delay award of a contract when a protest is received prior to award unless the agency makes a written determination that there are "urgent and compelling reasons" or that proceeding with award would be "in the best interest of the Government." Agencies are to delay performance of a contract when a protest is received within ten days after contract award or within five days after a debriefing date is offered by the contracting officer, whichever is later. Performance may, however, proceed if the agency makes the written determination of "urgent and compelling reasons" or "best interest of the Government."

There are no document discovery rules or rights, although the parties to the protest may exchange information to the extent permitted by law. An agency decision on the protest is due thirty-five days after the protest is filed, although that date is not a mandatory requirement and may be unilaterally extended by the agency.

Agency level protests are the least expensive and procedurally simplest protests to be filed and decided. It is, however, difficult for the protester to obtain the necessary government documents it may need to successfully pursue its protest. There are no provisions for a hearing or taking of depositions or testimony and the protest decision is made by an official of the agency alleged to have engaged in improper or illegal activity. It is a forum that provides some semblance of the possibility of obtaining an adequate remedy in protest situations, but one that does not provide for full development of a protest issue and record.

B. The Government Accountability Office

Note on GAO Protests

GAO provides a relatively informal, inexpensive, and quick forum for a protest. The protester — a disappointed bidder — files the protest. A protester may file a pre-award protest, typically complaining about the agency's solicitation, or a post-award protest, complaining about the agency's award.

As part of the Competition in Contracting Act of 1984 ("CICA"), the Comptroller General of the General Accounting Office ("GAO"), part of the legislative branch of government, was given statutory authority to decide a protest concerning an alleged violation of a procurement statute or regulation. 31 U.S.C. § 3552. Notwithstanding the specific statutory grant of protest authority, GAO has been hearing and deciding such protests for almost seventy-five years as part of the Comptroller General's role as auditor of the government for Congress with the power to "settle and adjust" claims against the United States. As a result, there is a well developed set of case law and decisions involving protests of procurement actions that have been relied upon by Congress, the courts, and executive branch agencies. Today, GAO remains a popular forum at which to file a bid protest, with thousands of protests being filed each year.

Note on GAO Bid Protest Procedure

In deciding bid protests, GAO considers whether federal agencies have complied with statutes and regulations controlling government procurements. As explained in "Bid Protests at GAO: A Descriptive Guide" published by the Office of General Counsel for GAO, an overview of the bid protest process at GAO is as follows:

> The bid protest process at GAO begins with the filing of a written protest. Unless the protest is dismissed because it is procedurally or substantively defective (e.g., the protest is untimely or the protest fails to clearly state legally sufficient grounds of protest), the contracting agency is required to file with GAO an agency report responding to the protest and to provide a copy of that report to the protester. The protester then has an opportunity to file written comments on the report. Other parties may be permitted to intervene, which means that they will also receive a copy of the report and will be allowed to file written comments on the report.

> During the course of a GAO protest, as appropriate, GAO may schedule status or other informal types of conferences to resolve procedural matters and to obtain information material to the disposition of the protest. GAO also may find that a hearing is necessary to resolve factual and legal issues raised in the protest. If it decides to hold a hearing, GAO will usually conduct a pre-hearing conference to decide the issues that will be considered at the hearing, to identify the witnesses who will testify at the hearing, and to settle procedural questions. After the hearing, all parties will be allowed to submit written comments on the hearing.

> After the record is complete, GAO will consider the facts and legal issues raised and will issue a decision, a copy of which will be sent to all parties participating in the protest. GAO may sustain the protest (that is, find that the agency violated a procurement statute or regulation and that the violation prejudiced the protester), in which case GAO will recommend appropriate corrective action. Alternatively, GAO may deny the protest or may dismiss the protest without reviewing the matter. GAO will issue its decision not later than 100 days from the date the protest was filed. The exact date on which GAO issues the decision depends on the urgency of the procurement, the complexity of the factual and legal issues raised in the protest, and GAO's work load.

"Bid Protests at GAO: A Descriptive Guide" published by the Office of General Counsel, United States General Accounting Office, GAO/OCG-96-24, Sixth Edition 1996 at 7–8.

GAO has promulgated fairly detailed regulations that govern the procedures of filing and pursuing a protest. *See* 4 CFR Part 21. The failure to follow the regulations will almost certainly result in a protest being summarily dismissed by GAO and the opportunity for corrective action being taken by the contracting agency will then be lost.

In order to file a protest at GAO, a person, represented either by himself or herself or by counsel, must be an "interested party" which means being an actual or prospective bidder or offeror with a direct economic interest in the procurement. Note that only bidders or offerors have standing to protest — subcontractors to a bidder to be prime contractor do not have standing.

Most GAO protests challenge the acceptance or rejection of a bid or proposal and the award or proposed award of a contract. GAO will also consider protests that allege defects in the solicitation such as unduly restrictive specifications that prevent a competitor from competing, omissions of required provisions, or ambiguous evaluation factors. GAO will not consider protests involving matters of: (1) contract administration; (2) Small Business Administration issues such as challenges as to whether a particular company qualifies as a small business concern; (3) procurements under section 8(a) of the Small Business Act involving the award of subcontracts to small disadvantaged businesses; (4) affirmative determinations of responsibility of the proposed or actual contractor; (5) violations of the procurement integrity laws; and (6) procurement actions taken by agencies other than those defined by section 3 of the Federal Property and Administrative Services of 1949, 40 U.S.C. § 472, such as the U.S. Postal Service, the Federal Deposit Insurance Corporation, and non-appropriated fund activities.

As is the case with an agency level protest, there is no particular prescribed form for filing a protest at GAO. The requirements for such a written protest follow those now established for agency level protests and include the following:

(1) The name, address, and telephone and fax numbers of the protester or its representative;

(2) The signature of the protester or its representative;

(3) The identification of the contracting agency and the solicitation and/or contract number;

(4) A detailed statement of the legal and factual grounds of protest, including copies of relevant documents;

(5) Information establishing that the protester is an interested party for the purposes of filing a protest;

(6) Information establishing the timeliness of the protest;

(7) The specific request for a ruling by the Comptroller General; and

(8) The form of relief requested.

In addition, the protest should identify any agency documents requested by the protester that are relevant to the protest grounds, a request for a protective order if documents that contain proprietary or confidential information are either submitted by the protester or requested from the agency, and a request for a hearing if the protester believes that there is a sufficient reason for having one.

Again, as is now the case with agency level protests, GAO follows very strict requirements for the filing of a timely protest. Protests alleging defects in the solicitation must be filed prior to the due date for bids or offers. All other protests must be filed not later than ten days after the basis for the protest is known except in the case of protests challenging a procurement conducted on the basis of competitive proposals. In that case, when a debriefing is requested and offered, the protest is to be filed within ten days after the date on which the debriefing was offered.

After a protest is filed, GAO will immediately notify the contracting agency of the protest. With the filing of the protest, the Competition in Contracting Act (CICA) stay kicks in. A pre-award protest will stay the issuance of the award; a post-award protest will stay performance of the contract. The agency may override the stay, with the applicable standards varying between pre- and post-award protests.

Specifically, if the contracting agency receives notice of the protest from GAO either prior to contract award or within ten days of contract award, the contracting agency is directed by 31 U.S.C. § 3553(c) to either withhold award or suspend award, unless the agency makes a written determination of "urgent and compelling" reasons for proceeding with the contract or a written determination that proceeding with the contract is in the best interests of the government. Once the contracting agency has received notice of the protest it will in turn, give notice of the protest to the awardee or if no award has been made, to all bidders or offerors which have a reasonable chance of receiving award. Those parties may advise GAO that they wish to intervene in the protest in order to have an opportunity to comment on the basis of the protest.

GAO has set forth its procedure on protests at 4 C.F.R. sec. 21. After receiving notice of a protest, the contracting agency is required to prepare an "agency report" that responds to the issues raised in the protest. The agency report is to be submitted within thirty days of the filing of the protest. The protester and each intervenor are then given ten days to file comments on the findings and determinations and legal arguments made in the agency report.

Documents covered by a protective order will be released only in accordance with the terms of the order. For example, if documents would reveal one bidder's proprietary documents, a protective order will only allow the other competitors' documents to be reviewed by the attorneys for parties, and the attorneys will be bound not to reveal the information to the competitors themselves. The GAO has a guide specifically about protective orders. This agency takes the protective order very seriously. It has imposed sanctions for violations of the protective order up to and including dismissal of the protest

The protester may request the production of additional agency documents. This is the basic form of discovery in this process. Conversely, the procuring agency may request that the protester produce relevant documents.

The protester and any intervenors may file "written comments" on the agency report, which are how they put the reasons why the agency should rule as they seek. Absent hearings, with the filing of the comments on the report, the record is considered closed and GAO may rule.

Before 1991, all that the GAO could do, hearing-wise, was a conference without a written record, testimony, or the examination or cross-examination of witnesses. Since 1991 amendments to the pertinent legislation, GAO may conduct a fact-finding hearing, although this is by no means universal. Witnesses may be requested by GAO to attend and answer relevant questions.

Once the record is complete, GAO will consider the protest and decide the case by means of a written decision issued by the Comptroller General. The decision must be issued within one hundred days of the protest being filed. As is often the case, supplemental protests are often filed by protesters after receipt of agency documents or the agency report that reveals additional grounds for alleged improprieties. GAO attempts to resolve these additional protests within the same one hundred day period, but may extend the decision date for the supplemental protests if necessary.

If GAO concludes in its written decision that the protested agency action does not comply with statute or regulation, GAO will recommend to the contracting agency any combination of the following remedies:

(1) Refrain from exercising options under the contract;

(2) Terminate the contract;

(3) Recompete the contract;

(4) Issue a new solicitation;

(5) Award a contract consistent with statute and regulation; or

(6) Such other recommendation(s) as GAO determines necessary to promote compliance.

The GAO decision sustaining the protest contains only *recommendations* to the agency for corrective action. As a result, although the vast majority of GAO recommendations are accepted, the contracting agency retains the right to take whatever corrective action it believes is necessary in order to correct defects found by GAO. This broad discretionary authority granted to contracting agencies by virtue of their position in the executive branch of government with the ultimate authority for spending money appropriated to them by Congress means that the protester may be successful in winning its battle that an agency violated procurement statutes or regulations, but more often than not will lose the war of actually being awarded the contract in dispute. Typically, the agency takes corrective action that either simply corrects a defect and permits the same outcome or recompetes the contract and makes an award decision consistent with its initial decision. This "winning the battle and losing the war" scenario should make pursuing a protest at GAO the consequence of a thoughtful process where all possibilities are presented by counsel and examined by the potential protester.

For further discussion of the issues in this subchapter, see: Robert E. Samuelson (II), *Late Is Late: Should The GAO Continue To Employ GAO Created Exceptions To The FAR?*, 2009 Army Law. 1 (Dec. 2009); Ryan Roberts, *Does Automatic Mean Automatic? The Applicability Of The CICA Stay To Task And Delivery Order Bid Protests*, 39 Pub. Cont. L.J. 641 (Spring 2010); 2009 Army Law. 1 (Dec. 2009); Kara M. Sacilotto, *Is The Game Worth The Candle? The Fate Of The CICA Override*, 45 Procrmt. Law. 3 (Fall 2009); Phillip E. Santerre, *The GAO Bid Protest: The First Thirty Day—A Procedural Guide For The Local Counsel*, 2009 Army Law. 55 (Apr. 2009); Robert S. Metzger & Daniel A. Lyons, Article, *A Critical Reassessment of the GAO Bid-Protest Mechanism*, 2007 Wis. L. Rev. 1225 (2007); Daniel I. Gordon, *Dismissals Of Bid Protests At The General Accounting Office*, 37 Procrmt. Law. 1 (Winter 2002).

Two GAO protest opinions follow. *Matter of: Network Security Technologies* addresses the important function in GAO protests of documents covered by a protective order. Protective orders has much more significance in GAO protests than in run-of-the-mill federal court cases, because protests often involve sensitive and proprietary information that the competing offerors in the protests could misuse absent such protection. *In re Bay Area Travel* addresses the important inclusion of awards of task and delivery orders among the awards that may be protested.

Matter of: Network Security Technologies, Inc.

B-290741.2 (Comp.Gen.), 2002 CPD P 193 (Comp.Gen.),
2002 WL 31538210 (Comp.Gen.)
COMPTROLLER GENERAL
November 13, 2002

DIGEST

1. GAO finds convincing evidence that protester sought to obtain for purposes of drafting its comments on the agency's report—and did obtain from its attorney, who was admitted to GAO protective order—information to which it was fully aware it was not entitled because the information was covered by protective order; while deciding this case on the merits, GAO provides notice that, in a future case, it may impose the sanction of dismissal to protect the integrity of GAO's bid protest process, where, as here, protester has abused that process.

2. Protest challenging awardee's past performance evaluation is denied where agency properly considered the past performance record of the various member firms of the joint venture proposed to perform the contract.

BACKGROUND

There are two aspects to the background of this procurement that are relevant to our decision—information regarding the solicitation and award process, which goes to the merits of NETSEC's arguments, and facts regarding NETSEC's and its counsel's actions in pursuing the protest.

The Procurement

The RFP sought proposals to create and operate a CIRC for the VA to ensure that computer security incidents are detected, reported, and corrected as quickly as possible, and with minimal impact on the availability and integrity of veterans services. In addition, the CIRC is to provide assurance that cyber security controls are in place to protect automated information systems from financial fraud, waste, and abuse. The RFP contemplated the award of a fixed-price, performance-based contract for a base year, with up to 9 option years.

Sixteen offerors submitted proposals, five of which, including NETSEC's and VAST's, were included in the competitive range. The offerors made oral presentations and engaged in discussions with the agency before submitting final proposal revisions. The final evaluations for VAST and NETSEC (the only proposals relevant here) were as follows:

	Technical	Past Performance	Price	Overall
NETSEC	Green	Light Blue	Yellow ($9.2 million)	Yellow
VAST	Blue	Dark Blue	Blue ($6.5 million)	Blue

In reaching its evaluation conclusions, the agency noted that NETSEC's proposal contained more weaknesses than strengths. For example, in the area of proposed proprietary tools, the agency found that the proposal lacked information on necessary customization, and provided a limited commitment of NETSEC's key personnel (90 days). Agency Report (AR), exh. 8, at 14. In contrast, the agency found that the VAST team had extensive experience in computer security; that its key personnel were likewise well-experienced and fully committed to perform for the base year; and that it had demonstrated the use of various tools. *Id.* at 15–16. With regard to price, NETSEC proposed the highest cost per hour of any of the vendors in the competitive range, and VAST proposed the lowest cost per hour. Because VAST's proposal had the highest technical rating and the lowest proposed price of all offerors, the agency determined that it represented the best value and awarded it the contract. After receiving notice of the award and a debriefing, NETSEC filed this protest challenging the evaluation and award decision.

NETSEC's Actions

The protest was originally filed on behalf of NETSEC in the name of Mr. Robert Kalchthaler, NETSEC's senior vice president. During the course of the development of the protest record, Mr. John Kitchings, NETSEC's contract administrator, acted as the protester's representative. Because NETSEC had filed its protest *pro se*, our Office did not issue a protective order in the matter, and NETSEC's copy of the agency report therefore did not include various source selection documents or VAST's proposal. *See* Bid Protest Regulations, 4 C.F.R. § 21.4(a) and (b) (2002). Instead, the agency submitted these source selection sensitive and proprietary documents to our Office for *in camera* review. 4 C.F.R. § 21.4(b). In the midst of the 10-day comment period following receipt of the agency report, NETSEC objected to this procedure and requested that we issue a protective order so that an attorney for NETSEC could review the withheld documents; we promptly did as NETSEC requested. While Mr. Kitchings is an attorney, he did not submit an application for admission to the protective order. NETSEC also elected not to have an attorney from the firm that usually represents the company submit an application for admission to the protective order. Instead, Mr. Kitchings retained an attorney who (according to Mr. Kitchings) was a "recent graduate of law school" and had been a member of the bar "for about 45 days." Video Transcript (VT) at 11:44. After submitting an application, NETSEC's retained counsel was admitted to the protective order 3 days before the comments were due. He subsequently received, among other documents, a copy of VAST's past performance proposal. On the day comments were due, our Office received comments not from retained counsel, but instead comments prepared by Mr. Kitchings and signed by Mr. Kalchthaler. The comments were not marked as protected.

While NETSEC's protest had made no references to the contents of VAST's proposal, NETSEC's comments included what appeared to be several direct references to the content of VAST's protected proposal as support for the firm's protest arguments. For example, it stated how "the proposals are titled on the cover page." The comments then stated that "[t]hroughout the VAST, LLC. proposal," a particular name for the awardee "is used quite frequently as being analogous to VAST, LLC." (NETSEC Comments at 2); and that "[a] close examination of the VAST, LLC. proposal, under the caption of past performance, will show a very polished evasion tactic on the issue of VAST, LLC's past performance.... For example, after naming the sham transaction d/b/a as VAST, LLC., the proposal smoothly reverted to the performance evaluations of the alleged limited liability company entities...." NETSEC Comments at 7.

On September 17, within 24 hours of receipt of the comments, Mr. John Linton, VAST's representative, advised our Office by telephone that he believed there had been a violation of the protective order, as evidenced by the fact that NETSEC's comments appeared to include several references to VAST's proprietary proposal. On that same date, 4 days after he had been admitted to the protective order, the retained counsel submitted a "Notice of Withdrawal" as NETSEC's counsel. Thereafter, we requested that VAST put its allegations in writing, and that NETSEC's (former) counsel and the firm's representatives (Messrs. Kitchings and Kalchthaler) submit statements in sworn, notarized form "at a minimum, covering the basis/origin of information for each reference in NETSEC's comments to VAST's proposal and the agency's evaluation of that proposal (e.g., pp. 2, 4, 5, 7–9, and 12)." Fax from GAO, Sept. 19, 2002. Subsequently, we requested that VAST respond to NETSEC's statements.

In response to our request, Mr. Kitchings initially declined to provide any explanation, invoking his "privileged rights not to divulge any information, discussions, and/or relationships concerning [retained counsel]." NETSEC Letter, Sept. 23, 2002. After our Office notified the parties that the protest was subject to dismissal due to the alleged violation, Mr. Kitchings submitted a statement. In this statement, Mr. Kitchings denies "knowledge of any alleged violations of the GAO Protective Order or any allegations of divulging any proposal information to anyone at NETSEC." Affidavit of Mr. John Kitchings, Sept. 24, 2002, ¶ 6. However, other than stating generally that the references to VAST's proposal were based on publicly available information obtained during his own investigation of several named trade journals, Mr. Kitchings' statement did not explain the origin of NETSEC's comments' specific references to the content of VAST's protected proposal.

In response to our request, NETSEC's former counsel provided a statement denying that he revealed "any of [the] information protected within the order." Affidavit of NETSEC's Former Counsel, Sept. 25, 2002, ¶ 12.

On November 7, 2002, at 10:00 a.m., our Office convened a hearing regarding the apparent inclusion of protected information in NETSEC's comments. Messrs. Kitchings and Kalchthaler attended, as did Mr. Linton and representatives from the VA. Although NETSEC's former counsel was invited to participate and had agreed to attend at a time that he specified, Mr. Kitchings informed our Office at the beginning of the hearing that the company's former counsel could not attend due to a previously scheduled deposition and the short notice of the hearing (the notice was faxed to the parties on November 1). In a letter received in our Office by fax at 11:54 a.m., nearly 2 hours after the hearing convened, the company's former counsel confirmed this explanation and advised us that, because he no longer represented NETSEC, he could not attend the hearing "gratis."

DISCUSSION OF NETSEC'S AND ITS COUNSEL'S ACTIONS
Protective Order Violation

The terms of our protective order limit "disclosure of certain material and information submitted in the … protest, so that no party obtaining access to protected material under this order will gain a competitive advantage as a result of the disclosure." Protective Order, Sept. 9, 2002. The order "applies to all material that is identified by any party as protected, unless [our Office] specifically provides otherwise," and strictly limits access to protected material only to those persons authorized under the order. Id. ¶¶ 1–3. The protective order also provides that "[e]ach individual covered under [the order] shall take all precautions necessary to prevent disclosure of protected material[; including but not limited] … to physically and electronically securing, safeguarding, and restricting access to the protected material in one's possession" and "[t]he confidentiality of protected material shall be maintained in perpetuity." Id. ¶ 6. Any violation of the terms of a protective order may result in the imposition of such sanctions as GAO deems appropriate. Id. ¶ 8; 4 C.F.R. § 21.4(d).

We find that the record establishes a violation of the protective order here. We note that, while the evidence in the record is to a large extent circumstantial in nature, it strongly supports our finding of a violation. The starting point in our analysis is the several references in NETSEC's comments to the particular wording used in VAST's protected proposal. In this regard, we reject as not credible Mr. Kitchings' assertion in his written statement that publicly available information was the origin of the references, and his hearing testimony, in response to our specific questions regarding the origin of the references, that he merely "speculated" and "concluded" that the VAST proposal contained this information based on the knowledge he gained from his investigation into VAST. VT at 11:47, 49, 51, 54–56, 58, 12:01, 03, 07.

* * *

Given this conclusion, it of course follows that NETSEC necessarily obtained the information from some source. There is no evidence in the record that VAST's proposal information was made available to NETSEC through the VA or VAST itself, and there is no reason to believe that this is the case. Neither Mr. Kitchings nor Mr. Kalchthaler has suggested that anyone at NETSEC obtained the VAST proposal information from VA or VAST employees, and neither testified that NETSEC obtained the information from any other source. VT at 11:47-48, 51, 12:50. Thus, while there is no direct evidence that retained counsel disclosed or failed to adequately safeguard the contents of VAST's past performance proposal, he remains as the only logical source of the information. The actions of Mr. Kitchings and the company's former counsel discussed above fully support this logical conclusion. To briefly recap, NETSEC's protest filing did not make any reference to information in VAST's proposal. NETSEC retained its counsel (after initially seeking protective order admission for Mr. Kitchings' spouse) only after learning that NETSEC's copy of the agency report did not include proprietary and source selection sensitive information concerning the VAST proposal. On September 16, NETSEC filed its comments containing the specific VAST proposal references. The next day, September 17, the same day that Mr. Linton advised our Office that NETSEC's comments appeared to evidence a violation of the protective order, the retained counsel advised us that he was withdrawing as NETSEC's counsel. In response to our initial request, Messrs. Kitchings and Kalchthaler declined to provide an explanation of the VAST proposal references, citing attorney-client privilege.

We are compelled by the facts to conclude that NETSEC's former counsel either disclosed protected information or did not adequately safeguard it from disclosure, in violation of our protective order. We would have preferred to hear that individual's testimony in response to our direct questioning before reaching our conclusion here; as noted above, however, he declined to appear at the hearing after initially indicating that he would attend. Based on his failure to appear, we draw an unfavorable inference against his position. 4 C.F.R. § 21.7(f).

NETSEC seems to believe that there could be no protective order violation because NETSEC does not consider VAST's different name designations to be proprietary, confidential, source-selection, or other information the release of which could result in a competitive advantage to one or more firms. Testimony of Mr. Kalchthaler, VT at 13:00-01; *see* 4 C.F.R. § 21.4(a). This argument reflects a misunderstanding of the provisions of protective orders issued by our Office. Although an individual admitted to a protective order may believe that certain information marked as protected cannot properly be protected because it is publicly available through other sources, that individual may not unilaterally disclose the information to individuals not admitted under the protective order. As clearly stated in the protective order, it "applies to all material that is identified by any party as protected, unless GAO specifically provides otherwise." Protective Order, ¶ 1. If a party were permitted to determine on its own that information marked as protected can nevertheless be released to persons not admitted to the protective order, the protections afforded by the protective order would become meaningless.

Abuse of Process

This case involves more than a protective order violation; our Regulations provide for the imposition of sanctions in the case of a violation, and we will consider appropriate sanctions against NETSEC's former counsel as a separate matter. Beyond the violation, we find that the record shows Mr. Kitchings actively sought, and obtained from the company's retained counsel, protected information, which he then used in pursuing NETSEC's protest. Again, the evidence in this regard is largely circumstantial. However, as discussed above, the circumstances strongly support our conclusion. Mr. Kitchings, who is himself an attorney, was aware that he was not permitted to view or possess the VAST proposal information released to retained counsel under the terms of our protective order. Mr. Kitchings nevertheless was able to obtain the VAST proposal information through retained counsel, as a result of either retained counsel's disclosure of the information, or his failure adequately to safeguard it.

The protective order process is essential to the proper functioning of the bid protest process as a whole. While the protective order applies primarily to those admitted under it (usually counsel to the private parties), where, as here, a protester's purposeful actions subvert that process, we believe it is appropriate to consider dismissing the protest to protect the integrity of our bid protest process. Fortunately, our experience is that the individuals concerned, both attorneys and non-attorneys, respect the process, and that we believe that the abuse apparent in this case is unprecedented. Nonetheless, we view our authority to impose dismissal or other sanctions as inherent, as do other fora.

DISCUSSION OF THE MERITS

* * *

The protest is denied.
Anthony H. Gamboa
General Counsel

Notes and Questions

1. GAO has published a *Guide to GAO Protective Orders* (2006). This deals with many aspects of the procedure for protective orders. It reflects the importance of the subject for GAO protest proceedings.

2. Note that the persons admitted to protective orders are typically the lawyers representing firms which would benefit from receiving the information their lawyers receive. Yet the lawyers must resist the urge to help the firms that pay their fees. It speaks well of the ethics of the government contract bar that this system works. On the other hand, it may fortify the principles of government contract lawyers that if they violate protective orders, while their client may suffer only briefly, they themselves may injure their long-term capacity to practice in their chosen professional specialty.

Matter of: In Re Bay Area Travel, Inc.; Cruise Ventures, Inc.; Tzell-AirTrak Travel Group, Inc.

B-400442, B-400547, B-400564, B-400442.2, B-400442.3, B-400547.2,
B-400547.3, B-400564.3, 2009 CPD P 65, 2008 WL 5784216 (Comp.Gen.)
November 5, 2008

DIGEST

1. GAO will review the issuance of task and delivery order in excess of $10,000,000 under indefinite-delivery/indefinite-quantity contracts to ensure that the "enhanced competition" requirements of the National Defense Authorization Act are met and to ensure that the evaluation is in accord with the solicitation and applicable procurement laws and regulations.

2. Protests challenging the issuance of three task orders for travel services are denied where the agency evaluated proposals consistent with the evaluation criteria stated in the solicitation and reasonably selected the higher technically rated, higher priced proposals.

DECISION

Bay Area Travel, Inc. of Brandon, Florida; Cruise Ventures, Inc. of Norfolk, Virginia; and Tzell-AirTrak Travel Group, Inc., a joint venture, of Bordenton, New Jersey, protest the issuance of three task orders to CW Government Travel, Inc. of Arlington, Virginia, issued by the Department of the Army under request for proposals (RFP) Nos. W91QUZ-08-R-0023, W91QUZ-08-R-0024, and W91QUZ-08-R-0025 for travel services to be provided to military travelers in "Defense Travel Area(s)" (DTA) 2, 3, and 4. The protesters contend that the agency improperly issued the task orders to an offeror whose proposals were higher in price, and that the agency is biased in favor of the awardee.

We deny the protests.

BACKGROUND

The protesters and awardee all hold indefinite-delivery/indefinite-quantity (ID/IQ) contracts to provide worldwide commercial travel office services to the Department of Defense (DoD). The Army conducted a series of task order competitions among ID/IQ contract holders pursuant to Federal Acquisition Regulation (FAR) Subpart 16.5 to acquire travel services for military personnel in various geographic areas called DTAs. At issue here are the task orders for DTAs 2, 3, and 4, all of which have been issued to CW.

* * *

The RFPs provided for the issuance of a single task order for each of the DTAs on a best value basis, considering the following evaluation factors: business approach, technical approach, past performance, and price. The solicitations provided that non-price evaluation factors, when combined, were "approximately equal to price"; price was stated to be "significantly more important" than any of the individual non-price factors alone. *See, e.g.,* RFP (DTA 2) at 31. Under the business approach and technical approach factors, proposals were given adjectival ratings of blue (outstanding), green (good), yellow (fair), pink (poor), or red (unacceptable). Under the past performance factor, proposals were rated blue (very low risk), green (low risk), yellow (moderate risk), red (high risk), or white (unknown risk). [FN7] The price factor was to be "weighted but not rated." Agency Report (AR) (DTA 2), Tab 37, Source Selection Decision, at 2–3.

* * *

Bay, Cruise, Tzell-AirTrak, and CW provided proposals in response to the RFPs for DTAs 2, 3, and 4. Discussions were held with each of the offerors in connection with each DTA, after which offerors submitted revised proposals. The revised proposals for each of the DTAs were evaluated by the same source selection evaluation board (SSEB) and source selection official (SSO) and were rated as follows:

* * *

CW's proposals were found to be the highest rated under the non-price factors for all of these DTAs. With regard to the business approach factor, CW's proposals were rated blue and were found to be superior to the protesters' proposals, including Cruise's proposals, which were the only ones of the protesters' proposals to receive blue ratings under this factor. Although the SSO favorably considered Cruise's "vast corporate experience of 24 years providing Federal and DoD commercial travel services," the SSO concluded that this "significant strength" in Cruise's proposals was outweighed by three significant strengths in CW's proposals, that is, CW's "over 50 years of experience as the travel management provider to all branches of the military" (including currently providing travel services to over 500 DoD and federal travel management centers), CW's proposed "comprehensive staffing plan," and CW's "detailed, well-defined implementation and transition approach." AR (DTA 2), Tab 37, Source Selection Decision, at 8; Tab 35-2, CW Final Consensus Report, at 2.... CW's proposals offered:

> highly trained personnel with a thorough knowledge and understanding of DoD policies procedures, and regulations as evidenced by its senior staff averaging 14 years of travel industry experience and more than 25 years of DoD management experience, and its travel agents having, on average, more than 20 years of specific military and Government travel experience.

Id. at 9.

* * *

CW's proposals were also found to be superior to the protesters' proposals with respect to the past performance factor, as reflected in the blue ratings that CW's proposals received and the green ratings that the protesters' proposals received. The SSO noted that CW currently provides travel services to military personnel on a worldwide basis under contracts that are similar in scope and magnitude to the DTAs here. For this work, CW received "positive responses to its delivery of quality services," "satisfactory comments in its ability to respond to contract performance issues in a timely manner," and "provided services within cost while meeting all contract requirements." *Id.* at 9.

* * *

The SSO considered offerors' pricing and selected CW for issuance of all three DTA task orders based on her conclusion that CW's proposals presented the "best overall value" to the government. AR (DTA 2), Source Selection Decision, at 16; AR (DTA 3), Tab 40, Source Selection Decision, at 14; AR (DTA 4), Tab 39, Source Selection Decision, at 16. In support of her determination, the SSO specifically noted that the benefits provided by CW's proposals under the non-price factors outweighed the additional cost of all other lower-priced proposals. AR (DTA 2), Source Selection Decision, at 9–10, 13, 15; AR (DTA 3), Source Selection Decision, at 9, 11, 13; AR (DTA 4), Source Selection Decision, at 12, 15–16.

Bay, Cruise, and Tzell-AirTrak protested the issuance of the task orders to CW for all three DTAs, contending that the agency gave too little weight to the price factor, performed an unreasonable evaluation, and engaged in a "pattern" of bias in favor of CW.

JURISDICTION

As a preliminary matter, the agency asserts that this Office is not authorized to consider the issues raised in the protests due to the limitations of the Federal Acquisition Streamlining Act of 1994 (FASA), 10 U.S.C. sect. 2304c (2006).[12] However, as discussed below, this Office's consideration of the protest issues is authorized by the recent enactment of section 843 of the National Defense Authorization Act of Fiscal Year 2008 (NDAA), Pub. L. 110-181, 122 Stat. 3, 236–39 (2008), which modified FASA's prior limitations on task order

---

12. Specifically, although FASA provided that, when placing task orders pursuant to multiple award ID/IQ contracts, all contractors with such contracts "shall be provided a fair opportunity to be considered," FASA limited protests of task order awards to assertions that the order increased the scope, period, or maximum value of the contract under which the order was issued. 10 U.S.C. sect. 2304c(b), (d).

protests. Specifically, the NDAA provides that protests of task order awards are not authorized "except for ... a protest of an order valued in excess of $10,000,000." 122 Stat. 237.

The agency acknowledges that the NDAA not only modified FASA's prior limitations on protests, but further, in order to meet the "fair opportunity to be considered" requirements, the NDAA requires that, for orders in excess of $5,000,000, procuring agencies must, among other things: (1) provide potential competitors with a clear statement of the agency's requirements; (2) disclose the significant factors and subfactors, along with their relative importance, that the agency expects to consider; and (3) provide a written statement documenting the basis for the task order award where, as here, award is to be made on a "best value" basis. *Id.* The agency further acknowledges that the NDAA authorizes protests challenging an agency's failure to comply with these "fair opportunity to be considered" requirements. Army's Legal Memorandum (DTA 2) at 9.

Nevertheless, the agency maintains that GAO is only permitted to review whether the "process" for issuing task orders is followed—that is, whether solicitations identify the agency's requirements, whether solicitations contain evaluation criteria, and whether best value award decisions are documented; GAO is not permitted to review the agency's "judgments" or otherwise review the reasonableness of the agency's evaluation and award decision. Army's Legal Memorandum (DTA 2) at 4. Thus, the agency asserts that although the NDAA's provisions permit a protester to challenge an agency's failure to *inform* offerors regarding the ground rules under which a task order competition will be conducted, it does not authorize a protest that challenges the agency's failure to actually *follow* those rules.

We reject the agency's arguments. Initially, as noted above, the NDAA authorizes "a protest of an order valued in excess of $10,000,000." 12 Stat. 237. The Competition in Contracting Act of 1984 (CICA), as modified by FASA, specifically defines the term "protest," as follows:

> The term "protest" means a written objection by an interested party to any of the following:
>
> (A) A solicitation or other request by a Federal agency for offers for a contract for the procurement of property or services.
>
> (B) The cancellation of such a solicitation or other request.
>
> (C) An award or proposed award of such a contract.
>
> (D) A termination or cancellation of an award of such a contract, if the written objection contains an allegation that the termination or cancellation is based in whole or in part on improprieties concerning the award of the contract.

31 U.S.C. sect. 3551(1) (2000).

In the context of CICA and FASA, and our Office's well established practices and procedures employed to implement the protest jurisdiction conferred by those statutes, we view the NDAA's authorization to consider "a protest of an order valued in excess of $10,000,000" as providing the same substantive protest jurisdiction conferred by those statutes. In this regard, we find no basis to conclude that, in enacting the NDAA and authorizing certain task order protests, Congress intended to establish a system under which an agency is obligated to advise offerors of the bases for task order competition, and enforces that requirement through authorization of bid protests, but which provides no similar enforcement authority to ensure that agencies actually act in accordance with the guidance they are required to provide to offerors. Rather, consistent with this Office's past practice and CICA's provisions that define a protest as an "objection ... to ... an award or proposed award," we view the NDAA's authorization to consider protests of task orders in excess of $10,000,000 as extending to protests asserting that an agency's award decision failed to reasonably reflect the ground rules established for the task order competition. Accordingly, our review of the protests here includes our assessment of whether the agency's source selection decisions were reasonably consistent with the terms of the solicitation and applicable procurement laws and regulations. *Triple Canopy, Inc.,* B-310566.4, Oct. 30, 2008, 2008 CPD para. __ at 5–7.

DISCUSSION

The protesters contend that the agency did not give sufficient weight to the price factor and failed to adequately document the best value tradeoff among proposals. The protesters argue that because price was the most important factor, the agency was precluded from making award to a higher-priced proposal.[13] Protest (DTA 2) at 10; Protest (DTA 3) at 3, 8–9; Protest (DTA 4) at 5, 8–9. As discussed below, we find the agency's evaluation to be consistent with the solicitation, reasonable, and sufficiently documented.

* * *

The protesters maintain that the evaluations are tainted by a "pattern" of bias, based in large part on the protesters' complaint that the agency has issued all of the DTA task orders (that is, for DTAs 1, 2, 3, 4, and 6) to CW despite CW's higher proposed prices. Because government officials are presumed to act in good faith, we do not attribute unfair or prejudicial motives to them on the basis of inference or supposition. *Ameriko Maint. Co.,* B-253274, B-253274.2, Apr. 25, 1993, 93-2 CPD para. 121 at 5. Thus, the protesters must provide credible evidence clearly demonstrating bias and that the agency's bias translated into action that unfairly affected the protesters' competitive positions. *Advanced Scis., Inc.,* B-259569.3, July 3, 1995, 95-2 CPD para. 52 at 17. The protesters have not shown that the agency's conduct of this procurement was motivated by bias. The mere fact that the protesters previously failed to receive task orders from the agency does not demonstrate bias. Moreover, as discussed above, the selection of CW for these DTA task orders was reasonable and supported by the record.

The protests are denied.

Gary L. Kepplinger
General Counsel

C. The Court of Federal Claims

For further discussion of the issues of this subchapter, see: Raymond M. Saunders, Patrick Butler, *A Timely Reform: Impose Timeliness Rules For Filing Bid Protests At The*

---

13. The protesters contend that the agency's failure to properly consider price and perform a more detailed cost-technical tradeoff violates FAR sections 15.303(b)(4) (describing a source selection authority's responsibilities in a negotiated procurement), 15.305 (describing proposal evaluation requirements in a negotiated procurement), 15.308 (describing source selection decision requirements in a negotiated procurement), and 15.101 and subsequent provisions (describing best value and tradeoff requirements). Protesters' Comments (DTA 2) at 8. However, FAR Subpart 16.5 expressly provides that the competition requirements of FAR Part 6 and the policies in Subpart 15.3 do not apply to the ordering process involving ID/IQ contracts. FAR sect. 16.505(b)(1)(ii). Although the protesters argue that excluding the "policies" of FAR Subpart 15.3 does not prohibit the import of the "procedures" set forth in those provisions, we conclude that FAR Part 15 procedures do not, as a general rule, govern task and delivery order competitions conducted under FAR Part 16. Instead, we will review task order competitions to ensure that the competition is conducted in accordance with the solicitation and applicable procurement laws and regulations. *Triple Canopy, Inc., supra,* at 7.

Court Of Federal Claims, 39 Pub. Cont. L.J. 539 (Spring 2010); Lawrence S. Sher, *Protest, Claim Or Both? Taking Advantage Of Dual Jurisdiction In The U.S. Court Of Federal Claims*, 23 No. 25 Westlaw J. Gov't Cont. 3 (Apr. 19, 2010); Frederick W. Claybrook (Jr.), *Please Check Your Crystal Ball At The Door—A Call For The Judiciary In Bid Protest Actions To Let Agencies Do Their Job*, 38 Pub. Cont. L.J. 375 (Winter 2009).; James J. McCullough, Catherine E. Pollack, Timothy W. Staley, Third Year Of COFC Postaward Bid Protest Jurisdiction: A Work In Progress, 42 GC ¶ 138 (Apr. 12, 2000).

Impresa Construzioni Geom. Domenico Garufi, Plaintiff-Appellant, v. United States, Defendant-Appellee

United States Court of Appeals, Federal Circuit, 2001
238 F.3d 1324

Opinion in Chapter 2

Notes and Questions

1. What do protesters lose and what do they gain by suing in the Court of Federal Claims? They may face a much more expensive proceeding, for one thing. Yet, they gain a much bigger procedural opportunity with much fuller discovery and a greater opportunity for an evidentiary trial. For an example, see *United International Investigative Services Inc. v. United States and MVM, Inc.*, 1998 WL 378878 (Fed. Cl.). A protester won in challenging an award on the ground that the agency had engaged in illegal re-scoring and downgrading of its technical proposal. Discussing the outcome, counsel for the successful protester gave much credit to the court's permitting discovery and hearing testimony in a three-day trial. See "Proposal Evaluation: Agency Illegally Allowed One Evaluator to Re-Score, Downgrade Proposal, Court Says," 70 BNA Fed. Cont. Rep. 87 (July 20, 1998).

2. Discussion of Congress' ability to alter Article III jurisdiction of federal courts has obviously much greater meaning in the government contracting context than in some other contexts. In regard to the federal courts' ability to hear controversial cases about constitutional rights, there have been far more threats and debates in recent decades than actual completed instances of Congress using its power to reduce federal court jurisdiction, tartly described as "court-curbing." Why is Congress willing and able, with little political controversy, to alter the government contract jurisdiction of the Court of Federal Claims and to abolish that jurisdiction of the district courts?

3. Formerly, another forum for filing and prosecuting bid protests was in a U.S. District Court. District courts did not have an active role in adjudicating bid protests until the D.C. Circuit decided the landmark case of *Scanwell Laboratories, Inc. v. Shaffer*, 424 F.2d 850 (D.C. Cir. 1970). Thirty years later, district court jurisdiction over bid protest was sunsetted on January 1, 2001 pursuant to section 12 of the Administrative Dispute Resolution Act of 1996, Public Law 104-320. *See* Peter Verchinski, Note, *Are District Courts Still a Viable Forum for Bid Protests?*, 32 Pub. Cont L.J. 393 (2003).

4. For a discussion of the case's standard of review, see: Steven W. Feldman, The Impresa Decision: Providing The Correct Standard Of Review For Affirmative Responsibility Determinations, 36 Procrmt. Law. 5 (Winter 2001)

COFC Bid Protest Practice

For the 1970s through the 1990s, protesters had a federal judicial forum in the district courts, but since then, the Court of Federal Claims (COFC) is the only federal judicial forum. The route to relief now used derives from the Federal Courts Improvement Act of 1982 (FCIA) and the Administrative Dispute Resolution Act of 1996 (ADRA). N ADRA, Congress intended to broaden the COFC's bid protest jurisdiction, to create national uniformity for judicial forums overseeing bid protests, and to create jurisdiction for the COFC over the full range of bid protest cases. (It created district court jurisdiction, but it sunsetted this in 2000.)

A protest in the COFC tends to cost much more than a GAO protest. Many considerations go into choice of forum between GAO and COFC. Among other factors, some think the contractor has a more independent and, hence, potentially favorable forum in an independent court. For another consideration, the GAO's process involves the automatic stay for up to 100 days, whereas the COFC does not have an automatic stay, just the opportunity to seek a preliminary injunction. Conversely, when an agency overrides the GAO stay, the protester may turn to the Court of Federal Claims for review of the agency's decision to override. *Ramco Servs. Group, Inc. v. United States*, 185 f. Cir. 1999).

The COFC case starts when the contractor files a complaint. As with the GAO, the agency prepares a record. Other bidders may intervene, and the COFC routinely allows them to do so. As at the GAO, a party may apply for a protective order for confidential or proprietary information.

At the COFC, the Administrative Procedures Act (APA) standard applies to protest— looking for a violation of a procurement statute or regulation in connection with a procurement or a proposed procurement; or, for an arbitrary or capricious act or an abuse of discretion. The protester must demonstrate the error competitively prejudiced it. The COFC issued General Order No. 38 in 19989 to establish standard practices in bid protests, and this is now embodied in Appendix C to the Rules of the United States Court of Federal Claims (RCFC).

This forum resolves most protests through a motion for summary judgment upon the administrative record. The COFC permits the taking of depositions and in theory might grant broader discovery than the GAO. However, in fact the normal discovery procedures available in other types of judicial proceedings are not generally available to protesters. The COFC focuses on Administrative Procedure Act review, so what generally matters is just what the agency had before it as an administrative recover, not what can be found out by discovery. Only when the administrative record is deficient or inadequate will the court permit limited discovery.

A protest may proceed to a trial or final hearing on the merits. This addresses remaining factual disputes. The court also may hold a less costly and expeditious "paper trial," which resembles a ruling on cross motions for summary judgment but allows the court to resolve issues of fact.

Broad remedial powers, including an injunction against an agency proceeding with performance, may be applied by the COFC. Its standards are the usual ones: for preliminary injunctive relief it considers the protesters likelihood to succeed on the merits, irreparable harm to the protester, substantial harm to the government, and the public interest.

For further information, see see Steven Feldman, *Government Contract Guidebook*, § 19 (Thomson Reuters, 4th ed. 2010); *Concentrated Course in Government Contracts: Chapter 3 Remedies of Unsuccessful Offerors: Bid Protests, Small Business Appeals & Court Actions* (2007).

Chapter 16

Disputes and Other Remedies

To someone familiar with the remedy procedures for basic (private) contract law, the remedy procedures for government contract law come as a shock. Rarely does the government allow cases with contractors to proceed like simple private contract cases, with aggrieved contractors and the government suing each other in the nearest court of general jurisdiction. On the contrary, government contract remedy procedures seem more the product of elaborate administrative law, with its many special aspects designed to channel and shape the controversies between private and public actors.

This area of law starts with the existence of an array of highly specialized tribunals, like the boards of contract appeals. Cases cannot begin without a series of required preliminary steps commonly referred to in administrative law as tests of ripeness and "exhaustion," a technical word for the requisite sequence of actions which, coincidentally, expresses well the litigants' likely state of mind before they are through.

Moreover, the remedy procedures for government contract law derive from a long and tortuous history, having been changed frequently and radically by Congressional enactments, some quite recent. Those specialized tribunals do not exist because someone sat down and developed a structured master plan, nor by some teleologically purposeful evolution of the common law, but by a series of historical accidents as repaired by the intermittent intervention of statutory alterations.

The chapter looks at the mechanisms for aggrieved contractors to litigate their claims against the government through the disputes process. The Contract Disputes Act of 1978 imposes an array of constraints on contractors as to what claims, when, and how they can present. Moreover, the disputes process provides for claims to receive a decision from contracting officers and then constrains all subsequent proceedings in the boards of contract appeals and the Court of Federal Claims by the content of that contracting officer decision.@text:A section at the end treats the procedure for suspension and debarment—curtailing a contractor's opportunity to make contracts with the government. This procedure takes on special importance today. Large businesses depend on a high level of government contracting. Some managers may stray into criminal abuses. This procedure works out the extent to which the government maintains its level of contracting with such businesses, notwithstanding such offenses.

For further discussion of the subjects of this chapter, see: the periodic surveys such as the annual *Year in Review: Analysis of Significant Federal Circuit Government Contracts Decisions* in the Public Contract Law Journal, the *Contract and Fiscal Law Developments—The Year in Review* in the Army Lawyer, and the *Cases and Recent Developments* in the Federal Circuit Bar Journal; Edward J. Kinberg, *The Upcoming Explosion In Government Contract Litigation*, 57 Fed. Law. 42 (Oct. 2010); Peter D. Ting, *Practice Pointers: A Primer On Effective Presentation Of An Appeal Before The Armed Services Board Of Contract Appeals*, 44 Procrmt. Law. 3 (Spring 2009); Thomas L. McGovern (III), Daniel P. Graham, Stuart B. Nibley, *A Level Playing Field: Why Congress Intended The Boards Of Contract Ap-*

peals To Have Enforceable Subpoena Power Over Both Contractors And The Government, 36 Pub. Cont. L.J. 495 (Summer 2007); Steven L. Schooner, *Fear of Oversight: The Fundamental Failure of Businesslike Government*, 50 Am. U. L. Rev. 627 (2001); Richard H. Seamon, *Separation of Powers and the Separate Treatment of Contract Claims Against the Federal Government for Specific Performance*, 43 Vill. L. R. 155 (1998); Michael J. Davidson, *10 U.S.C. § 2408: An Unused Weapon in the Procurement Fraud Wars*, 26 Pub. Cont. L.J. 181 (1997); Paul Frederic Kirgis, *Section 1500 and the Jurisdictional Pitfalls of Federal Government Litigation*, 47 Am. U. L. Rev. 301 (1997).

A. Disputes

Note on Disputes

After contract award and during performance, the government has a dispute process which has evolved to channel the variety of disagreements over contracts into an orderly procedure for resolution. While the contractor continues to perform and the government continues to pay, the contractor makes a certified claim and obtains from the contracting officer a final decision rejecting that claim. Then, the contractor who disagrees with the decision chooses whether to take the matter to the agency board of contract appeals or to the Court of Federal Claims.

Historically, the disputes process goes back a long way, but it received a comprehensive restructuring in the Contract Disputes Act ("CDA") of 1978. The CDA put all the boards of contract appeals on a uniform statutory footing. It gave structure to the contracting officer's powers, the types of claims subject to the disputes process, the time limits for the process, and the respective appeal rights of the government and the contractors. The CDA works together with the standard Disputes Clause in government contracts (FAR 52.233) to create a remarkably uniform government-wide process.

Perhaps the single highest set of goals of the disputes process resembles that of the exhaustion requirement in administrative law. The disputes process makes the contractor give full notice to the government so that it can take early remedial action. This process pushes the contractor to negotiation with contracting officers to resolve the disagreement at the administrative level. Moreover, the disputes process prevents the contractor from rushing prematurely into the contract appeals boards or the courts, overloading those tribunals with unnecessary matters.

Besides such general exhaustion purposes, the disputes process has specific aspects that confine what might otherwise be a difficult mess of a disagreement's paperwork, centered around two important documents: the certified claim and the final decision. On the contractor's side, the claim, if above the threshhold, must be "certified." This requires the contractor, instead of making loose, vague, or overbroad claims, to assert a quite specific sum. It takes considerable legal judgment to gauge just how much support a claim needs in order for certification to be proper. This contrasts with, say, the relatively free hand with which a tort plaintiff might pick the figure in her complaint's damages clause.

On the government's side, the contracting officer must issue a final decision. This insures careful thought on both sides, since the contractor must usually make a deliberate, considered effort to get the contracting officer beyond simply rejecting the contractor's request and instead to formally issue a final decision, and since the contracting officer anticipates the prospect of the subsequent challenge in another forum to that final decision. The FAR defines the contents of the final decision, which should cover such points as describing the claim, referring to the pertinent contract provisions, stating the factual areas of agreement or disagreement, and giving the supporting rationale for the decision. It formally notifies the contractor of its appeal rights.

The student familiar with basic (private) contract law will recognize that the disputes process ties in to the orderly processes for handling uncertainty or partial breach. That is, there are ways besides cancellation or repudiation for the parties to a private contract to handle a disagreement. Basic contracts courses today often treat the procedure under UCC § 2-609 for seeking assurances of performance, as a way of handling uncertainty or partial breach while giving a chance for the completion of the contract if satisfactory assurances of performance are, in fact, forthcoming. Still, it is far from routine in the context of private contracts for major disagreements to get resolved without at least a threat, if not the actuality, of one side or the other cancelling or repudiating.

In contrast, by the disputes process, the law of government contracts has raised to a high and elaborate art the handling of disagreement in the course of continuing performance of a contract. On the contractor's side, the Disputes Clause of a government contract sternly forbids a refusal to perform. On the government's side, the very fact that the government has not chosen to resort to termination (either for convenience or for default) signals the government's desire to continue mutual performance and payment. Thus, the disputes process takes the disagreement off for slow, thorough adjudication, while performance continues as though there were no disagreement at all.

An important procedural issue has concerned the extent to which formal dispute is necessary to support an appeal. Of course, in most contracts a stream of demands for payment occur in the form of routine vouchers or invoices and the FAR precludes considering these routine demands to amount, in themselves, to sufficient "claims" to support a formal dispute. Making every routine demand into a "claim" would sacrifice all the value of exhaustion, as neither the contractor nor the government would be making the efforts they should prior to the matter heading on down the formal disputes path. On the other hand, an experiment by the Federal Circuit in the 1990s with creating new, higher requirements for what constituted enough formal disagreement to be a "claim" was ended with the *Reflectone* decision. Accordingly, that decision is the proper starting point for understanding the balance in the disputes process between requiring enough exhaustion and enough pointed disagreement and asking too much exhaustion and disagreement before taking a billing controversy up to the litigating level.

For further discussion of the issues in this section, see: McKenna Long & Aldridge LLP & Ronald Kienlen, *Government Contract Disputes* (Thomson Reuters 2010); Peter C. Latham, Government Contract Disputes (2d ed. 1986); Dorothy E. Terrell, Kathryn T. Muldoon, *The Rise Of The Performance Evaluation: New Developments In Contractor Challenges To Adverse Evaluations Under The Contract Disputes Act*, 45 Procrmt. Law. 3 (Winter 2010); Scott E. Huttmacher, *Government Contracting Disputes: It's Not All About The Money*, 2009 Army Law. 31 (Aug. 2009); Marko W. Kipa, Keith R. Szeliga, Jonathan S. Aronie, *Conquering Uncertainty In An Indefinite World: A Survey Of Disputes Arising Under IDIQ Contracts*, 37 Pub. Cont. L.J. 415 (Spring 2008); Michael Davidson, *Claims Involving Fraud: Contracting Officer Limitations During Procurement Fraud Investigations*, Army Lawyer, Sept. 2002, at 21.

Disputes Clause
(Oct 1995)

(a) This contract is subject to the Contract Disputes Act of 1978, as amended (41 U.S.C. 601–613).

(b) Except as provided in the Act, all disputes arising under or relating to this contract shall be resolved under this clause.

(c) "Claim," as used in this clause, means a written demand or written assertion by one of the contracting parties seeking, as a matter of right, the payment of money in a sum certain, the adjustment or interpretation of contract terms, or other relief arising under or relating to this contract. A claim arising under a contract, unlike a claim relating to that contract, is a claim that can be resolved under a contract clause that provides for the relief sought by the claimant. However, a written demand or written assertion by the Contractor seeking the payment of money exceeding $100,000 is not a claim under the Act until certified as required by subparagraph (d)(2) of this clause. A voucher, invoice, or other routine request for payment that is not in dispute when submitted is not a claim under the Act. The submission may be converted to a claim under the Act, by complying with the submission and certification requirements of this clause, if it is disputed either as to liability or amount or is not acted upon in a reasonable time.

(d) (1) A claim by the Contractor shall be made in writing and, unless otherwise stated in this contract, submitted within 6 years after accrual of the claim to the Contracting Officer for a written decision. A claim by the Government against the Contractor shall be subject to a written decision by the Contracting Officer.

   (2) (i) Contractors shall provide the certification specified in subparagraph (d)(2)(iii) of this clause when submitting any claim—

   (A) Exceeding $100,000 ...

   (ii) The certification requirement does not apply to issues in controversy that have not been submitted as all or part of a claim.

   (iii) The certification shall state as follows: "I certify that the claim is made in good faith; that the supporting data are accurate and complete to the best of my knowledge and belief; that the amount requested accurately reflects the contract adjustment for which the Contractor believes the Government is liable; and that I am duly authorized to certify the claim on behalf of the Contractor."

   (3) The certification may be executed by any person duly authorized to bind the Contractor with respect to the claim.

(e) For Contractor claims of $100,000 or less, the Contracting Officer must, if requested in writing by the Contractor, render a decision within 60 days of the request. For Contractor-certified claims over $100,000, the Contracting Officer must, within 60 days, decide the claim or notify the Contractor of the date by which the decision will be made.

(f) The Contracting Officer's decision shall be final unless the Contractor appeals or files a suit as provided in the Act.

(g) If the claim by the Contractor is submitted to the Contracting Officer or a claim by the Government is presented to the Contractor, the parties, by mutual consent, may agree to use ADR....

(h) The Government shall pay interest on the amount found due and unpaid ...

(i) The Contractor shall proceed diligently with performance of this contract, pending final resolution of any request for relief, claim, appeal, or action arising under the contract, and comply with any decision of the Contracting Officer.

Reflectone, Inc., Appellant, v.
John H. Dalton, Secretary of the Navy, Appellee

United States Court of Appeals, Federal Circuit
60 F.3d 1572 (1995)

Before ARCHER, Chief Judge, SKELTON, Senior Circuit Judge, NIES, NEWMAN, MAYER, MICHEL, PLAGER, LOURIE, CLEVENGER, RICH, RADER, SCHALL and BRYSON, Circuit Judges.

Opinion for the court filed by Circuit Judge MICHEL. Concurring opinion filed by Circuit Judge NIES.

MICHEL, Circuit Judge.

Reflectone, Inc. (Reflectone) appeals from the decision of the Armed Services Board of Contract Appeals (Board) dismissing Reflectone's appeal for lack of subject matter jurisdiction. Reflectone, Inc., ASBCA No. 43081, 93-1 BCA ¶ 25,512, 1992 WL 302847 (1992). The Board held that Reflectone had not submitted a "claim" within the meaning of the Contract Disputes Act of 1978 (CDA), 41 U.S.C. §§ 601–13 (1988 & Supp. V 1993), as interpreted in the Federal Acquisition Regulation (FAR), because a dispute over the amount of money Reflectone asserted it was owed did not predate Reflectone's June 1, 1990 Request for Equitable Adjustment (REA), the purported claim. Board jurisdiction is grounded in the CDA which authorizes Board review only of a contracting officer's final decision on a "claim." The CDA, however, does not define "claim." Because we conclude that FAR 33.201 (1988), which alone defines "claim" for purposes of the CDA, does not require a pre-existing dispute as to either amount or liability when, as here, a contractor submits a non-routine "written demand ... seeking, as a matter of right, the payment of money in a sum certain," FAR 33.201, we hold that Reflectone's REA was a CDA "claim" and, therefore, the Board has jurisdiction. Accordingly, we reverse the dismissal and remand for adjudication of Reflectone's appeal from the contracting officer's decision on its merits.

BACKGROUND

On April 15, 1988, Reflectone entered into a $4,573,559 fixed price contract with the Naval Training Systems Center in Orlando, Florida, requiring Reflectone to update helicopter weapon system trainers. The contract called for delivery of the first trainer on February 15, 1989, with the other three trainers to follow at three-month intervals. In a letter dated December 14, 1988, Reflectone advised the contracting officer (CO) that delivery of certain equipment was being delayed by late, unavailable or defective government-furnished property. In response, the Navy denied responsibility for the delay and issued a cure notice warning Reflectone that unless the condition endangering timely delivery of the equipment was eliminated within thirty days, the Navy might terminate the contract for default.

On January 17, 1989, Reflectone again wrote the CO that the delays were the fault of the government and requested an extension of the contract delivery schedule. Subsequently, the Navy modified two of the original four delivery dates but reserved its right to seek additional compensation for delay. After Reflectone advised the Navy that it would be unable to meet even the extended delivery dates due to faulty government-furnished property, the CO indicated on May 5, 1989, that Reflectone was delinquent on the contract and that the Navy would seek compensation for the delay. Between May 1989 and April 1990, the contract delivery schedule was modified at least three more times and each time the Navy reserved the right to make a claim against Reflectone for delay. In response, Reflectone continued to inform the Navy that it considered the government to have caused all delays and that it would claim relief once the full economic impact of the delay was known.

On June 1, 1990, Reflectone submitted an REA to the CO demanding $266,840 for costs related to government-caused delay with respect to twenty-one enumerated items. Reflectone's President and CEO certified the REA and requested a decision from the CO. In the initial review of the REA, completed on January 15, 1991, the CO denied sixteen of the twenty-one items in their entirety, estimated entitlement in the remaining five items at $17,662, and advised Reflectone that a counterclaim and set-off, exceeding the amount requested by Reflectone, was being prepared. On March 19, 1991, the CO rendered a final decision indicating that the government's position remained the same and advising Reflectone of its right to appeal to the Board.

Reflectone appealed the CO's final decision to the Board, which held that the REA was not a "claim" within the meaning of the Contract Disputes Act and, therefore, it did not have jurisdiction over the appeal. The Board relied on language from Dawco Constr., Inc. v. United States, 930 F.2d 872, 878 (Fed.Cir.1991), stating, "A contractor and the government contracting agency must already be in dispute over the amount requested." Dawco also states "The [CDA] and its implementing regulation require that a 'claim' arise from a request for payment that is 'in dispute.' " Id. The Board interpreted Dawco as holding that no demand for payment could be a claim unless the amount of the payment had been put in dispute. The Board reasoned that because Reflectone first requested a specific amount from the government in the REA, no dispute over the amount existed prior to the REA and, therefore, the REA could not be a claim according to its interpretation of Dawco.

* * *

On appeal to this court, a divided, three-judge panel affirmed the Board's dismissal decision, accepting its interpretation of Dawco and its rationale, in an opinion dated September 1, 1994, now vacated. Reflectone, Inc. v. Kelso, 34 F.3d 1031 (Fed.Cir.) (withdrawn from bound volume), vacated, 34 F.3d 1039 (Fed.Cir.1994). Due to the exceptional public importance of the issue of first impression presented by this case concerning the proper definition of a CDA "claim," we granted Reflectone's Suggestion for Rehearing In Banc.Fed. Cir.R. 35.

* * *

ANALYSIS

I

A. FAR 33.201 Does Not Require That A Payment Demanded In A Non-Routine Submission Be In Dispute Before The Submission To A Contracting Officer Can Be A "Claim"

Under the CDA, a final decision by a CO on a "claim" is a prerequisite for Board jurisdiction. Sharman Co. v. United States, 2 F.3d 1564, 1568–69 (Fed.Cir.1993) (reviewing jurisdictional scheme of CDA). Because the CDA itself does not define the term "claim,"[1]

---

1. The CDA, 41 U.S.C. § 605(a) (1988), states in relevant part:
All claims by a contractor against the government relating to a contract shall be in writing and shall be submitted to the contracting officer for a decision. All claims by the government against a contractor relating to a contract shall be the subject of a decision by the contracting officer.

we must assess whether a particular demand for payment constitutes a claim, based on the FAR implementing the CDA, the language of the contract in dispute, and the facts of the case. Garrett v. General Elec. Co., 987 F.2d 747, 749 (Fed.Cir.1993). The FAR defines "claim" as:

> [1] a written demand or written assertion by one of the contracting parties seeking, as a matter of right, the payment of money in a sum certain, the adjustment or interpretation of contract terms, or other relief arising under or relating to the contract.... [2] A voucher, invoice, or other routine request for payment that is not in dispute when submitted is not a claim. [3] The submission may be converted to a claim, by written notice to the contracting officer as provided in 33.206(a), if it is disputed either as to liability or amount or is not acted upon in a reasonable time.

FAR (48 C.F.R. §) 33.201 (emphasis added). The issue is whether sentence [2] adds a requirement to those stated in sentence [1] that applies to all submissions.

The government and the Board would require that before Reflectone's REA can qualify as a claim, it be preceded by a dispute over entitlement to and the amount of a demand for payment. According to the government, this requirement is mandated by the language of FAR 33.201. In order to explore whether a CDA "claim" requires a dispute which pre-dates the submission to the CO, we requested that the following question be addressed by the in banc briefs.

> Did Dawco Constr., Inc. v. United States, 930 F.2d 872 (Fed.Cir.1991), properly conclude that a Contract Disputes Act (CDA) "claim" as defined in FAR 33.201 requires a pre-existing dispute between a contractor and the government when the claim is in the form of a "written assertion ... seeking, as a matter of right, the payment of money in a sum certain" or other contract relief per the first sentence of the FAR definition, or does that requirement only apply when the claim initially is in the form of a "routine request for payment"?

We answer the first half of this question in the negative and the second half in the affirmative. We hold that sentence [1] of FAR 33.201 sets forth the only three requirements of a non-routine "claim" for money: that it be (1) a written demand, (2) seeking, as a matter of right, (3) the payment of money in a sum certain. That sentence simply does not require that entitlement to the amount asserted in the claim or the amount itself already be in dispute when the document is submitted. The subsequent sentence does not add another requirement to a non-routine submission.

FAR 33.201 does not mention a dispute until the fourth sentence, sentence [2], which provides, "[a] voucher, invoice, or other routine request for payment that is not in dispute when submitted is not a claim." Routine requests for payment, too, are "written demand[3] ... seeking, as a matter of right, payment of money in a sum certain" and, therefore, appear to fall within the definition of claim recited in sentence [1] of FAR 33.201. However, the FAR explicitly excludes from the definition of "claim" those "routine request[s] for payment" that are not in dispute when submitted to the CO.[2] Nevertheless, nothing in the definition suggests that other written demands seeking payment of a sum certain as a matter of right, i.e., those demands that are not "routine request[s] for pay-

---

2. The distinction excluding routine requests for payment from the definition of "claim" relieves COs from the requirement of issuing a CDA final decision on each and every voucher that the government is obligated to pay under the express terms of the contract during its ordinary progression, including "progress payments." The process for converting such routine requests, if disputed, into claims assures that only those submissions that need final decisions will require them.

ment," also must be already in dispute to constitute a "claim." Moreover, that the regulation specifically excludes only undisputed routine requests for payment from the category of written demands for payment that satisfy the definition of "claim" implies that all other written demands seeking payment as a matter of right are "claims," whether already in dispute or not. The inclusion of only one exception to the definition of "claim"—undisputed, routine requests—implies the exclusion of any others. See United States v. Koonce, 991 F.2d 693, 698 (11th Cir.1993) (applying canon of statutory construction inclusio unius est exclusio alterius).

Our holding today that the FAR requires a "claim" to be a written demand seeking a sum certain (or other contract relief) as a matter of right, but not necessarily in dispute, is consistent with the ordinary meaning of the term "claim": "a demand for something due or believed to be due." Webster's Ninth New Collegiate Dictionary 244 (1990). That the demand is made as a matter of right constitutes the essential characteristic of a "claim" according to both the FAR and the dictionary definitions. See Essex Electro Eng'rs, Inc. v. United States, 960 F.2d 1576, 1580–81 (Fed.Cir.) ("[T]he dictionary definition of 'claim' supports the reasonableness of the requirement that the money be sought as a matter of right."), cert. denied, 506 U.S. 953, 113 S.Ct. 408, 121 L.Ed.2d 333 (1992). Nothing in the common definition of "claim," however, requires a pre-existing dispute before a demand as a matter of right can be a claim. Indeed, everything suggests the contrary.

Moreover, as Reflectone points out, it is illogical to require a dispute before a demand for payment rightfully due can be a "claim" because to have a dispute the contractor first must make a demand as a matter of right, i.e., a claim, that is then refused. Furthermore, neither the CDA, its legislative history, nor the FAR, nor its history, suggests that a dispute must pre-date the contractor's submission of the claim to the CO when the claim is in the form of a non-routine demand as of right.

The government argues, nevertheless, that a close reading of the regulation demonstrates that a "claim" always requires a pre-existing dispute. The government's analysis begins correctly by acknowledging that sentence [1] of the FAR, defining "claim" as "a written demand ... seeking, as a matter of right, the payment of money in a sum certain" appears to include vouchers, invoices and other routine requests for payment. According to the government, because the regulation later makes clear that the drafters intended to exclude routine requests for payment from the definition of "claim" unless they are in dispute, the question becomes one of distinguishing between non-routine written demands seeking the payment of a sum certain as a matter of right and "routine request[s] for payment." The government next asserts, incorrectly, that it is the existence of a dispute which distinguishes a non-routine "claim" from a routine request for payment and, therefore, every "claim" must involve a pre-existing dispute.

The government's interpretation of the FAR must fail, as a matter of logic, because it recognizes only two categories of potential claims, undisputed routine requests for payment, which do not satisfy the definition, and disputed non-routine written demands seeking payment as a matter of right, which do. This interpretation ignores a third category, undisputed, non-routine written demands seeking payment as a matter of right. Under the literal language of the FAR, however, the critical distinction in identifying a "claim" is not between undisputed and disputed submissions, but between routine and non-routine submissions.

To read the dispute requirement of sentence [2] of FAR 33.201 as applying to all submissions for payment, as the government suggests, one would have to construe every demand for payment as a matter of right as a "routine request for payment." However, this is clearly not so. For instance, an REA is anything but a "routine request for payment." It is a remedy payable only when unforeseen or unintended circumstances, such as government modification of the contract, differing site conditions, defective or late-delivered government property or issuance of a stop work order, cause an increase in contract performance costs. Pacific Architects and Eng'rs Inc. v. United States, 491 F.2d 734, 739, 203 Ct.Cl. 499 (1974). A demand for compensation for unforeseen or unintended circumstances cannot be characterized as "routine." The Supreme Court has confirmed the nonroutine nature of an REA by equating it with assertion of a breach of contract. Crown Coat Front Co. v. United States, 386 U.S. 503, 511, 87 S.Ct. 1177, 1181, 18 L.Ed.2d 256 (1967) ("With respect to claims arising under the typical government contract, the contractor has agreed in effect to convert what otherwise might be claims for breach of contract into claims for equitable adjustment."). Thus, an REA provides an example of a written demand for payment as a matter of right which is not "a routine request for payment" and, therefore, it satisfies the FAR definition of "claim" whether or not the government's liability for or the amount of the REA was already disputed before submission of the REA to the CO.[3]

A routine request for payment, on the other hand, is made under the contract, not outside it. For example, a voucher or invoice is submitted for work done or equipment delivered by the contractor in accordance with the expected or scheduled progression of contract performance. Similarly, progress payments are made by the government when the contractor completes predetermined stages of the contract. An REA can hardly be compared to an invoice, voucher or progress payment.

Thus, we hold that FAR 33.201 does not require that "a written demand ... seeking, as a matter of right, the payment of money in a sum certain" must already be in dispute when submitted to the CO to satisfy the definition of "claim," except where that demand or request is a "voucher, invoice or other routine request for payment." ... FAR 33.201, viewed as a whole, establishes a framework in which written demands seeking a sum certain as a matter of right are CDA "claims" with the only exception of "routine request[s] for payment" which may be converted to claims by the existence of a dispute and compliance with other requirements of conversion in FAR 33.206(a). Routine requests are a subset of all written demands for payment. Special requirements apply to the subset, but not to the rest of the set.

Reflectone's REA is clearly "a written demand or written assertion by one of the contracting parties seeking, as a matter of right, the payment of money in a sum certain." Reflectone, a contracting party, submitted a written document to the CO demanding the payment of $266,840 which it asserted the government owed for delaying performance of the contract by furnishing defective goods. The submission was certified and requested a CO decision. Consequently, Reflectone's REA satisfies all the requirements listed for a CDA "claim" according to the plain language of the first sentence of FAR 33.201. The REA is not a "routine request for payment" and, therefore, the fourth sentence of the FAR definition does not apply here to require, inter alia, a pre-existing dispute as to either liability or amount. Because we conclude that Reflectone's REA is a "claim" according to the

---

3. We do not hold, however, that every non-routine submission constitutes a "claim" under the FAR. Those submissions which do not seek payment as a matter of right are not claims, a definition which excludes, for example, cost proposals for work the government later decides it would like performed. See Essex Electro Eng'rs, 960 F.2d at 1581–82 (excluding cost proposals and inspection reports from the FAR definition of a CDA "claim").

FAR, we further conclude that the Board has jurisdiction to review the CO's denial of Reflectone's REA.

* * *

CONCLUSION

We hold that properly construed for its plain meaning, the language of FAR 33.201 does not require that a payment demand contained in a purported CDA claim be in dispute before being submitted for decision to the CO unless that demand is a "voucher, invoice or other routine request for payment." To the extent that Dawco and cases relying on Dawco can be read to suggest otherwise, they are overruled. We further hold that Reflectone's REA satisfies the definition of "claim," and, therefore, we reverse the Board's dismissal for lack of jurisdiction and remand this case to the Board for further proceedings on Reflectone's appeal consistent with this opinion.

[Concurring opinion omitted.]

Notes and Questions

1. *Reflectone* focuses on the existence of a "claim" that is ripe enough in terms of the amount of agency consideration and rejection. In some respects, the government's arguments as recited in the opinion sound phrased almost in delicate euphemisms. Do you understand the government's legitimate arguments for requiring a high level of agency consideration and rejection for a "claim," as hinted at when the government says that it would help for the contracting officer to have more opportunities to request clarification? How does it affect the power relationship of contracting officer and contractor not to require that highly formal level of agency consideration and rejection as a predicate for appeal? What happens to the contracting officer's power when the contractor has both the right and the temptation to appeal over her head that much faster?

2. Another requirement for a dispute under the Contract Disputes Act (41 U.S.C. sec. 601 et seq.) is that an asserted demand exceeding $100,000 must be certified. The submitting contractor is required to certify that the claims are made in good faith, are based on accurate and complete data, and that the sum certain requested accurately reflects the adjustment for which the party seeks payment (sec. 605(a)(1)). Certification can be effected by anyone with authority to bind the contractor regarding the claim, which must be submitted within six years of accrual. See *H. L. Smith, Inc. v. Dalton*, 49 F.3d 1563 (Fed. Cir. 1995); *Newport News Shipbuilding and Dry Dock Co. v. Garrett*, 6 F.3d 1547 (Fed. Cir. 1993); *Reliance Insurance Co v. United States*, 27 Fed. Cl. 815 (1993); *Mediax Interactive Technologies, Inc.*, ASBCA No. 43961 (1993).

3. The concept of what constitutes a "claim" remains elusive. The Contract Disputes Act, 41 U.S.C. §§ 601–613, simply requires that claims be written and submitted to the contract officer for a decision. 41 U.S.C. § 605(a). The FAR specifies further that

> Claim, as used in this clause, means a written demand or written assertion by one of the contracting parties seeking, as a matter of right, the payment of money in a sum certain, the adjustment or interpretation of contract terms, or other relief under or relating to the contract. FAR 52.233.1 (April 1984).

The contractor is further required to include details of the relevant facts of the contract at issue, as well as the basis and amount of the claim, to give the contract officer sufficient information upon which to render a decision. *Appeal of Automated Power Systems*, DOTCAB No. 2928 (1998). There is no need, however, for the contractor to specifically demand the contract officer's final decision. The subjective intent of the claimant in making the submission will suffice to meet the CDA claim test. *D.C. Cab and Taxi Dispatch*, VABCA No. 5482 (1998).

Note on CBCA, ASBCA, and COFC Disputes Procedure

Each of the fora that may review government contract disputes has its own procedures. In some respects, these procedures correspond to those in the federal courts. In other respects, these fora have their own procedures. The Civilian Board of Contract Appeals (CBCA) and the Armed Services Board of Contract Appeals (ASBCA)—the "boards of contract appeals" (BCAs)—share similar procedure. More attending to the precise specific provisions about jurisdictions, it is useful to tell a general version, combining aspects of different for an overall picture.

A case at the BCAs starts with a final decision by the contracting officer (CO), followed by the filing of a notice of appeal by the contractor (now the "appellant"). Soon the appellant files a complaint, stating the key facts and the underlying legal theories, such as the claim's basis in contract provisions. The contracting officer organizes and compiles Rule 4 (as the ASBCA styles it) file, containing all the pertinent documents—the CO's decision, the contract, correspondence, and any transcripts or affidavits. Copies of this go out to the BCA and the parties. Less key, the contracting officer may also compile a litigation file for the trial attorneys, with his case analysis, witness statements, and legal memoranda.

As the case proceeds, the parties may use the methods of discovery: depositions, written interrogatories, requests for documents, and making requests for admission. Subpoenas and motions may be used, including motions for summary judgment. There are various alternative ways to resolve the case: submission without hearing, small claims, accelerated and expedited proceedings, or alternative dispute resolution.

Ultimately, the case may go to a hearing. The parties should be ready to prove their cases as in federal courts. Hearings can vary from lasting only hours to continuing for weeks or months. They often occur at the BCA's headquarters in the Washington DC, area, although they may travel to more convenient places around the country. A single trial judge sits at the hearing. After posthearing briefs, the court drafts and issues an opinion.

A case about a dispute in the Court of Federal Claims (COFC) starts similarly, although with the notable difference that a contractor has only 90 days after the CO's final decision to file with a BCA but a full year to file with the COFC. The agency prepares a comprehensive litigation report which is similar to, but not the equivalent of, the Rule 4 report in the BCA. Discovery occurs as in the BCAs, although with distinctions such as the COFC's unique power to issue a "call" to the procuring agency.

For further information, see Peter D. Ting, *Practice Pointers: A Primer on Effective Presentation of an Appeal Before the Armed Services Board of Contract Appeals*, Procurement Lawyer, Spring 2009, at 3; Michael J. Schaengold & Robert S. Brams, *A Guide to the Civilian Board of Contract Appeals*, 07-8 Briefing Papers 1; Michael J. Schaengold & Robert S. Brums, *Choice of Forum for Contract Claims: Court v. Board/Edition II*, 06-6 Briefing Papers 1; Gary J. Suttles, *After the Contracting Officer's Final Decision, Your Contractor Sues—Now What?*, Cont. Mngmt, August 2003, at 6.

Bonneville Associates, Plaintiff, v.
The United States, Defendant, v.
Camco Construction Co., Third Party Defendant
No. 92-21C.
30 Fed.Cl. 85
United States Court of Federal Claims
Nov. 22, 1993

MARGOLIS, Judge.

This government contracts case comes before the court on defendant's motion to dismiss for lack of subject matter jurisdiction. The plaintiff, Bonneville Associates ("Bonneville"), contracted with the defendant, acting through the General Services Administration ("GSA"), for the repair and sale of an office building. Disputes arose regarding certain contractual obligations of Bonneville. After receiving a final decision of the contracting officer and filing a notice of appeal with the General Services Administration Board of Contract Appeals ("GSBCA"), plaintiff withdrew its notice of appeal and brought an action involving the same operative facts in this court.

Defendant argues that the contract is subject to the Contract Disputes Act, 41 U.S.C. §§ 601 *et seq.*, because it involved both the repair and sale of real property. Defendant further argues that 41 U.S.C. § 609 and the Election Doctrine bind plaintiff to its decision to appeal the final decision of the contracting officer to the GSBCA, and that this court lacks jurisdiction to hear plaintiff's claim....

After a careful review of the record and after hearing oral argument, this court grants defendant's motion to dismiss for lack of subject matter jurisdiction.

FACTS

The material facts are uncontested. On September 30, 1987, Bonneville entered into a contract with GSA for the repair and sale of an office building in Las Vegas, Nevada. GSA purchased the building for $9,908,452. The parties agreed that $1,708,452 of the contract price would be withheld for improvements to the building by Bonneville. These funds were to be paid to Bonneville as the repair work was completed. Of the amount withheld by GSA, $500,000 remains unpaid.

The parties disputed certain mechanical and structural improvements to the building to be performed by plaintiff. Specifically, Bonneville and GSA attempted to resolve disputes concerning floor strengthening and leveling, additional cooling capacity, duct work and acoustical insulation, and certain warranty issues. Inability to resolve the disputes led to an August 21, 1991 final decision of the contracting officer demanding $5,195,069 from Bonneville, allegedly representing the cost to defendant of correcting deficiencies in the building.

The contracting officer's final decision notified Bonneville of its right to appeal the decision to either the GSBCA within 90 days, or to the United States Court of Federal Claims within twelve months. Bonneville filed a notice of appeal with the GSBCA on November 19, 1991. The GSBCA docketed the appeal on November 26, 1991. Bonneville filed a motion to withdraw its GSBCA appeal on January 8, 1992, and the GSBCA dismissed the appeal without prejudice on January 17, 1992. On January 13, 1992, Bonneville filed this action.

DISCUSSION

The issue is whether the Contract Disputes Act ("Act") covers the contract between Bonneville and GSA, thus binding plaintiff to the Act's procedural rules and conferring jurisdiction on the GSBCA. If this case is subject to the Contract Disputes Act, 41 U.S.C. §609 and the Election Doctrine require dismissal of plaintiff's case for lack of subject matter jurisdiction. Section 609 provides that a contractor may bring an action on a claim in the Court of Federal Claims in lieu of appealing the decision of a contracting officer to an agency board. 41 U.S.C. §609(a)(1). Conversely, if this case is not covered by the Contract Disputes Act, then defendant's motion must be denied because the GSBCA was without jurisdiction over plaintiff's claim.

The contract was a dual-purpose agreement for both the repair and sale of an office building. The disputes concern the plaintiff's obligations under the repair and construction clauses of the contract.

Section 8(d) of the Act provides that the boards of contract appeals "shall have jurisdiction to decide any appeal from a decision of a contracting officer ... relative to a contract." 41 U.S.C. §607(d). Section 3 of the Act limits the types of contracts to which the statute applies:

§602. Applicability of law

(a) Executive agency contracts

Unless otherwise specifically provided herein, this chapter applies to any express or implied contract (including those of the nonappropriated fund activities described in sections 1346 and 1491 of title 28) entered into by an executive agency for—

(1) the procurement of property, *other than real property in being;*

(2) the procurement of services;

(3) *the procurement of construction, alteration, repair or maintenance of real property;* or,

(4) the disposal of personal property.

41 U.S.C. §602 (emphasis added).

Plaintiff contends that this case clearly fits within the section 602(a)(1) exception for the procurement of real property and that the Act does not apply....

Assuming, *arguendo,* that the section 602(a)(1) exception excludes all contracts for procurement of real property in being from the Act's coverage, this court's inquiry is not ended. The contract was not merely for the procurement of real property in being; it was for the *repair* and sale of an office building. Section 602(a)(3) of the Act expressly brings contracts for the "construction, alteration, repair or maintenance of real property" within the statute. Therefore, one purpose of the dual-purpose contract is specifically covered by the Act....

... [T]his court finds that the plaintiff's claim is covered by the Act. @text:Accordingly, this court next considers the applicability of the Election Doctrine.

> The Court of Claims recognized that, although the Contract Disputes Act provides a contractor with a choice of forums in which to contest an adverse decision by the contracting officer, the contractor is precluded by the Contract Disputes Act from pursuing its claim in both forums. Once a contractor makes a binding election under the Election Doctrine to appeal the contracting officer's adverse decision to the appropriate board of contract appeals, that election must stand and the contractor can no longer pursue its claim in the alternate forum. Under the Election Doctrine, the binding election of forums is an "either-or" alternative, and, as such, does not provide a contractor with dual avenues for contesting a contracting officer's adverse decision.

National Neighbors, Inc. v. United States, 839 F.2d 1539, 1542 (Fed.Cir.1988). Once this court finds that a plaintiff appealed a contracting officer's final decision to a board, "the only remaining issue is whether that election was 'informed, knowing and voluntary.' "*Mark Smith Constr. Co., Inc. v. United States,* 10 Cl.Ct. 540, 544 (1986) (citations omitted).

Plaintiff was advised that the contracting officer's decision was a final decision and that plaintiff had a right to appeal the decision to the GSBCA within 90 days or to the Court of Federal Claims within 12 months. *See* 41 U.S.C. § 609(a). Bonneville filed a timely notice of appeal with the GSBCA and its decision was "informed, knowing and voluntary." Under these circumstances, this court dismisses plaintiff's case pursuant to the Election Doctrine. *See, e.g., Prime Constr. Co., Inc. v. United States,* 231 Ct.Cl. 782, 784 (1982).

CONCLUSION

Because the contract is covered by the Contract Disputes Act, this court is without subject matter jurisdiction. The case must be dismissed pursuant to the Election Doctrine. The defendant's motion to dismiss is granted. The clerk will dismiss the complaint without prejudice. No costs.

Notes and Questions

This case points to some of the implicit realities of the dispute litigation system after the contracting officer has denied what the contractor wants, and the contractor has a "claim" (in *Reflectone* terms). At that point, the CDA gives the contractor an important choice, to appeal to the Board of Contract Appeals for that department, or to the Court of Federal Claims. Most contractors prefer the boards, but some prefer the court, and either way, each has its weighty reasons for making that choice of forum. In some respects procedure before the boards is a little more informal and, hence, can be less expensive. Once the contractor chooses, an "Election Doctrine" precludes their changing their mind and going to the other forum.

Any number of questions can arise, such as the one in this case about mixed contracts involving real estate and construction. Other potentially complex questions concern the procedures for when a contracting officer delays ruling on a claim; the government's claims against the contractor, and the government's ability to counterclaim; and interest on claims.

B. Alternative Dispute Resolution

Alternative Dispute Resolution ("ADR") in government contracting law consists of using methods such as mediation and arbitration, among others, to resolve protests and disputes without the full-scale proceedings previously described. For example, a protester and a contracting officer might agree to attempt to resolve the protest through mediation, i.e., working with a neutral third party who facilitates negotiation or even evaluates the two sides' proposals, thereby hopefully obviating the need for a decision by the agency, or GAO, or a court, on the protest. Or, a contractor and a contracting officer might agree to resolve a dispute through arbitration, a binding decision by a neutral arbitrator, rather than go through the disputes process up to the boards of contract appeals or the courts

In the 1990s, there was a marked increase in the use of ADR to resolve protests and disputes. Partly, Congress and senior levels of the contracting agencies encouraged greater use of ADR. Partly, both contracting officers and contractors found that ADR sometimes works better than litigation.

The trend toward ADR began with the Administrative Dispute Resolution Act ("ADRA") of 1990, Pub. L. 101-552, 104 Stat. 2736 (1990), a statute initially set to expire but subsequently reauthorized. FAR provisions implement ADRA. ADRA's fostering of ADR for disputes got implemented by the boards of contract appeals giving procedural instructions to the parties whenever an appeal is docketed, as well as by encouragement of ADR by the Court of Federal Claims and most of the federal district courts. More encouragement came by Executive Order 12979 (Oct. 25, 1995), and by agency policy statements.

ADR methods include partnering, which is just a better relationship between the parties; mediation, which can be either facilitative or evaluative; minitrials, which are truncated but moderately formal adversarial information exchanges heard by the parties' representatives as a way of fostering settlement; and arbitration, in which neutral third parties make binding decisions. Until the 1990s, the government had resisted arbitration, raising constitutional issues since arbitrators make decisions without receiving appointments pursuant to the Appointments Clause (the way, say, judges or agency heads do). However, the Department of Justice issued a legal memorandum, subsequently followed by a decision of the Court of Federal Claims, which upheld arbitration provided certain criteria were present. *Tenaska Washington Partners II, L.P. v. United States*, 34 Fed. Cl. 434 (1995).

In the course of a solicitation that produces a protest or a contract disagreement that produces a dispute, the decisive moment comes when the two sides decide to use an ADR method to resolve the protest or dispute and carry out that decision by an ADR Agreement. The ADR Agreement selects the method and the neutral participant (mediator or arbitrator), provides for information exchange and procedures, protects confidentiality, and may anticipate settlement. Once a disagreement gets resolved, the neutral participant prepares a written instrument setting forth the resolution. The parties must then carry out those terms.

For further discussion, see: Jeffrey M. Senger, *Advocacy In Mediation With The Government*, 61 Disp. Resol. J. 50 (Nov. 2006/Jan. 2007); Sarah A. Wight, No Out For The Federal Government: Enforcing Contractual Arbitration Clauses In Federal Government False Claims Actions, 2002 J. Disp. Resol. 227 (2002); Robert J. Gomez, Mediating Government Contract Claims: How It Is Different, 32 Pub. Cont. L.J. 63 (Fall 2002); Laurence J. Zielke, *Arbitrating Miller Act Claims and Problems in Enforcing an Award Under the Federal Arbitration Act*, 24 Pub. Cont. L.J. 401 (1995); Stephen G. Lee, *Hiring the Cheapest Piper: Arbitration of Subcontract Disputes by Boards of Contract Appeals*, 23 Pub. Cont. L.J. 105 (1993).

C. Liquidated Damages

DJ Manufacturing Corporation, Plaintiff-Appellant, v. The United States, Defendant-Appellee

No. 95-5128
United States Court of Appeals, Federal Circuit
86 F.3d 1130
June 12, 1996

Before CLEVENGER, Circuit Judge, NIES, Senior Circuit Judge, and BRYSON, Circuit Judge.

BRYSON, Circuit Judge.

DJ Manufacturing Corporation (DJ) appeals from a decision of the United States Court of Federal Claims granting summary judgment to the government. DJ argued that the liquidated damages clause in the contract between the parties was unenforceable as a penalty. The trial court rejected that argument, DJ Mfg. Corp. v. United States, 33 Fed. Cl. 357 (Fed.Cl.1995), as do we.

I

In January 1991, the government solicited an offer from DJ for 283,695 combat field packs to support troops who were then participating in Operation Desert Storm. The solicitation documents set forth a delivery schedule, sought accelerated delivery if possible, and provided for liquidated damages for late delivery. The parties negotiated a contract, which became effective on February 14, 1991. Like the underlying solicitation documents, the contract provided that, for each article delivered after the date fixed in the contract, liquidated damages would be assessed at 1/15 of one percent of the contract price for each day of delay.

DJ missed several delivery deadlines. In accordance with the liquidated damages clause, the government withheld payment in the amount of $663,266.92, a reduction of about 8 percent of the total contract price of $8,493,828.

DJ filed suit in the Court of Federal Claims to recover the withheld amount, contending that the liquidated damages clause constituted an unenforceable penalty. The government moved for summary judgment. In support of its motion, the government submitted a declaration by an Army logistics management specialist, who stated that possession of the field packs was essential to the troops' combat readiness. In addition, the government submitted a declaration from the contracting officer, who stated that all contracts for items to be used in Operation Desert Shield/Desert Storm contained liquidated damages clauses for late delivery because of the need to get war items to the soldiers quickly.

In response to the government's motion, DJ produced an affidavit of its president, who stated that the rate set forth in the liquidated damages clause "does not seem related to any specific need with respect to the item in question or the time-frame, but, rather, seems to be a fairly standard rate used in many solicitations for many different items." The affidavit listed several other government contracts and solicitations that allegedly contained clauses setting liquidated damages at the same rate. DJ argued that there was therefore a disputed issue of material fact as to whether the contracting officer had "used a standard rate, historically employed by [the agency]" and had made "no attempt to forecast just compensation."

The Court of Federal Claims granted the government's motion. At the outset, the court held that DJ bore the burden of establishing that the liquidated damages clause was unenforceable, and that in order to avoid summary judgment DJ had to point to evidence raising a triable question of fact with respect to that issue. The court then recited the rule that a liquidated damages clause is enforceable if the harm that would be caused by a breach is difficult to estimate and the amount or rate fixed as liquidated damages is a reasonable forecast of the loss that may be caused by the breach.

As to the first element, the court characterized this case as presenting "a paradigmatic example of a situation where accurate estimation of the damages resulting from delays in delivery is difficult, if not impossible." As to the second element, the court rejected DJ's argument that in order to determine the reasonableness of the liquidated damages, it was necessary to inquire into the process that the contracting officer followed in reaching the amount that was inserted into the contract. The inquiry, the court explained, is an objective one. "The proper inquiry focuses on whether the amount itself is a reasonable forecast, not whether, as [DJ] seems to suggest, the individual responsible for proposing the rate engaged in a reasonable attempt to forecast damages." Because DJ failed to offer any evidence that the liquidated damages rate agreed upon in the contract was "greater than that which the government could reasonably suffer as a result of the delayed delivery of the field packs," the court granted the government's motion and ordered DJ's complaint to be dismissed.

II

By fixing in advance the amount to be paid in the event of a breach, liquidated damages clauses save the time and expense of litigating the issue of damages. Such clauses "serve a particularly useful function when damages are uncertain in nature or amount or are unmeasurable," Priebe & Sons v. United States, 332 U.S. 407, 411, 68 S.Ct. 123, 126, 92 L.Ed. 32 (1947), which is often the case when there is a delay in the completion of a contract for the government. Id.; United States v. Bethlehem Steel Co., 205 U.S. 105, 120, 27 S.Ct. 450, 455–56, 51 L.Ed. 731 (1907); Jennie-O Foods, Inc. v. United States, 580 F.2d 400, 413, 217 Ct.Cl. 314 (1978) ("Costs to the public convenience and the temporary thwarting of the public goals … are hard to measure with precision.").

When damages are uncertain or difficult to measure, a liquidated damages clause will be enforced as long as "the amount stipulated for is not so extravagant, or disproportionate to the amount of property loss, as to show that compensation was not the object aimed at or as to imply fraud, mistake, circumvention or oppression." Wise v. United States, 249 U.S. 361, 365, 39 S.Ct. 303, 304, 63 L.Ed. 647 (1919); see United States v. Bethlehem Steel Co., 205 U.S. at 121, 27 S.Ct. at 456 ("The amount is not so extraordinarily disproportionate to the damage which might result from the [breach], as to show that the parties must have intended a penalty and could not have meant liquidated damages."). With that narrow exception, "[t]here is no sound reason why persons competent and free to contract may not agree upon this subject as fully as upon any other, or why their agreement, when fairly and understandingly entered into with a view to just compensation for the anticipated loss, should not be enforced." Wise v. United States, 249 U.S. at 365, 39 S.Ct. at 304; see also Sun Printing & Publishing Ass'n v. Moore, 183 U.S. 642, 674, 22 S.Ct. 240, 253, 46 L.Ed. 366 (1902) (except where "the sum fixed is greatly disproportionate to the presumed actual damages," a court "has no right to erroneously construe the intention of the parties, when clearly expressed, in the endeavor to make better contracts for them than they have made for themselves").

A party challenging a liquidated damages clause bears the burden of proving the clause unenforceable. See Jennie-O Foods, Inc. v. United States, 580 F.2d at 414; Farmers Export Co. v. M/V Georgis Prois, Etc., 799 F.2d 159, 162 (5th Cir.1986). That burden is an exacting one, because when damages are uncertain or hard to measure, it naturally follows that it is difficult to conclude that a particular liquidated damages amount or rate is an unreasonable projection of what those damages might be. See Restatement (Second) of Contracts § 356 cmt. b (1981) ("The greater the difficulty either of proving that loss has occurred or of establishing its amount with the requisite certainty … the easier it is to show that the amount fixed is reasonable."); 5 Samuel Williston, A Treatise on the Law of Contracts § 783 (W. Jaeger ed. 1961).

While some state courts are hostile to liquidated damages clauses, federal law "does not look with disfavor upon 'liquidated damages' provisions in contracts." Priebe & Sons, Inc. v. United States, 332 U.S. at 411, 68 S.Ct. at 126. The few federal cases in which liquidated damages clauses have been struck down provide some indication of how rare it is for a federal court to refuse to enforce the parties' bargain on this issue. For example, in Priebe & Sons, Inc. v. United States, the Supreme Court struck down a liquidated damages clause when it was "certain when the contract was made" that the breach in question "plainly would not occasion damage." 332 U.S. at 413, 68 S.Ct. at 126. The contract in Priebe contained two liquidated damages clauses: one for delay in the delivery of eggs and a second for failure to have the eggs inspected and ready for delivery by a specific time prior to the delivery date. The contractor was late in meeting the inspection requirement, but delivered the eggs on time. Thus, only the second liquidated damages clause was at issue in the case. As the Court viewed that clause, a delay in inspection that did not result in a delay in delivery could not cause any loss to the government. At the same time, however, the Court stated that if the breach had involved "failure to get prompt performance when delivery was due," the Court would have had "no doubt of the validity of the provision for 'liquidated damages' when applied under those circumstances." Id. at 412, 68 S.Ct. at 126.

Another case, equally unusual, involved a liquidated damages clause in a lease. In that case, Kothe v. R.C. Taylor Trust, 280 U.S. 224, 50 S.Ct. 142, 74 L.Ed. 382 (1930), the lessee agreed that the filing of a petition for bankruptcy against him would be deemed a breach, and that the lessor would be entitled to recover damages for the breach in an amount equal to the rent due for the remaining term of the lease. The Court held that the amount stipulated "is so disproportionate to any damage reasonably to be anticipated in the circumstances disclosed that we must hold the provision is for an unenforceable penalty." 280 U.S. at 226, 50 S.Ct. at 143. In reaching that conclusion, the Court made clear that it was influenced by the fact that the clause would take effect only in the event of the lessee's bankruptcy, and thus that the parties "were consciously undertaking to contract for payment to be made out of the assets of a bankrupt estate—not for something which the lessee would be required to discharge" and that enforcing the clause would be contrary to the purposes of the Bankruptcy Act. Id. at 226–27, 50 S.Ct. at 143.

In more conventional cases, when the amount of prospective damages are difficult to determine at the outset and the parties agree upon a fixed amount or rate to pay in the event of a breach, thereby bypassing the trouble and expense of litigating the damages issue, federal courts have regularly upheld liquidated damages clauses....

III

In light of these principles, the trial court was correct to grant summary judgment to the government. DJ argues that the government should bear the burden of proving the clause enforceable and that the evidence before the trial court did not establish the government's right to recovery as a matter of law. That argument, however, flies in the face of settled law regarding the burden of proof and the standards for granting summary judgment.

As noted above, it was DJ's burden to prove that the liquidated damages clause was unenforceable. When a party moves for summary judgment on an issue as to which the other party bears the burden of proof, the moving party need not offer evidence, but may obtain summary judgment merely by pointing out to the court "that there is an absence of evidence to support the nonmoving party's case." Celotex Corp. v. Catrett, 477 U.S. 317, 325, 106 S.Ct. 2548, 2554, 91 L.Ed.2d 265 (1986); see Conroy v. Reebok Int'l, Ltd., 14 F.3d 1570, 1575, 29 USPQ2d 1373, 1377 (Fed.Cir.1994); Avia Group Int'l, Inc. v. L.A. Gear Calif., Inc., 853 F.2d 1557, 1560, 7 USPQ2d 1548, 1551 (Fed.Cir.1988).

The only evidence that DJ produced at the summary judgment stage was the affidavit of its president, which alleged that the liquidated damages rate was a "standard" rate, rather than a rate selected specifically for the field pack contract. In addition, DJ relies on the declaration of the contracting officer, which stated that the liquidated damages clause was put into the field pack contract, as well as other contracts for items to be used in Operations Desert Shield/Desert Storm "due to the almost overwhelming need to get war items, such as field packs, into the soldiers' possession as soon as possible."

Neither of those two items of evidence raises an issue of material fact requiring a trial. DJ argues that the contracting officer's statement about the need to get war items into the soldiers' possession quickly shows that the liquidated damages clause was designed to be a "spur to performance" and thus was an unenforceable penalty. That assertion, however, is at odds with several Supreme Court decisions, which make clear that a liquidated damages clause is not rendered unlawful simply because the promisee hopes that it will have the effect of encouraging prompt performance by the promisor. In Robinson v. United States, for example, the Court explained that in the case of construction contracts, "a provision giving liquidated damages for each day's delay is an appropriate means of inducing due performance, or of giving compensation, in case of failure to perform." 261 U.S. at 488, 43 S.Ct. at 421 (emphasis added). Similarly, in Wise v. United States, the Court stated that courts should "look with candor, if not with favor," on liquidated damages clauses "as promoting prompt performance of contracts and adjusting in advance, and amicably, matters the settlement of which through courts would often involve difficulty, uncertainty, delay and expense." 249 U.S. at 366, 39 S.Ct. at 304 (emphasis added). And in United States v. Bethlehem Steel Co., the Court held that a liquidated damages clause may provide "security for the proper performance of the contract as to time of delivery" unless the amount of the liquidated damages is "extraordinarily disproportionate to the damage which might result from the [breach]." 205 U.S. at 121, 27 S.Ct. at 456 (emphasis added).

In support of its assertion that an intention to "spur performance" converts a liquidated damages clause into an unenforceable penalty, DJ cites Priebe & Sons, Inc. v. United States. That case, however, does not stand for such a broad proposition. As noted above, the liquidated damages clause at issue in Priebe & Sons served no compensatory function at all, since there was no possibility that the breach at issue would result in any compensable loss. Thus, the liquidated damages clause was struck down because it served "only as an added spur to performance," and because it constituted "an exaction of punishment for a breach which could produce no possible damage." 332 U.S. at 413, 68 S.Ct. at 127 (emphasis added).

There is no inconsistency in a promisee's seeking assurance of performance through a guarantee of fair compensation for breach. As Williston noted with respect to standard (and legitimate) liquidated damages provisions, "there can be no doubt that these provisions are intended not merely as a provision for an unfortunate and unexpected contingency but also to secure the promisee in the performance of the main obligation and to make the promisor more reluctant to break it." 5 Samuel Williston, supra, § 778, at 692. In this respect, at least, Corbin was in agreement. See 5 Arthur J. Corbin, Corbin on Contracts § 1058, at 339–40 (1964 ed.) ("The purpose of providing for a money payment in case of breach, whether it be called a penalty, a forfeiture, liquidated damages, or merely a sum of money, is primarily to secure the performance promised.... Penalties are said to be in terrorem to induce performance as promised; in large measure the same is true of liquidated damages."). What the policy against penalties is designed to prevent is a penal sanction that is so disproportionate to any damage that could be anticipated that it seeks "to enforce performance of the main purpose of the contract by the compulsion of this very disproportion." 5 Samuel Williston, supra, § 776, at 668 (emphasis added). Nothing that DJ offered or pointed to in the evidence before the trial court remotely suggested that the liquidated damages clause in this case is of that character.

DJ's second argument is that the evidence before the trial court raised a triable issue of fact as to whether the contracting officer set the liquidated damages rate based on a particularized assessment of the facts of this contract. In making that argument, DJ relies on 48 C.F.R. § 12.202(b), which directs that the "rate of liquidated damages used must be reasonable and considered on a case-by-case basis since liquidated damages fixed without any reference to probable actual damages may be held to be a penalty, and therefore unenforceable."

Contrary to DJ's assertion, section 12.202(b) does not create a rule of substantive law requiring a liquidated damages clause to be struck down unless the liquidated damages rate is specially tailored to the particular contract in advance. Section 12.202(b) merely recognizes that a court may refuse to enforce a liquidated damages clause if the liquidated damages amount or rate is shown not to be reasonably related to the actual damages that the promisee could suffer as a result of a breach, and it advises that care should be taken to ensure that the rate or amount is not unreasonable in light of the possible actual damages that could flow from breach. The regulation thus appears to be designed for internal guidance rather than to create rights in contracting parties. In any event, our predecessor court has held that the language on which DJ relies does not require that liquidated damages clauses be "tailor-made for each individual contract." Young Assocs., Inc. v. United States, 471 F.2d at 622 (construing an identically worded predecessor to 48 C.F.R. § 12.202(b) and rejecting the plaintiff's argument that liquidated damages clause is invalid because "no 'case-by-case' consideration was given to the rate of liquidated damages"). Instead, the test is objective; regardless of how the liquidated damage figure was arrived at, the liquidated damages clause will be enforced "if the amount stipulated is reasonable for the particular agreement at the time it is made." Young Assocs., Inc. v. United States, 471 F.2d at 622. See also Higgs v. United States, 546 F.2d at 377 (standard five percent earnest money forfeiture upheld as reasonable liquidated damages, even though not specifically tailored to a particular contract); Hughes Bros., Inc. v. United States, 134 F.Supp. 471, 474, 133 Ct.Cl. 108 (1955) (liquidated damages clause that provided for uniform liquidated damages for a variety of breaches upheld, even though "it had the result that in individual instances there were discrepancies between the stipulated damages and the damages that may actually have been anticipated"). The trial court was therefore correct in holding that it is unnecessary to inquire into the process that the contracting officer followed in arriving at the liquidated damages figure that was put forth in the solicitation and agreed to in the contract.

Finally, DJ argues that there was a triable issue as to whether the liquidated damages rate that the parties agreed upon in the field pack contract was unreasonable. Once again, DJ bore the burden of pointing to evidence establishing a material factual dispute on that issue, and the trial court correctly held that DJ failed to carry that burden.

The damages that are likely to flow from delays in the delivery of goods is often difficult to assess, particularly when the goods are to be produced in the uncertain setting of wartime. See Priebe & Sons, Inc. v. United States, 332 U.S. at 412, 68 S.Ct. at 126; United States v. Bethlehem Steel Co., 205 U.S. at 120–21, 27 S.Ct. at 455–56; Young Assocs., Inc. v. United States, 471 F.2d at 621 ("The Government's damages stemming from delayed receipt of the supplies or construction it ordered are normally hard to measure, and it is usually reasonable to establish some fixed monetary substitute for calculation by trial."). As the Third Circuit put the matter in United States v. Le Roy Dyal Co., 186 F.2d 460, 463 (3d Cir.1950), cert. denied, 341 U.S. 926, 71 S.Ct. 797, 95 L.Ed. 1357 (1951), "[i]n dealing with some matters pertaining to governmental activities, the question of ascertaining how much pecuniary loss is caused by failure of one contracting with the government to keep his promise is especially difficult." To illustrate the point, that court cited a colorful English case that is closely analogous here (id.):

> But how much damage could accrue to the Spanish government because a shipyard failed to deliver, at the time agreed upon, four torpedo-boat destroyers? This question was involved in testing the validity of a provision for liquidated damages for delay in the House of Lords decision in Clydebank Engineering and Shipbuilding Co., Ltd. v. Castaneda. How could the damages be accurately determined? As Lord Halsbury said in an opinion upholding the provision ..."in order to do that properly and to have any real effect upon any tribunal determining that question, one ought to have before one's mind the whole administration of the Spanish Navy."

See also 5 Arthur L. Corbin, supra, § 1072, at 402 ("Since the injury caused by [delay in performance] is nearly always difficult to determine, the courts strongly incline to accept the estimate [in a liquidated damages clause] as reasonable and to enforce it").

In this case, not only did DJ fail to raise a triable question with respect to the difficulty of forecasting damages at the outset, but it also failed to raise any factual issue casting doubt on the reasonableness of the stipulated damages rate. Nor is there anything inherently unreasonable about that rate—a reduction in the contract price of 1/15 of one percent per day, or two percent per month, on a contract that was supposed to be completed within a period of only a few months. In fact, the decision of our predecessor court in Pacific Hardware & Steel Co. v. United States, 49 Ct.Cl. 327, 1914 WL 1416 (1914), provides strong support for the reasonableness of the liquidated damages rate selected in this case. The military supply contract at issue in Pacific Hardware contained a liquidated damages clause providing for a deduction of 1/10 of one percent of the contract price for each day of delay after the scheduled delivery date (a slightly higher rate than the liquidated damages rate at issue in this case). Noting that a month's delay would result in the withholding of only three percent of the contract price, the court ruled (49 Ct.Cl. at 334):

> This basis of ascertaining the damages, if we are to treat it as such, does not appear to be unreasonable or oppressive. It indicates, we think, that the parties had in mind the inherent difficulty of proving actual damages and the differences that might arise between the parties in making settlements if there were delays in delivery. The representatives of the Government on the one hand could reason that it was desirable to have a provision in the contract which would render unnecessary any differences in settlement; while the contractor on the other hand could reason that such a course was preferable, because if for no other reason it would eliminate the delays incident to lawsuits brought to secure settlements.

In addition to being of roughly the same dimension as the liquidated damages rate in this case, the rate in Pacific Hardware also appears to have been a "standard" rate, as there were at least two other contemporaneous Court of Claims decisions upholding liquidated damages clauses containing the same liquidated damages rate of 1/10 of one percent per day. See Morris v. United States, 50 Ct.Cl. 154 (1915); Crane Co. v. United States, 46 Ct.Cl. 343 (1911). Despite the "standard" nature of the rate, the Court of Claims found the rate to be reasonable in all three cases. In this case, likewise, DJ has failed to point to any reason to believe that the liquidated damages rate of 1/15 of one percent per day agreed upon by the parties is so exorbitant in light of the prospective injury to the government that it is plainly penal in nature and therefore may not be enforced.

AFFIRMED.

Notes and Questions

1. The opinion fairly reflects the very low level of success that government contractors have in challenging liquidated damage clauses. Clearly a contractor gets nowhere simply by complaining that the liquidated damage clause was boilerplate in no way tailored to an estimate, crude or otherwise, of the actual damages. What would it take for a contractor to get at least a hearing? Suppose the contractor had a declaration from the functional equivalent of the government's declarant, e.g., a former Army logistics management specialist who stated that late delivery could be expected to produce actual damage of well under one percent per month owing (hypothetically) to the Army having stockpiles of what it was procuring. Or suppose the contractor's president declared, from a market survey, that the Army could hire contractors to produce faster than scheduled by paying one percent more per month, showing that the Army could put a ceiling on any actual damage that way. Would either of these suffice?

2. In contrast to sanctions like termination for default or debarment, liquidated damages seems more non-normative in its straightforwardly monetary quality. Could it be argued that liquidated damages permit—as private contract law remedies do, but government contract law penalties do not—the operation of the doctrine of efficient breach? That is, could DJ, as it fell behind schedule, make the rational judgment that it was more efficient to breach and to pay liquidated damages than to cancel some other (hypothetical) more lucrative private contract it was fulfilling? Moreover, from the government's perspective, note how much easier it is to administer liquidated damages—simply by the contracting officer doing a calculation and making a withholding from payment—that it is to terminate for default or to debar. So, to either side, does it matter that much how uneven or disproportionate the liquidated damages are to estimated actual damages, so long as they give clear guidance to the contractor and administrative simplicity to the government?

D. Set-Off

H.T. Johnson, Acting Secretary of the Navy, Appellant, v. All-State Construction, Inc., Appellee

No. 02-1442.

329 F.3d 848

United States Court of Appeals, Federal Circuit

May 21, 2003

Before RADER, LINN and DYK, Circuit Judges.

DYK, Circuit Judge.

The Secretary of the Navy ("the Navy") appeals the decision of the Armed Services Board of Contract Appeals ("Board") in favor of All-State Construction ("All-State" or "the contractor"). *All-State Constr., Inc.*, ASBCA No. 50,586, 02-1 B.C.A. (CCH) 31,794, at 157,019-21 (Feb. 21, 2002). This case presents the question of whether the Navy was entitled to withhold progress payments from All-State. The Navy offers two justifications for the withholding: (1) that the government is entitled to withhold progress payments when a default termination is imminent; and (2) that the government is entitled to withhold progress payments pursuant to its common-law right of set-off and also pursuant to section 1.12.2.b. of the contract. We disagree with the Navy's first theory, but agree with the second. Accordingly, we reverse the Board's decision and remand.

BACKGROUND

On September 30, 1994, the Navy awarded All-State a fixed-price contract valued at $982,000 for the construction of a hazardous waste storage facility. The contract required completion by May 13, 1995. The Navy unilaterally extended the period for completion to September 12, 1995. The extension was based, in part, on the unavailability of the site during a portion of that period. The project was not completed by the extended completion date.

In response to revised construction schedules submitted by All-State, the Navy sent letters dated October 31, 1995, and August 5, 1996, informing All-State that the Navy was forbearing termination of the contract for default while reserving the right to later terminate the contract for default and to assess liquidated damages. The August 5 letter provided a revised completion date of November 14, 1996. However, in a "Show Cause Notice" dated October 4, 1996, the Navy indicated that "[a]t present it is apparent that the work will not be completed by 14 November 1996." (J.A. at 22.) The notice further stated that "[s]ince you have failed … to make progress toward completing the work by 14 November 1996, the Government is considering terminating the contract under the provisions for default of this contract." *Id.*

On October 9, 1996, All-State submitted an invoice requesting payment of $120,878.67, representing compensation for 34 percent completion of the project less reimbursement previously received. There is no claim on this appeal that the progress payment had not been earned. The Board specifically found that the amount of the claimed progress payment was an "undisputed earned amount for completed work." *All-State,* 02-1 B.C.A. (CCH) at 157,020. However, the claimed progress payment amount was less than the government's pending claim for $180,900 in liquidated damages. *Id.* On October 16, 1996, the contracting officer informed All-State that he was recommending termination of the contract for default. On October 18, 1996, the Navy contracting officer refused payment of the October 9, invoice because "[t]he amount to be retained for liquidated damages exceeds the amount of the invoice." *Id.* The contract was terminated for default on November 26, 1996.

On March 28, 1997, All-State appealed the Navy's default termination of the contract to the Board. The complaint included four counts, all requesting that the termination be treated as a termination for the convenience of the government.

* * *

All-State moved for summary judgment on all four counts. The Board granted summary judgment in favor of All-State on the fourth count, finding that the Navy breached the contract by retaining 38 percent of the amount that All-State had earned. The Board held that Federal Acquisition Regulation ("FAR")§ 52.232-5(d) as incorporated in the contract limited the permissible retention of progress payments to 10 percent of the amount earned. The Board concluded that the contract was terminated for the convenience of the Navy and that All-State's obligation to perform was discharged. The Board stated "[i]n view of this result, we need not address the issues in the other counts." *All-State,* 02-1 B.C.A. (CCH) at 157,021. The Navy timely appealed.

DISCUSSION

* * *

The sole issue on appeal is whether the Navy's failure to make the progress payment operated as a breach of contract because the amount withheld was more than ten percent of the earned amount.

I

The Navy first argues that it permissibly withheld the progress payment because it was considering terminating the contract for default, and default termination was imminent. Thus, the Navy's position is that, when the government is about to declare a default termination, it is discharged from its contractual obligation to make progress payments because of the possibility that the contractor owes breach damages to the government. We conclude that, in the absence of a contract clause permitting such action, the Navy had no such authority.

The Navy does not cite any provision of the contract or regulation as authorizing it to withhold the progress payment in anticipation of a default determination. Instead, the Navy argues that "[t]he purpose of progress payments is to provide the contractor with the funds that he needs to continue performance," a purpose that was vitiated by the impending default. (Appellant's Br. at 7–8.) The FAR, as incorporated into the contract, expressly defines the government's contract termination rights for default. 48 C.F.R. § 52.249-10 (1984). There is no *regulation*, however, *permitting* the government to withhold progress payments when the government is considering declaring a default termination. The government has no right to withhold progress payments simply because it is considering a termination for default, except to the extent of the government's contractual ten percent retainage rights.

* * *

II

The government alternatively argues that it was entitled to withhold progress payments by virtue of its common law right of set-off, which it urges is specifically recognized in the language of this contract. The seminal case recognizing the government's set-off rights is the Supreme Court's decision in *United States v. Munsey Trust Co.*, 332 U.S. 234, 108 Ct.Cl. 765, 67 S.Ct. 1599, 91 L.Ed. 2022 (1947). In *Munsey*, the government had retained percentages of the progress payments due to the contractor on six contracts. *Id.* at 237, 67 S.Ct. 1599. The contractor defaulted on a subsequent contract, resulting in damages to the government, which the government set off against the retained progress payments. *Id.* The Court held that "[t]he government has the same right [of set-off] "which belongs to every creditor, to apply the unappropriated moneys of his debtor, in his hands, in extinguishment of the debts due to him." "*Id.* at 239, 67 S.Ct. 1599.

This court and our predecessor court have repeatedly recognized the government's right of set-off.

* * *

The set-off right applies to government claims both under other contracts, *see William Green*, 477 F.2d at 936, and under the same contract, *Cecile*, 995 F.2d at 1054.

Of necessity, the contractor here recognizes that the government has broad set-off rights, but makes a number of arguments as to why the government's set-off rights did not justify the withholding under the circumstances in this case.

First, the contractor argues that the government's set-off right is defeated by the FAR provision concerning progress payments ("the Retainage Clause"), which was incorporated in All-State's contract with the Navy. In other words, the contractor argues that the government surrendered its set-off right. The Board agreed, stating that if the contract is "interpreted as permitting the retention, before substantial completion of the work, of liquidated delay damages in excess of the express limit in the FAR [Retainage] clause, it is in violation of the FAR clause which is mandated by regulation, and the Government cannot by law benefit from it." *All-State*, 02-1 B.C.A. (CCH) at 157,020-21 (citing *Beta Sys., Inc. v. United States*, 838 F.2d 1179, 1185 (Fed.Cir.1988)). The Retainage Clause provides:

> If the Contracting Officer finds that satisfactory progress was achieved during any period for which a progress payment is to be made, the Contracting Officer shall authorize payment to be made in full. *However, if satisfactory progress has not been made, the Contracting Officer may retain a maximum of 10 percent of the amount of the payment until satisfactory progress is achieved.* When the work is substantially complete, the Contracting Officer may retain from previously withheld funds and future progress payments that amount the Contracting Officer considers adequate for protection of the Government and shall release to the Contractor all the remaining withheld funds. Also, on completion and acceptance of each separate building, public work, or other division of the contract, for which the price is stated separately in the contract, payment shall be made for the completed work without retention of a percentage.

48 C.F.R.§ 52.232-5(e) (1989) (emphasis added). We do not agree that the right of set-off was limited by this provision.

Both the Supreme Court and this court have made clear that the government's set-off right can be defeated only by explicit language. As we stated in *Applied*: "it is well settled that the government retains its setoff right *unless there is some explicit statutory or contractual provision that bars its exercise.*" 144 F.3d at 1476 (emphasis added) (citing *Munsey Trust*, 332 U.S. at 239, 67 S.Ct. 1599; *Marre v. United States*, 117 F.3d 297, 302 (5th Cir.1997)); *see also Cecile*, 995 F.2d at 1055.

* * *

The Retainage Clause here does not contain explicit language defeating the government's common law set-off right, but rather narrowly limits the scope of the government's retainage rights "if satisfactory progress has not been made ... [to] a maximum of 10 percent of the amount of the payment until satisfactory progress is achieved." 48 C.F.R. § 52.232-5(e) (1989). One purpose of contract "retainage is [as] an incentive to complete the contract." *Fireman's Fund Ins. Co. v. United States*, 909 F.2d 495, 498 (Fed.Cir.1990). Retainage rights also serve to protect the interests of the government against potential defaults by the contractor. *Nat'l Sur. Corp. v. United States*, 118 F.3d 1542, 1545 (Fed.Cir.1997); *Pigeon*, 27 Ct.Cl. at 175–76 (noting that retainage is used as indemnity by the government). No proof is required that the contractor has committed a breach of the contract, as the withholding is permitted to secure against possible future breaches or undiscovered prior breaches.

Common law set-off rights serve an entirely different purpose, "to apply the unappropriated moneys of his debtor, in his hands, in extinguishment of the debts due to him." *Gratiot v. United States*, 40 U.S. 336, 370, 15 Pet. 336, 10 L.Ed. 759 (1841). The set-off right is not an indemnity against a possible future breach, but rather offsets a current payable debt. Section 32.611 of the FAR (though not incorporated in this contract), in fact, recognizes the government's right to set off and makes no reference to the ten percent limit on retainage. 48 C.F.R. § 32.611 (1994).[3] The very existence of § 32.611 thus

---

3. FAR § 32.611, entitled Routine setoff provides:
    If a disbursing officer is the responsible official for collection of a contract debt, or is

demonstrates that the FAR provision at issue here, 48 C.F.R. § 52.232-5, was not designed to limit the government's set-off right.

While not determinative, we note also that the contract expressly limited the government's obligation to pay in clause 1.12.2 ("the Set-Off Clause"), which provides:

> The obligation of the Government to make any of the payments required under any of the provisions of this contract shall, in the discretion of the Officer in Charge of Construction, be *subject to ... [a]ny claims which the Government may have against the Contractor under or in connection with this contract.*

(J.A. at 19) (emphasis added). This provision also does not limit the government's right to set off only to funds the government has retained under FAR § 52.232-5(d). Instead, it refers to "[a]ny claims which the Government may have against the Contractor."

The contractor also argues that the government did not properly exercise its set-off right. All-State's argument regarding the procedure that the government must follow when effectuating a set-off is based on *Citizens Bank of Maryland v. Strumpf*, 516 U.S. 16, 116 S.Ct. 286, 133 L.Ed.2d 258 (1995), in which the Supreme Court stated that "a setoff has not occurred until three steps have been taken: (i) a decision to effectuate a setoff, (ii) some action accomplishing the setoff, and (iii) a recording of the setoff." *Id.* at 19, 116 S.Ct. 286. *The contracting officer here took all of these actions.* In withholding the progress payment, the government stated that it would not make the progress payment because "[t]he amount to be retained for liquidated damages exceeds the amount of the invoice." (J.A. at 27.) This notice satisfied each of the three requirements. It reflected "a decision to effectuate a setoff"; it reflected an act to accomplish the set-off; and it recorded the set-off. This case is quite unlike *Citizens Bank,* where the party purporting to perform the set-off, in fact, did not seek to "permanently and absolutely" retain the funds. 516 U.S. at 19, 116 S.Ct. 286. Instead, the party sought only to temporarily retain the funds. The government here did seek to permanently and absolutely retain the funds in settlement of the liquidated damages owed it.

The contractor argues that the set-off cannot precede a "final" decision by the contracting officer, meaning apparently a final decision to terminate the contract. In fact, the FAR provisions incorporated in the contract clearly contemplate a claim for liquidated damages either at the time of the default termination or earlier. Under FAR § 49.402-7, "[i]f a contract is terminated for default *or if a course of action in lieu of termination for default is followed* (see 49.402-4), the contracting officer shall promptly ascertain and make demand for any liquidated damages to which the Government is entitled under the contract." 48 C.F.R. § 49.402-7(a) (1994) (emphasis added). The allowable courses of action under FAR § 49.402-4 included "[p]ermit[ing] the contractor, the surety, or the guarantor, to continue performance of the contract under a revised delivery schedule." *Id.* § 49.402-4(a). Thus, the contracting officer's request for liquidated damages using the set-off procedure was proper, whether or not a final default termination notice had issued.

---

notified of the debt by the responsible official and has contractor invoices on hand for payment, the disbursing officer shall make an appropriate setoff. The disbursing officer shall give the contractor an explanation of the setoff. To the extent that the setoff reduces the debt, the explanation shall replace the demand prescribed in 32.610.
48 C.F.R. § 32.611 (1983).

Similarly, the contractor argues that the withholding of the progress payment was improper because the contractor was still performing under the contract. According to the contractor, the government breached "at the moment the Government assert[ed] setoff threats against progress payments on a contract on which the contractor is still progressing, despite the fact that the contractor may itself [have been] in default on [the] contract." (Appellee's Br. at 43–44.) For this proposition the contractor cites *William Green*, 477 F.2d at 938. However, the government's breach in *William Green* was predicated on the fact that "[t]here were ... no liquidated damages and no excess construction costs which could properly be offset against the [contracts]. *Id.* at 937. The government's refusal to make the progress payments in that case was therefore improper. *Id.* at 938. [Here, by contrast, no such determination has been made.]

Thus, the Navy under the contract had the right to set off any amounts due as liquidated damages. The exercise of that right cannot breach the contract, and cannot be the basis for defeating the default termination, or converting the default termination to a termination for convenience.

CONCLUSION

For the foregoing reasons, the judgment of the Board is reversed and the matter is remanded for further proceedings consistent with this decision.

REVERSED AND REMANDED.

E. Suspension and Debarment

Suspension and debarment constitute a mechanism by which the government formally decides not to do business with particular contractors for a period of time. This may arise either out of ethical issues of the kinds just discussed, or issues demonstrating contractor irresponsibility that may not involve a primarily ethical dimension, e.g., heavy-duty incompetent failures to perform. However, a debarment does involve the public imposition of a particular status upon a contractor, so that it kicks in some of the legal constraints that apply to normative judgments. Moreover, the procurement lawyer uses an understanding of suspension and debarment in two ways: to handle such cases, and to advise on how not to end up in that situation.

For the government, this constitutes a radical, but sometimes necessary, decision to deny itself the benefits of doing business with a particular contractor. For the contractor, this constitutes a very serious change of status, particularly if much or most of its economic activity comes from government sources. On both sides, apart from the economic impact, suspension and debarment constitute a major normative statement by the government against a contractor who has engaged in wrongdoing. Resort to that sanction signifies a strong governmental and societal stance against such wrongdoing, which may, depending on one's perspective and the pertinent factors, be considered either just and right to obtain respect for the law, or harsh and oppressive in its impact.

Suspension and debarment follow government-wide procedures laid down in FAR Part 9.4. A classic situation occurs when a contractor faces a fraud investigation. The government may immediately suspend the contractor to await the results of the investigation. Suspension can occur on limited evidence, such as the mere indictment (without adjudication) on the criminal fraud charges. The government may or may not give advance notice of a proposed suspension, and there may or may not be a hearing at which the contractor can oppose the suspension. While there are no hard and fast rules about duration, suspension would often, in the absence of debarment proceedings, be a matter of weeks or months, not more.

Suppose that the fraud investigation produces strong evidence of serious wrongdoing by a contractor, such as suffices for the contractor to plead guilty to felony fraud charges. The government may follow up that criminal conviction by initiating a debarment proceeding, seeking to preclude a contractor from receiving new contract awards for a specified time, usually not more than three years. In that proceeding, the government puts forth its basis for debarment and the contractor may both counter that basis and raise mitigating factors.

Government contracting lawyers obviously have a large role in fashioning, or defending, suspension and debarment proceedings. Moreover, awareness of these ultimate sanctions influences all the preliminary steps taken in situations of potentially serious charges against contractors. For example, counsel for a contractor may urge that it implement compliance procedures, make voluntary disclosures, cooperate with investigations, admit wrongdoing, and negotiate civil settlements and even criminal pleas, all with an eye to persuading the government not to push hard in the end for suspension and debarment.

For further discussions of the subject of this section, see: Christopher R. Yukins, *Ethics In Procurement: New Challenges After A Decade Of Reform,* 38 Procrmt. Law. 3 (Spring 2003); James J. McCullough, Abram J. Pafford, *Government Contract Suspension & Debarment—What Every Contractor Needs To Know,* 45 GC ¶ 465 (Nov. 19, 2003); Anthony H. Anikeeff, *Integrity & Business Ethics In Federal Contracting: Avoiding The "Blacklisting" Minefield,* 48 Fed. Law. 42 (Mar./Apr. 2001); Gary Krump, *The VA's Suspension/Debarment Program,* 33 Procurement Law., Spring 1998, at 10; Paul Griffin, *Debarment for Federal Contractors Who Knowingly Hire Unauthorized Alien Workers,* 10 Geo. Immgr. L.J. 532 (1996); Steven D. Gordon, *Suspension and Debarment from Federal Programs,* 23 Pub. Cont. L.J. 573 (1994); Edwin J. Tomko & Kathy C. Weinberg, *After the Fall: Conviction, Debarment, and Double Jeopardy,* 21 Pub. Cont. L.J. 355 (1992); Brian D. Shannon, *The Government-wide Debarment and Suspension Regulations After a Decade,* 21 Pub. Cont. L.J. 370 (1992).

United States of America, Plaintiff-Appellee, v. Fred L. Hatfield, Sr., d/b/a HVAC Construction Company, Incorporated, Defendant-Appellant

United States Court of Appeals, Fourth Circuit
108 F.3d 67
Decided March 7, 1997

Before MURNAGHAN and NIEMEYER, Circuit Judges, and HARVEY, Senior United States District Judge for the District of Maryland, sitting by designation.

Affirmed and remanded by published opinion.

NIEMEYER, Circuit Judge:

This case presents the question of whether a debarred government contractor may be prosecuted criminally for the same fraudulent conduct that led to the debarment. The defendant, arguing that his debarment constituted punishment, asserts that the Double

Jeopardy Clause of the Fifth Amendment bars his subsequent criminal prosecution. Because we conclude that debarment is civil and remedial, we reject the argument and affirm the district court's order refusing to dismiss his indictment.

In a twelve-count indictment, the government charges that over a period of several years beginning in September 1990, Fred L. Hatfield, Sr., doing business as HVAC Construction Company, made false and fraudulent statements to the government. The indictment charges that on several occasions when bidding for government work, Hatfield fraudulently misrepresented that he had never had a government contract terminated for default. It also charges that in performing government contracts, Hatfield had on various occasions made certifications for payment that fraudulently stated that work had been performed and that payments had been made to his subcontractors. The government further charges that on one occasion Hatfield presented a false subcontractor invoice.

This conduct alleged in the government's indictment was also the basis for Hatfield's earlier debarment from government contracting. In July 1994, the Department of the Army debarred Hatfield and his companies from all government contracting for a period of 26 months. That debarment, Hatfield claims, cost Hatfield and his company $1,147,227 in attorneys fees, lost profits, and out-of-pocket expenses. He attributes the majority of that assessment to lost profits and his own unpaid compensation.

Hatfield filed a motion to dismiss the indictment, arguing that under United States v. Halper, 490 U.S. 435, 109 S.Ct. 1892, 104 L.Ed.2d 487 (1989), his debarment constituted punishment because it caused him far more loss than the loss sustained by the government. Accordingly, he argued, his current prosecution would result in a second punishment in violation of the Double Jeopardy Clause. From the district court's order denying Hatfield's motion to dismiss the indictment, this interlocutory appeal followed.

The Double Jeopardy Clause, which provides, "nor shall any person be subject for the same offence to be twice put in jeopardy of life or limb," U.S. Const. amend. V, prohibits not only successive criminal prosecutions but also successive punishments for the same offense. Thus, if the government's debarment of Hatfield and his companies constituted punishment for double jeopardy purposes, he is entitled to have his subsequent criminal prosecution dismissed. As Hatfield argues, it does not matter whether the debarment preceded or succeeded the criminal prosecution. If both are punishment, the second proceeding is barred. See United States v. Reed, 937 F.2d 575, 576 n. 3 (11th Cir.1991); United States v. Bizzell, 921 F.2d 263, 267 (10th Cir.1990). If, on the other hand, debarment is a civil proceeding, it does not implicate the Double Jeopardy Clause because that clause prohibits "two criminal trials [or] two criminal punishments." One Lot Emerald Cut Stones v. United States, 409 U.S. 232, 235, 93 S.Ct. 489, 492, 34 L.Ed.2d 438 (1972). To determine whether debarment is civil or criminal, we look to (1) whether the procedure was designed to be remedial, and (2) whether the remedy provided, even if designated as civil, "is so unreasonable or excessive that it transforms what was clearly intended as a civil remedy into a criminal penalty." Id. at 237, 93 S.Ct. at 493; see also United States v. Ursery, ___ U.S. ___ , ___ , 116 S.Ct. 2135, 2147, 135 L.Ed.2d 549 (1996); United States v. One Assortment of 89 Firearms, 465 U.S. 354, 362, 104 S.Ct. 1099, 1104–05, 79 L.Ed.2d 361 (1984).

Debarment is the action taken against a contractor to exclude it from government contracting for a specified period. See 48 C.F.R. § 9.403. The action is an agency proceeding which is "as informal as is practicable, consistent with the principles of fundamental fairness." 48 C.F.R. § 9.406-3(b)(1). The cause for debarment, if not based on a conviction or judgment, must be established by "a preponderance of the evidence." 48 C.F.R. § 9.406-

3(d)(3). Finally, debarment cannot be imposed to punish but only to serve the remedial goal of protecting the government. See 48 C.F.R. §9.402(b).

There can be little doubt that debarment was designed to be a civil proceeding. By its own procedural rules, it may not be imposed for punishment, but only to protect the government in its dealings with contractors. See id. Moreover, its procedures are informal and the proof demanded is by a preponderance of the evidence. See 48 C.F.R. §9.406-3(b)(1), (d)(3). Finally, the remedial purpose is linked to specific conduct that relates to the protection of the government from fraud, neglect, nonperformance, or other conduct lacking integrity, with a focus on the "present responsibility" of the contractor. 48 C.F.R. §9.406-2; see also United States v. Bizzell, 921 F.2d 263, 267 (10th Cir.1990) ("debarment constitutes the rough remedial justice permissible as a prophylactic governmental action" (internal quotation marks omitted)); cf. Ursery, ___ U.S. ___ , ___ , 116 S.Ct. at 2148 (even though in rem civil forfeiture has "certain punitive aspects," it is designed to serve important nonpunitive goals and is, therefore, a remedial sanction).

We also believe that debarment for 26 months is not so "unreasonable or excessive" as to transform what is designed as a civil remedy into a criminal penalty. Hatfield is accused of fraudulently misrepresenting material facts on numerous occasions over a span of years, and of overstating a subcontractor's billing by more than $10,000. These facts raise a serious question about his "present responsibility" as an honest and dependable contractor to the government. In United States v. Glymph, 96 F.3d 722 (4th Cir.1996), where the facts are strikingly similar—Glymph was debarred for knowingly supplying the government with parts that did not conform to purchase order specifications—we rejected the argument that a four-year debarment was "overwhelmingly disproportionate" where the government paid more than $40,000 for nonconforming parts. See id. at 725–26. We so held even though the regulations provide that generally debarment should not exceed three years. See 48 C.F.R. §9.406-4; see also Glymph, 96 F.3d at 725 n.*. We believe the holding of Glymph controls the disposition of this case. The government estimates that Hatfield caused direct losses between $40,000 and $60,000, which does not take into account victims and losses sustained by subcontractors and suppliers whom Hatfield did not pay. In these circumstances, the 26-month debarment was not so unreasonable or excessive as to transform the remedial sanctions into a criminal penalty.

For the same reasons given in Ursery, we believe that debarment here is not subject to the same type of "particularized assessment" which Halper requires for fixed-amount penalties. That is, the government does not seek the return of a particular quantity of funds but instead seeks to protect the quality of its acquisition programs. Of course, the debarred contractor may quantify its losses in terms of potential profits, and the government may even be able to attach a number to much of the reason for debarment. For instance, we identified a $40,000 loss in nonconforming parts in Glymph. See 96 F.3d at 726. But the government may also debar a contractor for nonmonetary causes such as those affecting the responsibility of a contractor or for disreputable business practices. See 48 C.F.R. §9.406-2(a)(5), (c). Where the sanction and the purposes it seeks to achieve are qualitative rather than merely quantitative, the Halper inquiry is inapplicable. Instead, the question becomes the one raised in Ursery—whether the debarment is in effect so unreasonable and excessive, i.e. so punitive, that we must, from the "clearest proof" conclude that the proceeding is not civil but criminal in nature. See Ursery, ___ U.S. ___ , 116 S.Ct. at 2148–49.

In the case before us, Hatfield has not carried the burden of demonstrating with clearest proof that his 26-month debarment is disproportionate to the benefits received by the government in protec ting it against the effects of willful failures to perform in accordance with the terms of government contracts, the effects of a history of failures to perform, and the adverse effect of having the government contract with an irresponsible contractor. See 48 C.F.R. § 9.406-2(b)(1), (c); § 9.402(b); see also Glymph, 96 F.3d at 725–26. Indeed, we doubt that any debarment within the three-year guideline established in the regulations, see 48 C.F.R. § 9.406-4, could present a case sufficiently punitive to implicate the Double Jeopardy Clause. Cf. Glymph, 96 F.3d at 725 n.* (holding a four-year debarment not to be of constitutional significance).

Accordingly, we affirm the district court's order denying Hatfield's motion to dismiss the indictment in this case. The case is remanded for further proceedings.

Notes and Questions

1. Is it a fair comparison, as to proportionality that the government estimates that Hatfield caused losses of $40,000–$60,000, while Hatfield pegs the cost of debarment over $1 million? Or is that a comparison of apples and oranges? What Hatfield loses in lost profits, presumably some other contractor gains.

2. While the opinion explains that the government does not inflict (criminal) punishment, surely debarment has a normative dimension and a deterrant effect on potential wrongdoers. So, how much due process shold be provided? Enough to match the potent effect it has on the contractor? Or less so as not to clog the wheels of efficient government action to safeguard the fisc from plainly bad contractors?

3. There came a time at the end of the big 1980s defense buildup, when quite a large percentage of the top 100 Defense Department contractors were under investigation for crimes or had even been convicted. At the time, the Defense Department, with some support from the Justice Department, successfully argued that to debar many of these would hurt the government. So instead, the government put an emphasis on foregoing debarment when contractors would develop an internal control system for abuse. Critics in public interest groups and in Congress regarded this as a sellout. Was it?

4. A contractor's criminal conviction is cause for debarment, but even a convicted contractor still has a due process opportunity to oppose debarment and may succeed in doing so. *Present* responsibility (lack of which may be inferred from past acts) is the applicable test. In making debarment determinations, the FAR obliges the debarring official to consider the following factors: What self-policing and internal control mechanisms were put in place by the contractor prior to the government investigation; whether the contractor itself alerted the government agency to the cited conduct; the degree of cooperation between the government and the contractor; any restitution agreements; whether appropriate disciplinary actions were taken with respect to wrongdoers; implementation of remedial steps; overhaul of review and control procedures and ethics training programs; whether the contractor has had time to eliminate the circumstances that led to cause for debarment; and whether the contractor acknowledges the severity of the misconduct.

5. Once the government has notified the contractor of a debarment determination, the burden shifts to the contractor to establish that the decision was arbitrary or capricious, or that mitigating factors (including but not limited to those described above) were not considered. See For a further discussion of this issue, see Gary Krump, *The VA's Suspension/Debarment Program,* 33 Procurement Lawyer, Spring 1998, at 10; Brian D. Shannon, *Debarment and Suspension Revisited: Fewer Eggs in the Basket?* 44 Cath. U. L. Rev. 363 (1995); Steven D. Gordon, *Suspension and Debarment From Federal Programs,* 23 Pub. Cont. L.J. 573 (1994); 10 USC § 2393; FAR 9.403 (definitions); 9.406-1(lists mitigating

factors); *S.D. Carruthers Sons, Inc.*, DBCA No. 95-A-124-D17, 1996 WL 368751 (debarment vacated on review of mitigating factors).

Sameena Inc., an Oregon corporation dba Samtech Research; Sameena Ali; Mirza Ali, Plaintiffs-Appellants, v. United States Air Force; v. Carol Moore; Steve Bangs; Alan Schoenberg; Maxwell Air Force Base; Pilson; Mike Thomason, Defendants-Appellees.

No. 97-15252
United States Court of Appeals, Ninth Circuit
147 F.3d 1148
Decided July 6, 1998

Before: D. W. NELSON, BOOCHEVER, and REINHARDT, Circuit Judges.

D.W. NELSON, Circuit Judge:

This case arises from a contractor's alleged attempts to defraud the government and the government's efforts to bar the contractor from bidding on future government projects. The appellants bring civil rights and common-law tort claims against a number of individual employees of the United States Air Force (the "Air Force") and argue that the Air Force's decision to debar them for a period of fifteen years was arbitrary and capricious, in violation of the Administrative Procedure Act ("APA"), codified in pertinent part at 5 U.S.C. § 704. The district court dismissed the claims against the individual defendants and granted summary judgment in favor of the Air Force on the APA claims. We have jurisdiction pursuant to 28 U.S.C. § 1291. Although we affirm the dismissal of the claims against the individual defendants, we reverse the district court's summary judgment because we conclude that the Department of the Air Force (the "Air Force") violated the appellants' constitutional right to due process when it denied them an evidentiary hearing, as required by 48 C.F.R. § 9.406-3(b)(2).

FACTUAL AND PROCEDURAL BACKGROUND

In February 1992, the Social Security Administration ("SSA") solicited bids from computer suppliers for a quantity of microcomputer workstations. University Systems, Inc. ("USI"), a California-based corporation of which Appellant Mirza Ali was Chief Executive Officer, submitted a proposal to the SSA in April 1992. USI's bid was deemed competitive, and USI provided the SSA with samples of its products for further evaluation.

During this process, questions arose regarding whether a mouse device included in the proposal was manufactured in compliance with the Trade Agreements Act of 1979, 19 U.S.C. §§ 2501–2582. While this matter was being investigated, it was discovered that two USI officers had submitted a fraudulent letter to the SSA. The SSA consequently eliminated USI from consideration for the workstation contract.

Subsequently, the United States Department of Health and Human Services ("HHS"), of which the SSA is part, commenced "debarment" proceedings against USI and four of its officers, including Mirza Ali, seeking to disqualify them from submitting government contract proposals for three years. On February 2, 1994, USI, Mirza Ali, and the other USI officers were debarred from government contracting through February 18, 1996.

Mirza Ali's wife, Appellant Sameena Ali, is president and sole director of Appellant Sameena Inc. ("Sameena"), which was incorporated in February 1993 by Keith Griffen, a USI officer. Each of the appellants uses aliases: Sameena Ali sometimes goes by "Sameena

Ikbal." Mirza Ali sometimes goes by "Zulfiqar Eqbal." Sameena Inc. operates under the assumed name "Samtech Research, Inc." ("Samtech").

Like USI, Samtech supplied computer workstations to government agencies. In June 1995, an Alabama-based contracting squadron of the Air Force issued a contract solicitation for laptop computers. An amendment to the solicitation indicated that the buyer was V. Carol Moore.

Samtech submitted a proposal to Moore in July 1995. Included in Samtech's proposal was a certification that neither Samtech nor any of its principals was debarred or proposed for debarment at that time. The certification defined "principals" as "officers; directors; owners; partners; and persons having primary management or supervisory responsibilities within a business entity." Because the Air Force solicitation required that bidders have at least three years of experience as a government contractor, Samtech's proposal also included a list of "Government Contract Awards." Among them was a contract with the United States Department of Energy (the "DoE contract") that Sameena had obtained in 1994 through a novation from USI.

In response to a query, Samtech sent Moore a letter in September 1995 explaining that Samtech "started doing business with the Federal Government by acquiring a contract for the supply of ADP equipment to the United States Department of Energy in 1992." On further investigation, Moore discovered that the contract actually had been awarded to USI in 1992 and had only been novated to Samtech in 1994. Moore also obtained bank documents indicating that "Sameena Ikbal" and "Zulfiqar Eqbal" were authorized to make withdrawals from Samtech's accounts and were, respectively, "President/Secretary" and "Vice President" of the corporation. This information appeared to Moore to contradict the statements made in Samtech's contract proposal.

On the basis of these apparent misrepresentations, Samtech was deemed ineligible for the Air Force contract. Moreover, in December 1995, the Air Force Contracting Officer, Gladys McBride, submitted a recommendation that Samtech be debarred. McBride appended the entire administrative file to her recommendation, including an affidavit by Moore describing her investigations.

On December 26, 1995, Sameena Inc., Samtech, Sameena Ali, and Mirza Ali ("the appellants") were notified that they had been proposed for debarment (and, in Mirza Ali's case, an "extension" of debarment). The notices were accompanied by memoranda setting forth the grounds for the proposed debarments. The notices also invited the appellants to submit information and argument in opposition to the debarment.

The appellants included in their response a letter dated February 21, 1996, from an official at Samtech's bank. The letter stated that the document indicating that Zulfiqar Eqbal was Vice President of Samtech—a bank signature card—had been "corrected" after the bank was informed "that Eqbal was not a corporate officer" of Sameena or Samtech. The submission also included copies of checks written on Sameena's bank accounts. A number of these checks were signed by "Zulfiqar Eqbal" and were made out to a variety of payees, including physicians, a sports club, and Eqbal (Mirza Ali) himself. The appellants' submission also requested an evidentiary hearing on the issue of Mirza Ali's role at Samtech. Notwithstanding the submission, and without an evidentiary hearing, the Air Force issued a final decision in June 1996 to debar Sameena/Samtech and Sameena Ali—and to extend Mirza Ali's debarment—until December 2010. The debarment was based on findings that the appellants had (1) made false statements regarding Samtech's experience as a contractor, (2) provided false certifications that none of Samtech's principals was debarred, and (3) participated in a scheme to avoid the effects of USI's debarment.

On August 30, 1996, the appellants filed two complaints in the United States District Court for the Northern District of California. The first complaint, brought by Mirza Ali against HHS and against six agency employees in their individual capacities, focused on Ali's initial debarment and sought declaratory relief and damages. The second complaint, brought by Mirza Ali, Sameena Ali, and Sameena/Samtech against the Air Force and seven Air Force employees in their individual capacities, focused both on the debarment of Sameena/Samtech and Sameena Ali and on the extension of Mirza Ali's debarment.

This second complaint made substantially the same allegations as the first, even though it was directed at entirely different defendants. The appellants alleged (1) that the individual Air Force officials had conspired to violate their civil rights and had committed several common-law torts and (2) that the Air Force's decision to debar them was arbitrary and capricious and should be set aside pursuant to the APA.

In an order filed December 11, 1996, the district court dismissed the claims against the individual defendants for lack of personal jurisdiction and, alternatively, on the grounds that the appellants had failed either to plead conspiracy with sufficient particularity or to comply with the Federal Tort Claims Act, 28 U.S.C. §§ 1346(b), 2671–2680. The court also granted summary judgment to the Air Force on the APA claims. The appellants timely appeal. We affirm the district court's dismissal of the claims against the individual defendants but reverse the summary judgment in favor of the Air Force.

* * *

ANALYSIS

* * *

The Supreme Court has long recognized that a federal agency is obliged to abide by the regulations it promulgates. See Vitarelli v. Seaton, 359 U.S. 535, 545, 79 S.Ct. 968, 3 L.Ed.2d 1012 (1959); Service v. Dulles, 354 U.S. 363, 372, 77 S.Ct. 1152, 1 L.Ed.2d 1403 (1957); Accardi v. Shaughnessy, 347 U.S. 260, 267, 74 S.Ct. 499, 98 L.Ed. 681 (1954). An agency's failure to follow its own regulations "tends to cause unjust discrimination and deny adequate notice" and consequently may result in a violation of an individual's constitutional right to due process. NLRB v. Welcome-American Fertilizer Co., 443 F.2d 19, 20 (9th Cir.1971); see also United States v. Newell, 578 F.2d 827, 834 (9th Cir.1978). Where a prescribed procedure is intended to protect the interests of a party before the agency, "even though generous beyond the requirements that bind such agency, that procedure must be scrupulously observed." Vitarelli, 359 U.S. at 547, 79 S.Ct. 968 (Frankfurter, J., concurring); see also Note, Violations by Agencies of Their Own Regulations, 87 Harv. L. Rev. 629, 630 (1974) (observing that agency violations of regulations promulgated to provide parties with procedural safeguards generally have been invalidated by courts).

The Federal Acquisition Regulation ("FAR") establishes a system of uniform policies and procedures governing acquisitions by all executive agencies. See 48 C.F.R. § 1.101. In recognition of the "serious nature of debarment," see 48 C.F.R. § 9.402, the FAR sets out detailed procedures to ensure that this sanction, which is intended to safeguard the integrity of the acquisitions process, itself is applied in conformity with "principles of fundamental fairness." 48 C.F.R. § 9.406-3(b). Accordingly, the FAR provides:

> [I]f it is found that the contractor's submission in opposition raises a genuine dispute over facts material to the proposed debarment, agencies shall also—(i) Afford the contractor an opportunity to appear with counsel, submit documentary evidence, and confront any person the agency presents.

48 C.F.R. § 9.406-3(b)(2). Thus, in the event of a genuine factual dispute, the FAR clearly establishes that a contractor facing debarment is entitled to an evidentiary hearing.

The appellants claim that they raised a genuine issue of material fact with regard to Mirza Ali's position at Sameena/Samtech. They contend that Ali was mistakenly listed as Vice President of the company on the bank signature card discovered by Moore and that the February 1996 letter from the bank supports that contention. Accordingly, they claim that they were entitled under the FAR to an evidentiary hearing on the matter.

The district court rejected the appellants' claims on two grounds. First, the court found the letter from the bank to be inconclusive. The court pointed out that the letter merely acknowledged that the bank had issued a new signature card deleting Eqbal's name, and that it had made this "correction" after being informed that Zulfiqar Eqbal was not a corporate officer. The district court suggested that the letter had little probative value because it was sent after debarment proceedings against the appellants already had commenced.

Second, the district court observed that the operative factual question informing the debarment decision was not whether Ali/Eqbal was Vice President of Sameena/Samtech but, rather, whether he exercised control over the business. As the court noted, the Debarring Official found that Ali had written business-related and personal checks on Samtech's account and had stated on the telephone that he was project manager for government solicitations. Based on that evidence, the Debarring Official concluded, "[I]t is clear that Mr. Eqbal had full authority to expend Samtech's resources and bind the company." Because the district court found that "[n]othing plaintiffs submitted created a dispute as to this issue," it concluded that they were not entitled to an evidentiary hearing.

The district court failed, however, to acknowledge evidence submitted by the appellants that calls into question whether Ali/Eqbal was a principal of Sameena/Samtech. The appellants submitted evidence that Ali/Eqbal was Vice President of a Hong Kong corporation also called Samtech and that his position there had likely caused the confusion involving the signature cards. The appellants also submitted evidence indicating that Ali/Eqbal held no official position with Sameena/Samtech other than bookkeeper and that the writing of checks was consistent with that position. The appellants denied that Ali/Eqbal had represented himself to be a project manager or any other type of corporate officer. They explained that the checks made out to and signed by Eqbal were not for his personal use and were not issued at his discretion. Finally, the appellants challenged the government to produce any document indicating that Ali/Eqbal had actually acted in the capacity of a principal with regard to control over the company's decisionmaking process. Thus, although the appellants' submission does not establish that the Debarring Official acted arbitrarily or capriciously in determining that Ali/Eqbal was a principal of Samtech/Sameena, it does raise a genuine factual dispute regarding the issue.

The appellants requested an evidentiary hearing to address this question. The Debarring Official decided, however, that a hearing was unwarranted, finding the appellants' denials of the charges against them to be "unsupported by credible evidence." We do not doubt that the Air Force is in a better position than this Court to assess the credibility of the evidence offered by the appellants. We are convinced, however, that an evidentiary hearing would have been the appropriate forum in which to make such an assessment, particularly in view of the serious consequences attaching to a debarment of 15 years. The FAR states unambiguously that such a hearing "shall" be afforded if genuine factual disputes arise. Accordingly, we conclude that the Air Force violated the appellants' constitutional right to due process in failing to comply with binding regulations and that the appellants are entitled to such a hearing on remand. As Justice Frankfurter observed in a similar context, "He that takes the procedural sword shall perish with that sword." Vitarelli, 359 U.S. at 547, 79 S.Ct. 968 (Frankfurter, J., concurring).

CONCLUSION

For the foregoing reasons, we AFFIRM the district court's dismissal of the appellants' claims against the individual defendants. However, we REVERSE the summary judgment in favor of the Air Force and REMAND to the district court with instructions to remand this matter to the Air Force. The Air Force should hold an evidentiary hearing, pursuant to 48 C.F.R. § 9.406-3(b)(2), to address whether Mirza Ali/Zulfiqar Eqbal was a principal of Sameena/Samtech.

AFFIRMED in part, REVERSED in part and REMANDED. Each party shall bear its own costs.

Notes and Questions

1. This case is a triumph of procedure. How would it look to someone who cared more about results than procedure? Suppose you were the Air Force officer who had put together the case against Ali/Eqbal. Would you view a Ninth Circuit reversal and the need for an evidentiary proceeding as wonderful triumphs of justice or as rewarding culpable parties for hiring lawyers to come up with delaying tactics?

2. Note the total lack of deference. The Ninth Circuit reaches past the district court's affirmance to an intense review of the Air Force Debarring Official that accords him no respect at all. A driving force is the sense that a fifteen year debarment is so intense that it raises serious due process concerns. Note the contrast with the *Hatfield* case, where the court upheld (against a different kind of challenge, to be sure) a debarment of 26 months. Also, the Air Force tried to do this debarment on the quick and easy with just a paper record. Within the government, it presumably seemed virtuous to move swiftly to debar Ali/Eqbal as a repeat offender who had resumed offending before his previous debarment even ended. Outside the government, doing it just on a paper record looked to the Ninth Circuit more indolent than virtuous.

Chapter 17

False Claims and Defective Pricing

Two issues bring forth high-powered enforcement proceedings. False claims against the government bring forth the machinery of the False Claims Act. This has a pair of important parts: the procedures applicable in all False Claims Act cases, however brought; and, the special procedures that allow individual whistleblowers or "relators" to file their own "qui tam" cases.

Another issue that brings forth high-powered enforcement proceedings consists of defective pricing. This operates in certain cases in which the contractor fails to provide the information required by the Truth in Negotiation Act, or to inform the government of certain kinds of pricing which do not give the government an appropriate price in light of what the contractor charges its other customers. TINA requires certain kinds of government contractors to provide "cost or pricing data," so that the government's contracting officers can ascertain that the government is paying a reasonable price. Failure to provide required data can constitute "defective pricing" warranting government recovery of overpayments when audits subsequently uncover these. As would be expected from this combination of mandatory-disclosure, audits, and price-control systems, TINA requires much attention from lawyers.

For further discussion of the subjects in this chapter, see the cites in the specific subchapters, and see: Bradley J. Sauer, *Deterring False Claims In Government Contracting: Making Consistent Use Of 18 U.S.C. § 287*, 39 Pub. Cont. L.J. 897 (Summer 2010); Thomas L. Harris, *Alternate Remedies & The False Claims Act: Protecting Qui Tam Relators In Light Of Government Intervention And Criminal Prosecution Decisions*, 94 Cornell L. Rev. 1293 (July 2009); Michael Davidson, Claims Involving Fraud: Contracting Officer Limitations During Procurement Fraud Investigations, 2002 Army Law. 21 (Sept. 2002); Charles Tiefer & Heather Akehurst-Krause, *Risky Business: Medicare's Vulnerability to Selection Games of Managed Care Providers*, 28 U. Balt. L. Rev. 319 (1999); William E. Kovacic, *Whistleblower Lawsuits As Monitoring Devices in Government Contracting*, 29 Loy. L.A. L. Rev. 1799 (1996); Neal A. Cooper, *Third Party Liability or the False Claims Act: It Is Time for Consultants To Pay the Price For Their Bad Advice*, 29 J. Marshall L. Rev. 923 (1996).

A. False Claims Act/Qui Tam

Note on False Claims Act

The government faces an overwhelming challenge in contractor fraud resulting in a highly significant subfield of law particularly as to one procedural mechanism, the civil false claims act suit. Contract fraud derives part of its significance from its large scale. On the health care procurement side, it has been estimated that fraud and waste amount to 10% of government spending, or $25 billion. Just as important, fraud represents an open-ended threat. The nature of fraud adapts and changes to circumvent the government's efforts at control; it undermines the government's programs over and above the sheer loss of funding; and, as one of the key components of public corruption, it undermines the legitimacy and capacity to function of any government in general and of a democratic government in particular since fraud, like other corruption, reduces faith in the constitutionally and popularly legitimated officials. In an era in which numerous governments, from the Soviet Union to the Suharto regime in Indonesia, have fallen in part due to the undermining and paralyzing effects of state corruption, government contract fraud represents a threat far beyond even its large numbers.

Of course, the government has many procedural responses to fraud. Many are preventive measures, like open competition in acquisition decisions, inspection of delivered supplies, and active auditing of claims for payment. Others are fairly straightforward variations on familiar procedures, namely, criminal prosecutions for violations of the criminal fraud statute and terminations for contractors behaving fraudulently.

What is most worthy of attention in the fraud context is the unique civil litigation channel established by the False Claims Act. The False Claims Act has two aspects: the aspects common to all cases, regardless of who brings them; and, the unique "qui tam" aspect that a case can be initiated and even pursued to completion by a private party, such as a whistleblower, seeking a recovery on behalf of the government. These two aspects deserve separate treatment and each is represented by an important case in this section: *Aerodex*, illustrating the aspects common to all false claim cases, and *Rockwell*, illustrating the special aspects of a whistleblower suit.

Historically, the False Claims Act was first enacted in 1863 as a response to rampant contractor fraud during the Civil War, and many major cases, including *Aerodex*, proceeded under the law as it existed in 1863–1986. However, the explosive growth in importance of the Act occurred through its amendments in 1986, somewhat as part of the reaction of the mid-1980s to defense procurement scandals. After its initial employment predominantly against defense fraud, the 1990s saw a rapid growth of the statute's use against fraud in government health care contracting. This casebook uses a number of additional False Claims Act opinions in other chapters, notably in the chapter on specialized contracting, precisely because the False Claims Act has had such importance for government health care contracting.

The False Claims Act cases may seem like a sharp break from other aspects of government contracting. Other cases about contractor performance typically arise through the disputes process, following the orderly path of claims presented to contracting officers, final decisions by contracting officers, appeals, and consideration on a record largely created out of the regular documentation of the contracting process. The government personnel who present the government's side typically have a regular participating role in the contracting process, representing further continuity between the contracting process and the disputes case. In sum, the disputes case is an appeal from the contracting process, but deferential toward it and largely shaped by it.

In contrast, the False Claims Act case is a distinct break from the contracting process, not an effort to keep continuity with it, but a deliberate effort to respond to an apparent breakdown in the ordinary contracting process by mounting a highly independent response. The False Claims Act case proceeds only in federal district court, a deliberately independent, nonspecialized tribunal without any particular institutional sympathy toward the folkways of contracting officers and contractors. Moreover, the False Claims Act creates its own record, concerned with keeping sharp the tools for piercing through ingenious deception rather than taking on faith the contractor's adherence to basic norms. A sharp change also occurs in the personnel who participate: representing the government's interests are either Justice Department attorneys or even whistleblower's attorneys, who view the contracting officers as witnesses rather than clients.

The rough treatment received by contractors in this process has led them as a class to fight back politically against civil fraud enforcement. Defense contractors and health care providers have waged somewhat distinct struggles over the years against the fraud enforcement process in general and the civil fraud statute in particular. Such contractors argue that the civil fraud procedure exposes them to harsh penalties—both high damages and the label of defrauder—for what they contend are often relatively innocent mistakes.

Given the many uncertainties of government contracting, contractors urge, it is unfair to subject them to a punitive procedure that breaks so sharply with the ordinary contracting context. Contractors argue that they must often act in reliance on one form or another of informal or unspoken government guidance, or on common sense or commercial practicality, that affords them inadequate protection in the unforgiving procedures used in a civil fraud case. Moreover, they urge, it is inefficient as well, for it separates the government contracting sector from the general commercial marketplace. They argue such government-unique burdens make government contracting an area in which only a limited number of contractors prepared to operate in more self-protective, more defensive, more expensive ways, will take on work. This situation makes not only for interesting policy debates, but, of course, for a great deal of litigation for government contract lawyers.

For further discussions of the subject of this section, see: Joe R. Whatley (Jr.), Thomas J. Butler, *Update On Government Contract Litigation: The False Claims Act And Beyond*, 56 Fed. Law. 39 (Jan. 2009); Alan Tauber, The Susceptibility Of Municipalities To Suit Under The False Claims Act, 33 Pub. Cont. L.J. 625 (Spring 2004); C. Stanley Dees and Christopher C. Bouquet, *Beyond "Diminished Value": New Challenges in the Law of Civil False Claims Act Damages*, 25 Pub. Cont. L.J. 597 (1996).

1. Civil False Claims Act

The Civil False Claims Act, 31 U.S.C. 3719, has a number of prongs. Its most important one subjects to liability a person who knowingly presents a false or fraudulent claim to the government. Another important prong subjects a person who knowingly uses a false record or statement to get a false or fraudulent claim paid (a "false record") case. This removes the defense that the person did not directly and personally submit a claim to the government, for example, a fraudulent borrower of a government-guaranteed loan, whose only direct dealings are with the lending bank.

A false claim has three key elements: (1) a claim, that is (2) false and fraudulent, and (3) a level of intent. From the previous discussions in other contexts of what a "claim" is, it will come as no surprise that there is much law on this subject, with an important distinction being that mere bids or proposals to contract are not "claims." What is "false and fraudulent" has much in common with fraud in private contracting. However, many disputes have occurred over the extent to which contractors can raise as a defense that government officials had knowledge of or even approved what they did, with the government insisting that its officials cannot excuse fraud, and the contractors arguing that something is not fraudulent if it could not and did not mislead government officials. As for the intent level, the use of the term "knowingly" in the statute suggests a higher intent requirement than actually exists. The 1986 amendments made recklessness sufficient, so that an official who takes what the legislative history calls a "head-in-the-sand" attitude when submitting false claims is liable.

Contractors found guilty of a false claim pay triple damages. Moreover, even if the actual damages were low or nominal, the statute imposes liability to statutory damages.

The first case, *Aerodex*, is a classic illustration of how the False Claims Act empowers the government once it uncovers a deliberate falsehood, to overcome a number of seemingly plausible contractor defenses to liability and to high damage figures.

For further discussion of the subjects of this subchapter, see: Robert Salcido, *The 2009 False Claims Act Amendments: Congress' Efforts To Both Expand And Narrow The Scope Of The False Claims Act*, 39 Pub. Cont. L. J. 741 (Summer 2010); Andrew L. Hurst, *Civil False Claims Act Of 2003*, 51 Fed. Law. 26 (Jan. 2004).

United States of America, Plaintiff-Appellee, v. Aerodex, Inc., et al., Defendants-Appellants

United States Court of Appeals, Fifth Circuit
No. 71-2801. 469 F.2d 1003
Nov. 2, 1972

Before PHILLIPS, THORNBERRY and RONEY, Circuit Judges.

RONEY, Circuit Judge:

This case is about aircraft engine bearings. In 1962 Aerodex, Inc. contracted to sell certain aircraft parts to the Navy Department. Three hundred master rod bearings for the Curtiss-Wright R1820 engine were included in the sale. The bearings delivered were not those specified in the contract. The district court, 327 F.Supp. 1027, held that the invoices submitted by Aerodex for payment for these bearings were "false claims for payment" within the meaning of the Federal False Claims Act, 31 U.S.C.A. § 231 (1970). The government was awarded $381,838.36 with interest. We reverse as to Defendant Tonks and remand with directions to modify the amount of the judgment against Aerodex and Crawford.

At the time pertinent to this lawsuit, the Commercial Division of Aerodex, Inc. was engaged in the purchase and sale of spare aircraft parts. Defendant Raymond Tonks was president and general manager of Aerodex, and defendant Frank J. Crawford was vice president in charge of the Commercial Division.

On September 18, 1962, Crawford submitted to the U.S. Navy Aviation Supply Office a bid by Aerodex to sell 300 master rod bearings, Curtiss-Wright part number 171815, at a price of $90.00 each. This bid was accepted and was incorporated as a part of a contract entered into between Aerodex and the Aviation Supply Office on October 6, 1962.

As several of the contract provisions are crucial to this appeal, we set them out in full:

SPECIFICATIONS

Articles furnished from stocks of surplus material are acceptable under this contract provided that the articles so furnished meet the following requirements:

1. All articles furnished must be identified by the applicable Curtiss Wright Corporation, Wright Aeronautical Division part numbers ... and must conform to the requirements of the respective drawings for said articles.

* * *

3. All articles furnished … must be in new, unused condition.

INSPECTION AND ACCEPTANCE

* * *

At destination all delivered articles shall be subjected to 100% final inspection by the O & R shop for conformance to the applicable data, drawings and specifications required in the manufacture of said articles. Inspection shall include magnaflux or Zyglo or the equivalent thereof.…

UNSATISFACTORY MATERIAL

Any articles delivered which have been determined by the receiving activity to have failed to conform to the applicable specifications and drawings or which are otherwise considered unsuitable for intended use shall be returned, at the Contractor's expense, for replacement. The necessary replacement articles shall then be shipped, all transportation charges paid, to the destinations specified herein. If any of the articles returned to the Contractor are not replaced, the total amount due to be paid under this contract shall be reduced by the contract value of the returned article or articles.

The bearings supplied by Aerodex to the Navy under this contract were not P/N [part number] 171815 bearings. They were P/N 117971 and 117971Y10 bearings which had been reworked by Aerodex employees. The rework consisted of replacing the metallic overlay on the inside diameter of each bearing. After reworking, each bearing was reidentified with P/N 171815. To the naked eye, the reworked bearings were indistinguishable from new, unused P/N 171815 bearings.

Aerodex' reworked bearings were received and accepted at the Jacksonville Naval Air Station without the "100% final inspection" required by the contract. A number of them were installed in aircraft engines. When the Navy subsequently discovered that the bearings were not the ones contracted for, it removed and replaced those which had been installed. This "retrofit" operation cost $160,919.18. That amount was added to the contract price of $27,000 and the total doubled as provided in the False Claims Act. This, together with the $2,000 statutory penalty for each of the three invoices, resulted in the $381,838.36 judgment for the government.

I. Liability Under the False Claims Act

The defendants make a two-pronged attack on the district court's finding of liability under the False Claims Act. They allege that the evidence was (1) legally insufficient in that it did not show the necessary element of scienter, and (2) factually insufficient in that it did not demonstrate the individual defendants' personal knowledge and participation in the alleged fraudulent performance of the contract. The law is settled in this Circuit that to show a violation of the False Claims Act the evidence must demonstrate "guilty knowledge of a purpose on the part of [the defendant] to cheat the Government," United States v. Priola, 272 F.2d 589, 594 (5th Cir. 1959), or "knowledge or guilty intent," United States v. Ridglea State Bank, 357 F.2d 495, 498 (5th Cir. 1966).

The test is easily stated but difficult to apply in the circumstances of this case.

(a) The Mislabeled Parts

A master rod bearing for the R1820 engine is a cylindrical sleeve approximately 3 1/4 inches in length and 3 1/4 inches in diameter. The bearing is composed of steel, with a silver plating material on both the inside and outside surfaces. The inside of the bearing is further coated with a microscopically thin metallic overlay. The inside diameter of the bearing performs the function of a bearing surface which permits the free rotation of the crankshaft within the master rod bearing. This permits the crankshaft to rotate, turning the propellor. Failure of the bearing causes complete engine failure.

The bearing denominated P/N 117971 is impossible to distinguish visually from bearing P/N 171815 but has two basic differences. One difference is hardness of the steel in the shell backing; the P/N 117971 is made of a low carbon steel, while P/N 171815 is made of a harder, high carbon steel. The other difference lies in the composition of the metallic overlay used to line the inside diameter of the bearings: bearing P/N 117971's overlay consists of a lead and indium composition, while the overlay used in P/N 171815 is a lead-tin composition. Aerodex replaced the lead-indium overlay with lead-tin prior to renumbering the P/N 117971 bearings. This reworking did not change the hardness or composition of the bearings' steel shell.

Defendants do not deny that the bearings they sold to the Navy were reworked and renumbered. They argue, nevertheless, that their actions constituted no violation of the False Claims Act. They allege that all military and factory publications available to them showed that both P/N 117971 and P/N 171815 were approved for use in the R1820 engine and that the entire aviation industry at that time considered the two bearings to be interchangeable. Defendants argue, therefore, that they could not have had the requisite intent to "cheat" the government.

We think this argument requires too restrictive a reading of the False Claims Act. The mere fact that the item supplied under contract is as good as the one contracted for does not relieve defendants of liability if it can be shown that they attempted to deceive the government agency. In United States v. National Wholesalers, 236 F.2d 944 (9th Cir. 1956), cert. denied, 353 U. S. 930, 77 S.Ct. 719, 1 L.Ed.2d 724 (1957), the defendant contracted to deliver to the Army a number of Delco-Remy generators. Unable to procure these generators, National Wholesalers had substitutes manufactured and attached spurious "Delco-Remy" labels to them. Although the substitute generators performed according to contract specifications, liability under the False Claims Act was held to attach because of the deliberate misbranding.

We think that the deliberate mislabeling in the case at bar, coupled with the fact that the parts delivered did not actually meet the specifications of the contract, compels a finding of liability under the Act. If defendants had, in fact, believed that the reworked P/N 117971 bearings were interchangeable with the P/N 171815 bearings that they had contracted to deliver, they could easily have requested permission from the Navy to deliver the substitute parts or, at least, could have disclosed to the Navy the manner in which they thought they could comply with the contract. The failure to do so indicates nothing less than an intention to deceive.

II. Failure to Inspect

The government admits that the Navy did not perform the "100% final inspection" called for by the contract. Defendants proved at trial that a simple and inexpensive non-destructive test, the Rockwell Hardness Test, would have shown that the bearings did not meet contract specifications.

The inspection clause in the contract does not, however, insulate appellants from liability for fraud. First, a reading of the clause shows that it is for the government's benefit and imposes no duty on the government in favor of the appellants. Second, Article 5, the inspection article, provides that inspection is not conclusive "as regards latent defects, fraud, or such gross mistakes as to amount to fraud." This provision embodies the established rule that, even where final inspection is the obligation of the government, such obligation does not absolve a contractor on liability for fraud....

In addition, appellants failed to prove that 100% inspection would necessarily have included a Rockwell Hardness Test. Since hardness of the steel used in the bearing is controlled at the manufacturing level and is the same for all bearings of a given part number, the appearance of that part number on the bearing gives notice of the bearing's hardness. Thus, only upon suspicion of fraudulent misnumbering would an inspector conduct a Rockwell Hardness Test.

The lower court was correct in holding that the contract "could not be relied upon by the defendants to escape liability because such an interpretation would allow a supplier to escape liability for any deception where the inspection was not made but the deception discovered by other means—an obviously unfair and unintended result." This holding also applies to the defendants' reliance on the regulations.

III. Measure of Damages

The question raised on this appeal as to the measure of damages applied by the district court is difficult to resolve because there appears to be no precedent against which to judge the facts of this case.

The district court computed damages by first adding the contract price of the bearings, $27,000.00, to the $160,919.18 cost incurred in removing and replacing the P/N 117971 bearings which had been installed in aircraft engines. This sum, $187,919.18, was then doubled under the statutory formula in the False Claims Act which imposes liability for the submission of a false claim in "double the amount of damages which the United States may have sustained by reason of doing or committing such act ..." 31 U.S.C.A. § 231 (1970).

The cases that have considered the application of this statute's double damage provision have generally been of two kinds. One line of cases involves an overpricing for what was sold and delivered to the government. Here the damage sustained by the United States is the difference between the reasonable cost of the goods sold and the price the government actually paid for the goods, and recovery is double that amount. See, e. g., United States v. Foster Wheeler Corp., 447 F.2d 100 (2d Cir. 1971); United States v. Ben Grunstein & Sons Co., 137 F.Supp. 197 (D. N.J. 1956); United States v. American Packing Corp., supra.

In the other line of cases, the government has been billed and has paid for a greater quantity of goods or services than it has received. The basis for the double damage recovery is then the amount it paid for the goods that were short in delivery. See, e. g., United States v. Koenig, 144 F.Supp. 22 (E.D. Pa. 1956).

These cases all differ somewhat from this one because they involve a quantitative measure, a difference between what the government paid and what it should have paid for goods that were acceptable. None involved consequential damages incurred as a result of defective goods.

Upon careful analysis, we hold that the language of the False Claims Act does not include consequential damages resulting from delivery of defective goods. The statute assesses double damages attributable to the "act," which in this case is the submission of the false vouchers. The submission of these vouchers was not the cause of the government's consequential damages. The delivery and installation of the bearings in the airplanes, not the filing of the false claim, caused the consequential damages.

In a case of this kind, damages under the False Claims Act must be measured by the amount wrongfully paid to satisfy the false claim. United States v. Woodbury, 359 F.2d 370 (9th Cir. 1966); United States v. American Packing Corp., supra.

Toepleman v. United States, 263 F.2d 697 (4th Cir.), cert. denied sub nom. Cato Bros., Inc. v. United States, 359 U. S. 989, 79 S.Ct. 1119, 3 L.Ed.2d 978 (1959), relied upon by the government, is not authority to the contrary, in Toepleman, the defendants had obtained crop support loans from the Commodity Credit Corporation by fraudulently representing that the cotton collateral of the pledged promissory notes had been produced by the makers of the notes. The government had sold the collateral for less than the total amount of the loans, and the Fourth Circuit permitted the government to recover double the foreclosure deficiency under the False Claims Act. Toepleman's reasoning is inapposite here, because the damages were in no way consequential, i. e., additional losses incurred as proximate results of the act of submitting a fraudulent loan application. Rather, the government was permitted to double the amount still owing on the fraudulently obtained loans. In this respect, Toepleman closely resembles both lines of False Claims Act cases, as an example of the government being either overcharged for the correct quantity of goods or charged for goods short in delivery.

We think that a proper application of the double damage provision limits the government's claim to the amount that was paid out by reason of the false claim. We treat the matter as if the claims for $27,000 for P/N 171815 bearings were false because those bearings were never delivered. The government paid $27,000 for bearings it did not receive. This amount must be doubled, and the $2,000 statutory penalty must be added for each of the three invoices. The correct amount recoverable under the False Claims Act, consequently, is $60,000.00, and the judgment for $381,838.36 is reversed.

IV. Breach of Warranty

The consequential damage award to the government can be sustained on another theory. The district court found that Aerodex committed a breach of warranty in delivering to the government bearings which were at variance with those required by the contract. The issue is whether Aerodex has an adequate defense to the recovery of damages for that breach of warranty.

The warranty provisions of the contract are contained in Clause 33, which reads in pertinent part:

(a) Notwithstanding inspection and acceptance by the Government of articles furnished under this contract or any provision of this contract concerning the conclusiveness thereof, the Contractor warrants that at the time of delivery (i) all materials delivered under this contract will be free from defects in material or workmanship and will conform with the specifications, and all other requirements of this contract;....

(b) Within one year after the delivery of any article under this contract, written notice may be given by the Government to the Contractor of any breach of the warranties in paragraph (a) of this clause as to such article. Within a reasonable time after such notice, the Contracting Officer may either (i) require the prompt correction or replacement of any article or part thereof (including preservation, packaging, packing, and marking) that did not at the time of its delivery conform with the requirements of this contract within the meaning of paragraph (a) of this clause, or thereafter does not so conform in consequence of any such breach; or (ii) retain such article, whereupon the contract price thereof shall be reduced by an amount equitable under the circumstances and the Contractor shall promptly make appropriate repayment....

* * *

(e) The remedies afforded the Government by paragraph (b) of this clause shall be exclusive as to any breach of the warranties in paragraph (a) of this clause, except any such breach involving latent defects, fraud, or such gross mistakes as amount to fraud.

The government did not pursue either of the remedies afforded by subparagraph (b) of Clause 33. This omission does not provide Aerodex with a defense to the breach of warranty claim, however, because cases of fraud are specifically excepted from exclusivity under subparagraph (e).

Aerodex' main contention is that the government's failure to conduct the "100% final inspection" precludes it from any remedy for the breach of warranty.

Aerodex makes the following arguments to support its position:

[a] The damages were not foreseeable, since Aerodex could not have known that the government would not make the required inspections;

[b] The government cannot recover damages which it could have avoided by the exercise of reasonable diligence;

[c] The language of the "inspection" and "unsatisfactory material" clauses of the contract is repugnant to the warranty clause, and since the former are typed while the latter is printed, the former clauses must be given precedence, making rejection and return of nonconforming bearings the government's exclusive remedy; and

[d] The Christian doctrine required the government to perform tests required by specific Armed Services regulations.

These arguments are irrelevant because the breached warranty was an express one. Aerodex expressly warranted that the delivered bearings were of a specific serial number, when in truth they were not. The general rule is that a buyer is entitled to rely upon the express warranty of the seller, especially where the warranty is descriptive and the defects are not readily apparent, and the buyer's failure to inspect constitutes no defense for the seller. 8 S. Williston on Contracts § 973 (1964); 46 Am.Jur. Sales § 330 (1943); 77 C. J.S. Sales § 311(b) (1952); Refinery Equipment, Inc. v. Wickett Refining Co., 158 F.2d 710 (5th Cir. 1947). The government was therefore entitled to rely solely upon Aerodex' express warranty describing the bearings, and its failure to inspect the delivered bearings is of no legal consequence.

* * *

Reversed and remanded with directions.

Notes and Questions

1. Note the high penalties. (Under the statute at the time, damages were doubled. Subsequently, the statute was amended, and damages are now trebled.) A contract price of $27,000 yielded fraud penalties over $381,000, reduced on remand. Did you follow how they were calculated and, in particular, the existence of a $2,000 statutory penalty? In effect, the False Claims Act deals with the problem of the financial attractiveness of government contract fraud by arranging a lot of monetary punishment for those who are caught.

Over the years, the Supreme Court has devoted much attention to the issues posed by statutory penalties. It upheld such penalties under a statute akin to the False Claims Act against a challenge under the Fifth Amendment in *Rex Trailer Co. v. United States*, 350 U.S. 148 (1956). At one point, the Court temporarily established that civil penalties under the False Claims Act, imposed upon a defendant already sanctioned in a criminal fraud case could run afoul of the Double Jeopardy Clause. *United States v. Halper*, 490 U.S. 435 (1989). However, the Court subsequently disavowed the analysis in that case, finding that the Double Jeopardy Clause only dealt with successive criminal punishments. *Hudson v. United States*, 522 U.S. 93 (1997). Still, the Supreme Court found in criminal contexts that too high a forfeiture could violate the Excessive Fines Clause of the Constitution. *United States v. Bakajakian*, 524 U.S. 321 (1998).

This tension between the high and sometimes multiple penalties that the Civil False Claims Act allows, and the circumstances which in one respect or another contractors argue to be relatively benign, adds extra drive to the many debates about the False Claims Act.

2. One of those debates has concerned whether an element of False Claims Act liability is that there be some injury to the government. In this case, the contractor made the argument it supplied bearings that, although mislabeled, were interchangeable with the ones specified in the contract. Why does the court reject that argument? While the argument that the fraud did not injure the government fails when made in the unappealing circumstances of deliberate mislabeling, that by no means laid the argument to rest. For example, suppose a contractor building missiles creates false inspection records. Assume, for purposes of argument, that the missiles themselves are perfectly adequate and would have passed the most rigorous inspection, and the contractor misbehaved, not in the making of the missiles, but only in the inspecting. What does the government buy: the product or the inspection records? Consider this analysis:

> An economic analysis of the "false testing" cases is that the Government loses the "insurance" value, a concretely valuable aspect of quality control, inherent in a fully operative product testing and certification system. The Government loses something it pays competing producers to provide; the fraudulent producer frees itself from something its competitors would have counted as one of their costs to provide. Another way, more of a regulatory analysis, for understanding the "false testing" cases is that they involve loss of the governmental interest expressed by the FAR's contractor self-inspection clauses....

Charles Tiefer & Michael Blumenfeld, *Qui Tam Recovery Without "Actual Damages,"* 6 FCA & Qui Tam Q. Rev., July 1996, at 23, 25.

3. Another of the debates has concerned the defense that the contracting officers themselves in one way or another participated in, approved, knew of, or at least allowed the allegedly fraudulent activity. In this case, that argument takes the form that mandatory government inspections should have caught the mislabeling. That sounds like a weak form of the argument, but it catches the contractor's essential sense that government contracting is not a distant, formal, arms-length activity, but a close-knit activity. Higher management in the government contractor may well consider it a service to both sides to take off excessive layers of controls of the lower levels of production, and to depend on a known form of government inspection to do the policing, or on some other known government form of supervision or advice to provide guidance. The argument is certainly made, in a stronger form than in this case, by hospitals whose alleged fraud consists of how their billing personnel describe medical procedures: if the reviewers of those bills for the government are giving advice about proper billing, why cannot the hospitals rely on it?

4. Yet another of the debates has concerned the False Claims Act's burden of proof. In a criminal fraud case, the government must prove fraud beyond a reasonable doubt; and,

in some civil situations, plaintiffs must prove accusations by the standard of clear and convincing evidence. However, the False Claims Act only imposes on the government the burden of proof by a preponderance of the evidence. 31 U.S.C. § 3731(c). For this as for other effective aspects of the Act, its proponents cite the peculiar problem that fraud, particularly fraud on the government, is self-concealing and that the ability of contractors to avoid or to disguise evidence of fraud necessitates a not-too-high burden of proof.

United States of America, ex rel. Mary Hendow; Julie Albertson, Plaintiffs-Appellants, v. University of Phoenix, Defendant-Appellee

United States Court of Appeals, Ninth Circuit.
No. 04-16247, 461 F.3d 1166
Argued and Submitted Feb. 15, 2006
Filed Sept. 5, 2006

Before: HALL, SILVERMAN, and GRABER, Circuit Judges.

Opinion

HALL, Senior Circuit Judge:

The False Claims Act makes liable anyone who "knowingly makes, uses, or causes to be made or used, a false record or statement to get a false or fraudulent claim paid or approved by the Government." 31 U.S.C. § 3729(a)(2). In this case, relators have raised allegations that the University of Phoenix knowingly made false statements, and caused false statements to be made, that resulted in the payment by the federal Department of Education of hundreds of millions of dollars. Despite this axiomatic fit between the operative statute and the allegations made, respondent claims that relators' legal theory holds no water. The district court agreed, dismissing the suit for failure to state a claim upon which relief can be granted. We reverse.

I.

When an educational institution wishes to receive federal subsidies under Title IV and the Higher Education Act, it must enter into a Program Participation Agreement with the Department of Education (DOE), in which it agrees to abide by a panoply of statutory, regulatory, and contractual requirements. One of these requirements is a ban on incentive compensation: a ban on the institution's paying recruiters on a per-student basis. The ban prohibits schools from "provid[ing] any commission, bonus, or other incentive payment based directly or indirectly on success in securing enrollments or financial aid to any persons or entities engaged in any student recruiting or admission activities or in making decisions regarding the award of student financial assistance." 20 U.S.C. § 1094(a)(20). This requirement is meant to curb the risk that recruiters will "sign up poorly qualified students who will derive little benefit from the subsidy and may be unable or unwilling to repay federally guaranteed loans." *United States ex rel. Main v. Oakland City Univ.,* 426 F.3d 914, 916 (7th Cir.2005), *cert. denied,* 547 U.S. 1071, 126 S.Ct. 1786, 164 L.Ed.2d 519 (2006). The ban was enacted based on evidence of serious program abuses. *See* S.Rep. No. 102-58, at 8 (1991) ("Abuses in Federal Student Aid Programs") (noting testimony "that contests were held whereby sales representatives earned incentive awards for enrolling the highest number of student[s] for a given period"); H.R.Rep. No. 102-447, at 10, *reprinted in* 1992 U.S.C.C.A.N. 334, 343 (noting that the "new provisions include prohibiting the use of commissioned sales persons and recruiters").

This case involves allegations under the False Claims Act that the University of Phoenix (the University) knowingly made false promises to comply with the incentive compensation ban in order to become eligible to receive Title IV funds. Appellants, Mary Hendow and Julie Albertson (relators), two former enrollment counselors at the University, allege that the University falsely certifies each year that it is in compliance with the incentive compensation ban while intentionally and knowingly violating that requirement. Relators allege that these false representations, coupled with later claims for payment of Title IV funds, constitute false claims under 31 U.S.C. § 3729(a)(1) & (a)(2).

First, relators allege that the University, with full knowledge, flagrantly violates the incentive compensation ban. They claim that the University "compensates enrollment counselors ... based directly upon enrollment activities," ranking counselors according to their number of enrollments and giving the highest-ranking counselors not only higher salaries but also benefits, incentives, and gifts. Relators allege that the University also "urges enrollment counselors to enroll students without reviewing their transcripts to determine their academic qualifications to attend the university," thus encouraging counselors to enroll students based on numbers alone. Relator Albertson, in particular, alleges that she was given a specific target number of students to recruit, and that upon reaching that benchmark her salary increased by more than $50,000. Relator Hendow specifically alleges that she won trips and home electronics as a result of enrolling large numbers of students.

Second, relators allege considerable fraud on the part of the University to mask its violation of the incentive compensation ban. They claim that the University's head of enrollment openly brags that "[i]t's all about the numbers. It will always be about the numbers. But we need to show the Department of Education what they want to see." To deceive the DOE, relators allege, the University creates two separate employment files for its enrollment counselors—one "real" file containing performance reviews based on improper quantitative factors, and one "fake" file containing performance reviews based on legitimate qualitative factors. The fake file is what the DOE allegedly sees. Relators further allege a series of University policy changes deliberately designed to obscure the fact that enrollment counselors are compensated on a per-student basis, such as altering pay scales to make it less obvious that they are adjusted based on the number of students enrolled.

Third and finally, relators allege that the University submits false claims to the government. Claims for payment of Title IV funds can be made in a number of ways, once a school signs its Program Participation Agreement and thus becomes eligible. For instance, in the Pell Grant context, students submit funding requests directly (or with school assistance) to the DOE. In contrast, under the Federal Family Education Loan Program, which includes Stafford Loans, students and schools jointly submit an application to a private lender on behalf of the student, and a guaranty agency makes the eventual claim for payment to the United States only in the event of default. Relators allege that the University submits false claims in both of these ways. They claim that the University, with full knowledge that it is ineligible for Pell Grant funds because of its violation of the incentive compensation ban, submits requests for those funds directly to the DOE, resulting in a direct transfer of the funds into a University account. They further claim that the University, again with knowledge that it has intentionally violated the incentive compensation ban, submits requests to private lenders for government-insured loans.

On May 20, 2004, the district court dismissed the relators' complaint with prejudice under Federal Rule of Civil Procedure 12(b)(6) for failure to state a claim. Relators appealed on June 15, 2004. The United States Department of Justice submitted a brief as amicus curiae supporting the reversal of the district court.

* * *

II.

The district court below rejected both of relators' theories for why they have validly alleged that the University submitted false or fraudulent claims to the government in violation of the False Claims Act. First, the court rejected relators' claim under the "false certification" theory, as treated by this court in *United States ex rel. Hopper v. Anton,* 91 F.3d 1261, 1266 (9th Cir.1996), because the operative statute here "only requires that [the University] enter into an agreement, and does not require a certification." Second, the district court rejected relators' claim under the "promissory fraud" theory, because they did not "identif[y] any certification which is a prerequisite for [the University] to receive federal funds." These rulings conflated the proper analysis of False Claims Act liability, and so we will discuss the relevant theories in more detail.

In an archetypal *qui tam* False Claims action, such as where a private company overcharges under a government contract, the claim for payment is itself literally false or fraudulent. *See Anton,* 91 F.3d at 1266. The False Claims Act, however, is not limited to such facially false or fraudulent claims for payment. *See id.* Rather, the False Claims Act is "intended to reach all types of fraud, without qualification, that might result in financial loss to the Government." *United States v. Neifert-White Co.,* 390 U.S. 228, 232, 88 S.Ct. 959, 19 L.Ed.2d 1061 (1968). More specifically, in amending the False Claims Act in 1986, Congress emphasized that the scope of false or fraudulent claims should be broadly construed:

> [E]ach and every claim submitted under a contract, loan guarantee, or other agreement which was originally obtained by means of false statements or other corrupt or fraudulent conduct, or in violation of any statute or applicable regulation, constitutes a false claim.

S.Rep. No. 99-345, at 9 (1986), *reprinted in* 1986 U.S.C.C.A.N. 5266, 5274.

* * *

A. False Certification

Many different courts have held that a claim under the False Claims Act can be false where a party merely falsely certifies compliance with a statute or regulation as a condition to government payment. *See, e.g., id.* at 786; *Mikes v. Straus,* 274 F.3d 687, 697–700 (2d Cir.2001); *United States ex rel. Quinn v. Omnicare Inc.,* 382 F.3d 432, 441 (3d Cir.2004). The leading case on false certification in the Ninth Circuit is *United States ex rel. Hopper v. Anton.*

* * *

In *Anton,* we explained the theory of false certification, identifying two major considerations: " '(1) whether the false statement is the cause of the Government's providing the benefit; and (2) whether any relation exists between the subject matter of the false statement and the event triggering Government's [sic] loss.' " *Id.* at 1266 (quoting John T. Boese, *Civil False Claims and Qui Tam Actions* 1-29 to 1-30 (1995)). We also held that "[m]ere regulatory violations do not give rise to a viable FCA action," but rather, "[i]t is the false *certification* of compliance which creates liability when certification is a prerequisite to obtaining a government benefit." *Id.* at 1266–67 (emphasis in original). From the principles underlying these two statements, we created four conditions necessary to succeed on the false certification theory of False Claims Act liability.

Second, we emphasized the central importance of the scienter element to liability under the False Claims Act, holding that false claims must in fact be "false when made." *Id.* (citing *United States v. Shah,* 44 F.3d 285, 290 (5th Cir.1995)). In fact, we held, "[f]or a certified statement to be 'false' under the Act, it must be an intentional, palpable lie." *Id.* (citing *Hagood v. Sonoma County Water Agency,* 81 F.3d 1465, 1478 (9th Cir.1996)). We also noted that "some request for payment containing falsities made with scienter (i.e., with knowledge of the falsity and with intent to deceive) must exist." *Id.* at 1265. In short, we made clear that a palpably false statement, known to be a lie when it is made, is required for a party to be found liable under the False Claims Act.

We note that the University and the district court below have taken our holdings to mean that the word "certification" has some paramount and talismanic significance, apparently believing that a palpably false *statement* does not bring with it False Claims liability, while a palpably false *certification* will. This facile distinction would make it all too easy for claimants to evade the law. The Fourth Circuit rightly noted that False Claims liability attaches "*because of the fraud* surrounding the efforts to obtain the contract or benefit status, or the payments thereunder." *Harrison,* 176 F.3d at 788 (emphasis added). That the theory of liability is commonly called "false certification" is no indication that "certification" is being used with technical precision, or as a term of art; the theory could just as easily be called the "false statement of compliance with a government regulation that is a precursor to government funding" theory, but that is not as succinct. Furthermore, because the word "certification" does not appear in 31 U.S.C. §3729(a)(1) or (a)(2), there is no sense in parsing it with the close attention typically attending an exercise in statutory interpretation. So long as the statement in question is knowingly false when made, it matters not whether it is a certification, assertion, statement, or secret handshake; False Claims liability can attach.

Third, we held that the false statement or course of conduct must be material to the government's decision to pay out moneys to the claimant. This is plain from our focus on "(1) whether the false statement is the cause of the Government's providing the benefit; and (2) whether any relation exists between the subject matter of the false statement and the event triggering Government's [sic] loss." *Anton,* 91 F.3d at 1266. We also stated that the relevant certification of compliance must be both a "prerequisite to obtaining a government benefit," *id.,* and a "*sine qua non* of receipt of [government] funding," *id.* at 1267. We further held that the government funding must be "conditioned" upon certifications of compliance. *Id.*

This approach has been followed by a number of other circuits to adopt the false certification theory of false claims liability. *See Mikes,* 274 F.3d at 699 (holding that false certification theory applies when "governing federal rules ... are a precondition to payment"); *United States ex rel. Thompson v. Columbia/HCA Healthcare Corp.,* 125 F.3d 899, 902 (5th Cir.1997) (holding that false claims liability attaches only "where the government has conditioned payment of a claim upon a claimant's certification of compliance with ... a statute or regulation"); *Ab-Tech Constr., Inc. v. United States,* 31 Fed.Cl. 429, 434 (Fed.Cl.1994) (holding that false statement of compliance must be "critical to the decision to pay"), *aff'd,* 57 F.3d 1084 (Fed.Cir.1995). Once again, we note that there is no special significance to the term "certification" in determining materiality; the question is merely whether the false certification — or assertion, or statement — was relevant to the government's decision to confer a benefit.

Fourth and most obviously, for a false statement or course of action to be actionable under the false certification theory of false claims liability, it is necessary that it involve an actual *claim,* which is to say, a call on the government fisc. This is self-evident from the statutory language, of course, which requires a "claim paid or approved by the Government." 31 U.S.C. §3729(a)(2). In *Anton,* the case involved direct receipt of federal funding, but we agree with the Fourth Circuit that a claim arises whenever the government is asked to "pay out money or to forfeit moneys due." *Harrison*, 176 F.3d at 788.

* * *

III.

Thus, as the above analysis shows, under either the false certification theory or the promissory fraud theory, the essential elements of False Claims Act liability remain the same: (1) a false statement or fraudulent course of conduct, (2) made with scienter, (3) that was material, causing (4) the government to pay out money or forfeit moneys due. The question remaining is whether relators in this case have alleged facts satisfying all four of these elements.

* * *

C. Materiality

Most of the argument in this case centers on whether and how much the University's alleged fraud was material to the government's decision to disburse federal funds. The parties argue at length over, for instance, the enforcement power of the DOE, and whether its authority to take "emergency action"—to withhold funds or impose sanctions where it has information that statutory requirements are being violated—means that the statutory requirements are causally related to its decision to pay out moneys due.

These questions of enforcement power are largely academic, because the eligibility of the University under Title IV and the Higher Education Act of 1965—and thus, the funding that is associated with such eligibility—is *explicitly* conditioned, in three different ways, on compliance with the incentive compensation ban. First, a federal statute states that in order to be eligible, an institution must

> enter into a program participation agreement with the Secretary [of Education]. The agreement *shall condition* the initial and continuing eligibility of an institution to participate in a program *upon compliance* with the following requirements … [including the incentive compensation ban.]

20 U.S.C. § 1094(a) (emphasis added). Second, a federal regulation specifies:

> An institution may participate in any Title IV, HEA program … *only if* the institution enters into a written program participation agreement with the Secretary.… A program participation agreement *conditions* the initial and continued participation of an eligible institution in any Title IV, HEA program *upon compliance* with the provisions of this part [such as the incentive compensation ban.]

34 C.F.R. § 668.14(a)(1) (emphasis added). Third and finally, the program participation agreement itself states:

> The execution of this Agreement [which contains a reference to the incentive compensation ban] by the Institution and the Secretary is a *prerequisite* to the Institution's initial or continued participation in any Title IV, HEA program.

(emphasis added). All of the emphasized phrases in the above passages demonstrate that compliance with the incentive compensation ban is a necessary condition of continued eligibility and participation: compliance is a "prerequisite" to funding; funding shall occur "only if" the University complies; funding shall be "condition[ed] … upon compliance." These are not ambiguous exhortations of an amorphous duty. The statute, regulation, and agreement here all explicitly condition participation and payment on compliance with, among other things, the precise requirement that relators allege that the University knowingly disregarded.

* * *

IV.

Accordingly, because relators in this case have properly alleged (1) a false statement or fraudulent course of conduct, (2) made with scienter, (3) that was material, causing (4) the government to pay out money or forfeit moneys due, their cause of action under the False Claims Act survives a motion to dismiss, and the decision of the district court is

REVERSED.

Notes and Questions

1. Many opinions have wrestled with the main question in this case: what rule violations amount to a false claim? This court makes the answer seem straightforward: as long as the false statement is a "prerequisite" or a "condition" of payment, it justifies a false claim case.

2. How is that question different from materiality? Could a statement be false on a subject that was important (material) to the government without being a prerequisite or condition of payment?

2. "Qui Tam" Provisions

The most unique and dynamic feature of the False Claims Act consists of its provision for whistleblowers to initiate lawsuits on behalf of the government. If Jane Q. Citizen knows of fraud by Government Contractor Inc., she files a suit as a relator, captioned "United States ex rel. Jane Q. Citizen v. Government Contractor Inc." ("Ex rel." stands for "ex relator," signifying that Ms. Citizen is filing on behalf of the United States.) Congress has given her the incentive of a share of the recovery. This mechanism, newly envigorated by the Act's 1986 Amendments, brought forth hundreds of qui tam lawsuits with extensive recoveries for the Treasury.

For government contracts lawyers, the challenge comes in understanding the unusual aspects of the qui tam mechanism which can be loosely separated into two parts: the mechanics of how a relator suit works and the particular "public disclosure" jurisdictional barrier by which the FCA limits such suits.

Starting with the mechanics, suppose Ms. Citizen works for GC, Inc., and discovers that the company was doing what Aerodex was found to be doing, mislabeling aircraft parts. Ms. Citizen goes to a lawyer who evaluates whether the case has enough merit to bring. If so, the lawyer files a complaint presenting the case against GC, Inc., under seal, with Ms. Citizen as the "relator." The FCA requires that the lawyer furnish the complaint together with a disclosure statement of useful evidence of the fraud to the Civil Division of the Department of Justice. A public interest group that promotes the use of the Act, Taxpayers Against Fraud, the False Claims Act Legal Center, in Washington, D.C., has published a description of this process, entitled "Qui Tam Practitioner's Guide: Evaluating and Filing a Case," May 1997.

With the complaint and disclosure statement in hand, the Justice Department decides whether it will intervene. Often it tasks the agency inspector general or auditors to evaluate the claim, and makes its decision from a calculation of whether the case merits the investment of the government's limited resources for handling such suits. If the Justice Department decides to intervene, typically the case then goes forward largely the way a false claims case proceeds that had no relator at all, namely, the Justice Department takes the lead in discovery and trial. If the government successfully obtains a recovery through settlement or judgment, the relator receives a share of the proceeds between 15 and 25%, plus reasonable attorney's fees and costs.

If the Justice Department decides not to intervene, the relator, Ms. Citizen, can still proceed with the case. This time, the relator and her attorney themselves conduct discovery and trial. In this situation, if she obtains a recovery by settlement or judgment, that recovery still goes to the Treasury, but she gets a larger share, between 25 and 30%. 31 U.S.C. § 3730(d)(2).

The other part of the unique aspects of the qui tam case consists of the "public disclosure" jurisdictional barrier that limits such suits. In a word, if a fraud has already been publicly disclosed, a qui tam relator cannot sue regarding it. This barrier does not apply to the government; a fraud could receive national headlines and the government can still sue. However, a private qui tam relator could not initiate a suit on such a famous fraud, regardless of the merit of the case, because of the statutory barrier. Congress wanted to encourage more relators to uncover fraud, not simply more relators to sue about frauds that had already been uncovered before they sued. The "public disclosure" barrier has an exception for the "original source" of the information, so that if Ms. Citizen first disclosed her company's fraud, then even after the disclosure she can file suit.

Extensive litigation has occurred over the "public disclosure" rule. Contractors prize it as a defense, since it focuses on the relators, a group that contractors consider as having pronounced shortcomings. On the other hand, as a defense it has nothing to do with whether the allegations of fraud have merit, so relators scorn it as a mere technicality. Because of its importance as the special defense against relators, the "public disclosure" barrier has taken on some of the controversiality of all the other previously noted issues surrounding the False Claims Act, such as those concerning the measure of damages and the burden of proof, even though those issues concern relator-initiated and government-issued cases alike.

For further discussion of the subjects of this subsection, see: Barry M. Landy, *Deterring Fraud To Increase Public Confidence: Why Congress Should Allow Government Employees To File Qui Tam Lawsuits*, 94 Minn. L. Rev. 1239 (Apr. 2010); Nathan D. Sturycz, *The King And I?: An Examination Of The Interest Qui Tam Relators Represent And The Implications For Future False Claims Act Litigation*, 28 St. Louis U. Pub. L. Rev. 459 (2009); Christopher W. Myers, *The False Claims Act Clarification Act: An End To The FCA's Bar On Parasitic Qui Tam Actions?*, 44 Procrmt. Law. 7 (Spring 2009); Kenneth G. English, *Government Complicity & A Government Contractor's Liability In Qui Tam & Tort Cases*, 33 Pub. Cont. L.J. 649 (Spring 2004); James J. Gallagher, Barbara J. Bacon, *Was FAR 31.205-47 Properly Extended To Cover Qui Tam Defense Costs?*, 38 Procrmt. Law. 1 (Spring 2003); Robert L. Vogel, *The Public Disclosure Bar Against* Qui Tam *Suits*, 24 Pub. Cont. L.J. 477 (1995); Robert L. Vogel, *Eligibility Requirements for Relators Under* Qui Tam *Provisions of the False Claims Act*, 21 Pub. Cont. L.J. 593 (1992).

Vermont Agency of Natural Resources, Petitioner, v. United States ex rel. Stevens

No. 98-1828
Supreme Court of the United States
529 U.S. 765
Argued Nov. 29, 1999
Decided May 22, 2000

Justice SCALIA delivered the opinion of the Court.

This case presents the question whether a private individual may bring suit in federal court on behalf of the United States against a State (or state agency) under the False Claims Act, 31 U.S.C. §§ 3729–3733.

I

Originally enacted in 1863, the False Claims Act (FCA) is the most frequently used of a handful of extant laws creating a form of civil action known as *qui tam*. As amended, the FCA imposes civil liability upon "[a]ny person" who, *inter alia*, "knowingly presents, or causes to be presented, to an officer or employee of the United States Government ... a false or fraudulent claim for payment or approval." 31 U.S.C. § 3729(a). The defendant is liable for up to treble damages and a civil penalty of up to $10,000 per claim. *Ibid.*

An FCA action may be commenced in one of two ways. First, the Government itself may bring a civil action against the alleged false claimant. § 3730(a). Second, as is relevant here, a private person (the "relator") may bring a *qui tam* civil action "for the person and for the United States Government" against the alleged false claimant, "in the name of the Government." § 3730(b)(1). If a relator initiates the FCA action, he must deliver a copy of the complaint, and any supporting evidence, to the Government, § 3730(b)(2), which then has 60 days to intervene in the action, §§ 3730(b)(2), (4). If it does so, it assumes primary responsibility for prosecuting the action, § 3730(c)(1), though the relator may continue to participate in the litigation and is entitled to a hearing before voluntary dismissal and to a court determination of reasonableness before settlement, § 3730(c)(2).

If the Government declines to intervene within the 60-day period, the relator has the exclusive right to conduct the action, § 3730(b)(4), and the Government may subsequently intervene only on a showing of "good cause," § 3730(c)(3). The relator receives a share of any proceeds from the action—generally ranging from 15 to 25 percent if the Government intervenes (depending upon the relator's contribution to the prosecution), and from 25 to 30 percent if it does not (depending upon the court's assessment of what is reasonable)—plus attorney's fees and costs. §§ 3730(d)(1)–(2).

Respondent Jonathan Stevens brought this *qui tam* action in the United States District Court for the District of Vermont against petitioner Vermont Agency of Natural Resources, his former employer, alleging that it had submitted false claims to the Environmental Protection Agency (EPA) in connection with various federal grant programs administered by the EPA. Specifically, he claimed that petitioner had overstated the amount of time spent by its employees on the federally funded projects, thereby inducing the Government to disburse more grant money than petitioner was entitled to receive. The United States declined to intervene in the action....

II

We first address the jurisdictional question whether respondent Stevens has standing under Article III of the Constitution to maintain this suit. See *Steel Co. v. Citizens for a Better Environment*, 523 U.S. 83, 93–102, 118 S.Ct. 1003, 140 L.Ed.2d 210 (1998).

As we have frequently explained, a plaintiff must meet three requirements in order to establish Article III standing. See, *e.g., Friends of Earth, Inc. v. Laidlaw Environmental Services (TOC), Inc.*, 528 U.S. 167, ——, 120 S.Ct. 693, 704, 145 L.Ed.2d 610 (2000). First, he must demonstrate "injury in fact"—a harm that is both "concrete" and "actual or imminent, not conjectural or hypothetical." *Whitmore v. Arkansas*, 495 U.S. 149, 155, 110 S.Ct. 1717, 109 L.Ed.2d 135 (1990) (internal quotation marks and citation omitted). Second, he must establish causation—a "fairly ... trace[able]" connection between the alleged injury in fact and the alleged conduct of the defendant. *Simon v. Eastern Ky. Welfare Rights Organization*, 426 U.S. 26, 41, 96 S.Ct. 1917, 48 L.Ed.2d 450 (1976). And third, he must demonstrate redressability—a "substantial likelihood" that the requested relief will remedy the alleged injury in fact. *Id.*, at 45, 96 S.Ct. 1917....

Respondent Stevens contends that he is suing to remedy an injury in fact suffered by the United States. It is beyond doubt that the complaint asserts an injury to the United States—both the injury to its sovereignty arising from violation of its laws (which suffices to support a criminal lawsuit by the Government) and the proprietary injury resulting from the alleged fraud. But "[t]he Art. III judicial power exists only to redress or otherwise to protect against injury *to the complaining party.*" *Warth v. Seldin,* 422 U.S. 490, 499, 95 S.Ct. 2197, 45 L.Ed.2d 343 (1975) (emphasis added); see also *Sierra Club v. Morton,* 405 U.S. 727, 734–735, 92 S. Ct. 1361, 31 L.Ed.2d 636 (1972).

It would perhaps suffice to say that the relator here is simply the statutorily designated agent of the United States, *in whose name* (as the statute provides, see 31 U.S.C. § 3730(b)) the suit is brought—and that the relator's bounty is simply the fee he receives *out of the United States' recovery* for filing and/or prosecuting a successful action on behalf of the Government. This analysis is precluded, however, by the fact that the statute gives the relator himself an interest *in the lawsuit,* and not merely the right to retain a fee out of the recovery. Thus, it provides that "[a] person may bring a civil action for a violation of section 3729 *for the person and for the United States Government,*" § 3730(b) (emphasis added); gives the relator "the right to continue as a party to the action" even when the Government itself has assumed "primary responsibility" for prosecuting it, § 3730(c)(1); entitles the relator to a hearing before the Government's voluntary dismissal of the suit, § 3730(c)(2)(A); and prohibits the Government from settling the suit over the relator's objection without a judicial determination of "fair[ness], adequa[cy] and reasonable[ness]," § 3730(c)(2)(B). For the portion of the recovery retained by the relator, therefore, some explanation of standing other than agency for the Government must be identified.

There is no doubt, of course, that as to this portion of the recovery—the bounty he will receive if the suit is successful—a *qui tam* relator has a "concrete private interest in the outcome of [the] suit." *Lujan, supra,* at 573, 112 S.Ct. 2130. But the same might be said of someone who has placed a wager upon the outcome. An interest unrelated to injury in fact is insufficient to give a plaintiff standing....

We believe, however, that adequate basis for the relator's suit for his bounty is to be found in the doctrine that the assignee of a claim has standing to assert the injury in fact suffered by the assignor. The FCA can reasonably be regarded as effecting a partial assignment of the Government's damages claim. Although we have never expressly recognized "representational standing" on the part of assignees, we have routinely entertained their suits, see, *e.g., Poller v. Columbia Broadcasting System, Inc.,* 368 U.S. 464, 465, 82 S. Ct. 486, 7 L.Ed.2d 458 (1962); *Automatic Radio Mfg. Co. v. Hazeltine Research, Inc.,* 339 U.S. 827, 829, 70 S. Ct. 894, 94 L.Ed. 1312 (1950); *Hubbard v. Tod,* 171 U.S. 474, 475, 19 S.Ct. 14, 43 L.Ed. 246 (1898)—and also suits by subrogees, who have been described as "equitable assign[ees]," L. Simpson, Law of Suretyship 205 (1950), see, *e.g., Vimar Seguros y Reaseguros, S.A. v. M/V Sky Reefer,* 515 U.S. 528, 531, 115 S.Ct. 2322, 132 L.Ed.2d 462 (1995); *Musick, Peeler & Garrett v. Employers Ins. of Wausau,* 508 U.S. 286, 288, 113 S. Ct. 2085, 124 L.Ed.2d 194 (1993). We conclude, therefore, that the United States' injury in fact suffices to confer standing on respondent Stevens.

We are confirmed in this conclusion by the long tradition of *qui tam* actions in England and the American Colonies....

Qui tam actions appear to have originated around the end of the 13th century, when private individuals who had suffered injury began bringing actions in the royal courts on both their own and the Crown's behalf....

Qui tam actions appear to have been as prevalent in America as in England, at least in the period immediately before and after the framing of the Constitution....

We think this history well nigh conclusive with respect to the question before us here: whether *qui tam* actions were "cases and controversies of the sort traditionally amenable to, and resolved by, the judicial process." *Steel Co.*, 523 U.S., at 102, 118 S. Ct. 1003. When combined with the theoretical justification for relator standing discussed earlier, it leaves no room for doubt that a *qui tam* relator under the FCA has Article III standing.[8] We hold that a private individual has standing to bring suit in federal court on behalf of the United States under the False Claims Act, 31 U.S.C. §§ 3729–3733....

It is so ordered.

[Separate opinions on other issues are omitted.]

Notes and Questions

1. The *Stevens* case resolved a persistent controversy during the fourteen years following the strengthening of the False Claims Act and its qui tam mechanism by 1986 amendments. Initially, the Supreme Court granted certiorari in the case on a relatively narrow federalism issue, and then suddenly, ten days before argument, informed counsel to address the broad Article III issue unanimously resolved in this opinion. Combined this with Justice Scalia, who has elaborated his own views on Article III, deciding to write this opinion, and there are many tea leaves to read. Some observers believe he positioned himself to write the upholding of qui tam standing as an occasion to limit other kinds of standing, such as that of citizen plaintiffs pursuant to the environmental laws. For discussion, see Charles Tiefer, "Surprise Order in Qui Tam Case May Foretell a Scalia Surprise," Legal Times, Nov. 29, 1999, at 52; Myriam E. Gilles, *Representational Standing:* U.S. ex rel. Stevens *and the Future of Public Law Litigation*, 89 Cal. L. Rev. 315 (2001).

2. Note how the opinion refers to the injury of the United States that is partially assigned to the suing relator as a "proprietary injury resulting from the alleged fraud." The word proprietary is used in a non-narrow sense, since this case, like many similar cases, occurred regarding a federal grant rather than a federal contract. Even so, the opinion sets off the field of government contract (and grant) law—the realm of such "proprietary injury"—from other fields, like securities or consumer protection law, in which the United States has no proprietary interest. Government contract law thereby becomes a field in which the government's special "proprietary" injury meant, at least in this instance, greater constitutional flexibility in devising remedial systems, a point of interest in the rest of this chapter.

3. *Stevens* obviously took some, but not all, the steam out of the constitutional opposition to qui tam. What is the meaning of the Article II issue set apart in footnote 8? How would Article II challenges to the qui tam statute fare after an Article III challenge was unanimously rejected? For a case illustrating the application of the False Claims Act, see *United States ex rel. Plumbers and Steamfitters Local Union No. 38 v. C. W. Roen Construction Co.*, 183 F.3d 1088 (9th Cir. 1999), provided in the chapter on Policies, subchapter on Labor Standards.

---

8. In so concluding, we express no view on the question whether *qui tam* suits violate Article II, in particular the Appointments Clause of § 2 and the "take Care" Clause of § 3....

Rockwell International Corp. et al. v. United States et al.

No. 05-1272
Supreme Court
127 S.Ct. 1397
Argued Dec. 5, 2006
Decided March 27, 2007

SCALIA, J., delivered the opinion of the Court in which ROBERTS, C.J., and KENNEDY, SOUTER, THOMAS and ALITO, JJ. Joined. STEVENS, J. filed a dissenting opinion in which GINSBURG, J., joined. BREYER, J. took no part in the consideration or decision of the case.

Justice SCALIA delivered the opinion of the Court.

The False Claims Act, 31 U.S.C. §§ 3729–3733, eliminates federal-court jurisdiction over actions under § 3730 of the Act that are based upon the public disclosure of allegations or transactions "unless the action is brought by the Attorney General or the person bringing the action is an original source of the information." § 3730(e)(4)(A). We decide whether respondent James Stone was an original source.

I

The mixture of concrete and pond sludge that is the subject of this case has taken nearly two decades to seep, so to speak, into this Court. Given the long history and the complexity of this litigation, it is well to describe the facts in some detail.

A

From 1975 through 1989, petitioner Rockwell International Corp. was under a management and operating contract with the Department of Energy (DOE) to run the Rocky Flats nuclear weapons plant in Colorado.

* * *

From November 1980 through March 1986, James Stone worked as an engineer at the Rocky Flats plant. In the early 1980's, Rockwell explored the possibility of disposing of the toxic pond sludge that accumulated in solar evaporation ponds at the facility, by mixing it with cement. The idea was to pour the mixture into large rectangular boxes, where it would solidify into "pondcrete" blocks that could be stored onsite or transported to other sites for disposal.

Stone reviewed a proposed manufacturing process for pondcrete in 1982. He concluded that the proposal "would not work," App. 175, and communicated that conclusion to Rockwell management in a written "Engineering Order." As Stone would later explain, he believed "the suggested process would result in an unstable mixture that would later deteriorate and cause unwanted release of toxic wastes to the environment." *Ibid.* He believed this because he "foresaw that the piping system" that extracted sludge from the solar ponds "would not properly remove the sludge and would lead to an inadequate mixture of sludge/waste and cement such that the 'pond crete' blocks would rapidly disintegrate thus creating additional contamination problems." *Id.*, at 290.

Notwithstanding Stone's prediction, Rockwell proceeded with its pondcrete project and successfully manufactured "concrete hard" pondcrete during the period of Stone's employment at Rocky Flats. It was only after Stone was laid off in March 1986 that what the parties have called "insolid" pondcrete blocks were discovered. According to respondents, Rockwell knew by October 1986 that a substantial number of pondcrete blocks were insolid, but DOE did not become aware of the problem until May 1988, when several pondcrete blocks began to leak, leading to the discovery of thousands of other insolid blocks. The media reported these discoveries, 3 Appellants' App. in Nos. 99-1351, 99-1352, 99-1353 (CA10), pp. 889-38 to 889-39; and attributed the malfunction to Rockwell's reduction of the ratio of concrete to sludge in the mixture.

In June 1987, more than a year after he had left Rockwell's employ, Stone went to the Federal Bureau of Investigation (FBI) with allegations of environmental crimes at Rocky Flats during the time of his employment.

* * *

Stone provided the FBI with 2,300 pages of documents, buried among which was his 1982 engineering report predicting that the pondcrete-system design would not work. Stone did not discuss his pondcrete allegations with the FBI in their conversations.

* * *

Based in part on information allegedly learned from Stone, the Government obtained a search warrant for Rocky Flats, and on June 6, 1989, 75 FBI and Environmental Protection Agency agents raided the facility. The affidavit in support of the warrant included allegations (1) that pondcrete blocks were insolid "due to an inadequate waste-concrete mixture," App. 429, (2) that Rockwell obtained award fees based on its alleged "'excellent'" management of Rocky Flats, *id.,* at 98, and (3) that Rockwell made false statements and concealed material facts in violation of the Resource Conservation and Recovery Act of 1976 (RCRA), 90 Stat. 2811, 42 U.S.C. § 6928, and 18 U.S.C. § 1001. Newspapers published these allegations. In March 1992, Rockwell pleaded guilty to 10 environmental violations, including the knowing storage of insolid pondcrete blocks in violation of RCRA. Rockwell agreed to pay $18.5 million in fines.

B

In July 1989, Stone filed a *qui tam* suit under the False Claims Act. That Act prohibits false or fraudulent claims for payment to the United States, 31 U.S.C. § 3729(a), and authorizes civil actions to remedy such fraud to be brought by the Attorney General, § 3730(a), or by private individuals in the Government's name, § 3730(b)(1). The Act provides, however, that "[n]o court shall have jurisdiction over an action under this section based upon the public disclosure of allegations or transactions ... from the news media, unless the action is brought by the Attorney General or the person bringing the action is an original source of the information." § 3730(e)(4)(A). An "original source" is "an individual who has direct and independent knowledge of the information on which the allegations are based and has voluntarily provided the information to the Government before filing an action under this section which is based on the information." § 3730(e)(4)(B).

Stone's complaint alleged that Rockwell was required to comply with certain federal and state environmental laws and regulations, including RCRA; that Rockwell committed numerous violations of these laws and regulations throughout the 1980's; and that, in order to induce the Government to make payments or approvals under Rockwell's contract, Rockwell knowingly presented false and fraudulent claims to the Government in violation of the False Claims Act, 31 U.S.C. § 3729(a). As required under the Act, Stone filed his complaint under seal and simultaneously delivered to the Government a confidential disclosure statement describing "substantially all material evidence and information" in his possession, § 3730(b)(2). The statement identified 26 environmental and safety issues, only one of which involved pondcrete.

* * *

The Government initially declined to intervene in Stone's action, but later reversed course, and in November 1996, the District Court granted the Government's intervention. Several weeks later, at the suggestion of the District Court, the Government and Stone filed a joint amended complaint. As relevant here, the amended complaint alleged that Rockwell violated RCRA by storing leaky pondcrete blocks, but did not allege that any defect in the piping system (as predicted by Stone) caused insolid pondcrete.

* * *

II

Section 3730(e)(4)(A) provides that

"[n]o court shall have jurisdiction over an action under this section based upon the public disclosure of allegations or transactions in a criminal, civil, or administrative hearing, in a congressional, administrative, or Government Accounting Office report, hearing, audit, or investigation, or from the news media, unless the action is brought by the Attorney General or the person bringing the action is an original source of the information." (Footnote omitted.)

As discussed above, § 3730(e)(4)(B) defines "original source" as "an individual who [1] has direct and independent knowledge of the information on which the allegations are based and [2] has voluntarily provided the information to the Government before filing an action under this section which is based on the information." As this case comes to the Court, it is conceded that the claims on which Stone prevailed were based upon publicly disclosed allegations within the meaning of § 3730(e)(4)(A). The question is whether Stone qualified under the original-source exception to the public-disclosure bar.

We begin with the possibility that little analysis is required in this case, for Stone asserts that Rockwell conceded his original-source status. Rockwell responds that it conceded no such thing and that, even had it done so, the concession would have been irrelevant because § 3730(e)(4) is jurisdictional. We agree with the latter proposition.

* * *

III

We turn to the first requirement of original-source status, that the relator have "direct and independent knowledge of the information on which the allegations are based." 31 U.S.C. § 3730(e)(4)(B). Because we have not previously addressed this provision, several preliminary questions require our attention.

A

First, does the phrase "information on which the allegations are based" refer to the information on which the *relator's allegations* are based or the information on which the *publicly disclosed allegations* that triggered the public-disclosure bar are based? The parties agree it is the former.

* * *

The sense of the matter offers strong additional support for this interpretation. Section 3730(e)(4)(A) bars actions based on publicly disclosed allegations whether or not the information on which those allegations are based has been made public. It is difficult to understand why Congress would care whether a relator knows about the information underlying a publicly disclosed allegation (*e.g.,* what a confidential source told a newspaper reporter about in solid pondcrete) when the relator has direct and independent knowledge of different information supporting the same allegation (*e.g.,* that a defective process would inevitably lead to insolid pondcrete). Not only would that make little sense, it would raise nettlesome procedural problems, placing courts in the position of comparing the relator's information with the often *unknowable* information on which the public disclosure was based. Where that latter information has not been disclosed (by reason, for example, of a reporter's desire to protect his source), the relator would presumably be out of court. To bar a relator with direct and independent knowledge of information underlying his allegations just because no one can know what information underlies the similar allegations of some other person simply makes no sense.

* * *

B

Having determined that the phrase "information on which the allegations are based" refers to the relator's allegations and not the publicly disclosed allegations, we confront more textual ambiguity: *Which* of the relator's allegations are the relevant ones? Stone's allegations changed during the course of the litigation, yet he asks that we look only to his original complaint. Rockwell argues that Stone must satisfy the original-source exception through all stages of the litigation.

In our view, the term "allegations" is not limited to the allegations of the original complaint. It includes (at a minimum) the allegations in the original complaint *as amended*. The statute speaks not of the allegations in the "original complaint" (or even the allegations in the "complaint"), but of the relator's "allegations" *simpliciter*. Absent some limitation of §3730(e)(4)'s requirement to the relator's *initial* complaint, we will not infer one. Such a limitation would leave the relator free to plead a trivial theory of fraud for which he had some direct and independent knowledge and later amend the complaint to include theories copied from the public domain or from materials in the Government's possession. Even the Government concedes that new allegations regarding a fundamentally different fraudulent scheme require reevaluation of the court's jurisdiction. See Brief for United States 40; Tr. of Oral Arg. 40.

* * *

The Government objects that this approach risks driving a wedge between the Government and relators. It worries that future relators might decline to "acquiesc[e]" in the Government's tactical decision to narrow the claims in a case if that would eliminate jurisdiction with respect to the relator. Brief for United States 44. Even if this policy concern were valid, it would not induce us to determine jurisdiction on the basis of information underlying allegations that he no longer makes.

IV

Judged according to the principles set forth above, Stone's knowledge falls short. The only false claims ultimately found by the jury (and hence the only ones to which our jurisdictional inquiry is pertinent to the outcome) involved false statements with respect to environmental, safety, and health compliance over a one-and-a-half-year period between April 1, 1987, and September 30, 1988. As described by Stone and the Government in the final pretrial order, the only pertinent problem with respect to this period of time for which Stone claimed to have direct and independent knowledge was insolid pondcrete. Because Stone was no longer employed by Rockwell at the time, he did not know that the pondcrete was insolid; he did not know that pondcrete storage was even subject to RCRA; he did not know that Rockwell would fail to remedy the defect; he did not know that the insolid pondcrete leaked while being stored onsite; and, of course, he did not know that Rockwell made false statements to the Government regarding pondcrete storage.

Stone's prediction that the pondcrete would be insolid because of a flaw in the piping system does not qualify as "direct and independent knowledge" of the pondcrete defect. Of course a *qui tam* relator's misunderstanding of *why* a concealed defect occurred would normally be immaterial as long as he knew the defect actually existed. But here Stone did not *know* that the pondcrete failed; he *predicted* it. Even if a prediction can qualify as direct and independent knowledge in some cases (a point we need not address), it assuredly does not do so when its premise of cause and effect is wrong. Stone's prediction was a failed prediction, disproved by Stone's own allegations. As Stone acknowledged, Rockwell was able to produce "concrete hard" pondcrete using the machinery Stone said was defective. According to respondents' allegations in the final pretrial order, the insolidity problem was caused by a new foreman's reduction of the cement-to-sludge ratio in the winter of 1986, long after Stone had left Rocky Flats.

* * *

Because Stone did not have direct and independent knowledge of the information upon which his allegations were based, we need not decide whether Stone met the second requirement of original-source status, that he have voluntarily provided the information to the Government before filing his action.

V

Respondents contend that even if Stone failed the original-source test as to his pondcrete allegations, the Government's intervention in his case provided an independent basis of jurisdiction. Section 3730(e)(4)(A) permits jurisdiction over an action based on publicly disclosed allegations or transactions if the action is "brought by the Attorney General." Respondents say that any inquiry into Stone's original-source status with respect to amendments to the complaint was unnecessary because the Government had intervened, making this an "action brought by the Attorney General." Even assuming that Stone was an original source of allegations in his initial complaint, we reject respondents' "intervention" argument.

The False Claims Act contemplates two types of actions. First, under § 3730(a), "[i]f the Attorney General finds that a person has violated or is violating section 3729, the Attorney General may bring a civil action under this section against the person." Second, under § 3730(b), "[a] person may bring an action for a violation of section 3729 for the person and for the United States Government." When a private person brings an action under § 3730(b), the Government may elect to "proceed with the action," § 3730(b)(4)(A), or it may "declin[e] to take over the action, in which case the person bringing the action shall have the right to conduct the action," § 3730(b)(4)(B). The statute thus draws a sharp distinction between actions brought by the Attorney General under § 3730(a) and actions brought by a private person under § 3730(b). An action brought by a private person does not become one brought by the Government just because the Government intervenes and elects to "proceed with the action."

It is so ordered.

Justice BREYER took no part in the consideration or decision of this case.

Justice STEVENS, with whom Justice GINSBURG joins, dissenting.

Any private citizen may bring an action to enforce the False Claims Act, 31 U.S.C. §§ 3729–3733, unless the information on which his allegations are based is already in the public domain. Even if the information is publicly available, however, the citizen may still sue if he was an "original source" of that information. § 3730(e)(4)(A) ("No court shall have jurisdiction over an action under this section based upon the public disclosure of allegations or transactions ... unless the action is brought by the Attorney General or the person bringing the action is an original source of the information"). Because I believe the Court has misinterpreted these provisions to require that an "original source" in a *qui tam* action have knowledge of the actual facts underlying the allegations on which he may ultimately prevail, I respectfully dissent.

In my view, a plain reading of the statute's provisions — specifically, §§ 3730(e)(4)(A) and (B) — makes clear that it is the information underlying the publicly disclosed allegations, not the information underlying the allegations in the relator's complaint (original or amended), of which the relator must be an original source. Moreover, the statute's use of the article "an," rather than "the," in describing the original source indicates that the relator need not be the *sole* source of the information.

By contrast, the majority's approach suggests that the relator must have knowledge of actual facts supporting the theory ultimately proven at trial — in other words, knowledge of the information underlying the prevailing claims. See *ante*, at 1409 (limiting the relevant jurisdictional inquiry to those "false claims ultimately found by the jury"). I disagree. Such a view is not supported by the statute, which requires only that the relator have "direct and independent knowledge" of the information on which the publicly disclosed allegations are based and that the relator provide such information to the Government in a timely manner. As I read the statute, the jurisdictional inquiry focuses on the facts in the public domain at the time the action is commenced. If the process of discovery leads to amended theories of recovery, amendments to the original complaint would not affect jurisdiction that was proper at the time of the original filing.

In this case, as the Court points out, the fact that Rockwell was storing thousands of insolid pondcrete blocks at the Rocky Flats facility had been publicly disclosed by the news media before Stone filed this lawsuit. *Ante,* at 1402, 1403. In my view, the record establishes that Stone was an original source of the allegations publicly disclosed by the media in June 1989, even though he thought that the deterioration of the pondcrete blocks would be caused by poor engineering rather than a poor formula for the mixture. The search warrant that was executed on June 6, 1989, and the Federal Bureau of Investigation (FBI) affidavit that was released to the news media on June 9, 1989, were both based, in part, on interviews with Stone and on information Stone had provided to the Government, including the 1982 Engineering Order.

With respect to earlier media coverage of the pondcrete leakage discovery in May 1988, however, Stone's status as an original source is less obvious. Stone first went to the FBI with allegations of Rockwell's environmental violations in March 1986. He subsequently met with several FBI agents over the course of several years. *Id.,* at 180–182. During those meetings he provided the FBI with thousands of pages of documents, including the Engineering Order, in which he predicted that the pondcrete system design would not work. On the basis of that record, it seems likely that Stone (1) had "direct and independent knowledge of the information on which the [publicly disclosed] allegations [we]re based" and (2) voluntarily provided such information to the Government before filing suit. It is, however, his burden to establish that he did so. Because there has been no finding as to whether Stone was an original source as to those public disclosures, I would vacate and remand for a determination whether Stone was in fact an original source of the allegations publicly disclosed by the media in 1988 and 1989.

* * *

Notes and Questions

1. Should the original source barrier be high or low? How one answers that question often seems to depend on how, generally, one views the False Claims Act and the qui tam

mechanism. Proponents champion qui tam as summoning forth additional help from whistleblowers in the fight against fraud and want a low threshold barrier; opponents decry the mechanism as subjecting government contractors to unnecessary attacks by fee-seeking lawyers and want a high barrier.

2. Is there a fundamental tension built into the public disclosure barrier because it does not make the merits (or lack thereof) of the relator's allegations an element of the jurisdictional test? Or, does that tension get resolved because the Justice Department evaluates, in at least some sense, the merits of the relator's allegations in deciding whether to intervene, and such intervention obviates application of the jurisdictional test?

Schindler Elevator Corporation, Petitioner, v. United States ex rel. Daniel Kirk

Supreme Court of the United States
131 S.Ct. 1885
No. 10-188
Argued March 1, 2011
Decided May 16, 2011

Opinion

Justice THOMAS delivered the opinion of the Court.

The False Claims Act (FCA), 31 U.S.C. §§ 3729–3733, prohibits submitting false or fraudulent claims for payment to the United States, § 3729(a), and authorizes *qui tam* suits, in which private parties bring civil actions in the Government's name, § 3730(b)(1). This case concerns the FCA's public disclosure bar, which generally forecloses *qui tam* suits that are "based upon the public disclosure of allegations or transactions ... in a congressional, administrative, or Government Accounting Office report, hearing, audit, or investigation." § 3730(e)(4)(A) (footnote omitted). We must decide whether a federal agency's written response to a request for records under the Freedom of Information Act (FOIA), 5 U.S.C. § 552, constitutes a "report" within the meaning of the public disclosure bar. We hold that it does.

I

Petitioner Schindler Elevator Corporation manufactures, installs, and services elevators and escalators. In 1989, Schindler acquired Millar Elevator Industries, Inc., and the two companies merged in 2002.

Since 1999, Schindler and the United States have entered into hundreds of contracts that are subject to the Vietnam Era Veterans' Readjustment Assistance Act of 1972 (VEVRAA). That Act requires contractors like Schindler to report certain information to the Secretary of Labor, including how many of its employees are "qualified covered veterans" under the statute. 38 U.S.C. § 4212(d)(1). VEVRAA regulations required Schindler to agree in each of its contracts that it would "submit VETS-100 Reports no later than September 30 of each year." 48 CFR § 52.222-37(c) (2008); see also § 22.1310(b).

Respondent Daniel Kirk, a United States Army veteran who served in Vietnam, was employed by Millar and Schindler from 1978 until 2003. In August 2003, Kirk resigned from Schindler in response to what he saw as Schindler's efforts to force him out.

In March 2005, Kirk filed this action against Schindler under the False Claims Act, which imposes civil penalties and treble damages on persons who submit false or fraudulent claims for payment to the United States. 31 U.S.C. § 3729(a). The FCA authorizes both civil actions by the Attorney General and private *qui tam* actions to enforce its provisions. § 3730. When, as here, the Government chooses not to intervene in a *qui tam* action, the private relator stands to receive between 25% and 30% of the proceeds of the action. § 3730(d)(2).

In an amended complaint filed in June 2007, Kirk alleged that Schindler had submitted hundreds of false claims for payment under its Government contracts. According to Kirk, Schindler had violated VEVRAA's reporting requirements by failing to file certain required VETS-100 reports and including false information in those it did file. The company's claims for payment were false, Kirk alleged, because Schindler had falsely certified its compliance with VEVRAA. Kirk did not specify the amount of damages he sought on behalf of the United States, but he asserted that the value of Schindler's VEVRAA-covered contracts exceeded $100 million.

To support his allegations, Kirk pointed to information his wife, Linda Kirk, received from the Department of Labor (DOL) in response to three FOIA requests. Mrs. Kirk had sought all VETS-100 reports filed by Schindler for the years 1998 through 2006. The DOL responded by letter or e-mail to each request with information about the records found for each year, including years for which no responsive records were located. The DOL informed Mrs. Kirk that it found no VETS-100 reports filed by Schindler in 1998, 1999, 2000, 2002, or 2003. For the other years, the DOL provided Mrs. Kirk with copies of the reports filed by Schindler, 99 in all.

Schindler moved to dismiss on a number of grounds, including that the FCA's public disclosure bar deprived the District Court of jurisdiction. See § 3730(e)(4)(A). The District Court granted the motion, concluding that most of Kirk's allegations failed to state a claim and that the remainder were based upon the public disclosure of allegations or transactions in an administrative "report" or "investigation." 606 F.Supp.2d 448 (S.D.N.Y.2009).

The Court of Appeals for the Second Circuit vacated and remanded. 601 F.3d 94 (2010). The court effectively held that an agency's response to a FOIA request is neither a "report" nor an "investigation" within the meaning of the FCA's public disclosure bar. See *id.*, at 103–111 (agreeing with *United States ex rel. Haight v. Catholic Healthcare West,* 445 F.3d 1147 (C.A.9 2006), and disagreeing with *United States ex rel. Mistick PBT v. Housing Auth. of Pittsburgh,* 186 F.3d 376 (C.A.3 1999)). We granted certiorari, 561 U.S. ___, 131 S.Ct. 63, 177 L.Ed.2d 1152 (2010), and now reverse and remand.

II

Schindler argues that "report" in the FCA's public disclosure bar carries its ordinary meaning and that the DOL's written responses to Mrs. Kirk's FOIA requests are therefore "reports." We agree.

A

1

Adopted in 1986, the FCA's public disclosure bar provides:

> "No court shall have jurisdiction over an action under this section based upon the public disclosure of allegations or transactions in a criminal, civil, or administrative hearing, in a congressional, administrative, or Government Accounting Office report, hearing, audit, or investigation, or from the news media, unless the action is brought by the Attorney General or the person bringing the action is an original source of the information." 31 U.S.C. § 3730(e)(4)(A) (footnote omitted).

This broad ordinary meaning of "report" is consistent with the generally broad scope of the FCA's public disclosure bar.

* * *

2

Nor is there any textual basis for adopting a narrower definition of "report." The Court of Appeals, in holding that FOIA responses were not "reports," looked to the words "hearing, audit, or investigation," and the phrase "criminal, civil, [and] administrative hearings." It concluded that all of these sources "connote the synthesis of information in an investigatory context" to "serve some end of the government." 601 F.3d, at 107; cf. Brief for Respondent 30, n. 15 ("Each is part of the government's ongoing effort to fight fraud"). Applying the *noscitur a sociis* canon, the Court of Appeals then determined that these " 'neighboring words' " mandated a narrower meaning for "report" than its ordinary meaning. 601 F.3d, at 107.

* * *

We emphasized in *Graham County* that "*all* of the sources [of public disclosure] listed in § 3730(e)(4)(A) provide interpretive guidance." 559 U.S., at ___, 130 S.Ct., at 1404. When all of the sources are considered, the reference to "news media" — which the Court of Appeals did not consider — suggests a much broader scope. *Ibid.*

The Government similarly errs by focusing only on the adjectives "congressional, administrative, or [GAO]," which precede "report." Brief for United States as *Amicus Curiae* 18. It contends that these adjectives suggest that the public disclosure bar applies only to agency reports "analogous to those that Congress and the GAO would issue or conduct." *Ibid.* As we explained in *Graham County,* however, those three adjectives tell us nothing more than that a "report" must be governmental. See 559 U.S., at ___ , n. 7, 130 S.Ct., at 1403, n. 7. The governmental nature of the FOIA responses at issue is not disputed.

Finally, applying the ordinary meaning of "report" does not render superfluous the other sources of public disclosure in § 3730(e)(4)(A). Kirk argues that reading "report" to mean "something that gives information" would subsume the other words in the phrase "report, hearing, audit, or investigation." Brief for Respondent 23. But Kirk admits that hearings, audits, and investigations are processes "to *obtain* information." *Ibid.* (emphasis added). Those processes are thus clearly different from "something that *gives* information." Moreover, the statute contemplates some redundancy: An "audit," for example, will often be a type of "investigation."

* * *

B

A written agency response to a FOIA request falls within the ordinary meaning of "report." FOIA requires each agency receiving a request to "notify the person making such request of [its] determination and the reasons therefor." 5 U.S.C. § 552(a)(6)(A)(i). When an agency denies a request in whole or in part, it must additionally "set forth the names and titles or positions of each person responsible for the denial," "make a reasonable effort to estimate the volume of any [denied] matter," and "provide any such estimate to the person making the request." §§ 552(a)(6)(C)(i), (F). The DOL has adopted more detailed regulations implementing FOIA and mandating a response in writing. See 29 CFR § 70.21(a) (2009) (requiring written notice of the grant of a FOIA request and a description of the manner in which records will be disclosed); §§ 70.21(b)–(c) (requiring a "brief statement of the reason or reasons for [a] denial," as well as written notification if a record "cannot be located or has been destroyed" (italics deleted)). So, too, have other federal agencies. See, *e.g.,* 28 CFR § 16.6 (2010) (Dept. of Justice); 43 CFR § 2.21 (2009) (Dept. of Interior); 7 CFR § 1.7 (2010) (Dept. of Agriculture). Such an agency response plainly is "something that gives information," a "notification," and an "official or formal statement of facts."

Any records the agency produces along with its written FOIA response are part of that response, "just as if they had been reproduced as an appendix to a printed report." *Mistick,* 186 F.3d, at 384, n. 5. Nothing in the public disclosure bar suggests that a document and its attachments must be disaggregated and evaluated individually. If an allegation or transaction is disclosed in a record attached to a FOIA response, it is disclosed "in" that FOIA response and, therefore, disclosed "in" a report for the purposes of the public disclosure bar.

The DOL's three written FOIA responses to Mrs. Kirk, along with their attached records, are thus reports within the meaning of the public disclosure bar. Each response was an "official or formal statement" that "[gave] information" and "notif[ied]" Mrs. Kirk of the agency's resolution of her FOIA request.

III

A

* * *

1

The drafting history of the public disclosure bar does not contradict our holding. As originally enacted in 1863, the FCA placed no restriction on the sources from which a *qui tam* relator could acquire information on which to base a lawsuit. See *Graham County,* 559 U.S., at ___, 130 S.Ct., at 1411. Accordingly, this Court upheld the recovery of a relator, even though the Government claimed that he had discovered the basis for his lawsuit by reading a federal criminal indictment. See *United States ex rel. Marcus v. Hess,* 317 U.S. 537, 63 S.Ct. 379, 87 L.Ed. 443 (1943). In response, Congress amended the statute to preclude such "parasitic" *qui tam* actions based on "evidence or information in the possession of the United States ... at the time such suit was brought." 559 U.S., at ___ 130 S.Ct. at 1411 (internal quotation marks omitted). Then, in 1986, Congress replaced the so-called Government knowledge bar with the narrower public disclosure bar. *Id.,* at ___, 130 S.Ct. at 1411.

The Court of Appeals concluded that it would be inconsistent with this drafting history to hold that written FOIA responses are reports. The court reasoned that doing so would "essentially resurrect, in a significant subset of cases, the government possession standard ... repudiated in 1986." 601 F.3d, at 109.

We disagree with the Court of Appeals' conclusion. As a threshold matter, "the drafting history of the public disclosure bar raises more questions than it answers." *Graham County, supra,* at ___, 130 S.Ct., at 1407. In any event, it is hardly inconsistent with the drafting history to read the public disclosure bar as operating similarly to the Government knowledge bar in a "subset of cases." 601 F.3d, at 109. As we have observed, "[r]ather than simply repeal the Government knowledge bar," the public disclosure bar was "an effort to strike *a balance* between encouraging private persons to root out fraud and stifling parasitic lawsuits." 559 U.S., at ___, 130 S.Ct., at 1407 (emphasis added).

If anything, the drafting history supports our holding. The sort of case that Kirk has brought seems to us a classic example of the "opportunistic" litigation that the public disclosure bar is designed to discourage. *Ibid.* (internal quotation marks omitted). Although

Kirk alleges that he became suspicious from his own experiences as a veteran working at Schindler, anyone could have filed the same FOIA requests and then filed the same suit. Similarly, anyone could identify a few regulatory filing and certification requirements, submit FOIA requests until he discovers a federal contractor who is out of compliance, and potentially reap a windfall in a *qui tam* action under the FCA. See Brief for Chamber of Commerce of the United States of America et al. as *Amici Curiae* 20 ("Government contractors ... are required to submit certifications related to everything from how they dispose of hazardous materials to their affirmative action plans" (citing 40 U.S.C. § 3142 and 29 U.S.C. § 793)).

2

* * *

The DOL's three written FOIA responses in this case, along with the accompanying records produced to Mrs. Kirk, are reports within the meaning of the public disclosure bar. Whether Kirk's suit is "based upon ... allegations or transactions" disclosed in those reports is a question for the Court of Appeals to resolve on remand. The judgment of the United States Court of Appeals for the Second Circuit is reversed, and the case is remanded for further proceedings consistent with this opinion.

It is so ordered.

Justice KAGAN took no part in the consideration or decision of this case.

Justice GINSBURG, with whom Justice BREYER and Justice SOTOMAYOR join, dissenting.

The Veteran Era Veterans' Readjustment Assistance Act of 1972 (VEVRAA) requires federal contractors to certify, each year, the number of "qualified covered veterans" they employ and related information. 38 U.S.C. § 4212(d); 48 CFR §§ 22.1310(b) and 52.222-37(c) (2008). Respondent Daniel A. Kirk, a Vietnam War veteran and a former employee of petitioner Schindler Elevator Corporation (Schindler), had cause to believe, based on his own experience and observations, that Schindler failed to meet VEVRAA's annual information-reporting requirements. To confirm and support his on-the-job observations, Kirk obtained, through several Freedom of Information Act (FOIA) requests to the Department of Labor (DOL), copies of Schindler's VEVRAA filings. The DOL responses revealed that, in some years, Schindler filed no information, while in some other years, the corporation filed false information. Armed with the DOL's confirmation of his own impressions, Kirk commenced suit against Schindler under the federal False Claims Act (FCA), 31 U.S.C. § 3729 *et seq.*

In a carefully developed, highly persuasive opinion, the Second Circuit explained why a federal agency's response to a FOIA request should not automatically qualify as a "report, hearing, audit, or investigation" preclusive of a whistleblower's lawsuit under the public disclosure bar of the FCA, § 3730(e)(4). I would affirm the Second Circuit's judgment as faithful to the text, context, purpose, and history of the FCA's public disclosure bar.

The Court finds no "textual basis" for the Second Circuit's interpretation of the statutory language. *Ante,* at 1891 — 1892. But the Court of Appeals' opinion considered text as well as context. Leaving aside the term "report," the court explained:

> "All of the other terms in [§ 3730(e)(4)(A)'s] list of enumerated sources connote the synthesis of information in an investigatory context. '[C]riminal, civil, [and] administrative hearings,' for instance, all entail a government inquiry into a given subject, here into an alleged case of fraud. Similarly, government 'hearing[s and] audit[s]' are processes by which information is compiled with the concerted aim of deepening a government entity's knowledge of a given subject or, often, determining whether a party is in compliance with applicable law.…

"In this context, the term 'report' most readily bears a narrower meaning than simply 'something that gives information.' Rather, it connotes the compilation or analysis of information with the aim of synthesizing that information in order to serve some end of the government, as in a 'hearing' or 'audit.' It does not naturally extend to cover the mechanistic production of documents in response to a FOIA request made by a member of the public." 601 F.3d 94, 107 (2010) (citations omitted).

* * *

By ranking DOL's ministerial response an "administrative ... report," akin to a "Government Accounting Office report," § 3730(e)(4)(A) (footnote omitted), the Court weakens the force of the FCA as a weapon against fraud on the part of Government contractors. Why should a whistleblower attentive to the heightened pleading standards of Federal Rule of Civil Procedure 9(b) be barred from court if he seeks corroboration for his allegations, as Kirk did, through a FOIA request simply for copies of a contractor's filings? After today's decision, which severely limits whistleblowers' ability to substantiate their allegations before commencing suit, that question is worthy of Congress' attention.

B. TINA and Defective Pricing

For discussion of the subjects in this subchapter, see: Steven M. Masiello, Phillip R. Seckman, *Managing Subcontract Defective Pricing Liability*, 04-10 Briefing Papers 1 (2004); Richard C. Johnson, *Identifying "Subcontractors" Under TINA and Access-to-Records Statutes: Filling an Annoying Gap in Government Contracts Jurisprudence*, 32 Pub. Cont. L.J. 739 (2003); see: Richard C. Johnson, *Identifying "Subcontractors" Under TINA & Access To Records Statutes: Filling An Annoying Gap In Government Contracts Jurisprudence*, 32 Pub. Cont. L.J. 739 (Summer 2003); Carl L. Vacketta & Susan H. Pope, *Commercial Item Contracts: When Is a Government Contract Term or Condition Consistent with "Standard" or "Customary" Commercial Practice?*, 27 Pub. Cont. L.J. 291 (1998); Richard J. Wall & Christopher B. Pockney *Revisiting Commercial Pricing Reform*, 27 Pub. Cont. L.J. 315 (1998); Steven A. Kaufman & Clayton S. Marsh, *The Law of Defective Pricing: Its Shape and Fit with Commercial Law*, 19 Pub. Cont. L.J. 559 (1990).

Truth in Negotiations Act
Steven Feldman, *Government Contract Guidebook*
(Thomson Reuters, 4th ed. 2010)

In general

In 1962, Congress passed the Truth in Negotiations Act (TINA). The purpose of the Act is to put the government on an equal footing with contractors in contract negotiations by requiring contractors to provide the government with an extremely broad range of cost or pricing information relevant to the expected costs of contract performance. TINA, as amended, and the implementing procurement regulations require prime contractors and subcontractors in certain circumstances to submit cost or pricing data to the government and to certify that, to the best of their knowledge and belief, the data submitted are current, accurate, and complete. These rules have had a significant impact on government contractors: where the contractor submits inaccurate, incomplete, or noncurrent data, the contractor will be subject to contractual, civil, and even possible criminal liability.

The enactment, in October of 1994, of the Federal Acquisition Streamlining Act (FASA) had a significant impact on the operation of TINA. Along with FASA's key mandate of streamlining and consolidating federal acquisition laws, one of the statute's major goals was facilitating the government's access to products developed in the commercial sector. To accomplish this, FASA implemented a number of significant changes to TINA, including (a) raising the dollar threshold for TINA's application, (b) making the exceptions to the requirement to obtain cost or pricing data mandatory, (c) broadening several of these exceptions and making them less mechanical, (d) creating a "commercial item" exception, and (e) encouraging Contracting Officers to determine price reasonableness based on information other than cost or pricing data whenever possible.

* * *

Exceptions and waivers

TINA provides exceptions from its cost or pricing data submission requirements for prime contracts and contract modifications where the price negotiated is based on (a) adequate price competition, (b) prices set by law or regulation, or (c) the procurement of a commercial item. In addition, in exceptional cases, the head of the contracting activity may waive TINA requirements.

Exceptions and waivers—Adequate price competition

The first basis for exemption—"adequate price competition"—has resulted in much confusion over the years. Under the current FAR, price competition can exist even if only one offer is received from a responsible, responsive offeror provided there was a reasonable expectation, based on market research or other assessment, that two or more responsible offerors, competing independently, would submit priced offers in response to the solicitation's expressed requirement. Price competition is presumed to be adequate except under circumstances delineated in the FAR. Thus, assuming that a responsible offeror submits a responsive offer, in a competitive environment, the key to finding price competition is whether the contract is to be awarded to the offeror whose proposal represents the best value where price is a substantial factor in the source selection.

* * *

"Cost or pricing data" defined

TINA defines the term "cost or pricing data" as follows:

> [A]ll facts that, as of the date of agreement on the price of a contract (or the price of a contract modification), or, if applicable consistent with [*10 U.S.C.A. § 2306(e)(1)(B)*], another date agreed upon between the parties, a prudent buyer or seller would reasonably expect to affect price negotiations significantly. Such term does not include information that is judgmental, but does include the factual information from which a judgment was derived.

Under the above definition of cost or pricing data, the contractor must disclose as "facts" the data forming the basis for any judgment, projection, or estimate. The nondisclosure of this data will render the submission incomplete or inaccurate.

The "date of price agreement" means the "handshake" date, even if no legal contract exists at that time. Data are required to be current as of the time of price agreement. Although some reasonable "lag time" is inherent between the time when data are submitted and the time of price agreement, a contractor's failure to disclose labor rates that were available when prices were negotiated will constitute defective pricing. However, new or changed facts occurring after the "handshake" date need not be disclosed.

"Significant" information necessarily excludes data on which a contractor cannot reasonably have been expected to rely in formulating its price. But whether data are significant for TINA purposes must be analyzed on a case-by-case basis. Thus in one case, information concerning the number of employees that would be performing under a follow-on contract was considered cost or pricing data, and in another, vendor discounts—to which the government would not have been entitled—were considered significant. But, a contractor was not required to supply information on "every price discount it provided to its customers ever."

The concept of a "significant effect" on the price negotiations has been interpreted broadly. For example, in one case it was held that $20,000 out of a target price of $15 million was "significant." In another, an impact of $5,527 on a total price of $2.7 million was considered significant. But sums of $33 and $146.80 in the context of a government claim of $3.9 million were considered insignificant. The Defense Contract Audit Agency Contract Audit Manual provides some guidance on the subject. It states that potential price adjustments of 5% or $50,000, whichever is less, should normally be considered immaterial and pursued only when (1) a contractor's deficient estimating practices have resulted in recurring defective pricing, or (2) the potential price adjustment is due to a systematic deficiency that affects all contracts priced during the period.

* * *

Submission of data

In October 1997, Standard Forms 1411 and 1448 for submitting and seeking exemptions from submitting cost or pricing data were both eliminated. The FAR still requires submission of essentially identical information but permits it to be submitted in the prime's or subcontractor's own format or in whatever alternate format may be specified in the solicitation.

There are few definite rules regarding what constitutes a proper submission of cost or pricing data. At a minimum, there must be a reasonable identification of the data. Data vagueness (e.g., using only general terms in revealing lower vendor costs when viewed against the other numerous and detailed price quotations) can lead to a finding that there was no meaningful disclosure. Generally a contractor cannot escape liability for defective cost or pricing data by proving merely that the government should have been aware that the data were defective. However, a contractor is not obligated to analyze the impact of a raw data update where the government is equally capable of analyzing the data.[

* * *

Submission of data—When submitted

TINA requires that data be submitted before the award of a contract or modification expected to exceed the statutory price thresholds, but the FAR requires that data be submitted or identified in writing by the time of agreement on price or another time agreed upon by the parties "as close as practicable to the date of agreement on price." More than one submission of data may be necessary to comply with TINA and the implementing regulations, including a submission with the initial proposal and the updating of the data during negotiations. Many cautious contractors perform "sweeps" (an updating of all cost or pricing data after the conclusion of negotiations but before the execution of the "Certificate of Current Cost or Pricing Data") to ensure that all relevant data in the contractor's possession when negotiations were concluded have, in fact, been submitted to the government. Contractors customarily furnish any additional data discovered as a result of the sweep with their executed certificate. (Prudent prime contractors require their subcontractors to engage in similar sweeps, and include any additional subcontractor data in their supplemental data submissions.) The Federal Circuit has held, with respect to understatements of costs discovered during a sweep, that data discovered before certification had to be disclosed and could not be used as an offset, but data discovered after certification could be used as an offset against price reductions for other defective pricing.

* * *

Submission of data — Subcontractor data

Cost or pricing data is required for the award of a subcontract at any tier, if the contractor and each higher tier subcontractor were required to submit cost or pricing data. Any contractor or subcontractor that is required to submit cost or pricing data also shall obtain and analyze cost or pricing data before awarding any subcontract, purchase order, or modification expected to exceed the cost or pricing data threshold, unless an exception applies to the action. The exceptions in this setting are the same as those applicable to prime contractors.

The threshold applicable to subcontractor cost or pricing data is $10 million or more, *or* both more than the cost or pricing data threshold (using the same rules as applicable to prime contract actions) and more than 10% of the prime contractor's proposed price, unless the contracting officer believes such submission is unnecessary.

Under TINA, a subcontractor must certify that the cost or pricing data it submits are accurate, complete, and current. A prime contractor is liable to the extent defective subcontractor (or prospective subcontractor) data cause an increase in price, costs, or fee to the government.

Requiring cost or pricing data

TINA requires not only that contractors submit all cost or pricing data significant to price negotiations at the time of agreement on price, it also requires that they certify that, to the best of their knowledge and belief, the data submitted to the government are accurate, complete, and current. The FAR requires that the contractor do so in a prescribed "Certificate of Current Cost or Pricing Data."

* * *

Liability for defective data

The "Price Reduction for Defective Cost or Pricing Data" clause states that if "any price, including profit or fee ... was increased by any significant amount" because the contractor or subcontractor submitted data "that were not complete, accurate, and current as certified," the contract's "price or cost shall be reduced accordingly." The contractor's liability is usually measured as the difference between the actual contract price based on the defective data and the price that would have been negotiated had accurate, complete, and current data been disclosed. The FAR also provides that the government is entitled to "recovery of any overpayment plus interest on the overpayments." In addition, if the contractor or subcontractor knowingly or intentionally submitted defective data, it may be liable for a wide variety of civil and criminal penalties, including fines, imprisonment, and suspension and debarment from contracting with the government.

The government has the burden of proof in a defective pricing data case. The elements of the claim are: (1) the information is "cost or pricing data" under TINA; (2) the data were not disclosed, or meaningfully disclosed, to a proper government representative, and (3) the government relied on the defective data and shows by some reasonable method the amount by which the final negotiated price was overstated. After the government establishes a prima facie case, the contractor will have the burden to rebut the presumption that the natural and probable consequences of the defective data was an overstated contract price.

As stated above, the reliance element is a critical part of any defective pricing case. Frequently, the government's conduct during negotiations will be determinative in concluding whether the requisite reliance was present. For instance, where the government negotiators manifested a lack of confidence in one aspect of the contractor's data and developed their own data based upon the contractor's actual costs, the government failed to establish that the contractor data "would have been of major importance in price negotiations." Furthermore, where negotiations indicated that the government would not have relied on a learning curve, its contention that a learning curve should have been applied to labor cost figures was rejected.

The government's right to a price adjustment will not be affected by any of the following circumstances:

(i)   The contractor or subcontractor was a sole source supplier or otherwise was in a superior bargaining position;

(ii) The contracting officer should have known that the cost or pricing data in issue were defective even though the contractor or subcontractor took no affirmative action to bring the character of the data to the attention of the contracting officer;

(iii) The contract was based on an agreement about the total cost of the contract and there was no agreement about the cost of each item procured under such contract; or

(iv) Cost or pricing data were required, but the contractor or subcontractor did not submit a Certificate of Current Cost or Pricing Data relating to the contract.

Even where the contractor has submitted defective cost or pricing data, the contractor may be entitled to an offset under limited circumstances

---

Appeal of University of California, San Francisco
1996 WL 681971 (V.A.B.C.A.), 97-1 BCA 28,642, VABCA No. 4661
November 25, 1996

OPINION BY ADMINISTRATIVE JUDGE McMICHAEL

On Cross Motions for Summary Judgment

The University of California, San Francisco (UCSF or Contractor) appeals a claim by the Department of Veterans Affairs (VA or Government) seeking to recover certain sums paid to the Contractor under a series of six extensions to a negotiated firm fixed price contract for anesthesiology services. Alleging that the Contractor failed to supply certified cost and pricing data to support its 27% price increase in contract extensions, the VA final decision sought to recover $169,400, the difference between "what was paid to UCSF and the amount reflected [in] UCSF's payroll records."

UCSF has filed a MOTION FOR SUMMARY JUDGMENT asserting that the Government may not recover moneys paid because the contract did not contain a "Price Reduction for Defective Cost or Pricing Data" clause....

FINDINGS OF FACT

For approximately nine years the Government had been negotiating annual contracts with UCSF for the "Scarce Medical Specialist Services" of anesthesiologists which were furnished to the VA Medical Center, San Francisco (VAMC).... In a technical review of the proposed 1990 Contract, as required by VA Acquisition Regulation (VAAR) 801.602-70, officials at VA Central Office in Washington, DC approved the contract with UCSF subject to a number of revisions, including insertion of FAR Clause 52.215-22. (R4, tab 4) Notwithstanding this conditioned approval, the 1990 Contract as executed did not include FAR Clause 52.215-22, PRICE REDUCTION FOR DEFECTIVE COST OR PRICING DATA, as required by FAR 15.804-8(a)....

During this same period, UCSF transmitted to the VA on April 8, 1991, "cost and pricing documentation" in connection with RFP 662-20-91 (the proposed 1991 Contract). (R4, tab 16) The information, in the form of a letter from Dr. Ronald Miller, Chairman of UCSF's Department of Anesthesia, was directed to Jerry Prescott, a contract specialist at the San Francisco VAMC who was acting as contracting office liaison for negotiation of the new scarce medical services contract. (Prescott Aff. at 1).... Dr. Miller concluded by stating that there was "no indirect cost associated with this contract" and that he hoped that he had answered any "questions regarding the basis for the $726,997 annual contract price." ...

By letter dated July 23, 1991, the Western Regional Director of the Veterans Health Services and Research Administration (VHA) informed the Medical Center that the proposed scarce medical specialist contract with UCSF had been disapproved based on a June 7th memorandum from Dr. McDonald, the Chairman of the Sharing Contract Committee in Washington. Questions were raised about why the anesthesiologists who would be performing the work could not be identified, and about the composition of fringe benefits for which a "breakdown ... with respect to each professorial level" was needed. As for the requested administrative costs, Dr. McDonald said that he interpreted this as an "indirect cost," adding:

> The total of $77,196.66 as administrative or indirect cost is far more than any possible cost for performing the activity specified by Dr. Miller in his letter. As a matter of policy, VA cannot pay for administrative, overhead, or indirect cost for these personal contracts ... Indirect costs and overhead only can be included if they are a part of the operation. In this instance, schedules are made out by VA and all operation factors conducted in VA by VA personnel. Hence, personal contracts, such as this contract, incurs no indirect or administrative costs.

* * *

The continued funding of the anesthesiology scarce medical services contract by a series of 90 day extensions for over a year had attracted the attention of the VA's Office of Inspector General.... On August 28, 1992, David Sumarl, Regional Manager of the VA OIG Regional Office of Audit in Seattle, Washington transmitted a final "Report of Audit, Anesthesiology Services Contract VA Medical Center San Francisco." (R4, tab 45) The report concluded that the 1990 Contract extensions were "not managed in accordance with VA policy" and that the VAMC staff "did not properly use cost or pricing data to set the contract price" with the result that it "paid excessive charges on the contract." The report noted that, during calendar year 1991, the VA paid UCSF $715,000 through the four separate extensions to the 1990 Contract. This represented a 27% increase to the 1990 Contract price, although the "contracted level of services remained the same." (R4, tab 45 at 6) The report states that it could not "determine with certainty" why the price increase was agreed to on the extensions, observing that the "file did not contain any documentation to support" the new price.

The OIG report said that the "most important aspect" of its audit methodology was a comparison of what "VA paid for contract anesthesiology services to the cost UCSF incurred in providing the services" because:

> VA can pay only for direct medical services. SMS [Scarce Medical Services] contracts cannot be used to pay for administrative support, research, supplies, or any other expense not directly related to patient care. The applicable law (38 U.S.C. 7409) does not give VA medical centers authority to use SMS contractors to purchase any types of services other than medical services.

* * *

The OIG report recommended that action be taken to recover the excessive charges…, and on March 17, 1995, VA Contracting Officer Judy Infusino issued a final decision demanding recovery of $169,400 in "overpayments" under Contract V662P-4744 which "occurred on a series of … contract extensions between January 1, 1991 and June 30 [sic, July 31], 1992." (R4, tab 46)

In her final decision the CO said the overpayments were identified during an OIG audit which found the 27% increase in contract price for the interim extensions "was not supported with certified cost or pricing data" and further, that the "audit also determined that UCSF funded unallowable administrative costs with the 27% increase." "[I]n support of the Contracting Officer's final decision," CO Infusino stated that UCSF "did not provide certified cost or price data to support the proposed price" of the contract extension and that the "IG determined that from January 1, 1991, to July 31, 1992, there was a difference of $169,400 between what was paid to UCSF and the amount reflected [in] UCSF's payroll records."

These funds were used for "administrative support for research in academic activities of the contracted anesthesiologists and were not authorized by the contract." CO Infusino concluded that:

> The VAMC Contracting Officer acted outside the scope of his authority by granting UCSF's 27% price increase without requesting certified cost or pricing data or granting an exemption to the requirement. The Contracting Officer's failure to request certified cost or pricing data, or to grant an exemption does not relieve UCSF of responsibility … UCSF knew or should have known that in accordance with FAR 15.804-2(a)(1)(ii), cost or pricing data is required on all contract actions and modifications exceeding $100,000.…

* * *

DISCUSSION
I.

In its MOTION FOR SUMMARY JUDGMENT, Appellant initially observes that the Government is seeking a defective pricing adjustment in the pending appeal even though neither the 1990 Contract nor any of the 6 extensions thereto, totaling 16 months, contained the Price Reduction for Defective Cost of Pricing Data clause as outlined in 48 CFR s 52.215-22. Although the Contract did require the Contractor to submit certified cost or pricing information, UCSF argues that the Government's entitlement to a cost reduction is "not automatic or granted by the [Truth in Negotiations Act (TINA)] itself," but rather is "based solely upon having included the proper [price reduction] clause in the contract." (App. Mot. at 9) As for the possible incorporation of that clause into the contract as a matter of law pursuant to G.L. Christian & Associates v. United States, 312 F.2d 418 (Ct.Cl.), reh'g denied 320 F.2d 345, cert. denied 375 U.S. 954 (1963), Appellant notes the "judicious" application of the Christian doctrine by Courts and Boards which have limited it "to clauses which advance particularly significant public policies." Such significant public policies do not, in its view, apparently include defective pricing clauses.

In any event, Appellant argues that the Christian doctrine is "inapplicable" where, "as here, the CO has discretion as to whether or not the clause must be included," citing IBI Sec. Serv. v. United States, 19 Cl. Ct. 106 (1989), aff'd without op. 918 F.2d 188 (Fed Cir. 1990). In the case before us, the Contracting Officer "appears to have determined that UCSF was exempt from application of TINA." That is, in a contract for anesthesiologist services, it is "reasonable to assume that the CO determined UCSF was exempt from the requirement to submit certified cost or pricing data because the Contract price was based on established market prices of commercial items sold in substantial quantities to the general public." (App. Mot. at 10–11)

The Government in its OPPOSITION TO MOTION FOR SUMMARY JUDGMENT, argues that the Truth in Negotiations Act is "mandatory" with respect to noncompetetively negotiated contracts such as Scarce Medical Services contracts, and that the defective pricing clause required by TINA reflects a "significantly ingrained strand of public procurement policy." Thus, Christian doctrine principles would clearly incorporate such an omitted clause into the contract, a position which is also supported by existing case authority. Moreover, the Contracting Officer "could not waive the requirements of TINA by omission or inaction." The record is clear that the "CO did not apply any exemptions of TINA nor did the agency head grant a wavier of the Act." (Gov't Opp. at 42)

In Christian, the Government terminated a housing contract and the Appellant sought to recover anticipated but unearned profits under a breach theory, noting that the contract did not include a standard "termination for convenience" clause limiting its recovery for profits to work actually completed. The Government argued that the contract should be read as if it did contain a termination for convenience clause noting that procurement regulations "issued under statutory authority" required such a clause be inserted into the contract. In reviewing the history of the termination for convenience clause the court found the profit limitation contained therein to be "a deeply ingrained strand of procurement policy" and concluded that "the Defense Department and the Congress would be loath to sanction a large contract which did not provide the power to terminate and at the same time proscribe anticipated profits if termination did occur." G.L. Christian, 312 F.2d at 426. It also found that Appellant was an "experienced contractor" who "could not have been wholly unaware" of the prospects of a termination for convenience of the Government. Unearned profits have not been paid for such terminations "[f]or many years" and it was "probable too that [the Contractor] knew of that general policy." Accordingly, the court found it "fitting and legally proper for the clause to be "incorporated into [the contract] by operation of law" Id. at 427

On a motion for rehearing and reargument, the Court stated that it was important that "procurement policies set by higher authority not be avoided or evaded (deliberately or negligently) by lesser officials, or by a concert of contractor and contracting officer." It added:

> To accept plaintiff's pleas that a regulation is powerless to incorporate a provision into a new contract would be to hobble the very policies which the appointed rule makers considered significant enough to call for mandatory regulation. Obligatory Congressional enactments are held to govern federal contracts because there is a need to guard the dominant legislative policy against ad hoc en-

croachment or dispensation by the executive. There is a comparable need to protect the significant policies of superior administrators from sapping by subordinates. Like other individuals who deal with the Federal Government, potential contractors can validly be bound to discover the published directives telling them the limits and scope of the agreements the Government can make. (citations omitted)

320 F.2d at 351

The Christian doctrine was recently considered in two Federal Circuit cases. In General Engineering & Machine Works v. O'Keefe, 991 F.2d 775, 779 (Fed. Cir. 1993), the court reaffirmed that "the Christian doctrine applies to mandatory contract clauses which express a significant or deeply ingrained strand of public procurement policy." It affirmed a decision incorporating a requirement for separate cost pools into a contract. The regulation requiring separate cost pools was determined to be "sufficiently ingrained" in public procurement policy because it deterred double payments and "thus discouraged the unnecessary and wasteful spending of government money." Id. at 780

In S.J. Amoroso Construction Co., Inc., 12 F.3d 1072 (Fed.Cir.1993), the Court affirmed the incorporation into a contract of Buy American Act requirements which the parties had stricken. Initially observing that "[a]pplication of the Christian doctrine turns not on whether the clause was intentionally or inadvertently omitted," the court emphasized that that Buy American Act itself required that "[e]very contract for construction ... shall contain a provision" with respect to materials, supplies and articles manufactured in the United States. Thus:

> The statute alone, therefor, evidences a significant and deeply ingrained strand of public procurement policy sufficient to require incorporation of the clause prescribed ... as a matter of law. In addition, the procurement regulations themselves have reflected this significant statutory policy for over 25 years.

Id. at 1076.

In considering the applicability of the Christian doctrine to the case at hand, it should be recognized that the Truth in Negotiations Act, first enacted almost 35 years ago, requires certified disclosure of cost or pricing data for certain negotiated contracts and mandates, in pertinent part, that:

> A prime contract (or change or modification to a prime contract) under which a certificate ... is required, shall contain a provision that the price of the contract to the United States ... shall be adjusted to exclude any significant amount by which ... such price was increased because the contractor ... submitted defective cost or pricing data.

41 U.S.C. §254d (emphasis added).

We are thus presented with not only a long standing policy but one that has as its basis, an explicit statutory mandate requiring that such contracts contain a price reduction provision which is to operate in the event defective cost or pricing data is submitted. As the court stated in M-R-S Manufacturing Company v. United States, 492 F.2d 835, 842 (Ct.Cl.1974):

> [T]he purpose of then Truth in Negotiations Act was to avoid excessive costs that result from a contractor having in his possession accurate, complete, and current information when the Government does not possess the same data.

Incorporation of the defective pricing clause into negotiated contracts in order to protect the taxpayer's dollar from "excessive costs" and "unnecessary and wasteful spending" is, in our view, a "deeply ingrained strand of procurement policy." Moreover, failure to incorporate this clause into the contract by operation of law would be a failure to "guard the dominant legislative policy against ad hoc encroachment or dispensation by the executive." Appellant's citation of IBI Sec. Serv. v. United States, 19 Cl. Ct. 106 (1989), aff'd without op. 918 F.2d 188 (Fed. Cir. 1990) does not support its position. As that court stated, "[t]he Christian doctrine is available only when relevant statutory or regulatory provisions are required to be included in an agency's contracts." Id. at 109. But as we have previously observed, the price reduction provisions in issue here have been required to be included in the contract by both statute and regulation for over 35 years. See also Palmetto Enterprises, ASBCA No. 22839, 79-1 BCA p. 13,736 (TINA provisions incorporated by operation of law under the *Christian* doctrine).

It should also be pointed out that here, as in the G.L. Christian case, it is "probable" that the contractor "knew of the general policy" concerning the requirement for a defective pricing clause. UCSF had a nine year history of negotiated contracts with the VA which contained the price reduction clause for defective pricing. Even the 1990 contract from which the clause was omitted, required the submission of certified cost and pricing data which should have alerted this "experienced contractor" that consequences were intended to flow from the submission of defective cost or pricing data.

* * *

Notes and Questions

1. Just what did UCSF not disclose to the government? UCSF stands accused of slipping through 27% price increases that turned out to be for "administrative support for research in academic activities of the contracted anesthesiologists." Described one way, that is a sinister overcharging of the government for something it would never knowingly pay. Described another way, anesthesiologists who engage in research and teaching charged the payer for medical service, that is, the government, an added price to cover the costs of their research; that is exactly what everyone (except government auditors, perhaps) expects of such university hospital physicians. To put it differently, the physicians were not caught siphoning off government money for a corrupt reason. If you were the research anesthesiologists caught up in years of government auditing cases, what would you think of government contract law?

2. At first glance, nothing could differ more from the original circumstances that brought forth TINA than this UCSF case. TINA arose from scandals involving defense procurement, particularly of high-cost, high-technology aerospace items. UCSF concerns procuring the services of a few medical professionals. What do the original reasons for TINA have in common with the facts of UCSF? To put it differently, why does the government believe it needs disclosure of kinds of "cost or pricing data" that private-sector buyers do not typically obtain from sellers? Does it have to do with unique vulnerabilities of the government (regardless of what the government buys)? Or with a breakdown of market discipline in certain categories of purchases (regardless of who, public or private, makes such purchases)?

3. How would you argue as a matter of justice on UCSF's behalf? The Veteran's Administration sought competent service of a highly expensive medical specialty, anaesthesiology, in the high-cost location of San Francisco, at $73/hour, which may be described as a very low price. UCSF found a billing method that met the government's need, at the government's price, with what presumably was an acceptable quality. Was UCSF bad not to explain fully to the government how it did that? Could UCSF argue that at least some

of the government officials involved must have known and acquiesced? Is the "defective pricing" case a method by which auditors, acting afterwards, penalize government contractors simply for sensible "don't ask, don't tell" billing arrangements with quite willing contracting officers? On the other hand, much of government contract law aims to limit the ability of contracting officers to enter into cozy arrangements, regardless of how sensible they seem to those who enter into them.

4. How would you argue as a matter of classic economic policy on UCSF's behalf? Critics charge that TINA, by requiring special disclosures to the government, tends to create a separate and higher-cost sector of government suppliers. Those willing to supply the government's special paperwork needs, the argument goes, make up for their costs or take advantage of the lack of competitors in this isolated sector either by charging more or by providing less, but not by providing more at a lower price. What would these critics anticipate that the Veteran's Administration will get in the future: more honest anaesthesiological services, or just more heavily papered and expensive and lower-quality services?

Appeal of Honeywell Federal Systems, Inc.
Under Basic Ordering Agreement No. DAAB07-81-G-6156
March 26, 1992

OPINION BY ADMINISTRATIVE JUDGE STEMPLER

This is a timely appeal from a contracting officer's decision asserting a Government claim for defective pricing against appellant in the amount of $10,500,000. The Contract Disputes Act is applicable. The Government has moved for summary judgment on three legal entitlement issues. They are:

1. Did the Government's contracting officers act outside the scope of their authority when they permitted Appellant to withhold cost or pricing data when prices were determined for future use for orders placed against the subject Basic Ordering agreement?

STIPULATED UNDISPUTED FACTS

1. In April 1979, the Army competitively awarded contract No. DAHC26-79-C-0011 to Management & Technical Services Co. 'GE/MATSCO,' a subsidiary of General Electric Co., to provide a decentralized automated service support system ('DAS-3'). The DAS-3, a van-mounted (mobile) data processing unit, would be fielded world-wide to provide inventory and stock control capability to Army field commanders. The DAS-3 program was predicated on the use of commercial, off-the-shelf computers. Because of the mobility of the systems, the Army adopted a 'self-maintenance' philosophy for the DAS-3 program and, therefore, spare parts kits were included as line items in the competitive contract awarded to GE/MATSCO.

2. By firm-fixed price subcontract No. 167-H0029, GE/MATSCO procured 'Level 6 ' commercial computers and associated spare parts to be used for the DAS-3 program from appellant's predecessor in interest, Honeywell Information Systems, Inc. ('Honeywell'). The term of the subcontract was June 1979 to May 1991.

3. In or about late 1980 or early 1981, the Army began negotiations with appellant for a direct Basic Ordering Agreement ('BOA,') excluding GE/MATSCO, for DAS-3 spare parts. The Army sought such an agreement with Honeywell and fifteen other DAS-3 original equipment manufacturers, intending to gain the price benefits generally realized by 'breaking out' the procurement of spare parts in this manner.

4. At or prior to the time of the negotiations, the Army was aware that Honeywell did not sell the spare parts at issue separately, since most commercial customers chose to obtain spare parts as part of maintenance agreements which encompassed the provision of spare parts as necessary. Generally, the spare parts used during maintenance were not priced separately but rather Honeywell charged an established lump sum rate for the work. Honeywell did maintain a price list, known as the 'Master Parts Price List,' for parts in its inventory. This list was 'published' in the sense that, upon request, a commercial customer would be allowed to view it at Honeywell's location. Relevant portions of this list could also be sent to customers on request.

5. Honeywell did not sell spare parts separately to commercial customers in substantial quantities.

6. Honeywell spare parts were also available for purchase by Government agencies under Honeywell's then-current General Service Administration ('GSA') Automated Data Processing Equipment 'ADPE' Multiple Award Schedule ('MAS') contract. In that regard, Honeywell's GSA ADPE MAS contract incorporated by reference Honeywell's published Master Parts Price List for commercial customers. The spare parts sought by the Army under the BOA remained available for purchase by Government agencies under Honeywell's GSA ADPE MAS contracts throughout the period of the BOA at prices based on Honeywell's published Master Parts Price List for commercial customers.

7. The Army prepared a draft BOA in early 1981. The designated contracting officer ('CO') for the BOA at this time was Captain Carol L. Anstey. By a memorandum dated 28 January 1981, CO Anstey recommended pre-award approval of the BOA to the U.S. Army Communications-Electronic Command (hereinafter referred to as 'CECOM') Awards Committee. On 31 March 1981, the Awards Committee of CECOM recommended award of the BOA to Honeywell.

21. Honeywell responded to CO Satterfield's request for support of its claim for exemption under TINA by letter dated 15 March 1982, stating, essentially, that:

> a. Proof of commerciality for DAS-3 spares being ordered under the BOA was unnecessary, since those spares were used in Basic Level 6 end-item computer equipment and the Level 6 end-item equipment was available on Honeywell's GSA DPE MAS contract.
>
> b. The spare parts were found in Honeywell's published Master Parts Price List for commercial customers, hence further proof of commerciality was not required.

22. Under cover of its 15 March 1982 letter, Honeywell also submitted a DD Form 633-7, entitled 'Claim for Exemption from Submission of Cost or Pricing,' which listed data relative to previous sales of DAS-3 spares as 'NOT AVAILABLE.' The DD Form 633-7 did provide, however, sales data for Honeywell's Level 6 'Mini Computer Equipment,' which showed sales of the equipment for the period 1 January 1980 to 31 December 1980 as 89.5% to the general public and 10.5% to the Government.

23. In response to CO Satterfield's request, DCAA issued Audit Report No. 6151-2F2100412-0594, dated 4 May 1982, which stated in pertinent part:

> 2. Circumstances Affecting the Examination. The contractor could not provide us with supporting data which would enable us to perform a proper evaluation of its claim for exemption from submission of certified cost or pricing data covering the various parts proposed under the subject basic ordering agreement. The results of our audit are therefore qualified to the extent that the lack of supporting data may have an adverse effect on the results of our audit.

3. Conclusion

... The contractor stated that the proposed parts were not normally sold by themselves (separately) to commercial customers but instead the contractor supplied these parts as a part of maintenance services (a package) for a predetermined contract price. As stated in Paragraph 2, "Circumstances Affecting the Examination," we were unable to evaluate the contractor's claim for an exemption of cost or pricing data. The contractor could not provide us with adequate sales data in order to determine whether contractor's proposed prices are, or are based on, established catalog or market prices of commercial items sold in substantial quantities to the general public or are prices set by law or regulation as required by DAR 3-807.3(e). Therefore, we do not consider the proposal to be acceptable as a basis for negotiation of a price.

In view of the contractor's statement that the proposed spare parts are not normally sold to commercial customers, we believe it appropriate to request the contractor to submit cost or pricing data for the proposed spare parts ...

26. On 28 June 1982, CO Satterfield executed a 'Determination as to Reasonableness of Price,' stating:

Prices determined by the use of an established Pricelist which was generated by Honeywell Information Systems, Inc. was subject to audit by DCAA (audit Report 6141-2F210041-S1-2-0687 [sic] attached). The results of this audit have determined that the prices offered to the Government are the same as those offered to Honeywell's most preferred customers. The parts purchased with this delivery order are a part of the Level 6 end item equipment which is on the GSA contract.

27. CO Satterfield's Determination reflected his conclusion that Honeywell was entitled to a commerciality exception under TINA, see 10 U.S.C. sec. 2306a(b)(1)(B), and his decision to dispense with the submission by Honeywell of cost or pricing data in connection with BOA DOs.

42. During February 1985, Captain Carl Tegen replaced CO Walsh as the CECOM CO responsible for negotiating the successor BOA.

43. During negotiations of the successor BOA, Honeywell did not submit certified cost or pricing data. This was consistent with its actions since March 1982 when dealing with CO Satterfield on DO No. 0007.

44. CO Tegen elevated appellant's failure to provide cost and pricing data for the new BOA to higher Government levels. This culminated in its elevation to the attention of the Department of Defense ('DOD') Inspector General ('IG') on or about 5 July 1985.

45. During 1985 Honeywell began making efforts to, and subsequently did, alter its accounting system to permit future compliance with Cost Accounting Standards ('CAS') and the submission and certification of cost or pricing data. As a result of these changes and further discussions with CECOM, Honeywell furnished cost or pricing data for DAS-3 spares for the new BOA.

46. Acting in response to a CECOM request, the DOD IG conducted a review of the prices the Government had paid to Honeywell under the subject BOA. The DOD IG found: 'CECOM granted an improper exemption because Honeywell's claimed commercial catalog spare parts were not supportable as commercial items and the prices set for the spare parts had no direct relationship to Honeywell's costs to produce or purchase the items.' Based on this finding and its review of certain Honeywell cost data, the DOD

IG concluded that: 'Honeywell overpriced spare parts sold to CECOM under contract DAAB07-81-C-6156 by a net of $10.5 million.'

47. By letter dated March 22, 1988, the Army forwarded to Honeywell a draft of the DOD IG's Audit Report. On the basis of the draft report's conclusion that CECOM had improperly exempted Honeywell from the submission of cost or pricing data, and consistent with the approach recommended by the draft report (and the final DOD IG Audit Report) the Army requested a 'voluntary refund' of $10,500,000 from Honeywell for alleged overpricing on the BOA.

49. Upon Honeywell's refusal to comply with the Army's request for a voluntary refund, the final decision which is the subject of the instant appeal was issued by then BOA CO Gregory Coben on September 18, 1989. In his final decision, CO Coben (a) alleged that the determinations by prior BOA COs to exempt Honeywell from submission of cost or pricing data were improper and (b) claimed that the lack of Honeywell cost or pricing data had increased prices under the BOA by $10,500,000.

50. HFS initiated the instant appeal of the final decision by its Notice of Appeal filed December 6, 1989.

DECISION

The first issue presented by the parties for decision in their motions is whether the BOA COs acted outside the scope of their authority when they granted Honeywell's (HFS) commerciality exemptions from the requirement to submit cost or pricing data to support its proposals for the delivery orders under the BOA. The Government contends that the relevant statute (10 U.S.C. sec. 2306 (f)(1)) and the relevant regulations (DAR sec. 3-807) mandated that Honeywell submit cost or pricing data and that the BOA COs exceeded their authority by granting the exemptions.

* * *

Further, the Government argues that the COs, in effect, waived the statute and regulatory requirements and that they had no authority to do that and therefore the COs' actions were an abuse of discretion.

* * *

The statute provides in relevant part:

* * *

> Provided, that the requirements of this subsection need not be applied to contracts or subcontracts where the price negotiated is based on adequate price competition, established catalog or market prices of commercial items sold in substantial quantities to the general public, prices set by law or regulation or, in exceptional cases, where the head of the agency determines that the requirement of this subsection may be waived and states in writing his reasons for such determination.

(10 U.S.C. sec. 2306(f)(2))

The regulations governing this issue are lengthy and are set forth in relevant part in the appendix to this opinion.

The Government is correct that contractors dealing with COs assume the risk that the COs' actions are within the scope of their authority. Federal Crop Insurance v. Merrill, 332 U.S. 380 (1947); The American Aerospace Technology Corp., ASBCA No. 36049, 89-3 BCA par. 22,100. Further, the Government is correct that COs have no authority to waive mandatory statutory or regulatory requirements. Paul E. Lehman, Inc. v. U.S., 673

F.2d 352 (Ct. Cl. 1982); Singer Company, Librascope Division v. U.S., 576 F.2d 905 (Ct. Cl. 1978); M-R-S Manufacturing Company v. U.S., 492 F.2d 835 (Ct. Cl. 1974); Numax Electronics, Inc., ASBCA No. 29186, 85-3 BCA par. 18,396; Beech Aircraft Corporation, ASBCA No. 25388, 83-1 BCA par. 16,532. The statute and regulations, however, in this instance, specifically provide for the exemption at issue and it is undisputed that the BOA COs had the authority to exercise their discretion and judgment in granting or denying the exemptions. The relevant statute is quoted above. The regulatory instructions that accompany the DAR 7-104.29 provide in relevant part:

> The following clause [DAR 7-104.29 Price Reduction for Defective Cost or Pricing Data] shall be inserted in negotiated contracts which when entered into exceed [the statutory amount], except where the price is based on adequate price competition, established catalog or market prices of commercial items sold in substantial quantities to the general public, or prices set by law or regulation.

* * *

Whether or not to grant a commerciality exemption is clearly within the discretion of a CO, and is part of his duty to secure a fair and reasonable price on a case-by-case basis. Sperry Flight Systems—Division of Sperry Rand Corporation, ASBCA No. 17375, 74-1 BCA par. 10,648; aff'd, 548 F.2d 915 (Ct. Cl. 1977); cf., Resource Consultants, Inc., GSBCA No. 8342-P, 86-2 BCA par. 18,942 (discretionary with CO to determine if cost or pricing data is needed in protest situation); cf., Digital Equipment Corporation, B-219435, 85-2 CPD par. 456 (within CO discretion to grant commerciality exemption in protest situation). What the Government really complains of is that it now believes that the BOA COs exercised their judgment and discretion poorly and the Government would like to substitute the current CO's discretion and decisions on the exemption question for those determinations made by the BOA COs years ago. Clearly, in arguing that the BOA COs had no authority, the Government is confusing authority with judgment. There is no hint of fraud, bad faith or collusion in the BOA COs' determinations to grant the exemptions. The BOA COs clearly made reasoned independent decisions to grant the exemptions and there is sufficient evidence in the record to establish that these decisions had support. The BOA COs' decision process included: (1) the COs' examination of HFS' Master Parts Price List, (2) consideration of HFS' GSA ADPE BOA, (3) seeking legal advice, (4) requesting information from HFS, (5) requesting DCAA audits and (6) making written commerciality exemption decisions. If the BOA COs had the authority to made 'correct' determinations on the exemption issue, they had authority to make 'incorrect' ones. We will not, as the Government requests, measure authority by the results obtained rather than the scope of actual authority granted. Broad Avenue Laundry and Tailoring v. U.S., 681 F.2d 746 (Ct. Cl. 1982); Liberty Coat Company, ASBCA Nos. 4119, 4138, 4139, 57-2 BCA par. 1576. The BOA COs made determinations to grant the exemptions and such determinations were squarely within their authority and are binding on successor COs. Bell Helicopter Company, ASBCA No. 17776, 74-1 BCA par. 10,411.

We hold that the BOA COs did not act outside the scope of their authority in granting the exemptions and refuse to re-examine the specifics of the decisions to determine, in hindsight, if they were correct or incorrect. Accordingly, the Government is bound by the COs' determinations.

In view of our answer to the first issue, we do not reach the second or third issues.

CONCLUSION

The Government's motion for summary judgment is denied. The appellant's cross-motion for summary judgment is granted. The appeal is sustained.

Notes and Questions

1. The case concerns one simple question: Did Honeywell get to retain the benefit of a Contracting Officer's exempting it from TINA? However, consider the great variety and diversity of arguments on that question. How many different arguments can you find in each of these subcategories:

- what is a commercial market for purposes of government supply;
- whether Honeywell was truly in a commercial market as to spare parts;
- how much authority a CO should have, vis-a-vis (1) the DCAA, and (2) later COs; and
- how much repose—that is, protection against later review of earlier actions—should government contractors have.

2. Do you understand what the DCAA thought about giving Honeywell an exemption in 1982? The CO did not explain why he decided to give the exemption despite the DCAA's thoughts. Later, the DCAA seemed to get its revenge, though not in the end. Can you picture the changing Defense Department background of this case? Honeywell received its exemption during the heydey of defense suppliers in the early 1980s, during the major increase in defense spending that started with the American reaction to the U.S.S.R.'s invasion of Afghanistan in 1979 and reached peak levels during the Reagan Administration. Contracting officers had large budgets that they were under pressure to convert into defense supplies. Then, as years passed, scandals began breaking about overcharging of the government, including on such matters as spare or extra parts. New laws, regulations, and policies went into place to address those scandals. As more years went by, cases like this one gradually worked their way through the slow sequence of auditing, disputes, and litigation in an entirely different defense spending climate than the one at the time of the original spending spree.

3. Since the Honeywell decision, statuory and regulatory changes have expanded the commercial exemption from TINA. Regulations now provide the following:

> 48 C.F.R. 15.403-1 Prohibition on obtaining cost or pricing data (10 U.S.C. 2306a and 41 U.S.C. 254b).
>
> (b) Exceptions to cost or pricing data requirements. The contracting officer shall not require submission of cost or pricing data to support any action (contracts, subcontracts, or modifications) (but may require information other than cost or pricing data to support a determination of price reasonableness or cost realism)—
>
> (3) When a commercial item is being acquired (see standards in paragraph (c)(3) of this subsection);
>
> * * *
>
> (c) Standards for exceptions from cost or pricing data requirements—
>
> (3) Commercial items. Any acquisition for an item that meets the commercial item definition in 2.101, or any modification, as defined in paragraph (c)(1) or (2) of that definition, that does not change the item from a commercial item to a non-commercial item, is exempt from the requirement for cost or pricing data.

* * *

The regulation's definitional section, 48 C.F.R. 2.101, specifies that commercial items include those which are sold or offered for sale, lease, or license to the general public, including those with minor modifications, and meet the exception if they are publicly available at or before the delivery date of a government solicitation.

4. Something else changed during the course of this case Honeywell. Paragraph 45 says: "45. During 1985 Honeywell began making efforts to, and subsequently did, alter its accounting system to permit future compliance with Cost Accounting Standards ('CAS') and the submission and certification of cost or pricing data. As a result of these changes and further discussions with CECOM, Honeywell furnished cost or pricing data for DAS-3 spares for the new BOA." Do you understand Honeywell's changeover, not just on this contract, but on a large-scale basis? What would you have had to do, if you were the lawyer at Honeywell in charge of that changeover?

Congressional Intent and Commercial Products

Charles Tiefer & Ron Stroman, The Procurement Lawyer, Spring 1997, at 22

In enacting the Federal Acquisition Reform Act (FARA) of 1996, Congress carefully balanced its intent to continue partially "deregulating" commercial acquisition with the need for requiring competitive purchasing, directing contractor disclosure, and maintaining government remedies for overpayments. The enactment process for FARA presents a challenge in understanding congressional intent. Procurement reform laws typically have emerged from Congress after a relatively open process. FARA was passed in the 104th Congress, however, fairly suddenly on the heels of the Federal Acquisition Streamlining Act (FASA) enacted a year earlier. During a three-month conference committee in late 1995, Congress worked out .a number of FARA's complex aspects in internal discussions from which few details emerged. FARA became law through a compromise process involving both the legislative and executive branches that is not easy to follow without careful study.

What Was the Congressional Intent?

This article attempts to identify clearly the congressional intent in passing FARA by focusing on the provisions in FARA connected with commercial product acquisition, particularly with vendors' duties to provide information on pricing. This article begins with House passage and Senate preparation for conference and further reviews the process of the all-important three-month conference (September to December 1995) before the bill eventually became law as Division D of the 1996 Defense Authorization Act. Also addressed are several sections of FARA concerning "full and open competition," simplified commercial product acquisitions below a dollar threshold, and section 4201 concerning price reasonableness disclosures — even after government contractors have been exempted from the requirements of the Truth in Negotiation Act (TINA).

The enactment of FASA, signed into law on October 13, 1994, was the culmination of several initiatives.

FASA was the most comprehensive procurement reform in a decade. In the late 1980s and early 1990s, the House Committee on Government Operations under Chairman John Conyers conducted extensive oversight on procurement problems. The Clinton administration undertook an effort to implement reform as part of Vice President Gore's National Performance Review — popularly known as "Reinventing Government". Another initiative resulted from activities of the Defense Department and the Armed Services

Committees, symbolized by the well-known Section 800 Advisory Panel and its extensive report.

In the emerging area of procurement of commercial products, FASA expanded the exceptions requiring cost and pricing data under the Truth in Negotiations Act (TINA). FASA relaxed the previous requirements qualify for the "catalog or market pricing" exception to TINA by creating a new category of commercial product exception requiring only a "substantial quantity" of an item's sales be to the general public. Throughout 1995 and 1996 federal agencies worked to implement FASA's provisions by promulgating regulations on commercial product acquisition.

A month after FASA's enactment, the November 1994 election brought in the 104th Congress and a new majority party in each chamber. The incoming House Chair, Representative Clinger, and the incoming Democratic Member, Representative Collins, of the renamed House Committee on Government Reform and Oversight, had established themselves as effective legislators, interested in successful enactments rather than failed crusades. Thus, where the 104th Congress had difficulty in enacting a number of pieces of legislation, it was able to enact FARA due to an existing bipartisan philosophy. This philosophy emphasized competition and market effectiveness—with deregulation of commercial acquisition on one side and continuation of necessary pricing, product, and procurement integrity safeguards on the other.

* * *

FARA Section 4201-Commercial Product Exception

This section will address section 4201 of FARA, the commercial item exception to TINA's requirement for cost or pricing data, and, specifically, the exception in that exception, namely, the surviving requirements for vendors of commercial products to submit "other information." The exception to the exception arose because contracting officers must ensure that the government obtains a "reasonable" price.

When Congress defines the commercial product exception narrowly, as under TINA and even under FASA, it applies only to products in which the market is comparatively closer to being "perfect"—that is, the existence of competition forces prices to be reasonable even without disclosures to contracting officers. Conversely, when Congress defines the commercial product exception more broadly, as the House did in H.R. 1670, it applies to products in which the market is further from perfection and competition, by itself, is not safeguarding the market.

Reliance on Deregulation

In the House-passed bill, the expansion of the commercial exception from TINA's certified cost and pricing data disclosure included a very limited commitment to requiring compensating submission of other price reasonableness information. The limited commitment appeared in the bill's section 201(d) nonmandatory allowance of FAR provisions covering information that "contracting officers *may* consider on price reasonableness."

The House's view in section 201(d) was consistent with other provisions expressing great confidence in commercial product deregulation to replace traditional government protections. The House bill included a very broad provision for deregulated or—simplified—acquisition of commercial products. Section 202 extended "simplified" acquisition to commercial items without any dollar ceiling, even when this involved sole source acquisition. The committee report noted that "the Committee is aware that some have expressed a concern that there is no dollar threshold," but "[t]he purchase of a commercial item logically lends itself to simplified procedures because there exists a yardstick in the commercial marketplace against which to measure price and product quality and to serve as a surrogate for government-unique procedures."

Conference Committee Begins Work

The conference began its work in late September and early October through the exchange of Senate and House proposals. The first step was the Senate's formulation of proposals in areas covered by the House bill but not addressed by any Senate-passed bill. In many respects, the Senate position, as one would expect from the Senate's reliance upon Senators Cohen and Levin, leaned toward the reliance on "full and open competition" and toward balanced changes in current government protections. Regarding commercial items, the Senate's proposals centered on a narrow concept of "commercially available off-the-shelf products, "sold in substantial quantities in the commercial marketplace," and "offered to the Government, without modification, in the same form in which it is sold in the commercial marketplace." The FASA regulatory relaxations would be applied only for these "off-the-shelf" commercial items.

Mid-October 1995 was a dramatic time in the Congress. As the major budget proposals left committee and headed for the floor, the head-on clash between Congress and the president drew nearer, and the feeling in some quarters that the president and his party could be ignored in the legislative process subsided to a certain degree. The House definitely wanted to achieve a procurement law, not just an unproductive fight over an unenacted bill. Accordingly, at the end of mid-October, the House came back with an omnibus package proposal that sought to bridge the gap between the House-passed bill and the Senate's initial conference proposals. This began with the revision of the definition of competition, in which the House dropped the wording that had been the target of the Collins amendment with the intent of preserving the "full and open competition" language.

For the specific area of what became section 4201, the House proposal kept to its comparatively broad definition of commercial products, rather than adopting the Senate's narrow "off-the-shelf" view. The House provided that even where commercial products fit this new TINA exception, however, the agency head might nevertheless require submission of certified cost or pricing data where necessary for evaluating price reasonableness as long as the head of the procuring activity offered written justification. Moreover, even when the vendor did not have to submit certified cost or pricing data, the contracting officer might require submission of other data to the extent necessary to determine price reasonableness.

The Senate was required to make the final counterproposal at the end of October that became—in large measure—the conference report. The statement of the managers accompanying the conference report showed the influence of Senator Cohen in the following words: "This provision makes no change to the requirement for full and open competition or to the definition of full and open competition."

Senate Maintains "Off-the-Shelf" Provisions

The compromise involved a limited adherence to the Senate's early position of limiting the "commercial" relaxation to "off-the-shelf" products. The Senate still tried, in what became section 4202, to maintain the "off-the-shelf" position. However, it gave that up in what became section 4201. Specifically, the Senate counterproposal, like the final provision as enacted, stated that the contracting officer "shall require submission of data than certified cost or pricing data to the extent necessary to determine the reasonableness of the price" and that for the new commercial product exception, "the data submitted *shall* include, at a minimum, appropriate information on the prices at which the same item or similar items have previous been sold…."

With that, the House and Senate almost had a deal. The back-and-forth over simplified procedures for competitive acquisitions had still not been resolved with the House attempting to avoid a dollar ceiling and the Senate adhering to the narrow category of "off-the-shelf" products. The final compromise is codified in section 4202 that put a ceiling of $5 million and sunset the provision to expire after three years. The conference report was filed on December 13, 1995. The bill went through some uncertainties from being tied to a defense bill that was vetoed on unrelated grounds. Nevertheless, the conference version was placed aboard a new vehicle and it became law when the Congress passed, and the president signed on February 10, 1996, the Defense Department appropriation for FY 1996. At that point, public interest turned to how FARA would be implemented.

After the enactment of FASA, Senator Bingaman's article on the law's origins and development concluded with some "lessons for the future—ideas matter—details matter—analysis matters—bipartisanship matters—administration support matters." Nothing has happened in the last two years to question the significance of ideas, details, and analysis. This article confirms the Senator's comments about the significance of bipartisanship and administration support. The concept of producing bills acceptable to only one party does not apply to procurement reform, a highly technical and, to the public, arcane area. There, as Senator Bingaman wrote, "[w]hen you undertake to change a large number of existing statutes, you are likely to face opposition from those who have supported those laws. In this circumstance, bipartisan support is crucial to overcome opposition.…"

Analysis

Congress's intent in FARA to retain mandatory information-submission requirements for price reasonableness while easing TINA's burdens is symbolic of the debate over the direction of procurement reform. There was always an exception for commercial products in TINA. When Congress first enacted TINA in 1962, however, the exception was simply a pragmatic one. In later years a major thrust developed toward relaxing statutory and regulatory requirements for commercial procurement. The leading articulations of this thrust are too well known to require extended recitation. At its strongest, the commercial products "movement" served well in showing how TINA's requirements might simply amount to an undesirable entry barrier for commercial product vendors, actually lessening competition, raising costs, and impeding efficient procurement.

Pressure to Reduce Regulations

As the relaxation of regulatory requirements for "commercial" products expands beyond the area of true markets, the thrust to relax the requirements becomes less arguable as a policy matter. It then begins to appear as a thinly disguised effort to lower the protections of the Treasury against unreasonable vendor prices. Even at the peak of procurement reform sentiment, Congress would not do that.

As the procurement regulation enters and contracting officers implement FASA and FARA in years to come, they will often face pressures, either industrywide or from particular vendors, to relax various regulatory protections in the name of commercial product acquisition. An example is the continuing dispute between contracting agencies and industry over protections against overpricing. The largest scale dispute concerns the elaborate law surrounding the various remedies, both civil and criminal, for defective or fraudulent pricing. Knowing submission of fraudulent cost or pricing information will be treated as such by Inspectors General. Of course, the government has a difficult burden in making a fraud case out of complex aspects of disputed pricing questions.

Congress showed only measured and limited willingness in FARA to allow the undermining of price reasonableness by rolling back informational requirements. Accordingly, it raises serious questions of congressional intent to expect agencies to roll back other protections against overpricing based on generalized "commercial products" notions. For example, there has been a debate within the Public Contract Law Section about GSA's price reduction clause for its multiple award schedule. GSA supports that clause based on a 1995 Inspector General study and a 1993 GAO report. Without getting into the details of the debate, this review of the congressional intent in FARA shows the measured manner with which Congress approaches such issues. Provisions on such subjects had to obtain strong bicameral and bipartisan support and made little progress without extensive consultation with the administration. For all the desire to relax the entry barriers for commercial products, there was a strong competing awareness that there was a need to protect the government from the possibility of overpricing.

Conclusion

FARA stands out as a notable accomplishment for the 104th Congress. It must not be read, however, as a statement going further than congressional intent. The bill emerged from an elaborate conference consideration in which the thrust toward relaxing regulatory requirements in the initial version of the House bill was tempered by the need to build bicameral and bipartisan rapport and to consult with the administration. Where the commercial market was imperfect, that tempering took the form of the changes worked out with the Senate and placed in the final version.

FARA considerably relaxed the requirements of TINA for submission of certified price and cost data in carefully measured fashion. The proposal to relax all mandatory requirements for submission of price reasonableness information were considered and rejected.

———————

Michael W. Wynne, Secretary of the Air Force, Appellant, v. United Technologies Corporation, Appellee

No. 05-1393
United States Court of Appeals, Federal Circuit
463 F.3d 1261
Aug. 28, 2006

Before NEWMAN, Circuit Judge, CLEVENGER, Senior Circuit Judge, and SCHALL, Circuit Judge.

CLEVENGER, Senior Circuit Judge.

The Secretary of the Air Force (Air Force) appeals from the reconsideration decision of the Armed Services Board of Contract Appeals (Board) denying the Air Force's claim for a contract price reduction for a six-year, multi-billion dollar contract with United Technologies Corporation, Pratt & Whitney (UTech). *See In re United Techs. Corp.*, ASBCA Nos. 51410, 53089, 53349, 05-1 BCA ¶ 32,860 (Jan. 19, 2005) (*Reconsideration Decision*). The Air Force claims that UTech furnished defective cost or pricing data in connection with both its initial price proposal and its Best and Final Offer (BAFO) for the contract, such that the Air Force was entitled to a contract price reduction under the Truth in Negotiations Act (TINA), 10 U.S.C. § 2306(f) (1983). Because we agree with the Board that the Air Force did not establish that it relied upon the defective cost or pricing data to its detriment, we *affirm*.

I

TINA requires that when a government contract is expected to exceed a certain value, a contractor must submit "cost or pricing data ... [and] certify that, to the best of his knowledge and belief, the cost or pricing data he submitted was accurate, complete and current...." 10 U.S.C. § 2306(f)(1). In addition, TINA requires that a contract price be "adjusted to exclude any significant sums by which it may be determined ... that such price was increased because the contractor ... furnished cost or pricing data which ... was inaccurate, incomplete, or noncurrent." § 2306(f)(2). In other words, the government will be awarded a contract price adjustment when the government proves that a contractor furnished defective cost or pricing data and "the [g]overnment relied on the overstated costs to its detriment." *Singer Co., Librascope Div. v. United States*, 217 Ct.Cl. 225, 576 F.2d 905, 914 (1978) When it is determined that a contractor furnished defective data, there is a *rebuttable presumption* that the defective data resulted in "an overstated negotiated contract price.... for it is reasonable to assume that the government negotiators relied upon the data supplied by the contractor and that this data affected the negotiations." *Sylvania Elec. Pros., Inc. v. United States*, 202 Ct.Cl. 16, 479 F.2d 1342, 1349 (1973). However, *if that presumption of causation is rebutted*, the government can only prevail upon proof that it relied upon the defective data to its detriment in agreeing to the contract price.

In the instant case, the Air Force sought a contract price reduction in the amount of roughly $300 million, claiming that UTech furnished defective cost or pricing data in connection with both the initial price proposal, which was made on August 17, 1983, and the BAFO, which was made on December 5, 1983. In an initial decision, the Board determined that although certain of the Air Force claims did not constitute defective cost or pricing data, UTech had made a number of undisclosed mistakes which did constitute defective cost or pricing data. *Appeals of United Techs. Corp.*, ASBCA Nos. 51410, 53089, 53349, 04-1 BCA ¶ 32,556 (Feb. 27, 2004) (*Initial Decision*). The Board further determined that the Air Force had relied on this defective data to its detriment. However, the Board found that although the defective data had caused an increase in the contract price in some instances, it had caused a decrease in the contract price in other instances and that the contract price reductions to which the Air Force was entitled were exceeded by the offsets to which UTech was entitled. Consequently, the Board found that the Air Force did not prove "that it is entitled to an affirmative recovery due to appellant's defective cost or pricing data." *Id.*, slip op. at 39.

Upon reconsideration, UTech challenged the Board's *Initial Decision*, arguing that the Board's reliance analysis improperly focused on the Air Force's audit of the data submitted with the initial price proposal. *Reconsideration Decision*, slip op. at 2–3. UTech argued that the Air Force did not accept UTech's initial price proposal, dated August 17, 1983. Rather, the Air Force accepted UTech's BAFO, dated December 5, 1983, for the base year of the contract, Fiscal Year 1985 (FY 85), and accepted revised versions of that offer for the subsequent years of the contract, Fiscal Years 1986–1990 (FYs 86–90). Because each of the Air Force's claims were based upon its acceptance of the BAFO and subsequent revised offers, UTech argued that the Board's "inquiry as to causation should properly focus on whether the [Air Force] relied on the defective BAFO cost or pricing data to award the contract and to determine that the offered prices were fair and reasonable." *Id.*, slip op. at 2.

* * *

With respect to the contract price for FY 85, which was based upon the BAFO, the Board found as a matter of fact that "neither the Defense Contract Audit Agency (DCAA), the [Air Force] price analyst, the contracting officer (CO) nor the cost panel reviewed the BAFO cost or pricing data prior to award." *Id.* The Board found that the language in the Record of Acquisition Action (RAA) and attachments, which allegedly showed reliance on the defective cost or pricing data, was "seriously undercut by the concession of the RAA author … that he did not recall reviewing any of appellant's BAFO cost or pricing data." *Id.* The Board also found that the RAA did not discuss any specific BAFO cost or pricing data relied upon by the Air Force price analyst or the cost panel. In addition, the Board found that the Air Force failed to provide evidence indicating that the BAFO data was reviewed by any government person prior to award. Although the Air Force price analyst and the CO testified that they relied on the fact that the BAFO data furnished by appellant were current, accurate, and complete, the Board found that "this testimony— given roughly 17 years after the fact—was lacking in specificity and was unpersuasive." *Id.* Noting that "[w]e are hard pressed to understand how the AF could have relied on BAFO cost or pricing data—defective or otherwise—that no one reviewed[,]" the Board concluded that the Air Force had not shown reliance upon the defective cost or pricing data, and that "it failed to show that appellant's defective BAFO cost or pricing data caused an increase in contract price for the base year of the contract." *Id.*

With respect to the contract price for FYs 86–90, the Board noted that the Air Force did not exercise its contract options under the same terms and conditions contained within the BAFO, but instead sought more advantageous offers from UTech and a competitor each year.

* * *

Thus, the Board held that the Air Force could not recover on any of its TINA claims, as it failed to establish reliance upon the allegedly defective cost or pricing data. As a result, the Board declined to address the Air Force's motion for reconsideration on its denied claims, in which the Air Force alleged that the Board erred in the *Initial Decision* when it found that certain of its claims did not constitute defective cost or pricing data. *Id.,* slip op. at 5–6 n. 3.

The Air Force appeals the *Reconsideration Decision*, and we have jurisdiction pursuant to 28 U.S.C. § 1295(a)(10) (2000).

II

* * *

The issue before this court is whether the Board erred in the *Reconsideration Decision*. On appeal, the Air Force does not contest any of the factual findings underlying the *Reconsideration Decision*, but instead claims that the Board applied the law incorrectly. In particular, the Air Force argues that it is never necessary to establish that it relied upon the defective cost or pricing data to its detriment, as it is sufficient to establish that the contract price offered by UTech was calculated using the defective cost or pricing data.

We disagree. Section 2306(f) of Title 10 requires modification of a contract price where "such [contract] price was increased because the contractor … furnished cost and pricing data which … was inaccurate, incomplete, or noncurrent." As we noted in *Singer,* "[t]he ultimate question … is whether [the contractor] adequately disclosed to the Government the "accurate, complete, and current" … costs.… [and] whether the Government *relied* on the overstated costs to its detriment." 576 F.2d at 914 (emphasis added). In other words, a contract price has been increased by defective cost or pricing data when the government relied on the defective data to its detriment in agreeing to the contract price.

* * *

The Air Force cites to *Sylvania* and *Lockheed Aircraft Corp., Lockheed-Georgia Co. Division v. United States,* 193 Ct.Cl. 86, 432 F.2d 801, 806 (1970), for the proposition that "the causation element of TINA may be established merely by demonstrating a causal link between the defective data and the final contract price." Appellant's Br. at 45–46. However, in *Sylvania,* we found that this causal link was established because the contractor failed to rebut the presumption that "the government negotiators relied upon the data supplied by the contractor and that this data affected the negotiations." 479 F.2d at 1349. Thus, we affirmed the Board's factual finding that the government relied upon the inaccurate data. *Id.* Similarly, in *Lockheed,* we found that the requisite causal link existed because, in agreeing to the contract price, the government had relied upon its own audit, which had in turn relied upon the defective pricing. 432 F.2d at 806 ("Whether the Air Force thus relied on its own audit, as opposed to Midwestern's records, is immaterial.... [The] Air Force audit was based on the information in the Kardex file, which we have found to be deficient when measured against the requirements of the Defective Pricing Clause...."). Thus, in both *Sylvania* and *Lockheed,* this court found that the government had relied upon the defective cost or pricing data at issue.

Indeed, in 1986, Congress considered and rejected amendments to TINA that would have eliminated the reliance requirement. The legislative history of the 1986 amendments recognized that, as the law stood, the government could not recover on a TINA claim if it did not rely on the allegedly defective cost or pricing data to its detriment:

> Existing law has been interpreted to require that, in order to recover under TINA, the contractors' failure to disclose must have resulted in the government's being misled into agreeing to a price greater than it would have agreed to had the correct information been provided. Accordingly, *if a contractor proves that the government did not rely on the cost and pricing data submitted by the contractor* or that, even if it had known the correct information, the government would not have been able to negotiate a better price, *the government could not recover.*

H.R.Rep. No. 99-718, at 260 (1986) (emphases added). The proposed bill would have changed the rebuttable presumption of reliance upon defective pricing data into a conclusive presumption of reliance. *Acquisition Reform-1986: Hearing on H.R. 4548 Before the H. Acquisition and Procurement Policy Panel of the Armed Servs. Comm.,* 99th Cong. 444–45 (1986) (statement of Mr. Vander Schaaf, Deputy Inspector General, Department of Defense) (proposing changing TINA to read that "[i]t shall be *conclusively presumed* that the Government relied on all cost or pricing data furnished by the contractor ...") (emphasis added).

However, Congress rejected the proposed amendment; rather than altering TINA to create a conclusive presumption of reliance, Congress codified the reliance requirement as a defense to a TINA claim. National Defense Authorization Act for Fiscal Year 1987, Pub.L. No. 99-661, § 952, 100 Stat 3816, 3945–49 (codified at 10 U.S.C. § 2306a(d)(2) (1986)). Thus, as of 1986, TINA explicitly stated that "[i]n determining for purposes of a contract price adjustment ... whether, and to what extent, a contract price was increased because the contractor (or a subcontractor) submitted defective cost or pricing data, it shall be a defense that the United States *did not rely* on the defective data submitted by the contractor or subcontractor." 10 U.S.C. § 2306a(d)(2) (1986) (current version at 10 U.S.C. § 2306a(e)(2)).

In short, the Air Force was entitled to a rebuttable presumption that any defective cost or pricing data affected its agreement to the contract price and thus actually caused an increase in the contract price. However, once UTech rebutted this presumption of causation, the Air Force was required to establish that it actually relied on the defective data to its detriment. The Air Force did not assert any additional evidence or arguments establishing such reliance before either the Board or this court. Thus, the *Reconsideration Decision* was not in error.

* * *

The Board's *Reconsideration Decision* is affirmed.

Notes and Questions:

1. Does a contractor cheat the public and get away with it when the contractors show mere lack of reliance in the government?

2. Why will government have a hard time proving reliance?

3. In a complex sequel, United Technologies was found liable under the False Claims Act, but without damages. *U.S. v. United Technologies Corp.,* 626 F.3d 313 (6th Cir. 2010).

Chapter 18

Ethics

The topic of integrity in government contract law has become increasingly important over time. From the beginning of the republic, the contracting system has wrestled with the diverse ill-effects of this tension, namely, how that quest for gain can undermine the sacred public trust, and induce corruption, collusion, favoritism, conflicts of interest, and as many other noisome impairments of integrity as the imagination can conjure. The remedies began with some relatively narrow criminal provisions and the associated common-law questions. Scandals at each stage in procurement history, especially the Civil War, the defense expansion of the 1950s and 1960s, and the renewed defense expansion of the 1980s, have brought statutory and regulatory refinements in the control of such impairments of integrity. Somewhat in parallel, a system of suspension and debarment of contractors lacking in responsibility has also developed, as protection of the procurement system from the troubles expected in further dealings with particular contractors.

Broadly speaking, the subject of ethics in government contracting encompasses a wide array of ethical or normative restrictions imposed on government officials or businesses involved in such contracting. These restrictions concern a fundamental polarity. On the one hand, the public has high expectations for a system of public officials engaged in the dispensing of official funds, a sacred public trust. On the other hand, the public does not, as a general matter, impose the same level of expectations on private contractors, for which an unmitigated self-interested quest for gain, pursued by every allowed means, is tolerated as the route to overall economic efficiency.

At various times, and notably in the 1990s and 2000s, a somewhat countervailing set of considerations has also come into play. Contractors argue that too much of the wrong kinds of ethical restrictions not only accomplish little, but do particular harm to a procurement system. Such restrictions may clog the system with red tape and paperwork, limit desirable competition, and create a higher-cost, lower-efficiency enclave separated from the general marketplace. Moreover, both ethical and debarment rulings can have such stigmatizing and otherwise deleterious impact, as to necessitate a high measure of procedural rights before their imposition lest they become unfair instruments of oppression.

In any event, the life of the law is the clash of attack and defense, and if the lawyers for the government (or, sometimes, for protesting non-awardees) hurl charges about integrity in the thunderous tone of the aroused public conscience, the lawyers for the contractor in the defendant's posture must answer back with the equally righteous call for fairness and due process.

This chapter can only provide an introduction to the numerous complex aspects of procurement integrity. It starts with a section on the basic prohibited forms of rank corruption, bribery, gratuities, and kickbacks. Next, it discusses conflicts of interest and restrictions, and access to information, in procurement. Finally, it addresses debarment, which the tension between the government's need to protect itself from the irresponsible contractor, and the contractor's potentially facing a shut-off, if business from the government really matters, of what sustains its very existence.

For further discussion of the subject of this section, see the cites for each particular subchapter, and see: Sandeep Kathuria, *Best Practices For Compliance With The New Government Contractor Compliance And Ethics Rules Under The Federal Acquisition Regulation*, 38 Pub. Cont. L.J. 803 (Summer 2009); Richard J. Bednar, *The Fourteenth Major Creedmore Lecture*, 175 Mil. L. Rev. 286 (2003)(largely concerning integrity and fraud issues); Michael Davidson, *Claims Involving Fraud: Contracting Officer Limitations During Procurement Fraud Investigations*, Army Lawyer, Sept. 2002, at 21; Steven L. Schooner, *Fear of Oversight: The Fundamental Failure of Businesslike Government*, 50 Am. U. L. Rev. 627 (2001).

A. Bribery, Gratuities, and Kickbacks

Of course, concerns about basic forms of public corruption date back into English law, and Congress established criminal prohibitions against those basic forms in the 1800s. In basic terms, officials take bribes in taking a payment as the quid pro quo for an official act. Officials take gratuities in taking a payment for or because of an official act, e.g., a payment after a decision as an expression of gratitude, a "tip" or gratuity, for it. The decisions of procurement officers constitute quintessential official acts, potential magnets for bribes or gratuities because they offer such concrete profit as a motivation for such payments. Prime contractors take kickbacks in taking back a payment from a subcontractor for favorable treatment..

The case law on the basic forms of public corruption offers a number of illuminating lessons. Defending or prosecuting basic corruption law cases does not provide that large a part of the practice of the typical government or private procurement lawyer. However, such law creates a foundation for the rest of the often subtle and complex public integrity rules, and these can pop up at any point in procurement. By advising on those more complex public integrity rules, procurement lawyers can help contractors strive hard for profits without crossing the line into wrongdoing.

Moreover, these cases shed a particular light upon the difficult questions of the distinctions and boundaries between public and private in the realm of procurement. Although corrupt practices involving public officials seems both morally offensive and highly dangerous to responsible government, comparatively less concern, either moral or practical, attends similar practices involving private figures. Just why is that? Suppose a salesman for ordinary medical supplies pays off the buying officers for two hospitals and gets caught. Since it is just a minor offense to do so at the private hospital, why does the exact same behavior, with the same effect, become, at the public one, a serious felony?

Each of the particular cases in this section also has its own special illumination of the procurement world. In the first case, the Air Force has largely privatized the functions involved in the procurement itself where the bribery occurs. Hence, the case illustrates just how privatization of procurement works in contemporary practice.

In the second case, regarding a kickback scheme, the Supreme Court dissects elaborately the intermeshed workings of private contracting and subcontracting. Hence, the case illustrates how subcontracting, although not itself contracting with the government, comes to an important degree under government contracting law. Also, the case addresses, when

Congress enacts a criminal provision to punish lapses in integrity, the provision_s civil implications for the government_s rights vis-a-vis violators. This is particularly important as to large government contractors, where the management at some level may credibly dispute any involvement or awareness in an integrity lapse, and the government must decide, not only how to punish the lapse, but what to do about the contract.

United States of America, Plaintiff-Appellee, v. Ronnie Brunson Kenney, Defendant-Appellant

United States Court of Appeals for the Eleventh Circuit
No. 98-2128
185 F.2d 1217
Aug. 26, 1999

Before ANDERSON, Chief Judge, BLACK, Circuit Judge, and FORRESTER , District Judge.

PER CURIAM:

Ronnie Brunson Kenney appeals his conviction for soliciting a gratuity as a public official in violation of 18 U.S.C§ 201(c)(1)(B).... We conclude that Appellant's assignments of error are unavailing and therefore affirm his conviction.

I. PROCEDURAL BACKGROUND

Appellant was charged in a three-count indictment arising out of the United States District Court for the Northern District of Florida, Panama City Division. In the indictment, Appellant was charged with three separate counts of soliciting a bribe as a public official in violation of 18 U.S.C. § 201(b)(2)(A).... On August 25, 1997, a jury was impaneled and trial began....

On August 29, 1997, the jury returned verdicts of guilty of the lesser included offense of soliciting a gratuity under Counts 1 and 3 and not guilty as to Count 2. Appellant was sentenced on January 13, 1998 before Judge Hinkle. Appellant was sentenced to two concurrent terms of eighteen months of probation, ten months of which are to be served in home detention. In addition, Appellant was fined $40,000 and ordered to pay a $200.00 special assessment. The imposition of sentence was stayed pending appeal, and Appellant filed a timely notice of appeal on January 26, 1998.

II. FACTS

A. *The Edge-Marker Contract and Appellant's Duties with Respect to It*

Appellant was an employee of BDM International, Inc. ("BDM"), and his official job title was "Manager, Rapid Runway Repair Branch." BDM is a large publicly traded company that, among other things, does extensive government contract work with the Department of Defense. In 1988, BDM received a Systems Integration Support Contract from the United States Air Force. Pursuant to this contract, BDM provided manpower to supplement Air Force Functions. As part of the support provided, BDM supplied acquisition management and engineering personnel to assist the Air Force Civil Engineering Services Agency in procuring and approving materials and equipment. Pursuant to this general contract, BDM employees were assigned to assist in specific ongoing Air Force projects, or tasks.

In September of 1992, officials at Tyndall Air Force Base in Florida awarded a contract to Starflite Boats of Niceville, Florida, pursuant to which Starflite would provide the Air Force with a runway edge-marker system for its runway repair program. An edge marker is used to mark runway damage on a combat zone airfield and consists of a Styrofoam reflector mounted on top of a thirty inch by forty-eight inch rubber mat. Also, as part of the contract, Starflite was to ship the edge markers in wooden shipping containers intended to last fifteen years. As part of its bid, Starflite suggested the possibility of manufacturing more durable and less expensive boxes out of fiberglass.

After the contract was awarded, a post-award conference was held. Among other things, the purpose of this meeting was to finalize the details of the performance of the contract, introduce the principal of Starflite, Mr. Brown, to the people with whom he would be working during the administration of the contract, and establish channels of communication. The minutes from this conference show that it was chaired by Sue Harris, the Air Force contract administrator. These minutes also show that the contracting officer for this contract was Larry G. Edwards, the project manager was Douglas A. Orlando, and Lt. Col. Michael C. Chatham was the officer in charge of the project. All of these individuals were Air Force employees. In addition, pursuant to the BDM-Air Force contract, Appellant was assigned by BDM to serve as its Acquisition Manager to support the performance of this contract.

At the post-award conference, Appellant was introduced to Mr. Brown as the day-to-day contact on the project, and Mr. Brown was told that if anything came up, he should contact Appellant. (R2-47.) Mr. Brown was also informed that Appellant would serve as the "eyes and ears" of the Air Force during the administration of the contract and would report the status of the contract, progress made, and any problems encountered by Starflite. As a result, Mr. Brown believed that Appellant was the engineer on the project and had the authority to approve or disapprove most anything concerning the project. (R2-46.)

In reality, as Acquisition Manager Appellant did not have final decision-making authority and could not bind the government. He did, however, advise decision makers with respect to certain technical issues involved in the edge-marker contract. According to the task description for this project, Appellant's job responsibilities included the provision of "program management, field test support, technical reviews and support for technical meetings when requested by the Chief, Airfield Systems Branch in support of the MOS Marking program." *See* Record Excerpt 773A. In addition, testimony at trial described Appellant's role, variously, as: Providing "technical data … to the people in the government who were making decisions regarding the procurement" and to provide advice based upon that information (R4-489-91; R5-636); processing or evaluating information for use by others in making official government decisions (R4-492; R5-636); functioning as the "eyes and ears" for the Air Force throughout the performance of the contract (R4-519; R3-238); ensuring that the contractor used specified products in the prescribed manner to get the prescribed product, or, in other words, managing the performance of the contract (R2-47); and providing technical advice to support the government in their acquisition of civil engineering systems for the Air Force. (R3-342). Ms. Harris also testified that Appellant held a position of official federal trust. (R3-269.)

In addition, the testimony indicates that Appellant's recommendations and advice were given great weight by those Air Force officials in the position to make procurement decisions. (R3-238; R3-331; R4-512-13.) The evidence shows that, on at least one occasion, Ms. Harris adopted Appellant's recommendation. Appellant had input in at least two decisions to substitute equivalent components. (R2-71; R3-329–30.) Also, Mr. Brown testified that when he spoke to Ms. Harris and Mr. Edwards about substituting an equivalent rubber mat for that specified in the contract, both stated that the approval of the equivalent would be Appellant's decision. Finally, although Appellant's salary was not paid by Air Force, testimony indicates that his salary is paid by BDM directly from funds it receives from the government in payment for services under the contract. (R3-352.)

B. *The Solicitations*

It is alleged in the indictment that in November of 1992, Appellant suggested to Mr. Brown that Mr. Brown could cut costs by using a different brand of rubber mats than that specified in the contract. Appellant offered to approve the change if Mr. Brown would pay him one-half of the cost savings. In addition, in March of 1992, Appellant and Mr. Brown discussed Mr. Brown's preference for using cheaper fiberglass shipping boxes rather than the wooden ones specified in the contract. Again, Appellant told Mr. Brown he could have the contract modified if Mr. Brown would pay him $100.00 per box. At a later date, the contract was in fact modified to allow for the use of the fiberglass boxes. Further, an equivalent mat was eventually used, although not the original equivalent sought by Mr. Brown. Mr. Brown, however, never paid the above-described sums. Instead, he reported Appellant's solicitations to Air Force officials.

After Mr. Brown's report, the Federal Bureau of Investigation (FBI) and the Air Force conducted a joint investigation and on May 24, 1993 recorded an incriminating conversation between Mr. Brown and Appellant on both video and audio tape. Thereafter, the investigation was put on hold for the duration of the contract because law enforcement officials wanted to observe Appellant actually receiving illegal payments. The investigation was also delayed due to health problems suffered by Appellant. Eventually, however, investigators closed the investigation in late 1996 and Appellant was indicted on June 26, 1997. Count one of the indictment related to the change in the contract specifications regarding rubber mats; count two alleged a general promise by Appellant to direct Air Force business to Starflite Boats in return for cash payments; and count three pertained to the change in the contract specifications regarding fiberglass boxes.

III. DISCUSSION

Appellant's first and third enumerations of error regarding the pre-indictment delay and the failure of the government to prove an allegation in the indictment are meritless and may be disposed of without discussion. Appellant's contentions regarding his motion to dismiss and the jury instructions, however, require a bit more attention.

A. *Denial of the Motion to Dismiss*

As stated above, in his first enumeration of error, Appellant contends that the district court improperly denied his motion to dismiss on the grounds that he is not a "public official" as defined by the statute under which he was convicted.

18 U.S.C. § 201 provides that it is unlawful for a "public official" to, among other things, demand, seek, or accept anything of value in return for being influenced in an official act. *See* 18 U.S.C.§ 201(b)(2). This statute also makes it illegal to seek, receive, or accept anything of value for or because of an official act performed or to be performed. *See* 18 U.S.C.§ 201(c)(1)(B). The term "public official" is defined as:

> Member of Congress, Delegate, or Resident Commissioner, either before or after such official has qualified, or an officer or employee or person acting for or on behalf of the United States, or any department, agency or branch of Government thereof, including the District of Columbia, in any official function, under or by authority of any such department, agency, or branch of Government, or a juror.

18 U.S.C. § 201(a)(1).

In *Dixson v. United States,* 465 U.S. 482, 104 S.Ct. 1172, 79 L.Ed.2d 458 (1984), the Supreme Court held that this definition extends beyond merely government employees and contractors to include private individuals who "occupy a position of public trust with official federal responsibilities." *Id.* at 496, 104 S.Ct. 1172. Such an individual, however, "must possess some degree of official responsibility for carrying out a federal program or policy" to be considered a public official. *Id.* at 499, 104 S.Ct. 1172.

In the instant case, Appellant contends that he did not occupy a position of public trust with official federal responsibilities. Appellant bases this contention on the fact that his job merely consisted of "making non-binding recommendations based on technical data." Appellant's Brief at 30. In addition, Appellant points out that he was not in a position to authorize changes in the contract or make decisions binding on the government and relies upon internal Department of Defense Policies that identify "inherently governmental functions" that may not be delegated to private contractors such as himself.

Although this circuit has not addressed the scope of the term "public official" in circumstances such as these, the findings of several of our sister circuits are instructive. In *United States v. Hang,* 75 F.3d 1275 (8th Cir.1996), the Eighth Circuit found that an eligibility technician for an independent public corporation organized under Minnesota law and established for the purpose of administering federal programs and funds was a public official. The defendant's duties in *Hang* included screening applications to verify whether the applicants were entitled to preferences for low-income housing and placing them on a waiting list. The defendant did not, however, have authority actually to rent an apartment. In affirming the defendant's conviction for receiving bribes in exchange for accelerating the application process, the Eighth Circuit found that the defendant occupied a position of public trust in that he was "on the front line in the effort to provide affordable housing to eligible families." *Id.* at 1280. In addition, the court held that the defendant's job involved official federal responsibilities in that the agency he worked for was organized for the exclusive purpose of implementing federal programs; was subject to federal oversight; and the defendant himself had a great deal of responsibility in determining who would receive available housing in that he was ultimately responsible for the accuracy of the applicants' files and the approval of his recommendations were largely *pro forma. Id.*

Similarly, in *United States v. Madeoy,* 912 F.2d 1486 (D.C.Cir.1990), *cert. denied,* 498 U.S. 1105, 111 S.Ct. 1008, 112 L.Ed.2d 1091 (1991), the District of Columbia Circuit upheld the conviction of a VA-approved fee appraiser for accepting bribes as a public official. The defendant in *Madeoy* conducted real estate appraisals for the purpose of obtaining Federal Housing Administration-insured loans. Despite the existence of a VA regulation stating generally that appraisers are not agents of the government and had no authority to bind the government, the court found the defendant to be a public official. In so finding, the court noted that it was on the defendant's recommendation, subject to only limited review, that the government guaranteed loans. *See also United States v. Velazquez,* 847 F.2d 140 (4th Cir.1988) (applying the statute to a county deputy sheriff who was responsible for supervising federal inmates); *United States v. Strissel,* 920 F.2d 1162, 1165–66 (4th Cir.1990) (finding the executive director of a local housing authority to be a public official); *United States v. Ricketts,* 651 F.Supp. 283 (S.D.N.Y.1987) (applying the statute to a supervisor in an organization that contracted with the Bureau of Prisons).

These cases make it clear that in order to be considered a public official a defendant need not be the final decision maker as to a federal program or policy. Rather, it appears to be sufficient that the defendant is in a position of providing information and making recommendations to decision makers as long as the defendant's input is given sufficient weight to influence the outcome of the decisions at issue. Based upon such reasoning, this court finds that Appellant was indeed acting as a public official.

Appellant's position was one of public trust in that his advice and the information he provided was relied upon by officers of the Air Force in making decisions pertaining to the procurement of equipment. In addition, it is clear from the record that Appellant acted as the primary liaison between Starflite and the Air Force and could not have done so without some federal responsibility. Appellant's job also included federal responsibilities in that he was responsible for monitoring and providing information regarding the technical aspects of the edge-marker contract. In providing such information, the evidence shows that his opinion was highly regarded, the decision makers relied upon his technical expertise and deferred to him on many day-to-day decisions. Like the defendants in *Hang* and *Madeoy*, although Appellant did not exercise the final judgment on contracting decisions, the information and recommendations he provided served as the basis for many of those decisions. As a result, it is clear that, in the performance of his duties, Appellant had some official responsibility for the carrying out of a government program.

Nor does the existence of the Department of Defense policies relied upon by Appellant alter this conclusion. These policies do not purport to define what is an official responsibility as that term is used in § 201. Rather, they merely provide guidance as to what functions must be performed by government employees and those that may be out-sourced to contractors such as Appellant. Therefore, they do not provide any guidance as to whether the functions performed by Appellant can be seen as including federal responsibility. As a result, the court hereby AFFIRMS the district court's denial of Appellant's motion to dismiss.

B. *Jury Instructions*

Appellant's final enumeration of error alleges that the jury instructions inaccurately stated the law with respect to the definition of "public official." ... The district judge in the instant case drafted jury instructions on the definition of a public official that combine some aspects from the statutory definition of the term with elements from the case law and hypothetical examples. Specifically, the jury was instructed:

> A "public official" ... is any person who acts for or on behalf of the United States, that is, a person who possesses some degree of official responsibility for carrying out a federal program or policy. This includes someone who, acting for or on behalf of the government, either (a) makes official governmental decisions himself or herself, or (b) makes recommendations regarding official governmental decisions, or (c) processes or evaluates information for use by others in the making of official governmental decisions.

> A "public official" need not be an employee of the federal government or of any government at all; a person who acts for or on behalf of the federal government pursuant to a contract or other business relationship can be a "public official," just as a government employee can be a "public official." The term "public official" thus includes an employee of a private corporation who acts for or on behalf of the federal government pursuant to a contract.

Record Excerpt 26 at 10.

Appellant asserts that examples (b) and (c) above are vague, open-ended, and left the jury no choice but to find him to be a public official. We concede that these examples could be construed as overbroad. When read in conjunction with the preceding language requiring the jury to find that Appellant possessed some official responsibility, however, we find that they accurately reflect the meaning of "public official" as we have construed that term above. Accordingly, although the jury instructions may not be as precise as we would like, we cannot say that the district judge abused his discretion in this regard.

IV. CONCLUSION

After careful consideration of the arguments presented on appeal, we conclude that Appellant is not entitled to relief. Accordingly, we AFFIRM the findings of the district court.

Notes and Questions

1. On first glance, the offering of the corrupt payment itself seems so reprehensible and debilitating that any kind of legal defense constitutes mere pettifoggery about technicalities. However, the line of cases that started with *Dixson* and extends to this case brings out forcefully some real tensions on this issue. The same "corrupt payment" to persons who perform some mundane task in a private setting does not trigger heavy penalties or major law enforcement efforts. If this defendant had been a purchasing manager, performing the exact same task at a private airfield, much less severe penalties and lesser law enforcement efforts would have attended the same pressure by him for baksheesh.

Looking at some of the examples in the cases this opinion cites as precedents. Had those receiving payments as tenant application-screeners or mortgage appraisers been in the private sector, again, much less severe penalties and lesser law enforcement efforts would have attended the same behaviors. What justifies coming down so hard, yet so selectively, on payments to the public procurement managers, tenant application screeners, or property appraisers, and not private ones—practical considerations about the institutional vulnerability of public government and spending, or, moral ones about the distinctive nature of the public trust?

2. On the other hand, before one scoffs at how arbitrarily these laws work or the historical accidents that generated them, consider that many of the world's countries find themselves plagued with corrupt governments, which they can neither shake off nor cleanse, and which drag down not just their governance but their whole society. The United States is blessed that, compared to many other countries, its procurement stays relatively honest. Does the lack of corruption owe to the legal system or to something in the societal culture—or does that distinction have any meaning?

3. The bribery and gratuities laws arose historically not so much from some logical systematic reasoning effort as might occur in the perfect creation of a fresh system, but from public and Congressional indignant but sporadic reactions to the successive scandals of each particular new era. For example, government contracts now typically include a standard clause prohibiting payment of a contingent fee or commission to those helping to obtain the contract. Congress mandated this clause in response to the particular "five per center" scandals of the early 1950s. In general, gratuities statutes and laws reflect the higher standards of the public sector. [In the private sector, "tipping"—that is, providing gratuities after performance of a service—is by no means regarded even as reprehensible, let alone criminal. Quite the contrary, those who receive good service in fine private establishments, and fail to leave a tip, probably offend public morality considerably more than those who do leave one.]

United States, Petitioner, v. Acme Process Equipment Company

Supreme Court of the United States
385 U.S. 138
Decided Dec. 5, 1966

Mr. Justice BLACK delivered the opinion of the Court.

The respondent, Acme Process Equipment Company, brought this action against the United States in the Court of Claims to recover damages for breach of a contract under which Acme undertook through itself and subcontractors to manufacture 2,751 75-mm. recoilless rifles for about $337 per rifle. Among other defenses, the United States alleged that it had rightfully canceled its contract with Acme because three of Acme's principal employees had accepted compensation for awarding subcontracts in violation of the Anti-Kickback Act set out in part below.[1] The Court of Claims found, as facts, that the kickbacks had been paid as alleged and that this was the ground on which the United States had canceled the prime contract with Acme, but construed the Act as not authorizing the cancellation. 171 Ct. Cl. 324, 347 F. 2d 509. We hold that it does.

I.

In October 1952, Acme hired Harry Tucker, Jr., and his associate, James Norris, for the purpose of establishing and managing a new division of the company to handle government contracts. Norris was made general manager of production with authority to submit bids, sign government contracts, and award subcontracts. Tucker was placed in charge of sales, government contracts, and expediting subcontract operations. Prior to this time Tucker had entered into a contract with All Metals Industries, Inc., under which he was to receive a commission for all sales to customers, including Acme, procured by him. Tucker's employment contract with Acme specifically stated that he represented and would continue to represent firms in other lines of business, but Acme did not consult with any of his other clients at the time Tucker was hired.

Late in October, Tucker advised his superiors at Acme of the proposed Army contract for rifles, and at Tucker's suggestion, Acme submitted a bid of $337 per rifle. Since Acme's bid was the lowest, the Army began negotiations with Acme culminating in the award of the contract in January 1953. The negotiations were handled by Tucker and Norris for Acme. Since it was contemplated that the project would be largely subcontracted, leaving to Acme only the final finishing and assembly of components, the Army expressed a keen interest in Acme's proposed subcontractors. Not only did it review Acme's subcontracting plans and require Acme to notify it of changes in those plans during the final stages of negotiation, but the contract eventually awarded required government approval of all subcontracts in excess of $25,000. All Metals, because its proposed subcontract amounted to one-third of the amount of the prime contract, actually participated in the negotiations between Acme and the Army.

During this period of negotiation two other developments took place. Tucker obtained agreements from two other potential subcontractors to pay him commissions on any or-

---

1. Section 1 of the Anti-Kickback Act, 60 Stat. 37, as amended, 74 Stat. 740, 41 U.S.C. § 51, provides in pertinent part:

'That the payment of any fee, commission, or compensation of any kind or the granting of any gift or gratuity of any kind, either directly or indirectly, by or on behalf of a subcontractor, … (1) to any officer, partner, employee, or agent of a prime contractor holding a negotiated contract entered into by any department, agency, or establishment of the United States for the furnishing of supplies, materials, equipment or services of any kind whatsoever … as an inducement for the award of a subcontract or order from the prime contractor … is hereby prohibited. The amount of any such fee, commission, or compensation … shall not be charged, either directly or indirectly, as a part of the contract price charged by the subcontractor to the prime contractor…. The amount of any such fee, cost, or expense shall be recoverable on behalf of the United States from the subcontractor the recipient thereof by setoff … or by an action in an appropriate court of the United States….'

Section 4 of the Act, 41 U.S.C. § 54, provides:

'Any person who shall knowingly, directly or indirectly, make to receive any such prohibited payment shall be fined not more than $10,000 or be imprisoned for not more than two years, of both.'

ders he could procure from Acme. Army contracting officers warned Acme's president, Joshua Epstein, that Tucker was suspected of having engaged in contingent-fee arrangements with other government contractors.

Finally, Acme was awarded the prime contract. Although the price was fixed at $337 per rifle, the contract contained a price redetermination clause under which, after 30% of the rifles were delivered, the parties could negotiate the price on past and future shipments upward or downward, with an upper limit of $385 per rifle. Within a few weeks after the prime contract was awarded, All Metals and the other two companies with which Tucker had prior kickback arrangements obtained subcontracts from Acme. Tucker was paid his kickbacks, but, apparently unsatisfied with the amount of his payoff, he got Jack Epstein, the superintendent of the chief Acme plant and the son of Acme's president and principal stockholder, to join the kickback conspiracy. Together Epstein and Tucker threatened to cancel All Metals' subcontract unless it paid $25,000 to a dummy corporation owned by Tucker, Norris, and Epstein for fictitious consulting services. All Metals reluctantly acceded to the shakedown. The amountpaid to Tucker, Norris, and Epstein was charged to Acme through an increase in the subcontract price.

Although they knew that Tucker was representing other companies and had been notified of the Army's suspicions of Tucker's involvement in contingent fee arrangements, other officials of Acme were not aware of the kickback activities of Tucker, Norris, and Epstein until late in 1953. At that time, Acme's president caused the resignation of the three suspected officials.

In 1956 Tucker, Norris, and Epstein were indicted for violation of the then Anti-Kickback Act, 60 Stat. 37. After presentation of the Government's case, the District Court granted the defendants' motion for acquittal on the ground that the Act—which at that time embraced only 'cost-plus-a-fixed-fee or other cost reimbursable' government contracts— did not apply to Acme's contract, a fixed-price contract with a provision for limited price redetermination. The court found the defendants' actions 'despicable and morally reprehensible, but unfortunately within the narrow letter of the law.' The court recommended that Congress amend the Anti-Kickback Act 'to include as a crime the vicious and immoral type of conduct that has been exhibited in this case.' United States v. Norris, Crim. No. 18535 (D.C.E.D.Pa.), April 14, 1956.

The District Court's opinion did indeed spur the Comptroller General to recommend amendatory legislation and in 1960 the Anti-Kickback Act was amended to apply to all 'negotiated contracts.' The civil provision of the amended Act was made retroactive to allow government recovery of kickbacks 'whether heretofore or hereafter paid or incurred by the subcontractor.'

II.

The Anti-Kickback Act, as originally passed in 1946 and as amended in 1960, provides two express sanctions for its violation: (1) fine or imprisonment for one who makes or receives a kickback, and (2) recovery of the kickback by the United States. The Court of Claims held, and it is argued here, that had Congress wanted 'to provide the additional remedy of contract annulment, it could have done so' by express language, 347 F.2d, at 521, 171 Ct.Cl. 343, and of course it could have. But the fact that it did not see fit to provide for such a remedy by express language does not end the matter. The Anti-Kickback Act not only 'prohibited' such payments, but clearly expressed a policy decidedly hostile to them. They were recognized as devices hurtful to the Government's procurement practices. Extra expenditures to get subcontracts necessarily add to government costs in cost-plus-a-fixed-fee and other cost reimbursable contracts. And this is also true where the prime contract is a negotiated fixed-price contract with a price redetermination clause, such as the prime contract is here. The kickbacks here are passed on to the Government in two stages. The prime contractor rarely submits his bid until after he has tentatively lined up his subcontractors. Indeed, as here, the subcontractors frequently participate in negotiation of the prime contract. The subcontractor's tentative bid will, of course, reflect the amount he contemplates paying as a kickback, and then his inflated bid will be reflected in the prime contractor's bid to the Government. At the renegotiation stage, where the prime contractor's actual cost experience is the basis for price redetermination, any kickbacks, paid by subcontractors and passed on to the prime contractor after the prime contract is awarded, will be passed on to the Government in the form of price redetermination upward.[5]

Acme argues, however, that the express provision for recovery of kickbacks is enough to protect the Government from increased costs attributable to them. But this argument rests on two false assumptions. The first is that kickbacks can easily be detected and recovered. This is hardly the case. Kickbacks being made criminal means that they must be made—if at all—in secrecy. Though they necessarily inflate the price to the Government, this inflation is rarely detectable. This is particularly true as regards defense contracts where the products involved are not usually found on the commercial market and where there may not be effective competition. Such contracts are generally negotiated and awarded without formal advertising and competitive bidding, and there is often no opportunity to compare going prices with the price negotiated by the Government. Kickbacks will usually not be discovered, if at all, until after the prime contract is let. The second false assumption underlying Acme's argument is that the increased cost of the Government is necessarily equal to the amount of the kickback which is recoverable. Of course, a subcontractor who must pay a kickback is likely to include the amount of the kickback in his contract price. But this is not all. A subcontractor who anticipates obtaining a subcontract by virtue of a kickback has little incentive to stint on his cost estimates. Since he plans to obtain the subcontract without regard to the economic merits of his proposal, he will be tempted to inflate that proposal by more than the amount of the kickback. And even if the Government could isolate and recover the inflation attributable to the kickback, it would still be saddled with a subcontractor who, having obtained the job other than on merit, is perhaps entirely unreliable in other ways. This unreliability in turn undermines the security of the prime contractor's performance—a result which the public cannot tolerate, especially where, as here, important defense contracts are involved.

III.

In *United States v. Mississippi Valley Co.,* 364 U.S. 520, 563, 81 S.Ct. 294, 316, 5 L.Ed.2d 268, the Court recognized that 'a statute frequently implies that a contract is not to be enforced when it arises out of circumstances that would lead enforcement to offend the essential purpose of the enactment.' The Court there approved the cancellation of a government contract for violation of the conflict-of-interest statute on the ground that 'the sanction of nonenforcement is consistent with and essential to effectuating the public policy embodied in' the statute. Ibid. We think the same thing can be said about cancellation here....

---

5. This is precisely what happened here before the Government canceled Acme's contract. Acme in 1953 submitted cost data for price redetermination purposes that included the charges of the five subcontractors which had paid kickbacks to Acme's employees. These subcontracting charges in turn included the amounts paid as kickbacks. Had the kickbacks not been discovered and the contract not been canceled, Acme would have been able to use these costs to renegotiate the price per rifle from $337 to $385. Such price redetermination could have cost the Government about $132,000 more on the entire contract.

There is likewise no merit to the Court of Claims' distinction of the Mississippi Valley Co. case on the ground that there the criminal provision of the conflict-of-interest statute was violated whereas here the kickback conspirators were acquitted of violating the Anti-Kickback Act as it existed when the kickbacks occurred, prior to 1960. As we have seen, Acme's employees were acquitted on the technical ground that Acme's prime contract was not a 'cost reimbursable' contract to which the Act then expressly applied. It is unnecessary for us to decide whether this holding was correct.[7] For whether the kickbacks here contravened the narrow letter of the criminal law, strictly construed, they clearly were violative of the public policy against kickbacks first expressed by Congress in 1946. If Congress then limited the reach of the Act to cost reimbursable contracts, it was only because other types of negotiated contracts were rarely in use then. Though the recent extensive use of other forms of negotiated contracts led Congress in 1960 to amend the Act to cover clearly these types of contracts and to close the technical loophole opened by the acquittal of Acme's employees, the congressional policy against all kickbacks was not changed. Congress merely reiterated its recognition of the evil and sought to correct the letter of the law to effectuate its long-standing policy. In making the civil remedy of the 1960 Act retroactive, Congress clearly indicated that there had been no basic change in the public policy against kickbacks.

* * *

The judgment of the Court of Claims is reversed with directions to sustain the United States' right to cancel the prime contract.

It is so ordered.

Notes and Questions

1. Whereas the bribery and gratuity statutes apply, in the procurement context, to those directly involved in contracting between the government and its prime contractor, the anti-kickback law applies centrally to the relations between the contractor and its subcontractors. Recall that the government leaves most of the price relationship between fixed-price contractors, and their subcontractors, as to commercial items, to the ways of the private market, including what are understood as its relaxed standards as to formalities and incentives. Why treat this part of subcontracting differently?

2. As with bribes, on first glance, the corrupt payment itself seems so reprehensible and debilitating as described in this opinion that any kind of legal defense constitutes mere pettifoggery about technicalities. However, part of that owes to the loaded term, "kickback." In fact, fee- or commission-splitting in complex ways during teaming and joint venturing are common in the commercial world. Keep in mind that a typical setting for what contractors might call complex payment-sharing, and prosecutors would call kickbacks, would be construction work. Is it worth the federal government's scarce enforcement resources, or a complex system of regulations and prohibitions, to corral those who continue local norms about routine minor construction when they perform federal projects?

3. The Warren Court decided this case in 1966. It followed its own seminal *Missippi Valley* opinion in 1961, and Congressional reforms of the early 1960s, all pushing ethics and procurement reform. Also, the Court ruled at the peak of its general willingness, throughout its legislative interpretation cases, to find additional causes of action and

---

7. See *United States v. Barnard, 255 F.2d 583,* cert. denied, *358 U.S. 919, 79 S.Ct. 287, 3 L.Ed.2d 238,* holding that a fixed-price contract with provision for unlimited price redetermination is a 'cost reimbursable' contract.

remedies against business in order to fill in, expansively, what it considered as gaps left by Congress in statutory schemes. The Supreme Court of the 1990s and thereafter has had much less eagerness to infer the existence of implied causes of action and to create implied remedies. Now the Justices tend to say that if federal law enforcers want more authority, they can ask Congress for it. Would today's Supreme Court, deciding this case on a blank slate, read the statute the way the 1966 Court did?

4. The case identifies some of the history up to that point of the anti-kickback law. In 1986, Congress passed a new Anti-Kickback Act to close up loopholes and revitalize controls on kickbacks. It broadly defined kickbacks. And, it extended to any type of government contract, obviating the previous question of whether what the opinion says would apply equally to fixed-price commercial contracting and subcontracting. See United States v. Kruse, 101 F. Supp. 2d 410 (E.D. Va. 2000)(providing of interest-free loans is an illegal kickback). Now, it applies even without proof the kickbacking subcontractor knew any of what it did, would go towards a federal contract. United States v. Purdy, 144 F.2d 241 (2d Cir. 1998). In the context of health care, an even strongers set of provisions, the Stark Acts, apply, from fear that medical providers' judgments—for example, whether to order lucrative but unnecessary tests—will be distorted by the conflicts of interest from participation in payments made for their provision.

B. Conflicts of Interest, Restricted Information

Congress and executive authorities have created a structure of procurement ethics considerably beyond the age-old concerns with corrupt payments. Contemporary law also concerns conflicts of interest, such as can arise when today's government officials involved in procurement become tomorrow's government contractor employees, and vice-versa. On the one hand, critics fear that a "revolving door" means sweetheart deals provided to contractors because of connections, favors, the anticipation of favors, and other undermining of independence. On the other hand, in some sectors like sophisticated defense contracting, there are values other than independence. A degree of rotation between the defense contractors and the military, some would argue, promotes a coordination that produces a more effective and workable procurement. Denying those with experience the ability to move back and forth would deprive both the government and the private sector of what may be the largest and best pools of personnel with useful, perhaps even essential, experience, capacities, and attitudes.

Another set of issues concerns the question of information obtained by contractors. Naturally, contractors strive to learn all they legitimately can about what the government wants or their competitors have to offer. On the other hand, the famous "Ill Wind" law enforcement project after the defense buildup of the 1980s uncovered extensive and shocking rings of contractors, consultants, and government employees sharing information that made a mockery out of the competitive system. Congress reacted by enacting a first, strict version of the Procurement Integrity Act, which it amended it in 1996 to relax some of the aspects that had come to seem excessive

For further discussion of the issues of this subchapter, see: Allen B. Coe, *18 U.S.C. §207(A)(1) "Lifetime Representation Ban" Opinions: A Lifetime's Work For Agency Ethics Officials And Advisors*, 63 A.F. L. Rev. 129 (2009); Julian S. Greenspun, *1988 Amendments to Federal Procurement Policy Act: Did the "Ill Wind" Bring an Impractical Overreaction that May Run Afoul of the Constitution?*, 19 Pub. Cont. L. J. 393 (1990); Paul G. Dembling

& Herbert E. Forrest, *Government Service and Private Compensation—Conflict of Interests*, 20 Geo. Wash. L. Rev. 174, 264 (1951, 1952).

United States of America, Plaintiff-Appellee, v. Eugene Donald Schaltenbrand, Defendant-Appellant

United States Court of Appeals, Eleventh Circuit
930 F.2d 1554
May 13, 1991

ON PETITION FOR REHEARING

Before TJOFLAT, Chief Judge, KRAVITCH, Circuit Judge, and GODBOLD, Senior Circuit Judge.

KRAVITCH, Circuit Judge:

* * *

Defendant-Appellant Colonel Eugene Schaltenbrand appeals his conviction of two violations of the government employee conflict of interest statutes. Specifically, he was convicted under 18 U.S.C. § 208(a), which prohibits government employees from working on projects in which they have a financial interest, and 18 U.S.C. § 207(a), which prohibits former government employees from representing private parties before the government on matters in which they previously worked for the government. We affirm the section 208(a) conviction and reverse the section 207(a) conviction.

FACTS

In early 1987, the United States Air Force was engaged in a program to sell certain C-130 aircraft to friendly countries. These aircraft were being phased out of the American fleet because they were no longer cost effective to keep as a means of primary defense. One aspect of the program was to develop a system of maintenance and support for the aircraft through a private defense contractor.

Colonel Carl McPherson served as the System Program Manager of the project. To assist him on the project, McPherson requested the activation of Schaltenbrand, a reserve officer who was available at the time for extended service. From February 17, 1987 through May 1, 1987, Schaltenbrand was activated nine times for short periods of duty, usually lasting two to five days, with one period of sixteen days. Air Force records show that some of these periods were designated "active" duty, while some were designated "inactive" duty. During periods of inactive duty, Schaltenbrand was not paid, but was required to wear his uniform and received credit towards retirement.

In March 1987, Schaltenbrand was sent to Peru to do a site survey, the purpose being to determine the needs of that country so that the Air Force could better tailor a package of aircraft and support for it. While Schaltenbrand was in Peru, discussions between the Air Force and Mexico were progressing rapidly, and McPherson sent Schaltenbrand to Mexico to perform a site survey there also. Shortly after Schaltenbrand's return from Mexico, McPherson requested that Schaltenbrand be activated for a sixty-day period to work exclusively on the Air Force's deal with Mexico (the "Mexican Project"). McPherson made this request on March 25, 1987, but the sixty-day period did not actually begin until May 3, 1987. According to McPherson, Schaltenbrand was to be his "right-hand man" on the Mexican Project.

In early April 1987, Schaltenbrand attended a meeting concerning the Mexican Project. The purpose of the meeting was to discuss the Mexican site survey and to hear a proposal from Teledyne Brown Engineering ("TBE"), a private contractor that had been selected by the Mexican government as the likely provider of support for the aircraft being sold to Mexico. At that time, TBE's contract for the project had not been finalized. Following the meeting, Schaltenbrand spoke with Harold Timmons, TBE's vice president and representative at the meeting. Schaltenbrand informed Timmons that he was interested in working for TBE after his duty with the Air Force ended. Schaltenbrand told Timmons that he thought he was well qualified to assist TBE with its potential contract for the Mexican Project, and Timmons suggested that Schaltenbrand fill out an application and send it to TBE's personnel department. He also mentioned that Schaltenbrand should discuss with the Air Force any potential conflicts of interest that might arise.

Schaltenbrand sent a resume to TBE's personnel department and also travelled to TBE's offices in Huntsville, Alabama to further discuss the possibility of employment. On the day of his visit to TBE, Schaltenbrand apparently was listed on Air Force records as on "inactive" duty. Schaltenbrand spoke with Timmons about his qualifications, and Timmons explained what TBE was looking for. TBE had done some advertising for the position and was seeking someone to lead TBE's Mexican team. In addition to flight experience, TBE wanted someone who could speak Spanish. Schaltenbrand told Timmons that he had thought about that, and that he would take a course in Spanish in order to be qualified. No salary discussions took place at that time.

Schaltenbrand's sixty-day period of duty ended on July 1, 1987, but he was activated for short periods on several occasions throughout August and September. Although the record is unclear as to the description of his duties during these later periods, it does not appear that he was significantly involved in the Mexican Project. On or about September 21, 1987, Schaltenbrand contacted TBE and informed it that he had another offer of employment, and therefore needed to know whether TBE was going to offer him a job. On September 21, TBE offered him the position that he had discussed with Timmons in April. . . .

Schaltenbrand accepted TBE's offer on September 25 and began work on September 28.

In his new capacity as a TBE employee, Schaltenbrand attended a meeting at the Air Force base on November 4, 1987 concerning the Mexican Project. The meeting was considered a "status conference." At this time, TBE still had not formalized its contract on the project. Dale Weaver was the TBE spokesperson at the meeting and requested that Schaltenbrand accompany him because Schaltenbrand would be responsible for implementing the plans discussed at the meeting. Aside from discussing some delivery schedules, there is no evidence that Schaltenbrand made any other contributions to the meeting. . . .

DISCUSSION

Section 208

Schaltenbrand first challenges his conviction under 18 U.S.C. § 208(a). That section provides:

> [W]hoever, being an officer or employee of the executive branch of the United States Government, . . . participates personally and substantially . . . in a . . . particular matter in which, to his knowledge, he, . . . or any person or organization with whom he is negotiating or has any arrangement concerning prospective employment, has a financial interest . . . [shall be guilty of a felony].

The parties do not dispute that Schaltenbrand was an officer of the executive branch or that he participated personally and substantially in the Mexican Project. Thus, the only issue with respect to section 208(a) is whether or not his conduct in obtaining his position with TBE amounted to "negotiation" under the statute. Unfortunately, this term is not defined in the statute.

This court recently addressed the definition of "negotiation" under section 208(a) and stated that "the terms 'negotiating' and 'arrangement' are not exotic or abstruse words requiring detailed etymological study or judicial analysis. They are common words of universal usage. People of ordinary intelligence would have fair notice of the conduct proscribed by the statute." *United States v. Hedges,* 912 F.2d 1397, 1403 (11th Cir.1990) (quoting *United States v. Conlon,* 628 F.2d 150, 154 (D.C.Cir.1980), *cert. denied,* 454 U.S. 1149, 102 S.Ct. 1015, 71 L.Ed.2d 304 (1982)).

Not surprisingly, Schaltenbrand urges a rather rigid definition of negotiation. He points to the language in *Black's Law Dictionary,* which states:

> Negotiation is process of submission and consideration of offers until acceptable offer is made and accepted. The deliberation, discussion, or conference upon the terms of a proposed agreement; the act of settling or arranging the terms and conditions of a bargain, sale, or other business transaction.

Black's Law Dictionary 934 (5th ed. 1979) (citations omitted).... Schaltenbrand argues that he had submitted an application to TBE, but TBE did not make him an offer until after he was finished with the Mexican Project. Stating that "[n]egotiating is like doing the Tango—there may be some dispute over who is going to lead, but it still takes two," he argues that no negotiations took place because TBE had not yet shown interest on its side.

Schaltenbrand contends that *Hedges* supports his argument that "negotiation" cannot take place until an offer is made. Although the *Hedges* court found that negotiation had taken place, Schaltenbrand notes that in that case the employer had proposed a salary for the prospective employee, and the prospective employee had countered with a higher salary proposal. *See Hedges,* 912 F.2d at 1403.

Contrary to the interpretation urged by Schaltenbrand, we conclude his actions were not only consistent with the definitions quoted above, but were also consistent with the reasoning in *Hedges.* As an Air Force reserve officer, Schaltenbrand approached TBE about the possibility of employment. TBE responded that he should fill out an application. After submitting an application, he was invited by TBE to come to its offices for an interview. During the interview, Schaltenbrand and TBE discussed the necessary qualifications to fill a particular position. TBE stressed that they needed someone who spoke Spanish. Schaltenbrand replied that he would learn to speak Spanish. Some months later, he received the exact position he had discussed at the interview.

The above circumstances clearly indicate active interest on both sides. The two parties were not engaged in mere general discussions, but had a specific position in mind and discussed the qualifications of the position in detail. Moreover, when TBE suggested that Schaltenbrand did not meet all of the qualifications, he responded that he would remedy that problem. Schaltenbrand contends that because *TBE* did not make a formal offer, no negotiations took place. Here, Schaltenbrand seems to forget his own argument that negotiations "take two"—clearly if it takes two to negotiate, there should not be a requirement as to who must make their offer first. Schaltenbrand initiated the dialogue, and TBE invited him to its offices and pursued the matter further. To require that the statute does not apply until the moment when a formal offer is made is to read the statute too narrowly....

This reading of the term "negotiate" is consistent with the purpose of the statute. In discussing the history of the statute, the *Hedges* court stated:

> In the seminal case of the *United States v. Mississippi Valley Generating Co.,* 364 U.S. 520, 548, 81 S.Ct. 294, 308–10, 5 L.Ed.2d 268, 288–89 (1961), in consider-

ing Section 208's predecessor statute, 18 U.S.C. § 434, the Supreme Court reviewed the legislative history of the conflict of interest statute. It observed that
"[t]he obvious purpose of the statute is to insure honesty in the Government's
business dealings by preventing federal agents who have interests adverse to those
of the Government from advancing their own interests at the expense of the public welfare." Although the statute, enacted in 1863, has been reenacted several
times, "the broad prohibition contained in the original statute has been retained
throughout the years."

Hedges, 912 F.2d at 1401–02. Despite the Supreme Court's broad reading of the statute,
Congress amended the statute in 1962 with the intent to make it even broader. *See United
States v. Irons,* 640 F.2d 872, 878 (7th Cir.1981). With regard to the specific term "negotiate," the *Hedges* court found that "[t]he term is to be broadly construed." *Hedges,* 912 F.2d
at 1403. Other courts have also reached this conclusion. *See Conlon,* 628 F.2d at 155.

Schaltenbrand also argues that if his definition of negotiation is not adopted, the court
should at least hold that the term is ambiguous and apply the rule of lenity. Schaltenbrand
relies on the recent Supreme Court case of *United States v. Crandon,* 494 U.S. 152, 110
S.Ct. 997, 108 L.Ed.2d 132 (1990), which applied the rule of lenity to another government conflict of interest provision. We simply note that *Hedges,* which was decided several months after *Crandon,* specifically addressed the issue of lenity with respect to the term
"negotiate" and found that the term was not ambiguous. Our reasoning above is clearly
consistent with the *Hedges* holding on this issue.

Section 207

Schaltenbrand also was convicted under 18 U.S.C. § 207(a). Section 207(a) prohibits
former officers of the executive branch from knowingly acting "as agent or attorney for,
or otherwise represent[ing], any other person (except the United States), in any formal or
informal appearance before" any department of the United States in connection with any
contract in which the former government employee participated personally and substantially while employed by the government. Again, there is no dispute that Schaltenbrand
had been an officer of the executive branch or that he was involved personally and substantially in the Mexican Project.

Although the statute prohibits acting as "agent or attorney for, or otherwise represent[ing]," the indictment in this case stated only that Schaltenbrand "did act as agent" for
TBE and failed to allege that he "otherwise represent [ed]" TBE. Based on the language
in the indictment, Schaltenbrand could only be convicted of a violation of § 207(a) if the
government proved beyond a reasonable doubt that he acted as an agent at the November 4, 1987 meeting. *See United States v. Figueroa,* 666 F.2d 1375 (11th Cir.1982). The term
"agent" is not defined in the statute, and we have discovered no cases interpreting the
term as it pertains to the statute.

Agency is defined as "the fiduciary relation which results from the manifestation of
consent by one person to another that the other shall act on his behalf and subject to his
control, and consent by the other so to act." Restatement (Second) of Agency § 1(1) (1958).
The "principal" is "[t]he one for whom action is to be taken," *id.* § 1(2), and the "agent"
is "[t]he one who is to act." *Id.* § 1(3). This court has stated that "an essential characteristic of an agency is the power of the agent to commit his principal to business relationships with third parties...." *Griffin v. United States,* 588 F.2d 521, 528 (5th Cir.1979)....

The above evidence shows only that Schaltenbrand attended the November 4 meeting
as an employee of TBE, and that he did not participate other than to discuss delivery
schedules. The government produced no evidence to show that TBE had given Schal-

tenbrand authority to make any binding decisions on its behalf. Moreover, the government produced no evidence to show that TBE had held out Schaltenbrand as one who could make binding commitments on its behalf or that it had permitted Schaltenbrand to so hold himself out. The government's evidence on this point is especially meager in light of the other stipulations indicating that TBE's spokesperson at the meeting was Weaver, and that Weaver had asked Schaltenbrand to accompany him to the meeting "in order to listen." Based on this record, we reject the government's argument that Schaltenbrand acted as "agent" at the meeting. In light of this holding, we need not address Schaltenbrand's other arguments with respect to section 207(a).

* * *

CONCLUSION

In accordance with the above discussion, we AFFIRM the conviction for Count I. We REVERSE the conviction for Count II, direct entry of acquittal, and VACATE the sentence imposed as to that count.

Notes and Questions

1. It is a challenge for those studying procurement integrity to keep in mind the historical contexts in which the laws, rules, and doctrines arose, but, a sense of the context of origin helps. This opinion looks back at the 1961 *Mississippi Valley* case about conflicts of interest, which, like the *Acme* about kickbacks, construed the pre-1960 statutory system. Then, it construes the Congressional reforms pushed by the Kennedy Administration in 1962, from a reaction to the national sense that the 1950s had been a period of insensitivity to ethical considerations by the federal government in general, and by procurement, particularly military procurement, in particular. Ironically, no one at the time had expressed this out more forcefully than President Eisenhower—himself the great military leader of World War II—in his famous 1960 warning of a "military-industrial complex" with undue influence. Conversely, because the case deals with the 1962 Act, it does not involve the further wave of statutory reforms from the mid-1980s, like the Procurement Integrity Act, responding to the scandals of the defense buildup of the 1980s.

2. What do you think of the way the court upholds the conviction for Schaltenbrand's participation when negotiating for a job, but reverses the second count about his then being an agent of his employer after taking that job? Did the court reach a sort of compromise verdict of partial conviction and partial acquittal, or do you accept its reasoning that he was proven to commit one offense and not the other?

3. Two different gray areas came together here: the former (or reserve) military officer going to work for the military contractor, and the American military contractor in a government-approved sale of military items to foreign countries. Given how common both situations and others like them are, so that public and private clients of the procurement lawyer will want and expect to go right up to the line on them, could you give advice that would enable them to do so without crossing over that line?

Matter of: Loral Western Development Labs

General Accounting Office
B-256066
May 5, 1994

Loral Western Development Labs protests the award of a cost-plus-award fee, level-of-effort contract to HRB Systems, Inc. under request for proposals (RFP) No. MDA904-93-

R-I001, issued by the National Security Agency (NSA), Maryland Procurement Office, for the agency's Worldwide Software Lifecycle Support Program. Loral asserts that NSA ... failed to consider that HRB violated the procurement integrity provisions of the Office of Federal Procurement Policy Act.

We deny the protest.

BACKGROUND

The RFP contemplated award of the Worldwide Software Lifecycle Support contract (WSLSC) for a base year and 3 option years. The contractor is required to provide specified labor categories and associated hours necessary to perform highly-skilled support services at locations inside the continental United States (CONUS) and outside the continental United States (OCONUS). The services include professional engineering, software support and maintenance, technical support, configuration management, and documentation required to supervise and support the performance of these services.

* * *

The RFP provided for award to the responsible offeror which submitted the proposal most advantageous to the government and stated that proposals would be evaluated against the following criteria: technical/personnel, management, and cost. Technical was weighted 50 percent, management 15 percent, and cost 35 percent. Under the technical factor, personnel qualifications and personnel availability were listed as subfactors and each was worth 25 percent of the evaluation score. Under the cost factor, the RFP stated that the evaluation would consider evaluated cost, worth 15 percent, and cost realism, worth 20 percent.

NSA received proposals from Loral and HRB. After evaluating the offers, conducting discussions with both offerors and receiving and evaluating best and final offers (BAFO), NSA determined that the RFP did not accurately reflect its needs and issued amendment No. 4 to the solicitation which deleted the phase-in plan, changed the basis of award, decreased the level-of-effort and provided HRB and Loral with written discussion questions. After evaluating the responses to the discussion questions, NSA provided Loral with additional cost and technical questions and requested both offerors to submit second BAFOs by November 23. NSA received, evaluated, and scored the BAFOs.... The evaluation board recommended award to HRB based on the difference in point scores and, consistent with the RFP, recognized that the point scores took into account the technical/management evaluation factors and cost. The source selection authority reviewed the evaluation results and agreed that HRB should be selected for award. The contract was awarded to HRB and this protest followed.

* * *

PROCUREMENT INTEGRITY

Loral protests that NSA failed to follow applicable procurement regulations in awarding the contract to HRB in the face of an alleged violation of the procurement integrity provisions of the Office of Federal Procurement Policy Act, 41 U.S.C§ 423 (1988 and Supp. IV 1992). Loral explains that in September 1993, after the first BAFOs had been evaluated, a Loral employee informed Loral management that an HRB employee stated that he had been told by HRB management that Loral's proposal was approximately $8 million lower than HRB's and that a second round of BAFOs would be requested. Loral states that it informed the agency of this "rumor" and was told that the alleged violation was being investigated by the Inspector General.

Loral complains that the agency improperly made award to HRB before the investigation was completed. Loral further complains that even if the agency could properly award the contract to HRB while the investigation was pending, it failed to obtain approval from a level higher than the contracting officer before doing so as required by the Federal Acquisition Regulation (FAR). Finally, Loral argues that since its proposal was in fact about $8 million lower in cost than HRB's and since a second round of BAFOs was requested, it is clear that there was a violation of the act and that HRB had Loral proprietary information. According to Loral, HRB thus should not have received the award because HRB was able to use this information to revise its cost and technical proposals to offset Loral's lower cost.

Under FAR § 3.104.11(a), if the contracting officer learns of a violation or possible violation of the procurement integrity provisions of the act, he or she must determine if the violation has an impact on the pending award. If the contracting officer determines that there is no impact, he or she may proceed with the procurement with the concurrence of a designated official. FAR § 3.104.11(a)(1). The designated official must then refer the matter to the head of the contracting agency who reviews all available information and determines what action to take, including whether to advise the contracting officer to continue with the procurement, initiate an investigation, refer the matter for criminal investigation, or determine if a violation occurred. FAR § 3.104.11(b). If the head of the contracting agency determines that a violation occurred before an award was made, he or she may cancel the procurement, disqualify an offeror, or take other appropriate action. FAR § 3.104.11(d). If the head of the contracting agency decides that a violation occurred after an award has been made, he or she may void the contract, effect appropriate contractual remedies, or refer the matter to the debarment official. Id.

The regulations specifically provide the head of the contracting agency with a number of options when a possible violation is reported. These include advising the contracting officer to continue with the procurement and initiating an investigation.

We find that the agency acted consistently with the FAR in conducting the procurement once it was aware of the alleged violation. When Loral informed the agency that it had heard a rumor that HRB knew its cost was $8 million lower than Loral's and that a second round of BAFOs would be requested, the agency referred the matter to the Chief of the Maryland Procurement Office, an official higher than the contracting officer. The chief instructed the contracting officer to request both offerors to execute special procurement integrity certificates stating that they were not aware of any violations of the procurement integrity provisions of the act.

Finally, he determined that there was no reason to stop the procurement because at the time the alleged violations were classified only as rumors. Thus, as required by FAR § 3.104.11(a)(1), the contracting officer continued with the procurement only after being advised by a higher level official to do so. Also as required by the FAR, the matter was referred to the head of the contracting agency who considered the matter before the contract was awarded to HRB. Before the award was made, the head of the contracting agency, with the contracting officer and the Chief of the Maryland Procurement Office, reviewed the issue and determined, as permitted by FAR § 3.104.11(b), that there was no basis to conclude that there was a violation of the act. They reached this conclusion because HRB had not acted on the information—that is, HRB did not raise its price, because Loral never provided any further information, and because the offerors executed the special procurement integrity certificates. They also considered that the issue was still under investigation. Thus, the agency followed the requirements of the FAR in deciding to award the contract.

Finally, while Loral argues that the facts show that there was a procurement integrity violation, NSA reports that the investigation is still pending before the Defense Criminal Investigation Service. Accordingly, we will not consider this issue further.

The protest is denied.

Robert P. Murphy
Acting General Counsel

Notes and Questions

1. The opinion deals with aspects of the regulations pursuant to the Procurement Integrity Act (PIA). See 41 U.S.C. sec. 423. This act grew out of the "Ill Wind" scandal, in which contractors benefitted from inside information. The original version of the PIA in 1988 was amended in 1996. It targets two things, information disclosure, and contacts about post-employment As to the first, it circumscribes the disclosure or receipt of procurement information. Chiefly, it seeks to prevent disclosure of contractor proposal information or source selection information, like rankings or evaluation of proposals. That is the issue in NKF.

2. Second, it restricts acceptance of employment by former agency officials with, or employment contacts between agency officials and government contractors. It has mandatory reporting requirements for officials with personal and substantial participation in acquisitions. And, it bans certain persons, like those deeply involved in source selection, for a year from compensation by an awardee. In this respect, it is part of the controls on conflicts of interests in the 1962 legislation.

3. In contrast to the indignant and tough response in some opinions on integrity matters, this opinion reacts coolly and declines to interfere with a procurement award. What does this opinion tell about the possibility that integrity rules might get pushed so far that they do as much harm as good? If the integrity rules at issue here had gotten pushed to extreme strictness, would the government lose out on the ordinary criteria for deciding on awardees—price and technical factors—and instead ended up having to accept inferior bidders who behave in a nicer way?

Note on Revolving Door Standards

Statutes and regulations, often the result of procurement scandals, have imposed an elaborate set of restrictions on present and former government employees relations with post-government employment. Congress first enacted the Ethics in Government Act in 1962, responding to scandals during the Eisenhower Administration. After Watergate, Congress enacted the Ethics in Government Act of 1978. Scandals of the Reagan Administration led to the Ethics Reform Act in 1989. Responding to the Darleen Druyan scandal during the Bush Administration, Congress enacted a provision in the FY 2008 Defense Authorization to tighten up post-employment rules. The Office of Government Ethics has given regulatory guidance about the application of the many strictures.

Breaking the restrictions from into categories, ethics rules restrict employment discussions by government employees with their post-government employers. Section 208 of the Ethics Reform Act of 1989 restricts government employees from participating in a "particular matter" involving firm with which he is negotiating prospective employment. Obviously this applies to government contracting personnel involved in a particular contract who are negotiating a job with the contractor.

Section 207 of the Ethics Reform Act of 199 restricts former government employees from lobbying for a one-year, two-year, or lifetime period, depending on the facts. Lobbying includes appearances before, or communications to, the government. That life-time ban applies to lobbying with respect to a "particular matter" in which the former employees were "personally and substantially" participating while in the government. The two-year ban applies to lobbying with respect to a particular matter that was under their "official responsibility."

In contrast to the lifetime ban, which only applies for matters that actually had their hands-on participation, so to speak, the two-year ban applies to whatever they had with their broad authority. Lastly, the one-year ban applies to lobbying on any matter in the department or agency in which they served. Although these are lobbying restrictions with broad applicability, obviously they apply to former government contracting personnel lobbying on contracts that were in their own participation, their official responsibility, or their department, respectively.

The Procurement Integrity Act (PIA) focuses more narrowly on procurement activity than the Ethics Reform Act. First, the PIA imposes restrictions on a government employee participating in a procurement who is in contact with an offeror of employment. A contractor wrongly doing this also faces penalties. Second, the PIA restricts the hiring of former procurement officials for a year after they dealt with that contract.

Additionally, the NDAA FY2008 provision, requires Department of Defense (DoD) senior officials, for the two years after they leave service, to request a written opinion from an ethics official about prospective work for a DoD contractor.

C. Organizational Conflicts of Interest

Filtration Development Co., LLC, Plaintiff, v. The United States, Defendant

United States Court of Federal Claims
60 Fed.Cl. 371
Originally Filed Under Seal April 13, 2004
Reissued For Publication April 27, 2004

OPINION and ORDER

FUTEY, Judge.

This post-award bid protest case is before the court on the parties' corresponding cross-motions for judgment on the administrative record, as well as plaintiff's request for a permanent injunction. Difficult questions pertaining to balancing the level of deference that should be afforded to military decisions with the enforcement of statutory and regulatory procurement laws are addressed herein. In this regard, the parties have raised numerous persuasive and thought provoking arguments which can be categorized into three pre-dominate sections. First, the parties dispute whether the contracting officer (CO) adhered to pertinent Organizational Conflict of Interest (OCI) regulations.

* * *

Factual Background

Throughout the opinion, repeated references are made to engine inlet barrier filter (IBF) systems and so-called "A kits" and "B kits" which comprise the bulk of the system. The Army, defendant, has been on notice for several years, and it is undisputed, that the installation of a filter system significantly reduces damage caused by the ingestion of sand and foreign particles. The Army has twice sought to develop a solution, but both attempts proved unsuccessful. In this context, the IBF is attached to the UH-60 Blackhawk helicopter engine. The UH-60 helicopters to which the filter system will be attached are primarily scheduled to head toward the harsh desert terrain in Iraq. The helicopters being replaced in the combat theater were heavily damaged by the conditions.

* * *

Pursuant to a previously awarded contract, No. DAAH23-02-C-0006 (Blackhawk Production Contract), Sikorsky Aircraft Company (Sikorsky) is responsible for designing, developing and manufacturing the UH-60 Blackhawk helicopter. On July 23, 2003, under a different contract, Sikorsky was directed to conduct an engine filtration trade study. The trade study contemplated that Sikorsky would evaluate, in addition to two concepts chosen at its discretion, a design concept developed by Aerospace Filtration Systems (AFS), a division of Westar Corporation (Westar). In August 2003, however, the trade study was suspended and Sikorsky was directed to immediately begin incorporating the AFS design.

The parties contest two factual aspects of the August 2003 decision. First, the parties dispute whether Sikorsky was specifically directed to use the AFS design. In this regard, while the December 2003 contract modification does not expressly acknowledge such a requirement, two separate statements in the administrative record lead to an opposite conclusion. Second, the parties dispute how the suspension came about. In the same statements referenced above, defendant contends that the decision to suspend the trade study was the result of an Army directive requiring that the acquisition of IBFs be expedited. As plaintiff correctly points out, however, the actual August 2003 directive is not included in the administrative record.

October 2003 proved to be an extremely important month in the context of this procurement. On October 9, 2003, a directive was issued in which the Army concluded that "installation of BLACK HAWK main engine barrier filters was required for … deployment not later than [March 2004] to ensure required readiness in theater." Further, the CO attended several meetings with Utility Helicopters Project Management Office (UHPMO) personnel and it was estimated that the number of aircraft scheduled for deployment, and in turn, the number of IBF kits needed, was 240.

The Army invoked the unusual and compelling urgency exception to full and open competition to procure the IBFs. 10 U.S.C. § 2304(c)(2); 48 C.F.R. § 6.302-2(a)(2). The Justification and Approval (J & A) executed on November 5, 2003, and approved on November 10, 2003, provided that the United States Army Aviation Missile Command "propose[d] to acquire, utilizing an acquisition method other than full and open competition, 240 IBF Desert Kits." The J & A also noted, *inter alia*, that (1) the kits would substantially reduce engine deterioration, (2) Sikorsky was the only contractor that could complete the assignment within the requisite time frame, and (3) "[s]ince these operations began, 400 engines have been removed/replaced at an approximate cost of $300 [million]." In addition, the J & A provided that the IBF kits will be labeled "Special Mission Kits and … will be flown under an Airworthiness Release (AWR)." The total cost of the procurement was estimated at $40.8 million.

As these events occurred, antecedent and parallel events giving rise to plaintiff's OCI claim were also taking form. In May 2000, Westar was the recipient of an Omnibus 2000 contract (O2K). Under the contract's Statement of Work, Westar was responsible for performing systems engineering and technical direction (SETA) tasks. Westar's contemplated responsibilities under the O2K specifically included "Propulsion Systems/Technology." In addition, according to plaintiff, Westar has received four task orders under the O2K in connection with the propulsion system for the UH-60 Blackhawk helicopter. Task Order 23 has drawn the most attention from the parties. Although the particulars of Task Order 23 are laid out in detail in the administrative record, defendant has conceded that the "scope of work under Task Order 23 includes '[p]ropulsion systems support' with respect to 'engine barrier filters.' " Defendant's main objection to both the O2K and the accompanying task orders is not premised on the scope of work, rather defendant argues that the documents do not show the work that was actually tasked or performed under the contract.

In a report dated May 16, 2003, Westar noted that it had "[p]repared for and participated in meetings to generate Propulsion-related project ideas. Explored Westar capabilities and problem areas in the Army aircraft fleet to plan future projects." Plaintiff argues that what occurred next was a result of the above-mentioned work, whereas defendant maintains that the proximity of the two events was pure coincidence. On May 27, 2003, AFS made a presentation to the Army concerning "Inlet Barrier Filter (IBF) Systems for the H-60 Helicopter Main Engine Inlet."

Returning to the fall of 2003, the various COs' actions in response to OCI concerns warrant attention. After the trade study was suspended in August 2003, a CO for the O2K apparently recognized the conflict and sought to implement precautionary measures. The extent of the CO's actions are reflected in the administrative record through two unsigned and unapproved mitigation plans. The CO for the IBF contract, following correspondence from plaintiff's counsel, twice discussed the allegations of an OCI with Army personnel. The CO was informed that the Army had recognized the conflict and that the appropriate measures were in place. On the basis of these representations, the CO concluded that a significant potential OCI did not exist.

On December 15, 2003, the Army executed a contract modification to Sikorsky's Blackhawk Production Contract and procured, *inter alia*, 183 "A kits" and 150 B kits. The deliveries are scheduled to take place from March through July of 2004, with an incentive for accelerated deliveries. As of the date of this opinion, several developments have transpired. The IBF kit design was finalized and an airworthiness release certificate was issued. In addition, although it does not appear that the overall delivery schedule will be affected, the initial deliveries have been pushed back approximately three weeks due to unexpected engineering difficulties.

Prior to the December 15, 2003, contract modification being finalized, plaintiff had met with Army officials on several occasions to express its interest in providing IBF systems for the UH-60 Blackhawk helicopter. Despite the inquiries, meetings, phone calls, and emails, its efforts were to no avail. Plaintiff filed suit in this court on December 18, 2003. The court immediately placed the matter on an expedited schedule. After the parties completed their briefings, the court held oral argument on defendant's motion to dismiss for failure to state a claim upon which relief can be granted. Given the need for an expeditious resolution of the matter, defendant filed the administrative record on January 28, 2004. On February 2, 2004, the court denied defendant's motion to dismiss reasoning that it could exercise jurisdiction over plaintiff's allegations of procedural violations of CICA as well as OCI regulations. Defendant supplemented the administrative record on February 24, 2004. The parties filed simultaneous cross-motions for judgment on the administrative record on February 26, 2004. The parties filed their responses on March 4, 2004, and their replies on March 11, 2004. The court held oral argument on March 31, 2004.

In the interim, on March 2, 2004, plaintiff filed an amended complaint. In its prayer for relief, plaintiff, in pertinent part, asks the court for: (1) declaratory judgment that the procurement was in contravention of law and regulation; (2) permanent injunction limiting the current procurement to only the minimum amount necessary to satisfy the current emergency situation; (3) permanent injunction directing defendant to procure any amount over the minimum on a competitive basis; (4) permanent injunction preventing defendant or Sikorsky from awarding any subsequent contracts to either Westar or its affiliates for a time period no shorter than the duration of Westar's current O2K; and (5) permanent injunction precluding AFS from participating in the re-instituted trade study.

Discussion

* * *

I. Organizational Conflict of Interest

Plaintiff advances a litany of arguments purporting to demonstrate violations of OCI regulations. Plaintiff maintains that the CO failed to adhere to procedural requirements. Plaintiff asserts that the CO did not take any actions to address the OCI until after plaintiff's counsel brought the issue to her attention. Plaintiff contends that the CO's determination that no significant potential OCI existed was unreasonable. Further, plaintiff avers that the CO cannot abdicate her responsibilities under the Federal Acquisition Regulations (FAR) simply because government personnel represented that the conflict had been addressed through the submission of mitigation plans. In this regard, plaintiff maintains that the mitigation plans were inadequate and that there is no evidence that the mitigation plans were executed. Building upon its argument that a significant OCI existed, plaintiff contends that the CO failed to obtain approval for a mitigation plan from the appropriate personnel.

Defendant asserts that the CO fully complied with her responsibilities under the FAR. Defendant contends that the CO was only required to act before the time of contract award, which she did. Defendant maintains that the CO properly consulted government personnel first in examining a possible conflict. Defendant also avers that because the government personnel had implemented appropriate precautionary measures, the CO's conclusion that no significant conflict of interest existed was reasonable. Further, defendant asserts that once the CO determined that no significant OCI was present, no further action was required on her part.

The responsibility for ascertaining whether an actual or potential conflict of interest exists generally rests with the CO. 48 C.F.R. §9.504(a). The CO is instructed to "[i]dentify and evaluate potential organizational conflict of interest *as early in the acquisition process as possible....*" *Id.* §9.504(a)(1) (emphasis added). For assistance in making this determination, the CO "should obtain the advice of counsel and the assistance of appropriate technical specialists...." *Id.* §9.504(b); see also *id.* §9.506(a) (explaining that the CO "first should seek the information from within the Government ..."). The CO is not required to take additional steps if there is a determination that no significant conflict exists. *Id.* §9.506(b); see also *id.* §9.504(d) ("The [CO's] judgment need be formally documented only when a substantive issue concerning potential [OCIs] exists."). If the CO determines that a significant potential OCI may be present, however, certain steps must be taken before a solicitation is issued. *Id.* §9.506(b). Amongst these steps, the CO must proffer a "recommended course of action for avoiding, neutralizing, or mitigating the conflict" to the head of the contracting activity or the chief of the contracting office. *Id.* §9.506(b)(1); see also *id.* §9.504(c). The conflict must be resolved in the appropriate fashion prior to the contract being awarded. *Id.* §§9.506(d)(3), 9.504(a)(2); see also *LeBoeuf, Lamb, Greene & MacRae, LLP v. Abraham,* 347 F.3d 315, 321 (D.C.Cir.2003). A CO's determination regarding whether the acquisition involves a significant conflict will be overturned only on a showing of unreasonableness. *Informatics Corp. v. United States,* 40 Fed.Cl. 508, 513 (1998).

The identification of the OCI in this case did not occur "as early in the acquisition process as possible...." 48 C.F.R. § 9.504(a)(1). There was no recognition of any conflict in May 2003 when the Army began its discussions with AFS, despite clear signs that AFS was a division of Westar. Likewise, in August 2003, noticeably lacking were any conflict concerns when UHPMO suspended the trade study and directed Sikorsky to "immediately begin design activity to incorporate the AFS filter system onto UH-60 aircraft." Although defendant argues that the CO complied with her obligations because she determined that a significant OCI did not exist prior to the contract modification being executed, defendant overlooks that Sikorsky was incorporating AFS's design from August 2003 until October 2003 without any properly approved OCI safeguards. Contrary to defendant's assertions, such an assessment concerning any possible significant OCI would not have been overly premature. The FAR expressly contemplates that when analyzing significant potential OCIs, the determination occur prior to a solicitation being issued. 48 C.F.R. § 9.506(b). Further, the multiple unsigned mitigation plans contained in the administrative record do little to support defendant's position that the conflict was resolved prior to contract award.

The CO's determination that a significant OCI did not exist is contradicted by the record. The CO did properly contact other government personnel to apprise her of the situation. 48 C.F.R. § 9.506(a). Those personnel informed her that they recognized the potential for a conflict of interest. Their conclusion was buttressed by Westar's submission of at least two proposed mitigation plans. It is, therefore, safe to conclude that all those involved recognized the significant conflict. The CO, however, exceeded her authority by concluding that the appropriate safeguards were in place to eliminate the conflict. According to the FAR, that is not a decision the CO is empowered to make. 48 C.F.R. § 9.506(b). The authority to "[a]pprove, modify, or reject the [recommended course of action for avoiding, neutralizing, or mitigating the conflict]" rests with the chief of the contracting office. *Id.* § 9.506(b)–(d). Accordingly, the CO failed to abide by the procedures set forth in § 9.506.

Plaintiff also maintains that Westar, through AFS, is precluded from providing the IBF kits because Westar provides SETA services under its O2K. Plaintiff contends that Westar possesses an unfair competitive advantage through its access to information not available to other bidders, in particular source selection information. Further, plaintiff avers a significant OCI exists in light of Westar's vested interest in having AFS supply the IBF kits. Plaintiff also asserts that prejudice is presumed upon a finding of an actual OCI.

Defendant avers that there is no significant OCI because Westar never actually performed any work under either the O2K or the task orders in connection with the UH-60 Blackhawk helicopter or its propulsion system. Relying on the same line of reasoning, defendant argues that an actual OCI did not arise. Defendant also maintains that plaintiff's "unfair competitive advantage" argument is based on nothing more than speculation and borders on frivolous.

Given the "highly influential and responsible position" of contractors performing systems engineering and technical direction, 48 C.F.R. § 9.505-1(b), the FAR contains the following explicit prohibition:

> A contractor that provides systems engineering and technical direction for a system but does not have overall contractual responsibility for its development, its integration, assembly, and checkout, or its production *shall not* (1) be awarded a contract to supply the system or any of its major components or (2) be a subcontractor or consultant to a supplier of the system or any of its major components.

Id. § 9.505-1(a) (emphasis added); see also *Vantage Assocs., Inc. v. United States,* 59 Fed.Cl. 1, 10 (2003). Defendant appears to concede that Westar contracted to provide SETA services for the UH-60 propulsion system, but devotes significant attention to arguing that Westar did not perform any work pertaining to IBFs under the O2K. Specifically, defendant maintains that Task Order 23 only enumerates the work that could have been performed and does not enumerate the work that was actually performed. Defendant also submits a declaration that provides that Westar "did not received [sic] any taskings under their O2K contract task orders to provide any support, analysis, evaluation, development, or any other effort in connection with Engine [IBFs] on the UH-60 Blackhawk aircraft." Defendant's argument misses the point.

The FAR prohibits a SETA contractor, as either a prime contractor or a subcontractor, from supplying any of the system's major components, without regard to whether work was performed as to that particular component. 48 C.F.R. § 9.508(a). The FAR's prohibition is clarified in the following illuminating example: "Company A *agrees to provide* systems engineering and technical direction for the Navy on the power plant for a group of submarines.... *Company A should not be allowed to supply any power plant components.*" 48 C.F.R. § 9.508(a) (emphasis added). Westar agreed to provide SETA services concerning UH-60 propulsion systems under its O2K. For example, Westar "[p]repared for and participated in meetings to generate Propulsion-related project ideas. Explored Westar capabilities and problem areas in the Army aircraft fleet to plan future projects." Westar also "[p]rovided input on the rewrite of the Airworthiness Impact Statement" and "[r]eviewed Standard Operating Procedures on the new Airworthiness Impact Statement Document." Applying the reasoning of § 9.508(a), Westar or its affiliates were categorically precluded from supplying any propulsion system components. Simply put, Westar was improperly "in a position to make decisions favoring its own products or capabilities." 48 C.F.R. § 9.505-1(b). Through its contractual obligation to provide SETA services and through AFS's contractual obligations to provide IBFs, Westar as an entity occupied an impermissible dual role and an actual OCI, therefore, arose. *Matter of: Aetna Gov't Health Plans, Inc.,* B-254397.15, 95-2 CPD ¶ 129, at 18, 1995 WL 449806, at *11 (Comp.Gen. July 27, 1995) (explaining that the entity's "dual role[ ] placed it in an actual organizational conflict of interest because of the prospect that it would be unable to render impartial advice ...").

Plaintiff is, therefore, entitled to benefit from the presumption of harm/prejudice. *Id.* at 12, 1995 WL 449806, at *11 (citing *NKF Eng'g, Inc. v. United States,* 805 F.2d 372, 376 (Fed.Cir.1986), *Compliance Corp. v. United States,* 22 Cl.Ct. 193 (1990), *aff'd,* 960 F.2d 157 (Fed.Cir.1992)); see also *Matter of: DZS/Baker LLC,* B-281224, 99-1 CPD ¶ 19, at 7, 1999 WL 46706, at *4 (Comp.Gen. Jan.12, 1999) ("[W]e note that there is a presumption of prejudice ... where a conflict of interest, other than a de minimis or insignificant matter is not resolved."). Although defendant maintains that the presumption can be rebutted through the implementation of adequate safeguards, the argument loses its persuasiveness given the court's conclusion concerning Westar's mitigation plans. While the court does not question the credibility or integrity of Westar to voluntarily comply with the recommended precautionary measures, the court cannot allow an unsigned and unapproved mitigation plan to stand. Therefore, a presumption of harm to the procurement process and prejudice accompanies Westar's dual role.

* * *

Lastly, the court declines to enter a permanent injunction precluding AFS from future competition for engine filters. Defendant argues that the court's review in bid protest cases is limited to applying the APA standard of review to the administrative record. Defendant, however, overlooks the fact that the basis for the future injunction would be a finding that the current procurement created an OCI on a future acquisition. The FAR expressly contemplates such review and indicates that "some restrictions on future activities of the contractor may be required." 48 C.F.R. § 9.502(c). Nevertheless, this is not the only provision in the FAR which guides the resolution of the issue. The FAR provides the following instruction: "[e]ach individual contracting situation should be examined on the basis of its particular facts and the nature of the proposed contract." *Id.* § 9.505. Further, the FAR permits the CO, after finding that it is in the best interest of the United States to do so, to award the contract despite the OCI upon obtaining a waiver from the head of the agency or a designee. *Id.* §§ 9.503, 9.504(e). Given that the court can envision a situation where such an option could be exercised, a permanent injunction excluding AFS from the re-instituted trade study and from future competition is inappropriate.

Conclusion

For the above-stated reasons, plaintiff has shown that the Army violated OCI regulations and exceeded the permissible bounds of 10 U.S.C. § 2304(c)(2). In light of plaintiff's burden of demonstrating its entitlement to the extraordinary remedy of permanent injunctive relief by clear and convincing evidence, and after "giv[ing] due regard to the interests of national defense and national security" as required by 28 U.S.C. § 1491(b)(3), the following is hereby ordered:

1) Defendant is entitled to procure 183 "A kits" and 150 "B kits" under its current invocation of the unusual and compelling urgency exception;

2) Any procurement in excess of 183 "A kits" and 150 "B kits" must be conducted on a competitive basis unless an independent justification for invoking an exception to full and open competition is provided;

3) AFS will not be enjoined from participating in the re-instituted trade study or from participating in future competition.

* * *

IT IS SO ORDERED.

Notes and Questions

1. Could Sikorsky and Westar dispute the wisdom of having overly strict OCI rules? How many companies likely have the expertise to perform their tasks? Consider the consolidation of the defense contractors since the end of the Cold War, and the tendency, as part of globalization, for the number of American providers of certain kinds of goods and services to shrink. Does the government deny itself access to vital and limited expertise and, perhaps, competition, by ruling out the use of the same company in different roles? On the other hand, with the privatizing drive pushing more judgment decisions among choices into private hands, potentially the same hands as are themselves among the choices, does OCI represent a vastly increased and alarming modern counterpart of the ethics issues that were predominant when there was a clearer line between public and private roles?

2. OCI problems have been divided into three groups, relating to the type of problem created: biased ground rules, unequal access to information, and impaired objectivity. Which is this case? Do we have a demonstration that this actual problem occurred, or is there only the potential for, or appearance of, such a problem? Can there be a middle ground, of reason to have a "presumption" of such a problem?

3. Important treatments of the evolution of the OCI rules were provided in Daniel Guttman, *Organizational Conflict of Interest and the Growth of Big Government*, 15 Harv. J. on Legis. 297 (1977–78); Daniel Guttman, *Governance by Contract: Constitutional Vi-*

sions: Time for Reflection and Choice, 33 Pub. Cont. L.J. 321 (2004). An insightful survey is Daniel I. Gordon, *Organizational Conflicts of Interest: A Growing Integrity Challenge*, 35 Pub. Cont. L.J. 35 (2005).

Note on Organizational Conflicts of Interest

Filtration Development Co. itself sketches the law of organizational conflicts of interests (OCI), which this note builds on. OCIs have become, relatively recently, the plague of government contracting. This is so because the government outsources far more broadly and diversely than ever before. Moreover, the government relies increasingly and intimately on vendors fraught with potential for OCIs, such as firms that provide personnel augmentation for the acquisition function itself.

The commentary has suggested OCIs fall roughly into three types. "Biased ground rules" arise when one contract sets ground rules for another. For example, a contractor's personnel write requirements for a solicitation upon which that contractor may compete. Next, "impaired objectivity" arise when a contractor may entail evaluating either its own performance, or evaluation of proposals, for another contract. Third, situations with "unequal access to information" arise when a contractor's role provides access to nonpublic information relevant to a new competition.

GAO has rendered dozens of decisions on protests of awards challenged on the ground of OCIs. These decisions have looked favorably at agencies' decisions to waif an OCI on the ground that it has been avoided or mitigated. Contractors facing potential OCIs have a duty to provide a mitigation plan. For example, they may erect a firewall between their employees working on one contract and those working on another. Or, they may find ways to equalize the access to information of the contractor who would start off with an advantage, and, other contractors. Among other principles, it is always better to develop a mitigation plan or other way to avoid OCIs in advance of the problems, rather than wait until the problems become acute.

Although GAO has most OCI cases, the Court of Federal Claims and the Federal Circuit have provided important opinions. The Federal Circuit decided *Axiom Resource Management v. United States*, 564 F.3d 1374 (Fed. Cir. 2009). A competitor challenged an award on OCI grounds. The Federal Circuit upheld the award, finding that the contracting officer could be expected to enforce the awardee's mitigation plan, and, that the officer had the legal tools to do so.

Congress has also taken a position on some aspects of OCIs. In section 207 of the Weapon Systems Acquisition Reform Act of 2009, P.L. 111-23, it required DFARS provisions to deal with potential OCIs in a number of areas. These included contractor's simultaneous ownership of business units performing systems engineering, professional services or management support — on the one hand — and business units competing to perform as prime contractor or supplier of a major subsystem, on the other.

For more, see Government Contract Compliance Handbook sec. 8.15 (4th ed.), available on Westlaw; and, *Industry and Watchdog Organizations Comment on DOD OCI Requirements*, 51 Gov. Cont. para. 426 (2009).

Chapter 19

Governmental Breach
and Takings

Special questions arise when the government acts toward contractors in ways that raise more issues than constructive change. These cases go beyond the normal realm of whether the government has followed its rules. They may raise the issue of whether the government has gone beyond constitutional lines and "taken" the private interest. The subject has assumed renewed interest in the wake of the Supreme Court's decision in the *Winstar* case that the government committed a taking by violating an agreement with a regulated bank.

The first section looks at Government breach. The second section looks at takings. Because the issue in these cases may go beyond substantive law and involve the government's powerful procedural defenses, the third section discusses sovereign immunity.

For further discussion, see Michael R. Rizzo, Virginia M. Gomez, *Erosion Of The Sovereign Acts Doctrine? How Recent Winstar And Spent Nuclear Fuel Litigation Impacts Government Contractors*, 42 Procrmt. Law. 3 (Spring 2007); Evan C. Zoldan, *All Roar And No Bite: Lion Raisins And The Federal Circuit's First Swipe At The NAFI Doctrine*, 36 Pub. Cont. L.J. 153 (Winter 2007); Joshua I. Schwartz, *Assembling* Winstar: *Triumph of the Ideal of Congruence in Government Contracts Law?*, 26 Pub. Cont. L.J. 481 (1997).

A. Governmental Breach

The government can breach in ways a private buyer would not, such as by a new statute or program effectively frustrating completion of existing contracts. This topic has a long history in the law, such as the seminal 1925 case when the United States was sued for breach for dishonoring a contract involving a sale of silk. The government defended successfully on the ground the breach resulted from a subsequent embargo on such transactions, notwithstanding that the government itself had imposed that embargo. *Horowitz v. United States*, 267 U.S. 458 (1925).

This topic received renewed attention focusing upon the interesting but exceedingly complex opinions in *United States v. Winstar*, 518 U.S. 839 (1996). Cases since *Winstar* now appear to have clarified somewhat the contemporary law This section provides a post-*Winstar* case, *Mobil*, followed by notes.

For further discussion, see: Seon J. Lee, Note, *Does* Mobil Oil *Weaken the Sovereign Defenses of Government Breach of Contract Claims? An Analysis of the Unmistakability Doctrine and the Sovereign Acts Doctrine*, 31 Pub. Cont. L.J. 559 (2002); Deena B. Bothello, Note, *An Unequal Balance: Repudiation and Restitution in* Mobil Oil Exploration & Producing Southeast, Inc. v. United States, 80 Ore. L. Rev. 1469 (2001); Deena B. Bothello, Note,

An Unequal Balance: Repudiation and Restitution in Mobil Oil Exploration & Producing Southeast, Inc. v. United States, 80 Ore. L. Rev. 1469 (2001).

Mobil Oil Exploration & Producing Southeast, Inc., Petitioner, v. United States

Supreme Court of the United States
Nos. 99-244, 99-253
530 U.S. 604
Argued March 22, 2000
Decided June 26, 2000.

Justice BREYER delivered the opinion of the Court.

Two oil companies, petitioners here, seek restitution of $156 million they paid the Government in return for lease contracts giving them rights to explore for and develop oil off the North Carolina coast. The rights were not absolute, but were conditioned on the companies' obtaining a set of further governmental permissions. The companies claim that the Government repudiated the contracts when it denied them certain elements of the permission-seeking opportunities that the contracts had promised. We agree that the Government broke its promise; it repudiated the contracts; and it must give the companies their money back.

I

A

A description at the outset of the few basic contract law principles applicable to this action will help the reader understand the significance of the complex factual circumstances that follow. "When the United States enters into contract relations, its rights and duties therein are governed generally by the law applicable to contracts between private individuals." *United States v. Winstar Corp.,* 518 U.S. 839, 895, 116 S.Ct. 2432, 135 L.Ed.2d 964 (1996) (plurality opinion) (internal quotation marks omitted). The Restatement of Contracts reflects many of the principles of contract law that are applicable to this action. As set forth in the Restatement of Contracts, the relevant principles specify that, when one party to a contract repudiates that contract, the other party "is entitled to restitution for any benefit that he has conferred on" the repudiating party "by way of part performance or reliance." Restatement (Second) of Contracts § 373 (1979) (hereinafter Restatement). The Restatement explains that "repudiation" is a "statement by the obligor to the obligee indicating that the obligor will commit a breach that would of itself give the obligee a claim for damages for total breach." *Id.,* § 250. And "total breach" is a breach that "so substantially impairs the value of the contract to the injured party at the time of the breach that it is just in the circumstances to allow him to recover damages based on all his remaining rights to performance." *Id.,* § 243.

∗ ∗ ∗

B

In 1981, in return for up-front "bonus" payments to the United States of about $156 million (plus annual rental payments), the companies received 10-year renewable lease contracts with the United States. In these contracts, the United States promised the companies, among other things, that they could explore for oil off the North Carolina coast and develop any oil that they found (subject to further royalty payments) provided that the companies received exploration and development permissions in accordance with various statutes and regulations to which the lease contracts were made "subject." App. to Pet. for Cert. in No. 99-253, pp. 174a–185a.

The statutes and regulations, the terms of which in effect were incorporated into the contracts, made clear that obtaining the necessary permissions might not be an easy matter. In particular, the Outer Continental Shelf Lands Act (OCSLA), 67 Stat. 462, as amended, 43 U.S.C. § 1331 *et seq.* (1994 ed. and Supp. III), and the Coastal Zone Management Act of 1972 (CZMA), 86 Stat. 1280, 16 U.S.C. § 1451 *et seq.,* specify that leaseholding companies wishing to explore and drill must successfully complete [various] procedures....

C

The events at issue here ... are the following:

1. In 1981, the companies and the Government entered into the lease contracts. The companies paid the Government $156 million in up-front cash "bonus" payments.

2. In 1989, the companies, Interior, and North Carolina entered into a memorandum of understanding. In that memorandum, the companies promised that they would submit an initial draft Exploration Plan to North Carolina before they submitted their final Exploration Plan to Interior....

4. On August 20, 1990, the companies submitted both their final Exploration Plan and their CZMA "consistency certification" to Interior.

5. Just two days earlier, on August 18, 1990, a new law, the Outer Banks Protection Act (OBPA), § 6003, 104 Stat. 555, had come into effect....

6. About five weeks later, and in light of the new statute, Interior wrote a letter to the Governor of North Carolina with a copy to petitioner Mobil. It said that the final submitted Exploration Plan "is deemed to be approvable in all respects." ... But, it noted, the new law, the "Outer Banks Protection Act (OBPA) of 1990 ... prohibits the approval of any Exploration Plan at this time." It concluded, "because we are currently prohibited from approving it, the Plan will remain on file until the requirements of the OBPA are met." In the meantime a "suspension has been granted to all leases offshore the State of North Carolina." *Ibid....*

7. In November 1990, North Carolina objected to the companies' CZMA consistency certification on the ground that Mobil had not provided sufficient information about possible environmental impact. A month later, the companies asked the Secretary of Commerce to override North Carolina's objection.

8. In 1994, the Secretary of Commerce rejected the companies' override request, relying in large part on the fact that the new [OBPA-created] Panel had found a lack of adequate information in respect to certain environmental issues.

9. In 1996, Congress repealed OBPA. § 109, 110 Stat. 1321-177.

D

In October 1992, after all but the two last-mentioned events had taken place, petitioners joined a breach-of-contract lawsuit brought in the Court of Federal Claims. On motions for summary judgment, the court found that the United States had broken its contractual promise to follow OCSLA's provisions.... A panel of the Court of Appeals for the Federal Circuit reversed, one judge dissenting.... We granted certiorari to review the Federal Circuit's decision.

II

... [T]he Government denies that it must refund the companies' money.

This is because, in the Government's view, it did not breach the contracts or communicate its intent to do so; [and] any breach was not "substantial"....

A

The Government's "no breach" arguments depend upon the contract provisions that "subject" the contracts to various statutes and regulations.... [After analyzing these,] [w]e conclude, for these reasons, that the Government violated the contracts....

The dissent argues that only the statements contained in the letter from Interior to the companies may constitute a repudiation because "the enactment of legislation is not typically conceived of as a 'statement' of anything to any one party in particular," and a repudiation requires a "statement by the obligor to the obligee indicating that the obligor will commit a breach." *Post,* at 2441, n. 4 (opinion of STEVENS, J.) (quoting Restatement § 250).... If the dissent means to invoke a special exception such as the "sovereign acts" doctrine, which treats certain laws as if they simply created conditions of impossibility, see *Winstar,* 518 U.S., at 891–899, 116 S.Ct. 2432 (principal opinion of SOUTER, J.); *id.,* at 923–924, 116 S.Ct. 2432 (SCALIA, J., concurring in judgment), it cannot do so here. The Court of Federal Claims rejected the application of that doctrine to this action, see 35 Fed. Cl., at 334–336, and the Government has not contested that determination here. Hence, under these circumstances, the fact that Interior's repudiation rested upon the enactment of a new statute makes no significant difference.

We do not say that the changes made by the statute were unjustified. We say only that they were changes of a kind that the contracts did not foresee. They were changes in those approval procedures and standards that the contracts had incorporated through cross-reference. The Government has not convinced us that Interior's actions were authorized by any other contractually cross-referenced provision. Hence, in communicating to the companies its intent to follow OBPA, the United States was communicating its intent to violate the contracts.

B

The Government next argues that any violation of the contracts' terms was not significant; hence there was no "substantial" or "material" breach that could have amounted to a "repudiation." In particular, it says that OCSLA's 30-day approval period "does not function as the 'essence' of these agreements." Brief for United States 37. The Court of Claims concluded, however, that timely and fair consideration of a submitted Exploration Plan was a "necessary reciprocal obligation," indeed, that any "contrary interpretation would render the bargain illusory." 35 Fed. Cl., at 327. We agree....

The Government's modification of the contract-incorporated processes was not technical or insubstantial. It did not announce an (OBPA-required) approval delay of a few days or weeks, but of 13 months minimum, and likely much longer. The delay turned out to be at least four years. And lengthy delays matter, particularly where several successive agency approvals are at stake....

The upshot is that, under the contracts, the incorporated procedures and standards amounted to a gateway to the companies' enjoyment of all other rights. To significantly narrow that gateway violated material conditions in the contracts. The breach was "substantia[l]," depriving the companies of the benefit of their bargain. Restatement § 243. And the Government's communication of its intent to commit that breach amounted to a repudiation of the contracts.

* * *

D

Finally, the Government argues that repudiation could not have hurt the companies. Since the companies could not have met the CZMA consistency requirements, they could not have explored (or ultimately drilled) for oil in any event. . . . This argument, however, misses the basic legal point. The oil companies do not seek damages for breach of contract. They seek restitution of their initial payments. Because the Government repudiated the lease contracts, the law entitles the companies to that restitution. . . . If a lottery operator fails to deliver a purchased ticket, the purchaser can get his money back—whether or not he eventually would have won the lottery. And if one party to a contract, whether oil company or ordinary citizen, advances the other party money, principles of restitution normally require the latter, upon repudiation, to refund that money. Restatement § 373. . . .

. . . And therefore the Government must give the companies their money back.

For these reasons, the judgment of the Federal Circuit is reversed. We remand the cases for further proceedings consistent with this opinion.

It is so ordered.

Justice STEVENS, dissenting.

Since the 1953 passage of the Outer Continental Shelf Lands Act (OCSLA), 43 U.S.C. § 1331 *et seq.,* the United States Government has conducted more than a hundred lease sales of the type at stake today, and bidders have paid the United States more than $55 billion for the opportunity to develop the mineral resources made available under those leases. The United States, as lessor, and petitioners, as lessees, clearly had a mutual interest in the successful exploration, development, and production of oil in the Manteo Unit pursuant to the leases executed in 1981. . . .

From the outset, however, it was apparent that the Outer Banks project might not succeed for a variety of reasons. Among those was the risk that the State of North Carolina would exercise its right to object to the completion of the project. That was a risk that the parties knowingly assumed. They did not, however, assume the risk that Congress would enact additional legislation that would delay the completion of what would obviously be a lengthy project in any event. I therefore agree with the Court that the Government did breach its contract with petitioners in failing to approve, within 30 days of its receipt, the plan of exploration petitioners submitted. As the Court describes, *ante,* at 2430, the leases incorporate the provisions of the OCSLA into their terms, and the OCSLA, correspondingly, sets down this 30-day requirement in plain language. 43 U.S.C. § 1340(c).

I do not, however, believe that the appropriate remedy for the Government's breach is for petitioners to recover their full initial investment. When the entire relationship between the parties is considered, with particular reference to the impact of North Carolina's foreseeable exercise of its right to object to the project, it is clear that the remedy ordered by the Court is excessive. I would hold that petitioners are entitled at best to damages resulting from the delay caused by the Government's failure to approve the plan within the requisite time. . . .

Notes and Questions

1. How much does *Mobil* turn on the specific circumstances—how the statutes and regulations that existed or were contemplated at the time of the lease, as which the lessee "assumed the risk" for how they would operate, compared in effect with those, particularly the OBPA, that later came into existence? How much does *Mobil* reflect a general view coming down either from the spirit of the age, or that of the Supreme Court, about

the government being less exceptional as a sovereign and more like other non-sovereign contracting parties4. How does the outcome in *Mobil* compare with the remedy given to a contractor terminated for convenience pursuant to the FAR?

2. Suppose the feedback from cases like *Mobil* arms opponents in Congress of new proposed legislation affecting existing contracts with new ammunition to forestall enactment. Is that good, because it makes the enactment of legislation depend upon full awareness and acceptance of its costs? Or is it bad, because of the one-way direction in which it operates? Namely, the public gets set back by the prospect it must pay the business world for the burdens bestowed by some new legislation. But, the public does not get correspondingly encouraged by any similar prospect to recover other windfall benefits bestowed on the business world.

3. Another subjects has been the "spent nuclear fuel" cases. Initial opinions held the government had breached its contract. *Me. Yankee Atomic Power Co. v. United States*, 225 F.3d 1336 (Fed. Cir. 2002). The courts held the government's failure to perfect to be a partial, not total, breach of the contract. *Ind. Mich. Power Co. v. United States*, 422 F.3d 1369 (Fed. Cir. 2005). The opinions discuss broad doctrines of breach and damages applicable in different statutory schemes. To some extent, this opinion and others have made cases for government breach follow closely the particulars of each distinct statutory scheme. They take over the distinction between damages for total breach and for partial breach lock, stock and barrel from common law.

B. Takings and Remedies

For further discussion of the subjects of this subsection, see: David R. Volosov, *Too Much Time, Too Little Power: Waivers Of Sovereign Immunity And Their Statutes Of Limitations*, 38 Pub. Cont. L.J. 761 (Spring 2009); Sarah M. Graves, *Winstar Wars—Revenge Of The Thrift: A Viable Model To Right A Decade Of Wrongs*, 36 Pub. Cont. L.J. 361 (Spring 2007); Gregory C. Sisk, *A Primer On The Doctrine Of Federal Sovereign Immunity*, 58 Okla. L. Rev. 439 (Fall 2005); Richard E. Speidel, *Contract Excuse Doctrine and Retrospective Legislation: The* Winstar *Case*, 2001 Wisc. L. Rev. 795; Joshua I. Schwartz, *Assembling* Winstar: *Triumph of the Ideal of Congruence in Government Contracts Law?*, 26 Pub. Cont. L.J. 481 (1997).

Note on Winstar *and Takings*

It makes sense to touch briefly on the leading case in this context, *United States v. Winstar*, 518 U.S. 839 (1996). In *Winstar*, a federal lending agency dealing with the savings and loan crisis induced healthy financial entities to take over ailing ones by agreeing to permit their intangible "goodwill" to satisfy capital reserve requirements. Congress thereafter enacted new legislation that, among other matters, forbid this practice, and the acquiring entities sued for breach of their contract with the federal agency. The Supreme Court, with badly divided opinions, held the government liable for breach. A plurality opinion by Justice Souter held the lending agency's agreement with the acquiring entities constituted a promise to indemnify them from losses from future legal changes.

Notably, *Winstar* addressed several special defenses the government may raise in such cases, including the "sovereign acts" defense that the government is not liable for the "public and general acts" it adopts in its sovereign capacity. The different opinions had different reasoning about why the sovereign acts defense did not apply, but, however they were to synthesize, they evidently downgraded new legislation as a complete government defense, in some circumstances, to a breach suit. Although the Court in *Mobil* took the sovereign acts defense as having been resolved in the court below, the issues that Mobil did address, reflect somewhat the post-*Winstar* sense downgrading new legislation as a complete government defense in breach cases.

For further discussion of *Winstar*, see; Joshua I. Schwartz, *Liability for Sovereign Acts: Congruence and Exceptionalism in Government Contracts Law*, 64 Geo. Wash. L. Rev. 633 (1996); Gilliam Hadfield, *Of Sovereignty and Contract: Damages for Breach of Contract by Government*, 8 S. Cal. Interdisciplinary L.J. 467 (1999).

On the subject of *Winstar* itself, the Federal Circuit has moved ahead in refining the cause of action, and the damages measures, for banks that acquired failing thrifts. Among the cases addressing the cause of action were *Citizens Federal Bank v. United States*, 474 F.3d 1314 (Fed. Cir. 2007); *Bluebonnet Savings Bank, F.S.B.*, 466 F.3d 1349 (Fed. Cir. 2006); *Fifth Third Bank of Western Ohio v. United States*, 402 F.3d 1221 (Fed. Cir. 2005); and, *Coast Federal Bank, FSB v. United States*, 323 F.3d 1035 (Fed. Cir. 2003).

Among important principles, the Federal Circuit has applied the "substantial factor," rather than "but-for," theory of causation. In doing so, it rejected the Government's argument that it should only allow damages that were attributable to and resulted entirely from the breach. That theory sometimes meand the bank recovered nothing. The Circuit allowed the bank to use the "jury verdict" method of determining damages, a standard discussed in the case in this book, *Dawco*—a standard that makes it much easier to establish damages. These cases upheld the verdicts of juries in favor of the acquiring banks.

Winstar and other cases in this chapter arise in contexts distinct from the goods and services government agreements under the Federal Acquisition Regulations. However, agreements of that kind can raise related issues. How do you think the following two disputes should come out? (1) After defense contractors enter into cost-reimbursement contracts, Congress enacts a cap on executive pay that can be charged to such contracts, applying to pay subsequently incurred under contracts already made. A contractor challenges this cap as unconstitutional. (2) Cost-reimbursement contracts include government reimbursement of the costs of contractor employee pension plan contributions. These receive elaborate regulation pursuant to the Cost Accounting Standards. In 1995, revisions of the relevant standards were promulgated. These may be triggered, after 1995, by contractor restructurings affecting government reimbursements before 1995. Contractors challenge such triggering.

As to both of these, see Charles Tiefer, *Did* Eastern Enterprises *Send Enterprise Responsibility South?*, 51 Ala. L. Rev. 1305 (2000). As to issues in this context, see Bernard W. Bell, *In Defense of Retroactive Laws*, 78 Tex. L. Rev. 235 (1999); Jill E. Fisch, *Retroactivity and Legal Change: The Equilibrium Model*, 110 Harv. L. Rev. 1055 (1997).

Huntleigh USA Corporation, Plaintiff, v.
The United States, Defendant

No. 03-2670C
United States Court of Federal Claims
Jan. 7, 2005

MARGOLIS, Senior Judge.

This action is before the Court on defendant's motion to dismiss Counts I and II of plaintiff's complaint. Plaintiff, Huntleigh USA Corporation ("Huntleigh"), filed a complaint against defendant, the United States, alleging two counts. First, plaintiff alleges that defendant violated the Takings Clause of the Fifth Amendment to the United States Constitution when it federalized airport security at all domestic commercial airports thereby displacing Huntleigh, who had previously provided these services to various air carriers. Second, plaintiff alleges that defendant violated§ 101(g) of the Aviation and Transportation Security Act, Pub.L. No. 107-71, 115 Stat. 597 (the "Act") (codified primarily in sections of Title 49 of the United States Code), which according to plaintiff requires the Transportation Security Administration ("TSA") to pay adequate compensation to private security screening companies for the loss of their contracts.

* * *

After careful consideration of the briefs and oral argument, the Court denies defendant's motion to dismiss Counts I and II.

FACTS

On November 19, 2001, in response to the September 11, 2001 hijackings, the United States Congress enacted the Aviation and Transportation Security Act, Pub.L. No. 107-71, 115 Stat. 597. The Act created the Transportation Security Administration and charged it with carrying out, among other things, civil aviation security functions, including security screening operations for passenger air transportation. Pub.L. No. 107-71,§ 101(a), 115 Stat. 597, 597–602. The Act shifted the responsibility for screening passengers and property boarding aircrafts from private companies to TSA. 49 U.S.C.§ 44901(a). To carry out this shift, the Act sets forth various deadlines that TSA was required to meet. Of importance to this action, TSA was required to: (1) assume civil aviation security functions and responsibilities not later than three months after the date of enactment of the Act (February 19, 2002),§ 101(g)(1), and (2) have a sufficient number of federalized screeners in place to screen all passengers and property that would be boarding aircrafts at all 429 domestic commercial airports not later than one year after the date of enactment of the Act (November 19, 2002),§ 110(c)(1). Thus, TSA had a nine-month period to transition from private screeners to federal screeners.

The Act set out two approaches that TSA could use in transitioning from private to federalized airport security screening. First, TSA could assume the rights and responsibilities of air carriers under existing screening contracts.§ 101(g)(2). Second, TSA could obtain, through agreements with air carriers, the assignment of existing screening contracts.§ 101(g)(3). Thus, if TSA chose to utilize either of these two approaches, it would essentially be taking the place of the air carriers with respect to their contracts with private screening companies. If TSA chose to use the second approach, the Act required that the agreements be entered into not later than 90 days after the date of enactment. Further, the Act mandated that the agreements be for one 180-day period, which could be extended for one 90-day period if the Under Secretary determined that such an extension was necessary.§ 101(g)(3)(B).

TSA ultimately chose a different approach. Under TSA's approach, private security companies submitted bids for interim contracts with the government, which remained in effect for up to the nine-month transition period.

Huntleigh is a private security company. Since 1988, Huntleigh has provided passenger and baggage screening at airports throughout the United States. At the time the Act was passed, Huntleigh had contracts with eight major airlines, and a number of smaller air carriers, to provide passenger and baggage screening services at 35 airports across the United States. Huntleigh's contract with each airline consisted of a core agreement, with addendums for each separate airport location. These contracts generally had a term of three years, with a provision for automatic renewal, which the airlines often invoked.

In July 2002, Huntleigh received notices from the government informing it that TSA would be replacing Huntleigh's screening checkpoints one by one. On July 23, 2002, the government terminated the first Huntleigh security checkpoint. Over the next four months, TSA terminated all of Huntleigh's additional checkpoints. By November 2002, TSA had fully federalized airport security screening. As a result, Huntleigh alleges it has been forced out of the airport security industry, but continues to provide some non-security related services to air carriers and airports, such as skycap services, baggage handling, and janitorial services. On November 14, 2003, Huntleigh filed a complaint with this Court.

DISCUSSION

I. *Standard of Review*

Count I of Huntleigh's complaint alleges that by federalizing airport security at all domestic commercial airports, the federal government has taken Huntleigh's security business for public use without providing just compensation, in violation of the Fifth Amendment to the United States Constitution. Specifically, Huntleigh contends that the government's actions constituted a taking of its (1) contracts and (2) goodwill and going-concern value.

* * *

II. *Count I — Takings Claim*

"Whether or not a taking has occurred is a question of law based on factual underpinnings." *Cienega Gardens v. United States*, 331 F.3d 1319, 1328 (Fed.Cir.2003) (citing *Bass Enters. Prod. Co. v. United States*, 133 F.3d 893, 895 (Fed.Cir.1998)). In analyzing a takings claim a court must undertake three separate inquiries. First, a court must determine whether the subject of the alleged taking is property for purposes of the Takings Clause. If it is, the court must then determine whether the government action constituted a compensable taking, that is, whether the government interference goes "too far." *Penn Central Transportation Co. v. New York City*, 438 U.S. 104, 124, 98 S.Ct. 2646, 57 L.Ed.2d 631 (1978) (laying out a three-factor analysis to assess whether a given regulation goes "too far" for purposes of the Takings Clause). Finally, if the court finds that a taking has occurred, it must determine the amount of just compensation.

* * *

A. Nature of Plaintiff's Claim

* * *

Despite the government's attempt to characterize plaintiff's claim, the Court finds that plaintiff has alleged that its business assets were taken, including its contracts, goodwill, and going-concern value. Defendant is mistaken in its characterization of plaintiff's claim, as plaintiff repeatedly states that by federalizing airport security at all the nation's airports, the government has taken its business assets. Accordingly, the Court will analyze whether Huntleigh's business assets are compensable property under the Fifth Amendment.

B. Contracts, Goodwill and Going-Concern Value

Plaintiff alleges that by virtue of the Act, the government has taken its business assets, including its long-term screening contracts, goodwill and going-concern value. The government admits that contracts are property. Therefore, plaintiff's allegation that it had a contractual right to provide screening services to various airlines sufficiently sets forth a property interest. *See Cienega Gardens*, 331 F.3d at 1329–30. The parties dispute, however, whether goodwill and going-concern value are property under the Takings Clause. Plaintiff cites *Kimball Laundry Co. v. United States,* a case where the Army temporarily condemned the plaintiff's laundry plant during World War II. 338 U.S. 1, 69 S.Ct. 1434, 93 L.Ed. 1765 (1949). There, the plaintiff asserted that it was entitled not only to compensation for the value of the use of its plant and equipment, but also for the "diminution in the value of its business due to the destruction of its "trade routes." " *Id.* at 8, 69 S.Ct. 1434.The term "trade routes," explained the court, served as a "general designation both for the lists of customers built up by solicitation over the years and for the continued hold of the Laundry upon their patronage." *Id.* In other words, the Laundry's going-concern value. Thus, the court found that the government was required to compensate the plaintiff for the going-concern value of its laundry business. *Kimball Laundry,* 338 U.S. at 12, 69 S.Ct. 1434.

* * *

III. *Takings Analysis*

The Court must now determine whether or not the government's action constitutes a compensable taking, that is, whether the government has gone "too far." *See Pennsylvania Coal Co. v. Mahon,* 260 U.S. 393, 415, 43 S.Ct. 158, 67 L.Ed. 322 (1922). In *Penn Central Transportation v. New York City,* 438 U.S. 104, 124, 98 S.Ct. 2646, 57 L.Ed.2d 631 (1978), the Supreme Court identified three factors that have significance in determining whether a government regulation constitutes a taking: (1) the character of the governmental action; (2) the extent to which the regulation had interfered with distinct investment-backed expectations; and (3) the economic impact of the regulation on the claimant.

A. The Character of the Governmental Action

Defendant argues that the character of the government's action should be considered "an exercise of the police power" directed at protecting the safety, health, and welfare of the communit[y]," "and accordingly, does not require compensation." *See Rith Energy, Inc. v. United States,* 270 F.3d 1347, 1352 (Fed.Cir.2001). Defendant points to Congress' conclusion that the airlines' screeners failed to adequately protect the public, and as a consequence, public safety required government-controlled screening. Defendant maintains that the government has always had an interest in protecting the safety of airline passengers and has dictated airline screening procedures since at least 1974, with the advent of the federal nationwide anti-hijacking program. Therefore, the government argues that Huntleigh's status as a screening contractor did not flow from its own development of that market.

* * *

In *Rith Energy,* the court held that the revocation of the plaintiff's mining permit was an exercise of the government's police power aimed at protecting the safety, health, and welfare of the community surrounding the mine site. 270 F.3d at 1352. By contrast, Huntleigh allegedly is a company that carried out its screening duties in compliance with federal law. Therefore, at this stage of the proceeding, this Court does not consider the nature of the government's action to have been an appropriate exercise of police power. Rather, this Court holds that the nature of the government's action is the type that may require compensation, such that plaintiff should have the opportunity to present evidence.

B. Government Interference with Reasonable Investment-Backed Expectations

The second factor of the takings analysis is the extent to which defendant has interfered with plaintiff's reasonable investment-backed expectations. Defendant asserts that because Huntleigh did business in a highly regulated industry, it did not possess any investment-backed expectations. Similar to its earlier argument, the government maintains that any property right that Huntleigh may have had was subject to a regulatory scheme intended to protect the public. The government argues that Huntleigh should have been aware that Congress would change the airline screening system if it concluded that the system was not performing effectively.

* * *

Huntleigh knew it was operating in a highly regulated industry and does not challenge the government's ability to regulate procedures within the industry. What Huntleigh challenges is the destruction of its business. Huntleigh claims that it had the expectation that it would not be eliminated from the industry by the government, and in reliance, had invested significant resources to meet its long-term contractual obligations. Huntleigh alleges that it expanded its infrastructure by hiring and training a workforce of more than 3,000 screeners. Furthermore, Huntleigh maintains that contracts with air carriers were generally for three years, and the airlines often automatically renewed for multiple consecutive terms. These are reasonable investment-backed expectations. Huntleigh should, as it asserts, have the opportunity to present evidence that the government's actions interfered with its reasonable investment-backed expectations.

C. Economic Impact of the Regulation

The third factor of the takings analysis is the economic impact of the regulation on the claimant. With regard to this factor, "[w]hat has evolved in the case law is a threshold requirement that plaintiffs show 'serious financial loss' from the regulatory imposition in order to merit compensation." *Cienega Gardens*, 331 F.3d at 1340 (citation omitted). Huntleigh asserts that is has suffered devastating losses, which for purposes of this motion the Court must accept as true.

* * *

CONCLUSION

For the foregoing reasons, the Court DENIES defendant's motion to dismiss Counts I and II.

Notes & Questions

1. Suppose TSA had followed the first path laid out in the statute. Suppose it took over the existing contracts between the airlines and Huntleigh and did not complete these until they had expired by their normal terms. What additional arguments would that give the government against calling this a "taking"?

2. Would it matter if the Huntleigh contracts were in a set-for of direct contracting with the government? For example, suppose the government employed private security contractors at military airports, one of which was Huntleigh. And, suppose the events in this case had taken place against that background. What additional arguments would this give the government?

C. Sovereign Immunity

The previous sections of this chapter discuss the main regular channels for remedies in government contracting cases. Of course, cases occur in various postures outside these main channels, raising the question of what regulates jurisdiction for such cases. For the cases seeking against the United States, the general bar to suit, which regulates jurisdiction, consists of sovereign immunity. This principle, handed down from English common law, holds that the United States, as sovereign, is immune from suit except when it consents to be sued, meaning, when Congress enacts a statute conferring jurisdiction over such suits. The Contract Disputes Act of 1978 exemplifies such statutory consent to suit, by allowing a contractor to sue the United States in what has been renamed the Court of Federal Claims—but only on the precise terms of the statute. For discussion of this issues in this subsection, see Gregory C. Sisk, Litigation with the Federal Government: Cases and Material (2000); Karen L. Manos, Government Contract Costs & Pricing, sec. 90:1 (2009)(available on Westlaw).

Periodically, a case that does not follow the regular channels of government contract litigation tests the nature of the exceptions to sovereign immunity. The *Blue Fox* opinion describes what happens in one such case.

Department of the Army, Petitioner, v. Blue Fox, Inc.

525 U.S. 255
Supreme Court of the United States, 1999

Chief Justice REHNQUIST delivered the opinion of the Court

An insolvent prime contractor failed to pay a subcontractor for work the latter completed on a construction project for the Department of the Army. The Department of the Army having required no Miller Act bond from the prime contractor, the subcontractor sought to collect directly from the Army by asserting an equitable lien on certain funds held by the Army. The Court of Appeals for the Ninth Circuit held that § 10(a) of the Administrative Procedure Act (APA), 5 U.S.C. § 702, waived the Government's immunity for the subcontractor's claim. We hold that § 702 did not nullify the long settled rule that sovereign immunity bars creditors from enforcing liens on Government property.

Participating in a business development program for socially and economically disadvantaged firms run by the Small Business Administration (SBA), the Department of the Army contracted with Verdan Technology, Inc., in September 1993, to install a telephone switching system at an Army depot in Umatilla, Oregon. Verdan, in turn, employed respondent Blue Fox, Inc., as a subcontractor on the project to construct a concrete block building to house the telephone system and to install certain safety and support systems.

Under the Miller Act, 40 U.S.C. §§ 270a-270d, a contractor that performs "construction, alteration, or repair of any public building or public work of the United States" generally must post two types of bonds. § 270a(a). First, the contractor must post a "performance bond … for the protection of the United States" against defaults by the contractor. § 270a(a)(1). Second, the contractor must post a "payment bond … for the protection of all persons supplying labor and material." § 270a(a)(2). The Miller Act gives the subcontractors and other suppliers "the right to sue on such payment bond for the amount, or the balance thereof, unpaid at the time of institution of such suit and to prosecute said action to final execution and judgment for the sum or sums justly due him." § 270b(a). Although the Army's original solicitation in this case required the contractor to furnish payment and performance bonds if the contract price exceeded $25,000, the Army later amended the solicitation, treated the contract as a "services contract," and deleted the bond requirements. Verdan therefore did not post any Miller Act bonds.

Blue Fox performed its obligations, but Verdan failed to pay it the $46,586.14 that remained due on the subcontract. After receiving notices from Blue Fox that it had not been fully paid, the Army nonetheless disbursed a total of $86,132.33 to Verdan as payment for all work that Verdan had completed. In January 1995, the Army terminated its contract with Verdan for various defaults and another contractor completed the Umatilla project. Blue Fox obtained a default judgment in tribal court against Verdan. Seeing that it could not collect from Verdan or its officers, it sued the Army for the balance due on its contract with Verdan in Federal District Court.

Predicating jurisdiction on 28 U.S.C. § 1331 and the APA, Blue Fox sought an "equitable lien" on any funds from the Verdan contract not paid to Verdan, or any funds available or appropriated for completion of the Umatilla project, and an order directing payment of those funds to it. Blue Fox also sought an injunction preventing the Army from paying any more money on the Verdan contract or on the follow-on contract until Blue Fox was paid. By the time of the suit, however, the Army had paid all amounts due on the Verdan contract, Blue Fox failed to obtain any preliminary relief, and the Army subsequently paid the replacement contractor the funds remaining on the Verdan contract plus additional funds.

On cross-motions for summary judgment, the District Court held that the waiver of sovereign immunity provided by the APA did not apply to respondent's claim against the Army.... In a split decision, the Court of Appeals for the Ninth Circuit reversed in relevant part.... The majority held that under this Court's decision in *Bowen v. Massachusetts,* 487 U.S. 879 (1988), the APA waives immunity for equitable actions. Based in part on its analysis of several of our cases examining a surety's right of subrogation, the majority held that the APA had waived the Army's immunity from Blue Fox suit to recover the amount withheld by the Army. The majority concluded that the lien attached to funds retained by the Army but owed to Verdan at the time the Army received Blue Fox notice that Verdan had failed to pay. The majority stated that "[t]he Army cannot escape Blue Fox equitable lien by wrongly paying out funds to the prime contractor when it had notice of Blue Fox unpaid claims." 121 F.3d, at 1363...."Absent a waiver, sovereign immunity shields the Federal Government and its agencies from suit." *FDIC v. Meyer,* 510 U.S. 471 (1994). Congress, of course, has waived its immunity for a wide range of suits, including those that seek traditional money damages. Examples are the Federal Tort Claims Act, 28 U.S.C. § 2671 *et seq.,* and the Tucker Act, 28 U.S.C. § 1491.[3] They are not involved here. Respondent sued the Army under § 10(a) of the APA, which provides in relevant part:

> "A person suffering legal wrong because of agency action, or adversely affected or aggrieved by agency action within the meaning of a relevant statute, is entitled to judicial review thereof. An action in a court of the United States seeking relief *other than money damages* and stating a claim that an agency or an officer or employee thereof acted or failed to act in an official capacity or under color of legal authority shall not be dismissed nor relief therein be denied on the ground that it is against the United States or that the United States is an indispensable party." 5 U.S.C. § 702 (emphasis added).

Respondent asks us to hold, as did the court below, that this provision, which waives the Government's immunity from actions seeking relief "other than money damages," allows

---

3. The Federal Tort Claims Act provides that, subject to certain exceptions, "[t]he United States shall be liable, respecting the provisions of this title relating to tort claims, in the same manner and to the same extent as a private individual under like circumstances." 28 U.S.C. § 2674. The Tucker Act grants the Court of Claims jurisdiction "to render judgment upon any claim against the United States founded either upon the Constitution, or any Act of Congress or any regulation of an executive department, or upon any express or implied contract with the United States, or for liquidated or unliquidated damages in cases not sounding in tort." 28 U.S.C. § 1491(a)(1). The Tucker Act also gives federal district courts concurrent jurisdiction over claims founded upon the same substantive grounds for relief but not exceeding $10,000 in damages. See § 1346(a)(2).

subcontractors to place liens on funds held by the United States Government for work completed on a prime contract. We have frequently held, however, that a waiver of sovereign immunity is to be strictly construed, in terms of its scope, in favor of the sovereign. See, *e.g., Lane v. Peña*, 518 U.S. 187, 192, 116 S.Ct. 2092, 135 L.Ed.2d 486 (1996) (citing cases); *Library of Congress v. Shaw*, 478 U.S. 310, 318, 106 S.Ct. 2957, 92 L.Ed.2d 250 (1986). Such a waiver must also be "unequivocally expressed" in the statutory text. See *Lane, supra,* at 192, 116 S.Ct. 2092. Respondent's claim must therefore meet this high standard.

Respondent argues, and the court below held, that our analysis of § 702 in *Bowen* compels the allowance of respondent's lien. We disagree....

... *Bowen's* interpretation of § 702 ... hinged on the distinction between specific relief and substitute relief, not between equitable and nonequitable categories of remedies....

It is clear from *Bowen* that the equitable nature of the lien sought by respondent here does not mean that its ultimate claim was not one for "money damages" within the meaning of § 702. Liens, whether equitable or legal, are merely a means to the end of satisfying a claim for the recovery of money. Indeed, equitable liens by their nature constitute substitute or compensatory relief rather than specific relief....

We accordingly hold that the sort of equitable lien sought by respondent here constitutes a claim for "money damages"; its goal is to seize or attach money in the hands of the Government as compensation for the loss resulting from the default of the prime contractor. As a form of substitute and not specific relief, respondent's action to enforce an equitable lien falls outside of § 702's waiver of sovereign immunity....

Instead, recognizing that sovereign immunity left subcontractors and suppliers without a remedy against the Government when the general contractor became insolvent, Congress enacted the Miller Act.... But the Miller Act by its terms only gives subcontractors the right to sue on the surety bond posted by the prime contractor, not the right to recover their losses directly from the Government.

Respondent contends that in several cases examining a surety's right of equitable subrogation, this Court suggested that subcontractors and suppliers can seek compensation directly against the Government. See, *e.g., Prairie State Bank v. United States,* 164 U.S. 227, 32 Ct.Cl. 614, 17 S.Ct. 142, 41 L.Ed. 412 (1896); *Henningsen v. United States Fidelity & Guaranty Co.,* 208 U.S. 404, 410, 28 S.Ct. 389, 52 L.Ed. 547 (1908); *Pearlman v. Reliance Ins. Co.,* 371 U.S. 132, 141, 83 S.Ct. 232, 9 L.Ed.2d 190 (1962) (stating that "the laborers and materialmen had a right to be paid out of the fund [retained by the Government]" and hence a surety was subrogated to this right); but see *Munsey Trust Co., supra,* at 241, 67 S.Ct. 1599 ("[N]othing is more clear than that laborers and materialmen do not have enforceable rights against the United States for their compensation"). None of the cases relied upon by respondent involved a question of sovereign immunity, and, in fact, none involved a subcontractor directly asserting a claim against the Government. Instead, these cases dealt with disputes between private parties over priority to funds which had been transferred out of the Treasury and as to which the Government had disclaimed any ownership. They do not in any way disturb the established rule that, unless waived by Congress, sovereign immunity bars subcontractors and other creditors from enforcing liens on Government property or funds to recoup their losses.

The judgment of the Court of Appeals is reversed, and the case is remanded for proceedings consistent with this opinion.

It is so ordered.

Notes and Questions

1. Many different visions of sovereign immunity have come forth over the years. It started as the principle that "the King can do no wrong," a sentiment about the government that obviously did not fit the democratic ideals of the United States about government of, by, and for the people rather than ruling over it. At times, it has fallen into disfavor, seen as a hoary old notion just being used to close the courthouse doors. The court below drew on such views, by citing the Administrative Procedure Act's broad waiver of sovereign immunity as part of a general thrust to tear down much-criticized barriers surrounding the federal government and the courts, and the jurisprudence of the Warren and (to a somewhat lesser but still significant extent) Burger Courts, epitomized by Justice Brennan's decision in *Bowen*, also aimed to open up the federal government and the courts. At other times—this opinion reflects one of them—those believing in firmly closing the courthouse doors have revived sovereign immunity and raised it up as a sturdy barrier wall with only narrow, limited, well-defined exceptions. Do you believe this closed-door view will endure, or, can the pendulum swing back yet again?

2. No brief discussion can do justice to the immense and complex structure of reasoning surrounding sovereign immunity and its exceptions. The opinion mentions that the Tucker Act creates an exception for cases founded on "express or implied contract." A distinction between "implied-in-fact" contracts, for which the act waives sovereign immunity, and "implied-in-law" contracts, for which it does not, by itself has spawned countless cases and further distinctions. See *Hercules, Inc. v. United States*, 516 U.S. 417 (1996). Do you know that distinction from basic first year contract law?

3. Suppose Blue Fox asserted its rights before the payment by the United States reached the prime contractor. Do its rights depend on precisely where that payment is, on the continuum between funds still completely within the general Treasury and funds completely in the pocket of the prime contractor? Or does the discussion of the Miller Act's policy basically mean that Congress intended subcontractors should find any and all relief only against either the contractor itself or a Miller Act bond?

Note on Sovereign Immunity and Choice of (Federal) Law

Of crucial importance to government contracting are (1) when the federal government lets itself be sued—i.e., the rules of sovereign immunity; and (2) the body of law that applies—i.e., the choice of (mainly) federal law. Looked at from one perspective, these are path-determined by the happenstances of historic evolution, rather than the result of a unified or rational design. That perspective has much validity as to the particular details.

However, looked at from another perspective, the law on this subject has broad unifying and rational principles. Congress's statutes waiving sovereign immunity have concentrated the contracting suits against the government in specific channels—the boards of contract appeals (and the GAO for protests), the Court of Federal Claims (COFC), and the Federal Circuit. Thereby, Congress has gained the advantages of unification and consistency in the law and in the measurement of damages; expertise in the forums; not overloading the Supreme Court with an impossible burden of taking on large numbers of these cases to keep the appellate law unified; and, the avoidance of the other downsides were these cases to be scattered before hundreds of federal judges around the country, many of whom regards such cases as tedious and unnecessary distraction from the rest of their heavy caseload. For example, had the *Blue Fox* case gone the other way, contract cases would go into district courts around the country instead of—if they may be brought at all—going into the COFC.

Similarly, the line between federal law and state law has produced an understandable division of labor overall, however much the drawing of particular lines may be controversial. The cases involving prime contractors and "closely involved" subcontractors comes under federal statutory and common law as applied in the boards of contract appeals (and the GAO for protests) and the COFC. It is the rare contracting case in these forums that applies much state law. By contrast, the typical suppliers and not-closely-involved subcontractors go into their state courts and apply state law seeking relief from prime contractors. These cases do not make law applicable to the federal government that would make for awkwardness.

Both sovereign immunity, and choice of law, warrant a closer look. First, looking closer at some specifics about sovereign immunity, sovereign immunity shields the federal government and its agencies and instrumentalities from suit unless waived by statute. Also, sovereign immunity bars the award against the United States of money damages, interest, or attorney's fees. The key relevant statutes are the Tucker Act and the Contract Disputes Act of 1978. By statutory waiver, the COFC has exclusive jurisdiction over non-tort claims against the United States that are founded, inter alia, on an express or implied contract. The Little Tucker Act grants the federal district courts concurrent jurisdiction over such claims not exceeding $10,000, which has not been a major factor in litigation over substantial government contracting claims.

The short simple distinction historically has been between the COFC, which had exclusive jurisdiction over money damages against the United States, and specific relief (e.g., injunctions), which district courts might have. Congress amended the Administrative Procedure Act in 1976 to grant the federal district courts jurisdiction over claims against the United States other than money damages by persons adversely affected by agency action for which there is no other adequate relief. That leaves certain kinds of relief affected by precisely how the line is drawn between money damages and specific relief.

Initially, in *Bowen v. Massachusetts,* 487 U.S. 879 (1988), the Court held that specific relief included an action for specific relief to obtain specific quantities of money which had been handed over by state Medicaid programs to the federal government. Then, in *Blue Fox* in 1999, (as discussed fully in the opinion itself), the Court held that an action to assert an equitable lien, in the district court, was barred by sovereign immunity.

Second, looking closer at choice of law, the Supreme Court has had to draw important government contracting lines about how far federal common law made by federal courts extends into the general economy governed by state law. From the New Deal on, the Supreme Court took a relatively expansive view of federal law. See cases from *Clearfield Trust Co. v. United States,* 318 U.S. 363 (1943), to *United States v. Kimbell Foods, Inc.,* 400 U.S. 715 (1979).

A turning point may have been reached in *Empire Healthchoice Assurance, Inc. v. McVeigh,* 547 U.S. 677 (2006). The Court's majority argues that its approach conforms to prior case law. However, the dissent points to a number of cases related to government contracts which followed *Clearfield.* Interestingly, the lineup of justices in the case did not follow the usual conservative-liberal distinction. The majority opinion joined by Chief Justice Robert and Justices Scalia and Thomas was written by Justice Ginsburg and joined by Justice Stevens—not at all of the same ideological stripe. The dissenting opinion by Justice Breyer and joined by Justice Souter was also joined by Justices Kennedy and Alito—again a very mixed cast. This lineup seems based on the justices' views on federal jurisdiction.

Index

(Page references indicate either that a note is found on the page or that a case or other multi-page item begins on the page.)